# New Perspectives

# Microsoft® 365®
# Office 2021®

## Intermediate

 Cengage

Australia • Brazil • Canada • Mexico • Singapore • United Kingdom • United States

**New Perspectives Series®, Microsoft®
Office 365® & Office 2021® Intermediate**
Jennifer Campbell, Patrick Carey, Ann Shaffer

SVP, Product: Erin Joyner

VP, Product: Thais Alencar

Product Director: Mark Santee

Senior Product Manager: Amy Savino

Product Assistant: Ciara Horne

Learning Designer: Zenya Molnar

Content Manager: Christina Nyren

Digital Delivery Quality Partner: Jim Vaughey

Developmental Editors: Robin Romer,
Michael Sanford, Mary Pat Shaffer

VP, Product Marketing: Jason Sakos

Director, Product Marketing: Danaë April

Executive Product Marketing Manager: Jill Staut

IP Analyst: Ann Hoffman

IP Project Manager: Anjali Kambli

Production Service: Lumina Datamatics, Inc.

Designer: Erin Griffin

Cover Image Source: Artur Debat/Getty Images

For product information and technology assistance, contact us at
**Cengage Customer & Sales Support, 1-800-354-9706 or
support.cengage.com.**

For permission to use material from this text or product, submit all requests online at **www.copyright.com.**

Library of Congress Control Number: 2022938338

Student Edition ISBN: 978-0-357-67212-9
K12 ISBN: 978-0-357-67214-3
Looseleaf ISBN: 978-0-357-67213-6*
*Looseleaf available as part of a digital bundle

**Cengage**
200 Pier 4 Boulevard
Boston, MA 02210
USA

Cengage is a leading provider of customized learning solutions with employees residing in nearly 40 different countries and sales in more than 125 countries around the world. Find your local representative at **www.cengage.com.**

To learn more about Cengage platforms and services, register or access your online learning solution, or purchase materials for your course, visit **www.cengage.com.**

**Notice to the Reader**

Printed at CLDPC, USA, 12-22

# BRIEF CONTENTS

# TABLE OF CONTENTS

## EXCEL MODULES

## ACCESS MODULES

### Module 5 Creating Advanced Queries and Enhancing Table Design
*Making the Clinic Database Easier to Use*. . . . . . . . . . . . . . . . . . . . . . . . . . **AC 5-1**

### Module 6 Using Form Tools and Creating Custom Forms
*Creating Forms for Lakewood Community Health Services* . . . . . . . . . . . . . . . . . . . . . **AC 6-1**

# Getting to Know Microsoft Office Versions

Cengage is proud to bring you the next edition of Microsoft Office. This edition was designed to provide a robust learning experience that is not dependent upon a specific version of Office.

Microsoft supports several versions of Office:

- **Office 365:** A cloud-based subscription service that delivers Microsoft's most up-to-date, feature-rich, modern productivity tools direct to your device. There are variations of Office 365 for business, educational, and personal use. Office 365 offers extra online storage and cloud-connected features, as well as updates with the latest features, fixes, and security updates.

- **Office 2021:** Microsoft's "on-premises" version of the Office apps, available for both PCs and Macs, offered as a static, one-time purchase and outside of the subscription model.

- **Office Online:** A free, simplified version of Office web applications (Word, Excel, PowerPoint, and OneNote) that facilitates creating and editing files collaboratively.

Office 365 (the subscription model) and Office 2021 (the one-time purchase model) had only slight differences between them at the time this content was developed. Over time, Office 365's cloud interface will continuously update, offering new application features and functions, while Office 2021 will remain static. Therefore, your onscreen experience may differ from what you see in this product. For example, the more advanced features and functionalities covered in this product may not be available in Office Online or may have updated from what you see in Office 2021.

For more information on the differences between Office 365, Office 2021, and Office Online, please visit the Microsoft Support site.

Cengage is committed to providing high-quality learning solutions for you to gain the knowledge and skills that will empower you throughout your educational and professional careers.

Thank you for using our product, and we look forward to exploring the future of Microsoft Office with you!

# Using SAM Projects and Textbook Projects

SAM Projects allow you to actively apply the skills you learned live in Microsoft Word, Excel, PowerPoint, or Access. Become a more productive student and use these skills throughout your career.

## To complete SAM Textbook Projects, please follow these steps:

SAM Textbook Projects allow you to complete a project as you follow along with the steps in the textbook. As you read the module, look for icons that indicate when you should download **sam**⬇ your SAM Start file(s) and when to upload **sam**⬆ the final project file to SAM for grading.

Everything you need to complete this project is provided within SAM. You can launch the eBook directly from SAM, which will allow you to take notes, highlight, and create a custom study guide, or you can use a print textbook or your mobile app.  Download IOS or Download Android.

To get started, launch your SAM Project assignment from SAM, MindTap, or a link within your LMS.

## Step 1: Download Files

- Click the "Download All" button or the individual links to download your **Start File** and **Support File(s)** (when available). You <u>must</u> use the SAM Start file.

- Click the Instructions link to launch the eBook (or use the print textbook or mobile app).

- Disregard any steps in the textbook that ask you to create a new file or to use a file from a location outside of SAM.

- Look for the SAM Download icon **sam**⬇ to begin working with your start file.

- Follow the module's step-by-step instructions until you reach the SAM Upload icon **sam**⬆.

- Save and close the file.

## Step 2: Save Work to SAM

- Ensure you rename your project file to match the Expected File Name.

- Upload your in-progress or completed file to SAM. You can download the file to continue working or submit it for grading in the next step.

## Step 3: Submit for Grading

- Upload the completed file to SAM for immediate feedback and to view the available Reports.

  - The **Graded Summary Report** provides a detailed list of project steps, your score, and feedback to aid you in revising and re-submitting the project.

  - The **Study Guide Report** provides your score for each project step and links to the associated training and textbook pages.

- If additional attempts are allowed, use your reports to assist with revising and resubmitting your project.

- To re-submit the project, download the file saved in step 2.

- Edit, save, and close the file, then re-upload and submit it again.

## For all other SAM Projects, please follow these steps:

To get started, launch your SAM Project assignment from SAM, MindTap, or a link within your LMS.

## Step 1: Download Files

- Click the "Download All" button or the individual links to download your **Instruction File**, **Start File**, and **Support File(s)** (when available). You <u>must</u> use the SAM Start file.

- Open the Instruction file and follow the step-by-step instructions. Ensure you rename your project file to match the Expected File Name (change _1 to _2 at the end of the file name).

## Step 2: Save Work to SAM

- Upload your in-progress or completed file to SAM. You can download the file to continue working or submit it for grading in the next step.

## Step 3: Submit for Grading

- Upload the completed file to SAM for immediate feedback and to view available Reports.

  - The **Graded Summary Report** provides a detailed list of project steps, your score, and feedback to aid you in revising and resubmitting the project.

  - The **Study Guide Report** provides your score for each project step and links to the associated training and textbook pages.

- If additional attempts are allowed, use your reports to assist with revising and resubmitting your project.

- To re-submit the project, download the file saved in step 2.

- Edit, save, and close the file, then re-upload and submit it again.

For additional tips to successfully complete your SAM Projects, please view our Common Student Errors Infographic.

WORD

## Objectives

**Session 5.1**
- Create a new document from a template
- Move through a document using Go To
- Use the thesaurus to find synonyms
- Customize a document theme
- Save a custom theme
- Select a style set
- Customize a style
- Change character spacing

**Session 5.2**
- Create a new style
- Inspect styles
- Reveal and compare text formatting details
- Review line and page break settings
- Generate and update a table of contents
- Create and use a template
- Create a Quick Part

# Working with Templates, Themes, and Styles

## Creating a Summary Report

## Case | Allied Startup Accelerator

The Allied Center for Business and Technology, in Atlanta, Georgia, is spearheading construction of the Allied Startup Accelerator. The facility will provide guidance to new, technically oriented companies that require the specialized kind of support needed in the fast-moving technology world. Hayden Lazlo, a project manager at the center, is responsible for creating a report designed to help generate interest in the accelerator. Hayden has asked you to help him prepare the report. He's also interested in learning more about Word templates, so he'd like you to do some research by opening a few templates and examining the styles they offer. Next, he wants you to modify the formatting currently applied to his report document, including creating a customized theme, modifying one of the styles, creating a new style, and adding a table of contents. Then he wants you to create a template that can be used for all reports produced by his organization, as well as a reusable text box containing the current mailing address and phone number for the Atlanta Center for Business and Technology, which his coworkers can insert into any Word document via the Quick Parts gallery.

## Starting Data Files

**Word5** → **Module**

NP_WD_5-1.docx
NP_WD_5-2.docx
Support_WD_5_Diamond.docx
Support_WD_5_Placeholder.docx

**Review**

NP_WD_5-3.docx
NP_WD_5-4.docx
Support_WD_5_Headings.docx
Support_WD_5_Writers.docx

**Case1**

NP_WD_5-5.docx

**Case2**

NP_WD_5-6.docx
NP_WD_5-7.docx

# Session 5.1 Visual Overview:

Theme colors, which are one component of a document's theme, are used in the document's styles to format headings, body text, and other elements.

Theme fonts, the second component of a document's theme, are used in the document's styles.

Collectively, all the styles available in a document are called a style set. This style set, named Word, is applied to all new documents by default.

A third component of a document's theme, **theme effects**, controls the look of the reflections, shadows, and other effects that you can add to shapes.

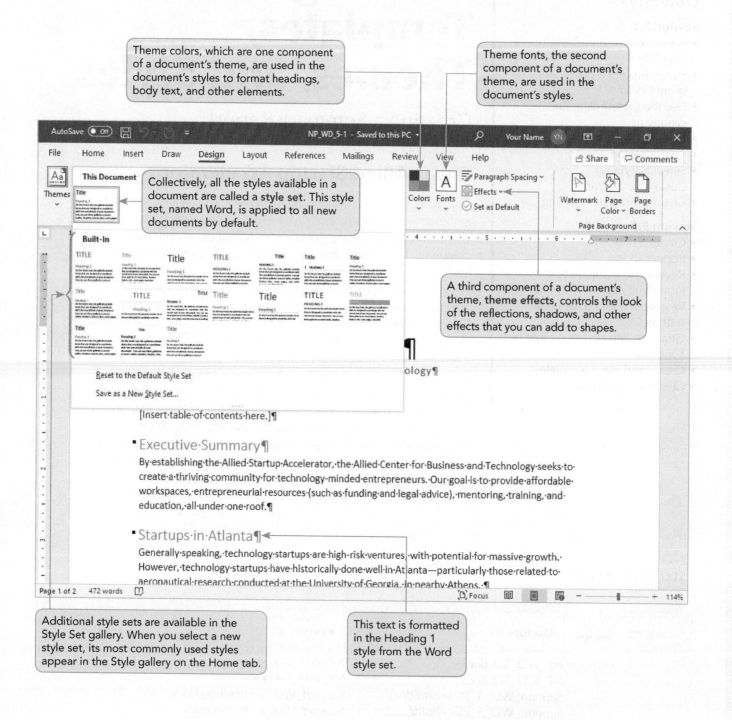

Additional style sets are available in the Style Set gallery. When you select a new style set, its most commonly used styles appear in the Style gallery on the Home tab.

This text is formatted in the Heading 1 style from the Word style set.

# Custom Themes and Style Sets

This style set, named Shaded, is applied to the document below. In the Shaded style set, the Heading 1 style formats text with blue paragraph shading and a white font color.

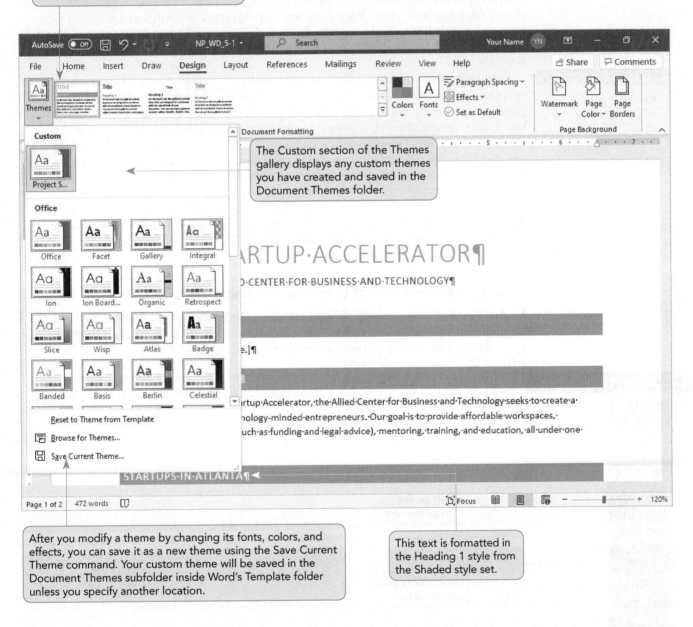

The Custom section of the Themes gallery displays any custom themes you have created and saved in the Document Themes folder.

After you modify a theme by changing its fonts, colors, and effects, you can save it as a new theme using the Save Current Theme command. Your custom theme will be saved in the Document Themes subfolder inside Word's Template folder unless you specify another location.

This text is formatted in the Heading 1 style from the Shaded style set.

# Creating a New Document from a Template

A template is a file that you use as a starting point for a series of similar documents so that you don't have to re-create formatting and text for each new document. A template can contain customized styles, text, graphics, or any other element that you want to repeat from one document to another. In this module, you'll customize the styles and themes in a Word document and then save the document as a template to use for future documents. Before you do that, however, you will investigate some of the ready-made templates available at Office.com.

When you first start Word, the Home screen in Backstage view displays a variety of templates available from Office.com. You can also enter keywords in the Search for online templates box to find templates that match your specific needs. For example, you could search for a calendar template, a birthday card template, or a report template.

**Tip**

Templates have the file extension .dotx to differentiate them from regular Word documents, which have the extension .docx.

Every new, blank document that you open in Word is a copy of the Normal template. Unlike other Word templates, the **Normal template** does not have any text or graphics, but it does include all the default settings that you are accustomed to using in Word. For example, the default theme in the Normal template is the Office theme. The Office theme, in turn, supplies the default body font (Calibri) and the default heading font (Calibri Light). The default line spacing and paragraph spacing you are used to seeing in a new document are also specified in the Normal template.

Hayden would like you to review some templates designed for reports. As you'll see in the following steps, when you open a template, Word actually creates a document that is an exact copy of the template. The template itself remains unaltered, so you can continue to use it as the basis for other documents.

### To review some report templates available on Office.com:

1. On the ribbon, click the **File** tab to open Backstage view, and then click **New** in the navigation pane. The New screen in Backstage view displays thumbnail images of the first page of a variety of templates. See Figure 5–1.

**Figure 5–1**   Featured templates on the New screen in Backstage view

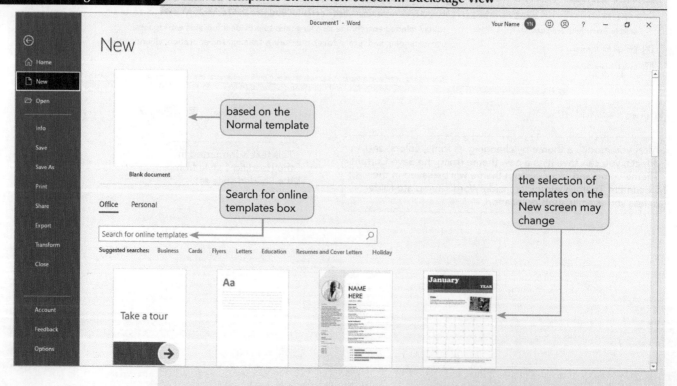

**Trouble?** If you just started Word, you'll see the list of templates on the Home screen. You'll be able to complete the next step using the Search for online templates box on the Home screen.

Below the Search for online templates box are template options available from Office.com. You've already used the Blank document template to open a new, blank document that is based on the Normal template. The list of templates changes as new templates become available, so your screen probably won't match Figure 5–1 exactly.

▶ 2. Click the **Search for online templates** box, type **report**, and then press **ENTER**. The New screen displays thumbnail images for a variety of report templates.

▶ 3. Click any report template. A window opens with a preview of the template. Note that the template indicates it is provided by Microsoft Corporation. Figure 5–2 shows the Student report with photo template.

**Figure 5–2** ▶ **Previewing a template**

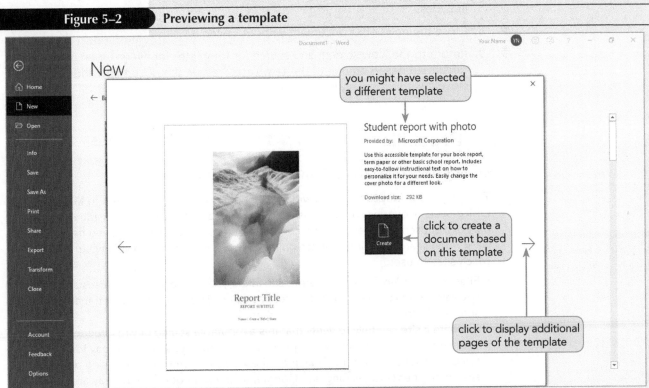

iStock.com/Turnervisual

You could click the Close button ☒ to close the preview window and browse other report templates, but Hayden asks you to continue investigating the current template.

4. Click the **Create** button. A new document based on the template opens. Depending on which template you selected, your document might include a cover page, a photo, and a number of content controls designed specifically for the template—similar to the content controls you've seen in other documents. The document also likely contains some placeholder text, a footer, and graphics. You might also see the Researcher pane open on the right side of the Word screen, ready to help you begin researching information for a report.

At this point, you could save the document with a new name and then begin revising it to create an actual report. But since your goal now is to review various templates, you'll close the document.

5. Close the document without saving any changes.

6. On the ribbon, click the **File** tab, and then click **New** in the navigation pane.

7. Search online for newsletter templates, open a document based on one of the templates, and then review the document, noting the various elements it includes.

8. Close the newsletter document without saving it.

9. Return to the New screen, and search for templates for flyers. Open a new document based on one of the templates, review the document, and then close it without saving it.

## Proskills

### Decision Making: Using Templates from Other Sources

The Office.com website offers a wide variety of templates that are free to Microsoft Office users. Countless other websites offer templates for free, for individual sale, as part of a subscription service, or a combination of all three. However, you need to be wary when searching for templates online. Keep in mind the following when deciding which sites to use:

- Files downloaded from the Internet can infect your computer with viruses and spyware, so make sure your computer has up-to-date antivirus and anti-malware software before downloading any templates.
- Evaluate a site carefully to verify that it is a reputable source of virus-free templates. Verifying the site's legitimacy is especially important if you intend to pay for a template with a credit card. Search for the website's name and URL using different search engines (such as Bing and Google) to see what other people say about it.
- Some websites claim to offer templates for free, when in fact the offer is primarily a lure to draw visitors to sites that are really just online billboards, with ads for any number of businesses completely unrelated to templates or Word documents. Avoid downloading templates from these websites.
- Many templates available online were created for earlier versions of Word that did not include themes, 3D models, or other advanced Word design features. Make sure you know what you're getting before you pay for an out-of-date template.

Now that you are finished reviewing report templates, you will open the document containing the report about the Allied Startup Accelerator.

**To open Hayden's report document:**

1.  Open the document **NP_WD_5-1.docx** from the Word5 > Module folder, and then save it as **NP_WD_5_Allied** in the location specified by your instructor.

2. Display nonprinting characters and the rulers, switch to Print Layout view if necessary, and then change the Zoom level to **120%**, if necessary. See Figure 5–3.

**Figure 5–3**　　**Report document**

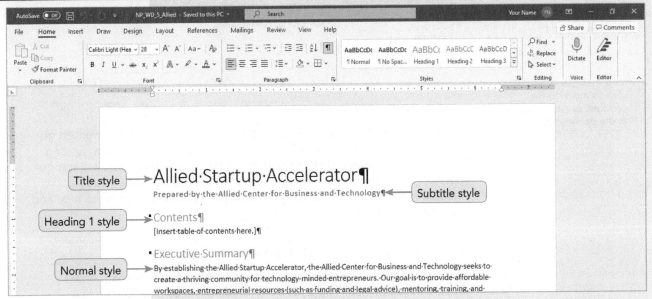

The report is formatted using the default settings of the Normal template, which means its current theme is the Office theme. Text in the report is formatted using the Title, Subtitle, Heading 1, Heading 2, and Normal styles. The document includes a footer containing "Allied Startup Accelerator" and a page number field.

Before you begin revising the document, you should review its contents. To get a quick overview of a document, it's helpful to use the Go To feature.

# Using Go To

The Go To tab in the Find and Replace dialog box allows you to move quickly among elements in a document. For example, you can use it to move from heading to heading, from graphic to graphic, or from table to table. In a long document, this is an efficient way to review your work. Although the document is not very long, you can still review its contents using Go To.

**To use the Go To feature to review the document:**

1. If necessary, press **CTRL+HOME** to move the insertion point to the beginning of the document.

2. On the ribbon, make sure the Home tab is displayed.

3. In the Editing group, click the **Find arrow** to display the Find menu, and then click **Go To**. The Find and Replace dialog box opens, with the Go To tab displayed. See Figure 5–4.

**Figure 5–4** 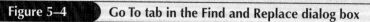 Go To tab in the Find and Replace dialog box

type additional information about the document element here

click the document element you want to go to

click to move to the previous or next instance in the document

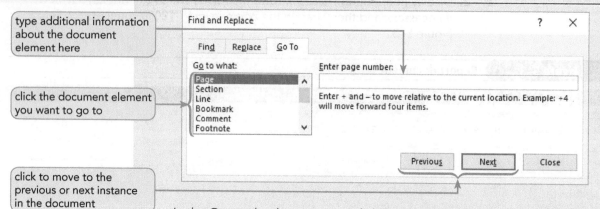

In the Go to what box, you can click the document element you want to go to. Then click the Next or Previous buttons to move back and forth among instances of the selected element in the document. You can also enter more specific information in the box on the right. For instance, when Page is selected in the Go to what box, you can type a page number in the box, and then click Next to go directly to that page.

Right now, Hayden would like to review all the headings in the document—that is, all the paragraphs formatted with a heading style.

4. Scroll down to the bottom of the Go to what box, click **Heading**, and then click the **Next** button. The document scrolls down to position the first document heading, "Contents," at the top of the document window.

5. Click the **Next** button again. The document scrolls down to display the "Executive Summary" heading at the top of the document window.

6. Click the **Next** button five more times to display the last heading in the document, "Saturn and Sun Investments," at the top of the document window.

7. Click the **Previous** button to display the "Chandra 3D Printing" heading at the top of the document window, and then close the Find and Replace dialog box.

## Insight

### Choosing Between Go To and the Navigation Pane

Both the Go To tab in the Find and Replace dialog box and the Navigation pane allow you to move through a document heading by heading. Although you used Go To in the preceding steps, the Navigation pane is usually the better choice for working with headings; it displays a complete list of the headings, which helps you keep an eye on the document's overall organization. However, the Go To tab is more useful when you want to move through a document one graphic at a time or one table at a time. In a document that contains a lot of graphics or tables, it's a good idea to use the Go To feature to make sure you've formatted all the graphics or tables similarly.

Next, before you begin formatting the document, Hayden asks you to help him find a synonym for a word in the text.

# Using the Thesaurus to Find Synonyms

In any kind of writing, choosing the right words to convey your meaning is important. If you need help, you can use the thesaurus in Word to look up a list of synonyms, or possible replacements, for a specific word. You can right-click a word to display a shortcut menu with a short list of synonyms or open the Thesaurus pane for a more complete list. Also, this list usually includes at least one antonym—that is, a word with the opposite meaning.

Hayden is not happy with the word "innovators" in the paragraph about Chandra 3D Printing because he thinks it's overused in writing about technical entrepreneurs. He asks you to find a synonym.

**To look up a synonym in the thesaurus:**

▶ **1.** In the third to last line on page 1, right-click the word **innovators**. A shortcut menu opens.

▶ **2.** Point to **Synonyms**. A menu with a list of synonyms for "innovators" is displayed, as shown in Figure 5–5.

**Figure 5–5** ▶ **Shortcut menu with list of synonyms**

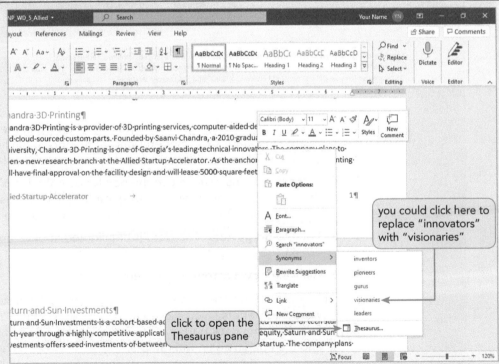

Hayden thinks one word in the list, "visionaries," is a good replacement for "innovators." You could click "visionaries" to insert it in the document in place of "innovators," but Hayden asks you to check the Thesaurus pane to see if it suggests a better option.

**3.** At the bottom of the shortcut menu, click **Thesaurus**. The Thesaurus pane opens on the right side of the document window, with the word "innovators" at the top and a more extensive list of synonyms below. The word "innovators" is also selected in the document, ready to be replaced. See Figure 5–6.

**Figure 5–6**    **Thesaurus pane**

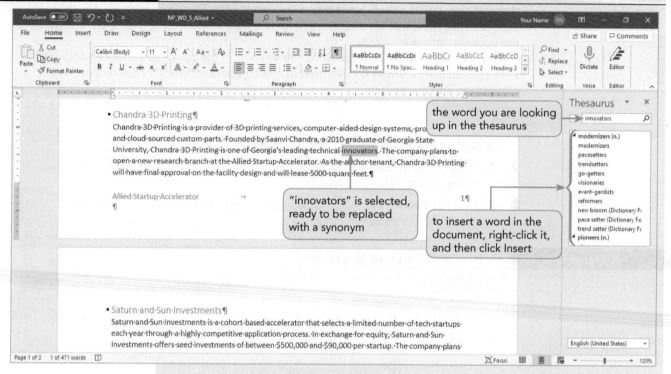

The synonym list is organized by different shades of meaning, with words related to the idea of "modernizers" at the top of the list. You can scroll down the list to see other groups of synonyms, and at least one antonym.

**4.** In the Thesaurus pane, move the pointer over the list of synonyms to display the scroll bar, scroll down to display other synonyms, as well as the antonym at the bottom of the list, and then scroll back up to the top of the list.

**5.** Point to **go-getters**. The word is highlighted in blue, and a down arrow ▼ appears to the right.

**6.** Click the **down arrow** ▼. A menu opens.

   **Trouble?** If the Thesaurus pane changes to display a set of synonyms for the word "go-getters," you clicked the word "go-getters" instead of just pointing at it. Click the Back button ◁ to redisplay the synonyms for "innovators," and then begin again with Step 5.

**7.** Click **Insert** to replace "innovators" with "go-getters" in the document, and then close the Thesaurus pane.

**8.** Save the document.

Now that the document text is finished, you can get to work on the formatting. You'll start by customizing the document theme.

# Customizing the Document Theme

A document theme consists of three main components—theme colors, theme fonts, and theme effects. A specific set of colors, fonts, and effects is associated with each theme, but you can mix and match them to create a customized theme for your document. This can be useful in specialized situations, such as when you need to create a series of documents that match an organization's preferred format for reports. After you create a customized theme, you can use it for all new reports that require that particular combination of fonts, colors, and effects.

Recall that the theme fonts are the fonts used in a document's styles. You see them at the top of the font list when you click the Font arrow in the Font group on the Home tab. The theme colors are displayed in the Theme Colors section of any color gallery. The colors used to format headings, body text, and other elements are all drawn from the document's theme colors. Theme effects alter the appearance of shapes. Because they are generally very subtle, theme effects are not a theme element you will typically be concerned with.

When you change the theme colors, fonts, or effects for a document, the changes affect only that document. However, you can also save the changes you make to create a new, custom theme, which you can then use for future documents.

Hayden's report document, which was based on the Normal template, is formatted with the Office theme—which applies a blue font color to the headings by default and formats the headings in the Calibri Light font. Hayden wants to select different theme colors and theme fonts to match the preferred formatting for reports created by the Allied Center for Business and Technology. He doesn't plan to include any graphics, so there's no need to customize the theme effects. You'll start with the theme colors.

## Changing the Theme Colors

As you have seen, theme colors, which are designed to coordinate well with each other, are used in the various document styles, including the text styles available on the Home tab. They are also used in shape styles, WordArt styles, and picture styles. So when you want to change the colors in a document, it's always better to change the theme colors rather than selecting individual elements and applying a new color to each element from a color gallery. That way you can be sure colors will be applied consistently throughout the document—for example, the headings will all be shades of the same color.

Reports created by the Allied Center for Business and Technology are typically emailed to many recipients, some of whom might choose to print the reports. To keep printing costs as low as possible for all potential readers of his report, Hayden wants to format his document in black and white. He asks you to apply a set of theme colors consisting of black and shades of gray.

### To change the theme colors in the document:

▶ **1.** Press **CTRL+HOME** to display the beginning of the document.

▶ **2.** On the ribbon, click the **Design** tab.

▶ **3.** In the Document Formatting group, move the pointer over the **Colors** button. A ScreenTip is displayed, indicating that the current theme colors are the Office theme colors.

4. Click the **Colors** button. A gallery of theme colors opens, with the Office theme colors selected at the top of the gallery. See Figure 5–7.

**Figure 5–7** Theme Colors gallery

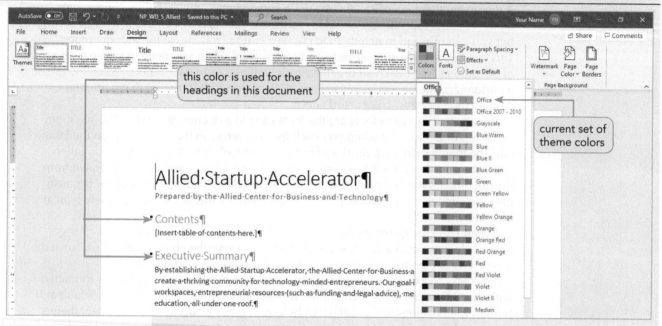

Each set of theme colors contains eight colors, with each assigned to specific elements. For example, the third color from the left is used for headings. The remaining colors are used for other types of elements, such as hyperlinks, page borders, shading, and so on.

**Trouble?** If you see additional theme colors at the top of the gallery under the "Custom" heading, then custom theme colors have been created and stored on your computer.

5. Move the pointer over the options in the gallery to observe the Live Preview of the colors in the document.

6. Near the top of the gallery, click the **Grayscale** color set, which is the third from the top. The document headings are now formatted in gray.

7. Save the document.

The new colors you selected affect only the report document. Your changes do not affect the Office theme that was installed with Word. Next, Hayden asks you to customize the document theme further by changing the theme fonts.

## Changing the Theme Fonts

As with theme colors, you can change the theme fonts in a document to suit your needs. Each theme uses two coordinating fonts—one for the headings and one for the body text. In some themes, the same font is used for the headings and the body text. When changing the theme fonts, you can select from all the font combinations available in any of the themes installed with Word.

## To select a different set of theme fonts for the document:

1. In the Document Formatting group, move the pointer over the **Fonts** button. A ScreenTip is displayed, indicating that the current fonts are Calibri Light for headings and Calibri for body text.

2. Click the **Fonts** button. The Theme Fonts gallery opens, displaying the heading and body font combinations for each theme.

3. Scroll down to review the fonts. Hayden prefers the Franklin Gothic set of theme fonts, which includes Franklin Gothic Medium for headings and Franklin Gothic Book for the body text.

4. In the Theme Fonts gallery, point to **Franklin Gothic** to display a Live Preview in the document. See Figure 5–8.

**Figure 5–8**     **Theme Fonts gallery**

5. Click **Franklin Gothic**. The Theme Fonts gallery closes, and the new fonts are applied to the document.

6. Save the document.

The changes you have made to the theme fonts for the document do not affect the original Office theme that was installed with Word and that is available to all documents. To make your new combination of theme fonts and theme colors available to other documents, you can save it as a new, custom theme.

## Insight

### Creating Custom Combinations of Theme Colors and Fonts

The theme color and font combinations installed with Word were created by Microsoft designers who are experts in creating harmonious-looking documents. It's usually best to stick with these preset combinations rather than trying to create your own set. However, in some situations you might need to create a customized combination of theme colors or fonts. When you do so, that set is saved as part of Word so that you can use it in other documents.

To create a custom set of theme colors, you click the Colors button in the Document Formatting group on the Design tab and then click Customize Colors to open the Create New Theme Colors dialog box, in which you can select colors for different theme elements and enter a descriptive name for the new set of theme colors. The custom set of theme colors will be displayed as an option in the Theme Colors gallery. To delete a custom set of colors from the Theme Colors gallery, right-click the custom color set in the gallery, click Delete, and then click Yes.

To create a custom set of heading and body fonts, you click the Fonts button in the Document Formatting group on the Design tab, click Customize Fonts, select the heading and body fonts, and then enter a name for the new set of fonts in the Name box. The custom set of theme fonts is displayed as an option in the Theme Fonts gallery. To delete a custom set of fonts from the Theme Fonts gallery, right-click the custom font set in the gallery, click Delete, and then click Yes.

## Saving a Custom Theme

You can save a custom theme to any folder, but when you save a custom theme to the default location—the Document Themes subfolder inside the Templates folder—it is displayed as an option in the Themes gallery. To delete a custom theme saved in the Document Themes folder, click the Themes button on the Design tab, right-click the theme, click Delete, and then click Yes.

Hayden asks you to save his combination of theme fonts and theme colors as a new custom theme, using "ACBT," the acronym for "Allied Center for Business and Technology," as part of the file name.

**To save the new custom theme:**

1. In the Document Formatting group, click the **Themes** button, and then click **Save Current Theme**. The Save Current Theme dialog box opens. See Figure 5-9.

| Figure 5-9 | Save Current Theme dialog box |

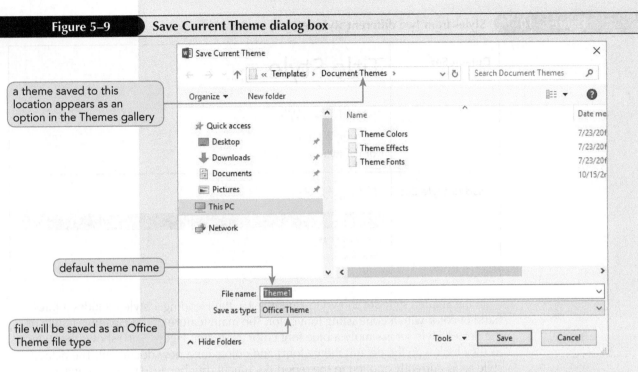

a theme saved to this location appears as an option in the Themes gallery

default theme name

file will be saved as an Office Theme file type

The Document Themes folder is the default location. The default theme name is "Theme1." You can select a different save location and enter a more meaningful theme name.

**2.** Navigate to the save location specified by your instructor.

**3.** Click in the File name box, type **NP_WD_5_Theme** and then click the **Save** button. The Save Current Theme dialog box closes.

Hayden plans to use the new theme to help standardize the look of all documents created in his department. When he is ready to apply it to a document, he can click the Themes button in the Document Formatting group on the Design tab, click Browse for Themes, navigate to the folder containing the custom theme, and then select the theme. If he wants to be able to access his theme from the Themes gallery instead, he will need to save it to the Document Themes folder first.

Hayden likes the document's new look, but he wants to make some additional changes. First, he wants to select a different style set.

## Selecting a Style Set

Recall that a style is a set of formatting options that you can apply to a specific text element in a document, such as a document's title, heading, or body text. So far, you have used only the default set of styles available in the Style gallery on the Home tab. You can access 16 additional style sets, or groups of styles, in the Style Set gallery, which is located in the Document Formatting group on the Design tab.

Each style set has a Normal style, a Heading 1 style, a Heading 2 style, and so on, but the formatting settings associated with each style vary from one style set to another. See Figure 5-10.

**Figure 5–10** **Styles from two different style sets**

| Default Set | Title Style |
| --- | --- |
| | Heading 1 style |
| | Heading 2 style |
| | **Normal style** |
| Shaded Style Set | TITLE STYLE |
| | HEADING 1 STYLE |
| | HEADING 2 STYLE |
| | Normal style |

In the Shaded style set shown in Figure 5–10, the Heading 1 style includes a thick band of color with a contrasting font color. The main feature of the Heading 1 style of the default style set is simply a blue font color. Note that Figure 5–10 shows the styles as they look with the default theme fonts and colors for a new document. The default style set is currently applied to the report document, but because you've changed the theme fonts and colors in the document, the colors and fonts in the document are different from what is shown in Figure 5–10. However, the styles in the report document still have the same basic look as the default styles shown in the figure.

Hayden asks you to select a style set for the report document that makes the Heading 1 text darker, so the headings are easier to read. Before you do that, you'll review the styles currently available in the Style gallery on the Home tab. Then, after you select a new style set, you'll go back to the Style gallery to examine the new styles.

**To review the styles in the Style gallery and select a new style set for the document:**

1. On the ribbon, click the **Home** tab.

2. In the Styles group, click the **More** button ⬇, and then review the set of styles currently available in the Style gallery. Note that the icon for the Heading 1 style indicates that it applies a light gray font color.

3. On the ribbon, click the **Design** tab.

4. In the Document Formatting group, click the **More** button ⬇ to open the Style Set gallery. Move the pointer across the icons in the gallery to display their ScreenTips and to observe the Live Previews in the document.

5. Point to the **Lines (Stylish)** style set, which is on the far-left side of the bottom row. In the Lines (Stylish) style set, the Heading 1 style applies a black font color, with a light gray line that spans the width of the document. See Figure 5–11.

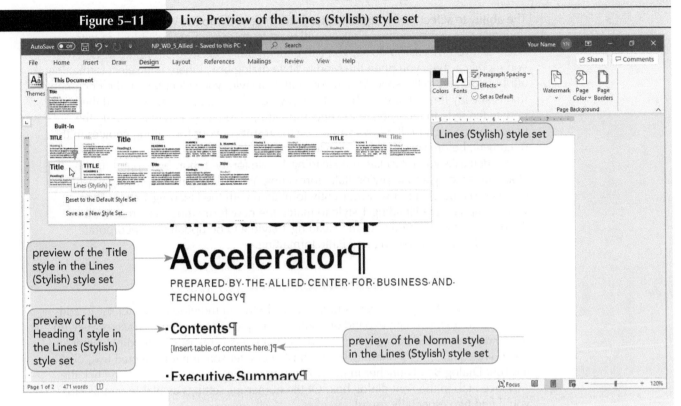

**Figure 5–11**    Live Preview of the Lines (Stylish) style set

Notice that the theme fonts you specified earlier—Franklin Gothic Medium for headings and Franklin Gothic Book for body text—are still applied, as are the Grayscale theme colors.

6. Click the **Lines (Stylish)** style set. The styles in the document change to reflect the styles in the Lines (Stylish) style set. You can verify this by looking at the Style gallery on the Home tab.

7. On the ribbon, click the **Home** tab.

8. In the Styles group, click the **More** button ⤓ to review the styles available in the Style gallery. The icon for the Heading 1 style indicates that it now applies a black font color. The style also applies a light gray underline, although that is not visible in the Style gallery icon.

9. Click anywhere in the document to close the Style gallery, and then save the document.

## Insight

### The Set as Default Button: A Note of Caution

The Set as Default button in the Document Formatting group on the Design tab saves the document's current formatting settings as the default for any new blank documents you create in Word. In other words, it saves the current formatting settings to the Normal template. You might find this a tempting option, but, as you will learn in Session 5.2, when working with styles, modifying the Normal template is almost never a good idea. Instead, a better option is to save a document with the formatting you like as a new template, which you can then use as the basis for future documents. Exercise similar caution with the Set as Default button in the Font dialog box, which allows you to change the default font for the Normal template.

# Customizing Styles

The ability to select a new style set gives you a lot of flexibility when formatting a document. However, sometimes you will want to customize an individual style to better suit your needs. To do so, you can either modify the style or update it. When you modify a style, you open the Modify Style dialog box, where you select formatting attributes to add to the style. When you update a style, you select text in the document that is already formatted with the style, apply new formatting to the text, and then update the style to incorporate the new formatting. Updating a style is usually the better choice because it allows you to see the results of your formatting choices in the document, before you change the style itself.

Hayden asks you to update the Heading 1 style for the report by expanding the character spacing and applying italic formatting. You will begin by applying these changes to a paragraph that is currently formatted with the Heading 1 style. Then you can update the Heading 1 style to match the new formatting. As a result, all the paragraphs formatted with the Heading 1 style will be updated to incorporate expanded character spacing and italic formatting.

## Changing Character Spacing

The term **character spacing** refers to the space between individual characters. To add emphasis to text, you can expand or contract the spacing between characters. As with line and paragraph spacing, space between characters is measured in points, with one point equal to 1/72 of an inch. To adjust character spacing for selected text, click the Font Dialog Box Launcher in the Font group on the Home tab, and then click the Advanced tab in the Font dialog box. Of the numerous settings available on this tab, you'll find two especially useful.

First, the Spacing box allows you to choose Normal spacing (which is the default character spacing for the Normal style), Expanded spacing (with the characters farther apart than with the Normal setting), and Condensed spacing (with the characters closer together than with the Normal setting). With both Expanded and Condensed spacing, you can specify the number of points between characters.

Second, the Kerning for fonts check box allows you to adjust the spacing between characters to make them look like they are spaced evenly. Kerning is helpful when you are working with large font sizes, which can sometimes cause evenly spaced characters to appear unevenly spaced. Selecting the Kerning for fonts check box ensures that the spacing is adjusted automatically.

**To add expanded character spacing and italic formatting to a paragraph formatted with the Heading 1 style:**

1. In the document, scroll down if necessary, and select the **Executive Summary** heading, which is formatted with the Heading 1 style.

2. Make sure the Home tab is selected on the ribbon.

3. In the Font group, click the **Font Dialog Box Launcher**. The Font dialog box opens.

4. Click the **Advanced** tab. The Character Spacing settings at the top of this tab reflect the style settings for the currently selected text. The Spacing box is set to Normal. The more advanced options, located in the OpenType Features section, allow you to fine-tune the appearance of characters.

5. Click the **Spacing arrow**, and then click **Expanded**. See Figure 5–12.

**Figure 5–12**     Changing character spacing in the Font dialog box

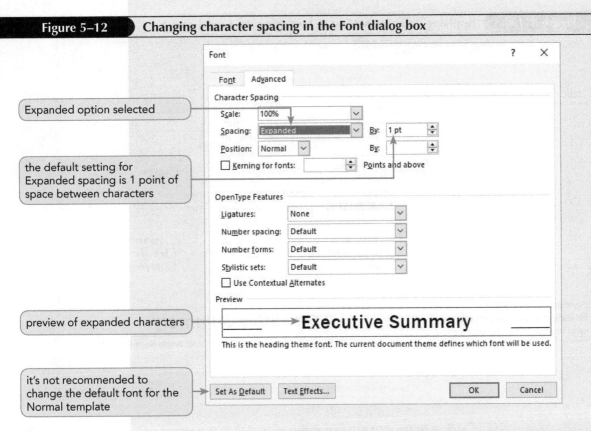

Expanded option selected

the default setting for Expanded spacing is 1 point of space between characters

preview of expanded characters

it's not recommended to change the default font for the Normal template

The By box next to the Spacing box indicates that each character is separated from the other by 1 point of space. You could increase the point setting, but in the current document, 1 point is fine. The Preview section shows a sample of the expanded character spacing.

Next, you need to apply italic formatting, which you could do from the Font group on the Home tab. But since you have the Font dialog box open, you'll do it from the Font tab in the Font dialog box instead.

**Tip**

Text formatted as hidden is visible only when nonprinting characters are displayed.

6. In the Font dialog box, click the **Font** tab.

   Here you can apply most of the settings available in the Font group on the Home tab and a few that are not available in the Font group—such as colored underlines and small caps (smaller versions of uppercase letters). You can also hide text from view by selecting the Hidden check box.

7. In the Font style box, click **Italic**. The Preview section of the Font tab shows a preview of the italic formatting applied to the "Executive Summary" heading. See Figure 5–13.

**Figure 5–13**   Applying italic formatting to text using the Font dialog box

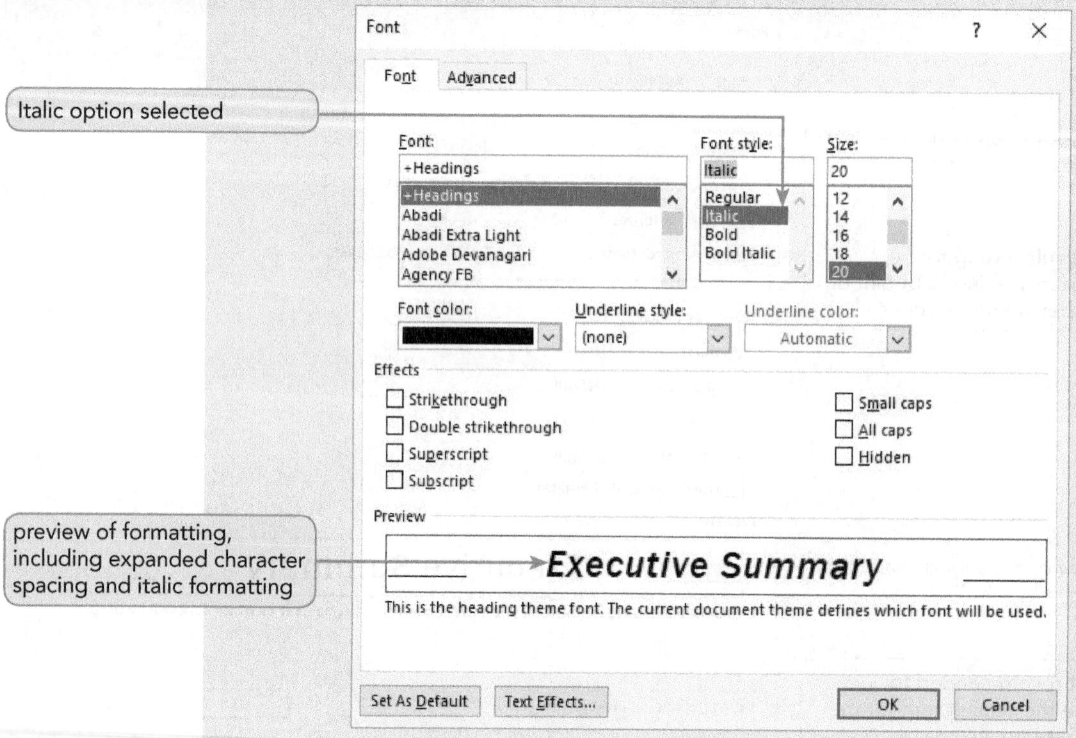

Italic option selected

preview of formatting, including expanded character spacing and italic formatting

The other font attributes associated with the Heading 1 style are also visible on the Font tab.

**8.** Click **OK** to close the Font dialog box. The selected heading is now italicized, with the individual characters spread slightly farther apart.

**9.** Click anywhere in the "Executive Summary" heading to deselect the text, and then save the document.

Now that the selected heading is formatted the way you want, you can update the Heading 1 style to match it. When working with styles, it's helpful to open the Styles pane to see more information about the styles in the current style set, so you'll do that next.

## Displaying the Styles Pane

The Styles pane shows you more styles than are displayed in the Style gallery. You can click a style in the Styles pane to apply it to selected text, just as you would click a style in the Style gallery.

The Styles pane provides detailed information about each style. In particular, it differentiates between character styles, paragraph styles, and linked styles. A **character style** contains formatting options that affect the appearance of individual characters, such as font style, font color, font size, bold, italic, and underline. When you click a character style, it formats the word that contains the insertion point or, if text is selected in the document, any selected characters.

A **paragraph style** contains all the character formatting options as well as formatting options that affect the paragraph's appearance—including line spacing, text alignment, tab stops, and borders. When you click a paragraph style, it formats the entire paragraph that contains the insertion point, or, if text is selected in the document, it formats all selected paragraphs (even paragraphs in which just one character is selected).

A **linked style** contains both character and paragraph formatting options. If you click in a paragraph or select a paragraph and then apply a linked style, both the paragraph styles and character styles are applied to the entire paragraph. If you apply a linked style to a selected word or group of words rather than to an entire paragraph, only the character styles for that linked style are applied to the selected text; the paragraph styles are not applied to the paragraph itself. All of the heading styles in Word are linked styles.

### To open the Styles pane to review information about the styles in the current style set:

1. Make sure the Home tab is selected on the ribbon.

2. In the Styles group, click the **Styles Dialog Box Launcher**. The Styles pane opens on the right side of the document window. See Figure 5–14.

**Figure 5–14**      **Styles pane**

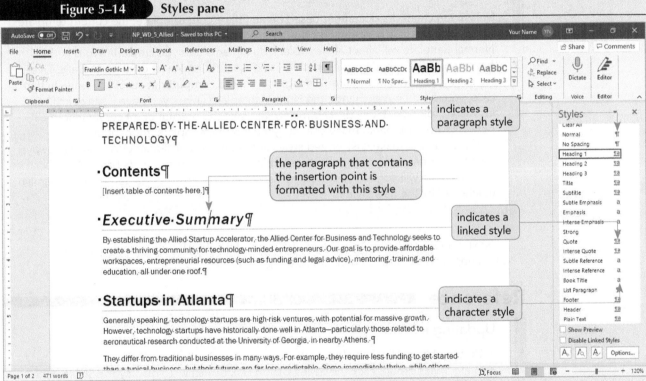

The outline around the Heading 1 style indicates that the insertion point is currently located in a paragraph formatted with that style. A paragraph symbol to the right of a style name indicates a paragraph style, a lowercase letter "a" indicates a character style, and a combination of both indicates a linked style. You can display even more information about a style by moving the pointer over the style name in the Styles pane.

3. In the Styles pane, move the pointer over **Heading 1**. An arrow is displayed to the right of the Heading 1 style name, and a ScreenTip with detailed information about the Heading 1 style opens below the style name.

The information in the ScreenTip relates only to the formatting applied by default with the Heading 1 style; it makes no mention of italic formatting or expanded character spacing. Although you applied these formatting changes to the "Executive Summary" heading, they are not yet part of the Heading 1 style.

You'll incorporate the new formatting into the Heading 1 style in the next section, when you update the style.

## Updating a Style

Word is set up to save all customized styles to the current document by default. In fact, when you update a style, you don't even have a choice about where to save it—the updated style is automatically saved to the current document, rather than to the current template. If for some reason you needed to save a customized style to the current template instead, you would need to modify the style using the Modify Style dialog box, where you could then select the New documents based on this template button to save the modified style to the current template.

## Insight

### Preserving the Normal Template

Unless you created a document based on an Office.com template, the current template for any document is probably the Normal template. Any changes you make to the Normal template will affect all new, blank documents that you create in Word in the future, so altering the Normal template is not something you should do casually. This is especially important if you are working on a shared computer at school or work. In that case, you should never change the Normal template unless you have been specifically instructed to do so. Many organizations even take the precaution of configuring their networked computers to make changing the Normal template impossible.

If you want to make customized styles available in other documents, you can always save the current document as a new template. All future documents based on your new template will contain your new styles. Meanwhile, the Normal template will remain unaffected by the new styles.

Next, you'll use the Styles pane to update the Heading 1 style to include italic formatting with expanded character spacing.

## Reference

### Updating a Style

- On the ribbon, click the Home tab.
- In the Styles group, click the Styles Dialog Box Launcher to display the Styles pane.
- In the document, apply formatting to a paragraph or group of characters.
- Click in the formatted paragraph (if you are updating a paragraph or linked style) or in the formatted group of characters (if you are updating a character style).
- In the Styles pane, right-click the style you want to update to display a shortcut menu.
- Click Update *Style* to Match Selection (where *Style* is the name of the style you want to update).

**The insertion point must be located in the "Executive Summary" heading to ensure that you update the Heading 1 style with the correct formatting.**

### To update the Heading 1 style:

▶ 1. In the document, make sure the insertion point is located in the paragraph containing the "Executive Summary" heading, which is formatted with the Heading 1 style.

▶ 2. In the Styles pane, right-click **Heading 1**. A menu opens with options related to working with the Heading 1 style. See Figure 5–15.

**Figure 5–15**    Heading 1 style menu

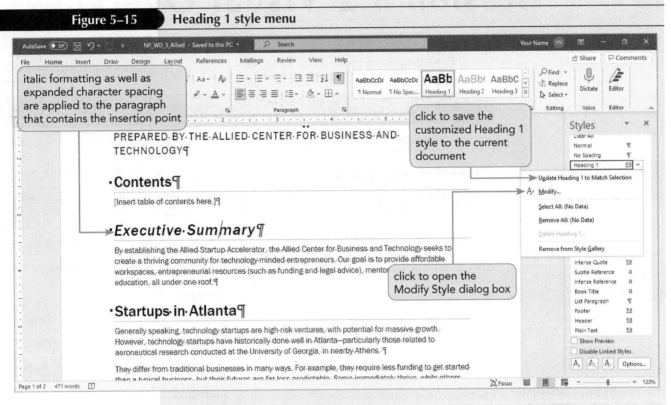

3. Click **Update Heading 1 to Match Selection**. The Heading 1 style is updated to reflect the changes you made to the "Executive Summary" heading. As a result, all the headings in the document formatted in the Heading 1 style now have italic formatting with expanded character spacing.

4. Save the document. The updated Heading 1 style is saved along with the document. No other documents are affected by this change to the Heading 1 style.

You can also use the Styles pane to create a new style for a document. You will do that in the next session.

## Review

### Session 5.1 Quick Check

1. What is a template?

2. Suppose you want to move through a document one graphic at a time. Should you use the Navigation pane or the Go To tab in the Find and Replace dialog box?

3. Explain how to change a document's theme fonts.

4. Explain how to select a new style set.

5. What template is applied to each new document by default?

6. What is the difference between a character style and a paragraph style?

# Session 5.2 Visual Overview:

Use the options in the Create New Style from Formatting dialog box to create a new style based on the formatting applied to selected text.

By default, each new style is based on the style originally applied to the selected text, but you can select a different style.

You should give your new style a descriptive name.

You can use these options to add additional formatting to the new style.

The new style will consist of all the formatting applied to the selected text, such as a green font color, bold, and italic formatting.

Clicking the Format button gives you access to more formatting options, including paragraph spacing and border options.

As when modifying an existing style, when creating a new style, it's usually best to save the style only to the current document.

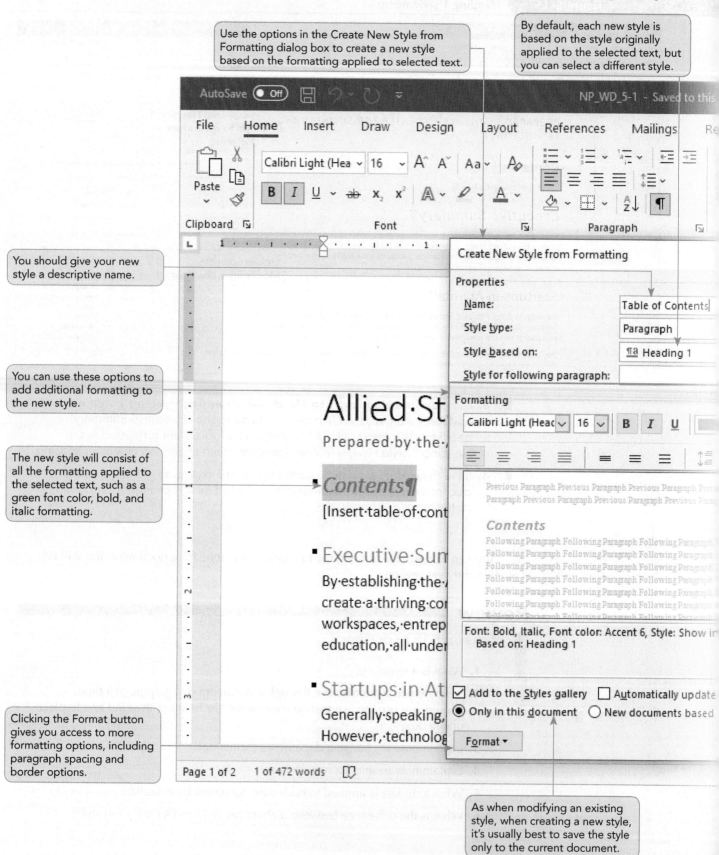

# Creating a New Style

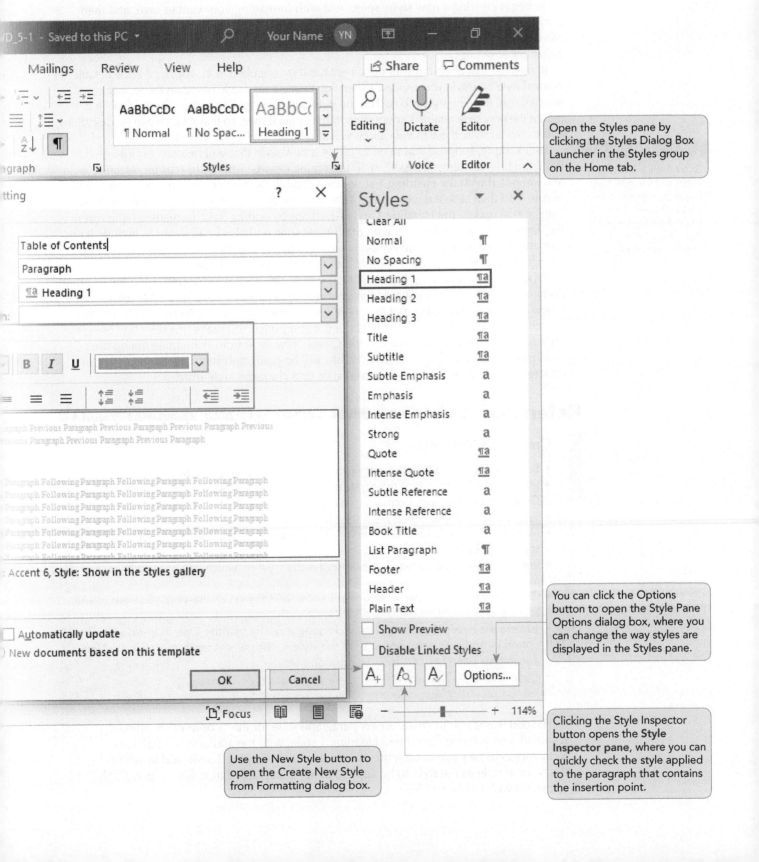

Open the Styles pane by clicking the Styles Dialog Box Launcher in the Styles group on the Home tab.

You can click the Options button to open the Style Pane Options dialog box, where you can change the way styles are displayed in the Styles pane.

Clicking the Style Inspector button opens the **Style Inspector pane**, where you can quickly check the style applied to the paragraph that contains the insertion point.

Use the New Style button to open the Create New Style from Formatting dialog box.

# Creating a New Style

Creating a new style is similar to updating a style, except that instead of updating an existing style to match the formatting of selected text, you save the text's formatting as a new style. By default, a new style is saved to the current document. You can choose to save a new style to the current template, but, as explained earlier, that is rarely advisable.

To begin creating a new style, select text with formatting you want to save, and then click the New Style button in the lower-left corner of the Styles pane. This opens the Create New Style from Formatting dialog box, where you can assign the new style a name and adjust other settings.

Remember that all text in your document has a style applied to it, whether it is the default Normal style or a style you applied. When you create a new style based on the formatting of selected text, the new style is based on the style originally applied to the selected text. That means the new style retains a connection to the original style, so that if you make modifications to the original style, these modifications will also be applied to the new style.

> **Tip**
>
> To break the link between a style and the style it is based on, click the Style based on arrow in the Create New Style from Formatting dialog box, and then click (no style).

For example, suppose you need to create a new style that will be used exclusively for formatting the heading "Budget" in all upcoming reports. You could start by selecting text formatted with the Heading 1 style, then change the font color of the selected text to purple, and then save the formatting of the selected text as a new style named "Budget." Later, if you update the Heading 1 style—perhaps by adding italic formatting—the text in the document that is formatted with the Budget style will also be updated to include italic formatting because it is based on the Heading 1 style. Note that the opposite is not true—changes to the new style do not affect the style on which it is based.

When creating a new style, you must also consider what will happen when the insertion point is in a paragraph formatted with your new style, and you then press ENTER to start a new paragraph. Typically, that new paragraph is formatted in the Normal style, but you can choose to have a different style applied if you prefer. You make this selection using the Style for following paragraph box in the Create New Style from Formatting dialog box.

In most cases, any new styles you create will be paragraph styles. However, you can choose to make your new style a linked style or a character style instead.

## Reference

### Creating a New Style

- Select the text with the formatting you want to save as a new style.
- In the lower-left corner of the Styles pane, click the New Style button to open the Create New Style from Formatting dialog box.
- Type a name for the new style in the Name box.
- Make sure the Style type box contains the correct style type. In most cases, Paragraph style is the best choice.
- Verify that the Style based on box displays the style on which you want to base your new style.
- Click the Style for following paragraph arrow, and then click the style you want to use. Normal is usually the best choice.
- To save the new style to the current document, verify that the Only in this document option button is selected; or to save the style to the current template, click the New documents based on this template option button.
- Click OK.

Hayden wants you to create a new paragraph style for the "Contents" heading. It should look just like the current Heading 1 style, with the addition of small caps formatting. He asks you to base the new style on the Heading 1 style and to select the Normal style as the style to be applied to any paragraph that follows a paragraph formatted with the new style.

## To format the "Contents" heading in small caps:

1. If you took a break after the last session, make sure the NP_WD_5_Allied .docx document is open in Print Layout view with the nonprinting characters and the ruler displayed. Confirm that the document Zoom level is set at 120% and that the Styles pane is docked on the right side of the document window.

2. Make sure the Home tab is selected on the ribbon.

3. In the document, select the **Contents** heading.

4. In the Font group, click the **Font Dialog Box Launcher**, and then, in the Font dialog box, click the **Font** tab, if necessary.

5. In the Effects section, click the **Small caps** check box to select it. See Figure 5–16.

**Figure 5–16**    Formatting the "Contents" heading

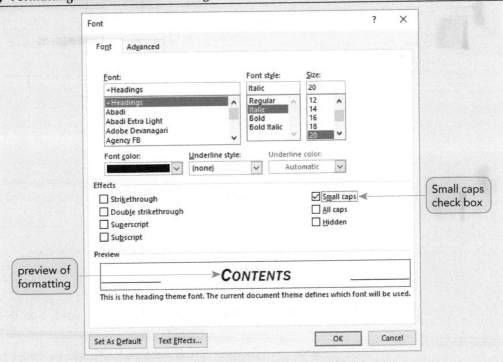

6. Click **OK**. The Font dialog box closes, and the "Contents" heading is formatted in small caps.

Now that the text is formatted the way you want, you can save its formatting as a new style.

## To save the formatting of the "Contents" heading as a new style:

1. Verify that the "Contents" heading is still selected.

2. In the lower-left corner of the Styles pane, click the **New Style** button A₊. The Create New Style from Formatting dialog box opens. A default name for the new style, "Style1," is selected in the Name box. The name "Style1" is also displayed in the Style for following paragraph box.

3. Type **Contents** to replace the default style name with the new one. The Style type box contains Paragraph by default, which is the type of style you want to create. The Style based on box indicates that the new Contents style is based on the Heading 1 style, which is also what you want. Notice that the Style for following paragraph box is now blank. You need to select the Normal style.

4. Click the **Style for following paragraph arrow**, and then click **Normal**. See Figure 5–17.

**Figure 5–17**    Creating a new style

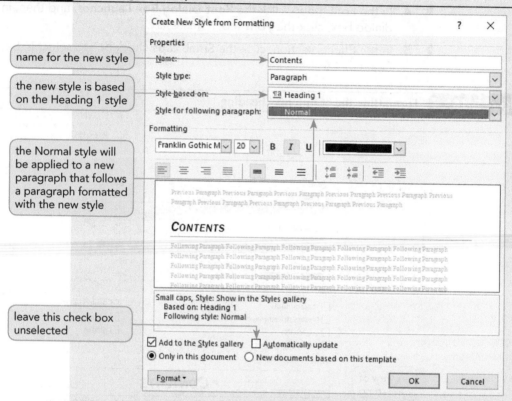

5. In the lower-left corner of the dialog box, verify that the Only in this document button is selected.

Note that, by default, the Automatically update check box is not selected. As a general rule, you should not select this check box because it can produce unpredictable results in future documents based on the same template.

If you plan to use a new style frequently, it's helpful to assign a keyboard shortcut to it. Then you can apply the style to selected text simply by pressing the keyboard shortcut.

**Tip**

To assign a keyboard shortcut to an existing style, right-click the style in the Styles pane, click Modify, click the Format button, and then click Shortcut key.

6. In the lower-left corner of the Create New Style from Formatting dialog box, click the **Format** button, and then click **Shortcut key** to open the Customize Keyboard dialog box. If you wanted to assign a keyboard shortcut to the Contents style, you would click in the Press new shortcut key box, press a combination of keys not assigned to any other function, and then click the Assign button. For now, you can close the Customize Keyboard dialog box without making any changes.

7. Click **Close**. You return to the Create New Style from Formatting dialog box.

8. Click **OK**. The Create New Style from Formatting dialog box closes. The new Contents style is added to the Style gallery and to the Styles pane. See Figure 5–18.

**Figure 5–18**    Contents style added to Style gallery and Styles pane

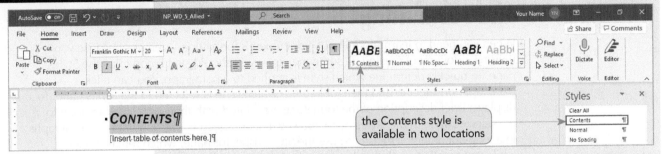

the Contents style is available in two locations

After you update a style or create a new one, you can create a custom style set that contains the new or updated style.

9. On the ribbon, click the **Design** tab.

10. In the Document Formatting group, click the **More** button ⬇, and then click **Save as a New Style Set**. The Save as a New Style Set dialog box opens, with the QuickStyles folder selected as the save location by default. Only style sets saved to the QuickStyles folder will appear in the Style Set gallery.

In this case, you don't actually want to create a new style set, so you can close the Save as a New Style Set dialog box.

11. Click **Cancel**, and then save the document.

# Insight

## Managing Your Styles

If you create a lot of styles, the Style gallery can quickly become overcrowded. To remove a style from the Style gallery without deleting the style itself, right-click the style in the Style gallery, and then click Remove from Style Gallery.

To delete a style entirely, open the Styles pane, and then right-click the style. What happens next depends on the type of style you are trying to delete. If the style was based on the Normal style, you can click Delete *Style* (where *Style* is the name of the style you want to delete), and then click Yes. If the style was based on any other style, you can click Revert to *Style* (where *Style* is the name of the style that the style you want to delete was based on), and then click Yes.

If you create a new style and then paste text formatted with your style in a different document, your new style will be displayed in that document's Style gallery and Styles pane. This means that a document containing text imported from multiple documents can end up with a lot of different styles. In that case, you'll probably reformat the document to use only a few styles of your choosing. But what do you do about the remaining, unused styles? You could delete them, but that can be time-consuming. It's sometimes easier to hide the styles that are not currently in use in the document. At the bottom of the Styles pane, click the Options button to open the Style Pane Options dialog box, click the Select styles to show arrow, and then click In current document.

The styles used in the report document are relatively simple. However, in a long document with many styles, it's easy to lose track of the style applied to each paragraph and the formatting associated with each style. In that case, it's important to know how to display additional information about the document's formatting.

# Displaying Information About Styles and Formatting

When you need to learn more about a document's formatting—perhaps because you're revising a document created by someone else—you should start by opening the Styles pane. To quickly determine which style is applied to a paragraph, you can click a paragraph (or select it) and then look to see which style is selected in the Styles pane. To display a brief description of the formatting associated with that style, you can point to the selected style in the Styles pane. However, if you need to check numerous paragraphs in a long document, it's easier to use the Style Inspector pane, which remains open while you scroll through the document and displays only the style for the paragraph that currently contains the insertion point. To see a complete list of all the formatting applied to a paragraph, you can use the **Reveal Formatting pane**. Within the Reveal Formatting pane, you can also choose to compare the formatting applied to two different paragraphs.

## Inspecting Styles

You can use the Style Inspector to examine the styles attached to each of the paragraphs in a document. When you are using the Style Inspector, it's also helpful to display the Home tab on the ribbon so the Style gallery is visible.

**To use the Style Inspector pane to examine the styles in the document:**

1. On the ribbon, click the **Home** tab.

2. On page 1, click anywhere in the **[Insert table of contents here.]** paragraph. The Normal style is selected in both the Style gallery and the Styles pane, indicating that the paragraph is formatted with the Normal style.

3. At the bottom of the Styles pane, click the **Style Inspector** button . The Style Inspector pane opens and is positioned next to the Styles pane. See Figure 5–19.

**Figure 5–19**    **Style Inspector pane**

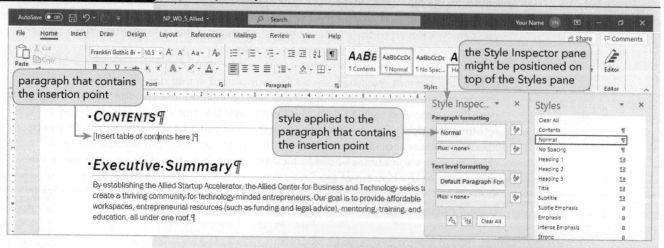

**Trouble?** If the Style Inspector pane on your computer is docked on the right side of the document window, drag it to position it to the left of the Styles pane.

In the Style Inspector pane, the top box under "Paragraph formatting" displays the name of the style applied to the paragraph that currently contains the insertion point.

▶ **4.** Press **CTRL+↓**. The insertion point moves down to the next paragraph, which contains the "Executive Summary" heading. The Style Inspector pane tells you that this paragraph is formatted with the Heading 1 style.

▶ **5.** Press **CTRL+↓** as necessary to move the insertion point down through the paragraphs of the document, observing the style names displayed in the Style Inspector pane as well as the styles selected in the Styles pane. Note that the bulleted paragraphs below the "Our Board of Directors" heading are formatted with the List Paragraph style. This style is applied automatically when you format paragraphs using the Bullets button in the Paragraph group on the Home tab.

▶ **6.** Scroll up, and select the paragraph **[Insert table of contents here.]**.

# Insight

### Finding Styles

Suppose you want to find all the paragraphs in a document formatted with a specific style. One option is to right-click the style in the Styles pane, and then click Select All *Number* Instances, where *Number* is the number of paragraphs in the document formatted with the style.

Another way to find paragraphs formatted with a particular style is by using the Find tab in the Find and Replace dialog box. If necessary, click the More button to display the Format button in the lower-left corner of the Find tab. Click the Format button, click Style, select the style you want in the Find Style dialog box, and then click OK. If you want to find specific text formatted with the style you selected, you can type the text in the Find what box on the Find tab, and then click Find Next to find the first instance. If, instead, you want to find any paragraph formatted with the style, leave the Find what box blank.

You can also use the Find and Replace dialog box to find paragraphs formatted with one style and then apply a different style to those paragraphs. On the Replace tab, click in the Find what box and use the Format button to select the style you want to find. Then, click in the Replace with box and use the Format button to select the style you want to use as a replacement. Click Find Next to find the first instance of the style, and then click Replace to apply the replacement style. As you've probably guessed, you can also type text in the Find what and Replace with boxes to find text formatted with a specific style and replace it with text formatted in a different style.

Next, Hayden wants you to use the Reveal Formatting panes to learn more about the formatting applied by the Normal and Heading 2 styles.

## Examining and Comparing Formatting in the Reveal Formatting Pane

You access the Reveal Formatting pane by clicking a button in the Style Inspector pane. Because the Reveal Formatting pane describes only formatting details without mentioning styles, it's helpful to keep the Style Inspector pane open while you use the Reveal Formatting pane.

### To examine formatting details using the Reveal Formatting pane:

1. At the bottom of the Style Inspector pane, click the **Reveal Formatting** button. The Reveal Formatting pane opens on top of the Styles pane, displaying detailed information about the formatting applied to the selected paragraph. It is positioned to the right of the Style Inspector pane and on top of the Styles pane in Figure 5–20, but on your computer it might be to the left of the Style Inspector pane.

| Figure 5–20 | Displaying formatting details in the Reveal Formatting pane |
|---|---|

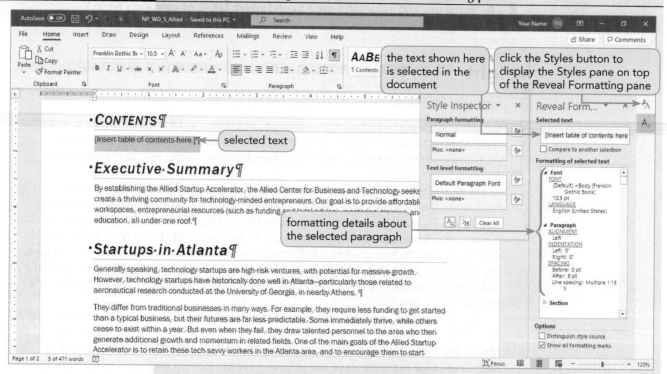

**Trouble?** If the Reveal Formatting pane on your computer is floating over the top of the document window, double-click the pane's title bar to dock the Reveal Formatting pane on top of the Styles pane.

The Formatting of selected text box displays information about the formatting applied to the paragraph that contains the insertion point. Note that this information includes no mention of the style used to apply this formatting, but you can still see the style's name, Normal, displayed in the Style Inspector pane.

Now that you have the Reveal Formatting pane open, you can use it to compare the formatting of one paragraph to another paragraph. Hayden asks you to compare text formatted with the Normal style to text formatted with the Heading 2 style.

## To compare the formatting of one paragraph to another:

1. In the Reveal Formatting pane, click the **Compare to another selection** check box to select it. The options in the Reveal Formatting pane change to allow you to compare the formatting of one paragraph to that of another. Under Selected text, both text boxes display the selected text, "[Insert table of contents here.]" This tells you that, currently, the formatting applied to the selected text is being compared to itself.

   Now you'll compare this paragraph to one formatted with the Heading 2 style.

2. In the document, scroll down to page 2 and select the heading text **Saturn and Sun Investments**, which is formatted with the Heading 2 style. The text "Saturn and Sun Investments" is displayed in the Reveal Formatting pane, in the text box below "[Insert table of contents here.]" The Formatting differences section displays information about the formatting applied to the two different paragraphs. See Figure 5–21.

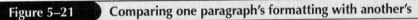

| Figure 5–21 | Comparing one paragraph's formatting with another's |
| --- | --- |

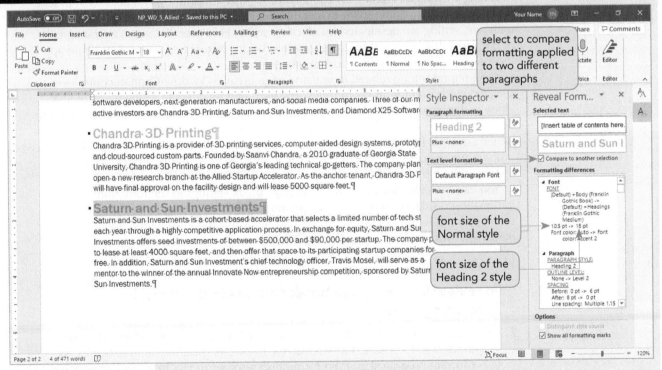

**Tip**

Text formatted in a white font is not visible in the text boxes at the top of the Reveal Formatting pane. To use the Reveal Formatting pane with white text, temporarily format it in black.

The information in the Reveal Formatting pane is very detailed. But, generally, if you see two settings separated by a hyphen and a greater than symbol, the item on the right relates to the text in the bottom box. For example, in the Font section, you see "10.5 pt -> 18 pt." This tells you that the text in the top text box, "[Insert table of contents here.]," is formatted in a 10.5-point font, whereas the text in the bottom text box, "Saturn and Sun Investments," is formatted in an 18-point font.

The Paragraph section of the Reveal Formatting pane provides some information about two important default settings included with all heading styles in Word—line and page break settings.

## Reviewing Line and Page Break Settings

By default, all the heading styles in Word are set up to ensure that a heading is never separated from the paragraph that follows it. For example, suppose you have a one-page document that includes a heading with a single paragraph of body text after it. Then suppose you add text before the heading that causes the heading and its paragraph of body text to flow down the page so that, ultimately, the entire paragraph of body text moves to page 2. Even if there is room for the heading at the bottom of page 1, it will move to page 2, along with its paragraph of body text. The setting that controls this is the **Keep with next** check box on the Line and Page Breaks tab in the Paragraph dialog box. By default, the Keep with next check box is selected for all headings.

A related setting on the same tab is the **Keep lines together** check box, which is also selected by default for all headings. This setting ensures that if a paragraph consists of more than one line of text, the lines of the paragraph will never be separated by a page break. This means that if one line of a paragraph moves from page 1 to page 2, all lines of the paragraph will move to page 2.

A nonprinting character in the shape of a small black square is displayed next to any paragraph for which either the Keep lines together setting or the Keep with next setting is selected. Because both settings are selected by default for all the heading styles (Heading 1 through Heading 9), you always see this nonprinting character next to text formatted with a heading style. By default, the Keep lines together setting and the Keep with next setting are deselected for all other styles. However, if you have a paragraph of body text that you want to prevent from breaking across two pages, you could apply the Keep lines together setting to that paragraph.

One helpful setting related to line and page breaks—Widow/Orphan control—is selected by default for all Word styles. The term **widow** refers to a single line of text alone at the top of a page. The term **orphan** refers to a single line of text at the bottom of a page. When selected, the **Widow/Orphan control** check box, which is also found on the Line and Page Breaks tab of the Paragraph dialog box, ensures that widows and orphans never occur in a document. Instead, at least two lines of a paragraph will appear at the top or bottom of a page.

You can see evidence of the line and page break settings in the formatting information displayed in the Reveal Formatting pane. Hayden asks you to check these settings for the report document. You'll start by displaying information about only the paragraph formatted with the Heading 2 style.

### To review line and page break settings in the Reveal Formatting pane:

1. In the Reveal Formatting pane, click the **Compare to another selection** check box to deselect it. The Reveal Formatting pane changes to display information only about the formatting applied to the text "Saturn and Sun Investments," which is currently selected in the document.

   The Style Inspector pane tells you that "Saturn and Sun Investments" is formatted with the Heading 2 style, so all the information in the Reveal Formatting pane describes the Heading 2 style.

2. In the Formatting of selected text box, scroll down to display the entire Paragraph section.

3. Review the information below the blue heading "LINE AND PAGE BREAKS." The text "Keep with next" and "Keep lines together" tells you that these two settings are active for the selected text. The blue headings in the Reveal Formatting pane are actually links that open a dialog box with the relevant formatting settings.

4. In the Formatting of selected text box, click **LINE AND PAGE BREAKS**. The Paragraph dialog box opens, with the Line and Page Breaks tab displayed. See Figure 5–22.

**Figure 5–22**    **Line and Page Breaks tab in the Paragraph dialog box**

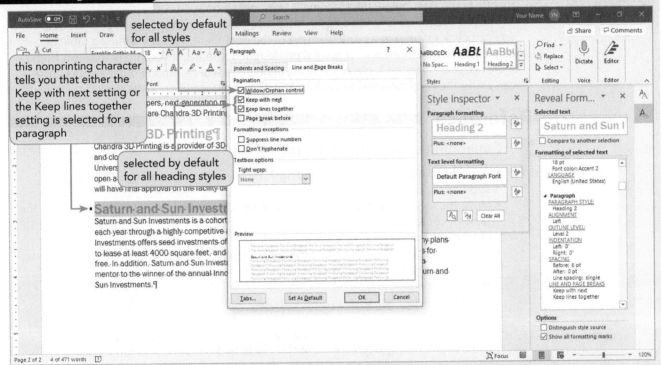

The settings on the tab are the settings for the selected paragraph, which is formatted with the Heading 2 style. The Widow/Orphan control, Keep with next, and Keep lines together check boxes are all selected, as you would expect for a heading style.

You are finished reviewing formatting information, so you can close the Paragraph dialog box and the Reveal Formatting pane.

5. In the Paragraph dialog box, click **Cancel**; and then, in the Reveal Formatting pane, click the **Close** button ☒.

6. In the Style Inspector pane, click the **Close** button ☒; and then, in the Styles pane, click the **Close** button ☒.

7. Click anywhere in the document to deselect the "Saturn and Sun Investments" heading.

You are almost finished working on Hayden's report. Your next task is to add a table of contents.

# Generating a Table of Contents

**Tip**

To delete a table of contents, click the Table of Contents button, and then click Remove Table of Contents.

You can use the Table of Contents button in the Table of Contents group on the References tab to generate a table of contents that includes any text to which you have applied heading styles. A **table of contents** is essentially an outline of the document. By default, in a table of contents, Heading 1 text is aligned on the left, Heading 2 text is indented slightly to the right below the Heading 1 text, Heading 3 text is indented slightly to the right below the Heading 2 text, and so on.

The page numbers and headings in a table of contents in Word are hyperlinks that you can click to jump to a particular part of the document. When inserting a table of contents, you can insert one of several predesigned formats. If you prefer to select from more options, open the Table of Contents dialog box where, among other settings, you can adjust the level assigned to each style within the table of contents.

## Reference

### Generating a Table of Contents

- Apply heading styles, such as Heading 1, Heading 2, and Heading 3, to the appropriate text in the document.
- Move the insertion point to the location in the document where you want to insert the table of contents.
- On the ribbon, click the References tab.
- In the Table of Contents group, click the Table of Contents button.
- To insert a predesigned table of contents, click one of the Built-In styles in the Table of Contents menu.
- To open a dialog box where you can choose from a variety of table of contents settings, click Custom Table of Contents to open the Table of Contents dialog box. Click the Formats arrow and select a style, change the Show levels setting to the number of heading levels you want to include in the table of contents, verify that the Show page numbers check box is selected, and then click OK.

The current draft of Hayden's report is fairly short, but the final document will be much longer. He asks you to create a table of contents for the report now, just after the "Contents" heading. Then, as Hayden adds sections to the report, he can update the table of contents.

**To insert a table of contents into the document:**

1. Scroll up to display the "Contents" heading on page 1.

2. Below the heading, delete the placeholder text **[Insert table of contents here.]**. Do not delete the paragraph mark after the placeholder text. Your insertion point should now be located in the blank paragraph between the "Contents" heading and the "Executive Summary" heading.

3. On the ribbon, click the **References** tab.

4. In the Table of Contents group, click the **Table of Contents** button. The Table of Contents menu opens, displaying a gallery of table of contents formats. See Figure 5–23.

Figure 5–23    Table of Contents menu

options for generating a table of contents made up of the document headings

option for generating a table of contents with placeholder text

click to open a dialog box where you can adjust the table of contents settings

The Automatic Table 1 and Automatic Table 2 options each insert a table of contents made up of the first three levels of document headings in a predefined format. Each of the Automatic options also includes a heading for the table of contents. Because Hayden's document already contains the heading "Contents," you do not want to use either of these options.

The Manual option is useful only in specialized situations, when you need to type the table of contents yourself—for example, when creating a book manuscript for an academic publisher that requires a specialized format.

You'll use the Custom Table of Contents command to open the Table of Contents dialog box.

5. Below the Table of Contents gallery, click **Custom Table of Contents**.

The Table of Contents dialog box opens, with the Table of Contents tab displayed. See Figure 5–24.

Figure 5–24    Table of Contents dialog box

text formatted with the Contents style is included in the table of contents

table of contents format will come from the document's template

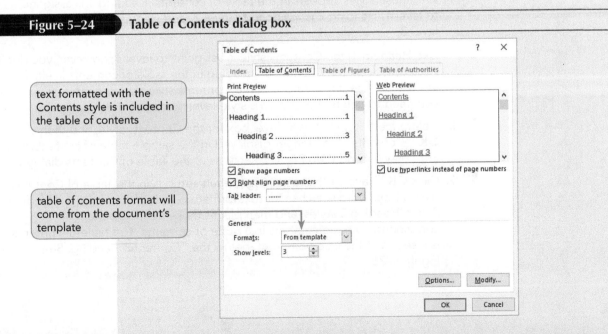

The Print Preview box on the left shows the appearance of the table of contents in Print Layout view, while the Web Preview box on the right shows what the table of contents would look like if you displayed it in Web Layout view. The Formats box shows the default option, From template, which applies the table of contents styles provided by the document's template.

In the Print Preview section, notice that the Contents heading style, which you created in Session 5.1, appears in the table of contents at the same level as the Heading 1 style.

6. In the lower-right corner of the Table of Contents dialog box, click the **Options** button. The Table of Contents Options dialog box opens. The Styles check box is selected, indicating that Word will compile the table of contents based on the styles applied to the document headings.

7. In the TOC level list, review the priority level assigned to the document's styles, using the vertical scroll bar, if necessary. See Figure 5–25.

**Figure 5–25** | **Checking the styles used in the table of contents**

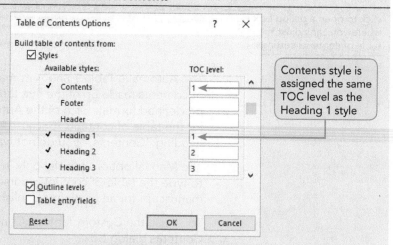

If the box next to a style name is blank, then text formatted with that style does not appear in the table of contents. The numbers next to the Contents, Heading 1, Heading 2, and Heading 3 styles tell you that any text formatted with these styles appears in the table of contents. Heading 1 is assigned to level 1, Heading 2 is assigned to level 2, and Heading 3 is assigned to level 3.

Like Heading 1, the Contents style is assigned to level 1; however, you don't want to include the "Contents" heading in the table of contents itself. To remove any text formatted with the Contents style from the table of contents, you need to delete the Contents style level number.

8. Delete the **1** from the TOC level box for the Contents style, and then click **OK**. "Contents" is no longer displayed in the sample table of contents in the Print Preview and Web Preview sections of the Table of Contents dialog box.

9. Click **OK** to accept the remaining default settings in the Table of Contents dialog box. Word searches for text formatted with the Heading 1, Heading 2, and Heading 3 styles, and then places those headings and their corresponding page numbers in a table of contents. The table of contents is inserted at the insertion point, below the "Contents" heading. See Figure 5–26.

**Figure 5–26** Table of contents inserted into document

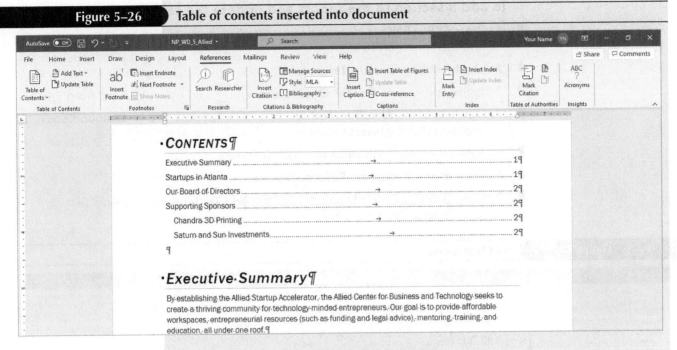

The text in the table of contents is formatted with the TOC styles for the current template. Depending on how your computer is set up, the table of contents might appear on a light gray background.

You can check the hyperlink formatting to make sure the headings really do function as links.

▶ 10. Press and hold **CTRL** while you click **Saturn and Sun Investments** in the table of contents. The insertion point moves to the beginning of the "Saturn and Sun Investments" heading near the bottom of page 2.

▶ 11. Save the document.

# Updating a Table of Contents

If you add or delete a heading in the document or add body text that causes one or more headings to move to a new page, you can quickly update the table of contents by clicking the Update Table button in the Table of Contents group on the References tab. To add text that is not formatted as a heading to the table of contents, you can select the text, format it as a heading, and then update the table of contents. However, if you already have the References tab displayed, it's more efficient to select the text in the document, use the Add Text button in the Table of Contents group to add a Heading style to the selected text, and then update the table of contents.

Hayden has information on a third participating organization saved as a separate Word file, which he asks you to insert at the end of the document. You will do this next and then add the new heading to the table of contents.

## To add a section to the report and update the table of contents:

1. Press **CTRL+END** to move the insertion point to the end of the document, and then press **ENTER**.

2. On the ribbon, click the **Insert** tab.

3. In the Text group, click the **Object arrow** ⬚▾, and then click **Text from File**.

4. Navigate to the **Word5 > Module** folder, click **Support_WD_5_Diamond.docx**, and then click the **Insert** button.

5. Select the paragraph **Diamond X25 Software**.

6. On the ribbon, click the **References** tab.

7. In the Table of Contents group, click the **Add Text** button. The Add Text menu opens. See Figure 5–27.

**Figure 5–27**   Add Text menu

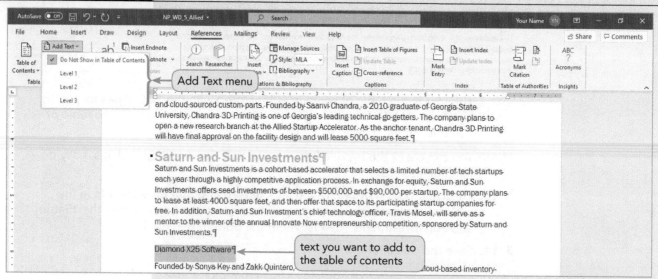

8. Click **Level 2**. The text is formatted with the Heading 2 style to match the headings for the sections about the other participating organizations. Now that the text is formatted with a heading style, you can update the table of contents.

9. Scroll up so you can see the table of contents, and then, in the Table of Contents group, click the **Update Table** button. The Update Table of Contents dialog box opens.

   You can use the Update page numbers only option button if you don't want to update the headings in the table of contents. This option is useful if you add additional content that causes existing headings to move from one page to another. In this case, you want to update the entire table of contents.

10. Click the **Update entire table** option button to select it, and then click **OK**. The table of contents is updated to include the "Diamond X25 Software" heading. See Figure 5–28.

Figure 5–28     **Updated table of contents**

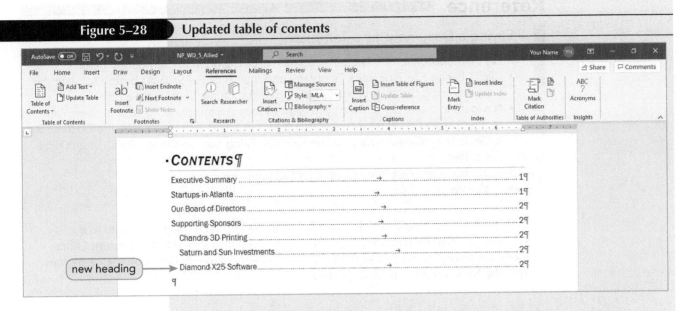

- **11.** In the document, scroll down below the "Our Board of Directors" heading on page 2, and replace "Cordelia May" with your first and last names.

- **12.** Press **CTRL+END** to move the insertion point to the last paragraph in the document, which is blank, and then press **DEL** to delete the blank paragraph.

- **13.** sam↑ Save the document.

Now that you are finished working on Hayden's report, he asks you to use the document to create a template that can be used for all reports issued by the Allied Center for Business and Technology.

# Saving a Document as a Template

If you frequently need to create a particular type of document, it's a good idea to create your own template for that type of document. Organizations often use templates to ensure that all employees use the same basic format for essential documents. When creating a template, you can save it to any folder on your computer. After you save it, you can open the template to revise it just as you would open any other document. You can also use the Save As option in Backstage view to create a new document based on the template, in which case Word Document will be selected as the file type in the Save As dialog box. If you want to be able to open a new document based on the template from the New screen, you need to save your template to the Custom Office Templates folder that is installed with Word.

# Reference

## Saving a Document as a Template

- On the ribbon, click the File tab, and then click Export in the navigation pane.
- Click Change File Type, click Template, and then click the Save As button to open the Save As dialog box with Word Template selected in the Save as type box.
- Navigate to the folder in which you want to save the template. To save the template to the Custom Office Templates folder that is installed with Word, click the Documents folder in the navigation pane of the Save As dialog box, and then click Custom Office Templates.
- In the File name box, type a name for the template.
- Click Save.

You will save the new Allied Center for Business and Technology template in the location specified by your instructor; however, you'll also save it to the Custom Office Templates folder so you can practice opening a new document based on your template from the New screen in Backstage view.

## To save the document as a new template:

1. Save the document to ensure that you have saved your most recent work.

**Tip**

You can also click the File tab, click Save As, and then select Word Template as the file type.

2. On the ribbon, click the **File** tab, and then click **Export** in the navigation pane.

3. Click **Change File Type**. The Export screen displays options for various file types you can use when saving a file. For example, you could save a Word document as a Plain Text file that contains only text, without any formatting or graphics. See Figure 5–29.

**Figure 5–29**    **Export screen with Change File Type options in Backstage view**

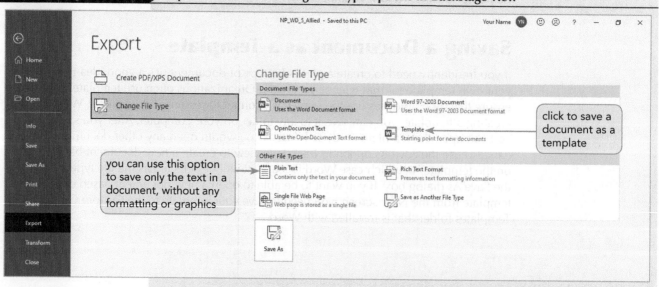

4. Under Change File Type, click **Template**, and then click the **Save As** button. The Save As dialog box opens with Word Template selected in the Save as type box.

5. If necessary, navigate to the location specified by your instructor. Next, you'll replace the selected, default file name with a new one.

6. In the File name box, type **NP_WD_5_Template**. See Figure 5–30.

| Figure 5–30 | Saving a document as a template |

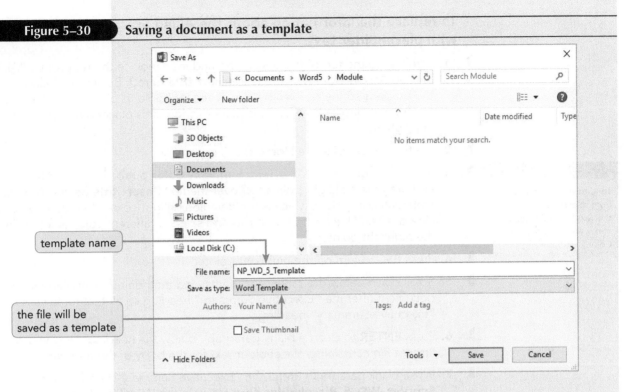

7. Click **Save**. The Save As dialog box closes, and the document, which is now a template with the .dotx file extension, remains open.

## Proskills

### Written Communication: Standardizing the Look of Your Documents

Large companies often ask their employees to use a predesigned template for all corporate documents. If you work for an organization that does not require you to use a specific template, consider using one anyway in order to create a standard look for all of your documents. A consistent appearance is especially important if you are responsible for written communication for an entire department because it ensures that colleagues and clients will immediately recognize documents from your department.

Be sure to use a professional-looking template. If you decide to create your own, use document styles that make text easy to read, with colors that are considered appropriate in your workplace. Don't try to dazzle your readers with design elements. In nearly all professional settings, a simple look is ideal.

To make the new template really useful to Hayden's colleagues, you need to delete the specific information related to the Allied Startup Accelerator and replace it with placeholder text explaining the type of information required in each section. In the following steps, you will delete the body of the report and replace it with some placeholder text. Hayden wants to use the current subtitle, "Prepared by the Allied Center for Business and Technology," as the subtitle in all reports, so there's no need to change it. However, the title will vary from one report to the next, so you need to replace it with a suitable placeholder. You'll retain the table of contents. When Hayden's colleagues use the template to create future reports, they can update the table of contents to include any headings they add to their new documents.

### To replace the information about the Allied Startup Accelerator with placeholder text:

1. Scroll up to the top of the document, and then replace the report title "Allied Startup Accelerator" with the text **[Insert title here.]**. Be sure to include the brackets so the text will be readily recognizable as placeholder text. To ensure that Hayden's colleagues don't overlook this placeholder, you can also highlight it.

2. On the ribbon, click the **Home** tab, if necessary.

3. In the Font group, click the **Text Highlight Color** button, and then click and drag the highlight pointer over the text **[Insert title here.]**. The text is highlighted in yellow, which is the default highlight color. Note that you could click the Text Highlight Color arrow and select a different color before using the highlight pointer.

4. Press **ESC** to turn off the highlight pointer.

5. Scroll down below the table of contents, and then delete everything in the document after the "Executive Summary" heading so all that remains is the "Executive Summary" heading.

6. Press **ENTER** to insert a blank paragraph below the heading. Now you can insert a file containing placeholder text for the body of the template.

7. In the blank paragraph under the "Executive Summary" heading, insert the **Support_WD_5_Placeholder.docx** file from the Word5 > Module folder included with your Data Files. See Figure 5–31.

**Figure 5–31** **Template with placeholder text**

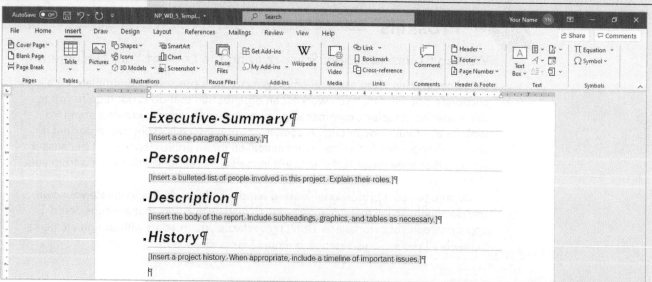

Scroll up to review the document, and notice that the inserted placeholder text is highlighted and the headings are all correctly formatted with the Heading 1 style. When Hayden created the Placeholder document, he formatted the text in the default Heading 1 style provided by the Office theme. But when you inserted the file into the template, Word automatically applied your updated Heading 1 style. Now you can update the table of contents.

8. On the ribbon, click the **References** tab.

▶ **9.** In the Table of Contents group, click the **Update Table** button. The table of contents is updated to include the new headings.

▶ **10.** On the Quick Access Toolbar, click the **Save** button 🖫 to save your changes to the template just as you would save a document.

At this point, you have a copy of the template stored in the location specified by your instructor. If you closed the template, clicked the File tab, and then opened the template again from the same folder, you would be opening the template itself and not a new document based on the template. If you want to be able to open a new document based on the template from the New screen, you have to save the template to the Custom Office Templates folder. You'll do that next. You can also open a new document based on a template by double-clicking the template file from within File Explorer. You'll have a chance to try that in the Case Problems at the end of this module.

**To save the template to the Custom Office Templates folder:**

▶ **1.** On the ribbon, click the **File** tab, and then click **Save As** in the navigation pane.

▶ **2.** Click **This PC** if necessary, and then click the **Browse** button to open the Save As dialog box.

▶ **3.** In the navigation pane of the Save As dialog box, click the **Documents** folder, and then, in the folder list on the right, double-click **Custom Office Templates**. See Figure 5–32.

**Figure 5–32**     Saving a template in the Custom Office Templates folder

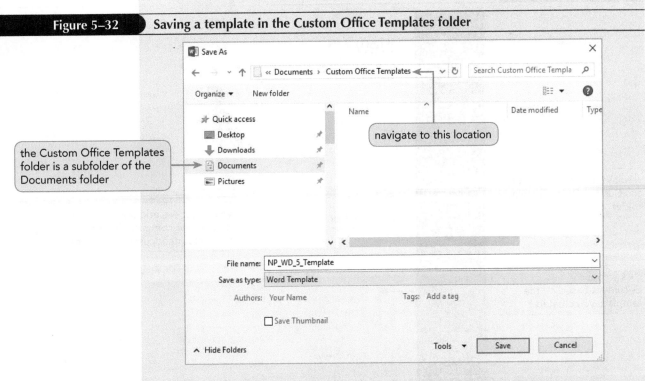

▶ **4.** Click the **Save** button to save the template to the Custom Office Templates folder and close the Save As dialog box.

▶ **5.** On the ribbon, click the **File** tab, and then click **Close** in the navigation pane to close the template, just as you would close a document.

The template you just created will simplify the process of creating new reports in Hayden's department.

# Opening a New Document Based on Your Template

Documents created using a template contain all the text and formatting included in the template. Changes you make to this new document will not affect the template file, which remains unchanged in the Custom Office Templates folder.

Hayden would like you to use the new template to begin a report on the Allied Center for Business and Technology's annual event promoting the importance of soft skills in technology fields.

**To open a new document based on the template you created:**

▶ **1.** On the ribbon, click the **File** tab, and then click **New** in the navigation pane.

▶ **2.** Note that the New screen in Backstage view includes two links—Office and Personal. The Office link is selected by default, indicating that the templates currently featured by Office.com are displayed. To open the template you just saved to the Custom Office Templates folder, you need to display the personal templates instead.

▶ **3.** Click **Personal**. The NP_WD_5_Template template is displayed as an option on the New screen. See Figure 5–33.

| Figure 5–33 | Opening a document based on the template you created |
| --- | --- |

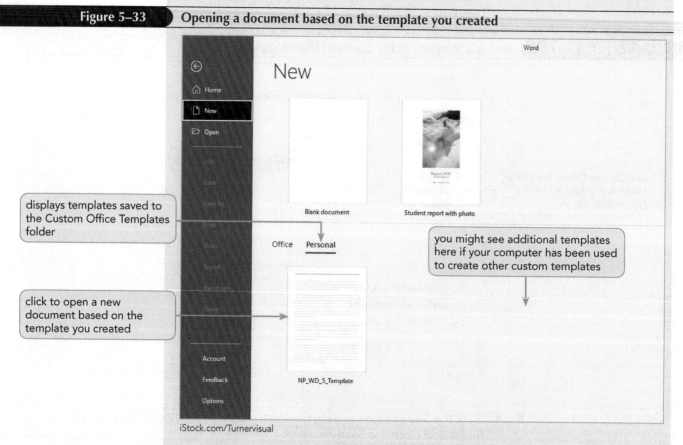

displays templates saved to the Custom Office Templates folder

you might see additional templates here if your computer has been used to create other custom templates

click to open a new document based on the template you created

iStock.com/Turnervisual

▶ **4.** Click **NP_WD_5_Template**. A new document opens, containing the text and formatting from the NP_WD_5_Template.dotx template.

▶ **5.** Delete the placeholder **[Insert title here.]** and type **Soft Skills Academy** in its place. If necessary, remove the yellow highlighting.

Hayden and his colleagues will add new material to this report later. For now, you can close it.

▶ **6.** Save the document as **NP_WD_5_SoftSkills** in the location specified by your instructor, and then close the document.

Next, to ensure that you can repeat the steps in this module if you choose to, you will delete the NP_WD_5_Template.dotx file from the Custom Office Templates folder. You can delete it from within the Open dialog box.

▶ **7.** On the ribbon, click the **File** tab, and then click **Open** in the navigation pane.

▶ **8.** Click the **Browse** button.

▶ **9.** In the navigation pane of the Open dialog box, click the **Documents** folder, and then double-click **Custom Office Templates**. The NP_WD_5_Template .dotx template is displayed in the file list.

▶ **10.** Right-click **NP_WD_5_Template.dotx** to display a shortcut menu, click **Delete**, and then click **Yes**.

The template file is removed from the file list.

▶ **11.** Click **Cancel** to close the Open dialog box, and then close Backstage view.

Creating a template makes it easy to create a series of similar documents. But what if you want to insert specific text such as an address or email address or a graphic such as a logo in many different documents? In that case, you can save the item as a Quick Part.

# Creating a New Quick Part

A **Quick Part** is reusable content that you create and that you can then insert into any document later with a single click in the Quick Parts gallery. For example, you might create a letterhead with your company's address and logo. To save the letterhead as a Quick Part, you select it and then save it to the Quick Parts gallery. Later, you can insert the letterhead into a document by clicking it in the Quick Parts gallery.

By default, a new Quick Part appears as an option in the Quick Parts gallery. However, you can assign a Quick Part to any gallery you want. For example, you could assign a text box Quick Part to the Text Box gallery so that every time you click the Text Box button on the Insert tab, you see your text box as one of the options in the Text Box gallery.

Quick Parts are just one type of a larger category of reusable content known as **building blocks**. All of the ready-made items that you can insert into a document via a gallery are considered building blocks. For example, preformatted headers, preformatted text boxes, and cover pages are all examples of building blocks. Some reference sources use the terms "building block" and "Quick Part" as if they were synonyms, but in fact a Quick Part is a building block that you create.

When you save a Quick Part, you always save it to a template; you can't save a Quick Part to an individual document. Which template you save it to depends on what you want to do with the Quick Part. If you want the template to be available to all new documents created on your computer, you should save it to the Building Blocks template. The **Building Blocks template** is a special template that contains all the building blocks installed with Word on your computer, as well as any Quick Parts you save to it. If you want to restrict the Quick Part to only documents based on the current template, or if you want to be able to share the Quick Part with someone else, you should save it to the current template. To share the Quick Part, you distribute the template to anyone who wants to use the Quick Part.

# Reference

### Creating and Using Quick Parts

- Select the text, text box, header, footer, table, graphic, or other item you want to save as a Quick Part.
- On the ribbon, click the Insert tab.
- In the Text group, click the Explore Quick Parts button, and then click Save Selection to Quick Part Gallery.
- In the Create New Building Block dialog box, replace the text in the Name box with a descriptive name for the Quick Part.
- Click the Gallery arrow, and then choose the gallery to which you want to save the Quick Part.
- To make the Quick Part available to all documents on your computer, select Building Blocks in the Save in box. To restrict the Quick Part to the current template, select the name of the template on which the current document is based.
- Click OK.

Hayden has created a text box containing the address and phone number for the Allied Center for Business and Technology. He asks you to show him how to save the text box as a Quick Part. He wants the Quick Part to be available to all new documents created on his computer, so you'll need to save it to the Building Blocks template.

### To save a text box as a Quick Part:

1. Open the document **NP_WD_5-2.docx** from the Word5 > Module folder, and then save it as **NP_WD_5_Address** in the location specified by your instructor.

2. Display nonprinting characters and the rulers, switch to Print Layout view, and then change the Zoom level to **120%**, if necessary.

3. Click the **text box** to select it, taking care to select the entire text box and not the text inside it. When the text box is selected, you'll see the anchor symbol in the left margin.

4. On the ribbon, click the **Insert** tab.

5. In the Text group, click the **Explore Quick Parts** button ▤ ▾. If any Quick Parts have been created on your computer, they will be displayed in the gallery at the top of the menu. Otherwise, you will see only the menu shown in Figure 5–34.

**Figure 5–34**    **Quick Parts menu, with no Quick Parts visible**

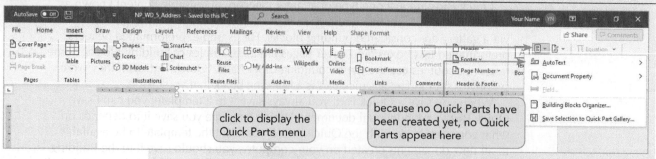

6. At the bottom of the menu, click **Save Selection to Quick Part Gallery**. The Create New Building Block dialog box opens. The name of this dialog box is appropriate because a Quick Part is a type of building block. See Figure 5–35.

**Figure 5-35**   Create New Building Block dialog box

the first two words in the text box are used as the name of the new building block by default

the new building block will be saved in the Quick Part gallery by default

Create New Building Block   ?   ×

Name:   Allied Center
Gallery:   Quick Parts
Category:   General
Description:
Save in:   Building Blocks
Options:   Insert content only

OK   Cancel

the new building block will be saved to the Building Blocks template by default

By default, the first two words in the text box, "Allied Center," are used as the default name for the new building block. You could type a new name, but Hayden is happy with the default. Also, the default setting in the Gallery box tells you that the new building block will be saved in the Quick Parts gallery. You could change this by selecting a different gallery name. The Save in box indicates that the Quick Part will be saved to the Building Blocks template, which means it will be available to all documents on your computer.

Hayden asks you to accept the default settings.

7. Click **OK** to accept your changes and close the Create New Building Block dialog box.

You've finished creating the new Quick Part. Now you can try inserting it in the current document.

### To insert the new Quick Part into the current document:

1. Press **CTRL+END** to move the insertion point to the end of the document.

2. In the Text group, click the **Explore Quick Parts** button. This time, the Quick Parts gallery is displayed at the top of the menu. See Figure 5-36.

**Figure 5-36**   New Quick Part in the Quick Parts gallery

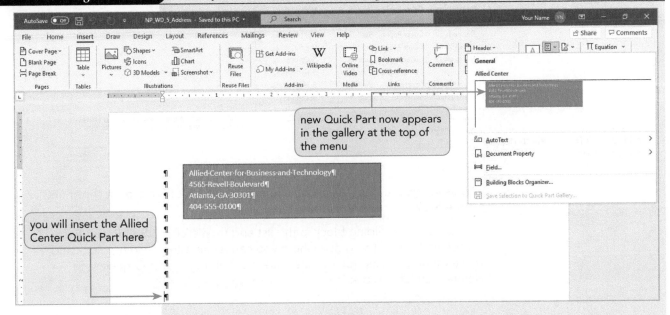

new Quick Part now appears in the gallery at the top of the menu

you will insert the Allied Center Quick Part here

Allied·Center·for·Business·and·Technology¶
4565·Revell·Boulevard¶
Atlanta,·GA·30301¶
404·555·0100¶

3. Click the **Allied Center** Quick Part. A copy of the orange text box is inserted at the end of the document, at the insertion point.

4. In the newly inserted text box, replace the phone number with your first and last names, and then save the document.

The new Quick Part is stored in the Quick Parts gallery, ready to be inserted into any document. However, after reviewing the Quick Part, Hayden has decided he wants to reformat the address text box and save it as a new Quick Part later. So you'll delete the Quick Part you just created.

**Tip**

To open the Building Blocks Organizer with a particular Quick Part selected, right-click the Quick Part in the Quick Parts gallery, and then click Organize and Delete.

### To delete a Quick Part:

1. In the Text group, click the **Explore Quick Parts** button and then click **Building Blocks Organizer** to open the Building Blocks Organizer dialog box. Here you see a list of all the building blocks, including Quick Parts, available in your copy of Word. See Figure 5–37.

| Figure 5–37 | Building Blocks Organizer dialog box |

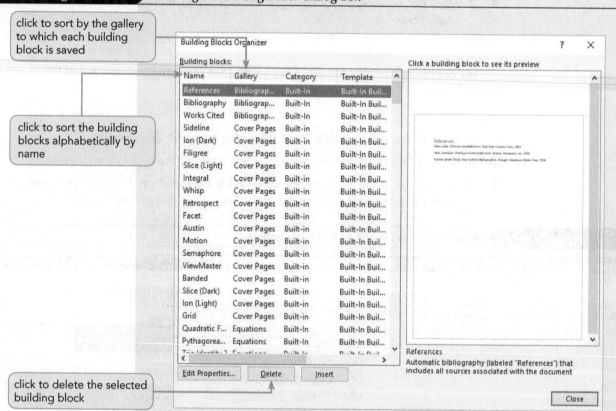

click to sort by the gallery to which each building block is saved

click to sort the building blocks alphabetically by name

click to delete the selected building block

The list on your computer will be somewhat different from the list shown in Figure 5–37.

You can click a building block in the list and then click the Edit Properties button to open a dialog box where you can rename the building block and make other changes. You can also use the Building Blocks Organizer to delete a building block.

▶ 2. Click the **Name** column header to sort the building blocks alphabetically by name, scroll down and click **Allied Center**, click the **Delete** button, and then click **Yes** in the warning dialog box. The Allied Center Quick Part is deleted from the list in the Building Blocks Organizer.

▶ 3. Click **Close**.

▶ 4. In the Text group, click the **Explore Quick Parts** button 📄▾, and verify that the Allied Center Quick Part is no longer displayed in the Quick Parts gallery.

Finally, to completely delete the Quick Part from the Building Blocks template, you need to save the current document. In the process of saving the document, Word will save your changes to the Building Blocks template, which controls all the building blocks available in your copy of Word. If you don't save the document now, you'll see a warning dialog box later, when you attempt to close the document. It's easy to get confused by the wording of this warning dialog box, and you might end up restoring your Quick Part rather than deleting it.

To avoid seeing this warning dialog box entirely, remember to save the current document after you delete a Quick Part.

▶ 5. Save the **NP_WD_5_Address.docx** document, and then close it.

Hayden is happy to know how to save Quick Parts to the Building Blocks template. He'll create a new Quick Part later and save it to a custom template so that he can make it available to everyone at the Allied Center for Business and Technology.

# Review

## Session 5.2 Quick Check

1. By default, is a new style saved to the current document or to the current template?

2. Explain how to create a new style.

3. What pane displays a complete list of the formatting applied to the paragraph that currently contains the insertion point?

4. Which setting on the Line and Page Breaks tab of the Paragraph dialog box ensures that if a paragraph consists of more than one line of text, the lines of the paragraph will never be separated by a page break?

5. What must you do to your document before you can create a table of contents for it?

6. Where should you save a custom template if you want to be able to access it from the New screen in Backstage view?

7. Define "building block" and give some examples.

# Practice

## Review Assignments

**Data Files needed for the Review Assignments: NP_WD_5-3.docx, NP_WD_5-4.docx, Support_WD_5_Headings.docx, Support_WD_5_Writers.docx**

Hayden's template is now used for all reports created by employees of the Allied Center for Business and Technology. Inspired by Hayden's success with the template, a project manager for the Allied Startup Accelerator Planning Commission, Malisa Kunchai, wants you to help with a report on construction plans for the new facility. After you format the report, she'd like you to save the document as a new template and then create a Quick Part. Complete the following steps:

1. Create a new document based on the Business report (Professional design) template from Office.com. (If you can't find that template, choose another.) Replace the title placeholder in the document with your name, and then save the document as **NP_WD_5_DocumentFromTemplate** in the location specified by your instructor. If you see a dialog box explaining that the document is being upgraded to the newest file format, click OK.

2. Close the document.

3. Open the document **NP_WD_5-3.docx** from the Word5 > Review folder included with your Data Files, and then save it as **NP_WD_5_Construction** in the location specified by your instructor.

4. Use the Go To feature to review all the headings in the document.

5. In the first line of the "History" section, use the Thesaurus pane to replace "excited" with a synonym. Use the third synonym in the list of words related to "happy."

6. Change the theme colors to Green, and then change the theme's fonts to the Franklin Gothic fonts.

7. Save the new colors and fonts as a theme named **NP_WD_5_ConstructionReportTheme** in the location specified by your instructor.

8. Change the style set to Lines (Simple).

9. Change the formatting of the "History" heading by adding italic formatting and by changing the character spacing so that it is expanded by 1 point between characters.

10. Update the Heading 1 style to match the newly formatted "History" heading.

11. Revise the "Scope" heading by changing the font size to 16 points, and then update the Heading 2 style to match the newly formatted "Scope" heading.

12. Create a new paragraph style for the "Contents" heading that is based on the Heading 1 style but that also includes Lime, Accent 3 paragraph shading. Name the new style **Contents**, select Normal as the style for the following paragraph, and then save the new style to the current document.

13. Open the Style Inspector pane, and check the style applied to each paragraph in the document. Then use the Reveal Formatting pane to compare the formatting applied to the "Contents" heading with the formatting applied to the "History" heading.

14. Delete the placeholder text directly below the "Contents" heading, and then insert a custom table of contents that does not include the Contents style. Except for excluding the Contents style, use the default settings in the Table of Contents dialog box.

15. Insert a blank paragraph at the end of the document, and then insert the **Support_WD_5_Writers.docx** file from the Word5 > Review folder. Add the text **Contributing Writers** to the table of contents as a Level 1 heading, and then delete the blank paragraph at the end of the document.

16. At the end of the report, replace "Student Name" with your first and last names.

17. Save your changes to the NP_WD_5_Construction.docx document.

18. Save the document as a Word Template named **NP_WD_5_ConstructionReportTemplate** in the location specified by your instructor.

19. On page 1, replace the title "CONSTRUCTING THE ALLIED STARTUP ACCELERATOR" with the placeholder text **[Insert title here.]** and then highlight the placeholder in the default yellow color.

20. Delete everything in the report after the blank paragraph after the table of contents.

21. In the blank paragraph below the table of contents, insert the **Support_WD_5_Headings.docx** file from the Word5 > Review folder.

22. In the Contributing Staff Members section, replace "Student Name" with your first and last names, and then update the table of contents.

23. Save the template, save it again to the Custom Office Templates folder, and then close it.

24. From the New screen in Backstage view, open a new document based on the template you just created, enter **Projections for Growth** as the document title, save the new document as **NP_WD_5_Projections** in the location specified by your instructor, and then close it.

25. Delete the **NP_WD_5_ConstructionReportTemplate.dotx** template from the Custom Office Templates folder.

26. Open the document **NP_WD_5-4.docx** from the Word5 > Review folder, and then save it as a Word Template named **NP_WD_5_AcceleratorAddressTemplate** in the location specified by your instructor.

27. Save the blue text box as a Quick Part named **Address**. Save it to the template named **NP_WD_5_AcceleratorAddressTemplate.dotx**, not to the Building Blocks template.

28. Save the template and close it.

# Apply

## Case Problem 1

**Data File needed for this Case Problem: NP_WD_5-5.docx**

**Robbins Morrow Aerospace Manufacturing**   Laqueta Porter is a project manager for Robbins Morrow Aerospace Manufacturing, a company that produces parts for small aircraft. The manufacturing team often takes on special projects for long-time customers. Management requires a comprehensive status report on each project every month. These reports can be quite long, so it's necessary to include a table of contents on the first page. Your job is to create a template that Laqueta and her fellow project managers can use when compiling their reports.

Complete the following steps:

1. Open the document **NP_WD_5-5.docx** from the Word5 > Case1 folder included with your Data Files, and then save it as **NP_WD_5_Status** in the location specified by your instructor.

2. Use Go To to review all the tables in the document.

3. Change the theme colors to Blue II, change the theme fonts to Arial, and then save the current theme as a custom theme named **NP_WD_5_StatusTheme** in the location specified by your instructor.

4. Change the style set to Basic (Stylish).

5. Format the "Contents" heading by changing the character spacing to Expanded, with 2 points of space between the expanded characters. Increase the font size to 22 points, add italic formatting, and then change the font color to one shade darker, using the Teal, Accent 6, Darker 50% font color. Update the Heading 1 style for the current document to match the newly formatted heading.

6. Create a new paragraph style for the company name at the top of the document that is based on the Heading 1 style but that also includes Turquoise, Accent 1, Lighter 40% paragraph shading; White, Background 1 font color; 24-point font size; and center alignment. Reduce the points of paragraph spacing before the paragraph to 0, and increase the points after the paragraph to 36. Name the new style **Company**. Select the Normal style as the style for the following paragraph, and save the style to the current document.

7. Remove the Company style from the Style gallery.

8. Below the "Contents" heading, replace the placeholder text with a custom table of contents that does not include the Company style.

9. In the document, delete the paragraph containing the "Contents" heading, and then update the table of contents to remove "Contents" from it.

10. Click in the paragraph before the table of contents, and increase the spacing after it to 24 points.

11. Add the "General Recommendations" heading, in the second to last paragraph of the document, to the table of contents at the same level as the "Project Summary" heading.

12. In the document's last paragraph, replace "ensuring" with a synonym. In the Thesaurus pane, use the second synonym in the list of words related to "safeguarding."

13. Save your changes to the document, and then save it as a template named **NP_WD_5_StatusTemplate** in the location specified by your instructor.

14. On page 3, save the complete "Scope Statement" section (including the heading, and the placeholder text) as a Quick Part named **Scope Statement**. Save the Quick Part to the **NP_WD_5_StatusTemplate.dotx** template.

15. Delete the complete "Scope Statement" section from the body of the template, including the heading and the placeholder text.

16. Update the table of contents to remove the "Scope Statement" heading.

17. Save the template to its current location, and then save the template again to the Custom Office Templates folder. Close the template.

18. Open a document based on your new template, and then save the new document as **NP_WD_5_StatusVectora** in the location specified by your instructor.

19. Replace the first placeholder with the current date, and then replace the second placeholder with **your name**. If necessary, remove the yellow highlighting from the date and your name. In the Project Summary table, replace "[Insert project name.]" with **Vectora 527 Rotor Bar** and then remove the yellow highlighting if necessary.

20. Above the "Progress" heading, insert the Scope Statement Quick Part.

21. Update the table of contents to include the new heading.

22. Save and close the document, and then delete the NP_WD_5_StatusTemplate.dotx file from the Custom Office Templates folder.

# Challenge

## Case Problem 2

**Data Files needed for this Case Problem: NP_WD_5-6.docx, NP_WD_5-7.docx**

**Chronos and Mercer Pharmaceuticals**    Blake Peralta is a technical writer at Chronos and Mercer Pharmaceuticals. Blake often uses Word styles in the reports and other publications he creates for the company, and he wants to learn more about managing styles. In particular, he wants to learn how to copy styles from one document to another. He's asked you to help him explore the Style Pane Options, Manage Styles, and Organizer dialog boxes. He would also like your help creating a Quick Part for a memo header. Complete the following steps:

1. Open the document **NP_WD_5-6.docx** from the Word5 > Case2 folder included with your Data Files, and then save it as **NP_WD_5_Memo** in the location specified by your instructor. This document contains the text you will eventually save as a Quick Part. It contains all the default styles available in any new Word document, as well as one style, named "Memorandum," which Blake created earlier. In the following steps, you will copy styles from another document to this document. For now, you can close it.

2. Close the NP_WD_5_Memo.docx document.

3. Open the document **NP_WD_5-7.docx** from the Word5 > Case2 folder, and then save it as **NP_WD_5_Styles** in the location specified by your instructor. This document contains styles created by Blake, which you will copy to the NP_WD_5_Memo.docx document. It also includes sample paragraphs formatted with Blake's styles, and one paragraph that you will format with a style later in this Case Problem.

✪ **Explore** 4. Open the Style Pane Options dialog box, and then change the settings so the Styles pane displays only the styles in the current document, in alphabetical order. Before closing this dialog box, verify that these settings will be applied only to the current document rather than to new documents based on this template.

✪ **Explore** 5. Open a new, blank document, and then use the Screenshot button in the Illustrations group on the Insert tab to create a screenshot of the NP_WD_5_Styles.docx document.

6. Copy the screenshot to the Clipboard, and then paste it in the blank paragraph at the end of the NP_WD_5_Styles.docx document, just as you would paste text that you had previously copied to the Clipboard. Close the document in which you created the screenshot without saving it.

✪ **Explore** 7. At the bottom of the Styles pane, click the Manage Styles button, and then click the Import/Export button to open the Organizer dialog box. Close the Normal template, and open the **NP_WD_5_Memo.docx** document instead. (*Hint*: On the right, under the In Normal box, click the Close File button, and then click the Open File button. In the Open dialog box, you'll need to display all files.)

✪ **Explore** 8. Copy the following styles from the NP_WD_5_Styles.docx document to the NP_WD_5_Memo.docx document: Company Name, Department, Documentation Heading, and Product Description. Then copy the Memorandum style from the NP_WD_5_Memo.docx document to the NP_WD_5_Styles.docx document.

9. Close the Organizer dialog box, and save your changes to the NP_WD_5_Memo.docx document when asked.

10. In the NP_WD_5_Styles.docx document, apply the Memorandum style to the text "Sample of Memorandum style."

11. Save the NP_WD_5_Styles.docx document, and then close it.

12. Open the NP_WD_5_Memo.docx document, and then review the list of styles in the Styles pane to locate the styles you just copied to this document from the NP_WD_5_Styles.docx document.

13. Apply the Company Name style to "Chronos and Mercer Pharmaceuticals" in the second paragraph.

14. Save the NP_WD_5_Memo.docx document, and then save it again as a template named **NP_WD_5_MemoTemplate** in the location specified by your instructor.

15. Select all of the text in the document, and then save it as a Quick Part named **Memo 1**. Save the Quick Part to the current template, not to the Building Blocks template.

16. Change the Paragraph shading for the first paragraph to the Turquoise, Accent 1 color, and then save the document text as a new Quick Part named **Memo 2**. Again, save the Quick Part to the current template.

17. Delete all the text from the template, save the NP_WD_5_MemoTemplate.dotx file, and then close it.

✪ **Explore** 18. Open a File Explorer window, and then navigate to the location where you saved the NP_WD_5_Memo_Template.dotx file. Open a new document based on the template by double-clicking the template's file name in File Explorer.

19. Save the new document as **NP_WD_5_SampleMemo** in the location specified by your instructor, insert the Memo 2 Quick Part in the document, and then save and close the document.

# Using Mail Merge

## Creating a Form Letter, Mailing Labels, and a Phone Directory

### Objectives

**Session 6.1**
- Insert a Date field
- Select a main document
- Create a data source
- Insert mail merge fields into a main document
- Create a mail merge rule
- Preview a merged document
- Complete a mail merge

**Session 6.2**
- Reopen a main document
- Edit a data source
- Sort and filter records
- Create mailing labels
- Create a phone directory
- Convert a table to text

## Case | Sun and Soul Wellness Resort

Amalia Ferreira manages the spa at Sun and Soul Wellness Resort, a luxury vacation destination in San Diego, California. The resort has just reopened its newly renovated spa facility. To encourage San Diego residents to patronize the spa, Amalia staffed a booth at several local community events and collected names and addresses of potential clients. Amalia plans to send a form letter to these people announcing the improvements to the spa and offering a free nutrition or fitness counseling appointment to anyone who shows a copy of the letter at the spa's front desk.

The form letter will also contain specific details for individual people, such as name and address. For people who indicated that they prefer yoga classes, the letter will include a sentence about the new yoga studios. For those who prefer weight lifting classes, the letter will include a sentence about the new weight room. Amalia has already written the text of the form letter. She plans to use the mail merge process to add the personal information for each person to the form letter. She asks you to revise the form letter by inserting a Date field in the document that will display the current date. Then she wants you to use the Mail Merge feature in Word to create customized letters. After you create the merged letters, Amalia would like you to create mailing labels for the envelopes and a directory of employee phone numbers. Finally, you'll convert some text to a table so that it can be used in a mail merge.

### Starting Data Files

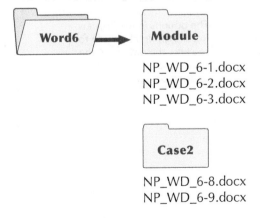

Word6 → **Module**

NP_WD_6-1.docx
NP_WD_6-2.docx
NP_WD_6-3.docx

**Review**

NP_WD_6-4.docx
NP_WD_6-5.docx
NP_WD_6-6.docx

**Case1**

NP_WD_6-7.docx

**Case2**

NP_WD_6-8.docx
NP_WD_6-9.docx

# Session 6.1 Visual Overview:

Use the Start Mail Merge button to select the type of main document you are creating. Possible types include letters, envelopes, emails, labels, and directories.

The Select Recipients button allows you to select an existing data source or create a new one in the New Address List dialog box.

The Mailings tab contains four groups of options that, working left to right, walk you through the process of creating a mail merge.

To complete the mail merge, you click the Finish & Merge button. This creates a new document, the merged document, which contains a separate copy of the main document for each record in the data source.

The Edit Recipient List button allows you to make changes to a data source.

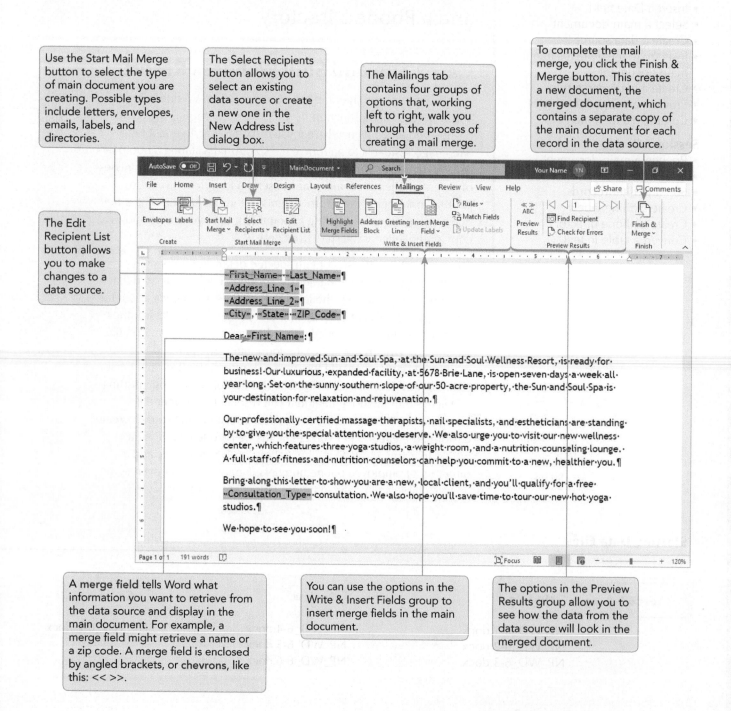

A merge field tells Word what information you want to retrieve from the data source and display in the main document. For example, a merge field might retrieve a name or a zip code. A merge field is enclosed by angled brackets, or **chevrons**, like this: << >>.

You can use the options in the Write & Insert Fields group to insert merge fields in the main document.

The options in the Preview Results group allow you to see how the data from the data source will look in the merged document.

# Mail Merge

A **data source** is a file that contains information, such as names and addresses, that is organized into fields and records; the merge fields cause the information in the data source to be displayed in the main document. You can use a Word table, an Excel spreadsheet, or other types of files as data sources, or you can create a new data source using the New Address List dialog box.

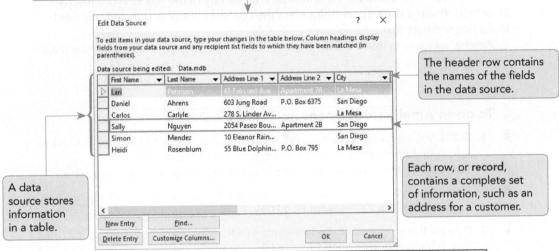

The header row contains the names of the fields in the data source.

Each row, or **record**, contains a complete set of information, such as an address for a customer.

A data source stores information in a table.

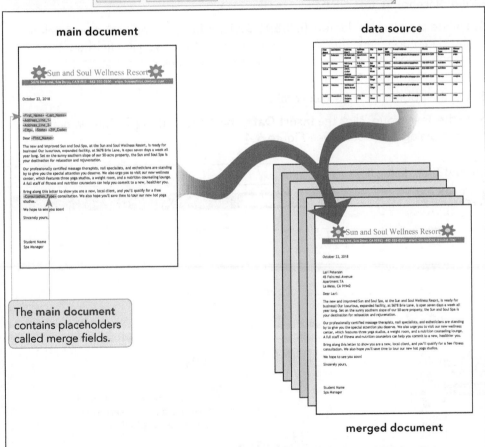

main document

data source

The main document contains placeholders called merge fields.

merged document

# Inserting a Date Field

A **Date field** is an instruction that tells Word to display the current date in a document. Although a Date field is not a merge field, it's common to use Date fields in mail merge documents to ensure that the main document always includes the current date. Every time you open a document containing a Date field, it updates to display the current date. To insert a Date field, you use the Date and Time dialog box to select from a variety of date formats. In addition to displaying the date with the current day, month, and year, you can include the current time and the day of the week. Word inserts a Date field inside a content control; unless the content control is selected, the field looks like ordinary text.

Amalia asks you to insert a Date field in her document before beginning the mail merge process.

**To open Amalia's document and insert a Date field:**

1. **sam↓** Open the document **NP_WD_6-1.docx** from the Word6 > Module folder included with your Data Files, and then save it as **NP_WD_6_MainDocument** in the location specified by your instructor.

2. Display nonprinting characters, switch to Print Layout view, display the rulers, and then set the Zoom level to **120%**.

3. Review the contents of the letter. Notice that the fourth paragraph includes the placeholder text "[INSERT DATE FIELD]."

4. Delete the placeholder text **[INSERT DATE FIELD]**, taking care not to delete the paragraph mark after the placeholder text. When you are finished, the insertion point should be located in the second blank paragraph of the document, with two blank paragraphs below it.

5. On the ribbon, click the **Insert** tab.

6. In the Text group, click the **Insert Data and Time** button. The Date and Time dialog box opens. See Figure 6–1.

**Figure 6–1    Date and Time dialog box**

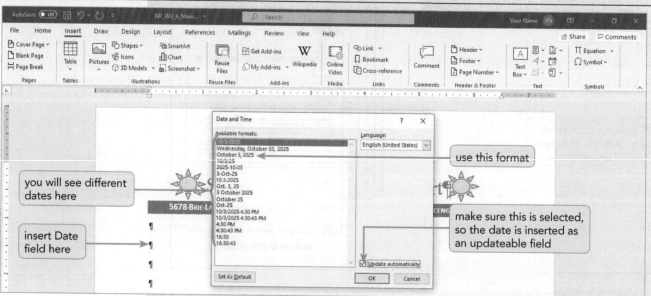

The Available formats list provides options for inserting the current date and time. In this case, you want to insert the date as a content control in a format that includes the complete name of the month, the date, and the year (for example, March 11, 2025).

**7.** In the Available formats list, click the third format from the top, which is the month, date, and year format.

**Tip**

If you use a date format that includes the time, you can update the time while the document is open by clicking the Update tab at the top of the content control.

**8.** If necessary, select the **Update automatically** check box so the date is inserted as a content control that updates every time you open the document.

**9.** Click **OK**. The current date is inserted in the document. At this point, it looks like ordinary text. To see the content control, you have to click the date.

**10.** Click the date to display the content control. If you closed the document and then opened it a day later, the content control would automatically display the new date. See Figure 6–2.

**Figure 6–2**    **Date field inside content control**

current date is displayed inside a content control

**11.** Scroll down to display the letter's closing, change "Amalia Ferreira" to your first and last names, and then scroll back up to the beginning of the letter.

**12.** Save the document.

Now that the document contains the current date, you can begin the mail merge process.

# Performing a Mail Merge

When you perform a mail merge, you insert individualized information from a data source into a main document. A main document can be a letter or any other kind of document containing merge fields that tell Word where to insert names, addresses, and other variable information from the data source. A main document can contain photos, shapes, SmartArt, tables, links to online videos, or any other type of non-text element. It can also be formatted with any theme or style set you want, or with any page layout options you want. For example, you could format a main document with custom margins, created by clicking the Margins button on the Layout tab, clicking Custom Margins, and then adjusting the Margins settings on the Margins tab of the Page Setup dialog box. In other words, the overall look of the main document is up to you, but you should take care to make sure it looks professional and is easy to read.

When you **merge** the main document with information from the data source, you produce a new document called a merged document. The Session 6.1 Visual Overview summarizes mail merge concepts.

Amalia's main document is the letter shown in the Session 6.1 Visual Overview. In this session, you will insert the merge fields shown in this letter. You'll also create Amalia's data source, which will include the name and address of each potential client. The data source will also include information about each person's preferred type of consultation (fitness or nutrition) and preferred type of fitness class (yoga or weight lifting).

You can perform a mail merge by using the Mail Merge pane, which walks you through the steps of performing a mail merge. You access the Mail Merge pane by clicking the Start Mail Merge button in the Start Mail Merge group on the Mailings tab and then clicking the Step-by-Step Mail Merge Wizard command on the menu. You can also use the options on the Mailings tab, which streamlines the process and offers more tools. In this module, you'll work with the Mailings tab to complete the mail merge for Amalia. The Mailings tab organizes the steps in the mail merge process so that you can move from left to right across the ribbon using the buttons to complete the merge.

## Starting the Mail Merge and Selecting a Main Document

The first step in the mail merge process is selecting the type of main document. Your choice of main document type affects the commands that are available to you later as you continue through the mail merge process, so it's important to make the correct selection at the beginning. In this case, you will use a letter as the main document.

**To start the mail merge process and select a main document:**

▶ **1.** On the ribbon, click the **Mailings** tab.

Notice that most of the buttons in the groups on the Mailings tab are grayed out, indicating the options are unavailable. These options become available only after you begin the mail merge process and select a data source.

▶ **2.** In the Start Mail Merge group, click the **Start Mail Merge** button. The Start Mail Merge menu opens, as shown in Figure 6–3.

**Figure 6–3**   **Start Mail Merge menu**

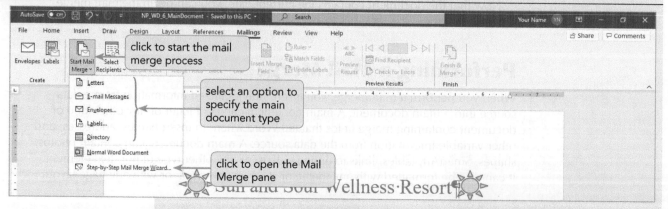

The first five options on the menu allow you to specify the type of main document you will create. Most of the options involve print items, such as labels and letters, but you can also select an email message as the type of main document. In this case, you'll create a letter.

3. Click **Letters**. The Start Mail Merge menu closes.

   Next, you need to select the list of recipients for Amalia's letter; that is, you need to select the data source.

4. In the Start Mail Merge group, click the **Select Recipients** button. The Select Recipients menu allows you to create a new recipient list, use an existing list, or select from Outlook Contacts (the address book in Outlook).

   Because Amalia hasn't had a chance to create a data source yet, she asks you to create one.

5. Click **Type a New List**. The New Address List dialog box opens, as shown in Figure 6–4.

---

**Figure 6–4** ▶ **New Address List dialog box**

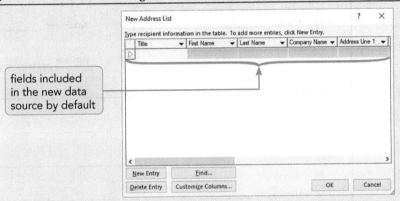

fields included in the new data source by default

The default fields for a data source are displayed in this dialog box. Before you begin creating the data source, you need to identify the fields and records Amalia wants you to include.

# Creating a Data Source

As described in the Session 6.1 Visual Overview, a data source is a file that contains information organized into fields and records. Typically, the data source for a mail merge contains a list of names and addresses, but it can also contain email addresses, phone numbers, and other data. Various kinds of files can be used as the data source, including an Excel workbook or an Access database. You can also use a file from another kind of database, such as one created by a company to store its sales information. For a simple mail merge project, such as a phone directory, you can use a table stored in a Word document.

When performing a mail merge, you'll usually select an existing data source file—created in another application—that already contains the necessary information. However, in this module, you'll create a new data source in Word and then enter the data into it so you can familiarize yourself with the basic structure of a data source. After creating the new data source, you'll save the file in its default format as an Access database file, with an .mdb file extension. Microsoft Outlook also uses MDB files to store contact information—in which case they are referred to as Microsoft Office Address Lists files.

When you create a new data source, Word provides a number of default fields, such as First Name, Last Name, and Company Name. You can customize the data source by adding new fields and removing the default fields that you don't plan to use. When creating a data source, keep in mind that each field name must be unique; you can't have two fields with the same name.

The Microsoft Office Address Lists file you will create in this session will contain information about Amalia's potential clients, including each person's name, address, preferred type of consultation (fitness or nutrition), and preferred type of fitness class (yoga or weight lifting). Figure 6–5 shows one of the forms Amalia used to collect the information.

**Figure 6–5**    **New client information card**

Sun and Soul Wellness Resort

Sign up for our mailing list to receive special offers and information about our newest services.

First Name_____  Last Name_____

Street Address _____  Apartment _____

City _____  Zip Code _____

Email Address _____

Home or mobile number _____

Preferred consultation _____

Preferred fitness class_____

The information on each form will make up one record in the data source. Each blank on the form translates into one field in the data source, as shown in Figure 6–6.

**Figure 6–6**    **Fields to include in the data source**

| Field Names | Description |
| --- | --- |
| First Name | Client's first name |
| Last Name | Client's last name |
| Address Line 1 | Client's street address |
| Address Line 2 | Additional address information, such as an apartment number |
| City | City |
| State | State |
| ZIP Code | Zip code |
| E-mail Address | Email address |
| Phone | Home or mobile number |
| Consultation Type | Preferred consultation type |
| Fitness Class | Preferred fitness class |

Even though you won't need email addresses or phone numbers to complete the mail merge, it's a good idea to include them in the data source. That way, Amalia can reuse the data source in future mail merges to send emails or when creating a directory of client phone numbers. When creating a data source, it's always wise to think ahead to possible future uses for it.

# Reference

### Creating a Data Source for a Mail Merge

- On the ribbon, click the Mailings tab.
- In the Start Mail Merge group, click the Select Recipients button, and then click Type a New List to open the New Address List dialog box.
- To select the fields for your data source, click the Customize Columns button to open the Customize Address List dialog box.
- To delete an unnecessary field, select it, click the Delete button, and then click Yes.
- To add a new field, click the Add button, type the name of the field in the Add Field dialog box, and then click OK.
- To rearrange the order of the field names, click a field name, and then click the Move Up button or the Move Down button.
- To rename a field, click a field name, click the Rename button to open the Rename Field dialog box, type a new field name, and then click OK to close the Rename Field dialog box.
- Click OK to close the Customize Address List dialog box.
- In the New Address List dialog box, enter information for the first record, click the New Entry button, and then enter the information for the next record. Continue until you are finished entering all the information for the data source, and then click OK to open the Save Address List dialog box.
- Type a name for the data source in the File name box. By default, Word will save the file to the My Data Sources folder unless you specify another save location. Click the Save button. The file is saved with the .mdb file extension.

You're ready to create the data source for the form letter using information Amalia has given you for three potential clients. However, before you begin entering information, you need to customize the list of fields to include only the fields Amalia requires.

### To customize the list of fields before creating the data source:

▶ 1. In the New Address List dialog box, click the **Customize Columns** button. The Customize Address List dialog box opens. Here you can delete the fields you don't need, add new ones, and arrange the fields in the order you want. You'll start by deleting some fields.

▶ 2. In the Field Names box, verify that **Title** is selected, and then click the **Delete** button. A message is displayed, asking you to confirm the deletion.

▶ 3. Click the **Yes** button. The Title field is deleted from the list of field names.

▶ 4. Continue using the Delete button to delete the following fields: **Company Name**, **Country or Region**, and **Work Phone**.

Next, you need to add some new fields. When you add a new field, it is inserted below the selected field, so you'll start by selecting the last field in the list.

▶ 5. In the Field Names box, click **E-mail Address**, and then click the **Add** button. The Add Field dialog box opens, asking you to type a name for your field. See Figure 6-7.

**Figure 6–7**   Add Field dialog box

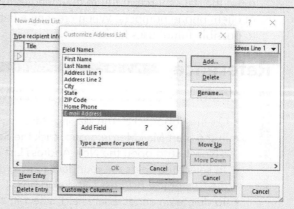

6. Type **Consultation Type** and then click **OK**. The field "Consultation Type" is added to the Field Names list.

7. Use the Add button to add the **Fitness Class** field below the Consultation Type field.

   Next, you need to move the E-mail Address field up above the Home Phone field, so that the fields are in the same order as they appear on the form shown in Figure 6–5.

8. Click **E-mail Address**, and then click the **Move Up** button. The E-mail Address field moves up, so it is now displayed just before the Home Phone field.

   Finally, because Amalia's form asks people to fill in a home or mobile phone number, you need to change "Home Phone" to simply "Phone."

9. Click **Home Phone**, and then click the **Rename** button to open the Rename Field dialog box.

10. In the To box, replace "Home Phone" with **Phone** and then click **OK** to close the Rename Field dialog box and return to the Customize Address List dialog box. See Figure 6–8.

**Figure 6–8**   Customized list of field names

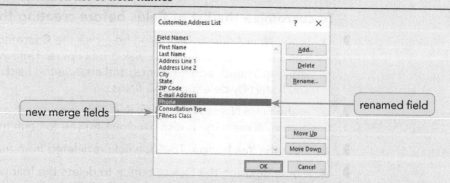

new merge fields

renamed field

11. Click **OK** in the Customize Address List dialog box to close it and return to the New Address List dialog box. This dialog box reflects the changes you just made. For instance, it no longer includes the Title field. The fields are listed in the same order as they appeared in the Customize Address List dialog box.

12. Use the horizontal scroll bar near the bottom of the New Address List dialog box to scroll to the right to display the Consultation Type and Fitness Class fields. See Figure 6–9.

Figure 6–9 | Changes made to New Address List dialog box

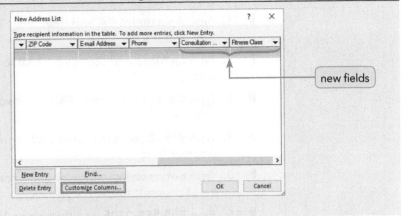

new fields

## Insight

### Organizing Field Names

Although the order of field names in the data source doesn't affect their placement in the main document, it's helpful to arrange field names logically in the data source so you can enter information quickly and efficiently. For example, you'll probably want the First Name field next to the Last Name field. To make it easier to transfer information from a paper form to a data source, it's a good idea to arrange the fields in the same order as on the form, just like you did in the preceding steps. Also, note that if you include spaces in your field names, Word will replace the spaces with underscores when you insert the fields into the main document. For example, Word transforms the field name "First Name" into "First_Name."

Now that you have specified the fields you want to use, you are ready to enter the information into the data source.

## Entering Data into a Data Source

Amalia has given you three completed new client information forms and has asked you to enter the information from the forms into the data source. You'll use the New Address List dialog box to enter the information. As you press TAB to move right from one field to the next, the dialog box will scroll to display fields that are not currently visible.

### To enter data into a record using the New Address List dialog box:

1. In the New Address List dialog box, scroll to the left to display the First Name field.

2. Click in the **First Name** field, if necessary, and then type **Lari** to enter the first name of the first person.

   Do not press SPACEBAR after you finish typing an entry in the New Address List dialog box.

**Tip**

You can press SHIFT+TAB to move the insertion point to the previous field.

3. Press **TAB** to move the insertion point to the Last Name field.

4. Type **Peterson** and then press **TAB** to move the insertion point to the Address Line 1 field.

5. Type **45 Faircrest Avenue** and then press **TAB** to move the insertion point to the Address Line 2 field.

6. Type **Apartment 7A** and then press **TAB** to move the insertion point to the City field.

7. Type **La Mesa** and then press **TAB** to move the insertion point to the State field.

8. Type **CA** and then press **TAB** to move the insertion point to the ZIP Code field.

9. Type **91942** and then press **TAB** to move the insertion point to the E-mail Address field.

10. Type **peterson@sample.cengage.com** and then press **TAB** to move the insertion point to the Phone field.

11. Type **858-555-0105** and then press **TAB** to move the insertion point to the Consultation Type field.

12. Type **fitness** and then press **TAB**. The insertion point is now in the Fitness Class field, which is the last field in the data source.

13. Type **yoga** and then stop. Do not press TAB.

14. Use the horizontal scroll bar to scroll to the left, and then review the data in the record. See Figure 6–10.

---

**Figure 6–10**    **Completed record**

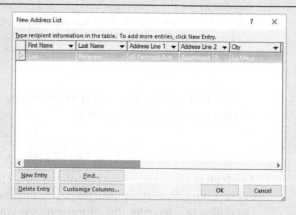

You have finished entering the information for the first record of the data source. Now you're ready to enter information for the next two records. You can create a new record by clicking the New Entry button, or by pressing TAB after you have finished entering information into the last field for a record. Note that within a record, you can leave some fields blank. For example, only two of the three new client forms include information for the Address Line 2 field.

**To add additional records to the data source:**

1. In the New Address List dialog box, click the **New Entry** button. A new, blank record is created.

2. Enter the information shown in Figure 6-11 for the next two records. To start the Carlos Carlyle record, press **TAB** after completing the Fitness Class field for the Daniel Ahrens record.

| Figure 6-11 | Information for records 2 and 3 |
| --- | --- |

| First Name | Last Name | Address Line 1 | Address Line 2 | City | State | ZIP Code | E-mail Address | Phone | Consultation Type | Fitness Class |
| --- | --- | --- | --- | --- | --- | --- | --- | --- | --- | --- |
| Daniel | Ahrens | 603 Jung Road | P.O. Box 6375 | San Diego | CA | 91911 | ahrens@sample.cengage.com | 760-555-0112 | nutrition | weights |
| Carlos | Carlyle | 278 S. Linder Avenue | | La Mesa | CA | 91942 | carlyle@sample.cengage.com | 619-555-0107 | nutrition | yoga |

Note that the Address Line 2 field should be blank in the Carlos Carlyle record.

**Trouble?** If you start a fourth record by mistake, click the Delete Entry button to remove the blank fourth record.

You have entered the records for three potential clients. Amalia's data source eventually will contain hundreds of records for spa clients. The current data source, however, contains the records Amalia wants to work with now. Next, you need to save the data source.

## Saving a Data Source

**Tip**

In File Explorer, the file type for a Microsoft Office Address Lists file is "Microsoft Access Database."

After you finish entering data for your new data source, you can close the New Address List dialog box. When you do so, the Save Address List dialog box opens, where you can save the data source using the default file type, Microsoft Office Address Lists.

**To save the data source:**

1. In the New Address List dialog box, click **OK**. The New Address List dialog box closes, and the Save Address List dialog box opens, as shown in Figure 6-12.

**Figure 6–12**    Saving the data source

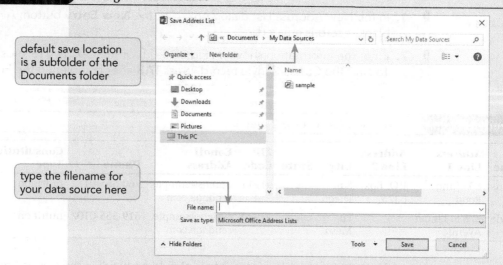

default save location is a subfolder of the Documents folder

type the filename for your data source here

The Save as type box indicates that the data source will be saved as a Microsoft Office Address Lists file. The File name box is empty; you need to name the file before saving it.

**2.** Click the **File name** box, if necessary, and then type **NP_WD_6_Data**.

Unless you specify another save location, Word will save the file to the My Data Sources folder, which is a subfolder of the Documents folder.

In this case, you'll save the data source in the same location in which you saved the main document.

**3.** Navigate to the location in which you saved the main document, and then click the **Save** button. The Save Address List dialog box closes, and you return to the main document.

The next step in the mail merge process is to add the necessary merge fields to the main document. For Amalia's letter, you need to add merge fields for the inside address, for the salutation, and for each person's preferred consultation type and fitness class.

## Proskills

### Decision Making: Planning Your Data Source

When creating a data source, think beyond the current mail merge task to possible future uses for your data source. For example, Amalia's data source includes both an E-mail Address field and a Phone field—not because she wants to use that information in the current mail merge project, but because she can foresee needing these pieces of information at a later date to communicate with her clients. Having all relevant client information in one data source will make it easier to retrieve and use the information effectively.

In some cases, you'll also want to include information that might seem obvious. For example, Amalia's data source includes a State field even though all of her current clients live in or around San Diego, California. However, she included a State field because she knows that her pool of addresses could expand sometime in the future to include residents of other states.

Finally, think about the structure of your data source before you create it. Try to break information down into as many fields as seems reasonable. For example, it's always better to include a First Name field and a Last Name field, rather than simply a Name field, because including two separate fields makes it possible to alphabetize the information in the data source by last name. If you entered first and last names in a single Name field, you could alphabetize only by first name.

If you're working with a very small data source, breaking information down into as many fields as possible is less important. However, it's very common to start with a small data source and then, as time goes on, find that you need to continually add information to the data source, until you have a large file. If you failed to plan the data source adequately at the beginning, the expanded data source could become difficult to manage.

You also need to consider the type of file you use to store your data source. In this session, you created a data source from within Word and saved it as a Microsoft Office Address Lists file. If you wanted, you could edit the file later in Microsoft Access, using its powerful data manipulation features. If you are more comfortable working in Excel, consider creating your data source in Excel instead, so that you can take advantage of its simpler data manipulation options.

# Inserting Merge Fields

When inserting merge fields into the main document, you must include proper spacing around the fields so that the information in the merged document will be formatted correctly. To insert a merge field, you move the insertion point to the location where you want to insert the merge field, and then click the Insert Merge Field arrow in the Write & Insert Fields group.

For Amalia's letter, you will build an inside address by inserting individual merge fields for the address elements. The letter is a standard business letter, so you'll place merge fields for the name and address below the date. Note that you could also insert the address as one address block field. But in these steps, you'll insert separate fields for each part of the address, so you can get some practice inserting fields.

### To insert a merge field in the main document:

1. Click in the second blank paragraph below the date.

2. In the Write & Insert Fields group, click the **Insert Merge Field arrow**.
   A menu opens with the names of all the merge fields in the data source.
   Note that the spaces in the merge field names have been replaced with underscores. See Figure 6–13.

Figure 6–13 **Insert Merge Field menu**

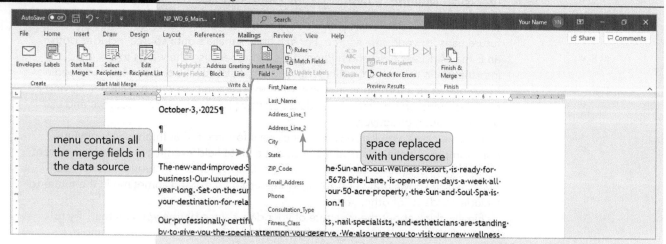

**Trouble?** If the Insert Merge Field dialog box opens, you clicked the Insert Merge Field button instead of the Insert Merge Field arrow. Close the dialog box and repeat Step 2.

3. Click **First_Name**. The Insert Merge Field menu closes, and the merge field is inserted into the document.

The merge field consists of the field name surrounded by double angled brackets << >>, also called chevrons.

**Trouble?** If you make a mistake and insert the wrong merge field, click to the left of the merge field, press DEL to select the field, and then press DEL again to delete it.

4. In the Write & Insert Fields group, click the **Highlight Merge Fields** button. The First_Name merge field is displayed on a gray background, making it easier to see in the document. See Figure 6–14.

**Tip**

You can only insert merge fields into a main document using the tools on the Mailings tab or in the Mail Merge pane. You cannot type merge fields into the main document—even if you type the angled brackets.

Figure 6–14 **First_Name merge field highlighted in main document**

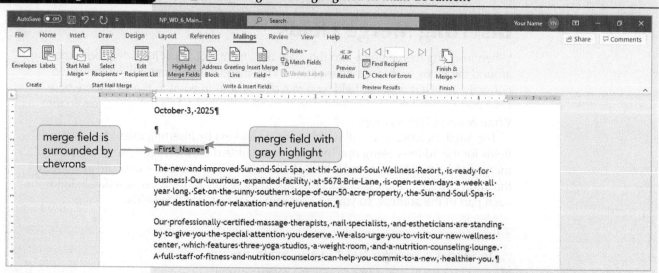

Later, when you merge the main document with the data source, Word will replace the First_Name merge field with information from the First Name field in the data source.

Now you're ready to insert the merge fields for the rest of the inside address. You'll add the necessary spacing and punctuation between the merge fields as well. You might be accustomed to pressing SHIFT+ENTER to start a new line in an inside address without inserting paragraph spacing. However, because your data source includes a record in which one of the fields (the Address Line 2 field) is blank, you need to press ENTER to start each new line. As you will see later in this Module, this ensures that Word hides the Address Line 2 field in the final merged document whenever that field is blank. To maintain the proper spacing in the main document, you'll adjust the paragraph spacing after you insert all the fields.

### To insert the remaining merge fields for the inside address:

▶ 1. Press **SPACEBAR** to insert a space after the First_Name merge field, click the **Insert Merge Field arrow**, and then click **Last_Name**.

▶ 2. Press **ENTER** to start a new paragraph, click the **Insert Merge Field arrow**, and then click **Address_Line_1**. Word inserts the Address_Line_1 merge field into the form letter.

▶ 3. Press **ENTER**, click the **Insert Merge Field arrow**, and then click **Address_Line_2**. Word inserts the Address_Line_2 merge field into the form letter.

▶ 4. Press **ENTER**, insert the **City** merge field, type **,** (a comma), press **SPACEBAR** to insert a space after the comma, and then insert the **State** merge field.

▶ 5. Press **SPACEBAR**, and then insert the **ZIP_Code** merge field. The inside address now contains all the necessary merge fields. See Figure 6–15.

| Figure 6–15 | Main document with merge fields for inside address |

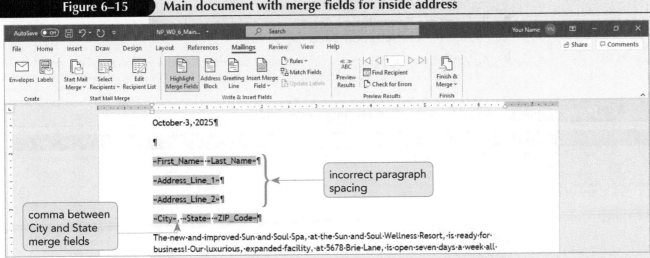

Next, you will adjust the paragraph spacing for the inside address.

▶ 6. Select the first three paragraphs of the inside address.

▶ 7. On the ribbon, click the **Home** tab.

▶ 8. In the Paragraph group, click the **Line and Paragraph Spacing** button [≡▾], and then click **Remove Space After Paragraph**. The paragraph spacing is removed, so that the paragraphs of the inside address are now correctly spaced.

You can now add the salutation of the letter, which will contain each person's first name. In the following steps, you'll get some practice combining text with merge fields. But keep in mind that you could also insert a greeting line by clicking the Greeting Line button in the Write & Insert Fields group. You could then use the options in the Insert Greeting Line dialog box to create a greeting that makes use of name fields in the data source.

### To insert the merge field for the salutation:

1. Insert a new paragraph after the ZIP_Code field, type **Dear** and then press **SPACEBAR**.

2. On the ribbon, click the **Mailings** tab.

3. In the Write & Insert Fields group, click the **Insert Merge Field arrow**, click **First_Name** to insert this field into the document, and then type **:** (a colon).

4. Save the document.

You'll further personalize Amalia's letter by including merge fields that will allow you to reference each person's preferred consultation type and fitness class.

### To add a merge field for the preferred consultation type:

1. If necessary, scroll down to display the paragraph that begins "Bring along this letter. . . ."

2. In the second line of the paragraph that begins "Bring along this letter," select the placeholder text **[CONSULTATION TYPE]**, including the brackets. You'll replace this phrase with a merge field. Don't be concerned if you also select the space following the closing bracket.

3. Insert the **Consultation_Type** merge field. Word replaces the selected text with the **Consultation_Type** merge field.

4. Verify that the field has a single space before it (on the preceding line) and after it. Add a space on either side if necessary. See Figure 6–16.

| Figure 6–16 | Main document after inserting merge fields |
| --- | --- |

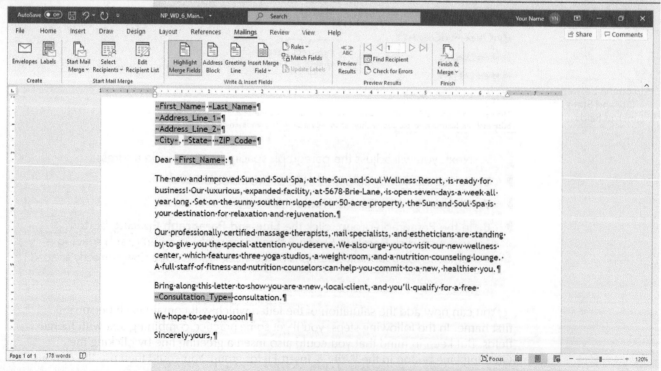

> **Trouble?** The text before and after the inserted merge fields might be marked with a blue underline because Word mistakenly identifies the text as a grammatical error. You can ignore the blue underlines.

> **5.** Save the document.

The main document now contains almost all the necessary merge fields. You need to add one more that displays one sentence for records that contain "yoga" in the Fitness Class field, and a different sentence for records that contain "weights" in the Fitness Class field. You can do that by creating a mail merge rule.

## Creating a Mail Merge Rule

A **mail merge rule** is an instruction that tells Word to complete a mail merge a certain way depending on whether a specific condition is met. For example, a condition could specify that a particular value must appear in one of the mail merge fields. This would allow you to create a mail merge rule that tells Word to skip a record in the data source if the ZIP Code field contains a particular zip code. Such a rule would be useful if you were creating letters announcing the grand opening of a new car wash and wanted to avoid sending letters to people who live in a distant zip code, because they live too far away to be likely clients.

One of the most useful type of mail merge rules is an **If. . . Then. . . Else rule**, which tells Word to choose between two options based on the contents of a particular field. In this case, Amalia wants to create a mail merge rule based on the contents of the Fitness Class field, which contains one of two possibilities: yoga or weights. It's easier to understand how an If. . . Then. . . Else rule works if you replace "Else" with "Otherwise." With this in mind, the basic logic of the rule Amalia wants you to create is shown in Figure 6–17. If the Fitness Class field contains the word "yoga" then Word will insert the sentence about the new hot yoga studios. Otherwise (that is, if the Fitness Class field contains "weights" instead of "yoga"), Word will insert the sentence about the new weight rooms. In this case, the line "The Fitness Class field contains the word yoga" is the condition.

**Figure 6–17**    Amalia's If. . . Then. . . Else rule

> **IF**
>
> The Fitness Class field contains the word *yoga*.
>
> **THEN**
>
> Insert the sentence *We also hope you'll save time to tour our new hot yoga studios.*
>
> **ELSE (OTHERWISE)**
>
> Insert the sentence *And by the way, feel free to spend an hour trying out our new weight room.*

In the following steps, you'll create a mail merge rule.

### To create an If. . . Then. . . Else mail merge rule:

> **1.** Click at the end of the paragraph that contains the <<Consultation Type>> field, and press **SPACEBAR** to insert a space after the period.

2.  In the Write & Insert Fields group, click the **Rules** button and then click **If. . . Then. . . Else** to open the Insert Word Field: IF dialog box. In the first row of boxes, you need to specify the condition that needs to be met in order for Word to insert the sentence about yoga studios.

3.  Click the **Field name arrow**, scroll down and then click **Fitness_Class**. By default, the Comparison box contains "Equal to" which is what you want. Now you need to specify what the Fitness Class field must contain in order for Word to display the sentence about hot yoga studios.

4.  Click the Compare to box and type **yoga**. Next, you need to type the sentence that you want Word to insert when the Fitness Class field contains the word "yoga."

5.  Click the **Insert this text** box, and then type **We also hope you'll save time to tour our new hot yoga studios.** Finally, you need to type the sentence that you want Word to insert when the Fitness Class field contains the word "weights."

6.  Click the **Otherwise insert this text** box, and then type **And by the way, feel free to spend an hour trying out our new weight room.** Your Insert Word Field: IF dialog box should match Figure 6–18.

| Figure 6–18 | Insert Word Field: IF dialog box |
| --- | --- |

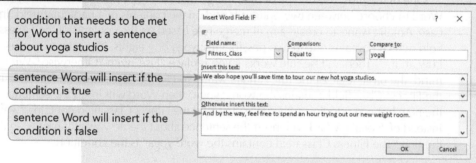

- condition that needs to be met for Word to insert a sentence about yoga studios
- sentence Word will insert if the condition is true
- sentence Word will insert if the condition is false

7.  Click **OK**. The sentence about the yoga studios is inserted into the document as a placeholder. When you complete the mail merge, the sentence included in the letters will vary, depending on the contents of the Fitness Class field. For now, you just need to make sure that the placeholder sentence is formatted to match the rest of the document.

8.  Triple-click in the paragraph to select the entire paragraph, click the **Home** tab, click the **Font arrow**, click **Trebuchet MS (Body)**, and then save the document. Now the entire paragraph is formatted in the same font.

9.  Click anywhere in the document. See Figure 6–19.

**Figure 6–19**    **Placeholder sentence formatted to match the rest of the paragraph**

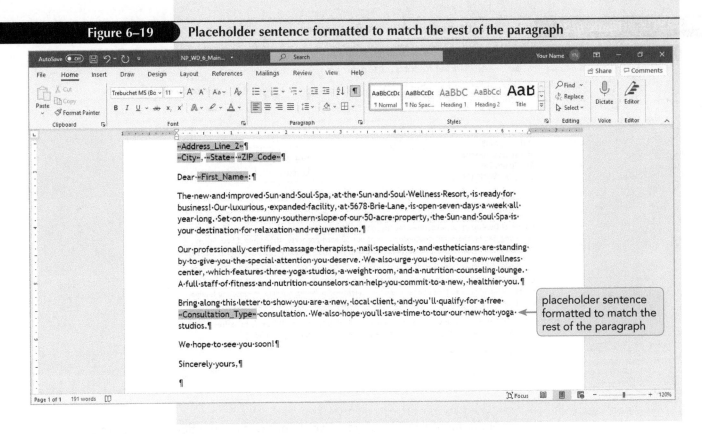

You've finished creating the mail merge rule. Your next step is to preview the merged document to see how the letter will look after Word inserts the information for each potential client.

# Previewing the Merged Document

When you preview the merged document, you can check one last time for any missing spaces between the merge fields and the surrounding text. You can also look for any other formatting problems, and, if necessary, make final changes to the data source.

**To preview the merged document:**

▶ **1.** Click the **Mailings** tab.

▶ **2.** In the Preview Results group, click the **Preview Results** button, and then scroll up to display the inside address. The data for the first record (Lari Peterson) replaces the merge fields in the form letter. On the ribbon, the Go to Record box in the Preview Results group shows which record is currently displayed in the document. See Figure 6–20.

Figure 6–20    **Letter with merged data for first record**

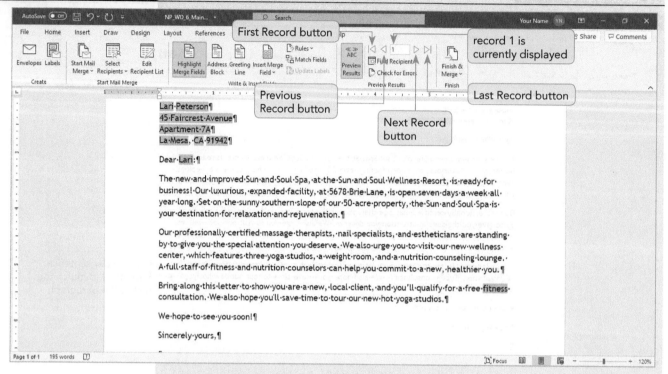

Note that the inside address, which includes information from the Address Line 2 field, contains a total of four lines.

3. Carefully check the Lari Peterson letter to make sure the text and formatting are correct, and make any necessary corrections. In particular, make sure that the spacing before and after the merged data is correct; it is easy to accidentally omit spaces or add extra spaces around merge fields.

4. In the Preview Results group, click the **Next Record** ▷ button. The data for Daniel Ahrens is displayed in the letter. As with the preceding record, the inside address for this record includes four lines of information.

5. Click the **Next Record** button ▷ again to display the data for Carlos Carlyle in the letter. In this case, the inside address includes only three lines of information. See Figure 6–21.

Figure 6–21    **Address for third record**

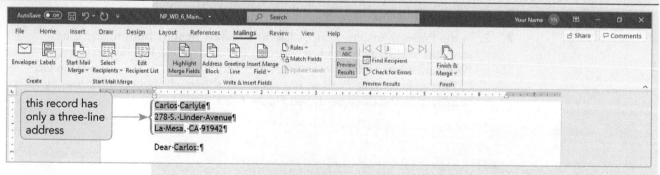

6. In the Preview Results group, click the **First Record** button ◁ to redisplay the first record in the letter (with data for Lari Peterson).

The main document of the mail merge is complete. Now that you have previewed the merged documents, you can finish the merge.

# Merging the Main Document and the Data Source

When you finish a merge, you can choose to merge directly to the printer. In other words, you can choose to have Word print the merged document immediately without saving it as a separate file. Alternatively, you can merge to a new document, which you can save using a new file name. If your data source includes an E-mail Address field, you can also create a mail merge in email format, generating one email for every email address in the data source.

Amalia wants to save an electronic copy of the merged document for her records, so you'll merge the data source and main document into a new document.

## To complete the mail merge:

▶ **1.** In the Finish group, click the **Finish & Merge** button. The Finish & Merge menu displays the three merge options. See Figure 6–22.

| Figure 6–22 | Finishing the merge |
| --- | --- |

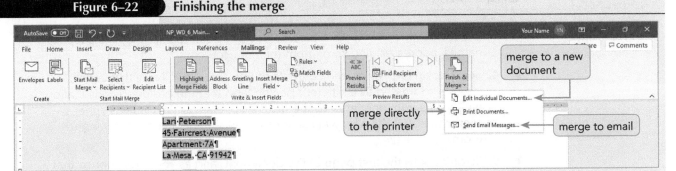

▶ **2.** In the Finish & Merge menu, click **Edit Individual Documents**. The Merge to New Document dialog box opens. Here, you need to specify which records to include in the merge. You want to include all three records from the data source.

▶ **3.** Verify that the **All** option button is selected, and then click **OK**. Word creates a new document named Letters1, which contains three pages—one for each record in the data source. See Figure 6–23.

**Figure 6–23**    Merged document

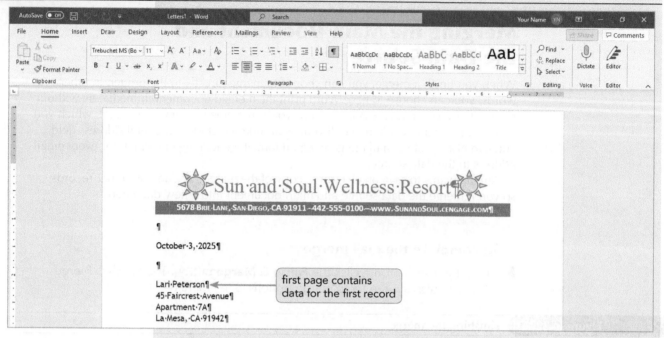

first page contains data for the first record

In this new document, the merge fields have been replaced by the specific names, addresses, and so on from the data source.

4. Scroll down and review the contents of the document. Note that each letter is addressed to a different person, and that the preferred consultation type varies from one letter to the next. Also, each letter contains either the sentence about the new yoga studios or the sentence about the weight room.

5. Scroll back to the first page of the document, and as you scroll, notice that the letters are separated by Next Page section breaks.

6. Save the merged document in the location specified by your instructor, using the file name **NP_WD_6_MergedLetters**.

7. **sam** ↑ Close the **NP_WD_6_MergedLetters.docx** document. The document named "**NP_WD_6_MainDocument.docx**" is now the active document.

After completing a merge, you need to save the main document. This ensures that any changes you might have made to the data source during the course of the mail merge are saved along with the main document.

8. **sam** ↑ Save and close the **NP_WD_6_MainDocument.docx** file.

Note that if you need to take a break while working on a mail merge, you can save the main document and close it. The data source and field information are saved along with the document. When you're ready to work on the merge again, you can open the main document and update the connection to the data source. You'll see how this works at the beginning of the next session, when you will learn how to use additional mail merge features.

## Review

### Session 6.1 Quick Check

1. Explain how to insert a Date field that updates automatically every time the document is opened.
2. Define the following:
   a. merge field
   b. record
   c. main document
   d. data source
3. List at least three types of files that you can use as data sources in a mail merge.
4. What is the first step in performing a mail merge?
5. Explain how to use the options on the Mailings tab to insert a merge field into a main document.
6. What button do you click to begin creating a mail merge rule?

# Session 6.2 Visual Overview:

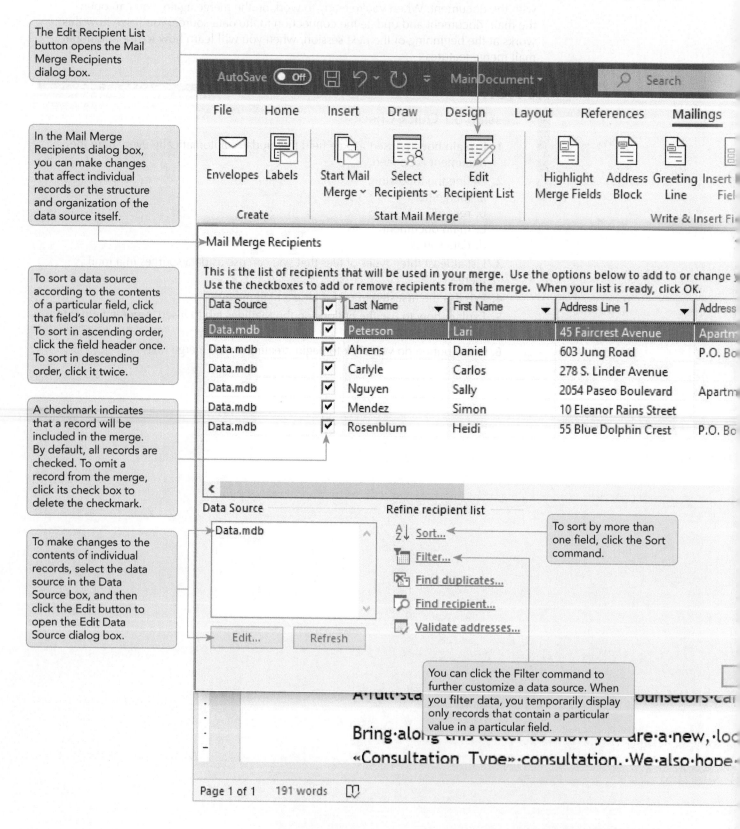

The Edit Recipient List button opens the Mail Merge Recipients dialog box.

In the Mail Merge Recipients dialog box, you can make changes that affect individual records or the structure and organization of the data source itself.

To sort a data source according to the contents of a particular field, click that field's column header. To sort in ascending order, click the field header once. To sort in descending order, click it twice.

A checkmark indicates that a record will be included in the merge. By default, all records are checked. To omit a record from the merge, click its check box to delete the checkmark.

To make changes to the contents of individual records, select the data source in the Data Source box, and then click the Edit button to open the Edit Data Source dialog box.

To sort by more than one field, click the Sort command.

You can click the Filter command to further customize a data source. When you filter data, you temporarily display only records that contain a particular value in a particular field.

# Editing a Data Source

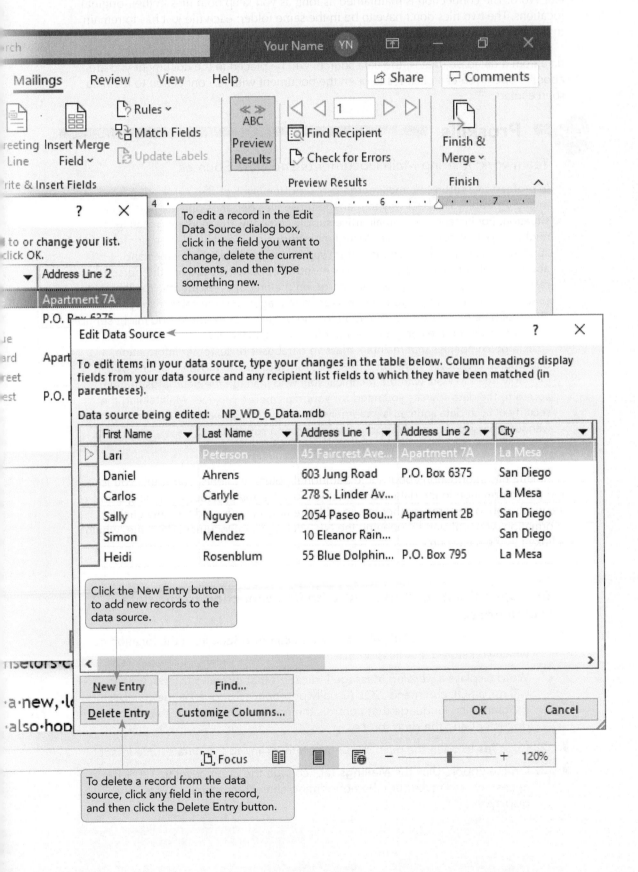

To edit a record in the Edit Data Source dialog box, click in the field you want to change, delete the current contents, and then type something new.

## Edit Data Source

To edit items in your data source, type your changes in the table below. Column headings display fields from your data source and any recipient list fields to which they have been matched (in parentheses).

Data source being edited:  NP_WD_6_Data.mdb

| First Name | Last Name | Address Line 1 | Address Line 2 | City |
|---|---|---|---|---|
| Lari | Peterson | 45 Faircrest Ave... | Apartment 7A | La Mesa |
| Daniel | Ahrens | 603 Jung Road | P.O. Box 6375 | San Diego |
| Carlos | Carlyle | 278 S. Linder Av... | | La Mesa |
| Sally | Nguyen | 2054 Paseo Bou... | Apartment 2B | San Diego |
| Simon | Mendez | 10 Eleanor Rain... | | San Diego |
| Heidi | Rosenblum | 55 Blue Dolphin... | P.O. Box 795 | La Mesa |

Click the New Entry button to add new records to the data source.

New Entry     Find...

Delete Entry     Customize Columns...     OK     Cancel

To delete a record from the data source, click any field in the record, and then click the Delete Entry button.

Focus   120%

# Reopening a Main Document

Performing a mail merge creates a connection between the main document file and the data source file. This connection persists even after you close the main document and exit Word. The connection is maintained as long as you keep both files in their original locations. The two files don't have to be in the same folder; each file just has to remain in the folder it was in when you first performed the mail merge.

When you reopen a main document, you see a warning dialog box explaining that data from a database (that is, the data source) will be placed in the document you are about to open. You can click Yes to open the document with its connection to the data source intact.

## Proskills

### Teamwork: Sharing Main Documents and Data Sources

In professional settings, a mail merge project often involves files originating from multiple people. The best way to manage these files depends on your particular situation. For instance, at a small office supply company, the marketing manager might supply the text of a main document introducing monthly sales on printer supplies, while the sales manager might supply an updated list of names and addresses of potential customers every month. Suppose that you are the person responsible for performing the mail merge on the first of every month. You'll be able to work more efficiently if you, the marketing manager, and the sales manager agree ahead of time on one storage location for the project. For example, you might set up a special folder on the company network for storing these files.

In large companies that maintain massive databases of customer information, a data source is typically stored at a fixed network location. In those situations, you'll probably need to work with the technical staff who manage the databases to gain access to the data sources you need for your mail merge projects. Maintaining the security of such data sources is extremely important, and you usually can't access them without a password and the appropriate encryption software.

Amalia has information about some additional potential clients. She wants you to add this information to the data source that you used in the previous mail merge, and she wants you to perform another merge with the new data. To add the new client information, you will start by opening the NP_WD_6_MainDocument.docx file, which is linked to the data source.

### To reopen the main document with its connection to the data source intact:

1. Open the document **NP_WD_6_MainDocument.docx** from the location in which you stored it in Session 6.1.

   Word displays a warning message indicating that opening the document will run a SQL command. SQL (usually pronounced *sequel*) is the database programming language that controls the connection between the main document and the data source.

2. Click **Yes** to open the main document with its link to the data source intact.

3. On the ribbon, click the **Mailings** tab, change the Zoom level to 120% if necessary, and make sure the nonprinting characters and the rulers are displayed.

The main document displays the data for the last record you examined when you previewed the merged document (Lari Peterson). You can alternate between displaying the merge fields and the information from the data file by toggling the Preview Results button on the Mailings tab.

**Trouble?** If you see the merge fields instead of the data for one of the records, skip to Step 5.

4. In the Preview Results group, click the **Preview Results** button to deselect it. The merge fields are displayed in the main document. At the beginning of the letter, the Date field, which is not a merge field, continues to display the current date.

5. If necessary, highlight the merge fields by clicking the **Highlight Merge Fields** button in the Write & Insert Fields group.

## Insight

### Maintaining, Breaking, and Reestablishing the Connection to a Data Source

As you have seen, when you reopen a main document, Word displays a warning dialog box, where you can click Yes to open the document with its connection to the data source intact. But what if you want to break the connection between the main document and the data source? One option is to click No in the warning dialog box. In that case, the main document opens with no connection to the data source. If the main document is currently open and already connected to the data source, you can break the connection by clicking Normal Word Document on the Start Mail Merge menu. You can reestablish the connection at any time by starting the mail merge over again and using the Select Recipients button to select the data source.

Keep in mind that you could also break the connection between a main document and its data source if you move one or both of the files to a different folder. Exactly what happens in this case depends on how your computer is set up and where you move the files. In the case of a broken connection, when you open the main document, you'll see a series of message boxes informing you that the connection to the data source has been broken. Eventually, you will see a Microsoft Word dialog box with a button labeled Find Data Source, which you can click, and then use the Select Data Source dialog box to locate and select your data source.

If you are creating mail merges for personal use, it's a good idea to either store the data source in the default My Data Sources folder or store the data source and the main document together—in a folder other than the My Data Sources folder. The latter option is best if you think you might need to move the files to a different computer. That way, if you do need to move them, you can move the entire folder.

## Editing a Data Source

After you complete a mail merge, you might need to make some changes to the data source and redo the merge. You can edit a data source in two ways—from within the program used to create the data source, or via the Mail Merge Recipients dialog box in Word. If you are familiar with the program used to create the data source, the simplest approach is to edit the file from within that program. For example, if you were using an Excel worksheet as your data source, you could open the file in Excel, edit it (perhaps by adding new records), save it, and then reselect the file as your data source. To edit the Microsoft Office Address Lists file that you created as a data source for this project, you can use the Mail Merge Recipients dialog box.

# Reference

## Editing a Microsoft Office Address Lists Data Source in Word

- Open the main document for the data source you want to edit.
- On the ribbon, click the Mailings tab.
- In the Start Mail Merge group, click the Edit Recipient List button.
- In the Data Source box in the Mail Merge Recipients dialog box, select the data source you want to edit, and then click the Edit button to open the Edit Data Source dialog box.
- To add a record, click the New Entry button, and then enter the data for the new record.
- To delete a record, click any field in the record, and then click the Delete Entry button.
- To add or remove fields from the data source, click the Customize Columns button, click Yes in the warning dialog box, make any changes, and then click OK. Remember that if you remove a field, you will delete any data entered into that field for all records in the data source.
- Click OK in the Edit Data Source dialog box, click Yes in the Microsoft Office Word dialog box, and then click OK in the Mail Merge Recipients dialog box.

Amalia would like you to add information for three new clients to the data source.

## To edit the data source by adding records:

1. In the Start Mail Merge group, click the **Edit Recipient List** button.

   The Mail Merge Recipients dialog box opens, displaying the contents of the data source that is currently connected to the main document—the NP_WD_6_Data.mdb file.

   This dialog box is designed to let you edit any data source, not just the one currently connected to the main document. To edit the NP_WD_6_Data.mdb file, you first need to select it in the Data Source box in the lower-left corner of the dialog box. If you had multiple data sources stored in the same folder as the NP_WD_6_Data.mdb file, you would see them all in this list box.

2. In the Data Source box, click **NP_WD_6_Data.mdb**. The file name is selected.

   Note that the file has the extension .mdb, which is the file extension for an Access database file—the default format for a data source created in Word. See Figure 6–24.

| Figure 6–24 | NP_WD_6_Data.mdb file selected in the Data Source box of the Mail Merge Recipients dialog box |

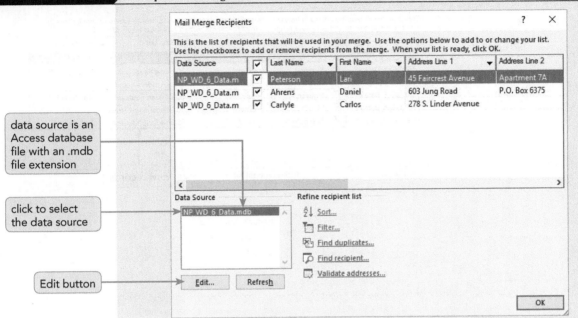

3. Click the **Edit** button. The Edit Data Source dialog box opens.

4. Click the **New Entry** button, and then enter the information for the three new records shown in Figure 6–25.

| Figure 6–25 | New client data |

| First Name | Last Name | Address Line 1 | Address Line 2 | City | State | ZIP Code | E-Mail Address | Phone | Consultation Type | Fitness Class |
|---|---|---|---|---|---|---|---|---|---|---|
| Sally | Nguyen | 2054 Paseo Boulevard | Apartment 2B | San Diego | CA | 92199 | nguyen@ sample. cengage.com | 858-555-0135 | fitness | weights |
| Simon | Mendez | 10 Eleanor Rains Street | | San Diego | CA | 91911 | mendez@ sample. cengage.com | 760-555-0102 | fitness | yoga |
| Heidi | Rosenblum | 55 Blue Dolphin Crest | P.O. Box 795 | La Mesa | CA | 91942 | rosenblum@ sample. cengage.com | 619-555-0199 | nutrition | yoga |

When you are finished, you will have a total of six records in the data source. Notice that the record for Simon Mendez contains no data in the Address Line 2 field.

5. Click **OK**, and then click the **Yes** button in the message box that asks if you want to update the NP_WD_6_Data.mdb file. (Note, you might have to wait a moment for the message box to appear.) You return to the Mail Merge Recipients dialog box, as shown in Figure 6–26.

Figure 6–26    New records added to data source

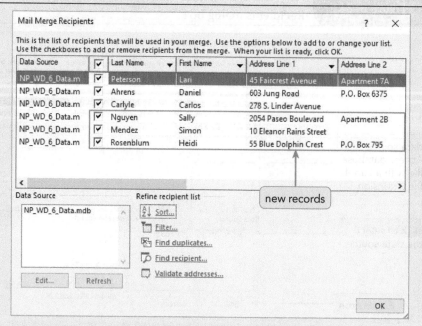

**Trouble?** If your records look different from those in Figure 6–26, select the data source, click the Edit button, edit the data source, and then click OK.

You'll leave the Mail Merge Recipients dialog box open so you can use it to make other changes to the data source.

# Sorting Records

You can sort, or rearrange, information in a data source table just as you can sort information in any other table. To quickly sort information in ascending order (*A* to *Z*, lowest to highest, or earliest to latest) or in descending order (*Z* to *A*, highest to lowest, or latest to earliest), click a field's heading in the Mail Merge Recipients dialog box. The first time you click the heading, the records are sorted in ascending order. If you click it a second time, the records are sorted in descending order.

To perform a more complicated sort, you can click the Sort command in the Mail Merge Recipients dialog box to open the Filter and Sort dialog box, where you can choose to sort by more than one field. For example, you could sort records in ascending order by last name, and then in ascending order by first name. In that case, the records would be organized alphabetically by last name, and then, in cases where multiple records contained the same last name, those records would be sorted by first name.

# Reference

## Sorting a Data Source by Multiple Fields

- On the ribbon, click the Mailings tab.
- In the Start Mail Merge group, click the Edit Recipient List button to open the Mail Merge Recipients dialog box.
- Click Sort to open the Sort Records tab in the Filter and Sort dialog box.
- Click the Sort by arrow, select the first field you want to sort by, and then select either the Ascending option button or the Descending option button.
- Click the Then by arrow, select the second field you want to sort by, and then select either the Ascending option button or the Descending option button.
- If necessary, click the Then by arrow, select the third field you want to sort by, and then select either the Ascending option button or the Descending option button.
- Click OK to close the Filter and Sort dialog box.
- Click OK to close the Mail Merge Recipients dialog box.

As Amalia looks through the letters to the potential clients in the merged document, she notices one problem—the letters are not grouped by zip codes. Currently, the letters are in the order in which people were added to the data source file. Amalia plans to use business mail (also known as bulk mail) to send her letters, and the U.S. Postal Service offers lower rates for mailings that are separated into groups according to zip code. She asks you to sort the data file by zip code and then by last name, and then merge the main document with the sorted data source.

## To sort the data source by zip code:

1. In the Mail Merge Recipients dialog box, click **Sort**. The Filter and Sort dialog box opens, with the Sort Records tab displayed.

2. Click the **Sort by arrow** to display a menu, scroll down in the menu, and then click **ZIP Code**. The Ascending button is selected by default, which is what you want.

3. In the Then by box, directly below the Sort by box, click the **Then by arrow**, and then click **Last Name**. See Figure 6–27.

**Figure 6–27**    **Sorting by zip code and by last name**

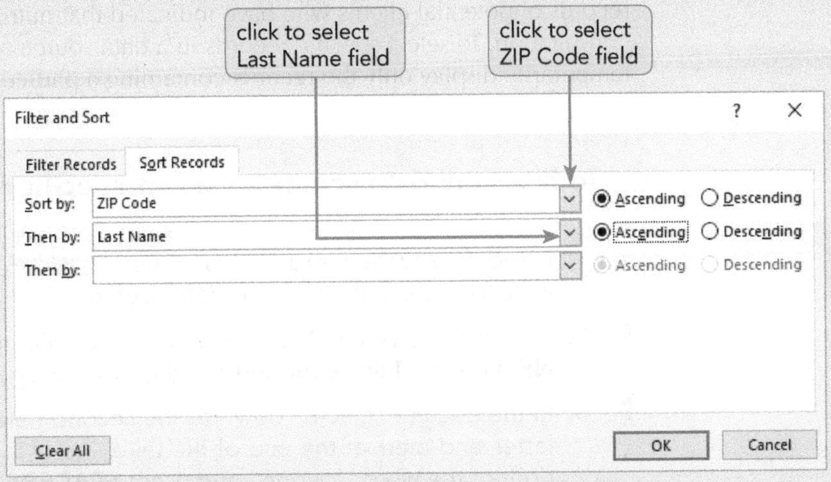

click to select Last Name field

click to select ZIP Code field

4. Click **OK**. Word sorts the records from lowest zip code number to highest, and then, within each zip code, it sorts the records by last name.

   In the Mail Merge Recipients dialog box, the record for Daniel Ahrens, with zip code 91911, is now at the top of the data source list. The record for Simon Mendez, which also has a zip code of 91911, comes second. The remaining records are sorted similarly, with the record for Sally Nguyen the last in the list. When you merge the data source with the form letter, the letters will appear in the merged document in this order.

5. Click **OK**. The Mail Merge Recipients dialog box closes.

6. On the Mailings tab, in the Preview Results group, click the **Preview Results** button. The data for Daniel Ahrens is displayed in the main document.

7. In the Finish group, click the **Finish & Merge** button, and then click **Edit Individual Documents**.

8. In the Merge to New Document dialog box, verify that the **All** option button is selected, and then click **OK**. Word generates the new merged document with six letters—one letter per page as before, but this time the first letter is addressed to Daniel Ahrens.

9. Scroll down and verify that the letters in the newly merged document are arranged in ascending order by zip code and then in ascending order by last name.

10. Save the new merged document in the location specified by your instructor, using the file name **NP_WD_6_MergedLetters2**, and then close it. You return to the NP_WD_6_MainDocument.docx file. Save the **NP_WD_6_MainDocument.docx** file, and keep it open for the next set of steps.

**Tip**

To omit an individual record from a merge, you can deselect the corresponding check box in the Mail Merge Recipients dialog box rather than using a filter.

Next, Amalia would like you to create a set of letters to send to potential clients who listed "nutrition" as their preferred type of consultation.

# Filtering Records

Amalia wants to inform potential clients that nutrition consultations are now available seven days a week. She asks you to modify the form letter and then merge it with the records of potential clients who have indicated that nutrition is their preferred type of consultation. To select specific records in a data source, you filter the data source to temporarily display only the records containing a particular value in a particular field.

## To filter the data source to select specific records for the merge:

1. In the Preview Results group, click the **Preview Results** button to deselect it and display the merge fields in the NP_WD_6_MainDocument.docx file instead of the data from the data source.

2. Save the NP_WD_6_MainDocument.docx with the new name **NP_WD_6_MainDocument2** in the location specified by your instructor.

3. In the document, scroll down to the second paragraph in the body of the letter, and then, at the end of the third line of that paragraph, click to the right of the word "lounge" and press **SPACEBAR** to insert a space between the "e" and the period.

4. Type **(with nutrition counselors available seven days a week)** and then verify that the sentence reads "...and a nutrition counseling lounge (with nutrition counselors available seven days a week)."

5. Save the document.

6. In the Start Mail Merge group, click the **Edit Recipient List** button to open the Mail Merge Recipients dialog box, and then scroll to the right so you can see the Consultation Type field.

7. In the header row, click the **Consultation Type arrow**. A menu opens, listing all the entries in the Consultation Type field, as well as a few other options. See Figure 6–28.

| Figure 6–28 | Filtering records in a data source |

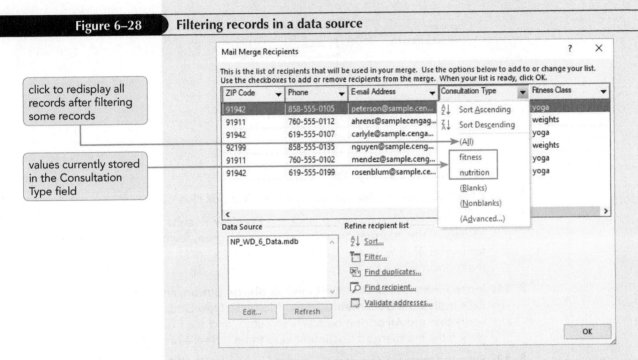

click to redisplay all records after filtering some records

values currently stored in the Consultation Type field

**Trouble?** If the records sort by Consultation Type, with the records for fitness at the top, you clicked the Consultation Type column header instead of the arrow. That's not a problem; you don't need to undo the sort. Repeat Step 6, taking care to click the arrow.

You can use the "(All)" option to redisplay all records after previously filtering a data source. The "(Advanced)" option takes you to the Filter Records tab in the Filter and Sort dialog box, where you can perform complex filter operations that involve comparing the contents of one or more fields to a particular value to determine whether a record should be displayed. In this case, however, you can use an option in this menu.

8. Click **nutrition**. Word temporarily hides all the records in the data source except those that contain "nutrition" in the Consultation Type field. See Figure 6–29.

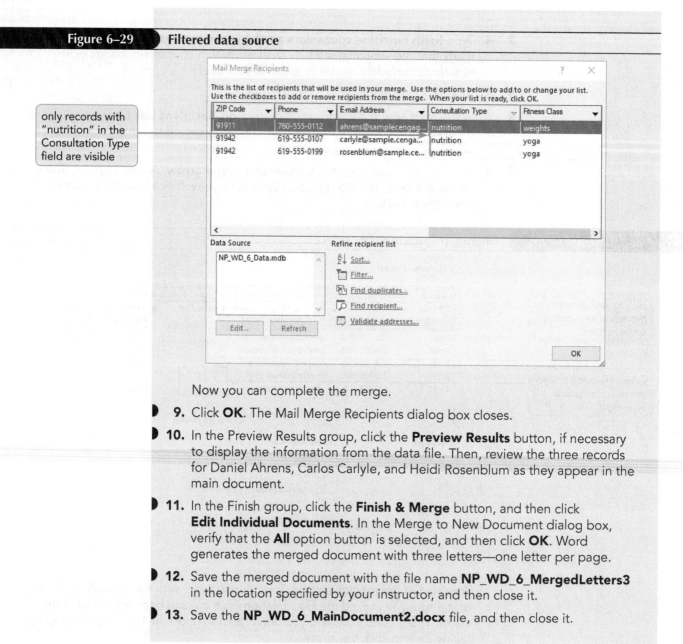

Figure 6-29    **Filtered data source**

only records with "nutrition" in the Consultation Type field are visible

Now you can complete the merge.

▶ **9.** Click **OK**. The Mail Merge Recipients dialog box closes.

▶ **10.** In the Preview Results group, click the **Preview Results** button, if necessary to display the information from the data file. Then, review the three records for Daniel Ahrens, Carlos Carlyle, and Heidi Rosenblum as they appear in the main document.

▶ **11.** In the Finish group, click the **Finish & Merge** button, and then click **Edit Individual Documents**. In the Merge to New Document dialog box, verify that the **All** option button is selected, and then click **OK**. Word generates the merged document with three letters—one letter per page.

▶ **12.** Save the merged document with the file name **NP_WD_6_MergedLetters3** in the location specified by your instructor, and then close it.

▶ **13.** Save the **NP_WD_6_MainDocument2.docx** file, and then close it.

Next, you'll create and print mailing labels for the form letters.

## Creating Mailing Labels

Amalia could print the names and addresses for the letters directly on envelopes, or she could perform a mail merge to create mailing labels. The latter method is easier because she can print 14 labels at once rather than printing one envelope at a time.

**Tip**

It is a good idea to print one page of a label document on regular paper so you can check your work before printing on the more expensive sheets of adhesive labels.

Amalia has purchased Avery® Laser Printer labels, which are available in most office-supply stores. Word supports most of the Avery label formats, allowing you to choose the layout that works best for you. Amalia purchased Avery 5162 Address Labels in 8 1/2 × 11-inch sheets that are designed to feed through a printer. Each label measures 4 × 1.33 inches. Each sheet contains seven rows of labels, with two labels in each row, for a total of 14 labels. See Figure 6–30.

**Figure 6–30**     **Layout of a sheet of Avery® 5162 Address Labels**

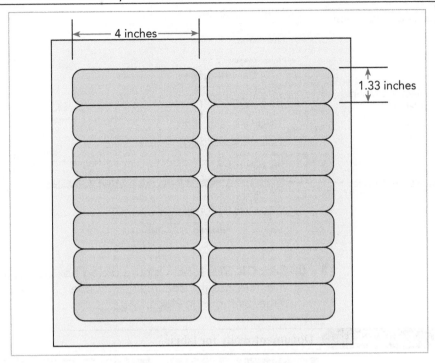

Performing a mail merge to create mailing labels is similar to performing a mail merge to create a form letter. You begin by selecting Labels as the type of main document and then you specify the brand and product number for the labels you are using. You will also need to specify a data source file. In this case, you'll use the Microsoft Office Address Lists data source file, NP_WD_6_Data.mdb, which you created and used in the form letter mail merges.

### To specify the main document for creating mailing labels:

▶ **1.** Open a new, blank document, and then save the document as **NP_WD_6_MainDocument3** in the location specified by your instructor.

▶ **2.** Make sure the rulers and nonprinting characters are displayed, and zoom out so you can see the whole page.

▶ **3.** On the ribbon, click the **Mailings** tab.

▶ **4.** In the Start Mail Merge group, click the **Start Mail Merge** button.

    At this point, if you wanted to merge to envelopes instead of labels, you could click Envelopes to open the Envelope Options dialog box, where you could select the envelope size you wanted to use. In this case, however, you want to merge to labels.

▶ **5.** Click **Labels**. The Label Options dialog box opens.

▶ **6.** Click the **Label vendors arrow** to display a list of vendors, scroll down, and then click **Avery US Letter**.

▶ **7.** Scroll down the Product number box, and then click **5162 Address Labels**. See Figure 6–31.

**Figure 6–31**    **Label Options dialog box**

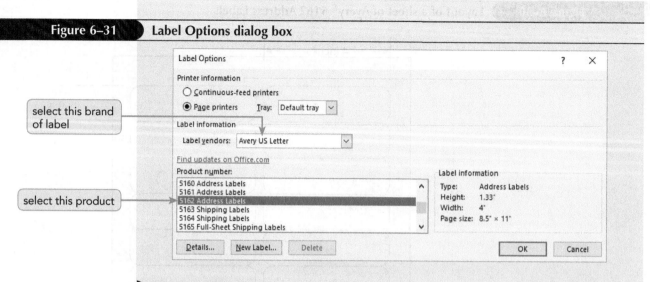

8. Click **OK**. The Label Options dialog box closes, and Word inserts a table structure into the document, with one cell for each of the 14 labels on the page, as shown in Figure 6–32.

**Figure 6–32**    **Document ready for labels**

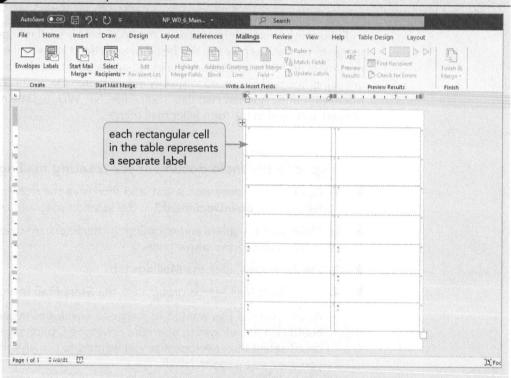

As with all table gridlines, these gridlines are visible only on the screen; they will not be visible on the printed labels.

**Trouble?** If you don't see the table gridlines, click the Layout contextual tab, and then, in the Table group, click the View Gridlines button to select it.

You have finished setting up the document. Next, you need to select the data source you created earlier. Note that the changes you made to the data source as a whole earlier in this session (sorting the records and selecting only some records) have no effect on the data source in this new mail merge. However, the changes you made to individual records (such as editing individual records or adding new records) are retained.

## To continue the mail merge for the labels:

1. In the Start Mail Merge group, click the **Select Recipients** button, and then click **Use an Existing List**. The Select Data Source dialog box opens.

2. Navigate to the location where you stored the NP_WD_6_Data.mdb file, select the **NP_WD_6_Data.mdb** file, and then click the **Open** button. The Select Data Source dialog box closes, and you return to the main document.

3. Change the Zoom level to **120%** so you can read the document. In each label except the first one, the code <<Next Record>> is displayed. This code tells Word to retrieve the next record from the data source for each label.

4. Verify that the insertion point is located in the upper-left label, and make sure the Mailings tab is still selected on the ribbon.

5. In the Write & Insert Fields group, click the **Address Block** button. The Insert Address Block dialog box opens. The left pane displays possible formats for the name in the address block. The default format, "Joshua Randall Jr.," inserts first and last names, along with the other address information, which is what Amalia wants. The Preview pane on the right currently shows the first address in the data source, which is the address for Lari Peterson.

6. In the Preview section of the Insert Address Block dialog box, click the **Next** button ▷. The record for Daniel Ahrens is displayed in the Preview pane, as shown in Figure 6–33. Note that you could also use the Insert Address Block dialog box to insert an inside address in a letter.

> **Tip**
>
> You can only use the Address Block merge field if you include a State field in your data source.

| **Figure 6–33** | **Previewing addresses in the Insert Address Block dialog box** |

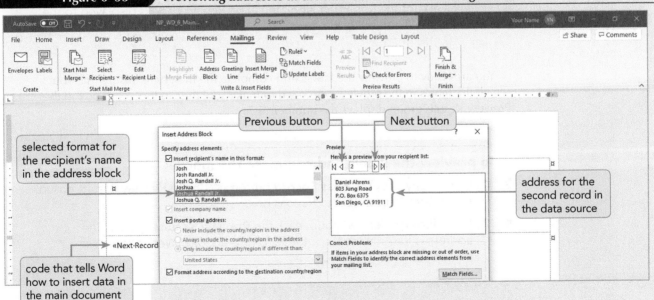

7. Click **OK**. The Insert Address Block dialog box closes, and an AddressBlock merge field is displayed in the upper-left label on the page. Next, you need to update the remaining labels to match the one containing the AddressBlock merge field.

8. In the Write & Insert Fields group, click the **Update Labels** button. The AddressBlock merge field is inserted into all the labels in the document, as shown in Figure 6–34.

**Figure 6–34**     Field codes inserted into document

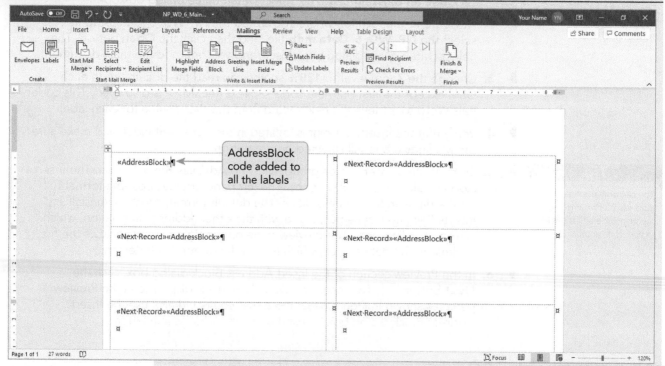

In all except the upper-left label, the Next Record code is displayed to the left of the AddressBlock merge field.

You are ready to preview the labels and complete the merge. To ensure that you see all the labels in the preview, you need to make sure the Go to Record box in the Preview Results group displays the number "1."

### To preview the labels and complete the merge:

1. If necessary, click the **First Record** button ◁ in the Preview Results group to display "1" in the Go to Record box.

2. In the Preview Results group, click the **Preview Results** button. The addresses for Amalia's six potential clients are displayed in the main document. See Figure 6–35.

**Figure 6–35**    Previewing addresses in labels

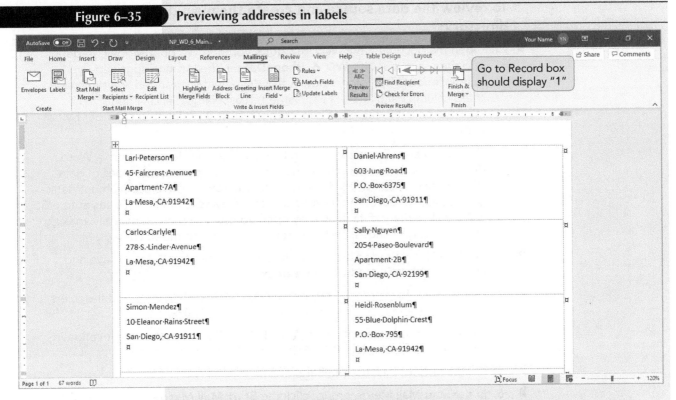

3. In the Finish group, click the **Finish & Merge** button, and then click **Edit Individual Documents**.

4. In the Merge to New Document dialog box, verify that the **All** option button is selected, and then click **OK**. The finished labels are inserted into a new document named Labels1.

5. Scroll through the document. The document contains space for 14 labels, but because the data source contains only six records, the new document only contains addresses for six labels.

6. In the upper-left label, change "Lari Peterson" to your first and last names, and then save the merged document as **NP_WD_6_MergedLabels** in the location specified by your instructor.

7. Close the **NP_WD_6_MergedLabels.docx** document, and then save and close the **NP_WD_6_MainDocument3.docx** file.

# Creating a Phone Directory

Next, Amalia wants you to create a phone directory for all spa employees. She has already created a Word document containing the phone numbers; you will use that document as the data source for the merge. You'll set up a mail merge as before, except this time you will select Directory as the main document type. Keep in mind that you should use a Word document as a data source only for a small-scale project like a directory. For letters, it's better to use an Access database, an Excel workbook, or a Microsoft Office Address Lists file. You'll start by examining the Word document that Amalia wants you to use as the data source, and then you'll create the main document.

### To review the data source and create the main document for the directory:

1. Open the document **NP_WD_6-2.docx** from the Word6 > Module folder, and then save it as **NP_WD_6_PhoneData** in the location specified by your instructor. The information in this document is arranged in a table with three column headings—"First Name," "Last Name," and "Phone." The information in the table has already been sorted in alphabetical order by last name.

   The Mail Merge Recipients dialog box does not display data from a Word document data source in the same way that it displays other types of data. Also, sorting and filtering does not work the same for Word document data sources as it does for other types of files. To avoid problems, it's easier to edit a Word document data source by opening the document separately, making any necessary changes, and then saving and closing the document.

2. Replace "Kiley Bradoff" with your first and last names, and then save and close the **NP_WD_6_PhoneData.docx** file.

3. Open a new, blank document, display nonprinting characters and the rulers, if necessary, and then change the Zoom level to **120%**.

4. Save the main document as **NP_WD_6_MainDocument4** in the location in which you saved the **NP_WD_6_PhoneData.docx** document.

5. On the ribbon, click the **Mailings** tab.

6. In the Start Mail Merge group, click the **Start Mail Merge** button, and then click **Directory**.

7. In the Start Mail Merge group, click the **Select Recipients** button, and then click **Use an Existing List** to open the Select Data Source dialog box.

8. In the dialog box, navigate to and select the Word document named **NP_WD_6_PhoneData.docx**, and then click the **Open** button.

You're ready to insert the fields in the main document. Amalia wants the directory to include the names at the left margin of the page and the phone numbers at the right margin, with a dot leader in between. Recall that a dot leader is a dotted line that extends from the last letter of text on the left margin to the beginning of the nearest text aligned at a tab stop.

### To set up the directory main document with dot leaders:

1. With the insertion point in the first line of the document, insert the **First_Name** merge field, press **SPACEBAR**, and then insert the **Last_Name** merge field.

2. In the Write & Insert Fields group, click the **Highlight Merge Fields** button. The First_Name and Last_Name merge fields are displayed on a gray background. Now you'll set a tab stop at the right margin (at the 5.5-inch mark on the horizontal ruler) with a dot leader.

3. On the ribbon, click the **Home** tab.

4. In the Paragraph group, click the **Paragraph Dialog Box Launcher** to open the Paragraph dialog box, and then in the lower-left corner of the Indents and Spacing tab, click the **Tabs** button. The Tabs dialog box opens.

**Tip**

You can click the Clear All button in the Tabs dialog box to delete all the tab stops in the document.

**5.** In the Tab stop position box, type **5.5** and then click the **Right** option button in the Alignment section.

**6.** Click the **2 .......** option button in the Leader section. See Figure 6–36.

**Figure 6–36**    Creating a tab with a dot leader

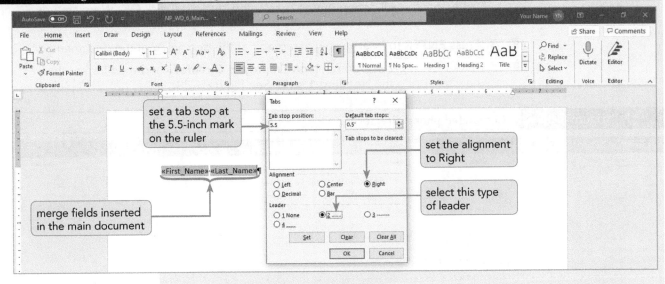

**7.** Click **OK**. Word clears the current tab stops and inserts a right-aligned tab stop at the 5.5-inch mark on the horizontal ruler.

**8.** Press **TAB** to move the insertion point to the new tab stop. A dotted line stretches from the Last_Name merge field to the right side of the page.

**9.** On the ribbon, click the **Mailings** tab.

Be sure to press ENTER here to ensure that each name and phone number is displayed on a separate line.

**10.** Insert the **Phone** merge field at the insertion point. The dot leader shortens to accommodate the inserted merge fields.

**11.** Press **ENTER**. The completed main document should look like the one shown in Figure 6–37.

**Figure 6–37**    Completed main document for the phone directory

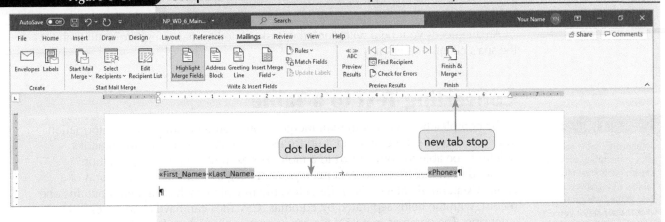

You are now ready to merge this file with the data source.

## To finish the merge for the phone directory:

1. In the Preview Results group, click the **Preview Results** button, and then review the data for the first record in the document.

2. In the Finish group, click the **Finish & Merge** button, and then click **Edit Individual Documents**. In the Merge to New Document dialog box, verify that the **All** option button is selected, and then click **OK**. Word creates a new document that contains the completed phone list.

3. Press **ENTER** to insert a new paragraph at the beginning of the document.

4. Click in the new paragraph, type **Employee Directory** and then format the new text using the **Heading 1** style. See Figure 6–38.

**Figure 6–38**    Completed phone directory

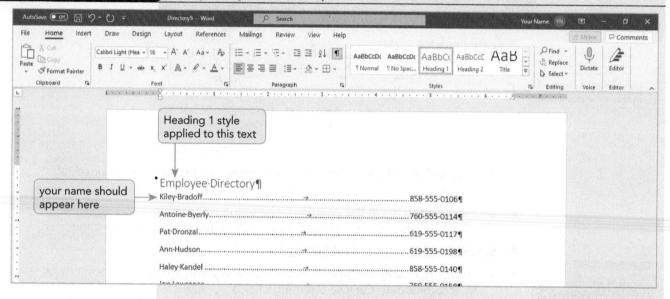

5. Save the document as **NP_WD_6_MergedDirectory** in the location in which you saved the main document, and then close it.

6. Save and close the **NP_WD_6_MainDocument4.docx** file.

Amalia needs your help with one other task related to managing information about the spa's clients and employees.

# Converting Text to a Table

To be completely proficient in mail merges, you should be able to take information from a variety of sources and set it up for use as a data source. In particular, it's helpful to be able to convert text to a table. For example, address information exported from email and contact management programs often takes the form of a **comma-separated values (CSV) file**, a text file in which each paragraph contains one record, with the fields separated by commas. CSV files can have a .txt or .csv file extension. The commas in a CSV file are known as **separator characters**, or sometimes delimiters.

You can use the Convert Text to Table command on the Table menu to transform text from a Word document or a CSV file into a table. But first you need to make sure the text is set up correctly; that is, you need to make sure that separator characters are used consistently to divide the text into individual fields. In a CSV file, commas are used as separator characters, but you might encounter a Word document that uses tab characters, or other characters, as separator characters. After you verify that separator characters are used consistently within a document, you need to make sure each paragraph in the document contains the same number of fields.

Upon conversion, each field is formatted as a separate cell in a column, and each paragraph mark starts a new row, or record. Sometimes a conversion might not turn out the way you expect. In that case, undo it, and then review the text to make sure each paragraph contains the same number of data items, with the items divided by the same separator character.

Amalia's assistant, who isn't familiar with Word tables, typed some information about new clients as text in a Word document. He forgot to include an email address and phone number for each client. Amalia wants to convert the text to a table and then add columns for the missing information. The next time the clients visit the spa, one of the assistants can ask for the missing information and then add it to the table.

### To convert text into a table:

1. Open the document named **NP_WD_6-3.docx** from the Word6 > Module folder, and then save it as **NP_WD_6_Table** in the location specified by your instructor.

2. Display nonprinting characters, if necessary, and then change the Zoom level to **120%**. See Figure 6–39.

| Figure 6–39 | Text with inconsistent separator characters |

The document consists of three paragraphs, each of which contains a client's name, address, city, state, zip code, preferred consultation type, and preferred fitness class. Some of the fields are separated by commas and spaces (for example, the address and the city), but some are separated only by spaces, with no punctuation character (for example, the first and last names). Also, the preferred consultation type and fitness class are enclosed in parentheses. You need to edit this information so that fields are separated by commas, with no parentheses enclosing the last two items.

**3.** Edit the document to insert a comma after each first name, city, and zip code, and then delete the parentheses in each paragraph.

Before you can convert the text into a table, you also need to make sure each paragraph includes the same fields. Currently, the first paragraph includes two pieces of address information—a street address and an apartment number, which is equivalent to an Address Line 1 field and an Address Line 2 field. However, the other paragraphs only include an Address Line 1 field.

**4.** In the second paragraph, click to the right of the comma after "Road," press **SPACEBAR**, and then type **,** (a comma).

**5.** In the third paragraph, click to the right of the comma after "Avenue," press **SPACEBAR**, and then type **,** (a comma). Now the second and third paragraphs each contain a blank field. See Figure 6–40.

| Figure 6–40 | Text set up for conversion to a table |
| --- | --- |

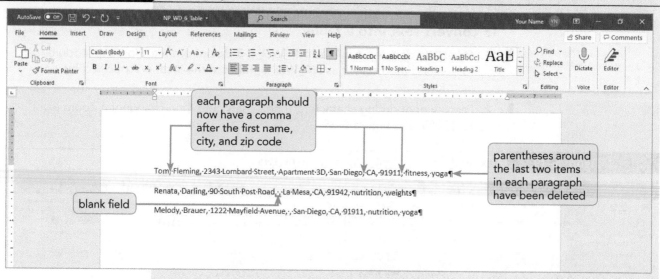

each paragraph should now have a comma after the first name, city, and zip code

parentheses around the last two items in each paragraph have been deleted

Tom, Fleming, 2343 Lombard Street, Apartment 3D, San Diego, CA, 91911, fitness, yoga¶

Renata, Darling, 90 South Post Road, , La Mesa, CA, 91942, nutrition, weights¶

blank field

Melody, Brauer, 1222 Mayfield Avenue, , San Diego, CA, 91911, nutrition, yoga¶

**6.** Press **CTRL+A** to select the entire document.

**7.** On the ribbon, click the **Insert** tab.

**8.** In the Tables group, click the **Table** button, and then click **Convert Text to Table**. The Convert Text to Table dialog box opens. See Figure 6–41.

| Figure 6–41 | Converting text to a table |
| --- | --- |

Convert Text to Table   ?   ×

Table size

Number of columns:   9

corresponds to nine pieces of information in each of the three paragraphs

Number of rows:   3

AutoFit behavior

◉ Fixed column width:   Auto

○ AutoFit to contents

○ AutoFit to window

Separate text at

○ Paragraphs   ◉ Commas

this option button is selected by default

○ Tabs   ○ Other:   -

OK   Cancel

Note that the Number of columns setting is 9, and the Number of rows setting is 3. This corresponds to the nine fields in each of the three paragraphs.

In the Separate text at section of the dialog box, you can choose from three possible separator characters—paragraphs, commas, and tabs. If the text in your document was separated by a character other than paragraphs, commas, or tabs, you could type the character in the box to the right of the Other button. In this case, though, the default option, Commas, is the correct choice because the information in each paragraph is separated by commas.

9. Click **OK**. The Convert Text to Table dialog box closes, and the text in the document is converted into a table consisting of nine columns and three rows.

10. Save the document.

Now that you have converted the text to a table, you need to finish the table by adding the columns for the phone numbers and email addresses and adding a header row to identify the field names.

### To finish the table by adding columns and a header row:

1. Switch to Landscape orientation, and then select the column containing the zip codes.

2. On the ribbon, click the **Layout** contextual tab for tables.

3. In the Rows & Columns group, click the **Insert Right** button twice to add two blank columns to the right of the column containing zip codes.

4. Select the table's top row, and then in the Rows & Columns group, click the **Insert Above** button.

5. Enter the column headings shown in Figure 6–42, and format the column headings in bold.

**Figure 6–42**    Table with new columns and column headings

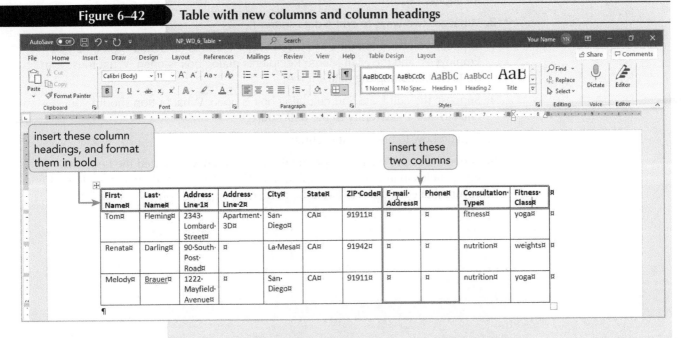

6. Save the **NP_WD_6_Table.docx** file, and then close it.

You have finished converting text into a table. Amalia can use the table later as the data source for another mail merge. As her business expands, she plans to continue to use the mail merge feature in Word to inform her clients about new offerings at the spa.

# Insight

## Combining Data with a Microsoft Office Address Lists File

If you have data in a Word file that you want to combine with data in a Microsoft Office Address Lists file, or any other Microsoft Access file, start by setting up the Word document as a table. That way, you can be sure that each record includes the same fields. You can also review the table quickly to confirm that you have entered data in the various fields in a consistent format. Once you are confident that you have set up the table correctly, you can begin the process of combining it with the Microsoft Office Address Lists file.

First, delete the heading row, and then convert the table back to text by clicking the Layout contextual tab, clicking Convert to Text in the Data group, clicking the Commas button, and then clicking OK. Next, save the Word file as a Plain Text file with the .txt file extension, and then close it. Finally, open the Microsoft Office Address Lists file in Access, click the External Data tab, click the New Data Source in the Import & Link group, click From File, and then click Text File. In the Get External Data—Text File dialog box, click the Append a copy of the records to the table button, click the Browse button to select the plain text file you created, click Open, click OK, click Finish, and then click Close. To display the expanded address list, double-click Office_Address_List in the All Access Objects pane.

# Review

## Session 6.2 Quick Check

1. Does the connection between a main document and its data source persist after you close the main document, if you keep both files in their original locations?

2. What are two ways to edit a data source?

3. Suppose you want to edit a Microsoft Office Address Lists data source named Employees, and the Mail Merge Recipients dialog box is open. What must you do to begin editing the data source?

4. Suppose the Edit Data Source dialog box is open. What button should you click to add a new entry to the data source?

5. Explain how to filter a data source.

6. Suppose you are creating a phone directory and have inserted the necessary merge fields in the first paragraph of the document. What do you need to do to ensure that each name and phone number is displayed on a separate line?

# Practice

## Review Assignments

**Data Files needed for the Review Assignments: NP_WD_6-4.docx, NP_WD_6-5.docx, NP_WD_6-6.docx**

The renovated spa at Sun and Soul Wellness Resort is a big hit with local residents as well as resort guests. Amalia has greatly expanded her local client base, and now she is adding a full schedule of fitness classes. Anyone who signs up for two months of classes also receives a wellness consultation. On the class sign-up form, clients can choose between a nutrition or fitness consultation. Now Amalia wants to send a letter inviting clients to reserve a time for their consultation. At the end of the letter, she wants to include one sentence promoting the spa's massage services, and another sentence promoting the spa's facial services, depending on which spa service the client prefers. She also needs to create an email directory of suppliers she deals with regularly. Finally, she needs to convert some additional client information into a table that she can use as a data source.

Complete the following steps:

1. Open the document **NP_WD_6-4.docx** from the Word6 > Review folder included with your Data Files, and then save the document as **NP_WD_6_ConsultationMainDocument** in the location specified by your instructor.
2. In the first paragraph, replace the placeholder text "[INSERT DATE FIELD]" with a Date field that displays the current month, day, and year—in the format March 11, 2025.
3. Begin the mail merge by selecting Letters as the type of main document.
4. Create a data source with the following fields in the following order: First Name, Last Name, Address Line 1, Address Line 2, City, State, ZIP Code, E-mail Address, Phone, Consultation Type, and Favorite Service. Remove any extra fields, and rename fields as necessary.
5. Create four records using the information shown in Figure 6–43.

**Figure 6–43    Information for new data source**

| First Name | Last Name | Address Line 1 | Address Line 2 | City | State | ZIP Code | E-mail Address | Phone | Consultation Type | Favorite Service |
|---|---|---|---|---|---|---|---|---|---|---|
| Calista | Cutler | 299 Eastley Avenue | Apartment 4A | La Mesa | CA | 91942 | calista@sample.cengage.com | 619-555-0176 | fitness | massage |
| Ruby | Pushkin | 821 Emerald Lane | | San Diego | CA | 31035 | ruby@sample.cengage.com | 760-555-0123 | nutrition | massage |
| Lupita | Morelo | 52 Red Earth Road | P.O. Box 2233 | La Mesa | CA | 91942 | lupita@sample.cengage.com | 619-555-0143 | fitness | facial |
| Marcus | Hesse | 933 Nakoma Way | | San Diego | CA | 31028 | marcus@sample.cengage.com | 760-555-0190 | nutrition | facial |

6. Save the data source as **NP_WD_6_ConsultationData** in the location in which you saved the main document.
7. Edit the data source to replace "Marcus Hesse" with your first and last names.
8. Sort the data source in ascending order by zip code and then by last name.
9. Replace the placeholder text "[INSERT INSIDE ADDRESS]" with an inside address consisting of the necessary separate merge fields. Adjust the paragraph spacing in the inside address as necessary.
10. In the salutation, replace the placeholder text "[INSERT FIRST NAME]" with the First_Name merge field.
11. In the body of the letter, replace the placeholder text "[INSERT CONSULTATION TYPE]" with the Consultation Type merge field.

12. At the end of the paragraph that begins "If you haven't sampled…" create an If. . . Then. . . Else mail merge rule that inserts one of two sentences as follows:
    - If the Favorite Service field contains "massage," then insert **Keep in mind our award-winning massage services are available at a 20% discount on Tuesdays and Thursdays.**
    - If the Favorite Service field contains "facial," then insert **Don't forget that your first facial is free as long as you sign up for three facials within two months.**

13. Adjust the formatting and spacing of the placeholder text inserted by the mail merge rule, as necessary.

14. Save your changes to the main document, and then preview the merged document. Correct any formatting or spacing problems.

15. Merge to a new document, save the merged document as **NP_WD_6_ConsultationMergedLetters** in the location in which you saved the main document, and then close the file.

16. Filter the data source to display only records for clients who requested a nutrition consultation, and then complete a second merge. Save the new merged document as **NP_WD_6_ConsultationMergedLetters2** in the location in which you saved the main document. Close all documents, saving all changes.

17. Open a new, blank document, and create a set of mailing labels using the vendor Avery US Letters and product number 5162. Save the main document as **NP_WD_6_SpaLabelsMainDocument** in the location in which you saved the **NP_WD_6_ConsultationData** file.

18. Select the **NP_WD_6_ConsultationData.mdb** file you created earlier in this assignment as the data source.

19. Insert an AddressBlock merge field in the "Joshua Randall Jr." format, and then update the labels.

20. Preview the merged labels, merge to a new document, and then save the new document as **NP_WD_6_MergedSpaLabels** in the location in which you saved the main document. Save and close all open documents.

21. Open the document **NP_WD_6-5**, and then save it as **NP_WD_6_SupplierData** in the location specified by your instructor. Change "Harvey Siska" to your first and last names, save the document, and close it.

22. Open a new, blank document, and then save it as **NP_WD_6_SupplierDirectory** in the location in which you saved the **NP_WD_6_SupplierData.docx** file. Create a directory main document. Select the **NP_WD_6_SupplierData.docx** file as the data source.

23. Set a right tab at 5.5 inches with a dot leader, and insert the necessary merge fields so that the directory shows a contact followed by a comma, followed by the company name and, on the right side of the page, the email address for each company. Merge to a new document, and then, at the top of the merged document, insert the heading **Vendor Contacts** formatted with the Heading 1 style. Save the merged document as **NP_WD_6_MergedSuppliers** in the location in which you saved the main document. Save and close all open documents.

24. Open the document **NP_WD_6-6.docx** from the Word6 > Review folder, and then save it as **NP_WD_6_ClientData** in the location specified by your instructor. Convert the data in the document to a table with eight columns. Insert a header row with the following column headers formatted in bold—**First Name**, **Last Name**, **Address Line 1**, **Address Line 2**, **City**, **State**, **ZIP code**, and **Consultation Type**. Replace "Tai Chen" with your first and last names. Save and close the document.

# Apply

## Case Problem 1

Data File needed for this Case Problem: NP_WD_6-7.docx

**Great West Coding Academy**   Deandre Baird is the executive director of Great West Coding Academy, a nonprofit institution in Las Vegas, Nevada, devoted to helping non-native English speakers learn to write programming code. As part of a new fund-raising campaign for the school, Deandre plans to send out customized letters to last year's donors, asking them to consider donating the same amount or more this year. He asks you to help him create the letters and the envelopes for the campaign.

Complete the following steps:

1. Open the document **NP_WD_6-7.docx** from the Word6 > Case1 folder, and then save it as **NP_WD_6_GWCAMainDocument** in the location specified by your instructor. In the closing, replace "Deandre Baird" with your first and last names.
2. In the first paragraph, replace the placeholder text "[INSERT DATE FIELD]" with a Date field that displays the current month, day, and year—in the format March 11, 2025.
3. Begin the mail merge by selecting Letters as the type of main document.
4. Create a data source with the following field names, in the following order—**Title**, **First Name**, **Last Name**, **Address Line 1**, **Address Line 2**, **City**, **State**, **ZIP code**, **E-mail Address**, and **Donation Amount**.
5. Enter the four records shown in Figure 6–44.

| Figure 6–44 | Four records for new data source |
| --- | --- |

| Title | First Name | Last Name | Address Line 1 | Address Line 2 | City | State | ZIP Code | E-mail Address | Donation Amount |
| --- | --- | --- | --- | --- | --- | --- | --- | --- | --- |
| Mr. | Tenzen | Sung | 844 Sumerdale Way | Unit 6 | Las Vegas | NV | 88901 | sung@sample.cengage.com | $2,500 |
| Mr. | Darryl | Fuhrman | 1577 Shanley Boulevard | Apartment 4C | Las Vegas | NV | 88105 | fuhrman@sample.cengage.com | $700 |
| Ms. | Susannah | Wilder | 4424 Rue Paris Avenue | | New Mesa | NV | 88133 | wilder@sample.cengage.com | $250 |
| Ms. | Cynthia | Borrego | 633 Hempstead Springs Road | | Las Vegas | NV | 89124 | borrego@sample.cengage.com | $300 |

6. Save the data source as **NP_WD_6_GWCAData** in the location in which you saved the main document.
7. Edit the data source to replace "Tenzen Sung" with your first and last names. Change the title to **Ms.** if necessary.
8. Sort the data source alphabetically by last name.
9. Build an inside address using separate merge fields. Remember to include the Title field. Adjust paragraph spacing as necessary.
10. Add a salutation using a Greeting Line field with the default settings on the appropriate line in the document. Verify that you deleted all placeholder text in the date paragraph, inside address, and the salutation.
11. In the paragraph that begins "In order to continue. . . ," insert the Donation_Amount merge field where indicated. Delete the placeholder text.
12. Save your changes to the NP_WD_6_GWCAMainDocument.docx file. Preview the merged document, and then merge to a new document.
13. Save the merged letters document as **NP_WD_6_GWCAMergedLetters** in the location in which you saved the main document, and then close it.

14. Save the NP_WD_6_GWCAMainDocument.docx file, and then close it.

15. Open a new, blank document, and then save it as **NP_WD_6_GWCAEnvelopes** in the location in which you saved the main document. The school has envelopes with a preprinted return address, so you don't need to type a return address. Begin the mail merge by selecting Envelopes as the type of main document, and then select Size 10 (4 1/8 × 9 1/2 in) as the envelope size in the Envelope Options dialog box.

16. For the data source, use the **NP_WD_6_GWCAData.mdb** file that you saved in Step 6. In the recipient address area of the envelope, insert an AddressBlock merge field in the format "Mr. Joshua Randall Jr."

17. Filter the records in the NP_WD_6_GWCAData.mdb file so that only records with Las Vegas addresses are included in the merge.

18. Merge to a new document.

19. Save the merged document as **NP_WD_6_GWCAMergedEnvelopes** in the location in which you saved the main document, and then close it. Save the main document and close it.

# Create

## Case Problem 2

**Data Files needed for this Case Problem: NP_WD_6-8.docx, NP_WD_6-9.docx**

**4SaleByMe Real Estate**   You have offered to help an older friend sell the home she has owned for 30 years. Instead of contracting with a real estate agent, you and your friend have decided to sell the house using the online listing service 4SaleByMe. For a small fee, the company will host a page on its website describing the home. It's up to you and your friend to generate interest by hosting open-house events, promoting the house's webpage through social media, and using mail merge to send out letters to members of a boating club who might be interested in the lake access the home provides, and also to members of a local biking club, who might be interested in the home's access to bike trails. To complete the mail merge tasks, you need to create a data source, write a letter, add merge fields, and create mailing labels. Finally, you need to diagnose some problems with a directory containing names of people who will be helpful to you while selling the house, and also create some labels that you want to use to send letters to the people in the directory.

Complete the following steps:

1. Open a new document and save it as **NP_WD_6_HouseData**.

2. Change the orientation to Landscape, and then create the table shown in Figure 6–45 and then enter data for four people. Use fictitious names and addresses from your area. For the Club field, enter **Boating** for two records and **Biking** for two records.

**Figure 6–45**   Table structure with field names for data source

| First Name | Last Name | Address Line 1 | Address Line 2 | City | State | ZIP Code | Club |
|------------|-----------|----------------|----------------|------|-------|----------|------|
|            |           |                |                |      |       |          |      |
|            |           |                |                |      |       |          |      |
|            |           |                |                |      |       |          |      |
|            |           |                |                |      |       |          |      |

3. Save the **NP_WD_6_HouseData.docx** document in the location specified by your instructor, and then close it.

4. Open a new blank document, and then save it as **NP_WD_6_HouseMainDocument** in the same location you saved the data file.

5. Begin the mail merge by selecting Letters as the type of main document.

6. Select the **NP_WD_6_HouseData.docx** file as the data source.

7. In the main document, change the top margin to 2.5 inches, to leave room for the 4SaleByMe Real Estate letterhead.

8. Write a letter to potential buyers that includes a date field. Also include an Address Block field and a Greeting Line field that are suitable for your data file. Assume that you will be using 4SaleByMe Real Estate letterhead, so there's no need to include a return address.

9. Include one paragraph explaining why you are writing the letter, and a second paragraph describing the house. Somewhere in the description, create a mail merge rule that displays the following text depending on the contents of the Club field:
   - If the Club field contains "Biking," insert the following in the document: **You are probably already familiar with the extensive bike trails in the area. The Seven Springs trail, which connects to four other trails, is only two minutes away by bike.**
   - If the Club field contains "Boating," insert the following in the document: **The popular Blue Ribbon boat ramp, on the shores of Lake Mendota, is a mere five minutes away by car. The ramp is free to state residents, so there's no need to rent a slip at a commercial marina.**

10. Include a complimentary close and a signature line, leaving space for your signature.

11. Sort the records in the data source in ascending order by last name.

12. Preview the merged document, and note that the lines of the inside address (inserted by the AddressBlock merge field) are spaced too far apart. Make any changes necessary so the inside address and the salutation include the appropriate amount of paragraph and line spacing.

13. Preview all the records in the document.

14. Merge to a new document. Save the merged document as **NP_WD_6_MergedHouseLetters** in the location in which you saved the main document.

15. Close all open documents, saving all changes.

16. Open the document **NP_WD_6-8.docx** from the Word6 > Case2 folder, and save it as **NP_WD_6_IncompleteLabels** in the location specified by your instructor. Attach a comment to the zip code in the first label that explains what error in the main document would result in a set of labels that includes information for only one record.

17. Change "Tony Flores" to your first and last name.

18. Save and close the document.

19. Open the document **NP_WD_6-9.docx** from the Word6 > Case2 folder, and save it as **NP_WD_6_IncompleteDirectory** in the location specified by your instructor. This merged directory will list people you'll need to contact at some point while trying to sell the house, along with each person's profession. The data source for this merged document included the following fields: First Name, Last Name, and Profession. Attach a comment to the name "Tony" that explains what error in the main document would result in a directory formatted like the one in the NP_WD_6_Directory.docx file.

20. Replace **Student Name** with your name, then save and close the document.

21. Save and close the document.

Module 7

## Objectives

**Session 7.1**
- Track changes in a document
- Compare and combine documents
- Accept and reject tracked changes
- Embed an Excel worksheet
- Modify an embedded Excel worksheet

**Session 7.2**
- Link an Excel chart
- Modify and update a linked Excel chart
- Create bookmarks
- Insert and edit hyperlinks
- Optimize a document for online viewing
- Create and publish a blog post

# Collaborating with Others and Integrating Data

## Preparing an Information Sheet

## Case | Movie Time Trivia

Rima Khouri is the marketing director for PYRAMID Games. The company is currently developing a new board game called Movie Time Trivia. Like many game companies, PYRAMID Games plans to use a crowdfunding website to raise the money required to finish developing and marketing its latest product. As part of her marketing effort, Rima also plans to email an information sheet about the fund-raising campaign to interested gamers she met at a recent gaming convention. Rima has asked James Benner, the company's development manager, to review a draft of the information sheet. While James is revising the document, Rima has asked you to work on another copy, making additional changes. When you are finished with your review, Rima wants you to merge James's edited version of the document with your most recent draft.

After you create a new version of the document for Rima, she wants you to add some fund-raising data from an Excel workbook. She also needs you to add a pie chart James created and optimize the information sheet for online viewing. Finally, Rima wants you to help her create a blog post in Word discussing the crowdfunding campaign.

## Starting Data Files

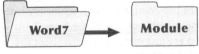

**Word7**  →  **Module**

NP_WD_7-1.docx
NP_WD_7-2.xlsx
NP_WD_7-3.docx
NP_WD_7-4.docx
Support_WD_7_Goals.xlsx
Support_WD_7_James.docx

**Review**

NP_WD_7-5.docx
NP_WD_7-6.xlsx
NP_WD_7-7.docx
Support_WD_7_Funding.xlsx
Support_WD_7_SportsJames.docx

**Case1**

NP_WD_7-8.docx
NP_WD_7-9.xlsx

**Case2**

NP_WD_7-10.docx
Support_WD_7_Aziz.docx
Support_WD_7_Tommy.docx

# Session 7.1 Visual Overview:

When you turn on Track Changes, Word marks the changes you make to the document with revision marks, or tracked changes.

When you point to a tracked change in the document, a ScreenTip displays the name of the reviewer who made the change, when the change was made, and what the change was.

A vertical line appears in the left margin next to text that has been changed in any way.

Inserted text appears with an underline and a contrasting color, with a different color for each person, or reviewer, who edits the document. Here, text inserted by Rima is red, and text inserted by James is blue.

Text with a comment attached is highlighted in color so you can easily see the reference point for the comment.

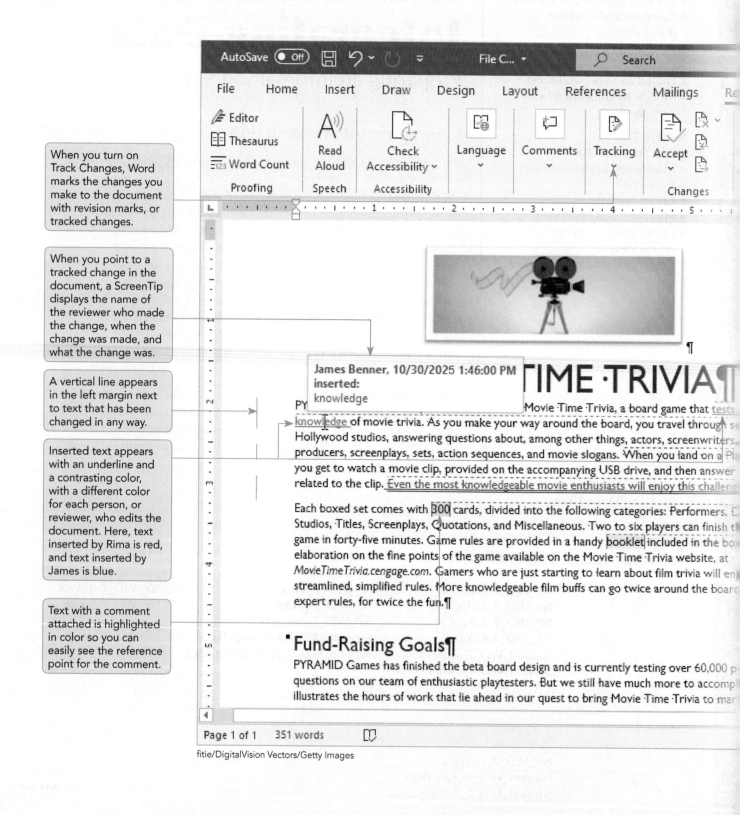

AutoSave ● Off ◻ ↺ ∨ ⟳ ≡     File C... ▾          ⌕ Search

File    Home    Insert    Draw    Design    Layout    References    Mailings    Re

Editor | Thesaurus | Word Count — Proofing
Read Aloud — Speech
Check Accessibility ∨ — Accessibility
Language ∨
Comments ∨
Tracking ∨
Accept ∨
Changes

**James Benner, 10/30/2025 1:46:00 PM inserted:**
knowledge

PY                                    Movie Time Trivia, a board game that tests
knowledge of movie trivia. As you make your way around the board, you travel through s
Hollywood studios, answering questions about, among other things, actors, screenwriters,
producers, screenplays, sets, action sequences, and movie slogans. When you land on a Pla
you get to watch a movie clip, provided on the accompanying USB drive, and then answer
related to the clip. Even the most knowledgeable movie enthusiasts will enjoy this challenge

Each boxed set comes with 300 cards, divided into the following categories: Performers, D
Studios, Titles, Screenplays, Quotations, and Miscellaneous. Two to six players can finish t
game in forty-five minutes. Game rules are provided in a handy booklet included in the bo
elaboration on the fine points of the game available on the Movie Time Trivia website, at
*MovieTimeTrivia.cengage.com.* Gamers who are just starting to learn about film trivia will en
streamlined, simplified rules. More knowledgeable film buffs can go twice around the boar
expert rules, for twice the fun.¶

## Fund-Raising Goals¶

PYRAMID Games has finished the beta board design and is currently testing over 60,000 p
questions on our team of enthusiastic playtesters. But we still have much more to accompl
illustrates the hours of work that lie ahead in our quest to bring Movie Time Trivia to mar

Page 1 of 1     351 words

fitie/DigitalVision Vectors/Getty Images

# Tracking Changes

The Review tab contains all the options you need for editing a document using tracked changes and comments.

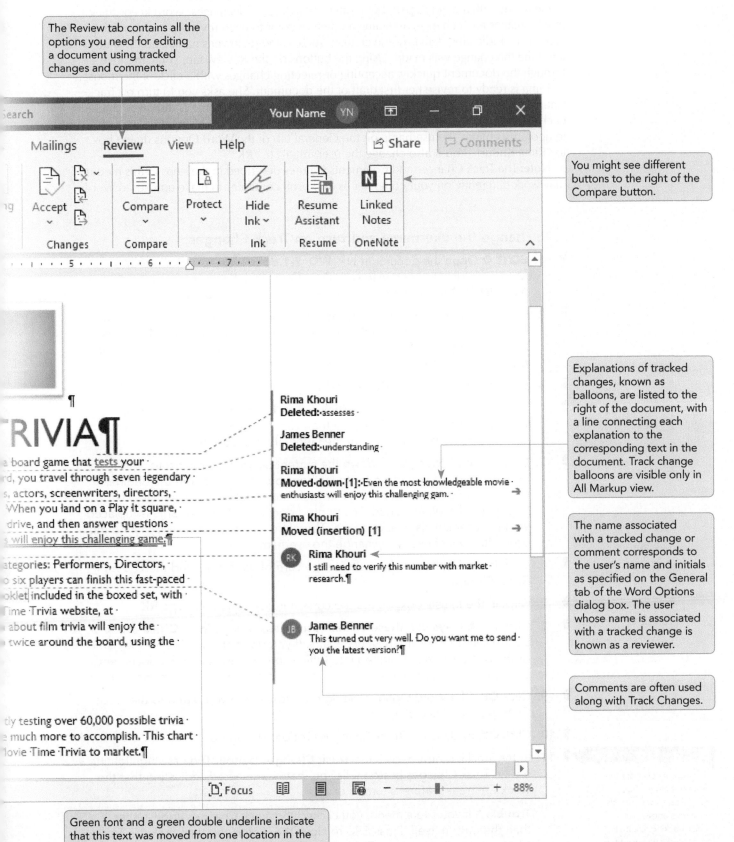

You might see different buttons to the right of the Compare button.

Explanations of tracked changes, known as balloons, are listed to the right of the document, with a line connecting each explanation to the corresponding text in the document. Track change balloons are visible only in All Markup view.

The name associated with a tracked change or comment corresponds to the user's name and initials as specified on the General tab of the Word Options dialog box. The user whose name is associated with a tracked change is known as a reviewer.

Comments are often used along with Track Changes.

Green font and a green double underline indicate that this text was moved from one location in the document and inserted in this new location.

# Editing a Document with Tracked Changes

The Track Changes feature in Word simulates the process of marking up a hard copy of a document with a colored pen, but it offers many more advantages. Word keeps track of who makes each change, assigning a different color to each reviewer and providing ScreenTips indicating details of the change, such as the reviewer's name and the date and time the change was made. Using the buttons on the Review tab, you can move through the document quickly, accepting or rejecting changes with a click of the mouse.

Rima is ready to revise her first draft of the document. She asks you to turn on Track Changes before you make the edits for her. To ensure that her name is displayed for each tracked change, and that your screens match the figures in this module, you will temporarily change the username on the General tab of the Word Options dialog box to "Rima Khouri." You'll also change the user initials to "RK."

**Note:** The Track Changes and Comments features described in the steps in this module may work differently on your computer as Microsoft continues to make updates to Word.

## To change the username and turn on Track Changes:

1. **sam** ↓ Open the document **NP_WD_7-1.docx** located in the Word7 > Module folder included with your Data Files, and then save the document as **NP_WD_7_Rima** in the location specified by your instructor.

2. Switch to Print Layout view if necessary, display the rulers and nonprinting characters, and change the document Zoom level to **110%**. You'll use this Zoom setting for the first part of this module to ensure that you can see all the tracked changes in the document.

3. On the ribbon, click the **Review** tab.

4. In the Tracking group, click the **Dialog Box Launcher** to open the Track Changes Options dialog box, and then click **Change User Name**. The Word Options dialog box opens, with the General tab displayed.

5. On a piece of paper, write down the current username and initials, if they are not your own, so you can refer to it when you need to restore the original username and initials later in this module. Although the user initials do not appear on the Word screen, in a printed document the username is replaced with the user initials to save space. Therefore, you should always change the user initials whenever you change the username.

6. Click in the **User name** box, delete the current username, and then type **Rima Khouri**.

7. Click in the Initials box, delete the current initials, and then type **RK**.

8. Click the **Always use these values regardless of sign in to Office** check box to insert a checkmark, if necessary. If you don't check this box, the name of the person currently signed into Office.com will appear in the document's tracked changes, no matter what username is entered in the User name box.

9. Click **OK**. The Word Options dialog box closes, and you return to the Track Changes Options dialog box.

10. Click **OK** to close the Track Changes Options dialog box.

11. In the Tracking group, click the **Track Changes** button. The gray highlighting on the Track Changes button tells you that it is selected, indicating that the Track Changes feature is turned on.

    **Trouble?** If you see a menu, you clicked the Track Changes arrow rather than the button itself. Press ESC to close the menu, and then click the Track Changes button to turn on Track Changes.

**Tip**

To prevent collaborators from turning off Track Changes, click the Track Changes arrow, click Lock Tracking, create a password if you want to use one, and then click OK.

**12.** In the Tracking group, verify that the Display for Review box displays "All Markup." This setting ensures that tracked changes are displayed in the document as you edit it.

**Trouble?** If the Display for Review box does not display "All Markup," click the Display for Review arrow, and then click All Markup.

**13.** In the Tracking group, click the **Show Markup** button, and then point to **Balloons**. See Figure 7–1.

| Figure 7–1 | Track Changes turned on |

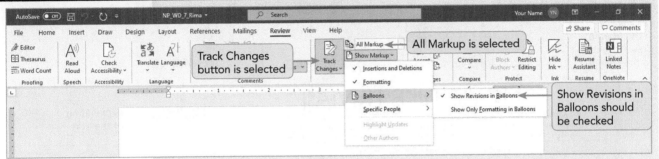

**14.** If you do not see a checkmark next to Show Revisions in Balloons, click **Show Revisions in Balloons** now to select it and close the menu. Otherwise, click anywhere in the document to close the menu.

Now that Track Changes is turned on, you can begin editing Rima's document. First, Rima needs to change the word "assesses" in the first sentence to "tests."

### To edit Rima's document and view the tracked changes:

**1.** In the line below the "Movie Time Trivia" heading, select the word **assesses** and then type **tests**. The new word ("tests") is displayed in color, with an underline. A vertical line is displayed in the left margin, drawing attention to the change. To the right of the document, the username associated with the change (Rima Khouri) is displayed, along with an explanation of the change. See Figure 7–2.

**Figure 7–2**     **Edit marked as tracked change**

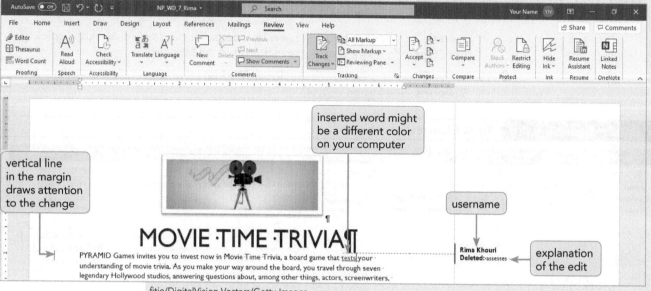

fitie/DigitalVision Vectors/Getty Images

2. Move the pointer over the newly inserted word "tests." A ScreenTip displays information about the edit, along with the date and time the edit was made.

3. Move the pointer over the explanation of the change to the right of the document. The explanation is highlighted, and the dotted line connecting the change in the document to the explanation turns solid. In a document with many tracked changes, this makes it easier to see which explanation is associated with which tracked change.

   Next, Rima wants you to move the second-to-last sentence in this paragraph to the end of the paragraph.

4. Press **CTRL**, and then click in the sentence that begins "Even the most knowledgeable…." The entire sentence is selected. Don't be concerned that the word "game" at the end of the sentence is misspelled. You'll correct that error shortly.

5. Drag the sentence to insert it at the end of the paragraph, and then click anywhere in the document to deselect it. See Figure 7–3.

**Figure 7–3**    Tracked changes showing text moved to a new location

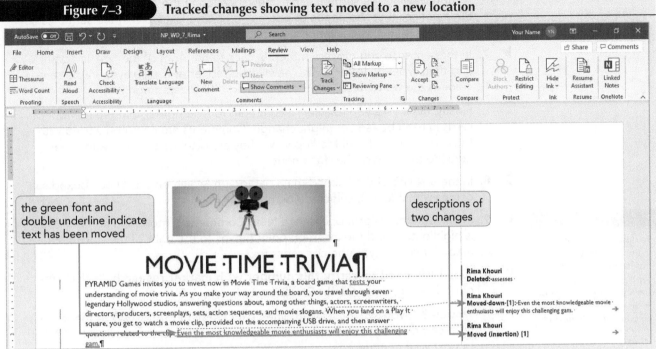

fitie/DigitalVision Vectors/Getty Images

The sentence is inserted with a double underline in green, which is the color Word uses to denote moved text. Word also inserts a space before the inserted sentence and marks the nonprinting space character as a tracked change. A vertical bar in the left margin draws attention to the moved text.

To the right of the document, descriptions of two new changes are displayed. The "Moved down [1]" change shows the text of the sentence that was moved. The "Moved (insertion) [1]" change draws attention to the sentence in its new location at the end of the paragraph.

A blue, right-facing arrow next to a tracked change explanation indicates that the change is related to another change. You can click the arrow to select the related change.

6. Next to the "Moved (insertion) [1]" change, click the blue, right-facing arrow →  to select the moved sentence in the "Moved down [1]" balloon. See Figure 7–4.

**Figure 7–4**    Selecting a related change

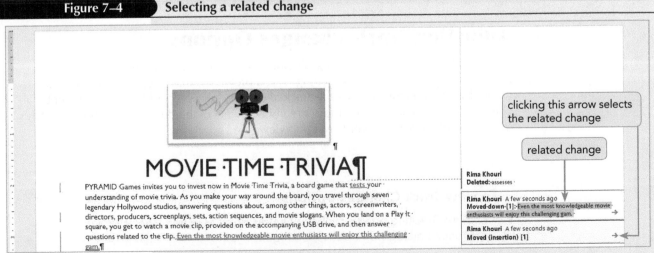

fitie/DigitalVision Vectors/Getty Images

After reviewing the sentence in its new location at the end of the paragraph, Rima notices that she needs to add an "e" to the last word in the sentence so that it reads "…this challenging game."

7. In the sentence you moved in Step 5, click to the right of the "m" in "gam," and then type the letter **e**. The newly inserted letter is displayed in the same color as the word "tests" at the beginning of the paragraph.

Finally, Rima asks you to insert a comment reminding her that the number of cards in each boxed set might change. Comments are commonly used with tracked changes. In All Markup view, they are displayed, along with other edits, to the right of the document.

8. In the first line of the second main paragraph (which begins "Each boxed set comes with 300…"), select the number **300**.

9. In the Comments group, click the **New Comment** button. The number "300" is highlighted, and the insertion point moves to the right of the document, ready for you to type the comment text.

10. Type **I still need to verify this number with market research.** (Include the period.) Then, press **CTRL+ENTER**. See Figure 7–5.

    **Trouble?** If you do not see the blue Post comment button ▶ in the lower-right corner of the comment balloon, you do not need to press CTRL+ENTER to post your comment.

**Figure 7–5**   Comment added to document

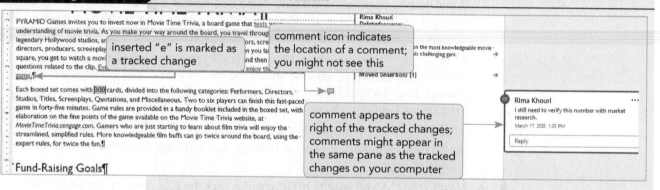

11. Save your document.

# Adjusting Track Changes Options

The default settings for Track Changes worked well as you edited Rima's document. However, you can change these settings if you prefer. For instance, you could choose not to display formatting changes as tracked changes, or you could select a different color for inserted text. To get a more streamlined view of the document, you can switch from All Markup view to Simple Markup view.

## To view Track Changes options:

1. In the Tracking group, click the **Dialog Box Launcher**. The Track Changes Options dialog box opens. See Figure 7–6.

**Figure 7–6**    **Track Changes Options dialog box**

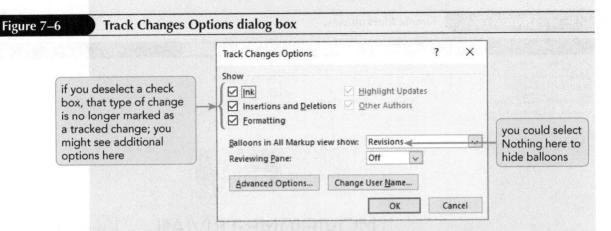

if you deselect a check box, that type of change is no longer marked as a tracked change; you might see additional options here

you could select Nothing here to hide balloons

The check boxes in the Show section control which types of edits are marked as tracked changes. For example, the Formatting check box is currently selected. If you didn't want formatting changes to be marked as tracked changes, you could deselect the Formatting check box. Note that Revisions is currently selected in the "Balloons in All Markup view show" box. To turn off the balloon feature, so that no track changes or comment balloons are displayed to the right of the document in All Markup view, you could select Nothing instead.

2. Click **Advanced Options**. The Advanced Track Changes Options dialog box opens.

   The options in this dialog box allow you to select the colors you want to use for various types of edits. For example, you can use the Color box next to the Insertions box to select a color to use for inserted text. Note that the default setting for Insertions, Deletions, Comments, and Formatting is By author. This means that Word assigns one color to each person who edits the document. When you are working with multiple reviewers, you should always retain the By author settings to ensure that you can easily distinguish the edits made by each reviewer.

3. Click **Cancel** to close the Advanced Track Changes Options dialog box, and then click **Cancel** or **Close** to close the Track Changes Options dialog box.

After reviewing the tracked changes with you, Rima decides the number of details shown in All Markup view makes the document too difficult to read. She wants you to switch to Simple Markup view instead and hide comments.

### To switch to Simple Markup view:

1. In the Tracking group, click the **Display for Review arrow**, and then click **Simple Markup**.

2. In the Comments group, click the **Show Comments** button if it is gray, to deselect it. Depending on the way Comments work on your computer, with the Show Comments button deselected, you might still see the comment in the margin, or you might see only an icon in the margin (see Figure 7-7).

   **Trouble?** If you do see the comment text *and* an icon, don't be concerned. You can still complete the steps that follow. The Comments feature in Word continues to evolve, so you might also find that it works differently over time. The point of this step is to alert you to the fact that in some installations of Word, you might not actually see the comment text, and instead see only an icon.

**Figure 7–7**   Simple Markup view

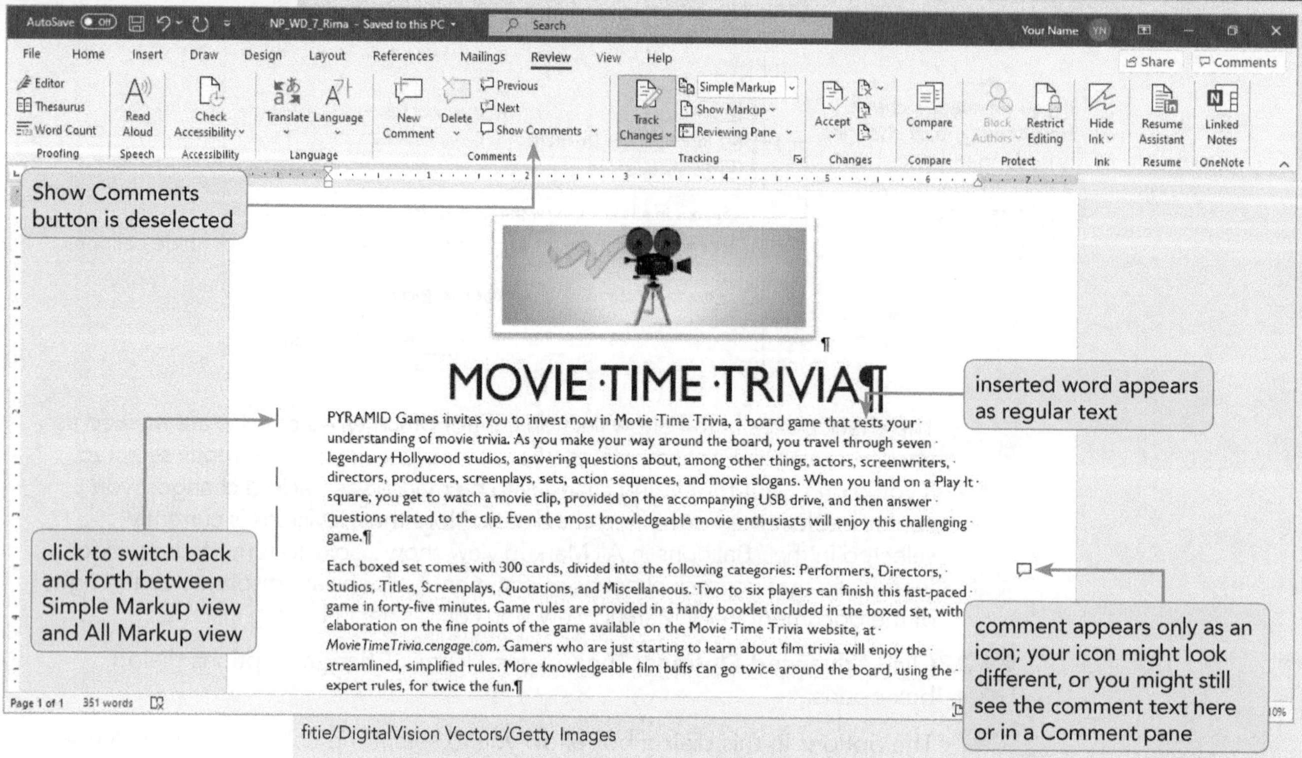

Show Comments button is deselected

inserted word appears as regular text

click to switch back and forth between Simple Markup view and All Markup view

comment appears only as an icon; your icon might look different, or you might still see the comment text here or in a Comment pane

fitie/DigitalVision Vectors/Getty Images

All of the tracked changes in the document are now hidden, and the comment balloon appears only as an icon in the right margin. The inserted word "tests" is in black font, like the surrounding text, as is the sentence you moved to the end of the paragraph. The only sign that the document contains tracked changes is the red vertical bar in the left margin. You can click a vertical bar to switch back and forth between Simple Markup view and All Markup view.

3. Click the red vertical bar to the left of the paragraph that begins "PYRAMID Games invites...." The document switches to All Markup view, with all the tracked changes visible. The vertical bar in the left margin changes from red to gray.

4. Click the gray vertical bar to the left of the paragraph that begins "PYRAMID Games invites...." The document switches back to Simple Markup view.

Rima has received James's edited copy of the first draft via email, and now she'd like your help in combining her edited copy of the NP_WD_7_Rima.docx document with James's copy.

# Comparing and Combining Documents

When you work in a collaborative environment with multiple people contributing to the same document, the Compare and Combine features in Word are essential tools. They allow you to see the difference between multiple versions of a document, with tracked changes highlighting the differences. The Compare and Combine features are similar, but they have different purposes.

The **Compare** feature, which is designed to help you quickly spot the differences between two copies of a document, is intended for documents that *do not* contain tracked changes. After it compares the two documents, Word notes the differences between the revised document and the original document with tracked changes, with all the tracked changes assigned to the username associated with the revised document.

The **Combine** feature, which is designed for documents that *do* contain tracked changes, allows you to see which reviewers made which changes. In a combined document, each reviewer's tracked changes are displayed, with each tracked change assigned to the reviewer who made that change. The Combine feature works well when you want to combine, or merge, two documents to create a third document. You can then combine additional reviewed versions of the document into this new document, until you have incorporated all the tracked changes from all your reviewers. Because the Combine feature allows you to incorporate more than two documents into one, it's the option you'll use most when collaborating with a group.

When you compare or combine documents, you select one document as the original and one as the revised document. Together, these two documents are known as the **source documents**. By default, Word then creates a new, third document, which consists of the original document's text edited with tracked changes to show how the revised document differs. The source documents themselves are left unchanged. If Word detects a formatting conflict—that is, if identical text is formatted differently in the source documents—Word displays a dialog box allowing you to choose which formatting you want to keep. You can choose to keep the formatting of the original document or the revised document, but not both. Occasionally, Word will display this formatting conflict dialog box even if both source documents are formatted exactly the same. If so, keep the formatting for the original document, and continue with the process of combining the documents.

# Reference

### Comparing and Combining Documents

- On the ribbon, click the Review tab.
- In the Compare group, click the Compare button.
- Click Compare to open the Compare Documents dialog box, or click Combine to open the Combine Documents dialog box.
- Next to the Original document box, click the Browse button, navigate to the location of the document, select the document, and then click the Open button.
- Next to the Revised document box, click the Browse button, navigate to the location of the document, select the document, and then click the Open button.
- Click the More button, if necessary, to display options that allow you to select which items you want marked with tracked changes, and then make any necessary changes.
- Click OK.

When you start combining or comparing documents, it's not necessary to have either the original document or the revised document open. In this case, however, the NP_WD_7_Rima.docx document, which you will use as the original document, is open. You'll combine this document with James's edited copy.

**Note:** The comparing and combining features described in the steps in this module may work differently on your computer as Microsoft continues to make updates to Word.

**To combine Rima's document with James's document:**

▶ **1.** Make sure you have saved your changes to the NP_WD_7_Rima.docx document.

▶ 2. In the Compare group, click the **Compare** button. A menu opens with options for comparing or combining different versions of a document.

▶ 3. Click **Combine**. The Combine Documents dialog box opens.

▶ 4. Click the **More** button. The dialog box expands to display check boxes, which you can use to specify the items you want marked with tracked changes.

**Trouble?** If the dialog box has a Less button instead of a More button, the dialog box is already expanded to show the check boxes for selecting additional options. In this case, skip Step 4.

▶ 5. In the Show changes section at the bottom of the dialog box, select the **New document** option button if necessary, so that Word will create a new, combined document rather than importing the tracked changes from the original document into the revised document, or vice versa.

▶ 6. Select any unchecked checkboxes in the Comparison settings section of the dialog box.

Now you need to specify the NP_WD_7_Rima.docx document as the original document. Even though this document is currently open, you still need to select it.

▶ 7. Next to the Original document box, click the **Browse** button ⬜ to open the Open dialog box.

▶ 8. If necessary, navigate to the location where you saved the NP_WD_7_Rima document, click **NP_WD_7_Rima.docx** in the file list, and then click the **Open** button. You return to the Combine Documents dialog box, where the file name "NP_WD_7_Rima" is displayed in the Original document box.

Next, you need to select the document you want to use as the revised document.

▶ 9. Next to the Revised document box, click the **Browse** button ⬜, navigate to the **Word7 > Module** folder included with your Data Files if necessary, select the document **Support_WD_7_James.docx**, and then click the **Open** button. The file name "Support_WD_7_James" is displayed in the Revised document box. See Figure 7–8.

**Figure 7–8**    **Selecting the original and revised documents**

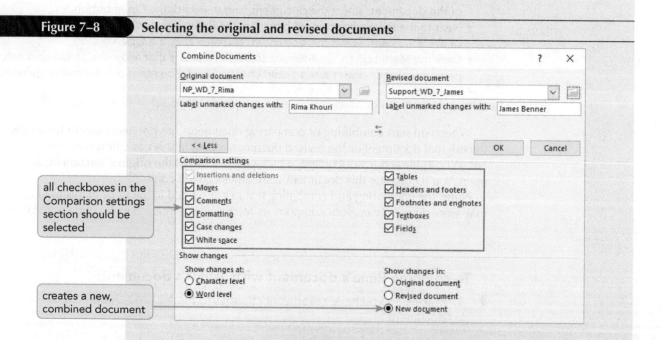

**10.** Click **OK**. The Combine Documents dialog box closes.

A new document opens. It contains the tracked changes from both the original document and the revised document.

At this point, depending on the previous settings on your computer, you might see only the new, combined document, or you might also see the original and revised documents open in separate windows. You might also see the Reviewing pane, with a list of all the changes, as shown in Figure 7–9.

**Figure 7–9    Two documents combined**

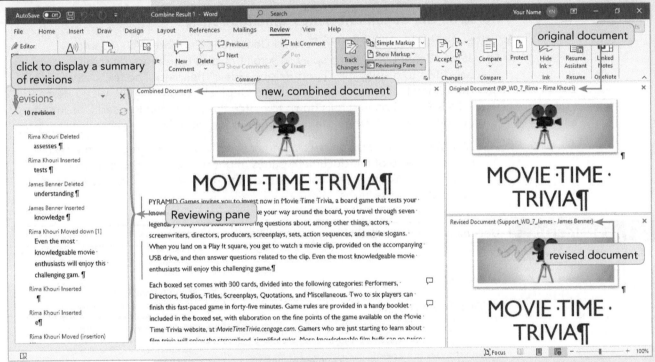

fitie/DigitalVision Vectors/Getty Images

Note that your combined document might have a different name than the one shown in Figure 7–9. For instance, it might be named "Document 1," instead of "Combine Result 1." Also, if you do see the Reviewing pane, don't be concerned if it is displayed at a different Zoom level than what you see in Figure 7–9. In the next few steps, you will make any adjustments necessary to ensure your screen looks similar (but possibly not identical to) Figure 7-9.

**11.** In the Compare group, click the **Compare** button, and then point to **Show Source Documents**.

**12.** If a checkmark appears next to Show Both, press ESC twice to close both menus; otherwise, click **Show Both**. Your screen should now match Figure 7–9.

**Trouble?** If the Reviewing pane is still not displayed, click the Reviewing Pane button in the Tracking group to display the Reviewing pane.

**Trouble?** If your Reviewing pane is displayed horizontally rather than vertically, as shown in Figure 7–9, click the Reviewing Pane arrow in the Tracking group, and then click Reviewing Pane Vertical.

Note that the combined document and the two source documents are all displayed in Simple Markup. Also, instead of Print Layout view, which you typically use when working on documents, the three documents are displayed in Web Layout view. You'll learn more about Web Layout view later in this module. For now, all you need to know is that in Web Layout view, the line breaks change to suit the size of the document window, making it easier to read text in the small windows.

It's helpful to have the source documents displayed when you want to quickly compare the two documents. For example, right now Rima wants to scroll down the documents to see how they differ. When you scroll up or down in the Revised Document pane, the other documents scroll as well.

### To scroll the document panes simultaneously:

▶ **1.** Move the pointer over the Revised Document (Support_WD_7_James – James Benner) pane to display its scroll bar, and then drag the scroll bar down to display the "Fund-Raising Goals" heading. The text in the Combined Document pane and in the Original Document (NP_WD_7_Rima - Rima Khouri) pane scrolls down to match the text in the Revised Document (Support_WD_7_James - James Benner) pane. See Figure 7–10.

**Trouble?** Depending on how Comments work on your computer, the text in one or more of the document panes might be formatted in a narrow column to make room for comments on the right. Ignore that, and continue completing these steps.

---

**Figure 7–10**    **Document panes scrolled to compare versions**

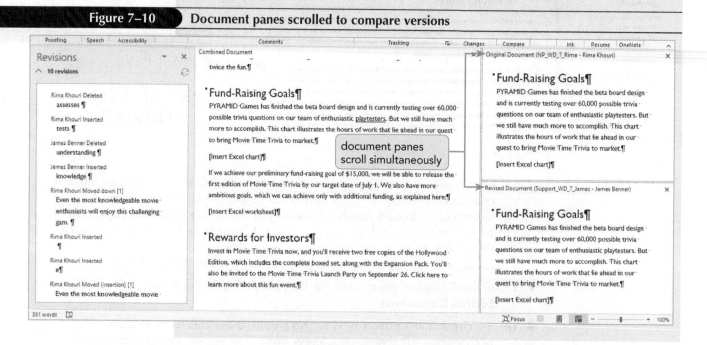

Now that you've reviewed both documents, you can hide the source documents to make the combined document easier to read. After you hide the source documents, you can review the edits in the Reviewing pane.

## To hide the source documents and review the edits in the Reviewing pane:

1. In the Compare group, click the **Compare** button, point to the **Show Source Documents** button, and then click **Hide Source Documents**. The panes displaying the original and revised documents close, and the combined document window switches to Print Layout view.

   **Trouble?** If the combined window does not switch to Print Layout view, click the Print Layout view button 📄 on the status bar.

2. Move the pointer over the list of edits in the Reviewing pane to display the vertical scroll bar, and then scroll down and review the list of edits. Notice that the document contains the edits you made earlier (under Rima's name) as well as edits made by James Benner.

   Rima prefers to review changes using All Markup view instead of the Reviewing pane.

**Tip**

To hide a reviewer's edits, click the Show Markup button in the Tracking group, point to Specific People, and then click the person's name.

3. In the Tracking group, click the **Reviewing Pane** button to deselect it. The Reviewing pane closes.

4. In the Tracking group, click the **Display for Review arrow**, and then click **All Markup**.

5. In the Tracking group, click the **Show Markup** button, point to Balloons, and then make sure **Show Revisions in Balloons** is selected.

6. Save the document as **NP_WD_7_Combined** in the location specified by your instructor.

7. In the Tracking group, click the **Track Changes** button to turn off Track Changes. This ensures that you won't accidentally add any additional edit marks as you review the document.

8. Change the Zoom level to **120%**.

# Insight

## Using Real-Time Co-Authoring to Collaborate with Others

Combining documents is a powerful way to incorporate the work of multiple people in one document. The only drawback to combining documents is that, typically, one person is charged with combining the documents, reviewing the tracked changes, and then making decisions about what to keep and what to delete. In some situations, it's more effective to give all team members the freedom to edit a document at the same time, with every person's changes showing up on everyone else's screen. You can accomplish this by saving a document to OneDrive and then sharing it using the co-authoring feature in Word.

To get started, click Share in the upper-right corner of the Word window to open the Share pane, and then save the document to OneDrive. Next, use the options in the Send link dialog box: (1) enter the email addresses for the people you want to share the document with, as well as a message inviting them to work on the document; or (2) create a sharing link, which you can then email to your collaborators, and which they can then click to open the document in the online version of Microsoft Office. After a delay of a few minutes or less, you and all of your collaborators can begin editing the document, while being able to see everyone else's changes to the document in real time.

Next, you will review the edits in the NP_WD_7_Combined.docx document to accept and reject the changes as appropriate.

# Accepting and Rejecting Changes

The document you just created contains all the edits from two different reviewers—Rima's changes made in the original document and James's changes as they appeared in the revised document. In the combined document, each reviewer's edits are displayed in a different color.

When you review tracked changes in a document, the best approach is to move the insertion point to the beginning of the document, and then navigate through the document one change at a time using the Next and Previous buttons in the Changes group on the Review tab. This ensures you won't miss any edits. As you review a tracked change, you can either accept the change or reject it.

## Reference

### Accepting and Rejecting Changes

- Move the insertion point to the beginning of the document.
- On the ribbon, click the Review tab.
- In the Changes group, click the Next button to select the first edit or comment in the document.
- To accept a selected change, click the Accept button in the Changes group.
- To reject a selected change, click the Reject button in the Changes group.
- To accept all the changes in the document, click the Accept arrow, and then click Accept All Changes.
- To reject all the changes in the document, click the Reject arrow, and then click Reject All Changes.

**To accept and reject changes in the NP_WD_7_Combined.docx document:**

1. Press **CTRL+HOME** to move the insertion point to the beginning of the document.

2. In the Changes group, click the **Next** button. To the right of the document, in a tracked change balloon, the deleted word "assesses" is selected, as shown in Figure 7–11.

| Figure 7–11 | First change in document selected |

fitie/DigitalVision Vectors/Getty Images

**Trouble?** If the insertion point moves to Rima's comment, you clicked the Next button in the Comments group instead of the Next button in the Changes group. Repeat Steps 1 and 2.

3. In the Changes group, click the **Accept** button. The tracked change balloon is no longer displayed, indicating that the change has been accepted. The inserted word "tests" is now selected in the document.

   **Trouble?** If you see a menu below the Accept button, you clicked the Accept arrow by mistake. Press ESC to close the menu, and then click the Accept button.

4. Click the **Accept** button. In a tracked change balloon to the right of the document, James's deletion of the word "understanding" is selected. See Figure 7–12.

| Figure 7–12 | Reviewing James's changes |
| --- | --- |

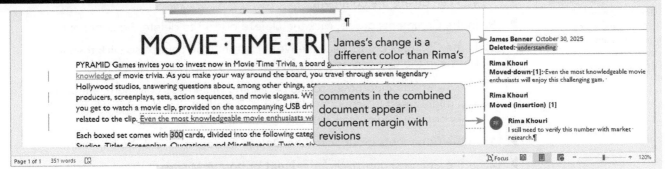

James deleted the word "understanding" and replaced it with the word "knowledge," which is displayed in the document as a tracked change. The inserted word, the tracked change balloon for the deleted word, and the icon in James's comment further down in the document are all the same color.

Because the word "knowledgeable" is used later in this same paragraph, Rima prefers to keep the original word, "understanding," so you need to reject James's change.

5. In the Changes group, click the **Reject** button to reject the deletion of the word "understanding." The tracked change balloon is no longer displayed, and the word "understanding" is restored in the document, to the left of the inserted word "knowledge," which is now selected. See Figure 7–13.

| Figure 7–13 | Document after rejecting change |
| --- | --- |

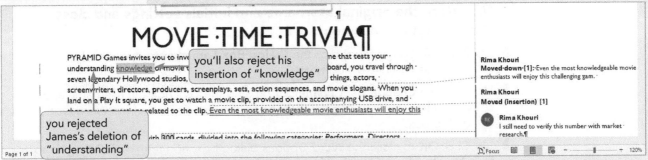

6. Click the **Reject** button. The inserted word "knowledge" is removed from the document. To the right of the document, in a tracked change balloon, the sentence that you moved is now selected.

7. Click the **Accept** button. The tracked change balloon containing the moved sentence and the related "Moved (insertion) [1]" tracked change balloon are no longer displayed. In the document, the sentence itself is displayed in black, like the surrounding text, indicating that the change has been accepted. Now the space before the moved sentence, which Word automatically inserted when you moved the sentence, is selected.

**Tip**

To accept all changes currently displayed (not necessarily all the changes in the document), click the Accept arrow, and click Accept All Changes Shown. To reject all changes shown, click the Reject arrow, and click Reject All Changes Shown.

8. Click the **Accept** button to accept the insertion of the space, and then click the **Accept** button again to accept the insertion of the letter "e" at the end of "gam."

   The insertion point moves to the beginning of Rima's comment. Rima has received final confirmation that 300 is indeed the correct number of cards, so you can delete the comment.

9. In the Comments group, click the **Delete** button to delete the comment.

10. In the Changes group, click the **Next** button. (You could also click the Next button in the Comments group since the next item is a comment.)

    The insertion point moves to the beginning of James's comment, although you might need to scroll down to see it. Rima has already seen a draft of the rules booklet, so you can delete the comment.

11. In the Comments group, click the **Delete** button to delete the comment.

12. In the Changes group, click the **Next** button. A Microsoft Word dialog box opens with a message indicating that there are no more comments or tracked changes in the document.

13. Click **OK** to close the dialog box.

14. At the end of the last paragraph in the document, click to the left of the period, insert a space if necessary, and type **or contact *your name***, where *your name* is your first and last name. When you are finished, the text should read "about this fun event or contact *your name*."

Now that you have finished editing and reviewing the document with tracked changes, you need to restore the original username and initials settings. Then you can close Rima's original document, which you no longer need.

**To restore the original username and initials settings and close Rima's original document:**

1. In the Tracking group, click the **Dialog Box Launcher** to open the Track Changes Options dialog box.

2. Click the **Change User Name** button, and then change the username and initials back to their original settings on the General tab of the Word Options dialog box.

3. Click **OK** to close the Word Options dialog box, and then click **OK** again to close the Track Changes Options dialog box.

4. On the taskbar, click the **Word** button, and then click the **NP_WD_7_Rima - Word** thumbnail to display the document.

5. Close the **NP_WD_7_Rima.docx** document.

6. Save the **NP_WD_7_Combined.docx** document, and then display the rulers.

7. On the ribbon, click the **Home** tab.

## Insight

### Checking for Tracked Changes

Once a document is finished, you should make sure it does not contain any tracked changes or comments. This is especially important in situations where comments or tracked changes might reveal sensitive information that could jeopardize your privacy or the privacy of the organization you work for.

You can't always tell if a document contains comments or tracked changes just by looking at it because the comments or changes for some or all of the reviewers might be hidden. Also, the Display for Review box in the Tracking group on the Review tab might be set to No Markup, in which case all tracked changes would be hidden. To determine whether a document contains any tracked changes or comments, open the Reviewing pane and verify that the number of revisions for each type is 0. You can also use the Document Inspector to check for a variety of issues, including leftover comments and tracked changes. To use the Document Inspector, click the File tab to display the Info tab, click Check for Issues, click Inspect Document, and then click the Inspect button.

Now that you have combined James's edits with Rima's, you are ready to add the Excel worksheet data and the pie chart to the document.

# Embedding and Linking Objects from Other Programs

The programs in Office are designed to accomplish specific tasks. As you've seen with Word, you can use a word-processing program to create, edit, and format documents such as letters, reports, newsletters, and proposals. On the other hand, Microsoft Excel, a **spreadsheet program**, allows you to organize, calculate, and analyze numerical data in a grid of rows and columns and to illustrate data in the form of charts. A spreadsheet created in Microsoft Excel is known as a **worksheet**. Each Excel file—called a **workbook**—can contain multiple worksheets. Throughout this module, a portion of an Excel worksheet is referred to as a **worksheet object**, and a chart is referred to as a **chart object**.

Sometimes it is useful to combine information created in the different Office programs into one file. For her document, Rima wants to use fund-raising goals from an Excel worksheet. She also wants to include an Excel chart that shows the hours of work remaining on the project. You can incorporate the Excel data and chart into Rima's Word document by taking advantage of **object linking and embedding**, or **OLE**, a technology that allows you to share information among the Office programs. This process is commonly referred to as **integration**.

Before you start using OLE, you need to understand some important terms. Recall that in Word, an object is anything that can be selected and modified as a whole, such as a table, picture, or block of text. Another important term, **source program**, refers to the program used to create the original version of an object. The program into which the object is integrated is called the **destination program**. Similarly, the original file that contains the object you are integrating is called the **source file**, and the file into which you integrate the object is called the **destination file**.

You can integrate objects by either embedding or linking. **Embedding** is a technique that allows you to insert a copy of an object into a destination document. You can double-click an embedded object in the destination document to access the tools of the source program, allowing you to edit the object within the destination document using the source program's tools. Because the embedded object is a copy, any changes you make to it are not reflected in the original source file and vice versa. For instance, you could embed data from a worksheet named Itemized Expenses into a Word document named Travel Report. Later, if you change the Itemized Expenses file, those revisions would not be reflected in the Travel Report document. The opposite is also true; if you edit the embedded object from within the Travel Report file, those changes will not be reflected in the source file Itemized Expenses. The embedded object retains no connection to the source file.

Figure 7–14 illustrates the relationship between an embedded Excel worksheet object in Rima's Word document and the source file.

| Figure 7–14 | Embedding an Excel worksheet object in a Word document |
| --- | --- |

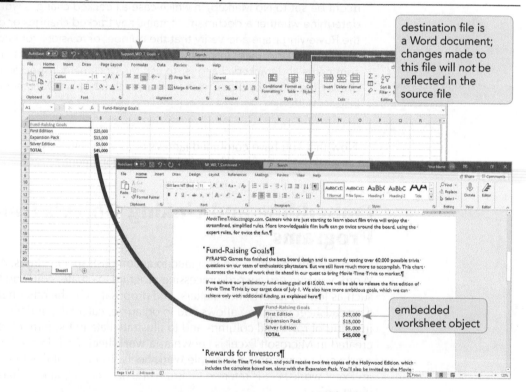

source file is an Excel workbook; changes made to this file will *not* be reflected in the destination file

destination file is a Word document; changes made to this file will *not* be reflected in the source file

embedded worksheet object

**Linking** is similar to embedding, except that the object inserted into the destination file maintains a connection to the source file. Just as with an embedded object, you can double-click a linked object to access the tools of the source program. However, unlike with an embedded object, changes to a linked object show up in both the destination file and the source file. The linked object in the destination document is not a copy; it is a shortcut to the original object in the source file.

Figure 7–15 illustrates the relationship between the data in James's Excel chart and the linked object in Rima's Word document.

**Figure 7–15**     Linking an Excel chart object to a Word document

source file is an Excel workbook; changes made to this file will be reflected in the destination file

destination file is a Word document; changes made to this file will be reflected in the source file

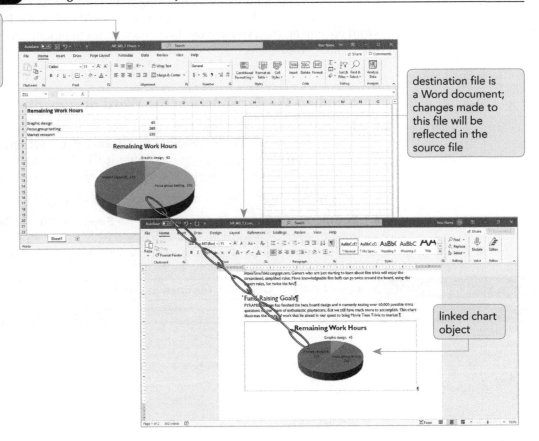

linked chart object

## Proskills

### Decision Making: Choosing Between Embedding and Linking

Embedding and linking are both useful when you know you'll want to edit an object after inserting it into Word. But how do you decide whether to embed or link the object? Create an embedded object if you won't have access to the original source file in the future, or if you don't need (or want) to maintain the connection between the source file and the document containing the linked object. Two advantages of embedding are that the source file is unaffected by any editing in the destination document, and the two files can be stored separately. You could even delete the source file from your disk without affecting the copy embedded in your Word document. A disadvantage is that the file size of a Word document containing an embedded object will be larger than the file size of a document containing a linked object.

Create a linked object whenever you have data that is likely to change over time and when you want to keep the object in your document up to date. In addition to the advantage of a smaller destination file size, both the source file and the destination file can reflect recent revisions when the files are linked. A disadvantage to linking is that you have to keep track of two files (the source file and the destination file) rather than just one.

## Embedding an Excel Worksheet Object

To embed an object from an Excel worksheet into a Word document, you start by opening the Excel worksheet (the source file) and copying the Excel object to the Office Clipboard. Then, in the Word document (the destination file), you open the Paste Special dialog box. In this dialog box, you can choose to paste the copied Excel object in a number of different forms. To embed it, you select Microsoft Excel Worksheet Object.

Rima wants to include the company's fund-raising goals in her document. If she needs to adjust numbers in the fund-raising goals later, she will need access to the Excel tools for recalculating the data. Therefore, you'll embed the Excel object in the Word document. Then you can use Excel commands to modify the embedded object from within Word.

### To embed the Excel data in the Word document:

1. Scroll down to the paragraph above the "Rewards for Investors" heading, and then delete the placeholder text [**Insert Excel worksheet**], taking care not to delete the paragraph mark after it. The insertion point should now be located in a blank paragraph above the "Rewards for Investors" heading.

    Now you need to open James's Excel file and copy the fund-raising data.

2. Start Microsoft 365 Excel, open the file **Support_WD_7_Goals.xlsx** located in the Word7 > Module folder included with your Data Files, and then maximize the Excel program window if necessary. See Figure 7–16.

| Figure 7–16 | Support_WD_7_Goals.xlsx file open in Excel |
| --- | --- |

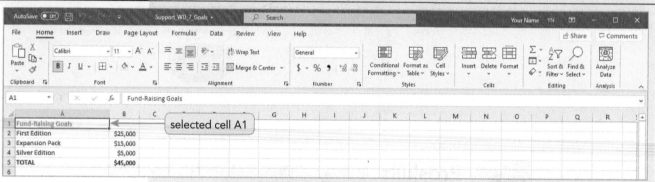

An Excel worksheet is arranged in rows and columns, just like a Word table. The intersection between a row and a column is called a **cell**; an individual cell takes its name from its column letter and row number. For example, the intersection of column A and row 1 in the upper-left corner of the worksheet is referred to as cell A1. Currently, cell A1 is selected, as indicated by its dark outline.

To copy the fund-raising data to the Office Clipboard, you need to select the entire block of cells containing the fund-raising data.

3. Click cell **A1** (the cell containing the text "Fund-Raising Goals"), if necessary, press and hold **SHIFT**, and then click cell **B5** (the cell containing "$45,000"). See Figure 7–17.

| Figure 7–17 | Fund-raising data selected in worksheet |
| --- | --- |

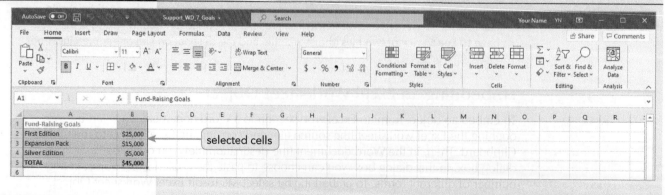

Now that the data is selected, you can copy it to the Office Clipboard.

Be sure to keep Excel open; otherwise, you won't have access to the commands for embedding the data in Word.

4. Press **CTRL+C**. The border around the selected cells has a moving, marquee effect, indicating that you have copied the data in these cells to the Office Clipboard. Next, you will switch to Word without closing Excel.

5. On the taskbar, click the **Word** button ▣ to return to the NP_WD_7_Combined.docx document. The insertion point is still located in the blank paragraph above the "Rewards for Investors" heading.

6. On the ribbon, click the **Home** tab, if necessary.

7. In the Clipboard group, click the **Paste arrow**, and then click **Paste Special** to open the Paste Special dialog box.

8. In the As list, click **Microsoft Excel Worksheet Object**. See Figure 7–18.

| Figure 7–18 | Paste Special dialog box |
| --- | --- |

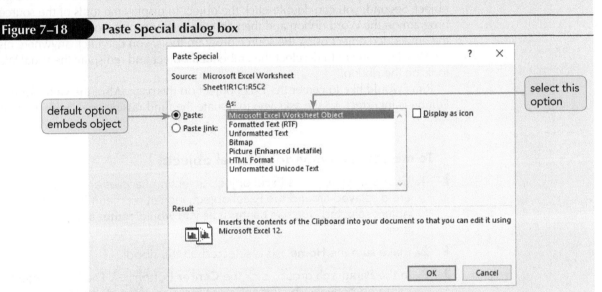

Next, you can choose to embed the Excel object or link it, depending on whether you select the Paste button (for embedding) or the Paste link button (for linking). The Paste button is selected by default, which is what you want in this case.

9. Click **OK**. The Excel worksheet object is inserted in the Word document, as shown in Figure 7–19.

| Figure 7–19 | Excel worksheet object embedded in Word document |
| --- | --- |

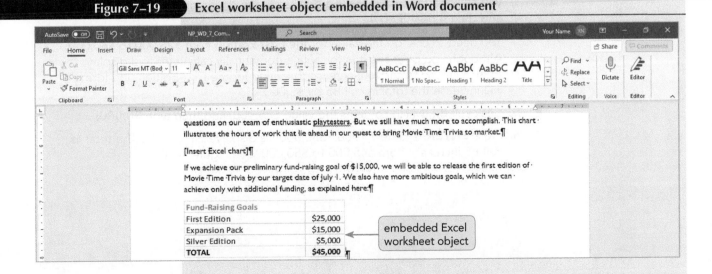

**Trouble?** If you don't see the top or bottom horizontal gridline in the embedded Excel object, don't be concerned. It won't affect the rest of the steps.

At this point, the Excel data looks like an ordinary table. But because you embedded it as an Excel worksheet object, you can modify it from within Word, using Excel tools and commands.

## Modifying an Embedded Worksheet Object

After you embed an object in Word, you can modify it in two different ways. First, you can click the object to select it, and then move or resize it just as you would a graphic object. Second, you can double-click the object to display the tools of the source program on the Word ribbon and then edit the contents of the object. After you modify the embedded object using the source program tools, you can click anywhere else in the Word document to deselect the embedded object and redisplay the usual Word tools on the ribbon.

Rima would like to center the Excel object on the page. Also, the value for the First Edition is incorrect, so she asks you to update the fund-raising goals with the new data.

**To modify the embedded Excel object:**

1. Click anywhere in the Excel object. Selection handles and a dotted outline are displayed around the Excel object, indicating that it is selected. With the object selected, you can center it as you would center any other selected item.

2. Make sure the **Home** tab is selected on the ribbon.

3. In the Paragraph group, click the **Center** button ≣. The Excel object is centered between the left and right margins of the document.

4. Double-click anywhere inside the Excel object. The object's border changes to resemble the borders of an Excel worksheet, with horizontal and vertical scroll bars, row numbers, and column letters. The Word tabs on the ribbon are replaced with Excel tabs.

   **Trouble?** If you don't see the Excel borders around the worksheet object, click outside the worksheet object to deselect it, and then repeat Step 4. If you still don't see the Excel borders, save the document, close it, reopen it, and then repeat Step 4.

   You need to change the value for the First Edition from $25,000 to $30,000. Although you can't see it, a formula automatically calculates and displays the total in cell B5. After you increase the value for the First Edition, the formula will increase the total in cell B5 by $5,000.

5. Click cell **B2**, which contains the value $25,000, and then type **30,000**.

6. Press **ENTER**. The new value "$30,000" is displayed in cell B2. The total in cell B5 increases from $45,000 to $50,000. See Figure 7–20.

**Figure 7–20**     **Revised data in embedded Excel object**

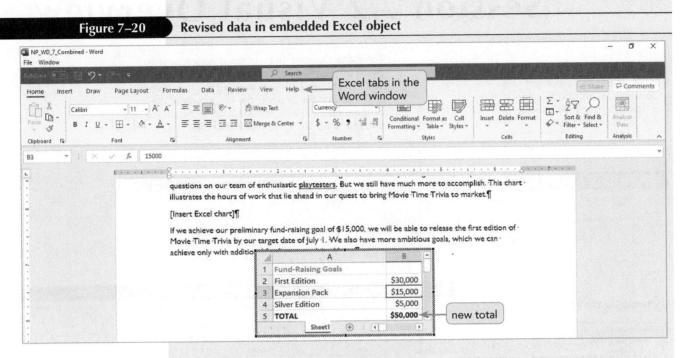

7. In the document, click outside the borders of the Excel object to deselect it. The Word tabs are now visible on the ribbon again.

8. On the taskbar, click the **Microsoft Excel** button [X] to display the Excel window.

    Because you embedded the Excel object rather than linking it, the First Edition value of $25,000 and the Total of $45,000 remain unchanged.

9. On the ribbon, click the **File** tab, and then click **Close** in the navigation pane without saving any changes. The Support_WD_7_Goals.xlsx workbook closes, but Excel remains open.

In this session, you worked with tracked changes in a document. You learned how to combine and compare documents, and you accepted and rejected tracked changes in a combined document. You also embedded an Excel Worksheet object in a Word document and modified the embedded worksheet object from within Word. In the next session, you'll learn how to link an object instead of embedding it. You'll also create bookmarks, insert and edit hyperlinks in a document, and optimize the document for online viewing. Finally, you'll learn how to create and publish a blog post.

## Review

### Session 7.1 Quick Check

1. How can you ensure that your name is displayed for each tracked change?

2. Explain how to turn on Track Changes.

3. Which provides a more streamlined view of a document's tracked changes, All Markup view or Simple Markup view?

4. What should you do before using the Next and Previous buttons to review the tracked changes in a document?

5. Explain the difference between a linked object and an embedded object.

6. How do you start editing an embedded Excel object in Word?

# Session 7.2 Visual Overview:

To link an Excel chart object to a Word document, you first need to open the Excel workbook that contains the chart.

The Paste Options menu offers different ways to paste text, a chart, or other items from a source file. You can choose between keeping the formatting of the source file or using the formatting of the destination file. Here, the Excel file is the source file, and the Word file is the destination file.

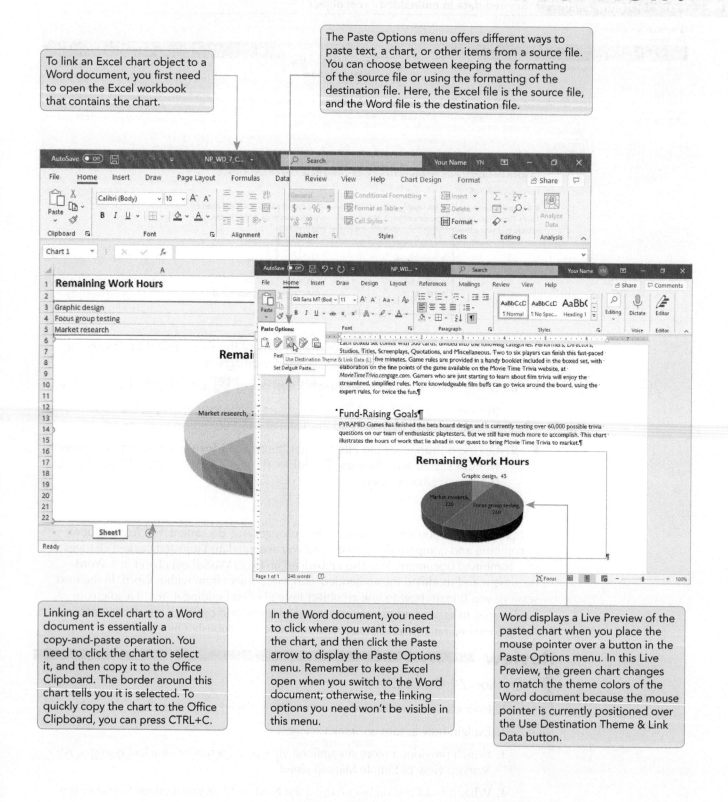

Linking an Excel chart to a Word document is essentially a copy-and-paste operation. You need to click the chart to select it, and then copy it to the Office Clipboard. The border around this chart tells you it is selected. To quickly copy the chart to the Office Clipboard, you can press CTRL+C.

In the Word document, you need to click where you want to insert the chart, and then click the Paste arrow to display the Paste Options menu. Remember to keep Excel open when you switch to the Word document; otherwise, the linking options you need won't be visible in this menu.

Word displays a Live Preview of the pasted chart when you place the mouse pointer over a button in the Paste Options menu. In this Live Preview, the green chart changes to match the theme colors of the Word document because the mouse pointer is currently positioned over the Use Destination Theme & Link Data button.

# Linking an Excel Chart Object

You can edit a linked chart object from within the Word document.

After you select the chart in the Word document, you click the Edit Data button on the Chart Design tab. This opens a spreadsheet window with the Excel source file displayed.

If the chart in the Word window does not change to reflect changes made to data in the spreadsheet window, you can click the Refresh Data button to update the chart in the Word window.

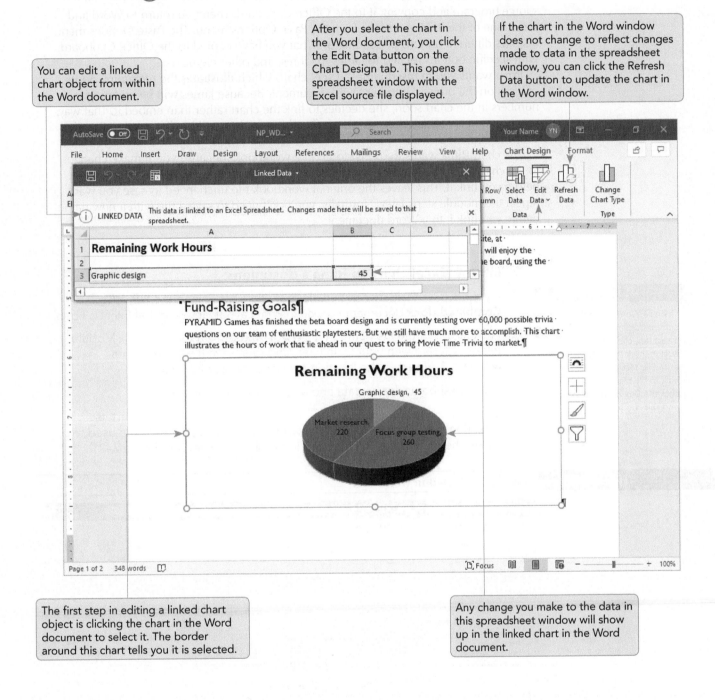

The first step in editing a linked chart object is clicking the chart in the Word document to select it. The border around this chart tells you it is selected.

Any change you make to the data in this spreadsheet window will show up in the linked chart in the Word document.

# Linking an Excel Chart Object

When you link an object to a Word document, you start by selecting the object in the source program and copying it to the Office Clipboard. Then you return to Word and select one of the linking options from the Paste Options menu. The Paste Options menu displays different options depending on what you have copied to the Office Clipboard, with specific options related to tables, pictures, and other elements.

Rima wants you to insert James's Excel chart, which illustrates the remaining hours of work on the project, into her Word document. Because James will be updating numbers in the chart soon, she decides to link the chart rather than embed it. That way, once the chart is updated in the source file, the new data will be displayed in Rima's Word document as well.

The chart Rima wants to use is stored in a workbook. Because you'll make changes to the chart after you link it, you will start by saving the workbook with a new name before you link it. This leaves the original workbook file unchanged in case you want to repeat the module steps later. Normally, you don't need to save a file with a new name before you link it to a Word document.

## To link the Excel chart to Rima's document:

**Tip**

To link a Word file to the current document: on the Insert tab, click the Object button, click the Create from File tab, select the Link to file check box, click the Browse button, and select the file.

1. If you took a break after the previous session, make sure the **NP_WD_7_Combined.docx** document is open in Print Layout view and that Excel is open.

2. In Excel, open the file named **NP_WD_7-2.xlsx** from the Word7 > Module folder included with your Data Files, and then save it with the name **NP_WD_7_Hours** in the location specified by your instructor.

   The worksheet includes data and a pie chart illustrating the data.

3. Click the rectangular chart border. Do not click any part of the chart itself. Selection handles appear on the chart border. The worksheet data used to create the chart is also highlighted in purple and blue. See Figure 7–21.

**Figure 7–21**    **Pie chart selected in worksheet**

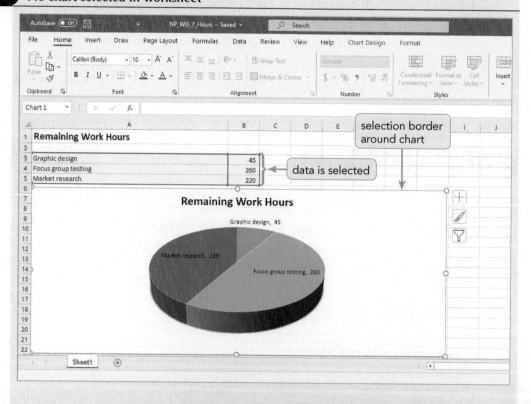

**Trouble?** If you see borders or handles around individual elements of the pie chart, you clicked the chart itself rather than the border. Click in the worksheet outside the chart border, and then repeat Step 3.

4.  Press **CTRL+C** to copy the pie chart to the Office Clipboard.

5.  On the taskbar, click the **Word button** 📄 to display the Word window with the NP_WD_7_Combined.docx document.

6.  On the ribbon, make sure the Home tab is selected.

7.  In the second paragraph after the "Fund-Raising Goals" heading, delete the placeholder text **[Insert Excel chart]** but not the paragraph symbol after it, and then verify that the insertion point is located in a blank paragraph between two paragraphs of text.

8.  In the Clipboard group, click the **Paste arrow** to display the Paste Options menu.

9.  Move the pointer over the icons on the Paste Options menu, and notice the changing appearance of the chart's Live Preview, depending on which Paste Option you are previewing.

    For linking, you can choose between the Use Destination Theme & Link Data option, which formats the chart with the teal, purple, and blue colors of the Word document's current theme, and the Keep Source Formatting & Link Data option, which retains the purple, blue, and orange colors of the Excel workbook. See Figure 7–22.

| Figure 7–22 | Linking options on the Paste Options menu |
| --- | --- |

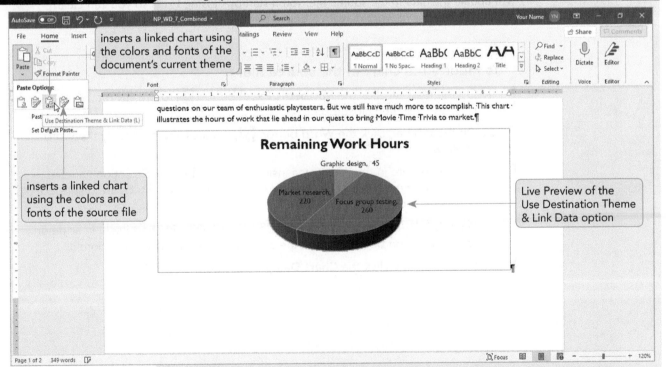

10. On the Paste Options menu, click the **Use Destination Theme & Link Data** button 📋. The chart is inserted in the document. It is formatted with the teal, purple, and blue colors and font of the Gallery theme used in the Word document.

Use the button's ScreenTip to verify you are about to click the Use Destination Theme & Link Data button. It's easy to click the wrong button on the Paste Options menu.

# Insight

## Storing Linked Files

When linking objects, it is important to keep the source and destination files in their original storage locations. If you move the files or the folders in which they are stored, you will disrupt the connection between the source file and the document containing the linked object because the shortcut in the destination file will no longer have a valid path to the source file.

For example, suppose you insert a linked Excel file into a Word document, and then later a colleague moves the Excel file to a different folder. The next time you open the Word document and try to update the linked object, you will see a dialog box explaining that the linked file is not available. At that point, you can make the link functional again by updating the path to the linked objects. To do so, click the File tab on the ribbon, and then click Info in the navigation pane, if necessary. On the Info screen, click Edit Links to Files. In the Links dialog box, click the link whose location has changed, click the Change Source button, and then navigate to the new location of the source file.

## Modifying the Linked Chart Object

The advantage of linking compared to embedding is that you can change the data in the source file, and those changes will automatically be reflected in the destination file as well.

Rima has received James's updated data about the total hours remaining on the project, and she wants the chart in her document to reflect this new information. You will update the data in the source file. You'll start by closing Excel so you can clearly see the advantages of working with a linked object.

### To modify the chart in the source file:

1. On the taskbar, click the **Microsoft Excel** button ▨ to display the Excel window, and then close Excel.

2. On the taskbar, click the **Word** button ▧ , if necessary, to display the Word window.

3. Click anywhere in the white area inside the chart border. Selection handles appear on the chart border, and the two chart contextual tabs are displayed on the ribbon.

   **Trouble?** If you see a selection border around the pie chart itself, in addition to the selection border around the chart and the title, you can ignore it.

4. On the ribbon, click the **Chart Design** tab. See Figure 7–23.

**Figure 7–23**    Chart selected in Word

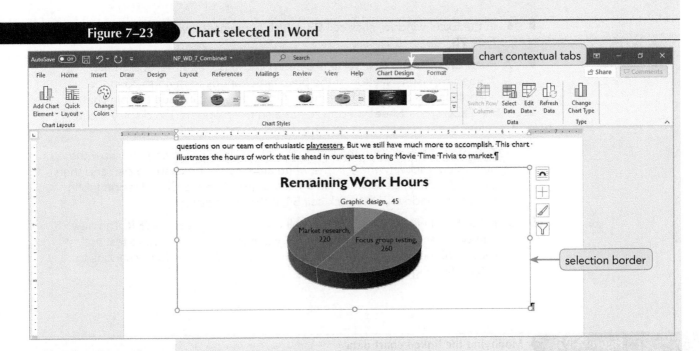

**Tip**

To edit the source file directly in Excel, click the Edit Data arrow to display a menu, and then click Edit Data in Excel.

5. In the Data group, click the **Edit Data** button. A spreadsheet that contains the chart data opens on top of the Word document.

Your spreadsheet might be larger or smaller than the one shown in Figure 7–24.

**Figure 7–24**    Spreadsheet window with chart data

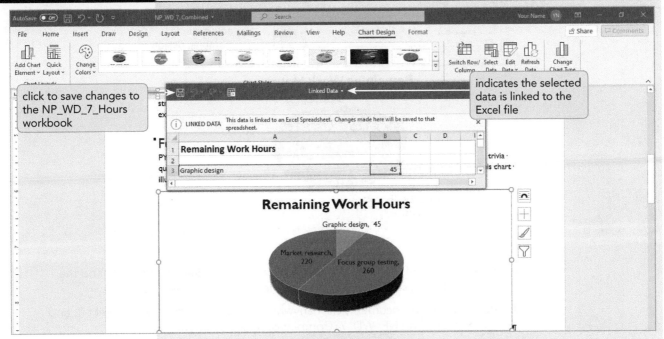

6. In the Excel window, click cell **B3**, which contains the value "45," and then type **75**.

7. Press **ENTER**. The new value is entered in cell B3, and the label in the "Graphic design" section of the pie chart changes from 45 to 75 in the linked chart in the Word document. Although you can't see the pie chart in the Excel spreadsheet window, it has also been updated to display the new value.

   **Trouble?** If the chart in the Word document does not change to show the new value, click anywhere in the white area inside the chart border, and then click the Refresh Data button in the Data group on the Chart Design tab in the Word window. Then, click cell B4 in the spreadsheet window.

8. In the Excel window, type **300** in cell B4, and then press **ENTER**. The new number is entered in cell B4, and the value in the "Focus group testing" section of the pie charts in both the Excel and Word windows changes to match. See Figure 7–25.

**Figure 7–25**    **Modifying the linked chart data**

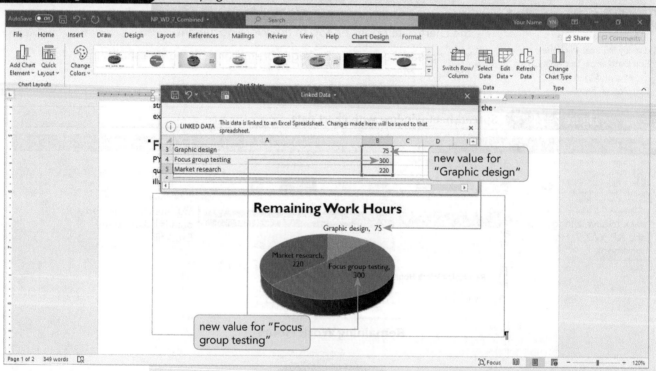

9. At the top of the spreadsheet window, click the **Save** button 🖫, and then click the **Close** button ✕ to close the spreadsheet window.

10. In the Word document, click anywhere outside the chart to deselect it, and then save the NP_WD_7_Combined.docx document.

When you edited the data in the spreadsheet window, you were actually editing the NP_WD_7_Hours.xlsx workbook. If you wanted, you could start Excel and open the NP_WD_7_Hours.xlsx workbook to verify that it contains the new values.

# Insight

### Editing a Linked Worksheet Object

The steps for editing a linked worksheet object are slightly different from the steps for editing a linked chart object. Start by right-clicking the linked worksheet object in Word, and then point to Linked Worksheet Object on the shortcut menu, and click Edit Link. This opens the workbook in Excel, where you can edit the data and save your changes. When you are finished, close the workbook, and then return to the Word document. If the data is not immediately updated within the Word document, right-click the linked worksheet object in the Word document to open a shortcut menu, and then click Update Link. When you open a Word document containing a linked worksheet object, you might see a dialog box asking if you want to update the document with the data from the linked files. Click Yes to continue.

Note that linked worksheet objects don't offer the formatting options of a Word table. To improve the appearance of a worksheet object, you can transform it into a regular Word table by breaking the link, as described later in this module. After you break the link, you can format the new table just as you would format any table.

Rima is finished with her work on the chart. She does not expect the data in it to change, so she wants to break the link between the Excel workbook and the Word document.

## Breaking Links

If you no longer need a link between files, you can break it. When you break a link, the source file and the destination file no longer have any connection to each other, and changes made in the source file do not affect the destination file. After breaking the link to the source file, you can change the formatting of a chart object from within the Word document, using the chart contextual tabs, but you can't make any changes related to the data shown in the chart. In the case of an Excel worksheet, after you break the link to the source file, the worksheet turns into a Word table.

# Reference

### Breaking a Link to a Source File

- On the ribbon, click the File tab.
- On the Info screen, scroll down if necessary, and then click Edit Links to Files to open the Links dialog box.
- In the list of links in the document, click the link that you want to break.
- Click the Break Link button.
- Click Yes in the dialog box that opens, asking you to confirm that you want to break the link.
- Click OK to close the Links dialog box.

Now, you will break the link between Rima's document and the NP_WD_7_Hours workbook.

### To break the link between the Word document and the Excel workbook:

1. On the ribbon, click the **File** tab, and then click **Info** in the navigation pane. Backstage view displays the Info screen.

2. Scroll down to display the lower-right corner of the Info screen, and then click **Edit Links to Files**. The Links dialog box opens with the only link in the document (the link to the NP_WD_7_Hours workbook) selected. See Figure 7–26.

**Figure 7–26**    **The Links dialog box**

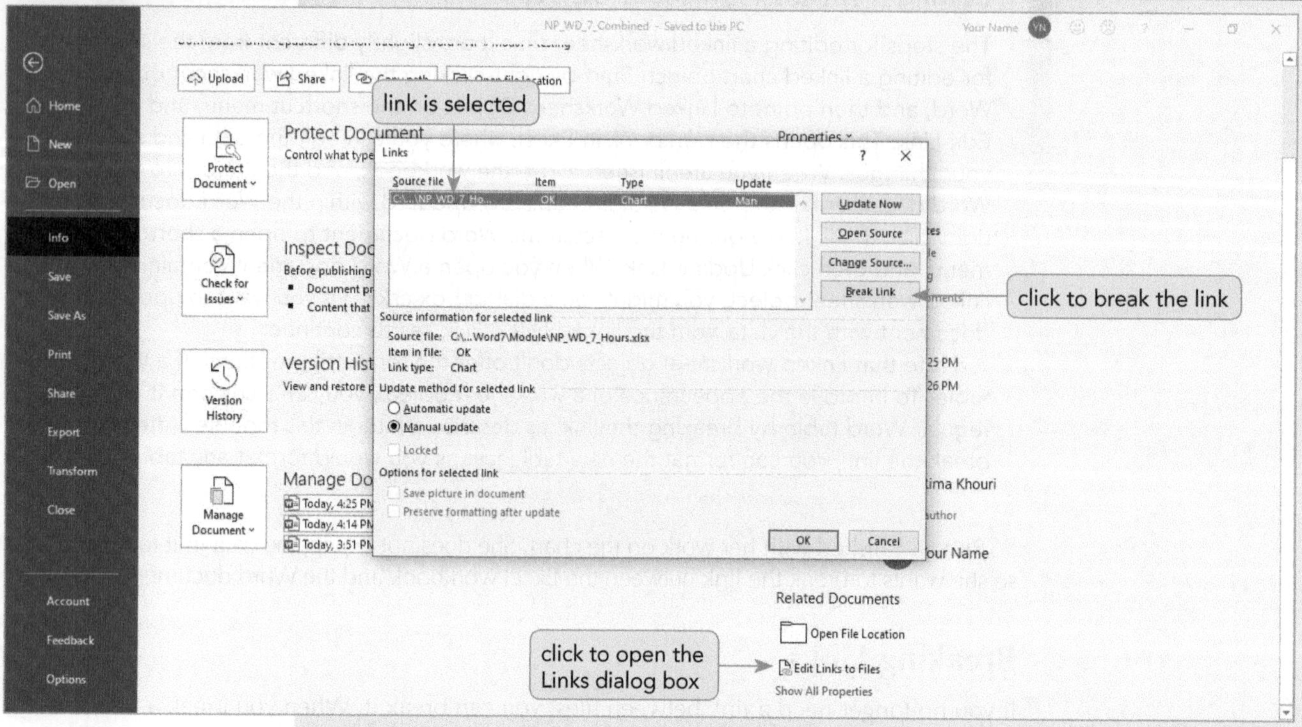

3. In the Links dialog box, click the **Break Link** button, and then click **Yes** in the dialog box that opens, asking if you are sure you want to break the link. The word "NULL" now appears under the heading Source file in the Links dialog box, indicating there is no source file for the chart in the document.

4. Click **OK** to close the dialog box. You return to the Info screen in Backstage view.

   With the link broken, you can no longer edit the Excel data from within Word. You can verify this by looking at the Chart Design tab.

5. At the top of the navigation bar, click the **Back** button ⊖ to close Backstage view and return to the document.

6. Click anywhere inside the chart border to select the chart.

7. On the ribbon, click the **Chart Design** tab, if necessary. Notice that the Edit Data button in the Data group is grayed out, indicating this option is no longer available.

8. Click anywhere outside the chart border to deselect it, and then save the document.

## Insight

### Using the Chart Tool in Word

The Chart tool in Word offers a simplified way to insert a chart in a document that does not involve opening Excel. To get started, click where you want to insert the chart, and then follow these steps:

1. Click the Chart button in the Illustrations group on the Insert tab.
2. In the left-hand pane of the Insert Chart dialog box, click the type of chart you want to create.
3. On the right side of the Insert Chart dialog box, select a chart style. For example, if you selected Column in step 2, you could choose a Stacked Column chart, a 3-D Stacked Column chart, or one of several other options.
4. Click OK to close the Insert Chart dialog box. The chart is added to the document, and a worksheet window opens above the chart.
5. In the worksheet window, enter row and column headings, and then enter data for your chart. The information you enter in the worksheet automatically appears in the chart window.
6. In the Word window, click the default chart title to select it, delete the text inside the title box, and replace it with an appropriate title.
7. Use the Chart Design tab to change the look of your chart. To change the chart colors, use the Change Colors button in the Chart Styles group. You can also select a new style in the Chart Styles group. Use the Add Chart Element button on the Chart Design tab to add, remove, or reposition a title, data labels, a legend, axes, gridlines, or other chart element. To add an outline to a chart element, right-click the element to display two shortcut menus, click the Outline button, and then click a color in the color palette.
8. Click outside the chart border to deselect the chart, close the worksheet window, and then close any extra formatting panes that might have opened while you were working on the chart.
9. To revise a chart, click it to select it, click the Chart Design tab, and then click the Edit Data button in the Data group to open a worksheet window containing the chart data.
10. To resize a chart to specific dimensions, select it, and then use the Size options on the Format tab.

# Using Hyperlinks in Word

**Tip**

Hyperlinks are commonly referred to as "links," but take care not to confuse them with the OLE links you worked with earlier in this module.

A hyperlink is a word, phrase, or graphic that you can click to jump to another part of the same document, to a separate Word document, to a file created in another program, or to a webpage. When used thoughtfully, hyperlinks make it possible to navigate a complicated document or a set of files quickly and easily. And as you know, you can also include email links in documents, which you can click to create email messages.

Rima wants you to add two hyperlinks to the document—one that jumps to a location within the document, and one that opens a different document.

## Inserting a Hyperlink to a Bookmark in the Same Document

Creating a hyperlink within a document is actually a two-part process. First, you need to mark the text you want the link to jump to—either by formatting the text with a heading style or by inserting a bookmark. A **bookmark** is an electronic marker that refers to specific text, a picture, or another object in a document. Second, you need to select the text that you want users to click, format it as a hyperlink, and specify the bookmark or heading as the target of the hyperlink. The **target** is the place in the document to which the link connects. In this case, Rima wants to create a hyperlink at the beginning of the document that targets the embedded Fund-Raising Goals Excel worksheet object near the end of the document. Figure 7–27 illustrates this process.

**Figure 7–27**   Hyperlink that targets a bookmark

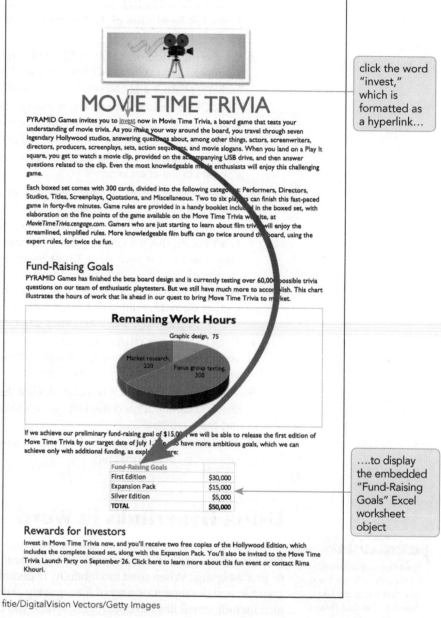

fitie/DigitalVision Vectors/Getty Images

To create a hyperlink in Rima's document, you'll first need to designate the worksheet object as a bookmark.

### To insert a bookmark:

1. Scroll down and click the "Fund-Raising Goals" worksheet object, on page 2. A dotted outline and handles are displayed around the worksheet object, indicating that it is selected.

2. On the ribbon, click the **Insert** tab.

**3.** In the Links group, click the **Bookmark** button. The Bookmark dialog box opens. You can now type the bookmark name, which cannot contain spaces.

**4.** In the Bookmark name box, type **Goals**. See Figure 7–28.

| Figure 7–28 | Creating a bookmark |
| --- | --- |

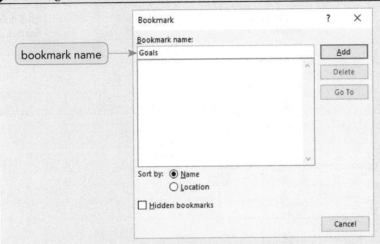

bookmark name →

**5.** Click the **Add** button. The Bookmark dialog box closes. Although you can't see any change in the document, the "Fund-Raising Goals" worksheet object has been designated as a bookmark.

**Tip**

To delete a bookmark, click it in the Bookmark dialog box, and then click the Delete button.

The bookmark you just created will be the target of a hyperlink, which you will create next.

## Reference

### Creating a Hyperlink to a Location in the Same Document

- Select the text, graphic, or other object that you want to format as a hyperlink.
- On the ribbon, click the Insert tab.
- In the Links group, click the Link button to open the Insert Hyperlink dialog box.
- In the Link to pane, click Place in This Document.
- In the Select a place in this document list, click the bookmark or heading you want to link to, and then click OK.

Rima wants you to format the word "invest" at the beginning of the document as a hyperlink that will target the bookmark you just created.

**Tip**

If you are storing your documents on OneDrive, then clicking the Links arrow displays a list of recent OneDrive documents. Click a document name to insert a link to it in the current document.

### To create and test a hyperlink to the bookmark:

**1.** Scroll up to page 1, and then, in the first line under the "Movie Time Trivia" heading, select the word **invest**.

**2.** In the Links group on the Insert tab, click the **Link** button. The Insert Hyperlink dialog box opens.

**3.** In the Link to pane, click **Place in This Document** to select it, if necessary. The "Select a place in this document" list shows the headings and bookmarks in the document. Here you can click the bookmark or heading you want as the target for the hyperlink.

▶ **4.** Under Bookmarks, click **Goals**. See Figure 7–29.

**Figure 7–29**    Inserting a hyperlink to a location in the same document

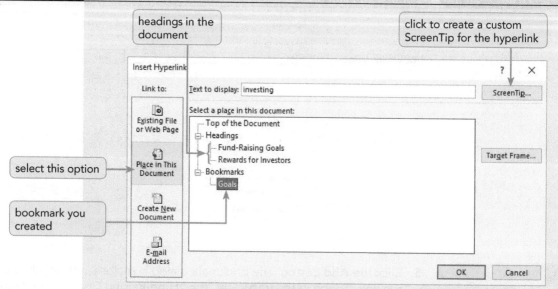

You can click the ScreenTip button to open the Set Hyperlink ScreenTip dialog box and type custom text for the hyperlink's ScreenTip, which appears when you place the pointer over the hyperlink in the document. In this case, however, Rima prefers to use the default ScreenTip.

**Tip**

To change a hyperlink's font color, open the Styles pane and modify the Hyperlink style.

▶ **5.** Click **OK**. The word "invest" is now formatted in the hyperlink style for the Gallery theme, which applies a red font color with an underline. The hyperlink targets the Goals bookmark that you created in the last set of steps. You can verify this by clicking the hyperlink.

▶ **6.** Move the pointer over the hyperlink **invest**. The default ScreenTip displays the name of the bookmark and instructions for following the link. See Figure 7–30.

**Figure 7–30**    Displaying the ScreenTip for a hyperlink

fitie/DigitalVision Vectors/Getty Images

▶ **7.** Press and hold **CTRL**, and then click the **invest** hyperlink. The insertion point jumps to the "Fund-Raising Goals" worksheet object on page 2.

8. Scroll up to review the "invest" hyperlink. It is now purple, which is the color for clicked links in the Gallery theme.

9. Save your document.

Next, you will create a hyperlink that jumps to a different document.

## Creating Hyperlinks to Other Documents

When you create a hyperlink to another document, you need to specify the document's file name and storage location as the hyperlink's target. The document can be stored on your computer or on a network; it can even be a webpage stored somewhere on the web. In that case, you need to specify the webpage's URL (web address) as the target. When you click a hyperlink to another document, the document opens on your computer, with the beginning of the document displayed. Keep in mind that if you move the document containing the hyperlink, or if you move the target document, the hyperlink will no longer work. However, if you create a hyperlink to a webpage on the Internet, the link will continue to work no matter where you store the document containing the hyperlink.

## Reference

### Creating a Hyperlink to Another Document

- Select the text, graphic, or other object you want to format as a hyperlink.
- On the ribbon, click the Insert tab.
- In the Links group, click the Link button to open the Insert Hyperlink dialog box.
- In the Link to pane, click Existing File or Web Page.
- To target a specific file on your computer or network, click the Look in arrow, navigate to the folder containing the file, and then click the file in the file list.
- To target a webpage, type its URL in the Address box.
- Click OK.

Rima wants to insert a hyperlink that, when clicked, will open a Word document containing details about the Movie Time Trivia Launch Party. You'll start by opening the document containing the party details and saving it with a new name.

### To create a hyperlink to a document with details about the Movie Time Trivia Launch Party:

1. Open the document **NP_WD_7-3.docx** located in the Word7 > Module folder included with your Data Files, save it as **NP_WD_7_Party** in the location specified by your instructor, and then close it.

2. In the NP_WD_7_Combined.docx document, scroll down to the end of the document, and then select the word **here** in the last sentence.

3. On the ribbon, click the **Insert** tab, if necessary.

4. In the Links group, click the **Link** button. The Insert Hyperlink dialog box opens.

5. In the Link to pane, click **Existing File or Web Page**. The dialog box displays options related to selecting a file or a webpage.

6. Click the **Look in arrow**, navigate to the location where you stored the NP_WD_7_Party.docx file, if necessary, and then click **NP_WD_7_Party** in the file list. See Figure 7-31.

**Figure 7–31** Inserting a hyperlink to a different document

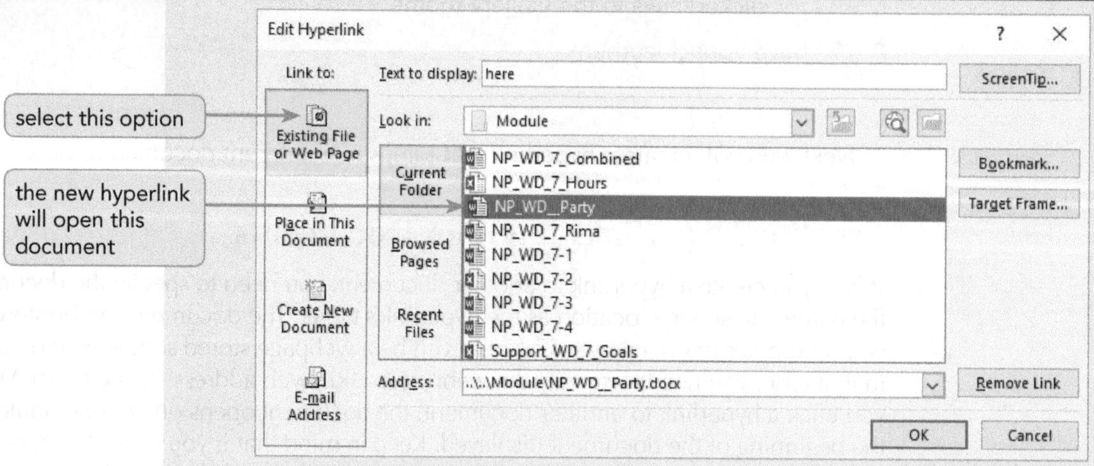

select this option

the new hyperlink will open this document

**7.** Click **OK**. The new "here" hyperlink is formatted in red with an underline. Now, you will test the hyperlink.

**8.** Press and hold **CTRL**, and then click the **here** hyperlink. The NP_WD_7_Party document opens. See Figure 7–32.

**Figure 7–32** NP_WD_7_Party document

**9.** Close the NP_WD_7_Party.docx document, and then return to the NP_WD_7_Combined.docx document. The link is now purple because you clicked it.

**10.** Save your document.

Now that you have finalized the document and added the necessary hyperlinks, you will optimize the document for online viewing by switching to Web Layout view and adding some formatting that is useful for documents that will be viewed online.

# Optimizing a Document for Online Viewing

When preparing a document intended solely for online distribution, you can focus on how the page will look on the screen, without having to consider how it will look when printed. This means you can take advantage of some formatting options that are visible only on the screen, such as a background page color or a background fill effect. You can also switch to **Web Layout view**, which displays a document as it would look in a web browser.

In Web Layout view, the text spans the width of the screen, with no page breaks and without any margins or headers and footers. The advantage of Web Layout view is that it allows you to zoom in on the document text as close as you want, with the text rewrapping to accommodate the new Zoom setting. By contrast, in Print Layout view, if you increase the Zoom setting too far, you end up having to scroll from side to side to read an entire line of text. The only downside to Web Layout view is that graphics may shift position as the text wrapping changes. However, these changes are only visible in Web Layout view. When you switch back to Print Layout view, you will see the original page layout.

Rima wants to switch to Web Layout view before she continues formatting the document.

**Tip**

Zooming in on text in Web Layout View is helpful when you have multiple panes open; the text wraps for easier reading.

### To switch to Web Layout view:

1. On the status bar, click the **Web Layout** button. The document text expands to span the entire Word screen.

2. Use the Zoom slider on the status bar to increase the Zoom setting to **160%**. The text rewraps to accommodate the new setting.

3. Scroll down and review the entire document, which no longer has any page breaks. See Figure 7–33.

**Figure 7–33**    **Document displayed in Web Layout view, zoomed to 160%**

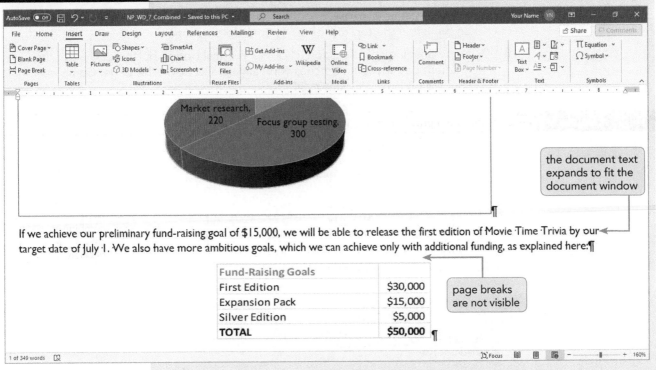

the document text expands to fit the document window

If we achieve our preliminary fund-raising goal of $15,000, we will be able to release the first edition of Movie Time Trivia by our target date of July 1. We also have more ambitious goals, which we can achieve only with additional funding, as explained here:¶

| Fund-Raising Goals | |
| --- | --- |
| First Edition | $30,000 |
| Expansion Pack | $15,000 |
| Silver Edition | $5,000 |
| **TOTAL** | **$50,000** |

page breaks are not visible

## Applying a Background Fill Effect

To make the document more eye-catching when it's displayed on a screen, Rima wants to add a background fill effect. A **background fill effect** is a repeating graphic element, such as a texture, a photo, or a color gradient, that is visible only when a document is displayed online. It's essential to use fill effects judiciously. In the hands of a trained graphic designer, they can be striking; if used carelessly, they can be garish and distracting. As a general rule, you should avoid using photos and textures and instead stick with simple colors or color gradients.

Rima decides to use a gradient background in shades of blue.

### To apply a background fill effect to the document:

1. On the ribbon, click the **Design** tab.

2. In the Page Background group, click the **Page Color** button. The Page Color gallery opens, with a menu at the bottom. You could click a color in the gallery to select it as a background color for the page. To select another type of background effect, you need to click Fill Effects.

3. Click **Fill Effects** to open the Fill Effects dialog box, and then click the **Gradient** tab, if necessary. Note that you could use other tabs in this dialog box to add a textured, patterned, or picture background.

4. In the Colors section, click the **Two colors** button. The Color 1 and Color 2 boxes and arrows are displayed.

5. Click the **Color 1 arrow**, and then click **Indigo, Accent 5, Lighter 80%**, the second color from the right in the second row of the Theme Colors section.

6. Click the **Color 2 arrow**, and then click **White, Background 1**, the first color on the left in the top row of the Theme Colors section.

7. In the Shading styles section, click the **Vertical** option button to change the gradient pattern so it stretches vertically up and down the page. Compare your dialog box to Figure 7-34.

**Figure 7-34**    Selecting a gradient background

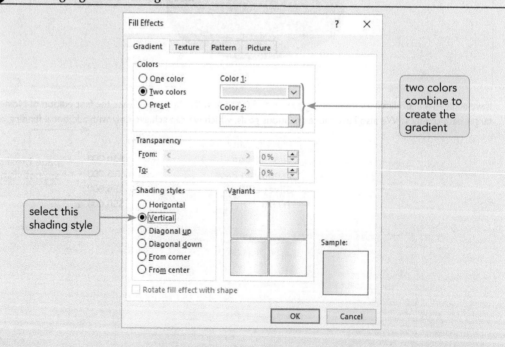

> **8.** Click **OK**. The document's background is now a gradient that varies between white and light blue.

> **9.** Scroll down, if necessary, so you can see the Fund-Raising Goals worksheet object.

The gradient background is light enough that you can still read the document text. However, to make the gridlines of the worksheet object easier to see, you can change the object's background color.

### To change the background for the Fund-Raising Goals worksheet object:

> **1.** Right-click the worksheet object to display a shortcut menu, and then click **Picture**. The Format Object dialog box opens, with the Picture tab displayed.

> **2.** Click the **Colors and Lines** tab to display settings related to the colors used in the worksheet object. In the Fill section, the Color box currently displays "No Color," indicating that the object's background is the same as the document's background.

> **3.** In the Fill section, click the **Color arrow**, and then click **White, Background 1**, the first color in the top row of the Theme Colors section.

> **4.** Click **OK** to close the Format Object dialog box. The worksheet object now has a white background, which makes the gridlines easier to see.

> **5.** Click outside the worksheet object to deselect it, and then save the document.

Next, you will add horizontal lines to separate the various sections of the document.

## Inserting Horizontal Lines

Horizontal lines allow you to see at a glance where one part of a document ends and another begins. Unlike background colors and fill effects, horizontal lines do appear in printed documents, along with the document text. However, they are commonly used in documents that are meant to be viewed only online.

Rima wants you to add a horizontal line before the "Fund-Raising Goals" heading and before the "Rewards for Investors" heading.

### To insert horizontal lines into the document:

> **1.** Scroll up and click at the beginning of the "Fund-Raising Goals" heading.

> **2.** On the ribbon, click the **Home** tab.

> **3.** In the Paragraph group, click the **Borders arrow** ⊞ ˇ to open the Borders gallery, and then click **Horizontal Line** to insert a default gray line.

  Rima wants to change the line's color. She also wants to make the line shorter, so it doesn't span the full page.

> **4.** Right-click the horizontal line to display a shortcut menu, and then click **Picture**. The Format Horizontal Line dialog box opens, with settings for

changing the line's width, height, color, and alignment. The current Width setting is 100%, meaning that the line spans the entire page from left to right. To leave a little space on each side, you need to lower the percentage.

5. Triple-click the **Width** box, and then type **75**. Because the Center alignment option at the bottom of the dialog box is selected by default, the shorter line will be centered on the page, with space to its left and its right.

6. Click the **Color arrow**, and then click **Indigo, Accent 5, Darker 50%**, the second color from the right in the bottom row of the Theme Colors section. The Color gallery closes, and the Use solid color (no shade) check box is now selected. See Figure 7-35.

**Figure 7-35**    **Format Horizontal Line dialog box**

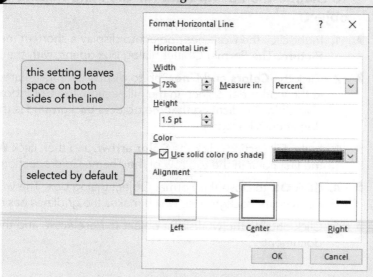

7. Click **OK**, and then click anywhere in the document to deselect the horizontal line. Your document should look similar to Figure 7-36.

**Figure 7-36**    **Newly inserted horizontal line**

Even the most knowledgeable movie enthusiasts will enjoy this challenging game.¶

Each boxed set comes with 300 cards, divided into the following categories: Performers, Directors, Studios, Titles, Screenplays, Quotations, and Miscellaneous. Two to six players can finish this fast-paced game in forty-five minutes. Game rules are provided in a handy booklet included in the boxed set, with elaboration on the fine points of the game available on the Movie Time Trivia website, at *MovieTimeTrivia.cengage.com*. Gamers who are just starting to learn about film trivia will enjoy the streamlined, simplified rules. More knowledgeable film buffs can go tw[...] the expert rules, for twice the fun.¶

*centered blue line spans 75% of the page*

## Fund-Raising Goals¶

PYRAMID Games has finished the beta board design and is currently testing over 60,000 possible trivia questions on our team of enthusiastic playtesters. But we still have much more to accomplish. This chart illustrates the hours of work that lie ahead in our quest to bring Movie Time Trivia to market.¶

**Remaining Work Hours**

Now, you can copy the line, and then insert it before the other heading.

**Tip**

To remove a horizontal line, click the line to select it, and then press DEL.

8. Click the horizontal line to select it, and then press **CTRL+C** to copy it to the Clipboard.

9. Scroll down, click to the left of the "R" in the "Rewards for Investors" heading, insert a new paragraph, format the new blank paragraph with the Normal style, and then press **CTRL+V** to insert the horizontal line before the heading.

10. Save the document.

You've finished formatting the NP_WD_7_Combined.docx document. Next, Rima needs to edit the hyperlink that opens the document with information about the launch party.

# Insight

## Saving a Word Document as a Webpage

Webpages are special documents designed to be viewed in a program called a **browser**. The browser included in Windows 10 is Microsoft Edge. Because webpages include code written in Hypertext Markup Language, or **HTML**, they are often referred to as HTML documents.

To create sophisticated webpages, you'll probably want to use a dedicated HTML editor, such as Adobe Dreamweaver. However, in Word you can create a simple webpage from an existing document by saving it as a webpage. When you do so, Word inserts HTML codes that tell the browser how to format and display the text and graphics. Fortunately, you don't have to learn HTML to create webpages with Word. When you save the document as a webpage, Word creates all the necessary HTML codes (called tags); however, you won't actually see the HTML codes in your webpage.

You can choose from several different webpage file types in Word. The Single File Web Page file type is a good choice when you plan to share your webpage only over a small network and not over the Internet. When you want to share your files over the Internet, it's better to use the Web Page, Filtered option, which breaks a webpage into multiple smaller files, for easier transmittal.

To save a document as a webpage, follow these steps:

1. Click the File tab, click Save as, and then click Browse to open the Save As dialog box.
2. Navigate to the location where you want to save the webpage.
3. If desired, type a new file name in the File name box.
4. Click the Save as type arrow, and then click one of the webpage file types.
5. Click the Save button. If you saved the document using the Web Page, Filtered option, click Yes in the warning dialog box.

Note that after you save a document as a webpage, Word displays it in Web Layout view.

# Editing Hyperlinks

Rima's document contains two hyperlinks—the "invest" link, which jumps to the Fund-Raising Goals worksheet object, and the "here" link, which jumps to the NP_WD_7_Party.docx document. To give all the Movie Time Trivia documents a coherent look, Rima saved a new version of the party invitation that is formatted with a fill effect. Now she wants you to edit the "here" hyperlink, so it opens this new version of the document. To make it possible to repeat these steps later if you want, you'll start by saving the formatted document with a new name.

## To edit the "here" hyperlink:

1. Open the document **NP_WD_7-4.docx** located in the Word7 > Module folder included with your Data Files, and then switch to Web Layout view, if necessary, so you can see the two-color gradient background.

2. Save the document as **NP_WD_7_FormattedParty** in the location specified by your instructor, and then close it.

3. In the NP_WD_7_Combined.docx document, scroll down to the end of the document, and then position the pointer over the **here** hyperlink near the end of the document to display a ScreenTip, which indicates that the link will jump to a document named NP_WD_7_Party.docx.

   **Trouble?** If you also see a ScreenTip that reads "Chart Area" you can ignore it.

4. Right-click the **here** hyperlink to open a shortcut menu, and then click **Edit Hyperlink**. The Edit Hyperlink dialog box opens. It looks just like the Insert Hyperlink dialog box, which you have already used. To edit the hyperlink, you select a different target file.

5. In the Link to pane, verify that the Existing File or Web Page option is selected.

6. Navigate to the location where you saved the NP_WD_7_FormattedParty document, if necessary, and then click **NP_WD_7_FormattedParty** in the file list.

7. Click **OK**. You return to the NP_WD_7_Combined.docx document.

8. Place the pointer over the hyperlink to display a ScreenTip, which indicates that the link will now jump to a document named NP_WD_7_FormattedParty.

9. Press and hold **CTRL**, and then click the **here** hyperlink. The NP_WD_7_FormattedParty.docx document opens.

10. sam↑ Close the **NP_WD_7_FormattedParty.docx** document, and then save and close the **NP_WD_7_Combined.docx** document.

## Proskills

### Teamwork: Emailing Word Documents

After you optimize a document for online viewing, you can share it with colleagues via email. To get started emailing a document, first make sure you have set up Microsoft Outlook as your email program. Then, in Word, open the document you want to email. On the ribbon, click the File tab, and then click Share in the navigation bar. On the Share screen, click Email, and then click either Send as Attachment or Send as PDF.

When you email documents, keep in mind the following:

- Many email services have difficulty handling attachments larger than 4 MB. Consider storing large files in a compressed (or zipped) folder to reduce their size before emailing them.

- Other word-processing programs and early versions of Word might not be able to open files created in the latest version of Word. To avoid problems with conflicting versions, you have two options. You can save the Word document as a rich text file (using the Rich Text File document type in the Save As dialog box) before emailing it; all versions of Word can open rich text files. Another option is to save the document as a PDF.

- If you plan to email a document that contains links to other files, remember to email all the linked files.

- Attachments, including Word documents, are sometimes used maliciously to spread computer viruses. Remember to include an explanatory note with any email attachment so that the recipient can be certain the attachment is legitimate. Also, it's important to have a reliable virus checker program installed if you plan to receive and open email attachments.

The new documents are just one way to share information about Movie Time Trivia. Rima also wants to write a blog post discussing the game's development. She asks you to help her create a blog post in Word.

## Creating and Publishing a Blog Post

Creating a blog post in Word is similar to creating a new Word document except that instead of clicking Blank document on the New screen in Backstage view, you click Blog post. Note that before you can publish your blog post using Word, you need to register a blog account with an Internet blog provider that is compatible with Microsoft Word.

Rima asks you to help her create a blog post about the development of the Movie Time Trivia game.

### To create and publish a blog post:

1. On the ribbon, click the **File** tab, and then click **New** in the navigation bar to display the icons for the various document templates.

2. Scroll down if necessary, and then click **Blog post**.

   **Trouble?** If Blog post is not listed on the New screen, click the Search for online templates box, type blog post, press ENTER, and then click the Blog post icon.

Word | Module 7 Collaborating with Others and Integrating Data

3. In the Blog post window, click the **Create** button, if necessary. A blank blog post opens. Assuming you have not previously registered for a blog account, you also see the Register a Blog Account dialog box.

   To register a blog account, you could click the Register Now button to open the New Blog Account dialog box. From there, you could follow the prompts to register your blog account. Rima will register her blog account later, so you can skip the registration step for now.

4. Click the **Register Later** button to close the dialog box.

5. At the top of the blog post, click the **[Enter Post Title Here]** placeholder, and then type **Movie Time Trivia**.

6. Click in the blank paragraph below the blog title, and then type **Movie Time Trivia is a board game that tests your knowledge of film trivia**. See Figure 7–37.

| Figure 7–37 | Blog post |
| --- | --- |

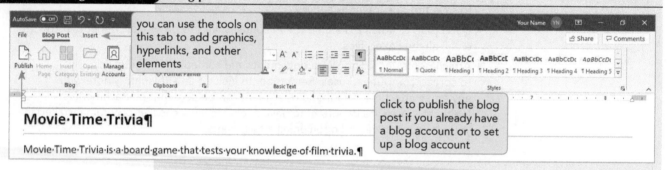

At this point, you could use the tools on the Insert tab to add hyperlinks, graphics, and other items to your blog post. Rima plans to add more text and some graphics to her blog post later. For now, you can save the post, and then explore options for publishing it.

7. Save the blog post as **NP_WD_7_Blog** in the location specified by your instructor. Note that a blog post is a regular Word document file, with a .docx extension.

8. On the Blog Post tab, in the Blog group, click the **Publish** button.

   Assuming you have not previously registered for a blog account, you see the Register a Blog Account dialog box again. At this point, you could click the Register an Account button and then follow the on-screen instructions to register a blog account and publish your blog. Because Rima plans to do that later, you can close the blog post for now.

   **Trouble?** If you see a menu below the Publish button, you clicked the Publish arrow instead of the Publish button. Press ESC, and then click the Publish button.

9. Click **Cancel** to close the Register a Blog Account dialog box, and then click **OK** in the Microsoft Word dialog box.

10. Close the blog post.

**Tip**

To add, remove, or change blog accounts, click the Manage Accounts button in the Blog group on the Blog Post tab.

Rima plans to write weekly blog posts describing the company's progress with the new game. Combined with the fact sheet, they will help generate interest in the company's crowd-sourcing effort.

# Insight

## Working with Saved and Unsaved Document Versions

By default, as you work on a document, versions of it are automatically saved every 10 minutes. To change how often a version is saved, click the File tab, click Options in the navigation bar, click Save in the navigation bar in the Word Options dialog box, and then change the number of minutes in the Save AutoRecover information every box.

If you want to open an autosaved version of the current document, click the File tab and then click Info to display the Info screen. If autosaved versions of the document are available, they are listed in the Manage Document section, along with the date and time each version was saved. Click a version to open it in Read Mode as a read-only document with "(Autorecovered Version)" in the title bar. At this point, you can save the document with a new name if you want. To compare an autosaved version with the current version of the document, right-click the version in the Manage Document section of the Info screen, and then click Compare with Current. To delete an autosaved version of a document, right-click the version in the Manage Document section of the Info screen, and then click Delete This Version.

If your computer shuts down unexpectedly with unsaved changes while a document is open, you might see a Recovered section in the Home screen the next time you start Word. To recover an unsaved version of a document, click Show Recovered Files in the Recovered section to create a new, blank document with the Document Recovery pane open. In the pane, click the unsaved version of the document that you want to open. You can also click the Manage Document button on the Info Screen, and then click Recover Unsaved Documents to display the Open dialog box with the folder that contains unsaved versions of files selected.

# Review

## Session 7.2 Quick Check

1. Describe two options on the Paste Options menu that allow you to control the formatting applied to a linked Excel chart.

2. What is the first step in creating a hyperlink to a location in the same document?

3. Are horizontal lines displayed on a printed page?

4. What is the difference between the way text is displayed in Web Layout view and the way it is displayed in Print Layout view?

5. Explain how to edit a hyperlink.

6. What do you need to do before you can publish a blog post?

# Practice

## Review Assignments

Data Files needed for the Review Assignments: NP_WD_7-5.docx, NP_WD_7-6.xlsx, NP_WD_7-7.docx, Support_WD_7_Funding.xlsx, Support_WD_7_SportsJames.docx

Rima is working on a document about a new game. She has written a draft of the document and has emailed it to James. While he reviews it, Rima asks you to turn on Track Changes and continue working on the document. Then, she can combine her edited version of the document with James's, accepting or rejecting changes as necessary. She also needs you to insert some data from an Excel worksheet as an embedded object and insert an Excel chart as a linked object. She then wants you to create a version of the document with hyperlinks, optimize the document for online viewing, and create a blog post. Complete the following steps:

1. Open the document **NP_WD_7-5.docx** located in the Word7 > Review folder included with your Data Files. Save the file as **NP_WD_7_SportsRima** in the location specified by your instructor.

2. Change the username to **Rima Khouri** and the user initials to **RK**, and then turn on Track Changes.

3. In the first paragraph below the title, move the sentence that begins "When you land on a Ref It square..." to the end of the paragraph, and then add an **s** to the word "drive" in that sentence so the text reads "...USB drives...."

4. In the second paragraph below the title, in the first line, attach a comment to the number "300" that reads **Should this be 325?**

5. Just before the period at the end of the document, add **or contact *your name*** (replacing *your name* with your first and last name) so that the sentence reads "Click here to learn more about this fun event or contact *your name*."

6. Save your changes to the NP_WD_7_SportsRima.docx document.

7. Combine the NP_WD_7_SportsRima.docx document with James's edited version, which is named **Support_WD_7_SportsJames.docx**. Use the NP_WD_7_SportsRima.docx document as the original document. If a message asks you which formatting changes to keep, select your document, and then continue with the merge.

8. Save the combined document as **NP_WD_7_SportsCombined** in the location specified by your instructor.

9. Turn off Track Changes, and then reject James's deletion of "chart" and his insertion of "graph." Accept all the other changes in the document. Delete all comments.

10. Change the username and initials back to their original settings, and then save the NP_WD_7_SportsCombined.docx document. Close the NP_WD_7_SportsRima.docx document, saving changes if you didn't save them earlier.

11. In the NP_WD_7_SportsCombined.docx document, replace the placeholder "[Insert Excel worksheet]" with the funding goals in the **Support_WD_7_Funding.xlsx** file. Include everything from cell A1 through cell B5. Insert the worksheet as an embedded object, and then close the Support_WD_7_Funding.xlsx file.

12. Center the embedded object, and then change the "Complete and Release Expansion Pack" value in the embedded worksheet object from $8,500 to **$7,500**.

13. Open the workbook **NP_WD_7-6.xlsx**, and then save it as **NP_WD_7_WorkHours** in the location specified by your instructor. Copy the pie chart to the Office Clipboard.

14. Return to the NP_WD_7_SportsCombined.docx document, and then replace the placeholder "[Insert Excel chart]" with a linked copy of the chart using the destination theme. If the label for the largest slice appears below the slice instead of on it, drag the chart's lower-right handle to increase the chart size slightly, until the label appears within the slice.

15. Save the NP_WD_7_SportsCombined.docx document, and then close it.

16. Return to the NP_WD_7_WorkHours.xlsx workbook in Excel. Edit the data in the workbook by changing the hours for focus group testing to **125**, and the hours for Research and question development to **300**. Save the workbook, and then close Excel.

17. Open the **NP_WD_7_SportsCombined.docx** document and review the chart. If it doesn't contain the new numbers, click the chart, and use the Refresh Data button to update the chart.

18. Save the NP_WD_7_SportsCombined.docx document, and then save the document with the new name **NP_WD_7_NoExcelLinks** in the location specified by your instructor.

19. Break the link to the Excel workbook, and then save the document.

20. Format the Excel worksheet object as a bookmark named **Funding**. In the first line of the third paragraph below the page title, format the phrase "Stadium Time Trivia Expansion Pack" as a hyperlink that targets the "Funding" bookmark. Test the hyperlink to make sure it works. Save the document.

21. Open the document **NP_WD_7-7.docx** from the Word7 > Review folder included with your Data Files, and then save the file as **NP_WD_7_ReleaseParty** in the location specified by your instructor. Close the NP_WD_7_ReleaseParty.docx document, and return to the NP_WD_7_NoExcelLinks.docx document.

22. In the last line of the document, format the word "here" as a hyperlink that targets the NP_WD_7_ReleaseParty.docx document. Test the hyperlink to make sure it works, and then close the NP_WD_7_ReleaseParty.docx document. Save the NP_WD_7_NoExcelLinks.docx document.

23. Switch to Web Layout view, and add a two-color gradient page color using Dark Teal, Text 2, Lighter 80% as Color 1 and White, Background 1 as Color 2—with the shading style set to Diagonal up.

24. Change the background color for the worksheet object to White, Background Color 1.

25. Insert a horizontal line in a new paragraph, formatted in the Normal style, before the "Our Goals" heading. Keep the default width, but change the color to Dark Teal, Text 2. Insert an identical horizontal line before the "Your Reward for Investing" heading.

26. Save and close the NP_WD_7_NoExcelLinks.docx document.

27. Create a new blog post without attempting to register a blog account. Save the blog post as **NP_WD_7_DevelopmentBlog** in the location specified by your instructor. Insert **Plans for New Games** as the post title, and then type the following as the text of the blog post: **PYRAMID Games is developing several new games focused on baseball and soccer.**

28. Save and close the NP_WD_7_DevelopmentBlog.docx file.

# Apply

## Case Problem 1

**Data Files needed for this Case Problem: NP_WD_7-8.docx, NP_WD_7-9.xlsx**

**Streamers Celebrations, LLC**   You recently started working as an event planner at Streamers Celebrations, LLC. You need to write a letter to a client that includes the budget for a corporate picnic. The budget is stored in an Excel workbook, and you want to embed the budget in the letter as an Excel worksheet object. After you embed the worksheet object, you need to make some edits to the document using Track Changes. Finally, the company owner is considering using Word to create posts for the company's events blog, so she asks you to create a sample blog post.

Complete the following steps:

1. Open the document **NP_WD_7-8.docx** from the Word7 > Case1 folder included with your Data Files. Save the file as **NP_WD_7_Picnic** in the location specified by your instructor.

2. In the signature line, replace "Student Name" with your name.

3. Delete the placeholder "[Insert Excel worksheet]" but not the paragraph symbol after it. When you are finished, there should be one blank paragraph before the paragraph that begins "Next week I suggest...."

4. Start Excel, open the workbook **NP_WD_7-9.xlsx** from the Word7 > Case1 folder included with your Data Files, and then save it as **NP_WD_7_PicnicBudget** in the location specified by your instructor.

5. Select the two-column list of items and amounts, from cell A6 through cell B10, and then copy the selection to the Clipboard.

6. Insert the worksheet data into the Word document in the blank paragraph that previously contained the placeholder text. Insert the data as a linked object that uses the destination styles.

7. Save the Word document, and then return to the NP_WD_7_PicnicBudget.xlsx workbook and close Excel.

8. Starting from within the Word window, edit the linked worksheet object to change the amount for food and beverages to **3,250**. (*Hint*: Remember that the steps for editing a linked worksheet object are different from the steps for editing a linked chart. Also, note that you don't need to type the dollar sign. Excel adds that automatically.) Save the workbook, close Excel, and then update the link in Word.

9. Save the NP_WD_7_Picnic.docx document, and then save it again as **NP_WD_7_PicnicNoLinks** in the location specified by your instructor.

10. Break the link in the **NP_WD_7_PicnicNoLinks.docx** document.

11. Format the budget table using the Grid Table 4 – Accent 5 table style.

12. If necessary, change the username to your first and last names, change the initials to your initials, and then turn on Track Changes.

13. At the beginning of the letter, replace "3/1/2025" with the current date using the format March 1, 2025.

14. In the inside address, change "Lane" to **Avenue**.

15. At the end of the paragraph that begins "Next week I suggest we visit…" add the sentence **In the meantime, please call if you have any questions.**

16. Save your changes to the NP_WD_7_PicnicNoLinks.docx document, and then save it with the new name **NP_WD_7_PicnicChangesAccepted** in the location specified by your instructor.

17. Turn off Track Changes, close the Reviewing pane if necessary, and then reject the replacement of "Avenue" for "Lane." Accept all the other changes in the document.

18. Return the username and initials to their original settings.

19. Save the NP_WD_7_PicnicChangesAccepted.docx document, and then close it.

20. Create a new blog post without attempting to register a blog account. Save the blog post as **NP_WD_7_InvitationsBlog** in the location specified by your instructor. Insert **Invitation Tips from Streamers Celebrations, LLC** as the post title, and then type the following as the text of the blog post: **You can use Word's 3-D models to add a little excitement to your event invitations. Here's just one example.**

21. Insert a stock 3D model of your choosing in a new paragraph below the sentence you typed in Step 20, and then select a different view of the model in the 3D Model Views group on the 3D Model tab.

22. Save and close the blog post.

# Challenge

### Case Problem 2

**Data Files needed for this Case Problem: NP_WD_7-10.docx, Support_WD_7_Aziz.docx, Support_WD_7_Tommy.docx**

**123 Project Management**   Kendall Aihara is the marketing manager for 123 Project Management, a consulting company that specializes in weekend project management seminars and week-long classes on specific topics. She is creating a series of fact sheets that she can email to potential students. The fact sheets will summarize course offerings at the school. Each fact sheet will also include a link to an Internet video about project management. Kendall has already emailed a draft of her first fact sheet to her two colleagues, Aziz and Tommy, and she now needs to combine their versions with hers to create a final draft. However, because Aziz forgot to turn on Track Changes before he edited the document, Kendall will need to compare her draft with his so that she can see his changes marked as tracked changes.

After she finishes accepting and rejecting changes, Kendall wants you to show her how to add a video to the document. A video production company is preparing a series of videos that she will eventually incorporate into her fact sheets before distributing them, but for now, she asks you to show her how to insert any video from the Internet. Finally, after the fact sheet is finished, Kendall would like you to help her create a chart that illustrates the average distance each client travels to 123 Project Management.

Complete the following steps:

1. Open the document **NP_WD_7-10.docx** from the Word7 > Case2 folder included with your Data Files, save it as **NP_WD_7_Kendall** in the location specified by your instructor, review the document to familiarize yourself with its contents, and then close it.

2. Open the document **Support_WD_7_Aziz.docx** from the Word7 > Case2 folder, review its contents, and then close it.

✦ **Explore** 3. Compare the NP_WD_7_Kendall.docx document with the Support_WD_7_Aziz .docx document, using NP_WD_7_Kendall.docx as the original document, and show the changes in a new document.

4. Review the new document to verify that Aziz's changes to Kendall's draft are now displayed as tracked changes, and then save the document as **NP_WD_7_AzizTrackedChanges** in the location specified by your instructor.

5. Open the document **Support_WD_7_Tommy.docx** from the Word7 > Case2 folder, review its contents, and then close it.

6. Combine the document Support_WD_7_Tommy with the NP_WD_7_AzizTrackedChanges document, using the Support_WD_7_Tommy file as the original document.

7. Save the new document as **NP_WD_7_FactSheet** in the location specified by your instructor.

8. Accept all changes in the document, turn off Track Changes, if necessary, and then use the Editor pane to correct any errors caused by missing spaces.

✦ **Explore** 9. Use Word Help to learn how to insert an Internet video in a document. Insert a blank paragraph at the end of the document, and then insert a video of a project management lecture. Take care to choose a video that is appropriate for a professional setting. After you insert the video in the document, click the Play button on the video image to test it. Press the Esc button to close the video window when you are finished watching it.

✦ **Explore** 10. In the Word document, size the video image just as you would an ordinary picture so that it fits on the first page.

11. Save the NP_WD_7_FactSheet.docx document, and close it and any other open documents.

12. Open a new, blank document, and then save it as **NP_WD_7_CommuteChart** in the location specified by your instructor.

13. Use the Chart tool in Word to create a bar chart. Select the 3-D Stacked Bar type. For the chart title, use **Student Commute Mileage**.

14. Include the data shown in Figure 7–38. To delete the default items in Column D, right-click the gray column D header and then click Delete.

**Figure 7–38**    Data for bar chart

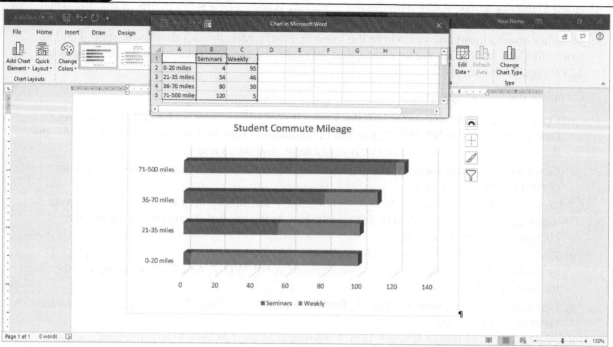

⊕ **Explore**  15. Close the spreadsheet window, and then format the chart with the Style 8 chart style.

16. Save and close all documents.

## Objectives

**Session 5.1**
- Copy worksheets between workbooks
- View a workbook in multiple windows
- Organize worksheets in a worksheet group
- Write a 3-D reference

**Session 5.2**
- Write an external reference
- Manage the security features of linked documents
- Create a hyperlink to a document source
- Link to an email address

**Session 5.3**
- Create and apply a named range
- Work with the scope of named ranges
- Create a workbook template

**EXCEL**

# Generating Reports from Multiple Worksheets and Workbooks

## Summarizing Profit and Loss Statements

## Case | Tibetan Grill

Gail Bailey is a financial officer for Tibetan Grill, a popular chain of Indian restaurants located across the country. As a financial officer, Gail needs to retrieve and combine financial statements from individual Tibetan Grill franchises into summary reports to be analyzed by the Board of Directors. Gail is currently working on an annual report of financial statements from eight Tibetan Grill restaurants located in Illinois and Iowa. You will help her combine data from multiple worksheets and workbooks into one workbook.

## Starting Data Files

| Excel5 → | Module | Review | Case1 |
|---|---|---|---|
| | NP_EX_5-1.xlsx | NP_EX_5-3.xlsx | NP_EX_5-4.xlsx |
| | NP_EX_5-2.xlsx | Support_EX_5_Peoria.xlsx | |
| | Support_EX_5_2020.xlsx | Support_EX_5_Region1.xlsx | |
| | Support_EX_5_2021.xlsx | Support_EX_5_Region2.xlsx | |
| | Support_EX_5_2022.xlsx | Support_EX_5_Region3.xlsx | |
| | Support_EX_5_2023.xlsx | Support_EX_5_Region4.xlsx | |
| | Support_EX_5_Grill08.xlsx | | |

**Case2**

NP_EX_5-5.xlsx
Support_EX_5_Fund01.xlsx
Support_EX_5_Fund02.xlsx
Support_EX_5_Fund03.xlsx
Support_EX_5_Fund04.xlsx
Support_EX_5_Fund05.xlsx

# Session 5.1 Visual Overview:

When worksheets are grouped, the workbook is in group-editing mode, and the word Group will appear in the title bar.

The New Window button creates multiple windows of the same workbook.

The Arrange All button lets you select how multiple windows are arranged on your screen.

In grouped worksheets, any edit made to one sheet is applied to all sheets in the group.

A worksheet group is the collection of two or more selected worksheets. In a worksheet group all selected sheet tabs are highlighted.

AutoSave ● Off    NP_EX_5_Tibetan.xlsx - 1 -...

File    Home    Insert    Draw    Page Layout    Formulas    Data    Review    View    Help

Sheet View | Workbook Views | Show | Zoom | 100% | Zoom to Selection | Window | Macros

Zoom        Macros

New Window | Arrange All | Freeze Panes | Split | Hide | Unhide

Window

B11          fx    324816

A

1   **Tibetan Grill**

2   Annual Profit & Loss Statement ending March 31, 2024

3

| | | Percent of Sales | Benchm |
|---|---|---|---|
| 4 | **SALES** | | |
| 5 | Food Sales  $  5,371,576 | 82.2% | |
| 6 | Beverage Sales  1,163,073 | 17.8% | |
| 7 | TOTAL SALES  6,534,649 | 100.0% | |
| 8 | | | |
| 9 | **COST OF GOODS SOLD** | | |
| 10 | Food Costs  1,669,965 | 31.1% | |
| 11 | Beverage Costs  324,816 | 27.9% | |
| 12 | TOTAL COST OF GOODS SOLD  1,994,781 | 30.5% | |
| 13 | | | |
| 14 | **PAYROLL COSTS** | | |
| 15 | Wages  1,740,000 | 26.6% | |
| 16 | Employee Benefits  414,000 | 6.3% | |
| 17 | Payroll Tax  220,845 | 3.4% | |
| 18 | TOTAL PAYROLL COSTS  2,374,845 | 36.3% | |
| 19 | | | |
| 20 | **PRIME COSTS**  4,369,626 | 66.9% | |
| 21 | | | |

◄    ►    ...    **Grill5-01**    **Grill5-02**    **Grill5-0:**    ...    ⊕

Ready

# Worksheet Groups and 3-D References

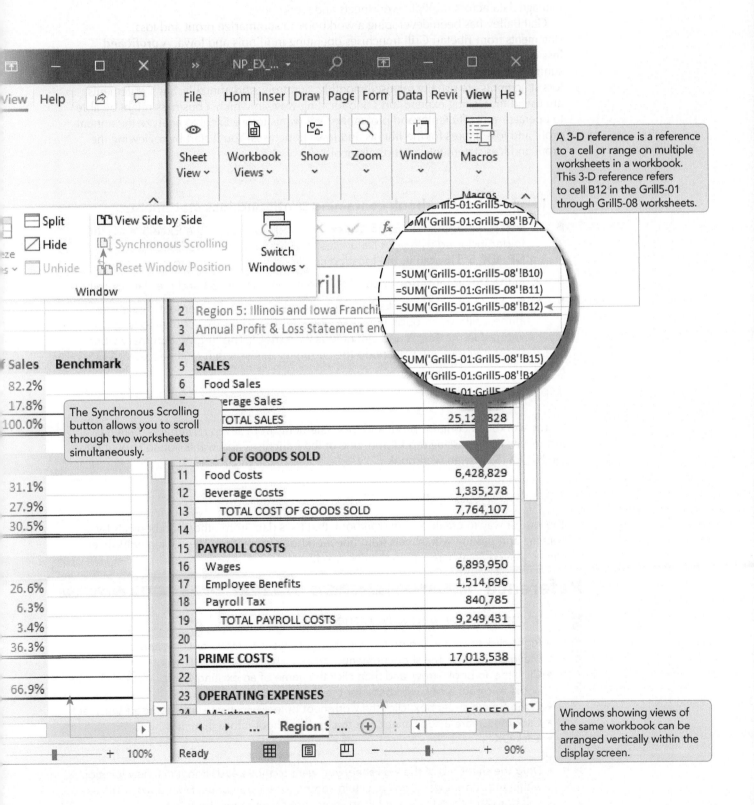

A **3-D reference** is a reference to a cell or range on multiple worksheets in a workbook. This 3-D reference refers to cell B12 in the Grill5-01 through Grill5-08 worksheets.

The **Synchronous Scrolling** button allows you to scroll through two worksheets simultaneously.

Windows showing views of the same workbook can be arranged vertically within the display screen.

=SUM('Grill5-01:Grill5-08'!B7)

=SUM('Grill5-01:Grill5-08'!B10)
=SUM('Grill5-01:Grill5-08'!B11)
=SUM('Grill5-01:Grill5-08'!B12) ◄

=SUM('Grill5-01:Grill5-08'!B15)

| | | |
|---|---|---|
| 2 | Region 5: Illinois and Iowa Franchi | |
| 3 | Annual Profit & Loss Statement en | |
| 4 | | |
| 5 | **SALES** | |
| 6 | Food Sales | |
| 7 | Beverage Sales | |
| | TOTAL SALES | 25,12 828 |
| 11 | Food Costs | 6,428,829 |
| 12 | Beverage Costs | 1,335,278 |
| 13 | TOTAL COST OF GOODS SOLD | 7,764,107 |
| 14 | | |
| 15 | **PAYROLL COSTS** | |
| 16 | Wages | 6,893,950 |
| 17 | Employee Benefits | 1,514,696 |
| 18 | Payroll Tax | 840,785 |
| 19 | TOTAL PAYROLL COSTS | 9,249,431 |
| 20 | | |
| 21 | **PRIME COSTS** | 17,013,538 |
| 22 | | |
| 23 | **OPERATING EXPENSES** | |
| 24 | Maintenance | 510 550 |

Split   View Side by Side
Hide   Synchronous Scrolling
Unhide   Reset Window Position
Switch Windows

Window

Sheet View   Workbook Views   Show   Zoom   Window   Macros

| Sales | Benchmark |
|---|---|
| 82.2% | |
| 17.8% | |
| 100.0% | |
| 31.1% | |
| 27.9% | |
| 30.5% | |
| 26.6% | |
| 6.3% | |
| 3.4% | |
| 36.3% | |
| 66.9% | |

# Working with Multiple Worksheets

So far, you have worked with formulas and functions that referenced cells in a single worksheet within a single workbook. However, data is often stored across several worksheets and workbooks. In this module you'll learn the skills you need to effectively manage data across multiple worksheets and workbooks.

Gail Bailey has been developing a workbook to summarize profit and loss statements from Tibetan Grill franchises operating in Illinois and Iowa. A **profit and loss (P&L) statement**, also called an **income statement**, is a financial statement that summarizes the income and expenses incurred during a specified interval. Profit and loss statements are usually released monthly, quarterly, and annually. Such statements are useful in tracking expenditures and locating ways in which a business might be able to operate more efficiently and profitably. Gail wants to use Excel to analyze the annual profit and loss figures for the Illinois and Iowa franchises. You'll start by reviewing the profit and loss statements for those franchises.

## To open the workbook containing profit and loss statements:

1. **sam↓** Open the **NP_EX_5-1.xlsx** workbook located in the **Excel5 > Module** folder included with your Data Files, and then save the workbook as **NP_EX_5_Tibetan** in the location specified by your instructor.

2. In the **Documentation** sheet, enter your name in cell B3 and the date in cell B4.

3. Review each of the worksheets in the workbook. P&L statements are stored in the Grill5-01 through Grill5-07 worksheets and financial definitions are entered in the Terms and Definitions worksheet. The Region Summary worksheet is where you will create the summary analysis that Gail needs.

4. Go to the **Grill5-01** worksheet.

The workbook contains profit and loss statements from seven restaurants. Gail has just received the missing report from one of the franchises and wants you to copy it into the NP_EX_5_Tibetan workbook.

## Copying a Worksheet

The easiest way to create a new workbook that uses data from other workbooks is by copying and pasting worksheets from one workbook to another. The copied worksheet can be placed anywhere within the new workbook.

# Reference

### Moving and Copying a Worksheet

- Right-click the sheet tab of the worksheet you want to move or copy, and then click Move or Copy on the shortcut menu.
- Click the To book arrow, and then click the name of an existing workbook or click (new book) to create a new workbook for the sheet.
- In the Before sheet box, click the worksheet before which you want to insert the sheet.
- Click the Create a copy check box to copy the sheet rather than moving it.
- Click OK.

*or*

- Drag the sheet tab of the worksheet you want to move and drop it in a new location within the current workbook or within another open workbook. Hold down CTRL as you drag and drop the sheet tab to copy rather than move the sheet.

Gail has provided you with a workbook showing the profit and loss statement from the Tibetan Grill franchise in Peoria, Illinois. You'll copy the worksheet in that workbook to the NP_EX_5_Tibetan workbook.

### To open the Peoria workbook:

1. Open the **Support_EX_5_Grill08.xlsx** workbook located in the **Excel5 > Module** folder included with your Data Files.

2. Go to the **Grill5-08** worksheet.

3. Right-click the **Grill5-08** sheet tab, and then click **Move or Copy** on the shortcut menu. The Move or Copy dialog box opens.

4. Click the **To book arrow**, and then click **NP_EX_5_Tibetan.xlsx** in the list.

5. In the Before sheet box, scroll down and click **Terms and Definitions** to place the Grill5-08 worksheet before the Terms and Definitions worksheet.

6. Click the **Create a copy** check box to place a copy of the Grill5-08 worksheet in the NP_EX_5_Tibetan workbook. See Figure 5–1.

> **Tip**
>
> You can create a new workbook and move or copy a sheet into that workbook by clicking (new book) in the To book list.
>
> Be sure to click the Create a copy check box to copy, not move, the worksheet.

**Figure 5–1**  Move or Copy dialog box

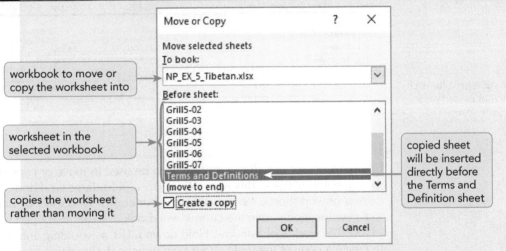

workbook to move or copy the worksheet into

worksheet in the selected workbook

copies the worksheet rather than moving it

copied sheet will be inserted directly before the Terms and Definition sheet

▶ 7. Click **OK**. The Grill5-08 worksheet is copied into the Tibetan workbook.

▶ 8. Close the **Support_EX_5_Grill08** workbook without saving changes.

▶ 9. Return to the **NP_EX_5_Tibetan** workbook and scroll through the sheets and verify that the Grill5-08 worksheet appears directly after the Grill5-07 sheet. See Figure 5–2.

| Figure 5–2 | Grill5-08 worksheet copied to the Tibetan workbook |
| --- | --- |

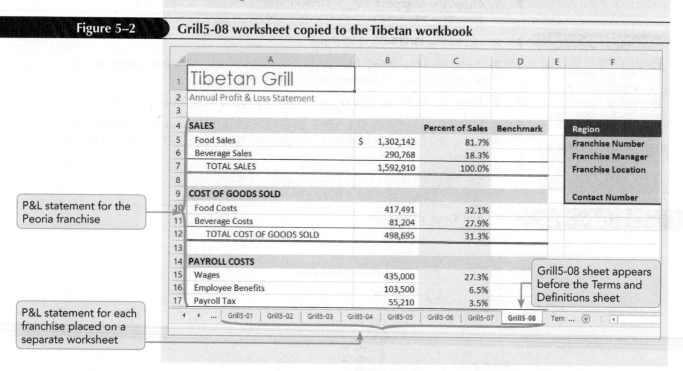

P&L statement for the Peoria franchise

P&L statement for each franchise placed on a separate worksheet

The Move or Copy dialog box can also be used to move or copy worksheets within the current workbook. This is particularly useful for large workbooks that contain dozens of worksheets. You can also move or copy a worksheet by dragging its sheet tab to a new location within the current workbook or to another open workbook displayed in a visible workbook window. Hold down CTRL as you drag and drop the sheet tab to create a copy of the sheet rather than moving it. Once you copy a worksheet into a different workbook, any changes you make to the copied worksheet do not appear in the original worksheet.

# Viewing a Workbook in Multiple Windows

When a workbook has several worksheets, you might find yourself constantly switching between sheets to compare data from different sheets. Instead, you can work on different parts of the workbook at the same time by displaying different sheets in separate windows. You do this with the New Window button in the Window group on the View tab.

Gail wants to compare all the franchises' income and expenses to determine whether any franchises are underperforming or exceeding expectations. Because each franchise's profit and loss statement is on a separate worksheet, Gail would have to switch between eight sheets to complete this analysis. Instead, you can create separate windows for different sheets.

**To create a new viewing window for the workbook:**

▸ **1.** On the ribbon, click the **View** tab to display the commands for viewing the workbook's contents.

▸ **2.** In the Window group, click the **New Window** button. A second window displaying the same workbook opens.

Two windows now display the same workbook. Excel distinguishes the different windows by adding a number after the file name in the title bar. In this case, the two windows for the NP_EX_5_Tibetan.xlsx workbook include the numbers 1 and 2. If you opened a third workbook window, the number 3 would appear after the file name, and so forth.

## Arranging Multiple Workbook Windows

When you have multiple windows, you can change how they are sized and arranged so you can see all windows at one time. When you use the Arrange All button in the Window group on the View tab, you can choose from the following four layout options, shown in Figure 5–3.

- **Tiled.** Resizes the height and width of windows to fill the screen in both horizontal and vertical directions likes floor tiles.
- **Horizontal.** Expands the width of the windows to fill the screen and places them in a single column.
- **Vertical.** Expands the height of the windows to fill the screen and places them in a single row.
- **Cascade.** Layers the windows in an overlapping stack.

**Figure 5–3**    **Workbook window layouts**

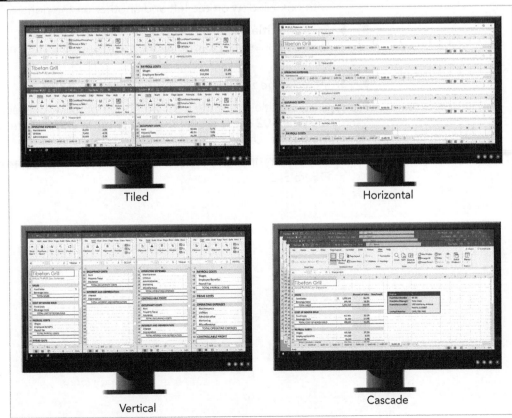

Tiled

Horizontal

Vertical

Cascade

Generally, you do not want to tile more than four windows at a time. With more windows, the contents become small and difficult to view. You'll use the Arrange All command to display the two windows of the NP_EX_5_Tibetan workbook in a vertical layout.

**To view the Tibetan workbook windows in a vertical layout:**

1. On the ribbon, click the **View** tab and then in the Window group, click the **Arrange All** button. The Arrange Windows dialog box opens.

2. Click the **Vertical** option button to select a vertical layout for the workbook windows.

3. Click the **Windows of active workbook** check box to select it. Now, only windows for the active workbook, and not any other open workbooks, will be arranged. See Figure 5–4.

**Figure 5–4**   Arrange Windows dialog box

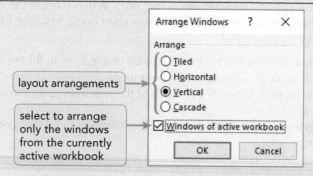

4. Click **OK**. The windows of the current workbook change to a vertical layout with one window on the left and another on the right.

5. Click the **title bar** of left workbook window to select it, and then click the **Grill5-01** sheet tab to display the profit and loss statement for the Chicago franchise.

6. Increase the zoom level of the worksheet to **120%**.

7. Click the title bar of the right workbook window to select it, and then click the **Grill5-02** sheet tab to display the profit and loss statement for the Des Moines franchise.

8. If necessary, increase the zoom level of the worksheet to **120%**. See Figure 5–5.

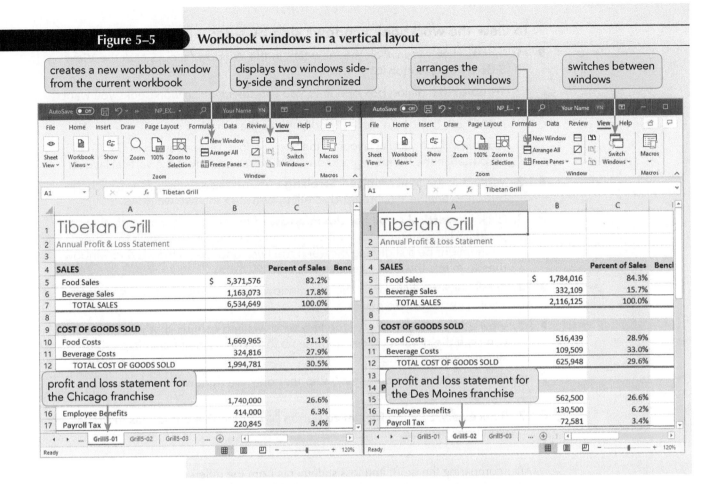

**Figure 5–5**   Workbook windows in a vertical layout

The two workbook windows allow you to compare the contents of one sheet with another. Because the windows are not maximized, more of the sheet contents area are hidden. You can deal with that problem with synchronized scrolling.

## Reference

### Arranging Multiple Workbook Windows

- To create a new window for the current workbook, on the View tab, in the Window group, click the New Window button.
- To arrange multiple workbook windows, on the View tab, in the Window group, click the Arrange All button, click an arrangement option button, click the Windows of active workbook check box to arrange only windows for the current workbook, and then click OK.
- To view two workbook windows side-by-side, on the View tab, in the Window group, click the View Side by Side button and select the workbook window to view along with the current window. If necessary, select the Synchronized Scrolling button to scroll both windows simultaneously.

## Using Synchronized Scrolling Between Windows

You can use synchronized scrolling in two windows that are viewed side by side. As you scroll the worksheet contents in one window, the scrolling is mirrored in the other window. Synchronized scrolling lets you more easily compare two worksheets whose contents extend beyond the workbook window. You'll use synchronized scrolling to review the two windows of the NP_EX_5_Tibetan workbook.

**To view the workbook windows side-by-side:**

▶ 1. In the active window, on the View tab, in the Windows group, click the **View Side by Side** button ⬚.

   **Trouble?** If a dialog box opens so you can select which workbooks you want to view side-by-side, you have multiple workbooks open. Select the window for NP_EX_5_Tibetan.xlsx - 2 workbook as the other window.

   **Trouble?** If the vertical layout of the two windows disappears, click the Arrange All button in the Window group on the View tab to restore the vertical layout.

▶ 2. Verify that the **Synchronized Scrolling** button ⬚ is selected. If not, click the button to enable synchronized scrolling between the two windows.

▶ 3. Click the **vertical scroll bar down arrow** of the left window to verify that the profit and loss statements for both franchises scroll up and down together. There might be a slight lag between the two windows as the second window tries to mirror the actions of the first.

▶ 4. Scroll horizontally through the left window, verifying the right window also scrolls horizontally to match it.

▶ 5. View other worksheets with the two windows and confirm that you can compare the profit and loss statements for other pairs of franchises using synchronized scrolling.

▶ 6. Close the left workbook window so that only the right workbook window is visible for the workbook.

▶ 7. If necessary, click the **Maximize** button ⬚ on the title bar to maximize the workbook window, filling the entire screen.

After comparing the profit and loss statements from the different franchises, Gail sees several errors. Each statement needs a subtitle specifying the end date on which the profit and loss numbers are calculated as well as a calculation of pretax profit for the year. Rather than fixing each worksheet individually, you can edit all the sheets simultaneously by grouping them.

# Working with Worksheet Groups

You can edit several worksheets simultaneously by grouping the worksheets. In a worksheet group, any changes made to one worksheet are automatically applied to all sheets in the group, including entering formulas and data, changing row heights and widths, applying conditional formats, inserting or deleting rows and columns, defining page layouts, and setting view options. Worksheet groups save time and improve consistency because identical actions are performed within several sheets at the same time.

# Reference

### Grouping and Ungrouping Worksheets

- To select an adjacent group, click the sheet tab of the first worksheet in the group, press and hold SHIFT, click the sheet tab of the last worksheet in the group, and then release SHIFT.
- To select a nonadjacent group, click the sheet tab of one worksheet in the group, press and hold CTRL, click the sheet tabs of the remaining worksheets in the group, and then release CTRL.
- To ungroup the worksheets, click the sheet tab of a worksheet that is not in the group; or right-click the sheet tab of one worksheet in the group, and then click Ungroup Sheets on the shortcut menu.

You'll group the profit and loss statements for the eight Tibetan Grill franchises.

### To group the Grill5-01 through Grill5-08 worksheets:

▶ **1.** Click the **Grill5-01** sheet tab to select that worksheet.

▶ **2.** Scroll the sheet tabs to the right until you see the sheet tab for the Grill5-08 worksheet.

▶ **3.** Hold down **SHIFT**, click the **Grill5-08** sheet tab, and then release **SHIFT**. All of the worksheets from the Grill5-01 worksheet and the Grill5-08 worksheet are selected. The sheet tab names are in bold and the word "Group" is added to the title bar as a reminder that you selected a worksheet group.

▶ **4.** Scroll the sheet tabs back to the front of the workbook, displaying the contents of the Grill5-01 worksheet. See Figure 5–6.

| Figure 5–6 | Grouped worksheets |
|---|---|

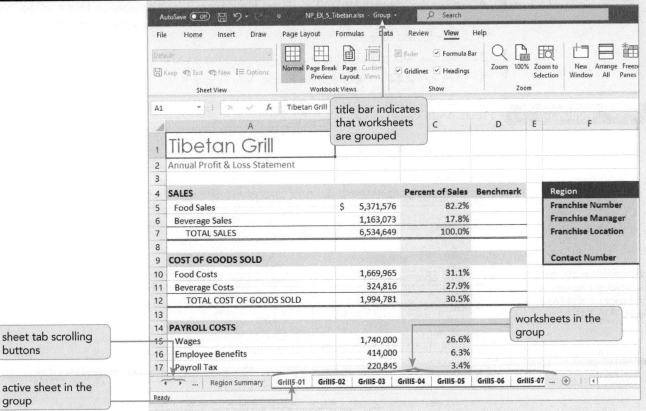

**Trouble?** If the sheets ungrouped, you probably clicked a sheet tab outside of the group. Repeat Steps 1 through 4 to regroup the sheets.

## Editing a Worksheet Group

With the worksheets selected as a single group, you can now edit all of them at the same time. Remember, any changes you make to one worksheet will be made to all sheets in the group. You will edit all of the sheets in the group now, adding a new subheading to each sheet and calculating the pretax profit for each franchise.

## To edit the worksheet group:

1. Make sure the **Grill5-01** worksheet is still the active sheet in the group, and then click cell **A2**. Cell A2 is selected in all the worksheets in the group.

2. In cell A2, change the subheading to **Annual Profit & Loss Statement ending March 31, 2024** to add the ending date, and then press **ENTER**. The subheading is updated for all worksheets in the group.

3. Scroll down and click cell **A43**, type **PRETAX PROFIT** as the label, and then press **TAB**. The label is added to all sheets in the group.

4. In cell **B43**, enter the formula **=B30-B36-B41** to subtract the total occupancy costs, interest, and depreciation from the franchise's controllable profit, and then press **TAB**. The pretax profit is $418,881.

5. In cell **C43**, enter the formula **=B43/B7** to calculate pretax profit divided by total sales, and then press **ENTER**. The pretax profit expressed as a percentage of total sales is 0.06410153.

6. Select the range **A29:D30**, click the **Home** tab on the ribbon, and then in the Clipboard group, click the **Format Painter** button to copy the format from the selected range.

7. Click cell **A42** to paste the copied format to the pretax figures you just calculated.

8. Click cell **A44** to deselect the range. See Figure 5–7.

| Figure 5–7 | Pretax profit calculations |
|---|---|

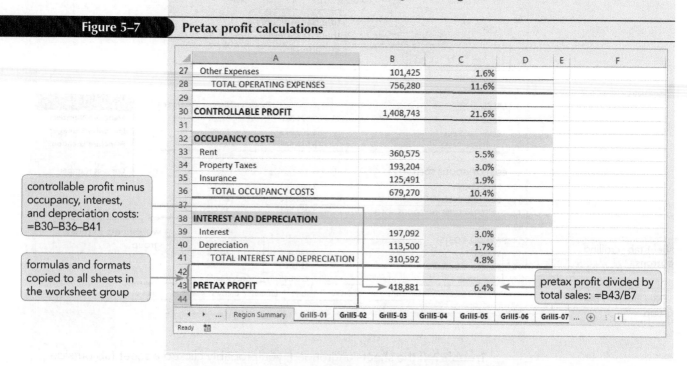

controllable profit minus occupancy, interest, and depreciation costs: =B30–B36–B41

formulas and formats copied to all sheets in the worksheet group

pretax profit divided by total sales: =B43/B7

The Chicago franchise's pretax profit as a percent of total sales is 6.4%, which is a good profit margin in the restaurant industry. Because you made these edits in a worksheet group, the text, data, and formulas you entered in the Grill5-01 worksheet also appear in the other sheets of the worksheet group. You'll review those other sheets to see the pretax profits and percentages in the other franchises.

**To view the pretax profits and percentages in the other sheets in the group:**

▶ 1. Click the **Grill5-02** sheet tab to view the profit and loss statement for the Des Moines franchise.

▶ 2. Scroll up the worksheet and verify that the subheading in cell A2 includes the date for the profit and loss statement.

▶ 3. Scroll down to row **43** and verify that the pretax profit for the Des Moines franchise is $179,261 with a percent of total sales value of 8.5%.

▶ 4. Click each of the other sheet tabs in the worksheet group to verify that the subheading in cell A2 was updated and the pretax profit and percentage appear in row 43.

As you can see from the different sheets in the worksheet group, only the franchise in Rockford, Illinois, showed a net loss for the last fiscal year. The other franchises showed pretax profits ranging from 1.4% to 8.5% of total sales.

## Ungrouping a Worksheet Group

Once you are finished with a worksheet group, you should ungroup the selected sheets so that all sheets start acting independently again. To ungroup worksheets, click the sheet tab of any sheet that is not part of the group. If the group includes all sheets in the workbook, clicking any sheet tab will ungroup the worksheets. You can also right-click any sheet tab in the selected group and click Ungroup Sheets on the shortcut menu.

You will ungroup the selected sheets in the worksheet group.

**To ungroup the sheets in the worksheet group:**

▶ 1. Right-click any **sheet tab** in the worksheet group to display the shortcut menu.

▶ 2. Click **Ungroup Sheets** on the shortcut menu.

▶ 3. Verify that the sheets are ungrouped and the word "Group" no longer appears in the title bar.

Be cautious when editing a worksheet group. If the layout and structure of the sheets are not the same, you might inadvertently overwrite important data in one of the worksheets. Also, remember to ungroup the worksheet group after you finish editing it. Otherwise, changes you intend to make to only one worksheet will be made to all the sheets in the group, potentially producing incorrect results.

## Insight

### Printing a Worksheet Group

Page layouts can be duplicated across multiple sheets. By grouping the worksheets, any of your choices for page orientation, margins, headers, footers, and other layout options will be applied to every other sheet in the group.

You can also print a worksheet group. To print a worksheet group, first group the sheets to be printed. Next, on the ribbon, click File to open Backstage view, and then click Print in the navigation bar. Then, on the Print screen, in the Settings section, verify that the Print Active Sheets option is selected. Finally, click the Print button to send the contents of all the worksheets in the group to the printer.

Gail reviewed the financial information from the eight Tibetan Grill franchises in Illinois and Iowa, and wants you to summarize the data from all of the franchises in a single worksheet.

# Writing 3-D References

So far, all the formulas and functions you created have used data stored on the same sheet. But as workbooks get larger and more complex, data can be spread across many sheets within the workbook. To analyze the data, you need to reference that data in other places.

## Referencing Cells in Other Worksheets

Formulas with references to cells on the same sheet can be thought of as 2-D (or 2-dimensional) references because they involve only the row address and the column address. A 3-D reference includes the row address, the column address, and the worksheet address, expressed within a single reference as:

`Sheet!Range`

where *Sheet* is the worksheet name and *Range* is the 2-D cell reference within that worksheet. The following expression references cell B10 on the Summary worksheet:

`Summary!B10`

If the worksheet title contains spaces, enclose the sheet name within a set of single quotation marks. The following expression uses this form to reference cell B10 on the Summary Report worksheet.

`'Summary Report'!B10`

The reference to a cell within a worksheet can be relative, absolute, or mixed so that the expression `'Summary Report'!$B$10` provides an absolute reference to cell B10 in the Summary Report worksheet.

## Applying 3-D References to Formulas and Functions

3-D cell references can be used within any Excel formula and function. For example, the following formula calculates the combined total of cell B10 from the Jan, Feb, Mar, Apr, and May worksheets.

`=Jan!B10+Feb!B10+Mar!B10+Apr!B10+May!B10`

Another way to reference several worksheets is to treat them as worksheet group starting from the group's first sheet and ending at the last sheet. The syntax of the worksheet group reference is

`FirstSheet:LastSheet!Range`

where *FirstSheet* is the first sheet in the group, *LastSheet* is the last sheet in the group, and *Range* is a cell range common to all sheets in the group. The following expression references cell B10 from all sheets in a group starting with the Jan worksheet and ending with the May worksheet:

`Jan:May!B10`

Any worksheet placed between the Jan and May sheets is part of the group reference. The following formula calculates the total of the B10 cells within the group:

`=SUM(Jan:May!B10)`

So, if the Feb, Mar, and Apr sheets are placed between the Jan and May worksheets in the workbook, they will be included in the calculation.

# Proskills

## Problem Solving: Managing 3-D Group References

Worksheet group references are based on the *current order* of worksheets in the workbook. Rearranging the worksheets will affect what values are included in the calculation. Here are some tips to keep in mind when you revised the structure of a workbook containing a reference to a worksheet group:

- If you insert a new sheet between the first and last sheets of the group, it automatically becomes part of the worksheet group reference.
- If you move a worksheet out from between the first and last sheets, it is no longer part of the worksheet group reference.
- If you move the positions of the first or last sheets, the worksheet group will automatically refer to the new position of the group within the workbook.
- If the first sheet in the group is deleted, the sheet to the right of the first sheet becomes the new first sheet in the worksheet group reference.
- If the last sheet in the group is deleted, the sheet to the left of the last sheet becomes the new last sheet in the worksheet group reference.

Keep in mind that relative references within the worksheets will not update if you change the structure of the sheets. For example, if you insert a new column B in the Jan through May worksheets, which moves cell B10 to cell C10 in those sheets, the formula remains =SUM(Jan:May!B10).

It's a good practice to use formulas that include a worksheet group reference only when you are confident that the sheet order and the row/column structure of the worksheets within the group will not change.

A 3-D reference can be used with most statistical functions, including the MIN, MAX, COUNT, AVERAGE, and MEDIAN functions. You can easily insert a 3-D reference in a formula by using your mouse to select the worksheet and then the cell range within the worksheet group.

# Reference

## Entering a 3-D Reference

- To create a 3-D reference to a range within a worksheet, enter

  *Sheet*!*Range*

  where *Sheet* is the worksheet name and *Range* is the cell address within that worksheet (enclose worksheet names that include spaces within a set of single quotes).
- To insert a 3-D reference in a formula, click the sheet tab of the worksheet, click the cell range in that worksheet, and then press ENTER.
- To copy the range from the worksheet, on the Home tab, in the Clipboard group, click the Paste arrow, and then click the Paste Link button.
- To create a 3-D reference to a range within a worksheet group, enter

  *FirstSheet*:*LastSheet*!*Range*

  where *FirstSheet* is the first sheet in the group, *LastSheet* is the last sheet in the group, and *Range* is a cell range common to all sheets in the group.
- To insert a 3-D reference to a range in a worksheet group, click the sheet tab of the first worksheet in the worksheet group, hold down SHIFT, click the tab for the last sheet in the group, release SHIFT, select the cell range in the selected worksheet group, and then press ENTER.

Gail wants you to determine the total food sales for all eight Tibetan Grill franchises. You will calculate that value using the SUM function with a 3-D cell reference.

## To calculate total food sales using a 3-D cell reference:

▶ **1.** Go to the **Region Summary** worksheet, and then click cell **B6** to select it.

▶ **2.** Type **=SUM(** to begin the SUM function.

▶ **3.** Click the **Grill5-01** sheet tab. The formula displayed in the formula bar is =SUM('Grill5-01'! showing the first worksheet used in the 3-D reference.

▶ **4.** Scroll the sheet tabs until the Grill5-08 sheet tab is visible.

▶ **5.** Press and hold **SHIFT**, click the **Grill5-08** sheet tab, and then release **SHIFT**. The formula changes to =SUM('Grill5-01:Grill5-08'! showing the entire worksheet group used in the reference.

▶ **6.** Click cell **B5** to complete the 3-D reference. The formula changes to =SUM('Grill5-01:Grill5-08'!B5 in the formula bar.

▶ **7.** Type **)** to complete the formula, and then press **ENTER**. The formula returns the value $20,599,586, which is the sum of food sales from all eight Tibetan Grill franchises in Illinois and Iowa.

▶ **8.** Click cell **B6** to select it. See Figure 5–8.

**Figure 5–8**    3-D reference in the SUM function

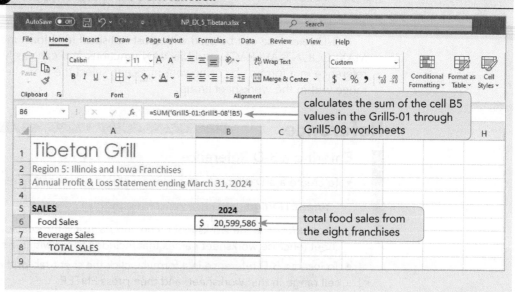

Rather than typing the SUM formula for the rest of the cells in the Region Summary worksheet, you can use AutoFill to copy the formula you created in cell B6. You will use AutoFill now to complete the summary statistics in the Region Summary worksheet.

## To calculate the totals for the rest of the worksheet:

1. With cell B6 still selected, drag the fill handle down to cell **B44**. The 3-D formula is copied down through the range B7:B44.

2. Click the **Auto Fill Options** button 📑, and then click the **Fill Without Formatting** option button. The cells return to their original formatting. Some cells that were blank now display the value 0.

3. In the range B6:B44, select all of the cells displaying 0 or -, and then press **DELETE** to clear the formulas from those cells.

4. Click cell **B44** to select it. The total pretax profit from all eight stores is $1,193,864. See Figure 5–9.

| Figure 5–9 | 3-D cell reference copied through Region Summary worksheet |

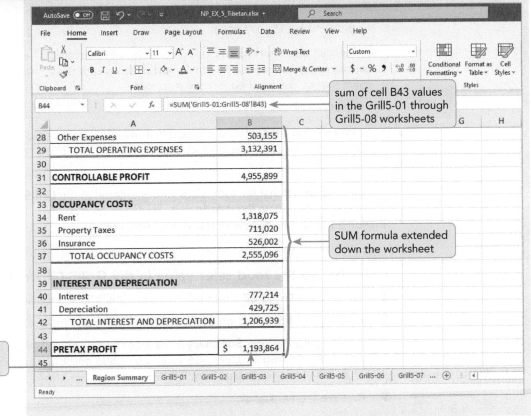

As with 2-D cell references, formulas with 3-D cell references update automatically when any of the values in a referenced worksheet cell change, making 3-D cell references a dynamic tool for analyzing data scattered across a workbook.

## Insight

### Wildcards and 3-D References

You can create flexible 3-D references by using wildcards. A **wildcard** is a symbol that represents any character, much as wildcards in poker can take on any card value. Two useful wildcards are the question mark (?) wildcard, which represents any single character and the asterisk (*) wildcard, which represents any string of characters. For example, to sum the value of cell B5 from all worksheets beginning with the text string "Grill", you could use the formula

```
=SUM('Grill*'!B5)
```

which would include worksheets named Grill5-01, Grill5-02, and so on in the calculation. If that wildcard expression includes worksheets you don't want to include, you can use the ? wildcard to narrow down the list of matching worksheets. In the following formula, only sheets that have names starting with 'Grill5-0' and followed by a single character would be included in the sum:

```
=SUM('Grill5-0?'!B5)
```

You can also omit any text string and use only wildcards. The following formula calculates the sum of cell B5 from any worksheet with three letters in its name, such as sheet names like Jan, Feb, Mar, and so forth:

```
=SUM('???'!B5)
```

When Excel encounters a wildcard in a worksheet reference, it automatically converts the reference to one in which the sheet name is explicitly entered.

Gail discovered that the food sales values entered in the Grill5-08 worksheet are incorrect. You'll update the data in that sheet, and then confirm that the values in the Region Summary worksheet updated automatically.

### To change the food sales value in the Grill5-08 worksheet:

1. Click the **Grill5-08** sheet tab to make Grill5-08 worksheet the active sheet.

2. Click cell **B5**, and then enter **1,322,142** as the correct value for food sales.

3. Go to the **Region Summary** worksheet and verify that the value in cell B6 increased from $20,599,586 to $20,619,586 and that the total pretax profit in cell B44 has increased from $1,193,864 to $1,213,864.

4. Save the workbook.

Gail now has a summary of the profit and losses for the restaurants in the Illinois/Iowa region over the past year. But how do those values compare to previous years? You will answer that question in the next session when you compare the profit and loss values in this workbook to profit and loss statements from other workbooks created over the past several years.

# Review

## Session 5.1 Quick Check

1. How do you create a worksheet group consisting of sheets that are not adjacent in a workbook?
2. Can a workbook have only one window?
3. How do you ungroup a worksheet group that consists of all the sheets in the workbook?
4. What is the 3-D cell reference to cell C20 in the Monday worksheet?
5. What is the absolute 3-D cell reference to cell C20 in the Monday worksheet?
6. What is the 3-D cell reference to cell C20 in the Monday through Friday worksheet group?
7. Write a formula that uses the MAX function to calculate the maximum value of cell C20 of the Monday through Friday worksheet group.

# Session 5.2 Visual Overview:

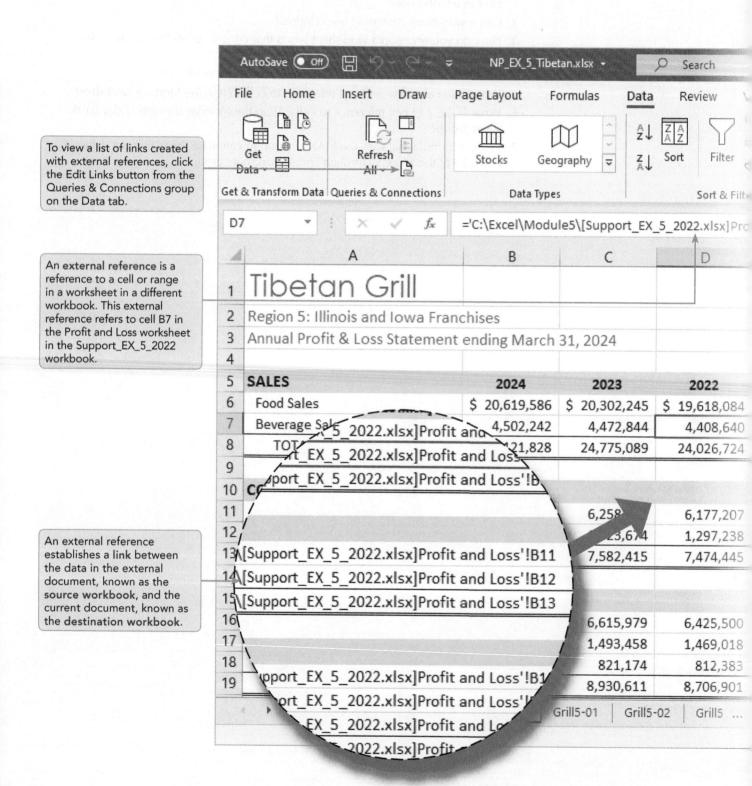

To view a list of links created with external references, click the Edit Links button from the Queries & Connections group on the Data tab.

An external reference is a reference to a cell or range in a worksheet in a different workbook. This external reference refers to cell B7 in the Profit and Loss worksheet in the Support_EX_5_2022 workbook.

An external reference establishes a link between the data in the external document, known as the **source workbook**, and the current document, known as the **destination workbook**.

AutoSave ● Off    NP_EX_5_Tibetan.xlsx    Search

File | Home | Insert | Draw | Page Layout | Formulas | Data | Review

Get Data | Refresh All | Stocks | Geography | Sort | Filter

Get & Transform Data | Queries & Connections | Data Types | Sort & Filte

D7    fx    ='C:\Excel\Module5\[Support_EX_5_2022.xlsx]Pro

|  | A | B | C | D |
|---|---|---|---|---|
| 1 | Tibetan Grill | | | |
| 2 | Region 5: Illinois and Iowa Franchises | | | |
| 3 | Annual Profit & Loss Statement ending March 31, 2024 | | | |
| 4 | | | | |
| 5 | SALES | 2024 | 2023 | 2022 |
| 6 | Food Sales | $ 20,619,586 | $ 20,302,245 | $ 19,618,084 |
| 7 | Beverage Sal_5_2022.xlsx]Profit and | 4,502,242 | 4,472,844 | 4,408,640 |
| 8 | TOT_EX_5_2022.xlsx]Profit and Loss | 21,828 | 24,775,089 | 24,026,724 |
| 9 | port_EX_5_2022.xlsx]Profit and Loss'!B | | | |
| 10 | CC | | | |
| 11 | | | 6,258 | 6,177,207 |
| 12 | | | 3,674 | 1,297,238 |
| 13 | [Support_EX_5_2022.xlsx]Profit and Loss'!B11 | | 7,582,415 | 7,474,445 |
| 14 | [Support_EX_5_2022.xlsx]Profit and Loss'!B12 | | | |
| 15 | [Support_EX_5_2022.xlsx]Profit and Loss'!B13 | | | |
| 16 | | | 6,615,979 | 6,425,500 |
| 17 | | | 1,493,458 | 1,469,018 |
| 18 | upport_EX_5_2022.xlsx]Profit and Loss'!B1 | | 821,174 | 812,383 |
| 19 | ort_EX_5_2022.xlsx]Profit and Loss'! | | 8,930,611 | 8,706,901 |

EX_5_2022.xlsx]Profit and Lo
2022.xlsx]Profit

Grill5-01 | Grill5-02 | Grill5

# External References and Links

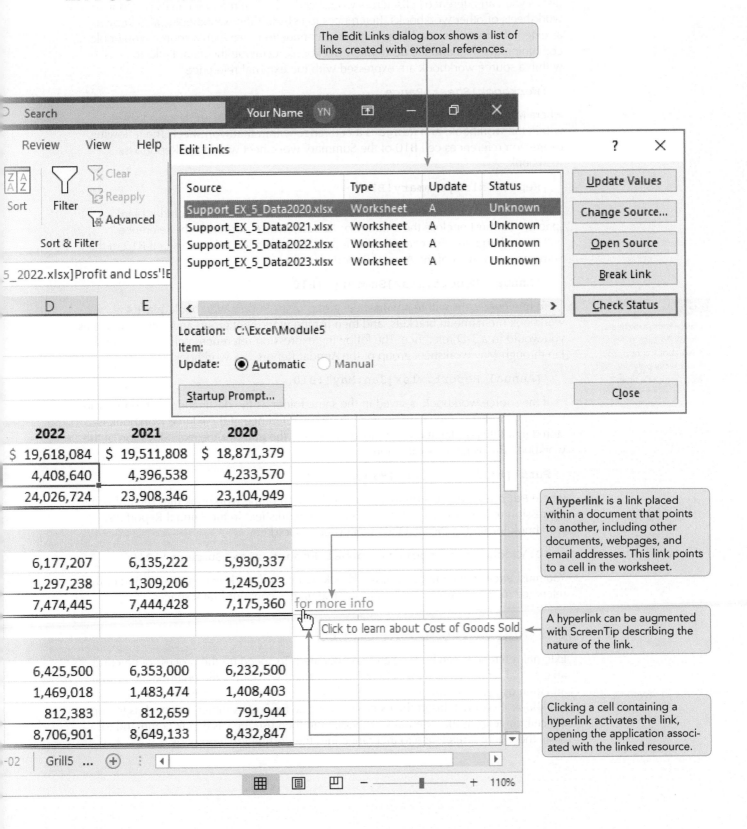

The Edit Links dialog box shows a list of links created with external references.

**Edit Links**

| Source | Type | Update | Status |
|---|---|---|---|
| Support_EX_5_Data2020.xlsx | Worksheet | A | Unknown |
| Support_EX_5_Data2021.xlsx | Worksheet | A | Unknown |
| Support_EX_5_Data2022.xlsx | Worksheet | A | Unknown |
| Support_EX_5_Data2023.xlsx | Worksheet | A | Unknown |

Update Values

Change Source...

Open Source

Break Link

Check Status

Location:   C:\Excel\Module5
Item:
Update:   ● Automatic   ○ Manual

Startup Prompt...                        Close

| 2022 | 2021 | 2020 |
|---|---|---|
| $ 19,618,084 | $ 19,511,808 | $ 18,871,379 |
| 4,408,640 | 4,396,538 | 4,233,570 |
| 24,026,724 | 23,908,346 | 23,104,949 |
| | | |
| 6,177,207 | 6,135,222 | 5,930,337 |
| 1,297,238 | 1,309,206 | 1,245,023 |
| 7,474,445 | 7,444,428 | 7,175,360 |
| | | |
| 6,425,500 | 6,353,000 | 6,232,500 |
| 1,469,018 | 1,483,474 | 1,408,403 |
| 812,383 | 812,659 | 791,944 |
| 8,706,901 | 8,649,133 | 8,432,847 |

for more info

Click to learn about Cost of Goods Sold

A hyperlink is a link placed within a document that points to another, including other documents, webpages, and email addresses. This link points to a cell in the worksheet.

A hyperlink can be augmented with ScreenTip describing the nature of the link.

Clicking a cell containing a hyperlink activates the link, opening the application associated with the linked resource.

# Linking to External Workbooks

Just as you can reference cells across worksheets, you can reference cells stored in worksheets of other workbooks. References to cells in other workbooks, also known as external references, establish a link, or a connection, between a source workbook containing the data and the destination workbook receiving the data. Links to cells within a source workbook are expressed with the external reference

`[Workbook]Sheet!Range`

where *Workbook* is the file name of the source workbook, *Sheet* is a worksheet within the workbook, and *Range* is a cell range within that worksheet. The following expression references cell B10 of the Summary worksheet within the Report.xlsx workbook.

`[Report.xlsx]Summary!B10`

If either the source workbook file name or the worksheet name includes blank spaces, you must enclose the entire [*Workbook*]*Sheet* portion of the reference within single quotes. For example, the following expression references cell B10 in the Summary worksheet of the Annual Report.xlsx file.

`'[Annual Report.xlsx]Summary'!B10`

**Tip**

Unlike with worksheets, there's no such thing as a workbook group. You can specify only one workbook at a time.

To reference cells within a worksheet group of the source workbook, place the workbook file name in brackets, and then list the worksheet group and cell reference as you would in a 3-D reference. The following expression references cell B10 within the Jan through May worksheet group of the Annual Report.xlsx workbook:

`'[Annual Report.xlsx]Jan:May'!B10`

If the source workbook is saved in the same folder as the destination workbook, you need to include only the workbook name in the reference. If the source workbook is stored in a different location, you need to include the **path**, or the exact location of the workbook file using the expression

`Path\[Workbook]Sheet!Range`

where *Path* is an expression that points to location of the workbook file. The following expression references cell B10 of the Summary worksheet in the Annual Report.xlsx workbook located in the C:\Documents\Reports folder:

`'C:\Documents\Reports\[Annual Report.xlsx]Summary'!B10`

You must enclose the entire path, workbook name, and worksheet name portion of the reference in single quotes if any one of those names contains blank spaces.

## Creating an External Reference

External references can be long and complicated. To speed up the process of entering an external reference as well as to avoid a mistake, you can begin entering the formula and then use your mouse to select the cell or cell range from an already opened workbook. Excel will insert the external reference for you. Another approach is to copy the cell range from the external workbook, and then use the Paste Link command to paste the external reference to that range into the destination workbook.

# Reference

### Entering an External Reference

- To create an external reference to a range from another workbook, enter

    `[Workbook]Sheet!Range`

    where *Workbook* is the file name of an Excel workbook, *Sheet* is a worksheet within that workbook, and *Range* is a cell range within that worksheet (enclose workbook or worksheet names that include spaces within a set of single quotes).
- To insert the external reference into a formula as you type, click the cell range from the source workbook and press ENTER.
- To enter the external reference into a formula, copy the range from the source workbook, in the destination workbook, on the Home tab, in the Clipboard group, click the Paste arrow, and then click the Paste Link button.
- To create an external reference to a source workbook stored at a different location than the destination workbook, enter

    `Path\[Workbook]Sheet!Range`

    where *Path* is the location of the folder containing the source workbook (enclose the path, workbook, or worksheet names that include spaces within a set of single quotes).

Gail wants you to create a link to the profit and loss statement in the previous year's report. You will use the Paste Link feature to insert this external reference.

### To insert an external reference to the previous year's data:

1. If you took a break after the previous session, make sure that the NP_EX_5_Tibetan workbook is open and the Region Summary worksheet is active.

2. Open the **Support_EX_5_2023.xlsx** workbook located in the **Excel5 > Module** folder included with your Data Files.

3. In the Profit and Loss worksheet, select the range **B5:B44** containing the previous year's profit and loss values.

4. On the Home tab, in the Clipboard group, click the **Copy** button to copy the data.

5. Return to the **NP_EX_5_Tibetan** workbook, and then click cell **C5** in the Region Summary worksheet to select it.

6. On the Home tab, in the Clipboard group, click the **Paste arrow** to open the Paste gallery, and then in the Other Paste Options section, click the **Paste Link** button 📋. Excel inserts links to the cells in the Support_EX_5_Data2023 workbook, starting with the formula =`'[Support_EX_5_Data2023.xlsx]Profit and Loss'!B5` in cell C5 and extending down through cell C44 showing the pretax profit from 2023.

7. Click the **column B** header to select the entire column, and then in the Clipboard group, click the **Format Painter** button to copy the format from that column.

8. Click the **column C** header to paste the copied formats.

9. Click cell **C5** to select it. See Figure 5–10.

> Make sure to use the Paste Link option so you paste the reference to the copied cells rather than pasting the cell values.

| Figure 5-10 | Formula with an external reference |

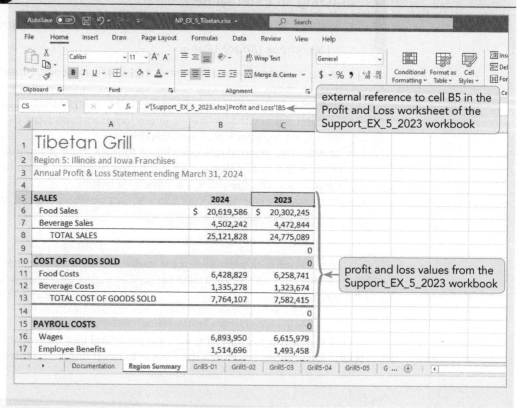

You learn that there has been an increase in total sales from the previous year, but there has also been an increase in the total cost of goods sold. Is this part of a trend? To find out, you'll retrieve more data from other years of profit and loss statements.

### To insert internal references to more years of data:

1. Repeat the previous set of steps, using the Paste Link command to create external references to the profit and loss values in the **Support_EX_5_2022.xlsx**, **Support_EX_5_2021.xlsx**, and **Support_EX_5_2020.xlsx** workbooks, placing the linked data in columns D through F. Several rows show zero or - because they contain formulas the reference empty cells in the source documents. You will remove those formulas.

2. Use **DELETE** on your keyboard to clear the zeros or - from rows 9, 10, 14, 15, 20, 22, 23, 30, 32, 33, 38, 39, and 43 in columns C through F of the Region Summary worksheet.

3. Scroll up the worksheet and click cell **F5** to select it. See Figure 5-11.

| Figure 5–11 | Profit and loss values from 2020 through 2024 |
| --- | --- |

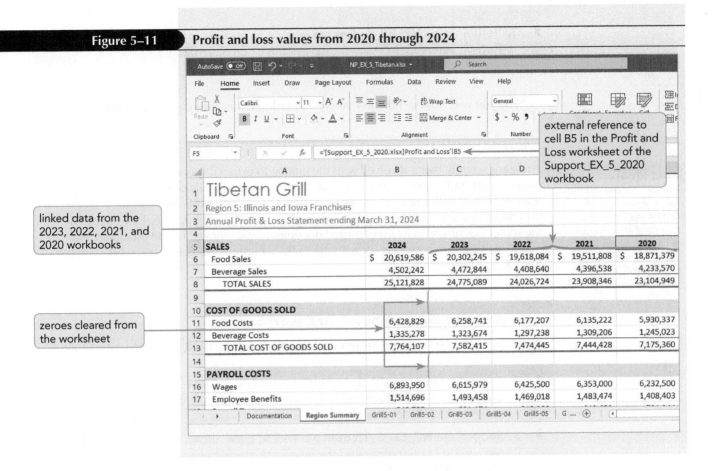

The annual profit and loss values show an interesting trend. Total sales have increased every year from the eight Illinois/Iowa franchises, rising from $23,104,949 in 2020 to $25,121,828 in 2024 (the range B8:F8). But pretax profits have decreased in the last year, dropping from $1,416,783 in 2023 (cell C44) to $1,213,864 in 2024 (cell B44). The decreased profit margin in the face of increasing sales indicates that rising costs are eating into profits. Gail also notices that payroll costs have increased by almost $320,000 from $8,930,611 in 2023 (cell C19) to $9,249,431 in 2024 (cell B19), which might be the important factor in the declining in profits. These are the types of insights that a workbook combining data from multiple worksheets and workbooks can provide.

## Updating Workbook Links

If both the destination and source workbooks are currently open, any changes you make to data in the source workbook will also be reflected in the destination workbook. Gail has a correction for the food sales value in the 2023 data. You'll make this edit in the source workbook.

### To edit the food sales value in the 2023 data source workbook:

1. Go to the **Support_EX_5_2023** workbook.

2. Make sure the **Profit and Loss** worksheet is the active sheet, and then in cell **B6**, change the entry from $20,302,245 to **$20,102,245** to correct the food sales value.

3. Return to the **NP_EX_5_Tibetan** workbook and verify that cell C6 in the Region Summary worksheet displays the value $20,102,245.

Next you will explore how to manage the links created by your external references.

## External References and Security Concerns

There are security issues involved with the linking to external source documents. It is possible you could open a workbook that contains links to malicious software. For that reason, Excel disables links to source documents unless you explicitly indicate that you trust the data source. Once you have indicated that you trust the source, Excel will add the source document to its list of trusted documents and you will not be prompted again.

You will explore how to work with the Excel security measures as you work with the NP_EX_5_Tibetan workbook.

### To open the linked Tibetan Grill workbooks:

1. Save the **NP_EX_5_Tibetan** and **Support_EX_5_2023** workbooks, and then close them.

2. Close the **Support_EX_5_2022**, **Support_EX_5_2021**, and **Support_EX_5_2020** workbooks, but do *not* save any changes that you may have inadvertently made during this session.

3. Reopen the **NP_EX_5_Tibetan** workbook. Excel shows a status message requesting confirmation that the links in this workbook are from known and trusted data sources.

4. Click the **Enable Content** button.

5. Close the **NP_EX_5_Tibetan** workbook without saving any changes you may have inadvertently made to the workbook.

6. Reopen the **NP_EX_5_Tibetan** workbook. Because you've already indicated that this is a trusted data source, you are not prompted to enable the external content. Instead the dialog box shown in Figure 5-12 opens.

**Figure 5-12**    Dialog box prompting for action on links to external files

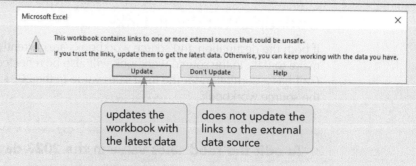

7. Click **Update** to update the links.

Excel prompts you to update the links every time you open the workbook to ensure that you are working with the most current data. But what happens after you open the document? If several people are working with a source document at the same time, the data might change from the time you first opened the workbook so that you are no longer working with the most current data. To deal with that problem, you can review and update all of the links currently active in your workbook.

## Reviewing Links Within a Workbook

A list of all links in your workbook is available in the Edit Links dialog box. For each link, the Edit Links dialog box shows the following information:

- **Source.** Indicates the source file for a given link
- **Type.** Identifies the type of source file, such as an Excel worksheet, a Word document, or a PowerPoint slideshow
- **Update.** Specifies how values are updated from the linked data source, where the letter *A* indicates the link is updated automatically upon opening the workbook, and *M* indicates that the link is updated manually in response to your request
- **Status.** Shows whether the data source has been accessed during the current session and if so, whether the link has been updated

Within the Edit Links dialog box, you can manually update each link, change a link's data source, open a link's data source, break the connection to the link's data source, or check the status of the link. You'll review the links in the NP_EX_5_Tibetan workbook.

### To review the links in the NP_EX_5_Tibetan workbook:

1. On the ribbon, click the **Data** tab to access commands for working with data.

2. In the Queries and Connections group, click the **Edit Links** button. The Edit Links dialog box opens, showing the four links in the workbook, their source file, the type of data source, how the data source is updated, and whether the link has been accessed during this session.

3. Click **Support_EX_5_2023.xlsx** (the last link) in the list.

4. Click **Update Values** to connect to the data source and update the values displayed in the workbook. The status for the Support_EX_5_2023.xlsx workbook changes from Unknown to OK, indicating that Excel has successfully accessed and updated it. See Figure 5–13.

**Figure 5–13**    Edit Links dialog box

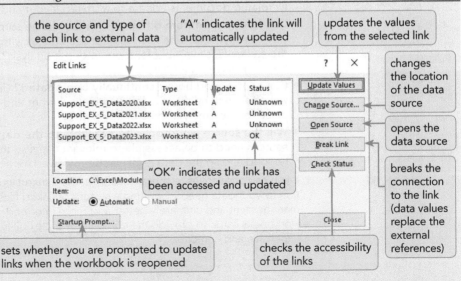

the source and type of each link to external data

"A" indicates the link will automatically updated

updates the values from the selected link

changes the location of the data source

opens the data source

breaks the connection to the link (data values replace the external references)

"OK" indicates the link has been accessed and updated

sets whether you are prompted to update links when the workbook is reopened

checks the accessibility of the links

5. Click **Check Status** to check the accessibility of all listed links. That status of the other links changes from Unknown to OK, indicating that they have also been accessed and updated.

6. Click **Close** to close the dialog box and return to the workbook.

## Managing Workbook Links

In some cases, you want to display only a "snapshot" of the data source at a single moment in time, as with financial statements that show final sales and expense figures at the end of the current month or year. To prevent a workbook from updating its content with data you don't want, you can break its link to the data source by clicking the Break Link button in the Edit Links dialog box. Breaking the link will remove the external references from your workbook, replacing them with the data values themselves.

Sometimes the source workbook that a workbook is linked to is renamed or moved. Such a situation can occur for organizations that are restructuring their file system or switching to a new file server. To keep workbook links active and updateable, click the Change Source button in the Edit Links dialog box, and then replace the link to the old location with a link to the data in its new location or with its new name. You do not need to use the Change Source button if the destination and source workbooks both move to a new location and their relative positions within the folder structure are unchanged. Using the Change Source button is necessary only if the location of the source workbook alone is changed.

## Proskills

### Decision Making: Deciding When to Link Workbooks

At most businesses, a team works together to assemble data used in formulating policy and making decisions. Linked workbooks provide one way to make information compiled by different people or departments accessible to the decision-makers. When choosing whether to create a structure of linked workbooks, consider the following questions:

- **Is a large workbook too difficult to use?** While it may appear simpler to just keep everything within a single file, such workbooks can quickly become large and unwieldy. It is often better to divide information among several workbooks, allowing teams to focus on their own areas of expertise. However, keep in mind that a workbook with many links can also take a long time to open and update.

- **Can separate workbooks share a common design and structure?** Workbooks from different stores, branches, or departments need to have a uniform structure to avoid errors in data entry and analysis. Someone needs to be responsible for ensuring that all related documents adhere to a shared layout and structure.

- **Can information from different workbooks be summarized?** Is there an obvious way to summarize data from several source files within a single workbook, leaving the source files available for more in-depth analysis? Would important information be lost in such a summary?

- **Can source workbooks continually be updated?** Users of the summary workbook will often assume that the information is current and accurate. Are mechanisms in place for the timely update of key data?

- **Will the source workbooks be available to the destination workbook?** Data sources need to be accessible to relevant users so that links can be updated as needed and so the data itself can be reviewed for accuracy and completeness.

If you can answer yes to these questions, then linked workbooks might be the solution to your data needs. Creating a system of linked files can lead to more reliable data management and ultimately better and more informed decisions. A system of linked workbooks can also provide the company with flexibility as data sources become more expansive and complex.

An external reference is only one type of link supported by Excel. You can create links to a wide variety of data sources.

# Creating Hyperlinks

Another type of link supported by Excel is a hyperlink, which is a text string or graphic image connected to a wide variety of resources, including:

- Websites
- Files on your computer, such as Word documents, PowerPoint presentations, text files, and PDF documents
- Cells and cell ranges within the current workbook
- Email addresses
- New documents created specifically as the source of the hyperlink

Clicking a hyperlink opens its linked resource using the application associated with that resource. So clicking a cell with a hyperlink to a website opens the website in your default browser; a hyperlink to a Word document opens the document file in Microsoft Word, and so forth. Hyperlinks are helpful in providing users with additional information not found in your workbook. For example, Gail can use hyperlinks to connect her workbook to Tibetan Grill's website or to an operation manual for franchise managers.

Excel recognizes website addresses and email addresses as links. So if you enter a website or email address into a cell, Excel will automatically convert that text into a hyperlink. For other types of links, you must manually define the type of link and its location.

> **Tip**
>
> You can create a hyperlink using the HYPERLINK function in which you specify the text of the link and the link's source.

## Linking to a Location Within a Workbook

You can manually create a link within a worksheet cell. Select the cell where you want to place the link. On the ribbon, click the Insert tab, and then in the Links group, click the Link button. The Insert Hyperlink dialog box opens. From the Insert Hyperlink dialog box, specify the type of resource to link to and the hyperlink text associated with that link. You can provide additional information about the hyperlink by adding a ScreenTip.

# Reference

### Working with Hyperlinks

- To create a hyperlink, select the text, graphic, or cell in which you want to insert the hyperlink. On the Insert tab, in the Links group, click the Hyperlink button. In the Insert Hyperlink dialog box, specify the link's location and the text as needed. Click the ScreenTip button to add a ScreenTip. Click OK.
- To create a hyperlink to a website or email address, type the address in a cell, and then press ENTER or TAB to convert the text into a hyperlink.
- To use a hyperlink, click the text, graphic, or cell containing the hyperlink; or right-click the hyperlink, and then click Open Hyperlink on the shortcut menu.
- To remove a hyperlink, right-click the hyperlink, and then click Remove Hyperlink on the shortcut menu.
- To edit a hyperlink, right-click the hyperlink, and then click Edit Hyperlink on the shortcut menu.

Gail thinks that some of the terms in the profit and loss statement might not be familiar to users. She asks you to create a hyperlink between those terms and their definitions on the Terms and Definitions worksheet. You'll create some of these hyperlinks now.

## To create hyperlinks to the Prime Costs and Controllable Profits entries in the Region Summary worksheet:

1. On the Region Summary worksheet, click cell **G21**, which is next to the data on prime costs.

2. On the ribbon, click the **Insert** tab, and then in the Links group, click the **Link** button. The Insert Hyperlink dialog box opens.

3. In the Text to display box, type **for more info** as the text of the hyperlink.

4. In the Link to section, click **Place in This Document** to display a list of places in the workbook you can link to.

5. In the Type the cell reference box, type **C16** as the cell reference, and then in the Or select a place in this document list, click **Terms and Definitions** to specify that the link be created to cell C16 in the Terms and Definitions worksheet. See Figure 5–14.

**Tip**

To link to a location in different workbook, click Existing File or Web Page, select the workbook file, click the Bookmark button, enter the cell reference, and then click OK.

**Figure 5–14**     Insert Hyperlink dialog box

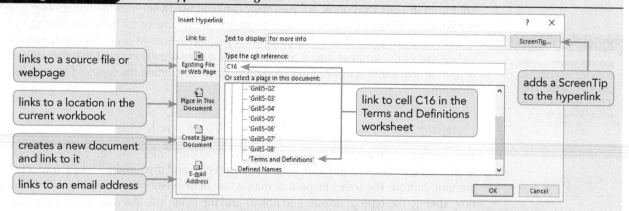

links to a source file or webpage

links to a location in the current workbook

creates a new document and link to it

links to an email address

link to cell C16 in the Terms and Definitions worksheet

adds a ScreenTip to the hyperlink

6. Click **ScreenTip** to open the Set Hyperlink ScreenTip dialog box.

7. In the ScreenTip text box, type **Click to learn more about Prime Costs** as the ScreenTip text, and then click **OK** to return to the Insert Hyperlink dialog box.

8. Click **OK** to insert the hyperlink into cell G21. The text "for more info" appears in cell G21, underlined and in green.

9. Repeat Steps 2 through 8 to link cell **G31** in the Region Summary worksheet to cell **C18** in the **Terms and Definitions worksheet** using **Click to learn more about Controllable Profit** as the ScreenTip text.

**Tip**

To change the style of hyperlink text, click the Cell Styles button in the Styles group on the Home tab, right-click the Hyperlink cell style, and then click Modify.

Excel indicates hyperlinked text by displaying the text in a green font and underlined. To use a link, click the cell containing the hyperlink. Excel will then jump to the linked location in the workbook. You will test the hyperlinks you created in cells G21 and G31 now.

## To use the hyperlinks you created:

**1.** Point to cell **G21** to view the ScreenTip for that hyperlink. See Figure 5–15.

**Figure 5–15**    **Hyperlink text within a worksheet**

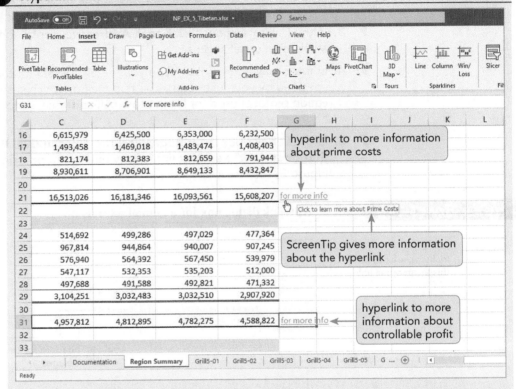

| Tip |
| --- |
| Only linked text within a cell is treated as a hyperlink; text extending beyond the cell's borders is not. |

**2.** Click cell **G21** to make cell C16 in the Terms and Definitions worksheet the active cell.

**3.** Read the definition of the Prime Costs definition entered in cell C16.

**4.** Return to the **Region Summary** worksheet and click cell **G31** to make cell C18 in the Terms and Definitions worksheet the active cell.

**5.** Read the definition of Controllable Profit and return to the **Region Summary** worksheet.

If you need to edit an existing hyperlink, right-click the cell, text, or graphic containing the link, and then click Edit Hyperlink on the shortcut menu to open the Edit Hyperlink dialog box. To remove a hyperlink, right-click the link, and then click Remove Hyperlink on the shortcut menu.

## Linking to an Email Address

You can make it easier for users to send you messages about your workbook by adding a hyperlink to your email address. Clicking a linked email address automatically opens the user's email program to a new message with your email address and a preset subject line already inserted. Gail wants you to add an email address to the Documentation sheet of the NP_EX_5_Tibetan workbook so users can easily submit questions and queries about the workbook's contents. You'll create this email link now.

## To link to an email address:

▶ **1.** Go to the **Documentation** sheet, and then click cell **B3** containing your name.

▶ **2.** On the Insert tab, in the Links group, click the **Link** button. The Insert Hyperlink dialog box opens.

▶ **3.** In the Link to section, click **E-mail Address** to display the options for creating a link to an email address.

▶ **4.** In the E-mail address box, type your email address (or the email address specified by your instructor). The text *mailto:*, which is an Internet communication protocol used for linking to email addresses, appears before the email address.

▶ **5.** In the Subject box, type **Regarding the Tibetan Grill Profit and Loss Statement** as the subject line of any email created using this link. See Figure 5–16.

| Figure 5–16 | Insert Hyperlink dialog box for an email address |
|---|---|

*mailto: prefix identifies this as an email link*

*email address*

*subject heading for the email message*

▶ **6.** Click the **ScreenTip** button, type **Email me for questions about the workbook** in the Set Hyperlink ScreenTip dialog box, and then click **OK**.

▶ **7.** In the Insert Hyperlink dialog box, click **OK** to insert the hyperlink in cell B3 of the Documentation sheet.

> **Tip**
> To select a cell containing a hyperlink without activating the link, right-click the cell.

▶ **8.** Click cell **B3** and verify that your email program opens to a new message with your email address and the subject line already filled in.

▶ **9.** Close the email message without sending it.

▶ **10.** Save the workbook.

Note that the hyperlinks you added are part of the workbook, but they won't appear in the Edit Links dialog box. That dialog box is used only for data values retrieved from external sources.

You've completed your work on external reference and links. In the next session, you will learn how to assign names to references to make it easier to write and understand formulas.

# Review

## Session 5.2 Quick Check

1. What is the external reference to cell C20 of the Final Report worksheet located in the Annual Statement.xlsx workbook?

2. What is the external reference to cell D10 of the Sunday worksheet located in the Weekly Report.xlsx workbook that is stored in the C:\Documents\ Reports folder?

3. When would you paste a copied cell using the Paste Link option?

4. How do you check the status of a link within the current workbook to determine whether the link's source file is accessible and up-to-date?

5. How does Excel indicate that a cell contains linked text?

6. What does Excel do when a hyperlink is clicked by the user?

# Session 5.3 Visual Overview:

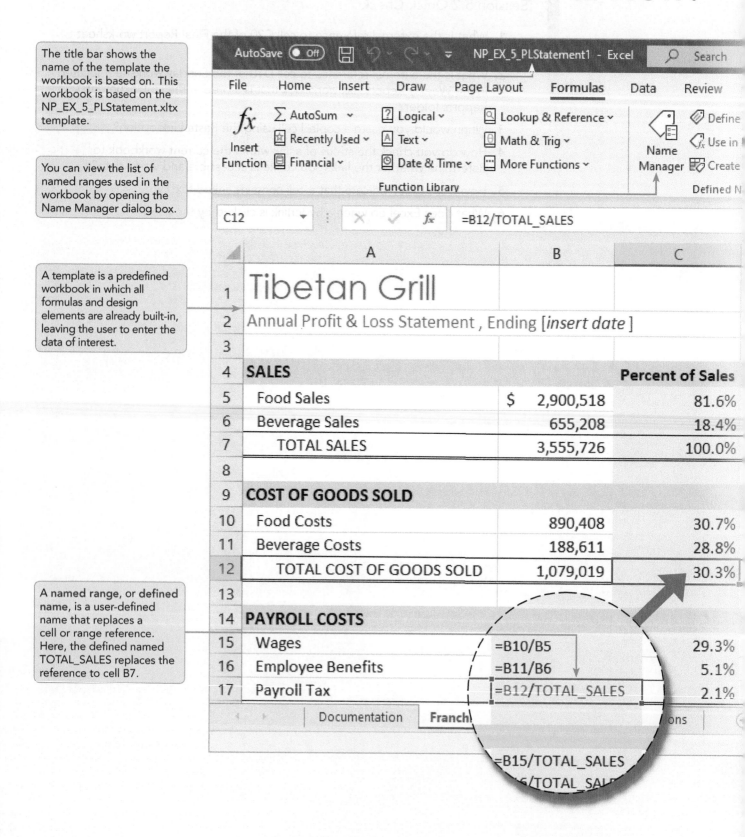

The title bar shows the name of the template the workbook is based on. This workbook is based on the NP_EX_5_PLStatement.xltx template.

You can view the list of named ranges used in the workbook by opening the Name Manager dialog box.

A template is a predefined workbook in which all formulas and design elements are already built-in, leaving the user to enter the data of interest.

A named range, or defined name, is a user-defined name that replaces a cell or range reference. Here, the defined named TOTAL_SALES replaces the reference to cell B7.

AutoSave ● Off    NP_EX_5_PLStatement1 - Excel    Search

File    Home    Insert    Draw    Page Layout    **Formulas**    Data    Review

Insert Function    ∑ AutoSum ˅    ? Logical ˅    Lookup & Reference ˅    Math & Trig ˅    More Functions ˅    Recently Used ˅    Text ˅    Date & Time ˅    Financial ˅

Name Manager    Define    Use in    Create    Defined N

Function Library

C12    fx    =B12/TOTAL_SALES

|  | A | B | C |
|---|---|---|---|
| 1 | Tibetan Grill | | |
| 2 | Annual Profit & Loss Statement , Ending [*insert date*] | | |
| 3 | | | |
| 4 | **SALES** | | **Percent of Sales** |
| 5 | Food Sales | $  2,900,518 | 81.6% |
| 6 | Beverage Sales | 655,208 | 18.4% |
| 7 | TOTAL SALES | 3,555,726 | 100.0% |
| 8 | | | |
| 9 | **COST OF GOODS SOLD** | | |
| 10 | Food Costs | 890,408 | 30.7% |
| 11 | Beverage Costs | 188,611 | 28.8% |
| 12 | TOTAL COST OF GOODS SOLD | 1,079,019 | 30.3% |
| 13 | | | |
| 14 | **PAYROLL COSTS** | | |
| 15 | Wages | =B10/B5 | 29.3% |
| 16 | Employee Benefits | =B11/B6 | 5.1% |
| 17 | Payroll Tax | =B12/TOTAL_SALES | 2.1% |

=B15/TOTAL_SALES
6/TOTAL_SAL

Documentation    Franch    ons

# Named Ranges and Templates

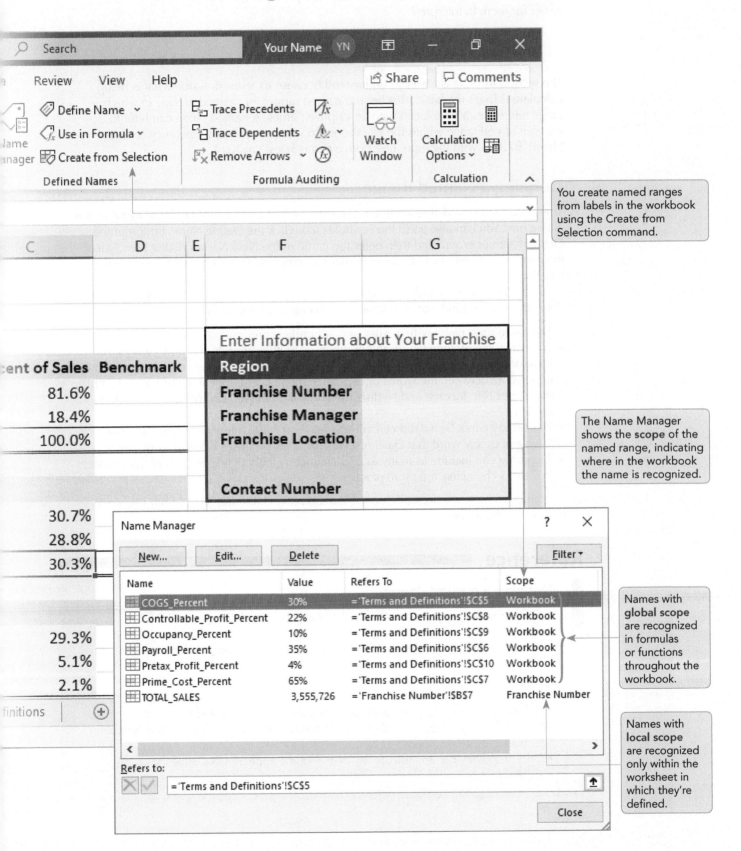

You create named ranges from labels in the workbook using the Create from Selection command.

The Name Manager shows the scope of the named range, indicating where in the workbook the name is recognized.

Names with **global scope** are recognized in formulas or functions throughout the workbook.

Names with **local scope** are recognized only within the worksheet in which they're defined.

# Simplifying Formulas with Named Ranges

If you are showing your workbook to other people, which of the following formulas is easier for them to interpret?

```
=B7 - B28

=Income - Expenses
```

The second formula is easier to understand because its terms describe what is being calculated. That's the basic idea behind named ranges, or defined names, in which range references are replaced with descriptive names. A named range can refer to any cell or cell range within the workbook, so you can replace a reference such as Sheet1!B7:B43 with the more descriptive name SalesData2024.

## Defining a Named Range

The simplest way to define a named range is to select a range and enter the name in the Name box. You can also go to the Formulas tab, click the Define Name button in the Defined Names group, and then enter the name in the New Names dialog box. Once the name is defined, it can be used in place of range references in any Excel formula or function.

The name you use should be short, meaningful, and descriptive of the range being defined. Keep in mind that any name you choose must follow these rules:

- The name must begin with a letter or _ (an underscore).
- The name can include letters and numbers as well as periods and underscores, but it cannot include other symbols or spaces. To distinguish multiword names, use an underscore between the words or capitalize the first letter of each word. For example, the names Net_Income and NetIncome are valid, but Net Income and Net-Income are not.
- The name cannot be a valid cell address (such as A20), a function name (such as Average), or any word that Excel reserves for other purposes (such as Print_Area).
- The name can include as many as 255 characters, although short, meaningful names of 5 to 15 characters are more practical.

Names are not case sensitive, so the named range Sales and SALES both reference the same cell address.

## Reference

### Defining a Named Range

- Select the range, type the name in the Name box, and then press ENTER.
or
- Select the range, and then on the Formulas tab, in the Defined Names group, click the Define Name button.
- Type a name in the Name box, and then click OK.
or
- Select the data values and labels you want used as named ranges.
- On the Formulas tab, in the Defined Names group, click the Create from Selection button.
- Click the check box to indicate where the labels appear in the selection.
- Click OK.

You will use named ranges as you analyze the profit and loss statements from the eight Tibetan Grill franchises. In the restaurant industry, incomes and expenses are often expressed in terms of their percent of total sales. For example, instead of only noting that the Chicago franchise has total payroll costs of $2,374,845, a profit and loss statement would also include the fact that Chicago's payroll costs were 36.3% of its total sales. This is done to compare restaurants operating in differently sized markets. The Tibetan Grill operating in Chicago should show a larger income, expense, and hopefully, profit, than a franchise operating in a smaller market like Rockford. But that doesn't mean the Chicago franchise is better managed. Expressing the profit and loss figures as a percent of total sales provides a way of determining whether the franchise is adequately managing its expenses regardless of the size of its market.

Gail entered industry benchmarks for different parts of the profit and loss statement in the Terms and Definitions worksheet. The worksheet shows a benchmark percentage for payroll costs of 35%, meaning that, regardless of the size of the market, a restaurant should spend no more than about 35% of its total sales income on payroll. You will create named ranges for these benchmark values so that you can display their values in the profit and loss statements for the eight franchises.

### To define a named range using the Name box:

1. If you took a break at the end of the previous session, make sure the NP_EX_5_Tibetan workbook is open.

2. Go to the **Terms and Definitions** worksheet, and then click cell **C5** containing 30% as the benchmark for cost of goods as a percentage of total sales.

3. Click the **Name box** to select the cell reference.

4. Type **COGS_Percent** as the name of the defined range, and then press **ENTER**. The COGS_Percent named range now points to cell C5 of the Terms and Definitions worksheet. See Figure 5–17.

| Figure 5–17 | Named range defined in the Name box |
| --- | --- |

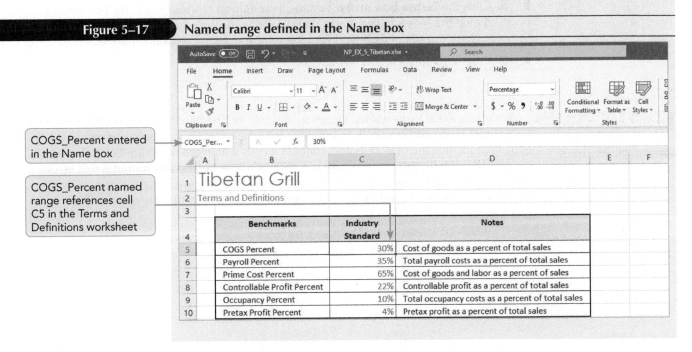

If you have many names to define, a more efficient approach is to use labels entered in the cells adjacent to the data cells as your names. The Create from Selection button in the Defined Names group on the Formulas tab automatically generates the named ranges based on the label text. In the Terms and Definitions worksheet, range B6:B10 contains other labels for the industry benchmarks, and the range C6:C10 contains the benchmark percent figures. You will use those labels to define named ranges for the values in the range C6:C10.

## To define named ranges using labels in adjacent cells:

**1.** In the Terms and Definitions worksheet, select the range **B6:C10** containing the industry benchmark labels and their associated values.

**2.** On the ribbon, click the **Formulas** tab, and then in the Defined Names group, click the **Create from Selection** button. The Create Names from Selection dialog box opens.

**3.** If necessary, click the **Left column** check box to insert a checkmark, leaving the other check boxes unselected. See Figure 5-18.

**Figure 5-18    Create Names from Selection dialog box**

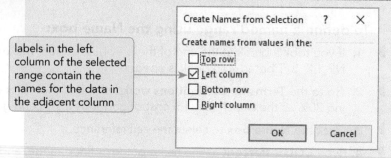

labels in the left column of the selected range contain the names for the data in the adjacent column

**4.** Click **OK** to define the named ranges.

**5.** Click the **Name box arrow** to see all six named ranges listed. These names match the labels in the range B5:B10. Because the names cannot contain spaces, the underscore ( _ ) replaced the spaces in the benchmark labels.

**6.** Press **ESC** to close the Name box.

By default, Excel treats named ranges as absolute cell references. However, the reference is dynamic. If you add new cells within the range the reference for the range name will expand to include the new cells and contract if cells within the range are deleted. If you remove all the cells, the named range will lose its reference and any formulas that invoke it will return the #REF error value. Finally, if you move the referenced cells to a new location, the reference for the named range is updated automatically so that the name will always point to your data.

**Proskills**

### Written Communication: Saving Time with Defined Names

Words can be more descriptive than numbers. This is especially true with cell references. Compared to the letter and number references for cells, a named range provides a more intuitive reference, which is increasingly important as the workbook becomes longer and more complex. Other advantages of named ranges are:

- Names such as TaxRate and TotalSales are more descriptive than cell references and are easier to remember and apply.
- Names in formulas clearly show users exactly what is being calculated. For example, a formula like =GrossPay−Deductions is more easily interpreted than =C15−C16.
- Names remain associated with their range. If a range is moved within the workbook, its name moves with it. Any formulas that contain the name automatically reference the new location.
- Named ranges operate like absolute cell references. If a formula containing a named range is moved or copied, the reference remains pointed to the correct range.

Using defined names saves time and gives everyone reviewing the worksheet a clearer understanding of what that worksheet is doing and what the results mean.

## Using Named Ranges in Formulas

A named range can be used in place of a cell reference in any Excel formula or function. So, the 3-D reference in the formula

```
=SUM('Sales Data'!E4:E20)
```

can be replaced with

```
=SUM(salesFigures)
```

where **salesFigures** refers to the 'Sales Data'!E4:E20 location.

You can insert names into a formula by typing them directly in the formula or by clicking the Use in Formula button in the Defined Names group on the Formulas tab.

Gail wants you to display the benchmark values within each franchise's profit and loss statement. To enter the formulas at the same time across all eight worksheets, you will group the eight worksheets and then create formulas using the named ranges you defined.

### To create formulas for the benchmark values:

1. Click the **Grill5-01** sheet tab, hold down **SHIFT**, click the **Grill5-08** sheet tab, and then release **SHIFT** to make the Grill5-01 through Grill5-08 worksheets a worksheet group.

2. Click cell **D12**, and then type **=** to begin the formula.

3. Type **cog** as the first letters of the COGS_Percent named range. As you type, a list of functions and named ranges that start with those letters appear. See Figure 5–19.

| Figure 5–19 | Named range being added to a formula |

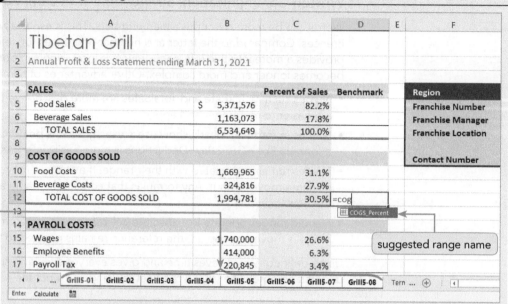

worksheets are grouped

suggested range name

Grill5-01  Grill5-02  Grill5-03  Grill5-04  Grill5-05  Grill5-06  Grill5-07  Grill5-08    Tern ...

4. Press **TAB** to complete the formula **=COGS_Percent**, and then press **ENTER**. The value 30.0% is displayed in cell D12, which is also the value of C5 in the Terms and Definitions worksheet.

5. In cell **D18**, enter **=Payroll_Percent** as the formula. The value 35.0% is displayed in the cell.

6. In cell **D20**, enter **=Prime_Cost_Percent** as the formula. The value 65.0% is displayed in the cell.

7. In cell **D30**, enter **=Controllable_Profit_Percent** as the formula. The value 22.0% is displayed in the cell.

8. In cell **D36**, enter **=Occupancy_Percent** as the formula. The value 10.0% appears in the cell.

9. In cell D43, enter **=Pretax_Profit_Percent** as the formula. The value 4.0% appears in the cell. See Figure 5–20.

**Figure 5–20    Named ranges used in formulas**

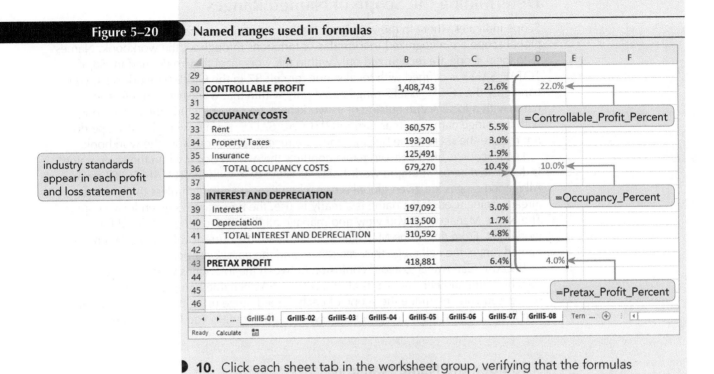

▶ **10.** Click each sheet tab in the worksheet group, verifying that the formulas containing named ranges are duplicated on every sheet in the group.

Comparing the franchise figures with the industry benchmarks helps Gail locate possible sources of trouble. For example, the Rockford franchise (Grill5-04), which showed a net loss during the past year, also spent 43% of its total sales on payroll, far exceeding the recommended 35% goal (cell D18).

Because total sales are involved in so many calculations in the profit and loss statements, Gail wants you to create a named range for total sales in each of the eight franchise profit and loss worksheets.

### To define a named range for total sales:

▶ **1.** In the worksheet group, click the **Grill5-01** sheet tab to make it the active sheet within the group.

▶ **2.** Select the range **A7:B7**. This selects the range in each worksheet in the group.

▶ **3.** On the ribbon, click the **Formulas** tab, and then in the Defined Names group, click the **Create from Selection** button. The Create Names from Selection dialog box opens.

▶ **4.** Make sure only the **Left column** check box is selected, and then click **OK**. The named range TOTAL_SALES associated with cell B7 is created for each worksheet in the group.

▶ **5.** On the formula bar, click the **Name box arrow** to display a list of defined names and verify that the new defined name TOTAL_SALES appears in the list of names.

Because the worksheets were grouped when you used the Create from Selection commands, the action of creating the named range TOTAL_SALES was duplicated on each of the grouped worksheets. So how does Excel manage eight TOTAL_SALES named ranges? That question brings up the issue of scope.

## Determining the Scope of Named Ranges

Scope indicates where in the workbook the named range is recognized. Names with global scope are recognized in formulas or functions throughout the workbook. Names with local scope are recognized only within the worksheet they're defined in. So, if TOTAL_SALES is defined with local scope for cell B7 in the Grill5-02 worksheet, you can apply the TOTAL_SALES range name only within that worksheet. To reference a name with a local scope outside of its worksheet, you must include the sheet along with the range name, such as Grill5-02!TOTAL_SALES. Names with global scope do not require the sheet name because they are recognized throughout the workbook.

Local scope is used to avoid name conflicts that would occur when the same name is duplicated across multiple worksheets, as is the case with the TOTAL_SALES name. All named ranges are given global scope when they are created unless that name is already being used. If the name is already in use, the new name is given local scope. The Name Manager lets you view and manage all the named ranges defined for a workbook. From the Name Manager, you can learn the current value stored with each named range, the cell range they reference, and the name's scope.

Because Gail wants to avoid confusion between the total sales value for one franchise and another, she wants all the TOTAL_SALES named ranges to have local scope. You can determine the scope of each named range using the Name Manager. You'll open the Name Manager to review the named ranges you have created.

### To open the Name Manager:

▶ **1.** If necessary, click the **Formulas** tab on the ribbon.

▶ **2.** In the Defined Names group, click the **Name Manager** button (or press **CTRL+F3**). The Name Manager dialog box opens. See Figure 5–21.

| Figure 5–21 | Name Manager dialog box |
| --- | --- |

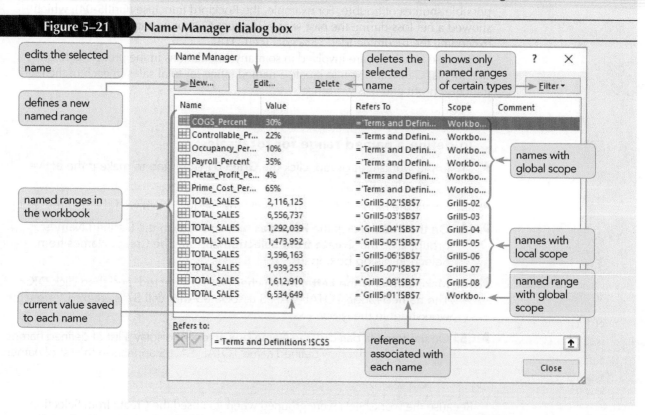

The Name Manager lists the 14 names defined for the workbook. The first six have global scope and point to ranges in the Terms and Definitions worksheet. The next eight are all named TOTAL_SALES and have local scope, confining them to use within the Grill5-02 through Grill5-08 worksheet. Only the TOTAL_SALES name from the Grill5-01 worksheet has global scope and can be referenced anywhere within the workbook.

The TOTAL_SALES name for the Grill5-01 worksheet has global scope because it was the first TOTAL_SALES name created when you were defining names in the worksheet group (Grill5-01 was the active sheet in that group). Once that named range had global scope, the other TOTAL_SALES names were forced to have local scope because the same name cannot be used more than once if it has global scope. If it did, Excel would have no way of resolving the conflict.

Gail wants the TOTAL_SALES name for the Grill5-01 worksheet to also have local scope to avoid confusion. You can't change the scope of a named range once it's created. Instead, you must delete and recreate the name using the Name Manager. You will use the Name Manager to delete and recreate the TOTAL_SALES name as a name with local scope for the Grill5-01 worksheet.

### To delete and recreate the TOTAL_SALES defined name:

1. In the Name Manager dialog box, click the **TOTAL_SALES** named range that references cell B7 in the Grill5-01 worksheet and has a current value of 6,534,649.

2. Click **Delete** to delete the TOTAL_SALES name, and then click **OK** in the dialog box that appears to confirm the deletion. The TOTAL_SALES name for the Grill5-01 worksheet no longer appears in the Name list.

3. Click **New** to open the New Name dialog box.

4. In the Name box, type **TOTAL_SALES** as the name for the new defined name, and then press **TAB**.

Make sure you select the worksheet from the Scope list box to create a named range of local scope.

5. In the Scope list, select **Grill5-01** as the worksheet. This specifies that scope of the TOTAL_SALES named range you are creating will be restricted to the Grill5-01 worksheet.

6. Press **TAB** twice to move to the Refers to box.

7. Click cell **B7** in the Grill5-01 worksheet. The reference ='Grill5-01'$B$7 appears in the Refers to box. See Figure 5–22.

**Figure 5–22**   New Name dialog box

name for the named range

scope of the name limited to the Grill5-01 worksheet

reference assigned to the named range

▶ **8.** Click **OK** to close the New Name dialog box and return to the Name Manager dialog box.

▶ **9.** Verify that the TOTAL_SALES name with the Scope value set to Grill5-01 appears in the list of named ranges.

▶ **10.** Click **Close** to close the Name Manager dialog box.

Next you will use the TOTAL_SALES range names in the calculations from the eight profit and loss statements.

## Insight

### Naming Constants

In addition to referencing ranges in a workbook, names can also store specific values. If you commonly use constants in your formulas, you can name the constant by completing the following steps:

1. In the Name Manager dialog box, click the New button. The New Name dialog box opens.
2. In the New name box, enter a name for the defined name.
3. In the Refers to box, enter the expression =*value* where *value* is the constant value stored in the defined name.
4. Click OK.

Once the constant is named, it can be used in any formula or function. For example, you can create a constant named salesTax that stores the value 0.05. Then the formula =B10*salesTax would multiply the value in cell B10 by 0.05. By storing named constants rather than using a worksheet cell, you can simplify your workbook and make it easier to write meaningful formulas and functions.

## Using Defined Names in Existing Formulas

Once you have defined a named range, you can have Excel replace all cell references in formulas and functions with the equivalent name. One advantage of such a substitution is that it makes your code easier to interpret.

To apply names to an existing set of formulas click the Apply Names command in the Defines Name button on the Formulas tab. This command cannot be used with a worksheet group. It can be applied only to ranges within individual sheets. You'll apply the TOTAL_SALES range names in formulas from the profit and loss statement from the eight Tibetan Grill franchises.

**To apply defined names to existing formulas in the profit and loss worksheets:**

▶ **1.** Right-click the **Grill5-01** sheet tab, and then click **Ungroup Sheets** on the shortcut menu.

▶ **2.** Save the workbook. You want to save before using the Apply Names command in case you make a mistake in the substitution.

▶ **3.** Select the range **C5:C43** containing the formulas that calculate the percent of total sales values.

▶ **4.** On the Formulas tab, in the Defined Names group, click the **Define Name arrow**, and then click **Apply Names**. The Apply Names dialog box opens.

▶ **5.** In the Apply names list, make sure **TOTAL_SALES** is selected. You want to replace every reference to cell B7 in the current worksheet with the TOTAL_SALES name.

▶ **6.** Verify that the **Ignore Relative/Absolute** check box is selected so that the name is applied whether cell B7 is referenced using an absolute or relative reference. See Figure 5–23.

**Figure 5–23**     Apply Names dialog box

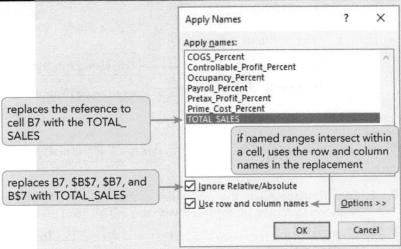

replaces the reference to cell B7 with the TOTAL_ SALES

if named ranges intersect within a cell, uses the row and column names in the replacement

replaces B7, $B$7, $B7, and B$7 with TOTAL_SALES

▶ **7.** Click **OK** to apply the named range to formulas in the selected cells.

▶ **8.** Click each cell in the range C5:C43 of the Grill5-01 worksheet, verifying that references to cell B7 have been replaced with TOTAL_SALES.

     **Trouble?** If the replacement was not made, you may have made a mistake when using the Apply Names command. Close the workbook without saving changes, reopen the workbook, and repeat Steps 3 through 7.

You cannot use the Apply Names command for worksheet groups. But, you can use the Find and Replace command to replace every occurrence of a cell reference with its equivalent defined name within a worksheet group. You'll use this technique to replace every reference to cell B7 with TOTAL_SALES in the remaining franchise profit and loss statements.

### To replace cell references with the TOTAL_SALES defined name:

▶ **1.** Save the workbook so that if you make a mistake, you can close the workbook without saving changes and then reopen the workbook and repeat this set of steps.

▶ **2.** Click the **Grill5-02** sheet tab, hold down **SHIFT**, click the **Grill5-08** sheet tab, and then release **SHIFT**. The Grill5-02 through Grill5-08 sheets are selected in a worksheet group.

▶ **3.** In the worksheet group, select the range **C5:C43**.

▶ **4.** On the ribbon, click the **Home** tab, in the Editing group, click the **Find & Select** button, and click **Replace**. The Find and Replace dialog box opens.

▶ **5.** Type **B7** in the Find what box, press **TAB**, and then type **TOTAL_SALES** in the Replace with box. See Figure 5–24.

| Figure 5–24 | Find and Replace dialog box |
| --- | --- |

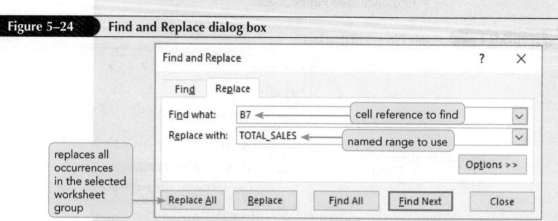

▶ **6.** Click **Replace All**. In the worksheet group, 161 occurrences of B7 in the selected formulas are replaced with the TOTAL_SALES defined name.

▶ **7.** Click **OK** in the message dialog box, and then click **Close** in the Find and Replace dialog box to return to the workbook.

▶ **8.** Examine the formulas in the C5:C43 range and verify that the references to cell B7 in the worksheet group have been replaced with the TOTAL_SALES name.

**Trouble?** If the cell references weren't changed to the defined name, you made a mistake in the steps. Close the workbook without saving changes, reopen the workbook, and then repeat Steps 2 through 7.

▶ **9.** sam↑ Ungroup the selected worksheets, and then save and close the workbook.

If a workbook has a lot of defined names, you might want a way to easily see all of the defined names. In addition to viewing the list of names in the Name Manager, you can paste a list of the defined names into a worksheet table. To create a list of defined names, click the Use in Formula arrow in the Defined Names group on the Formulas tab, and then click Paste Names. In the Paste Names dialog box that opens, click Paste List to paste a list of all the names and the ranges they reference. The pasted list will not be updated as you add, modify, or delete the names. So, be sure to paste the list of defined names only when your workbook is complete.

## Insight

### Indirect Referencing

A cell reference tells a formula or function exactly where to find the data it needs. However, some formulas need to retrieve data from several possible locations. An application might need the same SUM function to calculate the sum of values from the range C1:C10 in one case and from the range D1:D10 in another. Being able to change a cell reference without having to rewrite a formula is the purpose of **indirect referencing** in which the reference itself is a calculated value. Indirect references are created with the INDIRECT function

```
INDIRECT(ref_text, [a1])
```

where *ref_text* is a text string that specifies the reference address and *a1* is an optional argument specifying how that reference is written. For example, if cell A1 contains the text string C1:C10, then the expression

```
INDIRECT(A1)
```

is equivalent to typing the range reference C1:C10. So, nesting the INDIRECT function in the formula

```
=SUM(INDIRECT(A1))
```

is the equivalent to the formula =SUM(C1:C10). If the value of A1 is changed to the text string D1:D10, then the formula becomes the equivalent of =SUM(D1:D10), and so forth. You can also use a named range so that if the value of cell A1 is changed to TotalExpenses, the formula becomes the equivalent of =SUM(TotalExpenses), calculating the sum of the values referenced by named range TotalExpenses.

Using the INDIRECT function, you can make the same formula calculate the sum of any range in the workbook by changing the text string stored in cell A1. Paired with named ranges, indirect referencing can be used to create dynamic Excel applications in which the formulas themselves are modified even by users who have no training in writing Excel formulas and functions.

## Exploring Workbook Templates

This module began by looking at ways of collecting data from several workbooks. Now it examines how to ensure that those source workbooks employ an identical structure and design. Templates, or predesigned workbooks in which all the formulas and design elements are already built-in, are an easy way to ensure that a consistent design among workbooks. An additional advantage is that the end user will only focus on data entry because all of the structure, formatting, and formulas are already in place.

**Proskills**

### Teamwork: Using Excel Templates

A team working together will often need to create the same types of workbooks. Rather than each person or group designing a different workbook, each team member should create a workbook from the same template. The completed workbooks will then all have the same structure with identical formatting and formulas. Not only does this ensure consistency and accuracy, it also makes it easier to compile and summarize the results. Templates help teams work better together and avoid misunderstandings.

For example, a large organization may need to collect the same information from several regions. By creating and distributing a workbook template, each region knows what data to track and where to enter it. The template already includes the formulas, so the results are calculated consistently.

The following are just some of the advantages of using a template to create multiple workbooks with the same features:

- Templates save time and ensure consistency in the design and content of workbooks because all labels, formatting, and formulas are entered once.

- Templates ensure accuracy because formulas can be entered and verified once, and then used with confidence in all workbooks.

- Templates standardize the appearance and content of workbooks.

- Templates prevent data from being overwritten when an existing workbook is inadvertently saved with new data rather than saved as a new workbook.

If you are part of a team that needs to create the same type of workbook repeatedly, it's a good idea to use a template to both save time and ensure consistency in the design and content of the workbooks.

## Setting Up a Workbook Template

Any workbook can be turned into a template by just deleting all of the current data, leaving only the formulas and design elements. The data is left blank for end users to fill in at a later date when they start creating their own documents.

Gail is concerned that all of the franchise managers didn't complete their Profit and Loss reports in the same way, which made it more difficult to combine their results in a summary workbook. Gail has already created a workbook to use as a model for future reports and wants you to convert that workbook into a template. You'll open Gail's workbook now.

### To open Gail's workbook:

▶ 1. Open the **NP_EX_5-2.xlsx** workbook located in the **Excel5 > Module** folder included with your Data Files.

▶ 2. Review the **Documentation, Franchise Number**, and **Terms and Definitions** worksheets. Do not make any changes to the contents of those sheets. Figure 5–25 shows the contents of the Franchise Number worksheet.

| Figure 5–25 | Template for profit and loss statements |

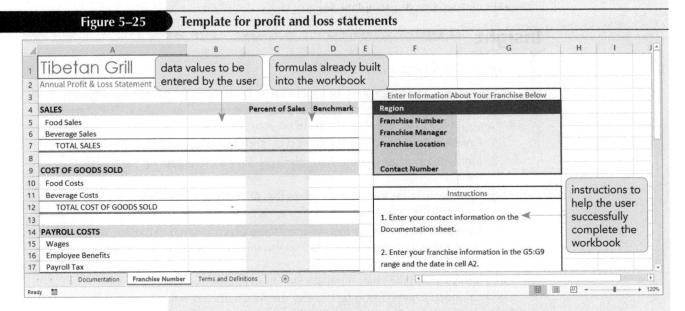

3. In each worksheet, scroll up to the top of the worksheet and click cell **A1**.

4. Click the **Documentation** sheet tab to make it the active sheet.

**Tip**

Good template designs assume users are not Excel experts and make it easy to fill out the workbook correctly.

The Franchise Number worksheet contains the framework Gail wants all franchises to use for their profit and loss reports. It does not include data values because those will be entered by the franchise managers. However, the worksheet does include all the formulas required to calculate sales and expense totals as well as percentages. The formulas in the worksheet use the TOTAL_SALES defined name to make the formulas easier to understand. Gail added detailed instructions about how the workbook should be filled out. Gail's email address is included as a hyperlink in case users want help completing the workbook.

Gail wants you to convert this workbook into a template. When you save the workbook as a template, Excel will save the file to the user's Custom Office Templates folder. An icon for the template will appear in the New screen in Background view so users can easily create workbooks based on the template design. However, you can save a template to any folder you choose. You'll save Gail's workbook as a template to a different folder.

**To save Gail's workbook as a template:**

1. On the ribbon, click the **File** tab to open Backstage view, and then in the navigation bar, click **Save As**. The Save As screen appears.

2. Click the **More options** link. The Save As dialog box opens.

3. In the File name box, type **NP_EX_5_PLStatement** as the file name for the template.

**Tip**

Excel template files have the .xltx file extension.

4. Click the **Save as type arrow**, and then click **Excel Template (*.xltx)** to save the file as a template. The default location for Excel templates, the Custom Office Templates folder, is displayed.

5. Navigate to the **Excel5 > Module** folder.

6. Click **Save** to save the template, and then close the file.

Now that you have created the template file, your next step is to create a new workbook based on this template design.

## Insight

### Creating a Chart Template

Templates can also be created for Excel charts. These chart templates store custom-ized chart designs that can be added as a new type in the chart gallery. Complete the following steps to save a chart template on your computer:

1. Create a chart, choosing the chart type and design of the chart elements.
2. Right-click the completed chart, and click Save as Template on the shortcut menu.
3. Enter a name for the chart template file. All chart template files have the *.crtx file extension.
4. Save the chart template file. All chart templates are saved in the Microsoft > Templates > Charts folder within your user account on your computer.

Once you've saved the chart template file, it will appear as an option in the Recommended Charts dialog box, under the All Charts tab in the Templates folder. Select the chart template to apply it to the next chart you create.

## Creating a Workbook Based on a Template

The great advantage of templates is that new workbooks are created based on the template design without altering the template file itself. As shown in Figure 5–26, each new workbook is a copy of the template design. Just as a blank workbook is named Book1, Book2, etc. based on the default "Book" template for new workbooks, files based on customized template are named *template*1, *template*2, etc. where *template* is the file name of the original template file.

**Figure 5–26**    **Workbooks created from a template**

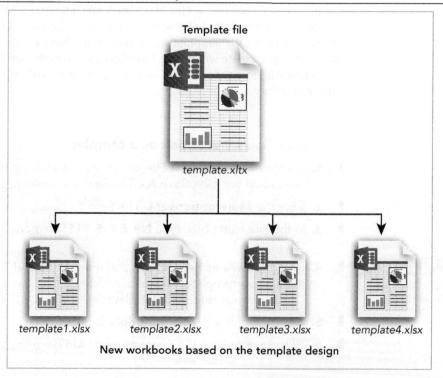

There are two ways to create a workbook based on a template. If you save the template file to the Custom Office Templates folder, the template is always available to you from the New screen in Backstage view, placed within the Personal section of the gallery of new file designs. Figure 5–27 shows how the NP_EX_5_PLStatement would appear in Backstage view.

| Figure 5–27 | New screen with templates |
|---|---|

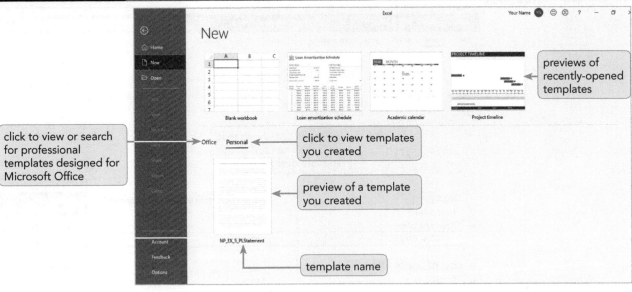

Clicking the template's icon in the gallery creates a new workbook based on the template design. You can also use one of the built-in templates displayed in the Featured gallery or use the Search box to search online for other templates created by professional designers.

When the template file is *not* stored in the Custom Office Templates folder, you can create a new workbook based on the template design by opening the template file from the File Explorer. You cannot use the Open screen in Backstage view of Excel because that would reopen the actual template file. Remember, you don't want users editing the template file, you only want to create new workbooks based on the template design.

You'll create a new workbook from the NP_EX_5_PLStatement template, and then enter some test data into it.

**To create a new workbook based on a PLStatement template:**

1. Open **File Explorer** and navigate to the **Excel5 > Module** folder containing your Data Files.

2. Double-click the **NP_EX_5_PLStatement** template file. A workbook named NP_EX_5_PLStatement1 opens in the workbook window.

3. Go to the **Franchise Number** worksheet.

4. In cell **B5**, enter **820,000** for the food sales, and then in cell **B6**, enter **210,000** for the beverage sales.

5. In cell **B10**, enter **210,000** for the food costs, and then in cell **B11**, enter **58,000** for the beverage costs.

6. In cell **B15**, enter **255,000** for wages, in cell **B16**, enter **52,000** for employee benefits, and then in cell **B17**, enter **24,000** for payroll tax. The worksheet automatically calculates the total sales, the total cost of goods sold, the total payroll costs, and the percent of total sales for each number. See Figure 5–28.

**Figure 5–28**    New workbook based on a template

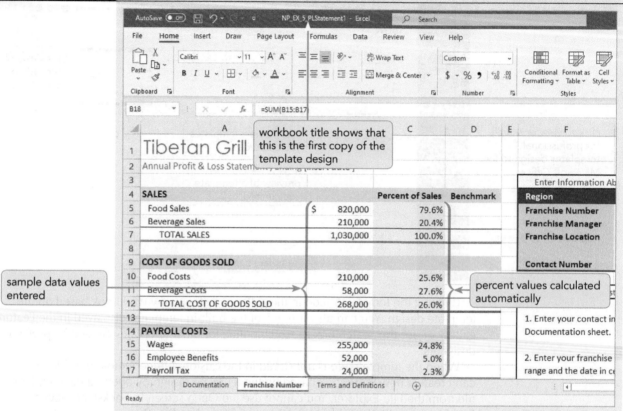

7. Save the workbook as **NP_EX_5_Franchise** in the location specified by your instructor, and then close the workbook.

If you want to edit the template file, you can reopen the file from the Open screen in Backstage view. Any changes you make to the template file will not be reflected in workbooks already created based on earlier versions of the template.

## Insight

### Copying Styles Between Templates

Consistency is a hallmark of professional documents. If you want to reuse the styles that you created for the workbook but don't want to recreate the entire workbook, you can copy only the styles from that template. To copy styles from one template to another:

1. Open the template with the styles you want to copy.
2. Open the workbook or template in which you want to place the copied styles.
3. On the Home tab, in the Styles group, click the Cell Styles button, and then click Merge Styles. The Merge Styles dialog box opens, listing the currently open workbooks and templates.
4. Select the workbook or template with the styles you want to copy, and then click OK to copy those styles into the current workbook or template.
5. If a dialog box opens, asking if you want to "Merge Styles that have the same names?", click YES.
6. Save the workbook with the new styles as the Excel Template file type.

Copying template styles is much faster and more accurate than trying to recreate all those styles in a new workbook document. However, the styles are not linked, so if you modify your design, you will have to recopy all the styles again.

Gail appreciates your work on the template and will forward the template to the franchise managers so that they can base their next profit and loss statements on its design.

## Review

### Session 5.3 Quick Check

1. Why is Report-Date not a valid named range?
2. What happens when you select a defined name in the Name box?
3. What is the difference between a defined name with global scope and one with local scope?
4. What is the expression to reference the local scope defined name TotalSales from the Final Report worksheet?
5. When would you create a template rather than just providing a coworker with the copy of your workbook?
6. What is displayed in the title bar for a workbook created from the EmployeeList.xltx template file?
7. By default, where does Excel store workbook templates?

# Practice

## Review Assignments

**Data Files needed for the Review Assignments: NP_EX_5-3.xlsx, Support_EX_5_Peoria.xlsx, Support_EX_5_Region1.xlsx, Support_EX_5_Region2.xlsx, Support_EX_5_Region3.xlsx, Support_EX_5_Region4.xlsx**

Gail wants to get a monthly sales and expense report from each franchise so that the company can catch issues early and offer suggestions to franchises that are underperforming. Gail started a summary workbook that will contain the collected data. She needs you to finalize the workbook. Complete the following:

1. Open the **NP_EX_5-3.xlsx** workbook located in the Excel5 > Review folder included with your Data Files. Save the workbook as **NP_EX_5_Report** in the location specified by your instructor.

2. In the Documentation sheet, in the range B3:B4, enter your name and the date.

3. Change your name to a hyperlink pointing to your email address using the subject heading **Monthly Sales and Expenses Report** for the message and **Email me for more info** as the ScreenTip text.

4. Open the **Support_EX_5_Peoria.xlsx** workbook located in the Excel5 > Review folder. Copy the Grill5-08 worksheet into the NP_EX_5_Report workbook, placing the worksheet at the end of the workbook.

5. Create a worksheet group from the Grill5-01 through Grill5-08 worksheets. In the worksheet group, select the nonadjacent range A7:B7,A11:B11,A16:B16, and then create named ranges from the selection using the labels in the left column.

6. Use the Name Manager to change the TOTAL_COST_ OF_ GOODS_SOLD, TOTAL_PAYROLL_COSTS, and TOTAL_SALES named ranges for the Grill5-01 worksheet from global scope to local scope by deleting those names and recreating them, limiting them to the scope of the Grill5-01 worksheet. Verify in the Name Manager that all the defined names in the workbook have local scope.

7. In the range B5:C17 of the Grill5-01 through Grill5-08 worksheets, replace the cell references to cells B7, B11, and B16 with the TOTAL_SALES, TOTAL_COST_OF_GOODS_SOLD, and TOTAL_PAYROLL_COSTS defined names. You can either use the Apply Names command or find and replace the cell reference with the range name.

8. In the Region Report worksheet, in cell F5, use the SUM function to calculate the sum of cell B5 in the Grill5-01 through Grill5-08 worksheet group, displaying the total income from food sales.

9. Use AutoFill to extend the formula in cell F5 through the range F5:F17. Fill without formatting in the range. Delete the zeros in cells F8 and F12.

10. Open the **Support_EX_5_Region1.xlsx** file located in the Excel5 > Review folder. Copy the range B5:B17 of the Region 1 worksheet, and then use the Paste Link command to paste the external reference to the copied cells in the range B5:B17 of the Region Report worksheet. Delete the zeroes in cells B8 and B12.

11. Repeat Step 10 for the Region 2 through Region 4 data located in the **Support_EX_5_Region2.xlsx** through **Support_EX_5_Region4.xlsx** workbooks, pasting their external references in the ranges C5:C17, D5:D17, and E5:E17, respectively. Delete the zeroes in rows 8 and 12.

12. Copy the Grill5-01 worksheet to a new workbook so you can create a template of the Sales and Expenses worksheet with all the data removed, but the formulas and formatting retained.

13. Save the NP_EX_5_Report workbook, and then close it.

14. In the new workbook you created in Step 12, make the following changes to the Grill5-01 worksheet:

    a. Change the worksheet name to **Franchise**.

    b. Change the text of cell A2 to **[Region] Monthly Sales and Expenses**.

    c. Delete the data in the nonadjacent range **B5:B6, B9:B10, B13:B15, F4:F9**.

15. Save the workbook as a template with the file name **NP_EX_5_Sales.xltx** in the location specified by your instructor.

16. Save and close all the workbooks you used in the Review Assignments.

# Apply

### Case Problem 1

**Data File needed for this Case Problem: NP_EX_5-4.xlsx**

**Medicina Medical Software**    Imani Emeka is the Social Media Manager for Medicina Medical Software, a tech company specializing in medical software for managing patient enrollments and hospital staffing. Imani is working on improving the company's visibility on social media and wants your help in maintaining a workbook tracking the company's monthly social media posts. Imani wants metrics on the number of posts made to social media, including the number of retweets, likes, mentions, clicks, and followers. Imani wants to determine whether the efforts to expand and improve the company's media presence are showing results. Complete the following.

1. Open the **NP_EX_5-4.xlsx** workbook located in the Excel5 > Case1 folder included with your Data Files. Save the workbook as **NP_EX_5_Medicina** in the location specified by your instructor.

2. In the Documentation sheet, in the range B3:B4, enter your name and the date.

3. The January through June worksheets contain the monthly social media logs. In each worksheet, change the entries in column C to hyperlinks by double-clicking each cell, and then pressing ENTER. (Note that you cannot make this change in a worksheet group.) Excel will automatically convert the cells to hyperlinks using the addresses stored into the cells. (Note that these fictional web addresses will not open real pages if clicked.)

4. One important social media metric is the number of engagements for each post where an individual is actively engaged in the post by retweeting the post, liking the post, mentioning the post in other forums, or clicking links within the post. In column I of the January through June worksheets, use the SUM function to calculate the total number of retweets, likes, mentions, and clicks. Do not include the number of followers in the total.

5. Another important social media metric is the Engagement Rate, which is the percentage of followers that are actively engaged with the post. In column J of the January through June worksheets, calculate the Engagement Rate by dividing the number of engagements by the number of followers for each post.

6. In the Metrics worksheet, calculate the following summary statistics:

   a. In cell C5, use the COUNT function to count the number of data values in column B of the January worksheet.

   b. In cell D5, use the SUM function to sum the total retweets in column D of the January worksheet.

   c. In cell D6, use the AVERAGE function to calculate the average number of retweets in column D of the January worksheet.

   d. Use AutoFill to copy the formulas from the range D5:D6 over the range D5:H6.

   e. In cell I5, use the AVERAGE function to calculate the average Engagement Rate from column J of the January worksheet.

7. Repeat Step 6 for February through June rows in the table to calculate summary statistics of the media metrics for each month.

8. Calculate summary statistics of the media metrics across all months by doing the following:

   a. In cell C19, use the COUNT function applied to column B of the January:June worksheet group to calculate the total number of posts made over the six month period.

   b. In cell D19, use the SUM function to sum up the total retweets in column D of January through June worksheets.

   c. In cell D20, use the AVERAGE function to average the number of retweets from column D of the January through June worksheets.

d. Use AutoFill to extend the formulas from the range D19:D20 over the range D19:H20.

e. In cell I19, use the AVERAGE function to calculate the average Engagement Rate from column J in the January through June worksheets.

9. Change the entries in cells B5, B7, B9, B11, B13, and B15 into hyperlinks that point to cell A1 of their respective monthly worksheets. For each hyperlink, add **View monthly posts** as the ScreenTip message.

10. Save the workbook, and then close it.

# Challenge

## Case Problem 2

**Data Files needed for this Case Problem: NP_EX_5-5.xlsx, Support_EX_5_Fund01.xlsx, Support_EX_5_Fund02.xlsx, Support_EX_5_Fund03.xlsx, Support_EX_5_Fund04.xlsx, Support_EX_5_Fund05.xlsx**

**Templeton Investments**   John Riegel is an accounts manager at Templeton Investments. John wants your help in creating an Excel workbook that can retrieve fund data from external workbooks and display summary statistics about those funds. The workbook should be accessible to non-Excel users. You'll use the INDIRECT function so that the user needs to enter only the symbol for the fund to get a summary report. The INDIRECT function is discussed in the "Indirect Referencing" InSight box. Complete the following.

1. Open the **NP_EX_5-5.xlsx** workbook located in the Excel5 > Case2 folder included with your Data Files. Save the workbook as **NP_EX_5_Templeton** in the location specified by your instructor.

2. In the Documentation sheet, enter your name in cell B3. Use an Excel function to enter the current date in cell B4.

3. Go to the Fund Lookup worksheet. In this sheet, you will create a lookup table with data drawn from external workbooks.

4. Open the **Support_EX_5_Fund01.xlsx** file located in the Excel5 > Case2 folder. Copy the data from the range E2:P2 of the Summary worksheet.

5. In the NP_EX_5_Templeton workbook, in the Fund Lookup worksheet, in the range A4:L4, paste a link to the data you copied.

6. Repeat Steps 4 and 5 using the data in the **Support_EX_5_Fund02.xlsx**, **Support_EX_5_Fund03.xlsx**, **Support_EX_5_Fund04.xlsx**, and **Support_EX_5_Fund05.xlsx** workbooks, pasting links to the copied data in the ranges A5:L5, A6:L6, A7:L7, and A8:L8 of the Fund Lookup worksheet.

7. Assign the named range **Fund_Lookup** to lookup table in the range A3:L8 of the Fund Lookup worksheet.

8. Copy the data in the range A2:C32 of the Summary worksheet in the Support_EX_5_Fund01 workbook. In the NP_EX_5_Templeton workbook, paste a link to the copied data in the range A3:C33 of the 30-Day Data worksheet.

9. Repeat Step 8 using data from Support_EX_5_Fund02, Support_EX_5_Fund03, Support_EX_5_Fund04, and Support_EX_5_Fund05 workbooks, pasting links to the copied data in the ranges D3:F33, G3:I33, J3:L33, and M3:O33 of the 30-Day Data worksheet.

10. Select the range A3:O33, and then create named ranges from the selection, using the labels in the top row. (*Hint:* Make sure only the Top row check box is selected.)

11. Go to the Statistics worksheet. In this worksheet, you will display information and summary statistics on a selected fund. In cell B4, enter the text **ORTFD** for the Ortus fund.

12. Select cell B4 and define a named range using **Symbol** as the name.

13. In cell B5, enter the VLOOKUP function to retrieve the name of the fund. Use the Symbol named range as the lookup value, the Fund_Lookup named range as the lookup table, 2 as the column to look up, and FALSE as the type of look up (exact match).

14. In the range B6:B15, repeat Step 13, inserting VLOOKUP functions for the remaining information on the selected fund, entering the next higher value as the column to look up (from 3 up to 12).

⊕ **Explore**  15. In cell B18, display the 30-day high value for the selected fund using the MAX function. Nest the INDIRECT function within the MAX function, using the named range Symbol as the input value for the INDIRECT function.

16. Repeat Step 15 using the MIN function in cell B19 to return the 30-day low of the selected fund and using the AVERAGE function in cell B20 to return the 30-day average of the selected fund.

⊕ **Explore**  17. In cell B21, calculate the average shares traded per day using the AVERAGE function. Nest the INDIRECT function within the AVERAGE function, using the argument **Symbol&"_Shares"** to reference the named range of shares traded for the selected fund.

18. Test the formulas you created by changing the value in cell B4 to **SNRFD**, **AIF**, **LTDX**, and then **IHGF**, verifying that a different set of information and summary statistics appears for each symbol.

⊕ **Explore**  19. In the Documentation sheet, in the range A8:B24, paste a list of the defined names used in the workbook. On the Formulas tab, in the Defined Names group, click the Use in Formula button, and then click Paste Names. In the Paste Name dialog box, click Paste List.

20. Save the NP_EX_5_Templeton workbook, and then close it. Close all other open workbooks without saving any changes.

## Objectives

**Session 6.1**
- Split a workbook window into panes
- Highlight and remove duplicate values in a data range
- Sort a data range by one or more fields
- Add subtotals to a data range

**Session 6.2**
- Find and select workbook cells
- Filter data based on one or more fields
- Create an advanced filter
- Convert a data range to an Excel table
- Work with table styles and table elements

**Session 6.3**
- Create and apply a slicer
- Calculate summary statistics with the SUBTOTAL function
- Design and create an interactive dashboard

# Managing Data with Data Tools

## Analyzing Employment Data

## Case | Orthographic

Jacek Baros is a Human Resources (HR) analyst for Orthographic, a company that produces 3-D imaging hardware and software with offices in Boston, Chicago, Denver, San Francisco, and Dallas. As an HR analyst, Jacek prepares employment reports and summaries. In doing these analyses, Jacek must deal with large amounts of employee data. You'll help Jacek complete a workbook that will provide an overview of the employee situation at Orthographic.

**EXCEL**

## Starting Data Files

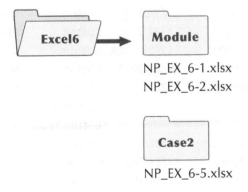

| Excel6 → | Module | Review | Case1 |
| --- | --- | --- | --- |
| | NP_EX_6-1.xlsx | NP_EX_6-3.xlsx | NP_EX_6-4.xlsx |
| | NP_EX_6-2.xlsx | | |

**Case2**

NP_EX_6-5.xlsx

# Session 6.1 Visual Overview:

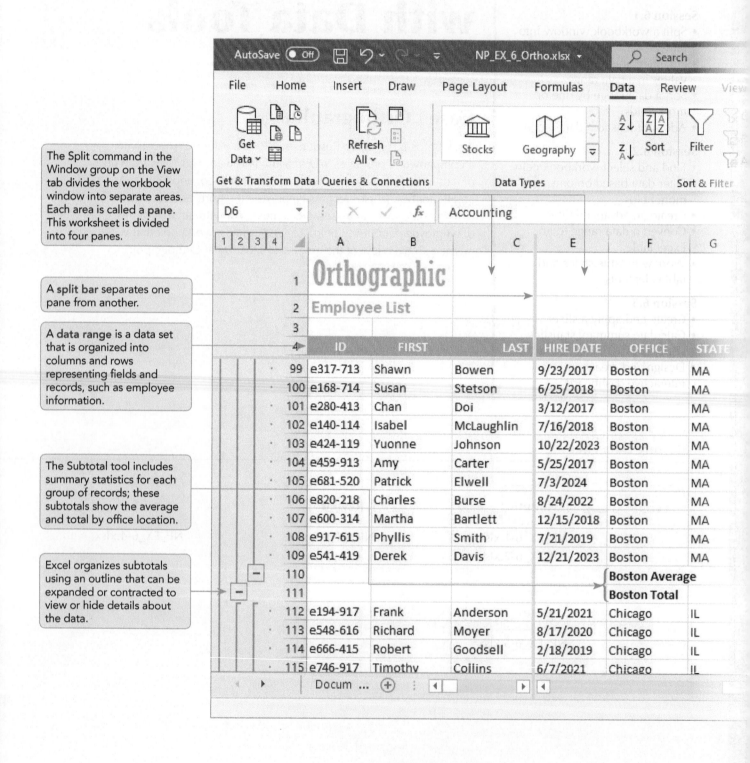

The Split command in the Window group on the View tab divides the workbook window into separate areas. Each area is called a pane. This worksheet is divided into four panes.

A split bar separates one pane from another.

A data range is a data set that is organized into columns and rows representing fields and records, such as employee information.

The Subtotal tool includes summary statistics for each group of records; these subtotals show the average and total by office location.

Excel organizes subtotals using an outline that can be expanded or contracted to view or hide details about the data.

| | ID | FIRST | LAST | HIRE DATE | OFFICE | STATE |
|---|---|---|---|---|---|---|
| 99 | e317-713 | Shawn | Bowen | 9/23/2017 | Boston | MA |
| 100 | e168-714 | Susan | Stetson | 6/25/2018 | Boston | MA |
| 101 | e280-413 | Chan | Doi | 3/12/2017 | Boston | MA |
| 102 | e140-114 | Isabel | McLaughlin | 7/16/2018 | Boston | MA |
| 103 | e424-119 | Yuonne | Johnson | 10/22/2023 | Boston | MA |
| 104 | e459-913 | Amy | Carter | 5/25/2017 | Boston | MA |
| 105 | e681-520 | Patrick | Elwell | 7/3/2024 | Boston | MA |
| 106 | e820-218 | Charles | Burse | 8/24/2022 | Boston | MA |
| 107 | e600-314 | Martha | Bartlett | 12/15/2018 | Boston | MA |
| 108 | e917-615 | Phyllis | Smith | 7/21/2019 | Boston | MA |
| 109 | e541-419 | Derek | Davis | 12/21/2023 | Boston | MA |
| 110 | | | | | Boston Average | |
| 111 | | | | | Boston Total | |
| 112 | e194-917 | Frank | Anderson | 5/21/2021 | Chicago | IL |
| 113 | e548-616 | Richard | Moyer | 8/17/2020 | Chicago | IL |
| 114 | e666-415 | Robert | Goodsell | 2/18/2019 | Chicago | IL |
| 115 | e746-917 | Timothy | Collins | 6/7/2021 | Chicago | IL |

Orthographic
Employee List

Cell D6: Accounting

NP_EX_6_Ortho.xlsx

# Data Ranges, Workbook Panes, and Subtotals

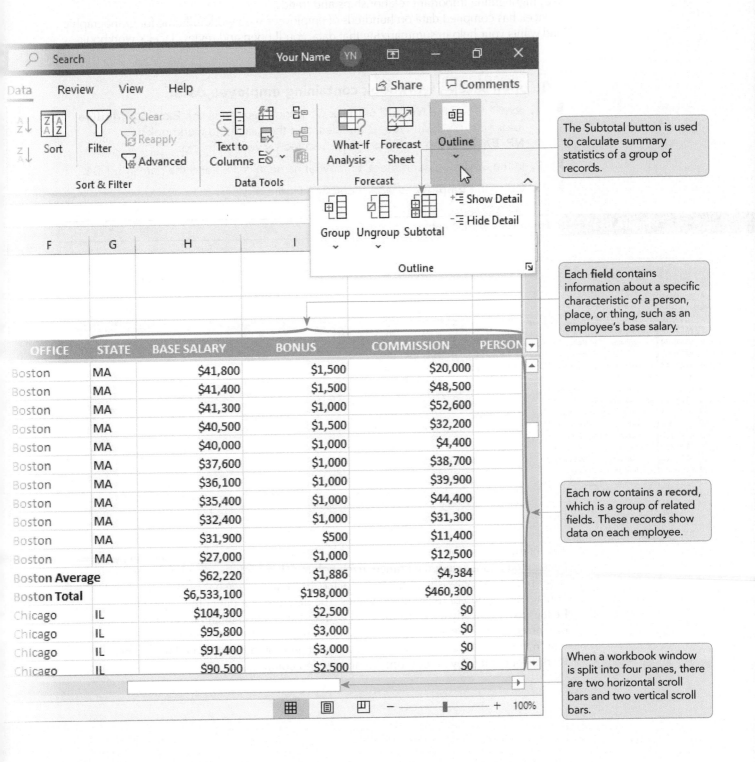

The Subtotal button is used to calculate summary statistics of a group of records.

Each **field** contains information about a specific characteristic of a person, place, or thing, such as an employee's base salary.

Each row contains a **record**, which is a group of related fields. These records show data on each employee.

When a workbook window is split into four panes, there are two horizontal scroll bars and two vertical scroll bars.

| OFFICE | STATE | BASE SALARY | BONUS | COMMISSION | PERSON |
|--------|-------|-------------|-------|------------|--------|
| Boston | MA | $41,800 | $1,500 | $20,000 | |
| Boston | MA | $41,400 | $1,500 | $48,500 | |
| Boston | MA | $41,300 | $1,000 | $52,600 | |
| Boston | MA | $40,500 | $1,500 | $32,200 | |
| Boston | MA | $40,000 | $1,000 | $4,400 | |
| Boston | MA | $37,600 | $1,000 | $38,700 | |
| Boston | MA | $36,100 | $1,000 | $39,900 | |
| Boston | MA | $35,400 | $1,000 | $44,400 | |
| Boston | MA | $32,400 | $1,000 | $31,300 | |
| Boston | MA | $31,900 | $500 | $11,400 | |
| Boston | MA | $27,000 | $1,000 | $12,500 | |
| Boston **Average** | | $62,220 | $1,886 | $4,384 | |
| Boston **Total** | | $6,533,100 | $198,000 | $460,300 | |
| Chicago | IL | $104,300 | $2,500 | $0 | |
| Chicago | IL | $95,800 | $3,000 | $0 | |
| Chicago | IL | $91,400 | $3,000 | $0 | |
| Chicago | IL | $90,500 | $2,500 | $0 | |

# Handling Data in Excel

Excel is a popular application for storing data and includes tools for managing and exploring that data. In this module, you will learn how to use Excel to handle large data sets, highlighting important relationships and trends.

Jacek has compiled data on hundreds of employees who work full time for Orthographic and wants your help in summarizing that data. You'll open and review Jacek's workbook.

### To open Jacek's workbook containing employee data:

1. **sam** ⬇ Open the **NP_EX_6-1.xlsx** workbook located in the **Excel6 > Module** folder included with your Data Files, and then save the workbook as **NP_EX_6_Ortho** in the location specified by your instructor.

2. In the Documentation sheet, enter your name in cell B3 and the date in cell B4.

3. Go to the **Employees** worksheet. See Figure 6–1.

| Figure 6–1 | Employees worksheet |
| --- | --- |

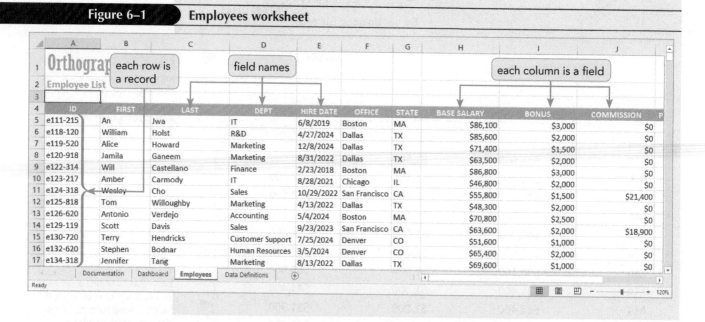

The information in the Employees worksheet is organized into a rectangular range of cells, or data range. In a data range, each column stores information known as a field describing a characteristic of a person, place, or thing and each row stores a record containing a group of related field values. The first row of a data range, known as the **header row**, typically contains the field names. Excel automatically recognizes data organized in this format and uses the labels in the header row to identify the columns within the range. To avoid confusion, a data range should be separated from other worksheet content by at least one blank row and column.

The field names for the employee data are in columns A through M of row 4 in the Employees worksheet. Jacek included fields for employee IDs, names, departments, dates of hire, office locations, wages (base salaries, bonuses, and commissions), personal days, sick days, and evaluation scores. Rows 5 through 538 contain 534 records providing detailed information on each employee.

With any data range, it's excellent practice to provide a **data definition table**, which lists the fields included with each record, the type of data stored in each field (such as numbers, text, or dates), and a short description of each field. A data definition table is useful for planning the kinds of data needed for an analysis and helping others who will use that data.

Jacek already entered a data definition table for the employee data. You will review that table to learn more about the data in the Employees worksheet.

### To view the data definition table for the Employees data:

▶ **1.** Go to the **Data Definitions** worksheet containing the data definition table. See Figure 6–2.

| Figure 6–2 | Data Definitions worksheet |

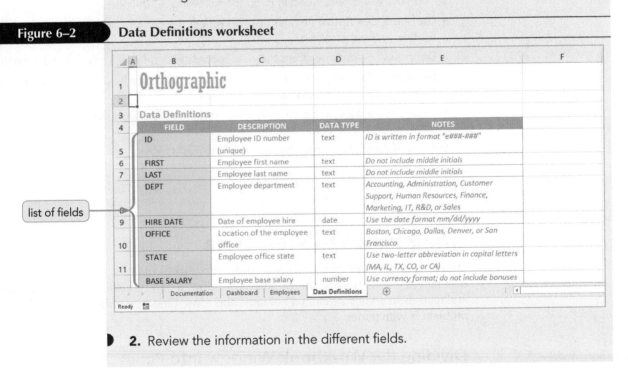

▶ **2.** Review the information in the different fields.

Next, you will study the contents of the Employees worksheet.

## Proskills

### Written Communication: Planning for Data Entry

Before entering data, you should plan how that data should be structured to best achieve your goals. Those goals help to determine the fields needed for each record. Consider each of the following:

- Who can view the data, and which fields contain confidential information available to a select few
- What questions you want answered, and what fields are required to generate those answers
- What reports you want generated for different audiences (supervisors, customers, directors, etc.)
- How often the data needs to be updated, and who is responsible for ensuring data accuracy

After you have identified the data needed and how it should be organized, you can set up your worksheet. Keep in mind the following guidelines:

- Use short, descriptive field names that reflect the content and fit more fields in the window without scrolling.
- Distinguish field names from the data records with different colors and font styles.
- Break fields into single units of information, such as one field for the city name and another field for the state name.
- Separate the data range from other information in the worksheet with at least one blank row and one blank column.

With careful and thorough planning, you will avoid having to redesign your worksheet after you start entering data.

## Using Panes to View Data

Data ranges can span thousands of records with dozens of fields. Because such large data ranges extend beyond the workbook window, it can be difficult to compare fields and records in widely separated columns and rows. One way of dealing with this problem is with panes.

### Dividing the Workbook Window into Panes

Excel can split the workbook window in up to four sections called panes with each pane offering a separate view into the worksheet. By scrolling through the contents of individual panes, you can compare cells from different sections of the worksheet side-by-side within the workbook window. To split the workbook window into four panes, select any cell or range in the worksheet, and then on the View tab, in the Window group, click the Split button. Split bars divide the workbook window along the top and left border of the selected cell or range. To split the window into two vertical panes displayed side-by-side, select any cell in the first row of the worksheet and then click the Split button. To split the window into two stacked horizontal panes, select any cell in the first column and then click the Split button.

# Reference

## Splitting the Workbook Window into Panes

- To split the workbook window into four panes, click any cell or range, and then click the Split button in the Window group on the View tab.
- To split the window into two vertical panes, select a cell in the first row, and then click the Split button.
- To split the window into two horizontal panes, select a cell in the first column, and then click the Split button
- To close the panes and return to one window, click the Split button again.

Jacek wants you to split the Employees worksheet into fours panes so you can more easily compare different parts of the worksheet.

## To split the Employees worksheet into four panes:

1. Go to the **Employees** worksheet and click cell **D5** to select it.

2. On the ribbon, click the **View** tab, and then in the Window group, click the **Split** button (or press **ALT,W,S**). Two split bars divide the workbook window into four panes with two sets of scroll bars along the horizontal and vertical edges of the workbook window.

> **Tip**
>
> To resize the panes, point to a pane split bar, and then use the double-headed split arrow to drag the split bar to a new location.

3. Drag the **lower vertical scroll bar** down until row 70 is aligned with the horizontal split bar. Notice that scrolling is synchronized between the lower-left and lower-right panes so that both panes show the same rows.

4. Drag the **right horizontal scroll bar** until column H is aligned with the vertical split bar. Scrolling between the upper-right and lower-right panes is also synchronized so that both panes show the same columns. See Figure 6–3.

### Figure 6–3    Workbook window split into four panes

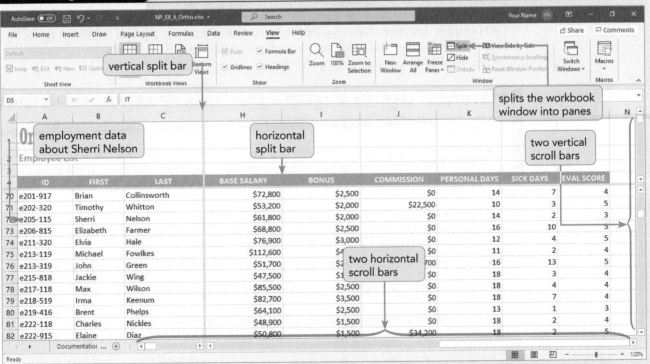

> **5.** Continue to drag the **lower vertical scroll bar** down until you can see row 538 in the workbook window. As you can see, you can view widely spaced areas in the different panes of the workbook window.

With the workbook window split into four panes, it is easy to read information about individual employees. For example, as you can see in Figure 6–3, Sherri Nelson is paid a base salary of $61,800 with a yearly bonus of $2,000. Reading this information without panes would be much more difficult because scrolling through the workbook window would have hidden those field names and values from view.

Splitting the workbook window affects only the active sheet or worksheet group. Other worksheets will remain unaffected. To return a worksheet to one pane, you remove the split. You'll change the Employees worksheet back to a single pane.

### To remove the split bars from the worksheet:

> **1.** Drag the **lower vertical scroll bar** up until you can see row 1 in the bottom two panes.

> **2.** On the View tab, in the Window group, click the **Split** button. The panes are removed, and the worksheet is again displayed within a single window.

**Tip**

You can also remove panes by double-clicking the split bar.

## Freezing Panes

Another way of viewing different sections of a worksheet is by freezing the split panes. When you **freeze** a pane, its contents are always visible though you cannot scroll within it. You can freeze the panes located to the top and left of a selected cell, allowing scrolling within the lower-right pane. You can freeze the top row of the worksheet, allowing scrolling for all rows in the pane below it. You can also freeze the first column of the worksheet, allowing scrolling for all columns in the pane to the right. Freezing panes is useful for worksheets with large data ranges like the Orthographic employee data. For example, you can freeze the top and left panes to keep the field names and a few select fields always in view. Then, the lower-right pane can be scrolled so you can display the data.

## Reference ▮

### Freezing Window Panes

- To split the workbook window into four panes with the top and left panes frozen, click the cell where you want to freeze panes to the top and left, and then on the View tab, in the Window group, click the Freeze Panes button and click Freeze Panes.
- To freeze the top row of the worksheet, click the Freeze Panes button, and then click Freeze Top Row.
- To freeze the first column of the worksheet, click the Freeze Panes button, and then click Freeze First Column.
- To remove the frozen panes, click the Freeze Panes button, and then click Unfreeze Panes.

You'll freeze the columns A through C and rows 1 through 4 to make scrolling through the worksheet easier as you continue to review the contents of the Employees worksheet.

### To freeze rows and columns in the Employees worksheet:

1. Scroll up the Employees worksheet so that cell A1 is visible in the upper-left corner of the worksheet.

2. Click cell **D5** to select it.

3. On the View tab, in the Window group, click the **Freeze Panes** button, and then click **Freeze Panes** on the menu that appears below the button. Narrow dividing lines appear between columns C and D and rows 4 and 5. Note that the worksheet has only one set of scrolling bars to scroll the contents in the lower-right pane.

4. Scroll down to row 210 and scroll to the right so that column H is displayed next to column C. Note that as you scroll through the worksheet, the contents of the first four rows and first three columns are locked in place.

5. Click cell **H210** to select the cell containing the base salary for Angeline Glover. See Figure 6–4.

| Figure 6–4 | Employees worksheet with frozen panes |
| --- | --- |

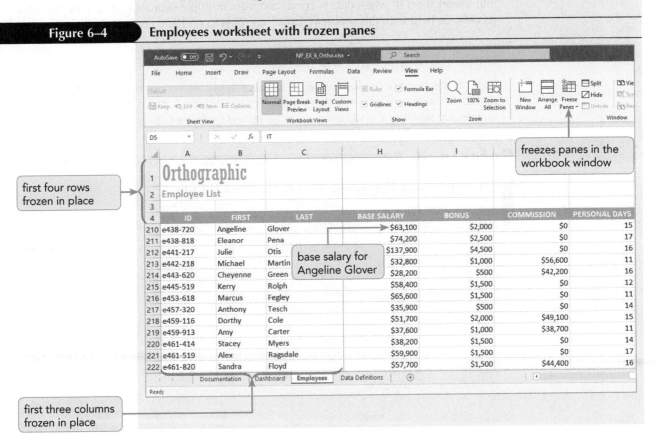

first four rows frozen in place

freezes panes in the workbook window

base salary for Angeline Glover

first three columns frozen in place

After you freeze the panes, the first option on the Freeze Panes button menu changes to Unfreeze Panes which releases the frozen panes and removes the panes from the workbook window. Now that you have viewed the contents of the Employees worksheet using panes, you will unfreeze and remove the panes.

**To unfreeze the panes in the workbook window:**

▶ **1.** On the View tab, in the Window group, click the **Freeze Panes** button. The first option is now Unfreeze Panes.

▶ **2.** Click **Unfreeze Panes** to remove the frozen panes from the workbook window.

▶ **3.** Scroll through the worksheet to verify that there are no frozen panes within the workbook window.

# Locating Duplicate Records

When a worksheet has a lot of data, data entry errors are almost sure to occur. One common error is creating a duplicate record in which the same record appears multiple times in the worksheet. Duplicate records can happen when several people enter data into a worksheet or when data is combined from multiple sources that include the same records. To help with this problem, Excel has tools to find and remove duplicated data.

## Highlighting Duplicate Values

You can use conditional formatting to locate a duplicate record by highlighting duplicate values within a selected range. Once you have located duplicate values, you can decide whether the value needs to be edited or deleted.

## Reference

### Highlighting Duplicate Values Within a Range

- Select the range you want to locate duplicate values within.
- On the Home tab, in the Styles group, click the Conditional Formatting button.
- On the conditional formatting menu, point to Highlight Cells Rules, and then click Duplicate Values.
- In the Duplicate Values dialog box, specify the highlighting style for duplicate values.
- Click OK.

Each employee at Orthographic is given a unique employee ID number. Jacek is worried that duplicate IDs might have entered by mistake and wants you to make sure that there are no duplicate values in the ID column. You will use conditional formatting to locate any duplicates.

**To highlight duplicate employee IDs in the Employees worksheet:**

▶ **1.** Click the **Name** box, type **A5:A538** as the range to select, and then press **ENTER**. All the ID values in column A are selected.

▶ **2.** On the ribbon, click the **Home** tab. In the Styles group, click the **Conditional Formatting** button, point to **Highlight Cell Rules**, and then click **Duplicate Values**. The Duplicate Values dialog box opens.

▶ **3.** Click **OK**. Cells that contain duplicate values are formatted with a light red fill with dark red text.

▶ **4.** Scroll down the worksheet until you can see rows 38 and 39. The red formatting in cells A38 and A39 highlight that these two employees have duplicate ID numbers. See Figure 6–5.

| Figure 6–5 | Conditional formatting highlights cells with duplicate values |
|---|---|

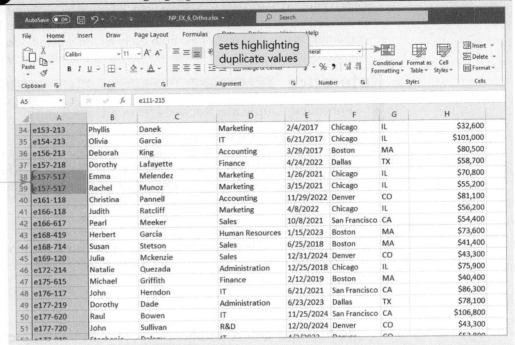

Emma Melendez and Rachel Munoz have the same employee IDs

Rachel Munoz's ID should have been entered as e157-617 and not e157-517. You'll correct this mistake now.

**5.** Click cell **A39**, and then enter **e157-617** as the ID value. Highlighting disappears from cells A38 and A39 because those IDs are no longer duplicates.

**6.** Scroll down the worksheet until you see duplicates highlighted. In rows 86 through 88, the employee record for Jennifer Rizzo is repeated three times. Jacek wants only one record per employee.

**7.** Drag the pointer over the **row 87** and **row 88** row headers to select both rows.

**8.** Right-click the selected rows, and then click **Delete** on the shortcut menu to remove these rows from the worksheet.

**9.** Scroll down the worksheet to rows 295 and 296. The employee record for Carmen Casares is duplicated.

**10.** Right-click the **row 296** row header, and then click **Delete** on the shortcut menu to remove row 296 from the worksheet.

**11.** Scroll down the worksheet to verify no other IDs are as duplicated.

**12.** Scroll back up to row 296, and then click cell **A295** to select it.

**Tip**

The conditional formatting rule will highlight duplicate values even if they are not adjacent to each other.

Carmen Casares is listed in both row 295 and row 296, although each listing has a different ID. Although it's not uncommon in a large company to have employees with the same name, these two records are completely identical except for the IDs. It would be extremely unlikely for two Carmen Casares to be hired on the same date in the same department at the same location for the same pay, not to mention reporting the same amount of personal and sick days and receiving the same employee evaluation score. Obviously, these are duplicate records in which the wrong ID was entered at some point, resulting in two records for the same employee. Jacek tells you that the second record has the incorrect employee ID and should be deleted. However, Jacek is concerned that the worksheet may contain other data entry errors like this.

## Removing Duplicate Records

One limit of using conditional formatting to locate duplicate records is that the process finds duplicate values only in a single field. It cannot highlight records that have several duplicated fields. In a worksheet with thousands of records, it would be extremely time-consuming to compare every field from every record. Instead, you can use the Remove Duplicates tool to locate and delete records that are duplicated across multiple fields.

## Reference

### Removing Duplicate Records from a Data Range

- Click any cell in the data range.
- On the Data tab, in the Data Tools group, click the Remove Duplicates button.
- Select the check boxes for the fields that you want to check for duplicates.
- Click OK to remove records containing duplicates of all of the selected fields.

Jacek asks you to remove records in which *all* the field values are duplicated except for the employee ID because it is extremely unlikely that two employees share every other possible employee characteristic. You will use the Remove Duplicates tool to remove those duplicate records.

### To find and delete duplicate records in the Employees worksheet:

▶ 1. On the ribbon, click the **Data** tab, and then in the Data Tools group, click the **Remove Duplicates** button ▦. The Remove Duplicates dialog box opens. All the employee data in the Employees worksheet is selected, and the dialog box lists the column labels in the first row of the range to identify the field names (ID through Eval Score).

 **Trouble?** If Excel shows the Remove Duplicates Warning dialog box, verify that the Expand the selection option button is selected and click the Remove Duplicates button.

▶ 2. Click the **ID** check box to deselect it, and then verify that every other field check box is selected. You deselected the ID field because you want to locate any delete duplicate records in which only the ID value is different while all other field values are identical. See Figure 6–6.

| Figure 6–6 | Remove Duplicates dialog box |

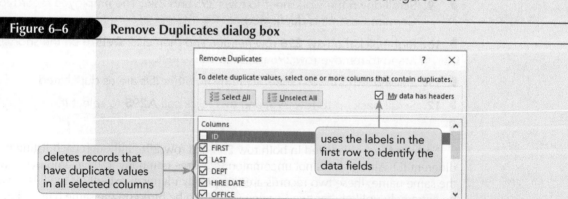

3. Click **OK** to remove the duplicate records. A dialog box opens, indicating that 1 duplicate record was found and deleted, leaving 530 unique records in the data range.

4. Click **OK** to close the dialog box and return to the worksheet.

5. Scroll to row **295** and verify that only one record exists for Carmen Casares.

**Tip**

If you delete records you did not intend to, click the Undo button on the Quick Access Toolbar (or press CTRL+Z).

Be *extremely cautious* when using the Remove Duplicates tool. You are *not* prompted to confirm deletion of duplicate records. Instead, Excel keeps the first instance of any duplicates it finds and deletes subsequent records. Make sure that you are deleting records based only on fields that should *never* be duplicated. For example, you wouldn't want to delete records in which the employee's first and last names are the same, because two people can share the same name.

Because you've found and corrected the duplicate records and IDs, you can remove the conditional formatting rule from the worksheet.

**To remove the Duplicate Values conditional formatting rule:**

1. On the ribbon, click the **Home** tab, and then in the Styles group, click the **Conditional Formatting** button.

2. At the bottom of the menu, click **Manage Rules**. The Conditional Formatting Rules Manager opens.

3. Click the **Show formatting rules for** box, and then click **This Worksheet** to show all of the conditional formats in the current sheet.

4. Click the **Duplicate Values** entry (the only conditional format in the worksheet), and then click **Delete Rule**. No rules appear in the dialog box.

5. Click **OK** to close the dialog box and return to the worksheet.

The data in the Employees worksheet is listed by the employee ID number. Jacek wants to arrange the data values in a different order. You can do that by sorting.

# Sorting Records in a Data Range

By default, records appear in the order in which they're entered. However, you can gain valuable insights into your data by arranging the records by one or more chosen fields. You can sort those fields in **ascending order** so that text entries are arranged alphabetically from A to Z, numeric values are sorted from smallest to largest, and date and time values are sorted from oldest to most recent. Excel can also sort the records in **descending order** so that text entries are sorted from Z to A, numeric values are sorted from largest to smallest, and dates and times are sorted from most recent to oldest.

## Sorting by a Single Field

You can sort any data range by any field in ascending or descending order. To sort data in ascending order by a single field or column, select any cell in that field or column. On the Data tab, in the Sort & Filter group, click the Sort A to Z button. To sort in descending order, click the Sort Z to A button.

# Reference

### Sorting Records in a Data Range

**To sort by a single field:**
- Click any cell in the field you want to sort by.
- On the Data tab, in the Sort & Filter group, click the Sort A to Z button or click the Sort Z to A button.

**To sort records by multiple fields:**
- Click any cell in the data range you want to sort.
- On the Data tab, in the Sort & Filter group, click the Sort button to open the Sort dialog box.
- Click the Sort by arrow and select a field to sort by. Click the Order arrow and select how the field should be sorted.
- For each additional field you want to sort by, click the Then by arrow to add a new row, click the Sort arrow and select a field, and then click the Order arrow and select how the field should be sorted.
- Click OK.

Jacek wants to know which employees have been with the company the longest. You will sort the data in the Employees worksheet in ascending order of the Hire Date field to answer that question.

**Tip**

You can click the Sort & Filter button in the Editing group on the Home tab to sort records by values in a single column.

### To sort the Employee data in ascending order by the Hire Date field:

1. Scroll up the worksheet and click cell **E5** to select a cell in the Hire Date column.

2. On the ribbon, click the **Data** tab.

3. In the Sort & Filter group, click the **Sort A to Z** button. The records are rearranged by the date the employees were hired with the earliest hire dates shown first. See Figure 6–7.

**Figure 6–7**    Data sorted based on a single column

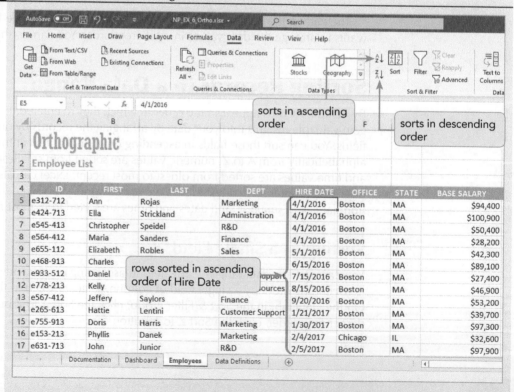

▶ **4.** Scroll down the worksheet to verify that the values in the Hire Date column appear in ascending order, ending with the most recent hiring dates.

This sort shows that employees who have been with Orthographic the longest were all hired in 2012 in Boston, which isn't surprising given that the company was formed in Boston that year and expanded over the next several years to offices across the country. Next, Jacek wants you to sort the data to find out which employee has the highest base salary and which employee received the largest end-of-year bonus.

**To sort the employee data by the Base Salary and Bonus fields:**

▶ **1.** Click cell **H5** to select a cell in the Base Salary field.

▶ **2.** On the Data tab, in the Sort & Filter group, click the **Sort Z to A** button to sort the employee records from the largest base salary to the smallest. The employee with the largest base salary is Paula Bernardi, an administrator from the San Francisco office, followed by Julie Otis, an administrator in the Chicago office.

▶ **3.** Click cell **I5** to select a value in the Bonus field, and then click the **Sort Z to A** button to sort the records in descending order of the Bonus field. Bennie Treadwell of the Chicago office IT department received the largest bonus with $5,000. Four employees received bonuses of $4,500.

The Sort A to Z and Sort Z to A buttons provide a fast way to sort your data. But they are limited to sorting by one field at a time. When you want to sort by multiple fields, you can use the Sort dialog box.

## Sorting by Multiple Fields

Sometimes you will want to sort by multiple levels of fields. For example, you might want to sort by base salary within a particular department to find the highest paid employees within that department. With sorts that involve multiple fields or columns, you identify one field as the **primary sort field** by which to initially sort the data and a second field as the **secondary sort field** for sorting data within the primary sort field. You can continue this process by identifying a third sort field for values within values of the first two fields and so forth.

Jacek wants to identify the highest-paid employees within each department at each office location. To retrieve that information, you will sort the employee data first by the Office field, then by Department within Office, and finally by Base Salary within Department.

**To sort the employee data by the Office, Dept, and Base Salary fields:**

▶ **1.** On the Data tab, in the Sort & Filter group, click the **Sort** button. The Sort dialog box opens. The selected data range is currently set to sort in descending order of the Bonus field. You will change that that first sort field the Office field.

▶ **2.** Click the **Sort by arrow** to display a list of fields in the data range, and then click **OFFICE** in the list. The first sort is now set the Office field.

3. Click the **Order arrow** to display the sort order options, and then click **A to Z** to sort the data in ascending order of office name. The first sort level is complete.

4. Click the **Add Level** button. A second sort level is added to the sort.

5. Click the **Then by arrow**, and then click **DEPT** to sort the values by department within office location. The sort order is already ascending, so you don't need to change it.

6. Click the **Add Level** button to add a third sort level, click its **Then by arrow** and click **BASE SALARY** to add the Base Salary as the third sort field, and then click its **Order arrow** and click **Largest to Smallest** to change the sort order to descending. See Figure 6–8.

| Figure 6–8 | Sort dialog box with three sorted fields |
|---|---|

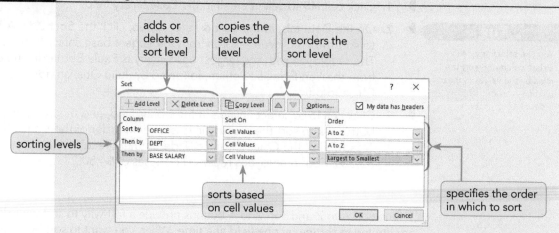

7. Click **OK** to sort the data in the Employees worksheet.

8. Scroll down the worksheet and verify that the data is sorted in ascending order by Office, then ascending order by department name within each office, and finally in descending order by base salary within each department. See Figure 6–9.

| Figure 6–9 | Employees sorted by the Office, Dept, and Base Salary fields |
|---|---|

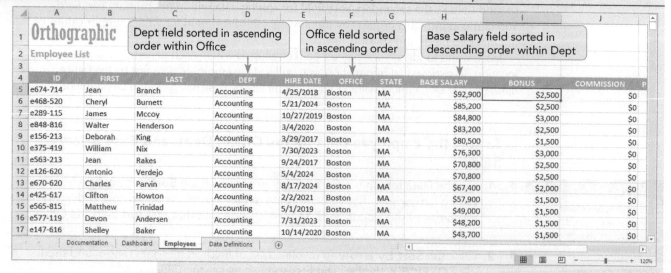

Excel supports 64 levels of sort fields, so you can continue to add more sorting levels as needed. However, you probably won't use more than three for most reports.

## Insight

### Choosing Sort Options

Typically, you sort a data range based on field values. You can also arrange data based on the formats applied to the cell, sorting the cells by the fill color, font color, and conditional formatting icon. To choose a different way of sorting, click the Sort On arrow in the Sort dialog box and select how you want the cells sorted.

All sorts assume that records are in rows and sort the data from top to bottom. If the records are in columns, you can change the sort orientation to sort the records from left to right. To do this, click the Options button in the Sort dialog box and change the orientation.

The default option for sorting text fields is to ignore capitalization so that values like "Chicago" and "CHICAGO" are sorted the same. To make the sort see different capitalization as unique entries, click the Options button in the Sort dialog box, and then click the Case Sensitive check box. If the records are sorted in ascending order, lowercase letters will be displayed first. For example, Chicago will come before CHICAGO.

## Sorting with a Custom List

So far, you have sorted data in ascending or descending order. However, some types of text data have their own special sort order. For example, the months of the year—January, February, March, and so on—and the days of week—Sunday, Monday, Tuesday, and so on—have a sort order that is neither alphabetical nor numeric. The Sort dialog box includes sort order options for month name and day name. But, for other sort orders, you can create a **custom list** that arranges the field values in the order you specify.

Jacek wants you to sort the Orthographic offices in the order they opened rather than alphabetically. Each office opened in a different year: Boston in 2016, Chicago in 2017, Denver in 2018, San Francisco in 2020, and Dallas in 2022. You'll create a custom list of those city names in that order and use it in your sort of the employee data.

**To create and apply a custom list to sorting:**

1. On the Data tab, in the Sort & Filter group, click the **Sort** button. The Sort dialog box opens.

2. In the Office field row, click the **A to Z** box, and then click **Custom List**. The Custom Lists dialog box opens.

3. Click **Add** to begin a new custom list.

**Tip**
Any custom list can be sorted in either ascending or descending order.

4. In the List Entries box, type **Boston** and press **ENTER**. Boston is added to the List Entries box.

5. Type the following city names, pressing **ENTER** after each name: **Chicago**, **Denver**, **San Francisco**, and **Dallas**. See Figure 6–10.

**Figure 6–10**    Custom Lists dialog box

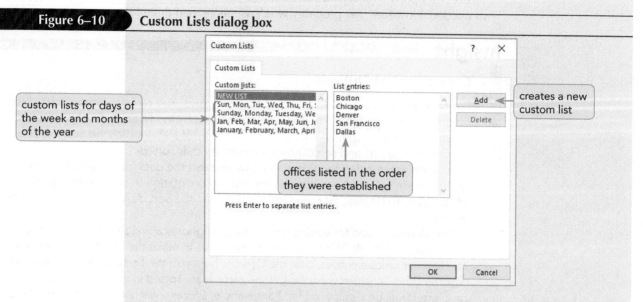

6. Click **OK** to create the list and return to the Sort dialog box. The Order box for the Office field shows the custom sort order: Boston, Chicago, Denver, San Francisco, and Dallas.

7. Click **OK** to apply this sort order to the employee data.

8. Scroll down the Employees worksheet and verify that employees are sorted in the new order with Boston employees listed first and Dallas employees listed last.

---

**Tip**

Any custom lists you create are available to and used by AutoFill.

Any custom list you create will remain part of your Excel settings and available to all other workbooks. If you want to remove a custom list, select the custom list in the Custom Lists dialog box, and click Delete. You will remove this custom list from your Excel settings.

### To delete a custom list:

1. On the Data tab, in the Sort & Filter group, click the **Sort** button. The Sort dialog box opens.

2. In the Office field row, click the **Boston, Chicago, Denver, San Francisco, Dallas** box, and then click **Custom List**. The Custom Lists dialog box opens.

3. In the Custom lists box, click **Boston, Chicago, Denver, San Francisco, Dallas**. The offices appear in the List entries box. You could edit the list entries if needed. Instead you want to delete the entire list.

4. Click **Delete** to delete the custom list, and then click **OK** in the dialog box that opens to confirm that you want to permanently delete this custom list.

5. Click **OK** in each dialog box to return to the Employees worksheet.

Even though you removed this custom list, the employee data is still sorted in the order that the Orthographic offices opened. The sort order will remain unchanged until you sort the data in a different way.

# Calculating Subtotals

Analyzing a large data range usually includes making calculations on the data. You can summarize the data by applying summary functions such as COUNT, SUM, and AVERAGE to the entire data range.

## Creating a Subtotal Row

Some analysis requires calculations on sections of a data range. To do this, you can add **subtotals**, which are summary functions that are applied to a part of a data range. For example, you can calculate a sum of the base salary for employees from each department or office. To calculate a subtotal, the data must first be sorted by a field, such as the Office or Dept field. Then the Subtotal tool will insert a new row wherever the field changes value and display the subtotal for the previous group of records.

# Reference

### Adding a Subtotal to a Data Range

- Sort the data range by the field where you want to place the subtotal values.
- On the Data tab, in the Outline group, click the Subtotal button.
- Click the At each change in arrow and select the field where the subtotals will be added to the data range.
- Click the Use function arrow and select the summary function to use in the subtotal calculation.
- In the Add subtotal to box, select the fields for which the subtotal will be calculated.
- Click OK to generate the subtotals.
- Use the outline buttons on the worksheet to expand and collapse groups within the data range.

Jacek wants you to calculate the total spent by each of the five offices on base salaries, bonuses, and commissions. You'll use the Subtotal button to add subtotal rows containing those statistics.

### To calculate the salary subtotal for each office:

▶ 1. On the Data tab, in the Outline group, click the **Subtotal** button. The Subtotal dialog box opens.

▶ 2. Click the **At each change in arrow**, and then click **OFFICE** in the list of fields to specify adding a subtotal for each Office field value.

▶ 3. If necessary, click the **Use function arrow**, and then click **Sum** to calculate the sum at each change in the Office field.

▶ 4. In the Add subtotal to box, click the **BASE SALARY, BONUS,** and **COMMISSION** check boxes to select them, and if necessary, click the **EVAL SCORE** check box to deselect it.

▶ 5. Verify that the **Replace current subtotals** and **Summary below data** check boxes are selected. See Figure 6–11.

**Figure 6–11**    **Subtotal dialog box**

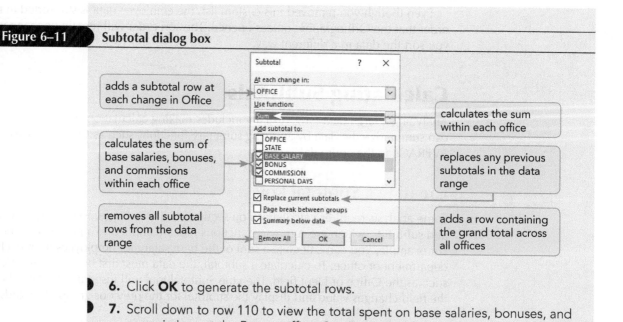

adds a subtotal row at each change in Office

calculates the sum of base salaries, bonuses, and commissions within each office

removes all subtotal rows from the data range

calculates the sum within each office

replaces any previous subtotals in the data range

adds a row containing the grand total across all offices

6. Click **OK** to generate the subtotal rows.

7. Scroll down to row 110 to view the total spent on base salaries, bonuses, and commissions at the Boston office. See Figure 6–12.

**Figure 6–12**    **Total compensation spent on employees in the Boston office**

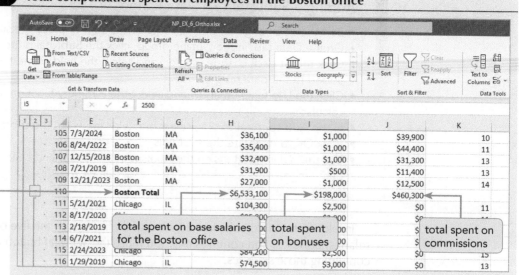

subtotal row inserted at the change in Office value

total spent on base salaries for the Boston office

total spent on bonuses

total spent on commissions

8. Continue to scroll down the worksheet to view the subtotals for offices in Chicago, San Francisco, Denver, and Dallas. Row 540 at the bottom of data range shows the grand total spent on commissions for all five offices.

The subtotal rows show that the Boston office spent $6,533,100 on base salaries, $198,000 on bonuses, and $460,300 on commissions. Other offices have similar totals. The grand total in row 540 shows that the entire company spent $32,803,000 on base salaries, $985,500 on bonuses, and $2,413,900 in commissions.

You can include several summary statistics in the subtotals row. Jacek wants this report to also include the average employee compensation in each office and across all offices. You'll add the AVERAGE function to the subtotal report.

## To add a second summary statistic to the employees subtotals:

▸ 1. On the Data tab, in the Outline group, click the **Subtotal** button. The Subtotal dialog box opens.

▸ 2. Click the **Use function arrow**, and then click **Average** in the list of summary statics.

Uncheck the Replace current subtotals check box so new statistics don't overwrite the current ones.

▸ 3. Click the **Replace current subtotals** check box to deselect it. This ensures that the averages are added to the current subtotal values instead of replacing them.

▸ 4. Click **OK** to add an average calculation to the subtotals.

▸ 5. Scroll down the worksheet and verify that each office shows the average and the total amount Orthographic spends on employee compensation. See Figure 6–13.

| Figure 6–13 | Sums and averages for the subtotal rows |

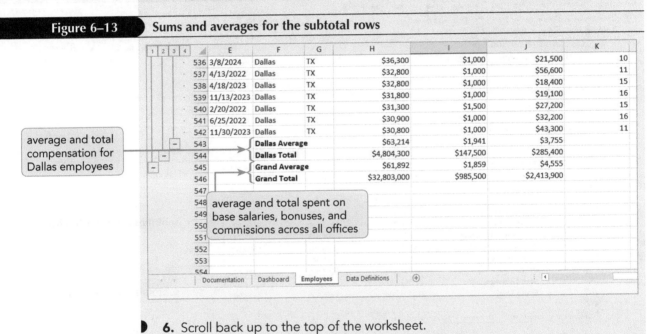

average and total compensation for Dallas employees

average and total spent on base salaries, bonuses, and commissions across all offices

▸ 6. Scroll back up to the top of the worksheet.

This report tells Jacek that across all offices, Orthographic pays its employees an average of $61,892 in base salary, $1,859 in bonuses, and $4,555 in commissions.

## Using the Subtotal Outline View

Rather than view detailed information on every field, you might want to view only summary statistics. The outline tool lets you control the level of detail displayed in the worksheet. The Employees worksheet has four levels in the outline of its data range. The topmost level, or Level 1, displays only the grand totals. Level 2 displays the total spent at each office. Level 3 displays both the total and average spent at each office. Finally, the bottommost level, Level 4, displays individual records. Clicking the outline buttons located to the left of the row numbers lets you choose how much detail you want to see in the worksheet. You will use the outline buttons to expand and collapse different sections of the data range.

### To expand and collapse the employee data outline:

1. Click the **Level 1 Outline** button [1] to collapse the outline. All of the rows between row 4 and row 545 are hidden. Only the grand average and grand total values for all offices are visible.

2. Click the **Level 2 Outline** button [2] to expand the outline to the second level. The totals for all offices as well as grand average and grand total are visible.

3. Click the **Level 3 Outline** button [3] to show the averages and totals for each office and for all offices. See Figure 6–14.

**Figure 6–14**    Sums and averages for each office and across offices

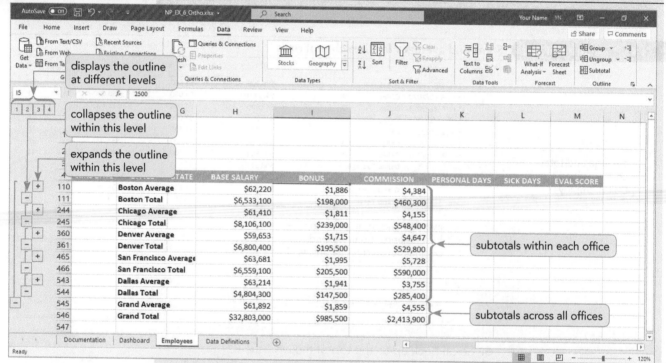

4. Click the **Show Detail** button [+] by row 465 to display employee records for only the San Francisco office. The outline expands to show rows 362 through 464. This lets you display select sections of the outline.

5. Click the **Hide Detail** [–] by row 465 to hide the rows 362 through 464 in the worksheet. The employee records from the San Francisco office are again hidden.

6. Click the **Level 4 Outline** button [4] to display all of the employee records. All of the rows from the data range are visible in the worksheet.

You have finished reviewing the employee records and the subtotals, so you can remove the subtotals from the worksheet. You will remove the subtotals now.

**To remove the subtotals from the Employees worksheet:**

▶ **1.** On the Data tab, in the Outline group, click the **Subtotal** button. The Subtotal dialog box opens.

▶ **2.** Click **Remove All**. The subtotals and the outline groups are removed from the worksheet.

▶ **3.** Save the workbook.

If at any time you wish to display the subtotals again or calculate different subtotals, you can rerun the Subtotal command.

## Insight

### Creating Manual Outlines

You can create outlines with any data range. Outlines can be applied to the range's rows or columns. To outline data, select the rows or columns you want to group and then click the Group button in the Outline group on the Data tab. Outline buttons appear in the worksheet. You can use these buttons to expand or collapse the outline. To remove the outlining, click the Ungroup button in the Outline group on the Data tab, and then click Clear Outline.

Many financial statements, such as profit and loss statements, already have subtotals. If you want to add outlining to a long and complicated financial statement, select anywhere within the statement and click the Group button and then click Auto Outline. The financial statement will automatically be grouped and outlined at each location of a subtotal.

You've completed your initial work with the employee records. In the next session, you will learn how to show subsets of the data range and how to convert a data range into an Excel table.

## Review

### Session 6.1 Quick Check

1. What is a field? What is a record?
2. If you split the worksheet into panes at cell E3, how many panes are created?
3. What are the three freeze pane options?
4. When highlighting duplicate values with a conditional format, do the duplicate values have to be adjacent to each other?
5. Why is it *not* a good idea for a company to treat employee records with duplicate first and last names as duplicate records?
6. When an ascending sort order is used, how is a date-time field sorted?
7. If you want to sort employees by the value of the Hire Date field within each value of the Dept field, which field is the primary sort field? Which is the secondary sort field?
8. Before you can add subtotals to a data range, what must you first do with the data?

# Session 6.2 Visual Overview:

Each Excel table is assigned a name that can be referenced elsewhere in the workbook.

An Excel table is a structured range of data that is managed independently from other data in the workbook.

Filtered rows, or records, are displayed in the worksheet. Records that do not match the filter criteria are hidden.

In an Excel table, the field or column names are referenced using the bracket notation. Here, the First and Last fields are referenced by [@FIRST] and [@LAST].

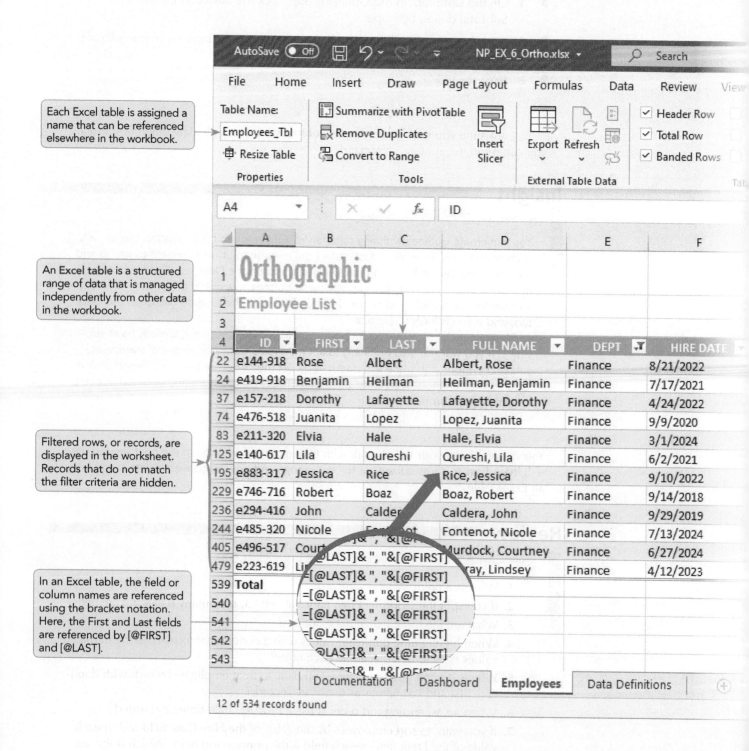

| | ID | FIRST | LAST | FULL NAME | DEPT | HIRE DATE |
|---|---|---|---|---|---|---|
| 22 | e144-918 | Rose | Albert | Albert, Rose | Finance | 8/21/2022 |
| 24 | e419-918 | Benjamin | Heilman | Heilman, Benjamin | Finance | 7/17/2021 |
| 37 | e157-218 | Dorothy | Lafayette | Lafayette, Dorothy | Finance | 4/24/2022 |
| 74 | e476-518 | Juanita | Lopez | Lopez, Juanita | Finance | 9/9/2020 |
| 83 | e211-320 | Elvia | Hale | Hale, Elvia | Finance | 3/1/2024 |
| 125 | e140-617 | Lila | Qureshi | Qureshi, Lila | Finance | 6/2/2021 |
| 195 | e883-317 | Jessica | Rice | Rice, Jessica | Finance | 9/10/2022 |
| 229 | e746-716 | Robert | Boaz | Boaz, Robert | Finance | 9/14/2018 |
| 236 | e294-416 | John | Calder | Caldera, John | Finance | 9/29/2019 |
| 244 | e485-320 | Nicole | Fontenot | Fontenot, Nicole | Finance | 7/13/2024 |
| 405 | e496-517 | Court | Murdock, Courtney | | Finance | 6/27/2024 |
| 479 | e223-619 | Li | ray, Lindsey | | Finance | 4/12/2023 |
| 539 | Total | | | | | |

Table Name:
Employees_Tbl

=[@LAST]& ", "&[@FIRST]

12 of 534 records found

# Filters and Excel Tables

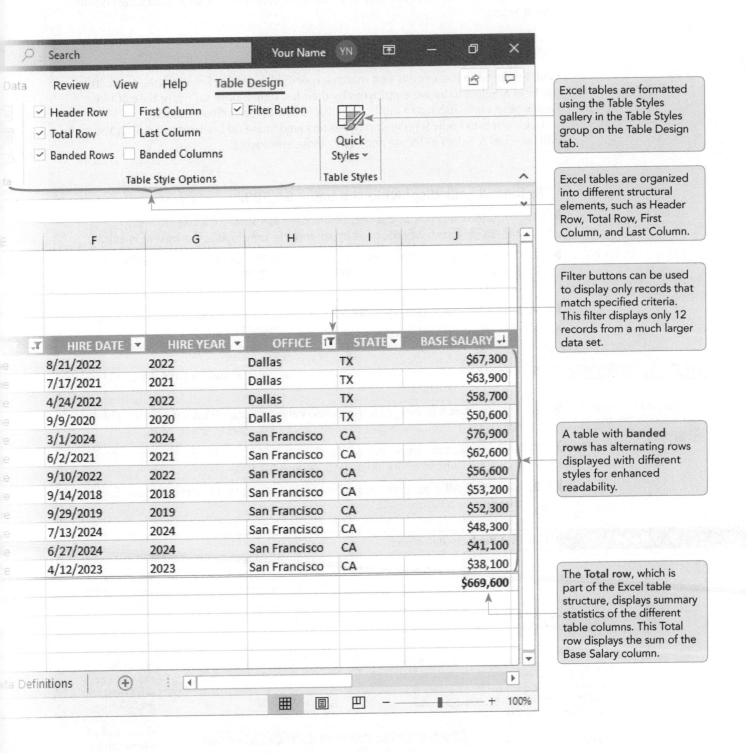

Excel tables are formatted using the Table Styles gallery in the Table Styles group on the Table Design tab.

Excel tables are organized into different structural elements, such as Header Row, Total Row, First Column, and Last Column.

Filter buttons can be used to display only records that match specified criteria. This filter displays only 12 records from a much larger data set.

A table with **banded rows** has alternating rows displayed with different styles for enhanced readability.

The **Total row**, which is part of the Excel table structure, displays summary statistics of the different table columns. This Total row displays the sum of the Base Salary column.

# Locating Cells Within a Worksheet

As the number of records grows within a data range, it becomes increasingly difficult to locate specific records. One way of locating records within a large data range is with Find & Select.

## Finding and Selecting Multiple Cells

Find & Select can locate cells that match a specified criterion. For example, you can use Find & Select to locate employees by their last name, base salary, or date of hire. Find & Select can also list multiple cells that satisfy the specified criterion.

Jacek wants to know which employees received year-end bonuses of $4,500. You will use Find & Select to locate and select those employees.

### To find all cells displaying the value $4,500:

1. If you took a break at the end of the previous session, make sure the NP_EX_6_Ortho workbook is open and the Employees worksheet is active.

2. On the ribbon, click the **Home** tab. In the Editing group, click the **Find & Select** button, and then click **Find** (or press **CTRL+F**). The Find and Replace dialog box opens.

3. In the Find what box, type **$4,500** as the value to locate.

4. Click **Options** if necessary to display an expanded list of find and replace options.

5. If necessary, click the **Within** box, and then click **Sheet** to limit the search to the current worksheet.

6. Click the **Look in** box, and then click **Values** to search based on the values displayed in the cells rather than the formulas used in those cells.

7. Click the **Match entire cell contents** check box to limit the search only to those cells whose entire displayed value is $4,500.

8. Click **Find All**. Four cells in the Employees worksheet match the specified criterion. See Figure 6–15.

**Figure 6–15**    **Find and Replace dialog box**

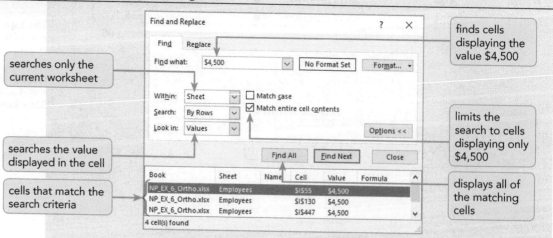

9.  Click the first entry in the list. Excel selects cell I55, the record for Rita Roden of the IT department in the Boston Office.

10. Click each of the other three entries in the list to view the records for Julie Otis, Paula Bernardi, and Michael Fowlkes, who each received a $4,500 end-of-the year bonus.

11. Click **Close** to close the Find and Replace dialog box.

The Find & Select command will select any cell that displays the value $4,500. It does not distinguish between fields.

### Finding Cells by Type

Find & Select can also locate cells based on criteria other than cell value, such as whether the cell contains a formula, constant, blank, or conditional formatting rule. To locate cells of a specific type, click the Find & Select button in the Editing group on the Home tab, and then click Go To Special. The Go To dialog box shown in Figure 6–16 opens.

---

**Figure 6–16    Go To Special dialog box**

The dialog box includes many ways to locate cells by types. For example, to select all of the records in a data range, click any cell in the data range, open the Go To Special dialog box, click the Current region option button, and then click OK. This approach is a big time-saver if you are working with a data range composed of thousands of records and dozens of fields.

## Filtering Data

Find & Select is a quick way of locating cells of a specific type within a worksheet and across worksheets. But, it does not search based on multiple criteria. To find records based on search criteria that involve multiple fields, you must filter the data.

## Filtering Based on One Field

Filtering data hides the rows whose values do not match the search criteria. Those rows are not removed from the worksheet. They can be redisplayed by removing the filter or applying a new filter. When you create a filter, Excel displays a filter button alongside each field name. By clicking the filter button, you can choose which values in that field to display, hiding the rows or records that do not match that value.

# Reference

### Filtering Data

- To add filter buttons to a data range or table, on the Data tab, in the Sort & Filter group, click the Filter button.
- To filter by a single field, click its filter button, click the check boxes for the values to include in the filter, and then click OK.
- To filter by a numeric field, click the filter button, click Number Filters, click the filter to apply, and then click OK.
- To filter by a date field, click the filter button, click Date Filters, click the filter to apply, and then click OK.
- To filter by a text field, click the filter button, click Text Filters, click the filter to apply, and then click OK.

Jacek wants to see a list that shows only employees in the Chicago office. You will filter the employee list.

### To filter the list to display only the Chicago records:

1. In the Employees worksheet, click cell **A5** to select a cell in the data range.

**Tip**

Select any cell within a data range to enable the Filter command for the entire range.

2. On the ribbon, click the **Data** tab, and then in the Sort & Filter group, click the **Filter** button. Filter buttons appear next to each field name in the range A4:M4.

3. In cell F4, click the **filter** button next to the Office field name. The filter menu opens, listing the five unique office values within the Office field. Currently all offices are displayed in the data range. See Figure 6–17.

**Figure 6–17** Filter criteria

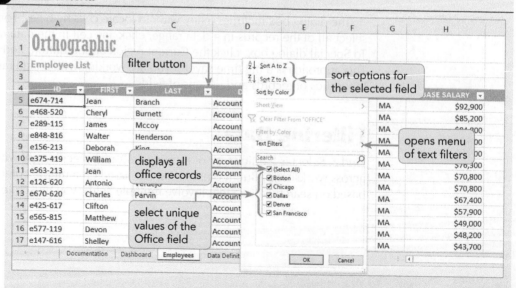

**4.** Click the **Select All** check box to deselect all the check boxes, and then click the **Chicago** check box. Only the Chicago office is selected.

**5.** Click **OK** to apply the filter. Only employees from the Chicago office appear in the worksheet. The records for other employees are hidden. See Figure 6–18.

| Figure 6–18 | Employee records for the Chicago office |
| --- | --- |

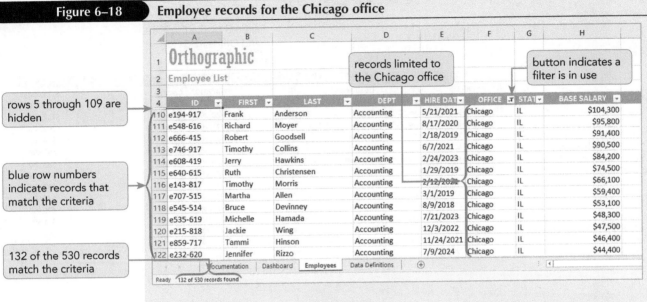

- rows 5 through 109 are hidden
- blue row numbers indicate records that match the criteria
- 132 of the 530 records match the criteria
- records limited to the Chicago office
- button indicates a filter is in use

**6.** Scroll down the worksheet to verify that only employees from the Chicago office are listed.

When a field or column is filtered, the filter button changes from ⊡ to ⊽ as a visual reminder that some of the data records are hidden because of the filter. The status bar also indicates the number of records that match the filter criteria. In this case 132 of the 530 records in the data range match the filter. Row numbers for records that match the criteria are displayed in blue.

## Filtering Based on Multiple Fields

You can filter a data range based on criteria from multiple fields. Each additional filter reduces the number of records displayed since a record has to fulfill all filter criteria to be selected. To use filters from multiple fields, select the filter button from other column headers in the data range.

Jacek wants you to add a filter to display only those Chicago employees working in the IT or R&D departments. You'll add that filter to the employees list.

### To add a second filter to the employee lists:

**1.** In cell **D4**, click the **filter** button next to the Dept field name. The filter menu opens.

**2.** Click the **Select All** check box to deselect all the department check boxes.

**3.** Click the **IT** and **R&D** check boxes to select only those two departments from the list.

**4.** Click **OK** to add this filter to the data range. The number of records found reduces to 35, which is the number of people employed in the IT or R&D departments of Chicago. See Figure 6–19.

Figure 6–19    IT and R&D employees from the Chicago office

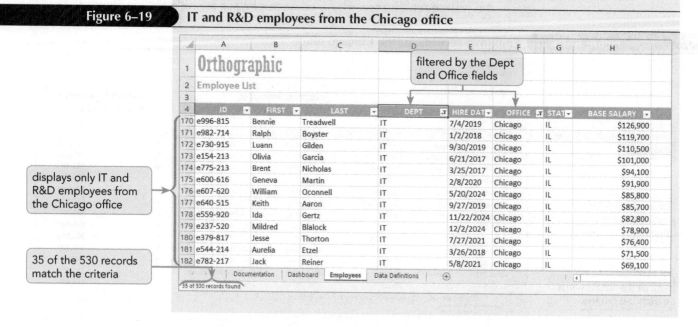

displays only IT and R&D employees from the Chicago office

35 of the 530 records match the criteria

The two filters you've applied have selected records based on field categories. You can also filter data based on date and time, numbers, and text.

## Using Criteria Filters

The filters created are limited to selecting records for fields matching a specific value or set of values. For more general criteria, you can create **criteria filters**, which are expressions involving dates and times, numeric values, and text strings. For example, you can filter the employee data to show only those employees hired within a specific date range or who receive a base salary above a certain amount. Figure 6–20 describes some of the criteria filters that you can apply to your data.

**Figure 6–20**     **Text, number, and date criteria filters**

| Filter | Criteria | Records Displayed |
|---|---|---|
| Text | Equals | Exactly match the specified text |
| | Does Not Equal | Do not exactly match the specified text |
| | Begins With | Begin with the specified text |
| | Ends With | End with the specified text |
| | Contains | Have the specified text anywhere |
| | Does Not Contain | Do not have the specified text anywhere |
| Number | Equals | Exactly match the specified number |
| | Greater Than or Equal to | Are greater than or equal to the specified number |
| | Less Than | Are less than the specified number |
| | Between | Are greater than or equal to and less than or equal to the specified numbers |
| | Top 10 | Are the top or bottom 10 (or the specified number) |
| | Above Average | Are greater than the average |
| Date | Today | Have the current date |
| | Last Week | Are in the prior week |
| | Next Month | Are in the month following the current month |
| | Last Quarter | Are in the previous quarter of the year (quarters defined as Jan, Feb, Mar; Apr, May, June; and so on) |
| | Year to Date | Are since January 1 of the current year to the current date |
| | Last Year | Are in the previous year (based on the current date) |

Jacek wants to further limit the employees list to include only those employees hired during 2024 and who have a base salary of at least $90,000 per year. You will use criteria filters now to add those two conditions to the worksheet.

**To filter the employee list for dates and values:**

1. In cell **E4**, click the **filter** button next to the Hire Date field name.

2. On the filter menu, point to **Date Filters**, and then click **After** in the date filter menu. The Custom AutoFilter dialog box opens.

**Tip**

You can also enter a date by clicking the calendar icon next to the input box and selecting a date from the calendar.

3. Click the upper-left **arrow**, click **is after or equal to**, press **TAB**, and then type **1/1/2024** as the first date in the filter.

4. Verify the **And** option button is selected.

5. Click the bottom-left **arrow**, click **is before or equal to**, press **TAB**, and then type **12/31/2024** as the last date in the filter. See Figure 6–21.

**Figure 6-21**    Custom AutoFilter dialog box

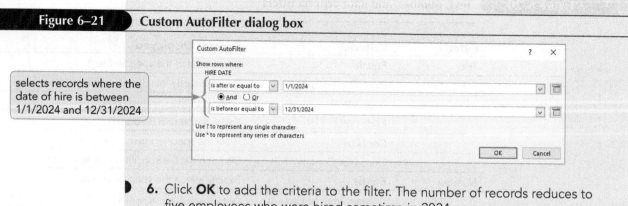

selects records where the date of hire is between 1/1/2024 and 12/31/2024

6. Click **OK** to add the criteria to the filter. The number of records reduces to five employees who were hired sometime in 2024.

7. In cell **H4**, click the **filter** button next to the Base Salary field name.

8. On the filter menu, point to **Number Filters**, and then click **Greater Than Or Equal To**. The Custom AutoFilter dialog box opens.

9. Type **90000** in the upper-right box, and then click **OK** to apply the filter. The worksheet displays only two records for the employees who also have a base salary greater than or equal to $90,000 who were hired in 2024 and who work in the IT or R&D departments of the Chicago office. See Figure 6–22.

**Figure 6-22**    Hire date and base salary added to the filter

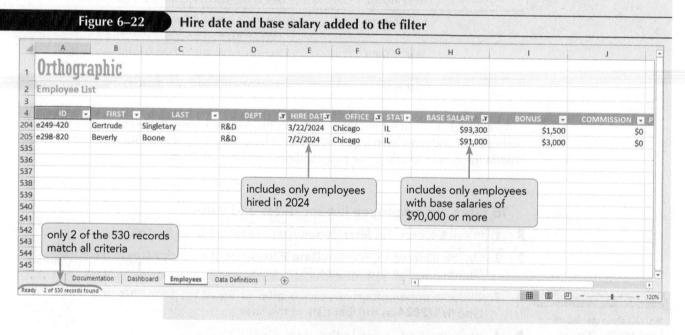

includes only employees hired in 2024

includes only employees with base salaries of $90,000 or more

only 2 of the 530 records match all criteria

Through the use of criteria filters, you can report to Jacek that only Gertude Singletary and Bevery Boone of the Chicago R&D department were hired during 2024 at base salaries greater than or equal to $90,000.

# Insight

## Exploring Text Filters

Text filters are useful for locating records based on all or part of a specified text string. If you want to match a certain pattern of characters within a text string, use the text filter options Begins With, Ends With, or Contains operators to filter a text field based on the characters the string starts with, ends with, or includes. The following are some text fields that can be applied to names and addresses:

- To match names like Smith, Smithe, or Smythe, use the Begins With text filter, matching all names which start with "Sm."

- To match names like Robertson, Anderson, Dawson, or Gibson, apply the Ends With text filter, matching all names that end with "son."

- To match addresses that share a common street name like 101 East Main St., 45B West Main St., or 778 West Main St., apply the Contains text filter, matching all street address containing "Main."

For more advanced text filters, you can use wildcard characters, which are symbols that match a character pattern. The ? character represents any single character and the * character represents any series of characters. For example, a text filter based on the criteria "Will?" will match any name starting with "Wil" followed by 0 or 1 character, like Will, Wills, or Wille, but not Williams. A text file based on the criteria "Wil*son" will match any name that starts with "Wil" and ends with "son" and has 0 or more characters in-between such as Wilson, Wilkerson, and Williamson.

## Clearing Filters

**Tip**

If you want to link the pasted records to the original data range, use the Paste Link option when pasting the selection.

After you have narrowed down a data range to a select few records, you can copy the data in the data range by selecting the visible rows and columns and pasting the selection to a new worksheet or workbook. This pastes only the selected records, ignoring any hidden rows or columns in the selection.

Once you have the information you need from the filtered data range, you can clear all the filters, revealing any hidden rows and columns. You'll clear the date filters from the employees list.

### To clear all the filters from the employees list:

1. On the Data tab, in the Sort & Filter group, click the **Clear** button to remove all the filters. All the records are redisplayed in the worksheet.

2. In the Sort & Filter group, click the **Filter** button. The filter buttons are removed from the field name cells in the worksheet.

If you want to clear only one filter out of multiple filters, click the filter button for that field, and then click Clear Filter on the filter menu.

## Applying an Advanced Filter

Filter buttons are limited to combining fields using the AND logical operator. For example, you searched records for employees in the Chicago office AND working in the IT or R& D departments AND hired during 2024 AND having a base salary of at least $90,000. If any one of those conditions is not met, the record fails the search criteria. You cannot use the filter buttons to create filters that combine fields with the OR logical operator, such as a filter that shows employees who work in the Chicago office (regardless of salary) OR make at least $90,000 a year (regardless of location).

**Advanced filtering** provides a way of writing more complicated filter criteria that involve expressions that combine fields using the AND and OR logical operators. To write an advanced filter, you must define a **criteria range** that lays out the specifications of the filter. Criteria ranges are placed in a table with the following structure:

1. Field names are listed in the first row of the table and must exactly match the field names from the data range. A field name can be repeated in the table.

2. Criteria for each field are listed in subsequent rows of the table.

3. Criteria within the same row are combined using the AND logical operator.

4. Criteria in different rows are combined using the OR logical operator.

Figure 6-23 show an example of a criteria range that contains three criteria entered in three rows.

**Figure 6-23** **Criteria range with three conditions**

employees in the Chicago Marketing department with base salaries between $70,000 and $80,000

| | A | B | C | D | E | F | G |
|---|---|---|---|---|---|---|---|
| 1 | OFFICE | DEPT | BASE SALARY | BASE SALARY | HIRE DATE | HIRE DATE | |
| 2 | Chicago | Marketing | >= 70000 | <= 80000 | | | |
| 3 | Dallas | | | | >=1/1/2024 | <=6/30/2024 | |
| 4 | Boston | | >=100000 | | | | |
| 5 | | | | | | | |

employees in the Boston office with base salaries greater than or equal to $100,000

employees in the Dallas office hired between 1/1/2024 and 6/30/2024

Three groups of employees would be matched by this advanced filter:

1. Employees in the Chicago Marketing department with base salaries between $70,000 and $80,000.

2. Employees in the Dallas office hired between 1/1/2024 and 6/30/2024.

3. Employees in the Boston office with a base salary of $100,000 or more.

Advanced filters can filter the data records in place as was done with the filter buttons or they can be used to copy records matching the filter criteria to a new location. If you copy the filtered records, all the columns from the data range satisfying the criteria will be copied in their current order and format. The copied values are not linked to the original values, so if you change your data values or the search criteria, you will have to copy the values again.

# Reference

## Applying an Advanced Filter

- Create a criteria range in which the field names are in the first row, criteria for each field are listed in subsequent rows, criteria within the same row are combined with the AND operator, and criteria in different rows are combined with the OR operator.
- On the Data tab, in the Sort & Filter group, click the Advanced button.
- Specify whether to filter the data in place or copy to another location.
- In the List range box, specify the range containing the data values. In the Criteria range box, specify the range containing the criteria.
- Click OK to apply the advanced filter.

Jacek has a colleague who wants a list of the employees in the Dallas accounting department with base salaries between $60,000 and $70,000 or employees in the Denver accounting department with base salaries between $80,000 and $90,000. You will use an advanced filter to find records satisfying either of these criteria.

**To enter the criteria range for an advanced filter:**

▶ **1.** Open the **NP_EX_6-2.xlsx** workbook located in the **Excel6 > Module** folder included with your Data Files and then save the workbook as **NP_EX_6_Filters** in the location specified by your instructor.

▶ **2.** In the **Documentation** sheet, enter your name in cell B3 and the date in cell B4.

▶ **3.** Go to the **Filters** worksheet. Jacek has already entered the field names for this advanced filter in this sheet.

▶ **4.** In cell **A6**, type **Dallas** as the office to include in the filter, press **TAB**, type **Accounting** in cell B6 as the department to include, press **TAB**, type **>=60000** in cell C6 as the minimum base salary to include, press **TAB**, type **<=70000** in cell D6 as the maximum base salary to include, and then press **ENTER**. The first row of the criteria range will filter the employee records to display only employees in the Dallas office who work in the Accounting department and have a base salary between $60,000 and $70,000.

▶ **5.** In the second row of the criteria range, type **Denver** in cell A7, press **TAB**, type **Accounting** in cell B7, press **TAB**, type **>=80000** in cell C7, press **TAB**, type **<=90000** in cell D7, and then press **ENTER**. See Figure 6–24.

| Figure 6–24 | Criteria range for matching accounting employees |

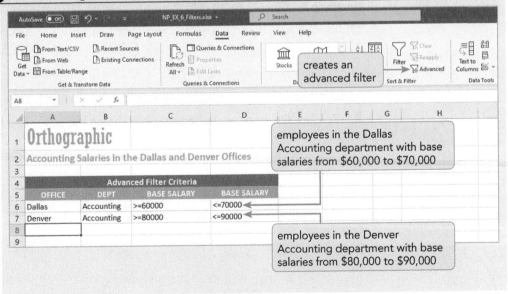

Next you will use an advanced filter to copy the records that match these criteria from the Employees worksheet in the NP_6_Ortho workbook to the Filters worksheet in the NP_6_Filters workbook.

## To copy the employee data with an advanced filter:

1. On the ribbon, click the **Data** tab, and then in the Sort & Filter group, click the **Advanced** button. The Advanced Filter dialog box opens.

2. Click the **Copy to another location** option button to copy matching records from the data range, and then press **TAB** to make the List range box active.

3. Go to the **Employees** worksheet in the **NP_EX_6_Ortho** workbook, click cell **A4**, and then press **CTRL+SHIFT+SPACEBAR** to select the entire data range. The external reference [NP_EX_6_Ortho.xlsx]Employees!$A$4:$M$534 appears in the List range box.

4. Press **TAB** to make the Criteria Range box active.

5. Select the range **A5:D7** containing the advanced filter criteria. The 3-D reference Filters!$A$5:$D$7 appears in the Criteria range box.

6. Press **TAB** to make the Copy to box active, and then click cell **A9** to specify the location for inserting the copied records. See Figure 6–25.

| Figure 6–25 | Advanced Filter dialog box |
| --- | --- |

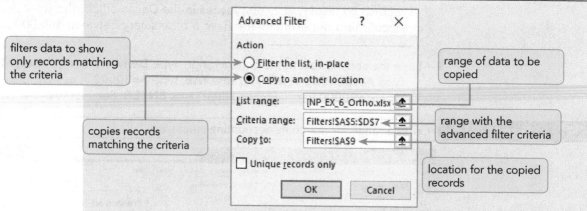

filters data to show only records matching the criteria

range of data to be copied

copies records matching the criteria

range with the advanced filter criteria

location for the copied records

7. Click **OK** to copy the records that match the advanced filter criteria. See Figure 6–26.

| Figure 6–26 | Advanced filter results |
|---|---|

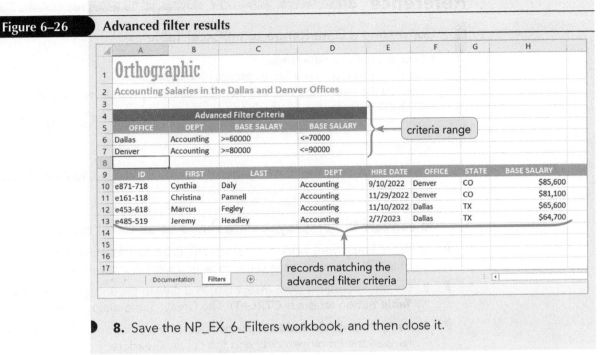

> **8.** Save the NP_EX_6_Filters workbook, and then close it.

Four employees match the specified criteria: Marcus Fegley and Jeremy Headley in the Dallas Accounting department, and Cynthia Daly and Christina Pannell in the Denver Accounting department.

# Creating an Excel Table

So far, you have relied on Excel to recognize that a range of cells with labels in the first row and data values in subsequent rows contained fields and records to be analyzed. To explicitly indicate that a range contains fields and records, you can create a structured range of data also known as an Excel table.

## Converting a Range to a Table

An Excel table is a range of data that is treated by Excel as a single object that can be managed independently from other data in the workbook. Excel tables support several features that are not available with data ranges, including:

- Sorting and filtering tools built into the table itself
- Table styles to format different features of the table, including banded rows and columns
- Automatic insertion of a totals row containing summary statistics for each field, which update as records are inserted or deleted
- Calculated values that use field names rather than cell references to make formulas easier to write and understand
- Named references to different parts of the table structure, including table columns, total rows, and header rows

Almost anything you can do with a data range, such as filtering and sorting, you can do with an Excel table. The main exception is that you *cannot* add subtotals to an Excel table because the table structure of field and records must be preserved, which doesn't allow for the insertion of subtotal rows.

# Reference

## Converting a Data Range to an Excel Table

- Click any cell in a data range.
- On the Insert tab, in the Tables group, click Tables.
- Confirm the data range and whether your data range contains headers.
- Click OK to create the Excel table.

Jacek asks you to convert the employee data to an Excel table. You'll do that now.

### To convert the employee data range to an Excel table:

1. In the Employees worksheet of the NP_EX_6_Ortho workbook, click cell **A4** to select a cell within the data range you want to convert to an Excel table.

2. On the ribbon, click the **Insert** tab, and then in the Tables group click the **Table** button (or press **CTRL+T**). The Create Table dialog box opens.

3. Verify that **=$A$4:$M$534** is specified as the data range. This range contains all the employee data and the column headers.

4. Verify that the **My tables has headers** check box is selected. This generates field names based on the labels in the first row of the selected range.

5. Click **OK** to convert the data range to a table. Filter buttons are added to each field name and banded rows distinguish one row from the next. The Table Design tab appears on the ribbon, which includes commands for formatting and analyzing the Excel table.

6. Click cell **A4** to remove highlighting from the entire table. See Figure 6–27.

Figure 6–27    Employees data converted to an Excel table

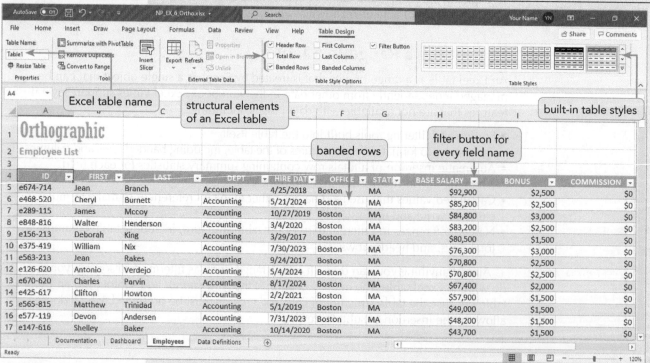

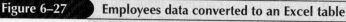

7. Scroll down the Employees worksheet. As you scroll further down the list, the field names replace the column letters, eliminating the need for freeze panes to keep the field names in view.

An Excel table has the following structural elements:

- **Header row**—The first row of the table containing the field names
- **Total row**—A row at the bottom of the table containing summary statistics for selected fields
- **First column**—The leftmost column of the table
- **Last column**—The rightmost column of the table
- **Banded rows**—The odd- and even-numbered rows of the table formatted differently to make records easier to distinguish
- **Banded columns**—The odd- and even-numbered columns of the table formatted differently to make fields easier to distinguish
- **Filter buttons**—Buttons next to each field name for filtering and sorting the table data

**Tip**

Include "Table" or "Tbl" as part of the table name to distinguish Excel tables from named ranges and other workbook objects.

An Excel table is automatically assigned a name that can be referenced in any formula. The first table is named Table1, the next is named Table2, and so forth. You can rename any table with a more meaningful and descriptive name. Table names must start with a letter or an underscore but can use any combination of letters, numbers, and underscores for the rest of the name. Table names cannot include spaces.

Jacek wants a more descriptive name for this table. You will rename Table1 as Employees_Tbl.

**To rename the Table1 Excel table:**

1. With the table still selected, on the ribbon, click the **Table Design** tab, if necessary.

2. In the Properties group, click the **Table Name** box.

3. Type **Employees_Tbl** as the new name, and then press **ENTER**. The Excel table is renamed.

**Tip**

You can edit the properties of the Excel table name using the Name Manager.

An Excel table name is added to the Name box with global scope, so you can go to an Excel table from any location in the workbook by selecting the table's name from the Name box just as you would for global named ranges. To convert an Excel table back to a data range, click the Convert to Range button in the Tools group on the Table Design tab.

## Using Table Styles

Because an Excel table is composed of structural elements, you can apply styles to different parts of the table. For example, you can create a special style for the table's first or last columns or the header row containing the field names. Excel also includes a gallery of built-in table styles that can be used to apply a professional look to the table. Jacek wants you to change the Excel table style to make it easier to read.

**To apply styles to the Employees_Tbl table:**

1. On the Table Design tab, in the Table Style Options group, click the **First Column** and **Last Column** check boxes to select those table elements.

2. Scroll through the worksheet and verify that values for the ID field in column A and the Eval Score field in column M are displayed in bold.

3. In the Table Style Options group, click the **First Column** and **Last Column** check boxes to deselect them. The boldface style applied to those two columns is removed.

4. In the Table Style Options group, click the **Banded Rows** check box to deselect it, and remove banded rows from the table. The table is harder to read this way, so Jacek wants you to add the banded rows back to the table.

5. Click the **Banded Rows** check box again to select it and add banded rows back to the table.

6. Click the **Filter Button** check box to remove the filter buttons from the Excel table, and then click the **Filter Button** check box again to redisplay them.

**Tip**

To remove table styles, click Clear in the Table Styles gallery.

7. In the Table Styles group, click the **More** button in the Table Styles gallery to display different styles that can be applied to the table.

8. Point to different styles in the Table Styles gallery. Live Previews shows how the Employees_Tbl table appears with those styles. See Figure 6–28.

**Figure 6–28    Live Preview of the Employees_Tbl table with a table style**

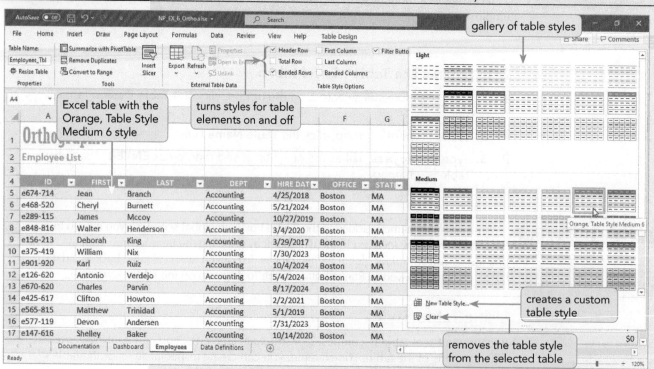

9. In the Table Styles gallery, click **Orange, Table Style Medium 6** to apply it to the Employees_Tbl table.

Table styles do not, by default, override the formatting applied to individual cells. So, if you format a cell or range those formats will be unaffected by your choice of table styles. To override a cell format with the table style, right-click the table style in the gallery, and then click Apply and Clear Formatting on the shortcut menu.

## Adding a Total Row

A useful table element for data analysis is the Total row, which is added to the end of the table after the last data record. The Total row calculates summary statistics, including the average, sum, minimum, and maximum of select fields within the table. The Total row is formatted with values displayed in bold and a double border line separating the data records from the Total row.

Jacek wants you to add summary statistics to the Employees_Tbl table. You'll calculate those statistics by adding a Total row.

### To add a Total Row to the Employees Excel table:

1. On the Table Design tab, in the Table Style Options group, click the **Total Row** check box to select it (or press **CTRL+SHIFT+T**). The Total row is added at the bottom of the table. Excel has already calculated the sum of the values in the Eval Score field.

2. Click the cell in the Total row for the BASE SALARY column. An arrow button appears. You use this button to select a summary statistic.

3. Click the **arrow**, and then click **Sum** in the list of summary statistics. The cell displays $32,803,000, which is the amount that company spent on base salaries.

4. Press **TAB** to move to the Bonus column in the Total row, click the **arrow**, and then click **Sum** in the list of statistics. The cell displays $985,500, which is the amount that Orthographic spent on bonuses.

5. Press **TAB** to move to the Commission column, click the **arrow**, and then click **Sum**. The cell displays $2,413,900, which is the amount the company spent on commissions.

6. Press **TAB** to move to the Personal Days column, click the **arrow**, and then click **Average**. The cell displays about 13.978 as the average number of personal days claimed by the employees.

7. In the Total row, for the Sick Days field, select **Average** from the list of statistics. The cell displays about 6.213 as the average number of sick days.

   The Total row already includes the sum of the Eval Score values, but that does not provide any relevant information to Jacek. Instead, Jacek wants to see the average evaluation score employees received.

8. In the Total row, change the Eval Score column to show **Average** as the statistic. The cell displays about 3.964 as the average evaluation score. See Figure 6–29.

**Figure 6–29**    Total row added to the Employees_Tbl table

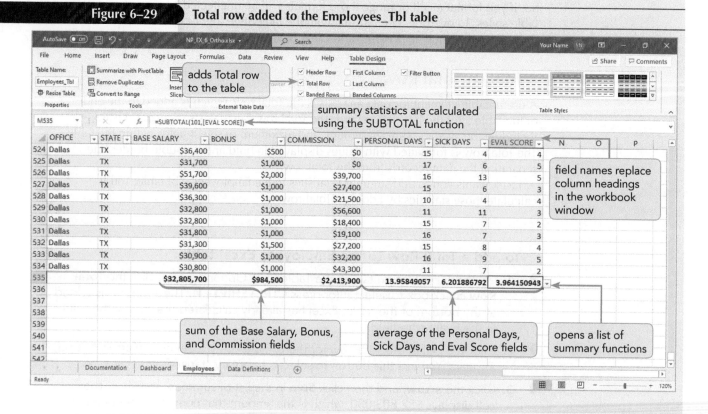

The values in the Total row automatically update to reflect any filters applied to the table. For example, if you filter the table to show only records from the Boston office, the Total row will show the sums and averages of employees from Boston.

## Adding and Deleting Records

When you add or delete records within an Excel table, the table adjusts to the new contents. The format applied to the banded rows updates to accommodate the new data set size. The calculations in the Total row reflect the new data.

Jacek wants you to edit the records in the Employees worksheet. Jean Rakes of the Accounting department in Boston is no longer with the company and Karl Ruiz has taken over that position. So you'll remove the record for Jean Rakes and replace it with a new record for Karl Ruiz.

**To modify the Employees_Tbl table by adding and deleting records:**

1. Scroll up the worksheet, click the **row 11** header containing the record for Jean Rakes.

2. On the ribbon, click the **Home** tab, and then in the Cells group, click the **Delete** button. The record for Jean Rakes is deleted from the table.

3. With row 11 still selected, in the Cells group, click the **Insert** button. A new row is added to the worksheet.

> **4.** In row 11, enter the following information to create the record for Karl Ruiz: **e901-920** in the ID field, **Karl** in the First field, **Ruiz** in the Last field, **Accounting** in the Dept field, **10/4/2024** in the Hire Date field, **Boston** in the Office field, **MA** in the State field, **$73,500** in the Base Salary field, **$1,500** in Bonus field, **$0** in the Commission field, **10** in the Personal Days field, **0** in the Sick Days field, and **4** in the Eval Score field.

In addition to adding or deleting table records, you can also add or delete table fields. You will modify the Employees_Tbl table by adding new fields containing formulas.

## Creating a Calculated Field

So far, all of the fields in the table contain entered values. A field can also contain a formula that references other fields in the table. Such a field is called a **calculated field**, and it updates automatically as other field values in the table change. Instead of cell references, formulas in a calculated field use field names enclosed in brackets as follows:

`[field]`

For example, the following formula adds the values of the Base Salary, Bonus, and Commission fields from all records in a table:

`=[Base Salary]+[Bonus]+[Commission]`

A formula can also include the name of the table by prefacing the field name with the table name as follows:

`table[field]`

The following formula returns the sum of the Base Salary values from all records in the Employees_Tbl table:

`=SUM(Employees_Tbl[Base Salary])`

With Excel tables, you enter the formula in only one record and it automatically applies to all records. This is faster than adding a formula to a data range, in which you copy and paste the formula across a range of cells.

An important symbol in calculated fields is the @ symbol, which refers to the current record or row within the table. The @ symbol is used in formulas that calculate values for each table record. For example, the following formula multiplies the value of the SalesPrice field by the UnitSold field within the table's current row:

`=[@SalesPrice]*[@UnitsSold]`

Jacek wants to add the Full Name field to the Employees_Tbl table. The Full Name field will display each employee's full name in the format *Last, First* using the formula:

`=[@Last] & ", " & [@First]`

The & symbol combines two text strings into one. You'll create the calculated field.

**To add the Full Name calculated field to the Employees_Tbl table:**

> **1.** Scroll up to the top of the worksheet, click the **Column D** header.

> **2.** On the Home tab, in the Cells group, click the **Insert** button. A new field named "Column1" is added to the table between the Last and Dept fields.

> **3.** Click cell **D4**, type **FULL NAME** as the descriptive name of this field, and then press **ENTER**.

> Be sure to enclose references to field or column names of an Excel table in square brackets.

4. In cell **D5**, type **=[@** to begin the structural reference. One advantage of Excel tables is that a list of field names appears as you type a formula. See Figure 6–30.

### Figure 6–30    Field name being entered in a structural reference

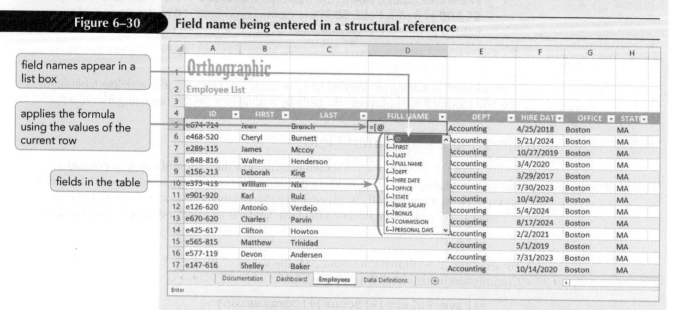

field names appear in a list box

applies the formula using the values of the current row

fields in the table

5. Press **DOWN ARROW** to highlight LAST in the list of field names, and then press **TAB**. The field name is added the structural reference.

6. Type **]** to close the reference to the Last field, press **SPACEBAR**, and then type **& ", " & [@** to enter the next part of the formula. Make sure you include a space directly after the comma. The list of field names in the table appears again after you type the bracket symbol.

7. Select **FIRST** in the list, press **TAB**, and then type **]** to finish the field reference.

8. Press **ENTER** to insert the formula. The formula applies to all the table records within Full Name field. See Figure 6–31.

### Figure 6–31    Values displayed for the Full Name calculated field

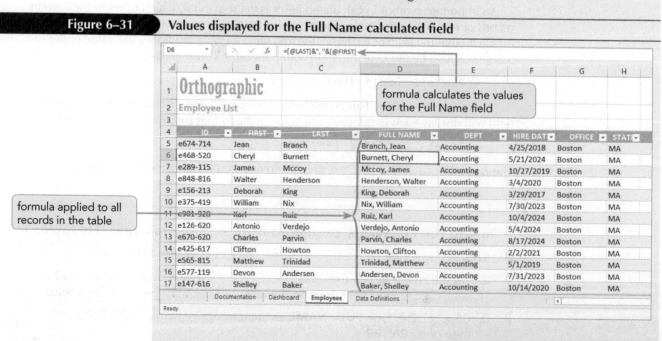

formula calculates the values for the Full Name field

formula applied to all records in the table

Jacek wants you to create a calculated field to display the year the employee was hired. You can extract the year value from a date using the YEAR function.

**To add the Hire Year field to the Employees_Tbl table:**

1. Click the **Column G** header, and then on the Home tab, in the Cells group, click the **Insert** button.

2. Click cell **G4**, type **HIRE YEAR** as the field name, and then press **ENTER**.

3. In cell **G5**, enter the formula **=YEAR([@[HIRE DATE]])** to extract the year value from the current row's Hire Date field, and then press **ENTER**. Excel displays the year values in date format, so they erroneously appear as 1905 dates. You'll reformat the values using the General format.

4. Press **CTRL+SPACEBAR** to select all the data records in the HIRE YEAR column.

5. On the Home tab, in the Number group, click the **Number Format arrow**, and then click **General**. The year value appears for each record.

6. Scroll back to the top of the worksheet and click cell **G5**.

**Tip**

You can select all the fields within a data row by pressing SHIFT+SPACEBAR.

## Structural References and Excel Tables

References to fields and elements in an Excel table are called **structural references** and are enclosed within square brackets [ ]. You've already seen a single field entered using the structural reference [field]. Structural references also exist for other parts of the table. For example, the header row is referenced with the expression [#Headers] and the Totals row is referenced with the expression [#Totals]. Structural references can also be nested inside one another. This expression uses nested structural references to reference a group of fields in the current row of the Excel table

[@[fieldFirst]:[fieldLast]]

where *fieldFirst* is the first field in the group and *fieldLast* is the last. For example, you can calculate the sum of the values in the Base Salary through Commission fields for the current row, including any fields between these two, with the formula

=SUM([@[Base Salary]:[COMMISSION]])

If you omit the @ symbol, the SUM function calculates the sum of the fields across all rows in the table.

Structural references are a powerful feature of Excel tables, but the syntax can be challenging. A simple way to enter a formula involving structural references is to select the fields with your mouse and let Excel enter the formula for you.

Jacek wants you to create a calculated field named Wages that calculates the sum of the Base Salary, Bonus, and Commission field for each employee record.

**To add the Wages field to the Employees_Tbl table:**

1. Click the **Column M** header, and then on the Home tab, in the Cells group, click the **Insert** button.

2. Click cell **M4**, type **WAGES** as the new field name, and then press **ENTER**.

3. In cell **M5**, type **=SUM(** to begin the formula.

4. Use your mouse to select the range **J5:L5**. Excel inserts the structural reference Employees_Tbl[@[BASE SALARY]:[COMMISSION]] to reference the Base Salary through Commission fields for the current employee record.

**5.** Type **)** to end the formula, and then press **ENTER**. The formula =SUM(Employees_Tbl[@[BASE SALARY]:[COMMISSION]]) is entered for every record, calculating every employees total wages. See Figure 6–32.

| Figure 6–32 | Calculated fields added to the Employees table |
|---|---|

M6    ▾  :  ✕  ✓  *fx*  =SUM(Employees_Tbl[@[BASE SALARY]:[COMMISSION]])  ◄

> year extracted from the Hire Date field using =YEAR([@[HIRE DATE]])

> formula calculates the values for the Wages field

> sum of the Base Salary through Commission fields calculated for each record

| | HIRE DATE | HIRE YEAR | OFFICE | STATE | BASE SALARY | BONUS | COMMISSION | WAGES | PERSONAL DAYS | SICK DAYS |
|---|---|---|---|---|---|---|---|---|---|---|
| 5 | 4/25/2018 | 2018 | Boston | MA | $92,900 | $2,500 | $0 | $95,400 | 15 | 6 |
| 6 | 5/21/2024 | 2024 | Boston | MA | $85,200 | $2,500 | $0 | $87,700 | 15 | 4 |
| 7 | 10/27/2019 | 2019 | Boston | MA | $84,800 | $3,000 | $0 | $87,800 | 17 | 3 |
| 8 | 3/4/2020 | 2020 | Boston | MA | $83,200 | $2,500 | $0 | $85,700 | 18 | 6 |
| 9 | 3/29/2017 | 2017 | Boston | MA | $80,500 | $1,500 | $0 | $82,000 | 13 | 9 |
| 10 | 7/30/2023 | 2023 | Boston | MA | $76,300 | $3,000 | $0 | $79,300 | 10 | 3 |
| 11 | 10/4/2024 | 2024 | Boston | MA | $73,500 | $1,500 | $0 | $75,000 | 10 | 0 |
| 12 | 5/4/2024 | 2024 | Boston | MA | $70,800 | $2,500 | $0 | $73,300 | 10 | 4 |
| 13 | 8/17/2024 | 2024 | Boston | MA | $67,400 | $2,000 | $0 | $69,400 | 13 | 7 |
| 14 | 2/2/2021 | 2021 | Boston | MA | $57,900 | $1,500 | $0 | $59,400 | 12 | 5 |
| 15 | 5/1/2019 | 2019 | Boston | MA | $49,000 | $1,500 | $0 | $50,500 | 13 | 7 |
| 16 | 7/31/2023 | 2023 | Boston | MA | $48,200 | $1,500 | $0 | $49,700 | 10 | 6 |
| 17 | 10/14/2020 | 2020 | Boston | MA | $43,700 | $1,500 | $0 | $45,200 | 15 | 8 |

Documentation | Dashboard | **Employees** | Data Definitions | ⊕

Ready    ▦  ▣  ▯  —  —  +  120%

**6.** Save the workbook.

Excel automatically updates formulas that involve structural references to reflect any changes made to the workbook. For example, if you change a field name any formula referencing that field will update automatically to use the new name.

## Proskills

### Problem Solving: Data Ranges vs. Excel Tables

As you've seen, you can do a great deal with data entered as either a data range or an Excel table. For managing a data set, Excel tables are much better than data ranges. Almost everything you can do with a data range, you can do with an Excel table. The only exception is subtotal rows, which you cannot add to an Excel table.

But Excel tables do even more than data ranges. In Excel tables, you can work with the structure of the data itself rather than with individual cells. This lets you create formulas that are easy to interpret because they use field names rather than cell references. Also, you can format different parts of the table with styles that update automatically as you add and delete rows in the table structure. The table structure itself helps to ensure data accuracy by preventing common data entry errors such as mistyping a cell reference. Finally, Excel tables are more easily read by other applications such as the Microsoft Access database program and the Microsoft Power BI data analytics service.

Despite these advantages, you do not want to replace every data range with an Excel table. Some data cannot be laid out in a table format and lack the structure that Excel tables require. You may find it more comfortable to work with data ranges and references, at least until you are more familiar with the table structure. But don't overlook Excel tables as a solution for data management challenges. The more Excel tools you master, the more you can accomplish for your company and organization.

In this session, you worked with Excel tables to analyze employee data for Jacek. In the next session, you will use slicers to create an interactive dashboard that Jacek can use to quickly and easily generate reports on the employee data.

# Review

## Session 6.2 Quick Check

1. What happens to worksheet rows that do not match the filter criteria? What happens to the data they contain?
2. When multiple filter buttons are used with a data range, how are criteria in different fields combined?
3. When would you use an advanced filter in place of the filter buttons?
4. What happens to banded rows in an Excel table when you insert or delete a row?
5. What is the reference to the Income field from the Employees table?
6. What is the formula to calculate the average of the Income field from the Employees table?
7. What is the structural reference to the table header row?

# Session 6.3 Visual Overview:

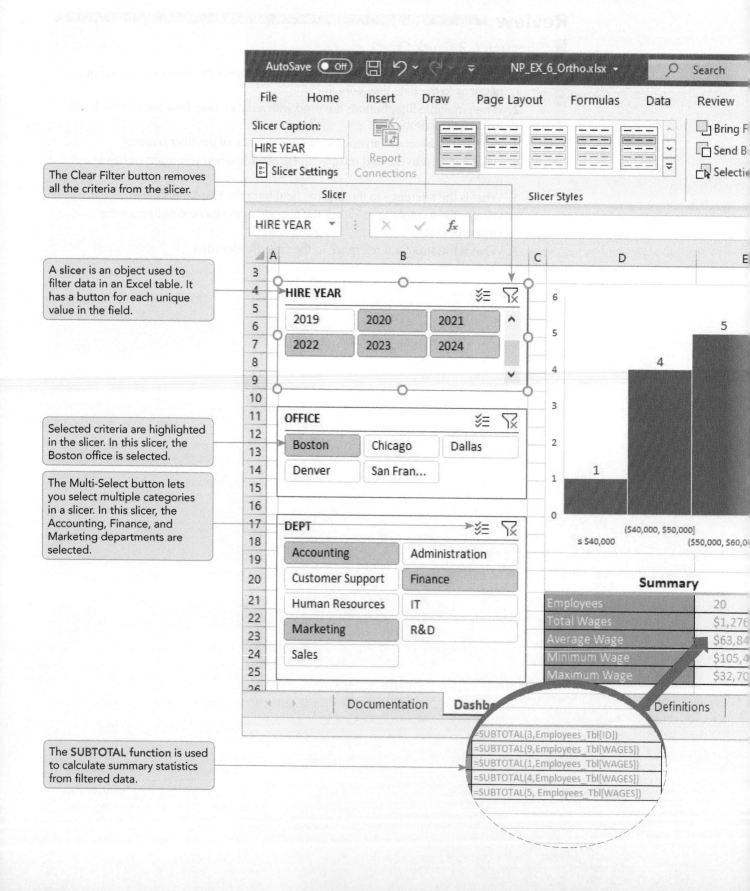

The Clear Filter button removes all the criteria from the slicer.

A slicer is an object used to filter data in an Excel table. It has a button for each unique value in the field.

Selected criteria are highlighted in the slicer. In this slicer, the Boston office is selected.

The Multi-Select button lets you select multiple categories in a slicer. In this slicer, the Accounting, Finance, and Marketing departments are selected.

The **SUBTOTAL** function is used to calculate summary statistics from filtered data.

# Slicers and Dashboards

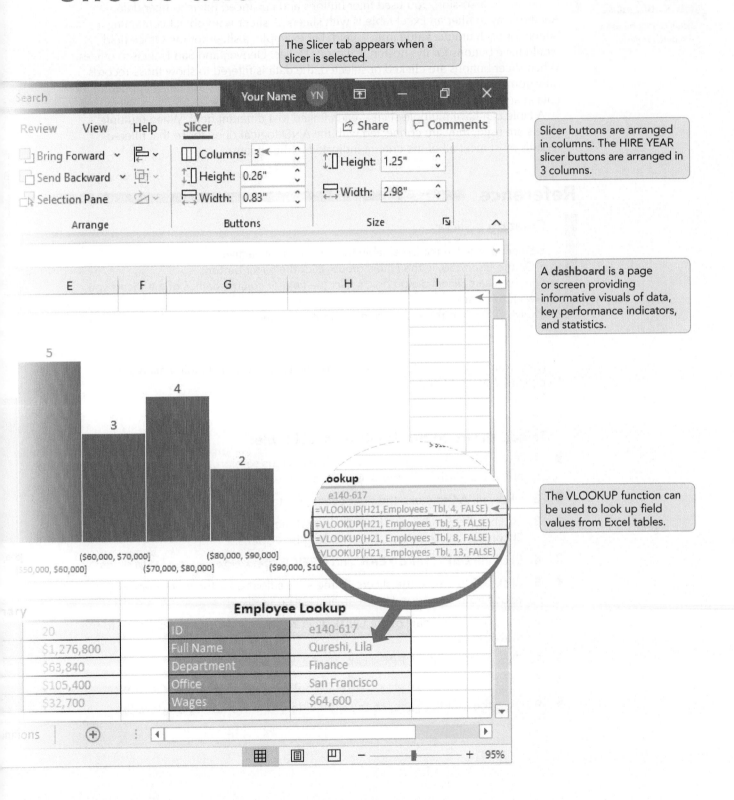

The Slicer tab appears when a slicer is selected.

Slicer buttons are arranged in columns. The HIRE YEAR slicer buttons are arranged in 3 columns.

A dashboard is a page or screen providing informative visuals of data, key performance indicators, and statistics.

The VLOOKUP function can be used to look up field values from Excel tables.

=VLOOKUP(H21,Employees_Tbl, 4, FALSE)
=VLOOKUP(H21, Employees_Tbl, 5, FALSE)
=VLOOKUP(H21, Employees_Tbl, 8, FALSE)
=VLOOKUP(H21, Employees_Tbl, 13, FALSE)

**Employee Lookup**

| ID | e140-617 |
|---|---|
| Full Name | Qureshi, Lila |
| Department | Finance |
| Office | San Francisco |
| Wages | $64,600 |

# Filtering Data with Slicers

In the previous session, you used filter buttons and advanced filters to filter data. Another way to filter an Excel table is with slicers. A slicer is an object containing a button for each unique value from a field. For example, a slicer for the Office field would have buttons for the Boston, Chicago, Dallas, Denver, and San Francisco offices. When slicer buttons are clicked or selected, the data is filtered to show those records only from the selected buttons. Slicers make it clear what filters are being applied to the data at any moment.

A table can have multiple slicers, each linked to a different field. When multiple slicers are used, they are connected with the AND logical operator so that filtered records must meet all of the criteria indicated in the slicers.

## Reference

### Creating a Slicer

- Select any cell in the Excel table to make the table active.
- On the Insert tab, in the Filters group, click the Slicer button.
- In the Insert Slicers dialog box, select the field or column names of the slicers you want to create.
- Click OK to add the slicers to the current worksheet.

Jacek wants you to create three slicers for the Employees_Tbl table linked to the Dept, Hire Year, and Office fields.

### To add slicers to the Employees_Tbl table:

1. If you took a break at the end of the previous session, make sure the NP_EX_6_Ortho workbook is open and the Employees worksheet is active.

2. Click cell **A4** to make the Employees_Tbl table active.

3. On the ribbon, click the **Insert** tab, and then in the Filters group, click the **Slicer** button. The Insert Slicers dialog box opens.

4. Click the **DEPT**, **HIRE YEAR**, and **OFFICE** check boxes in the list of fields.

5. Click **OK** to create the slicers. Three slicers float over the worksheet with values from the Dept, Hire Year, and Office fields.

6. Point to a blank part of the DEPT slicer to change the pointer changes to the Move pointer ⛶.

7. Click and drag the DEPT slicer cell over cell **A1**.

8. Drag the HIRE YEAR slicer to the right of the DEPT slicer over cell **C1**.

9. Drag the OFFICE slicer to the right side of the workbook window. See Figure 6–33.

**Figure 6–33**    Slicers added to the Employees_Tbl table

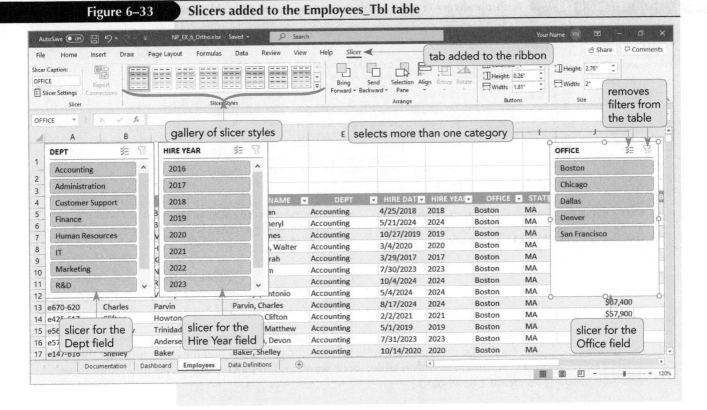

Each slicer shows the unique values for the selected field. The field name appears in the slicer title bar along with two buttons. The Multi-Select button ⌕ lets you select multiple slicer buttons. The Clear Filter button ⌕ clears the slicer filters from the table. When a slicer is selected, the Slicer tab appears on the ribbon. You use this tab to format slicers.

Jacek wants to see only those employees hired in the Denver Customer Support department from 2021 through 2024. You will use the three slicers to filter the Employees_Tbl table.

### To filter the Employees_Tbl table using slicers:

▶ **1.** In the DEPT slicer, click **Customer Support** to show only those employee records from the Customer Support department. Only 27 of the 530 records match this criterion.

▶ **2.** In the HIRE YEAR slicer, click the **Multi-Select** button ⌕ (or press **ALT+S**) so you can select multiple field categories.

▶ **3.** Click the **2016**, **2017**, **2018**, **2019**, and **2020** buttons to deselect them from the filter, leaving the 2021 through 2024 buttons selected. The number of found records reduces to 21.

▶ **4.** In the Office slicer, click the **Denver** button. Six employees match the filter criteria. Notice that the 2016 through 2019 buttons in the HIRE YEAR slicer are grayed out because they have no matching records in the table. The Denver office opened in 2020, so no employee records exist before that year. See Figure 6–34.

Figure 6–34    **Multiple slicers created to filter the Employees_Tbl table data**

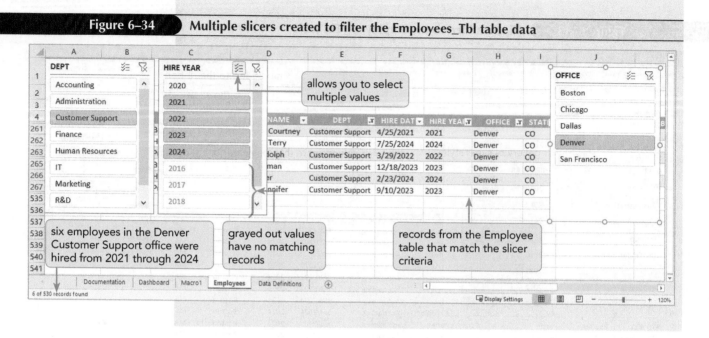

The slicers obscure much of the table data, making it difficult to read the records. Slicers can be moved to anywhere within the workbook and they will still filter the data records from their linked table. Jacek wants you to move these slicers to another sheet to create a dashboard.

## Insight

### Choosing Between Slicers and Filter Buttons

Slicers and filter buttons are two ways to filter data in an Excel table. Use slicers when data has a few distinct values that can be easily listed within the slicer. Also, use slicers when you want to perform data from a table on another worksheet.

Use filter buttons when you need to use criteria filters involving text, date, or numeric values. For example, use filter buttons to filter for records that fall within a specified time interval or for a specific range of incomes or expenses.

## Creating a Dashboard

A dashboard is a page or screen providing informative visuals of data, key performance indicators, and statistics. Most dashboards contain interactive tools to help users explore data under different conditions and assumptions. The term *dashboard* evokes the idea of an automobile dashboard that presents important information to the driver that can be quickly interpreted. Slicers are often used in dashboards because they provide a quick way to filter data.

Jacek included a Dashboard worksheet in the workbook. He wants you to place the three slicers you created in the Employees worksheet on this sheet. You'll cut and paste those slicers now.

### To move the slicers for the Employees_Tbl table to the Dashboard worksheet:

1. Click the **HIRE YEAR** slicer to select it. Sizing handles in the corners and along the sides of the selected object.

2. On the ribbon, click the **Home** tab, and then in the Clipboard group, click the **Cut** button (or press **CTRL+X**).

**Tip**

You can cut and paste slicers between worksheets; you cannot cut and paste slicers between workbooks.

3. Go to the **Dashboard** worksheet, click cell **B4** as the location for pasting the slicer, and then in the Clipboard group, click the **Paste** button (or press **CTRL+V**). The HIRE YEAR slicer is pasted into the worksheet.

4. Hold down **ALT** as you drag the lower-right sizing handle of the slicer to the lower-right corner of cell **B9**. The slicer resizes to cover the range B4:B9.

5. Repeat Steps 1 through 4 to cut and paste the **OFFICE** slicer to cover the range **B11:B15** on the Dashboard worksheet.

6. Repeat Steps 1 through 4 to cut and paste the **DEPT** slicer to cover the range **B17:B25** on the Dashboard worksheet. See Figure 6–35.

| Figure 6–35 | Slicers pasted onto the Dashboard worksheet |

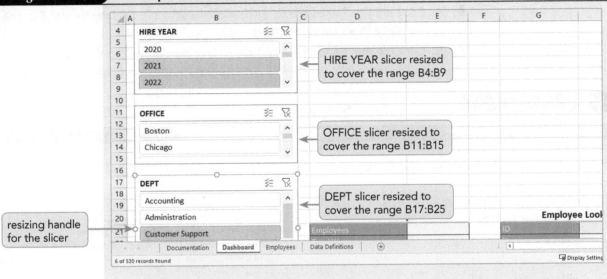

Even though the slicers are on a different worksheet, they will still filter the data in the Employees_Tbl table. Jacek wants you to test the slicers in their new location.

### To test the Employees_Tbl table slicers on the Dashboard worksheet:

1. In the HIRE YEAR slicer, select **2024** to limit the filter to employees hired in 2024.

2. In the OFFICE slicer, select **Chicago** to further limit the filter to employees hired at the Chicago office.

3. In the DEPT slicer, select **Accounting**. The message in the status bar indicates that 4 of 530 records were found.

4. Go to the **Employees** worksheet to view the records for the four employees who were hired in the Chicago Accounting department in 2024.

5. Return to the **Dashboard** worksheet.

## Formatting a Slicer

By default, slicer buttons are arranged in a single column. You can increase the number of the columns by formatting the slicer. Jacek suggest you increase the number of columns for the Hire Year, Office, and Dept slicers so that all of the buttons can be viewed together without needing to use the scroll bar. You will increase the number of columns now.

### To change the number of columns in the slicers:

▶ **1.** Click the title bar of the HIRE YEAR slicer to select it.

▶ **2.** On the ribbon, click the **Slicer** tab, and then in the Buttons group, click the **Columns** box.

▶ **3.** In the Columns box, change the value to **3**. The buttons in the HIRE YEAR slicer are laid out in three columns and three rows.

▶ **4.** Click the title bar of the OFFICE slicer to select it, and then enter **3** in the Columns box in the Buttons group.

▶ **5.** Click the title bar of the DEPT slicer, and then enter **2** in the Columns box. The three slicers now have all buttons visible without scrolling. See Figure 6-36.

**Figure 6-36**    **Formatted slicer layout**

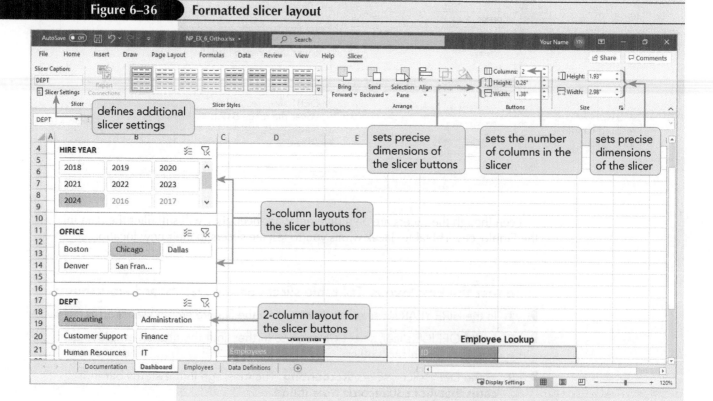

There are other ways to format a slicer's appearance using tools on the Slicer tab. You can set the exact size of the slicer and its buttons using the Height and Width boxes in the Buttons and Size groups. You can change the color scheme by selecting a slicer style from the Slicer Styles gallery. You can change the button order by clicking the Slicer Settings button in the Slicer group and then choosing the button sorting order (or create a custom sorting list) in the Slicer Settings dialog box. You can also change the slicer's title bar text from the field name to one of your own choosing by entering text in the Slicer Caption box in the Slicer group of the Slicer tab.

## Proskills

### Written Communication: Designing a Dashboard

A dashboard is designed to tell a story. It can be a springboard to reports providing more in-depth analysis, but fundamentally a dashboard needs to present useful information at a glance. As you create dashboards, keep in mind the following design tips:

- **Go Big. Go Bold.** Don't be afraid to use extremely large fonts and bright colors for important results. You want the viewer's eyes to be attracted to those results first, and you want those results to be remembered.
- **Start from the Upper-Left Corner.** Most people read from the top to the bottom and left to right, so put your most important information in the upper-left corner where it will be noticed first.
- **Keep It Simple.** Focus on a few key points, and keep the clutter of charts, graphics, and text to a minimum. You can always create additional dashboards.
- **Don't Let Color Overwhelm.** Keep the design of charts and graphics to a few complementary colors and be consistent in their use. Adding too many colors is distracting and reduces the impact of the dashboard.
- **Make It User Friendly.** The use and purpose of interactive tools like slicers and drop-down menus should be clear. You may not have room to explain how to use the dashboard.
- **Be Focused.** Settle on a few key points. If a chart or graphic doesn't relate to that idea, remove it or place it in a different dashboard.

As you design a dashboard, always keep your audience in mind. What are they looking for? The dashboard you present to a sales director might be very different from one you present to a marketing manager or an HR executive. A dashboard is most useful and has the greatest impact when it is tailored to the needs of your audience.

## Using the SUBTOTAL Function

Jacek wants the dashboard to display summary statistics on the employees matched by the slicers. The first summary statistic will count the number of employees listed in the filtered table. You'll use the COUNTA function to count the number of entries in the ID field of the Employees_Tbl table.

### To use the COUNTA function in the dashboard:

1. In each slicer's title bar, click the **Clear Filter** button to clear the filters. All 530 records are displayed in the Employees_Tbl table.

2. Click cell **E21**, and type the formula **=COUNTA(Employees_Tbl[ID])** to count the number of entries in the ID field. As you type the formula, the name of the Excel table and a list of fields within that table appear. You can use the TAB key to select the highlighted names provided by Excel.

3. Press **ENTER**. The formula returns 530, which is the number of records in the Employees_Tbl table.

4. In the OFFICE slicer, click **Boston**. The status bar indicates 105 employee records for the Boston office. However, the value in cell E21 is unchanged and still shows 530 as the number of employees.

Why does the dashboard show the same number of employees after limiting the employee list to the Boston office? The reason is that statistical functions like the COUNTA, AVERAGE, SUM, MAX, and MIN functions are applied to the *entire table*, regardless of any filter criteria. To count only records that match the filter criteria, you use the SUBTOTAL function

SUBTOTAL(*Function_Num, ref1,* [*ref2*], [*ref3*], …)

where *Function_Num* is the number corresponding to a statistical function, *ref1* is a reference to the data to be analyzed, and *ref2*, *ref3*, and so on are optional arguments for additional data references. Figure 6–37 lists some of the function numbers recognized by the SUBTOTAL function.

**Figure 6–37**    **Function numbers of the SUBTOTAL function**

| Function Number | Function | Function Number | Function |
| --- | --- | --- | --- |
| 1 | AVERAGE | 6 | PRODUCT |
| 2 | COUNT | 7 | STDEV |
| 3 | COUNTA | 8 | STDEVP |
| 4 | MAX | 9 | SUM |
| 5 | MIN | 10 | VAR |

**Tip**

To apply the SUBTOTAL function to data with manually hidden rows, add 100 to the function number.

The following formula uses the SUBTOTAL function with function number 3 to apply the COUNTA function only to records in the Employees_Tble table whose ID values match whatever filter criteria has been applied to the table:

=SUBTOTAL(3, Employees_Tbl[ID])

You've already worked with the SUBTOTAL function without realizing it when you had Excel calculate subtotals (refer back to Figure 6–12) and totals (refer back to Figure 6–29) in the Employees_Tbl table. Both calculations used the SUBTOTAL function.

# Reference

### Applying the SUBTOTAL Function

- To apply summary statistics records that match a filter criteria, apply the function

SUBTOTAL(*Function_Num, ref1,* [*ref2*], [*ref3*], …)

where *Function_Num* is an integer representing a statistical function to use in the subtotal calculation, *ref1* is a reference to the data to be analyzed, and *ref2*, *ref3*, etc. are optional arguments for additional data references.
- To calculate SUM from the filtered records of a table, set *Function_Num* to 9.
- To calculate AVERAGE from the filtered records, set *Function_Num* to 1.
- To calculate COUNT from the filtered records, set *Function_Num* to 2.
- To calculate COUNTA from the filtered records, set *Function_Num* to 3.

You'll use the SUBTOTAL function to calculate summary statistics from the Employees_Tbl table based on whatever records are selected the slicers on the dashboard.

## To apply the SUBTOTAL function:

▶ 1. Click cell **E21**, and then type **=SUBTOTAL(** to begin the formula. A list of function numbers for statistical functions appears.

▶ 2. Press **DOWN ARROW** to select 3. - COUNTA from the list, and then press **TAB** to insert 3 into the formula.

> Use the arrow keys or mouse to select the function number to ensure that you use the correct summary statistic.

▶ 3. Type **, Employees_Tbl[ID])** to complete the formula, and then press **ENTER**. The formula returns 105, which is the number of records that match the filter criteria in the slicers.

▶ 4. In cell **E22**, enter the formula **=SUBTOTAL(9, Employees_Tbl[WAGES])** to calculate the sum that Orthographic spends on wages for the 105 employees. The formula returns $7,193,100 as the total wages paid to the 105 employees.

▶ 5. In cell **E23**, enter the formula **=SUBTOTAL(1, Employees_Tbl[WAGES])** to calculate the average of those wages. The formula returns $68,506 as the average wage for Boston employees.

▶ 6. In cell **E24**, enter the formula **=SUBTOTAL(5, Employees_Tbl[WAGES])** to calculate the minimum wage paid to Boston employees. The formula returns $28,400 as the minimum wage.

▶ 7. In cell **E25**, enter the formula **=SUBTOTAL(4, Employees_Tbl[WAGES])** to calculate the maximum wage paid to Boston employees. The formula returns a maximum wage of $120,000. See Figure 6–38.

| Figure 6–38 | Summary statistics for Boston employees |
| --- | --- |

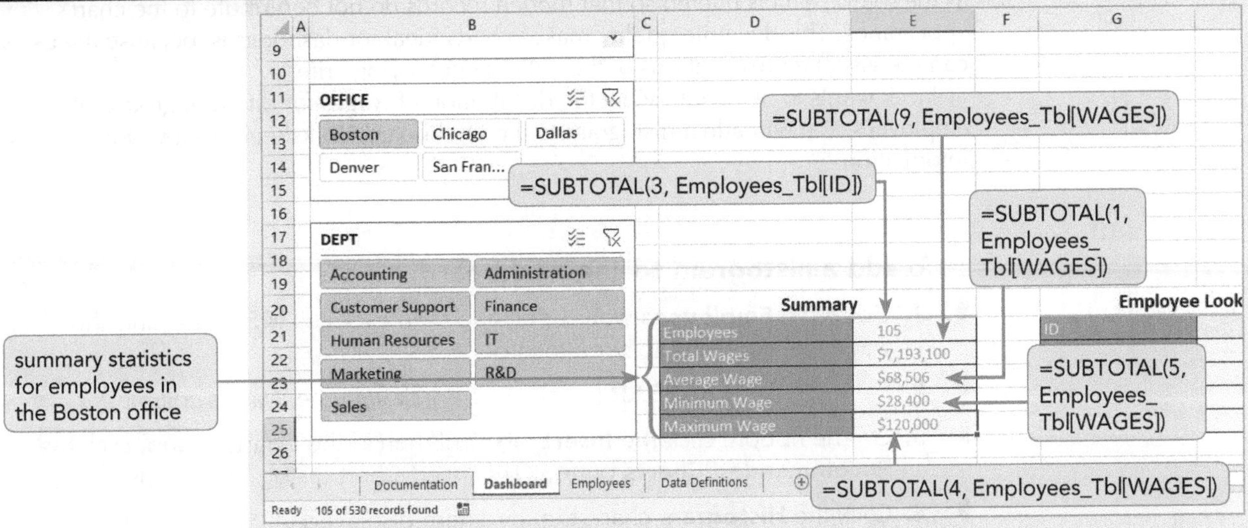

▶ 8. In the DEPT slicer, click **Accounting** to limit the report to only those employees in the Boston Accounting department. Because they use the SUBTOTAL function, the summary statistics in the range E21:E25 update to reflect the new filter criteria. See Figure 6–39.

**Figure 6–39**    Summary of employee wages for the Boston Accounting department

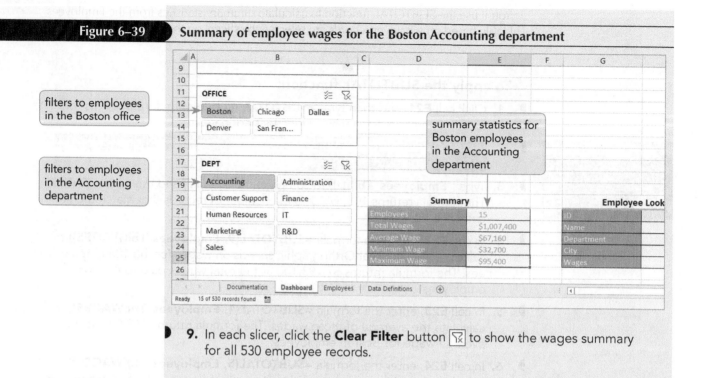

filters to employees in the Boston office

filters to employees in the Accounting department

summary statistics for Boston employees in the Accounting department

**9.** In each slicer, click the **Clear Filter** button 🔽 to show the wages summary for all 530 employee records.

In addition to the summary statistics, dashboards often contain informative charts. You will add charts to the dashboard next.

## Creating Dynamic Charts

Charts based on Excel tables are dynamic, which means they update automatically as the source data is filtered so that hidden records do not contribute to the chart's appearance. This dynamic quality makes charts ideal for dashboards, because the users can see visual representations of the data under varying criteria.

Jacek wants to be able to view the distribution of wages for different groups of employees. You will add a histogram to the Dashboard worksheet to show this information.

### To add a histogram to the dashboard:

**1.** Go to the **Employees** worksheet, and then click cell **M5** containing the wages in the first employee record.

**2.** Press **CTRL+SPACEBAR** to select all the data in the Wages column.

**3.** On the ribbon, click the **Insert** tab, and then in the Charts group, click the **Recommended Charts** button. The Insert Chart dialog box opens.

**4.** Click the **Histogram** chart, the third item displayed in the list of recommended charts, and then click **OK**. The histogram chart is created on the Employees worksheet.

**5.** On the ribbon, click the **Home** tab, and then in the Clipboard group, click the **Cut** button (or press **CTRL+X**).

**6.** Return to the **Dashboard** worksheet, click cell **D4**, and then in the Clipboard group, click the **Paste** button (or press **CTRL+V**) to paste the chart.

7. In the Dashboard worksheet, hold down **ALT** as you move and resize the histogram chart so it covers the range D4:H18. See Figure 6–40.

| Figure 6–40 | Histogram chart of the distribution of employee wages |

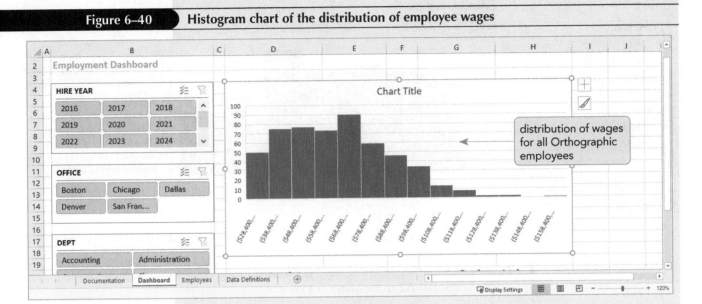

Jacek asks you to remove the chart title and gridlines and to change the bin intervals for the histogram chart. You'll change the axis scale to group the wages in intervals of $10,000 from $40,000 up to $100,000. Wages below or above that interval will be grouped together in the histogram.

### To format the histogram chart:

1. With the chart still selected, click the **Chart Elements** button, and then click the **Chart Title** and **Gridlines** check boxes to deselect them. The chart title and horizontal gridlines disappear from the chart.

2. Click the **Data Labels** check box to add show the number employees in each wage group on the chart.

3. Double-click the labels in the horizontal axis. The Format Axis pane opens.

4. In the Axis Options section, click the **Bin width** option button to set a bin width for the histogram intervals and, if necessary, type **10000** in the Bin width box.

5. Click the **Overflow bin** check box, and then type **100000** in the Overflow bin box.

6. Click the **Underflow bin** check box, and then type **40000** in the Underflow bin box.

7. On the ribbon, click the **Home** tab, and then in the Font group, click the **Font Size arrow** and click **8** to reduce the font size of the horizontal labels to 8 points. See Figure 6–41.

Figure 6-41        Formatted histogram chart

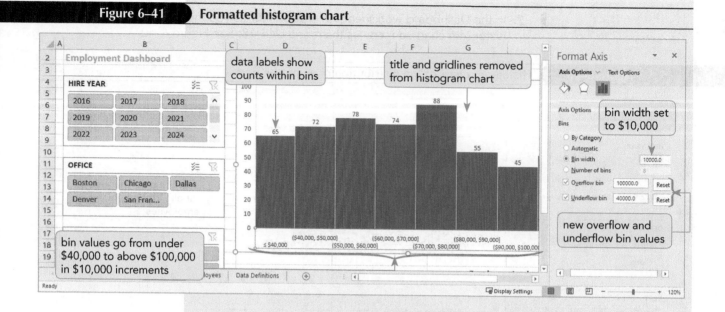

8. In the Format Axis pane, click the **Close** button [X] to close the pane, and then click cell **A2** to deselect the chart.

The histogram chart you created is dynamic and will show the distribution for employees based on the selected criteria. Jacek wants to view the distribution of wages for employees hired in the Finance department of any office in 2024.

### To view the distribution of wages for Finance department employees hired in 2024:

1. In the HIRE YEAR slicer, click the **2024** button to select that year. Only employees hired in 2024 are included in the chart.

2. In the DEPT slicer, click the **Finance** button to select only that category. Only the eight employees hired in 2024 that work in the Finance department are included in the chart. The summary statistics show that the average wage for these eight employees is $56,763. The histogram chart shows that one employee received less than $40,000 in wages and that three employees received from $70,000 to $80,000. The grayed-out Dallas button in the Office slicers indicates that the Dallas office did not hire anyone in its Finance department during 2024. See Figure 6-42.

**Figure 6–42**    Distribution of wages for Finance department employees hired in 2024

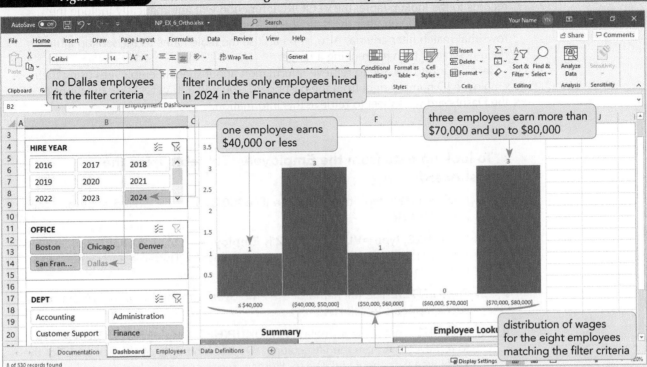

3. In each slicer, click the **Clear Filter** button ⌧ to display results for all Orthographic employees.

Using the slicers on the Dashboard worksheet Jacek can continue to explore the distribution of wages for different groups of employees at Orthographic.

## Insight

### Exploring Boxplots

Another way of showing the distribution of data values is with a boxplot. A boxplot is a schematic diagram of the distribution in which the location of the central 50% of the data is displayed as a box with edges at the 25th and 75th percentiles. Extending beyond the 25th and 75th percentiles are straight lines, or whiskers, that indicate the range of the data values. The median of the data set is displayed as a central line within the box. Extremely small or large values are displayed as open circles beyond the whiskers. A typical boxplot would appear as follows:

Boxplots are extremely useful charts for statisticians who want a quick overview of the data and as a way of identifying unusually small or large data values. You can create a boxplot from the Insert Chart dialog box by selecting the Box and Whisker chart type.

## Looking Up Data with Tables

Excel tables work well as lookup tables for the VLOOKUP function. As you add more records to the lookup table, the VLOOKUP function will automatically include the additional rows. If you filter the data, the lookup table will be restricted only to those rows that match filter criteria. Also, you can use the table name as the lookup table reference rather than referencing a range.

Jacek wants to be able to retrieve information about specific employees using their employee ID number right from the dashboard. You will add VLOOKUP functions to the Dashboard worksheet to retrieve this information.

### To look up data from the Employees_Tbl table from the dashboard:

1. Click cell **H21**, type the employee ID **e850-316** as the lookup entry, and then press **ENTER**.

2. In cell **H22**, type **=VLOOKUP(H21, Employees_Tbl, 4, FALSE)** to locate the record with the ID e850-316 from the Employees_Tbl table and retrieve the data from the fourth column (the Full Name column).

3. Press **ENTER**. The full name of the employee with the ID e850-316, Baros, Jacek, appears in cell H22.

4. In cell **H23**, enter the formula **=VLOOKUP(H21, Employees_Tbl, 5, FALSE)** to retrieve data from the fifth column (Dept) of the Employees_Tbl table for the employee with the ID e850-316. Human Resources is displayed in cell H23.

5. In cell **H24**, enter the formula **=VLOOKUP(H21, Employees_Tbl, 8, FALSE)** to retrieve data from the eighth column (Office) of the Employees_Tbl table for the employee with the ID e850-316. Denver is displayed in cell H24.

6. In cell **H25**, enter the formula **=VLOOKUP(H21, Employees_Tbl, 13, FALSE)** to retrieve data from the thirteenth column (Wages) of the Employees_Tbl table for the employee with the ID e850-316. The value $83,300 is displayed in cell H25. See Figure 6–43.

| Figure 6–43 | Data retrieved for a single employee |
| --- | --- |

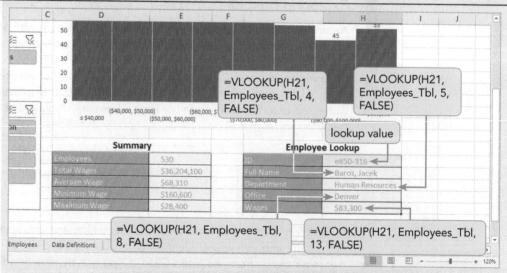

7. In cell **H21**, enter the employee ID **e140-617** to view information on Lila Qureshi and further test the VLOOKUP.

**Trouble?** If the lookup fails to retrieve the employee record, you probably mistyped the employee ID. Re-enter the value in cell H21 making sure you enter the ID correctly.

▶ **8. sam↑** Save the workbook, and then close it.

You've completed your work on the Employee dashboard. With this dashboard, Jacek can quickly retrieve payroll information for different groups of employees. By inserting even more slicers, Jacek can add more factors and depth to that analysis.

# Review

## Session 6.3 Quick Check

**1.** What are two reasons for using slicers rather than filter buttons to filter data?

**2.** What are two reasons for using filter buttons rather than slicers to filter data?

**3.** Can slicers be used with both data ranges and Excel tables?

**4.** Can slicers be moved to any worksheet or external workbook?

**5.** Write a formula to calculate the sum of the filtered values from the Sales Price field in the Sales_Result table.

**6.** Write a formula to calculate the average of the filtered values from the Sales Price field in the Sales_Result table.

**7.** Write a formula to retrieve the value from the third field in the Sales_Result table that exactly matches the lookup value in cell B10.

# Practice

## Review Assignments

**Data File needed for the Review Assignments: NP_EX_6-3.xlsx**

Jacek in the Human Resources department of Orthographic needs to track the hiring process for new recruits, from the initial application stage, through the interview stages, and culminating in a final offer of employment. Jacek compiled information on current candidates for positions in the soon-to-be-opened Atlanta office and wants you to develop reports and summaries of the recruitment efforts. Complete the following:

1. Open the **NP_EX_6-3.xlsx** workbook located in the Excel6 > Review folder included with your Data Files. Save the workbook as **NP_EX_6_Recruits** in the location specified by your instructor.

2. In the Documentation sheet, enter your name and the date in the range B3:B4.

3. Go to the Applications worksheet containing a list of applications made to the Atlanta office for 12 positions. The worksheet lists the dates that each applicant completed each stage of the recruitment process from the date the application was received, through the phone screening, manager interview, onsite interview, offer date, and acceptance date. The value #N/A indicates that the applicant did not pass to that recruitment stage. See the Table Data worksheet for a description of each field.

4. Use conditional formatting to locate records that have a duplicate Applicant ID in the range A5:A1043. Delete the second duplicate record. Do not remove the conditional formatting rule when you are finished.

5. One applicant record is duplicated for all fields except for the Applicant ID field. Use the Remove Duplicates command to remove the duplicate.

6. In the Applications worksheet, show how applicants are tracked through the recruitment process by sorting the data range by the Position field in A to Z order and then by Acceptance Date, Offer Date, Onsite Date, Manager Date, and finally Phone Date fields, with all dates sorted from newest to oldest. The sorted data should show applicants for each position that went farthest last.

7. Filter the data in the Applications worksheet to show only those records for which the value of the Hired field is Yes.

8. Copy the filtered values and paste them into the Hires worksheet starting at cell A4.

9. In the Hires worksheet, do the following:

   a. Sort the data in ascending order of the Position field.

   b. Add subtotal rows at each change in the value of the Position field, showing the average of the Base Salary field within each Position.

   c. Freeze panes at cell F5 so that you can scroll vertically and horizontally while keeping the data labels in view.

10. Return to the Applications worksheet and clear the filter from the data.

11. A colleague of Jacek's wants specific information about five hires to the IT and Marketing departments. Go to the IT and Marketing Hires worksheet and complete the following advanced filter:

    a. Complete the criteria range to create a list of new hires from the IT department with base salaries greater than $70,000 or from the Marketing department with base salaries greater than $60,000.

    b. Run the Advanced Filter using the copy data to another location option. Use the data in the range A4:N1041 of the Applications worksheet as the list range, the range A4:B6 in the IT and Marketing worksheet as criteria range, and cell D4 of the IT and Marketing Hires worksheet as the Copy to cell.

12. Return to the Applications worksheet, convert the data range to an Excel table, and then rename the table using **Recruits** as the name.

13. In the Recruits table, do the following:

    a. Insert a new field named **Full Name** between the Last Name and Position fields.

    b. In the Full Name field, enter the formula **=[@Last Name] & ", " & [@First Name]** to insert the applicants' full names.

c. Insert a new field after the Base Salary field named **Days to Hire** by entering the field name in cell P4.

d. In the Days to Hire field, use your mouse to enter a formula calculating the value of the Acceptance Date field in cell M5 minus the Application Date field in cell G5.

e. Apply the General number format to the result so that the values appear as days rather than dates and then resize the column to make the field name visible.

14. Insert a slicer for the Position field. Move the slicer to the Metrics worksheet and resize it to fit in the range B4:B13. Display the slicer buttons in two columns.

15. In the range E5:E10 of the Metrics worksheet, do the following to count the number of applicants who reach each stage of the recruitment process:

a. In cell E5, use the SUBTOTAL function with the COUNTA function to count the number of entries in the Applicant ID field of the Recruits table.

b. In cell E6, use the SUBTOTAL function with the COUNT function to count the number of values in the Phone Date field.

c. In cell E7, use the SUBTOTAL function with the COUNT function to count the number of values in the Manager Date field.

d. In cell E8, use the SUBTOTAL function with the COUNT function to count the number of values in the Onsite Date field.

e. In cells E9 and E10, use the SUBTOTAL function with the COUNT function to count the number of values in the Offer Date and Acceptance Date fields, respectively.

16. Jacek wants to track certain Key Performance Indexes (KPIs) that indicate the efficiency of the recruitment process. Calculate the following values:

a. In cell E11, calculate the number of applicants for each hire by dividing the value in cell E5 by the value in cell E10.

b. In cell E12, calculate the number of interviews for each hire by dividing the sum of the values in cells E7 and E8 by the value in cell E10.

c. In the range F6:F10, calculate the percent of the original applicants that survive to each step in the process by dividing the number of applicants that made it to each step by the value in cell E5.

d. In the range E5:E10, use conditional formatting to add orange data bars with a gradient fill to the values to show how the number of applicants is trimmed during recruitment.

17. In the Applications worksheet, create a Histogram chart of the data in the range P4:P1041 to the view the distribution of the number of days required for hiring new employees.

18. Do the following to the chart:

a. Move the chart to the Metrics worksheet, and then resize the chart to cover the range H4:M13.

b. Change the chart title to **Days to Hire** and add data labels to the bars in the histogram.

c. In the axis options, change the histogram's Bin width to 5 with an Overflow bin value of 50 and an Underflow bin value of 25.

19. Test the dashboard you created by showing the recruitment statistics for the Programmer, Systems Analyst, and Website Designer positions. The KPIs updated to reflect this subset of the data and the histogram changes to show the distributions of the number of days required to fill those three positions.

20. Save the workbook, and then close it.

# Apply

## Case Problem 1

**Data File needed for this Case Problem: NP_EX_6-4.xlsx**

**Seacation**  Alana Ngata is an inventory manager for Seacation, a major manufacturer and distributor of boating parts and tools. Alana uses Excel to help manage the inventory at Seacation warehouses, ensuring that products remain stocked and resupplied on a timely basis. At the Seacation warehouses, the products are located by row number and bin number. Alana wants a report that indicates how many of the warehouse items need restocking and at what cost. The report also must track restocking needs by row number and bin number. You will create a dashboard that will display the answers that Alana needs. Complete the following:

1. Open the **NP_EX_6-4.xlsx** workbook located in the Excel6 > Case1 folder included with your Data Files. Save the workbook as **NP_EX_6_Seacation** in the location specified by your instructor.

2. In the Documentation sheet, enter your name and the date in the range B3:B4.

3. Alana is concerned that the list of inventory items contains duplicate records. In the Inventory worksheet, use the Remove Duplicates tool to remove records for which every field value is duplicated. Verify that Excel reports that five duplicates are removed.

4. Convert the data range in the Inventory worksheet to an Excel table. Rename the table using **Inventory_Tbl** as the table name.

5. Sort the table by ascending order of the Warehouse, Bin, and Part ID fields.

6. Insert a new field named **Inventory Value** between the Stock Qty and Reorder Qty fields. Calculate the inventory value by using your mouse to enter the formula that multiplies the Unit Cost field (cell E5) by the Stock Qty field (cell F5). If necessary, format the values using the Currency format and resize the column to fit the data.

7. Click cell J4 and add a new field named **Restock** that you'll use to determine which items need to be restocked. Use your mouse to enter an IF function that displays a value of "Yes" if the Stock Qty field (cell F5) is less than or equal to the Reorder Qty field (cell H5) and "No" if it is not.

8. Click cell K4 and add the **Restock Indicator** field. Use your mouse to enter a formula that uses the IF function to display the value 1 if the Restock field (cell J5) equals "Yes" and the value 0 otherwise. Resize the column to fit the data.

9. Click cell L4 and add the **Restock Qty** field. In this field, determine the number of items to order for products that need to be restocked. Use your mouse to enter a formula equal to the Restock Indicator field (cell K5) times the difference between the Restock Level and Stock Qty fields (I5 – F5). Resize the column to fit the data.

10. Click cell M4 and add a new field named **Restock Cost** to calculate how much it will cost to restock the items that need restocking. Use your mouse to enter a formula that multiplies the Restock Qty field (cell L5) by the Unit Cost field (cell E5). Format the calculated values as currency and resize the column to fit the data.

11. Filter the Inventory_Tbl table to show only records where the Restock field equals "Yes." Copy the filtered table and paste it into the Restock List worksheet at cell A4.

12. In the Restock List worksheet, add subtotal rows at each change in the Warehouse field, showing the sum of the Restock Qty and Restock Cost fields.

13. Add a freeze pane to the Restock List worksheet at cell E5.

14. Return to the Inventory worksheet and clear the filter to redisplay all the records in the table.

15. Insert slicers for the Warehouse and Bin fields. Move the slicers to the Report worksheet. Place the Warehouse slicer over the range A4:A7 with 4 columns in the button layout. Place the Bin slicer in the range A9:A16 with 3 columns in the button layout.

16. Calculate the following summary statistics for the inventory data:

    a. In cell D5, apply the SUBTOTAL with the COUNTA function to count the number of records in the Part ID field of the Inventory_Tbl table.

    b. In cell D6, apply the SUBTOTAL function with the SUM function to the Stock Qty field to calculate the quantity of items in the warehouse.

c. In cell D7, apply the SUBTOTAL function with the SUM function to the Inventory Value field to calculate the total value of items in the warehouse.

d. In cell D8, apply the SUBTOTAL function with the SUM function to the Restock Indicator field to calculate the number of items requiring restocking.

e. In cell D9, calculate the difference between cells D5 and D8, returning the total number of items that do not require restocking.

f. In cell D10, apply the SUBTOTAL function with the SUM function to the Restock Cost field to calculate the total cost of restocking items that have low inventory.

17. Insert a pie chart of the data in the range C8:D9 and resize it to cover the range C11:D18. Remove the chart title and add data labels to the pie slices showing the percentage of items that need restocking.

18. Use the slicers to show results for items only in warehouse row 1 and bin 9.

19. Save the workbook, and then close it.

# Challenge

## Case Problem 2

**Data File needed for this Case Problem: NP_EX_6-5.xlsx**

**Mercy Field Clinic**   Craig Manteo is the Quality of Care manager at Mercy Field Clinic located in Knoxville, Tennessee. Craig wants to use Excel to monitor daily clinic appointments, looking at how many patients a doctor sees per day and how much time is spent with each patient. Craig is also interested in whether patients are experiencing long wait times within particular departments or with specific doctors. You've been given a worksheet containing the scheduled appointments from a typical day. Craig wants you to create a dashboard that can be used to summarize the appointments from that day. Complete the following.

1. Open the **NP_EX_6-5.xlsx** workbook located in the Excel6 > Case2 folder included with your Data Files. Save the workbook as **NP_EX_6_Mercy** in the location specified by your instructor.

2. In the Documentation sheet, enter your name and the date.

3. The Patient Log worksheet lists the entire day's appointments, from 8 am to 5 pm at four departments. Convert this data range into an Excel table using **Appointments** as the table name. Turn off the banded rows style.

4. In the Dept Lookup, Physician Lookup, and Patient Lookup worksheets, convert each data range to a table, naming them **Dept_Lookup**, **Physician_Lookup**, and **Patient_Lookup**, respectively. You'll use these tables to display names instead of IDs in the Appointments table.

5. In the Patient Log worksheet, use your mouse to enter formulas for the following calculated fields (resize the columns as needed):

   a. Between the Dept ID and Physician ID fields, insert the **Department** field, and then create an exact match lookup with the VLOOKUP function using the value of the Dept ID field in the Appointments table to retrieve the department name from column 2 of the Dept_Lookup table. (*Hint*: Remember with an exact match lookup to set the range_lookup argument to FALSE.)

   b. Between the Physician ID and Patient ID fields, insert the **Physician** field, and then create an exact match lookup with the VLOOKUP function using the Physician ID field to retrieve the physician name from column 2 of the Physician_Lookup table.

   c. Between the Patient ID and Patient Check In fields, insert the **Patient** field, and then create an exact match lookup using the Patient ID field to retrieve the patient name from column 2 of the Patient_Lookup table.

6. Insert the **Patient Wait** field in column K to calculate whether a patient had to wait past the scheduled appointment time. Use your mouse to enter the IF function to test whether the value of the Exam Start field (cell I5) is greater than the Appt Time Field (cell A5); if it is, return the value 1; otherwise, return the value 0. Format the calculated values with the General cell format.

7. Insert the **Wait Time** field in column L. Calculate how many minutes each patient had to wait by using your mouse to enter a formula that multiplies the value of the difference between the Exam Start (cell I5) and Appt Time (cell A5) fields by 24*60 (to express the difference in minutes). Format the calculated values with the General cell format.

8. Insert the **Visit Length** field in column M. Calculate the visit length in minutes by using your mouse to enter a formula that multiplies the difference between the Exam End and Exam Start fields by 24*60. Format the calculated values with the General cell format.

9. Insert slicers for the Department and Physician fields, and then move those slicers to the **Dashboard** worksheet. Resize the Department slicer to cover the merged range A4:D7. Resize the Physician slicer to cover the merged range A8:D16. Set the layout of both slicers to 5 columns.

✛ **Explore** 10. On the Slicer tab, in the Slicer group, in the Slicer Caption box, change the caption of the Department slicer to **Treating Department** and the caption of the Physician slicer to **Examining Physician**.

✛ **Explore** 11. Select the Department slicer, and then click the Slicer Settings button in the Slicer group to open the Slicer Settings dialog box. Click the Hide Items with no data check box to hide department names when they are not relevant to the dashboard report. Repeat for the Physician slicer.

12. Calculate the following summary statistics in the Dashboard worksheet:

a. In the merged cell A19, show the number of appointments behind schedule by applying the SUBTOTAL function with the SUM function to the Patient Wait field of the Appointments table.

b. In the merged cell B19, show the number of appointments that were on time by applying the SUBTOTAL function with the COUNT function to the Appt Time field of the Appointments table and subtracting the value of cell A19.

c. In the merged cell C19, use the SUBTOTAL function to calculate the average value of the Wait Time field in the Appointments table.

d. In the merged cell D19, use the SUBTOTAL function to calculate the average value of the Visit Length field in the Appointments table.

13. Insert a pie chart of the data in the range A18:B23, move the chart to cover the range A25:B34. Remove the chart legend but add Data Callouts data labels showing the percent of each category. (*Hint*: If you don't see two categories in the pie chart, on the Chart Design tab, in the Data group click the Switch Row/Column button.)

14. Create a histogram of the data in the Wait Time column in the Patient Log worksheet. Move the histogram to the Dashboard worksheet and then resize the chart to fit in the range C25:C34. Change the chart title to **Waiting Time**. Add data labels. Set the bin width to **5**, the Overflow bin value to **10**, and the Underflow bin value to **0**.

15. Create a histogram of the data in the Visit Length column in the Patient Log worksheet. Move the histogram to the Dashboard worksheet and resize it to fit in the range D25:D34. Change the chart title to **Length of Visit** and add data labels. Set the bin width to **10**, the Overflow bin value to **60**, and the Underflow bin value to **20**.

16. Test the slicer buttons by showing the results for Dr. Jacob Leiva of the Internal Medicine department.

17. Save the workbook, and then close it.

# Summarizing Data with PivotTables

EXCEL

## Preparing a Social Media Marketing Report

### Objectives

**Session 7.1**
- Do approximate match lookups
- Work with logical functions
- Calculate statistics with summary IF functions

**Session 7.2**
- Create a PivotTable
- Change a PivotTable layout
- Format a PivotTable

**Session 7.3**
- Create a PivotChart
- Apply a slicer to multiple PivotTables
- Create a timeline slicer

## Case | Syrmosta

Claire Christos is the social media marketing manager for the clothing company Syrmosta. Part of Claire's job is evaluating the impact of the company's presence on popular social media sites like Facebook, Twitter, and Instagram. Over the past 12 months, Syrmosta has instituted an ad campaign to increase its visibility on social media sites. Claire has received a workbook detailing the public's response to its social media posts. You'll help Claire summarize and analyze that market data.

### Starting Data Files

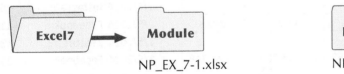

Excel7 → Module
NP_EX_7-1.xlsx

Review
NP_EX_7-2.xlsx

Case1
NP_EX_7-3.xlsx

Case2
NP_EX_7-4.xlsx

# Session 7.1 Visual Overview:

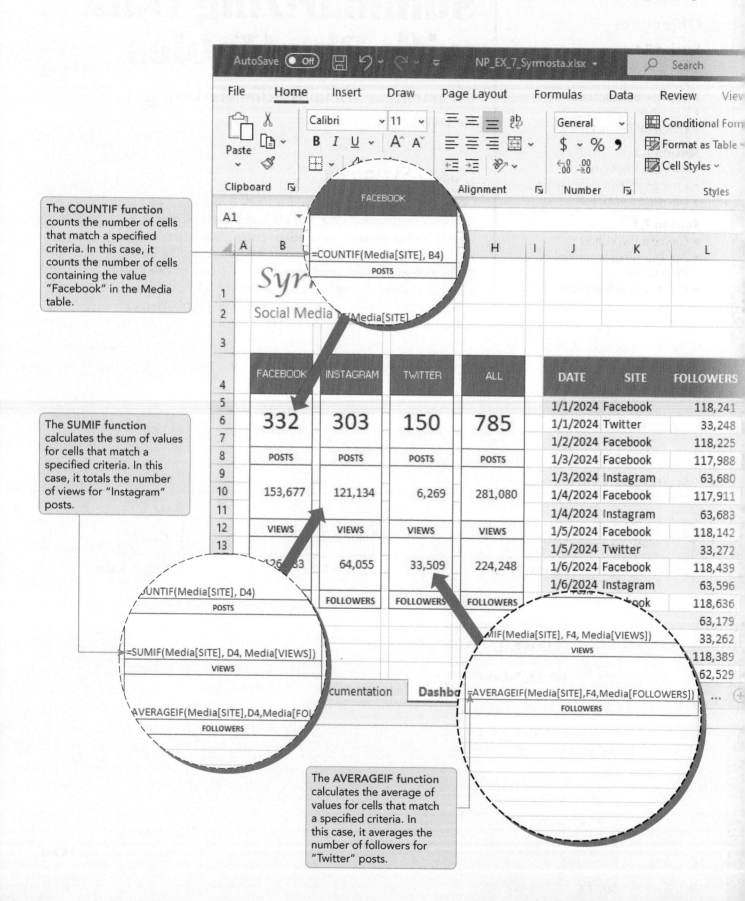

The **COUNTIF** function counts the number of cells that match a specified criteria. In this case, it counts the number of cells containing the value "Facebook" in the Media table.

The **SUMIF** function calculates the sum of values for cells that match a specified criteria. In this case, it totals the number of views for "Instagram" posts.

The **AVERAGEIF** function calculates the average of values for cells that match a specified criteria. In this case, it averages the number of followers for "Twitter" posts.

# Summary IF Functions and VLOOKUP

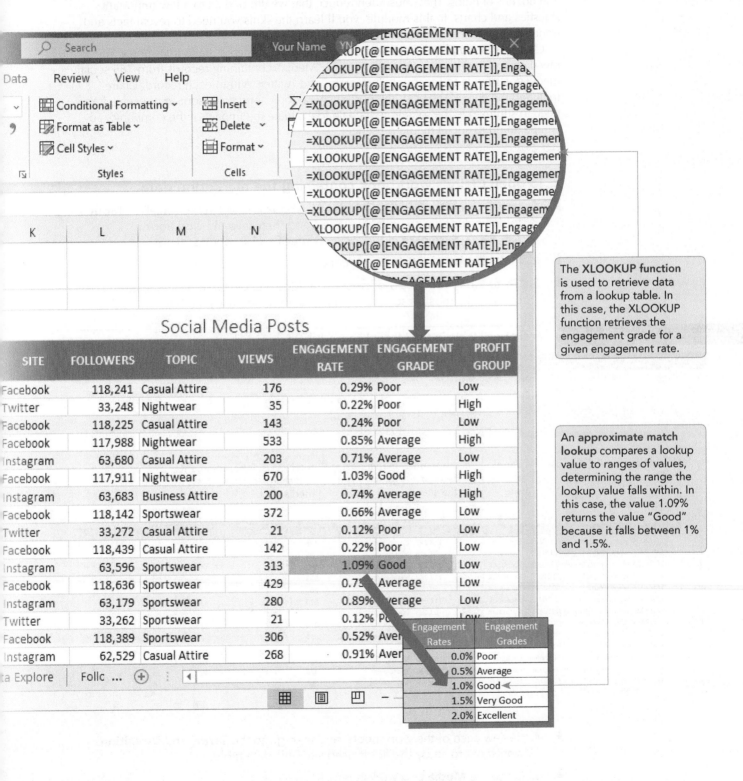

Search    Your Name    YN    =...[ENGAGEMENT R...
=...OKUP([@[ENGAGEMENT RATE]],E...
=...OOKUP([@[ENGAGEMENT RATE]],Engag...
=...XLOOKUP([@[ENGAGEMENT RATE]],Engage...
=XLOOKUP([@[ENGAGEMENT RATE]],Engagem...
=XLOOKUP([@[ENGAGEMENT RATE]],Engageme...
=XLOOKUP([@[ENGAGEMENT RATE]],Engagemen...
=XLOOKUP([@[ENGAGEMENT RATE]],Engagemen...
=XLOOKUP([@[ENGAGEMENT RATE]],Engageme...
=XLOOKUP([@[ENGAGEMENT RATE]],Engageme...
=XLOOKUP([@[ENGAGEMENT RATE]],Engagem...
=...XLOOKUP([@[ENGAGEMENT RATE]],Engage...
=...OKUP([@[ENGAGEMENT RATE]],Eng...
=...P([@[ENGAGEMENT RATE]]...

Data    Review    View    Help

Conditional Formatting ⌄    Insert ⌄    Σ
Format as Table ⌄    Delete ⌄
Cell Styles ⌄    Format ⌄

Styles    Cells

K    L    M    N

The **XLOOKUP function** is used to retrieve data from a lookup table. In this case, the XLOOKUP function retrieves the engagement grade for a given engagement rate.

## Social Media Posts

| SITE | FOLLOWERS | TOPIC | VIEWS | ENGAGEMENT RATE | ENGAGEMENT GRADE | PROFIT GROUP |
|---|---|---|---|---|---|---|
| Facebook | 118,241 | Casual Attire | 176 | 0.29% | Poor | Low |
| Twitter | 33,248 | Nightwear | 35 | 0.22% | Poor | High |
| Facebook | 118,225 | Casual Attire | 143 | 0.24% | Poor | Low |
| Facebook | 117,988 | Nightwear | 533 | 0.85% | Average | High |
| Instagram | 63,680 | Casual Attire | 203 | 0.71% | Average | Low |
| Facebook | 117,911 | Nightwear | 670 | 1.03% | Good | High |
| Instagram | 63,683 | Business Attire | 200 | 0.74% | Average | High |
| Facebook | 118,142 | Sportswear | 372 | 0.66% | Average | Low |
| Twitter | 33,272 | Casual Attire | 21 | 0.12% | Poor | Low |
| Facebook | 118,439 | Casual Attire | 142 | 0.22% | Poor | Low |
| Instagram | 63,596 | Sportswear | 313 | 1.09% | Good | Low |
| Facebook | 118,636 | Sportswear | 429 | 0.7... | Average | Low |
| Instagram | 63,179 | Sportswear | 280 | 0.89% | ...verage | Low |
| Twitter | 33,262 | Sportswear | 21 | 0.12% | Po... | Low |
| Facebook | 118,389 | Sportswear | 306 | 0.52% | Aver... | |
| Instagram | 62,529 | Casual Attire | 268 | 0.91% | Aver... | |

...a Explore    Follc ...    ⊕

An **approximate match lookup** compares a lookup value to ranges of values, determining the range the lookup value falls within. In this case, the value 1.09% returns the value "Good" because it falls between 1% and 1.5%.

| Engagement Rates | Engagement Grades |
|---|---|
| 0.0% | Poor |
| 0.5% | Average |
| 1.0% | Good ◄ |
| 1.5% | Very Good |
| 2.0% | Excellent |

# Using Lookup Functions

Often data analysts receive large data sets with hundreds or even thousands of records and dozens of fields. They must then reduce that wealth of data to a few important statistics and charts. In this module, you'll learn the skills you need to reveal facts and trends hidden within a mass of information.

Claire has a workbook containing results of a social media marketing survey. The raw data is stored in an Excel table named "Media" containing records from 785 social media posts made to Facebook, Instagram, and Twitter. Within each record, Claire included the date of the post, the post's general topic, and the response it received. You need to summarize the social media data to evaluate the impact of the company's ad campaign on its social media presence.

## To open Claire's workbook containing the marketing data:

1. **sam↓** Open the **NP_EX_7-1.xlsx** workbook located in the **Excel7 > Module** folder included with your Data Files, and then save the workbook as **NP_EX_7_Syrmosta** in the location specified by your instructor.

2. In the **Documentation** sheet, enter your name and the date.

3. Go to the **Media Log** worksheet. The Media Excel table on this sheet contains Syrmosta's social media posts from the past year. See Figure 7–1.

**Figure 7–1**        Media Excel table in the Media Log worksheet

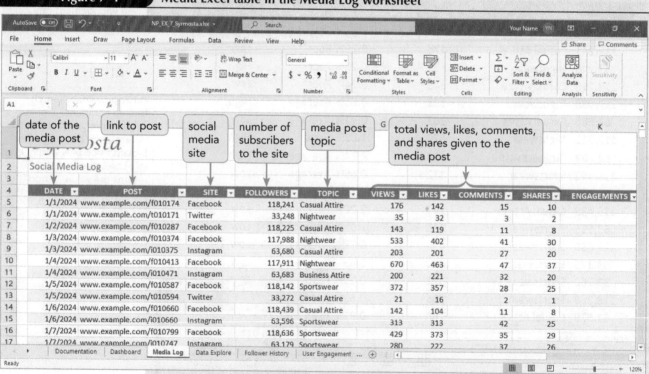

4. Review each of the worksheets, and then go to the **Terms and Definitions** worksheet to study the fields used with this data table.

5. Go to the **Media Log** worksheet.

Successful social media marketing is all about getting the user engaged. An engaged user is more likely to turn into a loyal customer. There are four general types of social media engagement with increasing levels of user involvement: (1) The user has viewed the social media post. (2) The user has indicated approval or "like" of the post. (3) The user has taken the time and effort to comment on the post. (4) The user has shared the post with others.

In the Media table, Claire recorded the total number of views, likes, comments, and shares for each social media post made in the last year. You will add another field that calculates the sum of these engagements for each post.

### To calculate the total engagements per post:

1. In the Media Log worksheet, click cell **K5** to select it.

2. Type **=SUM(** to begin the SUM function.

3. Use your mouse to select the range **G5:J5**. The field reference Media[@[VIEWS]:[SHARES]] is added to the formula to reference the Views through Shares field in the current row of the Media table.

4. Type **)** to complete the SUM function, and then press **ENTER**. Excel calculates the sum of the engagements for each post, returning a total of 343 engagements for the first post. See Figure 7–2.

| Figure 7–2 | Engagements calculated field added to the Media table |

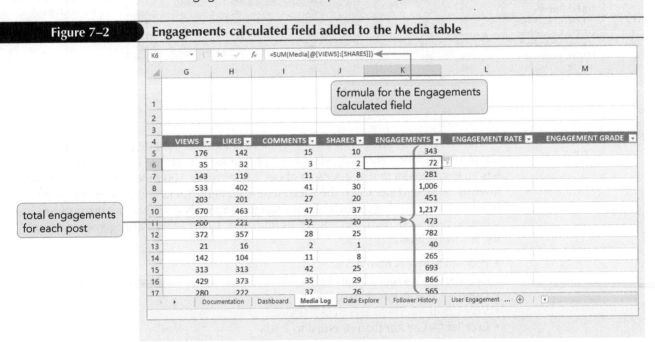

Claire is also interested in the engagement rate, which is the percentage of followers that engage with each post. The number of followers tells Claire how many subscribers a post might have, but the engagement rate shows how often they respond to the post's contents. You will calculate the engagement rate for each post by dividing the total engagements by total followers at the time the post was uploaded.

## To calculate the engagement rate per post:

1. In the Media Log worksheet, click cell **L5** to select it.

2. Type **=** to begin the formula, click cell **K5** to select the Engagements field, type **/** for division, click cell **E5** to select the Followers field, and then press **ENTER**. The formula =[@ENGAGEMENTS]/[@FOLLOWERS] is entered in the Engagement Rate column. See Figure 7–3.

**Figure 7–3     Engagement rate per post**

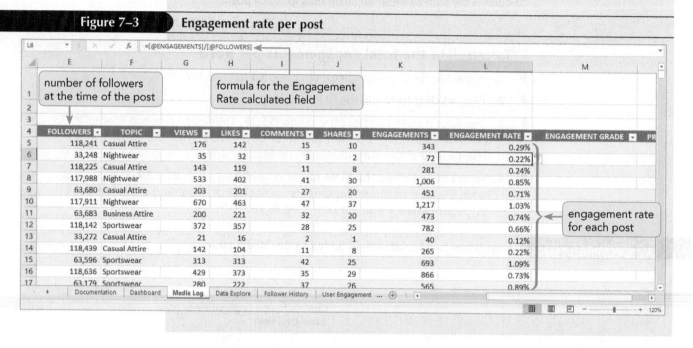

The first post, in row 5, has an engagement rate of 0.29% indicating that about 29 out of 10,000 followers engaged with the post in some way. The last post, in row 789, has an engagement rate of 2.49% or about 2.5 users per 100 followers. Are these rates low? The answer depends on the social media content. Social media sites for sports or politics typically have much higher engagements rates than this, but the fashion industry must work harder to engage its followers. Claire grades engagement rates at the following levels:

- Poor—0% to less than 0.5%
- Average—0.5% to less than 1.0%
- Good—1.0% to less than 1.5%
- Very Good—1.5% to less than 2.0%
- Excellent—Greater than or equal to 2.0%

Claire wants to show the engagement grade for each post. You will display the grade using an approximate match lookup.

## Creating Approximate Match Lookups

An approximate match lookup compares a lookup value to a range of values rather than a single, specific value. For example, an engagement rate of 0.38% would receive a "Poor" grade from Claire because it falls between 0% and 0.5%, and a value of 1.83% would receive a "Very Good" grade because it falls between 1.5% and 2.0%.

Approximate match lookups use a vertical lookup table or a horizontal lookup table. In a vertical lookup table, the range of values are in one column of the table and the return values are retrieved from another column. In a horizontal lookup table, the compare values are in one row of the table and the return values are retrieved from another row.

Claire wants to see the engagement grade for each post. You will add a vertical lookup table to the workbook that lists the ranges of engage rates in the first column and engagement grades in the second column.

## To create the vertical lookup table of engagement rates and grades:

1. Go to the **Lookup Tables** worksheet.

2. In the range **B5:B9**, enter the values **0.0%**, **0.5%**, **1.0%**, **1.5%**, and **2.0%** representing the lower end of each range of engagement rates in ascending order.

> Be sure to enter the approximate match lookup table values in ascending order using the lower end of each interval.

3. In the range **C5:C9**, enter **Poor**, **Average**, **Good**, **Very Good**, and **Excellent** as the grades for each interval of engagement rates. See Figure 7–4.

**Figure 7–4**    ▶    **Vertical lookup table for the engagement rate**

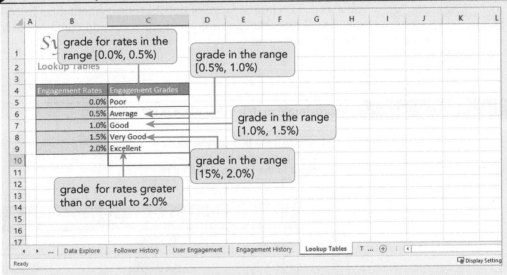

4. Select the range **B4:C9**.

5. On the ribbon, click the **Formulas** tab, and then in the Defined Names group, click the **Create from Selection** button.

6. Click the **Right column** check box to deselect it. Only the Top row check box is selected.

7. Click **OK**. The range names Engagement_Rates and Engagement_Grades are added to the workbook.

Once you have created a lookup table, you can use a lookup function to retrieve a value from that table using an approximate match lookup. Two lookup functions commonly found in Excel workbook are VLOOKUP and HLOOKUP.

The VLOOKUP function uses a vertical lookup table. The first column of the table contains the range of lookup values in ascending order. Each value listed is the *lower* end of the interval. The VLOOKUP function makes an approximate match by going down the first column to locate the cell containing the largest value that is less than or equal to the supplied value. Then the VLOOKUP function retrieves the value from a different column in the same row.

The HLOOKUP function uses a horizontal lookup table. The first row of the table contains the range of lookup values in ascending order. Like the vertical lookup table, each value listed is the *lower* end of the interval. An approximate match is made going left to right across the row until a cell containing the largest value that is less than or equal to the supplied value is found. The HLOOKUP function retrieves the value from another row in the same column.

The VLOOKUP and HLOOKUP functions have similar syntax:

```
VLOOKUP(lookup, array, col, [range_lookup=TRUE])

HLOOKUP(lookup, array, row, [range_lookup=TRUE])
```

where `lookup` is the value to look up, `array` references the cell range containing the lookup table, `col` and `row` are index numbers representing the column or row containing the values returned by the function, and `range_lookup` specifies whether to do an approximate match lookup (TRUE) for a range of values, or an exact match lookup (FALSE) to match a single specific value. If you do not specify a `range_lookup` value, an approximate match lookup is performed by default.

Figure 7–5 shows the VLOOKUP function finding an approximate match for a lookup value of 1.83% from a range of possible engagement rates listed in the table's first column. Notice that each entry in the first column contains the lower value of the range of engagement grades.

**Tip**

With exact match lookups, the data in the first column or row of the lookup table can be placed in any order.

**Figure 7–5    Approximate match using VLOOKUP**

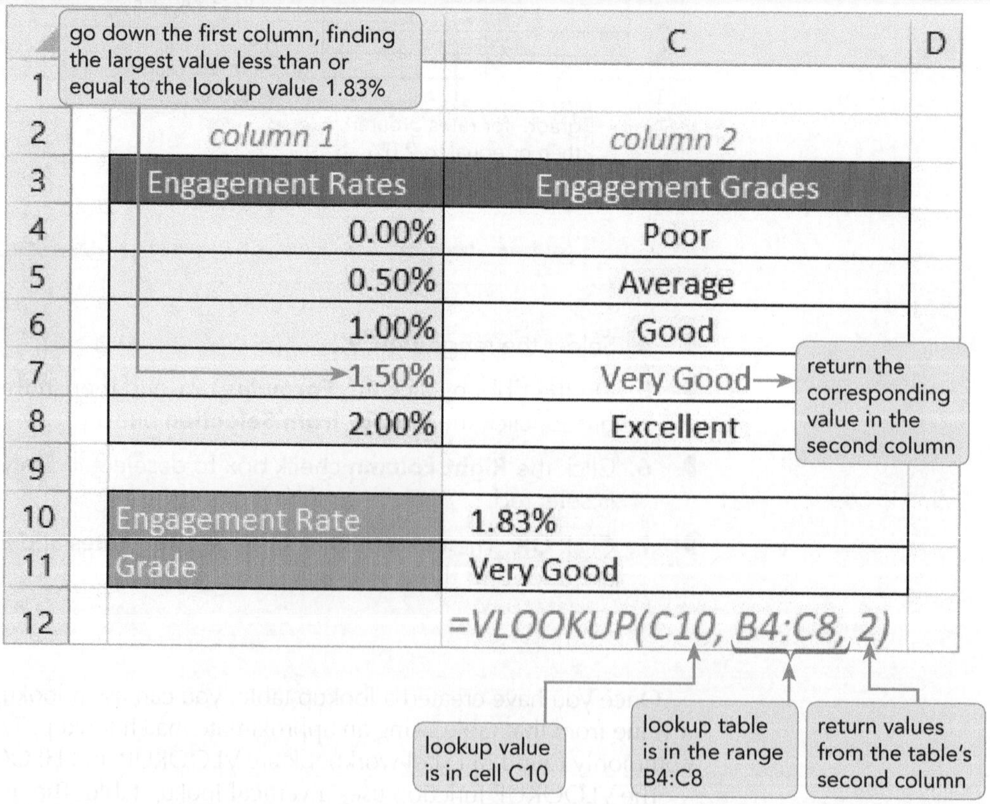

The HLOOKUP function would return the same result with the engagement rates placed in the first row of the lookup table and the grades placed in another row. The HLOOKUP function goes across the row of engagement rates, finding the largest rate that is less than or equal to 1.83%.

Another Excel lookup function is the XLOOKUP function. The XLOOKUP function has the following advantages over the VLOOKUP and HLOOKUP functions:

- Lookup tables can be arranged in either the vertical or horizontal direction.

- Lookup values can be in any column or row, not just the first column or row.

- Lookup values can be arranged in any order and not just ascending order.

- If no match is found, the XLOOKUP function can return a user-specified value instead of the default #N/A error value.

The syntax of the XLOOKUP function is:

```
XLOOKUP(lookup, array, return, [not_found], [match], [search])
```

where *lookup* is the value to look up, *array* is the column or row containing the lookup values, *return* is the column or row containing the return values, *not_found* is an optional value returned by the function if no match is found, *match* is the match mode used by the function, and *search* is the search mode used by the function. For example, the following XLOOKUP function searches the values in the range C1:C10, looking for a match to the value in cell A1. If a match is found, it returns the value in the corresponding row in the range E1:E10.

```
XLOOKUP(A1, C1:C10, E1:E10)
```

If no match is found, the function returns the error value #N/A. To provide a more friendly message, the following function displays the text string "no match" if no match is found:

```
XLOOKUP(A1, C1:C10, E1:E10, "no match")
```

By default, the XLOOKUP function searches for exact matches. If you don't want an exact match, you choose one of the following values for the optional *match* argument:

- *match* = 0    (default) Exact match; if none is found, returns #N/A, unless a value is specified by the *not_found* argument
- *match* = –1    Exact match; if none is found, returns the next smaller value (like approximate match lookups with the VLOOKUP and HLOOKUP functions)
- *match* = 1    Exact match; if none is found, returns the next larger value
- *match* = 2    Wildcard match using the *, ? and ~ symbols to locate a match

By default, XLOOKUP starts the search with the first entry in the column or row of lookup values and then proceeds down or to the right. You can specify a different direction for the search by adding one of the following optional *search* argument values to the function:

- *search* = 1    (default) Search starting from the first entry in the column or row of lookup values
- *search* = –1    Reverse search, starting from the last entry in the column or row of lookup values
- *search* = 2    Binary search using lookup values sorted in ascending order; returns invalid results if not sorted
- *search* = –2    Binary search using lookup values sorted in descending order; returns invalid results if not sorted

> **Tip**
>
> If you don't specify a *not_found* value, include a comma placeholder (, ,) to include values for the *match* or *search* arguments of the XLOOKUP function.

If you do not include values for the *match* and *search* arguments, the XLOOKUP function assumes the defaults and performs an exact match lookup starting with the first value in the specified lookup row or column. Figure 7–6 shows the XLOOKUP function performing an approximate match lookup in a vertical lookup table of engagement rates and grades.

**Figure 7–6**    **Approximate match using XLOOKUP**

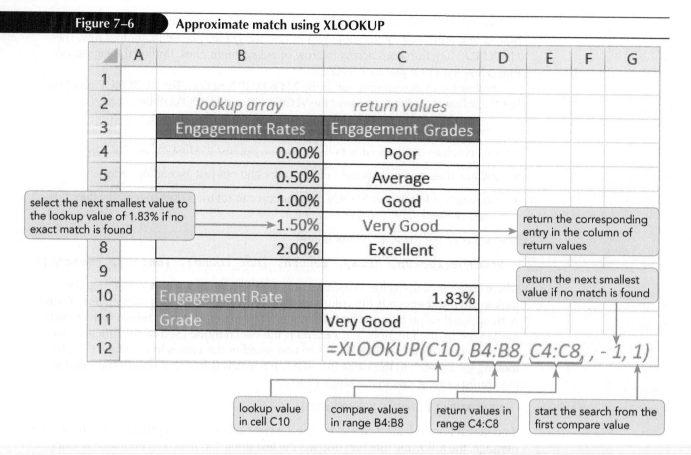

Because of its greater flexibility and power, you will use the XLOOKUP function to grade every social media post in the Media Log worksheet based on its engagement rate.

### To perform an approximate match lookup with the XLOOKUP function:

1. Go to the **Media Log** worksheet and click cell **M5**.

2. On the Formulas tab, in the Function Library group, click the **Lookup & Reference** button, scroll down the list of functions, and then click **XLOOKUP**. The Function Arguments dialog box opens.

3. Make sure the insertion point is in the Lookup_value box, and then click cell **L5** in the Media table. The cell reference [@[ENGAGEMENT RATE]] references the value of the Engagement Rate field in the current row.

4. Press **TAB** to move to the Lookup_array box, and then type **Engagement_Rates** to reference to lookup column contain the engagements rate you defined in the last set of steps.

5. Press **TAB** to move to the Return_array box, and then type **Engagement_Grades** to reference the column of grades associated with the range of engagement rates.

6. Press **TAB** twice to move to the Match_mode box, and then type **–1** to specify that XLOOKUP will return the next smallest value from the lookup table if no match is found. You will not specify a value for the Search_mode box, accepting the default method of a search starting with the first entry in the column of lookup values. See Figure 7–7.

| Figure 7–7 | Function arguments for an approximate match XLOOKUP function |

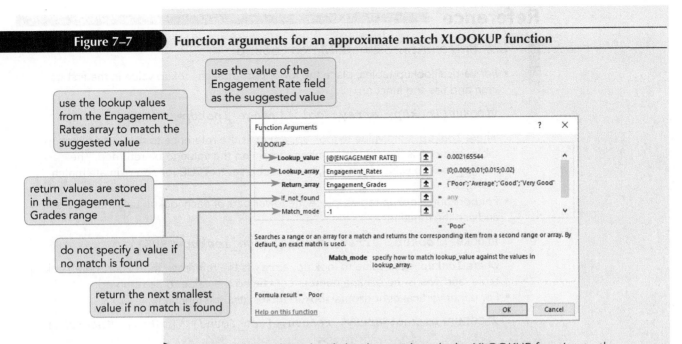

use the value of the Engagement Rate field as the suggested value

use the lookup values from the Engagement_Rates array to match the suggested value

return values are stored in the Engagement_Grades range

do not specify a value if no match is found

return the next smallest value if no match is found

7. Click **OK** to close the dialog box and apply the XLOOKUP function to the Engagement Grades field for all records in the table. See Figure 7–8.

| Figure 7–8 | Engagement grades retrieved by the XLOOKUP function |

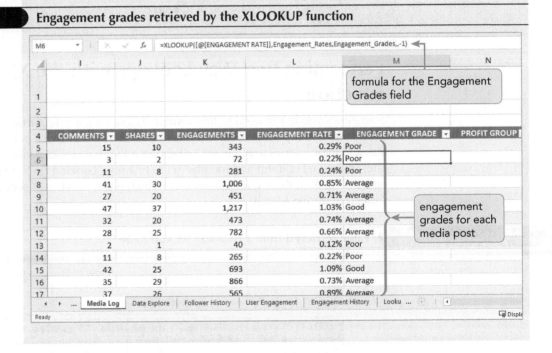

formula for the Engagement Grades field

engagement grades for each media post

A grade appears alongside each post based on the value of the engagement rate. Later, you'll explore how these grades differ based on the social media site and the content of post.

# Reference

### Creating an Approximate Match Lookup

- For vertical lookup tables, place the lower part of each lookup value in the first column and use the function

    VLOOKUP(*lookup, array, col,* [*range_lookup*=TRUE])

    where *lookup* is the value to look up, **array** is the reference to the vertical lookup table, and **col** is the column number containing the value to be returned. The **range_lookup** value is optional, but must be set to TRUE for approximate match lookups.
- For horizontal lookup tables, place the lower part of each lookup value in the first row and use the function

    HLOOKUP(*lookup, array, row,* [*range_lookup*=TRUE])

    where *lookup* is the value to look up, **array** is the reference to the horizontal lookup table, and **row** is the column number containing the value to be returned.
- For either vertical or horizontal lookup tables, use the function

    XLOOKUP(*lookup, array, return,* [*not_found*], [*match*], [*search*])

    where *lookup* is the value to look up, **array** is the column or row containing the lookup values, **return** is the column or row containing the return values, **not_found** is an optional value returned by the function if no match is found, **match** is the match mode used by the function, and **search** is the search mode used by the function.

## Performing Two-Way Lookups with the XLOOKUP Function

Sometimes you might need to find a value that occurs where a row and a column cross. A **two-way lookup table** has lookup values in both a row and a column with the return value at their intersection. Figure 7–9 shows a two-way lookup table that lists media sites in the first column and months in the first row. Looking up Instagram as the media site and MAR as the month returns 824, which is the number of social media shares on Instagram during March.

**Figure 7–9** | **Value retrieved from a two-way lookup table**

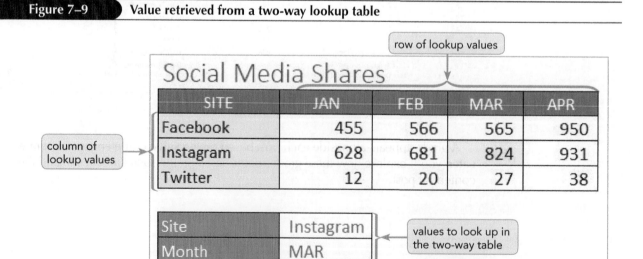

**Social Media Shares**

| SITE | JAN | FEB | MAR | APR |
|---|---|---|---|---|
| Facebook | 455 | 566 | 565 | 950 |
| Instagram | 628 | 681 | 824 | 931 |
| Twitter | 12 | 20 | 27 | 38 |

row of lookup values

column of lookup values

| Site | Instagram |
|---|---|
| Month | MAR |
| Media Share | 824 |

values to look up in the two-way table

return value

A useful feature of the XLOOKUP function is that it can return an array of values matching a given lookup value. For example, in Figure 7–10, the XLOOKUP function searches across the lookup table's first row and returns the monthly media shares that match the Instagram media site.

| Figure 7–10 | Array of values returned using XLOOKUP |

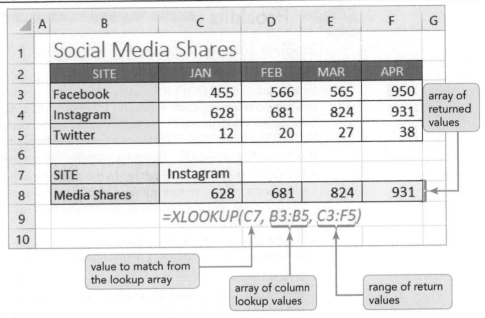

This XLOOKUP feature is useful with two-way tables because the array of return values can act as a lookup table for another XLOOKUP function by nesting one XLOOKUP function within another. The general syntax for returning a value from a two-way table using nested XLOOKUP functions is

XLOOKUP(*value1*, *column*, XLOOKUP(*value2*, *row*, *return*))

where *value1* is the value to be matched in the column of the two-way table, *value2* is the value to be matched in the row, *column* and *row* reference the column and row containing the lookup values, and *return* references the array of return values from the two-way table. Figure 7–11 shows how to apply nested XLOOKUP functions to retrieve media shares based on the name of the media site and the month. Notice that the array of values returned by the XLOOKUP function in Figure 7–10 appears as the lookup table in the outer XLOOKUP function.

| Figure 7–11 | Two-way lookup with nested XLOOKUP functions |

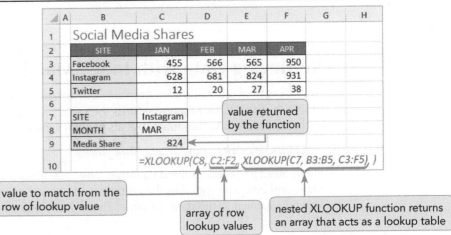

This process of nesting one XLOOKUP function within another can also be used with approximate match lookups in which the two-way table's row and column contain ranges of values rather than specific categories. For those types of tables, you will need to include argument values specifying how the XLOOKUP functions will search through the lookup values to find an approximate match.

## Proskills

### Problem Solving: Transitioning to XLOOKUP

The VLOOKUP and HLOOKUP functions are older Excel standards for retrieving lookup data. The XLOOKUP function is the newer standard and provides greater flexibility in retrieving data, especially for approximate match lookups. Because of the advantages associated with the XLOOKUP function, you might want to transition any VLOOKUP and HLOOKUP functions in your workbooks to the XLOOKUP function. However, keep in mind the following important differences between them:

- VLOOKUP and HLOOKUP reference the entire lookup table and retrieve values based on a column or row number. XLOOKUP references the column or row of lookup values and the column or row of return values. XLOOKUP does not use column or row numbers.

- VLOOKUP and XLOOKUP perform an approximate match lookup by default. XLOOKUP performs an exact match lookup by default.

- VLOOKUP and HLOOKUP require lookup values in the first column or row of the table. XLOOKUP allows lookup values placed anywhere. In fact, the lookup values and returns don't even have to be in the same table or in the same worksheet.

- VLOOKUP and HLOOKUP for approximate match lookups require lookup values sorted in ascending order with each value representing the lower end of a numeric interval. XLOOKUP allows lookup values to be arranged in any order with the *match* argument determining what constitutes a matching value.

- VLOOKUP or HLOOKUP do not support two-way lookups; instead you use the INDEX and MATCH functions. XLOOKUP supports two-way lookups using nested XLOOKUP functions.

- VLOOKUP and HLOOKUP must be edited if you revise the structure of a lookup table by inserting rows and columns. XLOOKUP automatically adjusts if you add or remove table rows and columns.

- VLOOKUP and HLOOKUP return the #N/A error value in the case of a failed match. XLOOKUP can return any specified value.

While XLOOKUP can do everything the VLOOKUP and HLOOKUP can do and more, the experienced Excel user should be comfortable with both approaches as they will both be encountered in many workbooks.

## Retrieving Data with Index Match Lookups

Another way of retrieving data from a two-way table is with the INDEX and MATCH functions. The INDEX function returns the value from a table by specifying a row index and column index within that table. Its general syntax is

```
INDEX(array, row_num, col_num)
```

where *array* references the data range, *row_num* specifies the row number within that array, and *col_num* specifies the column number. For example, the following INDEX function applied to the data shown in Figure 7–11 returns a value of 950, which is the number of media shares for Facebook during April located at the first row and fourth column of the array of media shares:

```
INDEX(C3:F5, 1, 4)
```

The MATCH function returns the position of a value found within a row or column. Its syntax is

```
MATCH(lookup_value, array, [match = 1])
```

where `lookup_value` is the value to locate, `array` is the row or column in which to search, and `match` is an optional argument specifying how the search should be conducted. The `match` argument has three values, similar to the `match` argument in the XLOOKUP function:

- `match = 1`    (default) An approximate match lookup that finds the largest value less than or equal to lookup value. The values must be arranged in ascending order.
- `match = 0`    An exact match. If none is found, returns #N/A.
- `match = -1`  An approximate match lookup that finds the smallest value greater than or equal to *lookup_value*. The values must be arranged in descending order.

For example, using the table shown in Figure 7–11, the following two expressions return values of 1 and 4, respectively, indicating the exact positions of the "Facebook" and "APR" values in the table's first column and first row:

```
MATCH("Facebook", B3:B5, 0)
```

```
MATCH("APR", C2:F2, 0)
```

You can nest the MATCH function within the INDEX function to return a specific value from a two-way lookup table. The general syntax is

```
INDEX(array, columnMatch, rowMatch)
```

where `array` is the array of return values, `columnMatch` is the MATCH function applied to the lookup values in the table's first column and `rowMatch` is a MATCH function applied to lookup values in the table's first row. For example, the following expression combines the INDEX and MATCH functions retrieve the return value for Facebook media posts in April:

```
INDEX(C3:F5, MATCH("Facebook", B3:B5, 0), MATCH("APR", C2:F2, 0))
```

Nested XLOOKUP functions and nested INDEX MATCH functions can both be used to retrieve values from a two-way table. Which approach you use is often a matter of personal preference.

# Insight

## Performing Partial Lookups with Wildcards

Partial lookups can be helpful when you're working with large data sets. A **partial lookup** matches a character pattern rather than a specific value. You use wildcards to create the character pattern for the lookup. For example, the following XLOOKUP function uses the * wildcard to match any string of characters that start with letters "WIL" using the lookup values in the LastNames array and returning values from the FirstNames array. If no match is found, the text string "No Name" is returned. The *match* argument value must equal 2 for XLOOKUP to interpret the wildcard symbols within the lookup value.

```
XLOOKUP("WIL*", LastNames, FirstNames, "No Name", 2)
```

Because XLOOKUP ignores case, values such as William, Willet, Will, or Willey would be matched by this function. Excel will choose the first match it encounters in the table even if other entries would match the wildcard pattern. To combine a wildcard character with a cell value, use the & character. For example, the following function looks up values starting with the text stored in cell B10:

```
XLOOKUP(B10&"*", LastNames, FirstNames, "No Name", 2)
```

Partial lookups can also be done with VLOOKUP or HLOOKUP by adding wildcard characters within the lookup value. The following VLOOKUP function uses wildcards to retrieve values of the second column in the UserNames table in which the values in the lookup column starts with the text string "WIL":

```
XLOOKUP("WIL*", UserNames, 2, FALSE)
```

Note that partial matches in VLOOKUP and HLOOKUP can be done only with exact match lookups, so the range_lookup argument must be set to FALSE.

# Exploring Logical Functions

Logical functions are used to set data values based on whether a condition is true or false. So far, you've only used the IF function

```
IF(logical_test, value_if_true, [value_if_false])
```

where **logical_test** is the condition that is either true or false, **value_if_true** is the value returned by the IF function if **logical_test** is true, and **value_if_false** is the function's value if **logical_test** is false. The IF function is limited to returning one of two possible results. To test for multiple conditions, returning different values for each condition, you can nest one IF function within the other, replacing the **value_if_false** argument with another IF function. For example, the following function uses two nested IF function to test the value of cell A1:

```
IF(A1 < 0.5%, "Poor", IF(A1 < 1%, "Average", "Good"))
```

If A1 is less than 0.5%, the function returns the value "Poor." Otherwise, the function tests for whether A1 is less than 1%. If that condition is true, the function returns the value "Average." And if that condition is false, the function returns the value "Good." By adding more nested IF functions, you can test for as many possible conditions as you want. However, at some point the collection of nested IF functions will become so convoluted that you're better off using a lookup table to match each condition to a different value.

## Reference

### Applying a Logical Function

- To test one condition against two possible outcomes, use

  `IF(logical_test, value_if_true, [value_if_false])`

  where **logical_test** is the condition that is either true or false, **value_if_true** is the value returned by the IF function if **logical_test** is true, and **value_if_false** is the function's value if **logical_test** is false.
- To test for multiple possible outcomes, use

  `IF(logical_test1, value_if_true1, logical_test2, value_if_true2, …)`

  where **logical_test1, logical_test2**, and so on are the different logical conditions, and **value_if_true1, value_if_true2**, and so on are the values associated with each condition, if true.
- To return a true value if any one of multiple conditions are true, use

  `OR(logical1, [logical2], [logical3], …)`

  where **logical1, logical2, logical3**, and so on are conditions which are either true or false.
- To return a true value only if all conditions are true, use

  `AND(logical1, [logical2], [logical3], …)`

## Using the IFS Function

Another way of working with multiple IF conditions is with the IFS function. The **IFS function** tests for multiple conditions without nesting and has the syntax

`IFS(logical_test1, value_if_true1, logical_test2, value_if_true2, …)`

where **logical_test1, logical_test2**, and so on are logical conditions, and **value_if_true1, value_if_true2**, and so on are the values associated with each condition, if the condition is true. This means that you could rewrite the nested IF function from earlier using the following IFS function that specifies three possible conditions for the value of cell A1:

`IFS(A1 < 0.5%, "Poor", A1 < 1%, "Average", A1 >= 1%, "Good")`

The IFS function doesn't include a default value if all the conditions are false. However, you can add a default condition to the end of the list by setting the final logical test to the value TRUE, as in the following expression:

`IFS(A1 < 0.5%, "Poor", A1 < 1%, "Average", TRUE, "Good")`

This IFS function will return a value of "Poor" if A1 is less than 0.5%. Otherwise, the function will return a value of "AVERAGE" if A1 is less than 1. But if neither of those conditions is met, the function will return a value of "Good."

## Combining Conditions with the OR and AND Functions

Another way of combining multiple conditions is with the OR function or the AND function. The **OR function** combines multiple conditions, returning a value of TRUE if *any* of the conditions are true. The **AND function** returns a value of TRUE if *all* of the conditions are true. The two functions have a similar syntax:

`OR(logical1, [logical2], [logical3], …)`
`AND(logical1, [logical2], [logical3], …)`

where *logical1*, *logical2*, *logical3*, and so on are conditions that are either true or false. For example, the following expression returns a value of TRUE if cell A1 equals 2 *or* if cell B1 equals 4 *or* if cell C1 equals 10:

```
OR(A1=2, B1=4, C1=10)
```

However, the following expression returns the value TRUE only if A1 equals 2 *and* B1 equals 4 *and* C1 equals 10:

```
AND(A1=2, B1=4, C1=10)
```

**Tip**

To switch a logical value between TRUE and FALSE, enclose the logical value within the NOT function.

The OR and AND functions can be nested within an IF function to provide a test involving multiple conditions. The following IF function tests three conditions enclosed within the AND function, returning the value "Pass" if A1 = 2 *and* B1 = 4 *and* C1=10; otherwise, it returns the value "Fail":

```
IF(AND(A1=2, B1=4, C1=10), "Pass", "Fail")
```

Claire wants to know whether the clothing product discussed in the media post is a high-profit or low-profit item. Clothes from the Business Attire or Nightwear categories are considered high-profit items for the company, and clothes from the Casual Attire or Sportswear categories are considered low-profit items. You'll add a field named Profit Group to the Media table, and then nest an OR function within an IF function to calculate the value of the Profit Group field for each record in the table.

### To nest the OR in an IF function to display the product's profitability:

1. In the Media Log worksheet, click cell **N5** to select it.

   Because this will be a complicated nested function, you will enter the formula starting with the innermost function.

2. On the Formulas tab, in the Function Library group, click the **Logical** button, and then click **OR**. The Function Arguments dialog box opens.

3. With the insertion point in the Logical1 box, click cell **F5** to enter the reference [@TOPIC] in the box, type **="Business Attire"** as the first logical condition, and then press **TAB** to go to the Logical2 box.

4. In the Logical2 box, click cell **F5** to enter the reference[@TOPIC], type **="Nightwear"** as the second logical condition.

5. Click **OK**. The formula is entered in the Profit Group column. Each record in the Profit Group column displays either TRUE or FALSE. FALSE appears in cell N5, TRUE appears in cell N6, FALSE appears in cell N7, and so forth.

6. Double-click cell **N5** to enter Edit mode. You will enclose the OR function in cell N5 within an IF function.

7. Click between the = symbol and OR, and then type **IF(** to begin inserting the IF function before the OR function.

8. Click the end of the formula, and then type **, "High", "Low")** to specify the two possible values that can appear depending on the value returned by OR function.

9. Press **ENTER**. The formula =IF(OR([@TOPIC]="Business Attire",[@TOPIC]="Nightwear"), "High", "Low") is added to every record in the Profit Group column. See Figure 7–12.

| Figure 7–12 | OR function nested within an IF function |

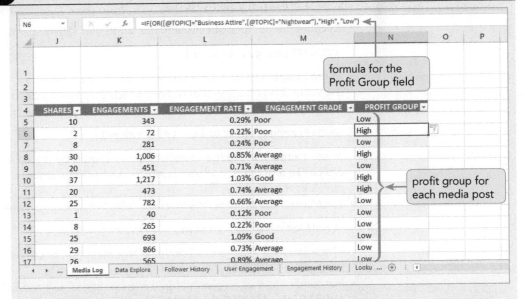

**Trouble?** If Excel reports a syntax error, you made a mistake when typing the formula. Clear the formulas from the Profit Group column, and then repeat Steps 1 through 9. Before pressing ENTER, make sure you have closed all quotation marks and matched opening and closing parentheses and brackets.

If you are still having trouble, clear the formulas from the Profit Group column, and then go to the Terms and Definitions worksheet. Copy cell G18, go back to the Media Log worksheet, and paste the formula into cell N5. Double-click cell N5, and then press ENTER to enter the formula for every record in the Media table.

The Media table is complete. Next, you will analyze the data in the table, starting by calculating summary statistics that tally the number of posts made to each social media site.

## Applying Summary IF Functions

Excel supports several functions that combine statistics like AVERAGE, SUM, and COUNT, with logical expressions, so that you calculate statistics only on those cells that match the logical condition.

# Reference

## Using a Summary IF Function

- To count the number of cells within a range that satisfy specified criteria, use

   COUNTIF(*range, criteria*)

   where **range** references the range of cells or table field to be counted and **criteria** is a value or a condition that defines which cells to include in the count.
- To calculate the sum of values for cells that satisfy specified criteria, use

   SUMIF(*range, criteria, [sum_range]*)

   where **range** is the range of cells to be evaluated by the criteria specified in the **criteria** argument, and *sum_range* is an optional argument that specifies the range of values to sum.
- To calculate the average of values for cells that satisfy specified criteria, use

   AVERAGEIF(*range, criteria, [average_range]*)

   where *average_range* is an optional argument that specifies the range of values to average.
- For conditions that involve multiple criteria ranges, use the COUNTIFS, SUMIFS, AVERAGEIFS, MAXIFS, and MINIFS functions.

## Conditional Counting with COUNTIF

Claire wants to know how many posts over the past year were made to Facebook, Instagram, and Twitter. You can use the COUNT function to count the number of social media posts, but that would include all records, regardless of the social media site. To count only those records that match a specified condition, you can create a **conditional count** using the COUNTIF function

   COUNTIF(*range, criteria*)

where **range** references the range of cells or table field to be counted and **criteria** is a value or a condition that defines which cells to include in the count. For example, the following expression counts the number of cells in the range D5:D789 whose value equals "Facebook":

   COUNTIF(D5:D789, "Facebook")

Rather than explicitly entering the criteria value, you can reference a cell containing that value. The following formula counts the numbers of cells in the range D5:D789 whose values equal the value stored in cell B10:

   COUNTIF(D5:D789, B10)

Figure 7–13 provides examples of other ways the COUNTIF function can be used for conditional counting.

| Figure 7–13 | Conditional counting with the COUNTIF function |

| Formula | Description |
|---|---|
| =COUNTIF(A1:A100, "Twitter") | Counts the cells in the A1:A100 range with the text, "Twitter" |
| =COUNTIF(Media[SITE], "Twitter") | Counts the records in the Media table whose Platform field value equals the text, "Twitter" |
| =COUNTIF(B1:B100, 25) | Counts the cells in the B1:B100 range that have a value of 25 |
| =COUNTIF(C1:C100, D10) | Counts the cells in the C1:C100 range with values equal to the value stored in cell D10 |
| =COUNTIF(E1:E100, "> 50") | Counts the cells in the E1:E100 range with values greater than 50 |
| =COUNTIF(Media[SHARES], ">=50") | Counts the records in the Media table whose Shares value is greater than or equal to 50 |
| =COUNTIF(F1:F100, ">=" & G10) | Counts the cells in the F1:F100 range with values greater than or equal to the value in cell G10 |
| =COUNTIF(Media[VIEWS], "> " & Popular) | Counts the records in the Media table where the value of the Views field is greater than the value stored in the Popular defined name |

Note that you can use the ampersand character (&) to combine text strings with cell values. For example, if cell A1 contains the value 50, then the expression "<=" & A1 is equivalent to the text string "<= 50". By storing conditional values within cells, you can use the COUNTIF function to calculate different conditions by changing those cell's values.

You will use the COUNTIF function to count the number of posts from each social media site, placing the formulas in the Dashboard worksheet.

### To do conditional counting with the COUNTIF function:

1. Go to the **Dashboard** worksheet and click cell **B11**.

2. Type **=COUNTIF(Media[SITE], B10)** to count the number of records in Media table where the value of the Site field equals the value stored in cell B10 (Facebook).

Tip

When entering the formula, use AutoComplete to select the table name (Media) and the field name (SITE) from the list.

3. Press **ENTER**. The formula returns 332, indicating that 332 posts were made to Facebook over the past 12 months.

4. Copy the formula in cell **B11** and paste it into cells **D11** and **F11** to count the number of posts made to the Instagram and Twitter sites. There were 303 posts to Instagram and 150 posts to Twitter.

5. In cell **H11**, enter the formula **=COUNTA(Media[SITE])** to calculate the total posts from all sites. The formula returns 785, which is also equal to the sum of cells B11, D11, and F11. See Figure 7–14.

| Figure 7-14 | COUNTIF function applied to the Media table |

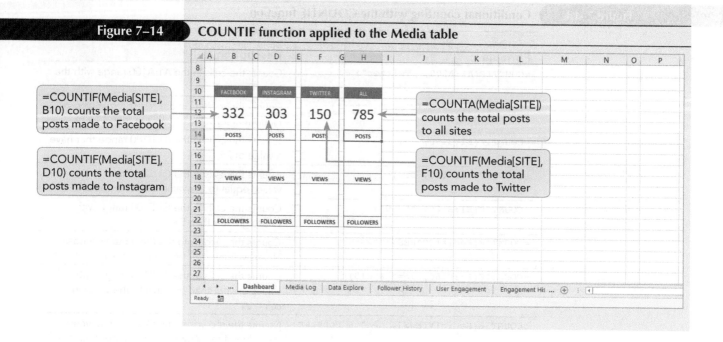

Note that the COUNTIF function makes no distinction between text values and numeric values unlike the COUNT function, which does not count text values.

## Calculating Conditional Sums with SUMIF

The SUMIF function calculates the sum of values that match specified criteria, creating a **conditional sum**. The syntax of the SUMIF function is

```
SUMIF(range, criteria, [sum_range])
```

where **range** is the range of cells to be evaluated by the criteria specified in the *criteria* argument, and *sum_range* is an optional argument that specifies the values to sum. The following expression uses the SUMIF function to calculate the sum of values in the range A1:A100, but only those cells whose value is greater than 50:

```
SUMIF(A1:A100, "> 50")
```

If you include the *sum_range* argument, the selected cells in that range will correspond to the selected cells in the criteria range. Figure 7-15 shows an example of using the SUMIF function to sum the values in the range E3:E12 whose cells correspond to cells in the criteria range (range C3:C12) with the value "Twitter."

**Figure 7–15**    Conditional sums with the SUMIF function

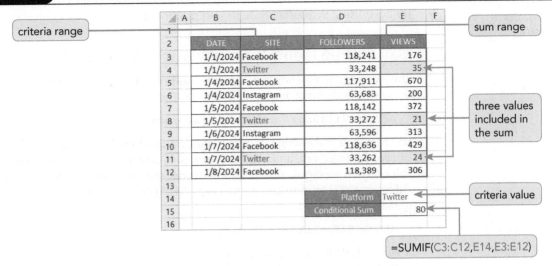

You will use the SUMIF function to calculate the total number of views for each social media site in Media table. You will use the SITE field as the criteria range and the VIEWS field as the sum range.

### To calculate a conditional sum with the SUMIF function:

▶ **1.** In the Dashboard worksheet, click cell **B15**.

▶ **2.** Type **=SUMIF(Media[SITE], B10, Media[VIEWS])** to sum the values from the Views field for records whose Site field value equals "Facebook" (cell B10).

▶ **3.** Press **ENTER**. The formula returns 153,677, which is the total number of views from posts made to Facebook over the past year.

▶ **4.** Copy the formula in cell **B15** and paste it into cells **D15** and **F15** to find the total views from posts made to Instagram and Twitter. The values 121,134 and 6,269 appear in cells D15 and F15, respectively.

▶ **5.** In cell **H15**, enter the formula **=SUM(Media[VIEWS])** to calculate the total views from all sites. The formula returns 281,080. See Figure 7–16.

**Figure 7–16**    SUMIF function applied to the Media table

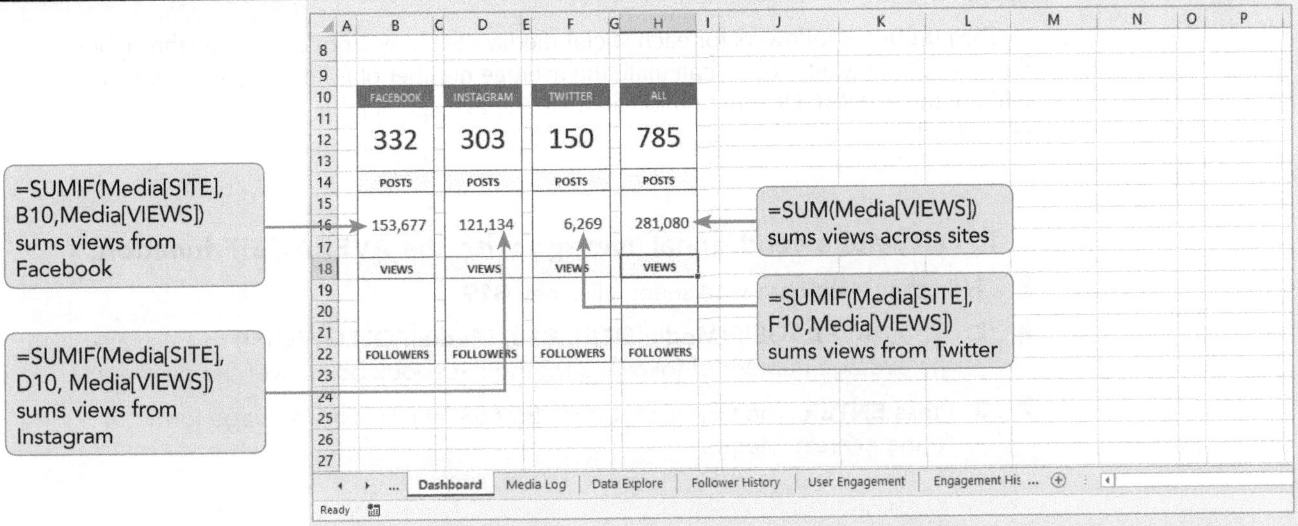

**Tip**

For more general matches, use wildcards in the criteria expression.

These calculations reveal that most views come from Facebook and Instagram, and very few come from Twitter. This indicates that those two sites might be better platforms for advertising Syrmosta products and promotions.

## Calculating Conditional Averages with AVERAGEIF

The AVERAGEIF function calculates a **conditional average** by taking the average only of those values that match specified criteria. The syntax of the AVERAGEIF function is

        AVERAGEIF(*range, criteria,* [*average_range*])

where **range** is the range of cells to be evaluated by the criteria specified in the **criteria** argument, and *average_range* is an optional argument that specifies the values to be averaged. The following expression uses the AVERAGEIF function to calculate the sum of values in the range A1:A100, but only those cells whose value is greater than 50:

        AVERAGEIF(A1:A100, "> 50")

If you include the *average_range* argument, Excel will calculate averages for cells in that range corresponding to values in the criteria range. Figure 7–17 shows how to apply the AVERAGEIF function to calculate the average of the values in the range D3:D12 but only for followers of the Facebook site.

**Figure 7–17** Conditional averages with the AVERAGEIF function

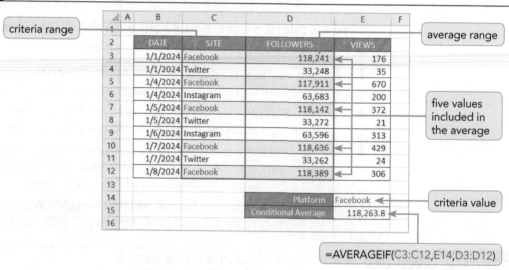

The number of followers for each social media site varies from day-to-day throughout the year. Claire wants you to calculate the average number of followers per post. You will use the AVERAGEIF function to calculate the average number of followers broken down by the social media site.

**To calculate a conditional average with the AVERAGEIF function:**

1. In the Dashboard worksheet, click cell **B19**.

2. Type **=AVERAGEIF(Media[SITE], B10, Media[FOLLOWERS])** to calculate the average number of followers for the Facebook posts over the past year.

3. Press **ENTER**. The formula returns 126,683, which is the average formatted to the nearest integer.

▶ **4.** Copy the formula in cell **B19** and paste it into cells **D19** and **F19** to calculate the average followers per post for Instagram and Twitter. The formulas return 64,055 and 33,509, respectively.

▶ **5.** In cell **H19**, enter the formula **=B19+D19+F19** to calculate the sum of the three averages. The average for all the three sites is 224,248. See Figure 7–18.

| Figure 7–18 | AVERAGEIF function applied to the Media table |

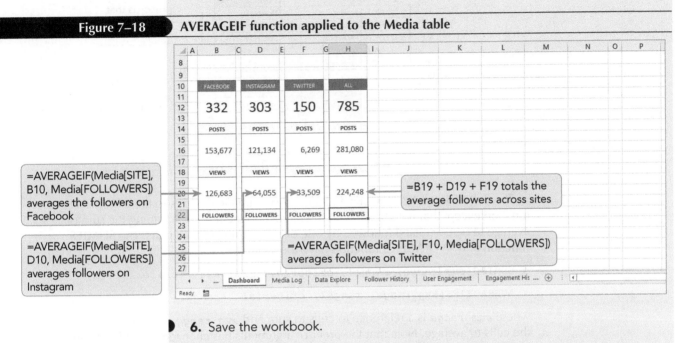

▶ **6.** Save the workbook.

Facebook is the most popular social media site for following news about Syrmosta. Your calculations show that an average post has almost 127,000 followers on Facebook, 64,000 followers on Instagram, and more than 33,000 followers on Twitter. The total number of followers is about 224,000.

## Using Summary IFS Functions

The COUNTIF, SUMIF, and AVERAGEIF functions support a single criteria argument. Excel also supports summary functions that allow for multiple criteria—COUNTIFS, SUMIFS, and AVERAGEIFS. To apply multiple criteria for a conditional count, use the **COUNTIFS function**

```
COUNTIFS(range1, criteria1, [range2], [criteria2] …)
```

where **range1** is the range in which to count cells indicated in **criteria1**; the optional arguments **range2**, **criteria2**, and so on are additional ranges and criteria for choosing which cells to count. You can include up to 127 range/criteria pairs. Each additional range must have the same number of rows and columns as *range1* and *criteria1*, though the ranges do not have to be adjacent.

Figure 7–19 shows conditional counting with two range/criteria pairs. Notice that the count includes only those records that satisfy *both* criteria.

**Figure 7-19**    Conditional counting with the COUNTIFS function

The SUMIFS and AVERAGEIFS functions have similar syntaxes to the COUNTIFS function except that both begin with a reference to the range containing the sum or average to be calculated followed by one or more criteria/range pairs. The **SUMIFS function** and **AVERAGEIFS function** have the syntax

SUMIFS(*sum_range, range1, criteria1,* [*range2*], [*criteria2*] …)

AVERAGEIFS(*avg_range, range1, criteria1,* [*range2*], [*criteria2*] …)

where **sum_range** is a reference to cells to sum and **avg_range** is a reference to the cells to average. Note that the order of arguments has changed from SUMIF and AVERAGEIF. In the SUMIF and AVERAGEIF functions, the range to be calculated is an optional argument listed last. With the SUMIFS and AVERAGEIFS functions, the range to be calculated is listed first and is required.

Figure 7–20 shows how to calculate conditional sums and averages using multiple range/criteria pairs. Once again, only those cells that match *all* criteria are included in the calculated result.

**Figure 7-20**    Sums and averages with multiple criteria

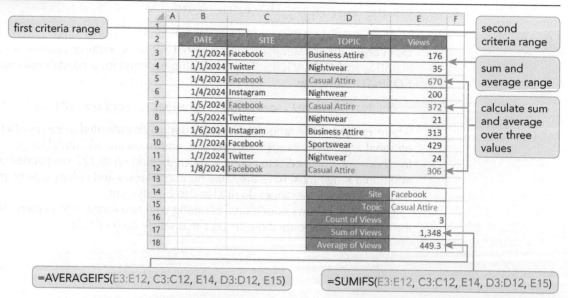

Finally, to calculate the minimum and maximum value in a range under multiple criteria, use the **MINIFS function** and the **MAXIFS function**, which have the syntax

```
MINIFS(min_range, range1, criteria1, [range2], [criteria2] …)
```

```
MAXIFS(max_range, range1, criteria1, [range2], [criteria2] …)
```

where *min_range* and *max_range* reference the cells in which to find the minimum and maximum value, subject to constraints specified in the range/criteria pairs.

The summary IFS functions calculate summary statistics based on several criteria. But that approach becomes cumbersome as you add more criteria ranges to the function. A better approach in those situations is to construct a PivotTable. You'll work with PivotTables in the next session.

# Review

## Session 7.1 Quick Check

1. A school gives out grades in the following ranges: F: 0 – < 60; D: 60 – < 70; C: 70 – < 80; B: 80 – < 90; A: 90 – 100. Create a vertical lookup table for this grade scale with the range values in the first column and the letter grades in the second.

2. What is the VLOOKUP function to perform an approximate match lookup for a test score of 83? Assume the lookup table is named GradeScale and the grades are in the second column.

3. What is the XLOOKUP function to perform an approximate match lookup for a test score of 83? Assume the column containing the lower end of the range of test scores is named TestScores and the range containing the grades is named Grades.

4. How does XLOOKUP differ from VLOOKUP in the placement of the column of lookup values?

5. How does XLOOKUP differ from VLOOKUP in how it handles failed matches?

6. What is the function to count the number of cells in the range B1:B50 that equal "B"?

7. What is the function to calculate the average of the cells in the range C1:C50 for which the adjacent cell in the range B1:B50 equals "B"?

8. What is the function to calculate the sum of the values in the range D1:D50 for which the adjacent value in the range A1:A50 equals "Senior" and the adjacent value in the range B1:B50 equals "B"?

# Session 7.2 Visual Overview:

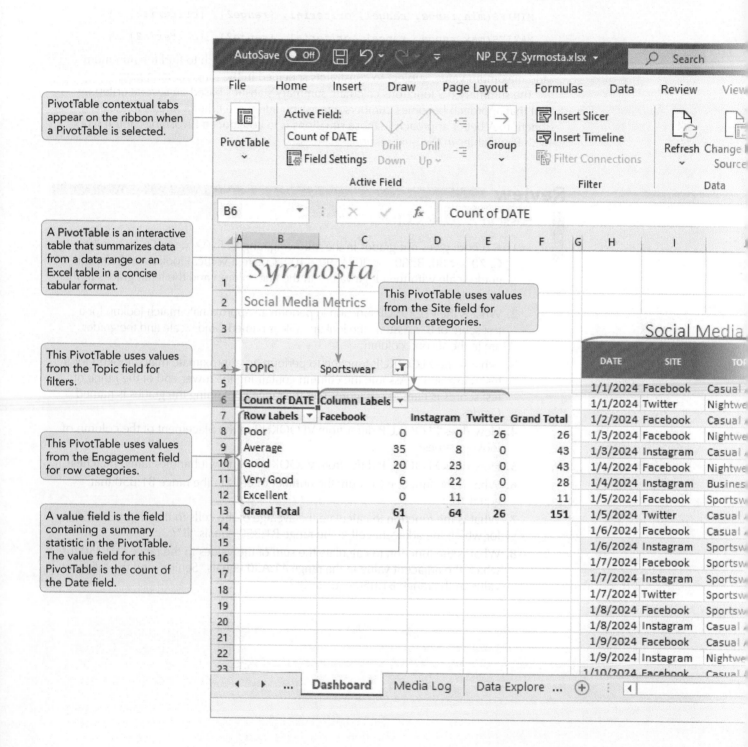

PivotTable contextual tabs appear on the ribbon when a PivotTable is selected.

A PivotTable is an interactive table that summarizes data from a data range or an Excel table in a concise tabular format.

This PivotTable uses values from the Topic field for filters.

This PivotTable uses values from the Site field for column categories.

This PivotTable uses values from the Engagement field for row categories.

A value field is the field containing a summary statistic in the PivotTable. The value field for this PivotTable is the count of the Date field.

| Count of DATE | Column Labels | | | |
|---|---|---|---|---|
| Row Labels | Facebook | Instagram | Twitter | Grand Total |
| Poor | 0 | 0 | 26 | 26 |
| Average | 35 | 8 | 0 | 43 |
| Good | 20 | 23 | 0 | 43 |
| Very Good | 6 | 22 | 0 | 28 |
| Excellent | 0 | 11 | 0 | 11 |
| Grand Total | 61 | 64 | 26 | 151 |

TOPIC    Sportswear

# PivotTables

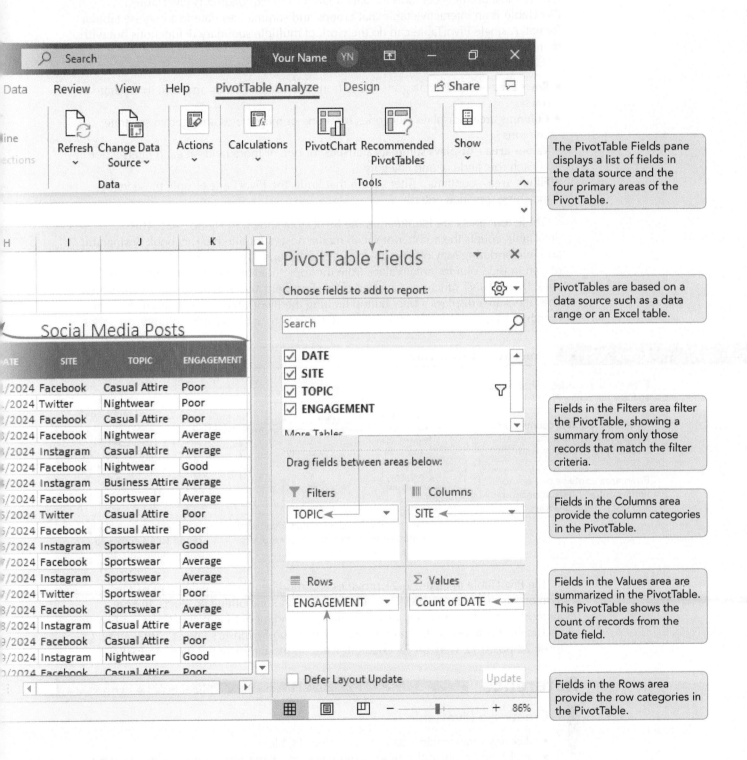

The PivotTable Fields pane displays a list of fields in the data source and the four primary areas of the PivotTable.

PivotTables are based on a data source such as a data range or an Excel table.

Fields in the Filters area filter the PivotTable, showing a summary from only those records that match the filter criteria.

Fields in the Columns area provide the column categories in the PivotTable.

Fields in the Values area are summarized in the PivotTable. This PivotTable shows the count of records from the Date field.

Fields in the Rows area provide the row categories in the PivotTable.

# Creating PivotTables

One of most useful Excel tools for data analysis and exploration is PivotTables. A PivotTable is an interactive table that groups and summarizes data in a concise tabular format. A single PivotTable can do the work of multiple summary IF functions but with more ease and flexibility.

Every PivotTable includes the following four primary areas:

- **Rows area**—displays category values from one or more fields arranged in separate rows
- **Columns area**—displays categories from one or more fields arranged in separate columns
- **Values area**—displays summary statistics for one or more fields at each intersection of each row and column category
- **Filters area**—contains a filter button that limits the PivotTable to only those values matching specified criteria

These four areas are identified in the PivotTable shown in Figure 7–21. This PivotTable counts the number of social media posts submitted to Facebook, Instagram, and Twitter during May broken down by the post topic. The social media sites are placed in the Columns area. Values from the Topic field are displayed in the Rows area. The COUNT function is applied to the Post field and displayed in the Values area. The Filters area displays a filter button limiting the PivotTable to data records from the month of May. A table also includes grand totals across all row and column categories.

| Figure 7–21 | Structure of a PivotTable |
|---|---|

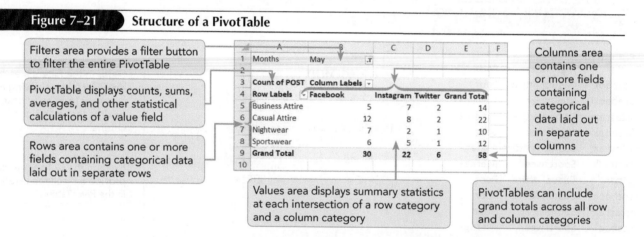

The PivotTable in Figure 7–21 provides a comprehensive breakdown of where Syrmosta is posting their messages and for what line of clothing products. In May, Syrmosta posted 58 times on social media sites, and more than half of those posts were on Facebook (30 posts). Of the 58 posts, 22 were on Syrmosta's line of casual attire. Of those 22 posts, 12 were on Facebook, 8 were on Instagram, and 2 were on Twitter.

# Reference

### Creating a PivotTable

- Click anywhere within a data range or Excel table.
- On the Insert tab, in the Tables group, click the PivotTable button; or on the Table Design tab, in the Tools group, click the Summarize with PivotTable button.
- Specify whether to insert the PivotTable in a new worksheet or at a cell location within an existing worksheet.
- Click OK.
- Drag fields from the field list on the PivotTable Fields pane and drop them on the Filters, Columns, Rows, or Values area boxes.

## Inserting a PivotTable

You can create a PivotTable from any data range or Excel table and insert the PivotTable within a new worksheet or an existing worksheet. To create a PivotTable, click in a data range or an Excel table, and then click the PivotTable button in the Tables group on the Insert tab. Excel reserves a space 3 columns wide by 18 rows tall for the initial PivotTable report. If the worksheet does not have enough empty space, you'll be prompted to overwrite the cell content.

Claire wants to analyze social media posts by site and product line. You'll create a PivotTable from the data in the Media table for this purpose.

### To create a PivotTable from the Media table:

1. If you took a break at the end of the previous session, make sure the NP_EX_7_Syrmosta workbook is open.

2. Go to the **Media Log** worksheet and click cell **B4** to select a cell in the Media table.

**Tip**

You can also click the Summarize with PivotTable button in the Tools group on the Table Design tab to open the Create PivotTable dialog box.

3. On the ribbon, click the **Insert** tab, and then in the Tables group, click the **PivotTable** button. The Create PivotTable dialog box opens.

4. Verify that **Media** appears in the Table/Range box. This specifies the Media table as the source for the PivotTable.

5. Click the **Existing Worksheet** option button, and then press **TAB** to move the insertion point into the Location box. You want to insert the PivotTable into the Data Explore worksheet starting at cell B6.

6. Click the **Data Explore** sheet tab, and then in the Data Explore worksheet, click cell **B6**. The 3-D reference 'Data Explore'!$B$6 is entered into the Location box. See Figure 7–22.

| Figure 7–22 | Create PivotTable dialog box |
| --- | --- |

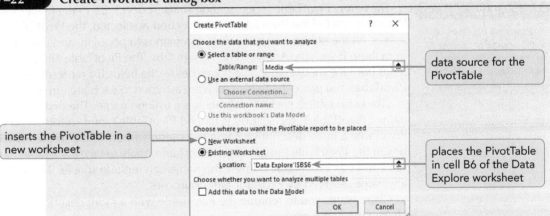

7. Click **OK**. The empty PivotTable report appears in the Data Explore worksheet. See Figure 7–23.

**Figure 7–23** Empty PivotTable report

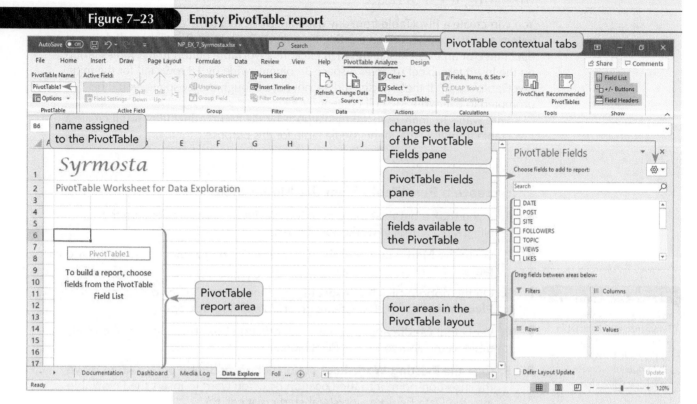

**Trouble?** If you do not see the PivotTable Fields pane, you need to display it. Click the PivotTable Analyze tab, and then in the Show group, click the Field List button.

**Tip**

You can click the Gear icon in the upper-right corner of the PivotTable Fields pane to choose a different layout of the area boxes.

The empty PivotTable report section starts from cell B6 in the Data Explore worksheet. When any part of the PivotTable report section is selected, the PivotTable contextual tabs appear on the ribbon. You can select commands to populate and format the PivotTable from these PivotTable Analyze and Design tabs. The PivotTable Fields pane shows the fields from the Media table. The boxes below the fields list represent the four areas of the PivotTable. You place the fields you want assigned to each area in these boxes.

Like Excel tables, each PivotTable has a unique name. The first PivotTable created is named PivotTable1, the second is named PivotTable2, and so forth. You can give each PivotTable a more descriptive name by entering a new name in the PivotTable Name box in the PivotTable group on the PivotTable Analyze tab. PivotTable names have the same rules as Excel table names: The name can include spaces. The name cannot be any name reserved by Excel for other purposes.

Claire wants you to rename the PivotTable with a more descriptive name. You will change the name now.

### To change the PivotTable name:

**Tip**

Always give PivotTables descriptive names so you can more easily reference them in your workbook.

1. On the PivotTable Analyze tab, in the PivotTable group, double-click the **PivotTable Name** box. The default name "PivotTable1" is selected.

2. Press **DELETE**, and then type **Explore PivotTable** as the new name.

3. Press **ENTER**. The PivotTable is renamed.

Next you will begin populating the PivotTable with the fields from the Media table.

## Creating a PivotTable Layout

The PivotTable layout is created by dragging fields from the field list into one of the four area boxes. This determines the basic structure of the PivotTable. There is no particular order that the areas of the table need to be filled in. Although it's often best to start with the field containing the data you want to summarize and then expand the PivotTable from there. Excel updates the PivotTable in the report area and does all the calculations to match your selections. Once the PivotTable layout is in place, you can fine-tune its format and appearance.

Claire wants this PivotTable to count the number of posts made to the different social media sites broken down by topic. You will start by placing the Post field in the Values area box, followed by the Site field in the Columns areas and the Topic field in the Rows area.

**To place fields in the Values, Columns, and Rows areas:**

▶  **1.** In the PivotTable Fields pane, point to **POST** in the field list to highlight it, and then drag the Post field into the Values areas box. "Count of POST" appears in the Values box and the PivotTable shows the count of the Posts field. See Figure 7–24.

| Figure 7–24 | Post field added to the Values area |
| --- | --- |

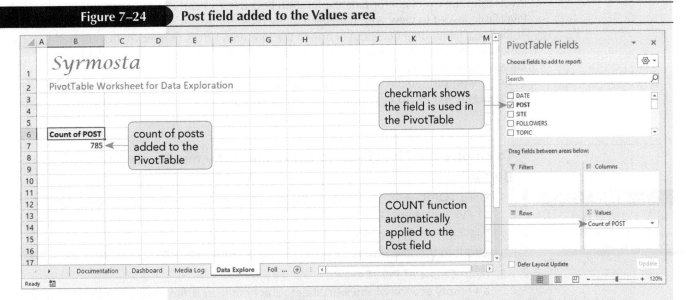

Tip

PivotTables by default use the COUNT function for non-numeric data placed in the Values area.

▶  **2.** Drag the **Site** field into the Columns area box. The number of posts is broken down by social media site, showing 332 posts made to Facebook, 303 posts made to Instagram, and 150 posts made to Twitter. These are the same numbers you calculated with the COUNTIF function (refer back to Figure 7–14), but the PivotTable does all those calculations for you.

▶  **3.** Drag the **Topic** field onto the Rows area box. The number of posts for each social media site is now broken out by topic. See Figure 7–25.

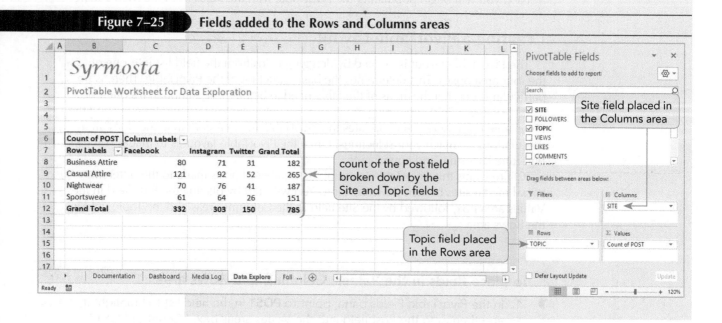

**Figure 7–25** Fields added to the Rows and Columns areas

## Modifying the PivotTable Layout

PivotTables are excellent for data exploration because you can quickly change the PivotTable layout to view your data from many different angles. To change the content of the PivotTable, drag fields out of any of the four area boxes to remove them from the table and drop new fields into the area boxes to add them. The PivotTable calculations are automatically updated to reflect the new layout.

Claire wants to see the sum of shares broken down by media site and profit group. You'll modify the PivotTable to show these calculations.

### To modify the PivotTable to show shares by media site and profit group:

1. Drag **TOPIC** from the Rows area box and drop the icon on an empty section of the worksheet. The Topic field is removed from the PivotTable.

2. Drag the **PROFIT GROUP** field from the field list into the Rows area box to add it to the PivotTable.

3. Drag **Count of POST** from the Values area box and drop the icon on an empty section of the worksheet. The Post field is removed from the PivotTable.

4. Drag the **SHARES** field from the field list into the Values area box. The sum of the Shares field is added to the PivotTable. PivotTables by default use the SUM function for numeric data placed in the Values area. See Figure 7–26.

| Figure 7–26 | Modified PivotTable |

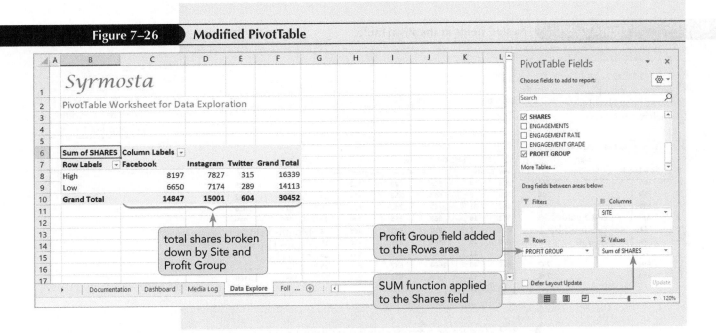

Over the past year, there was a total of 30,452 shares of Syrmosta social media posts. The row totals show the media shares were fairly evenly split between the high-profit and low-profit items, with high-profit items receiving slightly more shares across all media sites.

## Adding Multiple Fields to a Row or Column

PivotTables are not limited to a single field in the Rows or Columns area. You can place additional fields in each area, nesting one field within another. For example, placing the Profit Group field and then Site field in the Columns area would show values for each profit group divided into different media sites. The PivotTable will include subtotals for each profit group, so you can view summary statistics within and across the group levels.

Excel automatically provides subgroups for date fields. If values from a date field span several years, the dates are grouped by years and by quarters within years. If the dates cover a single year, the dates are automatically grouped by months.

Claire wants you to modify the PivotTable to show the Profit Group and Site fields in the Columns area and the Date field in the Rows area. You'll make these changes now.

### To nest fields within a PivotTable:

▶ 1. Drag **PROFIT GROUP** from the Rows area box and drop it into the Columns area box directly above the SITE field. Both the Profit Group field and the Site field appear in the PivotTable columns. Subtotals appear for each profit group and site.

▶ 2. Drag the **DATE** field from the field list and drop it into the Rows area box to add it to the PivotTable. A new field named Months is added to the PivotTable, which groups the dates in the PivotTable by month. See Figure 7–27. You can expand any month to view daily statistics.

**Figure 7–27**    **Nested fields in the PivotTable**

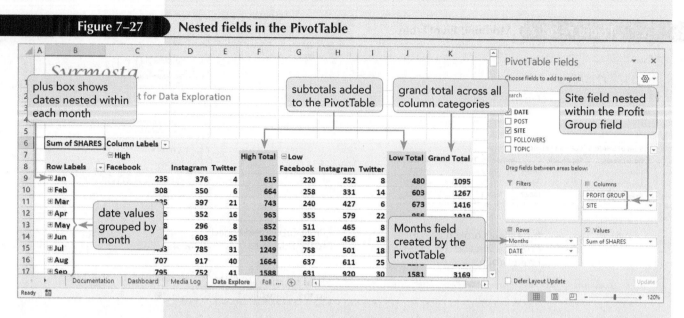

**3.** In the Rows area of the PivotTable, to the left of the Jan entry, click the **plus box** to expand the January group. The posts made for dates in January are displayed. Depending on your computer's configuration, dates might appear as 01-Jan, 02-Jan, and so forth. See Figure 7–28.

**Figure 7–28**    **Grouped field expanded**

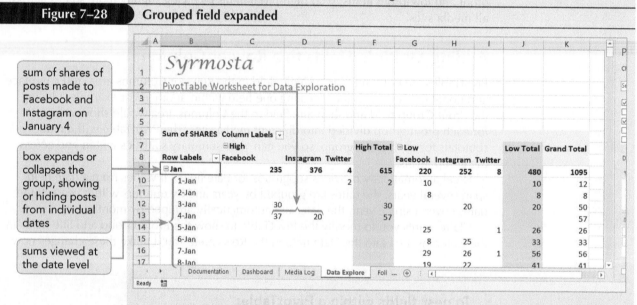

**4.** Click the **minus box** to left of the Jan entry to collapse the group, showing only the month totals.

**5.** Click the **Date** check box in the field list. The Date field is deselected, removing it from the PivotTable. The Months field remains, leaving only the monthly totals.

**6.** Click the **Profit Group** check box in the field list to remove that field from the PivotTable.

The PivotTable now shows the sum of the Shares field broken down by media site and month. Next you will explore how to filter the PivotTable data.

## Filtering a PivotTable

The Filters area is a quick way to filter PivotTable data. When you add a field to the Filters area, a filter button appears two rows above the upper-left corner of the table. You can then use the button to choose a value to filter the entire PivotTable by. For example, you can add a filter button for the Topic field, and then use the button to filter the PivotTable by one of the Topic values, such as Sportswear. Like the Columns and Rows area, the Filters area can contain multiple fields.

Claire wants the PivotTable to show a summary of the posts about Syrmosta's line of sportswear. You'll add the Topic field to the Filters area, and then use the filter button to show only posts dealing with sportswear.

### To add the Topic field to the Filters area:

**Tip**

To select multiple items, click the Select Multiple Items check box and then click each item to include in the filter.

1. Drag the **TOPIC** field from the field list and drop it in the Filters area box. A label and filter button are added to the range B4:C4.

2. Click the **filter** button in cell C4, and then click **Sportswear** from the list of topics.

3. Click **OK** to apply the filter to the PivotTable. See Figure 7–29.

**Figure 7–29**   Filtered PivotTable

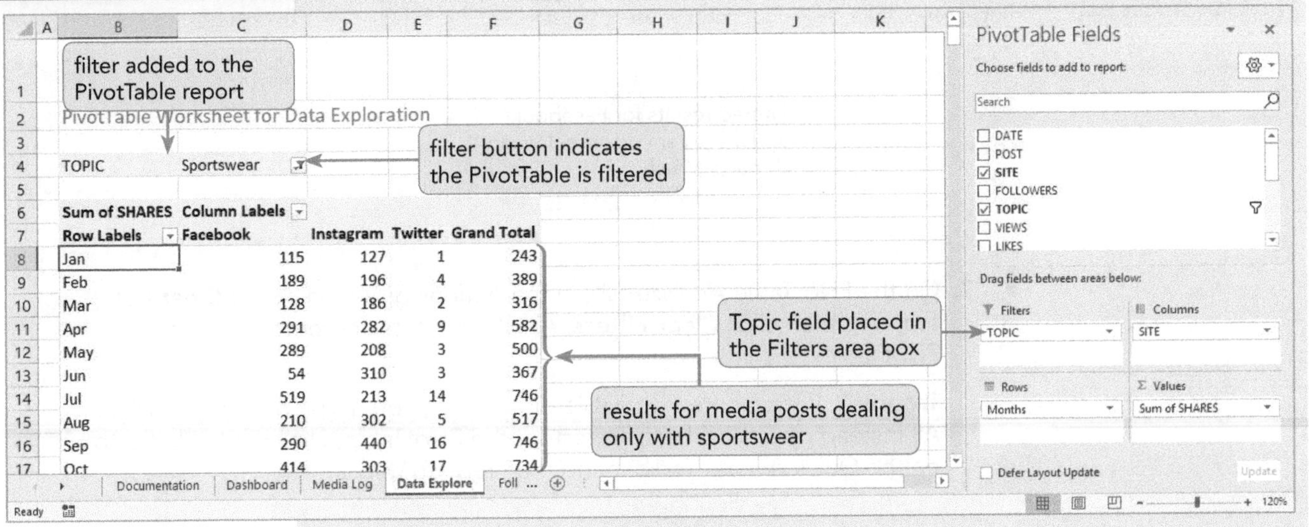

For more filter options, you can use the filter buttons next to the row and column labels in the PivotTable, choosing which row or column categories to include in the PivotTable. Claire wants you to limit the PivotTable to show only Facebook and Instagram posts for the months of January through March. You'll use the column and row labels filter buttons to do this.

## To filter the column and row categories:

1. In cell C6, click the **Column Labels filter** button. The filter menu opens.

2. Click the **Select All** check box to deselect it, and then click the **Facebook** and **Instagram** check boxes to select them.

3. Click **OK** to apply the filter to the column categories. Only Facebook and Instagram posts appear in the PivotTable.

4. In cell B7, click the **Row Labels filter** button. The filter menu opens.

5. Click the **Select All** check box to deselect it, and then click the **Jan**, **Feb**, and **Mar** check boxes to select them.

6. Click **OK** to apply the filter to the row categories. Only January, February, and March posts appear in the PivotTable. See Figure 7–30.

| Figure 7–30 | Filtered column and row categories |

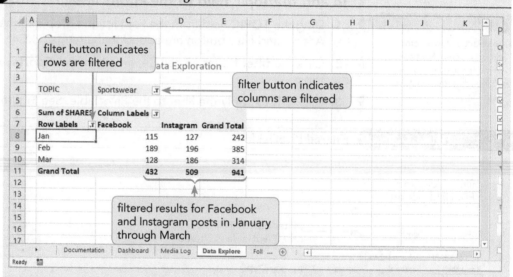

filter button indicates rows are filtered

filter button indicates columns are filtered

filtered results for Facebook and Instagram posts in January through March

7. On the PivotTable Analyze tab, in the Actions group, click the **Clear** button, and then click **Clear Filters**. All of the filters are removed from the PivotTable.

   **Trouble?** If the entire PivotTable disappears, you might have clicked Clear All instead of Clear Filters. To restore the PivotTable, click the Undo button on the Quick Access Toolbar and then repeat Step 7.

As you've seen, PivotTables are extremely flexible. With them you can quickly explore data from a variety of views without writing a single formula.

## Insight

### Choosing a Recommended PivotTable

If you're not sure what to include in a PivotTable or how to structure it, you can use the Recommend PivotTables tool. To use the tool, select any cell within a data range or Excel table, and then click the Recommended PivotTables button in the Tables group on the Insert tab. A gallery of PivotTable layouts suitable for that data opens. Choose the one you find most useful and relevant. The PivotTable is inserted on a new sheet in the workbook using the layout you selected.

# Formatting a PivotTable

You can format PivotTables to make them more visually appealing and the results easier to read. You should format a PivotTable after you have decided on its structure, layout, and content.

Claire wants PivotTables added to the Dashboard worksheet that provide a concise summary of Syrmosta's social media history. The first PivotTable will display the total number of views, likes, comments, shares, and engagements for Syrmosta social media posts. You'll add this table now.

### To create a PivotTable that summarizes social media engagement:

1. Go to the **Media Log** worksheet and click cell **B4** if necessary to select it.

2. On the ribbon, click the **Insert** tab, and then in the Tables group, click **PivotTable**. The Create PivotTable dialog box opens.

3. Click the **Existing Worksheet** option button, press **TAB**, click the **Dashboard** sheet tab, click cell **J11** on the Dashboard worksheet, and then click **OK**. A blank PivotTable Report is added to the Dashboard worksheet starting from cell J11.

4. On the PivotTable Analyze tab, in the PivotTable group, click the **PivotTable Name** box, type **Engagement Pivot**, and then press **ENTER**. The PivotTable is renamed.

5. Drag the **VIEWS**, **LIKES**, **COMMENTS**, **SHARES**, and **ENGAGEMENTS** fields from the field list into the Values area box in the order listed. The sum of each field is displayed in the PivotTable.

   When a PivotTable contains multiple value fields, Excel organizes those fields into an item called ∑Values, so you can place all value fields within a single location in the PivotTable. In this PivotTable, the ∑Values item is added to the Columns area so that each of the fields appears in a separate column.

6. Drag **∑Values** from the Columns area box and drop it in the Rows area box. The five fields are now placed in separate rows.

7. Drag the **SITE** field from the field list into the Columns area box to add the sums for each field by media site. The PivotTable shows the total number of views, likes, comments, shares, and engagements for Facebook, Instagram, and Twitter. See Figure 7–31.

**Figure 7–31**    Sum of social media engagements

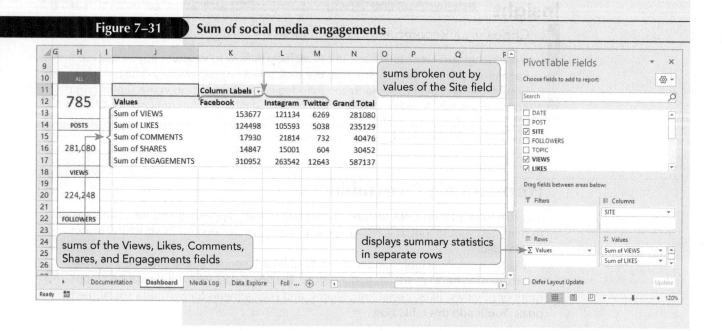

Next, you will format the contents of the PivotTable.

## Changing Labels and Number Formats

The label for each value field contains the summary function followed by the field name. For example, the first label in the Engagement Pivot PivotTable is "Sum of VIEWS," the second is "Sum of LIKES," and so forth. You can change these labels to any text except the name of a field used by the PivotTable. You can also modify the appearance of the summary statistics by changing the number format.

Claire wants the PivotTable labels changed to Viewed, Liked, Commented, Shared and Engaged. Claire also wants a thousands separator added to the calculated results to make the numbers easier to read. You will make these changes to the format of the five value fields now.

### To format the five PivotTable calculated value fields:

1. In cell J13 of the PivotTable, double-click the **Sum of VIEWS** label. The Value Field Settings dialog box opens so you can set the options for this value field.

2. Click the **Number Format** button. The Format Cells dialog box opens and contains only the Number tab.

3. In the Category box, click **Number**, enter **0** in the Decimal places box, click the **Use 1000 Separator (,)** check box, and then click **OK** to return to the Value Field Settings dialog box.

4. In the Custom Name box, change the text to **Viewed**. See Figure 7–32.

| Figure 7–32 | Value Field Settings dialog box |

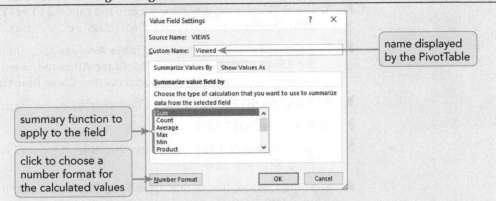

summary function to apply to the field

click to choose a number format for the calculated values

name displayed by the PivotTable

5. Click **OK**. The title in the PivotTable's first row changes to Viewed and the calculated sums in the first row have a thousands separator and no decimal places.

6. Repeat Steps 1 through 5 for the Sum of LIKES, Sum of COMMENTS, Sum of SHARES, and Sum of ENGAGEMENTS value fields, changing their names to **Liked**, **Commented**, **Shared**, and **Engaged** and changing the number formats to display zero decimal places and include a thousands separator. See Figure 7–33.

| Figure 7–33 | PivotTable with custom labels and number formats |

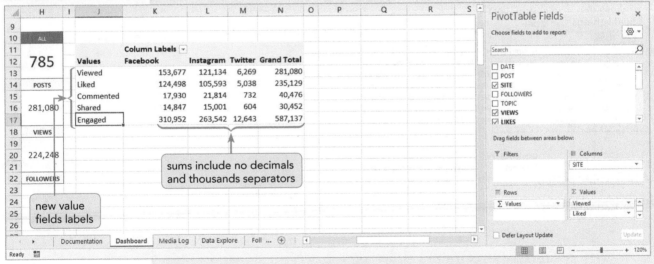

new value fields labels

sums include no decimals and thousands separators

Although you can format PivotTable values using the formatting commands on the Home tab, this formatting is lost if the PivotTable layout changes. Instead, you should format values using the Value Field Settings dialog box, which maintains the formats even when the PivotTable layout changes.

The next PivotTable Claire wants added to the dashboard will count the number of posts by social media site. You'll create and format this PivotTable, changing the label to "Total Posts." Rather than creating a new PivotTable from the Media table, you can copy the PivotTable that already exists on the Dashboard worksheet and then edit that new PivotTable.

## To create a PivotTable counting the number of social media posts:

1. In the Dashboard worksheet, copy the range **J11:N17** and paste it into cell **J20**. The Engagement Pivot PivotTable is duplicated.

2. On the ribbon, click the **PivotTable Analyze** tab, in the Actions group, click the **Clear** button, and then click **Clear All** to remove all the fields from the pasted PivotTable. If prompted, click the **Clear PivotTable** button.

3. Place the **SITE** field into the Columns area of the PivotTable.

4. Place the **POST** field in the Values area.

5. Double-click cell **J22** containing the label "Count of Post" to open the Value Field Settings dialog box.

6. In the Custom Name box, type **Total Posts** to revise the field label, and then click **OK**.

7. On the PivotTable Analyze tab, from the PivotTable group, click the **PivotTable Name** box, type **Total Posts Pivot** as the new name, and then press **ENTER**. See Figure 7–34.

| Figure 7–34 | Total posts by media site |

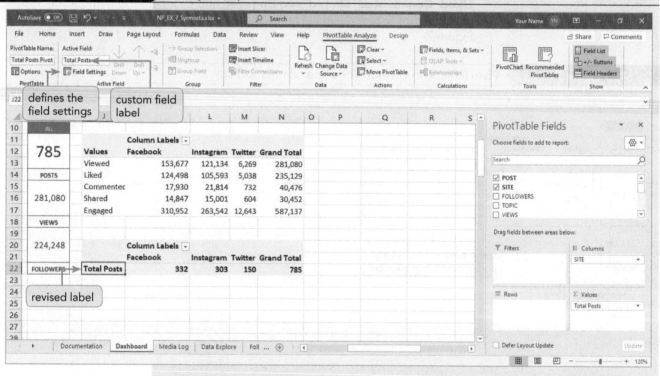

## Choosing a PivotTable Summary Function

By default, Excel uses the COUNT function to summarize non-numeric data and the SUM function for numeric data. However, sometimes you'll want to use different statistics in your analysis. You can choose a different summary function, such as AVERAGE, MIN, and MAX, from the Value Field Settings dialog box.

Claire wants to see a PivotTable showing the average engagement rate for each social media site added to the dashboard. You'll create that PivotTable now.

## To create a PivotTable of average engagement rates:

1. In the Dashboard worksheet, copy the range **J20:N22** and paste it into cell **J25**. The Total Posts Pivot PivotTable is duplicated.

2. Drag **Total Posts** out of the Values area, and then drag the **ENGAGEMENT RATE** field into the Values area.

3. On the ribbon, click the **PivotTable Analyze** tab, and then in the PivotTable Name box, enter **Engagement Rate Pivot** as the PivotTable name.

4. Double-click cell **J27** containing the "Sum of ENGAGEMENT RATE" label. The Value Field Settings dialog box opens.

5. In the list of summary statistics, click **Average**.

6. In the Custom Name box, type **Engaged Rate** as the new name.

7. Click the **Number Format** button. The Format Cells dialog box opens.

8. In the Category box, click **Percentage**, and then click **OK** in each dialog box to return to the worksheet. See Figure 7–35.

| Figure 7–35 | Average engagement rate by media site |
| --- | --- |

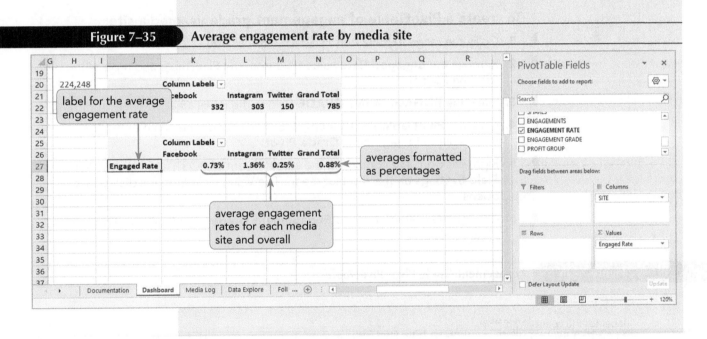

The Engagement Rate Pivot PivotTable shows that the highest average engagement rates are associated with posts on Instagram (1.36%) followed by Facebook (0.73%). Twitter has the lowest average engagement rate with 0.25%.

## Insight

### Moving a PivotTable

You can move any PivotTable to a new location in the workbook. To move a PivotTable within its current worksheet, select the entire PivotTable range and then drag the table to a new location, being careful not to overwrite other content in the process. To move a PivotTable to a different worksheet, click anywhere within the PivotTable to select it, and then click the Move PivotTable button in the Actions group on the PivotTable Analyze tab. The Move PivotTable dialog box opens so you can choose the new location for the PivotTable. You can create a new worksheet for the PivotTable or choose an existing worksheet in the workbook. You can also select the entire PivotTable and then use the Cut and Paste buttons in the Clipboard group on the Home tab to move the PivotTable within the workbook.

The last PivotTable Claire wants added to the dashboard will summarize the media posts by values of the Engagement Grade field. You will create this PivotTable now.

### To create a PivotTable of engagement grade vs. media site:

1. Copy the range **J25:N27** and paste it into cell **J30**.

2. Remove the **Engaged Rate** value field from the PivotTable and replace it with the **Post** field.

3. Place the **ENGAGEMENT GRADE** field in the Rows area.

4. Click the **PivotTable Analyze** tab, and then change the name of the PivotTable to **Engagement Grade Pivot**.

5. Right-click cell **J30** containing the label "Count of POST," and click **Value Field Settings** on the shortcut menu. The Value Field Settings dialog box opens.

6. Change the custom name to **Engagement Grades** and then click **OK**. See Figure 7–36.

| Figure 7–36 | Engagement Grade Pivot PivotTable |

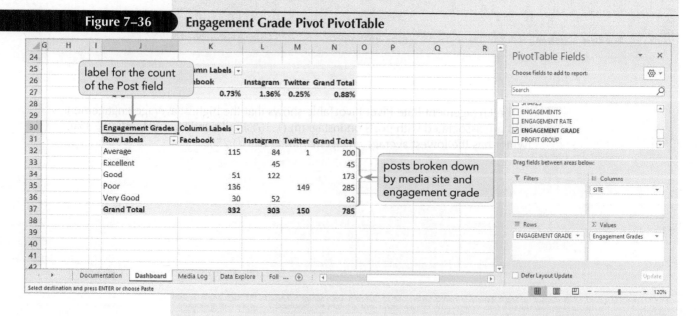

All of the posts that had an excellent grade of user engagement (where the engagement rate is above 2%) were on Instagram. On the other hand, of the 150 posts made on Twitter, 149 had poor engagement grades (an engagement rate less than 0.5%). The PivotTable contains several blank cells where there is no count of media posts. For example, no post made to Facebook had an excellent engagement response, so cell K33 is blank.

## Reordering PivotTable Categories

The categories listed in a PivotTable row or column follow a predefined order. Text categories are listed alphabetically. Date categories are arranged from the earliest date to the latest. If a custom list has been defined for the field, the categories appear in the order of the custom list. However, you can change the order of the categories at any point by typing the category names in whatever order you choose.

The categories for the Engagement Grade Pivot PivotTable are difficult to interpret because they are arranged alphabetically rather than in the order of user engagement. Claire wants them sorted from Poor up to Excellent. You'll rearrange the categories.

### To rearrange the Engagement Grade categories:

1. Click cell **J32** containing the Average category value.

2. Type **Poor** as the category name, and then press **ENTER**. The values for the Poor category are displayed in row 32 and the other categories are shifted down.

3. Click cell **J36** containing the Very Good category value.

4. Type **Excellent** as the category name, and then press **ENTER**. The Engagement Grade values are now listed in the order Poor, Average, Good, Very Good, and Excellent.

Make sure you type the category name exactly so the PivotTable can match it to the correct category.

Once you define the category order, that order becomes part of the **PivotTable cache**, which stores information about the PivotTable. If you move the Engagement Grade field to another area of the table or remove it and add it back in later, Excel will remember your preferred category order, so you will not have to redefine it.

## Insight

### Choosing a Report Layout

In addition to changing the structure of a PivotTable by moving fields into the different areas, you can change the overall table layout. PivotTables have possible three report layouts:

- **Compact Form**—(the default layout) places all fields from the Rows area in a single worksheet columns and indents values to distinguish nested fields from other fields.
- **Outline Form**—places each field in the Rows area in its own column and includes subtotals above every field category group.
- **Tabular Form**—places each field in the Rows area in its own column and includes subtotals below every group.

To switch between PivotTable layouts, click the Report Layout button from the Layout group on the Design tab. Choose the PivotTable layout that presents your data in the informative and effective format.

## Setting PivotTable Options

Several default values and behaviors are associated with PivotTables. For example, Excel automatically sorts the row and column categories and displays missing combinations within the PivotTable as blank cells. You can modify these defaults in the PivotTable Options dialog box.

Claire wants the Engagement Grade Pivot PivotTable to display zeros in place of blank cells to prevent confusion about the PivotTable values. Claire also doesn't want the PivotTable to display a Grand Total row because that information already appears in another PivotTable. Finally, Claire wants all the PivotTables in the Dashboard worksheet to maintain a constant width. Right now, the width of column J has varied with the addition of each PivotTable. You'll change these settings now.

### To set the PivotTable options:

1. On the PivotTable Analyze tab, in the PivotTable group click the **Options** button. The PivotTable Options dialog box opens.

2. On the Layout & Format tab, verify that the **For empty cells show** check box is selected, and then type **0** as the value to display for blank PivotTable cells.

3. Click the **Autofit column widths on update** check box to remove the checkmark. The row will remain the same width no matter how the PivotTables might change. See Figure 7–37.

---

**Figure 7–37**  **PivotTable Options dialog box**

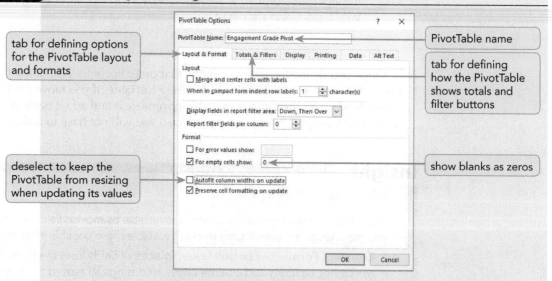

tab for defining options for the PivotTable layout and formats

PivotTable name

tab for defining how the PivotTable shows totals and filter buttons

deselect to keep the PivotTable from resizing when updating its values

show blanks as zeros

---

4. Click the **Totals & Filters** tab to display options for PivotTable totals and filters.

5. Click the **Show grand totals for columns** check box to deselect it.

6. Click **OK** to return to the worksheet and verify that the grand total row has been removed and blank cells are displayed as zeros.

7. Click cell **J25** to select the Engagement Rate Pivot PivotTable.

8. On the PivotTable Analyze tab, in the PivotTable group, click the **Options** button, click the **Autofit column widths on update** check box to deselect it, and then click **OK**. The PivotTable will not be resized.

9. Click cell **J20** to select the Total Posts Pivot PivotTable and then repeat Step 8 so the PivotTable will not resize.

10. Click cell **J11** to select the Engagement Pivot PivotTable, and then repeat Step 8 so that the PivotTable will not resize.

You can also remove grand total rows and columns by clicking the Grand Totals button in the Layout group on the Design tab, and selecting an option turn grand totals on or off for the rows and columns.

 **Proskills**

### Written Communication: Making PivotTables Accessible

Many companies and government agencies require documents to be accessible to users with visual impairments and special needs. Excel provides support for those users by making objects such as charts, graphics, and PivotTables accessible through alternate text.

To add alternate text to a PivotTable, open the PivotTable Options dialog box, and go to the Alt Text tab. On the Alt Text tab, you can specify a title for the alternate text. The title provides a brief description of the alternate text so that the user can decide whether to continue to review the PivotTable content. Below the title box, you can insert a description of the PivotTable. The description can be a general overview of the table's contents or a detailed summary of the PivotTable numbers and summary statistics. There is no character limit on alternate text, though a general guideline is to limit the summary to about 160 characters.

If you have to add alternate text to many objects in your workbooks, you can add the Alt Text command to the Quick Access Toolbar. For information on modifying the Quick Access Toolbar, refer to Excel Help.

## Setting the PivotTable Design

Just as you can apply built-in styles to Excel tables, there are built-in styles that you can apply to PivotTables. These styles are available in the PivotTable Styles gallery, which includes a variety of column and row colors. You can also set options such as adding banded rows and banded columns to the PivotTable design and whether to include column and row headings.

Another design feature you might want to remove are the filter buttons from the PivotTable's row and column areas. If you are preparing a final report in which you no longer need to filter the PivotTable data, you can hide this feature, giving your PivotTable a more compact and clean design.

Claire wants you to format the PivotTables on the Dashboard worksheet in preparation for the final report.

### To apply a design style to a PivotTable:

1. In cell **J10**, enter **USER RESPONSES** to label the top PivotTable, and then apply the **Accent3** cell style to cell J10.

2. Click cell **J11** to select the Engagement Pivot PivotTable.

**Tip**

You can hide the PivotTable Field pane by deselecting the Field List button in the Show group on the PivotTable Analyze tab.

3. On the ribbon, click the **PivotTables Analyze** tab, and then in the Show group, click the **Field Headers** button to deselect it. The Column Labels filter button disappears from the PivotTable.

4. Click the **Design** tab to display commands related to the layout and design of the PivotTable.

5. In the PivotTable Styles group, click the **More** button to open the PivotTable Styles gallery, and then in the Medium section, click the **Light Yellow, Pivot Style Medium 4** style located in the first row and fourth column of the Medium section.

6. In the PivotTable Style Options group, click the **Banded Rows** and **Banded Columns** check boxes to add gridlines to the PivotTable. See Figure 7–38.

**Figure 7–38**    **PivotTable with style and options**

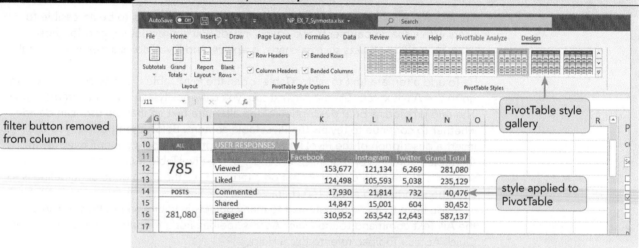

Claire wants all the PivotTables on the Dashboard worksheet to have the same look and design. You will repeat the formatting for the remaining PivotTables on the Dashboard worksheet.

**To complete the designs of the remaining PivotTables:**

1. In cell **J19**, enter **MEDIA POSTS** as the label, and then format that cell using the **Accent2** cell style.

2. Click cell **J20** to select the Total Posts Pivot PivotTable.

3. On the ribbon, click the **PivotTable Analyze** tab, and then in the Show group, click the **Field Headers** button to remove the Column Labels filter button.

4. On the ribbon, click the **Design** tab, in the PivotTable Styles group, click the **More** button, and then in the Medium section, click the **Light Orange, Pivot Style Medium 3** style in the gallery.

5. In the PivotTable Styles Options group, click the **Banded Rows** and **Banded Columns** check boxes to select them.

6. Repeat Steps 1 through 5 for the Engagement Rate Pivot PivotTable, inserting **ENGAGEMENTS** in cell J24 with the **Accent4** cell style and applying the **Lavender, Pivot Style Medium 5** style to the PivotTable.

**7.** Repeat Steps 1 through 5 for the Engagement Grade Pivot PivotTable, inserting **USER RESPONSES** in cell J29 with the **Accent6** cell style and applying the **Ice Blue, Pivot Style Medium 7** style to the PivotTable. See Figure 7–39.

| Figure 7–39 | Completed PivotTables in the Dashboard worksheet |
| --- | --- |

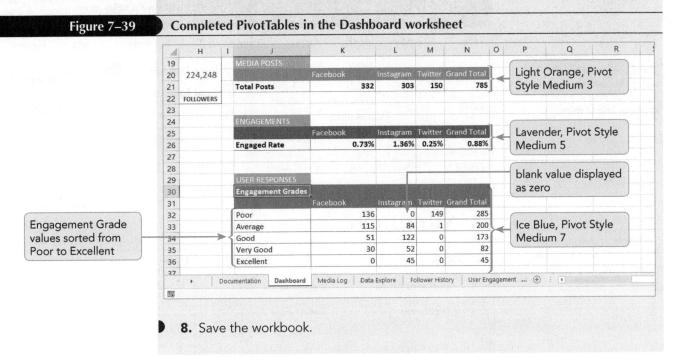

**8.** Save the workbook.

You've finished adding PivotTables to the dashboard. In the next session, you will complete the dashboard by adding PivotCharts and slicers to create a dashboard that users can interact with to explore Syrmosta's social media presence.

# Review

## Session 7.2 Quick Check

1. What is a PivotTable?
2. What are the four primary areas of a PivotTable?
3. What default statistic is used for non-numeric data in the Values area of the PivotTable?
4. What default statistic is used for numeric data in the Values area of the PivotTable?
5. By default, how does a PivotTable arrange the categories in a row or column?
6. What happens when you place a date field in a row or column area?
7. What are two ways of filtering a PivotTable?

# Session 7.3 Visual Overview:

The Report Connections button is used to connect a slicer or timeline to multiple PivotTables.

This slicer is used to filter PivotTables to show results from only posts about sportswear.

These PivotTables show filtered results.

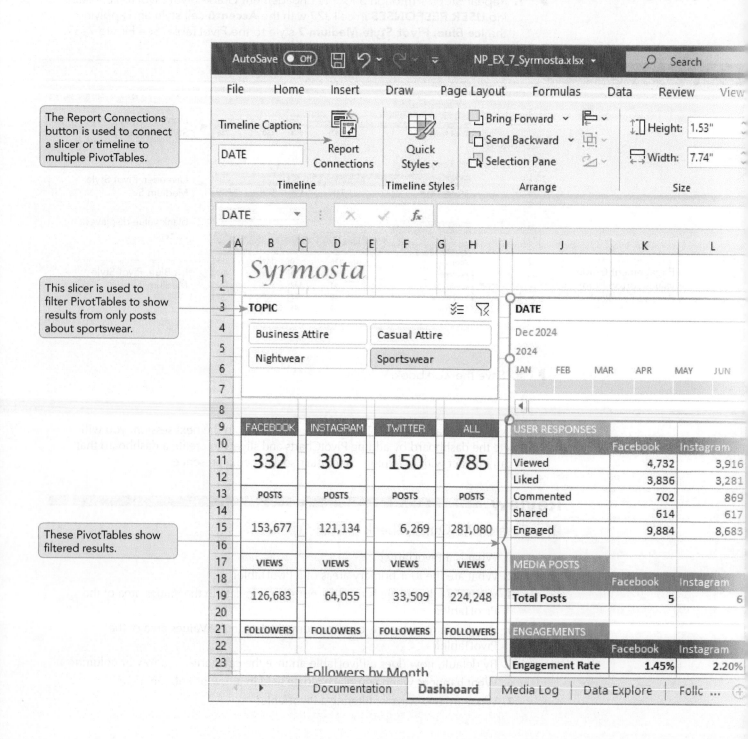

# PivotCharts and Slicers

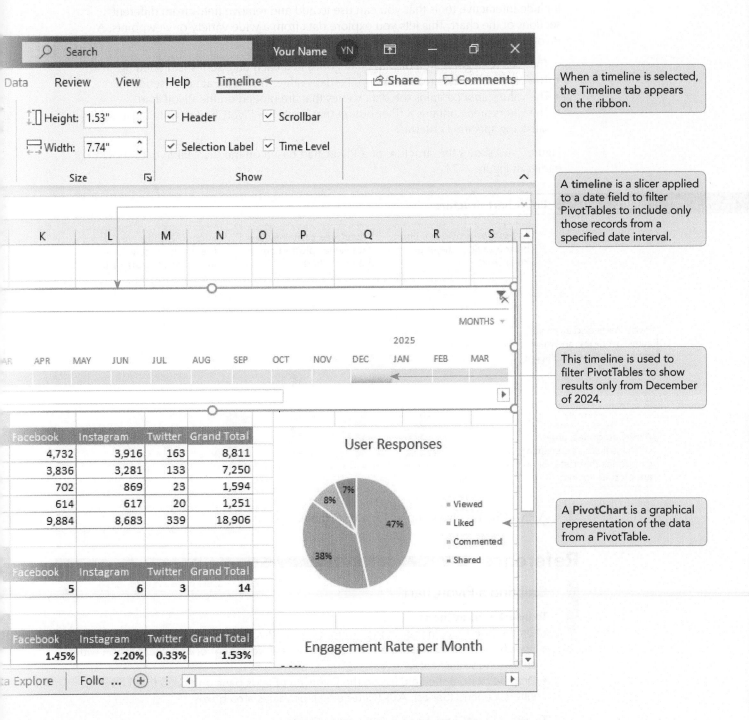

When a timeline is selected, the Timeline tab appears on the ribbon.

A **timeline** is a slicer applied to a date field to filter PivotTables to include only those records from a specified date interval.

This timeline is used to filter PivotTables to show results only from December of 2024.

A **PivotChart** is a graphical representation of the data from a PivotTable.

# Introducing PivotCharts

A PivotChart is a graphical representation of a PivotTable. Like PivotTables, PivotCharts include interactive tools that you can use to add and remove fields from different sections of the chart. This lets you explore data from a wide variety of viewpoints. A PivotChart has four primary areas:

- The Axis (Category) area displays categories that each data series is plotted against.
- The Legend (Series) area breaks up the data values into separate data series.
- The Values area contains the data values that are plotted on the PivotChart.
- The Filters area contains a filter button that limits the PivotChart to only those values satisfying specified criteria.

Figure 7–40 shows the structure of a PivotChart based on the PivotTable data shown earlier in Figure 7–21.

**Figure 7–40**    **PivotChart structure**

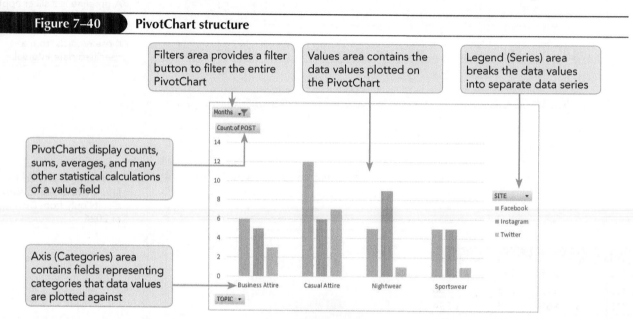

A PivotChart is always linked to a PivotTable.

# Reference

### Creating a PivotChart

**To insert a PivotChart:**
- On the Insert tab, in the Charts group, click the PivotChart button.
- Specify whether to insert the PivotChart in a new worksheet or at a cell location within an existing worksheet.
- Drag fields from the field list on the PivotChart Fields pane and drop them on the Filters, Legend (Series), Axis (Categories), or Values area boxes.

**To add a PivotChart to an existing PivotTable:**
- Select a PivotTable from the workbook.
- On the PivotTable Analyze tab, in the Tools group, click the PivotChart button.
- Select the PivotChart chart type.
- If necessary, move the PivotChart to a different worksheet than the PivotTable.

## Creating a PivotChart

A PivotChart is either created from an existing PivotTable or created at the same time as its PivotTable. The layouts of a PivotTable and PivotChart always mirror one another. Any changes you make to the structure and layout of a PivotTable affect the PivotChart, and vice versa.

Claire wants you to create a PivotChart using data from the Media table on the Media Log worksheet.

### To begin building a PivotChart:

▶ **1.** If you took a break at the end of the previous session, make sure the NP_EX_7_Syrmosta workbook is open.

▶ **2.** Go to the **Media Log** worksheet and click cell **B4** if necessary to select the Media table.

▶ **3.** On the ribbon, click the **Insert** tab, and then in the Charts group, click the **PivotChart** button. The Create PivotChart dialog box opens.

▶ **4.** Click the **Existing Worksheet** option button, press **TAB** to move to the Location box, click the **Follower History** sheet tab, and then click cell **B4** in the Follower History worksheet. The reference 'Follower History'!$B$4 appears in the Location box.

▶ **5.** Click **OK**. An empty PivotTable report and an empty PivotChart appear in the worksheet. See Figure 7–41.

| Figure 7–41 | Empty PivotTable report and PivotChart |
| --- | --- |

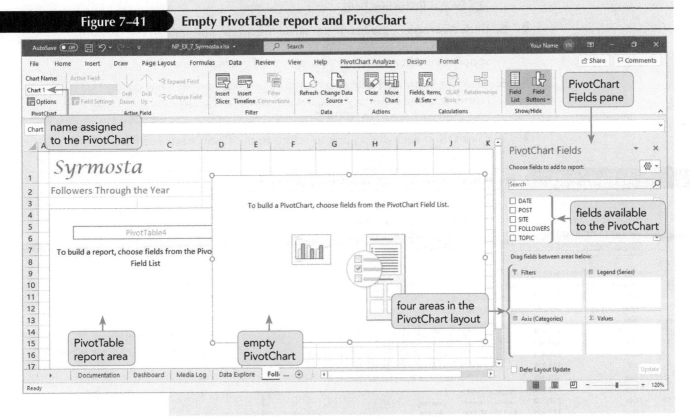

When a PivotChart is selected, the PivotChart Analyze, Design, and Format tabs appear on the ribbon. The Design and Format tabs include the same commands you've seen for working with other Excel charts. The PivotChart Analyze tab includes many of the same commands you've seen for working with PivotTables. So, once you know how to work with PivotTables and charts, you've already mastered many of the tools applicable to PivotCharts.

PivotCharts are built the same way as PivotTables: by choosing fields from the field list and dropping them into one of four PivotChart areas. Claire wants you to create a PivotChart line chart showing the average number of followers for each media site per month to determine whether the number of followers has increased over the past year. You will create this PivotChart layout now.

### To lay out the PivotChart contents:

Tip

By default, PivotCharts are initially formatted as column charts.

1. Drag the **FOLLOWERS** from the field list into the Values area box. The PivotChart becomes a column chart showing the sum of the Followers field. The PivotTable is also updated to show the value of that sum.

2. Drag the **SITE** field from the field list into the Legend (Series) area box. The column PivotChart and PivotTable update to show the sum of the Followers broken down by media site.

3. Drag the **DATE** field from the field list into the Axis (Categories) area box. The column PivotChart and PivotTable show the sum of the Followers field for each month of the year. The Date field is grouped, so you can ungroup individual months to view day-to-day values of the Followers field.

4. In the upper-left corner of the PivotChart, right-click the **Sum of FOLLOWERS** cell, and then click **Value Field Settings** on the shortcut menu. The Value Field Settings dialog box opens. Claire wants to the view the average of the Followers field.

5. Click **Average** in the list of statistical functions, and then in the Custom Name box, change "Average of Followers" to **Followers** followed by a blank space (to avoid a name conflict with the Followers field.

6. Click the **Number Format** button to open the Format Cells dialog box, click **Number** in the Category box, set the value of the Decimal place box to **0**, and then click the **Use 1000 Separator (,)** check box to select it.

7. Click **OK** in each dialog box to return to the PivotChart. See Figure 7–42.

| Figure 7–42 | PivotChart of the average followers per month |
| --- | --- |

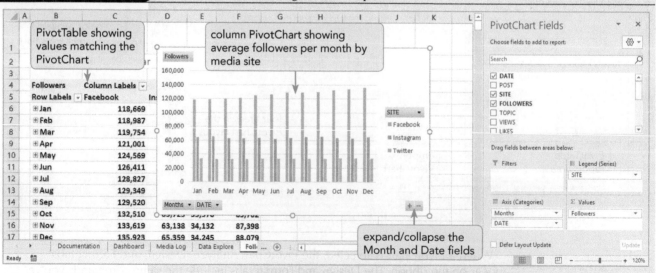

**Tip**

To use a chart type that is not a PivotChart, copy and paste the data from a PivotTable into a new data range and then create a regular chart from the pasted values.

Not every Excel chart type can be created as a PivotChart. You can create PivotCharts from only the Column, Line, Pie, Bar, Area, Surface, Radar chart types, and from Combo charts created from the preceding chart types. Claire thinks this data would be better displayed as a line chart. You'll change the chart type now.

### To change the chart type:

1. On the ribbon, click the **Design** tab to show commands for changing the design of the selected PivotChart.

2. In the Type group, click the **Change Chart Type** button. The Change Chart Type dialog box opens.

3. Click **Line** in the list of chart types, and then click **OK**. The PivotChart changes from a column chart to a line chart.

4. Next to the chart, click the **Chart Elements** button ⊞, click the **Chart Title** check box, type **Followers by Month** as the chart title, and then press **ENTER**. The chart title appears at the top of the chart.

5. Click the **Chart Elements** button ⊞, click the **Gridlines arrow**, and then click the **Primary Major Vertical** check box. Vertical gridlines appear on the chart.

6. In the Chart Elements menu ⊞, click the **Legend arrow**, and then click **Bottom**. The legend moves to the bottom of the chart. See Figure 7–43.

**Figure 7–43**    **Line PivotChart showing average followers per month**

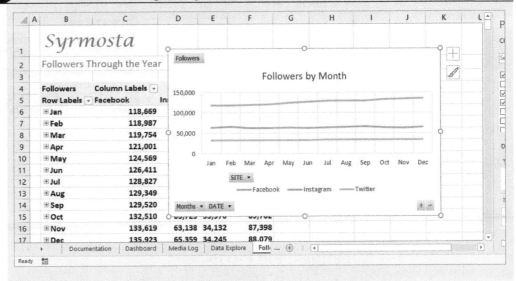

## Moving a PivotChart to Another Worksheet

The PivotTable and PivotChart do not need to be on the same worksheet (though they must be in the same workbook). Claire wants the PivotChart moved to the Dashboard worksheet to be displayed alongside other summary tables and charts. Before moving the chart, Claire wants you to give the PivotTable a descriptive name to distinguish it from other PivotTables you've already created for your workbook.

**To name and move the PivotChart:**

1. Click cell **B4** to make the PivotTable the active object in the workbook.

2. On the ribbon, click the **PivotTable Analyze** tab, and then in the PivotTable group, click the **PivotTable Name** box and enter **Followers by Month Pivot** as the name of the PivotTable.

3. Click the PivotChart to select it, click the **PivotChart Analyze** tab on the ribbon, and then in the Actions group, click the **Move Chart** button. The Move Chart dialog box opens.

4. Verify that the **Object in** option button is selected, click the **Object in** box, click **Dashboard** as the worksheet to place the PivotChart in, and then click **OK**. The PivotChart moves to the Dashboard worksheet.

5. In the Dashboard worksheet, move and resize the PivotChart to cover the range **B24:H36**. Claire is not going to revise the layout of this PivotChart, so you can hide the field buttons.

6. On the PivotChart Analyze tab, in the Show/Hide group, click the **Field Buttons** button to hide the field buttons. See Figure 7-44.

**Figure 7-44**    **Line PivotChart moved to the Dashboard worksheet**

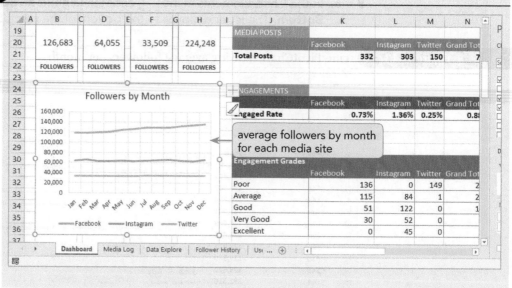

## Creating a Pie PivotChart

A media post is more successful when it elicits comments and shares, so Claire wants the dashboard to include a pie chart breaking down total user engagements by views, likes, comments, and shares. You'll create a PivotChart showing this information as a pie chart.

**To create the pie PivotChart showing the breakdown of user engagements:**

1. Go to the **Media Log** worksheet, click the **Insert** tab on the ribbon, and then in the Charts group, click the **PivotChart** button. The Create PivotChart dialog box opens.

2. Place the PivotChart on the existing **User Engagement** worksheet in cell **B4**, and then click **OK**. A blank PivotTable and a PivotChart appear on the User Engagement worksheet.

3. In the field list, click the **Views**, **Likes**, **Comments**, and **Shares** check boxes to add those fields to the Values area box.

4. Drag the **ΣValues** item from the Legend (Series) box to the Axis (Categories) box.

5. On the ribbon, click the **Design** tab, and then in the Type group, click the **Change Chart Type** button. The Change Chart Type dialog box opens.

6. Click **Pie** as the chart type, and then click **OK**. The PivotChart changes to a pie chart.

7. Double-click cell **B5**, change the value in the Custom Name box to **Viewed**, and then click **OK**.

8. Repeat Step 7 to change the label in cell **B6** to **Liked**, the label in cell **B7** to **Commented**, and the label in cell **B8** to **Shared**. See Figure 7–45.

| Figure 7–45 | Pie PivotChart of the engagement totals |
| --- | --- |

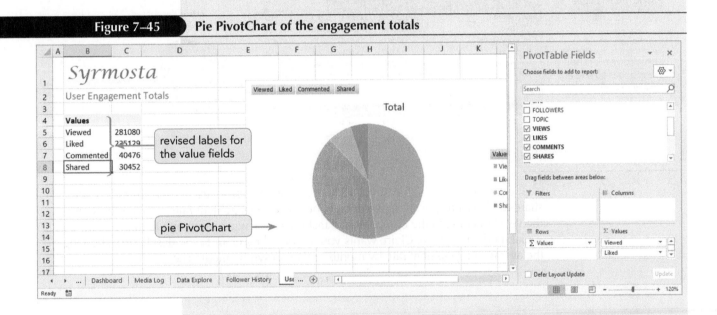

You'll move the pie chart to the Dashboard sheet and format it for Claire's report.

### To format the pie chart PivotChart:

1. Click the **PivotTable Analyze** tab, in the PivotTable group, click the **PivotTable Name** box, type **Engagement Pie Pivot** as the PivotTable name, and then press **ENTER**.

2. Click the Engagement Pie Pivot PivotChart to select it, click the **PivotChart Analyze** tab on the ribbon, in the Actions group, click the **Move Chart** button.

3. Move the PivotChart to the **Dashboard** worksheet, and then move and resize the Engagement Pie Pivot PivotChart to cover the range **P11:S21**.

4. On the ribbon, click the **PivotChart Analyze** tab, and then in the Show/Hide group, click the **Field Buttons** button to hide the field buttons on the chart.

5. Change the chart title to **User Responses**.

6. Click the **Design** tab, in the Chart Layouts group, click the **Quick Layout** button, and then click **Layout 6** to add data callouts to the pie chart.

7. In the Chart Styles group, click **Style 1** to add a white border around each slice. See Figure 7–46.

| Figure 7–46 | Formatted pie chart on the dashboard |

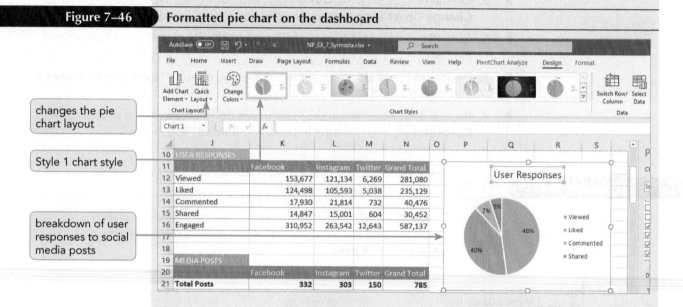

changes the pie chart layout

Style 1 chart style

breakdown of user responses to social media posts

The pie chart shows that about 12% of all user response are due to comments and shares. This is a respectable percentage, but is the engagement rate constant through the year? Recall that the company had instituted a new ad campaign to improve its social media presence. Claire wants you to add a line chart to the dashboard, showing the average engagement rate by month broken down by media site.

### To create a PivotChart of engagement rate per month:

1. Go to the **Media Log** worksheet, click the **Insert** tab on the ribbon, and then in the Charts group, click the **PivotChart** button.

2. Place the PivotTable/PivotChart on the **Engagement History** worksheet starting at cell **B4**.

3. Place the **SITE** field in the Legend (Series) area box, place the **DATE** field in the Axis (Categories) area box, and then place the **ENGAGEMENT RATE** field in the Values area box.

4. Change the PivotChart chart type to a **Line** chart.

5. Right-click cell **B4**, and then click **Value Field Settings** on the shortcut menu. The Value Field Settings dialog box opens.

6. Click **Average** in the list of functions.

7. Click the **Number Format** button, click **Percentage** in the Category box, and then click **OK** in each dialog box to return to the worksheet.

8. On the ribbon, click the **PivotTable Analyze** tab, and then in the PivotTable group, enter **Engagement Rate per Month Pivot** in the PivotTable Name box.

You'll move the line chart to the Dashboard worksheet and finish formatting it.

### To place the line chart in the Dashboard worksheet:

1. Move the line PivotChart to the Dashboard worksheet, and then resize the chart to cover the range **P23:S36**.

2. On the PivotChart Analyze tab, in the Show/Hide group, click the **Field Buttons** button to hide the field buttons.

3. Click the **Design** tab, in the Chart Layouts group, click the **Quick Layout** button, and then click the **Layout 3** layout to place the legend at the bottom of the chart.

4. Change the chart title to **Engagement Rate per Month**.

5. Close the PivotChart Fields pane. See Figure 7–47.

| Figure 7–47 | Chart of engagement rate per month |

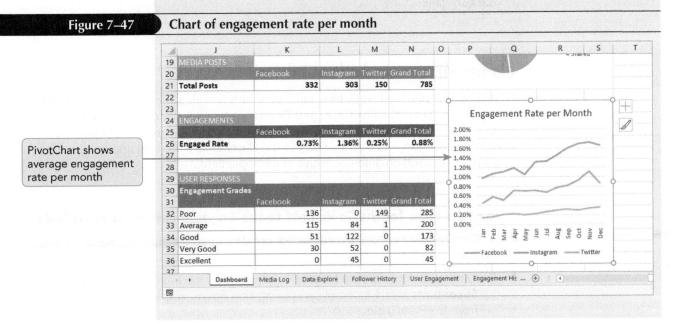

PivotChart shows average engagement rate per month

The line chart shows that average engagement rates generally increased throughout the year for all three media sites, except for a decrease in the last month Facebook posts. This favorable trend indicates to Claire that the ad campaign has increased customer interest and engagement.

## Insight

### Dynamic Referencing with the OFFSET Function

In working with data ranges and Excel tables, you referenced a range whose size and location were defined and static. In some Excel applications, you might need to reference a range whose size and location changes based on the need of the application. For example, a formula might need to reference data in the range A1:A10 on one occasion and the range C11:E15 on another occasion.

You can create references whose location and size change by using the OFFSET function

```
OFFSET(reference, rows, cols, [height], [width])
```

where *reference* points to cells in the workbook, *rows* and *cols* are the number of rows and columns to shift that reference, and *height* and *width* set the size of the new reference in terms of rows and columns. For example, the following expression shifts the A1:A10 reference 10 rows down and 2 columns across to point the range C11:C20:

```
OFFSET(A1:A10, 10, 2)
```

To resize the range to cover C11:E15, you specify the size of the new reference to be 5 rows high and 3 columns wide in the following expression:

```
OFFSET(A1:A10, 10, 2, 5, 3)
```

By modifying the parameters of the OFFSET argument, you can reference ranges of any location and size in a workbook, creating dynamic ranges that can change with your application.

## Using Slicers and PivotTables

Another way of filtering PivotTables and PivotCharts is with a slicer. By clicking a slicer button, you can limit the PivotTable and PivotChart to a select group of records. Claire wants to explore whether user engagement varies based on the topic of the post. To answer this question, you'll add a slicer to the Dashboard worksheet and use it to filter the PivotTable based on different values of the Topic field.

### To add a slicer for the Topic field to the Engagement Pivot PivotTable:

1. On the Dashboard worksheet, click cell **J11** to select the Engagement Pivot PivotTable.

2. On the ribbon, click the **Insert** tab, and then in the Filters group, click the **Slicer** button. The Insert Slicers dialog box opens, displaying a list of fields from the PivotTable.

3. Click the **TOPIC** check box, and then click **OK**. The TOPIC slicer appears on the Dashboard worksheet.

4. Move and resize the TOPIC slicer to cover the range **B4:H7**.

5. On the Slicer tab, in the Buttons group, change the value in the Columns box to **2** to arrange the slicer buttons in two rows and two columns.

6. In the TOPIC slicer, click the **Business Attire** button to filter the Engagement Pivot PivotTable to show only posts regarding business attire. The filtered PivotTable shows there were 100,603 engagements for posts dealing with business attire. See Figure 7–48.

| Figure 7–48 | Business Attire posts |
|---|---|

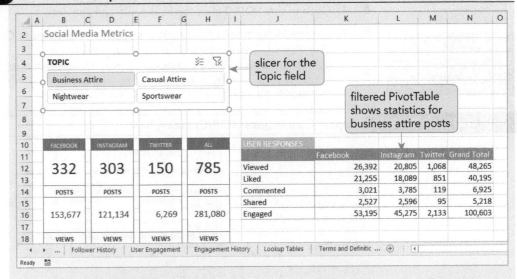

7. Click the **Nightwear**, **Casual Attire**, and **Sportswear** slicer buttons to filter the summary statistics for the other topic categories in the PivotTable.

8. Click the **Clear Filter** button 🗑 (or press **ALT+C**) to clear the filters and redisplay summary statistics for all topics.

The slicer made it possible to compare engagements across values of the Topic field. The highest number of total engagements occurs with posts on nightwear, which had 215,426 engagements. Claire wants to see how the other PivotTables and PivotCharts on the dashboard are affected by a change in topic.

## Applying a Slicer to Multiple PivotTables

The same slicer can be applied to multiple PivotTables (and their associated PivotCharts), allowing you to filter the entire dashboard based on criteria you choose. The PivotTables do not need to be in the same worksheet, only the same workbook. Note that a slicer is not applied directly to a PivotChart, only the PivotTable that PivotChart is based on.

## Reference

### Applying a Slicer to Multiple PivotTables

- Click the PivotTable slicer to select it.
- On the Slicer tab, in the Slicer group, click the Report Connections button.
- Click the check boxes for all the PivotTables to be associated with the slicer.
- Click OK.

Claire wants you to apply the slicer you created for the Topic field to all PivotTables and PivotCharts in the Dashboard worksheet.

## To apply a slicer to all the PivotTables in the dashboard:

1. Click in the **TOPIC** slicer to make sure it is selected.

2. On the Slicer tab, in the Slicer group, click the **Report Connections** button. The Report Connections (TOPIC) dialog box opens.

3. Click the check box for every PivotTable listed *except* the Explore PivotTable from the Data Explore worksheet. See Figure 7–49.

Select the PivotTables associated with the PivotCharts to filter both table and chart.

**Figure 7–49**　　**Report Connections (TOPIC) dialog box**

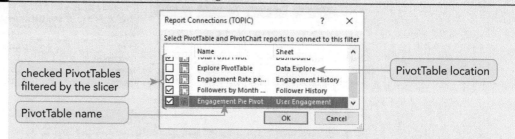

checked PivotTables filtered by the slicer

PivotTable name

PivotTable location

4. Click **OK** to apply the slicer to all selected PivotTables.

5. In the TOPIC slicer, click the **Business Attire**, **Casual Attire**, **Nightwear**, and then **Sportswear** buttons, and then confirm that all of the PivotTables and PivotCharts displayed in the Dashboard worksheet are filtered by the slicer.

6. Click the **Clear Filter** button  (or press **ALT+C**) to clear the filters from all the PivotTables and PivotCharts on the dashboard.

Your analysis shows that the highest engagement rates and the greatest increase in engagement rates occur with media posts on nightwear and sportswear. The engagements rates for business and casual attire are much lower. Although posts on business and casual attire show an increase in user engagement over the past 12 months, the increase is not as great as for nightwear and sportswear.

## Aa Proskills

### Problem Solving: Consolidating Data from Multiple Worksheets

This module worked with PivotTables whose data is stored within a single data range or Excel table. However, some projects require PivotTables that analyze data spread across several worksheets.

One way of summarizing, or consolidating, data from multiple worksheets is with the Consolidate Data command. Click the Consolidate button in the Data Tools group on the Data tab to open the Consolidate dialog box. From the Consolidate dialog box, first choose the function for consolidating the data, such as average, count, minimum, and maximum, among others. Then, select a list of ranges from different worksheets containing the data to be consolidated, including any row or column labels to identify the data. Excel will generate a table containing the statistical summary for the data from multiple worksheets.

Unlike PivotTables, the Consolidate command does not create an interactive table, so you must recreate the table each time you want to analyze your data from a different point of view. The consolidation table also does not interact with slicers or timelines, so you cannot filter the results. You can learn more about the Consolidate command in Excel Help.

**Tip**

Timeline slicers can be applied only to PivotTables and not to Excel tables.

## Creating a Timeline Slicer

Another type of slicer is a timeline slicer, which filters a PivotTable to include only those records from a specified date interval. For example, you can limit the PivotTables only to those results between January and April or for an interval of specific years.

## Reference

### Filtering a PivotTable with a Timeline Slicer

- Click anywhere in the PivotTable to select it.
- On the Insert tab, in the Filters group, click the Timeline button.
- Click the check boxes of the fields containing date values which you want to create timelines.
- Click OK.
- Format the size, position, and appearance of the timeline.
- Select intervals within the timeline to filter the PivotTable.

Claire is interested not just in the engagement rate, but also in the quality of the engagements. Are more users commenting on and sharing posts at the end of the year than at the beginning? To answer that question, you will add a timeline slicer to the dashboard and examine the number of views, likes, comments, and shares from different time intervals.

### To create the Date timeline slicer:

1. In the Dashboard worksheet, click cell **J11** to select the first PivotTable.

2. On the ribbon, click the **Insert** tab, and then in the Filters group, click the **Timeline** button. The Insert Timelines dialog box opens. There is only one field that contains date information.

3. Click the **DATE** check box, and then click **OK**. The DATE timeline slicer is inserted in the dashboard.

4. Move and resize the timeline slicer to cover the range **J4:S9**.

5. On the Timeline tab, in the Timeline group, click the **Report Connections** button. The Report Connections (DATE) dialog box opens.

6. Click the **Engagement Grade Pivot**, **Engagement Rate Pivot**, **Total Posts Pivot**, and **Engagement Pie Pivot** check boxes to select those PivotTables, and then click **OK**. See Figure 7–50.

**Figure 7–50**    Timeline connected to all PivotTables

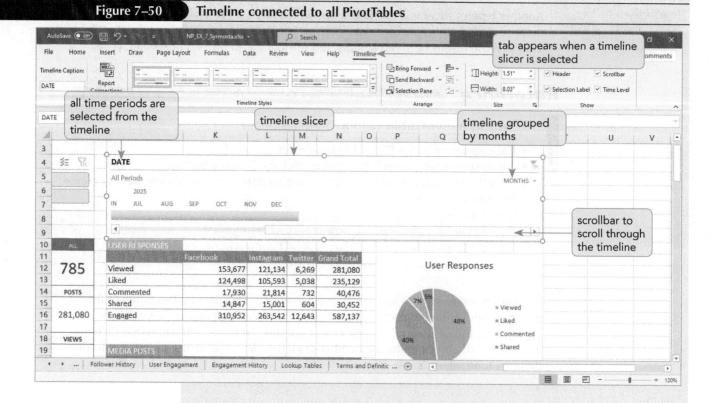

The timeline is laid out as a horizontal scroll bar grouped by months. You can filter the dashboard to show values only for specified time periods by selecting data ranges from the timeline. You'll filter the data on the dashboard by viewing the results for January 2024, and then you'll compare those values to the results for December 2024.

### To filter the timeline by dates:

1. Drag the timeline scroll bar to the left until you see JAN 2024 in the timeline slicer.

2. Click the **JAN** box located directly below JAN 2024, deselecting all the other months in the timeline. The PivotTables and PivotCharts show the January results. During the month of January 2024, there were 30,973 user engagements (cell N16), a total of 65 posts (cell N21), and an average engagement rate of 0.59% (cell N26). The pie chart shows that 5% of the engagements involved user comments and 4% involved user shares.

3. Click the **DEC** box from 2024 to select only that month. In that month, there were 65,594 engagements (cell N16), 73 posts (cell N21), and an average engagement rate of 1.02% (cell N26). The pie chart shows that 8% of the engagements involved user comments and 7% involved user shares. See Figure 7–51.

**Tip**

To select a range of months, click the selection box in the timeline and drag the left or right selection handles over the range of months you want to cover.

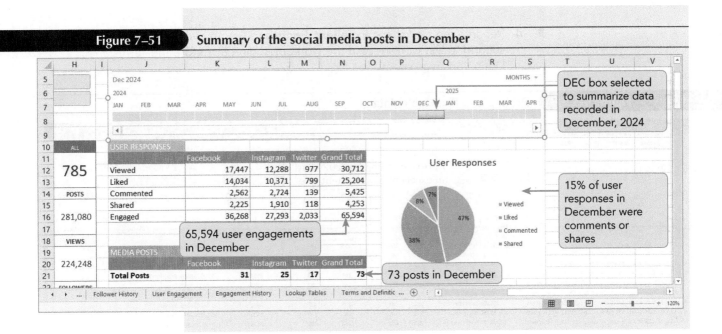

**Figure 7–51**    Summary of the social media posts in December

Comparing the January and December figures reveals that by the end of the year, more users were engaging with the company's social media posts and there were a higher percentage of active engagements in which users either commented on the posts or shared them with others. Claire can report that the ad campaign has had a positive impact on the company's social media presence.

# Drilling Down a PivotTable

A PivotTable summarizes data, but sometimes you will want to examine the data records themselves. You can do this by **drilling down** the PivotTable to display the records responsible for the PivotTable calculations. To drill down a PivotTable, double-click any cell within the table. Excel then opens a new sheet displaying the records used to calculate that PivotTable value.

From the filtered values on the dashboard, Claire has learned that in December there were nine posts in which user engagement was graded as excellent. Claire wants to study those posts to discover what might have made them so appealing to users. You will drill down the PivotTable to display those records.

### To drill down the Engagement Grade Pivot PivotTable:

▸ **1.** In the Dashboard worksheet, scroll down to the Engagement Grade Pivot PivotTable.

▸ **2.** Double-click cell **L36** containing the value 9, which is the number of Instagram posts that had an excellent grade of user engagement in December 2024. A new worksheet opens, containing the 9 relevant records. Some of the data is not visible in the columns.

▸ **3.** On the Home tab, in the Cells group, click the **Format** button, and then click **AutoFit Column Width**. The column widths expand to show all the data within each column.

> **4.** Rename the worksheet **Excellent Posts** and then move the sheet to be the second to last worksheet in the workbook, directly before the Terms and Definitions worksheet. See Figure 7–52.

**Figure 7–52**    **Drilling into PivotTable data**

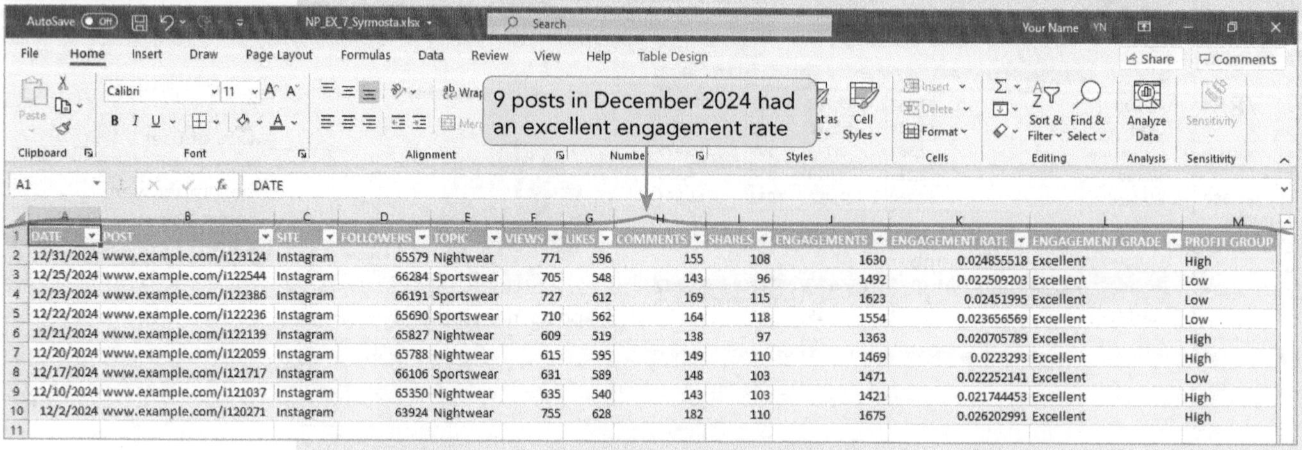

> **5.** sam↑ Save the workbook, and then close it.

Claire can use the contents of the Excellent Posts worksheet to further study what makes an effective media post. Note that the data retrieved through drilling down is not linked to the source data, so any changes made to the values in the data source, will not be reflected in the worksheet.

## Insight

### Refreshing PivotTable Data

The information in a PivotTable is connected to a data source, which can be a data range or Excel table. As you add more data to the data source or revise the data, the PivotTable is not updated to show the most current results. The PivotTable is not updated until you refresh it, forcing Excel to recreate the table using new data. To refresh the PivotTable, click the Refresh button in the Data group on the PivotTable Analyze tab.

You can modify the PivotTable settings to have Excel automatically update a PivotTable every time the workbook is opened. Select the PivotTable and then click the Options button in the PivotTable group on the PivotTable Analyze tab to open the PivotTable Options dialog box. On the Data tab, click the Refresh data when opening the file check box. Excel will then refresh the PivotTable each time the workbook is reopened. Note that whenever you refresh a PivotTable, *all* PivotTables that rely on the same data source get updated.

You've completed your work on the social media report. Using the interactive dashboard you created, Claire can quickly analyze social media metrics for any topic within any timeframe.

# Review

## Session 7.3 Quick Check

1. What are the four areas of a PivotChart?
2. Can you create a PivotChart without a PivotTable?
3. Can any Excel chart type be turned into a PivotChart?
4. How do you apply the same slicer to multiple PivotTables?
5. Can a timeline slicer be used with Excel tables as well as PivotTables?
6. When you do you need to refresh a PivotTable?

# Practice

## Review Assignments

**Data File needed for the Review Assignments: NP_EX_7-2.xlsx**

Claire continues to analyze social media metrics and needs to evaluate what factors might result in a successful Facebook post. Claire has compiled a list of Facebook posts that advertise company specials and business news. Claire wants to know whether user engagement is higher when the posts include photos and coupon offers. She also wants to determine whether certain days of the week are better than others to engage the user. Finally, Claire is mindful that users might ignore long posts and wants to examine whether word count has an impact on user engagement. Claire grades post length according to the table in Figure 7–53.

| Figure 7–53 | Lengths of Facebook posts |
| --- | --- |

| Character Count | Post Size |
| --- | --- |
| 0 – < 80 characters | short |
| 80 – < 160 characters | medium |
| 160 – < 240 characters | long |
| >= 240 characters | very long |

Complete the following:

1. Open the **NP_EX_7-2.xlsx** workbook located in the Excel7 > Review folder included with your Data Files. Save the workbook as **NP_EX_7_Facebook** in the location specified by your instructor.

2. In the Documentation sheet, enter your name and the date.

3. In the Lookup Tables worksheet, use the data in Figure 7–53 to complete the lookup table in the range B4:C8. Give the first column of values the defined name **Character_Lookup** and give the second column of values the defined name **Post_Lookup**.

4. In the Media Posts worksheet, in column G of the Facebook table, apply the XLOOKUP function to categorize the size of each post, using the value of the Characters field for the lookup value, the Character_Lookup range as the lookup array, and the Post_Lookup range as the return array. Do not specify the if_not_found argument, and use −1 for the match_mode argument.

5. In the Report worksheet, count the number of posts with and without photos and coupons as follows:

    a. In cell C15, use the COUNTIF function to count the number of records in the Photo field of the Facebook table equal to the "Photo" field value.

    b. In cell C16, calculate the difference between cell C14 and C15.

    c. In cell C18, count the number of records in the Coupon field equal to the "Coupon" field value.

    d. In cell C19 calculate the difference between cell C14 and C18.

6. Calculate the average engagement rate for posts with and without photos and coupons as follows:

    a. In cell C23, calculate the average engagement rate for posts with photos by using the AVERAGEIF function with the *Range* argument equal to Facebook[PHOTO], the *Criteria* argument equal to "Photo", and the *Average_Range* argument equal to Facebook[ENGAGEMENT RATE].

    b. In cell C24, calculate the average engagement rate for posts without posts by copying the formula in C23 and change the value of the **Criteria** argument to "No Photo".

    c. In cell C26, calculate the average engagement rate for posts with coupons by using the AVERAGEIF function with the **Range** argument equal to Facebook[COUPON], the *Criteria* argument equal to "Coupon", and the *Average_Range* argument equal to Facebook[ENGAGEMENT RATE].

   d. In cell C27, calculate the average engagement rate for posts without coupons by copying the formula in C26 and change the value of the *Criteria* argument to "No Coupon".

7. Create a PivotTable of the data in the Media Posts worksheet, placing the PivotTable in cell E12 of the Report worksheet.

8. Make the following changes to the PivotTable:

   a. Rename the PivotTable as **Day Pivot**.

   b. Place the Day field in the Rows area of the table, and then place the Post and Engagement Rate fields in the Values area. (Posts are in the left column of the PivotTable.)

   c. Change the label for the Count of Posts value field to **Posted**. Change the label for the Sum of Engagement Rate value field to **Engagement Rates** and display the average engagement rate as a percentage formatted to two decimal places.

   d. Apply the Light Green, Pivot Style Medium 7 to the PivotTable and turn on Banded Rows and Banded Columns.

   e. Modify the PivotTable options so that the Excel does *not* AutoFit column widths on update.

9. Copy the PivotTable in the range E12:G20 and paste it in cell E22, and then make the following changes to the PivotTable:

   a. Rename the PivotTable as **Size Pivot**.

   b. Replace the Day field in the Rows area with the Post Size field.

   c. Reorder the categories in the Rows area to the following order: short, medium, long, very long.

10. In the Media Posts worksheet, create a PivotChart from the data, placing the PivotTable/PivotChart in the Engagement Types worksheet in cell B4, and then do the following:

   a. Rename the PivotTable as **Engaged Pivot**.

   b. Place the Clicks, Likes, Comments, and Shares field in the Values area box.

   c. Rename the value fields as **Clicked**, **Liked**, **Commented**, and **Shared**.

   d. Move the ΣValues item into the Rows area box so that all values fields are displayed in separate rows.

11. Make the following changes to the PivotChart:

   a. Move the PivotChart to the Report worksheet, and then resize it to cover the range I12:L18.

   b. Change the chart type to a pie chart.

   c. Remove the field buttons and the chart title from the chart.

   d. Change the chart style to Style 8.

12. Create another PivotChart from the data in the Facebook table, place it in the Engagement History worksheet in cell B4, and then make the following changes:

   a. Rename the PivotTable as **History Pivot**.

   b. Place the Date field in the Rows area and the Engagement Rate field in the Values areas.

   c. Change the Engagement Rate value field settings to display the average of the Engagement Rate field as a percentage to two decimal places using **Engagement Rates** as the label.

   d. Change the PivotChart to a line chart. Remove the legend and field buttons from the PivotChart. Change the chart title to **Engagement Rates**.

   e. Move the PivotChart to the Report worksheet and resize it to cover the range I19:L27.

13. Click cell E12 to select the first PivotTable, add slicers for the Photo and Coupon fields, and then do the following:

   a. Move and resize the PHOTO slicer to cover the range B4:C6.

   b. Move and resize the COUPON slicer to cover the range B8:C11.

   c. Display both slicers with two columns.

   d. Set the report connections of both slicers to connect to every PivotTable in the workbook.

14. Click cell E12 to select the first PivotTable, insert a timeline using the Date field, and then do the following:

   a. Resize the timeline to cover the range E4:L10.

   b. Set the report connections of the slicer to connect to the Engaged Pivot, Day Pivot, and Size Pivot PivotTables.

15. Use the slicers to filter the Report worksheet to show only the social media metric for posts that involved photos and coupons and were posted in December 2024.

16. Display the posts that match these conditions by double-clicking cell G20 to drill down into the PivotTable. Rename the worksheet containing the drilled-down data **Drilled Data** and move the sheet after the Media Posts worksheet. Resize the column widths so that all of the data is visible.

17. Save the workbook, and then close it.

# Apply

## Case Problem 1

**Data File needed for this Case Problem: NP_EX_7-3.xlsx**

**STEM Mentors**   Robert Harshaw is an Events Coordinator for STEM Mentors, a company specializing in education software for high school STEM teachers. Every July, the company sponsors a conference to showcase its wares and provide informative speakers and workshops on technology in science and math education. After the conference, Robert compiles results from a survey to act as a guide for the next conference. You'll help Robert generate a report on the conference response. In the Survey Results worksheet, the answers to seven survey questions have been entered in an Excel table named Survey. The responses for the first four questions are the letters a through d, which represent responses from "very satisfied" to "very dissatisfied." The text of the survey questions is on the Survey Questions worksheet. Complete the following.

1. Open the **NP_EX_7-3.xlsx** workbook located in the Excel7 > Case1 folder included with your Data Files, and then save the workbook as **NP_EX_7_STEM** in the location specified by your instructor.

2. In the Documentation sheet enter your name and the date.

3. In the Survey Results worksheet, in the Workshops column, display text associated with answers to Q1 by clicking cell I6 and inserting the XLOOKUP function to do an exact match lookup with the Q1 field as the lookup value, the survey_lookup range as the lookup array, and the rating_lookup range as the return array.

4. Repeat Step 3 for the Speakers through Meals field, using values of the Q2 through Q4 fields. (*Hint*: You can use AutoFill to quickly enter the formulas for the Speakers through Meals fields.)

5. In the School column, display the type of school of each attendee (Public, Private, Online, or Tutor) by clicking cell M6 and inserting the XLOOKUP function to do an exact match lookup of values in the Q5 field from the school_lookup range, and returning values from the type_lookup range.

6. In the Prior Conferences column, indicate the number of conferences previously attended (0, 1, 2, and 3+) by clicking cell N6 and inserting the XLOOKUP function to do an approximate match lookup of the values in the Q6 field using the conference_lookup range as the lookup array and returning the value from the prior_lookup range. Set the match_mode value to −1.

7. In the Report worksheet, do the following:

   a. In cell B14, use the COUNTIF function to count the number of records in the Return field from the Survey table that equal "will return."

   b. In cell B15, calculate the difference between cell B11 and B14.

   c. In the range B18:B21, use the COUNTIF function to count the number of records of the School field in the Survey table that equal Public, Private, Online, and Tutor.

   d. In the range B24:B27, use the COUNTIF function to count the number of records in the Prior Conferences field of the Survey table that equal 0, 1, 2, and 3+.

   e. In cells C14, C15, C18:C21, and C24:C27, divide the counts you calculated for each response group by the total number of responses shown in cell B11 to express the values as percentages.

8. In the Survey Results worksheet, create a PivotChart, placing it in cell A4 of the PivotTables worksheet, and then do the following to analyze what factors might have contributed to a person deciding against returning to next year's conference:

   a. Name the PivotTable as **workshop pivot**.

   b. Place the Workshops field in the Columns area, the Return field in the Rows area, and the ID field in the Values area.

9. Make the following changes to the PivotChart:

   a. Move the chart to the Report worksheet to cover the range E7:I17.

   b. Change the chart type to the 100% Stacked Column chart.

   c. Remove the chart legend and field buttons from the chart.

   d. Add the chart title **Workshop Satisfaction** to the chart.

   e. Display the table associated with this chart by clicking the Data Tables check box in the Chart Elements menu. Verify that data table rows are arranged from top to bottom in the order Very Satisfied, Satisfied, Dissatisfied, and Very Dissatisfied.

10. Repeat Steps 8 and 9 to create a 100% Stacked column chart plotting the Speakers field against the Return field. Place the PivotTable in cell A10 on the PivotTables worksheet. Enter **speaker pivot** as the PivotTable name. Place the PivotChart in the range K7:O17 on the Report worksheet and add **Speaker Satisfaction** as the chart title.

11. Repeat Steps 8 and 9 to create a 100% Stacked column chart plotting the Facilities field against the Return field. Place the PivotTable in cell A16 on the PivotTables worksheet. Enter **facility pivot** as the PivotTable name. Place the PivotChart in the range E19:I29 on the Report worksheet and add **Facility Satisfaction** as the chart title.

12. Repeat Steps 8 and 9 to create a 100% Stacked column chart plotting the Meals field against the Return field. Place the PivotTable in cell A22 on the PivotTables worksheet. Enter **meal pivot** as the PivotTable name. Place the PivotChart in the range K19:O29 on the Report worksheet and add **Meal Satisfaction** as the chart title.

13. Click the first PivotChart to select it and then create a slicer for the School field. Move and resize the slicer to cover the range E2:O5 and then arrange the buttons in 4 columns. Connect the slicer to all four PivotTables in the workbook.

14. Use the School slicer to filter the PivotCharts to show only the summaries of the public school attendees.

15. Save the workbook, and then close it.

# Challenge

## Case Problem 2

**Data File needed for this Case Problem: NP_EX_7-4.xlsx**

**Blue Star Grocery**   Gina Ndaw, as a fleet manager for Blue Star Grocery, is responsible for managing the trucks and drivers that make deliveries to grocery stores in Colorado. Gina wants to analyze shipping data and track the delivery times and accumulated mileage of the company drivers. Gina has compiled a shipping log detailing the routes of four drivers from the past three months and needs your help creating the PivotTables and PivotCharts to analyze the data. Complete the following:

1. Open the **NP_EX_7-4.xlsx** workbook located in the Excel7 > Case2 folder included with your Data Files. Save the workbook as **NP_EX_7_Driving** in the location specified by your instructor.

2. In the Documentation sheet, enter your name and the date.

3. The Driving Log worksheet contains driving records of four Blue Star Grocery drivers. Each record in the Log table contains a separate segment of a daily trip by a driver and provides the date and times for each segment. In the Driving Time field, determine the time required for each

segment in hours by calculating the difference between the End Time field and the Start Time field and multiplying that difference by 24. (*Hint:* You can find the formula for this field in the Terms and Definitions worksheet.)

⊕ **Explore**  4. In the Time Goal field of the Log table, you will display the time it should take a driver to drive between cities (as determined by the company). To display that time value, use a nested XLOOKUP function. XLOOKUP should first use the value in the Start City field as the lookup value, and then search the Time_Start range in the Travel Times worksheet as the lookup array. For the return array, include a nested XLOOKUP function that uses the value in the End City field as its lookup value and searches the Time_End range as its lookup array. Finally, the nested XLOOKUP function returns the value in the Travel_Times range at the intersection of the start city and end city being looked up. (*Hint:* See the Terms and Definitions worksheet for help in constructing the function.)

5. In the Time Over field, calculate the amount by which the driver was over the recommended travel time in minutes by calculating the difference between the Driving Time field and the Time Goal field, and then multiplying that difference by 60.

⊕ **Explore**  6. In the Mileage field, use a nested XLOOKUP function to calculate the mileage for each segment driven. Refer to Step 4 as you create the function to first look for the Start City field value in the Distance_Start range in the Travel Distances worksheet. The nested XLOOKUP function should look for the End City field value in the Distance_End range and return the value at the intersection of the two in the Travel_Distances range. (*Hint:* You can refer to the Terms and Definitions worksheet if you need help in constructing the function.)

7. In the Driving Summary worksheet, Gina entered a formula in cell C10 to calculate the average daily mileage for the first driver. Copy the formula in cell C10 into the range C11:C13 to calculate the average daily mileage for the other three drivers.

8. In cell C16 of the Driving Summary worksheet, Gina has entered a formula to calculate the average daily driving time for the first driver. Copy the formula in cell C16 into the range C17:C19 to calculate the average daily driving times for the other drivers.

9. Gina wants to track the number of minutes the drivers are over their scheduled driving times. Use data in the Driving Log worksheet to create a PivotTable/PivotChart in the Driver Times worksheet in cell B4. Rename the PivotTable as **Driving Times Pivot**. Place the Time Over field in the Values area, place the Date field in the Rows area, and then remove the Months field from the Rows area.

10. Move the PivotChart to the Driving Summary worksheet, placing it in the range E9:G19. Change the chart type to a line chart. Remove the field buttons and the legend from the chart. Change the chart title to **Minutes Over Time Goal**.

11. Gina wants to track the daily distance driven by the drivers. In the Driving Log worksheet, create another PivotTable/PivotChart from the Log table, placing them in the Driver Miles worksheet in cell B4. Rename the PivotTable using **Driving Miles Pivot** as the name. Place the Mileage field in the Values area, place the Date field in the Rows area, and remove the Months field.

12. Move the PivotChart to the Driving Summary worksheet in the range I9:K19. Change the chart type to a line chart. Remove the field buttons and the chart legend. Change the title to **Distance in Miles**.

13. Insert a slicer for the Driver field in the range E4:K7. Display the slicer buttons in 4 columns and connect the slicer to both PivotTables.

14. Click each slicer button to verify that you can view time and distance charts for each individual driver over the past three months.

15. Driver D600-622 is new to the job, and Gina wants to know whether that driver's travel times have improved in the last three months. Use the slicer to display the charts for only that driver, displaying the general trend of the minutes over the company's time goals each day.

16. Save the workbook, and then close it.

# Performing What-If Analyses

## Maximizing Profits with the Right Product Mix

## Objectives

### Session 8.1
- Explore the principles of cost-volume-profit relationships
- Create a one-variable data table
- Create a two-variable data table

### Session 8.2
- Create and apply different Excel scenarios with the Scenario Manager
- Generate a scenario summary report
- Generate a scenario PivotTable report

### Session 8.3
- Explore the principles of a product mix
- Run Solver to calculate optimal solutions
- Create and apply constraints to a Solver model
- Save and load a Solver model

## Case | Athena Cycles

Roy Lockley is a sales analyst for Athena Cycles, a manufacturer of high-end bicycles for triathletes and cycling enthusiasts. Roy wants to use Excel to analyze the profitability of the company's line of bicycles to determine the number of each model the company must produce and sell to be profitable. Roy is interested in whether the company can increase its net income by reducing the selling price of the bikes to increase the sales volume or by increasing the sales price even if it means less sales. Roy also wants to determine whether the company can increase profits by promoting one model over another. To answer these questions, you will use the Excel what-if tools.

## Starting Data Files

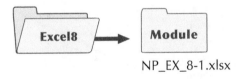

| Excel8 → | Module | Review | Case1 |
|---|---|---|---|
| | NP_EX_8-1.xlsx | NP_EX_8-2.xlsx | NP_EX_8-3.xlsx |

| Case2 |
|---|
| NP_EX_8-4.xlsx |

# Session 8.1 Visual Overview:

A one-variable data table performs several what-if analyses by specifying one input cell and several result cells.

Input cells are the cells that contain values that are used in formulas of a what-if analysis.

Input values are values in a data table that are based on input cells. The values in the range D6:D14 are based on the input cell B5.

Result values are values in a data table that come from formulas applied to one or more input values. The values in the range E6:G14 are calculated from the result cells in the range B25:B27.

Result cells are the cells that contain the outcome of formulas involving input cells.

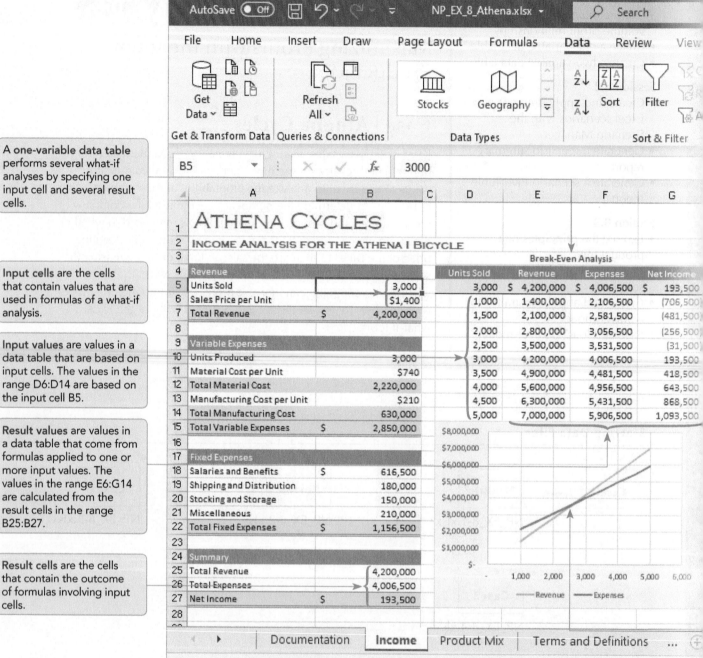

# Data Tables and What-If Analysis

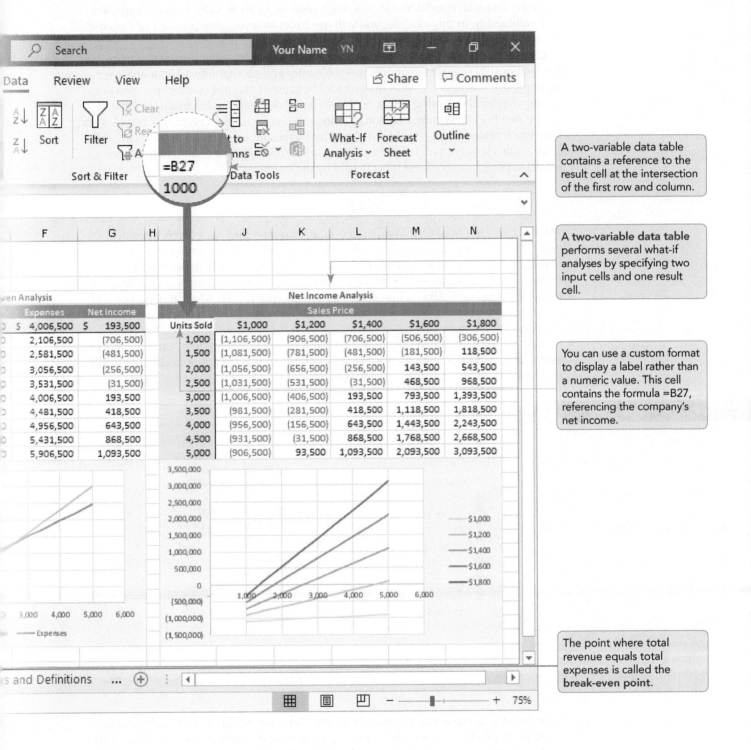

A two-variable data table contains a reference to the result cell at the intersection of the first row and column.

A two-variable data table performs several what-if analyses by specifying two input cells and one result cell.

You can use a custom format to display a label rather than a numeric value. This cell contains the formula =B27, referencing the company's net income.

The point where total revenue equals total expenses is called the break-even point.

Net Income Analysis

| Units Sold | Sales Price | | | | |
| --- | --- | --- | --- | --- | --- |
| | $1,000 | $1,200 | $1,400 | $1,600 | $1,800 |
| 1,000 | (1,106,500) | (906,500) | (706,500) | (506,500) | (306,500) |
| 1,500 | (1,081,500) | (781,500) | (481,500) | (181,500) | 118,500 |
| 2,000 | (1,056,500) | (656,500) | (256,500) | 143,500 | 543,500 |
| 2,500 | (1,031,500) | (531,500) | (31,500) | 468,500 | 968,500 |
| 3,000 | (1,006,500) | (406,500) | 193,500 | 793,500 | 1,393,500 |
| 3,500 | (981,500) | (281,500) | 418,500 | 1,118,500 | 1,818,500 |
| 4,000 | (956,500) | (156,500) | 643,500 | 1,443,500 | 2,243,500 |
| 4,500 | (931,500) | (31,500) | 868,500 | 1,768,500 | 2,668,500 |
| 5,000 | (906,500) | 93,500 | 1,093,500 | 2,093,500 | 3,093,500 |

# Understanding Cost-Volume Relationships

One of the most powerful features of Excel is the ability to explore the impact of changing financial conditions on outcomes such as revenue, sales volume, expenses, and profitability. In this module, you will use Excel to investigate a variety of "what-if" scenarios. You will begin by exploring Cost-Volume-Profit analysis.

**Cost-Volume-Profit (CVP) analysis** is a branch of financial analysis that studies the relationship between expenses, sales volume, and profitability. CVP analysis is an important business decision-making tool because it can help predict the effect of cutting overhead or raising prices on a company's net income. For example, Athena Cycles needs to determine a reasonable price to charge for the company's bicycles and how much added profit could be realized by increasing (or even decreasing) the sales price. In this session, you will focus on the sales and expenses related to the Athena I model, a popular entry-level bicycle sold by the company.

## Comparing Expenses and Revenue

The first component of CVP analysis is cost, or expense. There are three types of expenses—variable, fixed, and mixed. **Variable expenses** are expenses that change in proportion to production volume. For each additional bicycle the company produces, it spends more on parts, raw materials, and other expenses associated with manufacturing. Each Athena I produced by the company costs $740 in materials and $210 in manufacturing, for a total cost of $950 per unit. The company's total variable expenses are equal to the cost of producing each Athena I multiplied by the total number of bikes produced. Figure 8–1 shows a line graph of the total variable expense as it relates to production volume. From this graph, you learn that Athena Cycles will incur $4.75 million in variable expenses if it produces 5,000 Athena I bicycles.

| Figure 8–1 | Chart of variable expenses |
| --- | --- |

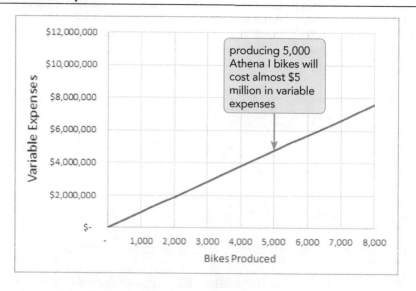

Athena Cycles sells the Athena I for $1,400, which is $450 more than the variable expense for producing each unit. At first glance, it might seem that the company earns a $450 profit on each sale, but that is incorrect. The sales price must also cover the company's fixed expenses. A **fixed expense** is an expense that must be paid regardless of sales volume. For example, the company must pay salaries and benefits for its employees as well as insurance, maintenance fees, and administrative overhead. Roy tells you that the Athena I model costs the company more than $1 million in fixed expenses that must be paid even if the company doesn't sell a single bike.

You can estimate total expense by adding variable and fixed expenses. The graph in Figure 8–2 shows the company's total expenses for a given number of Athena I bicycles produced each year. From this chart, you learn that if the company produces 5,000 Athena I bicycles, its total expense would be about $5.9 million. Of this, about $4.75 million represents variable expenses and about 1.15 million is from fixed expenses.

| Figure 8–2 | Chart of total expenses |

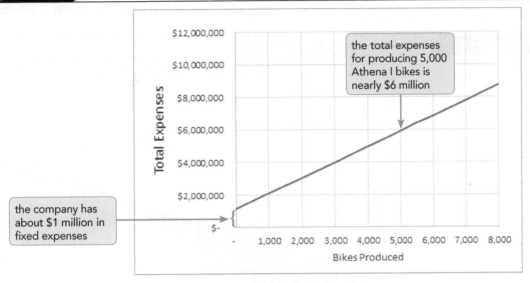

A third type of expense is a **mixed expense**, which is an expense that is part variable and part fixed. For example, if the salespeople at Athena Cycles receive commissions based on sales volume, their total compensation would be a mixed expense to the company because each salesperson has a fixed salary but also earns extra income as sales volume increases. You will not consider any mixed expenses in the analysis you'll prepare for Roy.

Because Athena Cycles is a highly specialized company with a select but loyal clientele, Athena Cycles sells almost all of what it produces. So, the company should bring in more revenue as it increases production. Figure 8–3 shows the increase in revenue in relation to the increase in sales volume. For example, selling 5,000 Athena I bicycles at an average price of $1,400 per bike would generate about $7 million in revenue.

| Figure 8–3 | Chart of revenue |

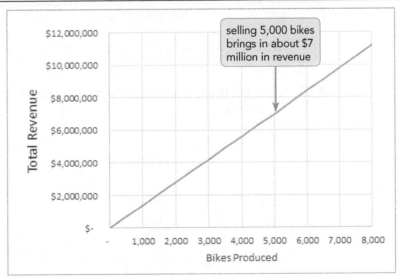

## Exploring the Break-Even Point

The point where total revenue equals total expenses is called the break-even point. For this reason, CVP analysis is sometimes called **break-even analysis**. The more bicycles Athena Cycles sells above the break-even point, the greater its profit. Conversely, when sales levels fall below the break-even point, the company loses money.

You can illustrate the break-even point by graphing revenue and total expenses against sales volume on the same chart. The break-even point occurs where the two lines cross. This type of chart, shown in Figure 8–4, is called a **Cost-Volume-Profit (CVP) chart**.

| Figure 8–4 | Break-even point in a CVP chart |

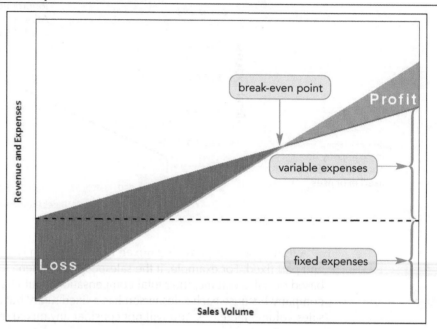

Roy prepared an income statement for the Athena I model that projects the revenue, variable expenses, and fixed expenses for next year's sales. You'll review Roy's data now. Later, you will use Roy's projections to calculate the break-even point for sales of the Athena I model.

### To review the income statement for the Athena I:

1. **sam** ↓ Open the **NP_EX_8-1.xlsx** workbook located in the **Excel8 > Module** folder included with your Data Files, and then save the workbook as **NP_EX_8_Athena** in the location specified by your instructor.

2. In the Documentation worksheet, enter your name and the date.

3. Go to the **Income** worksheet and review its contents and formulas. See Figure 8–5.

| Figure 8–5 | Income statement for the Athena I bicycle |
|---|---|

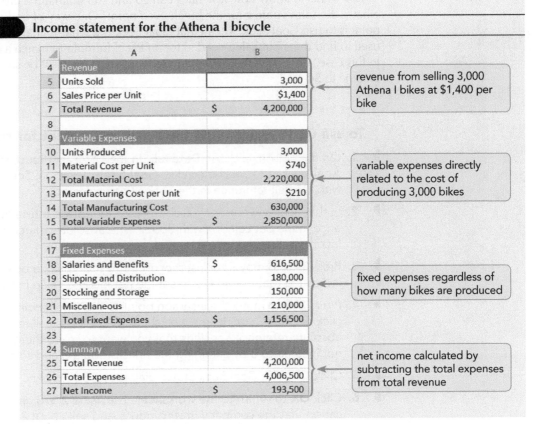

|  | A | B |
|---|---|---|
| 4 | Revenue | |
| 5 | Units Sold | 3,000 |
| 6 | Sales Price per Unit | $1,400 |
| 7 | Total Revenue | $    4,200,000 |
| 8 | | |
| 9 | Variable Expenses | |
| 10 | Units Produced | 3,000 |
| 11 | Material Cost per Unit | $740 |
| 12 | Total Material Cost | 2,220,000 |
| 13 | Manufacturing Cost per Unit | $210 |
| 14 | Total Manufacturing Cost | 630,000 |
| 15 | Total Variable Expenses | $    2,850,000 |
| 16 | | |
| 17 | Fixed Expenses | |
| 18 | Salaries and Benefits | $    616,500 |
| 19 | Shipping and Distribution | 180,000 |
| 20 | Stocking and Storage | 150,000 |
| 21 | Miscellaneous | 210,000 |
| 22 | Total Fixed Expenses | $    1,156,500 |
| 23 | | |
| 24 | Summary | |
| 25 | Total Revenue | 4,200,000 |
| 26 | Total Expenses | 4,006,500 |
| 27 | Net Income | $    193,500 |

- revenue from selling 3,000 Athena I bikes at $1,400 per bike
- variable expenses directly related to the cost of producing 3,000 bikes
- fixed expenses regardless of how many bikes are produced
- net income calculated by subtracting the total expenses from total revenue

As itemized in the Income worksheet, the company projects that it will sell 3,000 Athena Is for $1,400 each, generating $4.2 million in revenue. The variable expenses involved in producing those bicycles is $2.85 million and the company's fixed expenses are about $1.16 million. Based on this sales volume, the company would generate $193,500 in net income.

## Finding the Break-Even Point with What-If Analysis

What-if analysis lets you explore the impact of changing different values in a worksheet. You can use such an analysis to explore the impact of changing financial conditions on a company's profitability. Roy wants to know what the impact would be if the number of Athena I bicycles the company produces and sells rises to 4,000 or falls to 2,000.

### To perform what-if analysis for different sales volumes:

1. In cell **B5**, enter **4000** to change the units produced and sold value. Increasing the sales volume to 4,000 units, the net income of the company shown in cell B27 increases to $643,500.

2. In cell **B5**, enter **2000**. If the units produced and sold drop to 2,000, the net income shown in cell B27 becomes –$256,500. The company will lose money with that low of a sales volume.

3. In cell **B5**, enter **3000** to return to the original units produced and sold projection.

Roy wants to know how low sales can go and still maintain a profit. In other words, what is the sales volume for the break-even point? One way of finding the break-even point is to use Goal Seek. Recall that Goal Seek is a what-if analysis tool that can be used to find the input value needed for an Excel formula to match a specified value. In this case, you'll find out how many Athena I bicycles must be sold to set the net income to $0.

## To use Goal Seek to find the break-even point for the Athena I:

1. On the ribbon, click the **Data** tab. In the Forecast group, click the **What-If Analysis** button, and then click **Goal Seek**. The Goal Seek dialog box opens with the cell reference in the Set cell box selected.

2. In the Income worksheet, click cell **B27** to replace the selected cell reference in the Set cell box with $B$27. The absolute reference specifies the Net Income cell as the cell whose value you want to set.

3. Press **TAB** to move the insertion point to the To value box, and then type **0** indicating that the goal is to set the net income value in cell B27 to 0.

4. Press **TAB** to move the insertion point to the By changing cell box, and then click cell **B5** in the Income worksheet to enter the cell reference $B$5. The absolute reference specifies that you want to reach the goal of setting the net income to 0 by changing the units produced and sold value in cell B5.

5. Click **OK**. The Goal Seek Status dialog box opens once Excel finds a solution.

6. Click **OK** to return to the worksheet. The value 2,570 appears in cell B5, indicating that the company must produce and sell about 2,570 Athena I bicycles to break even. See Figure 8–6.

**Figure 8–6**    **Sales required to break even**

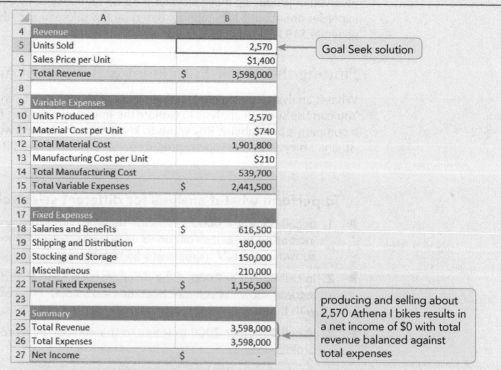

| | A | B |
|---|---|---|
| 4 | Revenue | |
| 5 | Units Sold | 2,570 |
| 6 | Sales Price per Unit | $1,400 |
| 7 | Total Revenue | $        3,598,000 |
| 8 | | |
| 9 | Variable Expenses | |
| 10 | Units Produced | 2,570 |
| 11 | Material Cost per Unit | $740 |
| 12 | Total Material Cost | 1,901,800 |
| 13 | Manufacturing Cost per Unit | $210 |
| 14 | Total Manufacturing Cost | 539,700 |
| 15 | Total Variable Expenses | $        2,441,500 |
| 16 | | |
| 17 | Fixed Expenses | |
| 18 | Salaries and Benefits | $        616,500 |
| 19 | Shipping and Distribution | 180,000 |
| 20 | Stocking and Storage | 150,000 |
| 21 | Miscellaneous | 210,000 |
| 22 | Total Fixed Expenses | $        1,156,500 |
| 23 | | |
| 24 | Summary | |
| 25 | Total Revenue | 3,598,000 |
| 26 | Total Expenses | 3,598,000 |
| 27 | Net Income | $        - |

Goal Seek solution

producing and selling about 2,570 Athena I bikes results in a net income of $0 with total revenue balanced against total expenses

7. Click cell **B5** and enter **3000** to return to the original units produced and sold projection.

Roy wants to continue to analyze the company's net income under different sales assumptions. For example, what would happen to the company's net income if sales increased to 5,000 bicycles? How much would the company lose if the number of sales fell to 1,500? How many bicycles must the company sell to reach a net income of exactly $500,000? You could continue to use Goal Seek to answer each of these questions in turn, but a more efficient approach is to use a data table.

# Working with Data Tables

A **data table** is an Excel table that displays the results from several what-if analyses. The table consists of input cells and result cells. The input cells contain the constants to be changed in a what-if analysis. The result cells contain calculated values that are impacted by the changing input values. In Excel, you can use one-variable data tables and two-variable data tables.

## Creating a One-Variable Data Table

A one-variable data table contains one input cell and any number of result cells. The range of possible values for the input cell is entered in the first row or column of the data table, and the corresponding result values appear in the subsequent rows or columns. One-variable data tables are particularly useful in business to explore how changing a single input value can impact several financial measures.

# Reference

### Creating a One-Variable Data Table

- In the upper-left cell of the table, enter a formula that references the input cell.
- In either the first row or the first column of the table, enter input values.
- For input values in the first row, enter formulas referencing result cells in the table's first column; for input values in the first column, enter formulas referencing result cells in the table's first row.
- Select the table (excluding any row or column headings).
- On the Data tab, in the Forecast group, click the What-If Analysis button, and then click Data Table.
- If the input values are in the first row, enter the cell reference to the input cell in the Row input cell box; if the input values are in the first column, enter the cell reference to the input cell in the Column input cell box.
- Click OK.

Figure 8–7 shows a one-variable data table for calculating the total revenue, expenses, and net income for units sold values that range from 2,000 up to 3,000 units in increments of 100 units. In this worksheet, cell B4 is the input cell and cells B13 through B15 contain the results cells. These cells correspond to columns D through G in the one-variable data table. With this table, you can, at a glance, compare the financial outcomes for different amounts of bicycles sold by the company. For example, you can see that between 2,500 and 2,600 units sold the net income goes from positive to negative. You've already determined that the break-even point occurs at around 2,570 units sold, but the one-variable data table gives you a broader picture.

**Figure 8–7**    One-variable data table example

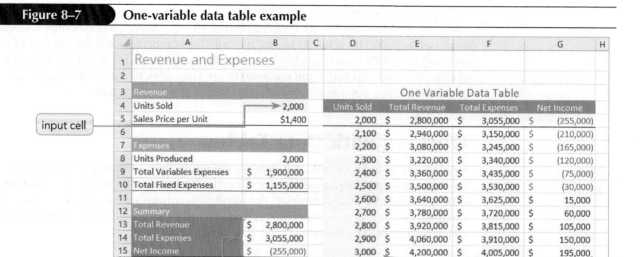

Roy wants to add a one-variable data table to the Income worksheet, with the units sold values going from 1,000 to 5,000 units in 500-unit increments. The first step is to set up the data table so that the first row of the table starts with a reference to the input cell in the worksheet, followed by references to one or more result cells.

**To set up the one-variable data table to examine the impact of changing sales volume:**

1. In cell **D3**, enter **Break-Even Analysis** as the table label, merge and center the range **D3:G3**, and then format the text with the **Heading 3** cell style.

2. In the range **D4:G4**, enter **Units Sold**, **Revenue**, **Expenses**, and **Net Income** as the labels, center the text in the selected cells, and then apply the **Accent 2** cell style to the cells.

3. In cell **D5**, enter the formula **=B5** to reference the input cell to be used in the data table.

4. In cell **E5**, enter the formula **=B25** to reference the result cell that displays the total revenue.

5. In cell **F5**, enter the formula **=B26** to reference the total expenses.

6. In cell **G5**, enter the formula **=B27** to reference the company's net income.

7. Format the range **E5:G5** using the **Accounting** format with no decimal places.

8. Format the range **D5:G5** with the **40% - Accent1** cell style and add a bottom border.

9. In the range **D6:D14**, enter Units Sold values from **1000** to **5000** in 500-unit increments, and then format the selected cells with the **Comma** style and no decimal places.

10. Select cell **D5**. See Figure 8–8.

**Figure 8–8**        Setup for the one-variable data table

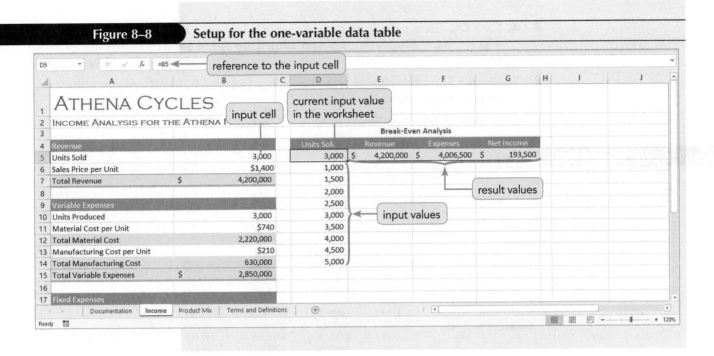

A one-variable data table is based on either a row input cell matching the values placed in the first row of the data table or a column input cell matching the values in the data table's first column. You want to find the revenue, expenses, and net income values for different units sold figures, so you will match the value from cell B5 to the units sold values in the first column of the data table.

## To complete the one-variable data table:

1. Select the range **D5:G14** containing the cells for the data table.

2. On the Data tab, in the Forecast group, click the **What-If Analysis** button, and then click **Data Table**. The Data Table dialog box opens.

3. Press **TAB** to move the insertion point to the Column input cell box, and then click cell **B5** in the Income worksheet to indicate that all the result values in the data table first column should be matched with cell B5. The absolute reference $B$5 appears in the Column input box. See Figure 8–9.

**Figure 8–9**        Data Table dialog box

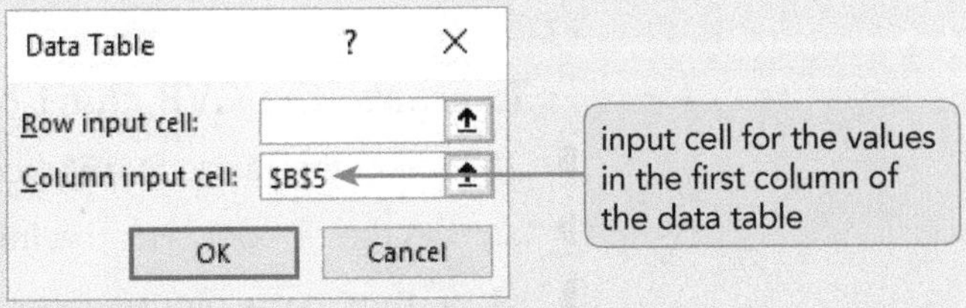

Data Table        ?    ✕

Row input cell:    [                ] ⬆

Column input cell:  $B$5 ◄    ⬆        input cell for the values in the first column of the data table

       OK          Cancel

4. Click **OK**. Excel completes the data table by entering the revenue, expenses, and net income for each units sold value specified in the data table's first column.

5. Use the Format Painter to copy the format from cell **B25** and apply it to the result values in the range **E6:G14**.

6. Select cell **G14**. See Figure 8–10.

**Figure 8–10**    Completed one-variable data table

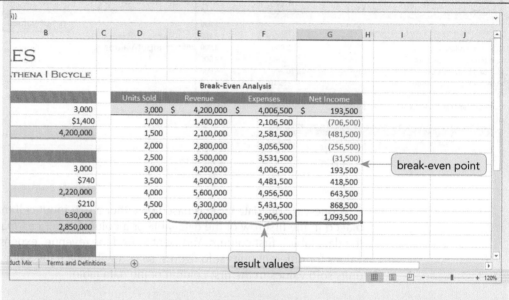

The data table shows the results of several what-if analyses simultaneously. For example, if 4,500 Athena I bicycles are sold, the revenue would be $6,300,000, but the total expenses would be $5,431,500, yielding a net income of $868,500.

## Charting a One-Variable Data Table

The one-variable data table provides the results of several what-if analyses, but the results are often clearer if you include a CVP chart along with the table. The chart gives a better picture of the relationship between sales volume, revenue, and expenses. You'll use a scatter chart to map out the revenue and total expenses against the total number of units sold.

### To create the CVP chart of the data table:

1. Select the range **D4:F14** containing the data you want to chart.

2. On the ribbon, click the **Insert** tab.

3. In the Charts group, click the **Insert Scatter (X, Y) or Bubble Chart** button , and then click **Scatter with Straight Lines** (the second option in the second row of the Scatter section). Each point in the data table is plotted on the chart and connected with a line. The break-even point occurs where the two lines cross.

4. Move and resize the chart so that it covers the range **D15:G27**.

5. Remove the chart title from the chart.

6. Change the fill color of the chart area to **Ice Blue, Accent 1, Lighter 80%**, and then change the fill color of the plot area to **White, Background 1**. See Figure 8–11.

| Figure 8–11 | Completed CVP chart |
| --- | --- |

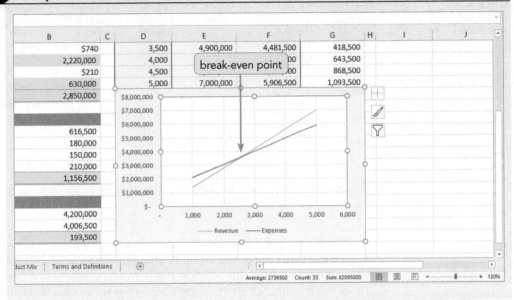

The line chart provides a visual representation of the break-even point that Roy can use in reports that he presents to other members of the Athena Cycles sales team.

## Modifying a Data Table

Data tables are dynamic, which means that changes in the worksheet data are automatically reflected in the data table result values. This includes changes to cells that are displayed in data table but are involved in the results calculations. Athena Cycles is considering lowering its prices to be more competitive with other manufacturers. Roy wants you to perform another what-if analysis that examines the effect of reducing sales price of the Athena I from $1,400 to $1,250. Changing the value in the Income worksheet will affect other results in the sheet, including the what-if analysis displayed in the one-variable data table and the break-even chart.

### To view the impact of changing the sales price:

1. In cell **B6**, enter **$1,250** to reduce the sales price of the Athena I. At this lower sales price, the break-even point moves to somewhere between 3,500 and 4,000 units—a fact reflected in both the data table and the CVP chart. See Figure 8–12.

| Figure 8–12 | Data table for the $1,250 sales price |

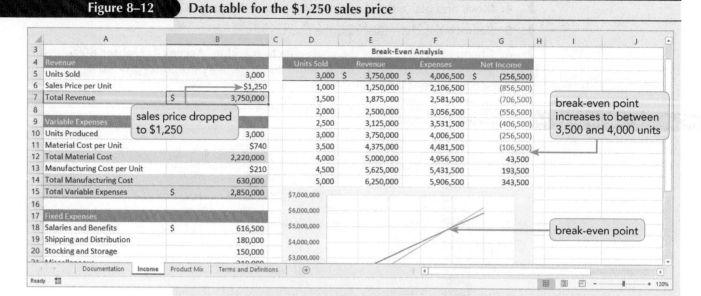

2. In cell **B6**, enter **$1,400** to return the sales price to its original value.

With a sales price set at $1,250, Athena Cycles will need to sell about 4,000 Athena I bicycles to break-even. You could continue to perform what-if analyses with different sales prices to explore the relationship between sales volume and sales price on the break-even point, but another approach is to create a two-variable data table.

## Insight

### Directly Calculating the Break-Even Point

A CVP chart is a useful visual tool for displaying the break-even point. You can also calculate the break-even point directly by using the following formula:

$$\text{break-even point} = \frac{\text{fixed expenses}}{\text{sales price per unit} - \text{variable expenses per unit}}$$

For example, with a sales price of $1,250, fixed expenses of $1,156,500, and variable expenses of $950 per unit, the following equation calculates the break-even point:

$$\text{break-even point} = \frac{1,156,500}{1,250 - 950} = 3,855$$

Athena Cycles would have to sell 3,855 Athena I bikes to break-even. If the company sells more than that number, the company will show a profit.

## Creating a Two-Variable Data Table

A two-variable data table lets you view the relationship between two input cells and one result cell. Figure 8–13 shows a two-variable data table that examines the impact of sales price and sales volume on the company's net income.

**Figure 8–13**    Two-variable data table example

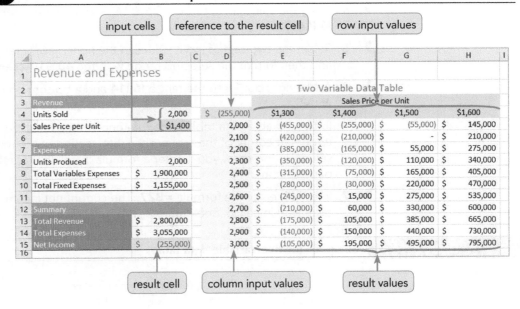

The two input cells are cell B4 and cell B5, containing the units sold and the sales price per unit. The first column of the data table displays a range of possible values for the first input cell (units sold) and the first row contains possible values for the second input cell (sales price). The result cell is cell D4—net income—and references the value in cell B15. The data table shows the net income for each combination of input values. For example, selling 2,200 bikes at $1,500 each will result in a net income of $55,000 (cell G7).

# Reference

### Creating a Two-Variable Data Table

- In the upper-left cell of the table, enter a formula that references the result cell.
- In the first row and first column of the table, enter input values.
- Select the table (excluding any row or column headings).
- On the Data tab, in the Forecast group, click the What-If Analysis button, and then click Data Table.
- Enter the cell reference to the first row input values in the Row input cell box, and then enter the cell reference to the first column input values in the Column input cell box.
- Click OK.

Roy wants you to examine the impact of the sales price and the yearly sales volume on the net income from selling the Athena I. You'll create a two-variable data table to do this.

### To set up the two-variable data table:

1. In cell I3, enter **Net Income Analysis**, merge and center the range I3:N3, and then format the merged range with the **Heading 3** cell style.

2. In cell I4, enter **Sales Price**, and then merge and center the range I4:N4.

3. In the range J5:N5, enter the possible sales prices **$1,000** through **$1,800** in increments of $200.

4. Copy the values in the range **D6:D14**, and then paste them into the range **I6:I14**.

5. Select the two sets of input values in the nonadjacent range **J5:N5, I6:I14**, and then format the selected range with the **40% - Accent1** cell style.

6. Add a right border to the range **I6:I14** and a bottom border to the range **J5:N5**.

In two-variable data tables, the reference to the result cell is placed in the upper-left corner of the table at the intersection of the row and column input values. In this case, you'll enter a formula in cell I5 that references the company's net income.

7. In cell **I5**, enter the formula **=B27**. The current net income value $193,500 is displayed in cell I5. See Figure 8–14.

| Figure 8–14 | Setup for the two-variable data table |
| --- | --- |

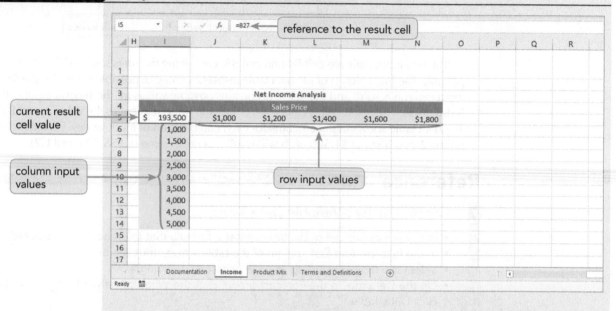

The two-variable data table is generated using the same Data Table command used with the one-variable data table, except that you specify both the row input cell (matched to the values in the first row of the table) and the column input cell (matched to the values in the table's first column).

## To generate the result values:

1. Select the range **I5:N14** containing the row input values, the column input values, and the reference to the result cell.

2. On the ribbon, click the **Data** tab. In the Forecast group, click the **What-If Analysis** button, and then click **Data Table**. The Data Table dialog box opens.

3. In the Row input cell box, type **B6** to reference the sales price from the income statement.

4. In the Column input cell box, type **B5** to reference the number of units sold from the income statement.

5. Click **OK**. The data table values appear in the range J6:N14.

6. Use the Format Painter to copy the formatting from cell **G14** to the range **J6:N14**.

7. Click cell **J6** to deselect the highlighted range. See Figure 8–15.

---

**Figure 8–15** ▶ **Completed two-variable data table**

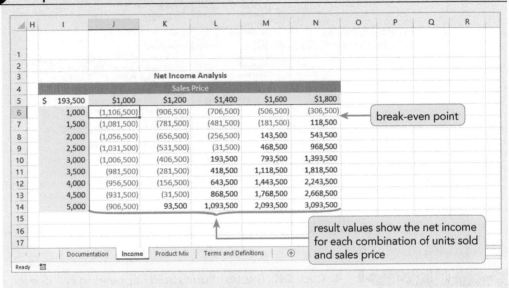

*Net Income Analysis*

| | Sales Price | | | | | |
|---|---|---|---|---|---|---|
| $ 193,500 | $1,000 | $1,200 | $1,400 | $1,600 | $1,800 | |
| 1,000 | (1,106,500) | (906,500) | (706,500) | (506,500) | (306,500) | ← break-even point |
| 1,500 | (1,081,500) | (781,500) | (481,500) | (181,500) | 118,500 | |
| 2,000 | (1,056,500) | (656,500) | (256,500) | 143,500 | 543,500 | |
| 2,500 | (1,031,500) | (531,500) | (31,500) | 468,500 | 968,500 | |
| 3,000 | (1,006,500) | (406,500) | 193,500 | 793,500 | 1,393,500 | |
| 3,500 | (981,500) | (281,500) | 418,500 | 1,118,500 | 1,818,500 | |
| 4,000 | (956,500) | (156,500) | 643,500 | 1,443,500 | 2,243,500 | |
| 4,500 | (931,500) | (31,500) | 868,500 | 1,768,500 | 2,668,500 | |
| 5,000 | (906,500) | 93,500 | 1,093,500 | 2,093,500 | 3,093,500 | |

result values show the net income for each combination of units sold and sales price

Documentation  **Income**  Product Mix  Terms and Definitions  ⊕

Ready

---

The break-even points for different combinations of price and units sold are easy to track because negative net income values are displayed in red and positive net income values are displayed in black. For example, if the sales price is set at $1,600, Athena Cycles must sell between 1,500 and 2,000 Athena I bicycles to break even. However, if the price is decreased to $1,000, no break-even point appears in the table, indicating that the company must sell much more than 5,000 Athena I bicycles to break even.

## Formatting the Result Cell

The reference to the result cell in the table's upper-left corner might confuse some users. To prevent that, you can hide the cell value using the custom cell format "*text*", where *text* is the text you want to display in place of the cell value. In this case, Ron wants you to use a custom format to display "Units Sold" instead of the value in cell I5.

### To apply a custom format to cell I5:

1. Right-click cell **I5**, and then click **Format Cells** on the shortcut menu (or press **CTRL+1**). The Format Cells dialog box opens.

2. If necessary, click the **Number** tab, and then in the Category box, click **Custom**.

> Be sure to use opening and closing quotation marks around the custom text.

**3.** In the Type box, select the format code text, and replace it with the text string **"Units Sold"** (including the quotation marks) as the custom text to display in the cell. See Figure 8–16.

**Figure 8–16** **Format Cells dialog box**

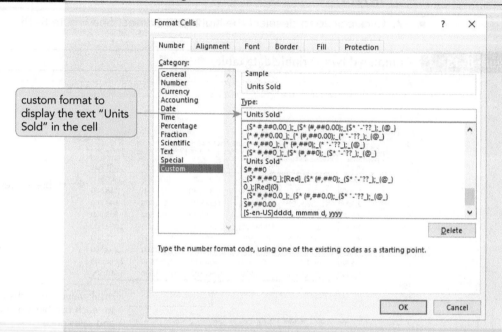

custom format to display the text "Units Sold" in the cell

> **Tip**
>
> You can also hide the reference to the result cell by applying the same font and fill color to the cell.

**4.** Click **OK**. The text "Units Sold" appears in cell I5 even though the cell's underlying formula is =B27.

**Trouble?** If "Units Sold" does not appear in cell I5, you probably didn't include the quotation marks in the custom format. Repeat Steps 1 through 4, making sure that you include both opening and closing quotation marks.

## Charting a Two-Variable Data Table

You can chart the values from a two-variable data table using lines to represent the different columns of the table. Roy wants you to create a scatter chart based on the two-variable data table you just created.

### To create a chart of the two-variable data table:

**1.** Select the range **I6:N14**. You'll plot this range on a scatter chart. You did not select the unit prices in row 5 because Excel would interpret these values as data values to be charted, not as labels.

**2.** On the ribbon, click the **Insert** tab. In the Charts group, click the **Insert Scatter (X, Y) or Bubble Chart** button ⌊⋅⋅⌋, and then click the **Scatter with Straight Lines** chart subtype (the second chart in the second row of the Scatter section).

3. Move and resize the chart so that it covers the range **I15:N27**.

4. Remove the chart title, and then position the chart legend to the right of the chart.

5. Change the fill color of the chart area to **Ice Blue, Accent 1, Lighter 80%**, and then change the fill color of the plot area to **White, Background 1**. See Figure 8–17.

| Figure 8–17 | Chart of net income values |
| --- | --- |

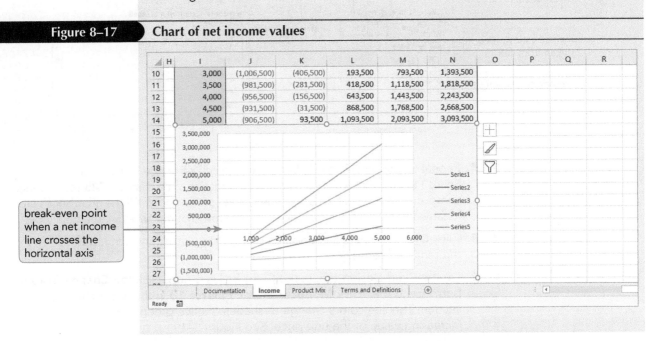

break-even point when a net income line crosses the horizontal axis

The chart shows a different trend line for each of the five possible values for unit price. However, the prices are not listed in the chart, and Excel uses generic series names (Series1, Series2, Series3, Series4, and Series5). To display the unit prices rather than the generic names in the chart, you must add the unit price values as series names.

**To edit the chart series names:**

1. On the Chart Design tab, in the Data group, click the **Select Data** button. The Select Data Source dialog box opens.

2. In the Legend Entries (Series) box, click **Series1**, and then click **Edit**. The Edit Series dialog box opens.

3. With the insertion point in the Series name box, click cell **J5** to insert the reference =Income!$J$5, and then click **OK**. The Select Data Source dialog box reappears with the Series1 name changed to $1,000. See Figure 8–18.

**Figure 8–18**    Select Data Source dialog box

edits the data source of the selected series

revised series name (taken from cell J5)

generic series names

Select Data Source                                               ?    ✕

Chart data range:                                                         ⬆

The data range is too complex to be displayed. If a new range is selected, it will replace all of the series in the
Series panel.

⬔ Switch Row/Column ⬳

Legend Entries (Series)                    Horizontal (Category) Axis Labels

☐ Add    ☐ Edit    ✕ Remove    △ ▽        ☐ Edit

☑ ➤ $1,000                                  1,000
☑ Series2                                   1,500
☑ Series3                                   2,000
☑ Series4                                   2,500
☑ Series5                                   3,000

Hidden and Empty Cells                                    OK        Cancel

**4.** Repeat Steps 2 and 3 to edit Series2 to use cell **K5** as the series name, edit Series3 to use cell **L5** as the series name, edit Series4 to use cell **M5** as the series name, and edit Series5 to use cell **N5** as the series name. All the chart series are renamed to match the sales price values in row 5 of the two-variable data table.

**5.** Click **OK**. The Select Data Source dialog box closes, and the legend shows the renamed series.

**6.** On the Chart Design tab, in the Chart Styles group, click the **Change Colors** button, and then click **Monochromatic Palette 10** in the Monochromatic section. The line colors change to shades of olive green, reflecting the increasing value of the unit price. See Figure 8–19.

**Figure 8–19**    Final chart of net income values

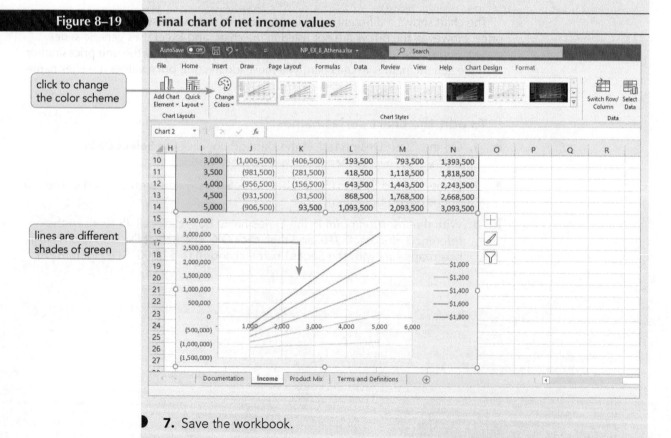

click to change the color scheme

lines are different shades of green

**7.** Save the workbook.

The chart shows how different unit prices will affect the relationship between sales volume and net income; where each line crosses the horizontal axis indicates the break-even point for that sales price. For example, the $1,600 line (the second highest of the five lines) crosses the horizontal axis near 1,800 units, indicating that with sales price of $1,600, the company will have to sell about 1,800 Athena I bicycles to break even.

## Insight

### Data Tables and Arrays

If you examine the cells in the two-variable data table you just created, you can see that every cell displays a different value even though it has the same formula: {=TABLE(B6, B5)}. This formula is an **array formula**, which performs multiple calculations in a single step, returning either a single value to one cell or multiple values to several cells. Array formulas are always enclosed within curly braces.

An array formula that returns a single value is {=SUM(B1:B10*C1:C10)}. This formula multiplies each cell in the range B1:B10 by the matching cell in the same row of the range C1:C10. The sum of those 10 products is then calculated and returned. To create this array formula, enter the formula =SUM(B1:B10*C1:C10) in the formula bar and then press CTRL+SHIFT+ENTER. Excel treats the formula as an array formula, adding the curly braces for you.

The TABLE function is an array function that returns multiple values to multiple cells. Other such functions include the TREND, MINVERSE, MMULT, and TRANSPOSE functions. To calculate multiple cell values, select the range, type the array formula, and then press CTRL+SHIFT+ENTER to enter the formula. Excel applies the array formula to all the selected cells.

Array formulas are a powerful feature of Excel. They can perform complex calculations within a single expression and extend a single formula over a range of cells. Use Excel Help to learn more about array formulas and the functions that support them.

So far, you have used what-if analysis with Goal Seek and data tables to analyze how the number of Athena I bikes sold and the sales price impact the company's net income. In the next session, you will use other what-if analysis tools to examine the impact of more than two input values on multiple result values.

## Review

### Session 8.1 Quick Check

1. Describe the difference between a variable expense and a fixed expense.
2. When does the break-even point occur?
3. What is a data table? What is an input cell? What is a result cell?
4. What is a one-variable data table? What is a two-variable data table?
5. How many result cells can you display with a one-variable data table? How many result cells can you display with a two-variable data table?
6. Cell E5 contains the formula =B10. You want to display the text "Profits" instead of the formula's value. What custom format would you use?
7. What is an array formula?

# Session 8.2 Visual Overview:

The Scenario Manager creates scenarios of several what-if analyses within the worksheet.

A scenario is a defined collection of changing cells used to perform a what-if analysis.

Cells whose values will change within each scenario are called changing cells.

Result cells are displayed in the scenario summary and scenario PivotTable reports.

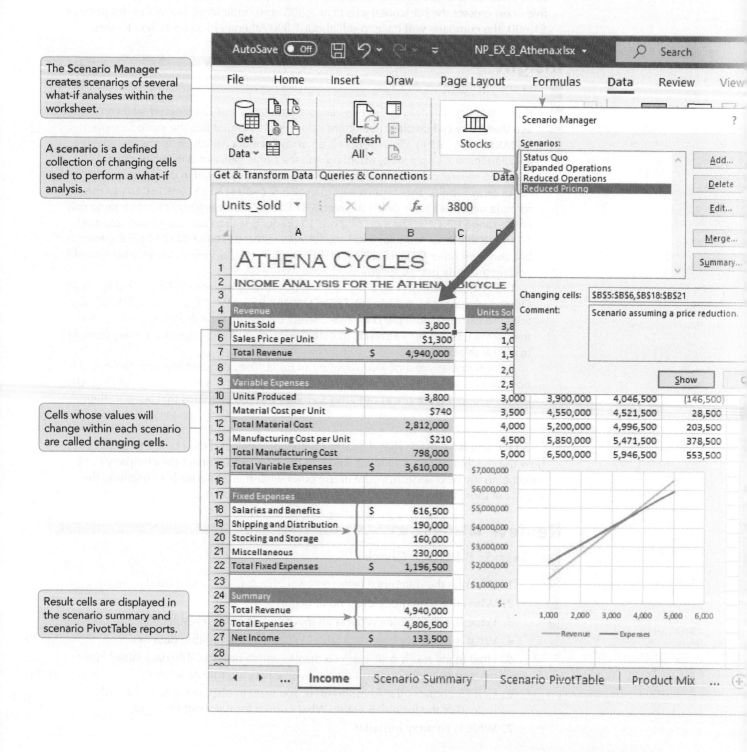

# What-If Scenarios

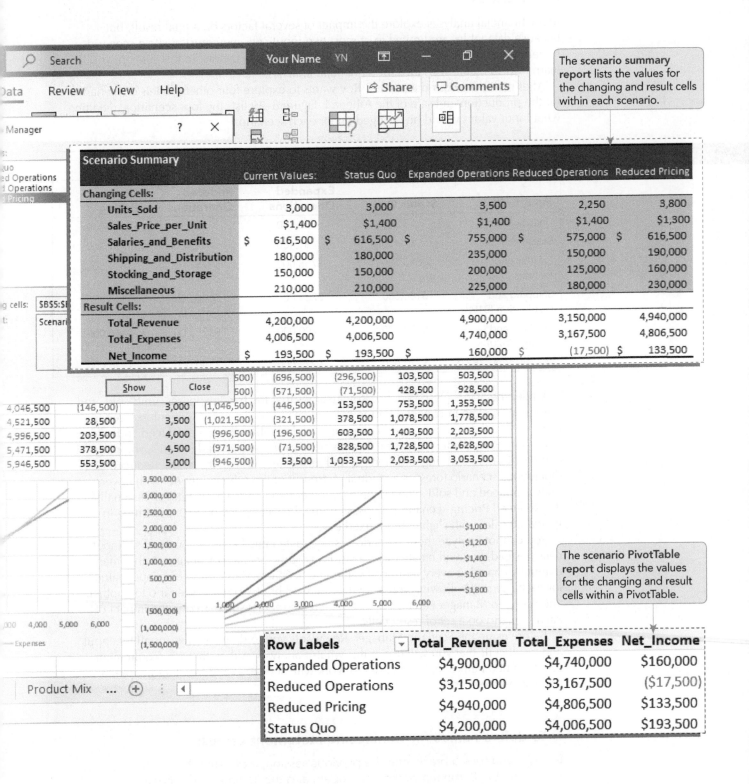

The scenario summary report lists the values for the changing and result cells within each scenario.

## Scenario Summary

| | Current Values: | Status Quo | Expanded Operations | Reduced Operations | Reduced Pricing |
|---|---|---|---|---|---|
| **Changing Cells:** | | | | | |
| Units_Sold | 3,000 | 3,000 | 3,500 | 2,250 | 3,800 |
| Sales_Price_per_Unit | $1,400 | $1,400 | $1,400 | $1,400 | $1,300 |
| Salaries_and_Benefits | $ 616,500 | $ 616,500 | $ 755,000 | $ 575,000 | $ 616,500 |
| Shipping_and_Distribution | 180,000 | 180,000 | 235,000 | 150,000 | 190,000 |
| Stocking_and_Storage | 150,000 | 150,000 | 200,000 | 125,000 | 160,000 |
| Miscellaneous | 210,000 | 210,000 | 225,000 | 180,000 | 230,000 |
| **Result Cells:** | | | | | |
| Total_Revenue | 4,200,000 | 4,200,000 | 4,900,000 | 3,150,000 | 4,940,000 |
| Total_Expenses | 4,006,500 | 4,006,500 | 4,740,000 | 3,167,500 | 4,806,500 |
| Net_Income | $ 193,500 | $ 193,500 | $ 160,000 | $ (17,500) | $ 133,500 |

[ Show ]  [ Close ]

| | | | | | | |
|---|---|---|---|---|---|---|
| | | 500) | (696,500) | (296,500) | 103,500 | 503,500 |
| | | 500) | (571,500) | (71,500) | 428,500 | 928,500 |
| 4,046,500 | (146,500) | 3,000 | (1,046,500) | (446,500) | 153,500 | 753,500 | 1,353,500 |
| 4,521,500 | 28,500 | 3,500 | (1,021,500) | (321,500) | 378,500 | 1,078,500 | 1,778,500 |
| 4,996,500 | 203,500 | 4,000 | (996,500) | (196,500) | 603,500 | 1,403,500 | 2,203,500 |
| 5,471,500 | 378,500 | 4,500 | (971,500) | (71,500) | 828,500 | 1,728,500 | 2,628,500 |
| 5,946,500 | 553,500 | 5,000 | (946,500) | 53,500 | 1,053,500 | 2,053,500 | 3,053,500 |

The scenario PivotTable report displays the values for the changing and result cells within a PivotTable.

Product Mix  ...  ⊕

| Row Labels | Total_Revenue | Total_Expenses | Net_Income |
|---|---|---|---|
| Expanded Operations | $4,900,000 | $4,740,000 | $160,000 |
| Reduced Operations | $3,150,000 | $3,167,500 | ($17,500) |
| Reduced Pricing | $4,940,000 | $4,806,500 | $133,500 |
| Status Quo | $4,200,000 | $4,006,500 | $193,500 |

# Exploring Financial Scenarios with Scenario Manager

Many financial analyses explore the impact of several factors on a final result, but because data tables are limited to at most two input cells, you must create a scenario to perform a what-if analysis that involves more than two factors. In this session, you'll learn how to create scenarios for a financial analysis.

After reviewing your data tables, Roy wants to explore four other models or scenarios for the production and sale of the Athena I. Figure 8–20 lists the four scenarios, detailing what input values would be changed under each scenario.

**Figure 8–20**    What-if scenarios

| Input Cells | Status Quo | Expanded Operations | Reduced Operations | Reduced Pricing |
|---|---|---|---|---|
| Units Sold (B5) | 3,000 | 3,500 | 2,250 | 4,000 |
| Sales Price (B6) | $1,400 | $1,400 | $1,400 | $1,300 |
| Salaries and Benefits (B18) | $616,500 | $755,000 | $575,000 | $616,500 |
| Shipping and Distribution (B19) | $180,000 | $235,000 | $150,000 | $190,000 |
| Stocking and Storage (B20) | $150,000 | $200,000 | $125,000 | $160,000 |
| Miscellaneous (B21) | $210,000 | $225,000 | $180,000 | $230,000 |

Under the Status Quo scenario, Roy assumes that the fixed expenses, units sold, and unit prices remain unchanged for the coming year. The Expanded Operations scenario assumes that the company will increase the total number of bikes produced and sold while at the same time increasing its expenditures on salaries and benefits, shipping and distribution, stocking and storage, and miscellaneous expenses. The Reduced Operations scenario foresees a gradual phase-out of the Athena I model with fewer units produced and sold accompanied by lower fixed costs for all categories. Finally, the Reduced Pricing scenario proposes cutting the sales price by $100, resulting in increased sales with slightly more fixed costs.

You cannot analyze these scenarios using a data table because you need six input cells. Instead, you will create the scenarios using the Scenario Manager. Rather than manually changing every input cell value, the Scenario Manager defines input values for each scenario, allowing you to switch the workbook from one scenario to another. The Scenario Manager can also be used to create reports summarizing the impact of each scenario on a set of result cells.

Before using the Scenario Manager, Roy wants you to define names for all the input and result cells that you will use in this what-if analysis. Although not a requirement, using defined names makes it easier to work with scenarios and for other people to understand the scenario reports.

## To define names for the income statement values:

1. If you took a break after the previous session, make sure the NP_EX_8_Athena workbook is open, and the Income worksheet is the active sheet.

2. In the Income worksheet, select the range **A5:B6,A18:B21,A25:B27**. You'll define names for each of these cells.

3. On the ribbon, click the **Formulas** tab, and then in the Defined Names group, click the **Create from Selection** button. The Create Names from Selection dialog box opens.

4. Click the **Left column** check box to insert a checkmark, if necessary, and then click any other check box that has a checkmark to deselect it.

5. Click **OK**. The cell values in column B are named using the labels in the corresponding cells in column A.

6. Click cell **A1** to deselect the range.

## Defining a Scenario

Now that you've defined the names used in the worksheet, you'll use the Scenario Manager to create scenarios based on the values shown in Figure 8–20. Each scenario includes a scenario name, a list of input or changing cells, and the values of each input cell under the scenario. The number of scenarios you can create is limited only by your computer's memory.

# Reference

### Defining a Scenario

- Enter the data values in the worksheet for the scenario.
- On the Data tab, in the Forecast group, click the What-If Analysis button, and then click Scenario Manager.
- Click Add in the Scenario Manager dialog box.
- In the Scenario name box, type a name for the scenario.
- In the Changing cells box, specify the changing cells.
- Click OK.
- In the Scenario Values dialog box, specify values for each input cell, and then click Add.
- Click OK.

You'll start by creating the Status Quo scenario, whose values match those currently entered in the workbook.

### To add the Status Quo scenario:

1. On the ribbon, click the **Data** tab. In the Forecast group, click the **What-If Analysis** button, and then click **Scenario Manager**. The Scenario Manager dialog box opens. No scenarios are defined yet.

2. Click **Add**. The Add Scenario dialog box opens.

3. In the Scenario name box, type **Status Quo**, and then press **TAB**. The cell reference in the Changing cells box is selected.

**Tip**

Scenarios are limited to a maximum of 32 changing cells.

The Scenario Manager refers to input cells as "changing cells" because these worksheet cells contain values that are changed under the scenario. Changing cells can be located anywhere in the current worksheet. You can type the range names or locations of changing cells, but it's faster and more accurate to select them with the mouse.

The changing cells for each of the four scenarios are:

- Cell B5: Units Sold
- Cell B6: Sales Price per Unit
- Cell B18: Salaries and Benefits
- Cell B19: Shipping and Distribution
- Cell B20: Stocking and Storage
- Cell B21: Miscellaneous

You'll specify these cells as the changing cells for the Status Quo scenario.

### To specify the changing cells for the Status Quo scenario:

▶ **1.** With the Changing cells box still active, select the nonadjacent range **B5:B6,B18:B21**. Absolute references for the range appear in the Changing cells box. These are the input cells.

▶ **2.** Press **TAB** to select the default text in the Comment box, and then type **Scenario assuming no change in values** in the Comment box. See Figure 8–21.

**Figure 8–21**    Edit Scenario dialog box

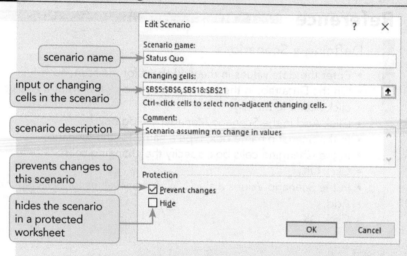

▶ **3.** Click **OK**. The Scenario Values dialog box opens so you can enter values for each changing cell you entered in the Changing cells box in the Edit Scenario dialog box. The Status Quo scenario values already appear in the dialog box because these are the current values in the workbook. See Figure 8–22.

**Figure 8–22**    Scenario Values dialog box

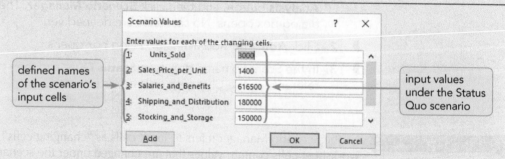

▶ **4.** Click **OK**. The Scenario Manager dialog box reopens with the Status Quo scenario listed in the Scenarios box. See Figure 8–23.

**Figure 8-23**    Scenario Manager dialog box

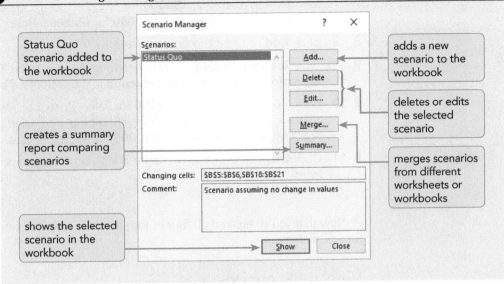

You'll use the same process to add the remaining three scenarios on Roy's list—Expanded Operations, Reduced Operations, and Reduced Pricing.

## To add the remaining scenarios:

1. Click **Add**. The Add Scenario dialog box opens.

2. In the Scenario name box, type **Expanded Operations**, press **TAB** twice to go the Comment box, and then type **Scenario assuming expanded operations** in the Comment box.

   Note that the nonadjacent range you selected for the Status Quo scenario appears in the Changing cells box. Because you want to use the same set of changing cells, you didn't edit the range.

3. Click **OK**. The Scenario Values dialog box for the Expanded Operations scenario opens.

4. Enter the following values, pressing **TAB** to move from one input box to the next: **3500** for Units_Sold, **1400** for Sales_Price_per_Unit, **755000** for Salaries_and_Benefits, **235000** for Shipping_and_Distribution, **200000** for Stocking_and_Storage, and **225000** for Miscellaneous.

   **Trouble?** If the Scenario Manager dialog box reopens, you probably pressed ENTER instead of TAB. Make sure that the Expanded Operations scenario is selected in the Scenarios box, click Edit, and then click OK to return to the Scenario Values dialog box. Enter the remaining values in the scenario, being sure to press TAB to move to the next input box.

5. Click **Add**. The Add Scenario dialog box reopens so you can enter the next scenario.

   **Trouble?** If the Scenario Manager dialog box reopens, you clicked OK instead of Add. Click Add in the Scenario Manager dialog box to return to the Add Scenario dialog box, and then continue with Step 6.

6. Type **Reduced Operations** in the Scenario name box, press **TAB** twice, type **Scenario assuming reduced operations** in the Comment box, and then click **OK**.

Be sure you enter the values for the scenario; do not simply accept the default values currently in the worksheet.

▶ 7. Enter **2250** for Units_Sold, **1400** for Sales_Price_per_Unit, **575000** for Salaries_and_Benefits, **150000** for Shipping_and_Distribution, **125000** for Stocking_and_Storage, and **180000** for Miscellaneous.

▶ 8. Click **Add** to enter the final scenario.

▶ 9. Type **Reduced Pricing** in the Scenario name box, press **TAB** twice, type **Scenario assuming a price reduction** in the Comment box, and then click **OK**.

▶ 10. Enter **4000** for Units_Sold, **1300** for Sales_Price_per_Unit, **616500** for Salaries_and_Benefits, **190000** for Shipping_and_Distribution, **160000** for Stocking_and_Storage, and **230000** for Miscellaneous.

▶ 11. Click **OK**. The Scenario Manager dialog box reappears with all four scenarios listed.

Now that you've entered all four of the scenarios, you can view their impact on the income statement.

## Viewing Scenarios

You can view the effect of each scenario by selecting that scenario in the Scenario Manager dialog box. You switch from one scenario to another by clicking Show in the Scenario Manager dialog box. You do not have to close the dialog box to switch scenarios. You'll start by viewing the results of the Expanded Operations scenario.

### To view the impact of the Expanded Operations scenario:

**Tip**

You can double-click a scenario name in the Scenario Manager dialog box to view that scenario.

▶ 1. In the Scenario Manager dialog box, in the Scenarios box, click **Expanded Operations**. The changing cells and the comment for the selected scenario appear at the bottom of the Scenario Manager dialog box.

▶ 2. Click **Show**. The values in the Income worksheet change to reflect the scenario.

▶ 3. Click **Close**. The Scenario Manager dialog box closes. The income statement for is updated to show expanded operations with increased fixed expenses. See Figure 8–24.

**Figure 8–24** Income statement under the Expanded Operations scenario

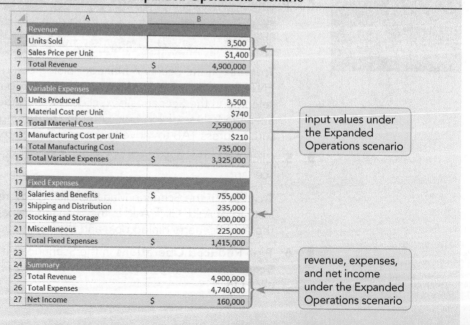

input values under the Expanded Operations scenario

revenue, expenses, and net income under the Expanded Operations scenario

**Trouble?** If the values in your income statement do not match those in the figure, you probably entered the values for the scenario incorrectly. You'll learn how to edit a scenario shortly, and can then enter the correct values.

Excel automatically changes the values of the six input cells to match the scenario. Under the Expanded Operations scenario, the company's net income in cell B7 declines from the current value of $193,500 to $160,000. You'll review the other scenarios.

**To view the impact of the remaining scenarios:**

1. On the Data tab, in the Forecast group, click the **What-If Analysis** button, and then click **Scenario Manager**. The Scenario Manager dialog box opens.

2. In the Scenarios box, double-click **Reduced Operations** to update the worksheet, and then click **Close** to close the Scenario Manager dialog box. Under the Reduced Operations scenario, the company will show a net loss of $17,500 in the sales of Athena I bikes.

3. Repeat Steps 1 and 2 to update the worksheet with the **Reduced Pricing** scenario. Under that scenario, the company would generate a net income of $203,500. Figure 8–25 shows the income statements under both scenarios.

**Figure 8–25**    Income statements under the Reduced Operations and Reduced Pricing scenarios

Reduced Operations                 Reduced Pricing

When you substitute a new scenario for the Status Quo scenario, all the worksheet values and charts are automatically updated. For example, under the Reduced Pricing scenario, the one-variable and two-variable data tables changed to reflect the new values of the input and result cells. The break-even point for the Reduced Pricing scenario is close to 3,500 units.

## Editing a Scenario

After you create a scenario, you can edit its assumptions to view other possible outcomes. When you edit a scenario, the worksheet calculations are automatically updated to reflect the revised input values.

The Reduced Pricing scenario results in the highest net income, but it relies on the company selling 4,000 Athena I bikes for $1,300 per model to generate a net income of $203,500. Roy is unsure whether the company can meet that sales goal at that sales price. He asks you to modify the Reduced Pricing scenario, reducing the total sales to 3,800 units to see how this impacts the company's profitability.

## To edit the Reduced Pricing scenario:

1. On the Data tab, in the Forecast group, click the **What-If Analysis** button, and then click **Scenario Manager**. The Scenario Manager dialog box opens.

2. In the Scenarios box, click **Reduced Pricing** if it is not already selected, and then click **Edit**. The Edit Scenario dialog box opens. You don't need to make any changes in this dialog box.

3. Click **OK**. The Scenario Values dialog box opens.

4. Change the Units_Sold value from 4000 to **3800**, and then click **OK** to return to the Scenario Manager dialog box.

5. Click **Show**, and then click **Close**. The Income worksheet updates to reflect the revised scenario, which results in net income decreasing from $203,500 to $133,500—a decline of $70,000. See Figure 8–26.

**Figure 8–26**    Revised Reduced Pricing scenario

| | A | B |
|---|---|---|
| 4 | Revenue | |
| 5 | Units Sold | 3,800 |
| 6 | Sales Price per Unit | $1,300 |
| 7 | Total Revenue | $ 4,940,000 |
| 8 | | |
| 9 | Variable Expenses | |
| 10 | Units Produced | 3,800 |
| 11 | Material Cost per Unit | $740 |
| 12 | Total Material Cost | 2,812,000 |
| 13 | Manufacturing Cost per Unit | $210 |
| 14 | Total Manufacturing Cost | 798,000 |
| 15 | Total Variable Expenses | $ 3,610,000 |
| 16 | | |
| 17 | Fixed Expenses | |
| 18 | Salaries and Benefits | $ 616,500 |
| 19 | Shipping and Distribution | 190,000 |
| 20 | Stocking and Storage | 160,000 |
| 21 | Miscellaneous | 230,000 |
| 22 | Total Fixed Expenses | $ 1,196,500 |
| 23 | | |
| 24 | Summary | |
| 25 | Total Revenue | 4,940,000 |
| 26 | Total Expenses | 4,806,500 |
| 27 | Net Income | $ 133,500 |

projected sales declines to 3,800 units

net income declines from $203,500 to $133,500

6. Open the Scenario Manager dialog box, and then double-click **Status Quo** in the Scenarios box to return the Income worksheet to the original values. Leave the Scenario Manager dialog box open.

# Creating Scenario Summary Reports

Although scenarios can help you make important business decisions, repeatedly switching between scenarios can become time-consuming. You can summarize all your scenarios in a single report, either as an Excel table or PivotTable. Roy wants you to create both types of reports with the four scenarios you generated for the company, starting with a summary report that appears as an Excel table.

# Reference

## Creating a Scenario Summary Report or a Scenario PivotTable Report

- On the Data tab, in the Forecast group, click the What-If Analysis button, and then click Scenario Manager.
- Click Summary.
- Click the Scenario summary or Scenario PivotTable report option button.
- Select the result cells to display in the report.
- Click OK.

To create a scenario summary report, you must identify which result cells you want to include in the report. Roy is interested in the following result cells—cell B25 (Total Revenue), cell B26 (Total Expenses), and cell B27 (Net Income). You'll display these values along with the values of the input cell defined by the scenario in your report.

## To create the scenario summary report:

1. In the Scenario Manager dialog box, click **Summary**. The Scenario Summary dialog box opens, allowing you to create a scenario summary report or a scenario PivotTable report. You want to create a scenario summary report.

2. Verify that the **Scenario summary** option button is selected.

3. Make sure that the reference in the Result cells box is selected, and then in the Income worksheet, select the range **B25:B27** to enter the range reference for the result cells you want to display in the report.

4. Click **OK**. The scenario summary report is inserted in the workbook as a new worksheet.

5. Move the Scenario Summary worksheet directly after the Income worksheet.

6. Increase the Zoom factor of the worksheet to **120%** to better view its contents. See Figure 8–27.

| Figure 8–27 | Scenario summary report |

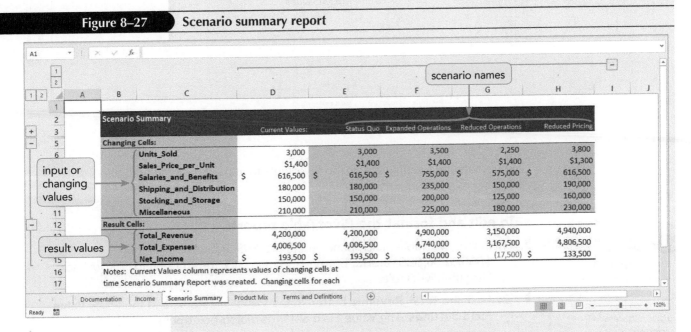

The scenario summary report displays the values of the changing cells and result cells under each scenario. Each scenario is listed by name, and the current worksheet values are also displayed. The report uses the defined names you created earlier to identify the changing and result cells, making the report simpler to interpret. The report also includes outline buttons to allow you expand and collapse different sections of the report, a useful feature when the scenarios involve many different input and result values.

Next, Roy wants you to compare the scenarios using a PivotTable report. As the name implies, a Scenario PivotTable report displays the results from each scenario as a PivotTable field within a PivotTable.

### To create the Scenario PivotTable report:

1. Go to the **Income worksheet** and open the Scenario Manager dialog box.

2. Click **Summary** to open the Scenario Summary dialog box, and then click the **Scenario PivotTable report** option button. You'll use the same result cells for this report.

3. Click **OK**. The Scenario PivotTable sheet is inserted in the workbook and contains the scenario values in a PivotTable.

4. Move the Scenario PivotTable worksheet after the Scenario Summary worksheet, and then change the zoom level of the worksheet to **120%**. See Figure 8–28.

**Figure 8–28**    Scenario PivotTable report

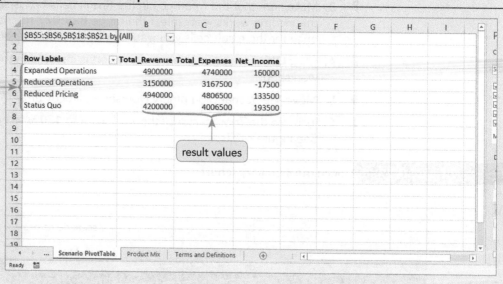

scenarios

result values

Roy wants you to edit the scenario PivotTable to make it easier to read.

### To edit and format the PivotTable report:

**Tip**

The PivotTable filter button is useful only when you have merged scenarios from multiple users and want to filter scenarios by user.

1. In the PivotTable Fields pane, in the FILTERS area box, click the **$B$5:$B$6,$B$18:$B...** button, and then click **Remove Field**. You will not filter the PivotTable.

2. Click the **Total_Revenue** button in the Values area box, and then click **Value Field Settings**. The Value Field Settings dialog box opens.

3. Click **Number Format** to open the Format Cells dialog box, click **Currency** in the Category box, change the number of decimal places to **0**, and then click the last entry **($1,234)** in the Negative numbers box to display negative currency values in a red font enclosed in parentheses.

4. Click **OK** in each dialog box to return to the worksheet. The currency format is applied to the Total_Revenue cells.

5. Repeat Steps 2 through 4 for the **Total_Expenses** and the **Net_Income** buttons in the Values box to apply the same currency format.

6. In cell A1, enter **Scenario PivotTable**, and then format the text with the **Title** cell style. See Figure 8–29.

| Figure 8–29 | Formatted PivotTable report |
| --- | --- |

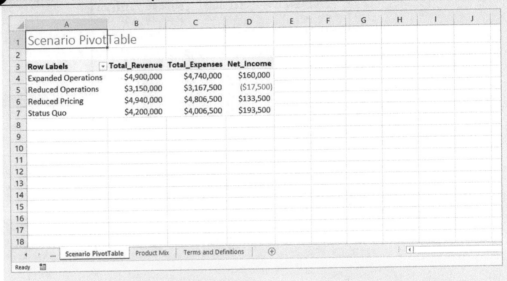

The Scenario Summary report and the Scenario PivotTable report are both static reports. If you alter the source data or the terms of the scenarios, those changes will not be reflected in either report. You will have to recreate the reports to view the impact of your edits.

Roy wants you to augment the Scenario PivotTable report with a chart of the scenario results. You'll add a PivotChart to the worksheet now.

**To create a PivotChart with the scenario results:**

1. Click cell **A3** to select the PivotTable.

2. On the ribbon, click the **PivotTable Analyze** tab, and then in the Tools group, click the **PivotChart** button. The Insert Chart dialog box opens.

3. On the All Charts tab, click the **Combo** chart type to create a combination chart.

4. Verify that the **Total_Revenue** and **Total_Expenses** series are displayed as clustered column charts and the **Net_Income** series is displayed as a line chart.

5. Click the **Secondary Axis** check box for the Net_Income series to chart those data values on a secondary axis.

▶ **6.** Click **OK** to create the chart.

▶ **7.** Move and resize the PivotChart to cover the range **A8:D19**.

▶ **8.** On the ribbon, click the **PivotChart Analyze** tab, and then in the Show/ Hide group, click the **Field Buttons** button. The field buttons in the chart are hidden.

▶ **9.** Position the chart legend at the bottom of the chart. See Figure 8–30.

**Figure 8–30** Scenario PivotChart

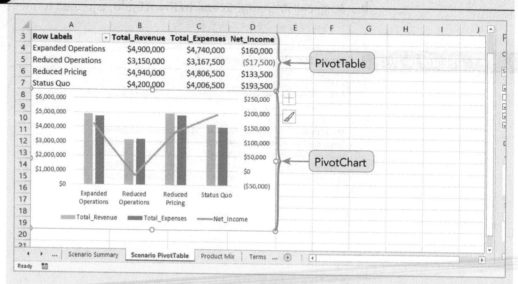

▶ **10.** Save the workbook.

Roy can now present an informative summary to the financial team at Athena Cycles. Using that report the team can determine whether other scenarios need to be explored. However, at the current time, the status quo appears to still offer the best outcome in terms of net income.

**Proskills**

### Teamwork: Merging Scenarios

In many businesses, several workbooks often track the same set of figures and evaluate the same set of scenarios. Colleagues can share scenarios by merging the scenarios from multiple workbooks into one workbook. The Scenario Manager dialog box includes a Merge button that you can use to merge scenarios from different workbooks. The scenarios will be merged into the active sheet, so they can be compared within a single document. It's easier to merge scenarios if all the what-if analyses on the different worksheets and workbooks are identical. All the changing cells from the merged scenario must correspond to changing cells in the active workbook and worksheet.

Once the scenarios are merged, they can be analyzed using a Scenario PivotTable report. One of the advantages of the Scenario PivotTable report over the Scenario Summary report is that you can use it with merged scenarios created by different users. For example, each member of the financial analysis team might propose different numbers for the various scenarios being considered. A Scenario PivotTable report can filter the four scenarios by user or show the average results across all users, giving the team a broader understanding of the various financial scenarios.

By sharing and merging scenarios, the team can more easily explore the impact of different financial situations, ensuring that everyone is always working from a common set of assumptions and goals.

In this session, you used scenarios to examine the impact of different financial scenarios on the profitability of the Athena I. However, the Athena I is just one of many models sold by Athena Cycles. In the next session, you'll explore how by promoting different models within its lineup, Athena Cycles can increase the profitability of its entire operation.

## Review

### Session 8.2 Quick Check

1. What is one advantage of scenarios over data tables?
2. What should you do before creating a scenario report to make the entries on the report easier to interpret?
3. What are changing cells in a scenario?
4. Where are the result cells in a scenario?
5. What are the two types of scenario reports?
6. When would you use the filter button in a Scenario PivotTable report?

# Session 8.3 Visual Overview:

Product mix is the combination of different products offered by a company for sale to the consumer.

Variable cells contain values that will be changed to reach an optimal solution. Here, the range B11:E11 contains variable cells.

Solver models can be stored within worksheet cells to be reloaded and used later.

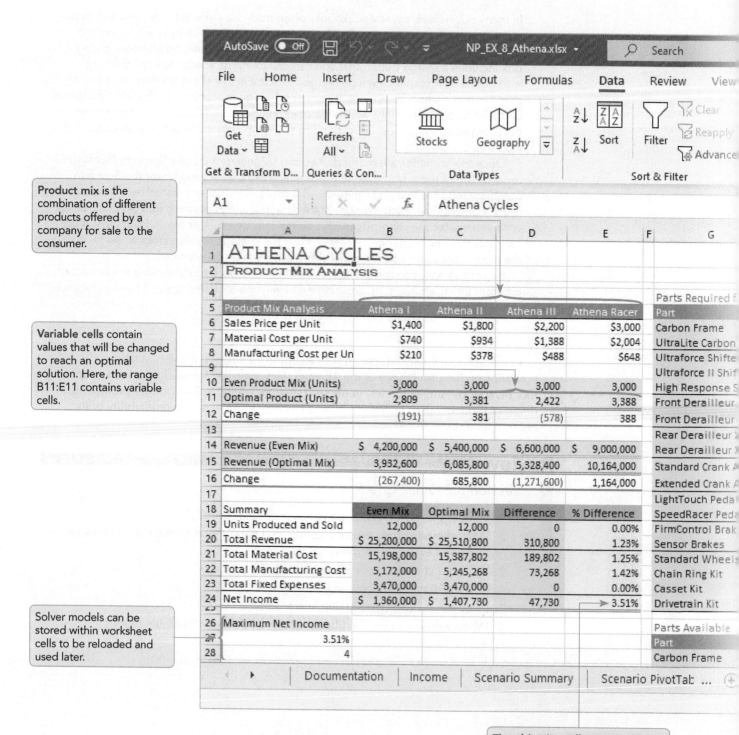

The objective cell contains a value to maximize, minimize, or set to a specific value. Here, cell E24 is the objective cell.

| Product Mix Analysis | Athena I | Athena II | Athena III | Athena Racer |
|---|---|---|---|---|
| Sales Price per Unit | $1,400 | $1,800 | $2,200 | $3,000 |
| Material Cost per Unit | $740 | $934 | $1,388 | $2,004 |
| Manufacturing Cost per Un | $210 | $378 | $488 | $648 |
| | | | | |
| Even Product Mix (Units) | 3,000 | 3,000 | 3,000 | 3,000 |
| Optimal Product (Units) | 2,809 | 3,381 | 2,422 | 3,388 |
| Change | (191) | 381 | (578) | 388 |
| | | | | |
| Revenue (Even Mix) | $ 4,200,000 | $ 5,400,000 | $ 6,600,000 | $ 9,000,000 |
| Revenue (Optimal Mix) | 3,932,600 | 6,085,800 | 5,328,400 | 10,164,000 |
| Change | (267,400) | 685,800 | (1,271,600) | 1,164,000 |

| Summary | Even Mix | Optimal Mix | Difference | % Difference |
|---|---|---|---|---|
| Units Produced and Sold | 12,000 | 12,000 | 0 | 0.00% |
| Total Revenue | $ 25,200,000 | $ 25,510,800 | 310,800 | 1.23% |
| Total Material Cost | 15,198,000 | 15,387,802 | 189,802 | 1.25% |
| Total Manufacturing Cost | 5,172,000 | 5,245,268 | 73,268 | 1.42% |
| Total Fixed Expenses | 3,470,000 | 3,470,000 | 0 | 0.00% |
| Net Income | $ 1,360,000 | $ 1,407,730 | 47,730 | 3.51% |

| Maximum Net Income | |
|---|---|
| | 3.51% |
| | 4 |

Parts Required f
Part
Carbon Frame
UltraLite Carbon
Ultraforce Shifte
Ultraforce II Shif
High Response S
Front Derailleur
Front Derailleur
Rear Derailleur X
Rear Derailleur X
Standard Crank A
Extended Crank A
LightTouch Peda
SpeedRacer Peda
FirmControl Brak
Sensor Brakes
Standard Wheels
Chain Ring Kit
Casset Kit
Drivetrain Kit

Parts Available
Part
Carbon Frame

Documentation | Income | Scenario Summary | Scenario PivotTab ...

# Optimal Solutions with Solver

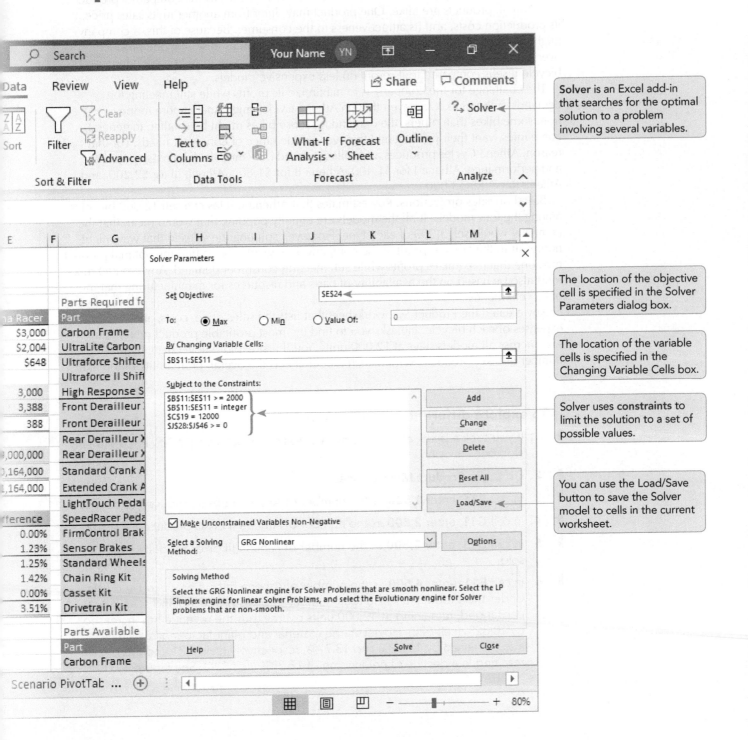

**Solver** is an Excel add-in that searches for the optimal solution to a problem involving several variables.

The location of the objective cell is specified in the Solver Parameters dialog box.

The location of the variable cells is specified in the Changing Variable Cells box.

Solver uses **constraints** to limit the solution to a set of possible values.

You can use the Load/Save button to save the Solver model to cells in the current worksheet.

# Optimizing a Product Mix

The combination of products offered by a company is known as the company's product mix. Not all products are alike. One product may differ from another in its sales price, its production costs, and its attractiveness to the consumer. Because of this, a company might find that it is profitable to devote more of its resources to selling one product over another. For example, Athena Cycles might make a larger profit on each high-end bicycle it sells compared to its profit on less expensive models.

The challenge for the company is to maximize its profits while still meeting the demands of the market. So even though Athena Cycles might make more money from some bikes than others, the demand for those bikes might be smaller. In general, companies want their product mix to cover a wide range of consumer needs. For that reason, Athena Cycles produces and sells four road bike models of increasing quality and performance: Athena I for $1,400, Athena II for $1,800, Athena III for $2,200, and Athena Racer for $3,000.

Based on sales projections, Roy estimates that Athena Cycles can sell 12,000 bicycles among the four models. If all the models are equally popular, that would mean that the company would sell 3,000 of each type. However, splitting the sales in that way might not result in the greatest profit to the company. Roy wants you to find the optimal product mix, one that maximizes profits while still meeting consumer demand. Any product mix must also be based on the availability of parts and resources for manufacturing that mix of bicycle models.

Roy created the Product Mix worksheet that lists the sales price, costs, and variable expenses of each bicycle. He asks you to find the most profitable product mix if total sales across all models stays at 12,000 units. You'll first explore how changing the number of bikes produced within each model affects the overall profitability of the line.

## To explore different product mixes:

1. If you took a break after the previous session, make sure the NP_EX_8_Athena workbook is open.

2. Go to the **Product Mix** worksheet.

3. In cell **B11**, enter **1,500** as the number of Athena I bikes produced and sold.

4. In cell **C11**, enter **2,500** as the number of Athena II bikes produced and sold.

5. In cell **D11**, enter **3,500** as the number of Athena III bikes produced and sold.

6. In cell **E11**, enter **4,500** as the number of Athena Racers produced and sold. Under this product mix, the total number of bikes produced and sold is unchanged, remaining at 12,000 units overall, but the revenue has increased by 10.32% (cell E20). However, the material and manufacturing costs have also increased by 13.97% and 13.77%, respectively (cells E21 and E22), resulting in a decline of net income of 17.28% (cell E24). See Figure 8–31.

| Figure 8–31 | Product mix assuming increasing sales for higher-end models |
| --- | --- |

bicycle models

| | A | B | C | D | E |
| --- | --- | --- | --- | --- | --- |
| 5 | Product Mix Analysis | Athena I | Athena II | Athena III | Athena Racer |
| 6 | Sales Price per Unit | $1,400 | $1,800 | $2,200 | $3,000 |
| 7 | Material Cost per Unit | $740 | $934 | $1,388 | $2,004 |
| 8 | Manufacturing Cost per Unit | $210 | $378 | $488 | $648 |
| 9 | | | | | |
| 10 | Even Product Mix (Units) | 3,000 | 3,000 | 3,000 | 3,000 |
| 11 | Optimal Product (Units) | 1,500 | 2,500 | 3,500 | 4,500 |
| 12 | Change | (1,500) | (500) | 500 | 1,500 |
| 13 | | | | | |
| 14 | Revenue (Even Mix) | $ 4,200,000 | $ 5,400,000 | $ 6,600,000 | $ 9,000,000 |
| 15 | Revenue (Optimal Mix) | 2,100,000 | 4,500,000 | 7,700,000 | 13,500,000 |
| 16 | Change | (2,100,000) | (900,000) | 1,100,000 | 4,500,000 |
| 17 | | | | | |
| 18 | Summary | Even Mix | Optimal Mix | Difference | % Difference |
| 19 | Units Produced and Sold | 12,000 | 12,000 | 0 | 0.00% |
| 20 | Total Revenue | $ 25,200,000 | $ 27,800,000 | 2,600,000 | 10.32% |
| 21 | Total Material Cost | 15,198,000 | 17,321,000 | 2,123,000 | 13.97% |
| 22 | Total Manufacturing Cost | 5,172,000 | 5,884,000 | 712,000 | 13.77% |
| 23 | Total Fixed Expenses | 3,470,000 | 3,470,000 | 0 | 0.00% |
| 24 | Net Income | $ 1,360,000 | $ 1,125,000 | (235,000) | (17.28%) |

sales price and cost for each model

product mix in which an equal number of model types are produced

product mix in which more higher-end models are produced and sold

revenue for each model under the two product mixes

results under the even product mix

results under the optimal product mix

net income decreases by 17.28%

total revenue increases by 10.32%

Next, you'll try a different product mix to see if you can increase the company's net income by producing more of the low-end models.

7. In the range **B11:E11**, enter the following values: **3,500**, **3,500**, **2,500**, and **2,500**. Under this product mix, even though the revenue declines by 3.97% (cell E20), the material and manufacturing costs decline even more (cells E21 and E22). resulting in an increase of net income by 9.78% (cell E24). See Figure 8–32.

**Figure 8-32**    Product mix assuming lower sales for higher-end models

| | A | B | C | D | E |
|---|---|---|---|---|---|
| 5 | Product Mix Analysis | Athena I | Athena II | Athena III | Athena Racer |
| 6 | Sales Price per Unit | $1,400 | $1,800 | $2,200 | $3,000 |
| 7 | Material Cost per Unit | $740 | $934 | $1,388 | $2,004 |
| 8 | Manufacturing Cost per Unit | $210 | $378 | $488 | $648 |
| 9 | | | | | |
| 10 | Even Product Mix (Units) | 3,000 | 3,000 | 3,000 | 3,000 |
| 11 | Optimal Product (Units) | 3,500 | 3,500 | 2,500 | 2,500 |
| 12 | Change | 500 | 500 | (500) | (500) |
| 13 | | | | | |
| 14 | Revenue (Even Mix) | $ 4,200,000 | $ 5,400,000 | $ 6,600,000 | $ 9,000,000 |
| 15 | Revenue (Optimal Mix) | 4,900,000 | 6,300,000 | 5,500,000 | 7,500,000 |
| 16 | Change | 700,000 | 900,000 | (1,100,000) | (1,500,000) |
| 17 | | | | | |
| 18 | Summary | Even Mix | Optimal Mix | Difference | % Difference |
| 19 | Units Produced and Sold | 12,000 | 12,000 | 0 | 0.00% |
| 20 | Total Revenue | $ 25,200,000 | $ 24,200,000 | (1,000,000) | (3.97%) |
| 21 | Total Material Cost | 15,198,000 | 14,339,000 | (859,000) | (5.65%) |
| 22 | Total Manufacturing Cost | 5,172,000 | 4,898,000 | (274,000) | (5.30%) |
| 23 | Total Fixed Expenses | 3,470,000 | 3,470,000 | 0 | 0.00% |
| 24 | Net Income | $ 1,360,000 | $ 1,493,000 | 133,000 | 9.78% |

product mix in which sales are greater for lower-end models

net income increases by 9.78%

total revenue decreases by 3.97%

A trial-and-error approach gives a quick financial picture under different scenarios, but it doesn't really get you any closer to answering the fundamental question, "Which product mix is the best?" Keep in mind that "best" doesn't simply mean the most profitable because the company still must meet consumer demand and be capable of manufacturing what has been ordered. To find the best solution to this problem, you need to use Solver.

# Finding the Optimal Solution with Solver

Solver is an **add-in**, which is a program that adds commands and features to Microsoft Office applications such as Excel. Solver works to find a numeric solution to a problem involving several input values, such as the problem of finding a product mix that maximizes profits. It can also be used for other problems such as scheduling employees subject to their availability or finding a travel route that minimizes time or distance traveled. Before you can use Solver, it must be activated.

# Reference

## Activating Solver

- On the Data tab, confirm whether Solver appears in the Analyze group. If it appears, Solver is already active. If it does not appear, continue with these steps.
- On the ribbon, click the File tab, and then click Options in the navigation bar.
- Click Add-ins in the left pane, click the Manage arrow, and then click Excel Add-ins.
- Click Go to open the Add-Ins dialog box.
- Click the Solver Add-in check box, and then click OK.
- Follow the remaining prompts to install Solver, if it is not already installed.

## Activating Solver

Solver is supplied with every desktop version of Microsoft Excel, but it might not be "turned on" or activated. You need to check whether Solver is already active on your version of Excel. If the Solver button does not appear in the Analyze group on the Data tab, the Solver add-in needs to be activated. If you are working on a network, you might need your instructor or network administrator to activate Solver for you. If you are working on a stand-alone PC, you can activate Solver yourself.

### To activate the Solver add-in:

1. On the ribbon, click the **Data** tab, and then look for the Analyze group and the Solver button. If you see the Solver button, as shown in Figure 8–33, Solver is active and you should read but not perform the rest of the steps in this section. If you don't see the Solver button, continue with Step 2.

| Figure 8–33 | Solver button in the Analyze group on the Data tab |
| --- | --- |

Solver is installed and active

2. On the ribbon, click the **File** tab, and then click **Options** at the bottom of the navigation bar. The Excel Options dialog box opens.

3. In the left pane, click **Add-ins**. Information about all the add-ins currently installed within Excel appears in the right pane.

4. If necessary, click the **Manage arrow** at the bottom of the dialog box, and then click **Excel Add-ins**.

5. Click **Go**. The Add-ins dialog box opens and displays a list of all the available Excel add-ins. Although these add-ins are available, they might not have been activated.

6. Click the **Solver Add-in** check box to insert a checkmark.

   **Trouble?** If you don't see Solver in the list of available add-ins, you may have to reinstall Excel on your computer. See your instructor or technical resource person for help.

7. Click **OK**. Solver is activated, and its button is added on the Data tab in the Analyze group.

**Tip**

You can also open the Excel Options dialog box by right-clicking the ribbon, and then clicking Customize the Ribbon on the shortcut menu.

Now that Solver is activated, you can use it to find the optimal product mix.

## Insight

### Excel Add-Ins

Solver is only one of many available Excel add-ins. Other add-ins provide the ability to perform statistical analyses, generate business reports, and produce interactive maps. You can also create your own add-ins using the Visual Basic for Applications (VBA) macro language. The process for activating other add-ins is the same as the process you used to activate the Solver add-in. Most third-party add-ins provide detailed instructions for their installation and use.

## Setting the Objective Cell and Variable Cells

Every Solver model needs an objective cell and one or more variable cells. An objective cell is a result cell that is maximized, minimized, or set to a specific value. A variable cell is an input cell that changes so that the objective cell can meet its defined goal.

In the Product Mix worksheet, cell E24, which displays the percent change in net income, is the objective cell whose value you want to maximize. The cells in the range B11:E11, which contain the number of bicycles of each model produced and sold by the company, are the variable cells whose values you want Solver to change to achieve an optimal result.

## Reference

### Setting Solver's Objective and Variable Cells

- On the Data tab, in the Analyze group, click the Solver button.
- In the Set Objective box, specify the cell whose value you want to set to match a specific objective.
- Click the Max, Min, or Value Of option button to maximize the objective cell, minimize the objective cell, or set the objective cell to a specified value, respectively.
- In the By Changing Variable Cells input box, specify the changing cells.

You will start Solver now and define the objective cell and the variable cells.

### To set up the Solver model:

1. On the Data tab, in the Analyze group, click the **Solver** button. The Solver Parameters dialog box opens with the insertion point in the Set Objective box.

2. Click cell **E24** in the Product Mix worksheet. The absolute reference to the cell appears in the Set Objective box.

3. Verify that the **Max** option button is selected. This option tells Solver to find the maximum value possible for cell E24.

4. Click the **By Changing Variable Cells** box, and then select the range **B11:E11** in the Product Mix worksheet. The absolute reference to this range tells Solver to modify the product mix values stored in these cells to maximize the value in cell E24. See Figure 8–34.

**Tip**

Changing cells can contain only constant values, not formulas.

**Figure 8–34**    Solver Parameters dialog box

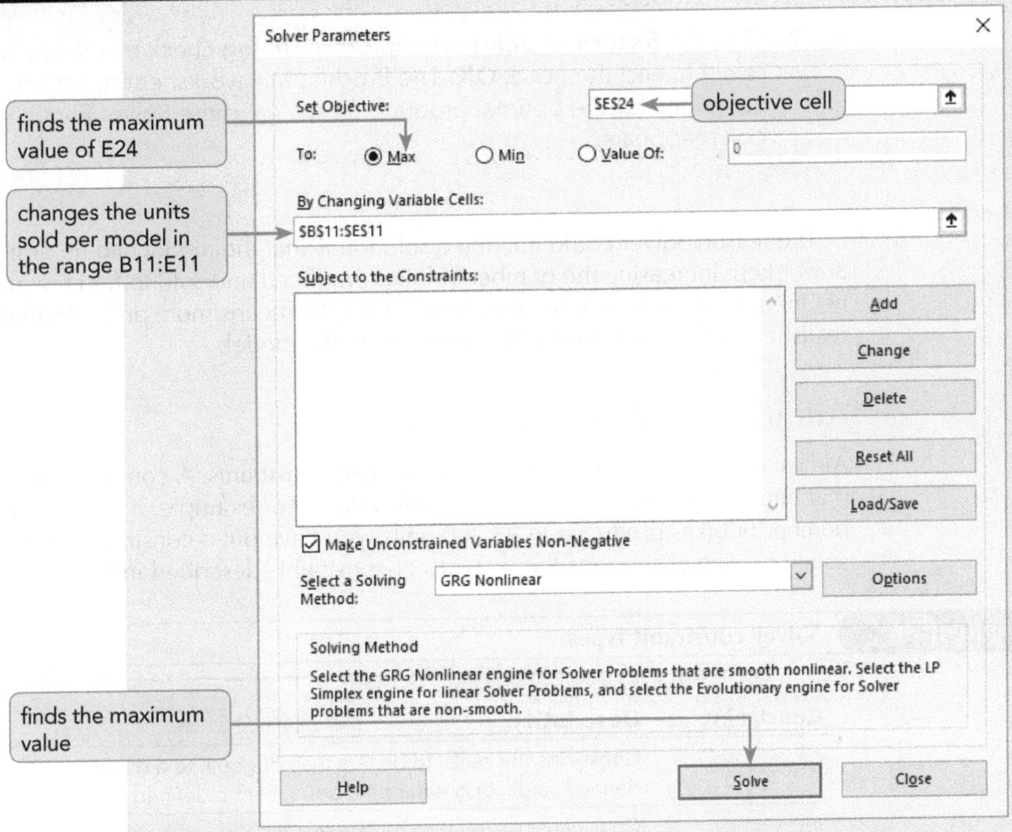

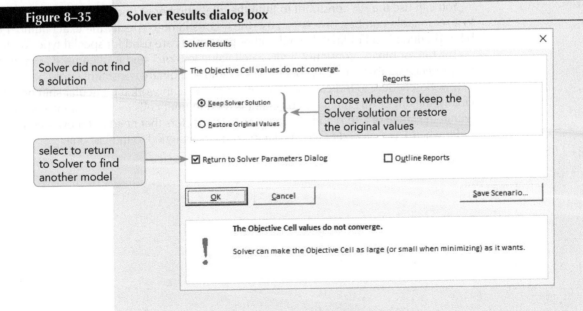

finds the maximum value of E24

changes the units sold per model in the range B11:E11

finds the maximum value

objective cell

5. Click **Solve**. Solver finds the optimal product mix by evaluating different product mix combinations. The Solver Results dialog box opens, reporting that Solver was not able to arrive at a solution. See Figure 8–35.

**Figure 8–35**    Solver Results dialog box

Solver did not find a solution

select to return to Solver to find another model

choose whether to keep the Solver solution or restore the original values

▶ **6.** Click the **Restore Original Values** option button to reset the original product mix numbers.

▶ **7.** Click the **Return to Solver Parameters Dialog** check box if necessary to select it, and then click **OK**. The Product Mix worksheet returns to the original values for the optimal product mix cell, and the Solver Parameters dialog box reappears.

The reason Solver could not find a solution is that the model had no limits. So, Solver kept increasing the number of bikes produced and sold to find the maximum net income, because selling more bikes generally means more profit. To find a more realistic solution, you must add constraints to the model.

## Adding Constraints to Solver

Almost every Solver model needs one or more constraints. A constraint is a condition that limits the solution to a set of possible values. For example, if you limit the total number of bikes produced to 12,000 units, you have put a constraint on the possible solutions. Solver supports the six types of constraints described in Figure 8–36.

**Figure 8–36**    **Solver constraint types**

| Constraint | Description |
| --- | --- |
| <= , = , >= | Constrains the cell(s) to be less than or equal to a defined value, equal to a defined value, or greater than or equal to a defined value |
| int | Constrains the cell(s) to be integers |
| bin | Constrains the cell(s) to binary values (0 or 1) |
| dif | Constrains the cells to be different integers within the range 1 to $n$, where $n$ is the number of cells in the constraint |

You can use the <= constraint to limit the total number of bikes produced and sold to a reasonable number, or you can use the = constraint to specify the exact number of bikes produced and ultimately sold. Other constraints are used for special types of data.

The bin, or binary, constraint limits a cell value to 0 or 1 and is often used to indicate the presence or absence of a property. For example, a binary constraint could be used in a work schedule to indicate whether an employee can work a particular shift or not. Finally, the dif, or All Different, constraint is used to limit cells to different integer values within the range of 1 to $n$ and is often applied for factors that need to follow a defined order when 1 is assigned to the first factor and $n$ is assigned to the last one.

# Reference

## Setting Constraints on the Solver Solution

- In the Solver Parameters dialog box, click Add.
- Enter the cell reference of the cell or cells containing the constraint.
- Select the constraint type (<=, =, >=, int, bin, or dif).
- Enter the constraint value in the Constraint box.
- Click OK to add the constraint and return to the Solver Parameters dialog box.
- Repeat for each constraint you want to add to the model.

Roy wants to set the total number of bikes produced and sold to exactly 12,000 units because that is the limit of the company's production capacity and what the market will bear. You will add an = constraint to Solver.

### To add the units sold constraint to Solver:

1. In the Solver Parameters dialog box, click **Add**. The Add Constraint dialog box opens with the insertion point in the Cell Reference box.

**Tip**

Constraints can be applied only to adjacent ranges. For a nonadjacent range, apply separate constraints to each part of the range.

2. Click cell **C19** in the Product Mix worksheet to enter the absolute cell reference to the Optimal Units Produced and Sold value.

3. Click the **arrow** next to the constraint type box (the center box), and then click = in the list to specify an equal to constraint.

4. In the Constraint box, type **12000**. This constraint limits cell C19 to be equal to 12,000. See Figure 8–37.

| Figure 8–37 | Add Constraint dialog box |

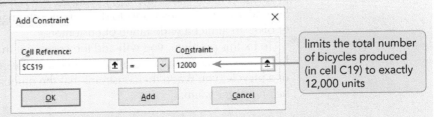

limits the total number of bicycles produced (in cell C19) to exactly 12,000 units

5. Click **OK**. The Solver Parameters dialog box reappears with the constraint $C$19 = 12000 added to the Subject to the Constraints box.

6. Click **Solve**. The Solver Results dialog box opens, indicating that the solution that Solver found satisfies the objective and constraints. Solver's solution, shown in the Product Mix worksheet, is that the company should produce only Athena II bicycles. See Figure 8–38.

**Figure 8–38**    Solver results with one constraint

under this solution, all of the production is used to create the Athena II model

total number of bikes produced is fixed at 12,000 units

| | A | B | C | D | E |
|---|---|---|---|---|---|
| 5 | Product Mix Analysis | Athena I | Athena II | Athena III | Athena Racer |
| 6 | Sales Price per Unit | $1,400 | $1,800 | $2,200 | $3,000 |
| 7 | Material Cost per Unit | $740 | $934 | $1,388 | $2,004 |
| 8 | Manufacturing Cost per Unit | $210 | $378 | $488 | $648 |
| 9 | | | | | |
| 10 | Even Product Mix (Units) | 3,000 | 3,000 | 3,000 | 3,000 |
| 11 | Optimal Product (Units) | - | 12,000 | - | - |
| 12 | Change | (3,000) | 9,000 | (3,000) | (3,000) |
| 13 | | | | | |
| 14 | Revenue (Even Mix) | $ 4,200,000 | $ 5,400,000 | $ 6,600,000 | $ 9,000,000 |
| 15 | Revenue (Optimal Mix) | - | 21,600,000 | - | - |
| 16 | Change | (4,200,000) | 16,200,000 | (6,600,000) | (9,000,000) |
| 17 | | | | | |
| 18 | Summary | Even Mix | Optimal Mix | Difference | % Difference |
| 19 | Units Produced and Sold | 12,000 | 12,000 | 0 | 0.00% |
| 20 | Total Revenue | $ 25,200,000 | $ 21,600,000 | (3,600,000) | (14.29%) |
| 21 | Total Material Cost | 15,198,000 | 11,208,000 | (3,990,000) | (26.25%) |
| 22 | Total Manufacturing Cost | 5,172,000 | 4,536,000 | (636,000) | (12.30%) |
| 23 | Total Fixed Expenses | 3,470,000 | 3,470,000 | 0 | 0.00% |
| 24 | Net Income | $ 1,360,000 | $ 2,386,000 | 1,026,000 | 75.44% |

Roy has several problems with this solution. First, the company cannot limit its production to only the Athena II because there is not enough demand for that model. Second, Athena Cycles wants to diversify its offerings by producing and selling a variety of bikes to attract a wide range of customers.

To fix this problem, you will add the constraint that the company must produce at least 2,000 units of each model. Also, because the company cannot produce a fraction of a bicycle, you'll add the constraint that the number of bikes produced and sold must be an integer value.

### To add more constraints to the model:

1. Click the **Restore Original Values** option button, verify that the **Return to Solver Parameters Dialog** check box is selected, and then click **OK** to return to the Solver Parameters dialog box.

2. Click **Add**. The Add Constraint dialog box opens with the insertion point in the Cell Reference box.

3. Select the range **B11:E11** in the Product Mix worksheet, select **>=** as the constraint type, and then enter **2000** in the Constraint box. This specifies that each value in the range B11:E11 must be greater than or equal to 2,000.

4. Click **Add** to add the constraint to the Solver model. The Add Constraint dialog box remains open, so you can create another constraint.

5. Select the range **B11:E11** in the Product Mix worksheet, and then select **int** as the constraint type. The word "integer" is added to the Constraint box, specifying that each value in the range B11:E11 must be an integer.

6.  Click **OK** to add the constraint to the model and return to the Solver Parameters dialog box. The Subject to the Constraints box now lists three constraints.

7.  Click **Solve**. Solver reports that it has found a solution that satisfies all of the constraints.

8.  Click the **Return to Solver Parameters Dialog** check box to remove the checkmark.

9.  Click **OK**. The Solver Results dialog box closes, and the Solver solution remains in the worksheet. See Figure 8–39.

| Figure 8–39 | Solver results with three constraints |
| --- | --- |

the company must produce at least 2,000 units of each model

| | A | B | C | D | E |
| --- | --- | --- | --- | --- | --- |
| 5 | Product Mix Analysis | Athena I | Athena II | Athena III | Athena Racer |
| 6 | Sales Price per Unit | $1,400 | $1,800 | $2,200 | $3,000 |
| 7 | Material Cost per Unit | $740 | $934 | $1,388 | $2,004 |
| 8 | Manufacturing Cost per Unit | $210 | $378 | $488 | $648 |
| 9 | | | | | |
| 10 | Even Product Mix (Units) | 3,000 | 3,000 | 3,000 | 3,000 |
| 11 | Optimal Product (Units) | 2,000 | 6,000 | 2,000 | 2,000 |
| 12 | Change | (1,000) | 3,000 | (1,000) | (1,000) |
| 13 | | | | | |
| 14 | Revenue (Even Mix) | $  4,200,000 | $  5,400,000 | $  6,600,000 | $  9,000,000 |
| 15 | Revenue (Optimal Mix) | 2,800,000 | 10,800,000 | 4,400,000 | 6,000,000 |
| 16 | Change | (1,400,000) | 5,400,000 | (2,200,000) | (3,000,000) |
| 17 | | | | | |
| 18 | Summary | Even Mix | Optimal Mix | Difference | % Difference |
| 19 | Units Produced and Sold | 12,000 | 12,000 | 0 | 0.00% |
| 20 | Total Revenue | $ 25,200,000 | $ 24,000,000 | (1,200,000) | (4.76%) |
| 21 | Total Material Cost | 15,198,000 | 13,868,000 | (1,330,000) | (8.75%) |
| 22 | Total Manufacturing Cost | 5,172,000 | 4,960,000 | (212,000) | (4.10%) |
| 23 | Total Fixed Expenses | 3,470,000 | 3,470,000 | 0 | 0.00% |
| 24 | Net Income | $  1,360,000 | $  1,702,000 | 342,000 | 25.15% |

net income increases by 25.15% under this solution

Solver's solution is a product mix in which 6,000 Athena IIs are produced and sold with 2,000 each of the other three models. Under this product mix, the company will show a net income of $1,702,000, which is a 25.15% increase over a product mix that has equal numbers of the four models.

Although this product mix is the most profitable to the company, production is limited by the number of available parts. In the range G27:J46, Roy included a table that tracks the parts each model requires, the quantity of each part currently available, and the number of parts remaining after the proposed production run. Figure 8–40 shows the parts usage under the optimal product mix you just found using Solver.

**Figure 8–40**    **Parts remaining after the proposed product mix**

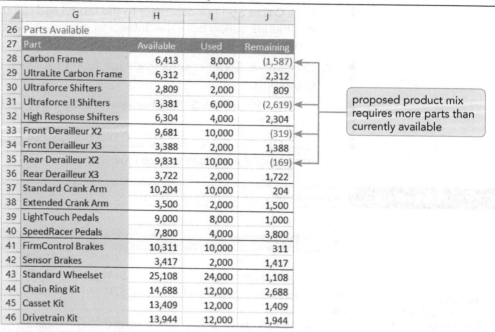

| | Available | Used | Remaining |
|---|---|---|---|
| 26 Parts Available | | | |
| 27 Part | Available | Used | Remaining |
| 28 Carbon Frame | 6,413 | 8,000 | (1,587) |
| 29 UltraLite Carbon Frame | 6,312 | 4,000 | 2,312 |
| 30 Ultraforce Shifters | 2,809 | 2,000 | 809 |
| 31 Ultraforce II Shifters | 3,381 | 6,000 | (2,619) |
| 32 High Response Shifters | 6,304 | 4,000 | 2,304 |
| 33 Front Derailleur X2 | 9,681 | 10,000 | (319) |
| 34 Front Derailleur X3 | 3,388 | 2,000 | 1,388 |
| 35 Rear Derailleur X2 | 9,831 | 10,000 | (169) |
| 36 Rear Derailleur X3 | 3,722 | 2,000 | 1,722 |
| 37 Standard Crank Arm | 10,204 | 10,000 | 204 |
| 38 Extended Crank Arm | 3,500 | 2,000 | 1,500 |
| 39 LightTouch Pedals | 9,000 | 8,000 | 1,000 |
| 40 SpeedRacer Pedals | 7,800 | 4,000 | 3,800 |
| 41 FirmControl Brakes | 10,311 | 10,000 | 311 |
| 42 Sensor Brakes | 3,417 | 2,000 | 1,417 |
| 43 Standard Wheelset | 25,108 | 24,000 | 1,108 |
| 44 Chain Ring Kit | 14,688 | 12,000 | 2,688 |
| 45 Casset Kit | 13,409 | 12,000 | 1,409 |
| 46 Drivetrain Kit | 13,944 | 12,000 | 1,944 |

proposed product mix requires more parts than currently available

Athena Cycles simply does not have the parts in stock to manufacture the bicycles in the proposed product mix. It lacks enough carbon frames, Ultraforce II Shifters, Front Derailleur X2s, and Rear Derailleur X2s. Roy asks you to add one more constraint that would limit the product mix only to those models for which Athena Cycles is equipped to produce in the specified quantities.

### To add a constraint limiting the product mix to the available parts:

1. On the Data tab, in the Analyze group, click the **Solver** button. The Solver Parameters dialog box opens showing the current Solver model.

2. Click **Add** to open the Add Constraint dialog box.

3. Select the range **J28:J46**, which contains the number of parts remaining after the production run, select **>=** as the constraint type, and then type **0** in the Constraint box to force all the values in the range J28:J46 to be greater than or equal to 0.

4. Click **OK**. The complete Solver model appears in the Solver Parameters dialog box. See Figure 8–41.

**Figure 8–41**    Final Solver model

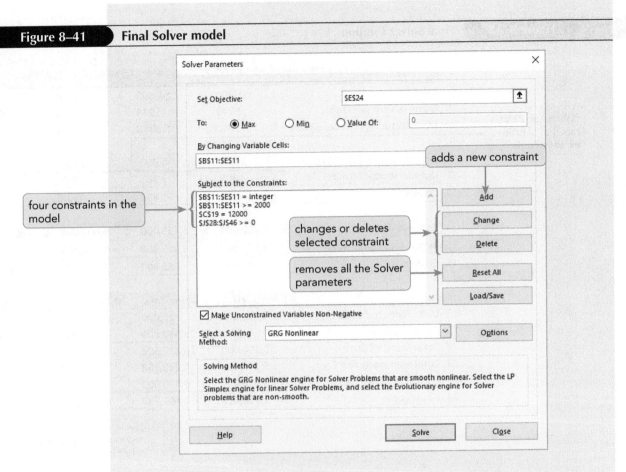

5. Click **Solve**, and then click **OK** in the Solver Results dialog box to accept the Solver solution and return to the worksheet.

6. Scroll to the top of the Product Mix worksheet to see the Solver results. See Figure 8–42.

Figure 8–42    Final Solver solution

optimal product mix that satisfies all constraints

| | A | B | C | D | E |
|---|---|---|---|---|---|
| 5 | Product Mix Analysis | Athena I | Athena II | Athena III | Athena Racer |
| 6 | Sales Price per Unit | $1,400 | $1,800 | $2,200 | $3,000 |
| 7 | Material Cost per Unit | $740 | $934 | $1,388 | $2,004 |
| 8 | Manufacturing Cost per Unit | $210 | $378 | $488 | $648 |
| 9 | | | | | |
| 10 | Even Product Mix (Units) | 3,000 | 3,000 | 3,000 | 3,000 |
| 11 | Optimal Product (Units) | 2,809 | 3,381 | 2,422 | 3,388 |
| 12 | Change | (191) | 381 | (578) | 388 |
| 13 | | | | | |
| 14 | Revenue (Even Mix) | $ 4,200,000 | $ 5,400,000 | $ 6,600,000 | $ 9,000,000 |
| 15 | Revenue (Optimal Mix) | 3,932,600 | 6,085,800 | 5,328,400 | 10,164,000 |
| 16 | Change | (267,400) | 685,800 | (1,271,600) | 1,164,000 |
| 17 | | | | | |
| 18 | Summary | Even Mix | Optimal Mix | Difference | % Difference |
| 19 | Units Produced and Sold | 12,000 | 12,000 | 0 | 0.00% |
| 20 | Total Revenue | $ 25,200,000 | $ 25,510,800 | 310,800 | 1.23% |
| 21 | Total Material Cost | 15,198,000 | 15,387,802 | 189,802 | 1.25% |
| 22 | Total Manufacturing Cost | 5,172,000 | 5,245,268 | 73,268 | 1.42% |
| 23 | Total Fixed Expenses | 3,470,000 | 3,470,000 | 0 | 0.00% |
| 24 | Net Income | $ 1,360,000 | $ 1,407,730 | 47,730 | 3.51% |

under the optimal product mix, net income increases by 3.51%

**7.** Scroll through the worksheet to verify that all four constraints are met, including the constraint that manufacturing the bicycles in the proposed product mix will not exceed the number of available parts.

Based on the Solver results, Athena Cycles can increase its profits by 3.51% and satisfy all of the constraints related to customer demand and available parts, by producing and selling 2,809 Athena Is, 3,381 Athena IIs, 2,422 Athena IIIs, and 3,388 Athena Racers. This is the best outcome in terms of maximizing profits that Roy can report to the company.

# Exploring the Iterative Process

Solver arrives at optimal solutions through an **iterative process**, in which Solver starts with an initial solution and uses that as a basis to calculate a new solution. If that solution improves the value of the objective cell, it will be used to generate the next solution; if it doesn't, Solver tries a different set of values as the starting point for the next step. Each step, or iteration, in this process improves the solution until Solver reaches the point where the new solutions are not significantly better than the solution from the previous step. At that point, Solver will stop and indicate that it has found an answer.

One way to think about this process is to imagine a terrain in which you want to find the highest point. The iterative process accomplishes this by following the terrain upward until the highest peak is scaled. The challenge with this approach is that you might simply find a nearby peak that is not the overall high point in the area. Solver refers to the overall high point as the **global optimum** and a nearby high point, which is not necessarily the highest overall point, as the **local optimum**.

To find the global optimum, you may want to rerun Solver using different initial values and then compare the solutions to determine which result represents the overall best solution. Solver also supports the following iterative methods:

**Tip**

For simple expressions, the Simplex LP method will always find the global optimum solution; that may not be the case with more complex expressions.

- The **Simplex LP method** is used for simple linear expressions involving only the operations of addition, subtraction, multiplication, and division.
- The **GRG Nonlinear method** is used for complicated expressions involving nonlinear functions such as some exponential and trigonometric functions.
- The **Evolutionary method** is used for complicated expressions that involve discontinuous functions that jump from one value to another.

If Solver fails to find a solution or you are not sure if its solution is the global optimum, you can try each method and compare the results to determine which solution is the best.

## Creating a Solver Answer Report

**Tip**

You cannot display sensitivity and limits reports when the Solver model contains integer constraints.

You can evaluate the solution the Solver produced through three different reports—an answer report, a sensitivity report, and a limits report. The **answer report** is probably the most useful because it summarizes the results of a successful solution by displaying information about the objective cell, changing cells, and constraints as well as the initial and final values in the worksheet. The **sensitivity report** and **limits report** are often used in science and engineering to investigate the mathematical aspects of the Solver result, allowing you to quantify the reliability of the solution.

As part of documenting the Solver solution, Roy wants you to create an answer report providing information on the process used to determine the optimal product mix. To ensure that the answer report includes information on the entire process, you'll change the current values in the range B11:E11 to assume a product mix with 3,000 of each model produced and sold.

### To create an answer report for the optimal product mix:

1. In the range **B11:E11**, enter **3,000** for each bike to set the product mix to an even distribution of production and sales among the four models.

2. On the Data tab, in the Analyze group, click the **Solver** button to open the Solver Parameters dialog box, and then click **Solve** to run Solver using the conditions you specified earlier.

3. In the Solver Results dialog box, click **Answer** in the Reports box, and then verify that the **Keep Solver Solution** option button is selected.

4. Click the **Outline Reports** check box so that Solver returns its report using the outline tools. See Figure 8–43.

| Figure 8-43 | Solver Results dialog box with the answer report selected |

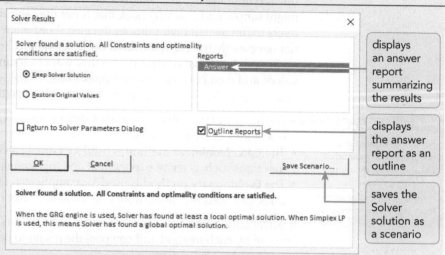

**5.** Click **OK** to accept the solution and generate the answer report in a separate sheet named Answer Report 1.

**6.** Move the **Answer Report 1** worksheet directly after the Product Mix worksheet, and then rename the worksheet as **Product Mix Report**. The answer report is long. With the outline tools turned on, some of the report is hidden.

**7.** Click the last three **expand outline** buttons [+] to view more detailed information about the variable cells and the constraints used in the solution. See Figure 8-44.

**Tip**

Answer reports are named Answer Report 1, Answer Report 2, and so on; the newest report has the next highest number.

| Figure 8-44 | Solver answer report |

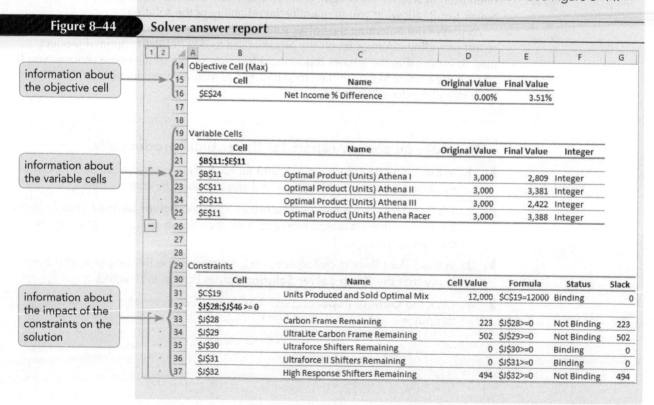

The answer report is divided into the following sections:

- The Title section (not shown in Figure 8-44) identifies the worksheet containing the Solver model, the date on which the report was created, and whether Solver found a solution.

- The Solver Engine section (not shown) provides technical information about how long Solver took to find a solution.
- The Solver Options section (not shown) lists the technical options used by Solver in arriving at a solution.
- The Objective Cell section provides the original and final value of the objective cell.
- The Variable Cells section lists the original and final values of the variable cells used in the solution.
- The Constraints section lists the constraints imposed on the solution by Solver.

The status of each constraint is listed as either Binding or Not Binding. A **binding constraint** is a constraint that must be included in the Solver model because it is a limiting factor in arriving at the solution. A **nonbinding constraint** is a constraint that did not need to be included as part of the Solver model. For example, the constraint that the number of units produced and sold be equal to 12,000 is a binding constraint that limited the solutions available to Solver. On the other hand, the constraint that the company produce and sell at least 2,000 of each type of bike turned out to be nonbinding. Once the company was limited to producing exactly 12,000 bicycles and was limited by the available parts on hand, the optimal product mix would have resulted in the company producing at least 2,000 units of each model anyway.

The last column in the Constraints section shows the slack for each constraint. The **slack** is the difference between the value in the cell and the value at the limit of the constraint, showing how close the constraint came to be a binding constraint. A binding constraint always shows a slack of 0, while nonbinding constraints show a nonzero value. For example, the slack for cell J28, the number of carbon frames remaining in stock, is 223, indicating that when Solver found the optimal product mix, there were still carbon frames left, ready to be used if needed. As a result, the availability of carbon frames was not a limiting factor in the solution.

## Proskills

### Decision Making: Choosing a What-If Analysis Tool

Part of performing an effective what-if analysis is deciding which what-if analysis tool to use. Each tool has its own set of advantages and disadvantages. Data tables are best used when you want to perform several what-if analyses involving one or two input cells and you need to display the analysis in a tabular format. Data tables can also be easily displayed as charts, providing a visual picture of the relationship between the input values and the result values. For what-if analyses involving more than two input cells, you must create a scenario. Scenario summary tables and scenario PivotTables can be used to obtain a quick snapshot of several possible outcomes, and scenarios can be merged and shared among several workbooks. Data tables and scenarios can provide a lot of information, but they cannot easily deliver a single solution or "best outcome." If you need to maximize or minimize a value, you must use Solver. You can also use Solver to set a calculated cell to a specific value. However, if you don't need to specify any constraints on your solution, it is generally quicker and easier to use Goal Seek.

## Saving and Loading Solver Models

You might want to apply different Solver models to the same data. For example, in addition to knowing what product mix maximizes the company's net income, Roy wants to know what product mix minimizes the company's total cost spent on materials. To determine this, you would create another Solver model, but creating a new model in the worksheet overwrites the previous model. You can save the Solver parameters within the worksheet to be retrieved later if needed.

# Reference

## Saving and Loading a Solver Model

- Open the Solver Parameters dialog box.
- Click Load/Save.
- Select an empty range containing the number of cells specified in the dialog box, and then click Save.
- Select the range containing the saved model, and then click Load.

Before running the second Solver problem for Roy, you'll store the parameters of the current model that maximizes the company's net income.

### To save the current Solver model:

1. Go to the **Product Mix** worksheet.

2. On the Data tab, in the Analyze group, click the **Solver** button. The Solver Parameters dialog box opens.

3. Click **Load/Save**. The Load/Save Model dialog box opens, specifying that you need to select an empty range with eight cells to store the model.

4. Select the range **A27:A34** in the Product Mix worksheet. You'll store the Solver parameters in this range.

5. Click **Save**. The information about the Solver model is entered in the range A27:A34, and the Solver Parameters dialog box reappears.

6. Click **Close** to close the Solver Parameters dialog box.

7. In cell **A26**, enter **Maximum Net Income** and then format that cell with the **40% - Accent 4** cell style. See Figure 8–45.

> Be sure the range of cells you select to save the Solver parameters is empty so you don't overwrite other information on the worksheet.

**Figure 8–45**   **Saved Solver model**

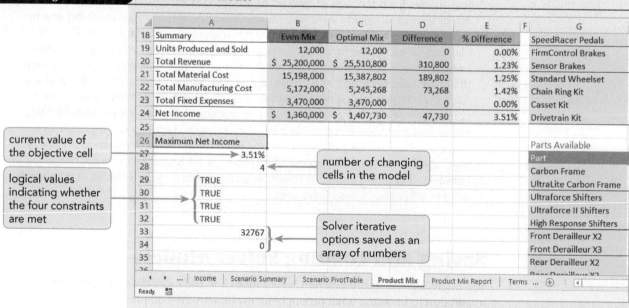

| | A | B | C | D | E | F | G |
|---|---|---|---|---|---|---|---|
| 18 | Summary | Even Mix | Optimal Mix | Difference | % Difference | | SpeedRacer Pedals |
| 19 | Units Produced and Sold | 12,000 | 12,000 | 0 | 0.00% | | FirmControl Brakes |
| 20 | Total Revenue | $ 25,200,000 | $ 25,510,800 | 310,800 | 1.23% | | Sensor Brakes |
| 21 | Total Material Cost | 15,198,000 | 15,387,802 | 189,802 | 1.25% | | Standard Wheelset |
| 22 | Total Manufacturing Cost | 5,172,000 | 5,245,268 | 73,268 | 1.42% | | Chain Ring Kit |
| 23 | Total Fixed Expenses | 3,470,000 | 3,470,000 | 0 | 0.00% | | Casset Kit |
| 24 | Net Income | $ 1,360,000 | $ 1,407,730 | 47,730 | 3.51% | | Drivetrain Kit |
| 25 | | | | | | | |
| 26 | Maximum Net Income | | | | | | Parts Available |
| 27 | | 3.51% | | | | | Part |
| 28 | | 4 | | | | | Carbon Frame |
| 29 | | TRUE | | | | | UltraLite Carbon Frame |
| 30 | | TRUE | | | | | Ultraforce Shifters |
| 31 | | TRUE | | | | | Ultraforce II Shifters |
| 32 | | TRUE | | | | | High Response Shifters |
| 33 | | 32767 | | | | | Front Derailleur X2 |
| 34 | | 0 | | | | | Front Derailleur X3 |
| 35 | | | | | | | Rear Derailleur X2 |
| 26 | | | | | | | Rear Derailleur X3 |

current value of the objective cell

number of changing cells in the model

logical values indicating whether the four constraints are met

Solver iterative options saved as an array of numbers

│ ‹ › … │ Income │ Scenario Summary │ Scenario PivotTable │ **Product Mix** │ Product Mix Report │ Terms … ⊕ ┊ ◂

Ready

The first parameter in cell A27 displays 3.51%, which is the value of the objective cell under this model. The second parameter in cell A28 displays 4, indicating the number of variable cells in the model. The next four cells display TRUE, indicating that the four constraints in the model are all satisfied in the Solver solution. If you later change some of the worksheet data so that it violates a constraint, the Solver parameter cells will display FALSE. These cells provide a quick visual check that all the model's conditions are still being met as the worksheet is modified. The final two cells, cells A27 and A28, are used to store the technical options for the iterative process by which Solver arrives at a solution (refer to the section titled, "Exploring the Iterative Process").

Now that you have saved this Solver model, you can create a second model to determine the product mix that minimizes the material cost of producing and selling these bicycles. Roy wants to know what product mix would result in the lowest material cost given that the company still wants to produce 12,000 bicycles and still wants to make at least 2,000 of each model. The objective cell for this model is cell C21 instead of cell E24.

### To determine the product mix that minimizes the total material cost:

1. In the range **B11:E11**, change the value of each cell to **3,000**.

2. Open the Solver Parameters dialog box.

3. With the Set Objective box selected, click cell **C21** in the Product Mix worksheet. This cell contains the total material cost under the Optimal product mix.

4. Click the **Min** option button. You want Solver to find the minimum value for cell C21. The changing cells and constraints you used to find the maximum net income remain unchanged for this model.

5. Click **Solve**. Solver finds the product mix that minimizes the total material cost.

6. Click **OK** to close the Solver Results dialog box and view the solution. See Figure 8–46.

**Figure 8–46**     Solution to minimizing total material costs

| | A | B | C | D | E |
|---|---|---|---|---|---|
| 5 | Product Mix Analysis | Athena I | Athena II | Athena III | Athena Racer |
| 6 | Sales Price per Unit | $1,400 | $1,800 | $2,200 | $3,000 |
| 7 | Material Cost per Unit | $740 | $934 | $1,388 | $2,004 |
| 8 | Manufacturing Cost per Unit | $210 | $378 | $488 | $648 |
| 9 | | | | | |
| 10 | Even Product Mix (Units) | 3,000 | 3,000 | 3,000 | 3,000 |
| 11 | Optimal Product (Units) | 2,809 | 3,381 | 3,491 | 2,319 |
| 12 | Change | (191) | 381 | 491 | (681) |
| 13 | | | | | |
| 14 | Revenue (Even Mix) | $ 4,200,000 | $ 5,400,000 | $ 6,600,000 | $ 9,000,000 |
| 15 | Revenue (Optimal Mix) | 3,932,600 | 6,085,800 | 7,680,200 | 6,957,000 |
| 16 | Change | (267,400) | 685,800 | 1,080,200 | (2,043,000) |
| 17 | | | | | |
| 18 | Summary | Even Mix | Optimal Mix | Difference | % Difference |
| 19 | Units Produced and Sold | 12,000 | 12,000 | 0 | 0.00% |
| 20 | Total Revenue | $ 25,200,000 | $ 24,655,600 | (544,400) | (2.16%) |
| 21 | Total Material Cost | 15,198,000 | 14,729,298 | (468,702) | (3.08%) |
| 22 | Total Manufacturing Cost | 5,172,000 | 5,074,228 | (97,772) | (1.89%) |
| 23 | Total Fixed Expenses | 3,470,000 | 3,470,000 | 0 | 0.00% |
| 24 | Net Income | $ 1,360,000 | $ 1,382,074 | 22,074 | 1.62% |

product mix that minimizes the total material costs

minimum total material cost based on the constraints

material costs decline 3.08% from the Even product mix model

The minimum material cost to the company is $14,729,298, which is $468,702 less than the material cost under the Even product mix. This is the optimal solution based on the constraints that the company must produce exactly 12,000 bicycles with 2,000 units of each model, and not exceed the available parts. You will save this model in the Product Mix worksheet.

### To save the model to minimize material costs:

▶ **1.** In cell **A36**, enter **Minimum Material Cost** and then format that cell with the **40% - Accent2** cell style.

▶ **2.** Open the Solver Parameters dialog box, and then click **Load/Save**. The Load/Save Model dialog box opens.

▶ **3.** Select the range **A37:A44** in the Product Mix worksheet to specify the eight cells in which to save the model.

▶ **4.** Click **Save**. The current Solver model is saved in the Product Mix worksheet.

▶ **5.** Click **Close** to close the Solver Parameters dialog box.

You have two Solver models saved in the Product Mix worksheet—the Maximum Net Income model and the Minimum Material Cost model. You can quickly reload each of these Solver models in the worksheet from the Solver Parameters dialog box.

Roy wants the final version of the worksheet to use the Solver model that maximizes net income for the company. You'll load and run the Maximum Net Income model.

### To load the Maximum Net Income model and run it:

▶ **1.** In the range **B11:E11**, change the values in each cell to **3,000** as the initial product mix.

▶ **2.** Open the Solver Parameters dialog box, and then click **Load/Save**. The Load/Save Model dialog box opens.

▶ **3.** In the Product Mix worksheet, select the range **A27:A34** containing the parameters of the Maximum Net Income model.

**Tip**

To combine the Solver model with the model currently used in the worksheet, click the Merge button.

▶ **4.** Click **Load** to load the Solver parameters from the worksheet. The Load Model dialog box opens, asking whether you want to replace the current model or merge the new model with the current model.

▶ **5.** Click **Replace**. The Solver Parameters dialog box appears. The parameters for the Maximum Net Income model have replaced the parameters for the Minimum Material Cost model with the objective cell set once again to cell E24 and the Max option button selected in the dialog box.

▶ **6.** Click **Solve**. Solver runs the Maximum Net Income model, and then the Solver Results dialog box opens.

▶ **7.** Click **OK** to keep the Solver solution and return to the Product Mix worksheet.

▶ **8.** **sam** ⬆ Save the workbook, and then close it.

By saving the Solver model parameters to cells on the worksheet, you can create as many models as you need to effectively analyze the data. You can then load and apply these different models to your analysis as new data is entered.

You have finished analyzing how Athena Cycles can maximize its profits from its line of road bicycles by modifying the product mix. Using data tables, Excel scenarios, and Solver models, you provided Roy with several pricing and production options to increase the company's net income or minimize material costs for the upcoming year.

# Review

## Session 8.3 Quick Check

1. What is an add-in?
2. What are three options for the objective cell using Solver?
3. What is an objective cell? What is a variable cell?
4. What are the six types of constraints you can put on a cell in a Solver model?
5. What is an iterative process?
6. What is the difference between a binding constraint and a nonbinding constraint?
7. In the Solver report, what is meant by the term "slack"?

## Practice

### Review Assignments

**Data File needed for the Review Assignments: NP_EX_8-2.xlsx**

Athena Cycles is planning to start a new line of mountain bikes. As you did with the company's line of road bikes, Roy wants you to perform a what-if analysis on the company's income statement for its mountain bike line, creating one-variable and two-variable data tables to determine the break-even point for sales. Roy also wants you to use Scenario Manager to explore the impact on the profitability of the line under different possible scenarios. Finally, you will calculate the product mix, among four different mountain bike models, that will result in the maximum net income to the company. Complete the following:

1. Open the **NP_EX_8-2.xlsx** workbook located in the Excel8 > Review folder included with your Data Files. Save the workbook as **NP_EX_8_Bikes** in the location specified by your instructor.
2. In the Documentation sheet, enter your name and the date.
3. In the Income Statement worksheet, in the range D5:G5, enter formulas that reference Units Sold value in cell B5 and the Revenue, Expenses, and Net Income values from the cells B25, B26, and B27.
4. In the range D6:D13, enter Units Sold values from 250 to 2,000 in 250-unit increments.
5. Create a one-variable data table in the range D5:G13 with cell B5 as the column input cell.
6. Create a Cost-Volume-Profit chart of the revenue and expenses values in the range D4:F13 of the one-variable data table. Resize the chart to cover the range D14:G27. Change the chart title to **CVP Analysis**.
7. Copy the Units Sold values from the range D6:D13 into the range I6:I13. In the range J5:N5, enter Sales Price values from $800 to $1,200 in $100 increments. In cell I5, enter a formula that references the net income value stored in cell B27. Format the value in cell I5 to display the text **Units Sold** rather than the net income value.
8. Create a two-variable data table in the I5:N13 range using cell B6 and the row input cell and cell B5 as the column input cell.
9. Select the range I6:N13 and create a scatter chart with straight lines of the data. Move and resize the chart to cover the range I14:N27. Format the chart as follows:
   a. Change the chart title to **Break-Even Analysis**.
   b. Change the name of each of the five data series from their default names to the Sales Price values in the cells J5 through N5.
   c. Move the chart legend to the right of the chart.
   d. Change the scale of the horizontal axis to go from 0 to 2,000 in 500-unit increments.
10. Use the Scenario Manager to store the three scenarios listed in Figure 8–47.

**Figure 8–47**    Mountain bike what-if scenarios

| Input Cells | Status Quo | Increased Production | Decreased Production |
|---|---|---|---|
| Units Sold | 1,200 | 1,500 | 1,000 |
| Sales Price | $900 | $800 | $950 |
| Salaries and Benefits | $175,000 | $175,000 | $145,000 |
| Shipping and Distribution | $72,000 | $90,000 | $60,000 |
| Stocking and Storage | $65,000 | $75,000 | $55,000 |
| Miscellaneous | $55,000 | $70,000 | $40,000 |

11. Create a scenario summary report of the three scenarios, displaying their impact on total revenue, total expenses, and net income. Move the worksheet directly after the Income Statement worksheet.

12. Create a Scenario PivotTable report of the three scenarios displaying the total revenue, total expenses, and net income under each scenario. Make the following changes to the PivotTable:

    a. Display Total Revenue, Total Expenses, and Net Income in Currency style with no decimals places and negative values displayed in red, enclosed within parentheses.

    b. Remove the filter from the PivotTable.

    c. Enter **Scenario Report** in cell A1 and format that cell with the Title cell style.

13. Add a PivotChart of the PivotTable displaying the data as combination chart positioned over the range A8:D20. Display the Total_Revenue and Total_Expenses fields as clustered columns, display the Net_Income field as a line chart on the secondary axis. Remove the field buttons from the chart and move the legend below the chart.

14. Move the Scenario PivotTable worksheet after the Scenario Summary worksheet.

15. The Product Line worksheet lists four mountain bikes produced and sold by Athena Cycles. Use Solver to find the product mix that maximizes the value in cell E24 by changing the values in the range B11:E11 under the following constraints:

    a. The total mountain bikes produced and sold as indicated in cell C19 must be exactly 5,000.

    b. The company needs to produce 1,000 or more of each model type, so the values in the range B11:E11 must be at least 1,000.

    c. The values in the range B11:E11 must be integers.

    d. The values in the range J28:J46 must be greater than or equal to zero because Athena Cycles cannot produce more mountain bikes than the available parts.

16. Save the Solver model you just created to the range A27:A34.

17. Change the values in the range B11:E11 to 1,000 units of each model, and then rerun Solver to find the product mix that minimizes the total material cost in cell C21 subject to the same constraints you used for the Maximum Net Income model.

18. Save the Solver model to the range A37:A44.

19. Restore the values in the range B11:E11 to 1,000 units of each model. Load the Maximum Net Income model into Solver, and then run Solver. Create an answer report with outline buttons enabled, and then move the Answer Report 1 worksheet after the Product Line worksheet.

20. Save the workbook, and then close it.

# Apply

## Case Problem 1

**Data File needed for this Case Problem: NP_EX_8-3.xlsx**

**Granite Life**   Brenda Castro is an Events Coordinator for the Granite Life insurance company. One event that the company sponsors is a three-day educational seminar on insurance and investing, which will take place in Provo, Utah, this year. Brenda wants to estimate the number of attendees and predict the net income from the event. Complete the following:

1. Open the **NP_EX_8-3.xlsx** workbook located in the Excel8 > Case1 folder included with your Data Files. Save the workbook as **NP_EX_8_Seminar** in the location specified by your instructor.

2. In the Documentation sheet, enter your name and the date.

3. Brenda wants to calculate a budget that assumes **200** people will attend the seminar at a cost of **$500** per person. In the Budget worksheet, enter these values in the range B5:B6. In cell B7, calculate the total revenue from attendance at the seminar by multiplying the number of attendees and the registration fee per attendee.

4. Each attendee will receive training materials costing **$150** and supplementary materials costing **$75**. Enter these values into the range B10:B11. In cell B12, calculate the total variable costs by multiplying the cost of the materials by the number of attendees.

5. In the range B15:B19, enter the fixed costs associated with the seminar. Providing computers and networking support for the entire seminar will cost **$1,400**. The speakers at the seminar will cost **$2,400** for their fees, **$2,000** for their travel, and **$950** for their lodging. Brenda estimates **$5,000** in miscellaneous expenses. In cell B20, calculate sum of these fixed costs.

6. The company must rent conference rooms large enough to accommodate the number of attendees. The lookup table in the range D5:E11 contains the room charges for seminars of in groups of 100 from 0 up to 500 or more. For example, to accommodate 0 to 100 people will cost the company $1,500. In cell B23, calculate the room costs by looking up the room rental fee based on the number of attendees (cell B5). (*Hint*: Use the XLOOKUP function to perform an approximate match lookup using the value in cell B5, the list of attendees in the AttendeeLookup range, the room fees in the RoomFees range, and the match mode set to −1.)

7. The more attendees, the less the hotel will charge per person to cater the seminar meals. In cell B24, calculate the total catering charge by using the XLOOKUP function to do an approximate match lookup with the value in B5, the lookup values in the AttendeeLookup range, the return values in the MealCatering range, and the match mode set to −1. Multiply the returned value by the value in B5.

8. The company also pays for seminar support staff. The larger the seminar, the higher the support staff fee. The lookup table in the range D23:E29 contains the staff fees for groups of different sizes. For example, a seminar of 0 to 100 people will incur a $150 staff fee. In cell B25, calculate the support cost by doing an approximate match lookup with the XLOOKUP function, using cell B5 as the lookup value, AttendeeLookup as the lookup range, SeminarSupport as the return range, and −1 as the match mode value.

9. In cell B26, calculate the total mixed costs by adding the room, meal, and support costs.

10. In cell B28, calculate the cost per attendee by dividing the sum of the variable costs (cell B12), fixed costs (cell B20), and mixed costs (cell B26) by the number of attendees (cell B5).

11. In cell B29, calculate the balance from the conference by subtracting the sum of the variable, fixed, and mixed costs from the total revenue (cell B7).

12. Create a one-variable data table of different seminar budgets. In cell G6, display the value of cell B5. In cell H6, display the value of B7. In cell I6, display the sum of cells B12, B20, and B26. In cell J6, display the value of cell B29. In the range G7:G16, enter the number of possible attendees ranging from 50 to 500 in increments of 50. Complete the data table with cell B5 as the column input cell, showing the total revenue, total costs, and balance under different numbers of attendees.

13. Create a CVP chart of the Total Revenue and Total Costs values using the data from the range G5:I16, the one-variable table, and then format the chart as follows:

    a. Move and resize the chart to cover the range G18:J29.

    b. Change the chart title to **CVP Analysis**.

    c. Change the scale of the horizontal axis to go from 0 to 500 in 100-unit increments.

14. Brenda wants to investigate the impact of different registration fees and number of attendees on the seminar balance. In cell L6, display the value of cell B29 formatted to display the text **Attendees**. In the range L7:L16, enter attendee values ranging from 50 to 500 in increments of 50. In the range M6:P6, enter registration fees of **$200**, **$300**, **$400**, and **$500**.

15. Create a two-variable data table in the range L6:P16, using cell B6 as the row input cell and cell B5 as the column input cell.

16. Create a scatter chart with straight lines of the data in the range L7:P16, and then make the following changes to the chart:

    a. Move and resize the chart to cover the range L18:P29.

    b. Change the chart title to **Balance Analysis**.

    c. Change the name of the four data series to match the registration fee values in cells M6, N6, O6, and P6.

    d. Change the scale of the horizontal axis to go from 0 to 500 in 100-unit increments.

17. Create scenarios for the other possible values for the input cells listed in Figure 8–48.

| Figure 8–48 | Seminar what-if scenarios |

| Changing Cell | Seminar 1 | Seminar 2 | Seminar 3 |
|---|---|---|---|
| Attendees | 200 | 300 | 150 |
| Registration Fee | $500 | $400 | $600 |
| Training Materials | $150 | $175 | $135 |
| Supplemental Materials | $75 | $100 | $55 |
| Computing Costs | $1,400 | $1,200 | $1,600 |
| Speaker Fees | $2,400 | $2,800 | $2,600 |
| Speaker Travel | $2,000 | $2,200 | $1,600 |
| Speaker Lodging | $950 | $1,200 | $1,000 |
| Miscellaneous | $5,000 | $4,500 | $4,800 |

18. Create a scenario summary report of the Seminar 1, Seminar 2, and Seminar 3 scenarios, show-ing the cost per person and balance from each seminar as the result. Move the sheet to the end of the workbook.

19. Show the results of Seminar 3 in the Budget worksheet.

20. Experience has taught Brenda that as the registration fee for the seminar increases, the number of attendees willing to pay decreases. Based on data from other seminars, Brenda has defined a relationship between attendance and registration fee, shown in the range R4:X21 on the Budget worksheet. In cell B5 of the Budget worksheet, change the number of attendees from a constant value to the following formula that projects the number of attendees for a given registration fee based on the value in cell B6. (*Hint*: Look at the formulas in the range S6:S21 to learn how to translate this equation into an Excel formula.)

$$Attendees = 1000 \times e^{-(fee/500)}$$

21. Use Solver to determine the registration fee in cell B6 that will maximize the balance value in cell B29 with the constraint that the registration fee should be an integer. Run Solver with an initial registration fee of $1,000.

22. Save the workbook, and then close it.

# Challenge

## Case Problem 2

Data File needed for this Case Problem: NP_EX_8-4.xlsx

**Hardin Medical Clinic**   Catherine Smythe is a personnel manager for Hardin Medical Clinic in Toledo, Ohio. Part of Catherine's job is to manage the weekly nursing schedule. The clinic employs 20 nurses—16 full-time and 4 part-time. The clinic needs 12 nurses on weekdays and 10 on week-ends. Catherine is working on the schedule for an upcoming week and is trying to accommodate all the vacation and sick-leave requests, while maintaining the required level of on-duty nurses. Catherine asks you to develop a schedule that meets the needs of the clinic and the requests of the nurses. Complete the following:

1. Open the **NP_EX_8-4.xlsx** workbook located in the Excel8 > Case2 folder included with your Data Files. Save the workbook as **NP_EX_8_Clinic** in the location specified by your instructor.

2. In the Documentation sheet, enter your name and the date.

3. In the Schedule worksheet, in the range D5:J24, enter **0** in all the cells. In this sheet, 0s and 1s indicate whether an employee is scheduled for a shift that day (0 indicates an employee is not scheduled, and 1 indicates an employee is scheduled).

4. In the range K5:K24, enter formulas to sum the total number of shifts worked by each employee from Monday through Sunday.

5. In the range L5:L24, calculate the total number of hours worked by each employee during the week by multiplying the number of shifts worked by 8 (each shift is eight hours long).

6. In the range D26:J26, enter the required shifts per day. The clinic requires 12 nurses on the weekdays, and 10 nurses on Saturday and Sunday.

7. In the range D27:J27, enter formulas to sum the total number of shifts scheduled for nurses on each day.

8. In the range D28:J28, enter formulas to calculate the difference between the number of nurses scheduled and the number of nurses required. A negative value indicates that not enough nurses are scheduled to cover that day's shifts.

9. In cell D30, calculate the total shortfall for the week by summing the daily shortfall values in the range D28:J28.

⊕ **Explore** 10. Create a Solver model that sets the value of cell D30 to 0 (indicating that all shifts are covered for every day of the week) by changing the values in the range D5:J24 under the following constraints:

   a. Add a binary constraint to force every value in the range D5:J24 to be either a 0 or a 1.

   b. Add a constraint to limit the total hours worked by each full-time employee to less than or equal to 40.

   c. Add a constraint to limit the total hours worked by each part-time employee to less than or equal to 24.

   d. Add a constraint to require that the difference values in the range D28:J28 all equal 0.

   e. Add more constraints based on the schedule requests in the range C5:C24 so that nurses are not scheduled to work shifts on days they have requested off. If a nurse has requested a day off, the cell corresponding to that day for that nurse must equal 0.

⊕ **Explore** 11. Run the Solver model using the Evolutionary method. (Solver might take a minute to arrive at a solution.) Confirm that the schedule generated by Solver fulfills all the requirements—all shifts are covered each day, no full-time nurse works more than 40 hours, no part-time nurse works more than 24 hours, and no nurse works on a requested day off.

12. Save the workbook, and then close it.

ACCESS

# Creating Advanced Queries and Enhancing Table Design

*Making the Clinic Database Easier to Use*

## Case | *Lakewood Community Health Services*

Lakewood Community Health Services, a nonprofit health clinic located in the greater Atlanta, Georgia area, provides a range of medical services to patients of all ages. The clinic specializes in chronic disease management, cardiac care, and geriatrics. Donna Taylor, the office manager for Lakewood Community Health Services, oversees a small staff and is responsible for maintaining records for the clinic's patients.

In order to best manage the clinic, Donna and her staff rely on electronic medical records for patient information, billing, inventory control, purchasing, and accounts payable. The Lakewood staff developed the Clinic database, which contains tables, queries, forms, and reports that Donna and other staff members use to track patient, visit, and billing information.

Donna is interested in taking better advantage of the power of Access to make the database easier to use and to create more sophisticated queries. For example, Donna wants to obtain lists of patients in certain cities. She also needs a summarized list of invoice amounts by city. In this module, you'll modify and customize the Clinic database to satisfy these and other requirements.

## STARTING DATA FILES

Access2 → Module
Clinic.accdb

Review
Supplier.accdb

Case1
School.accdb

Case2
Storm.accdb

# Session 5.1 Visual Overview:

A Select query selects the records in the fields that satisfy the criteria.

The tbl prefix tag identifies a table object.

The qry prefix tag identifies a query object.

The frm prefix tag identifies a form object.

The rpt prefix tag identifies a report object.

A calculated field contains an expression that calculates the values of the data in the field.

The design grid contains the fields and criteria that will be used in the query.

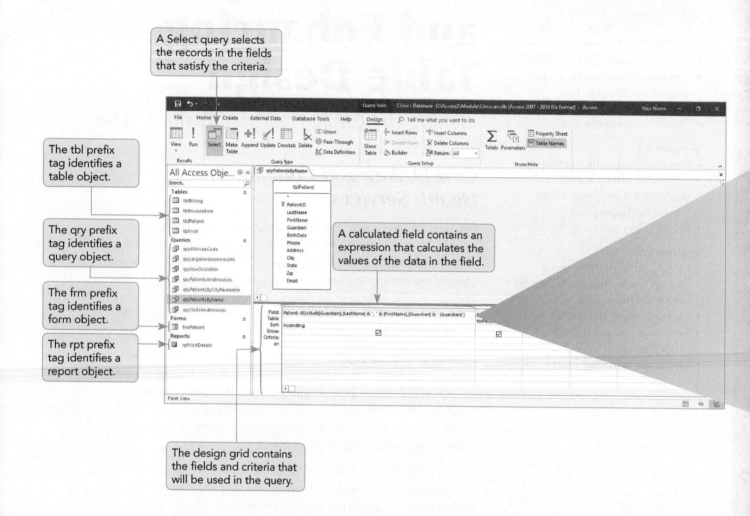

# Calculated Field

The name of the new calculated field is placed to the left of the expression, separated with a colon.

The IIf function tests a condition and returns one of two values. The function returns the first value if the condition is true and the second value if the condition is false.

The Expression Builder can be used to create an expression for a calculated field.

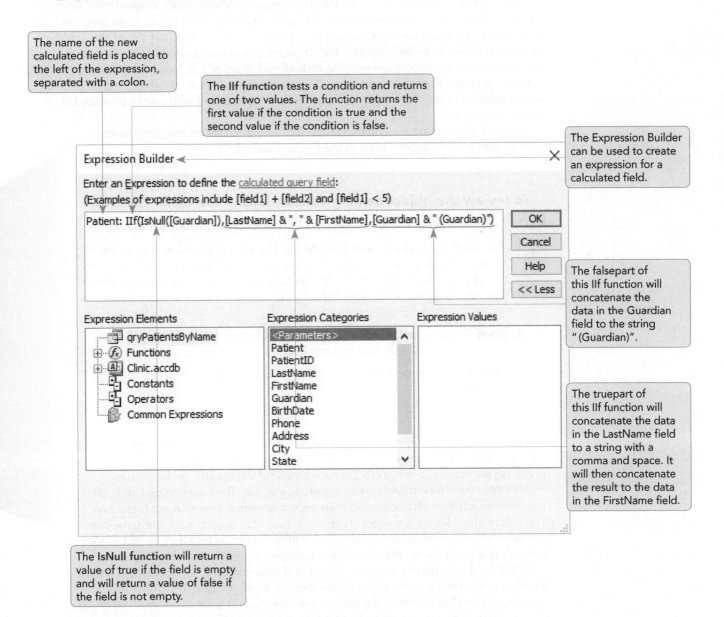

**Expression Builder**                                                      ✕

Enter an Expression to define the calculated query field:
(Examples of expressions include [field1] + [field2] and [field1] < 5)

Patient: IIf(IsNull([Guardian]),[LastName] & ", " & [FirstName],[Guardian] & " (Guardian)")

OK

Cancel

Help

<< Less

**Expression Elements**

- qryPatientsByName
- Functions
- Clinic.accdb
- Constants
- Operators
- Common Expressions

**Expression Categories**

<Parameters>
Patient
PatientID
LastName
FirstName
Guardian
BirthDate
Phone
Address
City
State

**Expression Values**

The falsepart of this IIf function will concatenate the data in the Guardian field to the string " (Guardian)".

The truepart of this IIf function will concatenate the data in the LastName field to a string with a comma and space. It will then concatenate the result to the data in the FirstName field.

The IsNull function will return a value of true if the field is empty and will return a value of false if the field is not empty.

# Reviewing the Clinic Database

Donna and her staff had no previous database experience when they created the Clinic database; they simply used the wizards and other easy-to-use Access tools. As business continued to grow at Lakewood Community Health Services, Donna realized she needed an expert to further enhance the database. She hired Reginald Morales, who has a business information systems degree and nine years of experience developing database systems. Reginald spent a few days reviewing the Clinic database, making sure it adhered to simple naming standards for the objects and field names to make his future work easier.

Before implementing the enhancements for Donna, you'll review the naming conventions for the object names in the Clinic database.

**To review the object naming conventions in the Clinic database:**

▶ **1.** Make sure you have the Access starting Data Files on your computer.

**Trouble?** If you don't have the starting Data Files, you need to get them before you can proceed. Your instructor will either give you the Data Files or ask you to obtain them from a specified location (such as a network drive). If you have any questions about the Data Files, see your instructor or technical support person for assistance.

▶ **2.** **sam**⬇ Start Access, and then open the **Clinic** database from the Access2 > Module folder where your starting Data Files are stored.

**Trouble?** If the security warning is displayed below the ribbon, click the Enable Content button.

As shown in Visual Overview 5.1, the Navigation Pane displays the objects grouped by object type. Each object name has a prefix tag—a tbl prefix tag for tables, a qry prefix tag for queries, a frm prefix tag for forms, and a rpt prefix tag for reports.

All three characters in each prefix tag are lowercase. The word immediately after the three-character prefix begins with an uppercase letter. Using object prefix tags, you can readily identify the object type, even when the objects have the same base name—for instance, tblPatient, frmPatient, and rptPatient. In addition, object names have no spaces, because other database management systems, such as SQL Server and Oracle, do not permit spaces in object and field names. It is important to adhere to industry standard naming conventions, both to make it easier to convert your database to another DBMS in the future, if necessary, and to develop personal habits that enable you to work seamlessly with other major DBMSs. If Lakewood Community Health Services needs to scale up to one of these other systems, using standard naming conventions means that Reginald will have to do less work to make the transition.

*Teamwork: Following Naming Conventions*

Most Access databases have hundreds of fields, objects, and controls. You'll find it easier to identify the type and purpose of these database items when you use a naming convention or standard. Most companies adopt a standard naming convention, such as the one used for the Clinic database, so that multiple people can develop a database, troubleshoot database problems, and enhance and improve existing databases. When working on a database, a team's tasks are difficult, if not impossible, to perform if a standard naming convention isn't used. In addition, most databases and database samples on websites and in training books use standard naming conventions that are similar to the ones used for the Clinic database. By following the standard naming convention established by your company or organization, you'll help to ensure smooth collaboration among all team members.

Now you'll create the queries that Donna needs.

# Using a Pattern Match in a Query

You are already familiar with queries that use an exact match or a range of values (for example, queries that use the > or < comparison operators) to select records. Many other operators are available for creating select queries. These operators let you build more complicated queries that are difficult to create with exact-match or range-of-values selection criteria.

Donna created a list of questions she wants to answer using the Clinic database:

- Which patients have the 404 area code?
- What is the patient information for patients located in Decatur, Smyrna, or Stone Mountain?
- What is the patient information for all patients except those located in Decatur, Smyrna, or Stone Mountain?
- What is the patient and visit information for patients in Decatur or Stone Mountain who either walked in without an appointment or who visited during November?
- What are the first and last names of Lakewood Community Health Services patients, or the guardian name if it is listed? Patients with guardians should not be contacted directly.
- What is the patient information for patients in a particular city? This query needs to be flexible to allow the user to specify the city.

Next, you will create the queries necessary to answer these questions. Donna wants to view the records for all patients whose area code is 404. To answer Donna's question, you can create a query that uses a pattern match. A **pattern match** selects records with a value for the designated field that matches the pattern of a simple condition value—in this case, patients with the 404 area code. You do this using the Like comparison operator.

The **Like comparison operator** selects records by matching field values to a specific pattern that includes one or more of these wildcard characters: asterisk (*), question mark (?), and number symbol (#). The asterisk represents any string of characters, the question mark represents any single character, and the number symbol represents any single digit. Using a pattern match is similar to using an exact match, except that a pattern match includes wildcard characters.

To create the new query, you must first place the tblPatient table field list in the Query window in Design view.

## To create the new query in Design view:

1. If necessary, click the **Shutter Bar Open/Close Button** 《 at the top of the Navigation Pane to close it.

2. On the ribbon, click the **Create** tab.

3. In the Queries group, click the **Query Design** button. The Show Table dialog box opens in front of the Query window in Design view.

4. Click **tblPatient** in the Tables box, click the **Add** button, and then click the **Close** button. The tblPatient table field list is added to the Query window, and the Show Table dialog box closes.

5. Drag the bottom border of the tblPatient field list down until you can see the full list of fields.

6. Double-click the **title bar** of the tblPatient field list to highlight all the fields, and then drag the highlighted fields to the first column's Field box in the design grid. Each field is placed in a separate column in the design grid, in the same order that the fields appear in the table. See Figure 5–1.

**TIP**

You can also double-click a table name to add the table's field list to the Query window.

### Figure 5–1    Adding the fields for the pattern match query

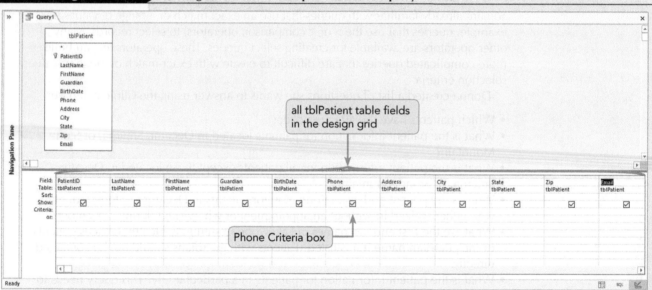

**Trouble?** If tblPatient.* appears in the first column's Field box, you dragged the * from the field list instead of the highlighted fields. Press DELETE, and then repeat Step 6.

Now you will enter the pattern match condition Like "404*" for the Phone field. The query will select records with a Phone field value of 404 in positions one through three. The asterisk wildcard character specifies that any characters can appear in the remaining positions of the field value.

**TIP**

If you omit the Like operator, it is automatically added when you run the query.

## To specify records that match the indicated pattern:

1. Click the **Phone Criteria** box, and then type **L**. The Formula AutoComplete menu displays a list of functions beginning with the letter L, but the Like operator is not one of the choices in the list. You'll finish typing the condition.

2. Type **ike "404\*"**. See Figure 5–2.

**Figure 5–2**   Record selection based on matching a specific pattern

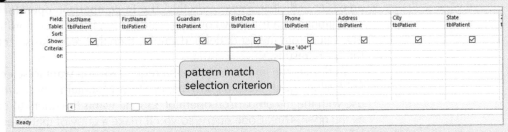

pattern match selection criterion

3. Click the **Save** button on the Quick Access Toolbar to open the Save As dialog box.

4. Type **qry404AreaCode** in the Query Name box, and then press **ENTER**. The query is saved, and the name is displayed on the object tab.

5. On the Query Tools Design tab, in the Results group, click the **Run** button. The query results are displayed in the query window. Seventeen records have the area code 404. See Figure 5–3.

**Figure 5–3**   tblPatient table records for phone numbers starting with 404

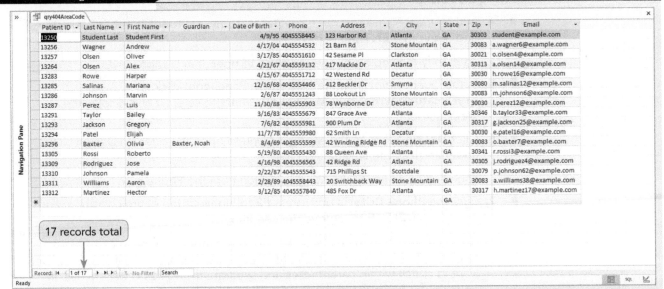

| Patient ID | Last Name | First Name | Guardian | Date of Birth | Phone | Address | City | State | Zip | Email |
|---|---|---|---|---|---|---|---|---|---|---|
| 13250 | Student Last | Student First | | 4/9/95 | 4045558445 | 123 Harbor Rd | Atlanta | GA | 30303 | student@example.com |
| 13256 | Wagner | Andrew | | 4/17/04 | 4045554532 | 21 Barn Rd | Stone Mountain | GA | 30083 | a.wagner6@example.com |
| 13257 | Olsen | Oliver | | 3/17/85 | 4045551610 | 42 Sesame Pl | Clarkston | GA | 30021 | o.olsen4@example.com |
| 13264 | Olsen | Alex | | 4/21/67 | 4045559132 | 417 Mackie Dr | Atlanta | GA | 30313 | a.olsen14@example.com |
| 13283 | Rowe | Harper | | 4/15/67 | 4045551712 | 42 Westend Rd | Decatur | GA | 30030 | h.rowe16@example.com |
| 13285 | Salinas | Mariana | | 12/16/68 | 4045554466 | 412 Beckler Dr | Smyrna | GA | 30080 | m.salinas12@example.com |
| 13286 | Johnson | Marvin | | 2/6/87 | 4045551243 | 88 Lookout Ln | Stone Mountain | GA | 30083 | m.johnson6@example.com |
| 13287 | Perez | Luis | | 11/30/88 | 4045555903 | 78 Wynborne Dr | Decatur | GA | 30030 | l.perez12@example.com |
| 13291 | Taylor | Bailey | | 3/16/83 | 4045555679 | 847 Grace Ave | Atlanta | GA | 30346 | b.taylor33@example.com |
| 13293 | Jackson | Gregory | | 7/6/82 | 4045555981 | 900 Plum Dr | Atlanta | GA | 30317 | g.jackson25@example.com |
| 13294 | Patel | Elijah | | 11/7/78 | 4045555980 | 62 Smith Ln | Decatur | GA | 30030 | e.patel16@example.com |
| 13296 | Baxter | Olivia | Baxter, Noah | 8/4/69 | 4045555599 | 42 Winding Ridge Rd | Stone Mountain | GA | 30083 | o.baxter7@example.com |
| 13305 | Rossi | Roberto | | 5/19/80 | 4045555430 | 88 Queen Ave | Atlanta | GA | 30341 | r.rossi3@example.com |
| 13309 | Rodriguez | Jose | | 4/16/98 | 4045556565 | 42 Ridge Rd | Atlanta | GA | 30305 | j.rodriguez4@example.com |
| 13310 | Johnson | Pamela | | 2/22/87 | 4045555543 | 715 Phillips St | Scottdale | GA | 30079 | p.johnson62@example.com |
| 13311 | Williams | Aaron | | 2/28/89 | 4045558443 | 20 Switchback Way | Stone Mountain | GA | 30083 | a.williams38@example.com |
| 13312 | Martinez | Hector | | 3/12/85 | 4045557840 | 485 Fox Dr | Atlanta | GA | 30317 | h.martinez17@example.com |
| * | | | | | | | | GA | | |

17 records total

Record: 1 of 17 | No Filter | Search

Note that Reginald removed the hyphens from the Phone field values; for example, 4045558445 in the first record used to be 404-555-8445. You'll modify the Phone field later in this module to format its values with hyphens.

6. If necessary, change the first record in the table, with Patient ID 13250, so the Last Name and First Name columns contain your last and first names, respectively, as shown in Figure 5–3.

7. Close the qry404AreaCode query.

Next, Donna asks you to create a query that displays information about patients who live in Decatur, Smyrna, or Stone Mountain. To produce the results Donna wants, you'll create a query using a list-of-values match.

# Using a List-of-Values Match in a Query

A **list-of-values match** selects records whose value for the designated field matches one of two or more simple condition values. You could accomplish this by including several Or conditions in the design grid, but the In comparison operator provides an easier and clearer way to do this. The **In comparison operator** lets you define a condition with a list of two or more values for a field. If a record's field value matches one value from the list of defined values, then that record is selected and included in the query results.

To display the information Donna requested, you want to select records if their City field value equals Decatur, Smyrna, or Stone Mountain. These are the values you will use with the In comparison operator. Donna wants the query to contain the same fields as the qry404AreaCode query, so you'll make a copy of that query and modify it.

**To create the query using a list-of-values match:**

▶ **1.** Open the Navigation Pane.

▶ **2.** In the Queries group on the Navigation Pane, right-click **qry404AreaCode**, and then click **Copy** on the shortcut menu.

   **Trouble?** If you don't see the qry404AreaCode query in the Queries group, press F5 to refresh the object listings in the Navigation Pane.

▶ **3.** Right-click the empty area in the Navigation Pane below the report and then click **Paste**.

▶ **4.** In the Query Name box, type **qryDecaturSmyrnaStoneMountainPatients**, and then press **ENTER**.

   To modify the copied query, you need to open it in Design view.

▶ **5.** In the Queries group on the Navigation Pane, right-click **qryDecaturSmyrnaStoneMountainPatients** to select it and display the shortcut menu.

▶ **6.** Click **Design View** on the shortcut menu to open the query in Design view, and then close the Navigation Pane.

   You need to delete the existing condition from the Phone field.

▶ **7.** Click the **Phone Criteria** box, press **F2** to highlight the entire condition, and then press **DELETE** to remove the condition.

   Now you can enter the criterion for the new query using the In comparison operator. When you use this operator, you must enclose the list of values you want to match within parentheses and separate the values with commas. In addition, for fields defined using the Short Text data type, you enclose each value in quotation marks, although the quotation marks are automatically added if you omit them. For fields defined using the Number or Currency data type, you don't enclose the values in quotation marks.

▶ **8.** Right-click the **City Criteria** box to open the shortcut menu, click **Zoom** to open the Zoom dialog box, and then type **In ("Decatur","Smyrna","Stone Mountain")**, as shown in Figure 5–4.

| Figure 5–4 | Record selection based on matching field values to a list of values |
|---|---|

list-of-values selection criteria

**TIP**

After clicking in a box, you can also open its Zoom dialog box by holding down SHIFT and pressing F2.

9. Click the **OK** button to close the Zoom dialog box, and then save and run the query. The recordset is displayed, which shows the 11 records with Decatur, Smyrna, or Stone Mountain in the City field.

10. Close the query.

Donna would also like a list of patients who do not live in Decatur, Smyrna, or Stone Mountain. You can provide her with this information by creating a query with the Not logical operator.

# Using the Not Logical Operator in a Query

The **Not logical operator** negates a criterion or selects records for which the designated field does not match the criterion. For example, if you enter Not "Decatur" in the Criteria box for the City field, the query results show records that do not have the City field value Decatur—that is, records of all patients not located in Decatur.

To create Donna's query, you will combine the Not logical operator with the In comparison operator to select patients whose City field value is not in the list ("Decatur","Smyrna","Stone Mountain"). The qryDecaturSmyrnaStoneMountainPatients query has the fields that Donna needs to see in the query results. Donna doesn't need to keep the qryDecaturSmyrnaStoneMountainPatients query, so you'll rename and then modify the query.

### To create the query using the Not logical operator:

**TIP**

You can rename any type of object, including a table, in the Navigation Pane using the Rename command on the shortcut menu.

1. Open the Navigation Pane.

2. In the Queries group, right-click **qryDecaturSmyrnaStoneMountainPatients**, and then on the shortcut menu, click **Rename**.

3. Position the insertion point after "qry," type **Non**, and then press **ENTER**. The query name is now qryNonDecaturSmyrnaStoneMountainPatients.

4. Open the **qryNonDecaturSmyrnaStoneMountainPatients** query in Design view, and then close the Navigation Pane.

   You need to change the existing condition in the City field to add the Not logical operator.

5. Click the **City Criteria** box, open the Zoom dialog box, click at the beginning of the expression, type **Not**, and then press **SPACEBAR**. See Figure 5–5.

**Figure 5–5**    **Record selection based on not matching a list of values**

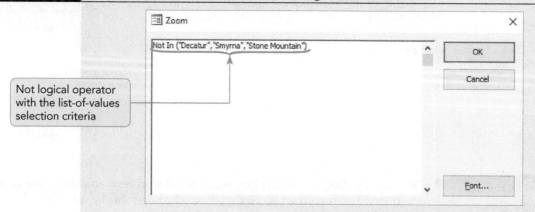

Not logical operator with the list-of-values selection criteria

6. Click the **OK** button, and then save and run the query. The recordset displays only those records with a City field value that is not Decatur, Smyrna, or Stone Mountain. The recordset includes a total of 41 patient records.

7. Scroll down the datasheet if necessary to make sure that no Decatur, Smyrna, or Stone Mountain patients appear in your results.

Now you can close and delete the query, because Donna does not need to run this query again.

8. Close the query, and then open the Navigation Pane.

9. Right-click **qryNonDecaturSmyrnaStoneMountainPatients**, click **Delete** on the shortcut menu, and then click **Yes** in the dialog box warning that deleting this object will remove it from all groups.

**TIP**

You can delete any type of object, including a table, in the Navigation Pane using the Delete command on the shortcut menu.

You now are ready to answer Donna's question about patients in Decatur or Stone Mountain who walked in without an appointment or who visited during the month of November.

## Using an AutoFilter to Filter Data

Donna wants to view the first and last names, cities, visit dates, walk-in statuses, and visit reasons for patients in Decatur or Stone Mountain who either walked in without an appointment or who visited during the month of November. The qryNovOrWalkin query contains the same fields Donna wants to view. This query also uses the Or logical operator to select records if the WalkIn field has a value of true or if the VisitDate field value is between 11/1/2020 and 11/30/2020. These are two of the conditions needed to answer Donna's question. You could modify the qryNovOrWalkin query in Design view to further restrict the records selected to patients located only in Decatur or Stone Mountain. However, you can use the AutoFilter feature to choose the city restrictions faster and with more flexibility. You previously used the AutoFilter feature to sort records, and you used Filter By Selection to filter records. Now you'll use the AutoFilter feature to filter records.

## To filter the records using an AutoFilter:

▶ 1. Open the **qryNovOrWalkin** query in Design view, and then close the Navigation Pane.

The true condition for the WalkIn field selects records for patients who walked in without an appointment, and the Between #11/1/2020# And #11/30/2020# condition for the VisitDate field selects records for patients whose visit date was in the month of November 2020. Although the WalkIn field is a yes/no field, these values are represented by true (yes) and false (no). Because the conditions are in two different rows, the query uses the Or logical operator.

If you wanted to answer Donna's question in Design view, you would add a condition for the City field, using either the Or logical operator—"Decatur" Or "Stone Mountain"—or the In comparison operator—In ("Decatur","Stone Mountain"). You'd place the condition for the City field in both the Criteria row and in the Or row. The query recordset would include a record only if both conditions in either row are satisfied. Instead of changing the conditions in Design view, though, you'll choose the information Donna wants using an AutoFilter.

▶ 2. Run the query, and then click the **arrow** on the City column heading to display the AutoFilter menu. See Figure 5–6.

| Figure 5–6 | Using an AutoFilter to filter records in the query recordset |
|---|---|

The AutoFilter menu lists all City field values that appear in the recordset. A checkmark next to an entry indicates that records with that City field value appear in the recordset. To filter for selected City field values, you uncheck the cities you don't want selected and leave checked the cities you do want selected. You can click the "(Select All)" check box to select or deselect all field values. The "(Blanks)" option includes null values when checked and excludes null values when unchecked. (Recall that a null field value is the absence of a value for the field.)

3. Click the **(Select All)** check box to deselect all check boxes, click the **Decatur** check box, scroll down the list, and then click the **Stone Mountain** check box.

    The two check boxes indicate that the AutoFilter will include only Decatur and Stone Mountain City field values.

4. Click the **OK** button. The AutoFilter displays the 8 records for patients in Decatur and Stone Mountain who walked in without an appointment or who had a visit in November. See Figure 5–7.

| Figure 5–7 | Recordset showing results of an AutoFilter |

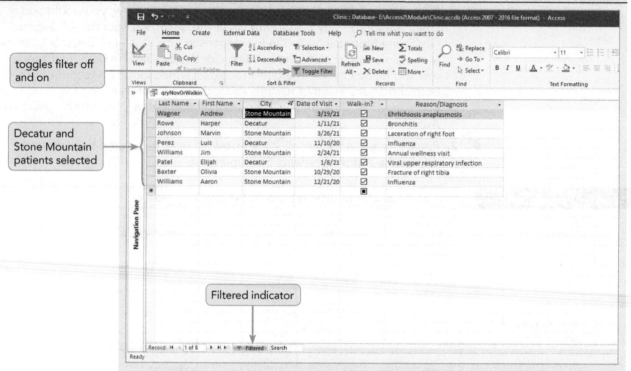

5. On the Home tab, in the Sort & Filter group, click the **Toggle Filter** button.

    The filter is removed, and all 41 records appear in the recordset.

6. Click the **Toggle Filter** button. The City filter is applied, displaying the 8 records for patients in Decatur and Stone Mountain.

7. Save the query and close it.

Next, Donna wants to view all fields from the tblPatient table, along with the patient name or the guardian name if the patient has a guardian.

# Assigning a Conditional Value to a Calculated Field

If a field in a record does not contain any information at all, it has a null value. Such a field is also referred to as a null field. A field in a record that contains any data at all—even a single space—is nonnull. Records for patients who do not have guardians have nonnull FirstName and LastName field values and null Guardian field values in the tblPatient table, while records for patients with guardians have nonnull values for all three fields. Donna wants to view records from the tblPatient table in order by the Guardian value, if it's nonnull, and at the same time in order by the LastName and then FirstName field values, if the Guardian field value is null. To produce this information for Donna, you need to create a query that includes all fields from the tblPatient table and then add a calculated field that will display the patient name—either the Guardian field value, which is entered using the format LastName, FirstName, or the LastName and FirstName field values, separated by a command and a space.

To combine the LastName and FirstName fields, you'll use the expression *LastName & ", " & FirstName*. The **& (ampersand) operator** is a concatenation operator that joins text expressions. **Concatenation** refers to joining two or more text fields or characters encapsulated in quotes. When you join the LastName field value to the string that contains the comma and space, you are concatenating these two strings. If the LastName field value is Trung and the FirstName field value is Grace, for example, the result of the expression *LastName & ", " & FirstName* is *Trung & ", " & Grace* which results in *Trung, Grace*.

## INSIGHT

### Using Concatenation

IT professionals generally refer to a piece of text data as a string. Most programming languages include the ability to join two or more strings using concatenation.

Imagine you're working with a database table that contains Title, FirstName, and LastName values for people who have made donations, and you've been asked to add their names to a report. You could add each individual field separately, but the data would look awkward, with each field in a separate column. Alternatively, you could create a calculated field with an expression that combines the fields with spaces into a more readable format, such as "Mr. Jim Sullivan." To do this, you would concatenate the fields with a space separator. The expression to perform this task might look like *=Title & " " & FirstName & " " & LastName*.

To display the correct patient value, you'll use the IIf function. The IIf (Immediate If) function assigns one value to a calculated field or control if a condition is true and a second value if the condition is false. The IIf function has three parts: a condition that is true or false, the result when the condition is true, and the result when the condition is false. Each part of the IIf function is separated by a comma. The condition you'll use is *IsNull(Guardian)*. The IsNull function tests a field value or an expression for a null value. If the field value or expression is null, the result is true; otherwise, the result is false. The expression *IsNull(Guardian)* is true when the Guardian field value is null and is false when the Guardian field value is not null.

For the calculated field, you'll enter *IIf(IsNull(Guardian),LastName & ", " & FirstName,Guardian & " (Guardian)")*. You interpret this expression as follows: If the Guardian field value is null, then set the calculated field value to the concatenation of the LastName field value, the text string ", " and the FirstName field value, which displays the patient's name. If the Guardian field value is not null, then set the calculated field value to the Guardian field value and the text string "(Guardian)" to indicate the displayed name is a patient's guardian.

Now you're ready to create Donna's query to display the patient name.

### To create the query to display the patient name:

1. Click the **Create** tab, and then in the Queries group, click the **Query Design** button. The Show Table dialog box opens on top of the Query window in Design View.

2. Click **tblPatient** in the Tables box, click the **Add** button, and then click the **Close** button. The tblPatient table field list is placed in the Query window, and the Show Table dialog box closes.

   Donna wants all fields from the tblPatient table to appear in the query recordset, with the new calculated field in the first column.

3. Drag the bottom border of the tblPatient field list down until all fields are visible, double-click the title bar of the tblPatient field list to highlight all the fields, and then drag the highlighted fields to the second column's Field box in the design grid. Each field is placed in a separate column in the design grid starting with the second column, in the same order that the fields appear in the table.

   **Trouble?** If you accidentally drag the highlighted fields to the first column in the design grid, click the PatientID Field box, and then in the Query Setup group, click the Insert Columns button. Continue with Step 4.

**TIP**

After clicking in a box, you can also open its Expression Builder dialog box by holding down CTRL and pressing F2.

4. Right-click the blank Field box to the left of the PatientID field, and then click **Build** on the shortcut menu. The Expression Builder dialog box opens.

   Donna wants to use "Patient" as the name of the calculated field, so you'll type that name, followed by a colon, and then you'll choose the IIf function.

5. Type **Patient:** and then press **SPACEBAR**.

6. Double-click **Functions** in the Expression Elements (left) column, and then click **Built-In Functions**.

Make sure you double-click instead of single-click the IIf function.

7. Scroll down the Expression Categories (middle) column, click **Program Flow**, and then in the Expression Values (right) column, double-click **IIf**. The IIf function is added with four placeholders to the right of the calculated field name in the expression box. See Figure 5–8.

| Figure 5–8 | IIf function inserted for the calculated field |
|---|---|

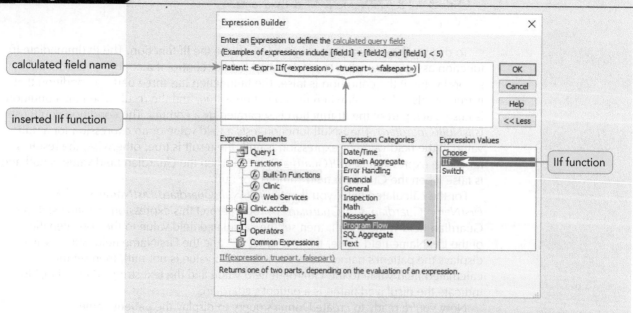

calculated field name

inserted IIf function

IIf function

The expression you will create does not need the leftmost placeholder (<<Expr>>), so you'll delete it. You'll replace the second placeholder (<<expression>>) with the condition using the IsNull function, the third placeholder (<<truepart>>) with the expression using the & operator and the FirstName and LastName fields, and the fourth placeholder (<<falsepart>>) with the expression using the & operator and the Nickname and LastName fields.

8. Click **<<Expr>>** in the expression box, and then press **DELETE**. The first placeholder is deleted.

9. Click **<<expression>>** in the expression box, and then click **Inspection** in the Expression Categories (middle) column.

10. Double-click **IsNull** in the Expression Values (right) column, click **<<expression>>** in the expression box, and then type **Guardian**. You've completed the entry of the condition in the IIf function. See Figure 5–9.

| Figure 5–9 | After entering the condition for the calculated field's IIf function |
| --- | --- |

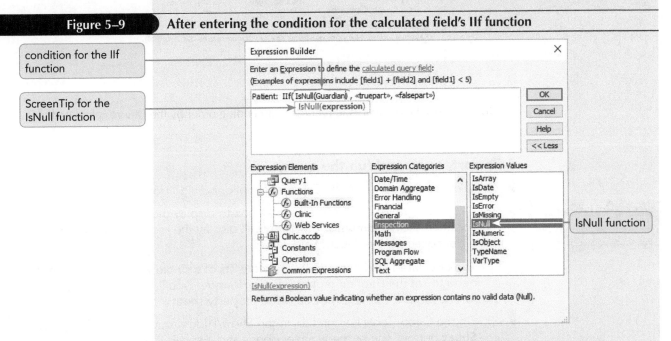

condition for the IIf function

ScreenTip for the IsNull function

IsNull function

After you typed the first letter of "Guardian," the Formula AutoComplete box displayed a list of functions beginning with the letter G, and a ScreenTip for the IsNull function was displayed above the box. The box closed after you typed the third letter, but the ScreenTip remains on the screen.

Instead of typing the field name of Guardian in the previous step, you could have double-clicked Clinic.accdb in the Expression Elements column, double-clicked Tables in the Expression Elements column, clicked tblPatient in the Expression Elements column, and then double-clicked Guardian in the Expression Categories column.

Now you'll replace the third placeholder and then the fourth placeholder.

11. Click **<<truepart>>**, and then type **LastName & ", " & FirstName**. Be sure you type a space after the comma within the quotation marks.

12. Click **<<falsepart>>**, and then type **Guardian & " (Guardian)"**. Be sure you type a space after the first quotation mark. See Figure 5–10.

| Figure 5–10 | Completed calculated field |
|---|---|

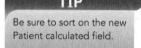
truepart expression

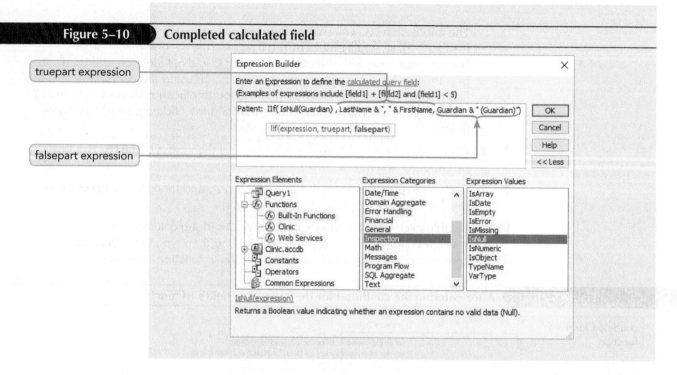
falsepart expression

Donna wants the query to sort records in ascending order by the Patient calculated field.

### To sort, save, and run the query:

1. Click the **OK** button in the Expression Builder dialog box to close it.

**TIP**

Be sure to sort on the new Patient calculated field.

2. Click the right side of the Patient Sort box to display the sort order options, and then click **Ascending**. The query will display the records in alphabetical order based on the Patient field values.

   The calculated field name of Patient consists of a single word, so you do not need to set the Caption property for it. However, you'll review the properties for the calculated field by opening its property sheet.

3. On the Query Tools Design tab, in the Show/Hide group, click the **Property Sheet** button. The property sheet opens and displays the properties for the Patient calculated field. See Figure 5–11.

| Figure 5–11 | Property sheet for the Patient calculated field |
|---|---|

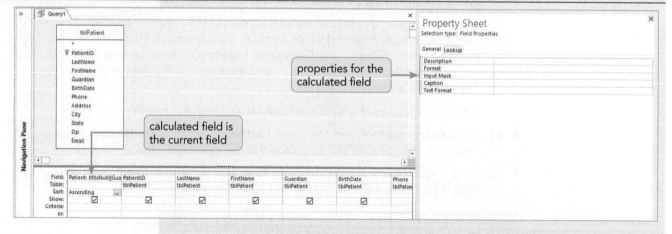
properties for the calculated field

calculated field is the current field

Among the properties for the calculated field, which is the current field, is the Caption property. Leaving the Caption property set to null means that the column name for the calculated field in the query recordset will be Patient, which is the calculated field name. The Property Sheet button is a toggle, so you'll click it again to close the property sheet.

4. Click the **Property Sheet** button again to close the property sheet.

5. Save the query as **qryPatientsByName**, run the query, and then resize the Patient column to its best fit. All records from the tblPatient table are displayed in alphabetical order by the Patient field. See Figure 5-12.

**Figure 5-12**    Completed query displaying the Patient calculated field

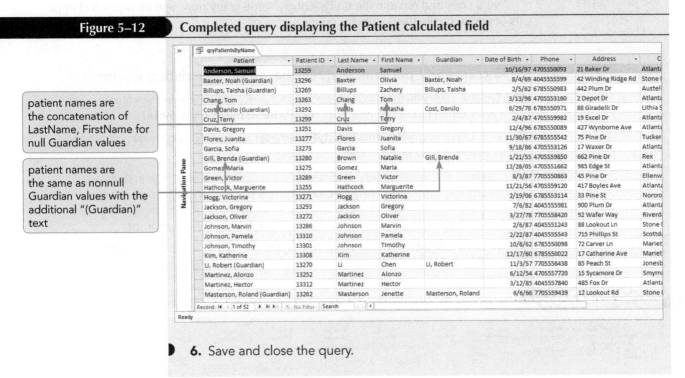

patient names are the concatenation of LastName, FirstName for null Guardian values

patient names are the same as nonnull Guardian values with the additional "(Guardian)" text

6. Save and close the query.

You're now ready to create the query to satisfy Donna's request for information about patients in a particular city.

# Creating a Parameter Query

Donna's next request is for records in the qryPatientsByName query for patients in a particular city. For this query, she wants to specify a city, such as Decatur or Stone Mountain, each time she runs the query.

To create this query, you will copy, rename, and modify the qryPatientsByName query. You could create a simple condition using an exact match for the City field, but you would need to change it in Design view every time you run the query. Alternatively, Donna or a member of her staff could filter the qryPatientsByName query for the city records they want to view. Instead, you will create a parameter query. A **parameter query** displays a dialog box that prompts the user to enter one or more criteria values when the query is run. In this case, you want to create a query that prompts for the city and selects only those patient records with that City field value from the table. You will enter the prompt in the Criteria box for the City field. When the query runs, it will open a dialog box and prompt you to enter the city. The query results will then be created, just as if you had changed the criteria in Design view.

REFERENCE

## Creating a Parameter Query

- Create a select query that includes all fields to appear in the query results.
- Choose the sort fields, and set the criteria that do not change when you run the query.
- Decide which fields to use as prompts when the query runs. In the Criteria box for each of these fields, type the prompt you want to appear in a dialog box when you run the query, and enclose the prompt in brackets.

You'll copy and rename the qryPatientsByName query now, and then you'll change its design to create the parameter query.

### To create the parameter query based on an existing query:

1. Open the Navigation Pane, copy and paste the qryPatientsByName query, and then name the new copy **qryPatientsByCityParameter**.

2. Open the **qryPatientsByCityParameter** query in Design view, and then close the Navigation Pane.

   Next, you must enter the criterion for the parameter query. In this case, Donna wants the query to prompt users to enter the city for the patient records they want to view. You need to enter the prompt in the Criteria box for the City field. Brackets must enclose the text of the prompt.

3. Click the **City Criteria** box, type **[Type the city:]** and then press **ENTER**. See Figure 5–13.

**Figure 5–13**    Specifying the prompt for the parameter query

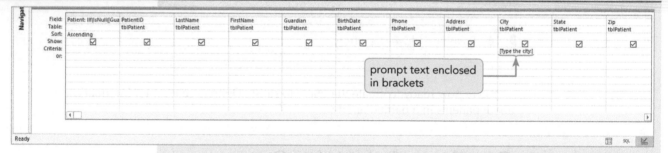

4. Save and run the query. A dialog box is displayed, prompting you for the name of the city. See Figure 5–14.

**Figure 5–14**    Enter Parameter Value dialog box

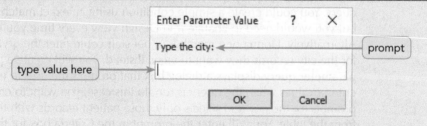

**TIP**

You must enter a value that matches the spelling of a City field value, but you can use either lowercase or uppercase letters.

The bracketed text you specified in the Criteria box of the City field appears above a box, in which you must type a City field value. Donna wants to see all patients in Decatur.

5. Type **Decatur**, press **ENTER**, and then scroll the datasheet to the right, if necessary, to display the City field values. The recordset displays the data for the three patients in Decatur. See Figure 5–15.

**Figure 5–15**    **Results of the parameter query**

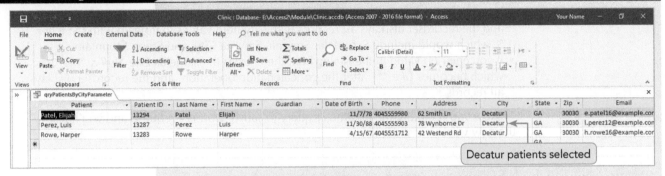

Donna asks what happens if she doesn't enter a value in the dialog box when she runs the qryPatientsByCityParameter query. You can run the query again to show Donna the answer to her question.

6. Switch to Design view, and then run the query. The Enter Parameter Value dialog box opens.

If you click the OK button or press ENTER, you'll run the parameter query without entering a value for the City field criterion.

7. Click the **OK** button. No records are displayed in the query results.

When you run the parameter query and enter "Decatur" in the dialog box, the query runs just as if you had entered "Decatur" in the City Criteria box in the design grid and displays all Decatur patient records. When you do not enter a value in the dialog box, the query runs as if you had entered "null" in the City Criteria box. Because none of the records has a null City field value, no records are displayed. Donna asks if there's a way to display records for a selected City field value when she enters its value in the dialog box and to display all records when she doesn't enter a value.

## Creating a More Flexible Parameter Query

Most users want a parameter query to display the records that match the parameter value the user enters or to display all records when the user doesn't enter a parameter value. To provide this functionality, you can change the value in the Criteria box in the design grid for the specified column. For example, you could change an entry for a City field from *[Type the city:]* to *Like [Type the city:] & "*"*. That is, you can prefix the Like operator to the original criterion and concatenate the criterion to a wildcard character. When you run the parameter query with this new entry, one of the following recordsets will be displayed:

- If you enter a specific City field value in the dialog box, such as *Smyrna*, the entry is the same as *Like "Smyrna" & "*"*, which becomes *Like "Smyrna*"* after the concatenation operation. That is, all records are selected whose City field values have Smyrna in the first six positions and any characters in the remaining positions. If the table on which the query is based contains records with City field values of Smyrna, only those records are displayed. However, if the table on which the query is based also contains records with City field values of Smyrna City, then both the Smyrna and the Smyrna City records would be displayed.
- If you enter a letter in the dialog box, such as *S*, the entry is the same as *Like "S*"*, and the recordset displays all records with City field values that begin with the letter S, which would include Scottdale, Smyrna, Smyrna City, and Stone Mountain.
- If you enter no value in the dialog box, the entry is the same as *Like Null & "*"*, which becomes *Like "*"* after the concatenation operation, and the recordset displays all records.

Now you'll modify the parameter query to satisfy Donna's request, and you'll test the new version of the query.

### To modify and test the parameter query:

▶ **1.** Switch to Design view.

▶ **2.** Click the **City Criteria** box, and then open the **Zoom** dialog box.

   You'll use the Zoom dialog box to modify the value in the City Criteria box.

▶ **3.** Click to the left of the expression in the Zoom dialog box, type **Like**, press **SPACEBAR**, and then press **END**.

▶ **4.** Press **SPACEBAR**, type **&**, press **SPACEBAR**, and then type **"*"** as shown in Figure 5–16.

   Be sure you type **"*"** at the end of the expression.

| Figure 5–16 | Modified City Criteria value in the Zoom dialog box |

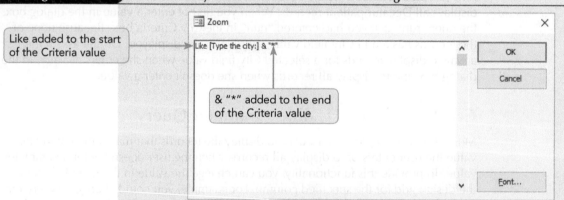

Like added to the start of the Criteria value

& "*" added to the end of the Criteria value

Now you can test the modified parameter query.

▶ **5.** Click the **OK** button to close the Zoom dialog box, save your query design changes, and then run the query.

   First, you'll test the query to display patients in Decatur.

6. Type **Decatur**, and then press **ENTER**. The recordset displays the data for the three patients in Decatur.

   Now you'll test the query without entering a value when prompted.

7. Switch to Design view, run the query, and then click the **OK** button. The recordset displays all 52 original records from the tblPatient table.

   Finally, you'll test how the query performs when you enter S in the dialog box.

8. On the Home tab, in the Records group, click the **Refresh All** button to open the Enter Parameter Value dialog box.

9. Type **S**, press **ENTER**, and then scroll to the right, if necessary, to display the City field values. The recordset displays the nine records for patients in Scottdale, Smyrna, and Stone Mountain.

10. Close the query.

11. If you are not continuing on to the next session, close the Clinic database, and then click the **Yes** button if necessary to empty the Clipboard.

The queries you created will make the Clinic database easier to use. In the next session, you'll use query wizards to create three different types of queries, and you'll use Design view to create a top values query.

## Session 5.1 Quick Check

REVIEW

1. According to the naming conventions used in this session, you use the _____ prefix tag to identify queries.

2. Which comparison operator selects records based on a specific pattern?

3. What is the purpose of the asterisk (*) in a pattern match query?

4. When do you use the In comparison operator?

5. How do you negate a selection criterion?

6. The _____ function returns one of two values based on whether the condition being tested is true or false.

7. When do you use a parameter query?

# Session 5.2 Visual Overview:

A crosstab query uses aggregate functions such as Sum and Count to perform arithmetic operations on selected records.

A simple query selects records from one or more tables that satisfy criteria.

A find duplicates query is a select query that finds duplicate records in a table or query.

A find unmatched query is a select query that finds all records in a table or query that have no related records in a second table or query.

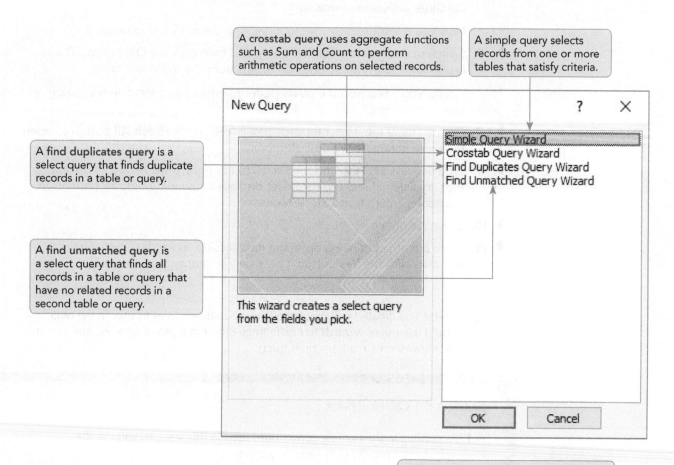

New Query

Simple Query Wizard
Crosstab Query Wizard
Find Duplicates Query Wizard
Find Unmatched Query Wizard

This wizard creates a select query from the fields you pick.

OK    Cancel

Each column and row intersection will display the sum of the InvoiceAmt values.

The selected field (InvoiceAmt) is used in the calculations for each column and row intersection.

This option determines whether to display an overall totals column in the crosstab query.

The crosstab query will display one column for the paid invoices and a second column for the unpaid invoices.

The crosstab query will display one row for each unique City field value.

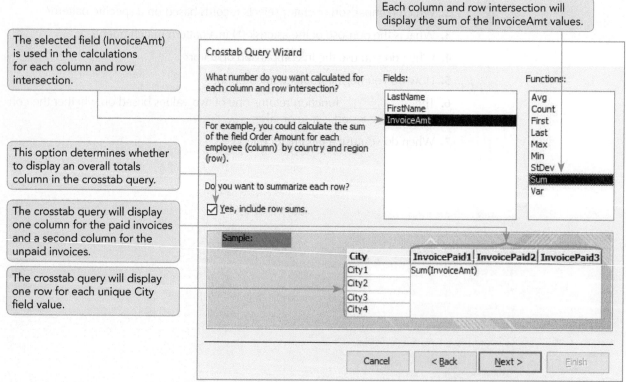

Crosstab Query Wizard

What number do you want calculated for each column and row intersection?

For example, you could calculate the sum of the field Order Amount for each employee (column) by country and region (row).

Do you want to summarize each row?

☑ Yes, include row sums.

Fields:
LastName
FirstName
InvoiceAmt

Functions:
Avg
Count
First
Last
Max
Min
StDev
Sum
Var

Sample:

| City | InvoicePaid1 | InvoicePaid2 | InvoicePaid3 |
|------|--------------|--------------|--------------|
| City1 | Sum(InvoiceAmt) | | |
| City2 | | | |
| City3 | | | |
| City4 | | | |

Cancel    < Back    Next >    Finish

# Advanced Query Wizards

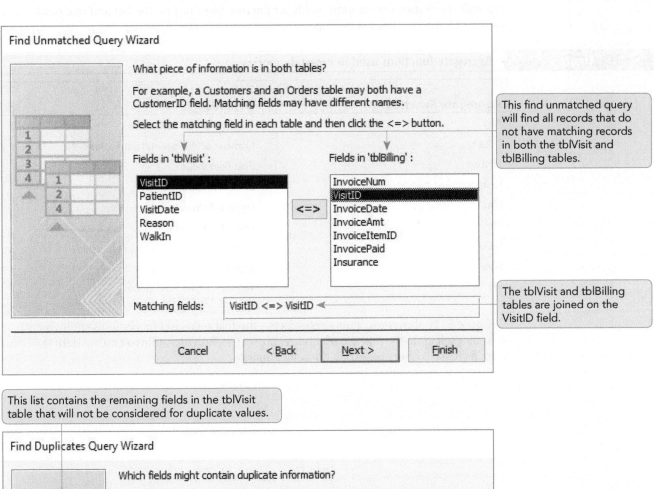

**Find Unmatched Query Wizard**

What piece of information is in both tables?

For example, a Customers and an Orders table may both have a CustomerID field. Matching fields may have different names.

Select the matching field in each table and then click the <=> button.

Fields in 'tblVisit' :

- VisitID
- PatientID
- VisitDate
- Reason
- WalkIn

Fields in 'tblBilling' :

- InvoiceNum
- VisitID
- InvoiceDate
- InvoiceAmt
- InvoiceItemID
- InvoicePaid
- Insurance

<=>

Matching fields:     VisitID <=> VisitID ◄

This find unmatched query will find all records that do not have matching records in both the tblVisit and tblBilling tables.

The tblVisit and tblBilling tables are joined on the VisitID field.

Cancel     < Back     Next >     Finish

This list contains the remaining fields in the tblVisit table that will not be considered for duplicate values.

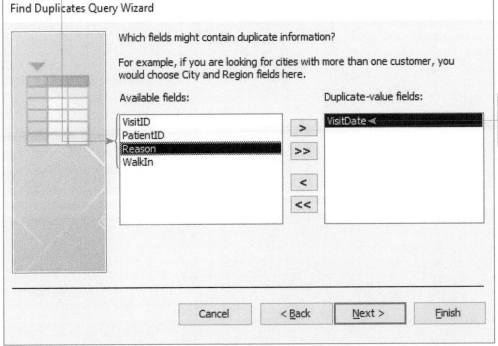

**Find Duplicates Query Wizard**

Which fields might contain duplicate information?

For example, if you are looking for cities with more than one customer, you would choose City and Region fields here.

Available fields:

- VisitID
- PatientID
- Reason
- WalkIn

Duplicate-value fields:

- VisitDate ◄

> >> < <<

This find duplicates query will find records that have the same VisitDate field value.

Cancel     < Back     Next >     Finish

# Creating a Crosstab Query

Donna wants to analyze the Lakewood Community Health Services invoices by city, so she can view the paid and unpaid invoice amounts for all patients located in each city. Crosstab queries use the aggregate functions shown in Figure 5–17 to perform arithmetic operations on selected records. A crosstab query can also display one additional aggregate function value that summarizes the set of values in each row. The crosstab query uses one or more fields for the row headings on the left and one field for the column headings at the top.

**Figure 5–17**    **Aggregate functions used in crosstab queries**

| Aggregate Function | Definition |
| --- | --- |
| Avg | Average of the field values |
| Count | Number of the nonnull field values |
| First | First field value |
| Last | Last field value |
| Max | Highest field value |
| Min | Lowest field value |
| StDev | Standard deviation of the field values |
| Sum | Total of the field values |
| Var | Variance of the field values |

Figure 5–18 shows two query recordsets—the first recordset (qryPatientsAndInvoices) is from a select query, and the second recordset (qryPatientsAndInvoicesCrosstab) is from a crosstab query based on the select query.

| Figure 5–18 | Comparing a select query to a crosstab query |

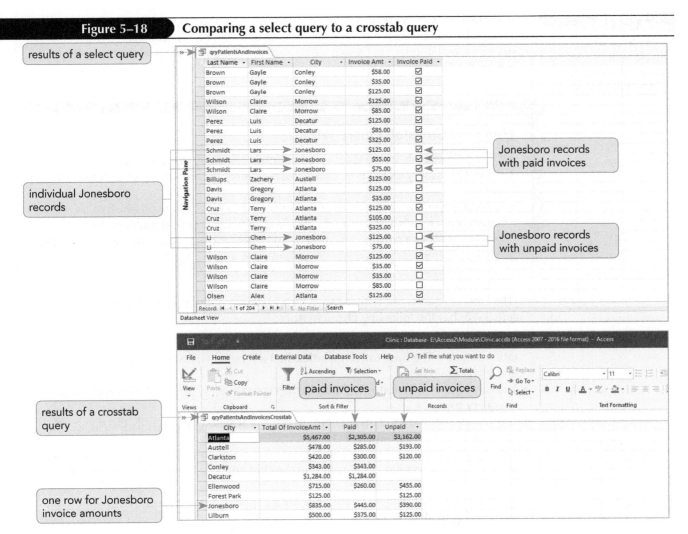

results of a select query

individual Jonesboro records

Jonesboro records with paid invoices

Jonesboro records with unpaid invoices

results of a crosstab query

one row for Jonesboro invoice amounts

The qryPatientsAndInvoices query, a select query, joins the tblPatient, tblVisit, and tblBilling tables to display selected data from those tables for all invoices. The qryPatientsAndInvoicesCrosstab query, a crosstab query, uses the qryPatientsAndInvoices query as its source query and displays one row for each unique City field value. The City column in the crosstab query identifies each row. The crosstab query uses the Sum aggregate function on the InvoiceAmt field to produce the displayed values in the Paid and Unpaid columns for each City row. An entry in the Total Of InvoiceAmt column represents the sum of the Paid and Unpaid values for the City field value in that row.

### Decision Making: Using Select Queries and Crosstab Queries

Companies use both select queries and crosstab queries in their decision making. A select query displays several records—one for each row selected by the select query— while a crosstab query displays only one summarized record for each unique field value. When managers want to analyze data at a high level to see the big picture, they might start with a crosstab query, identify which field values to analyze further, and then look in detail at specific field values using select queries. Both select and crosstab queries serve as valuable tools in tracking and analyzing a company's business, and companies use both types of queries in the appropriate situations. By understanding how managers and other employees use the information in a database to make decisions, you can create the correct type of query to provide the information they need.

**TIP**

Microsoft Access Help provides more information on creating a crosstab query without using a wizard.

The quickest way to create a crosstab query is to use the **Crosstab Query Wizard**, which guides you through the steps for creating one. You could also change a select query to a crosstab query in Design view using the Crosstab button in the Query Type group on the Query Tools Design tab.

**REFERENCE**

### Using the Crosstab Query Wizard

- On the Create tab, in the Queries group, click the Query Wizard button.
- In the New Query dialog box, click Crosstab Query Wizard, and then click the OK button.
- Complete the Wizard dialog boxes to select the table or query on which to base the crosstab query, select the row heading field (or fields), select the column heading field, select the calculation field and its aggregate function, and enter a name for the crosstab query.

The crosstab query you will create, which is similar to the one shown in Figure 5–18, has the following characteristics:

- The qryPatientsAndInvoices query in the Clinic database is the basis for the new crosstab query. The base query includes the LastName, FirstName, City, InvoiceAmt, and InvoicePaid fields.
- The City field is the leftmost column in the crosstab query and identifies each crosstab query row.
- The values from the InvoicePaid field, which is a Yes/No field, identify the rightmost columns of the crosstab query.
- The crosstab query applies the Sum aggregate function to the InvoiceAmt field values and displays the resulting total values in the Paid and Unpaid columns of the query results.
- The grand total of the InvoiceAmt field values appears for each row in a column with the heading Total Of InvoiceAmt.

Next you will create the crosstab query based on the qryPatientsAndInvoices query.

### To start the Crosstab Query Wizard:

1. If you took a break after the previous session, make sure that the Clinic database is open and the Navigation Pane is closed.

   **Trouble?** If the security warning is displayed below the ribbon, click the Enable Content button next to the security warning.

2. Click the **Create** tab on the ribbon.

3. In the Queries group, click the **Query Wizard** button. The New Query dialog box opens.

4. Click **Crosstab Query Wizard**, and then click the **OK** button. The first Crosstab Query Wizard dialog box opens.

You'll now use the Crosstab Query Wizard to create the crosstab query for Donna.

## To finish the Crosstab Query Wizard:

▶ **1.** In the View section, click the **Queries** option button to display the list of queries in the Clinic database, and then click **Query: qryPatientsAndInvoices**. See Figure 5–19.

| Figure 5–19 | Choosing the query for the crosstab query |

qryPatientsAndInvoices query selected

Queries option button selected

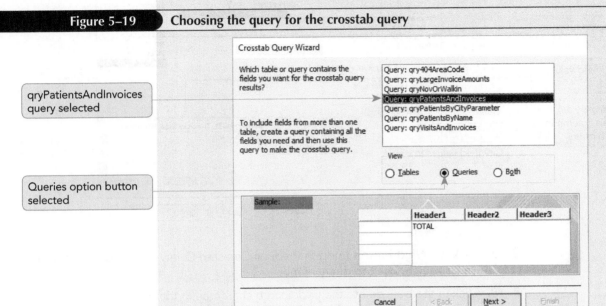

▶ **2.** Click the **Next** button to open the next Crosstab Query Wizard dialog box. This is the dialog box where you choose the field (or fields) for the *row* headings. Because Donna wants the crosstab query to display one row for each unique City field value, you will select that field for the row headings.

**TIP**

When you select a field, the sample crosstab query in the dialog box changes to illustrate your choice.

▶ **3.** In the Available Fields box, click **City**, and then click the **Select Single Field** button ⎡ **>** ⎤ to move the City field to the Selected Fields box.

▶ **4.** Click the **Next** button to open the next Crosstab Query Wizard dialog box, in which you select the field values that will serve as column headings. Donna wants to see the paid and unpaid total invoice amounts, so you need to select the InvoicePaid field for the column headings.

▶ **5.** Click **InvoicePaid** in the box, and then click the **Next** button.

In the next Crosstab Query Wizard dialog box, you choose the field that will be calculated for each row and column intersection and the function to use for the calculation. The results of the calculation will appear in the row and column intersections in the query results. Donna needs to calculate the sum of the InvoiceAmt field value for each row and column intersection.

▶ **6.** Click **InvoiceAmt** in the Fields box, click **Sum** in the Functions box, and then make sure that the "Yes, include row sums" check box is checked. The "Yes, include row sums" option creates a column showing the overall totals for the values in each row of the query recordset. See Figure 5–20.

| Figure 5-20 | Completed crosstab query design |

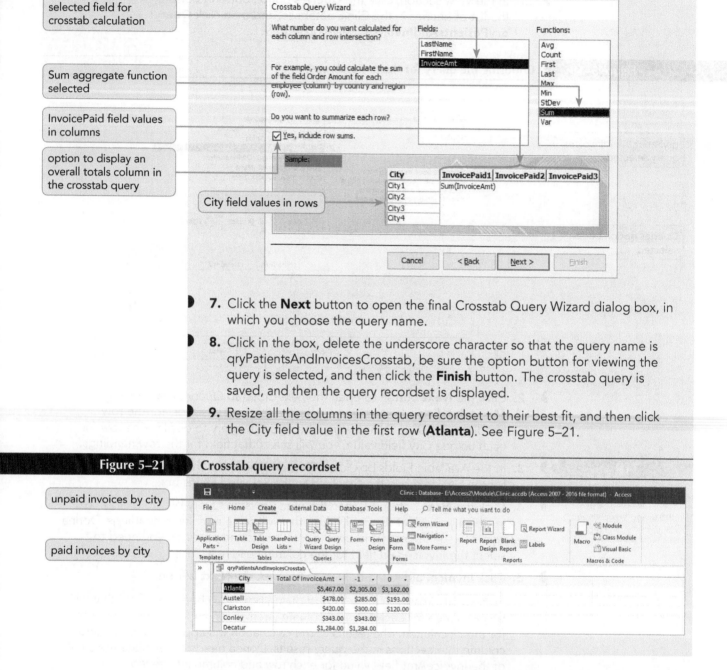

selected field for
crosstab calculation

Sum aggregate function
selected

InvoicePaid field values
in columns

option to display an
overall totals column in
the crosstab query

City field values in rows

> **7.** Click the **Next** button to open the final Crosstab Query Wizard dialog box, in which you choose the query name.

> **8.** Click in the box, delete the underscore character so that the query name is qryPatientsAndInvoicesCrosstab, be sure the option button for viewing the query is selected, and then click the **Finish** button. The crosstab query is saved, and then the query recordset is displayed.

> **9.** Resize all the columns in the query recordset to their best fit, and then click the City field value in the first row (**Atlanta**). See Figure 5-21.

| Figure 5-21 | Crosstab query recordset |

unpaid invoices by city

paid invoices by city

| City | Total Of InvoiceAmt | -1 | 0 |
|---|---|---|---|
| Atlanta | $5,467.00 | $2,305.00 | $3,162.00 |
| Austell | $478.00 | $285.00 | $193.00 |
| Clarkston | $420.00 | $300.00 | $120.00 |
| Conley | $343.00 | $343.00 | |
| Decatur | $1,284.00 | $1,284.00 | |

The query recordset contains only one row for each City field value. The Total Of InvoiceAmt column shows the total invoice amount for the patients in each city. The columns labeled -1 and 0 show the sum total paid (-1 column) and sum total unpaid (0 column) invoice amounts for patients in each city. Because the InvoicePaid field is a Yes/No field, by default, field values in datasheets, forms, and reports are displayed in a check box (either checked or unchecked), but a checked value is stored in the database as a -1 and an unchecked value as a 0. Instead of displaying check boxes, the crosstab query displays the stored values as column headings.

Donna wants you to change the column headings of -1 to Paid and 0 to Unpaid. You'll use the IIf function to change the column headings, using the expression *IIf(InvoicePaid, "Paid", "Unpaid")*—if the InvoicePaid field value is true (because it's a Yes/No field or a True/False field), or is checked, use "Paid" as the column heading;

otherwise, use "Unpaid" as the column heading. Because the InvoicePaid field is a Yes/No field, the condition *InvoicePaid* is the same as the condition *InvoicePaid = -1*, which uses a comparison operator and a value. For all data types except Yes/No fields, you must use a comparison operator in a condition.

### To change the crosstab query column headings:

1. Click the **Home** tab on the ribbon, and then switch to Design view. The design grid has four entries. See Figure 5–22.

**Figure 5–22    Crosstab query in the design grid**

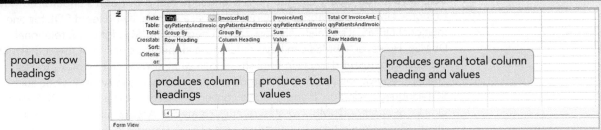

From left to right, the [City] entry produces the row headings, the [InvoicePaid] entry produces the column headings, the [InvoiceAmt] entry produces the totals in each row/column intersection, and the Total Of InvoiceAmt entry produces the row total column heading and total values. The field names are enclosed in brackets; the Total Of InvoiceAmt entry is the name of this calculated field, which displays the sum of the InvoiceAmt field values for each row.

You need to replace the Field box value in the second column with the IIf function expression to change the -1 and 0 column headings to Paid and Unpaid. You can type the expression in the box, use Expression Builder to create the expression, or type the expression in the Zoom dialog box. You'll use the last method.

2. Right-click the **InvoicePaid Field** box, and then open the Zoom dialog box.

3. Delete the InvoicePaid expression, and then type **IIf (InvoicePaid,"Paid","Unpaid")** in the Zoom dialog box. See Figure 5–23.

**Figure 5–23    IIf function for the crosstab query column headings**

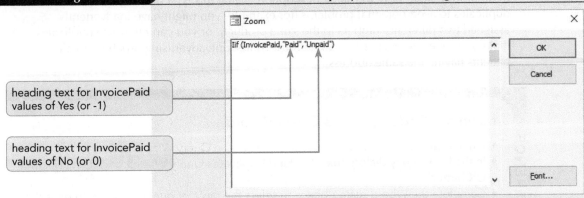

4. Click the **OK** button, and then save and run the query. The completed crosstab query is displayed with Paid and Unpaid as the last two column headings, in alphabetical order, as shown in Figure 5–18.

5. Close the query, and then open the Navigation Pane.

**TIP**

Point to an object in the Navigation Pane to display the full object name in a ScreenTip.

In the Navigation Pane, unique icons represent different types of queries. The crosstab query icon appears in the Queries list to the left of the qryPatientsAndInvoicesCrosstab query. This icon looks different from the icon that appears to the left of the other queries, which are all select queries.

**INSIGHT**

### Using Special Database Features Cautiously

When you create a query in Design view or with a wizard, an equivalent SQL statement is constructed, and only the SQL statement version of the query is saved. **SQL (Structured Query Language)** is a language that provides a standardized way to request information from a relational database system. If you learn SQL for one relational DBMS, it's a relatively easy task to begin using SQL for other relational DBMSs. However, DBMSs can have differences in their versions of SQL—somewhat like having different dialects in English—and in what additions they make to SQL. The SQL-equivalent statement created for a crosstab query in Access is one such SQL-language addition. If you need to convert an Access database to SQL Server, Oracle, or another DBMS, crosstab queries created in Access will not work in these other DBMSs. You'd have to construct a set of SQL statements in the other DBMS to replace the SQL statement automatically created by Access. Constructing this replacement set of statements is a highly technical process that only an experienced programmer can complete, so you should use special features of a DBMS judiciously.

Next, Donna wants to identify any visit dates that have the same visit dates as other patients because they might have potential scheduling difficulties.

To find the information Donna needs, you'll create a find duplicates query.

## Creating a Find Duplicates Query

A find duplicates query is a select query that finds duplicate records in a table or query. The **Find Duplicates Query Wizard** guides you through the steps for creating this type of query. A find duplicates query searches for duplicate values based on the fields you select when answering the Wizard's questions. For example, you might want to display all employers that have the same name, all students who have the same phone number, or all products that have the same description. Using this type of query, you can locate duplicates to avert potential problems (for example, you might have inadvertently assigned two different numbers to the same product), or you can eliminate duplicates that cost money (for example, you could send just one advertising brochure to all patients having the same address).

**REFERENCE**

### Using the Find Duplicates Query Wizard

- On the Create tab, in the Queries group, click the Query Wizard button.
- In the New Query dialog box, click Find Duplicates Query Wizard, and then click the OK button.
- Complete the Wizard dialog boxes to select the table or query on which to base the query, select the field (or fields) to check for duplicate values, select the additional fields to include in the query results, enter a name for the query, and then click the Finish button.

You'll use the Find Duplicates Query Wizard to create and run a new query to display duplicate visit dates in the tblVisit table.

## To create the query using the Find Duplicates Query Wizard:

1. Close the Navigation Pane, click the **Create** tab on the ribbon, and then, in the Queries group, click the **Query Wizard** button to open the New Query dialog box.

2. Click **Find Duplicates Query Wizard**, and then click the **OK** button. The first Find Duplicates Query Wizard dialog box opens. In this dialog box, you select the table or query on which to base the new query. You'll use the tblVisit table.

3. Click **Table: tblVisit**, and then click the **Next** button. The next Find Duplicates Query Wizard dialog box opens, in which you choose the fields you want to check for duplicate values.

4. In the Available fields box, click **VisitDate**, click the **Select Single Field** button  > to select the VisitDate field as the field to check for duplicate values, and then click the **Next** button. In the next Find Duplicates Query Wizard dialog box, you select the additional fields to display in the query results.

   Donna wants all remaining fields to be included in the query results.

5. Click the **Select All Fields** button  >> to move all fields from the Available fields box to the Additional query fields box, and then click the **Next** button. The final Find Duplicates Query Wizard dialog box opens, in which you enter a name for the query. You'll use qryDuplicateVisitDates as the query name.

6. Type **qryDuplicateVisitDates** in the box, be sure the option button for viewing the results is selected, and then click the **Finish** button. The query is saved, and then the 50 records for visits with duplicate visit dates are displayed. See Figure 5–24.

| Figure 5–24 | Query recordset for duplicate visit dates |

all records returned by the query share a visit date with other records

| Date of Visit | Visit ID | Patient ID | Reason/Diagnosis | Walk-in? |
|---|---|---|---|---|
| 10/26/20 | 1451 | 13309 | Laceration of right hand | ☑ |
| 10/26/20 | 1450 | 13272 | Influenza | ☑ |
| 11/3/20 | 1459 | 13276 | Asthma | ☐ |
| 11/3/20 | 1461 | 13250 | Dermatitis | ☑ |
| 11/10/20 | 1464 | 13276 | Osteoarthritis | ☐ |
| 11/10/20 | 1465 | 13287 | Influenza | ☑ |
| 11/16/20 | 1471 | 13269 | Hypertension | ☐ |
| 11/16/20 | 1472 | 13251 | Dermatitis | ☑ |
| 12/21/20 | 1492 | 13308 | COPD management visit | ☐ |
| 12/21/20 | 1493 | 13311 | Influenza | ☑ |
| 12/23/20 | 1496 | 13261 | Cardiac monitoring | ☐ |
| 12/23/20 | 1498 | 13263 | Fracture of right fifth metacarpal | ☑ |
| 12/23/20 | 1495 | 13310 | Rhinitis | ☑ |
| 1/7/21 | 1509 | 13273 | Annual wellness visit | ☑ |
| 1/7/21 | 1511 | 13285 | Dermatitis | ☐ |
| 1/7/21 | 1508 | 13305 | Viral upper respiratory infection | ☑ |
| 1/8/21 | 1513 | 13255 | Annual wellness visit | ☐ |
| 1/8/21 | 1514 | 13294 | Viral upper respiratory infection | ☑ |
| 1/15/21 | 1520 | 13267 | Annual wellness visit | ☐ |
| 1/15/21 | 1521 | 13280 | Osteoarthritis | ☑ |
| 1/25/21 | 1528 | 13285 | Annual wellness visit | ☐ |
| 1/25/21 | 1529 | 13270 | Pneumonia | ☑ |
| 1/26/21 | 1533 | 13291 | UTI | ☑ |
| 1/26/21 | 1531 | 13277 | Annual wellness visit | ☑ |

Record: 1 of 50   No Filter   Search

Datasheet View

7. Close the query.

Donna now asks you to find the records for patients with no visits. These are patients who have been referred to Lakewood Community Health Services but have not had a first visit. Donna wants to contact these patients to see if they would like to book initial appointments. To provide Donna with this information, you need to create a find unmatched query.

# Creating a Find Unmatched Query

A find unmatched query is a select query that finds all records in a table or query that have no related records in a second table or query. For example, you could display all patients who have had an appointment but have never been invoiced or all students who are not currently enrolled in classes. Such a query provides information for a medical office to ensure all patients who have received services have also been billed for those services and for a school administrator to contact the students to find out their future educational plans. The **Find Unmatched Query Wizard** guides you through the steps for creating this type of query.

## REFERENCE

### Using the Find Unmatched Query Wizard

- On the Create tab, in the Queries group, click the Query Wizard button.
- In the New Query dialog box, click Find Unmatched Query Wizard, and then click the OK button.
- Complete the Wizard dialog boxes to select the table or query on which to base the new query, select the table or query that contains the related records, specify the common field in each table or query, select the additional fields to include in the query results, enter a name for the query, and then click the Finish button.

Donna wants to know which patients have no visits. She will contact them to determine if they will be visiting Lakewood Community Health Services or whether they are receiving their medical services elsewhere. To create a list of patients who have not had a visit to the clinic, you'll use the Find Unmatched Query Wizard to display only those records from the tblPatient table with no matching PatientID field value in the related tblVisit table.

### To create the query using the Find Unmatched Query Wizard:

▶ 1. On the Create tab, in the Queries group, click the **Query Wizard** button to open the New Query dialog box.

▶ 2. Click **Find Unmatched Query Wizard**, and then click the **OK** button. The first Find Unmatched Query Wizard dialog box opens. In this dialog box, you select the table or query on which to base the new query. You'll use the qryPatientsByName query.

▶ 3. In the View section, click the **Queries** option button to display the list of queries, click **Query: qryPatientsByName** in the box to select this query, and then click the **Next** button. The next Find Unmatched Query Wizard dialog box opens, in which you choose the table that contains the related records. You'll select the tblVisit table.

▶ 4. Click **Table: tblVisit** in the box, and then click the **Next** button. The next dialog box opens, in which you choose the common field for both tables. See Figure 5-25.

| Figure 5–25 | Selecting the common field |
| --- | --- |

matching field in the tblVisit table

matching field in the qryPatientsByName query

click to confirm after selecting matching fields

matching fields will appear here

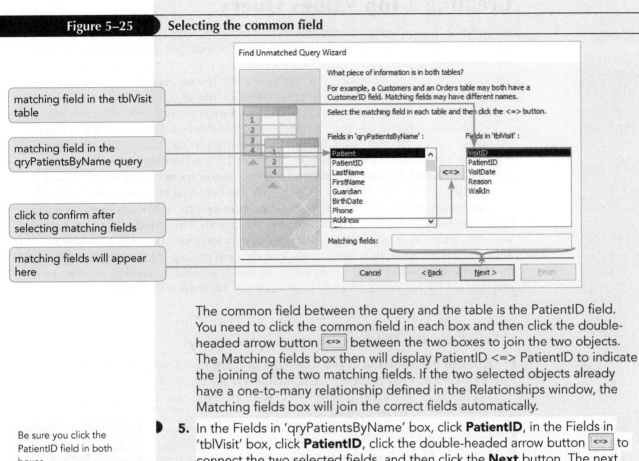

The common field between the query and the table is the PatientID field. You need to click the common field in each box and then click the double-headed arrow button <=> between the two boxes to join the two objects. The Matching fields box then will display PatientID <=> PatientID to indicate the joining of the two matching fields. If the two selected objects already have a one-to-many relationship defined in the Relationships window, the Matching fields box will join the correct fields automatically.

Be sure you click the PatientID field in both boxes.

5. In the Fields in 'qryPatientsByName' box, click **PatientID**, in the Fields in 'tblVisit' box, click **PatientID**, click the double-headed arrow button <=> to connect the two selected fields, and then click the **Next** button. The next Find Unmatched Query Wizard dialog box opens, in which you choose the fields you want to see in the query recordset. Donna wants the query record-set to display all available fields.

6. Click the **Select All Fields** button >> to move all fields from the Available fields box to the Selected fields box, and then click the **Next** button. The final dialog box opens, in which you enter the query name.

7. Type **qryInactivePatients**, be sure the option button for viewing the results is selected, and then click the **Finish** button. The query is saved, and then one record is displayed in the query recordset. See Figure 5–26.

| Figure 5–26 | Query recordset displaying one patient without a visit |
| --- | --- |

record for patients without visits

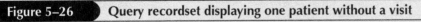
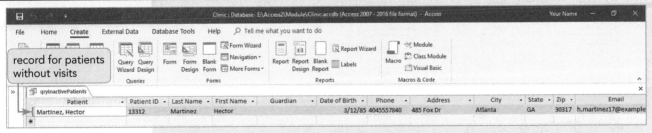

8. Close the query.

Next, Donna wants to contact those patients who have the highest invoice amounts to make sure that Lakewood Community Health Services is providing satisfactory service. To display the information Donna needs, you will create a top values query.

# Creating a Top Values Query

Whenever a query displays a large group of records, you might want to limit the number to a more manageable size by displaying, for example, just the first 10 records. The **Top Values property** for a query lets you limit the number of records in the query results. To find a limited number of records using the Top Values property, you can click one of the preset values from a list or enter either an integer (such as 15, to display the first 15 records) or a percentage (such as 20%, to display the first fifth of the records).

For instance, suppose you have a select query that displays 45 records. If you want the query recordset to show only the first five records, you can change the query by entering a Top Values property value of either 5 or 10%. If the query contains a sort, and the last record that can be displayed is one of two or more records with the same value for the primary sort field, all records with that matching key value are displayed.

Donna wants to view the same data that appears in the qryLargeInvoiceAmounts query for patients with the highest 25% invoice amounts. Based on the number or percentage you enter, a top values query selects that number or percentage of records starting from the top of the recordset. Thus, you usually include a sort in a top values query to display the records with the highest or lowest values for the sorted field. You will modify the query and then use the Top Values property to produce this information for Donna.

## To set the Top Values property for the query:

1. Open the Navigation Pane, open the **qryLargeInvoiceAmounts** query in Datasheet view, and then close the Navigation Pane. Nineteen records are displayed, all with InvoiceAmt field values greater than or equal to $150, in descending order by InvoiceAmt.

2. Switch to Design view.

3. On the Query Tools Design tab, in the Query Setup group, click the **Return** arrow (with the ScreenTip "Top Values"), and then click **25%**. See Figure 5–27.

| Figure 5–27 | Creating the top values query |

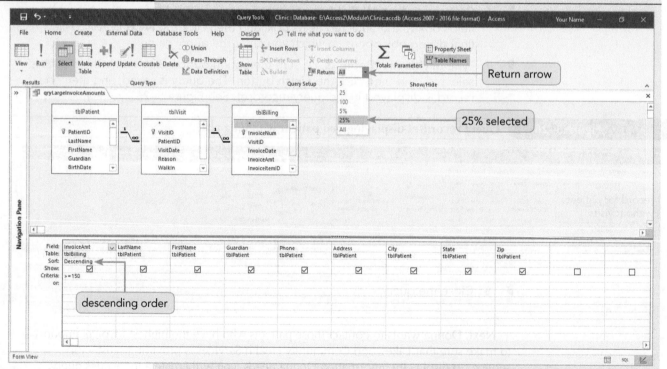

If the number or percentage of records you want to select, such as 15 or 20%, doesn't appear in the Top Values list, you can type the number or percentage in the Return box.

4. Run the query. Nine records are displayed in the query recordset; these records represent the highest 25% of invoice amounts (25% of the original 19 records). See Figure 5–28.

| Figure 5–28 | Top values query recordset |

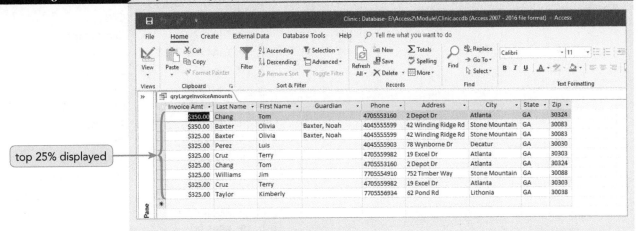

top 25% displayed

5. Save and close the query.

6. If you are not continuing on to the next session, close the Clinic database.

Donna will use the information provided by the queries you created to analyze the Lakewood Community Health Services business and to contact patients. In the next session, you will enhance the tblPatient and tblVisit tables.

## Session 5.2 Quick Check

REVIEW

1. What is the purpose of a crosstab query?

2. What are the four query wizards you can use to create a new query?

3. What is a find duplicates query?

4. What does a find unmatched query do?

5. What happens when you set a query's Top Values property?

6. What happens if you set a query's Top Values property to 2, and the first five records have the same value for the primary sort field?

# Session 5.3 Visual Overview:

The tblInvoiceItem table supplies the field values for the lookup field in the tblBilling table. A lookup field lets the user select a value from a list of possible values to enter data into the field.

**tblInvoiceItem**

| Invoice Item ID | Invoice Item |
|---|---|
| ⊞ DIA124 | EKG |
| ⊞ DIA157 | Radiograph |
| ⊞ DIA428 | Lab work |
| ⊞ DIA432 | Lab work - culture |
| ⊞ OST023 | Cast |
| ⊞ OST057 | Cast removal |
| ⊞ PRM784 | Pharmacy |
| ⊞ REP019 | Office visit |
| ⊞ REP245 | Phlebotomy |
| ⊞ REP289 | Physical therapy |
| ⊞ REP407 | Intravenous fluid therapy |
| ⊞ REP444 | Respiratory therapy |
| ⊞ REP556 | Supplies |
| ⊞ SUR071 | Minor surgery |
| ⊞ SUR088 | Suture removal |

The tblBilling table contains the lookup field.

The InvoiceItemID and InvoiceItem fields from the tblInvoiceItem table are used to look up InvoiceItemID values in the tblBilling table.

**tblBilling**

| Invoice Num | VisitID | Invoice Date | Invoice Amt | Invoice Item ID | Invoice Paid | Insurance | Click to Add |
|---|---|---|---|---|---|---|---|
| 26501 | 1450 | 10/27/2020 | $125.00 | Office visit | ☑ | $0.00 | |
| 26502 | 1450 | 10/27/2020 | $75.00 | EKG          DIA124 | | $0.00 | |
| 26503 | 1451 | 10/27/2020 | $125.00 | Radiograph          DIA157 | | $0.00 | |
| 26504 | 1451 | 10/27/2020 | $225.00 | Lab work          DIA428 | | $100.00 | |
| 26505 | 1451 | 10/27/2020 | $65.00 | Lab work - culture   DIA432 | | $0.00 | |
| 26508 | 1453 | 10/28/2020 | $125.00 | Cast          OST023 | | $0.00 | |
| 26509 | 1453 | 10/28/2020 | $45.00 | Cast removal          OST057 | | $100.00 | |
| 26510 | 1453 | 10/30/2020 | $35.00 | Pharmacy          PRM784 | | $0.00 | |
| 26511 | 1453 | 10/30/2020 | $55.00 | Office visit          REP019 | | $0.00 | |
| 26513 | 1458 | 10/30/2020 | $125.00 | Phlebotomy          REP245 | | $0.00 | |
| 26514 | 1458 | 10/30/2020 | $75.00 | Physical therapy          REP289 | | $0.00 | |
| 26515 | 1458 | 10/30/2020 | $350.00 | Intravenous fluid the REP407 | | $0.00 | |
| 26516 | 1458 | 10/30/2020 | $325.00 | Respiratory therapy   REP444 | | $0.00 | |
| 26518 | 1459 | 11/04/2020 | $125.00 | Supplies          REP556 | | $0.00 | |
| 26519 | 1459 | 11/04/2020 | $175.00 | Minor surgery          SUR071 | | $100.00 | |
| 26521 | 1461 | 11/04/2020 | $125.00 | Suture removal          SUR088 | | $0.00 | |
| 26522 | 1461 | 11/04/2020 | $65.00 | Phlebotomy          ☑ | | $0.00 | |
| | | | | Pharmacy          ☐ | | $0.00 | |

Values in the lookup field appear in alphabetical order, sorted by Invoice Item ID.

Only the InvoiceItemID values are stored in the InvoiceItemID field in the tblBilling table even though the user also sees the InvoiceItem values in the datasheet.

# Lookup Fields and Input Masks

The tblPatient table contains the field that displays values with an input mask. An **input mask** is a predefined format that is used to enter and display data in a field.

The Phone field uses an input mask to format displayed field values.

| tblPatient | | |
|---|---|---|
| **Field Name** | **Data Type** | |
| PatientID | Short Text | Primary key |
| LastName | Short Text | |
| FirstName | Short Text | |
| Guardian | Short Text | Guardian or billing contact |
| BirthDate | Date/Time | |
| Phone | Short Text | |
| Address | Short Text | |
| City | Short Text | |
| State | Short Text | |
| Zip | Short Text | |
| Email | Short Text | |

You can create an input mask for any field with a Short Text or Number data type.

The 9 character in an input mask indicates a digit or space in the field value whose entry is optional.

| General | Lookup |
|---|---|
| Field Size | 14 |
| Format | |
| Input Mask | 999\-000\-0000;; |
| Caption | |
| Default Value | |
| Validation Rule | |
| Validation Text | |
| Required | No |
| Allow Zero Length | Yes |
| Indexed | No |
| Unicode Compression | No |
| IME Mode | No Control |
| IME Sentence Mode | None |
| Text Align | General |

The \ indicates that the following character is a literal display character.

The character after the ;; indicates what character to display as the user is entering data. In this case the _ will be displayed.

The 0 character in an input mask indicates that only a digit can be entered and the entry is mandatory.

# Creating a Lookup Field

The tblBilling table in the Clinic database contains information about patient invoices. Donna wants to make entering data in the table easier for her staff. In particular, data entry is easier if they do not need to remember the correct InvoiceItemID field value for each treatment. Because the tblInvoiceItem and tblBilling tables have a one-to-many relationship, Donna asks you to change the tblBilling table's InvoiceItemID field, which is a foreign key to the tblInvoiceItem table, to a lookup field. A lookup field lets the user select a value from a list of possible values. For the InvoiceItemID field, a user will be able to select an invoice item's ID number from the list of invoice item names in the tblBilling table rather than having to remember the correct InvoiceItemID field value. The InvoiceItemID field value will be stored in the tblBilling table, but both the invoice item and the InvoiceItemID field value will appear in Datasheet view when entering or changing an InvoiceItemID field value. This arrangement makes entering and changing InvoiceItemID field values easier for users and guarantees that the InvoiceItemID field value is valid. A **Lookup Wizard field** uses the Lookup Wizard data type, which lets you create a lookup field in a table.

Donna asks you to change the InvoiceItemID field in the tblBilling table to a lookup field. You'll begin by opening the tblBilling table in Design view.

## To change the InvoiceItemID field to a lookup field:

1. If you took a break after the previous session, make sure that the Clinic database is open.

   **Trouble?** If the security warning is displayed below the ribbon, click the Enable Content button next to the warning.

2. If necessary, open the Navigation Pane, open the **tblBilling** table in Design view, and then close the Navigation Pane.

**TIP**

You can display the arrow and the menu simultaneously if you click the box near its right side.

3. Click the **Data Type** box for the InvoiceItemID field, click the arrow to display the list of data types, and then click **Lookup Wizard**. A message box appears, instructing you to delete the relationship between the tblBilling and tblInvoiceItem tables if you want to make the InvoiceItemID field a lookup field. See Figure 5–29.

**Figure 5–29**  **Warning message for an existing table relationship**

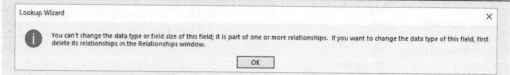

The lookup field will be used to form the one-to-many relationship between the tblBilling and tblInvoiceItem tables, so you don't need the relationship that previously existed between the two tables.

4. Click the **OK** button and then close the tblBilling table, clicking the **No** button when asked if you want to save the table design changes.

5. Click the **Database Tools** tab on the ribbon, and then in the Relationships group, click the **Relationships** button to open the Relationships window.

6. Right-click the join line between the tblBilling and tblInvoiceItem tables, click **Delete**, and then click the **Yes** button to confirm the deletion.

   **Trouble?** If the Delete command does not appear on the shortcut menu, click a blank area in the Relationships window to close the shortcut menu, and then repeat Step 6, ensuring you right-click the relationship line.

▶ **7.** Close the Relationships window.

Now you can resume changing the InvoiceItemID field to a lookup field.

### To finish changing the InvoiceItemID field to a lookup field:

▶ **1.** Open the **tblBilling** table in Design view, and then close the Navigation Pane.

▶ **2.** Click the right side of the **Data Type** box for the InvoiceItemID field, if necessary click the arrow, and then click **Lookup Wizard**. The first Lookup Wizard dialog box opens.

This dialog box lets you specify a list of allowed values for the InvoiceItemID field in a record in the tblBilling table. You can specify a table or query from which users select the value, or you can enter a new list of values. You want the InvoiceItemID values to come from the tblInvoiceItem table.

▶ **3.** Make sure the option for "I want the lookup field to get the values from another table or query" is selected, and then click the **Next** button to display the next Lookup Wizard dialog box.

▶ **4.** In the View section, click the **Tables** option button, if necessary, to display the list of tables, click **Table: tblInvoiceItem**, and then click the **Next** button to display the next Lookup Wizard dialog box. See Figure 5–30.

**Figure 5–30**    **Selecting the lookup fields**

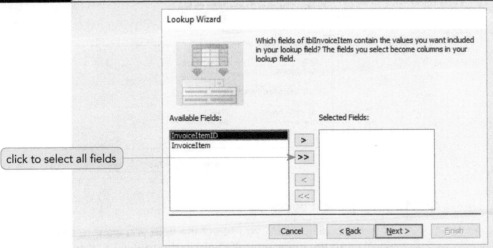

This dialog box lets you select the lookup fields from the tblInvoiceItem table. You need to select the InvoiceItemID field because it's the common field that links the tblInvoiceItem table and the tblBilling table. You must also select the InvoiceItem field because Donna wants the user to be able to select from a list of invoice item names when entering a new contract record or changing an existing InvoiceItemID field value.

▶ **5.** Click the **Select All Fields** button `>>` to move the InvoiceItemID and InvoiceItem fields to the Selected Fields box, and then click the **Next** button to display the next Lookup Wizard dialog box. This dialog box lets you choose a sort order for the box entries. Donna wants the entries to appear in ascending Invoice Item Description order. Note that ascending is the default sort order.

6. Click the **arrow** for the first box, click **InvoiceItem**, and then click the **Next** button to open the next dialog box.

In this dialog box, you can adjust the widths of the lookup columns. Note that when you resize a column to its best fit, the column is resized so that the widest column heading and the visible field values fit the column width. However, some field values that aren't visible in this dialog box might be wider than the column width, so you must scroll down the column to make sure you don't have to repeat the column resizing.

7. Click the **Hide key column** check box to remove the checkmark and display the InvoiceItemID field.

8. Click the Invoice Item ID column heading to select it. With the mouse pointer on the Invoice Item ID heading, drag it to the right of the Invoice Item column to reposition it.

9. Place the pointer on the right edge of the Invoice Item field column heading, and then when the pointer changes to the column resize pointer ✛, double-click to resize the column to its best fit.

10. Scroll down the columns, and repeat Step 9 as necessary until the Invoice Item column accommodates all contents, and then press **CTRL+HOME** to scroll back to the top of the columns. See Figure 5–31.

**Figure 5–31**    **Adjusting the width of the lookup column**

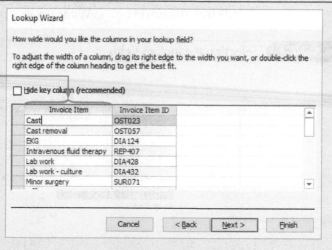

column adjusted to its best fit

11. Click the **Next** button.

In the next dialog box, you select the field you want to store in the table. You'll store the InvoiceItemID field in the tblBilling table because it's the foreign key to the tblInvoiceItem table.

12. Click **InvoiceItemID** in the Available Fields box if it's not already selected, and then click the **Next** button.

In the next dialog box, you specify the field name for the lookup field. Because you'll be storing the InvoiceItemID field in the table, you'll accept the default field name, InvoiceItemID.

13. Click the **Finish** button, and then click **Yes** to save the table.

The Data Type value for the InvoiceItemID field is still Short Text because this field contains text data. However, when you update the field, the InvoiceItemID field value will be used to look up and display in the tblBilling table datasheet both the InvoiceItem and InvoiceItemID field values from the tblInvoiceItem table.

In reviewing patient visits recently, Donna noticed that the InvoiceItemID field value stored in the tblBilling table for visit number 26521 is incorrect. She asks you to test the new lookup field to select the correct field value. To do so, you need to switch to Datasheet view.

## To change the InvoiceItemID field value:

1. Switch to Datasheet view, and then resize the Invoice Item ID column to its best fit.

   Notice that the Invoice Item ID column displays InvoiceItem field values, even though the InvoiceItemID field values are stored in the table.

2. For Invoice Num 26521, click **Phlebotomy** in the Invoice Item ID column, and then click the **arrow** to display the list of InvoiceItem and InvoiceItemID field values from the tblInvoiceItems table. See Figure 5–32.

| Figure 5–32 | List of InvoiceItem and InvoiceItemID field values |

Note that the column displaying InvoiceItem values in your list may be narrower than the values themselves, even though you resized the column. This bug should be fixed in a future version of Access.

The invoice item for visit 26521 should be Office Visit, so you need to select this entry in the list to change the InvoiceItemID field value.

3. Scroll through the list if necessary, and then click **Office visit** to select that value to display in the datasheet and to store the InvoiceItemID field value of REP019 in the table. The list closes, and "Office visit" appears in the Invoice Item ID column.

4. Save and close the tblBilling table.

Next, Donna asks you to change the appearance of the Phone field in the tblPatient table to a standard telephone number format.

## Using the Input Mask Wizard

The Phone field in the tblPatient table is a 10-digit number that's difficult to read because it appears with none of the special formatting characters usually associated with a telephone number. For example, the Phone field value for Gregory Davis, which appears as 6785550089, would be more readable in any of the following formats: 678-555-0089, 678.555.0089, 678/555-0089, or (678) 555-0089. Donna asks you to use the (678) 555-0089 style for the Phone field.

Donna wants the parentheses and hyphens to appear as literal display characters whenever users enter Phone field values. A literal display character is a special character that automatically appears in specific positions of a field value; users don't need to type literal display characters. To include these characters, you need to create an input mask, which is a predefined format used to enter and display data in a field. An easy way to create an input mask is to use the **Input Mask Wizard**, an Access tool that guides you in creating a predefined format for a field. You must be in Design view to use the Input Mask Wizard.

### To use the Input Mask Wizard for the Phone field:

▶ **1.** Open the **tblPatient** table, close the Navigation Pane, and then, if necessary, switch to Design view.

▶ **2.** Click the **Phone Field Name** box to make that row the current row and to display its Field Properties options.

▶ **3.** Click the **Input Mask** box in the Field Properties pane. The Build button ⊡ appears at the right edge of the Input Mask box.

▶ **4.** Click the **Build** button ⊡ in the Input Mask box. The first Input Mask Wizard dialog box opens. See Figure 5–33.

**Figure 5–33** **Input Mask Wizard dialog box**

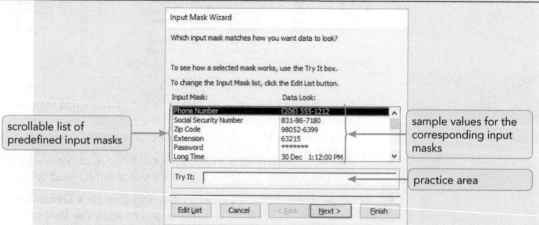

scrollable list of predefined input masks

sample values for the corresponding input masks

practice area

You can scroll the Input Mask box, select the input mask you want, and then enter representative values to practice using the input mask.

▶ **5.** If necessary, click **Phone Number** in the Input Mask box to select it.

6. Click the far left side of the **Try It** box. (\_\_\_) \_\_\_-\_\_\_ appears in the Try It box. As you type a phone number, the underscores, which are placeholder characters, are replaced.

   **Trouble?** If your insertion point is not immediately to the right of the left parenthesis, press ← until it is.

7. Type **6785550089** to practice entering a sample phone number. The input mask formats the typed value as (678) 555-0089.

8. Click the **Next** button. The next Input Mask Wizard dialog box opens. In it, you can change the input mask and the placeholder character. Because you can change an input mask easily after the Input Mask Wizard finishes, you'll accept all wizard defaults.

9. Click the **Finish** button, and then click to the right of the value in the Input Mask box to deselect the characters. The Input Mask Wizard creates the phone number input mask, placing it in the Input Mask box for the Phone field. See Figure 5–34.

| Figure 5–34 | Phone number input mask created by the Input Mask Wizard |

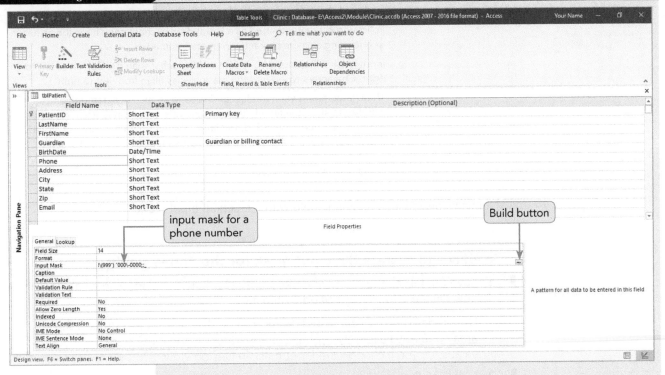

The characters used in a field's input mask restrict the data you can enter in the field, as shown in Figure 5–35. Other characters that appear in an input mask, such as the left and right parentheses in the phone number input mask, are literal display characters.

**Figure 5-35**    **Input mask characters**

| Input Mask Character | Description |
|---|---|
| 0 | Digit only must be entered. Entry is required. |
| 9 | Digit or space can be entered. Entry is optional. |
| # | Digit, space, or a plus or minus sign can be entered. Entry is optional. |
| L | Letter only must be entered. Entry is required. |
| ? | Letter only can be entered. Entry is optional. |
| A | Letter or digit must be entered. Entry is required. |
| a | Letter or digit can be entered. Entry is optional. |
| & | Any character or a space must be entered. Entry is required. |
| C | Any character or a space can be entered. Entry is optional. |
| > | All characters that follow are displayed in uppercase. |
| < | All characters that follow are displayed in lowercase. |
| " | Enclosed characters treated as literal display characters. |
| \ | Following character treated as a literal display character. This is the same as enclosing a single character in quotation marks. |
| ! | Input mask is displayed from right to left, rather than the default of left to right. Characters typed into the mask always fill in from left to right. |
| ;; | The character between the first and second semicolons determines whether to store the literal display characters in the database. If the value is 1 or if no value is provided, the literal display characters are not stored. If the value is 0, the literal display characters are stored. The character following the second semicolon is the placeholder character that appears in the displayed input mask. |

Donna wants to view the Phone field with the default input mask.

### To view and change the input mask for the Phone field:

1. Save the table, and then switch to Datasheet view. The Phone field values now have the format specified by the input mask.

   Donna decides that she would prefer to omit the parentheses around the area codes and use only hyphens as separators in the displayed Phone field values, so you'll change the input mask in Design view.

2. Switch to Design view.

   The input mask is set to !\(999") "000\-0000;;_. The backslash character (\) causes the character that follows it to appear as a literal display character. Characters enclosed in quotation marks also appear as literal display characters. (See Figure 5-35.) The exclamation mark (!) forces the existing data to fill the input mask from right to left instead of left to right. This does not affect new data. This applies only when data has already been entered in the table and a new input mask is applied. For instance, if the existing data is 5551234 and the input mask fills from left to right, the data with the input mask would look like (555) 123-4. If the input mask fills from right to left, the data with the input mask applied would look like ( ) 555-1234.

If you omit the backslashes preceding the hyphens, Access inserts them when you press TAB. However, Access does not add backslashes for other literal display characters, such as periods and slashes, so it's always best to type the backslashes. Since all of the existing data includes the area code, it will not make a difference whether the input mask applied to the data fills the data from left to right or from right to left, so you'll omit the ! symbol.

3. In the Input Mask box for the Phone field, change the input mask to **999\-000\-0000;;_** and then press **TAB**.

Because you've modified a field property, the Property Update Options button appears to the left of the Input Mask property.

4. Click the **Property Update Options** button . A menu opens below the button, as shown in Figure 5–36.

**Figure 5–36**    **Property Update Options button menu**

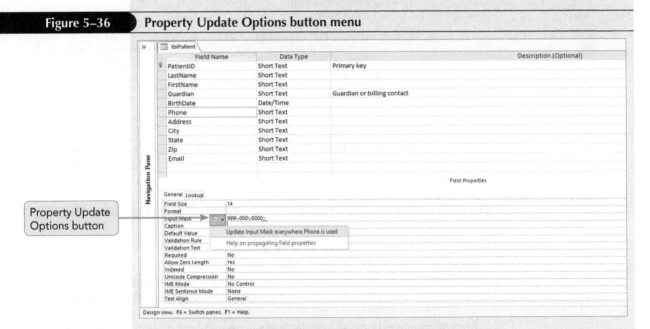

Property Update Options button

**Figure 5–37**    **Update Properties dialog box**

5. Click **Update Input Mask everywhere Phone is used**. The Update Properties dialog box opens. See Figure 5–37.

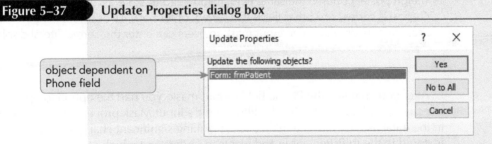

object dependent on Phone field

Because the frmPatient form displays the Phone field values from the tblPatient table, the Phone field's Input Mask property in this object will automatically be changed to your new input mask. If other form objects included the Phone field from the tblPatient table, they would be included in this dialog box as well. This capability to update control properties in objects when you modify a table field property is called **property propagation**.

Although the Update Properties dialog box displays no queries, property propagation also occurs with queries automatically. Property propagation is limited to field properties such as the Decimal Places, Description, Format, and Input Mask properties.

▶ 6. Click the **Yes** button, save the table, switch to Datasheet view, and then if necessary, resize the Phone column to its best fit. The Phone field values now have the format Donna requested. See Figure 5–38.

| Figure 5–38 | After changing the Phone field input mask |

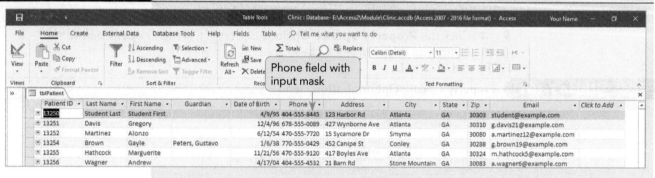

Because Donna wants her staff to store only standard 10-digit U.S. phone numbers for patients, the input mask you've created will enforce the standard entry and display format that Donna desires.

## Understanding When to Use Input Masks

An input mask is appropriate for a field only if all field values have a consistent format. For example, you can use an input mask with hyphens as literal display characters to store U.S. phone numbers in a consistent format of 987-654-3210. However, a multinational company would not be able to use an input mask to store phone numbers from all countries because international phone numbers do not have a consistent format. In the same way, U.S. zip codes have a consistent format, and you could use an input mask of 00000#9999 to enter and display U.S. zip codes such as 98765 and 98765-4321, but you could not use an input mask if you need to store and display foreign postal codes in the same field. If you need to store and display phone numbers, zip/postal codes, and other fields in a variety of formats, it's best to define them as Short Text fields without an input mask so users can enter the correct literal display characters.

After you changed the Phone field's input mask, you had the option to update, selectively and automatically, the Phone field's Input Mask property in other objects in the database. Donna is thinking about making significant changes to the way data is stored in the tblPatient table and wants to understand which other elements those changes might impact. To determine the dependencies among objects in an Access database, you'll open the Object Dependencies pane.

# Identifying Object Dependencies

An **object dependency** exists between two objects when a change to the properties of data in one object affects the properties of data in the other object. Dependencies between Access objects, such as tables, queries, and forms, can occur in various ways. For example, the tblVisit and tblBilling tables are dependent on each other because they have a one-to-many relationship. In the same way, the tblPatient table uses the qryPatientsByName query to obtain the Patient field to display along with the PatientID field, and this creates a dependency between these two objects. Any query, form, or other object that uses fields from a given table is dependent on that table. Any form or report that uses fields from a query is directly dependent on the query and is indirectly dependent on the tables that provide the data to the query. Large databases contain hundreds of objects, so it is useful to have a way to easily view the dependencies among objects before you attempt to delete or modify an object. The **Object Dependencies pane** displays a collapsible list of the dependencies among the objects in an Access database; you click the list's expand indicators to show or hide different levels of dependencies. Next, you'll open the Object Dependencies pane to examine the object dependencies in the Clinic database.

## To open and use the Object Dependencies pane:

1. Click the **Database Tools** tab on the ribbon.

2. In the Relationships group, click the **Object Dependencies** button to open the Object Dependencies pane, and then drag the left edge of the pane to the left until none of the items in the list are cut off.

3. If necessary, click the **Objects that depend on me** option button to select it, then click the **Refresh** link to display the list of objects. See Figure 5–39.

**Figure 5–39**  The Object Dependencies pane for the tblPatient table

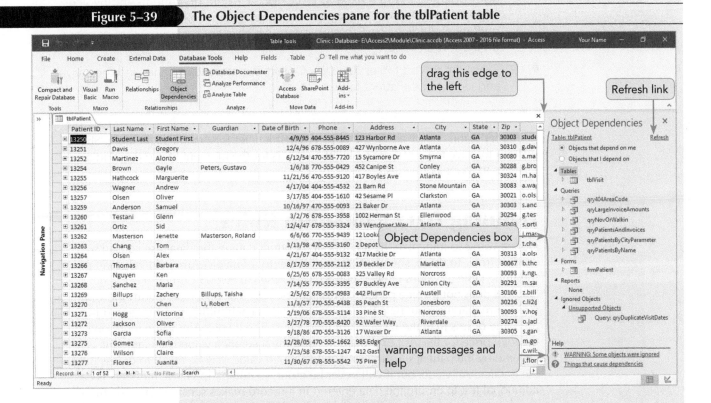

The Object Dependencies pane displays the objects that depend on the tblPatient table, the object name that appears at the top of the pane. If you change the design of the tblPatient table, the change might affect objects in the pane. Changing a property for a field in the tblPatient table that's also used by a listed object affects that listed object. If a listed object does not use the field you are changing, that listed object is not affected.

Objects listed in the Ignored Objects section of the box might have an object dependency with the tblPatient table, and you'd have to review them individually to determine if a dependency exists. The Help section at the bottom of the pane displays links for further information about object dependencies.

▶ **4.** Click the **frmPatient** link in the Object Dependencies pane. The frmPatient form opens in Design view. All the fields in the form are fields from the tblPatient table, which is why the form has an object dependency with the table.

▶ **5.** Switch to Form view for the frmPatient form. Note that the Phone field value is displayed using the input mask you applied to the field in the tblPatient table. This change was propagated from the table to the form.

▶ **6.** Close the frmPatient form, open the Navigation Pane, open the **tblVisit** table in Datasheet view, and then click the **Refresh** link near the top of the Object Dependencies pane. The Object Dependencies box now displays the objects that depend on the tblVisit table.

▶ **7.** Click the **Objects that I depend on** option button near the top of the pane to view the objects that affect the tblPatient table.

▶ **8.** Click the **Objects that depend on me** option button, and then click the right-pointing triangle expand indicator ▷ for the qryPatientsAndInvoices query in the Object Dependencies pane. The list expands to display the qryPatientsAndInvoicesCrosstab query, which is another query that depends on the tblVisit table.

▶ **9.** Close the tblVisit table, close the Object Dependencies pane, and then save and close the tblPatient table.

You let Donna know about the object dependencies for the tblPatient table. She decides to leave the tblPatient table the way it is for the moment to avoid making changes to forms or queries.

# Defining Data Validation Rules

Donna wants to minimize the amount of incorrect data in the database caused by typing errors. To do so, she wants to limit the entry of InvoiceAmt field values in the tblBilling table to values greater than $10 because Lakewood Community Health Services does not invoice patients for balances of $10 or less. In addition, she wants to make sure that the Insurance field value entered in each tblBilling table record is either the same or less than the InvoiceAmt field value. The InvoiceAmt value represents the total price for the visit or procedure, and the Insurance value is the amount covered by the patient's insurance. The Insurance value may be equal to or less than the InvoiceAmt value, but it will never be more, so comparing these numbers is an additional test to ensure the data entered in a record makes sense. To provide these checks on entered data, you'll set field validation properties for the InvoiceAmt field in the tblBilling table and set table validation properties in the tblBilling table.

## Defining Field Validation Rules

To prevent a user from entering an unacceptable value in the InvoiceAmt field, you can create a **field validation rule** that verifies a field value by comparing it to a constant or to a set of constants. You create a field validation rule by setting the Validation Rule and the Validation Text field properties. The **Validation Rule property** value specifies the valid values that users can enter in a field. The **Validation Text property** value will be displayed in a dialog box if a user enters an invalid value (in this case, an InvoiceAmt field value of $10 or less). After you set these two InvoiceAmt field properties in the tblBilling table, users will be prevented from entering an invalid InvoiceAmt field value in the tblBilling table and in all current and future queries and future forms that include the InvoiceAmt field.

You'll now set the Validation Rule and Validation Text properties for the InvoiceAmt field in the tblBilling table.

### To create and test a field validation rule for the InvoiceAmt field:

1. Open the **tblBilling** table in Design view, close the Navigation Pane, and then click the **InvoiceAmt Field Name** box to make that row the current row.

   To make sure that all values entered in the InvoiceAmt field are greater than 10, you'll use the > comparison operator in the Validation Rule box.

2. In the Field Properties pane, click the **Validation Rule** box, type **>10**, and then press **TAB**.

   You can set the Validation Text property to a value that appears in a dialog box that opens if a user enters a value not listed in the Validation Rule box.

3. In the Validation Text box, type **Invoice amounts must be greater than 10** as the message. See Figure 5–40.

| Figure 5–40 | Validation properties for the InvoiceAmt field |
| --- | --- |

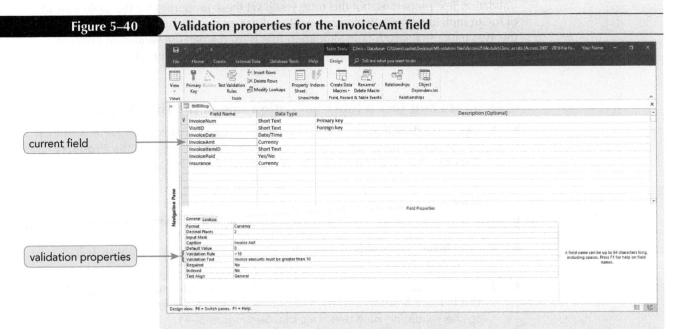

current field

validation properties

You can now save the table design changes and then test the validation properties.

▶ **4.** Save the table, and then click the **Yes** button when asked if you want to test the existing InvoiceAmt field values in the tblBilling table against the new validation rule.

The existing records in the tblBilling table are tested against the validation rule. If any existing record violated the rule, you would be prompted to continue testing or to revert to the previous Validation Rule property setting. Next, you'll test the validation rule.

▶ **5.** Switch to Datasheet view, select **$125.00** in the first row's InvoiceAmt field box, type **5**, and then press **TAB**. A dialog box opens containing the message "Invoice amounts must be greater than 10", which is the Validation Text property setting you created in Step 3.

▶ **6.** Click the **OK** button, and then press **ESC**. The first row's InvoiceAmt field reverts to its original value, $125.00.

▶ **7.** Close the tblBilling table.

Now that you've finished entering the field validation rule for the InvoiceAmt field in the tblBilling table, you'll enter the table validation rule for the date fields in the tblVisit table.

## Defining Table Validation Rules

To make sure that the Insurance field value that a user enters in the tblBilling table is not larger than the InvoiceAmt field value, you can create a **table validation rule**, which compares one field value in a table record to another field value in the same record to verify their relative accuracy. Once again, you'll use the Validation Rule and Validation Text properties, but this time you'll set these properties for the table instead of for an individual field. You'll use a table validation rule because this validation involves multiple fields. A field validation rule is used when the validation involves a restriction for only the selected field and does not depend on other fields.

**To create and test a table validation rule in the tblBilling table:**

Be sure "Table Properties" is listed as the selection type in the property sheet.

▶ **1.** Open the **tblBilling** table in Design view, close the Navigation Pane, and then on the Table Tools Design tab, in the Show/Hide group, click the **Property Sheet** button to open the property sheet for the table.

To make sure that each Insurance field value is less than or equal to the InvoiceAmt field value, you use the Validation Rule box for the table.

▶ **2.** In the property sheet, click the **Validation Rule** box.

▶ **3.** Type **Insur**, press **TAB** to select Insurance in the AutoComplete box, type **<= InvoiceAm**, and then press **TAB**.

▶ **4.** In the Validation Text box, type **Insurance coverage cannot be larger than the invoice amount** and then, if necessary, widen the Property Sheet pane so the Validation Rule text is visible. See Figure 5–41.

Figure 5–41    Setting table validation properties

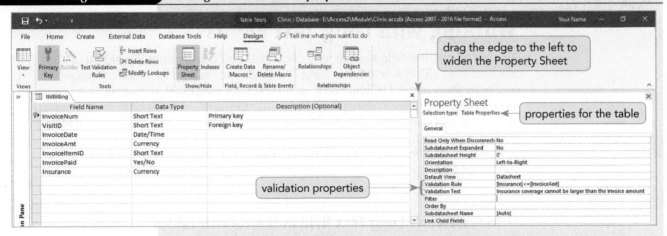

5. Close the property sheet, save the table, and then click the **Yes** button when asked if you want to test the existing dates in the tblBilling table against the new validation rule.

6. Switch to Datasheet view, and then click the Insurance column value in the first record.

7. Edit the Insurance value to change it to $150.00, and then press **TAB** to complete your changes to the record. A dialog box opens containing the message "Insurance coverage cannot be larger than the invoice amount," which is the Validation Text property setting you entered in Step 4.

   Unlike field validation rule violations, which are detected immediately after you finish a field entry and advance to another field, table validation rule violations are detected only when you finish all changes to the current record and advance to another record.

8. Click the **OK** button, and then press **ESC** to undo your change to the Insurance column value.

9. Close the tblBilling table.

**PROSKILLS**

*Problem Solving: Perfecting Data Quality*

It's important that you design useful queries, forms, and reports and that you test them thoroughly. But the key to any database is the accuracy of the data stored in its tables. The data must be as error-free as possible. Most companies employ people who spend many hours tracking down and correcting errors and discrepancies in their data, and you can greatly assist and minimize their problem solving by using as many database features as possible to ensure the data is correct from the start. Among these features for fields are selecting the proper data type, setting default values whenever possible, restricting the permitted values by using field and table validation rules, enforcing referential integrity, and forcing users to select values from lists instead of typing the values. Likewise, having an arsenal of queries—such as find duplicates and top values queries—available to users will expedite the work they do to find and correct data errors.

Based on a request from Donna, Reginald added a Long Text field to the tblVisit table. Next you'll review Reginald's work.

# Working with Long Text Fields

You use a Long Text field to store long comments and explanations. Short Text fields are limited to 255 characters, but Long Text fields can hold up to 65,535 characters. In addition, Short Text fields limit you to plain text with no special formatting, but you can define Long Text fields to store plain text similar to Short Text fields or to store rich text, which you can selectively format with options such as bold, italic, and different fonts and colors.

You'll review the Long Text field, named Comments, that Reginald added to the tblVisit table.

### To review the Long Text field in the tblVisit table:

1. Open the Navigation Pane, open the **tblVisit** table in Datasheet view, and then close the Navigation Pane.

2. Increase the width of the Comments field so most of the comments fit in the column.

   Although everything fits on the screen when using a screen of average size and resolution, on some computer systems, you need to freeze panes to view everything at once. On a smaller screen, if you scroll to the right to view the Comments field, you'll no longer be able to identify which patient applies to a row because the Patient ID column will be hidden. You may also see this effect if you shrink the size of the Access window. You'll freeze the Visit ID, Patient ID, and Date of Visit columns so they remain visible in the datasheet as you scroll to the right.

3. Click the **Visit ID column** selector, press and hold down **SHIFT**, click the **Date of Visit** column selector, and then release **SHIFT**. The Visit ID, Patient ID, and Date of Visit columns are selected.

4. On the Home tab, in the Records group, click the **More** button, and then click **Freeze Fields**.

5. If necessary, reduce the size of the Access window so not all columns are visible, and then scroll to the right until you see the Comments column. Notice that the Visit ID, Patient ID, and Date of Visit columns, the three leftmost columns, remain visible when you scroll. See Figure 5–42.

| Figure 5–42 | Freezing three datasheet columns |

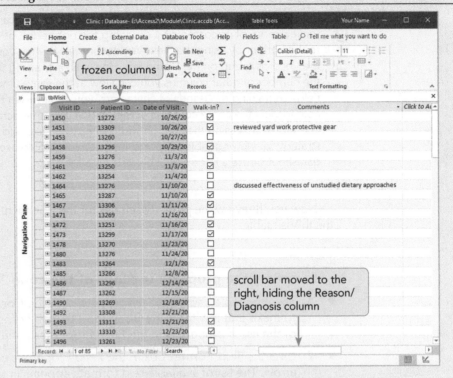

The Comments column is a Long Text field that Lakewood Community Health Services clinicians use to store observations and other commentary about each patient visit.

6. Scroll down if necessary so Visit ID 1557 is visible.

Note that the Comment for Visit ID 1557 displays rich text using a bold and green font. The Comments field values are partially hidden because the datasheet column is not wide enough. You'll view a record's Comments field value in the Zoom dialog box.

7. Click the **Comments** box for the record for Visit ID 1557, hold down **SHIFT**, press **F2**, and then release **SHIFT**. The Zoom dialog box displays the entire Comments field value.

8. Click the **OK** button to close the Zoom dialog box.

INSIGHT

## Viewing Long Text Fields with Large Contents in Datasheet View

For a Long Text field that contains many characters, you can widen the field's column to view more of its contents by dragging the right edge of the field's column selector to the right or by using the Field Width command when you click the More button in the Records group on the Home tab. However, increasing the column width reduces the number of other columns you can view at the same time. Further, for Long Text fields containing thousands of characters, you can't widen the column enough to be able to view the entire contents of the field at one time across the width of the screen. Therefore, increasing the column width of a Long Text field isn't necessarily the best strategy for viewing table contents. Instead, you should use the Zoom dialog box in a datasheet or use a large scrollable box on a form.

Now you'll review the property settings for the Comments field Reginald added to the tblVisit table.

### To review the property settings of the Long Text field:

1. Save the table, switch to Design view, click the **Comments Field Name** box to make that row the current row, and then, if necessary, scroll to the bottom of the list of properties in the Field Properties pane.

2. Click the **Text Format** box in the Field Properties pane, and then click its arrow. The list of available text formats appears in the box. See Figure 5–43.

| Figure 5–43 | Viewing the properties for a Long Text field |

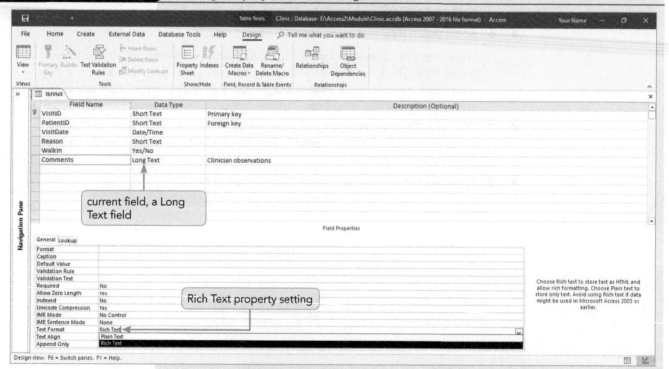

Reginald set the **Text Format property** for the Comments field to Rich Text, which lets you format the field contents using the options in the Font group on the Home tab. The default Text Format property setting for a Long Text field is Plain Text, which doesn't allow text formatting.

▶ **3.** Click the **arrow** on the Text Format box to close the list, and then click the **Append Only** box.

The **Append Only property**, which appears at the bottom of the list of properties, enables you to track the changes that you make to a Long Text field. Setting this property to Yes causes a historical record of all versions of the Long Text field value to be maintained. You can view each version of the field value, along with a date and time stamp of when each version change occurred.

You've finished your review of the Long Text field, so you can close the table.

▶ **4.** Close the tblVisit table.

When employees at Lakewood Community Health Services open the Clinic database, a security warning might appear below the ribbon, and they must enable the content of the database before beginning their work. Donna asks if you can eliminate this extra step when employees open the database.

# Designating a Trusted Folder

A database is a file, and files can contain malicious instructions that can damage other files on your computer or files on other computers on your network. Unless you take special steps, every database is treated as a potential threat to your computer. One special step that you can take is to designate a folder as a trusted folder. A **trusted folder** is a folder on a drive or network that you designate as trusted and where you place databases you know are safe. When you open a database located in a trusted folder, Access no longer displays a security warning. You can also place files used with other Microsoft Office programs, such as Word documents and Excel workbooks, in a trusted folder to eliminate warnings when you open them.

Because the Clinic database is from a trusted source, you'll specify its location as a trusted folder to eliminate the security warning when a user opens the database.

**To designate a trusted folder:**

▶ **1.** Click the **File** tab, and then click **Options** in the navigation bar. The Access Options dialog box opens.

▶ **2.** In the left section of the dialog box, click **Trust Center**. The Trust Center options are displayed in the dialog box.

▶ **3.** In the right section of the dialog box, click the **Trust Center Settings** button to open the Trust Center dialog box.

▶ **4.** In the left section of the Trust Center dialog box, click **Trusted Locations**. The trusted locations for your installation of Access and other trust options are displayed on the right. See Figure 5–44.

**Figure 5-44**    **Designating a trusted folder**

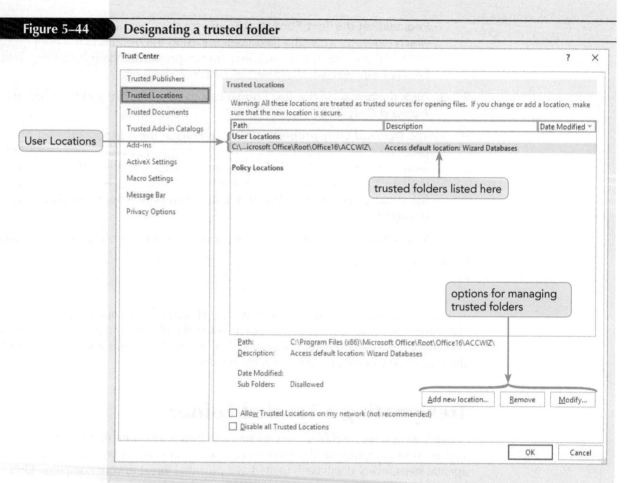

Existing trusted locations appear in the list at the top, and options to add, remove, and modify trusted locations appear at the bottom.

**Trouble?** Check with your instructor before adding a new trusted location. If your instructor tells you not to create a new trusted location, skip to Step 8.

5. Click the **Add new location** button to open the Microsoft Office Trusted Location dialog box.

6. In the Microsoft Office Trusted Location dialog box, click the **Browse** button, navigate to the Access2 > Module folder where your Data Files are stored, and then click the **OK** button.

You can also choose to designate subfolders of the selected location as trusted locations, but you won't select this option. By default, files in subfolders are not trusted.

7. Click the **OK** button. The Access2 > Module folder is added to the list of trusted locations.

8. Click the **OK** button to close the Trust Center dialog box, and then click the **OK** button to close the Access Options dialog box.

You've created several queries and completed several table design changes, so you should compact and repair the Clinic database. Reginald doesn't use the Compact on Close option with the Clinic database because it's possible to lose the database if there's a computer malfunction when the Compact on Close operation runs.

As a precaution, you'll make a backup copy of the database before you compact and repair it. Making frequent backup copies of your critical files safeguards your data from hardware and software malfunctions, which can occur at any time.

### To back up, compact, and repair the Clinic database:

1. Click the **File** tab on the ribbon, and then click the **Save As** menu item.

2. Click the **Back Up Database** option, and then click the **Save As** button. The Save As dialog box opens with a suggested filename of Clinic_date in the File name box, where date is the current date in the format year-month-day. For instance, if you made a backup on April 22, 2021, the suggested filename would be Clinic_2021-04-22.

3. Navigate to the location of a USB drive or other external medium, if available, and then click the **Save** button to save the backup file.

   Next, you'll verify that the trusted location is working.

4. Click the **File** tab on the ribbon, and then click the **Close** command to close the Clinic database.

5. Click the **File** tab on the ribbon, click **Open** on the navigation bar, and then click **Clinic.accdb** in the Recent list. The database opens, and no security warning appears below the ribbon because the database is located in the trusted location you designated.

   Next, you'll compact and repair the database.

6. Click the **File** tab on the ribbon, and then click the **Compact & Repair Database** button.

7. **sam**⬆ Close the Clinic database.

You've completed the table design changes to the Clinic database, which will make working with it easier and more accurate.

## REVIEW

### Session 5.3 Quick Check

1. What is a lookup field?

2. A(n) _____ is a predefined format you use to enter and display data in a field.

3. What is property propagation?

4. Define the Validation Rule property, and give an example of when you would use it.

5. Define the Validation Text property, and give an example of when you would use it.

6. Setting a Long Text field's Text Format property to _____ lets you format its contents.

7. A(n) _____ folder is a location where you can place databases that you know are safe.

PRACTICE

## Review Assignments

**Data File needed for the Review Assignments: Supplier.accdb**

Donna asks you to create several new queries and enhance the table design for the Supplier database. This database contains information about the vendors that Lakewood Community Health Services works with to obtain medical supplies and equipment for the center, as well as the vendors who service and maintain the equipment. Complete the following steps:

1. Open the **Supplier** database located in the Access2 > Review folder provided with your Data Files.
2. Modify the first record in the tblSupplier table datasheet by changing the ContactFirst and ContactLast Name field values to your first and last names, if necessary. Close the table.
3. Create a query called **qrySupplierNameAndAddress** that lists the following fields from the tblSupplier table: SupplierID, Company, City, State, and Zip. After you have created the query, use the AutoFilter feature of Access to list the suppliers in MD, PA, and VA only. Use the Toggle Filter button to remove and reapply the filter. Save and close the query.
4. Create a query to find all records in the tblSupplier table in which the City field value starts with the letter R. Display all fields in the query recordset, and sort in ascending order by the company name. Save the query as **qryRSelectedCities**, run the query, and then close it.
5. Make a copy of the qryRSelectedCities query using the new name **qryOtherSelectedCities**.
6. Modify the new query to find all records in the tblSupplier table in which the City field values are not Durham, Pittsburgh, or Richmond. Save and run the query, and then close it.
7. Create a query to find all records from the tblSupplier table in which the State value is GA, NC, or SC. Use a list-of-values match for the selection criteria. Display all fields in the query recordset, and sort in descending order by the company name. Save the query as **qrySelectedStates**, run the query, and then close it.
8. Create a query to display all records from the tblSupplier table, selecting the Company, City, and Phone fields, and sorting in ascending order by Company. Add a calculated field named **ContactName** as the last column that concatenates the ContactFirst value, a space, and the ContactLast value. If the contact has a nickname, use the nickname in place of the first name in the calculated field. Set the Caption property for the ContactName field to **Contact Name**. Save the query as **qryCompanyContacts**, run the query, resize the Contact Name column to its best fit, and then save and close the query.
9. Create a parameter query to select the tblSupplier table records for a State field value that the user specifies, using **Type the state**: as the prompt text. If the user doesn't enter a State field value, select all records from the table. Display the Company, Category, City, State, ContactFirst, ContactLast, and Phone fields in the query recordset, sorting in ascending order by City. Save the query as **qryStateParameter**. Run the query and enter no value as the State field value, and then run the query again and enter **WI** as the State field value. Close the query.
10. Create a crosstab query based on the tblSupplier table. Use the Category field values for the row headings, the SupplierID field values for the column headings, and the count of the Company field values as the summarized value. Include row sums. Save the query as **qrySupplierCategoryCrosstab**. Change the column heading for the total of each category to **Total of Companies**. Resize the Total of Companies column in the query recordset to its best fit, and then save and close the query.
11. Create a find duplicates query based on the tblProduct table. Select ProductName as the field that might contain duplicates, and select the ProductID, SupplierID, Price, and Units fields as additional fields in the query recordset. Save the query as **qryDuplicateProductTypes**, run the query, and then close it. Because the tblProduct table does not have any duplicate ProductName values, running this query should show that no duplicate records are found.
12. Create a find unmatched query that finds all records in the tblSupplier table that do not have a matching record in the tblProduct table. Select SupplierID as the information in both tables and choose Company, Phone, ContactFirst, ContactNickname, ContactLast, InitialContact, and

LatestContact as the fields for the query results. Specify **qryUnusedSuppliers** as the query name, view the results, and verify that one supplier is listed.

13. Create a query to display all records from the tblProduct table, selecting the ProductID, SupplierID, ProductName, and Price fields, and sorting in descending order by Price. Use the Top Values property to select the top 25 percent of records. Save the query as **qryTop25Price**, run the query, and then close it.

14. In the tblProduct table, change the SupplierID field to a lookup field. Select the Company field and then the SupplierID field from the tblSupplier table. Sort in ascending order by the Company field, do not hide the key column, make sure the Company column is the leftmost column, resize the lookup columns to their best fit, select SupplierID as the field to store in the table, and accept the default label for the lookup column. View the tblProduct table datasheet, resize the Supplier ID column to its best fit, test the lookup field without changing a value permanently, and then save and close the table.

15. Use the Input Mask Wizard to add an input mask to the Phone field in the tblSupplier table. The ending input mask should use periods as separators, as in 987.654.3210 with only the last seven digits required; do not store the literal display characters, if you are asked to do so. Update the Input Mask property everywhere the Phone field is used. Resize all columns in the datasheet to their best fit, and then test the input mask by typing over an existing Phone field value, being sure not to change the value by pressing ESC after you type the last digit in the Phone field.

16. Set a field validation rule on the Price field in the tblProduct table. Ensure that each product entered will have a price greater than zero. Should a user attempt to enter a value of zero, or less than zero, the following message should be displayed: **All prices must be greater than zero**. Test the field validation rule by modifying the price of the first item in the recordset to 0, and verify that the error message is displayed. Reset the value of the record to its original value. Save and close the tblProduct table.

17. Open the tblSupplier table, and then set a table validation rule on the tblSupplier table to ensure the initial contact date is prior to, or equal to, the latest contact date. If an invalid value is entered, the following message should be displayed: "Latest contact date cannot be prior to the initial contact date." Test the table validation rule by changing the latest contact date prior to the initial contact date in the first record. Advance to the next record, then verify that the error message is displayed. Reset the values of the first record to their original values. Save your changes to the tblSupplier table.

18. Open the tblProduct table, and then open the Object Dependencies pane for the tblProduct object. Click the Objects that depend on me option button, and then click the Refresh link if necessary to see the list of objects that depend upon the tblProduct table. Verify that the tblSupplier table depends upon the tblProduct table, as well as the following queries: qryEquipmentOrTempControl, qryFLSuppliers, qryHighPriceAndSterile, qryHighPriceWithDiscount, qryPriceStatistics, qryPriceStatisticsBySupplier, qryTop25Price, and qryUnusedSuppliers. (Note that various forms and reports will depend on the tblProduct table as well.) Close the Object Dependencies pane.

19. In the tblSupplier table, examine the Field Properties pane for the CompanyComments field. Verify that the Text Format property is set to Rich Text, and that the Append Only property is set to Yes. Close the tblSupplier table without saving changes.

20. Designate the Access2 > Review folder as a trusted folder. (*Note:* Check with your instructor before adding a new trusted location.)

21. Make a backup copy of the database, compact and repair the database, and then close it.

## Case Problem 1

**Data File needed for this Case Problem: School.accdb**

***Great Giraffe*** Jeremiah Garver is the operations manager at Great Giraffe, a career school in Denver, Colorado. Great Giraffe offers part-time and full-time courses in areas of study that are in high demand by industries in the area, including data science, digital marketing, and bookkeeping. Jeremiah created an Access database named School to store data about courses, registrations, and students. He wants to create several new queries and make design changes to the tables. Complete the following steps:

1. Open the **School** database located in the Access2 > Case1 folder provided with your Data Files.

2. Modify the first record in the tblStudent table datasheet by changing the First Name and Last Name column values to your first and last names, if necessary. Close the table.

3. Create a query to find all records in the tblStudent table in which the LastName field begins with H. Display the FirstName, LastName, City, and Phone fields in the query recordset, and sort in ascending order by LastName. Save the query as **qryLastNameH**, run the query, and then close it.

4. Create a query that finds all records in the tblCourse table with a Title value of Computer Science or Data Science. Use a list-of-values criterion and include the fields Title, StartDate, and HoursPerWeek in the query recordset, sorted in ascending order by StartDate. Save the query as **qryCompOrDataSci**, run the query, and then close it.

5. Create a query that finds all records in the tblStudent table in which the City field value is not equal to Denver. Display the FirstName, LastName, City, and Email fields in the query recordset, and sort in ascending order by City. Save the query as **qryNonDenver**, run the query, and then close it.

6. Create a query to display the InstanceID, TotalCost, and BalanceDue fields from the tblRegistration table and the Phone and Email fields from the tblStudent table. Find all records for which the BalanceDue value is greater than 0. Add a calculated field named **Payer** as the first column that concatenates FirstName, a space, LastName, and (student) if the BillingLastName field is null. Otherwise, the calculated field should concatenate BillingFirstName, a space, BillingLastName, and (billing). Sort the results on the calculated field in ascending order. Save the query as **qryBalanceContacts**, run the query, resize all columns to their best fit, and then save and close the query.

7. Create a parameter query to select the tblStudent table records for a City field value that the user specifies, using **Enter the city:** as the prompt text. If the user doesn't enter a City field value, select all records from the table. Display all fields from the tblStudent table in the query recordset. Save the query as **qryStudentCityParameter**. Run the query and enter no value as the City field value, and then run the query again and enter **Littleton** as the City field value. Close the query.

8. Create a find duplicates query based on the tblRegistration table. Select StudentID as the field that might contain duplicates, and select all other fields in the table as additional fields in the query recordset. Save the query as **qryDuplicateStudentRegistrations**, run the query, and then close it. Because the tblRegistration contains one student registered for two different courses, running this query should show that two records are found containing a duplicate StudentID.

9. Create a find unmatched query that finds all records in the tblStudent table for which there is no matching record in the tblRegistration table. Select the FirstName, LastName, Phone, and Email fields from the tblStudents table. Save the query as **qryUnregisteredStudents**, run the query, and then close it. Running this query should find five unmatched records.

10. Create a new query based on the tblStudent and tblRegistration tables. In the query recordset, display the FirstName, LastName, BillingFirstName, BillingLastName, Phone, and Email fields from the tblStudent table and the TotalCost and BalanceDue fields from the tblRegistration table. Sort in descending order by the BalanceDue field, and then use the Top Values property to select the top 5% of records. Save the query as **qryTopOutstandingBalances**, run the query, and then close it.

11. Use the Input Mask Wizard to add an input mask to the Phone field in the tblStudent table. The input mask should use periods as separators, as in 987.654.3210, with only the last seven digits required. Do not store the literal display characters if you are asked to do so, and apply the updated image mask everywhere it is used within the database. Resize the Phone column to its best fit, and then test the input mask by typing over an existing Phone column value, being certain not to change the value by pressing ESC after you type the last digit in the Phone column. Save and close the table.

12. Create a crosstab query based on the tblCourse table. Specify the HoursPerWeek values as the row headings and the Title field values as the column headings, calculate the InstanceID count, and include row sums. Save the query as **qryFullPartTimeCrosstab**, view the results, resize the columns as necessary, then save and close the query.

13. In the tblRegistration table, change the InstanceID field data type to Lookup Wizard. Select the Title, StartDate, and HoursPerWeek fields from the tblCourse table, sort in ascending order by Title, do not show the key column, resize the lookup columns to their best fit, select InstanceID as the field to store in the table, and accept the default label for the lookup column. View the tblRegistration datasheet, resize the InstanceID column to its best fit, test the lookup field without changing a field value permanently, and then close the table.

14. Define a field validation rule for the HoursPerWeek field in the tblCourse table. Acceptable field values for the HoursPerWeek field are values less than or equal to 40. Enter the message **Hours per week cannot be greater than 40** so it appears if a user enters an invalid HoursPerWeek field value. Save your table changes, and then test the field validation rule for the HoursPerWeek field; be certain the field values are the same as they were before your testing, and then close the table.

15. Define a table validation rule for the tblCourse table to verify that StartDate field values precede EndDate field values in time. Use **The course start date must come before the course end date** as the validation message. Save your table changes, and then test the table validation rule, making sure any tested field values are the same as they were before your testing.

16. Designate the Access2 > Case1 folder as a trusted folder. (*Note:* Check with your instructor before adding a new trusted location.)

17. Make a backup copy of the database, compact and repair the database, and then close it.

TROUBLESHOOT

## Case Problem 2

**Data File needed for this Case Problem: Storm.accdb**

***Drain Adopter***   Tandrea Austin manages the Drain Adopter program for the Department of Water and Power in Bellingham, Washington. The program recruits volunteers to regularly monitor and clear storm drains near their homes to ensure the drains are clear and unobstructed when large rainstorms are predicted. The program has been a hit with residents, and has increased the capacity of department staff to deal with other issues that arise during major storms.

Tandrea created an Access database to maintain information about the residents who have signed up for the program, the locations of selected storm drains throughout the city, and the inventory of supplies given to program participants, such as safety vests and gloves. To make the database easier to use, Tandrea wants you to create several queries and modify its table design. Complete the following steps:

1. Open the **Storm** database located in the Access2 > Case2 folder provided with your Data Files.

2. Change the first record in the tblVolunteer table datasheet so the FirstName and LastName field values contain your first and last names.

⚙ **Troubleshoot** 3. In the tblVolunteer table datasheet, examine the Phone field values. The input mask for this field displays an incorrect parenthesis character, and allows entry of a phone number with only seven digits. Change the input mask so it displays phone numbers using the format (987) 654-3210 and requires users to enter all 10 digits. Apply the updated image mask everywhere it is used within the database. Resize the Phone column to its best fit, and then test the input mask by typing over an existing Phone column value, being certain not to change the value by pressing ESC after you type the last digit in the Phone column. Save and close the table.

⚙ **Troubleshoot** 4. Open the qryNewestVolunteers query, and then examine the results in the datasheet. Tandrea wants the query to use the Top Values property to show only the five most recently signed up volunteers, but the datasheet currently displays eight results. Make changes to the query design so it shows only the top five results for this query, then save and close the query.

⚙ **Troubleshoot** 5. Open the qryTrainedOrSignupDate query, then examine the results in the datasheet. The third column, Expr1, is a calculated column. Tandrea wants this to show the word "trained" if the Trained field value is yes; otherwise, she wants to show the text "Signed up" followed by a space and the value of the SignupDate field. Currently the values are reversed, with dates showing for trained volunteers, and "trained" showing for untrained volunteers. Tandrea would also like the field to display the caption Status. Edit the calculated column to make the requested changes, then save and close the query.

6. Create a find duplicates query based on the tblDrain table. Select VolunteerID as the field that might contain duplicates, and select DrainID, MainStreet, and CrossStreet as additional fields in the query recordset. Save the query as **qryMultipleAdopters**, run the query, and then close it.

7. Create a find unmatched query that finds all records in the tblVolunteers table for which there is no matching record in the tblDrain table. Display the FirstName, LastName, Phone, Email, SignupDate, and Trained fields from the tblVolunteer table in the query recordset. Save the query as **qryVolunteersWithoutDrains**, run the query, and then close it.

8. Create a parameter query to select the tblDrain table records for a CrossStreet field value that the user specifies the starting characters for. If the user doesn't enter a CrossStreet field value, select all records from the table. Include the DrainID, MainStreet, CrossStreet, and Direction fields from the tblDrain table in the query recordset. Save the query as **qryCrossStreetParameter**. Run the query and enter no value as the start of the CrossStreet field value, and then run the query again and enter **44** as the start of the CrossStreet field value. Close the query.

9. Create a crosstab query based on the tblVolunteer table. Use the Trained field values for the row headings, the Zip field values for the column headings, and the count of the VolunteerID field values as the summarized value, and include row sums. Save the query as **qryTrainedVolunteersCrosstab**. Resize the columns in the query recordset to their best fit, and then save and close the query.

10. Create a query to find all records in the tblSupply table in which the SupplyID field value is Gloves01, Vest01LG, Vest01MD, or Vest01XL. Use a list-of-values criterion, and display all fields in the query recordset, sorted in ascending order by Description. Save the query as **qryClothingSupplies**, run the query, and then close it.

11. Create a query to find all records in the tblVolunteer table in which the Zip field value is not equal to 98225. Display the FirstName, LastName, Zip, Phone, and Email fields in the query recordset, and sort in ascending order by LastName. Save the query as **qryNon98225Volunteers**, run the query, and then close it.

12. In the tblDrain table, change the VolunteerID field data type to Lookup Wizard. Select the FirstName, LastName, and VolunteerID fields from the tblVolunteer table, sort in ascending order by VolunteerID, show the key column and move it to the right of the other two columns, resize the lookup columns to their best fit, select VolunteerID as the field to store in the table, and accept the default label for the lookup column. In Datasheet view, change the VolunteerID value for the first record to verify that the lookup functions correctly, then restore the original VolunteerID value for the first record. Save and close the table.

13. Define a field validation rule for the Direction field in the tblDrain table. Acceptable field values for the Direction field are NE, NW, SE, or SW. Use the message **Direction must be NE, NW, SE, or SW** to notify a user who enters an invalid Direction field value. Save your table changes, test the field validation rule for the Direction field, making sure any tested field values are the same as they were before your testing, and then close the table.

14. Designate the Access2 > Case2 folder as a trusted folder. (*Note:* Check with your instructor before adding a new trusted location.)

15. Make a backup copy of the database, compact and repair the database, and then close it.

MODULE **6**

# Using Form Tools and Creating Custom Forms

*Creating Forms for Lakewood Community Health Services*

ACCESS

## OBJECTIVES

**Session 6.1**
- Change a lookup field to a Short Text field
- View and print database documentation
- Create datasheet, multiple item, and split forms
- Modify a form and anchor form controls in Layout view

**Session 6.2**
- Plan, design, and create a custom form in Design view and in Layout view
- Select, move, align, resize, delete, and rename controls in a form
- Add a combo box to a form
- Add headers and footers to a form

**Session 6.3**
- Use a combo box in a form to find records
- Add a subform to a form
- Add calculated controls to a form and a subform
- Change the tab order in a form
- Improve the appearance of a form

## Case | *Lakewood Community Health Services*

Donna Taylor hired Reginald Morales to enhance the Clinic database, and he initially concentrated on standardizing the table design and creating queries for Lakewood Community Health Services. Donna and her staff created a few forms before Reginald came onboard, and Reginald's next priority is to work with Donna to create new forms that will be more functional and easier to use.

In this module, you will create new forms for Lakewood Community Health Services. In creating the forms, you will use many Access form customization features, such as adding controls and a subform to a form, using combo boxes and calculated controls, and adding color and special effects. These features make it easier for database users like Donna and her staff to interact with a database.

**STARTING DATA FILES**

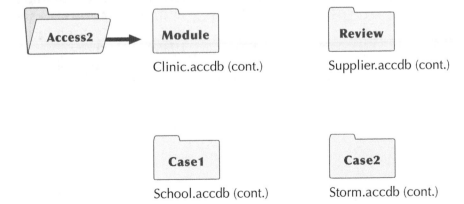

Access2 → Module
Clinic.accdb (cont.)

Review
Supplier.accdb (cont.)

Case1
School.accdb (cont.)

Case2
Storm.accdb (cont.)

# Session 6.1 Visual Overview:

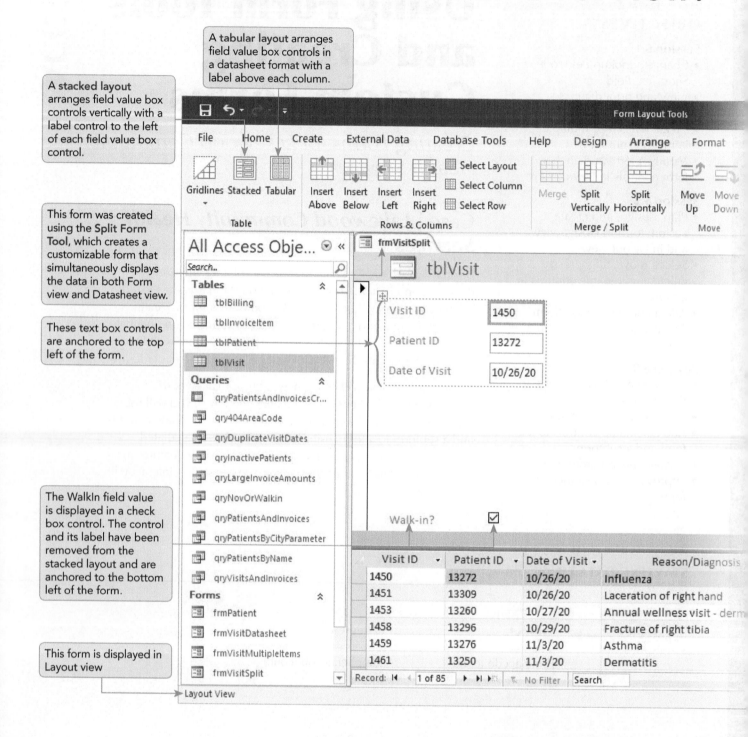

A tabular layout arranges field value box controls in a datasheet format with a label above each column.

A stacked layout arranges field value box controls vertically with a label control to the left of each field value box control.

This form was created using the Split Form Tool, which creates a customizable form that simultaneously displays the data in both Form view and Datasheet view.

These text box controls are anchored to the top left of the form.

The WalkIn field value is displayed in a check box control. The control and its label have been removed from the stacked layout and are anchored to the bottom left of the form.

This form is displayed in Layout view

# Anchoring Controls

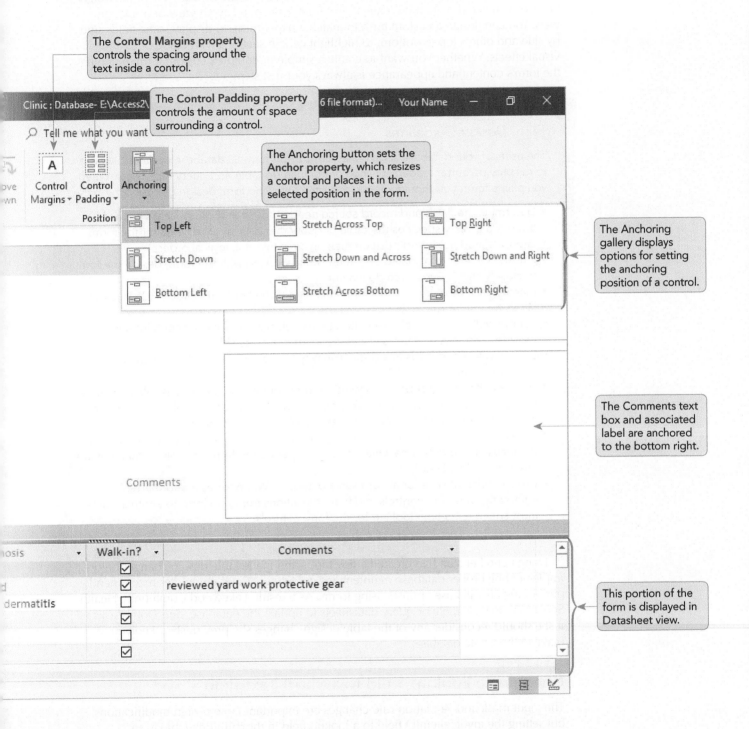

The **Control Margins** property controls the spacing around the text inside a control.

The **Control Padding** property controls the amount of space surrounding a control.

The Anchoring button sets the **Anchor** property, which resizes a control and places it in the selected position in the form.

The Anchoring gallery displays options for setting the anchoring position of a control.

The Comments text box and associated label are anchored to the bottom right.

This portion of the form is displayed in Datasheet view.

# Designing Forms

To create a **custom form**, you can modify an existing form in Layout view or in Design view, or you can design and create a form from scratch in Layout view or in Design view. You can design a custom form to match a paper form, to display some fields side by side and others top to bottom, to highlight certain sections with color, or to add visual effects. Whether you want to create a simple or complex custom form, planning the form's content and appearance is always your first step.

## Form Design Guidelines

The users of your database should use forms to perform all database updates because forms provide better readability and control than do table and query recordsets. When you plan a form, you should keep in mind the following form design guidelines:

- Determine the fields and record source needed for each form. A form's **Record Source property** specifies the table or query that provides the fields for the form.
- Group related fields and position them in a meaningful, logical order.
- If users will refer to a source document while working with the form, design the form to closely match the source document.
- Identify each field value with a label that names the field, and align field values and labels for readability.
- Set the width of each field value box to fully display the values it contains and to provide a visual cue to users about the length of those values.
- Display calculated fields in a distinctive way, and prevent users from changing and updating them.
- Use default values, list boxes, and other form controls whenever possible to reduce user errors by minimizing keystrokes and limiting entries. A control is an item, such as a text box or command button, that you place in a form or report.
- Use colors, fonts, and graphics sparingly to keep the form uncluttered and to keep the focus on the data. Use white space to separate the form controls so that they are easier to find and read.
- Use a consistent style for all forms in a database. When forms are formatted differently, with form controls in different locations from one form to another, users must spend extra time looking for the form controls.

Donna and her staff had created a few forms and made table design changes before implementing proper database maintenance guidelines. These guidelines recommend performing all database updates using forms. As a result, Lakewood Community Health Services won't use table or query datasheets to update the database, and Donna asks if she should reconsider any of the table design changes she previously asked you to make to the Clinic database.

## Changing a Lookup Field to a Short Text field

The input mask and validation rule changes are important table design modifications, but setting the InvoiceItemID field to a lookup field in the tblBilling table is an unnecessary change. A form combo box provides the same capability in a clearer, more flexible way. Many default forms use text boxes. A **text box** is a control that lets users type an entry. A **combo box** is a control that combines the features of a text box and a list box; it lets users either choose a value from a list or type an entry. A text box should be used when users must enter data, while a combo box should be used when there is a finite number of choices. Before creating the new forms for Donna, you'll change the data type of the InvoiceItemID field in the tblBilling table from a Lookup Wizard field to a Short Text field, so that you can create the relationship with referential integrity between the tblBilling and tblInvoiceItems tables.

## To change the data type of the InvoiceItemID field:

1. **sam** ↓ Start Access, and then open the **Clinic** database you worked with in the previous module.

   **Trouble?** If the security warning is displayed below the ribbon, click the Enable Content button.

**TIP**

You can press F11 to open or close the Navigation Pane.

2. Open the Navigation Pane, if necessary, open the **tblBilling** table in Design view, and then close the Navigation Pane.

3. Click the **InvoiceItemID** Field Name box, and then in the Field Properties pane, click the **Lookup** tab. The Field Properties pane displays the lookup properties for the InvoiceItemID field. See Figure 6–1.

**Figure 6–1**     Lookup properties for the InvoiceItemID field

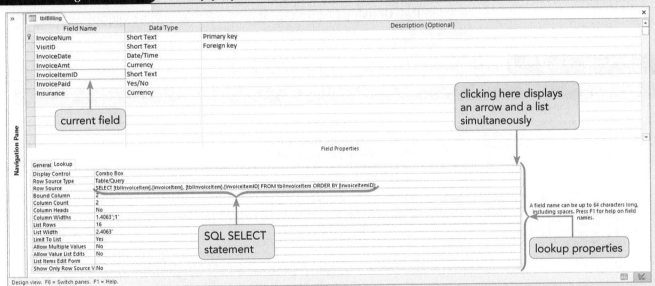

Notice the **Row Source property**, which specifies the data source for a control in a form or report or for a field in a table or query. The Row Source property is usually set to a table name, a query name, or a SQL statement. For the InvoiceItemID field, the Row Source property is set to a SQL SELECT statement.

To remove the lookup feature for the InvoiceItemID field, you need to change the **Display Control property**, which specifies the default control used to display a field, from Combo Box to Text Box.

4. Click the right end of the **Display Control** box, and then click **Text Box** in the list. All the lookup properties in the Field Properties pane disappear, and the InvoiceItemID field changes back to a standard Short Text field without lookup properties.

5. Click the **General** tab in the Field Properties pane, and notice that the properties for a Short Text field still apply to the InvoiceItemID field.

6. Save the table, switch to Datasheet view, resize the Invoice Item ID column to its best fit, and then click one of the Invoice Item ID boxes. An arrow does not appear in the Invoice Item ID box because the InvoiceItemID field is no longer a lookup field.

7. Save the table, and then close the tblBilling table.

Before you could change the InvoiceItemID field in the tblBilling table to a lookup field, you had to delete the one-to-many relationship between the tblInvoiceItem and tblBilling tables. Now that you've changed the data type of the InvoiceItemID field back to a Short Text field, you'll view the table relationships to make sure that the tables in the Clinic database are related correctly.

### To view the table relationships in the Relationships window:

1. Click the **Database Tools** tab, and then in the Relationships group, click the **Relationships** button to open the Relationships window. See Figure 6–2.

| Figure 6–2 | Clinic database tables in the Relationships window |
| --- | --- |

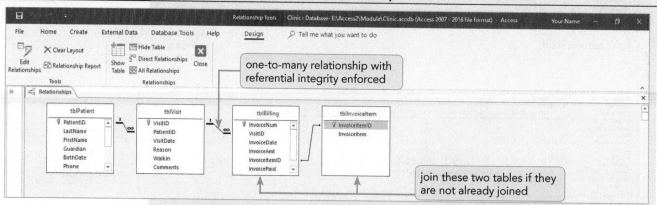

**Trouble?** If the order of the table field lists in your Relationships window do not match Figure 6–2, drag the table field lists to rearrange them so that they appear in the same left-to-right order shown in the figure.

The tblVisit table and the related tblBilling table have a one-to-many relationship with referential integrity enforced. You need to establish a similar one-to-many relationship between the tblInvoiceItem and tblBilling tables.

2. Double-click the **relationship line** between the tblBilling and tblInvoiceItem tables to open the Edit Relationships dialog box.

3. Click the **Enforce Referential Integrity** check box, click the **Cascade Update Related Fields** check box, and then click the **OK** button to close the dialog box. The join line connecting the tblInvoiceItem and tblBilling tables now indicates a one-to-many relationship with referential integrity enforced.

Donna is interested in documenting information on the objects and relationships between objects in the database in a form that she and her staff can use as a reference. In Access, you can create a report of the database relationships. You can also give Donna information on all the objects in the database using the Documenter.

# Creating a Relationship Report and Using the Documenter

From the Relationships window, you can create a Relationship report to document the fields, tables, and relationships in a database. You can also use the **Documenter**, another Access tool, to create detailed documentation of all, or selected, objects in a database. For each selected object, the Documenter lets you print documentation, such as the object's properties and relationships, and the names and properties of fields used by the object. You can use the documentation on an object, referred to as an Object Definition Report, to help you understand the object and to help you plan changes to that object.

**PROSKILLS**

*Written Communication: Satisfying User Documentation Requirements*

The Documenter produces object documentation that is useful to the technical designers, analysts, and programmers who develop and maintain Access databases and who need to understand the intricate details of a database's design. However, users who interact with databases generally have little interest in the documentation produced by the Documenter. Users need to know how to enter and maintain data using forms and how to obtain information using forms and reports, so they require special documentation that matches these needs; this documentation isn't produced by the Documenter, though. Many companies assign one or more users the task of creating the documentation needed by users based on the idea that users themselves are the most familiar with their company's procedures and understand most clearly the specific documentation that they and other users require. Databases with dozens of tables and with hundreds of other objects are complicated structures, so be sure you provide documentation that satisfies the needs of users separate from the documentation for database developers.

Next, you will create a Relationship report and use the Documenter to create documentation for the tblVisit table.

## To create the Relationship report:

▶ **1.** On the Relationship Tools Design tab, in the Tools group, click the **Relationship Report** button to open the Relationships for Clinic report in Print Preview. See Figure 6–3.

| Figure 6–3 | Relationships for Clinic report |
|---|---|

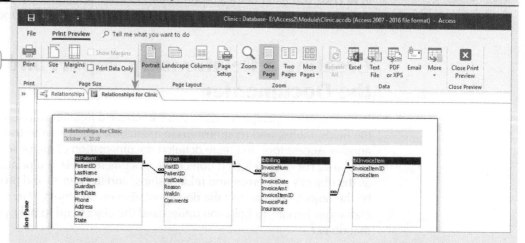

**2.** Right-click the **Relationships for Clinic** tab, and then click **Close** to close the tab. A dialog box opens and asks if you want to save the design of the report.

**3.** Click the **Yes** button to save the report, click the **OK** button to use the default report name Relationships for Clinic, and then close the Relationships window.

Donna wants to show her staff a sample of the information the Documenter provides.

**REFERENCE**

### Using the Documenter

- In the Analyze group on the Database Tools tab, click the Database Documenter button.
- In the Documenter dialog box, select the object(s) you want to document.
- If necessary, click the Options button to open the Print Table Definition dialog box, select specific documentation options for the selected object(s), and then click the OK button.
- Click the OK button to close the Documenter dialog box and open the Object Definition window in Print Preview.
- Print the documentation if desired, and then close the Object Definition window.

You will use the Documenter to create an Object Definition Report on the tblVisit table.

### To use the Documenter to create, save, and print an Object Definition report:

**1.** On the ribbon, click the **Database Tools** tab.

**2.** In the Analyze group, click the **Database Documenter** button to open the Documenter dialog box, and then click the **Tables** tab (if necessary). See Figure 6–4.

**Figure 6-4**    Documenter dialog box

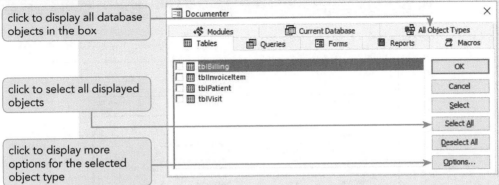

click to display all database objects in the box

click to select all displayed objects

click to display more options for the selected object type

3. Click the **tblVisit** check box, and then click the **Options** button. The Print Table Definition dialog box opens. In this dialog box, you select which documentation you want the Documenter to include for the selected table, its fields, and its indexes.

4. In the Include for Table section, make sure the **Properties**, **Relationships**, and **Permissions by User and Group** check boxes are all checked.

5. In the Include for Fields section, click the **Names, Data Types, and Sizes** option button (if necessary), then in the Include for Indexes section, click the **Names and Fields** option button (if necessary). See Figure 6-5.

**Figure 6-5**    Print Table Definition dialog box

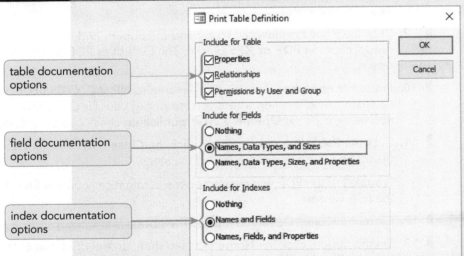

table documentation options

field documentation options

index documentation options

6. Click the **OK** button to close the Print Table Definition dialog box, and then click the **OK** button to close the Documenter dialog box. The Object Definition report opens in Print Preview.

7. On the Print Preview tab, in the Zoom group, click the **Zoom arrow**, and then click **Zoom 100%**. To display more of the report, you will collapse the ribbon.

8. On the right end of the ribbon, click the **Collapse the Ribbon** button ⌃, and then scroll down the report and examine its contents. See Figure 6-6.

| Figure 6–6 | Print Preview of the Object Definition report |

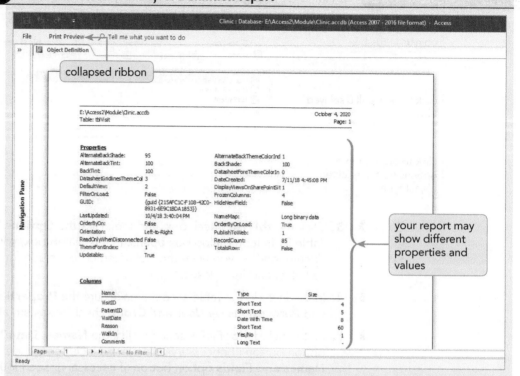

The Object Definition report displays table, field, and relationship documentation for the tblVisit table. Next, you'll export the report and save it as a PDF document.

9. Click the **Print Preview** tab to expand the ribbon, and then in the Data group, click the **PDF or XPS** button. The Publish as PDF or XPS dialog box opens.

10. In the File name box, change the filename to **NP_AC_6_ClinicDocumenter**, navigate to the location where you are saving your files, and then if necessary, click the **Open file after publishing** check box to unselect it.

11. Click the **Publish** button and then click the **Close** button in the Export – PDF dialog box to close without saving the steps.

    **Trouble?** If the PDF you created opens automatically during Step 11, close the PDF viewer.

12. Close the Object Definition report. The ribbon is still collapsed.

13. On the ribbon, click the **Home** tab, and then, on the right end of the ribbon, click the **Pin the ribbon** button ⊞ to expand and pin the ribbon again.

**TIP**

You can also collapse the ribbon by double-clicking any ribbon tab or by right-clicking a blank area of the ribbon and clicking Collapse the Ribbon on the shortcut menu.

The Clinic database currently contains the frmPatient form. The frmPatient form was created using the Form Wizard with some design changes that were made in Layout view including changing the theme, changing the form title color and line type, adding a picture, and moving a field. Next Donna would like you to create a form that allows her and her staff to see and modify the relevant data for patient visits. You will create this form using other form tools.

# Creating Forms Using Form Tools

You can create forms with and without subforms using the Form Wizard. You can create other types of forms using different form tools, namely the Datasheet tool, the Multiple Items tool, and the Split Form tool.

**PROSKILLS**

## Decision Making: Creating Multiple Forms and Reports

When developing a larger database application, it's not uncommon for the users of the database to be unsure as to what they want with respect to forms and reports. You may obtain some sample data and sample reports during the requirements-gathering phase that give you some ideas, but in the end, it is a good idea to have the users approve the final versions.

While you are actively developing the application, you might design different versions of forms and reports that you think will meet users' needs; later in the process, you might narrow the selection to a few forms and reports. Ultimately, you should ask the users to make the final choices of which forms and reports to incorporate into the database. By involving the users in the planning phase for forms and reports, the database is more likely to meet everyone's needs.

Donna has requested a form that her staff can use to work with information from the tblVisit table. Because her requirements at this point are vague, you'll create a selection of form designs for Donna to choose from. You'll create two simple forms that show the contents of the tblVisit table in a layout that resembles a table, and you'll create a custom form that Donna's staff may find a bit more user-friendly. First, you'll create the simple forms for Donna and her staff.

## Creating a Form Using the Datasheet Tool

You can create a simple form using the Datasheet Tool. The **Datasheet tool** creates a form in a datasheet format that contains all the fields in the source table or query. Donna might prefer this if she and her staff are very comfortable entering data in an Access table in Datasheet view. You'll use the Datasheet tool to create a form based on the tblVisit table. When you use the Datasheet tool, the record source (either a table or query) for the form must be open or selected in the Navigation Pane.

**To create the form using the Datasheet tool:**

1. Open the Navigation Pane, and then click **tblVisit**.

2. On the ribbon, click the **Create** tab.

3. In the Forms group, click the **More Forms** button, click **Datasheet**, and then, if necessary, close the Property Sheet. The Datasheet tool creates a form showing every field in the tblVisit table in a datasheet format. See Figure 6–7.

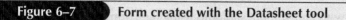

**Figure 6–7** Form created with the Datasheet tool

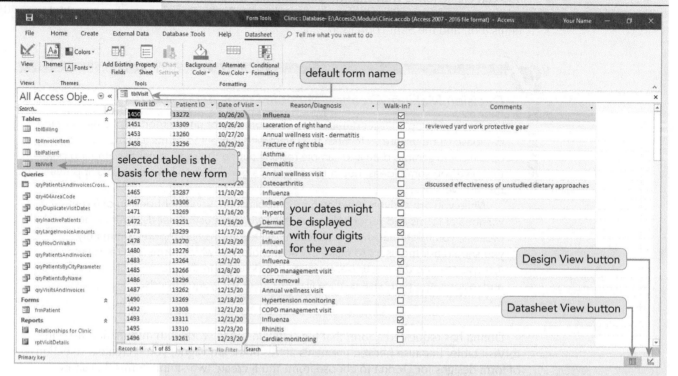

**Trouble?** Depending on your computer's settings, the dates in the Date of Visit column may be displayed with either two or four digits for the year. If your date format is different from that shown in the figures, it will not cause a problem.

The form resembles the Datasheet view for the table except that it does not include the expand buttons at the beginning of each row. The form name, tblVisit, is the same name as the table used as the basis for the form. Recall that each table and query in a database must have a unique name. Although you could give a form or report the same name as a table or query, doing so would likely cause confusion. Fortunately, using object name prefixes prevents this confusing practice, and you will change the name when you save the form.

As you know, when working with forms, you view and update data in Form view, you view and make simple design changes in Layout view, and you make simple and complex design changes in Design view. However, not all of these views are available for every type of form. For the form created with the Datasheet tool, you'll check the available view options.

4. On the Form Tools Datasheet tab, in the Views group, click the **View arrow**. See Figure 6–8.

**Figure 6–8** View options for a form created with the Datasheet tool

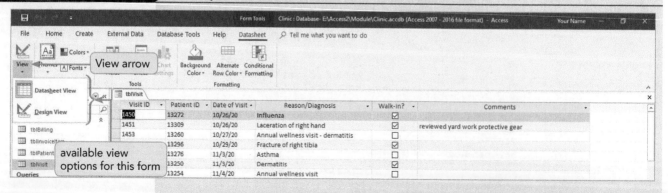

Notice Form view and Layout view are not options on the menu, which means that they are unavailable for this form type. Datasheet view allows you to view and update data, and Design view allows you to modify the form's layout and design. The buttons for accessing these two available views are also on the status bar.

You'll save this form to show Donna as one of the options for the forms for patient visits.

▶ **5.** Save the form as **frmVisitDatasheet**, and then close the form.

Donna might prefer a form created using the Multiple Items tool because it will provide a form with larger text boxes for displaying a record's field values.

## Creating a Form Using the Multiple Items Tool

The **Multiple Items tool** creates a customizable form that displays multiple records from a source table or query in a datasheet format. You'll use the Multiple Items tool to create a form based on the tblVisit table.

### To create the form using the Multiple Items tool:

▶ **1.** Make sure that the tblVisit table is selected in the Navigation Pane, and then click the **Create** tab.

▶ **2.** In the Forms group, click the **More Forms** button, and then click **Multiple Items**. The Multiple Items tool creates a form showing every field in the tblVisit table and opens the form in Layout view. See Figure 6–9.

| Figure 6–9 | Form created with the Multiple Items tool |
| --- | --- |

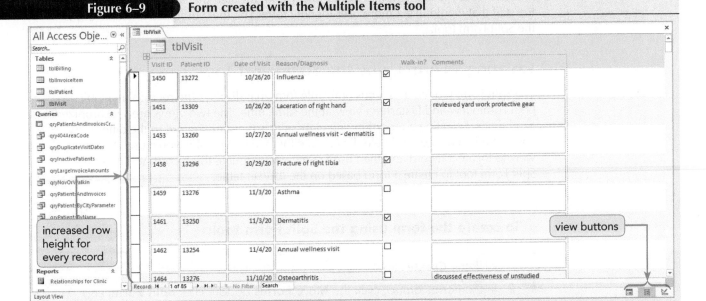

The new form displays all the records and fields from the tblVisit table in a format similar to a datasheet, but the row height for every record is increased compared to a standard datasheet. Unlike a form created with the Datasheet tool, which has only Datasheet view and Design view available, a Multiple Items form is a standard form that can be displayed in Form view, Layout view, and Design view, as indicated by the buttons on the right end of the status bar. You can also access these views for the forms created with the Multiple Items tool from the ribbon.

3. On the Form Layout Tools Design tab, in the Views group, click the **View arrow**. See Figure 6–10.

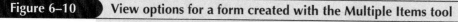

| Figure 6–10 | View options for a form created with the Multiple Items tool |

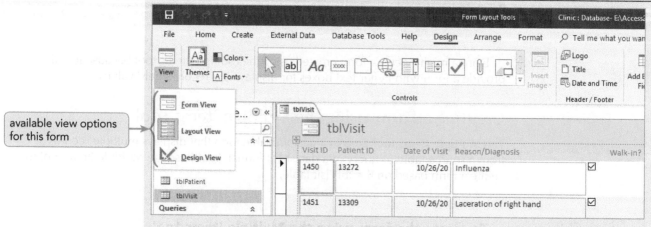

You'll want to show this form to Donna as one of the options, so you'll save it.

4. Save the form as **frmVisitMultipleItems**, and then close the form.

The final form you'll create to show Donna will include two sections, one providing the standard form inputs of field value boxes and the other section showing the table in Datasheet view. She might like this to satisfy both the staff that are more technical and the staff that would like a more user-friendly form. The tool you'll use to create this is the Split Form tool.

## Creating a Form Using the Split Form Tool

The Split Form tool creates a customizable form that displays the records in a table in both Form view and Datasheet view at the same time. The two views are synchronized at all times. Selecting a record in one view selects the same record in the other view. You can add, change, or delete data from either view. Typically, you'd use Datasheet view to locate a record and then use Form view to update the record. You'll use the Split Form tool to create a form based on the tblVisit table.

### To create the form using the Split Form tool:

1. Make sure that the tblVisit table is selected in the Navigation Pane, and then click the **Create** tab.

2. In the Forms group, click the **More Forms** button, click **Split Form**, and then close the Navigation Pane. The Split Form tool creates a split form that opens in Layout view and displays a form with the contents of the first record in the tblVisit table in the top section and a datasheet showing the first several records in the tblVisit table in the bottom section. In Layout view,

the form on top presents a record's fields in either a single column or in two columns, depending on the size of the Access window when the form was created. If you have a two-column layout, that won't affect your ability to complete the steps that follow. Figure 6–11 shows the single-column layout.

| Figure 6–11 | Form created with the Split Form tool |

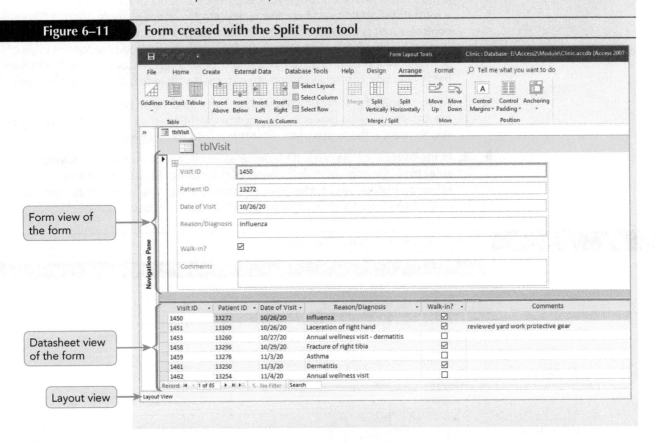

In Layout view, you can make layout and design changes to the form section and layout changes to the datasheet section of the split form.

## Modifying a Split Form in Layout View

In previous modules, you've modified forms using options on the Form Layout Tools Format tab. Additional options for modifying forms are available on the Form Layout Tools Arrange tab. When working with a split form, you use the options on the Form Layout Tools Design tab to add controls and make other modifications to the form section but not to the datasheet section. Also in this case, the options on the Arrange tab apply only to the form section and do not apply to the datasheet section.

Donna notices that first three field value boxes in the form, Visit ID, Patient ID, and Date of Visit, are much wider than necessary. You will resize these field value boxes, and you will also move and resize the Reason/Diagnosis field label and field value box.

## To resize field value boxes in the split form in Layout view:

1. On the ribbon, click the **Form Layout Tools Arrange** tab. The form's field label and field value boxes from the tblVisit table are grouped in a control layout. Recall that a control layout is a set of controls grouped together in a form or report so that you can manipulate the set as a single control. The control layout is a stacked layout, which arranges field value box controls vertically with a label control to the left of each field value box control in one or more vertical columns. You can also choose a tabular layout, which arranges field value box controls in a datasheet format with labels above each column.

   As you know, if you reduce the width of any field value box in a control layout, all the value boxes in the control layout are also resized. Donna wants you to reduce the width of the first three field value boxes only.

2. In the form, click the **Visit ID** label to select it, and then click the **layout selector** ⊞ in the upper-left corner of the control layout. An orange selection border, which identifies the controls that you've selected, appears around the labels and field value boxes in the form. See Figure 6–12.

| Figure 6–12 | Control layout selected in the form |
| --- | --- |

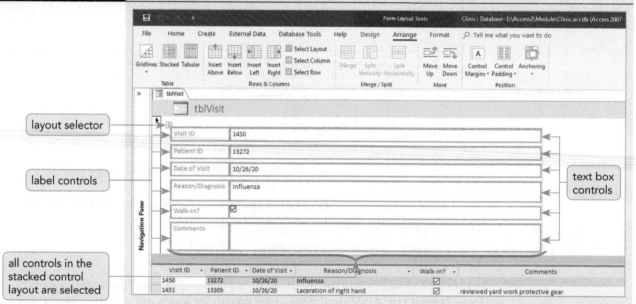

Next, you'll resize the field value boxes in the control layout.

3. Click the **VisitDate** field value box (containing the value 10/26/20) to deselect the control layout and select only the VisitDate field value box.

4. Position the pointer on the right border of the VisitDate field value box until the pointer changes to a horizontal resize pointer ↔, click and drag to the left until the right edge is just to the right of the VisitDate field value, and then release the mouse button. If you have a one-column layout, you've resized all five field value boxes. If you have a two-column layout, you've resized the three field value boxes on the left. Figure 6–13 shows the single-column layout.

| Figure 6–13 | Resized field value boxes in the control layout |

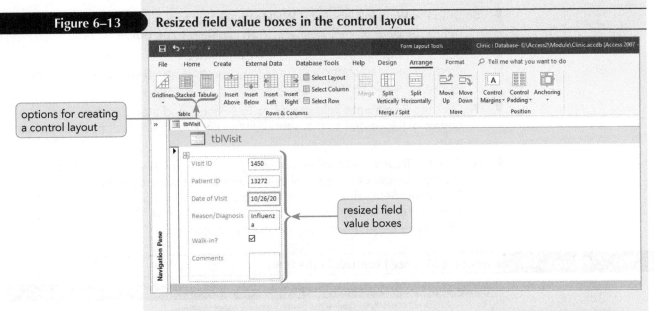

**Trouble?** If you resize the field value boxes too far to the left, number signs appear inside the PatientID and VisitDate value boxes, indicating the boxes are too small to display the full values. Repeat Step 4, this time dragging the right border of the field value box to the right until the values are visible inside these boxes.

With the one-column layout shown in Figure 6–13, the form has too much white space. To better balance the elements in the form, Donna suggests you move and resize the Reason/Diagnosis, Walk-in?, and Comments labels and field value boxes to a second column so that they fill this available space. To do this, you first need to remove these items from the stacked layout control.

### To remove field value labels and boxes from the layout control, and then move and resize them on the form:

1. Click the **Reason/Diagnosis** label, press and hold **CTRL**, click the **Reason** field value box, click the **Walk-in?** label, click the **WalkIn** check box, click the **Comments** label, and then click the **Comments** field value box to select all six controls, and then release **CTRL**.

2. Right-click the **Reason** field value box, point to **Layout** on the shortcut menu, and then click **Remove Layout**. You've removed the six selected controls from the stacked layout.

3. If your form has the single-column layout shown in Figure 6–13, make sure that the six controls are still selected, and then use the move pointer ⌖ to drag them up and to the right until the tops of the Reason label and field value box align with the tops of the VisitID label and field value box.

   **Trouble?** If your form already has a two-column layout, skip Step 3.

4. Click the **Walk-in?** label, press and hold **CTRL**, click the **WalkIn** check box, and then release **CTRL**. The Walk-in? label and the WalkIn check box are selected.

5. Drag the **Walk-in?** label and **WalkIn** check box to the left and position them below the Date of Visit label and VisitDate field value box.

6. Select the **Comments** label and the **Comments** field value box, and then drag the selected controls up until they are top-aligned with the Date of Visit label and VisitDate field value box.

7. Click the **Comments** field value box to select it, and then drag the right border of the control to the right until the field value box is about four inches wide.

8. Click the **Reason** field value box so that it's the only selected control, drag the right border of the control to the right until it is the same width as the Comments field value box, and then drag the bottom border down until it aligns with the bottom of the PatientID field value box. Compare your screen with Figure 6–14, making any necessary adjustments.

Figure 6–14    **Moved and resized controls in the form**

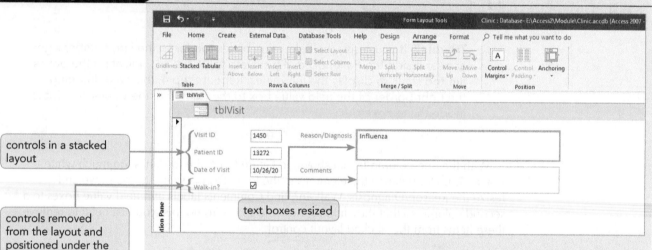

controls in a stacked layout

controls removed from the layout and positioned under the stacked layout controls

text boxes resized

**Trouble?** It won't cause any problems if the controls on your screen are in slightly different positions from the ones shown in the figure.

You do not usually need to change the default settings for the Control Margins property, which controls the spacing around the text inside a control, or the Control Padding property, which controls the spacing around the outside of a control. However, you'll explore the effects of changing these properties.

9. In the form, click the **Visit ID** label to select it, and then click the **layout selector** ⊞ to select the six controls that are still grouped in the stacked layout.

10. On the Arrange tab, in the Position group, click the **Control Margins** button, and then click **Medium**. The text inside the stacked layout controls moves down slightly.

11. Click the **Control Margins** button, click **Wide**, and observe the effect of this setting on the text inside the controls.

12. Click the **Control Margins** button again, and then click **Narrow**. Narrow is the default setting for the Control Margins property. Narrow is also the default setting for the Control Padding property.

Now that the form is complete and the controls are sized appropriately, you will save the form.

13. Save the form as **frmVisitSplit**.

Next, you'll anchor the controls on the form.

## Anchoring Controls in a Form

You can design forms that use the screen dimensions effectively when all the users of a database have the same-sized monitors and use the same screen resolution. How do you design forms when users have a variety of monitor sizes and screen resolutions? If you design a form to fit on large monitors using high screen resolutions, then only a portion of the controls in the form fit on smaller monitors with lower resolutions, forcing users to scroll the form. If you design a form to fit on smaller monitors with low screen resolutions, then the form is displayed on larger monitors in a small area in the upper-left corner of the screen, making the form look unattractively cramped. As a compromise, you can anchor the controls in the form. As shown in the Visual Overview for this session, as the screen size and resolution change, the Anchor property for a control automatically resizes the control and places it in the same relative position on the screen. Unfortunately, when you use the Anchor property, the control's font size is not scaled to match the screen size and resolution. Sometimes the results of anchoring controls work well, but sometimes the controls are spaced across a large screen, and the form may seem unorganized with controls moved to the corners of the screen.

Next, you'll anchor controls in the frmVisitSplit form. You can't anchor individual controls in a control layout; you can only anchor the entire control layout as a group. You've already removed the Reason/Diagnosis, Walk-in?, and Comments controls from the stacked layout so that you can anchor them separately from the stacked layout. Therefore, you'll have four sets of controls to anchor—the stacked layout is one set, the Reason/Diagnosis controls are the second set, the Comments controls are the third set, and the Walk-in? controls make up the fourth set.

### To anchor controls in the form:

1. Click the **Walk-in?** label, press and hold **CTRL**, and then click the **WalkIn** check box.

2. On the Arrange tab, in the Position group, click the **Anchoring** button to open the Anchoring gallery. See Figure 6–15.

**Figure 6–15**    The Anchoring gallery

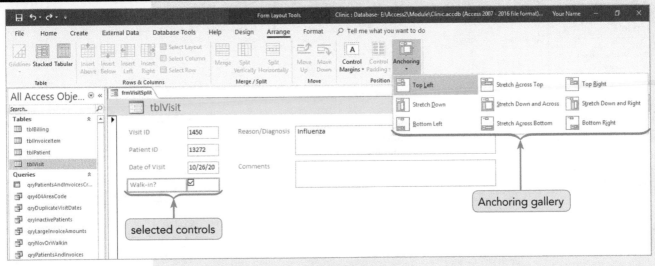

Four of the nine options in the Anchoring gallery fix the position of the selected controls in the top-left (the default setting), bottom-left, top-right, or bottom-right positions in the form. If other controls block the corner positions for controls you're anchoring for the first time, the new controls are positioned in relation to the blocking controls. The other five anchoring options resize (or stretch) and position the selected controls.

You'll anchor the Walk-in? controls in the bottom left, the Reason/Diagnosis controls in the top right, and the Comments controls in the bottom right.

▶ **3.** Click **Bottom Left** in the Anchoring gallery. The gallery closes, and the Walk-in? label and field value box move to the bottom-left corner of the form.

▶ **4.** Click the **Reason** field value box, in the Position group, click the **Anchoring** button, and then click **Top Right**. The Reason label and field value box move to the upper-right corner of the form.

▶ **5.** Anchor the Comments label and field value box to the Bottom Right.

Next, you'll increase the height of the form to simulate the effect of a larger screen for the form.

▶ **6.** Open the Navigation Pane. The four sets of controls on the left shift to the right because the horizontal dimensions of the form decreased from the left, and these four sets of controls are anchored to the left in the form. The Reason and Comments controls remain in the same position in the form.

▶ **7.** Position the pointer on the border between the form and the datasheet until the pointer changes to the vertical resize pointer ✛, and then drag down until only the column headings and the first row in the datasheet are visible. The bottom sets of controls shift down, because they are anchored to the bottom of the form, and the two sets of controls at the top remain in the same positions in the form. See Figure 6–16.

**Figure 6–16**    Anchored controls in a resized form

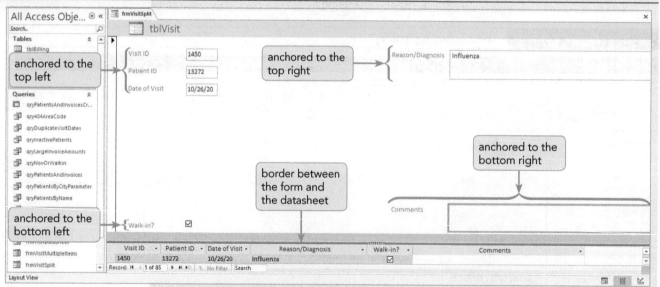

Finally, you'll use another anchoring option to resize the Comments text box as the form dimensions change.

▶ **8.** Click the **Comments** field value box (if necessary), in the Position group, click the **Anchoring** button, and then click **Stretch Down and Right**. Because the Comments field value box is already anchored to the bottom right, it can't stretch any more to the right, but it does stretch up while leaving the label in place, to increase the height of the box.

▶ **9.** Position the pointer on the border between the form and the datasheet until the pointer changes to the vertical resize pointer ✛, and then drag up to display several rows in the datasheet. The bottom set of controls shifts up, the bottom edge of the Comments field value box shifts up, and its height is reduced.

▶ **10.** Save the changes you've made to the form's design, close the form, and then, if you are not continuing on to the next session, close the Clinic database.

You've used form tools to create forms, and you've modified forms in Layout view. In the next session, you will continue your work with forms.

## Session 6.1 Quick Check

**REVIEW**

**1.** Which object(s) should you use to perform all database updates?

**2.** The _____ property specifies the data source for a control in a form or report or for a field in a table or query.

**3.** What is the Documenter?

**4.** What is the Multiple Items tool?

**5.** What is a split form?

**6.** As the screen's size and resolution change, the _____ property for a control automatically resizes the control.

# Session 6.2 Visual Overview:

The sizing handles located on the edges and corners are used to resize the control.

To move selected controls to the next nearest grid dot, press and hold CTRL, and then press the appropriate arrow key.

The larger handle in a control's upper-left corner is its move handle, which you use to move the control.

You can click the Detail section bar to select the entire Detail section.

The grid is the area with dotted and solid lines that helps you position controls precisely in a form.

The PatientID field value box is a combo box control.

The Comments field value box is a text box and a bound control, which is a control that is connected, or bound, to a field in the database.

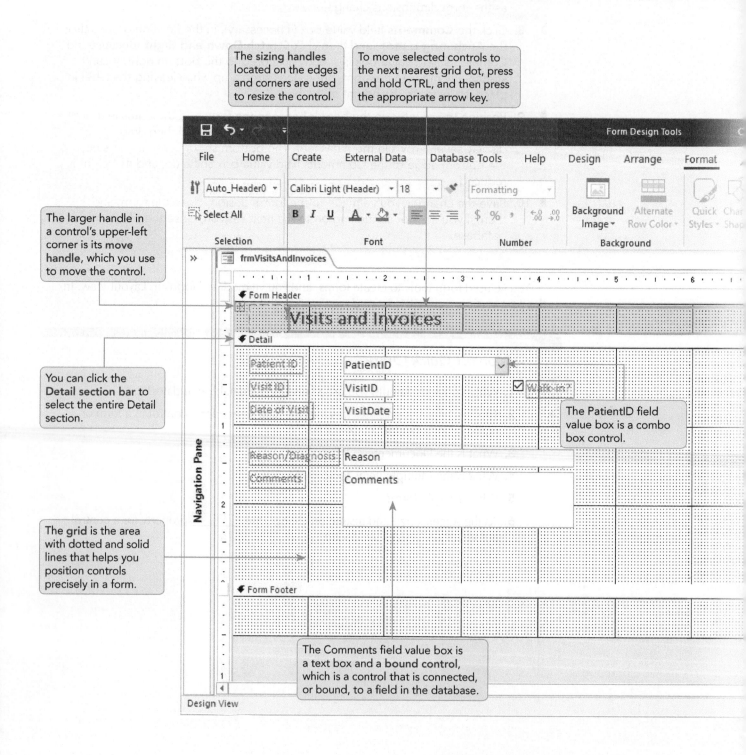

# Custom Form in Design View

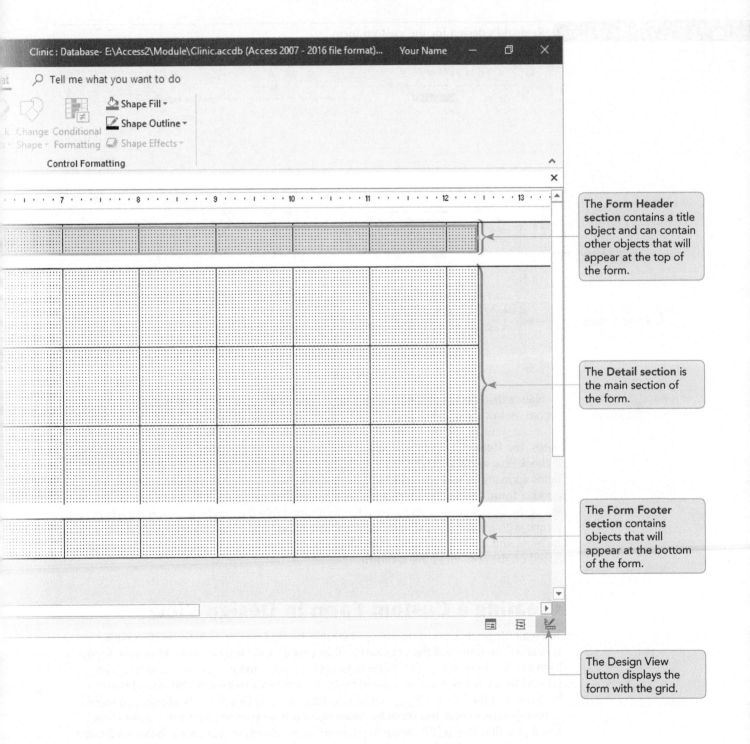

The **Form Header** section contains a title object and can contain other objects that will appear at the top of the form.

The **Detail section** is the main section of the form.

The **Form Footer** section contains objects that will appear at the bottom of the form.

The Design View button displays the form with the grid.

# Planning and Designing a Custom Form

Donna needs a form to enter and view information about Lakewood Community Health Services visits and their related invoices. She wants the information in a single form, and she asks Reginald to design a form for her review.

After several discussions with Donna and her staff, Reginald prepared a sketch for a custom form to display a patient visit and its related invoices. Reginald then used his paper design to create the form shown in Figure 6–17.

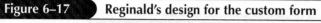

**Figure 6–17    Reginald's design for the custom form**

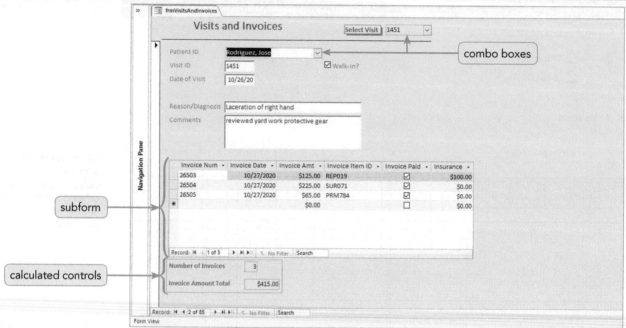

Notice that the top of the form displays a title and a combo box to select a visit record. Below these items are six field values with identifying labels from the tblVisit table; these fields are the PatientID, VisitID, WalkIn, VisitDate, Reason, and Comments fields. The PatientID field is displayed in a combo box, the WalkIn field is displayed as a check box, and the other field values are displayed in text boxes. The tblBilling table fields appear in a subform, which, as you know, is a separate form contained within another form. Unlike the tblVisit table data, which displays identifying labels to the left of the field values in text boxes, the tblBilling table data is displayed in datasheet format with identifying column headings above the field values. Finally, the Number of Invoices and Invoice Amount Total calculated controls in the main form display values based on the content of the subform.

# Creating a Custom Form in Design View

To create Reginald's custom form, you could use the Form Wizard to create a basic version of the form and then customize it in Layout and Design views. However, for the form that Reginald designed, you would need to make many modifications to a form created by a wizard. You can instead build the form in a more straightforward manner by creating it directly in Design view. Creating forms in Design view allows you more control and precision and provides more options than creating forms in Layout view. You'll also find that you'll create forms more productively if you switch between Design view and Layout view because some design modifications are easier to make in one view than in the other view.

# Working in the Form Window in Design View

You can use the Form window in Design view to create and modify forms. To create the custom form based on Reginald's design, you'll create a blank form, add the fields from the tblVisit and tblBilling tables, and then add other controls and make other modifications to the form.

The form you'll create will be a bound form. A **bound form** is a form that has a table or query as its record source. You use bound forms for maintaining and displaying table data. **Unbound forms** are forms that do not have a record source and are usually forms that help users navigate among the objects in a database.

## Creating a Form in Design View

- On the ribbon, click the Create tab.
- In the Forms group, click the Blank Form button to open the Form window in Layout view.
- Click the Design View button on the status bar to switch to Design view.
- Make sure the Field List pane is open, and then add the required fields to the form.
- Add other required controls to the form.
- Modify the size, position, and other properties as necessary for the fields and other controls in the form.
- Save the form.

Now you'll create a blank bound form based on the tblVisit table.

## To create a blank bound form in Design view:

▶ **1.** If you took a break after the previous session, make sure that the Clinic database is open and the Navigation Pane is open.

▶ **2.** On the ribbon, click the **Create** tab, and then, in the Forms group, click the **Blank Form** button. The Form window opens in Layout view.

▶ **3.** Click the **Design View** button 📐 on the status bar to switch to Design view, and then close the Navigation Pane.

▶ **4.** If the Field List pane displays the "No fields available to be added to the current view" message, click **Show all tables** to display the tables in the Clinic database, and then click the **plus sign** ⊞ next to tblVisit in the Field List pane to display the fields in the tblVisit table. See Figure 6–18.

**Figure 6–18**     **Blank form in Design view**

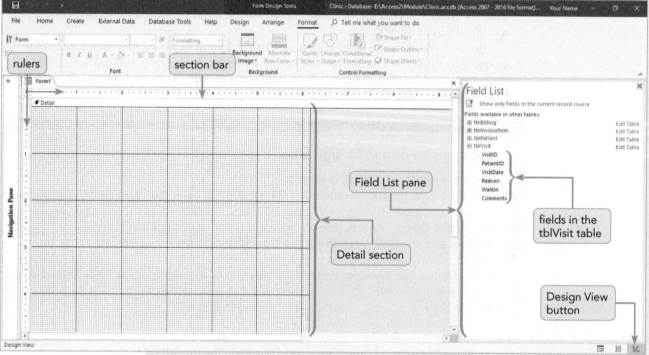

**Trouble?** If the tblVisit table in the Field List pane is not expanded to show the fields in the table, click the plus sign ⊞ next to tblVisit to display the fields.

Design view contains the tools necessary to create a custom form. You create the form by placing controls in the blank form. You can place three kinds of controls in a form:

- A bound control is connected, or bound, to a field in the database. The field could be selected from the fields in a table or query that are used as the record source. You use bound controls to display and maintain table field values.
- An **unbound control** is not connected to a field in the database. You use unbound controls to display text, such as a form title or instructions; to display lines, rectangles, and other objects; or to display graphics and pictures created using other software programs. An unbound control that displays text is called a **label**.
- A **calculated control** displays a value that is the result of an expression. The expression usually contains one or more fields, and the calculated control is recalculated each time any value in the expression changes.

To create bound controls, you add fields from the Field List pane to the Form window, and then position the bound controls where you want them to appear in the form. To place other controls in a form or a report, you use the tools in the Controls and Header/Footer groups on the Form Design Tools Design tab. The tools in the Controls group let you add controls such as lines, rectangles, images, buttons, check boxes, and list boxes to a form.

Design view for a form contains a Detail section, which is a rectangular area consisting of a grid with a section bar above the grid. You click the section bar to select the section in preparation for setting properties for the entire section. Some forms use Header, Detail, and Footer sections, but a simple form might have only a Detail section. The grid consists of dotted and solid lines that you use to position controls precisely in a form. In the Detail section, you place bound controls, unbound controls, and calculated controls in your form. You can change the size of the Detail section by dragging its borders. Rulers at the top and left edges of the Detail section define the horizontal and vertical dimensions of the form and serve as guides for placing controls in a form.

Your first task is to add bound controls to the Detail section for the six fields from the tblVisit table.

## Adding Fields to a Form

When you add a bound control to a form, Access adds a field value box and, to its left, an attached label. The field value box displays a field value from the record source. The attached label displays either the Caption property value for the field, if the Caption property value has been set, or the field name. To create a bound control, you first display the Field List pane by clicking the Add Existing Fields button in the Tools group on the Form Design Tools Design tab. Then you double-click a field in the Field List pane to add the bound control to the Detail section. You can also drag a field from the Field List pane to the Detail section.

The Field List pane displays the four tables in the Clinic database and the six fields in the tblVisit table. Next, you'll add bound controls to the Detail section for the tblVisit table's six fields.

### To add bound controls from the tblVisit table to the Detail section:

1. Double-click **VisitID** in the Field List pane. A bound text box control appears in the Detail section of the form. The Field List pane also lists the tblVisit table in the "Fields available for this view" section and the tblPatient and tblBilling tables in the "Fields available in related tables" section.

2. Repeat Step 1 for the **VisitDate**, **PatientID**, **Reason**, **Comments**, and **WalkIn** fields, in this order, in the Field List pane. Six bound controls—one for each of the six fields in the Field List pane—are added in the Detail section of the form. See Figure 6–19.

| Figure 6–19 | Bound controls added to the form |
| --- | --- |

You should periodically save your work as you create a form, so you'll save the form now.

▶ **3.** Click the **Save** button 🔲 on the Quick Access Toolbar. The Save As dialog box opens.

▶ **4.** With the default name selected in the Form Name box, type **frmVisitsAndInvoices**, and then press **ENTER**. The tab for the form now displays the form name, and the form design is saved in the Clinic database.

You've added the fields you need to the grid, so you can close the Field List pane.

▶ **5.** Click the **Form Design Tools Design** tab, and then, in the Tools group, click the **Add Existing Fields** button to close the Field List pane.

**INSIGHT**

### Strategies for Building Forms

To help prevent common problems and more easily recover from errors while building forms, you should keep in mind the following suggestions:

- You can click the Undo button one or more times immediately after you make one or more errors or make form adjustments you don't want to keep.
- You should back up your database frequently, especially before you create new objects or customize existing objects. If you run into difficulty, you can revert to your most recent backup copy of the database.
- You should save your form after you've completed a portion of your work successfully and before you need to perform steps you've never done before. If you're not satisfied with subsequent steps, close the form without saving the changes you made since your last save, and then open the form and perform the steps again.
- You can always close the form, make a copy of the form in the Navigation Pane, and practice with the copy.
- Adding controls, setting properties, and performing other tasks correctly in Access should work all the time with consistent results, but in rare instances, you might find that a feature doesn't work properly. If a feature you've previously used successfully suddenly doesn't work, you should save your work, close the database, make a backup copy of the database, open the database, and then compact and repair the database. Performing a compact and repair resolves most of these types of problems.

To make your form's Detail section match Reginald's design (Figure 6–17), you need to move the WalkIn bound control up and to the right. To do so, you must start by selecting the bound control.

## Selecting, Moving, and Aligning Form Controls

Six field value boxes now appear in the form's Detail section, one below the other. Each field value box is a bound control connected to a field in the underlying table, with an attached label to its left or right. Each field value box and each label is a control in the form; in addition, each pairing of a field value box and its associated label is itself a control. When you select a control, an orange selection border appears around the control, and eight squares, called handles, appear on the selection border's four corners and at the midpoints of its four edges. The larger handle in a control's upper-left corner is its move handle, which you use to move the control. You use the other seven handles, called sizing handles, to resize the control. When you work in Design view, controls you place in the form do not become part of a control layout, so you can individually select, move, resize, and otherwise manipulate one control without also changing the other controls. However, at any time you can select a group of controls and place them in a control layout—either a stacked layout or a tabular layout.

Based on Reginald's design for the custom form, shown in Figure 6–17, you need to move the WalkIn bound control up and to the right in the Detail section. The WalkIn bound control consists of a check box and an attached label, displaying the text "Walk-in?" to its right.

You can move a field value box and its attached label together. To move them, you place the pointer anywhere on the selection border of the field value box, but not on a move handle or a sizing handle. When the pointer changes to the move pointer ⁺⭢, you drag the field value box and its attached label to the new location. As you move a control, an outline of the control moves on the rulers to indicate the current position of the control as you drag it. To move a group of selected controls, point to any selected control until the pointer changes to the move pointer ⁺⭢, and then drag the group of selected controls to the new position. As you know, you can move controls with more precision by pressing the appropriate arrow key on the keyboard to move the selected control in small increments. To move selected controls to the next nearest grid dot, press and hold CTRL and then press the appropriate arrow key on the keyboard.

You can also move either a field value box or its label individually. If you want to move the field value box but not its label, for example, place the pointer on the field value box's move handle. When the pointer changes to the move pointer ⁺⭢, drag the field value box to the new location. You use the label's move handle in a similar way to move only the label.

You'll now arrange the controls in the form to match Reginald's design.

### To move the WalkIn bound control:

▶ **1.** If necessary, click the **Walk-in?** label box to select it. Move handles, which are the larger handles, appear on the upper-left corners of the selected label box and its associated bound control. Sizing handles also appear but only on the label box. See Figure 6–20.

| Figure 6–20 | Selected WalkIn bound control and label |

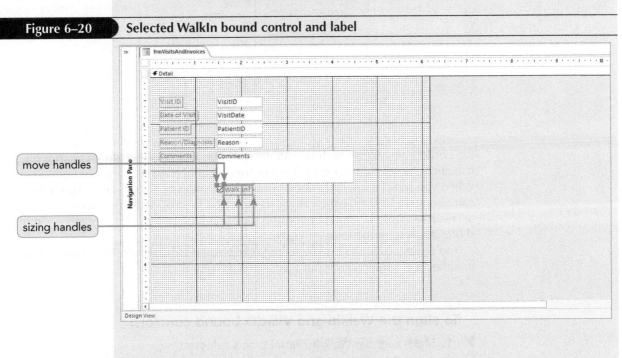

Be sure to position the pointer on one of the edges but not on a move handle or a sizing handle.

**2.** Position the pointer on the Walk-in? label box's orange selection border, but not on a move handle or a sizing handle, until the pointer changes to a move pointer ↖, drag the control up and to the right of the VisitID field value box, and then release the mouse button.

**3.** Press ↓ twice. The selected label box and its associated bound control move one grid dot in the direction of the arrow key with each key press. You can move a selected control using ↑, ←, and → as well.

**4.** Click the Undo button ↺ on the Quick Access Toolbar. The selected label box and bound control move back up one grid dot.

**5.** Click the Undo button ↺ two more times. The selected label box and bound control move back up one grid dot, and then move back to their original position.

**6.** Click the Redo button ↻. The label box and bound control return to the position where you dragged them.

**7.** Use any combination of dragging and arrow keys to position the WalkIn? label box and bound control as shown in Figure 6–21.

**Figure 6–21**    **Repositioned Walk-in? label and associated bound control**

selected label and associated bound control moved here

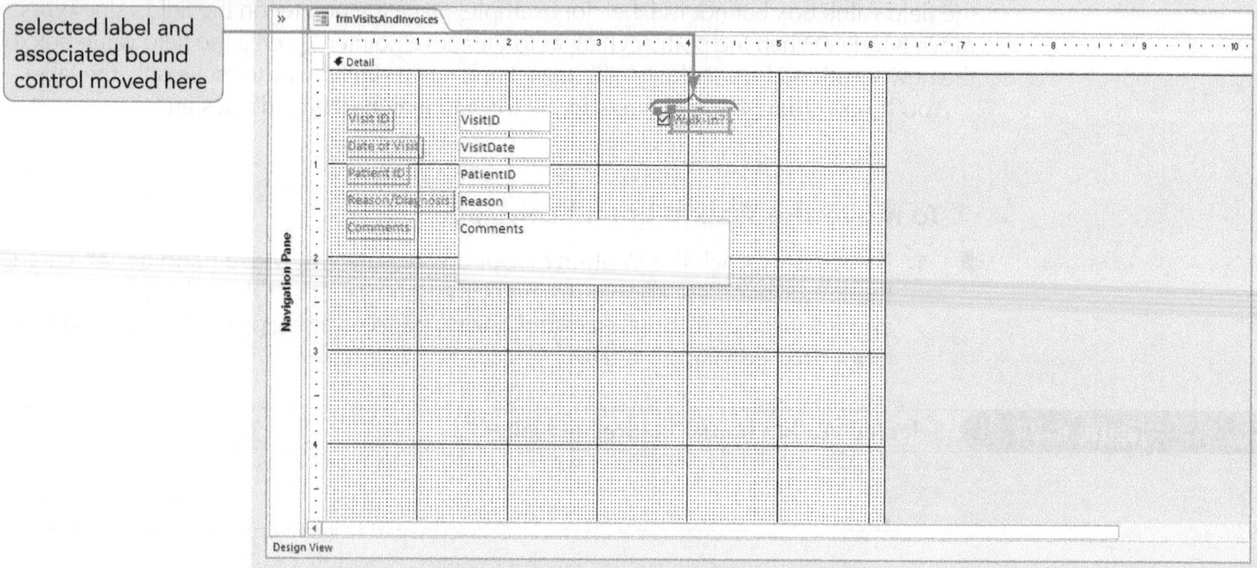

Now you need to top-align the WalkIn and VisitID bound controls (meaning their top borders are aligned with one another). When you select a column of controls, you can align the controls along their left or their right borders (left-align or right-align). When you select a row of controls, you can top-align or bottom-align the controls. You can also align To Grid, which aligns the selected controls with the dots in the grid. You access these five alignment options on the Form Design Tools Arrange tab or on the shortcut menu for the selected controls.

You'll use the shortcut menu to align the two bound controls. Then you'll save the modified form and review your work in Form view.

**To align the WalkIn and VisitID bound controls:**

**1.** Make sure the Walk-in? label box is selected.

2. Press and hold **SHIFT**, click the **WalkIn** check box, click the **VisitID** field value box, click the **Visit ID** label, and then release **SHIFT**. The four controls are selected, and each selected control has an orange selection border.

3. Right-click one of the selected controls, point to **Align** on the shortcut menu, and then click **Top**. The four selected controls are top-aligned. See Figure 6–22.

| Figure 6–22 | Aligned controls in the Detail section |

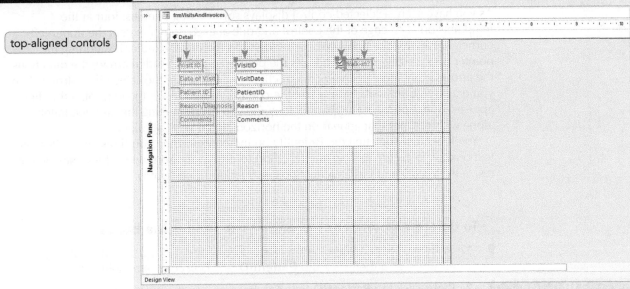

top-aligned controls

As you create a form, you should periodically save your modifications to the form and review your progress in Form view.

4. Save your form design changes, and then switch to Form view.

5. Click the **Next record** button ▶ to display the second record in the dataset (Visit ID #1451) in the form. See Figure 6–23.

| Figure 6–23 | Form displayed in Form view |

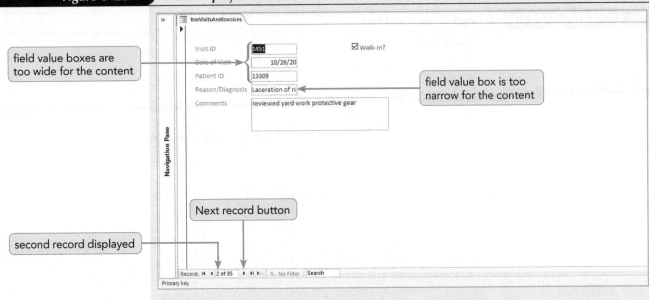

field value boxes are too wide for the content

field value box is too narrow for the content

Next record button

second record displayed

The value in the Reason field value box is not fully displayed, so you need to increase the width of the text box control. The VisitID and VisitDate text boxes are wider than necessary, so you'll reduce their widths. Also, the PatientID bound control consists of a label and a text box, but the plan for the form shows a combo box for the PatientID positioned below the WalkIn bound control. You'll delete the PatientID bound control, and then add it back to the form, this time as a combo box.

# Resizing and Deleting Controls

As you have seen, a selected control displays seven sizing handles: four at the midpoints on each edge of the control and one at each corner except the upper-left corner. Recall that the upper-left corner displays the move handle. Positioning the pointer over a sizing handle changes the pointer to a two-headed arrow; the directions the arrows point indicate in which direction you can resize the selected control. When you drag a sizing handle, you resize the control. As you resize the control, a thin line appears alongside the sizing handle to guide you in completing the task accurately, along with outlines that appear on the horizontal and vertical rulers.

You'll begin by deleting the PatientID bound control. Then you'll resize the Reason text box, which is too narrow and too short to display Reason field values. Next you'll resize the VisitID and VisitDate text boxes to reduce their widths.

## To delete a bound control and resize field value boxes:

1. Switch to Design view, click a blank area of the window to deselect all controls, and then click the **PatientID** text box control to select it.

**TIP**

If you want to delete a label but not its associated field value box, right-click the label, and then click Delete on the shortcut menu.

2. Right-click the **PatientID** text box to open the shortcut menu, and then click **Delete**. The label and the bound text box control for the PatientID field are deleted.

3. Click the **Reason** text box to select it.

4. Place the pointer on the middle-right handle of the Reason text box until it changes to a horizontal resize pointer ↔, and then drag the right border to the right until it is approximately the same width as the Comments text box. See Figure 6–24.

| Figure 6–24 | Resized Reason text box |
|---|---|

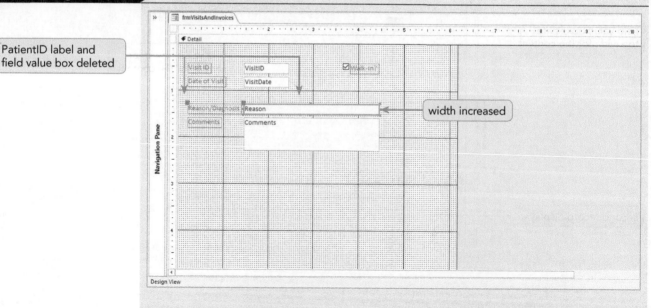

PatientID label and field value box deleted

width increased

Resizing controls in Design view is a trial-and-error process, in which you resize a control in Design view, switch to Form view to observe the effect of the resizing, switch back to Design view to make further refinements to the control's size, and continue until the control is sized correctly. It's easier to resize controls in Layout view because you can see actual field values while you resize the controls. You'll resize the other two text box controls in Layout view. The sizes of the VisitID and VisitDate controls will look fine if you reduce them to the same widths, so you'll select both boxes and resize them with one action.

5. Switch to Layout view, and then click the **VisitID** field value box (if necessary) to select it.

6. Press and hold **SHIFT**, click the **VisitDate** field value box (next to the label "Date of Visit") to select it, and then release the mouse button.

7. Position the pointer on the right border of the **VisitDate** field value box until the pointer changes to a horizontal resize pointer ↔, drag the border to the left until the field box is slightly wider than the field value it contains, and the value in the VisitID field is also visible, and then release the mouse button. See Figure 6–25.

Figure 6–25    **Resized field value boxes in Layout view**

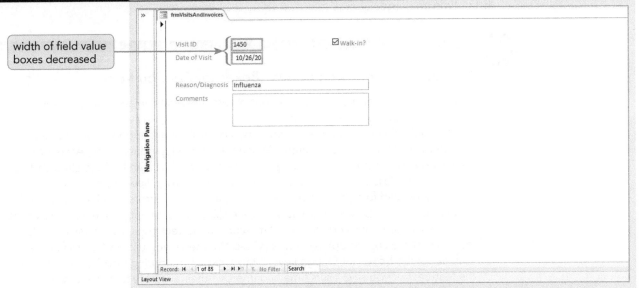

width of field value boxes decreased

**Trouble?** If you resized the field value boxes too far to the left, number signs will be displayed inside the VisitDate field value box. Drag the right border to the right slightly until the date value is visible.

8. Navigate through the first several records to make sure the first three field value boxes are sized properly and display the full field values. If any field value box is too small, select it, and then resize it as appropriate.

9. Save your form design changes, switch to Design view, and then deselect all controls by clicking a blank area of the window.

### Making Form Design Modifications

When you design forms and other objects, you'll find it helpful to switch frequently between Design view and Layout view. Some form modifications are easier to make in Layout view, other form modifications are easier to make in Design view, and still other form modifications can be made only in Design view. You should check your progress frequently in either Layout view or Form view, and you should save your modifications after completing a set of changes successfully.

Recall that you removed the lookup feature from the PatientID field because a combo box provides the same lookup capability in a form. Next, you'll add a combo box control for the PatientID field to the custom form.

# Adding a Combo Box Control to a Form

The tblPatient and tblVisit tables are related in a one-to-many relationship. The PatientID field in the tblVisit table is a foreign key to the tblVisit table, and you can use a combo box control in the custom form to view and maintain PatientID field values more easily and accurately than using a text box. Recall that a combo box is a control that provides the features of a text box and a list box; you can choose a value from the list or type an entry.

### Problem Solving: Using Combo Boxes for Foreign Keys

When you design forms, combo box controls are a natural choice for foreign keys because foreign key values must match one of the primary key values in the related primary table. If you do not use a combo box control for a foreign key, you force users to type values in the text box control. When they make typing mistakes, Access rejects the values and displays nonmatching error messages, which can be frustrating and make the form less efficient for users. Combo box controls allow users to select only from a list of valid foreign key values so that nonmatching errors are eliminated. At the same time, combo boxes allow users who are skilled at data entry to more rapidly type the values, instead of using the more time-consuming technique of choosing a value from the list the combo box control provides. Whenever you use an Access feature such as combo boxes for foreign keys, it takes extra time during development to add the feature, but you save users time and improve their accuracy for the many months or years they use the database.

You use the **Combo Box tool** in Design view to add a combo box control to a form. If you want help when adding the combo box, you can select one of the Control Wizards. A **Control Wizard** asks a series of questions and then, based on your answers, creates a control in a form or report. Access offers Control Wizards for the Combo Box, List Box, Option Group, Command Button, Subform/Subreport, and other control tools.

You will use the Combo Box Wizard to add a combo box control to the form for the PatientID field.

### To add a combo box control to the form:

**1.** Click the **Form Design Tools Design** tab, and then in the Controls group, click the **More** button ⏷ to open the Controls gallery. See Figure 6–26.

| Figure 6–26 | Controls gallery |
| --- | --- |

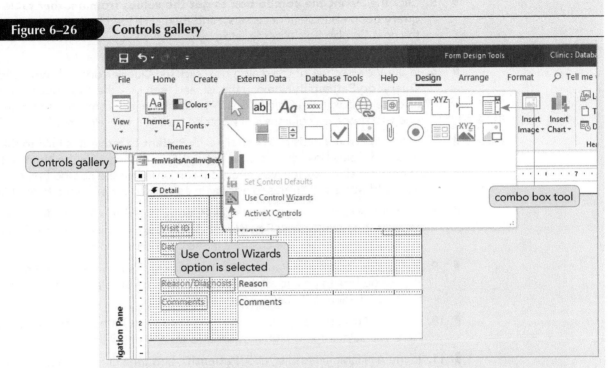

The Controls gallery contains tools that allow you to add controls (such as text boxes, lines, charts, and labels) to a form. You drag a control from the Controls gallery and place it in position in the grid. If you want to use the Combo Box Wizard to add a control, you need to select that option below the gallery.

**2.** In the gallery, make sure the Use Control Wizards option is selected (its icon should appear with a gray background) at the bottom of the Controls gallery.

**Trouble?** If the Use Control Wizards option is not selected, click Use Control Wizards to select it, and then click the More button ⏷ again to open the Controls gallery.

**3.** In the Controls gallery, click the **Combo Box** tool ▦. The Controls gallery closes.

Once you select the Combo Box tool (or most other tools in the Controls gallery) and move the mouse pointer into the Detail section of the form, the pointer changes to a shape that is unique for the control with a plus symbol in its upper-left corner. You position the plus symbol in the location where you want to place the upper-left corner of the control.

You'll place the combo box near the top of the form, below the WalkIn bound control, and then position it more precisely after you've completed the steps in the wizard.

**4.** Position the plus symbol of the pointer shape below the WalkIn bound control and at the 3.5-inch mark on the horizontal ruler, and then click the mouse button. A combo box control appears in the form, and the first Combo Box Wizard dialog box opens.

You can use an existing table or query as the source for a new combo box or type the values for the combo box. In this case, you'll use the qryPatientsByName query as the basis for the new combo box.

5. Click the **I want the combo box to get the values from another table or query** option button (if necessary), and then click the **Next** button to open the next Combo Box Wizard dialog box, in which you specify the source of information for the combo box.

6. In the View section of the dialog box, click the **Queries** option button, click **Query: qryPatientsByName** in the list, and then click the **Next** button. The next dialog box in the Combo Box Wizard lets you select the fields from the query to appear as columns in the combo box. You will select the first two fields.

7. In the Available Fields box, double-click **Patient** to move this field to the Selected Fields box, double-click **PatientID**, and then click the **Next** button. The next dialog box lets you choose a sort order for the combo box entries. Reginald wants the entries to appear in ascending order on the Patient field.

8. Click the **arrow** in the first box, click **Patient**, and then click the **Next** button to open the next Combo Box Wizard dialog box, in which you specify the appropriate width for the columns in the combo box control.

9. Resize the Patient and Patient ID columns to fit their content, scroll the list in the dialog box to ensure all the Patient values are visible, and if any are not, resize the Patient column as necessary.

10. Click the **Next** button to open the next dialog box in the Combo Box Wizard. Here you select the foreign key, which is the PatientID field.

11. In the Available Fields list, click **PatientID**, and then click the **Next** button. In this dialog box, you specify the field in the tblVisit table where the selected PatientID value from the combo box will be stored. You'll store the value in the PatientID field in the tblVisit table.

12. Click the **Store that value in this field** option button, click the arrow to display a list of fields, click **PatientID**, and then click the **Next** button.

   **Trouble?** If PatientID doesn't appear in the list, click the Cancel button, press DELETE to delete the combo box, click the Add Existing Fields button in the Tools group on the Form Design Tools Design tab, double-click PatientID in the Field List pane, press DELETE to delete PatientID, close the Field List pane, and then repeat Steps 1–12.

   In the final Combo Box Wizard dialog box, you specify the name for the combo box control. You'll use the field name of PatientID.

13. With the current text selected in the "What label would you like for your combo box?" box, type **PatientID** and then click the **Finish** button. The completed PatientID combo box control appears in the form.

You need to position and resize the combo box control, but first you will change the Caption property for the PatientID combo box label control so that it matches the format used by the other label controls in the form.

**REFERENCE**

*Changing a Label's Caption*

- Right-click the label to select it and to display the shortcut menu, and then click Properties to display the Property Sheet.
- If necessary, click the All tab to display the All page in the Property Sheet.
- Edit the existing text in the Caption box; or click the Caption box, press F2 to select the current value, and then type a new caption.

You want the label control attached to the combo box control to display "Patient ID" instead of "PatientID". You will change the Caption property for the label control next.

**To set the Caption property for the PatientID combo box's label control:**

**TIP**

After selecting a control, you can press F4 to open and close the Property Sheet for the control.

1. Right-click the **PatientID** label, which is the control to the left of the PatientID combo box control, and then click **Properties** on the shortcut menu. The Property Sheet for the PatientID label control opens.

   **Trouble?** If the Selection type entry below the Property Sheet title bar is not "Label," then you selected the wrong control in Step 1. Click the PatientID label in the form to change to the Property Sheet for this control.

2. If necessary, in the Property Sheet, click the **All** tab to display all properties for the selected PatientID label control.

   The Selection type entry, which appears below the Property Sheet title bar, displays the control type (Label in this case) for the selected control. Below the Selection type entry in the Property Sheet is the Control box, which you can use to select another control in the form and list its properties in the Property Sheet. Alternately, you can click a control in the form and modify its properties in the Property Sheet. The first property in the Property Sheet, the **Name property**, specifies the name of a control, section, or object (PatientID_Label in this case). The Name property value is the same as the value displayed in the Control box, unless the Caption property has been set. For bound controls, the Name property value matches the field name. For unbound controls, an underscore and a suffix of the control type (for example, Label) is added to the Name property setting. For unbound controls, you can set the Name property to another, more meaningful value at any time.

3. In the Caption box, click before "ID", press **SPACEBAR**, and then press **TAB** to move to the next property in the Property Sheet. The Caption property value changes to Patient ID, and the label for the PatientID bound label control displays Patient ID. See Figure 6–27.

**Figure 6–27**    **PatientID combo box and updated label added to the form**

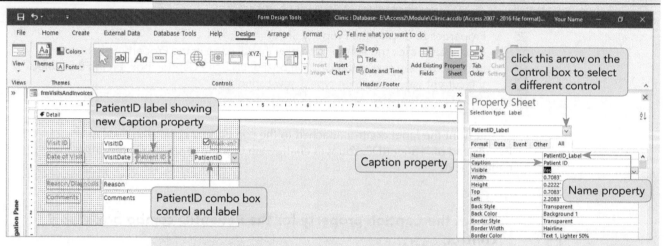

**Trouble?** Some property values in your Property Sheet, such as the Width and Top property values, might differ if your label's position differs slightly from the label position used as the basis for Figure 6–27. These differences cause no problems.

4. Close the Property Sheet, and then save your design changes to the form.

Now that you've added the combo box control to the form, you can position and resize it appropriately. You'll need to view the form in Form view to determine any fine-tuning necessary for the width of the combo box.

### To modify the combo box in Design and Layout views:

1. Click the **PatientID** combo box control, press and hold **SHIFT**, click the **Patient ID** label control, and then release **SHIFT** to select both controls.

   First, you'll move the selected controls above the VisitID controls. Then you'll left-align the PatientID, VisitID, VisitDate, Reason, and Comments labels; left-align the PatientID combo box control with the VisitID, VisitDate, Reason, and Comments text box controls; and then right-align the WalkIn label and check box control with the right edges of the Reason and Comments text box controls.

2. Drag the selected controls to a position above the VisitID controls. Do not try to align them.

3. Click in a blank area of the window to deselect the selected controls.

4. Press and hold **SHIFT** while you click the **Patient ID** label, the **Visit ID** label, **Date of Visit** label, **Reason/Diagnosis** label, and the **Comments** label, and then release **SHIFT**.

5. Click the **Form Design Tools Arrange** tab, in the Sizing & Ordering group, click the **Align** button, and then click **Left**. The selected controls are left-aligned.

6. Repeat Steps 4 and 5 to left-align the PatientID combo box, VisitID text box, VisitDate text box, Reason text box, and the Comments text box.

7. Click the **Walk-In?** label, press and hold **SHIFT**, click the **Reason** text box and **Comments** text box, and then release **SHIFT**.

8. In the Sizing & Ordering group, click the **Align** button, and then click **Right**. The selected controls are right-aligned.

9. Switch to Form view, and then click the **PatientID** arrow to open the combo box control's list box. Note that the column is not wide enough to show the full data values. See Figure 6–28.

**Figure 6–28** | **PatientID combo box and updated label in Form view**

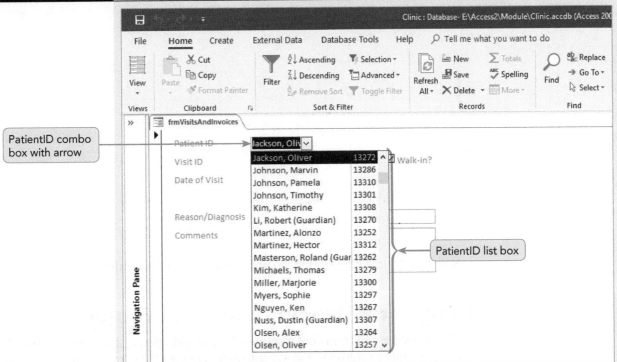

You need to widen the PatientID combo box so that that the widest value in the list is displayed in the combo box. You can widen the combo box in Layout view or in Design view. Because Form view and Layout view display actual data from the table rather than placeholder text in each bound control, these views let you immediately see the effects of your layout changes. You'll use Layout view instead of Design view to make this change because you can determine the proper width more accurately in Layout view.

10. Switch to Layout view, and then navigate to record 19. Masterson, Roland (Guardian), which is the patient name for this record, is one of the widest values that is displayed in the combo box. You want to widen the combo box so that it is a little bit wider than the value in record 19.

11. Make sure that only the combo box is selected, and then drag the right border to widen the combo box until the entire name of the patient is visible. See Figure 6–29.

Figure 6–29    Resized PatientID combo box in Layout view

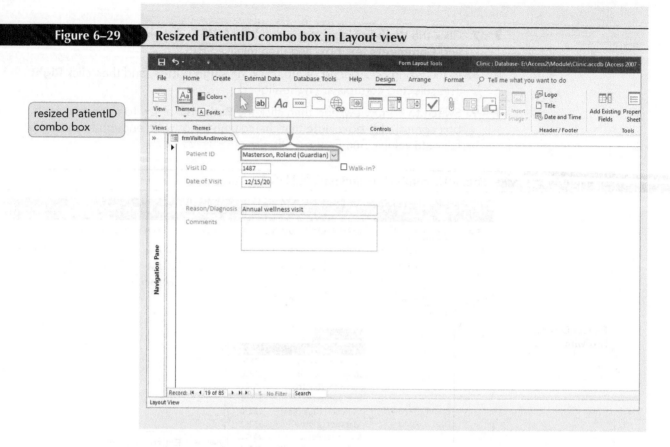

resized PatientID combo box

Now you'll add the title to the top of the form by adding a Form Header section.

# Using Form Headers and Form Footers

The Form Header and Form Footer sections let you add titles, instructions, command buttons, and other controls to the top and bottom of your form, respectively. Controls placed in the Form Header or Form Footer sections remain on the screen whenever the form is displayed in Form view or Layout view; they do not change when the contents of the Detail section change as you navigate from one record to another record.

To add either a form header or footer to your form, you must first add both the Form Header and Form Footer sections as a pair to the form. If your form needs one of these sections but not the other, you can remove a section by setting its height to zero, which is the same method you would use to remove any form section. You can also prevent a section from appearing in Form view or in Print Preview by setting its Visible property to "No." The **Visible property** determines if a control or section appears in Form view, in Print Preview, or when printed. You set the Visible property to Yes to display the control or section, and set the Visible property to No to hide it.

If you've set the Form Footer section's height to zero or set its Visible property to No and a future form design change makes adding controls to the Form Footer section necessary, you can restore the section by using the pointer to drag its bottom border back down or by setting its Visible property to Yes.

In Design view, you can add the Form Header and Form Footer sections as a pair to a form by right-clicking the Detail section selector, and then clicking Form Header/Footer. You also can click the Logo button, the Title button, or the Date and Time button in the Header/Footer group on the Form Design Tools Design tab or the Form Layout Tools Design tab. Clicking any of these three buttons adds the Form Header and Form Footer sections to the form and places an appropriate control in the Form Header section only. A footer section is added to the form, but with a height set to zero to one-quarter inch.

Reginald's design includes a title at the top of the form. Because the title will not change as you navigate through the form records, you will add the title to the Form Header section in the form.

## Adding a Title to a Form

You'll add the title to Reginald's form in Layout view. When you add a title to a form in Layout view, a Form Header section is added to the form and contains the form title. At the same time, a Page Footer section with a height setting of zero is added to the form.

### To add a title to the form:

▶ **1.** On the Form Layout Tools Design tab, in the Header/Footer group, click the **Title** button. A title consisting of the form name is added to the form and is selected.

You need to change the title.

▶ **2.** Type **Visits and Invoices** to replace the selected default title text. See Figure 6–30.

| Figure 6–30 | Title added to the form in the Form Header section |
| --- | --- |

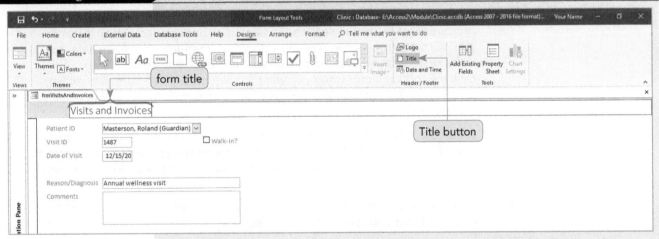

The title has a larger font size than the font used for the form's labels and field value boxes, but Reginald would like you to apply bold to increase its prominence.

▶ **3.** Click a blank area of the window, click the title control to select it, click the **Form Layout Tools Format** tab, and then in the Font group, click the **Bold** button ⓑ. The title is displayed in 18-point, bold text.

It is not obvious in Layout view that the title is displayed in the Form Header section, so you'll view the form design in Design view.

▶ **4.** Switch to Design view, and then click a blank area of the window to deselect all controls. The title is displayed in the Form Header section. See Figure 6–31.

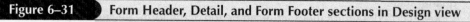

**Figure 6–31**     **Form Header, Detail, and Form Footer sections in Design view**

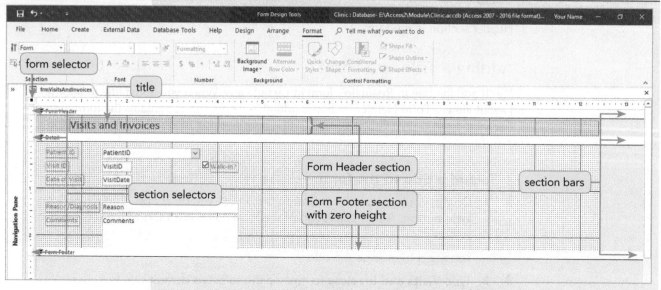

The form now contains a Form Header section that displays the title, a Detail section that displays the bound controls and labels, and a Form Footer section that is set to a height of zero. Each section consists of a **section selector** and a section bar, either of which you can click to select and set properties for the entire section, and a grid or background, which is where you place controls that you want to display in the form. The **form selector** is the selector at the intersection of the horizontal and vertical rulers; you click the form selector when you want to select the entire form and set its properties. The vertical ruler is segmented into sections for the Form Header section, the Detail section, and the Form Footer section.

A form's total height includes the heights of the Form Header, Detail, and Form Footer sections. If you set a form's total height to more than the screen size, users will need to use scroll bars to view the content of your form, which is less productive for users and isn't good form design.

▶ **5.** Save the design changes to the form, and then, if you are not continuing on to the next session, close the Clinic database.

So far, you've added controls to the form and modified the controls by selecting, moving, aligning, resizing, and deleting them. You've added and modified a combo box and added a title in the Form Header section. In the next session, you will continue your work with the custom form by adding a combo box control for use in finding records, adding a subform, adding calculated controls, changing form and section properties, and changing control properties.

*Session 6.2 Quick Check*

REVIEW

1. What is a bound form, and when do you use bound forms?
2. What is the difference between a bound control and an unbound control?
3. The _____ consists of the dotted and solid lines that appear in the Header, Detail, and Footer sections in Design view to help you position controls precisely in a form.
4. The larger handle in a selected object's upper-left corner is the _____ handle.
5. How do you move a selected field value box and its label at the same time?
6. How do you resize a control?
7. A(n) _____ control provides the features of a text box and a list box.
8. How do you change a label's caption?
9. What is the purpose of the Form Header section?

# Session 6.3 Visual Overview:

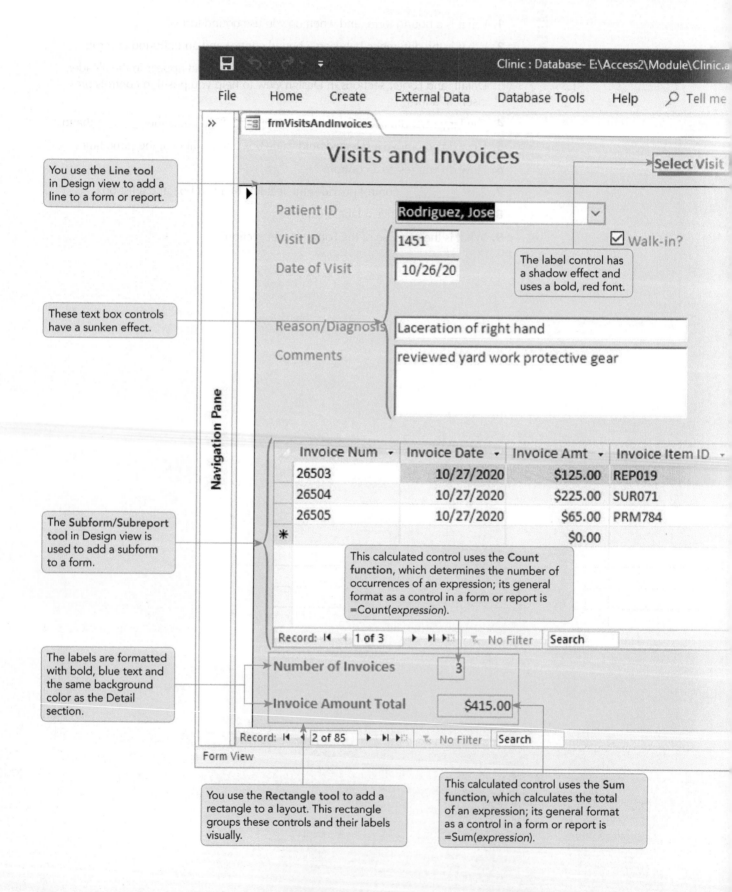

You use the Line tool in Design view to add a line to a form or report.

These text box controls have a sunken effect.

The Subform/Subreport tool in Design view is used to add a subform to a form.

The labels are formatted with bold, blue text and the same background color as the Detail section.

Clinic : Database- E:\Access2\Module\Clinic.a

File    Home    Create    External Data    Database Tools    Help    🔎 Tell me

frmVisitsAndInvoices

## Visits and Invoices

Select Visit

The label control has a shadow effect and uses a bold, red font.

Patient ID       Rodriguez, Jose

Visit ID         1451                                    ☑ Walk-in?

Date of Visit    10/26/20

Reason/Diagnosis  Laceration of right hand

Comments          reviewed yard work protective gear

| Invoice Num ▾ | Invoice Date ▾ | Invoice Amt ▾ | Invoice Item ID ▾ |
|---|---|---|---|
| 26503 | 10/27/2020 | $125.00 | REP019 |
| 26504 | 10/27/2020 | $225.00 | SUR071 |
| 26505 | 10/27/2020 | $65.00 | PRM784 |
| ✳ | | $0.00 | |

This calculated control uses the Count function, which determines the number of occurrences of an expression; its general format as a control in a form or report is =Count(expression).

Record: ◄ ◄ 1 of 3 ► ►► ►▦    ✎ No Filter    Search

Number of Invoices       3

Invoice Amount Total    $415.00

Record: ◄ ◄ 2 of 85 ► ►► ►▦    ✎ No Filter    Search

Form View

You use the Rectangle tool to add a rectangle to a layout. This rectangle groups these controls and their labels visually.

This calculated control uses the Sum function, which calculates the total of an expression; its general format as a control in a form or report is =Sum(expression).

# Custom Form in Form View

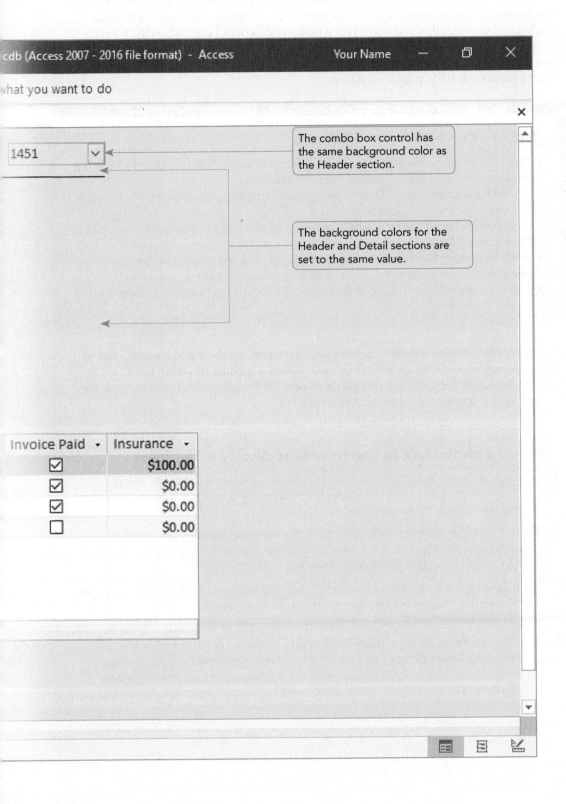

# Adding a Combo Box to Find Records

As you know, a combo box control is used to display and update data in a form. You can also use a combo box control to allow users to find records. You can use the Combo Box Wizard to create this type of combo box control. However, the Combo Box Wizard provides this find option for a combo box control only when the form's record source is a table or query. Before creating a combo box control to be used to find records, you should view the Property Sheet for the form to confirm the Record Source property is set to a table or query.

**REFERENCE**

### Adding a Combo Box to Find Records

- Open the Property Sheet for the form in Design view, confirm the record source is a table or query, and then close the Property Sheet.
- On the Form Design Tools Design tab, in the Controls group, click the More button, and then click the Combo Box tool.
- Click the location in the form where you want to place the control, and then open the Combo Box Wizard.
- In the first dialog box of the Combo Box Wizard, click the "Find a record on my form based on the value I selected in my combo box" option button.
- Complete the remaining Combo Box Wizard dialog boxes to finish creating the combo box control.

To continue creating the form that Reginald sketched, you will add a combo box to the Form Header section that will allow users to find a specific record in the tblVisit table to display in the form. But first you will view the Property Sheet to make sure the Record Source property is set to the tblVisit table.

### To add a combo box to find records to display in the form:

1. If you took a break after the previous session, make sure that the Clinic database is open, the frmVisitsAndInvoices form is open in Design view, and the Navigation Pane is closed.

2. To the left of the horizontal ruler, click the **form selector** ☐ to select the form, if necessary. The form selector changes to display a black square inside it ▣, indicating that the form is selected.

   **Trouble?** If the Form Header section bar instead turns black, you might have clicked the header selector button. Click the form selector button, which is just above the header selector button.

3. Click the **Form Design Tools Design** tab, in the Tools group, click the **Property Sheet** button, and then click the **All** tab in the Property Sheet, if necessary. The Property Sheet displays the properties for the form. See Figure 6–32.

**Figure 6–32**    Property Sheet for the form

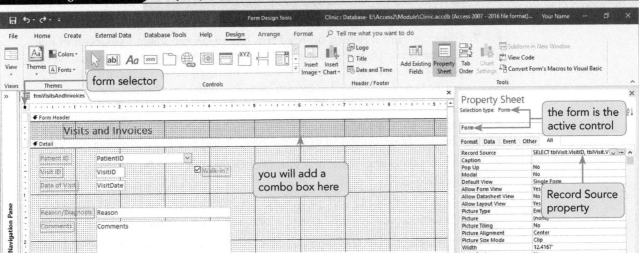

The Record Source property is set to a SQL SELECT statement, which is code that references a table. You need to change the Record Source property to a table or query, or the Combo Box Wizard will not present you with the option to find records in a form. You'll change the Record Source property to the tblVisit table because this table is the record source for all the bound controls you have added to the Detail section of the form.

4. In the Record Source box, click the **Record Source** arrow, click **tblVisit** in the list, and then close the Property Sheet.

You'll now use the Combo Box Wizard to add a combo box to the form's Form Header section, which will enable a user to find a record in the tblVisit table to display in the form.

5. On the Form Design Tools Design tab, in the Controls group, click the **More** button ▼ to open the Controls gallery, and then click the **Combo Box** tool 📑.

6. Position the plus symbol pointer at the top of the Form Header section at the 5-inch mark on the horizontal ruler (see Figure 6–32), and then click the mouse button. A combo box control appears in the Form Header section of the form, and the first Combo Box Wizard dialog box opens.

**Trouble?** If the Combo Box Wizard dialog box does not open, delete the new controls and try again, ensuring the plus symbol pointer is very near the top of the Form Header grid.

You will recall seeing this dialog box when you used the Combo Box Wizard in the previous session. The first dialog box in the Combo Box Wizard this time displays an additional option than what was available previously. This additional option, "Find a record on my form based on the value I selected in my combo box," is what you need to use for this combo box. (Recall in the last session you selected the first option, "I want the combo box to get the values from another table or query" when you used the Combo Box Wizard to create the PatientID combo box, allowing the user to select a value from a list of foreign key values from an existing table or query.) You would choose the second option if you wanted users to select a value from a short fixed list of values that don't change. For example, if Lakewood Community Health

Services wanted to include a field in the tblPatient table to identify the state in which the patient resides, you could use a combo box with this second option to display a list of states.

7. Click the **Find a record on my form based on the value I selected in my combo box** option button, and then click the **Next** button. The next Combo Box Wizard dialog box lets you select the fields from the tblVisit table to appear as columns in the combo box. You need to include only one column of values, listing the VisitID values.

8. Double-click **VisitID** to move this field to the Selected Fields box, and then click the **Next** button to open the next dialog box in the Combo Box Wizard.

9. In the dialog box, resize the VisitID column to its best fit, and then click the **Next** button.

   In the last dialog box in the Combo Box Wizard, you specify the name for the combo box's label. You'll use "Select Visit" as the label.

10. Type **Select Visit** and then click the **Finish** button. The completed unbound combo box control and its corresponding Select Visit label appear in the form. See Figure 6–33.

| Figure 6–33 | Unbound combo box added to the form |
| --- | --- |

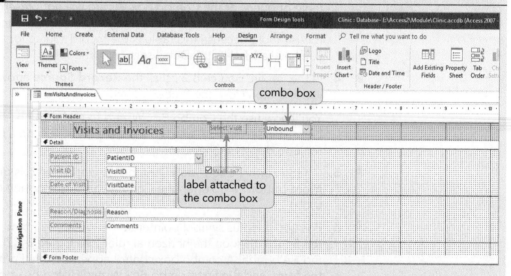

You'll move the attached label closer to the combo box control, and then you'll align the bottoms of the combo box control and its attached label with the bottom of the title in the Form Header section.

11. Click the **Select Visit** label, point to the label's move handle on the upper-left corner of the orange selection border, and then drag the label to the right until its right edge is two grid dots to the left of the combo box.

12. With the Select Visit label still selected, press and hold **SHIFT**, click the **combo box**, and then click the **Visit and Invoices** form title.

13. Right-click the selected controls, point to **Align** on the shortcut menu, and then click **Bottom**. The three selected controls are bottom-aligned. See Figure 6–34.

**Figure 6–34**    Aligned combo box control and form title

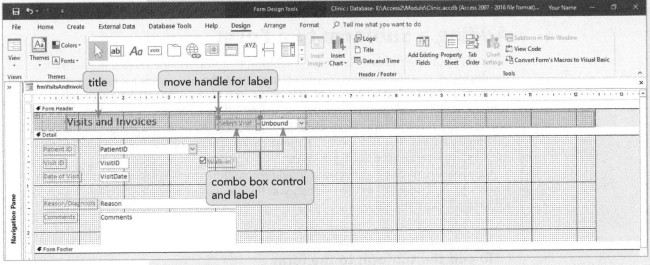

You'll save your form changes and view the new combo box control in Form view.

### To save the form and view the Select Visit combo box control:

1. Save the form design changes, and then switch to Form view.
2. Click the **Select Visit** arrow to display the list of Visit ID numbers. See Figure 6–35.

**Figure 6–35**    List of Visit IDs in the combo box

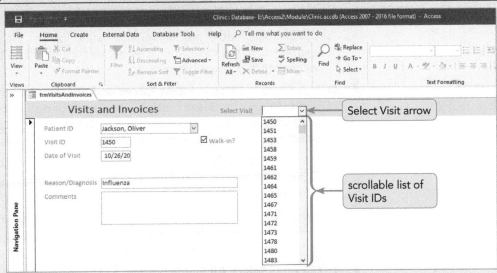

3. Scroll down the list, and then click **1467**. The current record changes from record 1 to record 10, which is the record for visit ID 1467.

   **Trouble?** If you see the data for record 1, the navigation combo box is not working correctly. Delete the combo box, check to ensure that you have set the Record Source for the form object correctly, and then repeat the previous set of steps to re-create the combo box.

The form design currently is very plain, with no color, formatting effects, or visual contrast among the controls. Before making the form more attractive and useful, though, you'll add the remaining controls: a subform and two calculated controls.

## Adding a Subform to a Form

Reginald's plan for the form includes a subform that displays the related invoices for the displayed visit. The form you've been creating is the main form for records from the primary tblVisit table (the "one" side of the one-to-many relationship), and the subform will display records from the related tblBilling table (the "many" side of the one-to-many relationship). You use the Subform/Subreport tool in Design view to add a subform to a form. You can create a subform from scratch, or you can get help adding the subform by using the SubForm Wizard.

You will use the SubForm Wizard to add the subform for displaying tblBilling table records to the bottom of the form. First, you'll increase the height of the Detail section to make room for the subform.

### To add the subform to the form:

1. Switch to Design view.

**TIP**

Drag slightly beyond the desired ending position to expose the vertical ruler measurement, and then decrease the height back to the correct position.

2. Position the pointer on the bottom border of the Detail section until the pointer changes to the vertical resize pointer ✛, and then drag the border down to the 5-inch mark on the vertical ruler.

3. On the Form Design Tools Design tab, in the Controls group, click the **More** button ▼ to open the Controls gallery, and then click the **Subform/Subreport** tool ▣.

4. Position the plus symbol of the pointer in the Detail section at the 2.5-inch mark on the vertical ruler and at the 1-inch mark on the horizontal ruler, and then click the mouse button. A subform control appears in the form's Detail section, and the first SubForm Wizard dialog box opens.

   You can use a table, a query, or an existing form as the record source for a subform. In this case, you'll use the related tblBilling table as the record source for the new subform.

5. Make sure the **Use existing Tables and Queries** option button is selected, and then click the **Next** button. The next SubForm Wizard dialog box opens, in which you select a table or query as the record source for the subform and select the fields to use from the selected table or query.

6. Click the **Tables/Queries arrow** to display the list of tables and queries in the Clinic database, scroll to the top of the list, and then click **Table: tblBilling**. The Available Fields box lists the fields in the tblBilling table.

   Reginald's form design includes all fields from the tblBilling table in the subform, except for the VisitID field, which you already placed in the Detail section of the form from the tblVisit table.

7. Click the **Select All Fields** button ⟩⟩ to move all available fields to the Selected Fields box, click **VisitID** in the Selected Fields box, click the **Remove Field** button ⟨ , and then click the **Next** button to open the next SubForm Wizard dialog box. See Figure 6–36.

**Figure 6–36**    Selecting the linking field

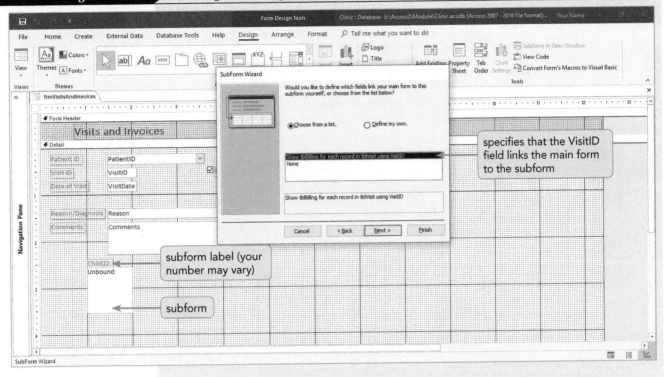

In this dialog box, you select the link between the primary tblVisit table and the related tblBilling table. The common field in the two tables, VisitID, links the tables. The form will use the VisitID field to display a record in the main form, which displays data from the primary tblVisit table, and to select and display the related records for that contract in the subform, which displays data from the related tblBilling table.

▶ 8. Make sure the **Choose from a list** option button is selected, make sure **"Show tblBilling for each record in tblVisit using VisitID"** is selected in the list, and then click the **Next** button. In the last SubForm Wizard dialog box, you specify a name for the subform.

▶ 9. Type **frmBillingSubform** and then click the **Finish** button. The completed subform appears in the Details section of the Form window; its label appears above the subform and displays the subform name.

▶ 10. Click a blank area of the window, and then save the form.

▶ 11. Switch to Form view, click the **Select Visit** arrow, and then click **1453**. The subform displays the four invoices related to visit ID 1453. See Figure 6–37.

| Figure 6–37 | The subform in Form view |

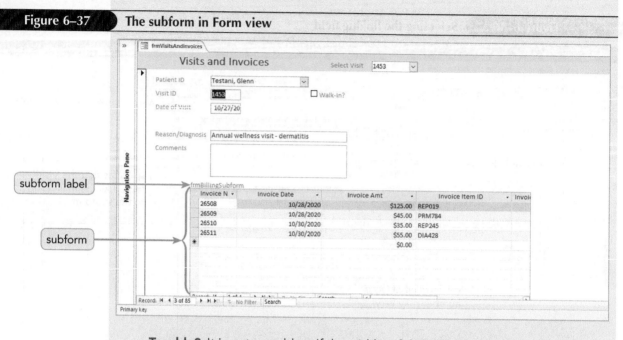

**Trouble?** It is not a problem if the widths of the columns in your datasheet differ or the position of your subform is not exactly as shown in Figure 6–37. You will resize columns and position the subform in the next set of steps.

After viewing the form, Reginald identifies some modifications he wants you to make. He wants you to resize the subform and its columns so that all columns in the subform are entirely visible and the columns are sized to best fit. Also, he asks you to delete the subform label, because the label is unnecessary for identifying the subform contents. You'll use Design view and Layout view to make these changes.

### To modify the subform's design and adjust its position in the form:

1. Switch to Design view. Notice that in Design view, the data in the subform control does not appear in a datasheet format as it does in Form view. That difference causes no problem; you can ignore it.

   First, you'll delete the subform label control.

2. Deselect all controls (if necessary), right-click the **frmBillingSubform** subform label control to open the shortcut menu, and then click **Delete**.

   Next, you'll align the subform control with the Comments label control.

3. Click the border of the subform control to select it, press and hold **SHIFT**, click the **Comments** label control, and then release **SHIFT**. The subform control and the Comments label control are selected. Next you'll left-align the two controls.

4. Right-click the **Comments** label control, point to **Align** on the shortcut menu, and then click **Left**. The two controls are left-aligned. Next, you'll resize the subform control in Layout view so that you can observe the effects of your changes as you make them.

5. Switch to Layout view, click the border of the subform to select it, and then drag the right border of the subform to the right until the Insurance column arrow is fully visible.

Before resizing the columns in the subform to best fit, you'll display record 22 in the main form. The subform for this record contains the related records in the tblBilling table with one of the longest field values.

6. Use the record navigation bar for the main form (at the bottom left of the form window) to display record 3, for visit number 1453, and then resize each column in the subform to its best fit.

Next, you'll resize the subform again so that its width matches the width of the resized columns.

7. Resize the subform so that its right border is aligned with the right border of the Insurance column, and then if necessary scroll down and resize the subform so it displays rows for eight records. See Figure 6–38.

8. Save your form design changes.

**Figure 6–38**    **Moved and resized subform**

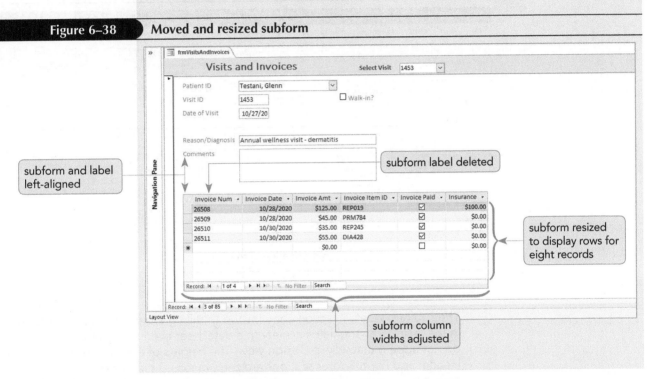

You've finished your work with the subform. Now you need to add two calculated controls to the main form.

# Displaying a Subform's Calculated Controls in the Main Form

**TIP**

You precede expressions with an equal sign to distinguish them from field names, which do not have an equal sign.

Reginald's form design includes the display of calculated controls in the main form that tally the number of invoices and the total of the invoice amounts for the related records displayed in the subform. To display these calculated controls in a form or report, you use the Count and Sum functions. The Count function determines the number of occurrences of an expression; its general format as a control in a form or report is =Count(*expression*). The Sum function calculates the total of an expression, and its general format as a control in a form or report is =Sum(*expression*). The number of invoices and total of invoice amounts are displayed in the subform's Detail section, so you'll need to place the calculated controls in the subform's Form Footer section.

## Adding Calculated Controls to a Subform's Form Footer Section

First, you'll open the subform in Design view in another window and add the calculated controls to the subform's Form Footer section.

**To add calculated controls to the subform's Form Footer section:**

1. Switch to Design view, click a blank area of the window to deselect any selected controls, right-click the subform's border, and then click **Subform in New Window** on the shortcut menu. The subform opens in its own tab in Design view. See Figure 6–39.

**Figure 6–39**    Subform in Design view

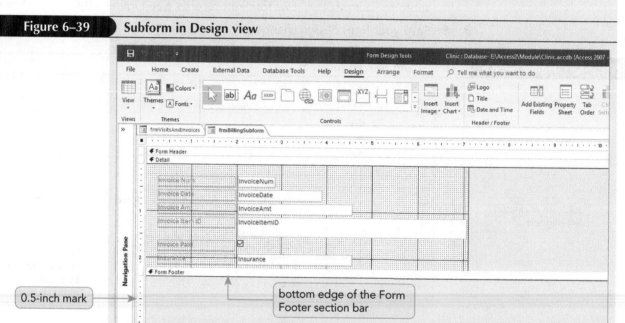

0.5-inch mark

bottom edge of the Form Footer section bar

The subform's Detail section contains the tblBilling table fields. As a subform in the main form, the fields appear in a datasheet even though the fields do not appear that way in Design view. The heights of the subform's Form Header and Form Footer sections are zero, meaning that these sections have been removed from the subform. You'll increase the height of the Form Footer section so that you can add the two calculated controls to the section.

2. Click the **Form Footer** section bar, position the pointer on the bottom border of the Form Footer section bar until the pointer changes to the vertical resize pointer ✛, and then drag the bottom border of the section down to the 0.5-inch mark on the vertical ruler.

   Now you'll add the first calculated control to the Form Footer section. To create the text box for the calculated control, you use the Text Box tool in the Controls group on the Form Design Tools Design tab. Because the Form Footer section is not displayed in a datasheet, you do not need to position the control precisely.

3. On the Form Design Tools Design tab, in the Controls group, click the **Text Box** tool [abl].

4. Position the plus symbol of the pointer near the top of the Form Footer section and aligned with the 1-inch mark on the horizontal ruler, and then

click the mouse button. A text box control and an attached label control appear in the Form Footer section. The text "Unbound" appears in the text box, indicating it is an unbound control.

Next, you'll set the Name and Control Source properties for the text box. Recall that the Name property specifies the name of an object or control. Later, when you add the calculated control in the main form, you'll reference the subform's calculated control value by using its Name property value. The **Control Source property** specifies the source of the data that appears in the control; the Control Source property setting can be either a field name or an expression.

5. Open the Property Sheet for the text box in the Form Footer section, click the **All** tab (if necessary), select the value in the Name box, type **txtInvoiceAmtSum** in the Name box, and then press **TAB** twice to move to the Control Source box.

6. In the Control Source box, type **=Sum(Inv**, press **TAB** to accept the rest of the field name of InvoiceAmt suggested by Formula AutoComplete, type **)** (a right parenthesis), and then press **TAB**. InvoiceAmt is enclosed in brackets in the expression because it's a field name. See Figure 6–40.

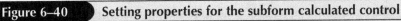

**Figure 6–40**     **Setting properties for the subform calculated control**

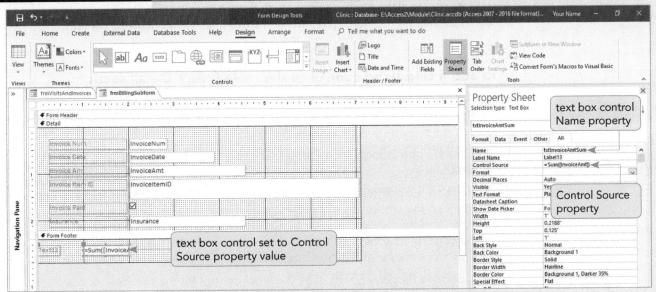

You've finished creating the first calculated control; now you'll create the other calculated control.

**TIP**

In the Name property, txtInvoiceNumCount, txt identifies the control type (a text box), InvoiceNum is the related field name, and Count identifies the control as a count control.

7. Repeat Steps 3 through 6, positioning the calculated field text box near the top of the Form Footer section aligned to the 3.5-inch mark on the horizontal ruler, setting the Name property value to **txtInvoiceNumCount**, and setting the Control Source property value to **=Count([InvoiceNum])**.

When you use the Count function, you are counting the number of displayed records—in this case, the number of records displayed in the subform. Instead of using InvoiceNum as the expression for the Count function, you could use any of the other fields displayed in the subform.

You've finished creating the subform's calculated controls.

▶ **8.** Close the Property Sheet, save your subform changes, and then close the subform. The active object is now the main form in Design view.

**Trouble?** The subform in the frmContractsAndInvoices form might appear to be blank after you close the frmInvoiceSubform form. This is a temporary effect; the subform's controls do still exist. Switch to Form view and then back to Design view to display the subform's controls.

▶ **9.** Switch to Form view. The calculated controls you added in the subform's Form Footer section are *not* displayed in the subform.

▶ **10.** Switch to Design view.

Next, you'll add two calculated controls in the main form to display the two calculated controls from the subform.

## Adding Calculated Controls to a Main Form

The subform's calculated controls now contain a count of the number of invoices and a total of the invoice amounts. However, notice that Reginald's design has the two calculated controls displayed in the main form, *not* in the subform. You need to add two calculated controls in the main form that reference the values in the subform's calculated controls. Because it's easy to make a typing mistake with these references, you'll use Expression Builder to set the Control Source property for the two main form calculated controls.

### To add a calculated control to the main form's Detail section:

▶ **1.** Adjust the length of the Detail section if necessary so that there is approximately 0.5 inch below the frmBillingSubform control. The Detail section should be approximately 5.5 inches.

▶ **2.** On the Form Design Tools Design tab, in the Controls group, click the **Text Box** tool [abl].

▶ **3.** Position the pointer's plus symbol below the frmBillingSubform at the 5-inch mark on the vertical ruler and aligned with the 1-inch mark on the horizontal ruler, and then click to insert the text box control and label in the form. Don't be concerned about positioning the control precisely because you'll resize and move the label and text box later.

▶ **4.** Open the Property Sheet, click the label control for the text box, set its Caption property to **Number of Invoices**, right-click the border of the label control, point to **Size** on the shortcut menu, and then click **To Fit**. Don't worry if the label control now overlaps the text box control.

You'll use Expression Builder to set a Control Source property for the text box control.

▶ **5.** Click the unbound text box control to select it, click the **Control Source** box in the Property Sheet, and then click the property's **Build** button [...] to open Expression Builder.

▶ **6.** In the Expression Elements box, click the **expand indicator** [+] next to frmVisitsAndInvoices, and then click **frmBillingSubform** in the Expression Elements box.

▶ **7.** Scroll down the Expression Categories box, and then double-click **txtInvoiceNumCount** in the Expression Categories box. See Figure 6-41.

| Figure 6–41 | Text box control's expression in the Expression Builder dialog box |

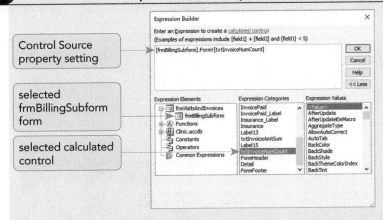

Instead of adding txtInvoiceNumCount to the expression box at the top, the Expression Builder changed it to [frmBillingSubform]. Form![txtInvoiceNumCount]. This expression displays the value of the txtInvoiceNumCount control that is located in the frmBillingSubform form, which is a form object.

You need to add an equal sign to the beginning of the expression.

**8.** Press **HOME**, type **=** (an equal sign), and then click the **OK** button. The Expression Builder dialog box closes, and the Control Source property is set.

Next, you'll add a second text box control to the main form, set the Caption property for the label control, and use Expression Builder to set the text box's Control Source property.

*Be sure you resize the label to its best fit.*

**9.** Repeat Steps 2 through 4 to add a text box to the main form, positioning the text box at the 3.5-inch mark on the horizontal ruler and approximately the 5-inch mark on the vertical ruler, and setting the label's Caption property to **Invoice Amount Total**.

**10.** Click the unbound text box control to select it, click the **Control Source** box in the Property Sheet, and then click the property's **Build** button ⋯ to open Expression Builder.

**11.** In the Expression Builder dialog box, type **=** (an equal sign), in the Expression Elements box, click the **expand indicator** ⊞ next to frmVisitsAndInvoices, click **frmBillingSubform** in the Expression Elements box, scroll down the Expression Categories box, and then double-click **txtInvoiceAmtSum** in the Expression Categories box.

**12.** Click the **OK** button to accept the expression and close the Expression Builder dialog box, close the Property Sheet, and save the form.

**13.** Click the **Collapse the Ribbon** button ⌃, switch to Form view, and then display the record for VisitID 1453. See Figure 6–42.

Figure 6–42    **Form with calculated controls**

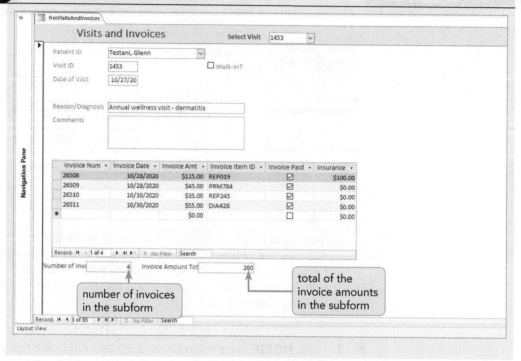

Now that the calculated controls are in the form, you will modify their appearance. You also will set additional properties for the calculated controls.

## Resizing, Moving, and Formatting Calculated Controls

In addition to resizing and repositioning the two calculated controls and their attached labels, you need to change the format of the rightmost calculated control to Currency and to set the following properties for both calculated controls.

- Set the Tab Stop property to a value of No. The **Tab Stop property** specifies whether users can use TAB to navigate to a control on a form. If the Tab Stop property is set to No, users can't tab to the control.
- Set the ControlTip Text property to a value of "Calculated total number of invoices for this patient visit" for the calculated control on the left and "Calculated invoice total for this patient visit" for the calculated control on the right. The **ControlTip Text property** specifies the text that appears in a ScreenTip when users position the mouse pointer over a control in a form.

Now you'll resize, move, and format the calculated controls and their attached labels.

### To size, move, and format the calculated controls and their attached labels:

1. Switch to Layout view, right-click the **Invoice Amount Total** calculated control, and then click **Properties** on the shortcut menu to open the Property Sheet.

2. Click the **All** tab in the Property Sheet (if necessary), set the Format property to **Currency**, and then close the Property Sheet. The value displayed in the calculated control changes from 260 to $260.00.

Now you'll resize and move the controls into their final positions in the form.

▶ **3.** Individually, reduce the widths of the two calculated controls by dragging the left border to the right to decrease the text box width so that they approximately match those shown in Figure 6–43.

| Figure 6–43 | Resized calculated controls and labels |

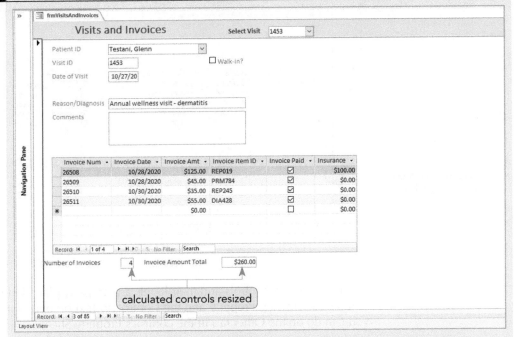

▶ **4.** Switch to Design view, select the **Number of Invoices** label and its related calculated control, and then use ➡ to move the label and its related text box to the right, aligning the left edge of the label with the left edge of the Comments label as closely as possible.

▶ **5.** Press ↑ to move the selected calculated control and its label until it is two grid dots from the bottom of the subform control.

▶ **6.** Lengthen the Detail section to approximately the 6-inch marker on the vertical ruler.

▶ **7.** Click the **Invoice Amount Total** label control, press **SHIFT**, click the corresponding calculated control text box, release **SHIFT**, and then drag the selected calculated control and its label to position them below and left-aligned with the Number of Invoices label control and its calculated control.

▶ **8.** Switch to Layout view.

**TIP**

In Design view you must use the move handle to move only a text box or its label, while in Layout view you can use either the move handle or the arrow keys.

▶ **9.** Click the **Invoice Amount Total** label control, and use the arrow keys to left-align the label control with the Number of Invoices label, select the **Invoice Amount Total** text box, and then use the arrows to left-align the calculated control text box with the Number of Invoices calculated control text box.

▶ **10.** Deselect all controls, switch to Form view, and then select record 1453. See Figure 6–44.

**Figure 6–44**     Calculated controls and labels aligned

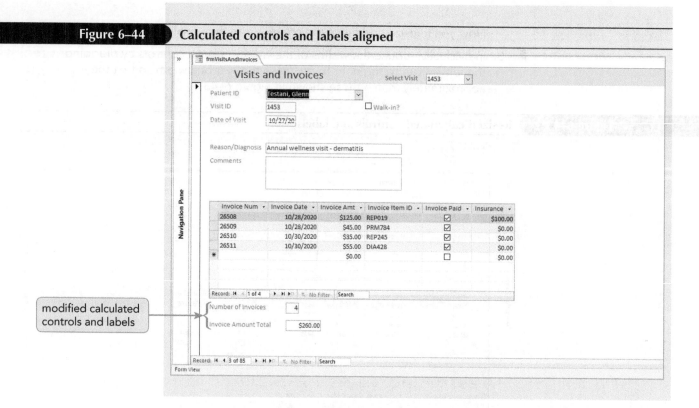

modified calculated controls and labels

The calculated controls and their labels are properly placed in the form. Next you will set the Tab Stop Property and the ControlTip Text property for both controls, which you can do on the Other tab in the control's Property Sheet.

### To set the Tab Stop Property and the ControlTipText property for the calculated controls:

1. Switch to Layout view, right-click the **Invoice Amount Total** calculated control, click **Properties** on the shortcut menu, and then click the **Other** tab in the Property Sheet.

2. Set the Tab Stop property to **No**, and then in the ControlTip Text box, specify **Calculated invoice total for this patient visit** as the value.

3. Click the **Number of Invoices** calculated control to display this control's properties in the Property Sheet, set the Tab Stop property to **No**, and then in the ControlTip Text box, specify **Calculated total number of invoices for this patient visit** as the value.

4. Close the Property Sheet, save your form design changes, switch to Form view, and then display visit 1453.

5. Position the pointer on the **Number of Invoices** box to display its ScreenTip, and then position the pointer on the **Invoice Amount Total** box to display its ScreenTip. You may have to pause while you position the pointer over the box, until the ScreenTip appears. See Figure 6–45.

| Figure 6–45 | ScreenTip for the calculated control |

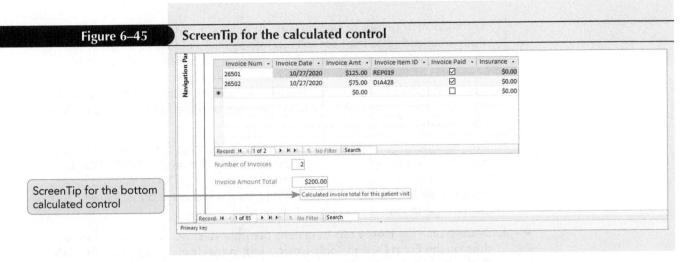

ScreenTip for the bottom calculated control

Reginald asks you to verify that users can't update the calculated controls in the main form and that when users tab through the controls in the form, the controls are selected in the correct order.

# Changing the Tab Order in a Form

Pressing TAB in Form view moves the focus from one control to another. A control is said to have **focus** when it is active and awaiting user action. The order in which the focus moves from control to control when a user presses TAB is called the **tab order**. Setting a logical tab order enables the user to keep his or her hands on the keyboard without reaching for the mouse, thereby speeding up the process of data entry in a form. Reginald wants to verify that the tab order in the main form is top-to-bottom, left-to-right. First, you'll verify that users can't update the calculated controls.

## To test the calculated controls and modify the tab order:

1. Select the value in the Number of Invoices box, and then type **8**. The Number of Invoices value remains unchanged, and the message "Control can't be edited; it's bound to the expression '[frmBillingSubform].[Form] ![txtInvoiceNumCount]'" is displayed on the status bar. The status bar message warns you that you can't update, or edit, the calculated control because it's bound to an expression. The calculated control in the main form changes in value only when the value of the expression changes in the subform.

2. Click the Invoice Amount Total box, and then type **8**. The value remains unchanged, and a message again is displayed on the status bar because you cannot edit a calculated control.

   Next, you'll determine the tab order of the fields in the main form. Reginald wants the tab order to be down and then across.

3. Select the value in the Visit ID box, press **TAB** to advance to the Date of Visit box, and then press **TAB** five more times to advance to the Reason/Diagnosis box, Comments text box, WalkIn check box, and PatientID combo box, in order, and then to the subform.

   Access sets the tab order in the same order in which you add controls to a form, so you should always check the form's tab order when you create a custom form in Layout or Design view. In this form you can see that the tab order is set such that the user will tab through the field value boxes in the main form before tabbing through the fields in the subform. In the main form, tabbing bypasses the two calculated controls because you set their Tab Stop properties to No, and you bypass the Select Visit combo box because it's an unbound control. Also, you tab through only the field value boxes in a form, not the labels.

The tab order Reginald wants for the field value boxes in the main form (top-to-bottom, left-to-right) should be the following: PatientID, VisitID, WalkIn, VisitDate, Reason, Comments, and then the subform. The default tab order doesn't match the order Reginald wants, so you'll change the tab order. You can change the tab order only in Design view.

4. Double-click the **Home** tab to restore the ribbon, switch to Design view, and then on the Form Design Tools Design tab, in the Tools group, click the **Tab Order** button. The Tab Order dialog box opens. See Figure 6–46.

---

**Figure 6–46**    **Tab Order dialog box**

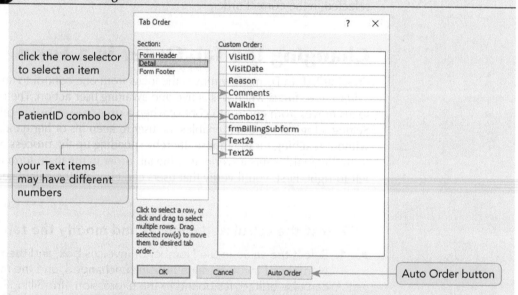

Because you did not set the Name property for the combo box control and the calculated controls, Access assigned them names that consist of the type of control and number; for example Combo12 for the PatientID combo box, Text24 for the Number of Invoices calculated control, and Text26 for the Invoice Amount Total calculated control as shown in Figure 6–46. (The numbers assigned to your controls might differ.) The Auto Order button lets you create a left-to-right, top-to-bottom tab order automatically, which is not the order Reginald wants. You need to move the Combo12 entry above the VisitID entry.

5. Click the **row selector** to the left of the Combo12 item (your number might differ), and then drag the row selector up to position it above the VisitID entry.

6. Click the row selector to the left of the WalkIn item, and then drag the row selector up to position it above VisitDate. The entries are now in the correct order. See Figure 6–47.

**Figure 6–47**    **Tab Order dialog box with corrected order**

**7.** Click the **OK** button to close the Tab Order dialog box, save your form design changes, and then switch to Form view.

**8.** Tab through the controls in the main form to make sure the tab order is correct, moving from the Patient ID box, to the Visit ID box, then to the Walk-in? check box, then to Date of Visit box, the Reason/Diagnosis box, the Comments box, and then finally to the subform.

**Trouble?** If the tab order is incorrect, switch to Design view, click the Tab Order button in the Tools group, change your tab order in the Tab Order dialog box to match the order shown in Figure 6–47, and then repeat Steps 7 and 8.

**PROSKILLS**

*Written Communication: Enhancing Information Using Calculated Controls*

For a small number of records in a subform, it's easy for users to quickly count the number of records and to calculate numeric total amounts when the form doesn't display calculated controls. For instance, when students have completed few courses or when people have made few tax payments, it's easy for users to count the courses and calculate the student's GPA or to count and total the tax payments. But for subforms with dozens or hundreds of records—for instance, students with many courses, or people with many tax payments—displaying summary calculated controls is mandatory. By adding a few simple calculated controls to forms and reports, you can increase the usefulness of the information presented and improve the ability of users to process the information, spot trends, and be more productive in their jobs.

You've finished adding controls to the form, but the form is plain looking and lacks visual clues organizing the controls in the form. You'll complete the form by making it more attractive and easier for Donna and her staff to use.

# Improving a Form's Appearance

The frmVisitsAndInvoices form has four distinct areas: the Form Header section containing the title and the Select Visit combo box, the six bound controls in the Detail section, the subform in the Detail section, and the two calculated controls in the Detail section. To visually separate these four areas, you'll increase the height of the Form Header section, add a horizontal line at the bottom of the Form Header section, and draw a rectangle around the calculated controls.

## Adding a Line to a Form

You can use lines in a form to improve the form's readability, to group related information, or to underline important values. You use the Line tool in Design view to add a line to a form or report.

**REFERENCE**

### Adding a Line to a Form or Report

- Display the form or report in Design view.
- On the Form Design Tools Design tab, in the Controls group, click the More button, and then click the Line tool.
- Position the pointer where you want the line to begin.
- Drag the pointer to the position for the end of the line, and then release the mouse button. If you want to ensure that you draw a straight horizontal or vertical line, press and hold SHIFT as you drag the pointer to draw the line.

You will add a horizontal line to the Form Header section to separate the controls in this section from the controls in the Detail section.

### To add a line to the form:

▶ 1. Switch to Design view, and then drag the bottom border of the Form Header section down to the 1-inch mark on the vertical ruler to make room to draw a horizontal line at the bottom of the Form Header section.

▶ 2. On the Form Design Tools Design tab, in the Controls group, click the **More** button ⤓, and then click the **Line** tool ◻.

▶ 3. Position the pointer's plus symbol at the left edge of the Form Header section just below the title.

▶ 4. Press and hold **SHIFT**, drag right to the 6-inch mark on the horizontal ruler, release the mouse button, and then release **SHIFT**. See Figure 6–48.

**Figure 6–48**        Line added to the form

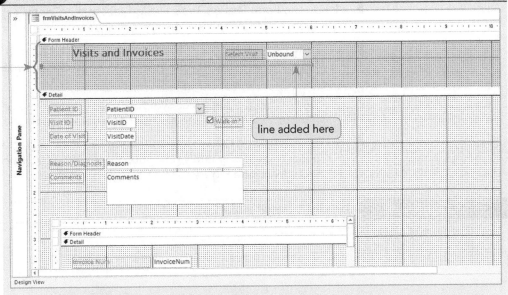

Form Header section height increased

line added here

**Trouble?** If the line is not straight or not positioned correctly, click the Undo button ↶ on the Quick Access Toolbar, and then repeat Steps 2 through 4. If the line is not the correct length, be sure the line is selected, press and hold SHIFT, and press ← or → until the line's length is the same as that of the line shown in Figure 6–48.

**5.** Drag the bottom border of the Form Header section up to just below the line.

**6.** Save your form design changes.

Next, you'll add a rectangle around the calculated controls in the Detail section.

## Adding a Rectangle to a Form

You can use a rectangle in a form to group related controls and to visually separate the group from other controls. You use the Rectangle tool in Design view to add a rectangle to a form or report.

### REFERENCE

**Adding a Rectangle to a Form or Report**

- Display the form or report in Design view.
- On the Form Design Tools Design tab, in the Controls group, click the More button, and then click the Rectangle tool.
- Click in the form or report to create a default-sized rectangle, or drag a rectangle in the position and size you want.

You will add a rectangle around the calculated controls and their labels to separate them from the subform and from the other controls in the Detail section.

## To add a rectangle to the form:

1. On the Form Design Tools Design tab, in the Controls group, click the **More** button ⍿ to open the Controls gallery, and then click the **Rectangle** tool ▢.

2. If necessary, scroll down the form so the two calculated controls and their labels are fully visible, with at least one grid dot between the bottom of the controls and the scroll bar.

3. Position the pointer's plus symbol approximately one grid dot above and one grid dot to the left of the Number of Invoices label.

4. Drag the pointer down and to the right to create a rectangle that that has all four sides approximately one grid dot from the two calculated controls and their labels. See Figure 6–49.

**Figure 6–49**    Rectangle added to the form

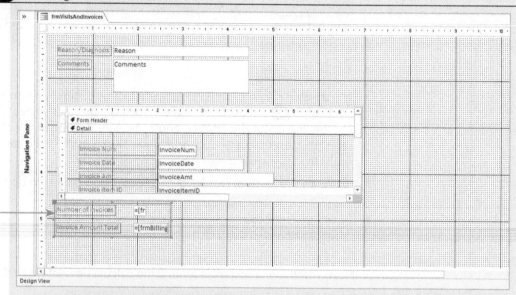

rectangle grouping the controls

**Trouble?** If the rectangle is not sized or positioned correctly, use the sizing handles on its selection border to adjust its size and the move handle to adjust its position.

Next, you'll set the thickness of the rectangle's lines.

5. Click the **Form Design Tools Format** tab.

6. In the Control Formatting group, click the **Shape Outline button**, point to **Line Thickness** at the bottom of the gallery, and then click **1 pt** line (second line from the top).

7. Click a blank area of the Form window to deselect the control.

Next, you'll add color and visual effects to the form's controls.

**TIP**

Using a theme can improve a form's appearance, but a theme doesn't provide the control you can achieve by setting individual properties in Design or Layout view.

## Modifying the Visual Effects of the Controls in a Form

Distinguishing one group of controls in a form from other groups is an important visual cue to the users of the form. For example, users should be able to distinguish the bound controls in the form from the calculated controls and from the Select Visit control in the Form Header section. You can modify the visual effects of a control in either Form

Design View or Form Layout View. You'll now use Form Design View to modify the controls in Reginald's form to provide these visual cues. You'll start by setting font properties for the calculated control's labels.

## To modify the format of the controls in the form:

1. Select the **Number of Invoices** label and the **Invoice Amount Total** label, using SHIFT to select multiple controls.

2. On the Form Design Tools Format tab, in the Font group, click the **Font Color button arrow** [A ▾], click the **Blue** color (row 7, column 8 in the Standard Colors palette), and then in the Font group, click the **Bold** button [B]. The labels' captions now appear in bold, blue font.

   Next, you'll set properties for the Select Visit label in the Form Header section.

3. If necessary, scroll up so the entire Form Header section is visible.

4. Select the **Select Visit** label in the Form Header section, change the label's font color to **Red** (row 7, column 2 in the Standard Colors palette), and then apply bold formatting.

   Next, you'll set the label's Special Effect property to a shadowed effect. The **Special Effect property** specifies the type of special effect applied to a control in a form or report. The choices for this property are Flat, Raised, Sunken, Etched, Shadowed, and Chiseled.

5. Open the Property Sheet for the Select Visit label, click the **All** tab (if necessary), set the Special Effect property to **Shadowed**, and then deselect the label. The label now has a shadowed special effect, and the label's caption appears in a red, bold font.

   Next, you'll set the Special Effect property for the bound control text boxes to a sunken effect.

6. Select the **VisitID** text box, the **VisitDate** text box, the **Reason** text box, and the **Comments** text box, set the controls' Special Effect property to **Sunken**, close the Property Sheet, and then deselect the controls.

   Finally, you'll set the background color of the Form Header section, the Detail section, the Select Visit combo box, and the two calculated controls. You can use the **Background Color button** in the Font group on the Form Design Tools Format tab to change the background color of a control, section, or object (form or report).

**TIP**

To set a background image instead of a background color, click the Background Image button in the Background group on the Form Design Tools Format tab.

7. Click the **Form Header** section bar.

8. On the Form Design Tools Format tab, in the Font group, click the **Background Color button arrow** [🎨 ▾], and then click the **Light Blue 2** color (row 3, column 5 in the Standard Colors palette). The Form Header's background color changes to the Light Blue 2 color.

9. Click the **Detail** section bar, and then in the Font Group, click the **Background Color** button to change the Detail section's background color to the **Light Blue 2** color.

10. Select the **Select Visit** combo box, **Number of Invoices** calculated control box, and the **Invoice Amount Total** calculated control box, set the selected controls' background color to the **Light Blue 2** color, and then deselect all controls by clicking to the right of the Detail section's grid.

11. Save your form design changes, switch to Form view, hide the ribbon, click the **Select Visit** arrow, and then click **1451** in the list to display this visit record in the form. See Figure 6–50.

Figure 6–50    **Completed custom form in Design view**

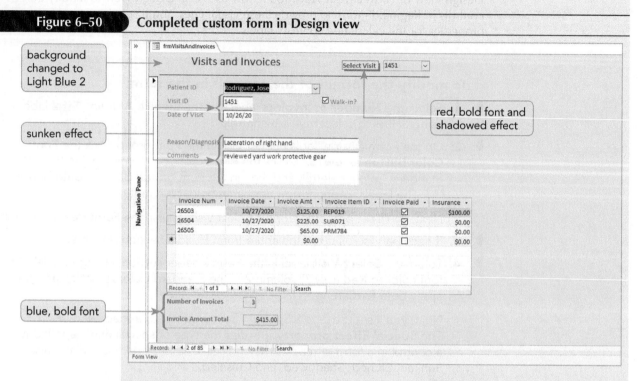

12. Test the form by tabbing between fields, navigating between records, and using the Select Visit combo box to find records, making sure you don't change any field values and observing that the calculated controls display the correct values.

13. **sam↑** Close the form, pin the ribbon, make a backup copy of the database, compact and repair the database, and then close the database.

### INSIGHT

### Applying Styles to Form and Report Controls

You can use the Quick Styles gallery to apply a built-in style reflecting a combination of several formatting options to a control in a form or report. To do this, select the control in either Layout or Design view, and then, on the Form or Report Design Tools Format tab, click the Quick Styles button in the Control Formatting group to display the Quick Styles gallery. Click a style in the gallery to apply it to the selected control.

You can also change the shape of a control in a form or report by clicking the Change Shape button in the Control Formatting group to display the Change Shape gallery, and then clicking a shape to apply it to the selected control.

Donna is pleased with the forms you have created. She will show these to her staff, and determine which of the forms will be most effective for using and managing the Clinic database.

**REVIEW**

### Session 6.3 Quick Check

**1.** To create a combo box to find records in a form with the Combo Box Wizard, the form's record source must be a(n) _____.

**2.** You use the _____ tool to add a subform to a form.

**3.** To calculate subtotals and overall totals in a form or report, you use the _____ function.

**4.** The Control Source property setting can be either a(n) _____ or a(n) _____.

**5.** Explain the difference between the Tab Stop property and tab order.

**6.** What is focus?

**7.** The _____ property has settings such as Raised and Sunken.

**PRACTICE**

## Review Assignments

**Data File needed for the Review Assignments: Supplier.accdb** (*cont. from Module 5*)

Donna wants you to create several forms, including a custom form that displays and updates companies and the products they offer. Complete the following steps:

1. Open the **Supplier** database you worked with in the previous module.
2. In the **tblProduct** table, remove the lookup feature from the SupplierID field, and then resize the Supplier ID column in the datasheet to its best fit. Save and close the table.
3. Edit the relationship between the primary tblSupplier and related tblProduct tables to enforce referential integrity and to cascade-update related fields. Create the relationship report, save the report as **rptRelationshipsForSupplier**, and then close it.
4. Use the Documenter to document the qryCompanyContacts query. Select all query options; use the Names, Data Types, and Sizes option for fields; and use the Names and Fields option for indexes. Export the report produced by the Documenter as a PDF file with the filename **NP_AC_6_SupplierDocumenter.pdf** and without saving the export steps, and then close the report.
5. Use the Datasheet tool to create a form based on the tblProduct table, save the form as **frmProductDatasheet**, and then close it.
6. Use the Multiple Items tool to create a form based on the qryDuplicateProductTypes query, save the form as **frmProductTypeMultipleItems**, and then close it.
7. Use the Split Form tool to create a split form based on the tblProduct table, and then make the following changes to the form in Layout view:
   a. Remove the two Units controls from the stacked layout and then reduce the width of the Units field value box by about half. Move the controls to the bottom left, and then anchor the two Units controls to the bottom left.
   b. Remove the four control pairs in the right column from the stacked layout, and then anchor the group to the bottom right. You may see a dotted border outlining the location of the previously removed controls. This may be automatically selected as well.
   c. Remove the ProductName control pair from the stacked layout, move them to the top right, and then anchor them to the top right.
   d. Reduce the widths of the ProductID and SupplierID field value boxes to a reasonable size.
   e. Change the title to **Product**, save the modified form as **frmProductSplitForm**, and then close it.
8. Use Figure 6–51 and the following steps to create a custom form named **frmSuppliersWithProducts** based on the tblSupplier and tblProduct tables.

**Figure 6-51**    Supplier database custom form design

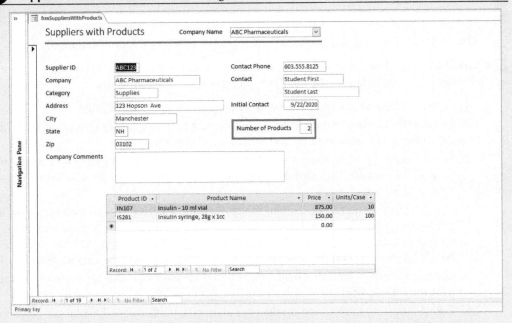

a.  Place the 12 fields from the tblSupplier table shown in Figure 6–51 at the top of the Detail section. Delete the Contact Last Name label, and change the caption for the Contact First Name label to **Contact**.

b.  Move the fields into two columns in the Detail section, as shown in Figure 6–51, resizing and aligning controls, as necessary, and increasing the width of the form.

c.  Add the title in the Form Header section.

d.  Make sure the form's Record Source property is set to tblSupplier, and then add a combo box in the Form Header section to find Company field values. In the Combo Box Wizard steps, select the Company and SupplierID fields, and hide the key column. Resize and move the control. Ensure the label displays the text "Company Name". Make sure the size of the Company Name field value box can accommodate the largest company name.

e.  Add a subform based on the tblProduct table, include only the fields shown in Figure 6–51, link with SupplierID, name the subform **frmPartialProductSubform**, delete the subform label, resize the columns in the subform to their best fit, and resize and position the subform.

f.  Create a calculated control in the subform that totals the number of products displayed, and then add a control to the main form that displays this calculated value. Set the main form control's Tab Stop property to No, and specify the text **Calculated number of products** for the ControlTip Text property.

g.  Add a line in the Form Header section, and add a rectangle around the calculated control and its label, setting the line thickness of both controls to 3 pt. Set the rectangle's color the same as the line's color.

h.  In the main form, use the Green 1 fill color (row 2, column 7 in the Standard Colors palette) for all form sections, and use the Black font color (row 1, column 2 in the Standard Colors palette) for all the label text, the calculated control, Company Name combo box, and the Title.

i.  Make sure the tab order is top-to-bottom, left-to-right for the main form text boxes.

9. Make a backup copy of the database, compact and repair the database, and then close the database.

## Case Problem 1

**Data File needed for this Case Problem: School.accdb (*cont. from Module 5*)**

**Great Giraffe**    Jeremiah Garver wants you to create several forms, including two custom forms that display and update data in the database. Complete the following steps:

1. Open the **School** database you worked with in the previous module.
2. Remove the lookup feature from the InstanceID field in the tblRegistration table, and then resize the Instance ID column to its best fit. Save and close the table.
3. Define a one-to-many relationship between the primary tblCourse table and the related tblRegistration table. Select the referential integrity option and the cascade updates option for this relationship.
4. Use the Documenter to document the qryStudentData query. Select all query options; use the Names, Data Types, and Sizes option for fields; and use the Names and Fields option for indexes. Export the report produced by the Documenter as a PDF file with the filename **NP_AC_6_StudentDataDocumenter.pdf** and without saving the export steps.
5. Use the Datasheet tool to create a form based on the tblCourse table, and then save the form as **frmCourseDatasheet**.
6. Create a custom form based on the qryBalanceContacts query. Display all fields from the query in the form. Create your own design for the form. Add a label to the bottom of the Detail section that contains your first and last names. Change the label's font so that your name appears in bold, blue font. Change the BalanceDue text box format so that the field value is displayed in bold, red font. Save the form as **frmBalanceContacts**.
7. Use Figure 6–52 and the following steps to create a custom form named **frmCoursesWithRegistrations** based on the tblCourse and tblRegistration tables.

Figure 6–52    **School database custom form design**

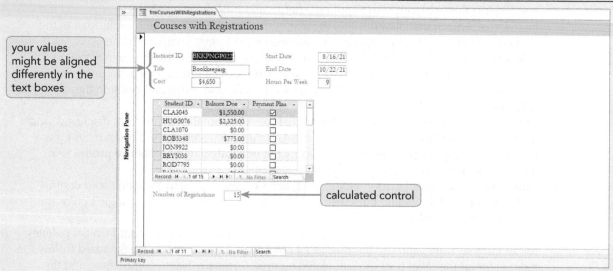

a. Place the fields from the tblCourse table shown in Figure 6–52 at the top of the Detail section, and edit the captions in the associated label controls as shown.
b. Selected fields from the tblRegistration table appear in a subform named **frmCoursesWithRegistrationsSubform**.
c. The calculated control displays the total number of records that appear in the subform. Set the text **Total number of students registered for this course** as the value of the calculated control's ControlTip Text property. Set the calculated control's Tab Stop property to **No**.

    d.   Apply the Organic theme to the frmCoursesWithRegistrations form only.

    e.   Save and close the form.

8. Make a backup copy of the database, compact and repair the database, and then close the database.

## Case Problem 2

**Data File needed for this Case Problem: Storm.accdb (*cont. from Module 5*)**

***Drain Adopter***   Tandrea Austin wants you to create several forms, including a custom form that displays and updates the location and information of drains that volunteers have signed up for. Complete the following steps:

1. Open the **Storm** database you worked with in the previous module.

2. Remove the lookup feature from the VolunteerID field in the tblDrain table, and then resize the Volunteer ID column to its best fit. Save and close the table.

3. Define a one-to-many relationship between the primary tblVolunteer table and the related tblDrain table. Select the referential integrity option and the cascade updates option for this relationship.

4. Use the Documenter to document the tblDrain table. Select all table options; use the Names, Data Types, and Sizes option for fields; and use the Names and Fields option for indexes. Export the report produced by the Documenter as a PDF file with the filename **NP_AC_6_DrainDocumenter.pdf** and without saving the export steps.

5. Create a query called **qryDrainsByVolunteer** that uses the tblVolunteer and tblDrain tables and includes the fields FirstName and LastName from the tblVolunteer table, and the fields DrainID, MainStreet, CrossStreet, and Direction from the tblDrain table.

6. Use the Multiple Items tool to create a form based on the qryDrainsByVolunteer query, change the title to **Drains by Volunteer**, and then save the form as **frmDrainsByVolunteerMultipleItems**.

7. Use the Split Form tool to create a split form based on the qryDrainsByVolunteer query, and then make the following changes to the form in Layout view.

    a.   Size each field value box as necessary to fit a reasonable amount of data.

    b.   Remove the MainStreet, CrossStreet, and Direction controls and their labels from the stacked layout, move these six controls to the right and then to the top of the form, and then anchor them to the top right.

    c.   Remove the DrainID control and its label from the stacked layout, and then anchor the pair of controls to the bottom left.

    d.   Change the title to **Drains by Volunteer**, and then save the modified form as **frmDrainsByVolunteerSplitForm**.

8. Use Figure 6–53 and the following steps to create a custom form named **frmSupply** based on the tblSupply table.

    a.   Make sure the form's Record Source property is set to tblSupply, and then add a combo box in the Form Header section to find SupplyID field values.

    b.   Add a calculated control that displays the total value of current inventory (cost multiplied by number on hand). *Hint*: Use the * symbol for multiplication. Set the calculated control's Tab Stop property to No, set the format to Currency, and use **Calculated value of stock on hand** as the ControlTip text value.

    c.   Add a line in the Form Header section, add a second line below it, and then add a second pair of lines near the bottom of the Detail section. Set the line thickness of all lines to 1 pt.

    d.   Use the Label tool to add your name below the pair of lines at the bottom of the Detail section.

    e.   For the labels in the Detail section, except for the Total Hours label and the label displaying your name, use the Aqua Blue 5 font color (row 6, column 9 in the Standard Colors palette) and make the text bold.

    f.   For the background fill color of the sections, the calculated control, and the Supply ID combo box, apply the Brown 2 color (row 3, column 10 in the Standard Colors palette).

    g.   Make sure the tab order is top-to-bottom, left-to-right for the main form field value boxes.

9.  Make a backup copy of the database, compact and repair the database, and then close the database.

---

**Figure 6–53**      **Storm database custom form design**

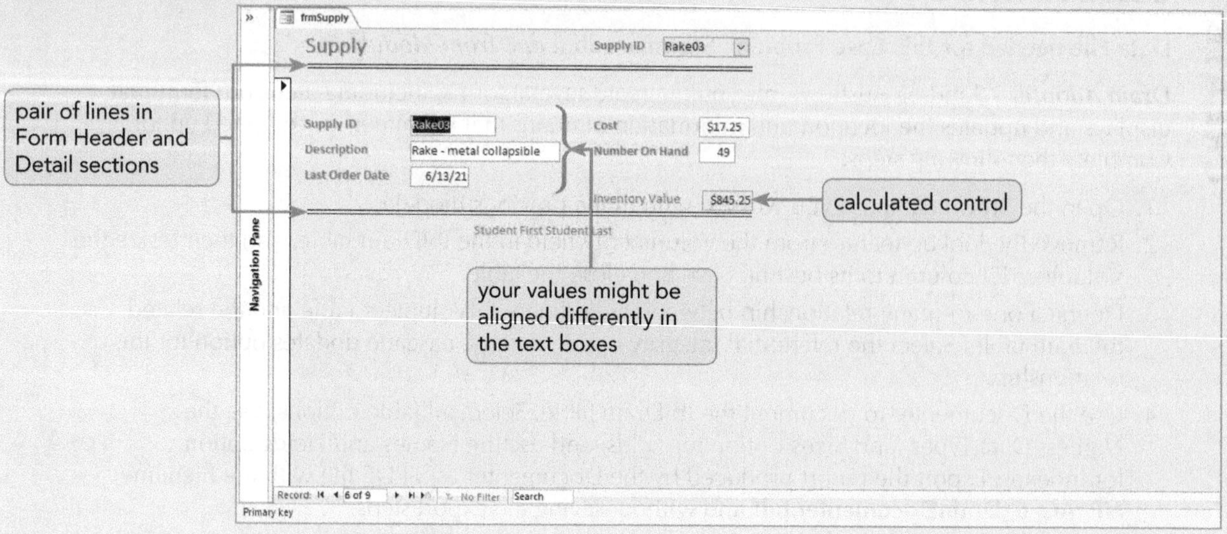

# Creating Custom Reports

*Creating Custom Reports for Lakewood Community Health Services*

## OBJECTIVES

**Session 7.1**
- View and filter a report in Report view
- Copy information from a report into a Word document
- Modify a report in Layout view
- Modify a report in Design view

**Session 7.2**
- Design and create a custom report
- Sort and group data in a report
- Add, move, resize, and align controls in a report
- Hide duplicate values in a report

**Session 7.3**
- Add the date and page numbers to a report's Footer section
- Add and format report titles
- Create and modify mailing labels

## Case | *Lakewood Community Health Services*

At a recent staff meeting, Donna Taylor, the office manager, indicated that she would like to make some changes to an existing report in the database. She also requested a new report that she can use to produce a printed list of all invoices for all visits.

In this module, you will modify an existing report and create the new report for Donna. In modifying and building these reports, you will use many Access features for customizing reports, including grouping data, calculating totals, and adding lines to separate report sections. These features will enhance the reports and make them easier for Donna and her staff to work with.

## STARTING DATA FILES

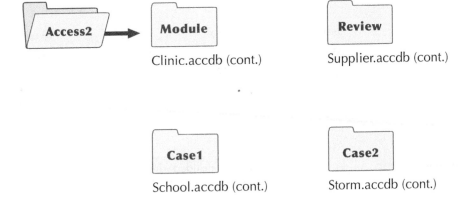

Access2 → Module
Clinic.accdb (cont.)

Review
Supplier.accdb (cont.)

Case1
School.accdb (cont.)

Case2
Storm.accdb (cont.)

# Session 7.1 Visual Overview:

A report title is placed in either the Report Header section or the Page Header section.

Each column in the report is a field from a table or query.

The report is grouped by PatientID.

Subtotals sum the values in the grouped columns.

The date appears in the Page Footer section at the bottom of every page in the report.

This report is displayed in Layout view.

The grand total is included when you add subtotals to the report.

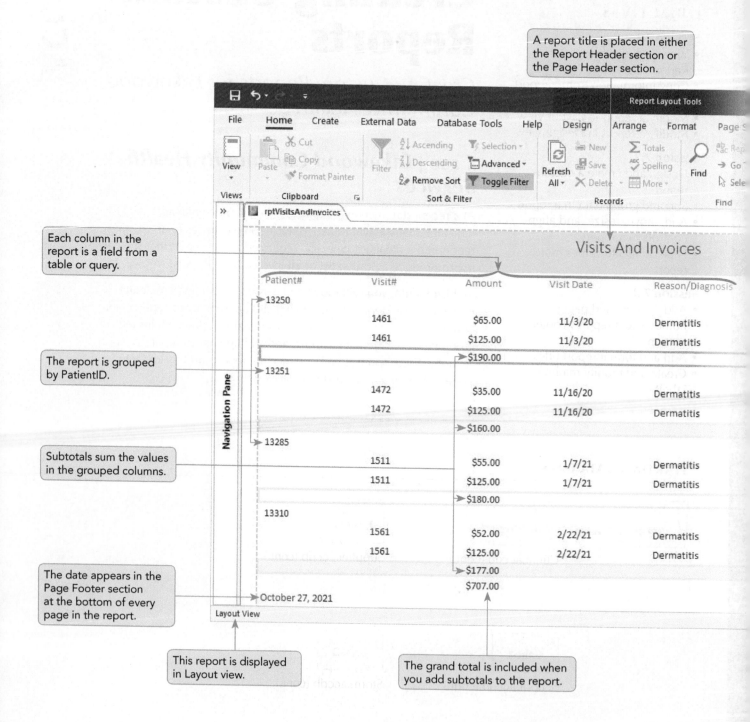

# Report Sections

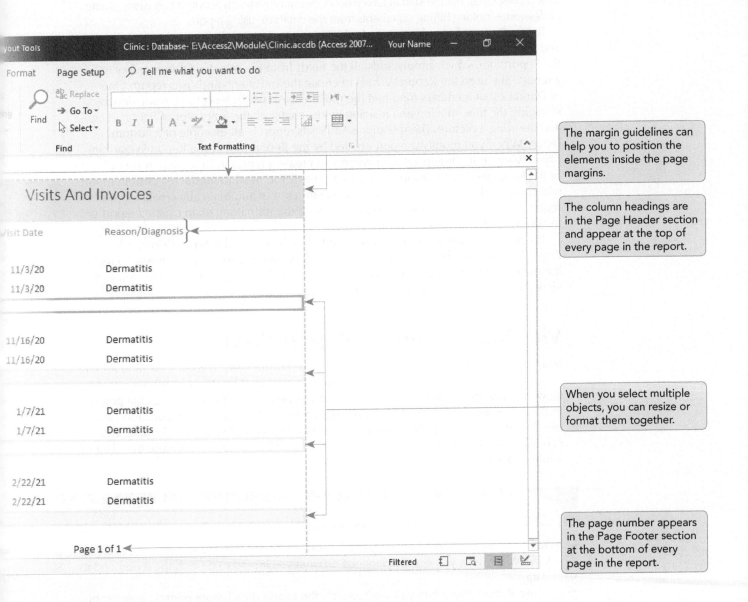

The margin guidelines can help you to position the elements inside the page margins.

The column headings are in the Page Header section and appear at the top of every page in the report.

When you select multiple objects, you can resize or format them together.

The page number appears in the Page Footer section at the bottom of every page in the report.

# Customizing Existing Reports

As you know, a report is a formatted output (screen display or printout) of the contents of one or more tables in a database. Although you can format and print data using datasheets, queries, and forms, reports offer greater flexibility and provide a more professional, readable appearance. For example, a billing statement created using a datasheet would not look professional, but the staff at Lakewood Community Health Services can easily create professional-looking billing statements from the database using reports.

Before Reginald Morales was tasked with enhancing the Clinic database, Donna and her staff created two reports. Donna created the rptVisitsAndInvoices report using the Report tool, which simply adds all the fields from the selected table or query to a report. She used the Report Wizard to create the rptPatientsAndVisits report. One of Donna's staff members modified the rptPatientsAndVisits report in Layout view by changing the title, moving and resizing fields, changing the font color of field names, and inserting a picture. The rptPatientsAndVisits report is an example of a custom report. When you modify a report created by the Report tool or the Report Wizard in Layout view or in Design view, or when you create a report from scratch in Layout view or in Design view, you produce a **custom report**. You need to produce a custom report whenever the Report tool or the Report Wizard cannot automatically create the specific report you need, or when you need to fine-tune the formatting of an existing report or to add controls and special features.

The rptVisitsAndInvoices report is included in the Clinic database. Donna asks Reginald to review the rptVisitsAndInvoices report and suggest improvements to make it more user friendly. You will make the changes Reginald suggests, but first, you will view and work with the report in Report view.

# Viewing a Report in Report View

You can view reports on screen in Print Preview, Layout view, Design view, and Report view. You've already viewed and worked with reports in Print Preview and Layout view. Making modifications to reports in Design view is similar to making changes to forms in Design view. **Report view** provides an interactive view of a report. You can use Report view to view the contents of a report and to apply a filter to its data. You can also copy selected portions of the report to the Clipboard and then use that data in another program.

---

**INSIGHT**

### Choosing the View to Use for a Report

You can view a report on screen using Report view, Print Preview, Layout view, or Design view. Which view you choose depends on what you intend to do with the report and its data.

- Use Report view when you want to filter the report data before printing a report or when you want to copy a selected portion of a report.
- Use Print Preview when you want to see what a report will look like when it is printed. Print Preview is the only view in which you can navigate the pages of a report, zoom in or out, or view a **multiple-column report**, which is a report that prints the same collection of field values in two or more sets across the page.
- Use Layout view when you want to modify a report while seeing actual report data.
- Use Design view when you want to fine-tune a report's design or when you want to add lines, rectangles, and other controls that are available only in Design view.

---

You'll open the rptVisitsAndInvoices report in Report view, and then you'll interact with its data in this view.

## To view and filter the rptVisitsAndInvoices report in Report view:

1. **sam** ⬇ Start Access, and then open the **Clinic** database you worked with in the previous two modules.

   **Trouble?** If the security warning is displayed below the ribbon, click the Enable Content button.

2. Open the Navigation Pane if necessary, double-click **rptVisitsAndInvoices**, and then close the Navigation Pane. The rptVisitsAndInvoices report opens in Report view.

   In Report view, you can view the report prior to printing it, just as you can do in Print Preview. Report view also lets you apply filters to the report before printing it. You'll apply a text filter to the rptVisitsAndInvoices report.

3. Scroll down to Patient ID 13252, which has four report detail lines for Visit ID 1585, right-click **Annual wellness visit** in the Reason column to open the shortcut menu, and then point to **Text Filters**. A submenu of filter options for the Text field opens. See Figure 7–1.

Figure 7–1    Filter options for a Text field in Report view

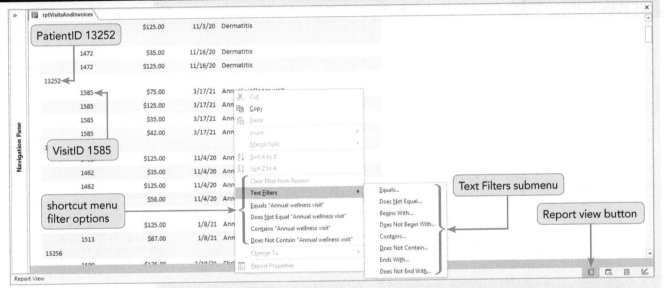

The filter options that appear on the shortcut menu depend on the selected field's data type and the selected value. Because you clicked the Reason field value without selecting a portion of the value, the shortcut menu displays filter options—various conditions using the value "Annual wellness visit"—for the entire Reason field value. You'll close the menus and select a portion of the Reason field value to explore a different way of filtering the report.

4. Click a blank area of the screen to close the menus.

5. For Patient ID 13252: Visit ID 1585, double-click **visit** in the Reason/Diagnosis column to select it, and then right-click **visit**. The filter options on the shortcut menu now apply to the selected text, "visit." Notice that the filter options on the shortcut menu include options such as "Ends With" and "Does Not End With" because the text you selected is at the end of the field value in the Reason/Diagnosis column.

6. On the shortcut menu, click **Contains "visit"**. The report content changes to display only those visits that contain the word "visit" anywhere in the Reason/Diagnosis column.

7. In the Reason/Diagnosis column, double-click the word **Annual** for the Visit ID 1585 report detail line for Patient ID 13252, right-click **Annual** to open the shortcut menu, and then point to **Text Filters**. The filter options now include the "Begins With" and "Does Not Begin With" options because the text you selected is at the beginning of the field value in the Reason/Diagnosis column.

Donna wants to view only those visits that contain the phrase "Annual wellness visit" in the Reason/Diagnosis column.

8. Click a blank area of the screen to close the menus, and then click in a blank area again to deselect the text.

9. In the report detail line for Visit ID 1585, right-click **Annual wellness visit** in the Reason/Diagnosis column, and then click **Equals "Annual wellness visit"** on the shortcut menu. Only the 15 invoices that contain the selected phrase are displayed in the report. See Figure 7–2.

| Figure 7–2 | Filter applied to the report in Report View |
| --- | --- |

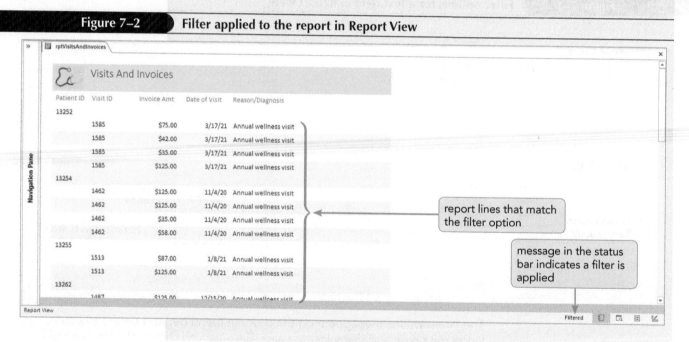

You can print the filtered report, or you can select the entire filtered report or a portion of it and copy it into another file so you can work with it in a different program.

## Copying and Pasting a Report into Word

Sometimes it is helpful to copy a filtered report or a portion of a filtered report into another file, such as a Word document or an Excel spreadsheet. This allows you to distribute the report electronically in a format that others can easily access, or you can print the filtered report to distribute on paper. When you copy information contained in an Access object such as a report, it is placed on the Clipboard. The Clipboard is a temporary storage area on your computer on which text or objects are stored when you cut or copy them, and its contents are available to all Windows programs. You can then paste the text or objects stored on the Clipboard into another file, such as a Word document or an Excel spreadsheet.

Donna would like you to create a Word document that contains the records from the Annual wellness visit filter so she can provide this information to the nurse who will follow up with these patients. Next, you'll copy the entire filtered report to the Clipboard.

## To copy the filtered report and paste it into a Word document:

**TIP**

You can press CTRL+A to select all items in the report.

1. Click to the left of the title graphic at the top of the report to select the report title control, drag down to the end of the last record in the report, and then release the mouse button to select the report title, field titles, and all of the records in the report. See Figure 7–3.

   **Trouble?** If you selected nothing, you clicked above the title graphic. Make sure the mouse pointer is to the left of the title graphic, but not above it, and then repeat Step 1.

   **Trouble?** If you selected only a portion of the report, press ESC to deselect your selection, and then repeat Step 1.

**Figure 7–3**    Selected filtered report in Report view

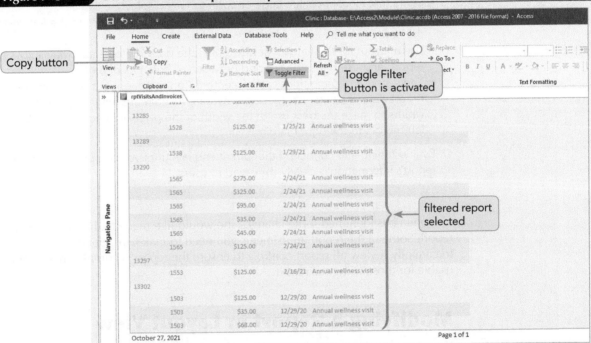

2. On the Home tab, in the Clipboard group, click the **Copy** button.

   You'll copy this report data into a Word document.

3. Open Word, and then in Backstage view, click **Blank document**. A blank Word document opens.

4. On the Home tab, in the Clipboard group, click the **Paste** button to paste the report data into the document.

5. Save the Word document with the filename **NP_AC_7_AnnualWellnessVisit** in the location where you are saving your files, and then close the NP_AC_7_AnnualWellnessVisit.docx document and exit Word. You return to Access with the rptVisitsAndInvoices filtered report in Report view.

6. To the right of the records, click a blank area of the window to deselect the report records, and then, in the Sort & Filter group, click the **Toggle Filter** button. The filters are removed from the report.

Viewing and working with a report in Report view often helps you to identify adjustments and modifications you can make to the report to enhance its readability. You can make modifications to a report in Layout view and Design view.

*Written Communication: Enhancing Reports Created by the Report Tool and the Report Wizard*

Creating a report using the Report tool or the Report Wizard can save time, but you should review the report to determine if you need to make any of the following types of common enhancements and corrections:

- Change the report title from the report object name (with an rpt prefix and no spaces) to one that has meaning to the users.
- Reduce the widths of the date and page number controls, and move the controls so that they are not printed on a separate page.
- Review the report in Print Preview, and, if the report displays excess pages, adjust the page margins and the placement of controls.
- Verify that all controls are large enough to fully display their values.
- Use page margins and field widths that display equal margins to the left and right of the data.
- Use a layout for the fields that distributes the data in a balanced way across the report, and use the same spacing between all columns of data.
- The report and page titles can be centered on the page, but do not center the report data. Instead, use spacing between the columns and reasonable column widths to make the best use of the width of the page, extending the data from the left margin to the right margin.

By fine-tuning and correcting the format and layout of your reports, you ensure the report's information is clearly conveyed to users.

Donna has identified some changes she would like made to the rptVisitsAndInvoices report. Some of the report adjustments you need to make are subtle ones, so you need to carefully review all report controls to ensure the report is completely readable and usable for those using the report.

# Modifying a Report in Layout View

You can make the report changes Donna wants in Layout view. Modifying a report in Layout view is similar to modifying a form in Layout view. When you open a report in Layout view, the Report Layout Tools Design, Arrange, Format, and Page Setup contextual tabs appear on the ribbon. You use the commands on these tabs to modify and format the elements of the report.

Donna wants you to decrease the width of columns and adjust the page margins in the report. She also wants you to rename some of the column headings, format the InvoiceAmt field values using the Standard format, resize the column headings, delete the picture from the Report Header section, remove the alternate row color from the detail and group header lines, and add a grand total of the InvoiceAmt field values. These changes will make the report more useful for Donna and her staff.

First, you will view the report in Layout view and observe how the information in the report is grouped and sorted.

## To view the report in Layout view:

1. On the status bar, click the **Layout View** button ⊞, and then scroll to the top of the report (if necessary).

2. On the Report Layout Tools Design tab, in the Grouping & Totals group, click the **Group & Sort** button to open the Group, Sort, and Total pane at the bottom of the window. The Group & Sort button is a toggle button; you click this button to open and close this pane as needed. See Figure 7–4.

| Figure 7–4 | Viewing the report in Layout view |
| --- | --- |

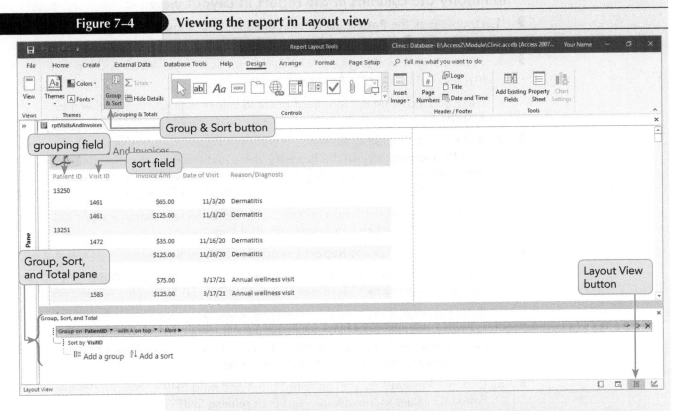

The rptVisitsAndInvoices report has a grouping field (the PatientID field) and a sort field (the VisitID field). At the bottom of the window, the **Group, Sort, and Total pane** provides you with the options to modify the report's grouping fields and sort fields and the report calculations for the groups. A **grouping field** is a report sort field that includes a Group Header section before a group of records having the same sort field value and a Group Footer section after the group of records. These sections are defined with section bars in Design view. A Group Header section usually displays the group name and the sort field value for the group. A Group Footer section usually displays subtotals or counts for the records in that group. The rptVisitsAndInvoices report's grouping field is the PatientID field, which is displayed in a Group Header section that precedes the set of visits for the Patient; the grouping field does not have a Group Footer section. The VisitID field is a secondary sort key, as shown in the Group, Sort, and Total pane.

Because you don't need to change the grouping or sort fields for the report, you'll close the pane and then make Donna's modifications to the report.

3. In the Grouping & Totals group, click the **Group & Sort** button to close the Group, Sort, and Total pane.

Now that you have an understanding of how the information in the report is grouped and sorted, you are ready to make the modifications to the report Donna has requested. First, you'll change the column headings for the first three columns to Patient#, Visit#, and Amount. Donna prefers to see all the detail data on one line, even when it means abbreviating column headings for columns whose headings are wider than the data. After reducing the column headings, you'll reduce the column widths, freeing up space on the detail lines to widen the Reason/Diagnosis column.

### To modify the columns in the report in Layout view:

1. Double-click the **Patient ID** column heading to change to editing mode, change it to **Patient#**, and then press **ENTER**.

2. Repeat Step 1 to change the Visit ID column heading to **Visit#** and the Invoice Amt heading to **Amount**.

   Next, you'll change the format of the field values in the Amount column to Standard.

3. Right-click any value in the Amount column to open the shortcut menu, click **Properties** to open the Property Sheet, set the Format property to **Standard**, and then close the Property Sheet. The Standard format uses comma separators and two decimal places, but no dollar signs.

   Now you'll widen the report margins. This will provide room on the printed page for staff to make handwritten notes if necessary.

4. On the ribbon, click the **Report Layout Tools Page Setup** tab.

5. In the Page Size group, click the **Margins** button, and then click **Wide**. This sets page margins to 1" on the top and bottom and 0.75" on the left and right.

   Sometimes when margins are decreased, some elements appear outside the margins, and this causes additional pages to be created in the report. This has occurred with the page number, and you'll fix that later. Now you'll adjust the widths of the columns to fit the data better.

6. Click the **Patient#** column heading, press and hold **SHIFT**, click one of the PatientID values in the column, and then release **SHIFT**. The Patient# column heading and all the values in this column are selected.

7. Position the pointer on the right border of the Patient# column heading selection box, and then when the pointer changes to the horizontal resize pointer ↔, drag the right border of the Patient# heading to the left until the border is just to the right of the # symbol in the column heading text. Now, you'll move the VisitID column to the left, closer to the Patient# column.

8. Click the **Visit#** column heading, press and hold **SHIFT**, click one of the VisitID values in the column, and then release **SHIFT**. The Visit# column heading and all the VisitID values in this column are selected.

9. Using the move pointer ⁺↕, drag the **Visit#** column to the left, until it is positioned such that the left border of the Visit# column heading selection box aligns with the right edge of the image in the report header. The column does not appear to move until you release the mouse button.

   **Trouble?** If the window scrolls to the bottom of the report after you release the mouse button in the drag operation, scroll back to the top of the report.

10. Drag the right edge of the Visit# column to the left to fit the column heading and the VisitID values.

Now you'll resize and move the Amount heading and InvoiceAmt values to the left, closer to the VisitID column, and then you'll move the Date of Visit and Reason/Diagnosis columns to the left, closer to the Amount column.

▶ **11.** Select the **Amount** column heading and the **InvoiceAmt** values in the column, and then drag the right border of the Amount column heading selection box to the left until it is positioned just to the right of the "t" in the column heading "Amount." The Amount column is resized to better fit the values in the column.

▶ **12.** With the Amount column heading and the InvoiceAmt values still selected, drag the column heading to the left until the left border of its selection box aligns with the letter "A" in the word "And" in the report's title.

▶ **13.** Select the **Date of Visit** column heading and the **VisitDate** values, and then resize and reposition the selected column heading and column of values as shown in Figure 7–5.

| Figure 7–5 | Resized columns in Layout view |

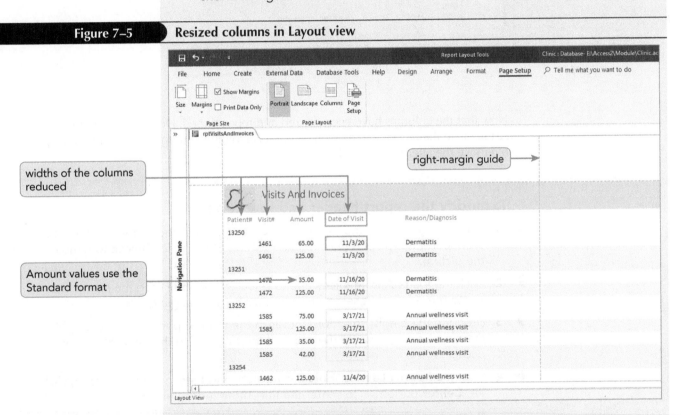

Now you'll move the column for the Reason field to the left and resize it to better fit the data, aligning it with the page's right margin.

▶ **14.** Select the **Reason/Diagnosis** column heading and field values, move them to the left, closer to the Date of Visit column, then resize the column heading and the column of values by dragging the right border of the selected items to the right margin of the report, as shown in Figure 7–6.

Figure 7–6    **Adjusted Reason/Diagnosis column width**

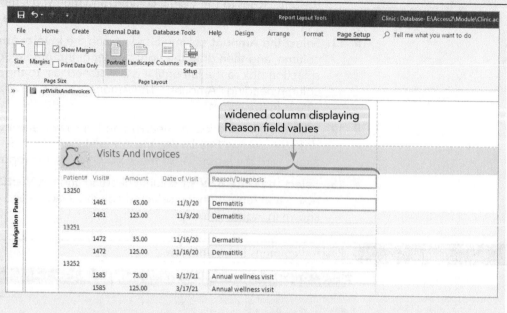

Now that the columns have been resized and repositioned, Donna asks you to make adjustments to the report header, which contains a picture and the report's title. You'll also remove the alternate row color.

### To modify the report header and row color:

1. If necessary, scroll to the top of the report, right-click the picture to the left of the report title to open the shortcut menu, and then click **Delete** to remove the picture.

2. Click the **Visits And Invoices** title to select it, and then drag the title to the left to position its left selection border at the left-margin guide.

3. Drag the title's right selection border to the right to position it at the right-margin guide to increase the width of the title box to the full width of the page.

4. Click the **Report Layout Tools Format** tab, and then in the Font group, click the **Center** button ☰ to center the title in the report header.

   Donna finds the alternate row color setting in the group header and detail lines distracting, and asks you to remove this formatting.

5. To the left of the first PatientID value in the first column, click to the left of the left-margin guide to select the group headers.

6. In the Background group, click the **Alternate Row Color** arrow to display the gallery of available colors, and then at the bottom of the gallery, click **No Color**. The alternate row color is removed from the PatientID group header rows.

   You've removed the alternate row color from the PatientID values in the report, and next you'll remove the alternate row color from the detail lines. Because the Alternate Row Color button is now set to "No Color," you can just click the button to remove the color.

**7.** Next to the first VisitID in the first PatientID record detail line, click to the left of the left-margin guide and then in the Background group, click the **Alternate Row Color** button to remove the alternate row color from the detail lines.

Donna's last change to the report is to add a grand total for the Amount field values. First, you must select the Amount column or one of the values in the column.

### To add a grand total to the report in Layout view:

**1.** In the first detail line for VisitID 1461, click **65.00** in the Amount column. The values in this column are all selected.

**2.** Click the **Report Layout Tools Design** tab, and then in the Grouping & Totals group, click the **Totals** button to display the Totals menu. See Figure 7-7.

| Figure 7-7 | The Totals menu |
|---|---|

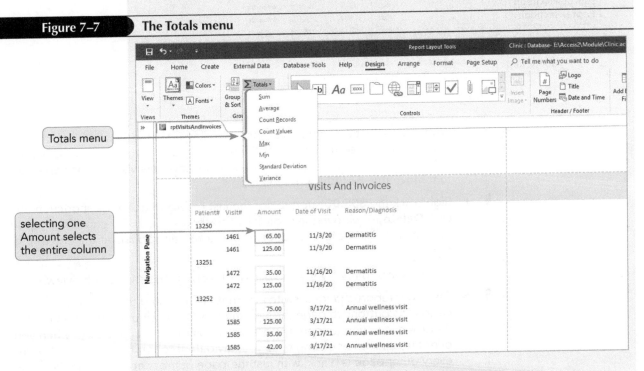

Totals menu

selecting one Amount selects the entire column

You can select one of the eight aggregate functions on the Totals menu to summarize values in the selected column. To calculate and display the grand total visit amount, you'll select the Sum aggregate function.

**3.** Click **Sum** in the Totals menu, scroll to the bottom of the report, and then if the last value in the Amount column displays as ######## instead of numbers, click ######## to select it, then drag the left selection border of the selected value to the left until the grand total of 22,223.00 is displayed.

Notice subtotals for each group of visits are displayed for each PatientID field value (355.00 for the last patient). See Figure 7-8.

**Trouble?** If the field value box still contains ###### after you resize it, increase the width again until the grand total value of 22,223.00 is visible.

**Figure 7-8**    **Report showing subtotals and a grand total of the InvoiceAmt field values**

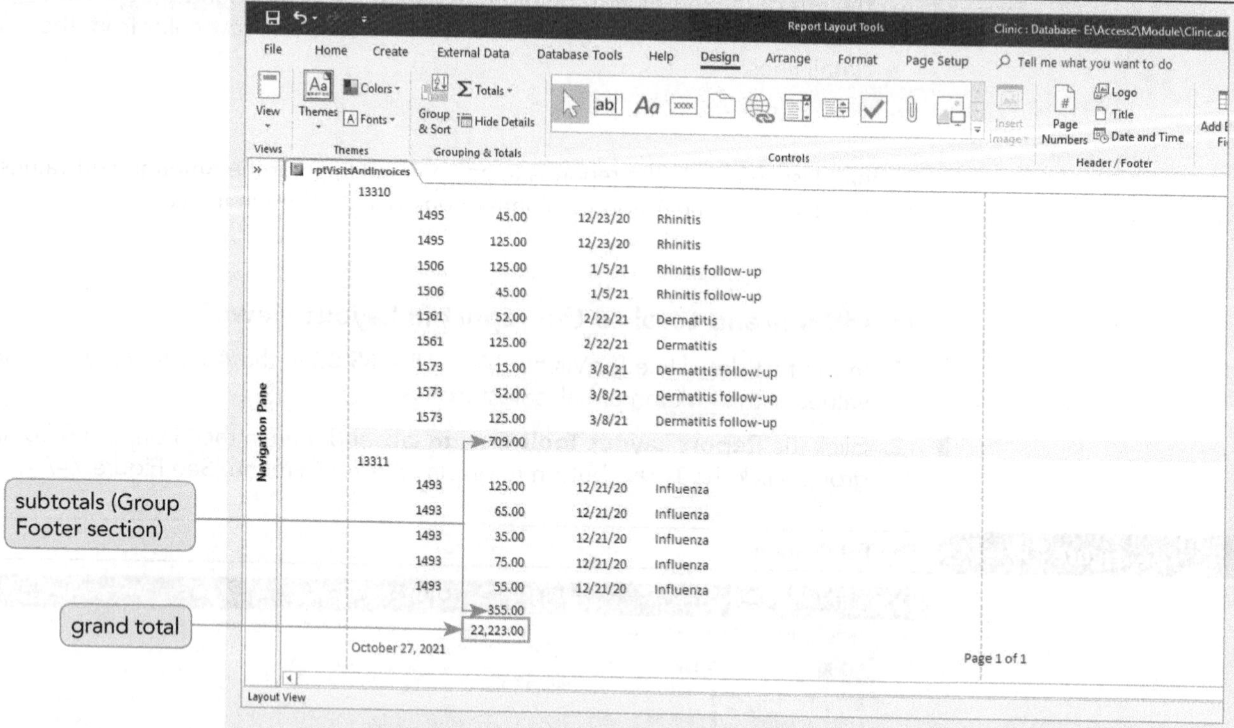

subtotals (Group Footer section)

grand total

When you select an aggregate function in Layout view, the results of the function are added to the end of the report, and subtotals for each grouping field are also added. Because some patients have few visits, Donna asks you to remove the subtotals from the report.

4. Right-click the **355.00** subtotal for the last record to open the shortcut menu, click **Delete** to remove the subtotals, and then scroll to the end of the report. You deleted the subtotals, but the grand total still appears at the end of the report.

   Donna wants to review the rptVisitsAndInvoices report in Print Preview.

5. Save your report changes, switch to Print Preview, and then use the navigation buttons to page through the report. Viewing the report in Print Preview allows you to identify possible problems that might occur when you print the report. For example, as you navigate through the report, notice that every other page is blank, with just the page number appearing in the footer.

6. Navigate to the second to last page of the report that shows the grand total line, and then click the **Zoom In** button ⊞ on the status bar to increase the zoom percentage to 110%. See Figure 7-9.

Figure 7-9    The rptVisitsAndInvoices report in Print Preview

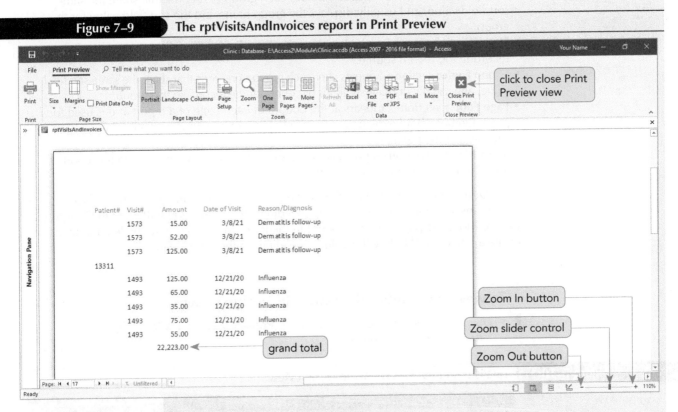

**Trouble?** Depending on the printer you are using, the last page of your report might differ. If so, don't worry. Different printers format reports in different ways, sometimes affecting the total number of pages and the number of records printed per page.

▶ **7.** On the status bar, click the **Zoom Out** button ⊟ to decrease the zoom percentage to 100%, and close the Print Preview view and display the report in Layout view.

As you saw in Print Preview, the page numbers are outside the right margin and are causing extra pages in the report. Therefore, you need to reposition the page number that appears at the bottom of each page. Donna suggests you move the page number box to the left so that its right edge is aligned with the right edge of Reason field value box in the Detail section, thereby eliminating the extra pages in the report. She also wants you to add a line below the column heading labels. Although you can make Donna's modifications in Layout view, you'll make them in Design view so you can work more precisely.

## Modifying a Report in Design View

Design view for reports is similar to Design view for forms, which you used in the previous module to customize forms. When you open a report in Design view, the Report Design Tools contextual tabs—Design, Arrange, Format, and Page Setup—appear on the ribbon.
A report in Design view is divided into seven sections:

- **Report Header section**—appears once at the beginning of a report and is used for report titles, company logos, report introductions, dates, visual elements such as lines, and cover pages.
- **Page Header section**—appears at the top of each page of a report and is used for page numbers, column headings, report titles, and report dates.

- **Group Header section**—appears before each group of records that share the same sort field value, and usually displays the group name and the sort field value for the group.
- **Detail section**—contains the bound controls to display the field values for each record in the record source.
- **Group Footer section**—appears after each group of records that share the same sort field value, and usually displays subtotals or counts for the records in that group.
- **Page Footer section**—appears at the bottom of each page of a report and is used for page numbers, brief explanations of symbols or abbreviations, or other information such as a company name.
- **Report Footer section**—appears once at the end of a report and is used for report totals and other summary information.

As Donna requested, you need to move the page number in the report, and you need to insert a line below the column headings. To do this, you will work in Design view to move the page number control in the Page Footer section to the left and then create a line control below the column headings in the Page Header.

### To view and modify the report in Design view:

1. Switch to Design view, and click the **Report Design Tools Design** tab, if necessary. See Figure 7–10.

| Figure 7–10 | rptVisitsAndInvoices report in Design view |
| --- | --- |

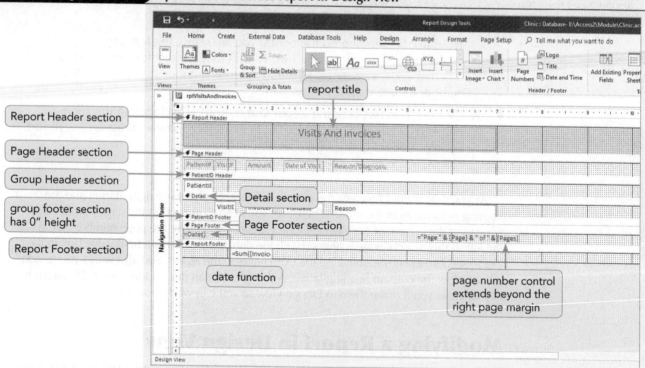

Notice that Design view for a report has most of the same components as Design view for a form. For example, Design view for forms and reports includes horizontal and vertical rulers, grids in each section, and similar buttons in the groups on the Report Design Tools Design tab.

Design view for the rptVisitsAndInvoices report displays seven sections: the Report Header section contains the report title; the Page Header section contains the column heading labels; the Group Header section (PatientID Header) contains the PatientID grouping field; the Detail section contains the bound controls to display the field values for each record in the record source (tblVisit); the Group Footer section (PatientID Footer) isn't displayed in the report; the Page Footer section contains the current date and the page number; and the Report Footer section contains the Sum function, which calculates the grand total of the InvoiceAmt field values.

You will now move the page number control in the Page Footer section so that it is within the report's right page margin. To guide you in this, recall you earlier resized and repositioned the Reason/Diagnosis column in Layout view so it aligned to the right margin of the page. Therefore, you will right-align the page number control to the Reason field value box in the Detail section.

2. Click the **Page Number** control to select it (the control on the right side of the Page Footer section), and then press ← to move the control to the left until the right border of its selection box is roughly aligned with the right edge of the Reason field value control box in the Detail section.

   **Trouble?** If the page number control overlaps the date control in the Report Footer section, don't worry about it. The contents of both will still be displayed.

3. With the Page Number control still selected, press and hold **SHIFT**, click the **Reason** field value control box in the Detail section, and then release **SHIFT**. Both controls are now selected.

4. Right-click one of the selected controls, point to **Align** on the shortcut menu, and then click **Right**. Both controls are now right-aligned.

   Finally, you'll create the line in the Page Header section.

5. Drag the bottom border of the Page Header section down to increase the height approximately half an inch. You'll resize this again after the line is created.

6. On the Report Design Tools Design tab, in the Controls group, click the **More** button ⬇, and then click the **Line** tool ⬛.

7. In the Page Header section, position the plus symbol of the Line tool pointer approximately two grid dots below the column header boxes, press and hold **SHIFT**, drag to the right page margin, and then release **SHIFT** to create a horizontal line that spans the width of the page. Holding SHIFT while drawing or extending a line snaps the line to either horizontal or vertical—whichever is nearest to the angle at which the line is drawn.

8. If necessary, drag the lower edge of the Page Header section up so it is approximately two grid dots below the line. See Figure 7–11.

**Figure 7–11**   Modified report in Design view

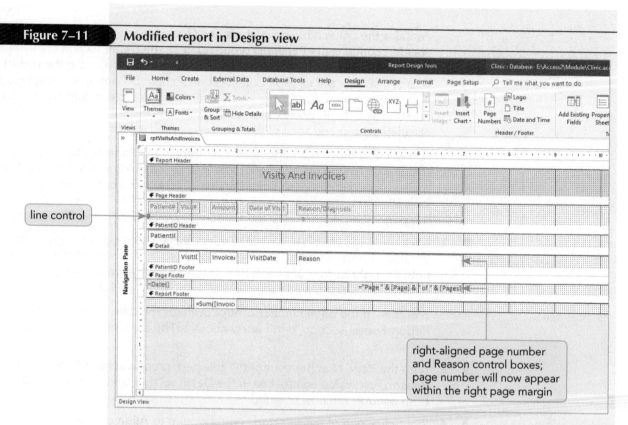

9. Save your report changes, switch to Print Preview, and then scroll and use the navigation buttons to page through the report, paying particular attention to the placement of the line in the Page Header section and the page number in the Page Footer section. The page number is right-aligned in the control box, so the text appears flush with the right margin. The data in the Reason field value text boxes are left-aligned, so this data does not appear flush with the right margin.

   **Trouble?** If you resize a field to position it outside the current margin, the report may widen to accommodate it, triggering a dialog box about the section width being greater than the page width. If this dialog box opens, click OK, manually move form elements as necessary so that no elements extend past 7 inches, and then adjust the report width to 7 inches.

   **Trouble?** If you position all report elements within the margins and still receive a message about the section width being greater than the page width, click OK, then click the Form Selector button where the rulers intersect, click the Error Checking Options button ⚠, and then on the menu, click Remove Extra Report Space.

10. Save and close the report.

11. If you are not continuing on to the next session, close the Clinic database.

Donna is happy with the changes you've made to the rptVisitsAndInvoices report. In the next session, you create a new custom report for her based on queries instead of tables.

## Session 7.1 Quick Check

**1.** What is a custom report?

**2.** Can a report be modified in Layout view?

**3.** Besides viewing a report, what other actions can you perform in Report view?

**4.** What is a grouping field?

**5.** List and describe the seven sections of an Access report.

# Session 7.2 Visual Overview:

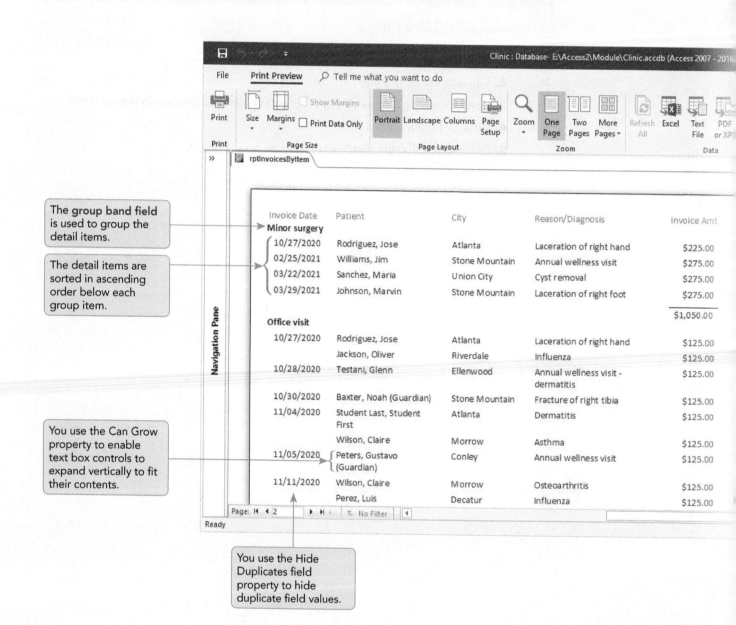

**The group band field is used to group the detail items.**

**The detail items are sorted in ascending order below each group item.**

**You use the Can Grow property to enable text box controls to expand vertically to fit their contents.**

**You use the Hide Duplicates field property to hide duplicate field values.**

# Form in Design View and Print Preview

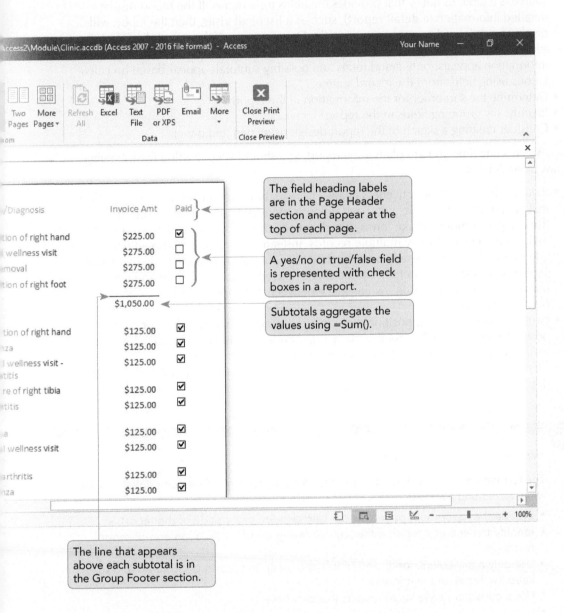

The field heading labels are in the Page Header section and appear at the top of each page.

A yes/no or true/false field is represented with check boxes in a report.

Subtotals aggregate the values using =Sum().

The line that appears above each subtotal is in the Group Footer section.

# Planning and Designing a Custom Report

Before you create a custom report, you should first plan the report's contents and its layout. When you plan a report, you should follow this general process:

- Determine the purpose of the report and its record source. Recall that the record source is a table or query that provides the fields for a report. If the report displays detailed information (a **detail report**), such as a list of all visits, then the report will display fields from the record source in the Detail section. If the report displays only summary information (a **summary report**), such as total visits by city, then no detailed information appears; only grand totals and possibly subtotals appear based on calculations using fields from the record source.
- Determine the sort order for the information in the report.
- Identify any grouping fields in the report.
- Consider creating a sketch of the report design using pen and paper.

At the same time you are planning a report, you should keep in mind the following layout guidelines:

- Balance the report's attractiveness against its readability and economy. Keep in mind that an attractive, readable, two-page report is more economical than a report of three pages or more. Unlike forms, which usually display one record at a time in the main form, reports display multiple records. Instead of arranging fields vertically as you do in a form, you usually position fields horizontally across the page in a report. Typically, you set the detail lines to be single-spaced in a report. At the same time, make sure to include enough white space between columns so the values do not overlap or run together.
- Group related fields and position them in a meaningful, logical order. For example, position identifying fields, such as names and codes, on the left. Group together all location fields, such as street and city, and position them in their customary order.
- Identify each column of field values with a column heading label that names the field.

## Written Communication: Formatting a Report

The formatting of a report impacts its readability. Keep in mind the following guidelines when formatting a report:

- Include the report title, page number, and date on every page of the report.
- Identify the end of a report either by displaying grand totals or an end-of-report message.
- Use only a few colors, fonts, and graphics to keep the report uncluttered and to keep the focus on the information.
- Use a consistent style for all reports in a database.

By following these report-formatting guidelines, you'll create reports that make it easier for users to conduct their daily business and to make better decisions.

After working with Donna and her staff to determine their requirements for a new report, Reginald prepared a design for a custom report to display invoices grouped by invoice item. Refer to the Session 7.2 Visual Overview, which details Reginald's custom report design in Print Preview.

The custom report will list the records for all invoices and will contain five sections:

- The Page Header section will contain the report title ("Invoices by Item") centered between the current date on the left and the page number on the right. A horizontal line will separate the column heading labels from the rest of the report page. From your work with the Report Wizard, you know that, by default, Access places the report title in the Report Header section and the date and page number in the Page Footer section. Donna prefers that the date, report title, and page number appear at the top of each page, so you need to place this information in the custom report's Page Header section.

- The InvoiceItem field value from the tblInvoiceItem table will be displayed in a Group Header section.
- The Detail section will contain the InvoiceDate, InvoiceAmt, and InvoicePaid field values from the tblBilling table; the Reason field value from the tblVisit table; the PatientName field value from the tblPatient table; and the Patient calculated field value from the qryPatientsByName query. The detail records will be sorted in ascending order by the InvoiceDate field.
- A subtotal of the InvoiceAmt field values will be displayed below a line in the Group Footer section.
- The grand total of the InvoiceAmt field values will be displayed below a double line in the Report Footer section.

Before you start creating the custom report, you need to create a query that will serve as the record source for the report.

## Creating a Query for a Custom Report

**TIP**

Create queries to serve as the record source for forms and reports. As requirements change, you can easily add fields, including calculated fields, to the queries.

As you know, the data for a report can come from a single table, from a single query based on one or more tables, or from multiple tables and/or queries. Donna's report will contain data from the tblInvoiceItem, tblBilling, tblVisit, and tblPatient tables, and from the qryPatientsByName query. You'll use the Simple Query Wizard to create a query to retrieve all the data required for the custom report and to serve as the report's record source. A query filters data from one or more tables using criteria that can be quite complex. Creating a report based on a query allows you to display and distribute the results of the query in a readable, professional format, rather than only in a datasheet view.

### To create the query to serve as the custom report's record source:

1. If you took a break after the previous session, make sure that the Clinic database is open and the Navigation Pane is closed.

2. On the ribbon, click the **Create** tab.

3. In the Queries group, click the **Query Wizard** button to open the New Query dialog box, make sure **Simple Query Wizard** is selected, and then click the **OK** button. The first Simple Query Wizard dialog box opens.

    You need to select fields from the tblInvoiceItem, tblBilling, tblVisit, and tblPatient tables and from the qryPatientsByName query, in that order.

4. In the Tables/Queries box, select **Table: tblInvoiceItem**, and then move the **InvoiceItem** field from the Available Fields box to the Selected Fields box.

5. In the Tables/Queries box, select **Table: tblBilling**, and then move the **InvoiceItemID, InvoiceDate, InvoiceAmt**, and **InvoicePaid** fields, in that order, from the Available Fields box to the Selected Fields box.

6. In the Tables/Queries box, select **Table: tblVisit**, and then move the **Reason** field from the Available Fields box to the Selected Fields box.

7. In the Tables/Queries box, select **Table: tblPatient**, and then move the **City** field from the Available Fields box to the Selected Fields box.

8. In the Tables/Queries box, select **Query: qryPatientsByName**, move the **Patient** calculated field from the Available Fields box to the Selected Fields box, and then click the **Next** button.

▶ 9. Make sure the **Detail (shows every field of every record)** option button is selected, and then click the **Next** button to open the final Simple Query Wizard dialog box.

▶ 10. Change the query name to **qryInvoicesByItem**, click the **Modify the query design** option button, and then click the **Finish** button. The query is displayed in Design view.

Next you need to set the sort fields for the query. The InvoiceItem field will be a grouping field, which means it's the primary sort field, and the InvoiceDate field is the secondary sort field.

### To set the sort fields for the query:

▶ 1. In the design grid, set the value in the InvoiceItem Sort box to **Ascending** and then set the value in the InvoiceDate Sort box to **Ascending**.

▶ 2. Lengthen the query and table field lists as necessary to view all fields, drag the tables if necessary to position them so the join lines between them are visible, and then save your query changes. The completed query contains eight fields from four tables and one query, and the query includes two sort fields, the InvoiceItem primary sort field and the InvoiceDate secondary sort field. See Figure 7–12.

**Figure 7–12**   **Completed qryInvoicesByItem query in Design View**

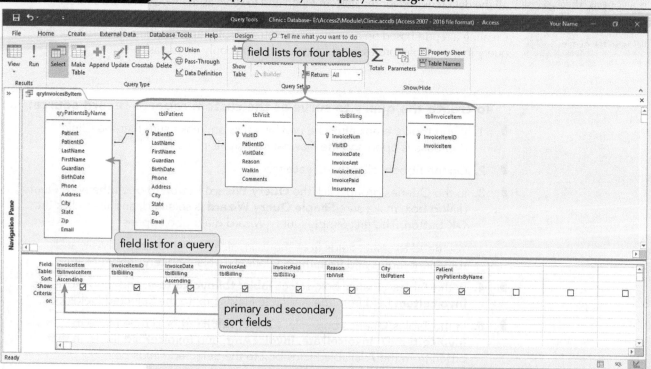

▶ 3. If necessary, click the **Query Tools Design** tab, run the query, verify that it returns 204 records, and then save and close the query.

You'll use the qryInvoicesByItem query as the record source for the custom report.

# Creating a Custom Report

Now that you've created the record source for the custom report, you could use the Report Wizard to create the report and then modify it to match the report design. However, because you need to customize several components of the report, you will create a custom report in Layout view and then switch between Layout and Design view to fine-tune the report.

**INSIGHT**

## Making Report Design Modifications

You perform operations in Layout and Design views for reports in the same way that you perform operations in these views for forms. These operations become easier with practice. Remember to use the Undo button when necessary, back up your database frequently, save your report changes frequently, work from a copy of the report for complicated design changes, and compact and repair the database on a regular basis. You can also display the report in Print Preview at any time to view your progress on the report.

You'll create a blank report in Layout view, set the record source, and then add controls to the custom report.

### To create a blank report and add bound controls in Layout view:

▶ 1. Click the **Create** tab, and then in the Reports group, click the **Blank Report** button. A new report opens in Layout view, with the Field List pane open, and the Report Layout Tools Design tab active on the ribbon. See Figure 7–13.

| Figure 7–13 | Blank report in Layout view |
|---|---|

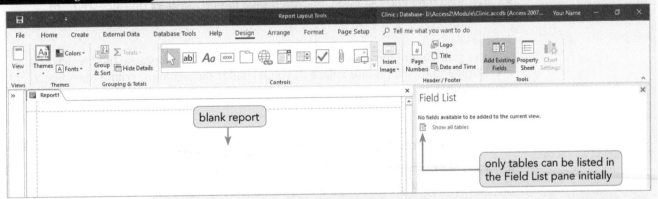

▶ 2. In the Tools group, click the **Property Sheet** button to open the Property Sheet for the report.

▶ 3. In the Property Sheet, click the **All** tab (if necessary), click the **Record Source** arrow, click **qryInvoicesByItem**, and then close the Property Sheet.

▶ 4. In the Tools group, click the **Add Existing Fields** button to open the Field List pane. The Field List pane displays the eight fields in the qryInvoicesByItem query, which is the record source for the report.

Referring to Reginald's report design, you'll add six of the eight fields to the report in a tabular layout, which is the default control layout when you add fields to a report in Layout view.

5. In the Field List pane, double-click **InvoiceItem**, and then, in order, double-click **InvoiceDate**, **Patient**, **City**, **Reason**, **InvoiceAmt**, and **InvoicePaid** in the Field List pane. The six bound controls are displayed in a tabular layout in the report. See Figure 7–14.

**Figure 7–14**    **After adding fields to the report in Layout view**

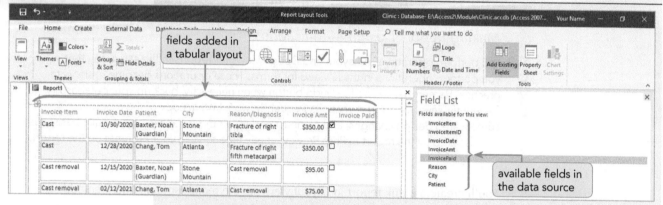

**Trouble?** If you add the wrong field to the report, click the field's column heading, press and hold SHIFT, click one of the field values in the column to select the column, release SHIFT, click the Home tab on the ribbon, and then in the Records group, click the Delete button to delete the field. If you add a field in the wrong order, click the column heading in the tabular layout, press and hold SHIFT, click one of the field values in the column, release SHIFT, and then drag the column to its correct position.

You are done working with the Field List pane.

6. Close the Field List pane, and then save the report as **rptInvoicesByItem**.

Next, you'll adjust the column widths in Layout view. Also, because the Invoice Amt and Invoice Paid columns are adjacent, you'll change the rightmost column heading to "Paid" to save space.

### To resize and rename columns in Layout view:

1. In the rightmost column, double-click **Invoice Paid**, delete **Invoice** and the following space, and then press **ENTER**.

2. Drag the right border of the Paid column heading selection box to the left to decrease the column's width so it just fits the column heading.

3. Repeat Step 2 to resize the InvoiceDate and InvoiceAmt columns.

4. Click the **Patient** column heading to select the column, and then drag the right edge of the selection box to the right to increase its width, until it accommodates the contents of all data in the column. (You might need to scroll through the report to ensure all Patient field values are visible.)

5. Repeat Step 4 to resize the Invoice Item, City, and Reason columns, if necessary, as shown in Figure 7–15. You'll fine-tune the adjustments and the spacing between columns later in Design view.

| Figure 7–15 | Resized and renamed columns in Layout view |

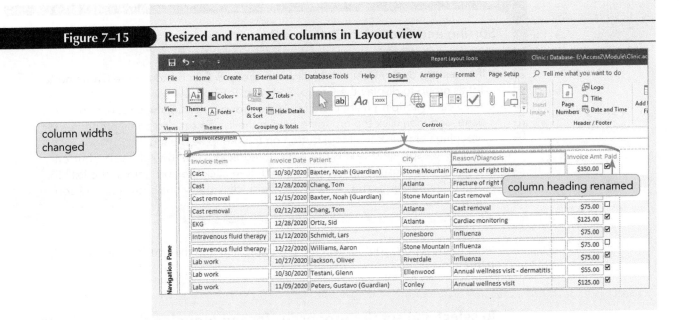

Next you need to add the sorting and grouping data to the report.

## Sorting and Grouping Data in a Report

In Access, you can organize records in a report by sorting them using one or more sort fields. Each sort field can also be a grouping field. If you specify a sort field as a grouping field, you can include a Group Header section and a Group Footer section for the group. A Group Header section typically includes the name of the group, and a Group Footer section typically includes a count or subtotal for records in that group. Some reports have a Group Header section but not a Group Footer section, some reports have a Group Footer section but not a Group Header section, and some reports have both sections or have neither section.

You use the Group, Sort, and Total pane to select sort fields and grouping fields for a report. Each report can have up to 10 sort fields, and any of its sort fields can also be grouping fields.

In Reginald's report design, the InvoiceItem field is a grouping field, and the InvoiceDate field is a sort field. The InvoiceItem field value is displayed in a Group Header section, but the InvoiceItem field label is not displayed. The sum of the InvoiceAmt field values is displayed in the Group Footer section for the InvoiceItem grouping field.

**REFERENCE**

## Sorting and Grouping Data in a Report

- Display the report in Layout view or Design view.
- If necessary, on the Design tab, click the Group & Sort button in the Grouping & Totals group to display the Group, Sort, and Total pane.
- To select a grouping field, click the Add a group button in the Group, Sort, and Total pane, and then click the grouping field in the list. To set additional properties for the grouping field, click the More button on the group field band.
- To select a sort field that is not a grouping field, click the Add a sort button in the Group, Sort, and Total pane, and then click the sort field in the list. To set additional properties for the sort field, click the More button on the sort field band.

Next, in the report, you'll select the grouping field and the sort field and set their properties.

## To select and set the properties for the grouping field and the sort field:

1. Switch to Design view, and then click the **Report Design Tools Design** tab, if necessary.

2. In the Grouping & Totals group, click the **Group & Sort** button to open the Group, Sort, and Total pane at the bottom of the Report window.

Be sure to click the Add a group button and not the Add a sort button.

3. In the Group, Sort, and Total pane, click the **Add a group** button, and then click **InvoiceItem** in the list. An empty Group Header section is added to the report, and group band options appear in the Group, Sort, and Total pane for this section.

4. In the Detail section, right-click the **InvoiceItem** text box control, point to **Layout**, then click **Remove Layout**.

5. With the InvoiceItem control still selected, press **CTRL+X** to cut the control and move it to the Clipboard, click the **InvoiceItem Header** bar, then press **CTRL+V** to paste the control into the Group Header. InvoiceItem is now a bound control in the report in a Group Header section that displays a field value box.

6. In the Page Header section, right-click the **InvoiceItem** label control, then click **Delete** on the shortcut menu. See Figure 7–16.

**Figure 7–16**     **InvoiceItem set as a grouping field in Design view**

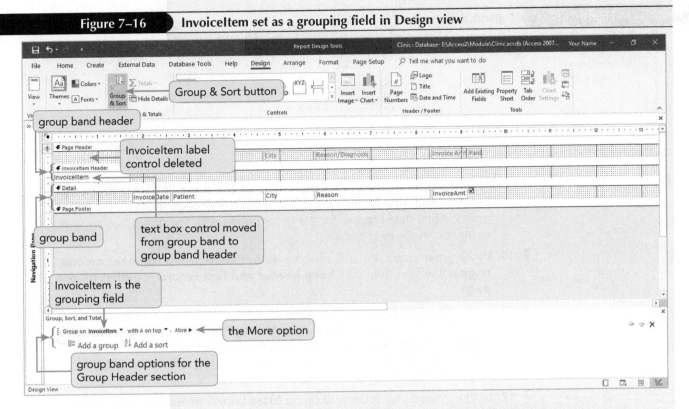

7. In the Group, Sort, and Total pane, click the **Group on InvoiceItem** group band to select it.

   The group band options in the Group, Sort, and Total pane contain the name of the grouping field (InvoiceItem), the sort order ("with A on top" to indicate ascending), and the More button, which you click to display more options for the grouping field. You can click the "with A on top" arrow to change to descending sort order ("with Z on top").

   Reginald's design specifies an additional ascending sort on the InvoiceDate field. Next, you'll select this field as a secondary sort field; the InvoiceItem grouping field is the primary sort field.

8. In the Group, Sort, and Total pane, click the **Add a sort** button, and then click **InvoiceDate** in the list. A sort band is added for the InvoiceDate field in the Group, Sort, and Total pane.

   Next, you'll display all the options for the InvoiceItem group band field and set group band options as shown in Reginald's report design.

9. In the Group, Sort, and Total pane, click **Group on InvoiceItem**, and then click the **More** button to display all group band options in an orange bar at the top of the Group, Sort, and Total pane. See Figure 7–17.

**Figure 7–17** Expanded group band

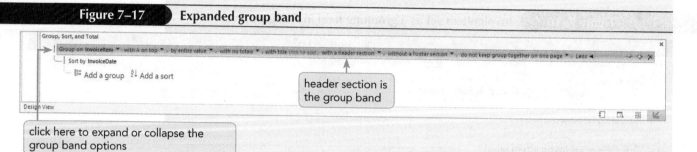

header section is the group band

click here to expand or collapse the group band options

Next you'll set the Keep Together property. The **Keep Together property** prints a group header on a page only if there is enough room on the page to print the first detail record for the group; otherwise, the group header prints at the top of the next page.

10. In the group band options, click the **do not keep group together on one page** arrow, and then click **keep header and first record together on one page**.

11. In the group band options, click the **More** button to expand the options (if necessary), click the **without a footer section** arrow, and then click **with a footer section**. A Group Footer section is added to the report for the InvoiceItem grouping band field, but the report will not display this new section until you add controls to it.

12. In the group band options, click the **More** button to expand the options (if necessary), click the **with no totals** arrow to open the Totals menu, click the **Total On** arrow, click **InvoiceAmt**, make sure **Sum** is selected in the Type box, click the **Show Grand Total** check box, click the **Show subtotal in group footer** check box, and then click a blank area of the report window to close the menu. This adds subtotals in the Amount column, at the bottom of each group.

13. In the group band options, click the **More** button to expand the options (if necessary). The group band options show the InvoiceAmt subtotals and a grand total added to the report. See Figure 7–18.

**Figure 7–18** Completed properties in the group band

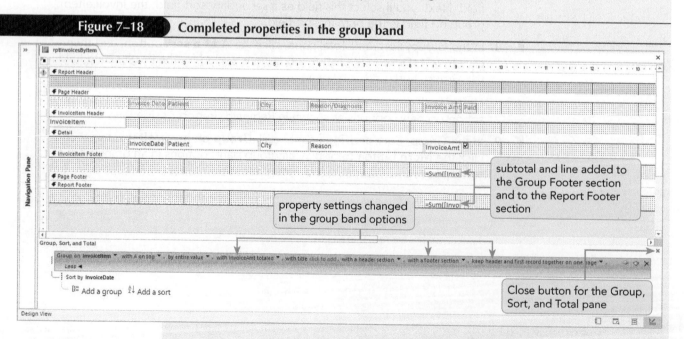

subtotal and line added to the Group Footer section and to the Report Footer section

property settings changed in the group band options

Close button for the Group, Sort, and Total pane

▶ **14.** Save your report changes, switch to Print Preview, and then use the navigation buttons to review each page until you reach the end of the report—noticing in particular the details of the report format and the effects of the Keep Together property. Also, notice that because of the space left by the grouping field after you moved it, the current report design prints the detail values across two pages.

Before you can move the detail values to the left onto one page, you need to remove all controls from the control layout.

### To remove controls from a control layout in Design view:

▶ **1.** Switch to Design view.

▶ **2.** Click the layout selector ⊞, which is located at the upper-left corner of the Page Header section, to select the entire control layout. An orange selection border, which identifies the controls that you've selected, appears around the labels and field value boxes in the report.

▶ **3.** Right-click one of the selected controls to open the shortcut menu, point to **Layout**, and then click **Remove Layout**. This removes the selected controls from the layout so they can be moved individually without affecting the other controls.

Next you'll move all the controls to the left except for the InvoiceItem field value box. You have to be careful when you move the remaining controls to the left. If you try to select all the column headings and the field value boxes, you're likely to miss the subtotal and grand total controls. The safest technique is to select all controls in the report, and then remove the InvoiceItem field value box from the selection.

▶ **4.** Click the **Report Design Tools Format** tab, and then in the Selection group click the **Select All** button. All controls in the report are now selected.

▶ **5.** Press and hold **SHIFT**, click the **InvoiceItem** control box in the InvoiceItem Header section to remove this control from the selection, and then release **SHIFT**.

▶ **6.** Press and hold ← to move the selected controls rapidly to the left edge of the report, and then release ←. See Figure 7–19.

**Figure 7–19**    Controls repositioned in the report

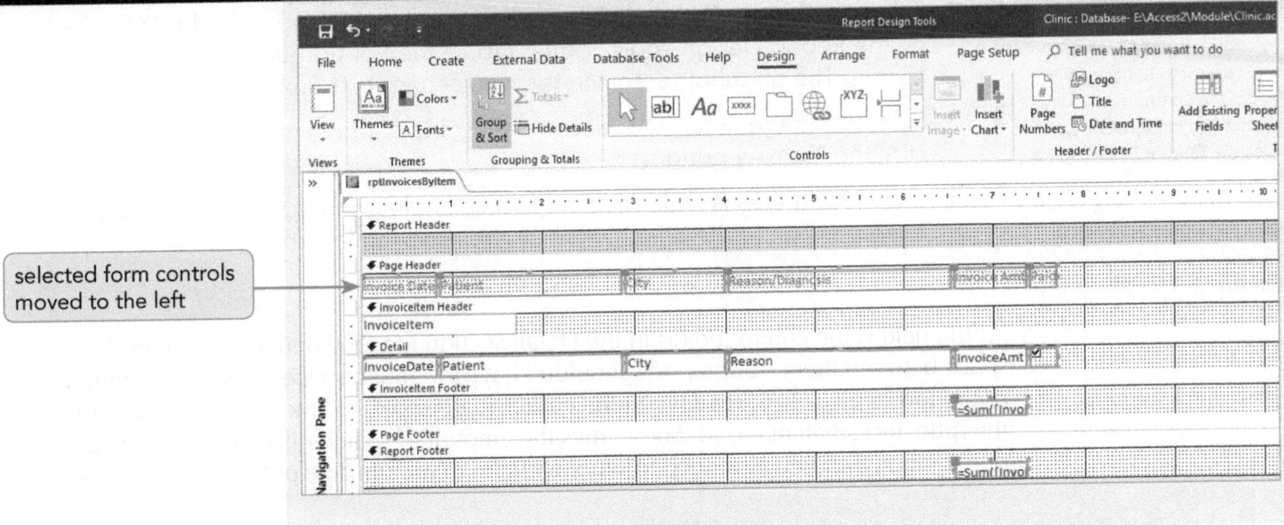

selected form controls moved to the left

The grand total of the InvoiceAmt field values is displayed at the end of the report, and subtotals are displayed for each unique InvoiceItem field value in the Group Footer section. It's possible for subtotals to appear in an orphaned footer section.

An **orphaned footer section** appears by itself at the top of a page, and the detail lines for the section appear on the previous page. When you set the Keep Together property for the grouping field, you set it to keep the group and the first detail record together on one page to prevent an **orphaned header section**, which is a section that appears by itself at the bottom of a page. To prevent both types of orphaned sections, you'll set the Keep Together property to keep the whole group together on one page.

In addition, you need to fine-tune the sizes of the field value boxes in the Detail section, adjust the spacing between columns, and make other adjustments to the current content of the report design before adding a report title, the date, and page number to the Page Header section. You'll make most of these report design changes in Design view.

# Working with Controls in Design View

As you learned when working with forms, Design view gives you greater control over the placement and sizing of controls than you have in Layout view and lets you add and manipulate many more controls; however, this power comes at the expense of not being able to see live data in the controls to guide you as you make changes.

The rptInvoicesByItem report has five sections that contain controls: the Page Header section contains the six column heading labels; the InvoiceItem Header section (a Group Header section) contains the InvoiceItem field value box; the Detail section contains the six bound controls; the InvoiceItem Footer section (a Group Footer section) contains a line and the subtotal control; and the Report Footer section contains a line and the grand total control.

You'll format, move, and resize controls in the report in Design view. The Group, Sort, and Total pane is still open, so first you'll change the Keep Together property setting.

## To set the report size:

1. In the Group, Sort, and Total pane, click the **More** button to display all group options, click the **keep header and first record together on one page** arrow, click **keep whole group together on one page**, and then click the **Close** button ☒ in the upper-right corner of the Group, Sort, and Total pane to close it.

   You'll start improving the report by setting the InvoiceItem label control to bold.

**TIP**

To copy formatting from one control to another, select the control whose format you want to copy, click the Format Painter tool on the Form Design Tools Format tab, and then click another control to apply the copied formatting.

2. Select the **InvoiceItem** text box in the InvoiceItem Header section, and then on the Report Design Tools Format tab, in the Font group, click the **Bold** button. The placeholder text in the InvoiceItem text box is displayed in bold.

3. Select the Page Setup tab, click the **Margins** button, and then if necessary click the **Narrow** button.

4. If the report area is wider than eight inches, drag the right border of any report section to the 8-inch mark on the horizontal ruler.

The field value control boxes in the Detail section are crowded together with little space between them. Your reports shouldn't have too much space between columns, but reports are easier to read when the columns are separated more than they are in the rptInvoicesByItem report. Sometimes the amount of spacing is dictated by the users of the report, but you also need to work with the minimum size of the form controls as well. To design this report to fit on a page with narrow margins, the report width will have to be 8.5 inches minus the left and right margins of 0.25 inches each, which results in a maximum report width of 8 inches (8.5"–0.25"–0.25"). This is the size you already applied to your report. Next you'll add some space between the columns while ensuring they still fit in the 8-inch report width. First, you'll resize the Invoice Date, Patient, and Reason columns, and then you'll arrange the columns. You'll size the corresponding heading and field value boxes for each column to be the same width.

## To move and resize controls in the report:

1. In the Page Header section, click the **Invoice Date** column heading, press and hold **SHIFT**, and then in the Detail section, click the **Invoice Date** control.

2. Drag the right side of the controls to the left to approximately the 3/4-inch mark on the ruler.

3. Switch to Layout view. The date values are displayed as a series of # symbols because the controls are too narrow to display them. It's often more efficient to resize controls to fit data in Layout view because you can instantly see whether the new size is appropriate for the data.

4. Click the **Invoice Date** column heading, press and hold **SHIFT**, and then click one of the **Invoice Date** field values to select all of the Invoice Date field values boxes.

5. Drag the right side of the controls to the right to increase the size of the field value boxes to fit the values and the heading text.

6. Click the Group Header text **Cast** at the top of the first page of the report to select all of the group header controls, then if necessary drag the right side of the control to the right until the text of the fourth group header, Intravenous fluid therapy, is fully visible. Intravenous fluid therapy is the longest group header in the report.

**TIP**

You can resize labels and controls added with the Label tool using the To Fit command, but you can't resize field value boxes using the To Fit method.

7. Switch to Design view, then Repeat Steps 1 and 2 to resize the Patient column heading and field values so the right edge is at the 2.5-inch mark on the ruler, and to resize the Reason column heading and field values so the right edge is at the 6-inch mark on the ruler. Reginald's design calls for the widths of these two items to be set to sizes that are narrower than their longest values, but you'll adjust formatting later to ensure that all contents are visible. See Figure 7–20.

**Figure 7–20**    Labels and controls resized in Design View

labels in Page Header section resized along with corresponding controls in Detail section

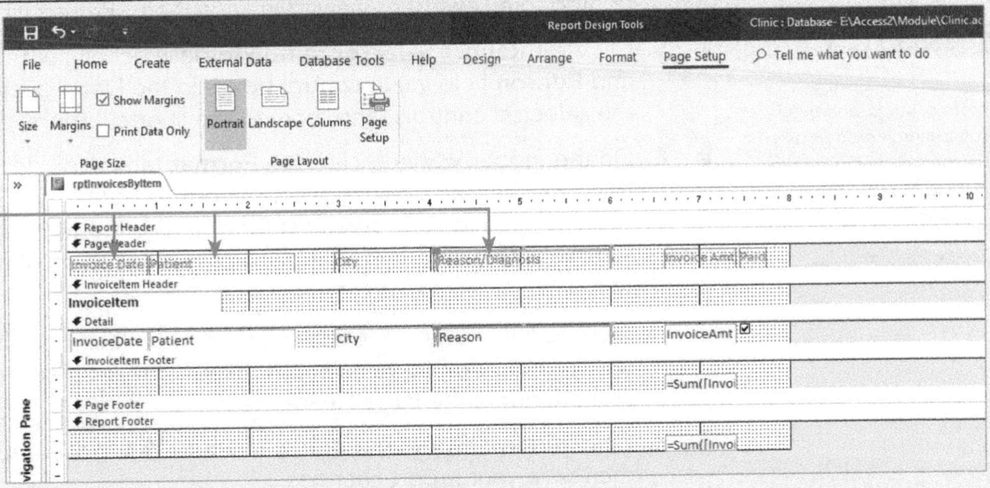

Next you'll adjust the spacing between the controls to distribute them evenly across the page.

### To redistribute controls in the report:

**TIP**

To delete a control in Report Design view, right-click the control, and then click Delete from the menu.

1. Click the **Report Design Tools Format** tab, and then in the Selection group, click the **Select All** button to select all controls.

2. Press and hold **SHIFT**, and click the **InvoiceItem** control in the Group Header to deselect it.

3. On the ribbon, click the **Report Design Tools Arrange** tab

4. In the Sizing & Ordering group, click the **Size/Space** button, and then click **Equal Horizontal**. The form controls are shifted horizontally so the spacing between them is equal. See Figure 7–21.

**Figure 7–21** **Equal horizontal spacing applied to form controls in Design view**

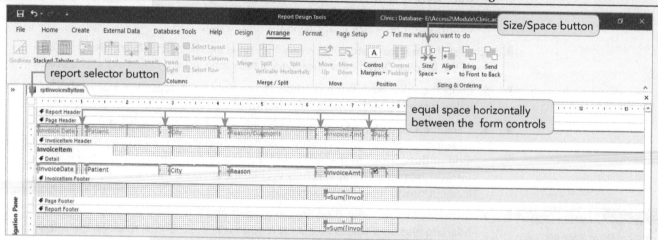

Because of the changes you made to the widths of the Patient and Reason field value boxes, they may not be wide enough to display the entire field value in all cases. For the Patient and Reason field value boxes, you'll set their Can Grow property to Yes. The **Can Grow property**, when set to Yes, expands a field value box vertically to fit the field value when the report is printed, previewed, or viewed in Layout and Report views.

**TIP**

You can select two or more controls, and then set common properties for the selected controls, instead of setting them one control at a time.

5. Click the **Report Selector** button to deselect all controls, select the **Patient** and **Reason** field value control boxes in the Detail section, right-click one of the selected controls, and then on the shortcut menu click **Properties**.

6. On the Property Sheet, click the **Format** tab, scroll down the Property Sheet to locate the Can Grow property, and then if the Can Grow property is set to Yes, set it to **No**. The default setting for this feature may not work properly, so to ensure the setting is applied correctly, you must make sure it is first set to No.

   **Trouble?** If you don't see the Can Grow property on the Format tab, double-check to ensure you've selected the Patient and Reason controls in the Detail section, not in the Page Header section.

7. Change the Can Grow property value to **Yes**, close the Property Sheet, and then save your report changes.

8. Switch to Print Preview, and then review every page of the report, ending on the last page. See Figure 7–22.

**Figure 7–22    Effect of setting the Can Grow property**

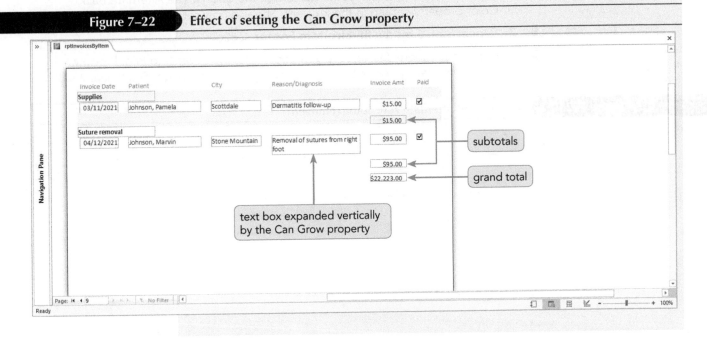

The groups stay together on one page, except for the groups that have too many detail lines to fit on one page. Where necessary, the Can Grow property expands the height of the Patient and Reason field value boxes.

Also, the lines that were displayed above the subtotals and grand total are no longer displayed, and the commas in the values are not fully visible. You'll add the totals lines back in the report and resize the field value boxes for the totals. First, Reginald thinks the borders around the field value boxes and the alternate row color are too distracting, so you'll remove them from the report.

### To remove the borders and alternate row color:

1. Switch to Design view.

2. Click the **Report Design Tools Format tab**, and then in the Selection group, click the **Select All** button.

3. Right-click one of the selected controls, and then click **Properties** on the shortcut menu to open the Property Sheet.

4. Click the **Format** tab (if necessary) in the Property Sheet, click the right side of the Border Style box, and then click **Transparent**. The transparent setting removes the borders from the report by making them transparent.

5. Click the **InvoiceItem Header** section bar, click the right side of the **Alternate Back Color** box in the Property Sheet, and then click **No Color** at the bottom of the gallery. This setting removes the alternate row color from the InvoiceItem Header section. You can also control the Alternate Back Color property using the Alternate Row Color button in the Background group on the Format tab, because the two options set the same property.

6. Click the **Detail** section bar, and then on the **Report Design Tools Format** tab, in the Background group, click the **Alternate Row Color button arrow**, and then click **No Color** at the bottom of the gallery. The Alternate Back Color property setting in the Property Sheet is now set to No Color.

7. Repeat Step 6 for the **InvoiceItem Footer** section.

8. Close the Property Sheet, save your report changes, switch to Print Preview, and review each page of the report, ending on the last page. See Figure 7–23.

Figure 7–23    **Borders and alternate row color removed**

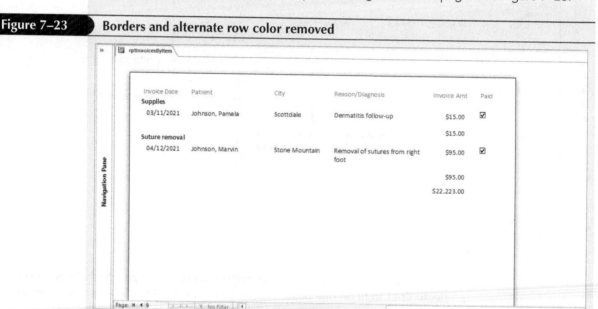

You still need to resize the subtotal and grand total field value boxes so that the comma separators are fully displayed. In addition, you'll add lines to separate the values from the subtotals and grand total.

### To resize the subtotals and grand totals field value boxes and add totals lines to the report:

1. Switch to Design view.

2. In the InvoiceItem Footer section, click the calculated control box to select it, and then drag the upper-middle sizing handle up to increase its height by one row of grid dots.

3. Repeat Step 2 to resize the calculated control box in the Report Footer section.

4. On the Report Design Tools Design tab, in the Controls group, click the **More** button ⏷ to open the Controls gallery.

5. Click the **Line** tool ◹, position the Line tool pointer's plus symbol in the InvoiceItem Footer section in the upper-left corner of the calculated control box, press and hold **SHIFT**, drag from left to right so the line aligns with the top border of the calculated control box and ends at the upper-right corner of the calculated control box, release the mouse button, and then release **SHIFT**.

6. In the Report Footer section, click the calculated control box, press ↓ two times to move the control down slightly in the section, and then deselect all controls.

7. In the Controls group, click the **More** button ⤓, click the **Line** tool ◻, position the pointer's plus symbol in the Report Footer section in the upper-left corner of the calculated control box, press and hold **SHIFT**, drag left to right so the line aligns with the top border of the calculated control box and ends at the upper-right corner of the calculated control box, release the mouse button, and then release **SHIFT**.

The grand total line should have two lines separating it from the rest of the report. Next, you'll copy and paste the line you just created in the Report Footer section, and then align the copied line into position.

8. Right-click the selected line in the Report Footer section, and then click **Copy** on the shortcut menu.

9. Right-click the **Report Footer** section bar, and then click **Paste** on the shortcut menu. A copy of the line is pasted in the upper-left corner of the Report Footer section.

10. Press ↓ two times to move the copied line down in the section, press and hold **SHIFT**, click the first line in the Report Footer section to select both lines, and then release **SHIFT**.

11. Right-click the selected lines to open the shortcut menu, point to **Align**, and then click **Right**. A double line is now positioned above the grand total box.

12. Save your report changes, switch to Print Preview, and then navigate to the last page of the report. See Figure 7–24.

**Figure 7–24**      **Total lines added to the report**

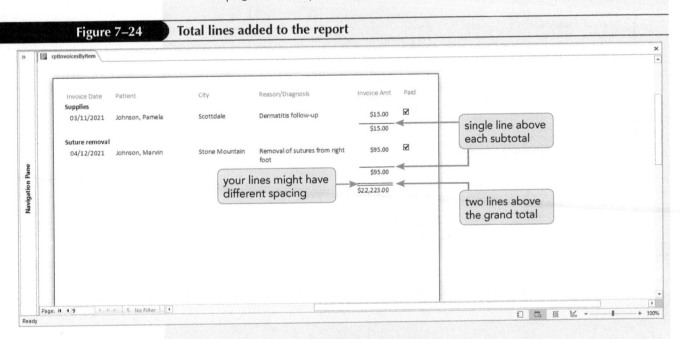

Your next design change to the report is to hide duplicate InvoiceDate field values in the Detail section. This change will make the report easier to read.

# Hiding Duplicate Values in a Report

You use the **Hide Duplicates property** to hide a control in a report when the control's value is the same as that of the preceding record in the group. You should use the Hide Duplicates property only on fields that are sorted. Otherwise it may look as if data is missing.

For the rptInvoicesByItem report, the InvoiceDate field is a sort field. Two or more consecutive detail report lines can have the same InvoiceDate field value. In these cases, Reginald wants the InvoiceDate field value to appear for the first detail line but not for subsequent detail lines because he believes it makes the printed information easier to read.

### To hide the duplicate InvoiceDate field values:

1. Switch to Design view, and then click a blank area of the window to deselect all controls.

2. Open the Property Sheet for the InvoiceDate field value box in the Detail section.

**TIP**

For properties offering a list of choices, you can double-click the property name repeatedly to cycle through the option in the list.

3. Click the **Format** tab (if necessary), scroll down the Property Sheet, click the right side of the **Hide Duplicates** box, and then click **Yes**.

4. Close the Property Sheet, save your report changes, switch to Print Preview, navigate to page 1 (the actual page you view might vary, depending on your printer) to the Lab work group to see the two invoice records for 01/27/2021. The InvoiceDate field value does not display for the second of the two consecutive records with a 01/27/2021 date. See Figure 7–25.

**Figure 7–25**    Report in Print Preview with hidden duplicate values

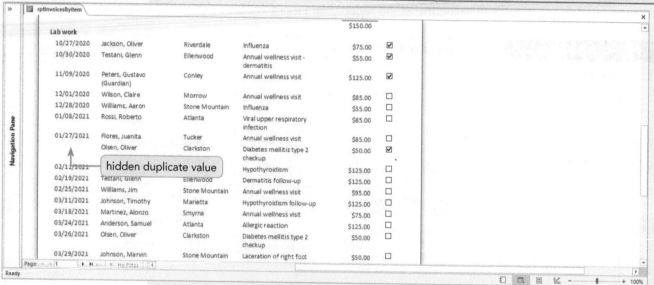

5. If you are not continuing on to the next session, close the Clinic database.

You have completed the Detail section, the Group Header section, and the Group Footer section of the custom report. In the next session, you will complete the custom report according to Reginald's design by adding controls to the Page Header section.

## Session 7.2 Quick Check

1. What is a detail report? A summary report?

2. The _____ property prints a group header on a page only if there is enough room on the page to print the first detail record for the group; otherwise, the group header prints at the top of the next page.

3. A(n) _____ section appears by itself at the top of a page, and the detail lines for the section appear on the previous page.

4. The _____ property, when set to Yes, expands a field value box vertically to fit the field value when a report is printed, previewed, or viewed in Layout and Report views.

5. Why might you want to hide duplicate values in a report?

# Session 7.3 Visual Overview:

The content in the Report Header section appears at the top of the first page of the report. This Report Header section has a height of 0" and no content.

The Date function displays the current date.

The Group Footer section's content appears at the bottom of each group.

The Report Footer section's content appears at the bottom of the last page of the report.

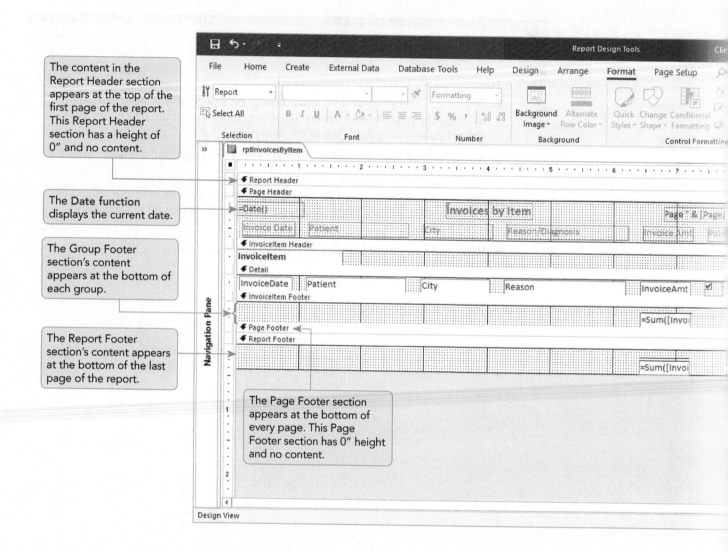

The Page Footer section appears at the bottom of every page. This Page Footer section has 0" height and no content.

# Custom Form in Design View

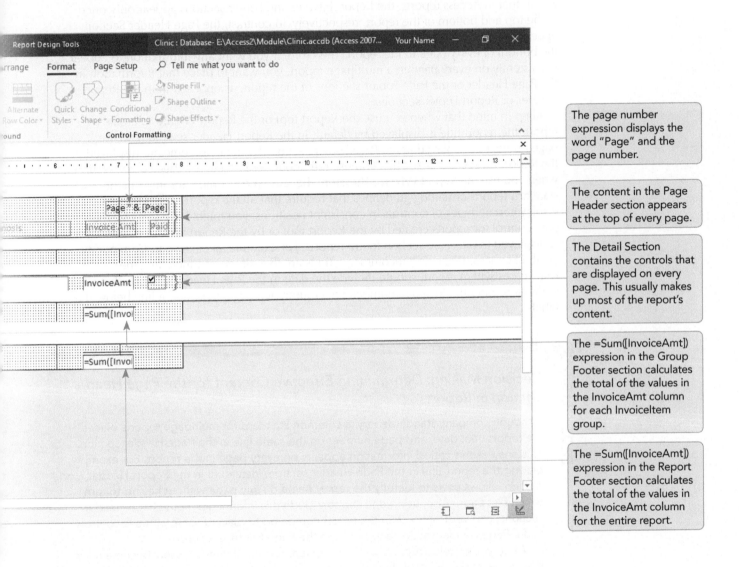

Report Design Tools

Clinic : Database- E:\Access2\Module\Clinic.accdb (Access 2007...    Your Name

arrange    **Format**    Page Setup    🔎 Tell me what you want to do

Alternate    Quick    Change Conditional    Shape Fill ▾
Row Color ▾    Styles ▾  Shape ▾ Formatting    Shape Outline ▾
ound    Shape Effects ▾

Control Formatting

· · · I · · · 6 · · · I · · · 7 · · · I · · · 8 · · · I · · · 9 · · · I · · · 10 · · · I · · · 11 · · · I · · · 12 · · · I · · · 13 · · ·

"Page" & [Page]

osis:    Invoice Amt    Paid

InvoiceAmt    ☑

=Sum([Invoi

=Sum([Invoi

The page number expression displays the word "Page" and the page number.

The content in the Page Header section appears at the top of every page.

The Detail Section contains the controls that are displayed on every page. This usually makes up most of the report's content.

The =Sum([InvoiceAmt]) expression in the Group Footer section calculates the total of the values in the InvoiceAmt column for each InvoiceItem group.

The =Sum([InvoiceAmt]) expression in the Report Footer section calculates the total of the values in the InvoiceAmt column for the entire report.

# Understanding Page Header and Page Footer Sections

Recall that in Access reports, the Report Header and Footer sections appear only once, at the top and bottom of the report, respectively. In contrast, the Page Header Section appears at the top of every page in the report, and the Page Footer Section appears at the bottom of every page in the report. Therefore, if you want any information to appear consistently on every page in a multipage report, you want to place that information in the Page Header or the Page Footer sections of the report, as opposed to in the Report Header or Report Footer sections.

Keep in mind that when you use the Report tool or the Report Wizard to create a report, the report title is displayed by default in the Report Header section, and the page number is displayed in the Page Footer section. The date and time are displayed in the Report Header section when you use the Report tool and in the Page Footer section when you use the Report Wizard. Therefore, because most companies implement standard report-formatting guidelines that require that all the reports in a database display certain types of controls in consistent positions, you might have to move the date control for reports created by the Report tool or by the Report Wizard so the date is displayed in the same section for all reports. For example, at Lakewood Community Health Services, Reginald's recommendations are that all reports, including the rptInvoicesByItem report, should include the date in the Page Header section, along with the report title, the page number, the column heading labels, and a line below the labels.

**PROSKILLS**

*Decision Making: Determining Effective Content for the Page Header Section in Reports*

Although company standards vary, a common standard for multipage reports places the report title, date, and page number on the same line in the Page Header section. This ensures this critical information appears on every page in the report. For example, placing the report title in the Page Header section, instead of in the Report Header section, allows users to identify the report name on any page without having to turn to the first page. Also, using one line to include this information in the Page Header section saves vertical space in the report compared to placing some of these controls in the Page Header section and others in the Page Footer section.

When you develop reports with a consistent format, the report users become more productive and more confident working with the information in the reports.

## Adding the Date to a Report

To add the date to a report, you can click the Date and Time button in the Header/Footer group on the Report Layout Tools or Report Design Tools Design tab. Doing so inserts the Date function in a control (without a corresponding label control) in the Report Header section. The Date function returns the current date. The format of the Date function is =Date(). The equal sign (=) indicates that what follows it is an expression; Date is the name of the function; the empty set of parentheses indicates a function rather than simple text.

### Adding the Date and Time to a Report

- Display the report in Layout or Design view.
- In Design view or in Layout view, on the Design tab, in the Header/Footer group, click the Date and Time button to open the Date and Time dialog box.
- To display the date, click the Include Date check box, and then click one of the three date option buttons.
- To display the time, click the Include Time check box, and then click one of the three time option buttons.
- Click the OK button.

In Reginald's design for the report, the date appears on the left side of the Page Header section. You'll add the date to the report and then cut the date from its default location in the Report Header section and paste it into the Page Header section. You can add the current date in Layout view or Design view. However, because you can't cut and paste controls between sections in Layout view, you'll add the date in Design view.

#### To add the date to the report:

1. If you took a break after the previous session, make sure that the Clinic database is open, that the rptInvoicesByItem report is open in Design view, and that the Navigation Pane is closed.

   First, you'll move the column heading labels down in the Page Header section to make room for the controls you'll be adding above them.

2. Increase the height of the Page Header section by dragging the Page Header's bottom border down until the 1-inch mark on the vertical ruler appears.

3. Select all six label controls in the Page Header section, and then move the controls down until the tops of the label controls are at the 3/8-inch mark on the vertical ruler. You may find it easier to use the arrow keys, rather than the mouse, to position the label controls.

   Reginald's report design calls for a horizontal line below the labels. You'll add this line next.

4. On the Report Design Tools Design tab, in the Controls group, click the **More** button ⬇, click the **Line** tool ◥, and then drag to create a horizontal line positioned one grid dot below the bottom border of the six label controls and spanning from the left edge of the Invoice Date label control and the right edge of the Paid label control.

5. Reduce the height of the Page Header section by dragging the bottom border of the section up until it touches the bottom of the line you just added.

6. In the Header/Footer group, click the **Date and Time** button to open the Date and Time dialog box, make sure the **Include Date** check box is checked and the **Include Time** check box is unchecked, and then click the third date format option button. See Figure 7–26.

**Figure 7–26**    Completed Date and Time dialog box

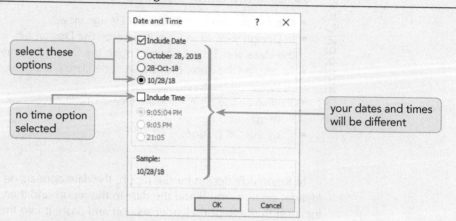

select these options

no time option selected

your dates and times will be different

> 7. Click the **OK** button. The Date function control is added to the right side of the Report Header section.

Next you'll move the Date function control to the Page Header section to match Reginald's design.

## To add the date to the Page Header section:

> 1. Click the **Date function** control box, and then click the **layout selector** in the upper-left corner of the Report Header section. The Date function control box is part of a control layout with three additional empty control boxes. See Figure 7–27.

**Figure 7–27**    Date function added to the Report Header section

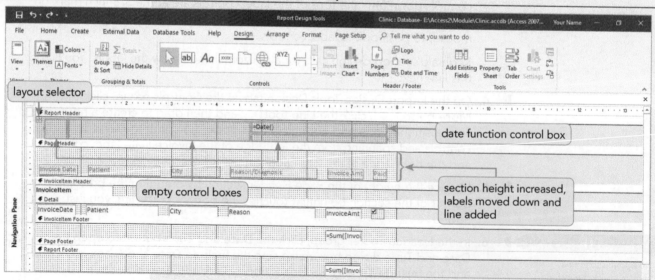

layout selector

date function control box

empty control boxes

section height increased, labels moved down and line added

You need to remove these controls from the control layout before you work further with the Date function control box.

2. Right-click one of the selected control boxes, point to **Layout** on the shortcut menu, and then click **Remove Layout**. The three empty cells are deleted, and the Date function control box remains selected.

The default size for the Date function control box accommodates long dates and long times, so the control box is much wider than needed for the date that will appear in the custom report. You'll decrease its width and move it to the Page Header section.

3. Drag the left border of the Date function control box to the right until it is 1 inch wide.

4. Right-click the selected **Date function** control box to open the shortcut menu, click **Cut** to delete the control, right-click the **Page Header** section bar to select that section and open the shortcut menu, and then click **Paste**. The Date function control box is pasted in the upper-left corner of the Page Header section.

> Be sure to paste the Date function control box in the Page Header section and not in the Report Header section.

5. Save your report changes, and then switch to Print Preview to view the date in the Page Header section. See Figure 7–28.

---

**Figure 7–28**     **Date in page header section in Print Preview**

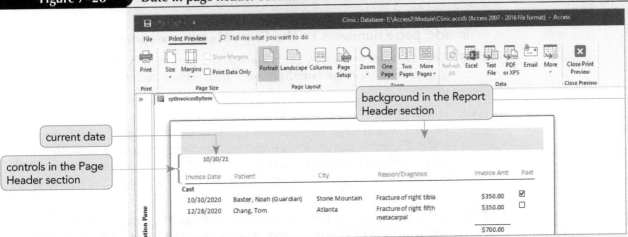

**Trouble?** Your year might appear with four digits instead of two digits as shown in Figure 7–28. Your date format might also differ, depending on your computer's date settings. These differences do not cause any problems.

Now that the date has been added to the Page Header section, you need to format and position it appropriately.

6. Switch to Design view, make sure the **Date function** control box is still selected, click the **Report Design Tools Format** tab, and then in the Font group, click the **Align Left** button.

7. In the Report Header section, drag the bottom border up to the top of the section so the section's height is reduced to zero.

If a report includes a control with the Date function, the current date will be displayed each time the report is run. If you instead want a specific date to appear each time the report is run, use a label control that contains the date, rather than the Date function.

You are now ready to add page numbers to the Page Header section.

## Adding Page Numbers to a Report

You can display page numbers in a report by including an expression in the Page Header or Page Footer section. On the Report Layout Tools or Report Design Tools Design tab, you can click the Page Numbers button in the Header/Footer group to add a page number expression. The inserted page number expression automatically displays the correct page number on each page of a report.

**REFERENCE**

### Adding Page Numbers to a Report

- Display the report in Layout or Design view.
- On the Design tab, click the Page Numbers button in the Header/Footer group to open the Page Numbers dialog box.
- Select the format, position, and alignment options you want.
- Select whether you want to display the page number on the first page.
- Click the OK button to place the page number expression in the report.

Reginald's design shows the page number displayed on the right side of the Page Header section, bottom-aligned with the date.

### To add page numbers to the Page Header section:

1. Click the **Report Design Tools Design** tab, and then in the Header/Footer group, click the **Page Numbers** button. The Page Numbers dialog box opens.

   You use the Format options to specify the format of the page number. Reginald wants page numbers to appear as Page 1, Page 2, and so on. This is the "Page N" format option. You use the Position options to place the page numbers at the top of the page in the Page Header section or at the bottom of the page in the Page Footer section. Reginald's design shows page numbers at the top of the page.

2. In the Format section, make sure that the **Page N** option button is selected, and then in the Position section, make sure that the **Top of Page [Header]** option button is selected.

   The report design shows page numbers at the right side of the page. You can specify this placement in the Alignment box.

3. Click the **Alignment** arrow, and then click **Right**.

4. Make sure the **Show Number on First Page** check box is checked, so the page number prints on the first page and all other pages as well. See Figure 7–29.

| Figure 7–29 | Completed Page Numbers dialog box |
| --- | --- |

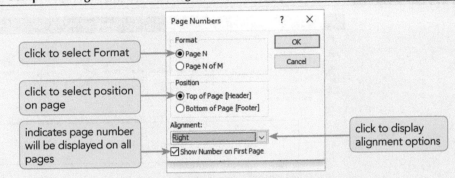

5. Click the **OK** button. A control box containing the expression =*"Page " &* *[Page]* appears in the upper-right corner of the Page Header section. The expression=*"Page " & [Page]* in the control box means that the printed report will show the word "Page" followed by a space and the page number. The page number control box is much wider than needed for the page number expression that will appear in the custom report. You'll decrease its width.

6. Click the **Page Number** control box, decrease its width from the left until it is 1 inch wide, and then move it to the left so its right edge aligns with the right edge of the Paid field value box. See Figure 7–30.

| Figure 7–30 | Page number expression added to the Page Header section |
| --- | --- |

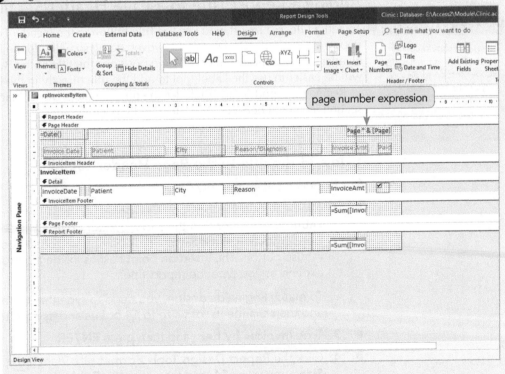

7. Save your report changes, and then switch to Print Preview. See Figure 7–31.

| Figure 7–31 | Date and page number in the Page Header section |

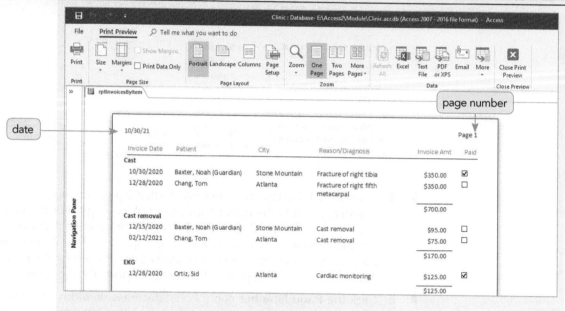

Now you are ready to add the title to the Page Header section.

## Adding a Report Title to a Page Header Section

To add a title to a report, you use the Title button in the Header/Footer group on the Report Design Tools Design tab. However, doing so will add the title to the Report Header section, and Reginald's design positions the title in the Page Header section. It will be easier to use the Label tool to add the title directly in the Page Header section.

Reginald's report design includes the title "Invoices by Item" in the Page Header section, centered between the date and the page number.

### To add the title to the Page Header section:

1. Switch to Design view.

2. On the Report Design Tools Design tab, in the Controls group, click the **Label** tool $Aa$, position the Label pointer's plus symbol at the top of the Page Header section at the 3-inch mark on the horizontal ruler, and then click the mouse button. The insertion point flashes inside a narrow box, which will expand as you type the report title.

   To match Reginald's design, you need to type the title as "Invoices by Item" and then change its font size to 14 points and its style to bold.

3. Type **Invoices by Item** and then press **ENTER**.

4. Click the **Report Design Tools Format** tab, in the Font group, click the **Font Size** arrow, click **14**, and then click the **Bold** button $B$.

5. Resize the label control box to display the full title, increase the height of the label control box by one grid dot, and move the label control box to the right so it is centered at the 4-inch mark. See Figure 7–32.

**Figure 7–32**    **Report title in the Page Header section**

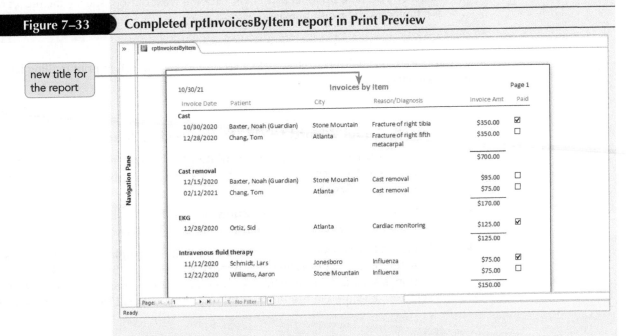

title font size

you can safely ignore the warning about the new label not being associated with a control

center handles align with the 4-inch mark

report title

**Trouble?** If a warning icon is displayed with ScreenTip text "This is a new label and is not associated with a control.", you can safely ignore it. A page heading does not need to be associated with a control.

Finally, you'll bottom-align the date, report title, and page number controls boxes. Yours might appear aligned already, but if not, this step will align the controls.

6. Select the **date**, **report title**, and **page number** control boxes in the Page Header section, right-click one of the selected controls, point to **Align,** and then click **Bottom**.

7. Save your report changes, and then switch to Print Preview to review the completed report. See Figure 7–33.

**Figure 7–33**    **Completed rptInvoicesByItem report in Print Preview**

new title for the report

8. Close the report.

Next, Donna wants you to create mailing labels that she can use to address materials to the patients seen by the Lakewood Community Health Services.

# Creating Mailing Labels

Donna needs a set of mailing labels printed for all patients so she can mail a marketing brochure and other materials to them. The tblPatient table contains the name and address information that will serve as the record source for the labels. Each mailing label will have the same format: first name and last name on the first line; address on the second line; and city, state, and zip code on the third line.

You could create a custom report to produce the mailing labels, but using the Label Wizard is an easier and faster way to produce them. The **Label Wizard** provides templates for hundreds of standard label formats, each of which is uniquely identified by a label manufacturer's name and product number. These templates specify the dimensions and arrangement of labels on each page. Standard label formats can have between one and five labels across a page; the number of labels printed on a single page also varies. Donna's mailing labels are manufactured by Avery and their product number is C2163. Each sheet contains 12 labels; each label is 1.5 inches by 3.9 inches, and the labels are arranged in two columns and six rows on the page.

**REFERENCE**

### Creating Mailing Labels and Other Labels

- In the Navigation Pane, click the table or query that will serve as the record source for the labels.
- On the Create tab, click the Labels button in the Reports group to start the Label Wizard and open its first dialog box.
- Select the label manufacturer and product number, and then click the Next button.
- Select the label font, color, and style, and then click the Next button.
- Construct the label content by selecting the fields from the record source and specifying their placement and spacing on the label, and then click the Next button.
- Select one or more optional sort fields, click the Next button, specify the report name, and then click the Finish button.

You'll use the Label Wizard to create a report Donna can use to print mailing labels for all patients.

### To use the Label Wizard to create the mailing label report:

1. Open the Navigation Pane, click **tblPatient** to make it the current object that will serve as the record source for the labels, close the Navigation Pane, and then click the **Create** tab.

2. In the Reports group, click the **Labels** button. The first Label Wizard dialog box opens and asks you to select the standard or custom label you'll use.

3. In the Unit of Measure section make sure that the **English** option button is selected, in the Label Type section make sure that the **Sheet feed** option button is selected, in the Filter by manufacturer box make sure that **Avery** is selected, and then in the Product number box, click **C2163**. See Figure 7–34.

**Figure 7–34**    Label wizard dialog box

select this Avery product number

make sure these options are selected

selected manufacturer

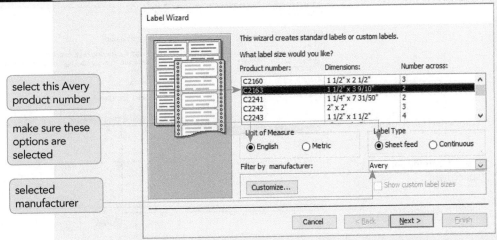

**TIP**

If your label manufacturer or its labels do not appear in the box, you can create your own custom format for them.

The top box shows the Avery product number, dimensions, and number of labels across the page for each of its standard label formats. You can display the dimensions in the list in either inches or millimeters by choosing the appropriate option in the Unit of Measure section. You specify in the Label Type section whether the labels are on individual sheets or are continuous forms.

4. Click the **Next** button to open the second Label Wizard dialog box, in which you choose font specifications for the labels.

Donna wants the labels to use 10-point Arial with a medium font weight and without italics or underlines. The font weight determines how light or dark the characters will print; you can choose from nine values ranging from thin to heavy.

5. If necessary, select **Arial** in the Font name box, **10** in the Font size box, and **Medium** in the Font weight box, make sure the Italic and the Underline check boxes are not checked and that black is the text color (bottom left in the Basic Colors gallery), and then click the **Next** button. The third Label Wizard dialog box opens, in which you select the data to appear on the labels.

Donna wants the mailing labels to print the FirstName and LastName fields on the first line, the Address field on the second line, and the City, State, and Zip fields on the third line. A single space will separate the FirstName and LastName fields, the City and State fields, and the State and Zip fields.

6. In the Available fields box, click **FirstName**, click the **Select Single Field** > button to move the field to the Prototype label box, press **SPACEBAR**, in the Available fields box click **LastName** (if necessary), and then click the **Select Single Field** > button. As you select fields from the Available fields box or type text for the label, the Prototype label box shows the format for the label. The braces around the field names in the Prototype label box indicate that the name represents a field rather than text that you entered.

**Trouble?** If you select the wrong field or type the wrong text, click the incorrect item in the Prototype label box, press the Delete key to remove the item, and then select the correct field or type the correct text.

7. Press **ENTER** to move to the next line in the Prototype label box, and then use Figure 7–35 to complete the entries in the Prototype label box. Make sure you type a comma and press SPACEBAR after selecting the City field, and then press SPACEBAR after selecting the State field.

**Figure 7–35**    Completed label prototype

Label Wizard

What would you like on your mailing label?

Construct your label on the right by choosing fields from the left. You may also type text that you would like to see on every label right onto the prototype.

Available fields:

Address
City
State
Zip
Email

Prototype label:

{FirstName} {LastName}
{Address}
{City}, {State} {Zip}

completed label format →

insert a comma and a space here →

insert a space here →

Cancel    < Back    Next >    Finish

8. Click the **Next** button to open the fourth Label Wizard dialog box, in which you choose the sort fields for the labels.

   Donna wants Zip to be the primary sort field and LastName to be the secondary sort field.

9. In the Available fields list, click the **Zip** field, click the **Select Single Field** ▸ button to select Zip as the primary sort field, click the **LastName** field, click the **Select Single Field** ▸ button to select LastName as the secondary sort field, and then click the **Next** button to open the last Label Wizard dialog box, in which you enter a name for the report.

10. Change the report name to **rptPatientMailingLabels**, and then click the **Finish** button. The report is saved, and the first page of the report appears in Print Preview. Note that two columns of labels appear across the page. See Figure 7–36.

**Figure 7–36**    Print Preview of mailing labels

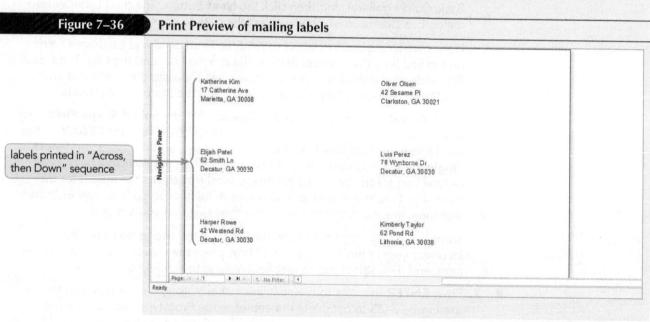

labels printed in "Across, then Down" sequence →

Katherine Kim
17 Catherine Ave
Marietta, GA 30008

Oliver Olsen
42 Sesame Pl
Clarkston, GA 30021

Elijah Patel
62 Smith Ln
Decatur, GA 30030

Luis Perez
78 Wynborne Dr
Decatur, GA 30030

Harper Rowe
42 Westend Rd
Decatur, GA 30030

Kimberly Taylor
62 Pond Rd
Lithonia, GA 30038

Page: 1    ▸ ▸I ▸    No Filter

Ready

The rptPatientMailingLabels report is a multiple-column report. The labels will be printed in ascending order by zip code and, within each zip code, in ascending order by last name. The first label will be printed in the upper-left corner on the first page, the second label will be printed to its right, the third label will be printed below the first label, and so on. This style of multiple-column report is the "across, then down" layout. Instead, Donna wants the labels to print with the "down, then across" layout because she prefers to pull the labels from the sheet in this manner. In this layout, the first label is printed, the second label is printed below the first, and so on. After the bottom label in the first column is printed, the next label is printed at the top of the second column. The "down, then across" layout is also called **newspaper-style columns** or **snaking columns**.

### To change the layout of the mailing label report:

1. Switch to Design view. The Detail section, the only section in the report, is sized for a single label.

   First, you'll change the layout to snaking columns.

2. On the ribbon, click the **Report Design Tools Page Setup** tab.

3. In the Page Layout group, click the **Page Setup** button to open the Page Setup dialog box, and then click the **Columns** tab. The Page Setup dialog box displays the column options for the report. See Figure 7–37.

   The options in the Page Setup dialog box let you change the properties of a multiple-column report. In the Grid Settings section, you specify the number of columns and the row and column spacing. In the Column Size section, you specify the width and height of each column set. In the Column Layout section, you specify the direction the information flows in the columns.

**Figure 7–37**    Columns tab in the Page Setup dialog box

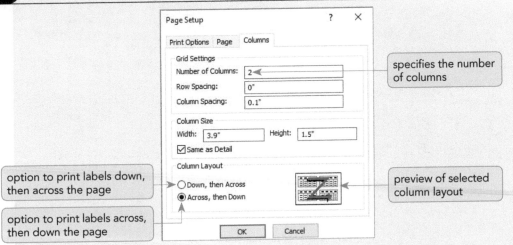

**TIP**

When you select a label using a manufacturer's name and product code, the options in the dialog box are set automatically.

4. Click the **Down, then Across** option button, and then click the **OK** button. You've finished the report changes, so you can now save and preview the report.

5. Save your report design changes, and then switch to Print Preview. The labels appear in the snaking columns layout.

   You've finished all work on Donna's reports.

6. **sam** ⬆ Close the report, make a backup copy of the database, compact and repair the database, and then close it.

Donna is very pleased with the modified report and the two new reports, which will provide her with improved information and expedite her written communications with patients.

## Session 7.3 Quick Check

1. What is the function and syntax to print the current date in a report?

2. How do you insert a page number in the Page Header section?

3. Must the page number reside only in the Page Header section?

4. Clicking the Title button in the Header/Footer group on the Report Design Tools Design tab adds a report title to the _____ section.

5. What is a multiple-column report?

## Review Assignments

**Data File needed for the Review Assignments: Supplier.accdb** *(cont. from Module 6)*

Donna wants you to create a custom report for the Supplier database that prints all companies and the products they offer. She also wants you to customize an existing report. Complete the following steps:

1. Open the **Supplier** database you worked with in the previous two modules.
2. Modify the **rptSupplierDetails** report by completing the following steps:
   a. Change the report title to **Lakewood Suppliers**.
   b. Remove the alternate row color from the detail lines in the report.
   c. Change the first column heading to **Supplier ID**. Change the fourth column heading to **First Name** and the fifth column heading to **Last Name**.
   d. In the Report Footer section, add a grand total count of the number of suppliers that appear in the report, make sure the calculated control box has a transparent border, and left-align the control with the left edge of the Company field value box. Left-align the count value in the calculated control box.
   e. Add a label that contains the text **Suppliers:** to the left of the count of the total number of suppliers, aligned to the left margin, and aligned with the bottom of the count calculated control box.
   f. Set the margins to Normal, and adjust the width of the grid to 7.5 inches. Adjust the width of the label control in the Report Header to span the width of the page, ending up one grid dot to the left of the width of the right margin.
   g. Move the page number control to the right until it is one grid dot to the left of the right margin. Right-align the page number value in the control box.
3. After you've completed and saved your modifications to the rptSupplierDetails report, filter the report in Report view, selecting all records that contain the word "supplies" in the Company field. Copy the headings and detail lines of the filtered report, and paste it into a new Word document. Save the document as **NP_AC_7_Supplies** in the location where you are storing your files. Close Word, save your changes to the Access report, and then close it.
4. Create a query that displays the Company and Category fields from the tblSupplier table and the ProductName, Price, and Units fields from the tblProduct table. Save the query as **qrySupplierProducts**, modify it to sort in ascending order by the first three fields in the query, and then save your changes.
5. Create a custom report based on the qrySupplierProducts query. Figure 7–38 shows a sample of the completed report. Refer to the figure as you create the report. Distribute the fields horizontally to produce a visually balanced report.

**Figure 7–38 Supplier database custom report**

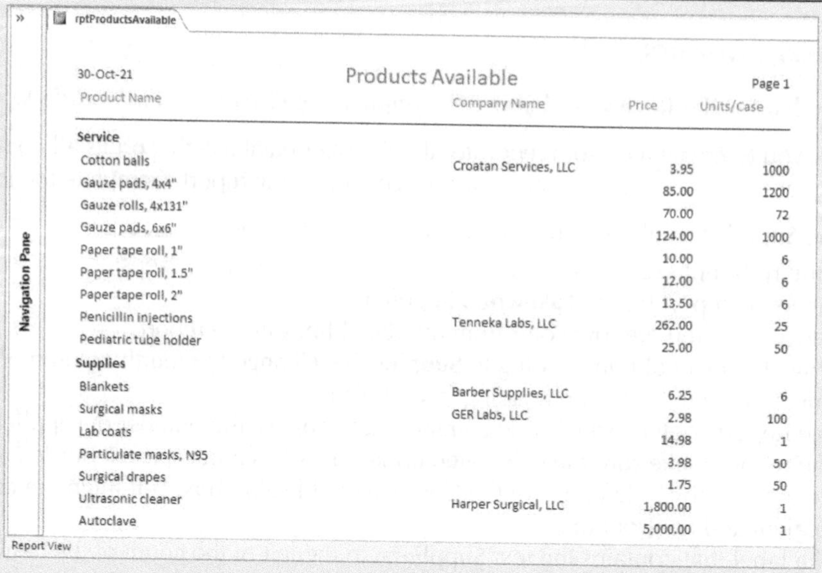

rptProductsAvailable

30-Oct-21 Products Available Page 1

| Product Name | Company Name | Price | Units/Case |
|---|---|---|---|
| **Service** | | | |
| Cotton balls | Croatan Services, LLC | 3.95 | 1000 |
| Gauze pads, 4x4" | | 85.00 | 1200 |
| Gauze rolls, 4x131" | | 70.00 | 72 |
| Gauze pads, 6x6" | | 124.00 | 1000 |
| Paper tape roll, 1" | | 10.00 | 6 |
| Paper tape roll, 1.5" | | 12.00 | 6 |
| Paper tape roll, 2" | | 13.50 | 6 |
| Penicillin injections | Tenneka Labs, LLC | 262.00 | 25 |
| Pediatric tube holder | | 25.00 | 50 |
| **Supplies** | | | |
| Blankets | Barber Supplies, LLC | 6.25 | 6 |
| Surgical masks | GER Labs, LLC | 2.98 | 100 |
| Lab coats | | 14.98 | 1 |
| Particulate masks, N95 | | 3.98 | 50 |
| Surgical drapes | | 1.75 | 50 |
| Ultrasonic cleaner | Harper Surgical, LLC | 1,800.00 | 1 |
| Autoclave | | 5,000.00 | 1 |

Report View

a. Save the report as **rptProductsAvailable**.
b. Use the Category field (from the tblSupplier table) as a grouping field, and use the Company field (from the tblSupplier table) as a sort field.
c. Hide duplicate values for the Company field.
d. Keep the whole group together on one page.
e. Remove the borders from the field value boxes.
f. Remove the alternate row color from the group header and detail line.
g. Add the Page title **Products Available** using an 18-point Calibri font, centered horizontally.
h. Apply a text filter for companies that contain "LLC" in the Company Name.

6. Create a mailing label report according to the following instructions:
   a. Use the tblSupplier table as the record source.
   b. Use Avery C2160 labels, and use the default font, size, weight, and color.
   c. For the prototype label, add the ContactFirst, a space, and ContactLast on the first line; the Company on the second line; the Address on the third line; and the City, a comma and a space, State, a space, and Zip on the fourth line.
   d. Sort by Zip and then by Company, and then name the report **rptCompanyMailingLabels**.
   e. Format the report with a down, then across page layout.
7. Make a backup copy of the database, compact and repair, and then close the Supplier database.

APPLY

## Case Problem 1

**Data File needed for this Case Problem: School.accdb *(cont. from Module 6)***

***Great Giraffe*** Jeremiah Garver wants you to create a custom report and mailing labels for the School database. The custom report will be based on the results of a query you will create. Complete the following steps:

1. Open the **School** database you worked with in the previous two modules.
2. Create a query that displays the Title and StartDate fields from the tblCourse table, and the SignupID, TotalCost, BalanceDue, and PaymentPlan fields from the tblRegistration table. Sort in ascending order by the Title and StartDate fields, and then save the query as **qryRegistrationPayments**.
3. Create a custom report based on the qryRegistrationPayments query. Figure 7–39 shows a sample of the first page of the completed report. Refer to the figure as you create the report.

| Figure 7–39 | School database custom report |

a.   Save the report as **rptRegistrationPayments**.
b.   Use the Title field as a grouping field.
c.   Hide duplicate values for the StartDate field.
d.   Keep the whole group together on one page.
e.   Use Wide margins and spacing to distribute the columns evenly across the page.
f.   Remove the alternate row color for all sections.
g.   Use black font for all the controls and a 2-point thickness for the lines.

4.  Use the following instructions to create the mailing labels:
a.   Use the tblStudent table as the record source for the mailing labels.
b.   Use Avery C2160 labels, and use the default font, size, weight, and color.
c.   For the prototype label, place FirstName, a space, and LastName on the first line; Address on the second line; and City, a comma and space, State, a space, and Zip on the third line.
d.   Sort by Zip and then by LastName, and then name the report **rptStudentLabels**.
e.   Format the report with a three-column, down, then across page layout.

5.  Make a backup copy of the database, compact and repair it, and then close the School database.

## Case Problem 2

**Data File needed for this Case Problem: Storm.accdb** *(cont. from Module 6)*

***Drain Adopter***   Tandrea Austin wants you to modify an existing report and to create a custom report and mailing labels for the Storm database. Complete the following steps:

1.  Open the **Storm** database you worked with in the previous two modules.
2.  Modify the **rptVolunteersAndDrains** report. Figure 7–40 shows a sample of the first page of the completed report. Refer to the figure as you modify the report.

**Figure 7–40**     **Storm database enhanced report**

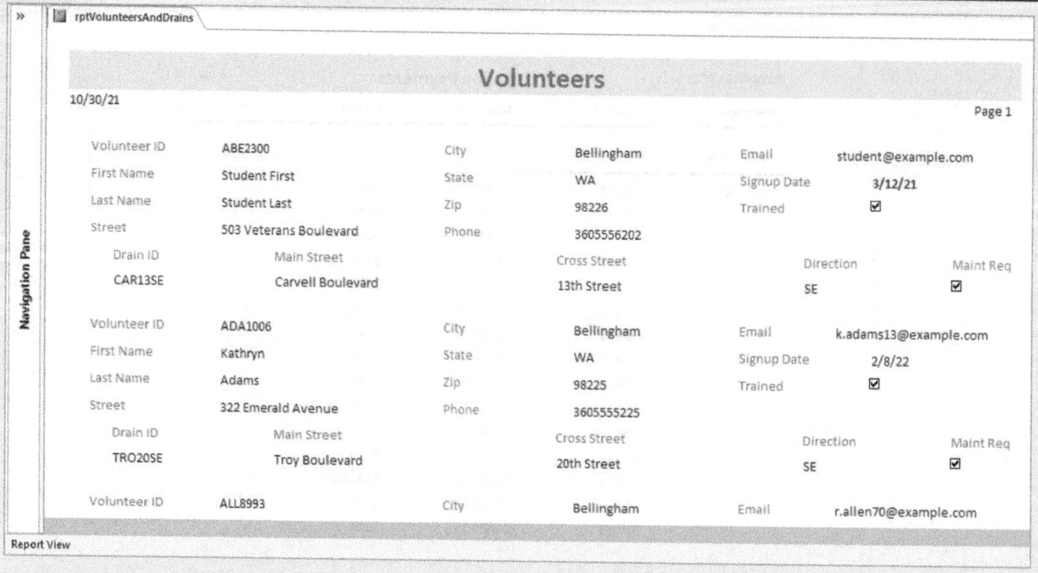

a.  Delete the picture at the top of the report.
b.  Set Narrow margins and a grid width of 10.5 inches.
c.  Center the report title at the 5.25-inch mark on the ruler, and ensure the text is "Volunteers", formatted in bold and 22-point font.
d.  Move the Maint Req column to the right margin, and use horizontal spacing to evenly distribute the columns.
e.  Remove the alternate row color from the detail lines in the report.
f.  Change the page number format from "Page n of m" to "Page n."
g.  Move the date and page number to the Page Header section.
h.  Change the date format to short date.
i.  Add a grand total control that calculates the total number of volunteers, and add a label with the text **Total volunteers**.

3.  Create a query that displays, in order, the DrainID, MainStreet, CrossStreet, and Direction fields from the tblDrain table, the FirstName and LastName fields from the tblVolunteer table. Sort in ascending order by the DrainID and LastName fields, and then save the query as **qryDrainsWithVolunteers**.

4.  Create a custom report based on the qryDrainsWithVolunteers query. Figure 7–41 shows a sample of the first page of the completed report. Refer to the figure as you create the report.

---

**Figure 7–41**    Storm database custom report

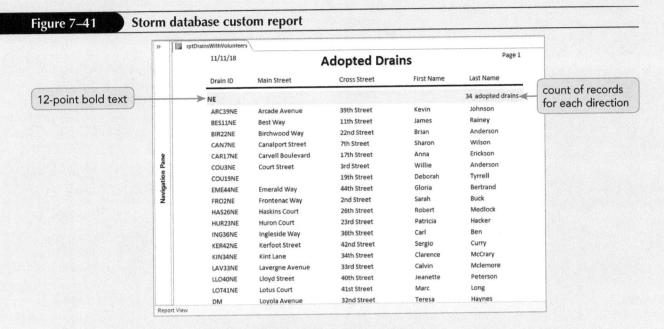

a. Save the report as **rptDrainsWithVolunteers**.
b. The Direction field (from the tblDrain table) is a grouping field.
c. The MainStreet field is a sort field.
d. Hide duplicate values for the MainStreet field.
e. Use Wide margins, and set the grid width to 7 inches. Size fields as shown, and distribute them horizontally using spacing to create a balanced look.
f. Set the background color for the group header and its controls to Blue, Accent 5, Lighter 80% (row 2, column 9 in the Theme Colors palette).
g. In addition to the total for each direction, give a grand total for all drains with the label **Total adopted drains:**.

5. Create a mailing label report according to the following instructions:
   a. Use the tblVolunteer table as the record source.
   b. Use Avery C2160 labels, use a 12-point font size, and use the other default font and color options.
   c. For the prototype label, place FirstName, a space, and LastName on the first line; Street on the second line; and City, a comma and a space, State, a space, and Zip on the third line.
   d. Sort by Zip and then by LastName, and then enter the report name **rptVolunteerMailingLabels**.
   e. Change the page layout of the rptVolunteerMailingLabels report to three snaking columns.

6. Make a backup copy of the database, compact and repair it, and then close the Storm database.

MODULE **8**

## OBJECTIVES

**Session 8.1**
- Export an Access query to an HTML document and view the document
- Import a CSV file as an Access table
- Use the Table Analyzer
- Import and export XML files
- Save and run import and export specifications

**Session 8.2**
- Create a tabbed subform using a tab control
- Create a chart in a tab control using the Chart Wizard
- Create and use an application part
- Export a PDF file
- Describe the difference between importing, embedding, and linking external objects
- Link data from an Excel workbook

# Sharing, Integrating, and Analyzing Data

*Importing, Exporting, Linking, and Analyzing Data in the Clinic Database*

## Case | *Lakewood Community Health Services*

Donna Taylor is pleased with the design and contents of the Clinic database. Donna feels that other employees would benefit from gaining access to the Clinic database and sharing data among the different applications employees use. Donna would also like to be able to analyze the data in the database.

In this module, you will import, export, and link data, and you will create application parts. You will also explore the charting features of Access.

## STARTING DATA FILES

**Access2** → **Module**

Clinic.accdb (*cont.*)
Support_AC_8_NewPatientReferrals.accdb
Support_AC_8_NewPatients.csv
Support_AC_8_Referral.xml
Support_AC_8_Volunteer.xlsx

**Review**

Supplier.accdb (*cont.*)
Support_AC_8_Ads.xlsx
Support_AC_8_Partners.accdb
Support_AC_8_Payables.csv
Support_AC_8_Payments.xml

**Case1**

School.accdb (*cont.*)
Support_AC_8_Company.xml
Support_AC_8_Instructor.csv
Support_AC_8_NewStudentReferrals.accdb
Support_AC_8_Room.xlsx

**Case2**

Storm.accdb (*cont.*)
Support_AC_8_Maintenance.xml
Support_AC_8_Suppliers.xlsx
Support_AC_8_Volunteers.csv

# Session 8.1 Visual Overview:

The field names from the table are used as XML tags to identify data.

Each piece of data is encapsulated in paired tags.

Access includes tools on the External Data tab for exporting data.

```
<tblReferral>
<PatientID>20001</PatientID>
<LastName>Santos</LastName>
<FirstName>Betty</FirstName>
<Guardian>Santos, Lee</Guardian>
<BirthDate>5/25/1920</BirthDate>
<Phone>4045552265</Phone>
<Street>643 Wellington Street</Street>
<City>Atlanta</City>
<State>GA</State>
<Zip>30303</Zip>
<Email>b.santos20@example.com</Email>
</tblReferral>
<tblReferral>
<PatientID>20002</PatientID>
<LastName>Fernandez</LastName>
<FirstName>Amy</FirstName>
<BirthDate>9/18/1943</BirthDate>
<Phone>4045551929</Phone>
<Street>935 Berteau Court</Street>
<City>Atlanta</City>
<State>GA</State>
<Zip>30303</Zip>
<Email>a.fernandez43@example.com</Email>
</tblReferral>
<tblReferral>
<PatientID>20003</PatientID>
<LastName>Brown</LastName>
<FirstName>William</FirstName>
<BirthDate>8/12/1966</BirthDate>
<Phone>4045555871</Phone>
<Street>104 North Greenleaf Court</Street>
<City>Atlanta</City>
<State>GA</State>
```

Access table exported as an XML file

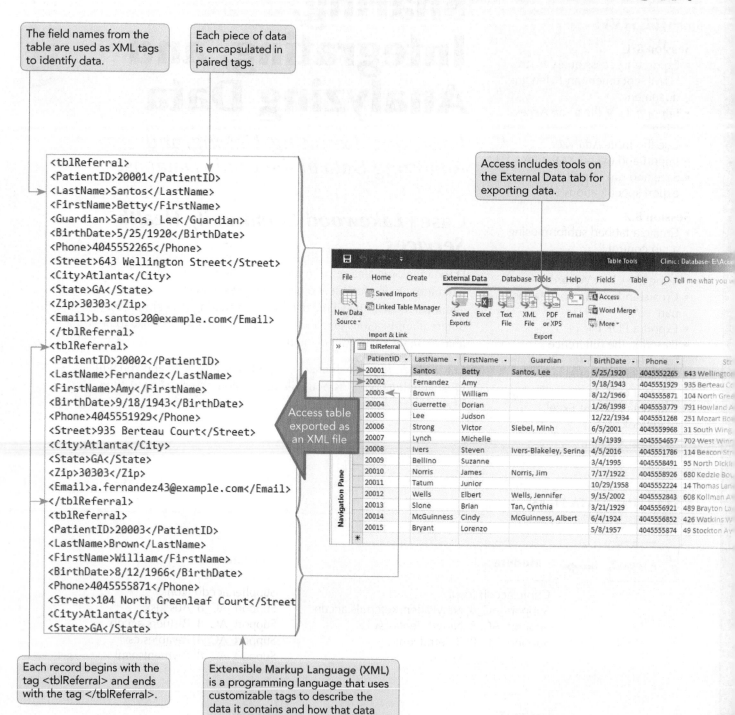

Each record begins with the tag <tblReferral> and ends with the tag </tblReferral>.

Extensible Markup Language (XML) is a programming language that uses customizable tags to describe the data it contains and how that data should be structured.

# Exporting Data to XML and HTML

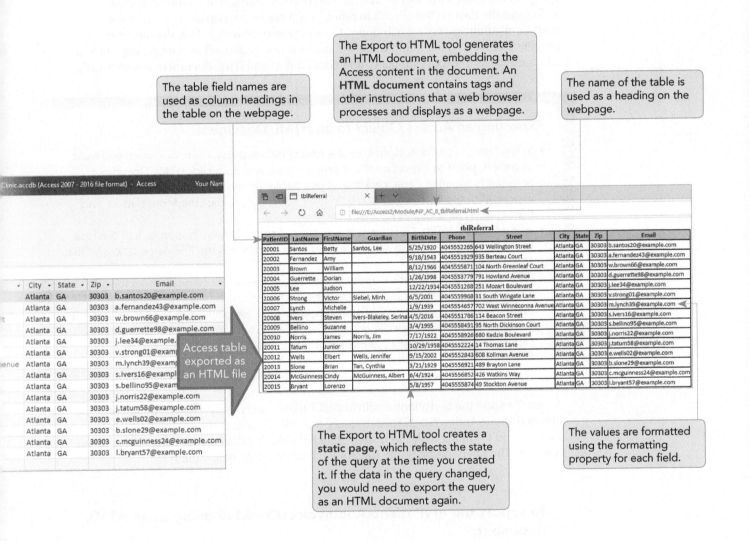

The table field names are used as column headings in the table on the webpage.

The Export to HTML tool generates an HTML document, embedding the Access content in the document. An **HTML document** contains tags and other instructions that a web browser processes and displays as a webpage.

The name of the table is used as a heading on the webpage.

Access table exported as an HTML file

The Export to HTML tool creates a **static page**, which reflects the state of the query at the time you created it. If the data in the query changed, you would need to export the query as an HTML document again.

The values are formatted using the formatting property for each field.

# Exporting an Access Query to an HTML Document

An HTML document contains tags and other instructions that a web browser, such as Google Chrome, Microsoft Edge, or Apple Safari, processes and displays as a webpage.

Donna wants to display the summary data in the qryPatientsAndInvoicesCrosstab query on the clinic's intranet so that all employees working in the office can view it. To store the data on the clinic's intranet, you'll create a webpage version of the qryPatientsAndInvoicesCrosstab query. Creating the necessary HTML document to provide Donna with the information she wants is not as difficult as it might appear. You can use Access to export the query and convert it to an HTML document automatically.

### Exporting an Access Object to an HTML Document

- In the Navigation Pane, right-click the object (table, query, form, or report) you want to export, point to Export on the shortcut menu, and then click HTML Document; or in the Navigation Pane, click the object (table, query, form, or report) you want to export, click the External Data tab, in the Export group, click the More button, and then click HTML Document.
- In the Export - HTML Document dialog box, click the Browse button, select the location where you want to save the file, enter the filename in the File name box, and then click the Save button.
- Click the Export data with formatting and layout check box to retain most formatting and layout information, and then click the OK button.
- In the HTML Output Options dialog box, if using a template, click the Select a HTML Template check box, click the Browse button, select the location for the template, click the template filename, and then click the OK button.
- Click the OK button, and then click the Close button.

You'll export the qryPatientsAndInvoicesCrosstab query as an HTML document. The qryPatientsAndInvoicesCrosstab query is a select query that joins the tblPatient, tblVisit, and tblBilling tables to display selected data associated with those tables for all invoices. The query displays one row for each unique City field value.

### To export the qryPatientsAndInvoicesCrosstab query as an HTML document:

1. **sam** ⬇ Start Access, and then open the **Clinic** database you worked with in the previous three modules.

   **Trouble?** If the security warning is displayed below the ribbon, click the Enable Content button.

2. Open the Navigation Pane (if necessary), right-click **qryPatientsAndInvoicesCrosstab** to display the shortcut menu, point to **Export**, and then click **HTML Document**. The Export - HTML Document dialog box opens.

3. Click the **Browse** button to open the File Save dialog box, navigate to the location where your Data Files are stored, select the text in the File name box, type **NP_AC_8_Crosstab**, make sure HTML Documents appears in the Save as type box, and then click the **Save** button. The File Save dialog box closes, and you return to the Export - HTML Document dialog box. See Figure 8–1.

| Figure 8–1 | Export - HTML Document dialog box |
| --- | --- |

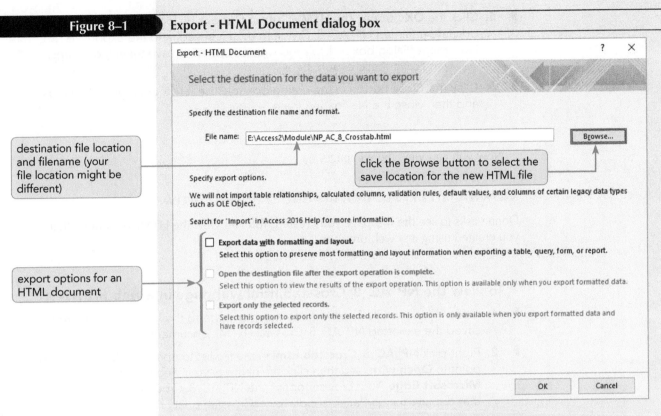

destination file location and filename (your file location might be different)

click the Browse button to select the save location for the new HTML file

export options for an HTML document

The dialog box provides options for exporting the data with formatting and layout, opening the exported file after the export operation is complete, and exporting selected records from the source object (available only when you select records in an object instead of selecting an object in the Navigation Pane). You need to select the option for exporting the data with formatting and layout; otherwise the HTML document created will be poorly formatted and difficult to read.

4. Click the **Export data with formatting and layout** check box to select it, and then click the **OK** button. The Export - HTML Document dialog box closes, and the HTML Output Options dialog box opens. See Figure 8–2. In this dialog box you specify the coding to be used to save the HTML file, and you also have the option to save the exported data in a pre-existing HTML document template. The default option, Default encoding, is selected.

| Figure 8–2 | HTML Output Options dialog box |
| --- | --- |

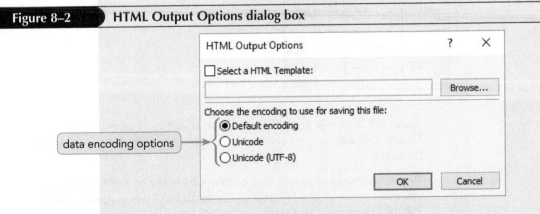

data encoding options

▶ **5.** Click the **OK** button. The HTML Output Options dialog box closes, the HTML document named NP_AC_8_Crosstab.html is saved, and the Export - HTML Document dialog box is displayed with an option to save the export steps. You won't save these export steps.

▶ **6.** Click the **Close** button in the dialog box to close it without saving the steps, and then close the Navigation Pane.

Now you can view the webpage.

## Viewing an HTML Document in a Web Browser

Donna asks to see the webpage you created. You can view the HTML document that you created using any web browser.

### To view the NP_AC_8_Crosstab.html webpage in a web browser:

▶ **1.** Open Windows File Explorer, and then navigate to the location where you saved the exported NP_AC_8_Crosstab HTML document.

▶ **2.** Right-click **NP_AC_8_Crosstab.html** in the file list to open the shortcut menu, point to **Open with**, and then click the name of your web browser, such as **Microsoft Edge**. Your browser opens the NP_AC_8_Crosstab.html webpage that displays the qryPatientsAndInvoicesCrosstab query results. See Figure 8–3.

| Figure 8–3 | **qryPatientsAndInvoicesCrosstab query displayed in Edge** |

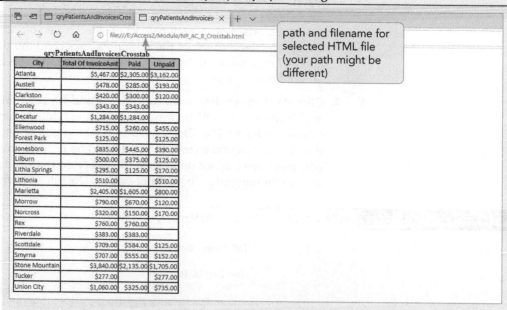

**Trouble?** You may see different column widths than the ones shown in Figure 8–3, depending on the size of your web browser window. This is not a problem.

Any subsequent changes that employees make to the Clinic database will not appear in the NP_AC_8_Crosstab.html webpage that you created because it is a static webpage—that is, it reflects the state of the qryPatientsAndInvoicesCrosstab query in the Clinic database at the time you created it. If data in the qryPatientsAndInvoicesCrosstab query changes, Donna would need to export the query as an HTML document again.

3. Close your browser, and then click the **Close** button $\boxed{\times}$ on the Windows File Explorer window title bar to close it and to return to Access.

   **Trouble?** If the Access window is not active on your screen, click the Microsoft Access program button on the taskbar.

Now that you've completed your work creating the webpage, Donna has a file containing information for new patients that she needs to add to the Clinic database. Instead of typing the information into new records, she asks you to import the data into the Clinic database.

# Importing a CSV File as an Access Table

Many people use Excel to manage a simple table, such as a table of contact information or product information. Donna has been maintaining an Excel workbook containing basic information for people who have signed up with the Lakewood Community Health Services clinic as patients but have not yet booked appointments. Recall that she could use the Excel button on the External Data tab to access the Import Spreadsheet Wizard and import the Excel worksheet data. However, in this case, Donna has already exported the Excel data to a CSV file. A **CSV (comma-separated values) file** is a text file in which commas separate values, and each line is a record containing the same number of values in the same positions. This is a common format for representing data in a table and is used by spreadsheet applications such as Excel as well as database applications. A CSV file can easily be imported into the Clinic database as a table. To do so, you use the Import Text Wizard, which you open by clicking the Text File button on the External Data Tab.

## Importing a CSV File into an Access Table

- On the External Data tab, in the Import & Link group, click the Text File button to open the Get External Data - Text File dialog box.
- Click the Browse button in the dialog box, navigate to the location where the file to import is stored, click the filename, and then click the Open button.
- Click the "Import the source data into a new table in the current database" option button, and then click the OK button.
- In the Import Text Wizard dialog box, click the Delimited option button, and then click the Next button.
- Make sure the Comma option button is selected. If appropriate, click the First Row Contains Field Names check box to select it, and then click the Next button.
- For each field, if necessary, select the column, type its field name and select its data type, and then click the Next button.
- Choose the appropriate option button to let Access create a primary key, to choose your own primary key, or to avoid setting a primary key, and then click the Next button.
- Type the table name in the Import to Table box, and then click the Finish button.

Donna's CSV file is named Support_AC_8_NewPatients.csv, and you'll import the data as a new table in the Clinic database.

## To view and import the CSV file as an Access table:

1. Open Windows File Explorer, navigate to the **Access2 > Module** folder included with your Data Files, right-click **Support_AC_8_NewPatients.csv** in the file list to open the shortcut menu, click **Open with**, and then click **Notepad**.

   **Trouble?** If Notepad isn't an option when you click Open with, click Choose another app, click Notepad in the How do you want to open this file dialog box that opens, and then click the OK button.

2. Examine the contents of the Support_AC_8_NewPatients.csv file. The file contains rows of data, with commas separating the individual pieces of data.

3. Close the Notepad window, and then close the File Explorer window. You return to the Access window.

   **Trouble?** If a dialog box appears prompting you to save the file, click Don't Save. You may have accidentally added or deleted a character, and you don't want to save this change to the file.

4. On the ribbon, click the **External Data** tab, and then in the Import & Link group, click **New Data Source**, point to **From File**, and then click the **Text File** button to open the Get External Data - Text File dialog box.

   **Trouble?** If the Export - Text File dialog box opens, you clicked the Text File button in the Export group. Click the Cancel button, and then repeat Step 4, being sure to select the New Data Source button in the Import & Link group.

5. Click the **Browse** button, navigate to the **Access2 > Module** folder included with your Data Files, click **Support_AC_8_NewPatients.csv**, and then click the **Open** button.

6. In the Get External Data - Text File dialog box, click the **Import the source data into a new table in the current database** option button (if necessary). The selected path and filename appear in the File name box. See Figure 8–4.

| Figure 8–4 | Get External Data - Text File dialog box |

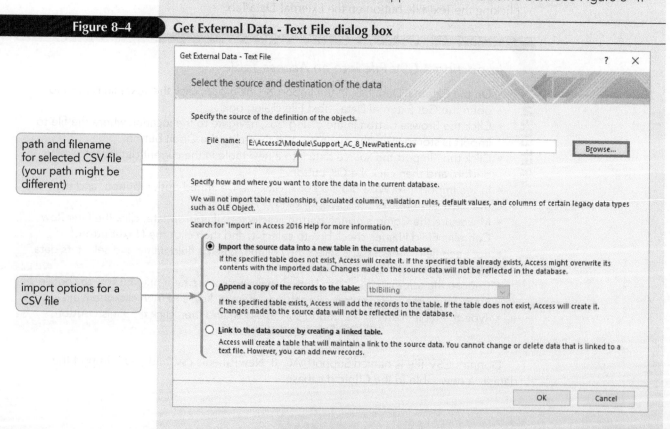

path and filename for selected CSV file (your path might be different)

import options for a CSV file

The dialog box provides options for importing the data into a new table in the database, appending a copy of the data to an existing table in the database, and linking to the source data. In the future, Donna wants to maintain the potential new patient data in the Clinic database, instead of using her Excel workbook, so you'll import the data into a new table.

7. Click the **OK** button to open the first Import Text Wizard dialog box, in which you designate how to identify the separation between field values in each line in the source data. The choices are the use of characters to separate, or delimit, the values, or the use of fixed-width columns with spaces between each column. The wizard has identified your file as delimited, which is correct.

8. Click the **Next** button to open the second Import Text Wizard dialog box, in which you specify the delimiter character. The choices are tab, semicolon, comma, space, or another character. The wizard has correctly identified that values are delimited by commas. See Figure 8–5.

| Figure 8–5 | Import Text Wizard dialog box specifying the delimiter for values in the CSV file |

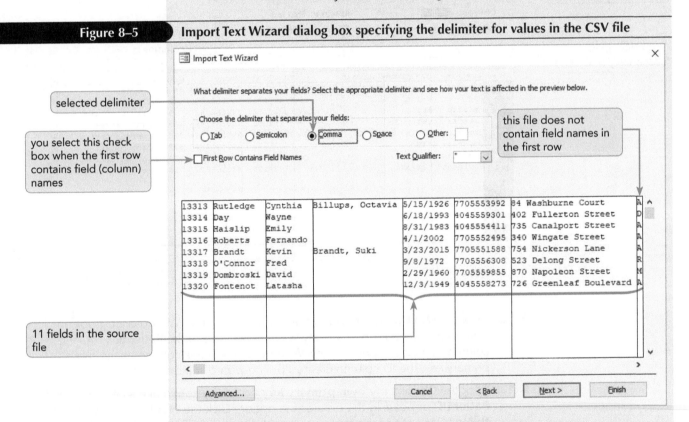

The CSV source file contains eight records with 11 fields in each record. A comma serves as the delimiter for values in each line (record), so the Comma option button is selected. The first row in the source file contains the first record, not field names, so the "First Row Contains Field Names" check box is not checked.

9. Click the **Next** button to open the third Import Text Wizard dialog box, in which you enter the field names and set other properties for the imported fields. You will import all fields from the source file and use the Short Text data type and default indexed settings for most fields, except for the data type of the BirthDate field.

▶ **10.** In the Field Name box, type **PatientID**, click the **Data Type** arrow, click **Short Text**, and then click **Field2** in the table list. The heading for the first column changes to PatientID (partially hidden) in the table list, and the second column is selected.

Be sure the data type for BirthDate is Date With Time, and the data type for Phone and Zip is Short Text.

▶ **11.** Repeat Step 10 for the remaining 10 columns, making sure Short Text is the data type for all fields, except for BirthDate, which should be Date With Time, typing **LastName**, **FirstName**, **Guardian**, **BirthDate**, **Phone**, **Address**, **City**, **State**, **Zip**, and **Email** in the Field Name box. See Figure 8–6.

| Figure 8–6 | Field names and options as specified in the Import Text Wizard |

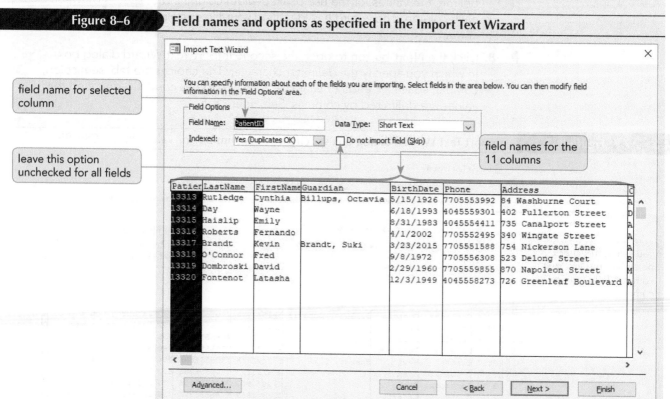

field name for selected column

leave this option unchecked for all fields

field names for the 11 columns

▶ **12.** Click the **Next** button to open the fourth Import Text Wizard dialog box, in which you select the primary key for the imported table. PatientID, the first column, will be the primary key. When you select this column as the table's primary key, the ID column created by the wizard will be deleted.

▶ **13.** Click the **Choose my own primary key** option button, make sure **PatientID** appears in the box for the option, click the **Next** button, type **tblNewPatients** as the table name in the Import to Table box, click the **I would like a wizard to analyze my table after importing the data** check box to select it, and then click the **Finish** button. An Import Text Wizard dialog box opens, asking if you want to analyze the table.

**TIP**

You can start the Table Analyzer Wizard directly by clicking the Database Tools tab and then clicking the Analyze Table button in the Analyze group.

▶ **14.** Click the **Yes** button to close the dialog box and start the Table Analyzer Wizard. You will continue working with this wizard in the next set of steps.

After importing data and creating a new table, you can use the Table Analyzer Wizard to analyze the imported table. The wizard identifies duplicate data in your table and displays a diagram and explanation in the dialog box describing the potential problem.

## Analyzing a Table with the Table Analyzer

Normalizing is the process of identifying and eliminating anomalies, or inconsistencies, from a collection of tables in the database. The **Table Analyzer** analyzes a single table and, if necessary, splits it into two or more tables that are in third normal form. The Table Analyzer looks for redundant data in the table. When the Table Analyzer encounters redundant data, it removes redundant fields from the table and then places them in new tables. The database designer must always review the analyzer results carefully to determine if the suggestions are appropriate.

### To use the Table Analyzer Wizard to analyze the imported table:

1. In the first Table Analyzer Wizard dialog box, click the first **Show me an example** button 🔅 , read the explanation, close the example box, click the second **Show me an example** button 🔅 , read the explanation, close the example box, and then click the **Next** button to open the second Table Analyzer Wizard dialog box. The diagram and explanation in this dialog box describe how the Table Analyzer solves the duplicate data problem.

2. Again, click the first **Show me an example button** 🔅 , read the explanation, close the example box, click the second **Show me an example** button 🔅 , read the explanation, close the example box, and then click the **Next** button to open the third Table Analyzer Wizard dialog box. In this dialog box, you choose whether to let the wizard decide the appropriate table placement for the fields, if the table is not already normalized. You'll let the wizard decide.

3. Make sure the **Yes, let the wizard decide** option button is selected, and then click the **Next** button. The wizard indicates that the City and State fields should be split into separate tables. Although this data is redundant, it is an industry practice to keep the city, state, and zip information with the address information in a table, so you'll cancel the wizard rather than split the table.

4. Click the **Cancel** button to close the Table Analyzer Wizard. You return to the final Get External Data - Text File dialog box, in which you specify if you want to save the import steps. You don't need to save these steps because you're importing the data only this one time.

5. Click the **Close** button to close the dialog box.

The tblNewPatients table is now listed in the Tables section in the Navigation Pane. You'll open the table to verify the import results.

### To open the imported tblNewPatients table:

1. Open the Navigation Pane, if necessary.

2. Double-click **tblNewPatients** to open the table datasheet, and then close the Navigation Pane.

3. Resize all columns to their best fit, and then click **13313** in the first row in the PatientID column to deselect all values. See Figure 8–7.

Figure 8–7 **Figure 8–7** Imported tblNewPatients table datasheet

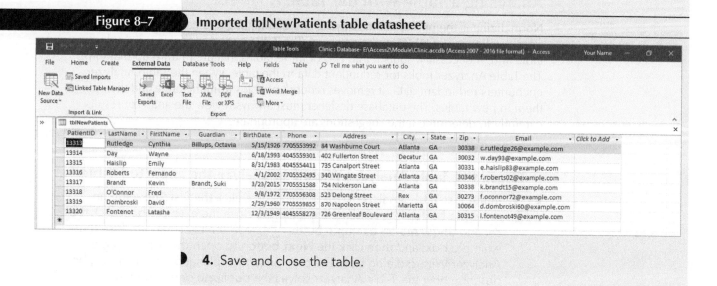

**4.** Save and close the table.

Next, Donna would like you to import data from another file containing new patient referrals from another health clinic. However, this data is not in an Access table; instead, it's stored in XML format.

# Working with XML Files

Lakewood Community Health Services occasionally receives patient referrals from other clinics. Donna was provided an XML document that contains patient contact information from another clinic, which she wants to add to the Clinic database. XML (Extensible Markup Language) is a programming language that is similar in format to HTML but is more customizable and is suited to the exchange of data between different programs. Unlike HTML, which uses a fixed set of tags to describe the appearance of a webpage, developers can customize XML to describe the data it contains and how that data should be structured.

PROSKILLS

*Teamwork: Exchanging Data Between Programs*

If all companies used Access, you could easily exchange data between any two databases. However, not all companies use Access. One universal and widely used method for transferring data between different database systems is to export data to XML files and import data from XML files. XML files are used to exchange data between companies, and they are also used to exchange data between programs within a company. For example, you can store data either in an Excel workbook or in an Access table or query, depending on which program is best suited to the personnel working with the data and the business requirements of the company. Because the XML file format is a common format for both Excel and Access—as well as many other programs—whenever the data is needed in another program, you can export the data from one program as an XML file and then import the file into the other program. When collaborating with a team of users or sharing database information with other organizations, always consider the characteristics of the programs being used and the best format for exchanging data between programs.

## Importing Data from an XML File

In Access, you can import data from an XML file directly into a database table. Donna's XML file is named Support_AC_8_Referral.xml, and you'll import it into a table called tblReferral in the Clinic database.

### Importing an XML File as an Access Table

- On the External Data tab, in the Import & Link group, click the New Data Source button, point to From File, and then click the XML File button to open the Get External Data - XML File dialog box; or right-click the table name in the Navigation Pane, point to Import, and then click XML File.
- Click the Browse button, navigate to the location of the XML file, click the XML filename, and then click the Open button.
- Click the OK button in the Get External Data - XML File dialog box, click the table name in the Import XML dialog box, click the appropriate option button in the Import Options section, and then click the OK button.
- Click the Close button; or if you need to save the import steps, click the Save import steps check box, enter a name for the saved steps in the Save as box, and then click the Save Import button.

Now you will import the Support_AC_8_Referral.xml XML document as an Access table.

### To import the contents of the XML document:

1. On the ribbon, click the **External Data** tab if necessary, and then in the Import & Link Group, click the **New Data Source** button, point to **From File**, and then click the **XML File** button. The Get External Data - XML File dialog box opens.

2. Click the **Browse** button to open the File Open dialog box, navigate to the **Access2 > Module** folder included with your Data Files, click **Support_AC_8_Referral.xml**, and then click the **Open** button. The selected path and filename now appear in the File name box.

3. Click the **OK** button. The Import XML dialog box opens. See Figure 8–8.

Figure 8–8    Import XML dialog box

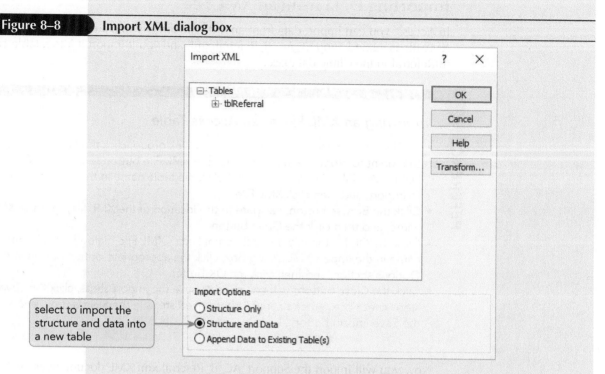

select to import the
structure and data into
a new table

From the XML file, you can import only the table structure to a new table,
import the table structure and data to a new table, or append the data in the
XML file to an existing table. You'll choose to import the data and structure
to a new table.

▶ **4.** Make sure the **Structure and Data** option button is selected, click
**tblReferral** in the box, and then click the **OK** button. The Import XML dialog
box closes, and the last Get External Data - XML File Wizard dialog box
is displayed. You'll continue to work with this dialog box in the next set of
steps.

## Saving and Running Import Specifications

If you need to repeat the same import procedure many times, you can save the steps for
the procedure and expedite future imports by running the saved import steps without
using a wizard. Because Donna will receive additional lists of patient referrals in the
future, you'll save the import steps so she can reuse them whenever she receives a
new list.

### To save the XML file import steps:

▶ **1.** In the Get External Data - XML File dialog box, click the **Save import steps**
check box to select it. The dialog box displays additional options for the save
operation. See Figure 8–9.

| Figure 8-9 | Save Import Steps dialog box in the Get External Data - XML File Wizard |
|---|---|

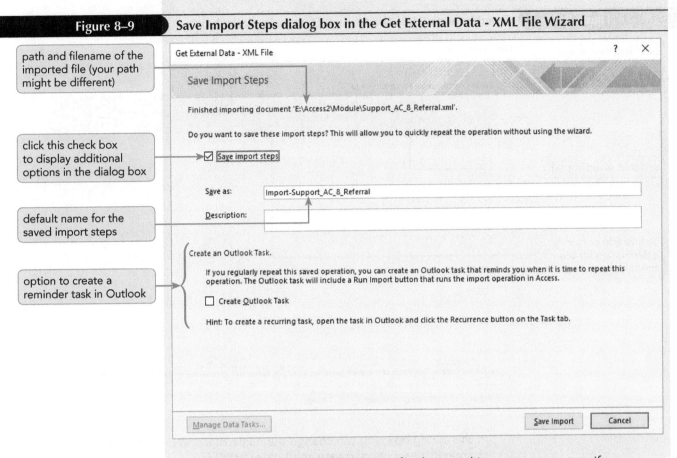

You can accept the default name for the saved import steps or specify a different name, and you can enter an optional description. If the import will occur on a set schedule, you can also create a reminder task in Microsoft Outlook. You'll accept the default name for the saved steps, and you won't enter a description or schedule an Outlook task.

2. Click the **Save Import** button. The import steps are saved as Import-Support_AC_8_Referral, the Get External Data - XML File dialog box closes, and the data from the Support_AC_8_Referral.xml file has been imported into the Clinic database with the name tblReferral. Before reviewing the imported table, you'll add a description to the saved import steps.

3. On the External Data tab, in the Import & Link group, click the **Saved Imports** button to open the Manage Data Tasks dialog box. See Figure 8-10.

**Trouble?** If the Saved Exports tab is displayed in the Manage Data Tasks dialog box, then you selected the Saved Exports button instead of the Saved Imports button. Click the Saved Imports tab in the dialog box.

**Figure 8–10**    Saved Imports tab in the Manage Data Tasks dialog box

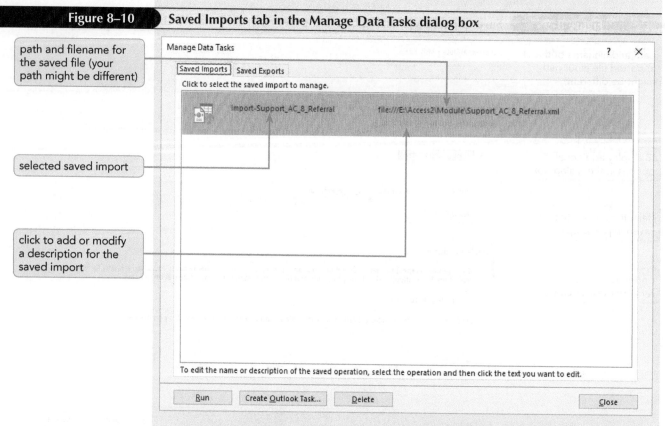

path and filename for the saved file (your path might be different)

selected saved import

click to add or modify a description for the saved import

In this dialog box, you can change the name of a saved import, add or change its description, create an Outlook task for it, run it, or delete it. You can also manage any saved export by clicking the Saved Exports tab. You'll add a description for the saved import procedure.

4. Click the **Click here to edit the description** link to open a box that contains an insertion point, type **XML file containing patient referrals from another clinic**, click an unused portion of the highlighted selection band to close the box and accept the typed description, and then click the **Saved Exports** tab. You have not saved any export steps, so no saved exports are displayed.

5. Click the **Close** button to close the Manage Data Tasks dialog box.

6. Open the Navigation Pane, double-click the **tblReferral** table to open the table datasheet, close the Navigation Pane, resize all columns to their best fit if necessary, and then click **20001** in the first row in the Patient ID column to deselect all values. See Figure 8–11.

| Figure 8-11 | Imported XML records in new tblReferral table |

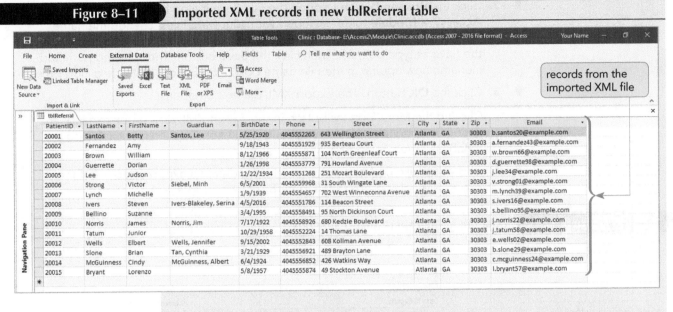

Next, Donna asks you to export the tblBilling table as an XML file.

## Exporting an Access Table as an XML File

Lakewood Community Health Services uses an accounting system that accepts data in XML files. Donna wants to export the tblBilling table as an XML file so it can be tested with the accounting system.

You'll export the tblBilling table as an XML file now.

### To export the tblBilling table as an XML file:

▸ **1.** Open the Navigation Pane (if necessary), right-click **tblBilling**, point to **Export** on the shortcut menu, and then click **XML File**. The Export - XML File dialog box opens.

2. Click the **Browse** button to open the File Save dialog box, navigate to the **Access2 > Module** folder included with your Data Files, change the name in the File name box to **NP_AC_8_Billing**, make sure **XML** is specified in the Save as type box, and then click the **Save** button. The selected path and filename now appear in the File name box in the Export-XML File dialog box.

3. Click the **OK** button. The Export XML dialog box opens.

Clicking the More Options button in the Export XML dialog box expands the dialog box and lets you view and select additional options for exporting a database object to an XML file.

4. Click the **More Options** button to display detailed export options in the Export XML dialog box. See Figure 8–12.

| Figure 8–12 | Data tab in the Export XML dialog box |
| --- | --- |

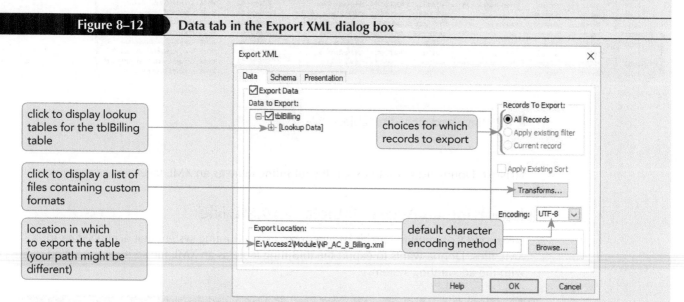

click to display lookup tables for the tblBilling table

click to display a list of files containing custom formats

location in which to export the table (your path might be different)

The Export Data check box, the Export Location box, and the Records To Export option group display the selections you made in the previous steps. You're exporting all records from the tblBilling table, including the data in the records and the structure of the table, to the NP_AC_8_Billing.xml file in the Access2 > Module folder. The encoding option determines how characters will be represented in the exported XML file. The encoding choices are UTF-8, which uses 8 bits to represent each character, and UTF-16, which uses 16 bits to represent each character. You can also click the Transforms button if you have a special file that contains instructions for changing the exported data.

The accounting software used by the center doesn't have a transform file and requires the default encoding, but Donna wants to review the tables that contain lookup data.

5. In the Data to Export box, click the **expand** icon ⊞ to the left of [Lookup Data], and then verify that the tblInvoiceItem check box and the tblVisit check box are not checked. Both the tblInvoiceItem table and tblVisit tables contain lookup data because they are in a one-to-many relationship with the tblBilling table. The accounting program requirements don't include any lookup data from the tblInvoiceItem table or tblVisit table, so you don't want the tblInvoiceItem check box or the tblVisit check box to be checked.

The Data tab settings are correct, so next you'll verify the Schema tab settings.

6. Click the **Schema** tab. See Figure 8–13.

**Figure 8–13**     Schema tab in the Export XML dialog box

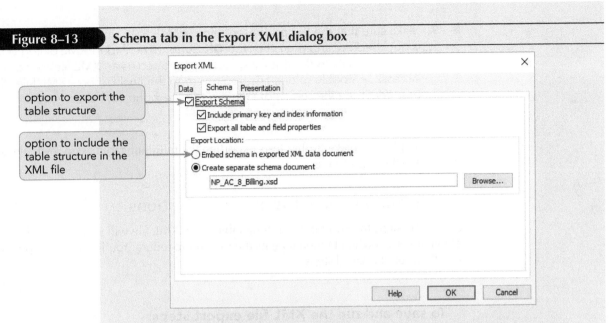

Along with the data from the tblBilling table, you'll be exporting its table structure, including information about the table's primary key, indexes, and table and field properties. An **XSD (XML Structure Definition) file** is a file that defines the structure of the XML file, much like the Design view of a table defines the fields and their data types. You can include this structure information in a separate XSD file, or you can embed the information in the XML file. The accounting software accepts a single XML file, so you'll embed the structure information in the XML file.

7. Click the **Embed schema in exported XML data document** option button. The Create separate schema document option button is now grayed out.

8. Click the **Presentation** tab. See Figure 8–14.

**Figure 8–14**     Presentation tab in the Export XML dialog box

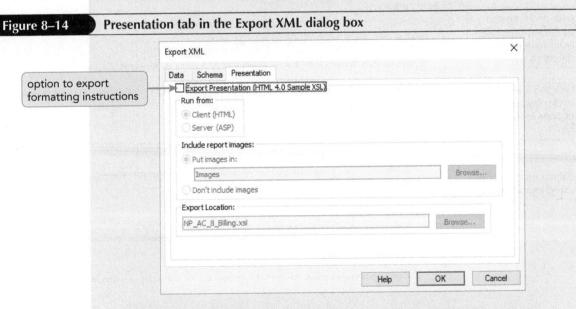

The Presentation tab options let you export a separate **XSL (Extensible Stylesheet Language) file** containing the format specifications for the tblBilling table data. The accounting software contains its own formatting instructions for any imported data, so you will not export an XSL file.

**9.** Make sure that the Export Presentation (HTML 4.0 Sample XSL) check box is not checked, and then click the **OK** button. The Export XML dialog box closes, the data in the tblBilling table is exported as an XML file to the Access2 > Module folder, and you return to the final Export - XML File dialog box. You'll see the results of creating this file in the next set of steps.

Donna plans to make further tests exporting the tblBilling table as an XML file, so you'll save the export steps.

## Saving and Running Export Specifications

Saving the steps to export the tblBilling table as an XML file will save time and eliminate errors when Donna repeats the export procedure. You'll save the export steps and then run the saved steps.

### To save and run the XML file export steps:

**1.** In the Export - XML File Wizard dialog box, click the **Save export steps** check box. The dialog box displays additional options for the save operation.

The dialog box has the same options you saw earlier when you saved the XML import steps. You'll enter a description, and you won't create an Outlook task because Donna will be running the saved export steps only on an as-needed basis.

**2.** In the Description box, type **XML file containing accounting entries from the tblBilling table**. See Figure 8–15.

| Figure 8–15 | Saving the export steps |
| --- | --- |

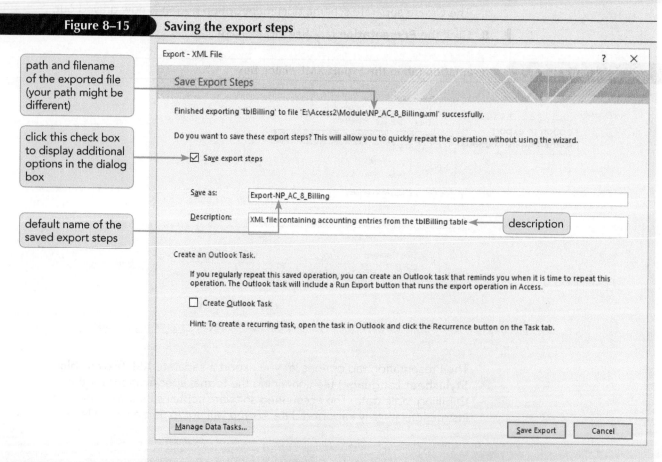

path and filename of the exported file (your path might be different)

click this check box to display additional options in the dialog box

default name of the saved export steps

Export - XML File                                                    ?    ✕

Save Export Steps

Finished exporting 'tblBilling' to file 'E:\Access2\Module\NP_AC_8_Billing.xml' successfully.

Do you want to save these export steps? This will allow you to quickly repeat the operation without using the wizard.

☑ Save export steps

Save as:    Export-NP_AC_8_Billing

Description:    XML file containing accounting entries from the tblBilling table    ◄— description

Create an Outlook Task.

If you regularly repeat this saved operation, you can create an Outlook task that reminds you when it is time to repeat this operation. The Outlook task will include a Run Export button that runs the export operation in Access.

☐ Create Outlook Task

Hint: To create a recurring task, open the task in Outlook and click the Recurrence button on the Task tab.

Manage Data Tasks...                                        Save Export        Cancel

3. Click the **Save Export** button. The export steps are saved as Export-NP_AC_8_Billing and the Export - XML File dialog box closes.

Now you'll run the saved steps.

4. Click the **External Data** tab (if necessary), and then in the Export group, click the **Saved Exports** button. The Manage Data Tasks dialog box opens with the Saved Exports tab selected. See Figure 8–16.

**Trouble?** If the Saved Imports tab is displayed in the Manage Data Tasks dialog box, then you selected the Saved Imports button instead of the Saved Exports button. Click the Save Exports tab in the dialog box.

| Figure 8–16 | Saved Exports tab in the Manage Data Tasks dialog box |

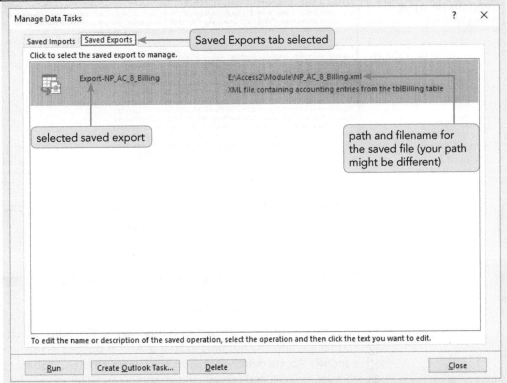

5. Verify that the Export-NP_AC_8_Billing export is selected, and then click the **Run** button. The saved procedure runs, and a message box opens, asking if you want to replace the existing XML file you created earlier.

6. Click the **Yes** button to replace the existing XML file. A message box informs you that the export was completed successfully.

7. Click the **OK** button to close the message box, and then click the **Close** button to close the Manage Data Tasks dialog box.

8. Open Windows File Explorer, navigate to the **Access2 > Module** folder included with your Data Files, right-click the **NP_AC_8_Billing.xml** XML file in the file list to open the shortcut menu, click **Open with**, and then click **Notepad**. See Figure 8–17.

Figure 8–17    NP_AC_8_Billing XML file in Notepad

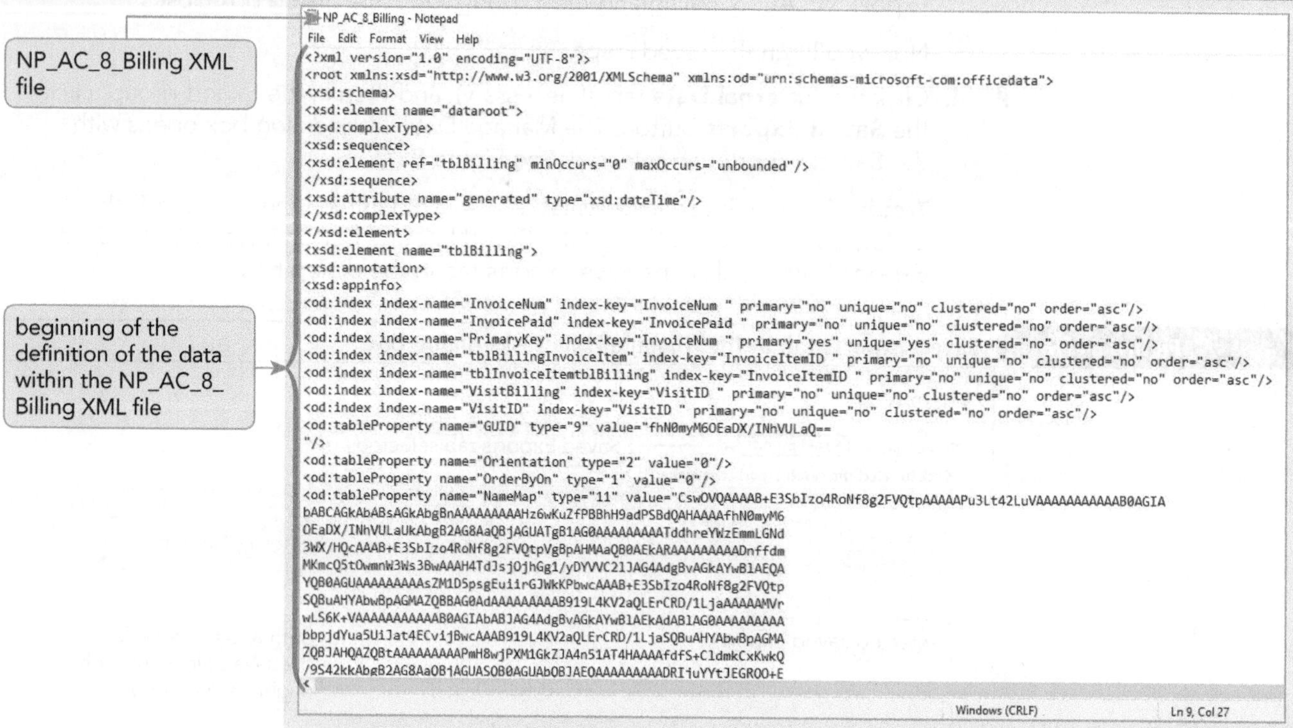

NP_AC_8_Billing XML file

beginning of the definition of the data within the NP_AC_8_Billing XML file

9. Close the Notepad window, and then close the File Explorer window.

10. If you are not continuing on to the next session, close the Clinic database.

## Importing and Exporting Data

**INSIGHT**

Access supports importing data from common file formats such as an Excel workbook, a text file, and an XML file. Additional Access options include importing an object from another Access database, importing data from other databases (such as Microsoft SQL Server, mySQL, and others), and importing an HTML document, an Outlook folder, or a SharePoint list.

In addition to exporting an Access object as an XML file or an HTML document, Access includes options for exporting data to another Access database, other databases (Microsoft SQL Server, mySQL), an Excel workbook, a text file, a Word document, a SharePoint list, or a PDF or XPS file. You can also export table or query data directly to Word's mail merge feature or export an object to an email message.

The steps you follow for other import and export options work similarly to the import and export steps you've already used.

You've imported and exported data, analyzed a table's design, and saved and run import and export specifications. In the next session, you will analyze data by working with a chart, creating and using an application part, linking external data, and adding a tab control to a form.

REVIEW

### Session 8.1 Quick Check

1. What is HTML?
2. What is an HTML template?
3. What is a static webpage?
4. What is a CSV file?
5. What is the Table Analyzer?
6. _____ is a programming language that describes data and its structure.

# Session 8.2 Visual Overview:

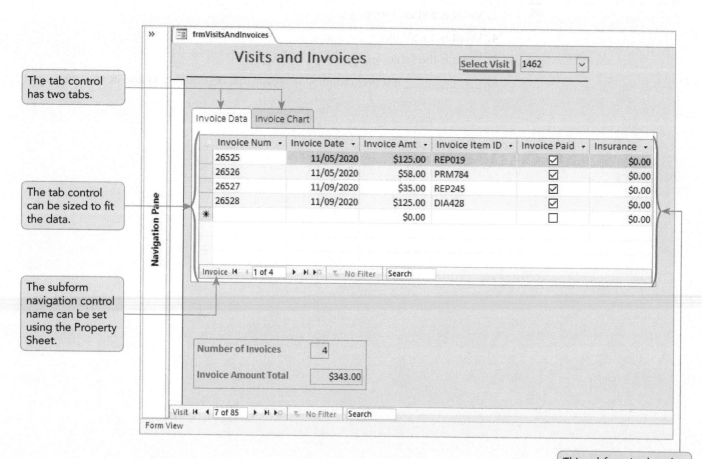

The tab control has two tabs.

The tab control can be sized to fit the data.

The subform navigation control name can be set using the Property Sheet.

This subform is placed as an object on the first page of the tab control.

# Tabbed Control with a Chart

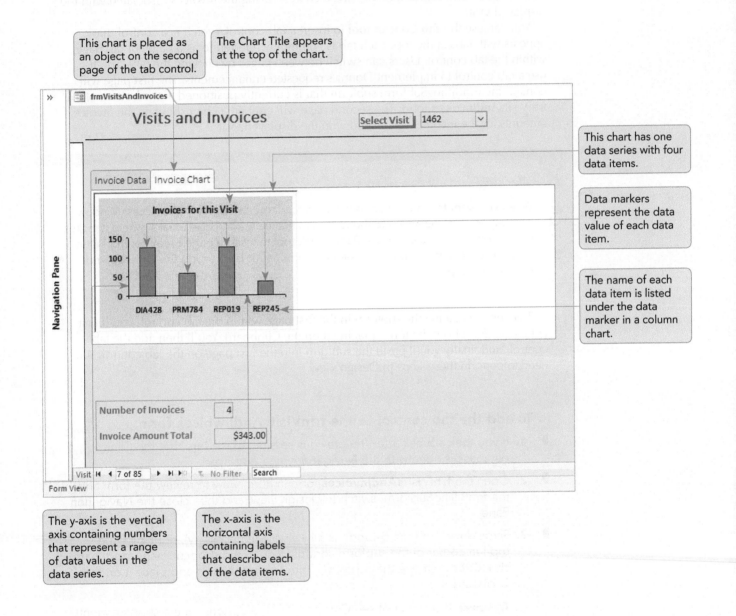

This chart is placed as an object on the second page of the tab control.

The Chart Title appears at the top of the chart.

This chart has one data series with four data items.

Data markers represent the data value of each data item.

The name of each data item is listed under the data marker in a column chart.

The y-axis is the vertical axis containing numbers that represent a range of data values in the data series.

The x-axis is the horizontal axis containing labels that describe each of the data items.

# Using a Tab Control in a Form

Donna wants you to enhance the frmVisitsAndInvoices form in the Clinic database to enable users to switch between different content. Recall the frmVisitsAndInvoices form currently contains a main form displaying Visit data and the frmBillingSubform subform displaying the information for the billed invoices related to a displayed visit. Specifically, Donna wants users to be able to choose between viewing the frmBillingSubform subform or viewing a chart showing the invoices associated with the displayed visit.

You can use the **Tab Control tool** to insert a tab control, which is a control that appears with tabs at the top. Each tab is commonly referred to as a page, or tab page, within the tab control. Users can switch between pages by clicking the tabs. You'll use a tab control to implement Donna's requested enhancements. The first page will contain the frmBillingSubform subform that is currently positioned at the bottom of the frmVisitsAndInvoices form. The second page will contain a chart showing the invoice amounts for the invoices associated with the displayed visit.

## INSIGHT

### Working with Large Forms

When you want to work with a form that is too large to display in the Access window, one way to help you navigate the form is to manually add page breaks, where it makes sense to do so. You can use the Page Break tool to insert a page break control in the form, which lets users move between the form pages by pressing the Page Up and Page Down keys.

To expedite placing the subform in the first page within the tab control, you'll first cut the subform from the form, placing it on the Clipboard. You'll then add the tab control, and finally you'll paste the subform into the first page on the tab control. You need to perform these steps in Design view.

### To add the tab control to the frmVisitsAndInvoices form:

1. If you took a break after the previous session, make sure that the Clinic database is open with the Navigation Pane displayed.

2. Open the **frmVisitsAndInvoices** form in Form view to review the form and the frmBillingSubform, switch to Design view, and then close the Navigation Pane.

3. Scroll down until the subform is fully visible (if necessary), right-click the top-left corner of the subform control to open the shortcut menu, and then click **Cut** to remove the subform control from the form and place it on the Clipboard.

   **Trouble?** If you do not see Cut as one of the options on the shortcut menu, you did not click the top edge of the subform control correctly. Right-click the top edge of the subform control until you see this option on the shortcut menu, and then click Cut.

4. Increase the length of the Detail section to **7.0** inches.

5. Select the **Number of Invoices** label and control, the **Invoice Amount Total** label and control, and the rectangle control surrounding them, and then move the selected controls below the 6-inch horizontal line in the grid.

6. On the Form Design Tools Design tab, in the Controls group, click the **Tab Control** tool ⬚.

7. Position the + portion of the Tab Control tool pointer in the Detail section at the 2.75-inch mark on the vertical ruler and three grid dots from the left edge of the form, and then click the mouse button. A tab control with two tabs is inserted in the form.

8. Right-click in the middle of the tab control, and then when an orange outline appears inside the tab control, click **Paste** on the shortcut menu. The subform is pasted in the tab control on the leftmost tab. See Figure 8–18.

**Figure 8–18     Subform in the tab control**

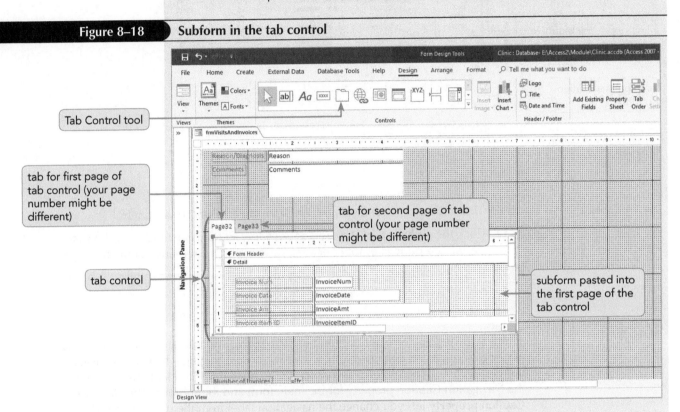

9. Switch to Form view, click the **Select Visit** arrow, click **1462** in the list, and then click **1462** in the Visit ID box to deselect all controls.

10. Scroll down to the bottom of the form. The left tab, which is labeled Page32 (yours might differ), is the active tab. See Figure 8–19.

**Figure 8–19**   **Subform in the tab control in Form view**

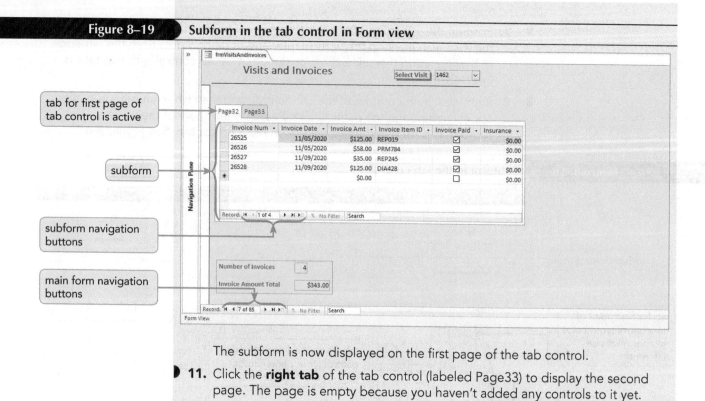

tab for first page of tab control is active

subform

subform navigation buttons

main form navigation buttons

The subform is now displayed on the first page of the tab control.

▶ **11.** Click the **right tab** of the tab control (labeled Page33) to display the second page. The page is empty because you haven't added any controls to it yet.

▶ **12.** Click the **left tab** of the tab control again to display the frmBillingSubform subform.

After viewing the form and subform in Form view, Donna's staff finds the two sets of navigation buttons confusing—they waste time determining which set of navigation buttons applies to the subform and which to the main form. To clarify this, you'll set the Navigation Caption property for the main form and the subform. The **Navigation Caption property** lets you change the navigation label from the word "Record" to another value. Because the main form displays data about visits and the subform displays data about invoices, you'll change the Navigation Caption property for the main form to "Visit" and for the subform to "Invoice."

You'll also set the Caption property for the tabs in the tab control, so they identify the contents of each page.

**To change the captions for the navigation buttons and the tabs:**

▶ **1.** Switch to Design view, and then click the main form's form selector to select the form control in the main form, open the Property Sheet to display the properties for the selected form control, click the **All** tab (if necessary), click the **Navigation Caption** box, and then type **Visit**. See Figure 8–20.

**Figure 8–20**    Navigation Caption property set for the main form

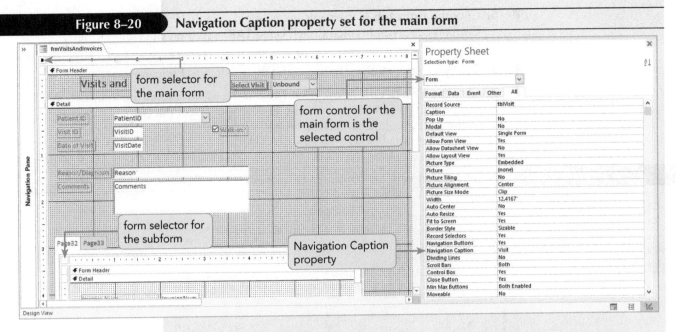

2. Click the **form selector** for the subform on the leftmost tab to select the subform, click the **form selector** for the subform again to select the form control in the subform and to display the Property Sheet for the selected form control, click the **Navigation Caption** box, and then type **Invoice**. Navigation buttons don't appear in Design view, so you won't see the effects of the Navigation Caption property settings until you switch to Form view. Before you do that, you will set the Caption property for the two tabs in the tab control.

3. Click the **left tab** in the tab control, and then click the **left tab** in the tab control again to select it.

4. In the Property Sheet, in the Caption box, type **Invoice Data** and then press **TAB**. The Caption property value now appears on the left tab in the tab control. See Figure 8–21.

**Figure 8–21**    Caption property set for the left tab of a tab control

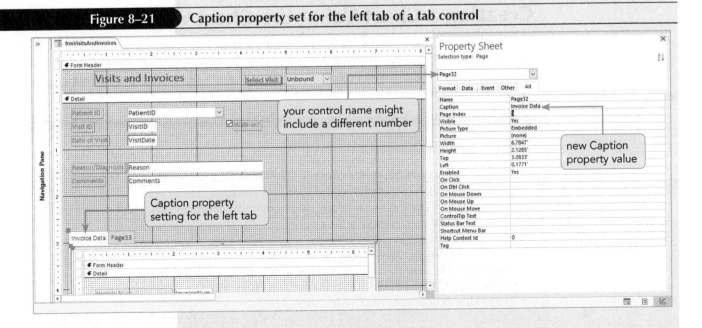

5. Click the **right tab** in the subform to select it, in the Property Sheet, in the Caption box, type **Invoice Chart**, press **TAB**, and then close the Property Sheet.

6. Save your form design changes, and then switch to Form view.

7. Click the **Select Visit** arrow, click **1462** in the list to display the information for this visit, click **1462** in the Visit ID box to deselect the text, and then scroll to the bottom of the form. The tabs and the navigation buttons now display the new caption values. See Figure 8-22.

**Figure 8-22**    **Modified report with tab control in Form view**

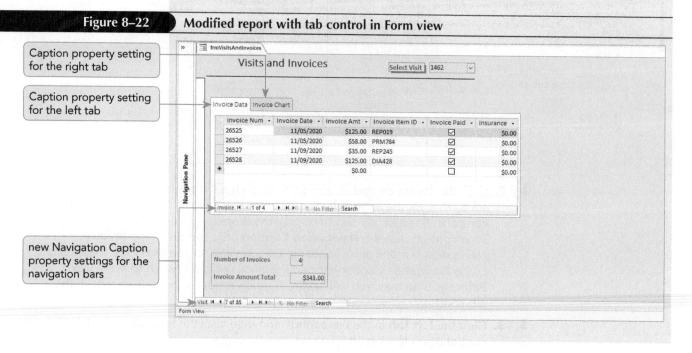

Next, Donna wants you to add a simple chart to the second page of the tab control. You will create the chart using the Chart Wizard.

# Creating a Chart Using the Chart Wizard

The Chart Wizard in Access guides you in creating a chart in a form or report based upon data contained in the database. Once the chart is created, you can modify and format the chart using Microsoft Graph, a simple graphing tool included in Microsoft Office 365.

**REFERENCE**

*Embedding a Chart in a Form or Report*

- On the Report Design Tools or Form Design Tools Design tab, click the More button in the Controls group, and then click the Chart tool.
- Position the + portion of the pointer in the form or report, and then click the mouse button to start the Chart Wizard.
- Navigate through the Chart Wizard dialog boxes to select the record source, fields, and chart type; specify a layout for the chart data; and select the fields that link the records in the database object to the chart's components, if necessary.
- In the Chart Wizard's last dialog box, enter a chart title, select whether to include a legend, and then click the Finish button.

The tblBilling table contains the information Donna wants displayed in chart form on the right tab in the tab control.

### To create a chart in the tab control using the Chart Wizard:

1. Switch to Design view, click the **Invoice Chart** tab in the tab control, then click the **Invoice Chart** tab again to select it, as indicated by the orange selection border.

Be sure to click the Chart tool in the Controls gallery and not the Insert Chart button.

2. On the Form Design Tools Design tab, in the Controls group, click the **Chart** tool in the Controls gallery, and then position the pointer in the tab control. When the pointer is inside the tab control, the rectangular portion of the tab control you can use to place controls is filled with the color black.

3. Position the + portion of the pointer in the upper-left corner of the black tab control, and then click the mouse button. A chart control appears in the tab control, and the first Chart Wizard dialog box opens, in which you select the source record for the chart.

   **Trouble?** If you don't see the Chart Wizard, you may have mistakenly clicked the Insert Chart button rather than the Chart tool in Step 2 above. Press Ctrl + Z to undo the chart creation, and then repeat Step 2 above, being sure to click the Chart tool in the Controls gallery rather than the Insert Chart button.

   Donna wants the chart to provide a simple visual display of the relative proportions of the invoice amounts for the invoice items for the currently displayed patient visit. You'll use the tblBilling table as the record source for the chart and select the InvoiceAmt and InvoiceItemID fields as the fields to use in the chart.

4. Click **Table: tblBilling** in the box listing the available tables, and then click the **Next** button to display the second Chart Wizard dialog box, in which you select the fields from the tblBilling table that contain the data to be used to create the chart.

The order of the items is important. Be sure to add InvoiceItemID first, then InvoiceAmt.

5. From the Available Fields box, add the **InvoiceItemID** and **InvoiceAmt** fields to the Fields for Chart box, in that order, and then click the **Next** button to display the third Chart Wizard dialog box, in which you choose the chart type.

6. Click the **Pie Chart** button (column 1, row 4) to select the pie chart as the chart type to use for Donna's chart. The box on the right displays a brief description of the selected chart type. See Figure 8–23.

| Figure 8–23 | Chart Wizard showing selected chart type |

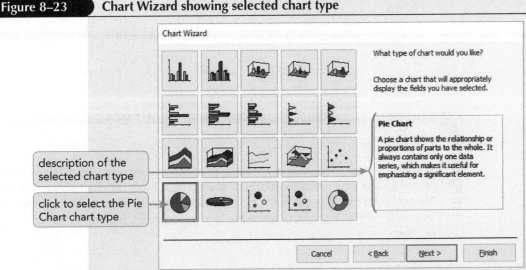

description of the selected chart type

click to select the Pie Chart chart type

7. Click the **Next** button to display the next Chart Wizard dialog box, which displays a preview of the chart and options to modify the layout of the data in the chart. You'll use the default layout based on the two selected fields.

8. Click the **Next** button to display the next Chart Wizard dialog box, which lets you choose the fields that link records in the main form (which uses the tblVisit table as its record source) to records in the chart (which uses the tblBilling table as its record source). You don't need to make any changes in this dialog box because the wizard has already identified VisitID as the common field linking these two tables. You can use the VisitID field as the linking field even though you didn't select it as a field for the chart.

9. Click the **Next** button to display the final Chart Wizard dialog box, in which you enter the title that will appear at the top of the chart and choose whether to include a legend in the chart.

10. Type **Invoices for this Visit**, make sure the **Yes, display a legend** option button is selected, and then click the **Finish** button. The completed chart appears in the tab control.

    You'll view the form in Form view, where it's easier to assess the chart's appearance.

11. Save your form design changes, switch to Form view, display Visit ID **1462** in the main form, click the **Invoice Chart** tab to display the chart, and then scroll down to the bottom of the form (if necessary). See Figure 8–24.

| Figure 8–24 | Pie chart in the tab control |
| --- | --- |

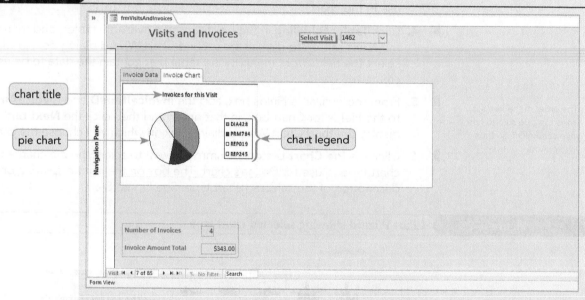

## Linking Record Sources

INSIGHT

The record source for a primary main form must have a one-to-many relationship to the record source for a related subform or chart. The subform or chart object has its Link Master Fields property set to the primary key in the record source for the main form and its Link Child Fields property set to the foreign key in the record source for the subform or chart.

After viewing the chart, Donna decides it needs some modifications. She wants you to change the chart type from a pie chart to a bar chart, remove the legend, and modify the chart's background color. To make these formatting changes, you'll switch to Design view. To modify the chart, you need to access the Microsoft Graph tools. You can double-click the chart to display the Microsoft Graph menu bar and toolbar on the ribbon and open the datasheet for the chart, or you can right-click the chart and use the shortcut menu to open the chart in a separate Microsoft Graph window.

## To edit the chart using Microsoft Graph tools:

1. Switch to Design view, right-click an edge of the chart object to open the shortcut menu, point to **Chart Object**, and then click **Open**. Microsoft Graph starts and displays the chart and datasheet in a separate window on top of the Access window. See Figure 8–25.

**Figure 8–25**     **Chart in the Microsoft Graph window**

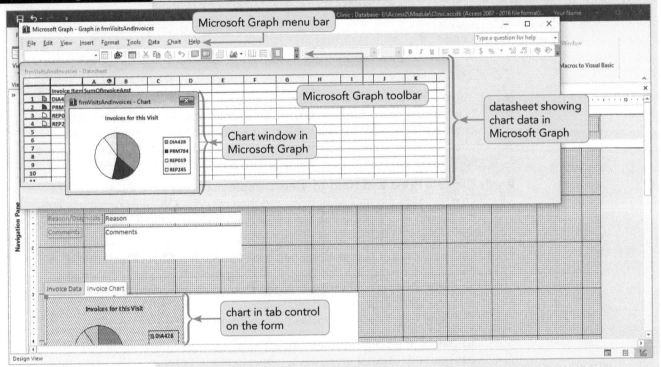

2. On the Microsoft Graph menu bar, click **Chart**, click **Chart Type** to open the Chart Type dialog box, and then click **Column** in the Chart type box to display the types of column charts. See Figure 8–26.

| Figure 8–26 | Microsoft Graph Chart Type dialog box |
| --- | --- |

click to create a custom chart type

selected chart type

subtypes of the selected chart type

description of selected chart subtype

click to view sample of selected chart subtype

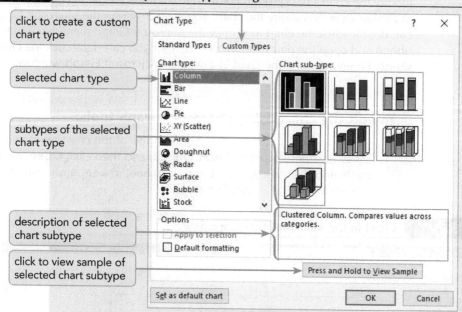

The column chart is the selected chart type, and the clustered column chart is the default chart subtype (row 1, column 1). A description of the selected chart subtype appears below the chart subtypes. You can create a custom chart by clicking the Custom Types tab. You can also use the Press and Hold to View Sample button to display a sample of the selected subtype.

3. Click the **Press and Hold to View Sample** button to view a sample of the chart, release the mouse button, and then click the **OK** button to close the dialog box and change the chart to a column chart in the Microsoft Graph window and in the tab control on the form.

4. On the Microsoft Graph menu bar, click **Chart**, click **Chart Options** to open the Chart Options dialog box, click the **Legend** tab to display the chart's legend options, click the **Show legend** check box to uncheck it, and then click the **OK** button. The legend is removed from the chart object in the Microsoft Graph window and in the tab control on the form.

To change the color or other properties of a chart's elements—the chart background (or chart area), axes, labels to the left of the y-axis, labels below the x-axis, or data markers (columnar bars for a column chart)—you need to double-click the chart element.

**TIP**

A data marker is a bar, dot, segment, or other symbol that represents a single data value.

5. In the Microsoft Graph Chart window, double-click one of the column data markers in the chart to open the Format Data Series dialog box, and then in the Area section, click the **orange** color (row 2, column 2) in the color palette. The sample color in the dialog box changes to orange to match the selected color. See Figure 8–27.

**Figure 8–27**    Format Data Series dialog box in Microsoft Graph

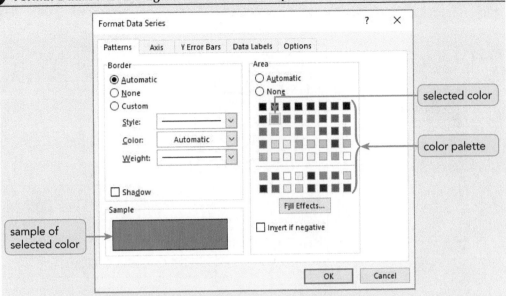

6. Click the **OK** button to close the dialog box. The color of the data markers in the chart in the Microsoft Graph window and in the form's tab control changes to orange.

   **Trouble?** If only one of the bars changed color, you selected one bar instead of the entire series. Click Edit, click Undo, and then repeat Steps 5 and 6.

7. In the Chart window, double-click the white chart background to the left of the title to open the Format Chart Area dialog box, in the Area section, click the **light orange** color (row 5, column 2) in the color palette, and then click the **OK** button. The chart's background color changes from white to light orange in the chart in the Microsoft Graph window and in the form's tab control.

8. Click **File** on the Microsoft Graph menu bar, and then click **Exit & Return to frmVisitsAndInvoices** to close the Microsoft Graph window and return to the form.

9. Save your form design changes, switch to Form view, display Visit ID **1462** in the main form, and then click the **Invoice Chart** tab to display the chart. Scroll down to the bottom of the form. See Figure 8–28.

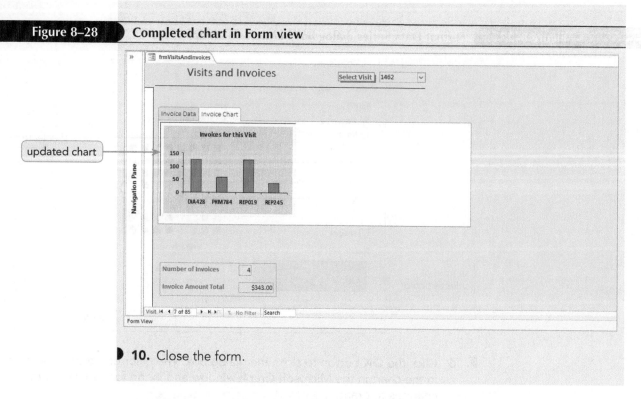

Figure 8–28    **Completed chart in Form view**

updated chart

**10.** Close the form.

Sometimes it is useful to use a table structure from one database in other databases. One option would be to import the table structure only from the database file into each subsequent database, a method you used in an earlier module. Another option is to create an application part in one database, which can then easily be included in any Access database file on your computer.

# Using Templates and Application Parts

A template is a predefined database that can include tables, relationships, queries, forms, reports, and other database objects and is used to create a new database file. On the New tab in Backstage view, a list of predefined templates is displayed. You can also create your own template from an existing database file. In addition to creating a database template, you can also create templates for objects using an **application part**, which is a specialized template for a specific database object that can be imported into an existing database. There are predefined application parts included with Access, and you can also create your own user-defined application part. Once you create a user-defined application part in one database, it is available to all Access databases created and stored on your computer.

You can use an application part to insert a predefined object from another database or template into an existing database. Like a template, an application part can contain tables, relationships, queries, forms, reports, and other database objects.

Donna would like to reuse a table structure from another database to create a new table in the Clinic database. You'll use the NewPatientReferrals.accdb database file to create an application part for the table structure, and then you'll import the new application part into the Clinic database to use to create a table of referrals from local pharmacies.

### To create an application part from a database file:

**1.** Click the **Create** tab, and then in the Templates group, click the **Application Parts** button to open the gallery of predefined application parts. See Figure 8–29.

Figure 8–29     Predefined application parts

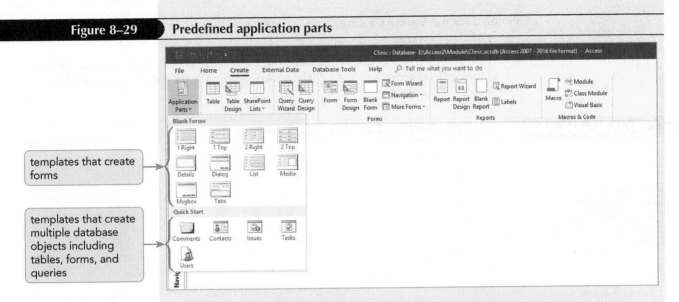

templates that create forms

templates that create multiple database objects including tables, forms, and queries

Note that there are Blank Forms and Quick Start Application Parts. If you or another user of your computer has created user-defined application parts, they also will appear in the gallery.

**2.** Close the Clinic database file.

**3.** Open the **Support_AC_8_NewPatientReferrals.accdb** database file from the **Access2 > Module** folder included with your Data Files, enabling the content if necessary.

When you save this file as a template, all database objects that are in the file will be included in the template file. This file contains only the tblReferral table.

**4.** Click the **File** tab to open Backstage view, and then in the navigation bar, click **Save As**.

**5.** In Database File Types section of the Save Database As list, click **Template**. See Figure 8–30.

Figure 8–30     Save As options in Backstage View

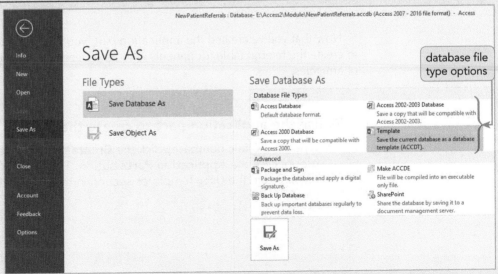

**6.** Click the **Save As** button. The Create New Template from This Database dialog box opens.

**7.** Click in the Name box, type **Referral**, click in the Description box, type **New patient referral**, and then click the **Application Part** check box to select it. See Figure 8–31.

Figure 8–31    **Create New Template from This Database dialog box**

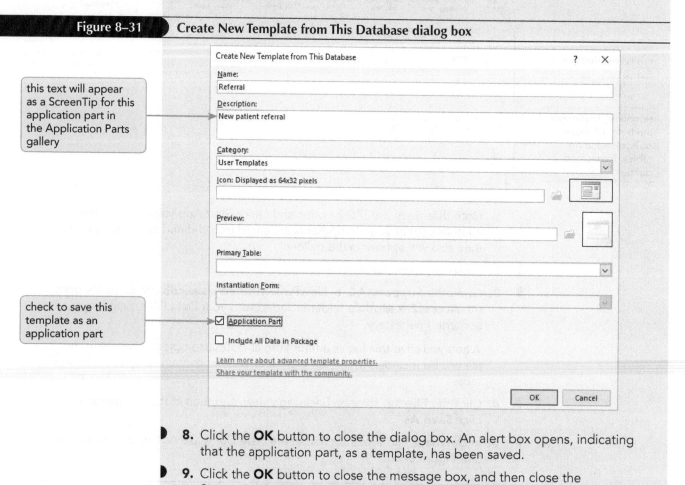

this text will appear as a ScreenTip for this application part in the Application Parts gallery

check to save this template as an application part

**8.** Click the **OK** button to close the dialog box. An alert box opens, indicating that the application part, as a template, has been saved.

**9.** Click the **OK** button to close the message box, and then close the Support_AC_8_NewPatientReferrals.accdb database.

Now that you've created the application part, you'll use it in the Clinic database to create the referral table for patients who have been referred to the clinic from local pharmacies.

## To use the application part to create the referral table:

**1.** Open the **Clinic** database, click the **Create** tab, and then in the Templates group, click the **Application Parts** button. The Referral template is displayed in the User Templates section in the Application Parts gallery. See Figure 8–32.

| Figure 8–32 | Referral template in Application Parts Gallery |
| --- | --- |

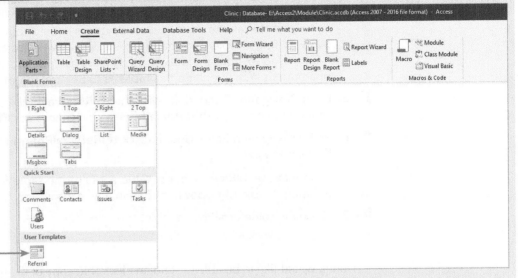

user-defined template added as an application part

2. Click **Referral**. The Create Relationship dialog box opens because the application part includes a table.

3. Click the **There is no relationship** option button. This indicates that the new table is not related to other tables in the current database. See Figure 8–33.

| Figure 8–33 | Create Relationship dialog box |
| --- | --- |

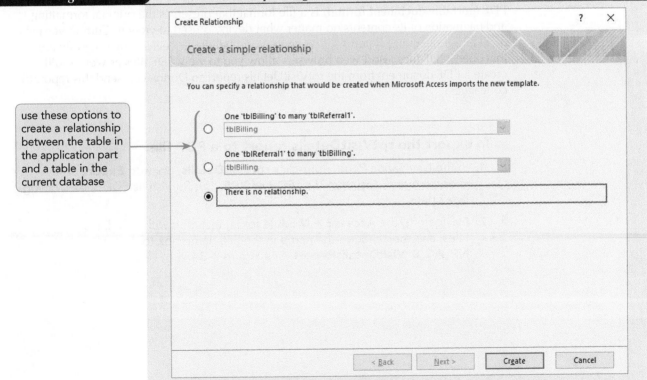

use these options to create a relationship between the table in the application part and a table in the current database

4. Click the **Create** button to insert the Referral database object into the current database, and then open the Navigation Pane.

Only the tblReferral table will be inserted into the current database because the Referral template contains only one database object, which is the tblReferral table. Because the Clinic database already contains a table called tblReferral, the newly inserted table is named tblReferral1, to avoid overwriting the table that already exists. The newly inserted tblReferral1 will be used to store the patient information for patients referred by local pharmacists. You'll rename this table as tblReferralPharm.

▶ **5.** In the Navigation Pane, right-click the **tblReferral1** table, click **Rename**, change the name to **tblReferralPharm**, and then press **ENTER**.

▶ **6.** In the Navigation Pane, double-click **tblReferralPharm** to open it in Datasheet view.

Note that the tblReferralPharm table contains the same fields as the tblReferral table but does not contain any records.

▶ **7.** Close the tblReferralPharm table.

Donna would like to be able to send an electronic copy of the rptVisitDetails report that other people can view on their computers, rather than distributing printed reports. You can export tables, queries, reports, and other database objects as files that can be opened in other programs such as Excel and PDF readers. Donna would like to distribute rptVisitDetails as a PDF and asks you to export the report in this format.

## Exporting a Report to a PDF File

**PDF (portable document format)** is a file format that preserves the original formatting and pagination of its contents no matter what device is used to view it. Current versions of all major operating systems for computers and handheld devices include software that opens PDF files. Most web browsers allow you to view PDF files as well. You'll create a PDF document from the rptVisitDetails report so Donna can send this report to colleagues.

### To export the rptVisitDetails report to a PDF file:

▶ **1.** In the Navigation Pane, right-click **rptVisitDetails**, point to **Export** on the shortcut menu, and then click **PDF or XPS**. The Publish as PDF or XPS dialog box opens.

▶ **2.** Navigate to the **Access2 > Module** folder included with your Data Files, and then change the name in the File name box to **NP_AC_8_VisitDetailsReport**. See Figure 8–34.

**Figure 8–34**     **Publish as PDF or XPS file dialog box**

the file structure of your computer drives and folders might differ

file size is reduced to minimize downloading time

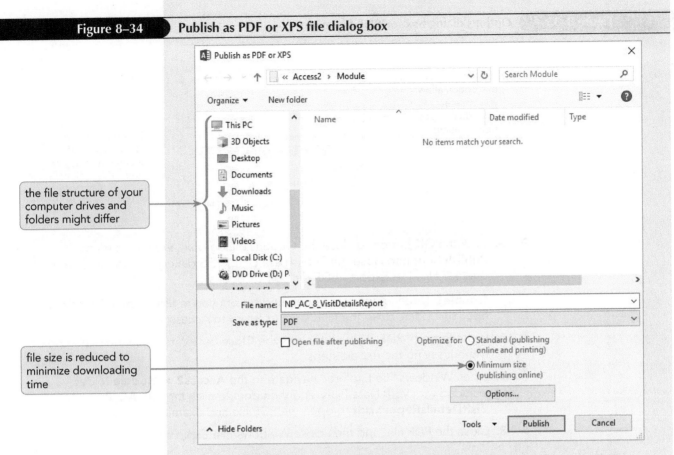

Donna would like people who are visually impaired to be able to use the PDF document with their screen readers. When a PDF file is saved using the minimum size option, there is no additional functionality for screen readers. You can include document structure tags that allow people using screen readers to navigate the document easily. Screen reader software voices the structure tags, such as a tag that provides a description of an image. Structure tags also reflow text so that screen readers understand the flow of information and can read it in a logical order. For instance, a page with a sidebar shouldn't be read as two columns; the main column needs to be read as a continuation of the previous page.

In order to add this functionality, you'll specify that document structure tags should be included.

3. Click the **Options** button. The Options dialog box opens.

4. Click the **Document structure tags for accessibility** check box to select it. See Figure 8–35.

Figure 8–35    Options dialog box for PDF file export

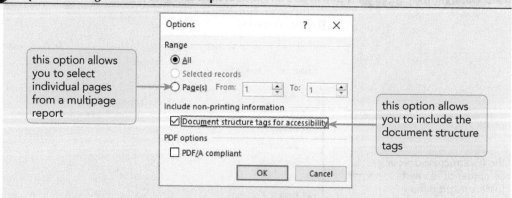

this option allows you to select individual pages from a multipage report

this option allows you to include the document structure tags

5. Click the **OK** button to close the Options dialog box, and then click the **Publish** button to close the Publish as PDF or XPS dialog box and to create the PDF file. The Export - PDF dialog box opens.

   **Trouble?** Depending on the operating system you're using, the PDF file may open. If it does, close the PDF file and return to Access.

6. In the Export - PDF dialog box, click the **Close** button to close the dialog box without saving the export steps.

7. Open Windows File Explorer, navigate to the **Access2 > Module** folder included with your Data Files, and then double-click the **NP_AC_8_ VisitDetailsReport.pdf** to open the PDF file and examine the results.

8. Close the PDF file, and then close Windows File Explorer.

Donna is pleased to know that she can export database objects as PDF files. Now she would like your help with one additional external data issue. Her staff maintains an Excel workbook that contains contact information for people who volunteer at Lakewood Community Health Services. Donna wants to be able to use this data in the Clinic database.

# Integrating Access with Other Applications

As you know, when you create a form or report in Access, you include more than just the data from the record source table or query. You've added controls such as lines, rectangles, tab controls, and graphics in your forms and reports to improve their appearance and usability. You can also add charts, drawings, and other objects to your forms and reports, but Access doesn't have the capability to create them. Instead, you create these objects using other applications and then place them in a form or report using the appropriate integration method.

When you integrate information between two files created using different software applications, the file containing the original information, or object, is called the **source file**, and the file in which you place the information from the source file is called the **destination file**. In Access there are three ways for you to integrate objects created by other applications—importing, embedding, and linking.

When you import an object, you include the contents of a file in a new table or append it to an existing table, or you include the contents of the file in a form, report, or field. In this module you imported CSV and XML files as new tables in the Clinic database, and the CSV and XML files you imported were created by other applications.

After importing an object into a destination file, it no longer has a connection to the original object in the source file or the application used to create it. Any subsequent changes you make to the object in the source file using the source application are not reflected in the imported object in the destination file.

When you **embed** an object from the source file into a form, report, or field in the destination file, you preserve its connection to the application used to create it in the source file, enabling you to edit the object, if necessary, using the features of the source application. However, any changes you make to the object are reflected only in the destination file in which it is embedded; the changes do not affect the original object in the source file from which it was embedded. Likewise, if you make any changes to the original object in the source file, these changes are not reflected in the embedded object in the destination file.

When you **link** an object to a form, report, or field in a destination file, you maintain a connection between the object in the destination file and the original object in the source file. You can make changes to a linked object only in the source file. Any changes you make to the original object in the source file using the source application are then reflected in the linked object in the destination file. To view or use the linked object in a form, report, or field in the destination file, you must first open the source file in the source application.

**PROSKILLS**

*Decision Making: Importing, Embedding, and Linking Data*

How do you decide which integration method to use when you need to include in an Access database data that is stored in another file created in a different application?

- You should choose to import an object when you want to copy an object from a file created using a different application into a table, form, or report in the Access database, *and* you want to be able to manipulate and work with that object using Access tools, *and* you do not need these changes to the imported object to be reflected in the original object in the source file.
- Conversely, you should choose to embed or link the object when you want to be able to edit the copied object in the table, form, or report using the application with which the source object was created. You should embed the object when you *do not* want your changes to the embedded object in the destination file to affect the original object in the source file. You should choose to link the object when you want the object in the destination file to always match the original object in the source file.

The decision to import, embed, or link to an object containing data depends on how you will use the data in your database and what connection is required to the original data. You should carefully consider the effect of changes to the original data and to the copied data before choosing which method to use.

## Linking Data from an Excel Worksheet

Donna's staff has extensive experience working with Excel, and one of her staff members prefers to use an Excel file named Support_AC_8_Volunteer.xlsx to maintain the data for people who volunteer at the clinic. However, Donna needs to reference the volunteer data in the Clinic database on occasion, and the data she's referencing must always be the current version of the data in the Support_AC_8_Volunteer.xlsx Excel file. Importing the Excel workbook data as an Access table would provide Donna with data that's quickly out of date unless she repeats the import steps each time the data in the Excel workbook changes. Therefore, you'll link the data in the Excel file to a table in the Clinic database. When the staff changes data in the Support_AC_8_Volunteer.xlsx Excel workbook, the changes will be reflected automatically in the linked version in the database table. In addition, Donna won't be able to update the volunteer data from the Clinic database, which ensures that only the staff members responsible for maintaining the Support_AC_8_Volunteer.xlsx Excel workbook can update the data.

### To link table data to an Excel file:

▶ **1.** Click the **External Data** tab, and then in the Import & Link group, click **New Data Source**, point to **From File**, and then click the **Excel** button. The Get External Data - Excel Spreadsheet dialog box opens.

   **Trouble?** If the Export - Excel File dialog box opens, you clicked the Excel button in the Export group. Click the Cancel button and then repeat Step 1, being sure to select the Excel button from the Import & Link group.

▶ **2.** Click the **Browse** button to open the File Open dialog box, navigate to the **Access2 > Module** folder included with your Data Files, click **Support_AC_8_Volunteer.xlsx**, click the **Open** button, and then click the **Link to the data source by creating a linked table** option button. This option links to the data instead of importing or appending it. The selected path and filename are displayed in the File name box. See Figure 8–36.

---

| **Figure 8–36** | **Linking to data in an Excel workbook** |

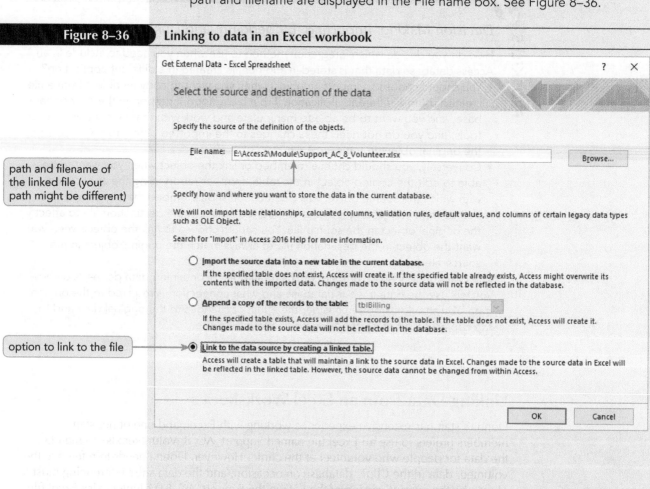

3. Click the **OK** button. The first Link Spreadsheet Wizard dialog box opens.

   The first row in the worksheet contains column heading names, and each row in the worksheet represents the data about a single volunteer.

4. Click the **First Row Contains Column Headings** check box to select it. See Figure 8–37.

**Figure 8–37**    **Link Spreadsheet Wizard dialog box**

option to use the first row in the worksheet as column heading names

data in the worksheet to be linked

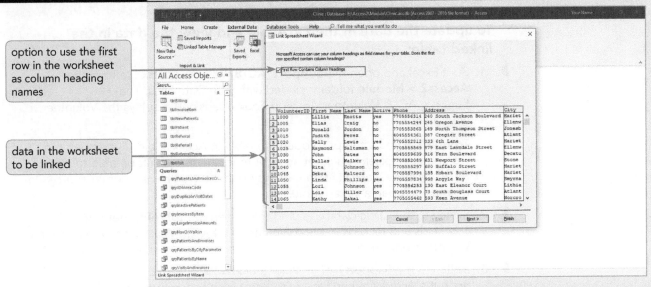

5. Click the **Next** button to open the final Link Spreadsheet Wizard dialog box, in which you choose a name for the linked table.

6. Change the default table name to **tblVolunteer** and then click the **Finish** button. A message box informs you that you've created a table that's linked to the workbook.

7. Click the **OK** button to close the message box. The tblVolunteer table is listed in the Navigation Pane, with an icon to its left indicating it is a linked table.

You can open and view the tblVolunteer table and use fields from the linked table in queries, forms, and reports, but you cannot update the data using the Clinic database. You can only update the data from the Excel workbook file. To open and view the tblVolunteer table in the Clinic database, you must first open and leave open the Excel file to which the table is linked.

Donna tells you that the volunteer Judith Perez had not been able to volunteer for a while, so her Active status was "no". She's now able to volunteer, and Donna would like to change her Active status to "yes". Next, you'll make a change to data in the Excel file and see the update in the linked table.

### To update the data in the Excel file and view the data in the linked table:

▶ **1.** Start Excel and open the **Support_AC_8_Volunteer.xlsx** file from the **Access2 > Module** folder included with your Data Files. The Support_AC_8_Volunteer.xlsx workbook opens and displays the Volunteer worksheet.

   **Trouble?** If you attempt to open the table in Access before you open the workbook in Excel, you'll get an error message and won't be able to open the workbook. Make sure you always open the workbook or other source file before you open a linked table.

▶ **2.** Switch to the Clinic database, and then open the **tblVolunteer** datasheet. The fields and records in the tblVolunteer table display the same data as the Volunteer worksheet.

▶ **3.** Switch to the Support_AC_8_Volunteer.xlsx Excel workbook, select the value **no** in the Active column for Judith Perez (row 5), type **yes** to replace the value, and then press **ENTER**.

▶ **4.** Switch to the Clinic database. The Active status for Judith Perez is now yes.

   **Trouble?** If the record is not updated in the tblVolunteer table in the Clinic database, click the record to show the update.

   You've completed your work for Donna and her staff.

▶ **5.** Close the tblVolunteer table in Access.

▶ **6.** Switch to the Support_AC_8_Volunteer.xlsx workbook, save your changes to the workbook, and then exit Excel.

▶ **7.** sam↑ Make a backup copy of the Clinic database, compact and repair the database, and then close it.

Knowing how to create tab controls and application parts, export data to PDF documents, and link to data maintained by other applications will make it easier for Donna and her staff to efficiently manage their data.

**REVIEW**

## Session 8.2 Quick Check

1. The _____ property lets you change the default navigation label from the word "Record" to another value.

2. What is the Microsoft Graph program?

3. What is a PDF file?

4. What is an application part?

5. What is the difference between an application part and a template?

6. How can you edit data in a table that has been linked to an Excel file?

PRACTICE

## Review Assignments

**Data Files needed for the Review Assignments: Supplier.accdb** (*cont. from previous module*), **Support_AC_8_Ads.xlsx, Support_AC_8_Partners.accdb, Support_AC_8_Payables.csv, and Support_AC_8_Payments.xml**

Donna wants you to integrate data in other files created with other applications with the data in the Supplier database, and she wants to be able to analyze the data in the database. Complete the following steps:

1. Open the **Supplier** database you worked with in the previous three modules.
2. Export the qrySupplierProducts query as an HTML document to the Access2 > Review folder provided with your Data Files, saving the file as **NP_AC_8_qrySupplierProducts** and exporting the data with formatting and layout. Save the export steps with the name **Export-NP_AC_8_ qrySupplierProducts**. Once saved, modify the description to be **HTML file containing the qrySupplierProducts query**.
3. Import the CSV file named Support_AC_8_Payables.csv, which is located in the Access2 > Review folder, as a new table in the database. Use the names in the first row as field names, use Currency as the data type for the numeric fields, choose your own primary key, name the table **tblPayables**, run the Table Analyzer, record the Table Analyzer's recommendation, and then cancel out of the Table Analyzer Wizard without making the recommended changes. Do not save the import steps.
4. Import the data and structure from the XML file named **Support_AC_8_Payments.xml**, which is located in the Access2 > Review folder included with your Data Files, as a new table named **tblPayments** in the database. Do not save the import steps, and then rename the table **tblPayment** (with no "s" on the end of the name).
5. Export the tblSupplier table as an XML file named **NP_AC_8_Supplier** to the Access2 > Review folder; do not create a separate XSD file. Save the export steps, and use the default name given.
6. Lakewood Community Health Services also pays for advertisements, and information on this activity is contained in an Excel file named Support_AC_8_Ads.xlsx. Create a table named **tblAds** in the Supplier database that links to the Support_AC_8_Ads.xlsx Excel file, which is located in the Access2 > Review folder included with your Data Files. Change the cost of the flyer for Ad 6 to **$89**, and save the workbook.
7. Modify the frmSuppliersWithProducts form in the following ways:
    a. Add a tab control to the bottom of the Detail section, so the left edge is aligned with the left edge of the Company Comments label, and then place the existing subform on the first page of the tab control.
    b. Change the caption for the left tab to **Product Data** and for the right tab to **Product Chart**.
    c. Change the caption for the main form's navigation buttons to **Supplier**.
    d. Add a chart to the second page of the tab control. Use the tblProduct table as the record source, select the ProductName and Price, use the 3-D Column Chart type (row 1, column 2), do not include a legend, and use **Products Offered** as the chart title.
    e. Change the chart to a 3-D Clustered Bar chart, and change the purple colored data markers to pink.
8. Export the tblPayment table as a PDF file called **NP_AC_8_Payments**, using document structure tags for accessibility. Do not save the export steps.
9. Open the Support_AC_8_Partners.accdb database from the Access2 > Review folder, and then create and implement an application part as follows:
    a. Create an application part called **Vendor** with the description **New Vendor**, and do not include the data.
    b. Close the Support_AC_8_Partners.accdb database.
    c. Open the **Supplier** database and import the Vendor application part, which has no relationship to any of the other tables. Open the tblNewVendor table to verify the structure has been imported, but does not contain any records.
10. Make a backup copy of the database, compact and repair the database, and then close it.

APPLY

## Case Problem 1

**Data Files needed for this Case Problem:** School.accdb (*cont. from previous module*), Support_AC_8_AddSubject.xml, Support_AC_8_NewStudentReferrals.accdb, Support_AC_8_Room.xlsx, and Support_AC_8_Subject.csv

***Great Giraffe***   Jeremiah Garver wants you to integrate data from other files created with different applications with the data in the School database, and he wants to be able to analyze the data in the database. Complete the following steps:

1. Open the **School** database you worked with in the previous three modules.
2. Export the rptCourseRosters report as a PDF document with a filename of **NP_AC_8_CourseRosters** to the Access2 > Case1 folder provided with your Data Files. Include the document structure tags for accessibility, and do not save the export steps.
3. Import the CSV file named Support_AC_8_Instructor.csv, which is located in the Access2 > Case1 folder, as a new table in the database. Use the names in the first row as field names, set the data type for the first two columns to Short Text and for the third and fourth columns to Yes/No, choose your own primary key, name the table **tblInstructor**, run the Table Analyzer, and record the Table Analyzer's recommendation, but do not accept the recommendation. Do not save the import steps.
4. Export the tblCourse table as an XML file named **NP_AC_8_Course** to the Access2 > Case1 folder; do not create a separate XSD file. Save the export steps.
5. Create a new table named **tblRoom** that is linked to the Support_AC_8_Room.xlsx Excel file, which is located in the Access2 > Case1 folder provided with your Data Files. Add the following new record to the Room workbook: Room Num **6**, Rental Cost **$275**, and Type **Private**.
6. Import the XML file named Support_AC_8_Company.xml file, which is located in the Access2 > Case1 folder included with your Data Files, adding the records to a new table named tblCompany. Do not save any import steps.
7. Modify the frmStudentsByCourse form in the following ways:
   a.  At the bottom of the Detail section, delete the Student label, then move the Student subform onto the first page of a new tab control. Align the tab control with the left edge of the Cost label and at the 2-inch mark on the vertical ruler.
   b.  Change the caption for the left tab to **Student Data** and for the right tab to **Student Chart**.
   c.  Change the caption for the main form's navigation buttons to **Course**.
   d.  Add a chart to the second page of the tab control. Use the tblRegistration table as the record source, select the BalanceDue and StudentID fields, use the Column Chart type (row 1, column 1), do not include a legend, and use **Outstanding Balances** as the chart title.
8. Open the **Support_AC_8_NewStudentReferrals.accdb** database from the Access2 > Case1 folder provided with your Data Files, and then create and work with an application part as follows:
   a.  Create an application part called **NewStudentContact** with the description **New student referrals**.
   b.  Close the Support_AC_8_NewStudentReferrals.accdb database.
   c.  Open the **School** database and import the **NewStudentContact** application part, which has no relationship to any of the other tables. Verify that the tblContact table is created and contains no data.
9. Make a backup copy of the database, compact and repair the database, and then close it.

CREATE

## Case Problem 2

**Data Files needed for this Case Problem:** Storm.accdb (*cont. from previous module*), Support_AC_8_CreditCard.xml, Support_AC_8_Maintenance.xml, Support_AC_8_Schedule.xlsx, Support_AC_8_Suppliers.xlsx, and Support_AC_8_Volunteers.csv.

***Drain Adopter***   Tandrea Austin wants you to integrate data from files created with other applications with the data in the Storm database, and she wants to be able to analyze the data in the database. Complete the following steps:

1. Open the **Storm** database you worked with in the previous three modules.

2. Export the qryVolunteersWithoutDrains query as an HTML document to the Access2 > Case2 folder using a filename of **NP_AC_8_UnmatchedVolunteers**. Save the export steps.

3. Export the rptDrainsWithVolunteers report as a PDF document with a filename of **NP_AC_8_Drains** to the Access2 > Case2 folder. Include the document structure tags for accessibility, and do not save the export steps.

4. Import the CSV file named Support_AC_8_Volunteers.csv, which is located in the Access2 > Case2 folder, as a new table in the database. Use the names in the first row as field names, set the data type for the first nine columns to Short Text, set the data type for the SignupDate column to Date With Time, set the data type for the Trained column to Yes/No, choose your own primary key, name the table **tblNewVolunteers**, run the Table Analyzer, and record the Table Analyzer's recommendation, but do not accept the recommendation. Do not save the import steps.

5. Import the data and structure from the XML file named Support_AC_8_Maintenance.xml, which is located in the Access2 > Case2 folder provided with your Data Files, as a new table. Save the import steps.

6. Export the tblSupply table as an XML file named **NP_AC_8_Supplies** to the Access2 > Case2 folder; do not create a separate XSD file. Save the export steps.

7. Create a new table named **tblSupplier** by linking to the Support_AC_8_Suppliers.xlsx Excel file, which is located in the Access2 > Case2 folder provided with your Data Files. For SupplierID 1004, change the ShippingCost value to **Free**.

8. Modify the frmVolunteersAndDrains form to include a tab control and named navigation tools as shown in Figure 8–38.

    a. At the bottom of the Detail section, delete the Drain label.

    b. Add a tab control to the bottom of the Detail section, and place the existing subform on the first page tab of the tab control.

    c. Change the caption for the left tab to **Drain Details** and for the right tab to **Status Summary**. Leave the main section of the right tab empty.

    d. Change the caption for the main form's navigation buttons to **Volunteer** and for the subform's navigation buttons to **Drain**.

**Figure 8–38**    **Customized frmVolunteersAndDrains form**

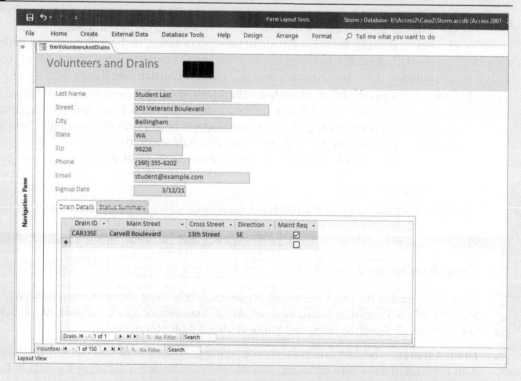

9. Make a backup copy of the database, compact and repair the database, and then close it.

## Objectives

**Session 3.1**
- Create and modify a SmartArt graphic
- Animate a SmartArt graphic
- Convert a SmartArt graphic to shapes
- Ungroup and group shapes
- Add an audio clip to a slide
- Create and modify a chart
- Insert and format text boxes
- Apply a WordArt style to text

**Session 3.2**
- Remove the background from a photo
- Apply an artistic effect to a photo
- Correct photos using photo editing tools
- Create a custom shape
- Rotate shapes with text
- Fill a shape with a texture and a custom gradient
- Check for accessibility issues and fix them
- Use the Selection pane

# Applying Advanced Formatting to Objects

## Formatting Objects in a Presentation for a Sales and Marketing Company

**POWERPOINT**

## Case | MBG Sales and Marketing

Kavita Goyal is a client operations manager for MBG Sales and Marketing, headquartered in Hattiesburg, Mississippi. After a customer service representative speaks to a client who has called to request support or describe a problem, the client receives a follow-up phone call asking them to describe their level of satisfaction with their service experience on a scale of one to five (from extremely satisfied to not at all satisfied). Kavita has noticed a decrease in the percentage of clients who are extremely or very satisfied and an increase in clients who are only somewhat satisfied. Kavita decided she needs to retrain her team so that they will provide greater satisfaction to clients. She asks for your help in enhancing her presentation.

In this module, you will create a SmartArt graphic and a chart and you will insert an audio clip. You will also create a text box, use WordArt styles, and rotate shapes containing text so that the text stays right-side up. You will edit pictures, create a custom shape, and apply advanced formatting to a shape. Finally, you will check the presentation for accessibility.

**Starting Data Files**

| PowerPoint3 → Module | Review |

NP_PPT_3-1.pptx
Support_PPT_3_Comment.m4a

NP_PPT_3-2.pptx
Support_PPT_3_Compliment.mp3
Support_PPT_3_FollowUp.jpg
Support_PPT_3_Form.jpg
Support_PPT_3_Respect.jpg

**Case1**

NP_PPT_3-3.pptx
Support_PPT_3_Recovery.mp3

**Case2**

NP_PPT_3-4.pptx

# Session 3.1 Visual Overview:

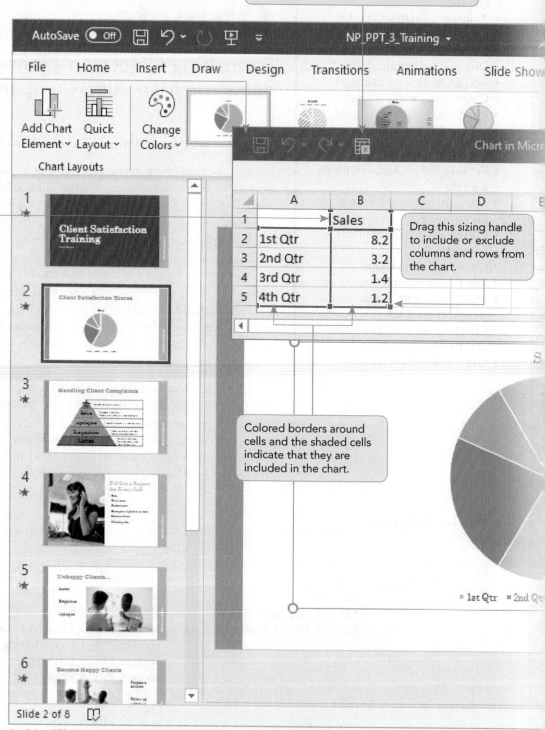

If you need additional tools, click the Edit Data in Microsoft Excel button to open the spreadsheet in an Excel workbook.

When you insert a chart, a spreadsheet appears in which you enter the data to create the chart. A **spreadsheet** (called a worksheet in Microsoft Excel) is a grid of cells that contain numbers and text.

As in a table, the intersection of a row and a column is a **cell**, and you add data and labels in cells. Cells in a datasheet are referenced by their column letter and row number. This cell is cell B1.

Drag this sizing handle to include or exclude columns and rows from the chart.

Colored borders around cells and the shaded cells indicate that they are included in the chart.

Jacob Lund/Shutterstock.com; fizkes/Shutterstock.com

# Creating a Chart on a Slide

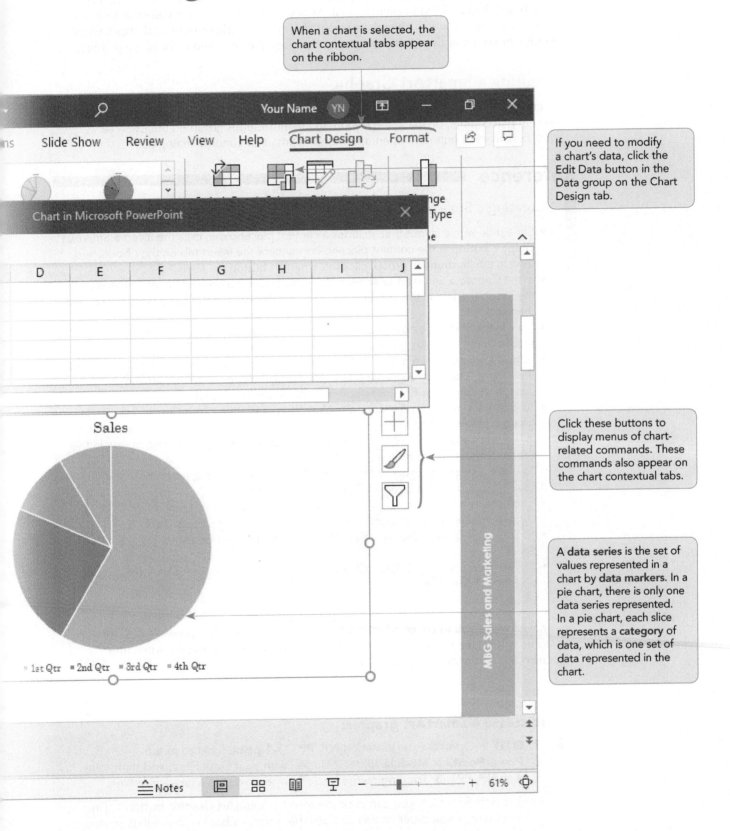

When a chart is selected, the chart contextual tabs appear on the ribbon.

If you need to modify a chart's data, click the Edit Data button in the Data group on the Chart Design tab.

Click these buttons to display menus of chart-related commands. These commands also appear on the chart contextual tabs.

A **data series** is the set of values represented in a chart by **data markers**. In a pie chart, there is only one data series represented. In a pie chart, each slice represents a **category** of data, which is one set of data represented in the chart.

# Working with SmartArt Graphics

In addition to creating a SmartArt graphic from a bulleted list, you can create one from scratch and then add text or pictures to it. As you have learned, once you create a SmartArt graphic, you can change its layout. You can also add or remove shapes from it; reorder, promote, or demote the shapes; and change the style and color of the graphic.

## Creating a SmartArt Graphic

To create a SmartArt graphic, you click the Insert a SmartArt Graphic button in a content placeholder, or, using the ribbon, in the Illustrations group on the Insert tab, click the SmartArt button to open the Choose a SmartArt Graphic dialog box.

## Reference

### Creating a SmartArt Graphic

- On a slide with a layout that includes a content placeholder, click the Insert a SmartArt Graphic button in the content placeholder; or click the Insert tab on the ribbon, and then in the Illustrations group, click the SmartArt button.
- In the Choose a SmartArt Graphic dialog box, select the desired SmartArt category in the list on the left, in the center pane, click the SmartArt graphic you want to use, and then click OK.
- Click in the text pane next to a bullet or click the placeholder text in one of the shapes in the SmartArt graphic, and then type the text for that shape.
- To add a shape, click a shape in the graphic, and then click the Add Shape button in the Create Graphic group on the SmartArt Design tab; or click after an item in the text pane, and then press ENTER to add a shape at the same level.
- To create a subitem for a shape, click the shape, and then in the Create Graphic group on the SmartArt Design tab, click the Add Bullet button; or click after an item in the text pane, press ENTER, and then press TAB or click the Demote button in the Create Graphic group on the SmartArt Design tab.
- To move a shape to a new position, click the shape to select it, and then in the Create Graphic group on the SmartArt Design tab, click the Move Up or Move Down button.
- To delete a shape or a subitem, click the shape to select it, and then press DELETE; or in the text pane, click the bullet next to the shape, and then press DELETE.
- To apply a style, click the SmartArt Design tab, and then click a style in the SmartArt Styles group.
- To change the colors, click the Change Colors button in the SmartArt Styles group, and then click a style.

Kavita wants you to create a SmartArt graphic on Slide 4 of her presentation. The graphic will list the steps Kavita wants the members of her team to take when they receive a call from an unhappy client.

**To create a SmartArt graphic:**

▶ 1. **sam** ↓ Open the presentation **NP_PPT_3-1.pptx**, located in the **PowerPoint3 > Module** folder included with your Data Files, and then save it as **NP_PPT_3_Training** to the location where you are saving your files.

   To insert SmartArt, you can click the Insert a SmartArt Graphic button 📄 in a content placeholder or you can use the SmartArt button in the Illustrations group on the Insert tab.

2. Display Slide 3 ("Handling Client Complaints"), and then in the content placeholder, click the **Insert a SmartArt Graphic** button ▦. The Choose a SmartArt Graphic dialog box opens.

3. In the list on the left, click **Relationship**, click the **Segmented Pyramid** layout, and then click **OK**. A SmartArt graphic in the shape of a pyramid in sections is inserted on the slide, and the SmartArt Design tab is selected on the ribbon. Kavita wants you to use a pyramid shape that has only one item on each level of the pyramid.

4. On the SmartArt Design tab, in the Layouts group, click the **More** button ⤵, and then click **More Layouts** to open the Choose a SmartArt Graphic dialog box.

5. In the list on the left, click **Pyramid**, click the **Basic Pyramid** layout, and then click **OK**. The SmartArt graphic layout is changed to a pyramid with one item of text in each of the three levels in the pyramid. The text is placeholder text.

6. On the SmartArt Design tab, in the Create Graphic group, click the **Text Pane** button to select it, if necessary. The text pane opens next to the graphic. See Figure 3–1. The insertion point is next to the first bullet in the text pane.

| Figure 3–1 | SmartArt graphic with the text pane open on Slide 3 |

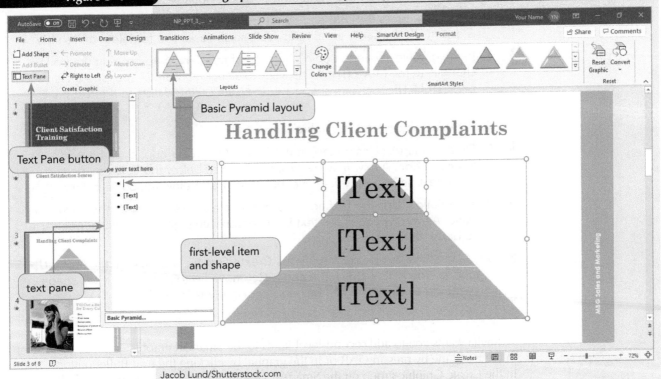

Jacob Lund/Shutterstock.com

Now that you've added the SmartArt graphic to the slide, you can add content to it. You will add first-level items to the graphic, and then reorder the shapes in the graphic by moving them up or down in the graphic and in the bulleted list in the text pane.

## To add text to the SmartArt graphic and move shapes:

1. With the insertion point in the first bulleted item in the text pane, type **Solve**. The text appears in the bulleted list in the text pane and in the top shape in the graphic.

2. In the text pane, next to the second bullet in the list, click **[Text]**. The placeholder text disappears, and the insertion point appears.

3. Type **Apologize**. The text "Apologize" replaces the placeholder text next to the second bullet in the text pane and appears in the middle shape in the graphic.

4. In the graphic, in the bottom shape, click **[Text]**, and then type **Empathize**. The text appears in both the shape and next to the third bullet in the text pane.

5. In the text pane, click after the word "Empathize", and then press **ENTER**. A new bullet is created below the Empathize bullet in the text pane. In the graphic, a new shape is added below the Empathize shape.

    **Trouble?** If a new line is inserted below "Empathize" in the bottom shape in the graphic instead of a new bullet, the insertion point was in the bottom shape of the graphic when you pressed ENTER. Press BACKSPACE to delete the new line, and then repeat Step 5, this time making sure you click in the text pane after the word "Empathize" before you press ENTER.

6. Type **Care**, press **ENTER**, and then type **Listen**. Kavita points out that "Care" is essentially the same as "Empathize", so she asks you to delete that shape.

7. In the graphic, move the pointer on top of the **Care** shape so that the pointer changes to the move pointer ⁺ₖ, click to select the Care shape, and then press **DELETE**. The Care shape and the Care bulleted item in the text pane are deleted.

8. In the graphic, select the **Solve** shape.

9. On the SmartArt Design tab, in the Create Graphic group, click the **Add Shape** button. A new first-level shape is added below the Solve shape and, in the text pane, a new first-level bullet appears below the Solve bullet.

10. Type **Follow Up**. The text appears in both the new shape and in the text pane. As you typed, all the text in the graphic changed to a smaller point size to better fit the text you typed.

11. On the SmartArt Design tab, in the Create Graphic group, click the **Move Up** button. The Follow Up shape and bullet move up to become the top shape in the graphic and the first bulleted item in the text pane.

Kavita wants you to add second-level items to the SmartArt graphic. You can do this in the text pane by pressing TAB or in the graphic by clicking the Add Bullet button in the Create Graphic group on the SmartArt Design tab. To change a shape or bullet from one level to another, you can click the Demote or Promote buttons in the Create Graphic group on the SmartArt Design tab.

## To add second-level shapes and bullets to the SmartArt graphic:

▶ **1.** In the graphic, click the **Listen** shape, and then in the Create Graphic group, click the **Add Bullet** button. In the graphic, a shape is added to the right of the Listen shape. In the text pane, a second-level bullet appears below the Listen bullet. See Figure 3–2.

| Figure 3–2 | Second-level shape added to the Listen shape |
|---|---|

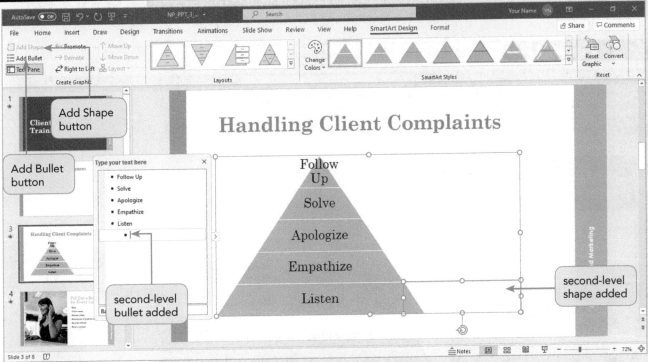

Jacob Lund/Shutterstock.com

▶ **2.** Type **Listen to the client.** in the new shape. The text appears in the new shape and next to the second-level bullet in the text pane.

▶ **3.** Press **ENTER**, and then type **Ask questions if you don't understand.** (including the period). The text is added as another second-level bullet.

▶ **4.** In the text pane, click after "Empathize", press **ENTER**, and then press **TAB**. A second-level bullet is created below the Empathize bullet in the text pane, and a new shape is added to the right of the Emphasize shape in the graphic.

▶ **5.** Type **Empathize with the client.**, press **ENTER**, and then type **Do not be condescending.** (including the period).

▶ **6.** In the graphic, click the **Apologize** shape, in the Create Graphic group, click the **Add Shape** button, and then click the **Demote** button. First, a shape was added below the Apologize shape. After you demoted the shape, the shape moved and appears to the right of the Apologize shape in the graphic. In the text pane, a second-level bullet appears below the Apologize bullet.

▶ **7.** Type **Apologize even if it is not our fault.** (including the period).

▶ **8.** Add a shape to contain second-level items next to the Solve shape, and then type the following two items into that new shape:

**Propose a solution.**

**Consult with Kavita if you need help.**

### Tip

To change the shapes in the graphic, select all the shapes, then in the Shapes group on the Format tab, click the Change Shape button to change the shapes to a different shape, or click the Larger or Smaller buttons to change the size of the shapes.

**Tip**

To reverse the direction of a SmartArt graphic so the first-level shapes appear in the opposite order, click the Right to Left button in the Create Graphic group on the SmartArt Design tab.

9. Add a shape to contain second-level items next to the Follow Up shape, and then type the following two items into that new shape:

**Get the contact's name.**

**Follow up within 14 days.**

Kavita asks you to delete the "Get the contact's name." second-level item.

10. In the text pane or in the shape next to the Follow Up shape, click before "Get the contact's name." and then press **DELETE** as many times as needed to delete the text and the bullet. Compare your screen to Figure 3–3.

**Figure 3–3** SmartArt with first and second levels

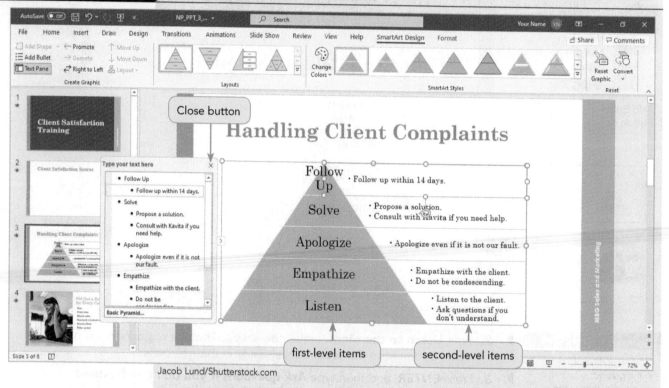

Jacob Lund/Shutterstock.com

11. In the text pane, click the **Close** button ☒. The text pane closes.

## Changing the Appearance of a SmartArt Graphic

You can change how a SmartArt graphic looks by applying a style and changing its colors. Kavita wants the pyramid to be more colorful.

### To apply a style to the SmartArt graphic and change its colors:

1. With Slide 3 ("Handling Client Complaints") displayed, on the SmartArt Design tab, in the SmartArt Styles group, click the **More** button ▾ to open the gallery of styles available for the graphic.

2. In the gallery, in the 3D section, click the **Inset** style. The style of the graphic changes to the Inset style, which gives the shapes a slightly three-dimensional look.

3. In the SmartArt Styles group, click the **Change Colors** button. A gallery of color styles opens.

4. Below Colorful, click the **Colorful – Accent Colors** style. Each shape in the pyramid is a different color.

SmartArt graphics contain multiple objects that are treated as a whole. This means that when you apply a style or other effect to the graphic, the effect is applied to the entire object. You can also apply formatting to individual shapes within the graphic if you want. You just need to select the specific shape first. You can also change the formatting of the text in SmartArt graphics.

You will change the color of the Listen shape, and then you will change the formatting of the text in the first-level shapes.

### To change the color of one shape and format the text in the SmartArt graphic:

1. In the SmartArt graphic, click the **Listen** shape. A selection box appears around the Listen shape in the graphic.

   **Trouble?** If the Listen shape is not selected, click it again.

2. Click the **Format** tab.

3. In the Shape Styles group, click the **Shape Fill** button, and then click the **Gray, Accent 6, Darker 25%** color (in the last column). The color of the Listen shape changes to the darker gray you selected.

4. In the bottom shape, double-click **Listen**, and then click the **Home** tab. The word "Listen" is selected.

5. In the Font group, click the **Font Size arrow**, and then click **44**. The font size of "Listen" changes to 44 points.

6. Change the font size of **Empathize** to **40** points, change the font size of **Apologize** and **Solve** to **36** points, change the font size of **Follow Up** to **20** points, and then click a blank area of the slide. See Figure 3–4.

| Figure 3–4 | SmartArt with formatted text |

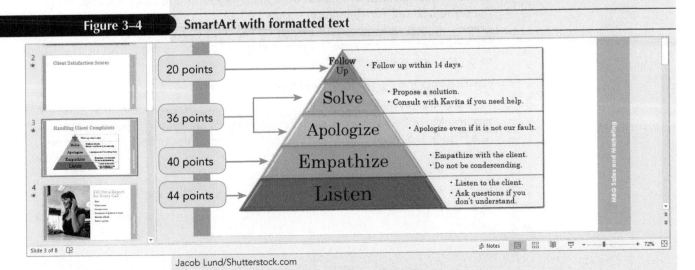

Jacob Lund/Shutterstock.com

## Animating a SmartArt Graphic

You animate a SmartArt graphic in the same way you animate any object. The default is for the entire object to animate as a single object. Similar to a bulleted list, after you apply an animation, you can use the Effect Options button to choose a different sequence effect.

Kavita wants each first-level shape in the SmartArt graphic to appear on the slide one at a time, followed by the associated second-level shape.

### To animate the SmartArt graphic:

▶ **1.** On Slide 3 ("Handling Client Complaints"), click the SmartArt graphic, and then click the **Animations** tab.

▶ **2.** In the Animation group, click the **Wipe** animation, click the **Effect Options** button, and then click **From Left**. The animation previews, and the SmartArt graphic wipes in from the left. An animation sequence icon appears above and to the left of the graphic.

▶ **3.** Click the **Effect Options** button again. The selected Sequence effect is As One Object.

▶ **4.** Click **Level at Once**, and then watch the preview. The first-level shapes appear all at the same time, followed by the second-level shapes. Two animation sequence icons appear, each overlapping other icons. This indicates that the animation indicated by the sequence icons that are below the top sequence icon on each stack is set to With Previous or After Previous. In this case, each of the first-level shapes would appear, one after the other, when you advance the slide show once. Then, each of the second-level shapes would appear, one after the other, when you advance the slide show once.

▶ **5.** Click the **Effect Options** button, click **Level One by One**, and then watch the preview. Each first-level shape appears one at a time, starting from the top. Then each second-level shape appears, again starting from the top. Ten animation sequence icons appear, indicating that each shape will appear, one at a time, when you advance the slide show. This means you would advance the slide show five times to display each of the first-level items, and then five more times to display each of the second-level items.

▶ **6.** Click the **Effect Options** button, click **One by One**, and then watch the preview. The top shape in the pyramid appears first, then the shape containing its second-level items appears. The rest of the shapes follow in the same fashion. Ten animation sequence icons appear to the left of the graphic. In this case, you would advance the slide show once to display the top first-level item, advance it again to display the top second-level item, and so on through the pyramid.

Kavita wants the pyramid to build from the bottom.

▶ **7.** Click the **1** animation sequence icon. In the Timing group on the Animations tab, the Move Earlier and Move Later commands are gray and not available. See Figure 3–5. This means that you cannot change the order of the selected animation.

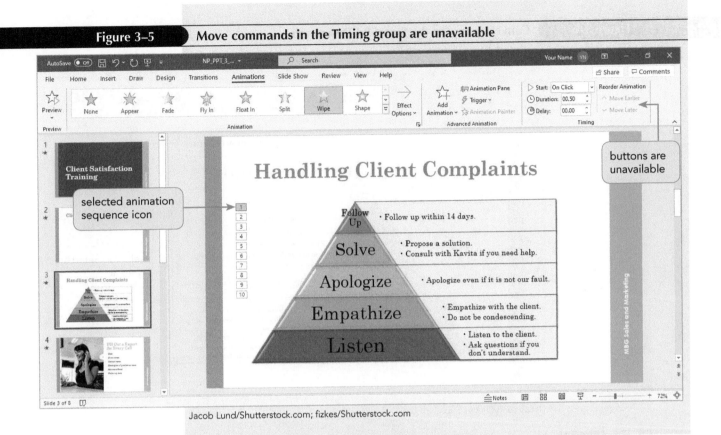

Figure 3–5          Move commands in the Timing group are unavailable

Jacob Lund/Shutterstock.com; fizkes/Shutterstock.com

Because you cannot change the order in which the shapes in the SmartArt graphic animate, you need to convert the SmartArt graphic bullets and sub-bullets to ordinary shapes. Then you can have the shapes on the bottom of the pyramid appear first, followed by the next shape and so on, building the pyramid from the bottom.

When you convert a SmartArt graphic into shapes, each shape in the graphic becomes an individual object, but all the shapes are grouped together. When objects are **grouped**, they are combined into one object.

You will convert the SmartArt graphic to shapes.

### To convert the SmartArt graphic to shapes:

1. Click the SmartArt graphic to select it, click the **SmartArt Design** tab, and then in the Reset group, click the **Convert** button. See Figure 3–6. The menu that opens contains two options. If you wanted to convert the graphic to a bulleted list, you would click Convert to Text. You want to convert the graphic to its individual shapes.

**Figure 3–6**     **Convert menu on the SmartArt Design tab**

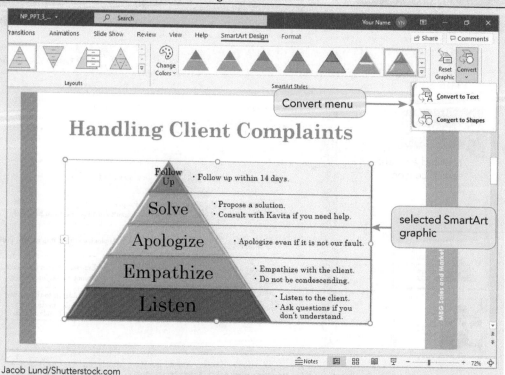

Jacob Lund/Shutterstock.com

**2.** On the menu, click **Convert to Shapes**. The SmartArt graphic is converted into shapes. On the ribbon, the SmartArt contextual tabs disappear, and the Shape Format contextual tab appears instead. A selection border appears around all of the shapes, indicating that they are grouped into one object. See Figure 3–7. The text in the first-level shapes was changed to white. On the ribbon, the Home tab is selected. First, you are going to change the text in the first-level shapes back to black.

**Figure 3–7**    SmartArt converted to shapes

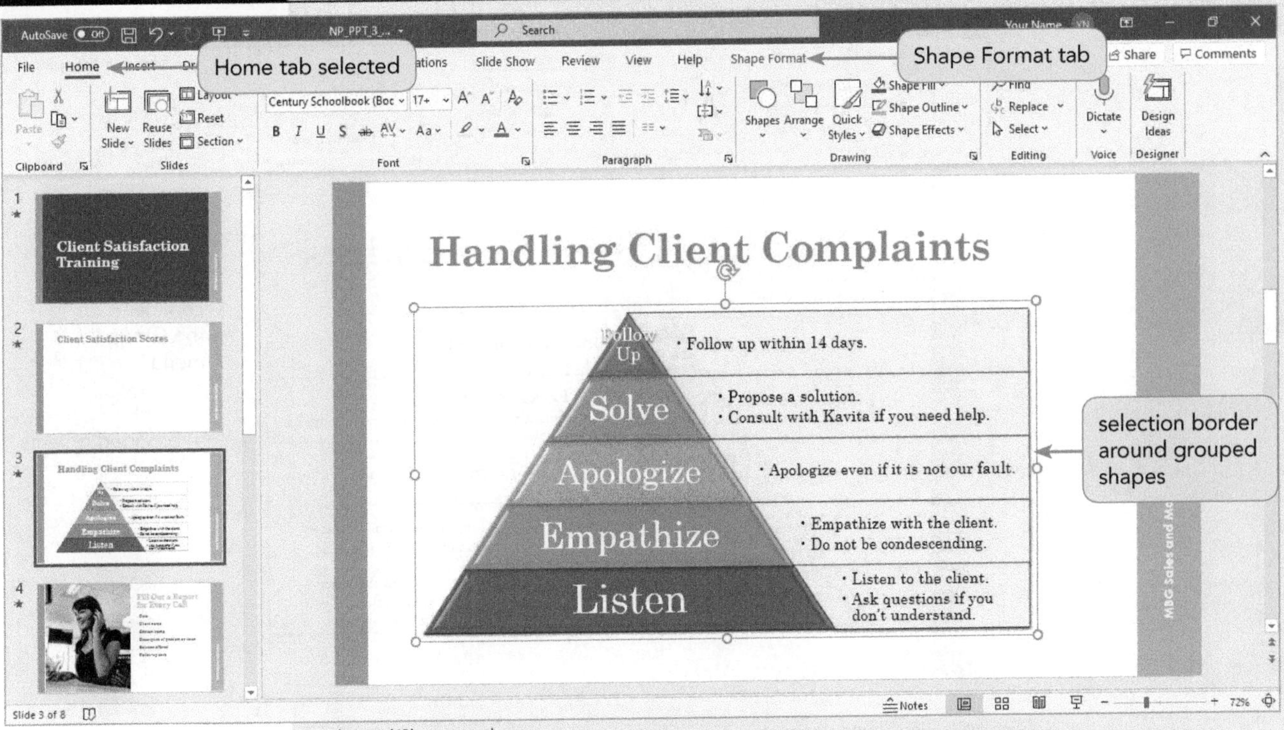

Jacob Lund/Shutterstock.com

> **3.** On the Home tab, in the Font group, click the **Font Color arrow** ![A] , and then click the **Black, Text 1** color. Because the entire grouped object was selected, all of the text changes to black.

> **4.** On the ribbon, click the **Animations** tab. In the Animation group, None is selected. When you converted the SmartArt graphic, the animation you had applied to the graphic was removed.

Kavita wants the second-level shapes to appear immediately after each first-level shape, as if the shapes were connected. To create this effect, you will first ungroup all the shapes. Next, you will group the shapes at each level, and then animate each group.

### To ungroup and group shapes:

> **1.** Click the **Shape Format** tab, and then in the Arrange group, click the **Group** button. A menu opens. See Figure 3–8. Because the objects are already grouped, the only command available is the Ungroup command.

Figure 3–8 **Group menu when a grouped object is selected**

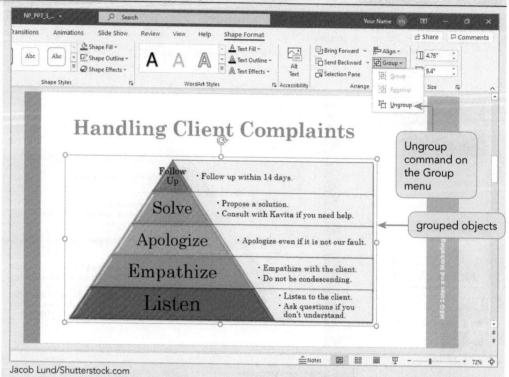

Jacob Lund/Shutterstock.com

2. On the menu, click **Ungroup**. The shapes are ungrouped, and each individual shape is selected. Next, you will group the Listen shape and the shape containing its subitems.

3. Click a blank area of the slide to deselect the shapes, click the **Listen** shape, press and hold **SHIFT**, click the shape to the right of the Listen shape, and then release **SHIFT**. The two shapes are selected.

4. On the Shape Format tab, in the Arrange group, click the **Group** button. The Group menu opens. This time, the Ungroup command is not available because the items are not yet grouped.

5. On the menu, click **Group**. The two shapes are grouped as one object and the selection border appears around both of them.

6. Working your way up the pyramid, use the **Group** command to group the two shapes in each level of the pyramid.

7. Click the grouped **Listen** shape, click the **Animations** tab, and then in the Animation group, click the **Wipe** entrance animation.

8. In the Animation group, click the **Effect Options** button, and then click **From Left**. The animation previews and the Listen shape and its subitems wipe on the screen from the left.

9. Starting with the Empathize group and working your way up the pyramid, apply the **Wipe** entrance animation with the **From Left** effect to each grouped object. When you are finished, the animation sequence icons should advance from 1 through 5 from the bottom of the pyramid to the top. See Figure 3–9.

| Figure 3–9 | Animations applied to the grouped shapes on Slide 3 |

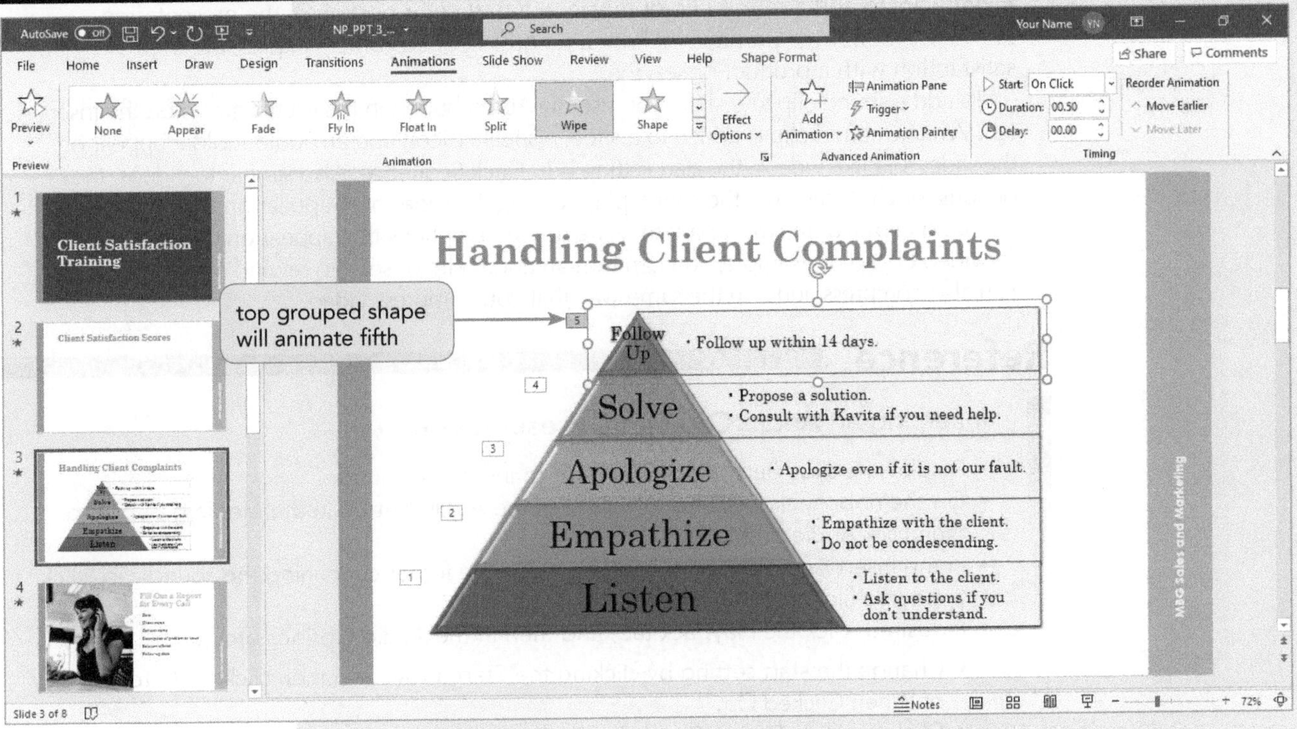

Jacob Lund/Shutterstock.com

**Trouble?** If the animation sequence icons are out of order, click the icon of the animation whose order you want to change, and then in the Timing group on the Animations tab, click the Move Earlier or Move Later button to move the animation earlier or later.

▶ **10.** Save the changes to the presentation.

## Insight

### Inserting Scalable Vector Graphics

In addition to shapes, you can insert icons. The icons are sorted into various categories, such as People, Education, Vehicles, Sports, and so on. To insert icons, click the Insert tab, and then in the Illustrations group, click the Icons button to open the Insert Icons dialog box. Click as many icons as you want to add to the slide, and then click Insert.

When you select an icon on a slide, the Graphic Format tab appears on the ribbon. Similar to the Shape Format tab, you can change the fill color, the outline color, weight, and style of an icon, or apply effects, such as shadows or bevels, to the icon. If you want to change to a different icon, you can click the Change Graphic button in the Change group.

An icon is a scalable vector graphic, which means the icon can be resized, rotated, or recolored without losing any quality. If you want to recolor or manipulate different parts of the icon, you need convert it to a shape or ungroup it. To do this, select the icon, and then in the Change group on the Graphic Format tab, click the Convert to Shape button. Then you can click each shape that makes up the icon and format it any way you want using the tools on the Shape Format tab.

# Adding Audio to Slides

Audio in a presentation can be used for a wide variety of purposes. For example, you might want to add a sound clip of music to a particular portion of the presentation to evoke emotion, or perhaps include a recording of customers expressing their satisfaction with a product or service.

To add a sound clip to a slide, you use the Audio button in the Media group on the Insert tab. When a sound clip is added to a slide, a speaker icon and an audio toolbar appear on the slide, and like videos, the start setting is In Click Sequence. Also similar to videos, the options for changing how the sound plays during the slide show appear on the Playback tab for audio clips. For the most part, they are the same options that appear on the Playback tab for video clips. For example, you can trim an audio clip or set it to rewind after playing. You can also compress audio in the same way that you compress video.

## Reference

### Inserting an Audio Clip into a Presentation

- Display the slide onto which you want to insert the sound.
- On the ribbon, click the Insert tab, click the Audio button in the Media group, and then click Audio on My PC.
- In the Insert Audio dialog box, navigate to the folder containing the sound clip, click the audio file, and then click Insert.
- If desired, click the Playback tab, and then in the Audio Options group:
  - Change the start setting by clicking the Start arrow, and then clicking Automatically or When Clicked On.
  - Click the Hide During Show check box to select it to hide the speaker icon during a slide show.
  - Click the Volume button, and then click a volume level or click Mute.
  - Click the Loop until Stopped check box to select it to play the audio clip continuously until the next action occurs.
  - Click the Rewind after Playing check box to rewind the clip to the beginning after it plays.
- If desired, click the Playback tab, and then in the Editing group:
  - Click the Trim Audio button, and then in the Trim audio dialog box, change the time in the Start Time or End Time boxes to change the point at which the audio clip starts or stops, and then click OK.
  - Increase the time in the Fade In or Fade Out boxes to fade the audio in or out at the beginning or end of the clip.

Kavita wants you to add a sound clip to the last slide in the presentation. The clip is a recording of a client who said that she was extremely satisfied with her customer service experience at MBG.

### To add a sound clip to Slide 6:

1. Display Slide 6 (the second "Pathway to Happy Clients" slide), and then click the **Insert** tab on the ribbon.

2. In the Media group, click the **Audio** button, and then click **Audio on My PC**. The Insert Audio dialog box opens.

3. Navigate to the **PowerPoint3 > Module** folder, click **Support_PPT_3_ Comment.m4a**, and then click **Insert**. A speaker icon appears in the middle of the slide with the audio toolbar below it, and the Playback tab is selected on the ribbon. See Figure 3–10. As with videos, the default Start setting is In Click Sequence.

**Tip**

To record an audio clip, click the Audio button in the Media group on the Insert tab, and then click Record Audio.

| Figure 3–10 | Speaker icon on Slide 6 |
| --- | --- |

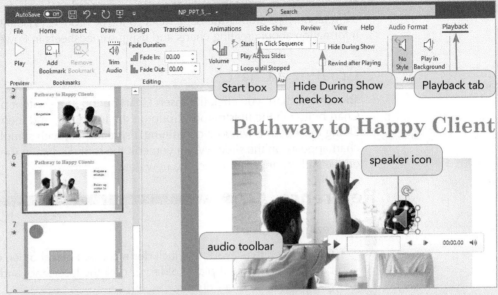

fizkes/Shutterstock.com

4. Drag the speaker icon to the lower-right corner of the slide so it is positioned at the bottom of the blue bar.

5. On the audio toolbar, click the **Play** button ▶. The sound clip, which is a comment from a satisfied client, plays. Kavita wants the clip to play automatically after the slide appears on the screen.

6. On the Playback tab, in the Audio Options group, click the **Start** arrow, and then click **Automatically**. Because the clip will play automatically, there is no need to have the sound icon visible on the screen during a slide show.

7. In the Audio Options group, click the **Hide During Show** check box to select it.

8. Save the changes to the presentation.

## Insight

### Playing Music Across Slides

You can add an audio clip to a slide and have it play throughout the slide show. On the Playback tab, in the Audio Styles group, click the Play in Background button. When you select this option, the Start setting in the Audio Options group is changed to Automatically, and the Play Across Slides, Loop until Stopped, and Hide During Show check boxes become selected. These setting changes ensure the audio clip will start playing when the slide appears on the screen during a slide show and will continue playing, starting over if necessary, until the end of the slide show. To change the settings so that the audio no longer plays throughout the slide show, click the No Style button in the Audio Styles group.

# Adding a Chart to a Slide

**Charts** are graphic elements that illustrate data using bars, columns, dots, lines, or other symbols to make the data easier to understand and to make it easier to see the relationships among the data. Refer to the Session 3.1 Visual Overview for more information about creating charts and using spreadsheets in PowerPoint.

## Creating a Chart

To create a chart, you click the Insert Chart button in a content placeholder or use the Chart button in the Illustrations group on the Insert tab, and then select a chart type. Doing this opens a window containing a spreadsheet with sample data, and a sample chart appears on the slide. When you edit the sample data in the spreadsheet, the chart on the slide changes to reflect the new data.

## Reference

### Creating a Chart

- On a slide with a layout that includes a content placeholder, click the Insert Chart button in the content placeholder; or click the Insert tab, and then, in the Illustrations group, click the Chart button.
- In the Insert Chart dialog box, click the desired chart type in the list on the left.
- In the row of styles, click the desired chart style, and then click OK.
- In the spreadsheet that opens, enter the data that you want to plot.
- If you need to chart fewer rows or columns than are shaded in the spreadsheet, drag the handle in the lower-right corner of the shaded area up to remove rows or to the left to remove columns.
- In the spreadsheet window, click the Close button.

Kavita wants you to create a chart on Slide 2 that illustrates the percentage of clients that are satisfied with their customer service encounters. A pie chart is a good choice when you want to show the relative size of one value compared to the other values and compared to the total set of values.

**To create a chart on Slide 2:**

1. Display Slide 2 ("Client Satisfaction Scores"). You can insert a chart by using the Insert Chart button ⊞ in a content placeholder or by clicking Chart in the Illustrations group on the Insert tab.

2. In the content placeholder, click the **Insert Chart** button ⊞. The Insert Chart dialog box opens. Column is selected in the list of chart types on the left, and the Clustered Column style is selected in the row of styles at the top and shown in the preview area. See Figure 3-11.

**Figure 3–11**    Insert Chart dialog box

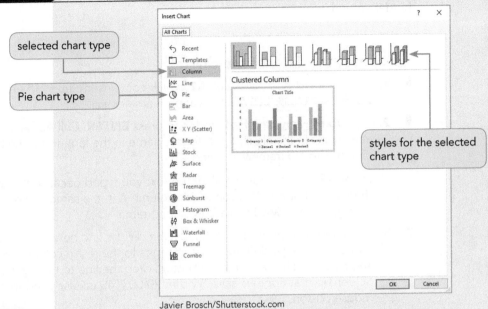

Javier Brosch/Shutterstock.com

**Tip**

After you insert a chart, you can click the Design Ideas button in the Designer group on the Design tab to open the Design Ideas pane with suggestions for the slide layout.

3. In the list of chart types, click **Pie**. The row of chart styles changes to pie chart styles. The Pie style is selected.

4. Click **OK**. A sample chart is inserted on Slide 2, and a small spreadsheet (sometimes called a datasheet) opens above the chart. In the spreadsheet, colored borders around the cells indicate which cells are included in the chart. At the bottom of the chart, the **legend** identifies how data is represented using colors or patterns. See Figure 3–12.

**Figure 3–12**    Spreadsheet and chart with sample data

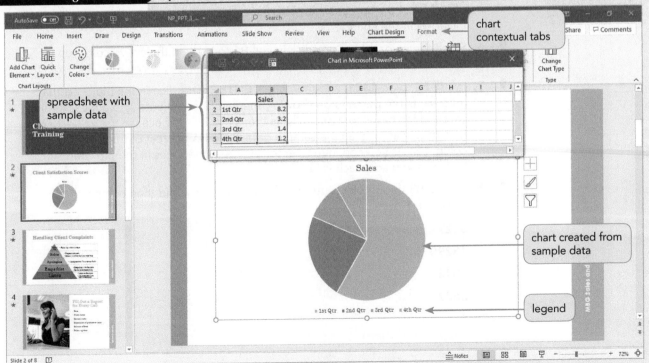

Jacob Lund/Shutterstock.com

To create the chart for Kavita's presentation, you need to edit the sample data in the spreadsheet. When you work with a spreadsheet, the cell that is selected is the **active cell**. When you enter data, it appears in the active cell. The active cell has a green border around it.

### To enter the data for the chart:

▶ 1. In the spreadsheet, click cell **A2**, which contains the text "1ˢᵗ Qtr". A green border surrounds cell A2, indicating it is selected.

▶ 2. Type **Extremely satisfied**, and then press **ENTER**. Cell A3 becomes the active cell. In the chart, the category name in the legend for the blue pie slice changes to "Extremely satisfied".

In cell A2, you cannot see all of the text you typed because the text is longer than the cell width. You can widen column A in the same manner that you change column widths in a PowerPoint table.

▶ 3. Move the pointer on top of the column divider line between the column A and column B headers so that it changes to the resize column width pointer ✛ , press and hold the mouse button, drag the line to the right until the ScreenTip that appears says "Width: 20.00 (145 pixels)", and then release the mouse button.

▶ 4. Enter the following in cells **A3** through **A5**, pressing **ENTER** after each entry:

**Very satisfied**

**Somewhat satisfied**

**Somewhat dissatisfied**

<table>
<tr><td>Tip</td></tr>
<tr><td>To add or remove a row or column from the chart, drag the small sizing handle at the bottom-right of the last column and last row of data in the spreadsheet.</td></tr>
</table>

▶ 5. In cell A6, type **Not at all satisfied**, and then press **ENTER**. The active cell is cell A7. In the chart, a new category name is added to the legend. Because there is no data for this new category in cell B6, a corresponding slice was not added to the pie chart. Although the shading and colored borders in the spreadsheet did not change, a small sizing handle appears in the corner of cell B6 in the spreadsheet. This indicates that the cells in this row will be included in the chart.

▶ 6. Scroll the spreadsheet up, click in cell **B1** to make it the active cell, type **Number**, and then press **ENTER**. The active cell is now cell B2.

▶ 7. In cell B2, type **1321**, and then press **ENTER**. The slice in the pie chart that represents the percentage showing the number of clients who are extremely satisfied increases to essentially fill the chart. This is because the value 1321 is so much larger than the sample data values in the rest of the rows in column B. As you continue to enter the data, the slices in the pie chart will adjust as you add each value.

▶ 8. In cells B3 through B6, enter the following values, and then compare your screen to Figure 3-13:

**3527**

**13290**

**7544**

**2637**

| Figure 3–13 | Spreadsheet and chart after entering data |

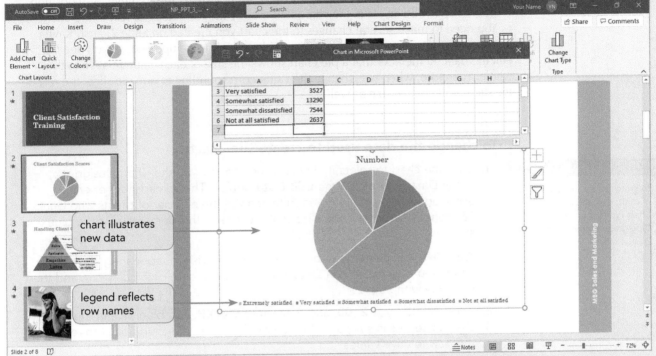

Jacob Lund/Shutterstock.com

Notice that the shading and colored borders in the spreadsheet now includes cells A6 and B6.

**9.** In the spreadsheet, click the **Close** button ✕. The spreadsheet closes.

**10.** Save the changes to the presentation.

## Proskills

### Decision Making: Selecting the Correct Chart Type

To use charts effectively, you need to consider what you want to illustrate with your data. Column charts use vertical columns and bar charts use horizontal bars to represent values. These types of charts are useful for comparing the values of items over a period of time or a range of dates or costs. Line charts and area charts use a line to connect points that represent values. They are effective for showing changes over time, and they are particularly useful for illustrating trends. Line and area charts are a better choice than column or bar charts when you need to display large amounts of information and exact quantities that don't require emphasis. Pie charts are used to show percentages or proportions of the parts that make up a whole. Treemap and sunburst charts also show the proportion of parts to a whole. These two chart types also show hierarchical data when the data is grouped into subcategories.

You can change a chart type after you create it. To do this, click the Change Chart Type button in the Type group on the Chart Design tab. The same dialog box appears as when you first create a chart.

## Modifying a Chart

Once a chart is on a slide, you can modify it by changing or formatting its various elements. For example, you can edit the data; apply a style; add, remove, or reposition chart elements; add labels to the chart; and modify the formatting of text in the chart.

You need to make several changes to the chart you created on Slide 2. First, Kavita informs you that one of the values she provided needs to be updated, so you need to edit the data. Remember that a pie chart shows the size of each value relative to the whole. Therefore, when you change the value corresponding to one pie slice, the rest of the slices will change size as well.

**Tip**

To switch to another type of chart, click the Change Chart Type button in the Type group on the Chart Design tab.

### To change the data used to create the chart:

1. Click the chart to select it, if necessary, and then on the Chart Design tab, in the Data group, click the **Edit Data** button. The spreadsheet opens again above the chart. You need to change the number of clients who were "Extremely satisfied". The slice that represents this percentage is the blue slice.

   **Trouble?** If a menu opened instead of a spreadsheet appearing above the chart, you clicked the Edit Data arrow. On the menu, click Edit Data, and then continue with Step 2.

2. Click cell **B2**, type **2100**, and then press **ENTER**. The blue slice in the pie chart increases in size, and the other slices in the pie chart adjust to reflect the new relative values.

3. On the spreadsheet, click the **Close** button ☒. The spreadsheet closes.

Next, Kavita wants you to make several formatting changes to the chart. She would like you to apply a different style to the chart and change its colors. There are several ways to do this. You can use the Quick Layout command, or you can change the style and apply a different palette of colors.

### To change the layout, style, and colors of the chart:

1. On the Chart Design tab, in the Chart Layouts group, click the **Quick Layout** button. A gallery of chart layouts specific to pie charts opens. Each layout includes different chart elements, such as the chart title and legend.

2. Point to several of the layouts to see which elements are added to the chart, and then click **Layout 1**. The category name and percentage of each slice are added as labels on the slices, and the legend is removed. With this layout, there is no need for the legend.

3. To the right of the chart, click the **Chart Styles** button 🖉. A gallery opens with the Style tab selected at the top.

4. Point to several of the styles to see the effect on the chart. In addition to changing the colors used, some of the styles include layouts and add or remove chart elements, similar to the Quick Layouts.

5. Click **Style 3**. This style adds the legend and a background that varies from very light gray to a darker gray. The labels that list the category names and percentages of each slice are still included. The labels overlap, but you will fix that in the next set of steps. See Figure 3–14.

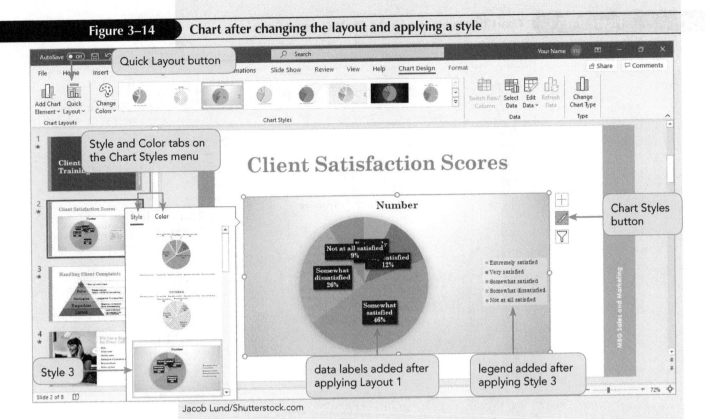

Figure 3-14    Chart after changing the layout and applying a style

Jacob Lund/Shutterstock.com

6. On the Chart Styles menu, click the **Color** tab at the top. A menu containing color palettes appears.

7. In the list, click **Colorful Palette 2**. The colors in the chart change to the colors specified in the palette you selected.

There is no need for a title on the chart because the slide title describes the chart. Because the pie slices are labeled with the category names and the percentage values, there is also no need for the legend. You will remove the title and the legend. Then you will reposition the labels on the chart.

## To remove, reposition, and format chart elements:

**Tip**

Double-click a chart element to open a pane that contains additional commands for modifying that element.

1. To the right of the chart, click the **Chart Elements** button ⊞. The Chart Styles menu closes, and the Chart Elements menu opens to the right of the chart. The Chart Title, Data Labels, and Legend check boxes are all selected, which means these elements are shown on the chart.

2. On the Chart Elements menu, move the pointer on top of **Chart Title** so that an arrow ▶ appears, and then click the **arrow** ▶. The Chart Title submenu opens. See Figure 3–15. The submenu contains two locations where you can place the chart title. The Above Chart option is selected. The submenu also contains the More Options command. If you click More Options, the Format Chart Title pane opens. That pane contains commands you can use to format the chart title.

**Figure 3–15**    Chart Title submenu on the Chart Elements menu

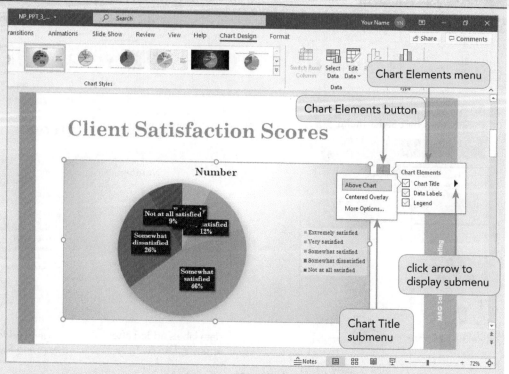

3.  On the Chart Elements menu, click the **Chart Title** check box. The check box is deselected, the submenu closes, and the chart title is removed from the chart.

4.  On the Chart Elements menu, move the pointer on top of **Legend**, and then click the **arrow** ▶ that appears. The Legend submenu opens listing four locations where you can position the legend.

5.  Click the **Legend** check box to deselect it. The legend is removed from the chart.

6.  On the Chart Elements menu, move the pointer on top of **Data Labels**, and then click the **arrow** ▶ to open the Data Labels submenu. This time, you will select a command on the submenu.

7.  On the submenu, click **Outside End**. The data labels are moved so that they are positioned next to each pie slice.

8.  Click the **Chart Elements** button ⊞ to close the menu.

9.  Click one of the data labels to select all of them, and then click the **Home** tab.

10. In the Font group, click the **Font** button, and then click **Century Gothic**.

11. In the Font group, click the **Font Size** button, and then click **11**.

12. Click the **Somewhat satisfied 46%** data label. The label you clicked is selected and the rest of the data labels are deselected.

13. Drag the **Somewhat satisfied 46%** data label so it is positioned in the center of the large, light-green slice.

    **Trouble?** If the label moves back to its original position, click the data label to select it, wait for several seconds, and then drag it again.

14. Drag the **Somewhat dissatisfied 26%** data label so it overlaps the dark blue slice.

**15.** Drag the **Very satisfied 12%** data label so its corner overlaps the light olive-green slice.

**16.** Drag the **Not at all satisfied 9%** data label so its corner overlaps the dark olive-green slice.

**17.** Drag the **Extremely satisfied 7%** data label so its corner overlaps the light blue slice and is approximately aligned with the "Not at all satisfied 9%" label. Compare your screen to Figure 3–16 and make any necessary adjustments so that your screen matches the figure.

| Figure 3–16 | Chart with modified data labels and the title and legend removed |

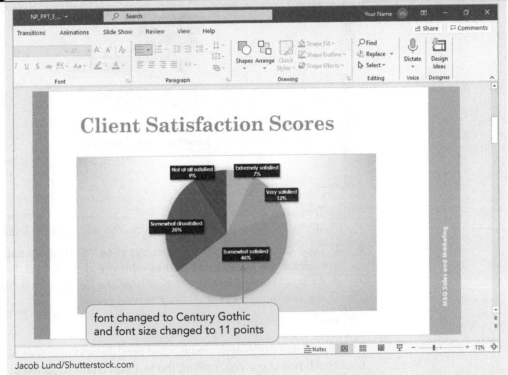

Jacob Lund/Shutterstock.com

**18.** Save the changes to the presentation.

# Inserting and Formatting Text Boxes

Sometimes you need to add text to a slide in a location other than in one of the text placeholders included in the slide layout. Two ways you can do this are to draw a shape and then add text to it, or add a special type of shape called a text box.

Ordinary shapes are filled with the Accent 1 color by default, but text box shapes have no fill when you create them. Therefore, when you place a shape over another object, it obscures the object behind it, while a text box shows the object through the background. With an ordinary shape, the text is center-aligned by default, but the text in a text box shape is left-aligned.

Regardless of the differences, after you create a text box, you can format the text box in all of the same ways you can format a shape, including adding a fill, adjusting the internal margins, and rotating and repositioning it.

Kavita wants you to add text on Slide 2 that describes the goal for her team for the next quarter. You will add a text box to accomplish this.

### To add a text box on Slide 2:

1. With Slide 2 ("Client Satisfaction Scores") displayed, click the **Insert** tab on the ribbon, and then in the Illustrations group, click the **Shapes** button.

2. In the Basic Shapes section, click the **Text Box** shape 🄰, and then move the pointer to the slide. The pointer changes to the draw text box pointer ↓.

3. Position the draw text box pointer ↓ below the left edge of the chart, and then click and drag to draw a text box as wide as the chart and about one-half-inch high. See Figure 3–17. The insertion point is in the text box.

**Figure 3–17**     Text box inserted on Slide 2

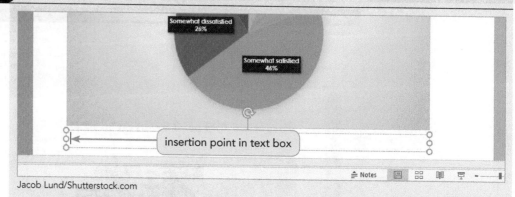

Jacob Lund/Shutterstock.com

> **Trouble?** If your text box is not the same size or is not positioned exactly as shown in Figure 3–17, don't worry. You will adjust it later.

4. Type **Goal is to make the largest slice "Extremely satisfied" and greatly reduce the number of clients who are dissatisfied.** (including the period). As you type the text in the text box, the height of the text box changes, and the additional text wraps to the next line.

Because you dragged to create a text box, the text box does not get wider no matter how much text you enter. Instead, the text you typed wrapped to new lines in the text box, and the height of the text box resized to accommodate the text you typed. If you had simply clicked to place the text box, the text box would have expanded horizontally as wide as necessary to accommodate the text you typed, even if it needed to flow off the slide. This differs from text boxes created from title and content placeholders and shapes with text in them. As you have seen, text boxes created from placeholders have the AutoFit feature applied to reduce the font size of the text to fit if you add more text than can fit in the placeholder. When you add text to a shape, if you add more text than can fit horizontally in that shape, the text wraps to the next line and then extends outside of the top and bottom of the shape if necessary.

Kavita thinks the text below the chart would look better if it were all on one line and italicized. You will change the text wrapping option so that the text does not wrap to the next line.

### To modify and reposition the text box:

1. Right-click the text box, and then on the shortcut menu, click **Format Shape**. The Format Shape pane opens to the right of the displayed slide. The pane contains two tabs at the top—Shape Options and Text Options—and buttons to display related commands on each tab. The Shape Options tab is selected. This tab contains categories of commands for formatting the shape, such as changing the fill or line. See Figure 3–18.

**Figure 3–18**   **Format Shape pane and text box with wrapped text**

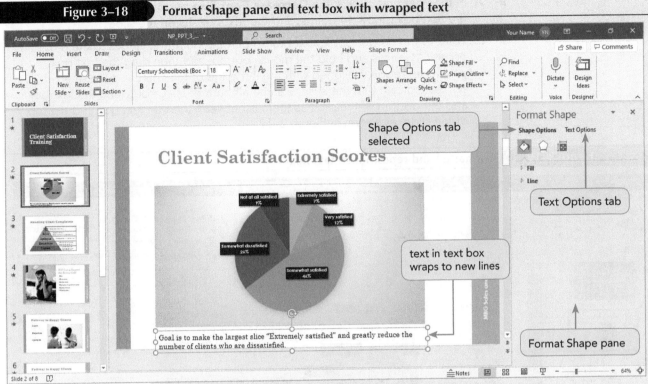

Jacob Lund/Shutterstock.com: fizkes/Shutterstock.com

2. In the Format Shape pane, click **Text Options** to display the Text Options tab. This tab contains commands for formatting the text in the text box.

3. Click the **Textbox** button 🖾. The Format Shape pane changes to show the Text Box section, containing options for formatting text in a text box. At the top of the pane, the Resize shape to fit text option button is selected. That is why the height of the text box increased when the text wrapped to a new line. Text and content placeholders have the Shrink text on overflow option button selected by default. And shapes other than text boxes have the Do not Autofit option button selected.

   First you want to change the wrap option so the text does not wrap in the text box.

4. Click the **Wrap text in shape** check box to deselect it. The text in the text box appears all on one line and overlaps the right edge of the slide. Next, you want to decrease the space between the first word in the text box and the left border of the box. In other words, you want to change the left margin in the text box.

   **Trouble?** If the Wrap text in shape check box is not selected, you clicked instead of dragging to create the text box in Step 3 in the previous set of steps. In this case, do not click the check box; leave it unselected.

5. Click the **Left margin** down arrow. The value in the box changes to 0", and the text shifts left in the text box.

6. On the slide, click the text box border to select all of the text in the text box, and then, in the Font group on the Home tab, click the **Italic** button 𝐼. The text in the text box is italicized.

**7.** In the Font group, click the **Decrease Font Size** button [A˅] twice. The text in the text box is now 14 points, and the text box fits on the slide.

**8.** Point to the border of the text box so that the pointer changes to the move pointer ⊹, press and hold the mouse button, and then drag the text box until its left edge is aligned with the left edge of the chart and the smart guides indicate that there is the same amount of space between the text box and the bottom of the slide as there is between the title text box and the top of the slide, as shown in Figure 3–19.

**Figure 3–19**    **Formatted and repositioned text box**

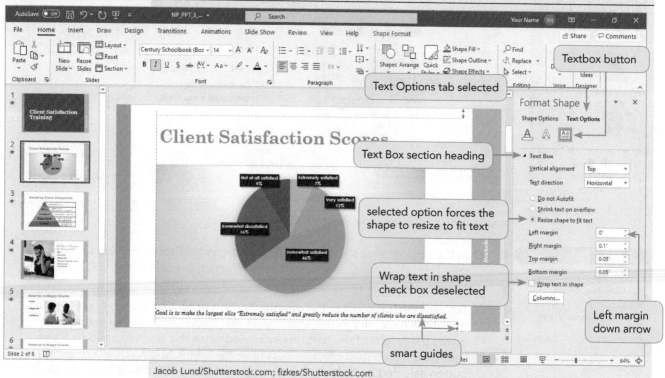

Jacob Lund/Shutterstock.com; fizkes/Shutterstock.com

**9.** Release the mouse button.

**10.** In the Format Shape pane, click the **Close** button [X], and then save the changes to the presentation.

# Applying WordArt Styles to Text

**WordArt** is formatted, decorative text in a text box. WordArt text has a fill color, which is the same as the font color, and an outline color. To create WordArt, you can insert a new text box by using the WordArt button in the Text group on the Insert tab or format an existing one by applying one of the built-in WordArt styles or using the Text Fill, Text Outline, and Text Effects buttons in the WordArt Styles group on the Format tab.

Kavita would like you to apply a WordArt style to the title of Slide 8.

## To apply a WordArt style to the title of Slide 8 and modify it:

1. Display Slide 8 ("100% Satisfaction"), click the title **100% Satisfaction**, and then click the title text box border. The entire text box is selected.

2. Click the **Shape Format** tab, and then in the WordArt Styles group, click the **More** button to open the WordArt gallery. See Figure 3–20.

**Figure 3–20    WordArt gallery**

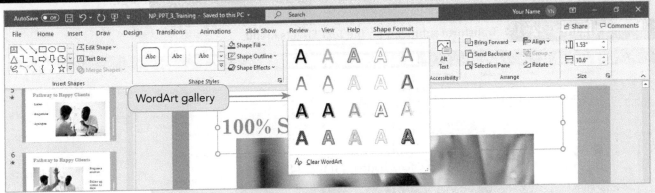

fizkes/Shutterstock.com

3. Click the **Pattern Fill: Brown, Dark Upward Diagonal Stripe; Hard Shadow** style (the last style in the last row). The title text is formatted with the style you selected in the WordArt gallery. This WordArt style doesn't really match the slide theme, so you will change it.

4. In the WordArt Styles group, click the **More** button , and then click the **Gradient Fill: Green, Accent color 5; Reflection** style (the second style in the second row). The style of the text changes to the style you chose. You want to change the color used in the gradient fill from green to blue.

5. In the WordArt Styles group, click the **Text Fill arrow**. The Theme Colors palette appears.

6. Click the **Ice Blue, Accent 1, Darker 50%** color. If you wanted to change the color of the outline of each letter, you would use the Text Outline button.

7. Click the **Home** tab, and then in the Paragraph group, click the **Center** button . See Figure 3–21.

**Figure 3–21    WordArt on Slide 8**

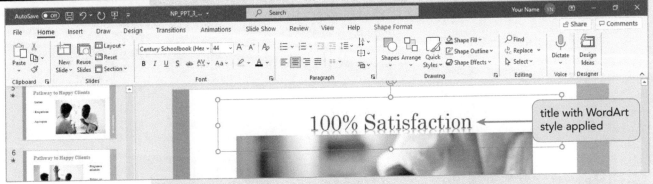

fizkes/Shutterstock.com

The shape of text in a text box can be transformed into waves, circles, and other shapes. To do this, you use the options located on the Transform submenu, which is accessed from the Text Effects menu on the Shape Format tab.

Kavita wants you to change the shape of the WordArt on Slide 8.

### To change the shape of the WordArt by applying a transform effect:

1. With the WordArt on Slide 8 selected, click the **Shape Format** tab.

2. In the WordArt styles group, click the **Text Effects** button, and then point to **Transform**. The Transform submenu appears. See Figure 3–22.

**Figure 3–22**      Transform submenu on the Text Effects menu

fizkes/Shutterstock.com

3. In the first row under Warp, click the **Square** effect. The effect is applied to the text in the text box. The WordArt text box is too large for the space.

4. In the Size group, click in the **Shape Height** box, type **0.7**, and then press **ENTER**. Compare your screen to Figure 3–23.

**Figure 3–23**     **Final WordArt**

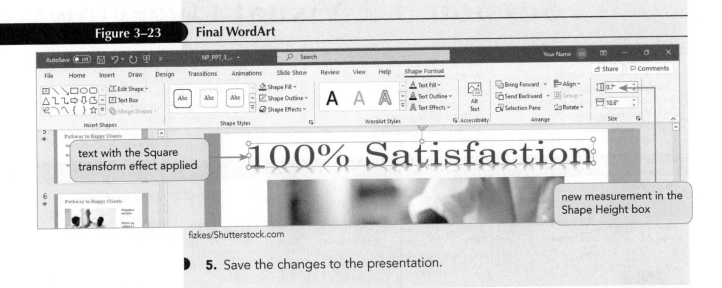

fizkes/Shutterstock.com

**5.** Save the changes to the presentation.

## Proskills

### Decision Making: Selecting Appropriate Font Colors

When you select font colors, make sure your text is easy to read during your slide show. Font colors that work well are dark colors on a light background or light colors on a dark background. Avoid red text on a blue background or blue text on a green background (and vice versa) unless the shades of those colors strongly contrast with each other. These combinations might look fine on your computer monitor, but they are almost totally illegible to an audience viewing your presentation on a screen in a darkened room. Also avoid using red/green or blue/yellow combinations, which many people with color blindness find illegible.

In this session, you created and modified a SmartArt graphic, and then you animated it and changed the effect options for the animation. You also converted a SmartArt graphic to shapes, ungrouped the shapes, and then grouped them in a different organization. You added an audio clip and WordArt to a slide. You learned how to create and modify a chart on a slide, and how to insert and format a text box. In the next session, you will continue modifying the presentation by creating a custom shape, formatting pictures and shapes, and making the presentation accessible.

## Review

### Session 3.1 Quick Check

1. How do you change the animation applied to a SmartArt graphic so that each shape animates one at a time?

2. What happens when you click the Play in Background button in the Audio Styles group on the Playback tab?

3. What happens when you group objects?

4. What is the start setting for an audio clip when you place it on a slide: In Click Sequence, Automatically, or When Clicked On?

5. What is a spreadsheet?

6. How do you identify a specific cell in a spreadsheet?

7. What is WordArt?

# Session 3.2 Visual Overview:

These buttons contain galleries of settings, which correspond to the galleries shown on the Presets buttons in the Presets buttons in the Format Picture pane.

When only a picture is selected, the Format Picture pane does not include any tabs, just buttons for displaying groups of commands.

The Format Picture pane contains the commands on the Picture Format tab and additional advanced options for formatting pictures.

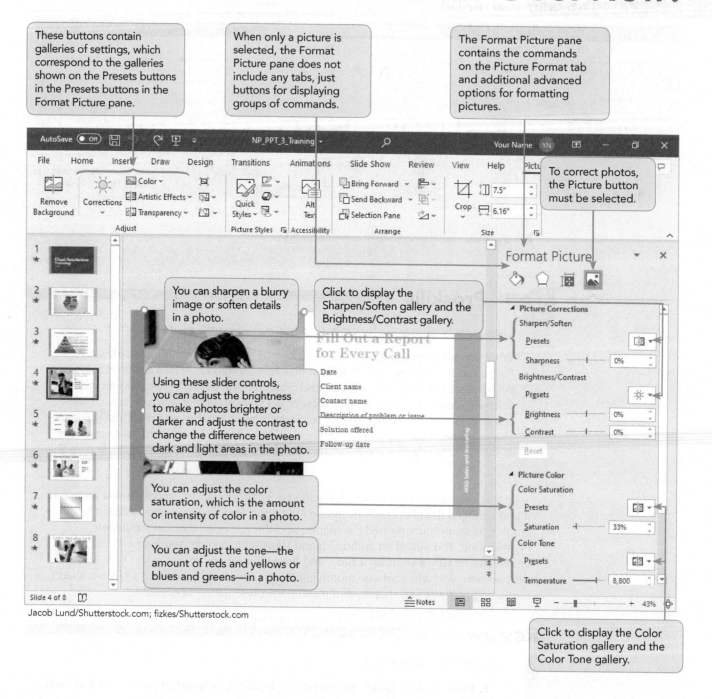

To correct photos, the Picture button must be selected.

You can sharpen a blurry image or soften details in a photo.

Click to display the Sharpen/Soften gallery and the Brightness/Contrast gallery.

Using these slider controls, you can adjust the brightness to make photos brighter or darker and adjust the contrast to change the difference between dark and light areas in the photo.

You can adjust the color saturation, which is the amount or intensity of color in a photo.

You can adjust the tone—the amount of reds and yellows or blues and greens—in a photo.

Click to display the Color Saturation gallery and the Color Tone gallery.

Jacob Lund/Shutterstock.com; fizkes/Shutterstock.com

# Formatting Shapes and Pictures

To use preset options in the Format Shape pane, you can use the Shape Fill and Shape Outline buttons.

In panes, click a tab to display the options on that tab. To create a custom gradient, the Shape Options tab must be selected.

The Format Shape pane contains the commands on the Shape Format tab and additional advanced options for formatting shapes.

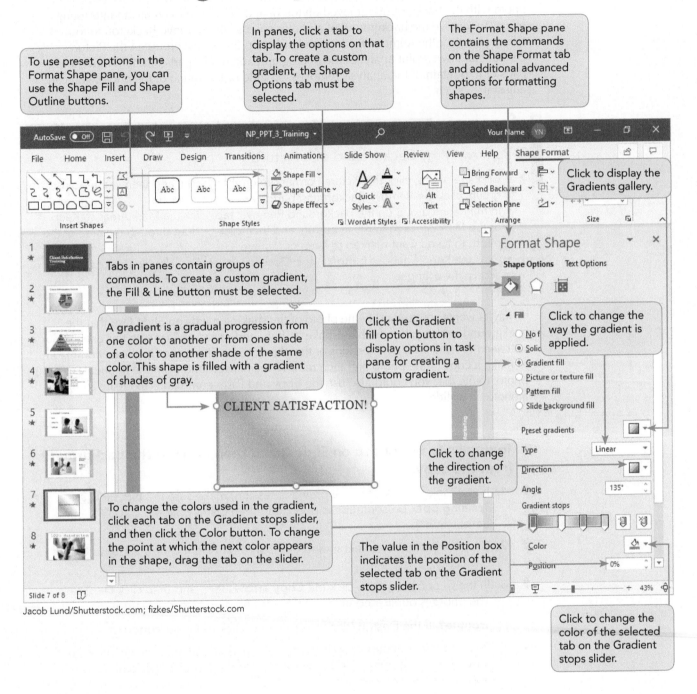

Click to display the Gradients gallery.

Tabs in panes contain groups of commands. To create a custom gradient, the Fill & Line button must be selected.

A gradient is a gradual progression from one color to another or from one shade of a color to another shade of the same color. This shape is filled with a gradient of shades of gray.

Click the Gradient fill option button to display options in task pane for creating a custom gradient.

Click to change the way the gradient is applied.

Click to change the direction of the gradient.

To change the colors used in the gradient, click each tab on the Gradient stops slider, and then click the Color button. To change the point at which the next color appears in the shape, drag the tab on the slider.

The value in the Position box indicates the position of the selected tab on the Gradient stops slider.

Click to change the color of the selected tab on the Gradient stops slider.

Jacob Lund/Shutterstock.com; fizkes/Shutterstock.com

# Removing the Background from Pictures

Sometimes a photo is more striking if you remove its background. You can also layer a photo with the background removed on top of another photo to create an interesting effect. To remove the background of a photo, you use the Remove Background tool. When you click the Remove Background button in the Adjust group on the Picture Format tab, PowerPoint analyzes the photograph and marks parts of it to remove and parts of it to retain. If the analysis removes too little or too much of the photo, you can adjust it.

## Reference

### Removing the Background of a Picture

- Click the photo, click the Picture Format tab on the ribbon, and then in the Adjust group, click the Remove Background button.
- In the Refine group on the Background Removal tab, click the Mark Areas to Keep or the Mark Areas to Remove button, and then click or drag through the area of the photo that you want marked to keep or remove.
- Click the Keep Changes button in the Close group or click a blank area of the slide to accept the changes.

Kavita wants you to modify the photo of the shaking hands on Slide 8 so that the background is blurry, but the handshake is sharp and in focus. To create this effect, you will need to work with two versions of the photo. You will use the Duplicate command to make a copy of the photo and then remove the background from the duplicate photo. (Note that you could also use the Copy and Paste commands to create a copy of a photo on a slide.)

**To duplicate the photo on Slide 8 and then remove the background from the copy:**

1. If you took a break after the previous session, make sure the **NP_PPT_3_Training.pptx** presentation is open, and then display Slide 8 ("100% Satisfaction").

2. Click the picture to select it, and then, on the ribbon, click the **Home** tab if necessary.

3. In the Clipboard group, click the **Copy arrow** ⬚⌄, and then click **Duplicate**. The photo is duplicated on the slide, and the duplicate is selected.

   **Trouble?** If the Design Ideas pane opens, click its Close button ✕.

4. Point to the selected duplicate photo so that the pointer changes to the move pointer ⬥, drag it left to position it to the left of the original photo so it appears in the blank space to the left of the slide border, and then scroll the window left so that you can see all of the duplicate photo.

5. With the duplicate photo selected, click the **Picture Format** tab on the ribbon.

6. In the Adjust group, click the **Remove Background** button. The areas of the photograph marked for removal are colored purple. A new tab, the Background Removal tab, appears on the ribbon and is the active tab. See Figure 3–24. You need to adjust the area of the photograph that is retained by using the Mark Areas to Keep and Mark Areas to Remove buttons in the Refine group on the Background Removal tab.

**Figure 3–24** | **Picture after clicking the Remove Background button**

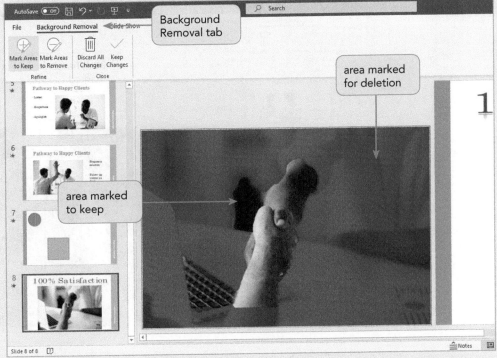

Background Removal tab

area marked for deletion

area marked to keep

fizkes/Shutterstock.com

7. In the Refine group, click the **Mark Areas to Keep** button if necessary. The pointer changes to the pencil pointer.

8. Drag the pencil pointer on the areas of the arm belonging to the top hand that are colored purple. A green line appears as you drag the pencil. After a moment, the green line disappears and the area you dragged the pointer along changes so it is no longer colored purple. The purple coloring might be removed from some of the other areas of the picture as well.

9. Drag the pencil pointer along the parts of the arm belonging to the bottom hand that are colored purple, and then drag over any other parts of the two arms and hands that are colored purple.

10. In the Refine group, click the **Mark Areas to Remove** button. The pointer is still the pencil pointer.

11. Drag the pencil pointer on the areas of the photo that are not colored purple but are part of the background. A red line appears as you drag the pencil pointer, and then the area you dragged over changes to purple to indicate it will be removed. Compare your modified picture to Figure 3–25. Your picture might not match Figure 3–25 exactly, but as long as most of the handshake is marked to keep and most of the background behind the handshake is colored purple, it's fine.

**Figure 3–25**     **Picture after marking areas to keep and remove**

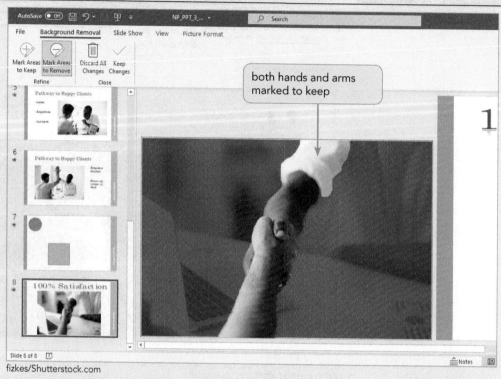

fizkes/Shutterstock.com

**12.** On the Background Removal tab, in the Close group, click the **Keep Changes** button. The changes you made are applied to the photograph, and the Background Removal tab is removed from the ribbon. Only the two hands and arms are visible now. See Figure 3–26.

**Figure 3–26**     **Duplicate picture with the background removed**

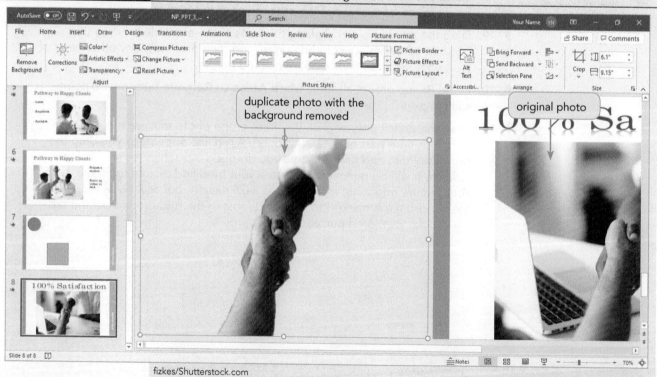

fizkes/Shutterstock.com

**Trouble?** If you want to make more adjustments to the photo, click the Remove Background button again, make the changes you want, and then repeat Step 12.

In the next section, you will complete the effect by modifying the original picture and then moving the picture with the background removed on top of the original picture.

# Editing Pictures

If photos you want to use in a presentation are too dark or require other fine-tuning, you can use PowerPoint's photo-correction tools to correct the photos. These photo-correction tools appear on the ribbon and in the Format Picture pane. Refer to the Session 3.2 Visual Overview for more information about correcting photos and the Format Picture pane.

One way you can edit pictures is to apply an artistic effect to make them look like they are paintings, black-and-white line drawings, under glass, and so on. On Slide 8 (the last slide), you will place the photo with the background removed on top of the original photo. Before you do this, you will apply an artistic effect to the original photo so that when the handshake is placed on top, it will stand out.

## To apply an artistic effect to the original photo on Slide 8:

▶ 1. On Slide 8 (the last slide), scroll right if needed so that you can see all of the original photo with the visible background, and then click the original photo.

▶ 2. Click the **Picture Format** tab if necessary, and then in the Adjust group, click the **Artistic Effects** button. See Figure 3–27.

| Figure 3–27 | Artistic Effects menu |

fizkes/Shutterstock.com

▶ 3. Click the **Glass** effect in the third row. The Glass effect is applied to the photo.

Next, you need to sharpen the photo on Slide 8 that has the background removed so that it is in sharper focus and soften the original photo. Then when you place the photo with the background removed on top of the original photo, there will be more contrast between the two photos.

### To sharpen and soften the photos on Slide 8:

1. On Slide 8 ("100% Satisfaction"), make sure the original photo with the background is still selected, and on the ribbon, the Picture Format tab is the active tab.

2. In the Adjust group, click the **Corrections** button. The options for sharpening and softening photos appear at the top of the menu.

3. Under Sharpen/Soften, click the **Soften: 50%** option. The edges of the objects in the picture are blurred and less distinct.

4. Scroll left, and then click the photo that you removed the background from.

5. In the Adjust group, click the **Corrections** button, and then under Sharpen/Soften, click the **Sharpen: 50%** option. The edges of the objects in the picture are sharper and clearer. Now you will place this photo with the background removed on top of the original photo with the Glass artistic effect and the soften effect applied.

6. Drag the photo with the background removed to the right and position it directly on top of the original photo with the artistic effect applied. Use the smart guides to ensure that it is positioned directly on top of the original photo, not centered horizontally on the slide. See Figure 3–28.

**Figure 3–28** **Final graphic on Slide 8**

fizkes/Shutterstock.com

Another correction you can make to photos is to change the brightness and contrast. Kavita thinks there is not enough contrast between the dark and light areas in the photos on Slides 5 and 6. You will correct this aspect of the photos.

### To change the contrast in the photo on Slides 5 and 6:

1. Display Slide 5 (the first "Pathway to Happy Clients" slide), and then click the photo to select it.

2. On the ribbon, click the **Picture Format** tab, and then in the Adjust group, click the **Corrections** button. The options for adjusting the brightness and the contrast of the photo are below the Sharpen/Soften options.

3. In the Brightness/Contrast section, click the **Brightness 0% (Normal) Contrast -20%** style (the third style in the second row). The contrast of the image changes. Because you chose a style with a Brightness percentage of 0%, the brightness of the photo is unchanged.

   You want to decrease the contrast just a little more. However, the gallery provides options that change the contrast in increments of 20 percent, which is more of an adjustment than you are looking for. For selecting a more precise contrast setting, you need to open the Format Picture pane.

**Tip**

Click the Transparency button in the Adjust group on the Picture Format tab to make the picture transparent.

4. Click the **Corrections** button again, and then click **Picture Corrections Options**. The Format Picture pane opens with the Picture button selected and the Picture Corrections section expanded.

5. Drag the **Contrast** slider to the left until the box next to the slider indicates -30%. The contrast decreases slightly. See Figure 3–29.

**Figure 3–29**   Contrast changed to -30%

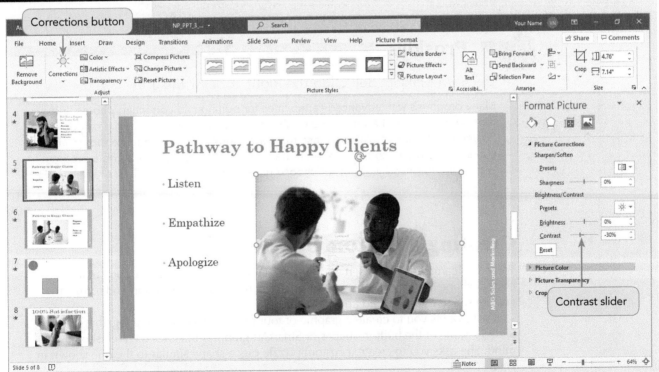

fizkes/Shutterstock.com; Jacob Lund/Shutterstock.com

> **Trouble?** If you can't position the slider exactly, click the up or down arrow in the box containing the percentage as needed, or select the current percentage and then type -30.
>
> ▶ **6.** Display Slide 6 (the second "Pathway to Happy Clients" slide), and then decrease the contrast of the picture on Slide 6 by **-30%** as well.
>
> ▶ **7.** Close the Format Picture pane.

Next, Kavita wants you to adjust the photo on Slide 4. She wants you to make the colors in the photo more realistic by reducing the saturation and the tone.

---

**To change the saturation and tone of the photo on Slide 4:**

▶ **1.** Display Slide 4 ("Fill Out a Report for Every Call"), click the photo to select it, and then click the **Picture Format** tab, if necessary.

▶ **2.** In the Adjust group, click the **Color** button. A menu opens with options for adjusting the saturation and tone of the photo's color.

▶ **3.** Under Color Saturation, click the **Saturation: 33%** option. The colors in the photo are now less intense.

▶ **4.** Click the **Color** button again.

▶ **5.** Under Color Tone, click the **Temperature: 8800K** option. More reds and yellows are added to the photo. The picture now looks like it was taken in an area with natural light.

▶ **6.** Save the changes to the presentation.

---

## Proskills

### Decision Making: Selecting the Right Tool for the Job

Many programs with advanced capabilities for editing and correcting photos and other programs for drawing complex shapes exist. Although the tools provided in PowerPoint for accomplishing these tasks are useful, if you need to do more than make simple photo corrections or create a simple shape, consider using a program with more advanced features, or choose to hire someone with skills in graphic design to help you.

## Creating a Custom Shape

You have learned how to insert and format shapes on slides. You can also create a custom shape by merging two or more shapes. Then you can position and format the custom shape as you would any other shape.

Kavita wants you to create a graphic of four puzzle pieces coming together on Slide 7. None of the built-in shapes or SmartArt graphics matches the idea she has in mind. She asks you to create a custom puzzle piece shape similar to the one shown in Figure 3–30.

**Figure 3–30**    **Kavita's sketch of the shape for Slide 7**

To create the custom shape for Kavita, you will merge shapes. Kavita already placed the shapes you need to use on Slide 7. To create the puzzle piece, you will first duplicate the circle shape.

**To arrange the shapes on Slide 7 so that you can create a custom shape:**

1. Display Slide 7 (the second to last slide), and then click the circle to select it.

2. On the Home tab, in the Clipboard group, click the **Copy arrow** ⬚ ▾, and then click **Duplicate**.

3. Drag the duplicated circle on top of the top border of the square so that the smart guides show that the center of the circle is aligned with the top of the square and the middle of the circle is aligned with the middle of the square.

4. Drag the other circle on top of the right border of the square so that the smart guides show that the center of the circle is aligned with the center of the square and the middle of the circle is aligned with the right edge of the square.

See Figure 3–31.

Make sure you position the circle as instructed in Step 4 or the final puzzle pieces will not fit together.

**Figure 3–31**    Shapes arranged to form the new shape

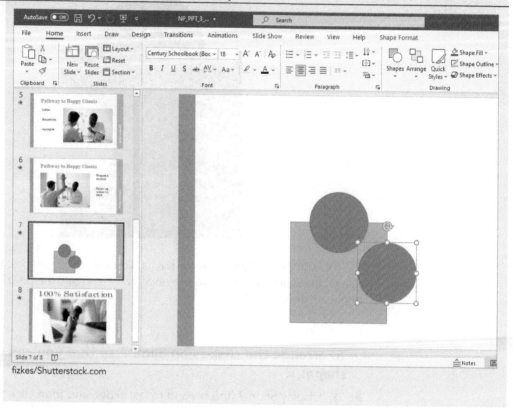

fizkes/Shutterstock.com

To create a custom shape, you use the commands on the Merge Shapes menu in the Insert Shapes group on the Shape Format tab. Each command has a different effect on selected shapes:

- **Union**—Merges selected shapes without removing any portions
- **Combine**—Merges selected shapes and removes the sections of the shapes that overlap
- **Fragment**—Separates overlapping portions of shapes into separate shapes
- **Intersect**—Merges selected shapes and removes everything except the sections that overlap
- **Subtract**—Removes the second shape selected, including any part of the first shape that is overlapped by the second shape

When you merge shapes, you place one shape on top of or touching another, and then you select the shapes. When you use the Union, Combine, Fragment, or Intersect command, the shape you select first determines the format of the merged shape. For example, if you select a red shape first and a blue shape second, and then you unite, combine, fragment, or intersect them, the merged shape will be red. When you use the Subtract command, the shape you select second is the shape that is removed.

To create the puzzle piece, you will use the Union command to combine the square and one of the circles. Then you will use the Subtract command to create the indented part of the puzzle piece.

## To merge the shapes:

1. Click the square shape, and then click the **Shape Format** tab. In the Insert Shapes group, the Merge Shapes button is gray and unavailable. At least two shapes need to be selected to use the commands on the Merge Shapes menu.

2. Press and hold **SHIFT**, click the circle shape at the top of the square, and then release **SHIFT**. The square and the top circle shape are now selected. In the Insert Shapes group, the Merge Shapes button is now available. Because you selected the square first, when you use the Union command, the merged shape will be filled with the fill color of the square.

3. In the Insert Shapes group, click the **Merge Shapes** button, and then click **Union**. The two shapes are merged into a new shape formatted the same blue color as the square shape. The merged shape is selected.

4. Press and hold **SHIFT**, click the circle shape on the right side of the square, and then release **SHIFT**. Because you selected the merged, blue shape first, the circle shape will be subtracted from the blue shape when you use the Subtract command.

5. In the Insert Shapes group, click the **Merge Shapes** button, and then click **Subtract**. The entire orange circle is removed and the part that had overlapped the blue merged shape was removed from the blue shape. See Figure 3–32.

**Figure 3–32**    **Merged shape**

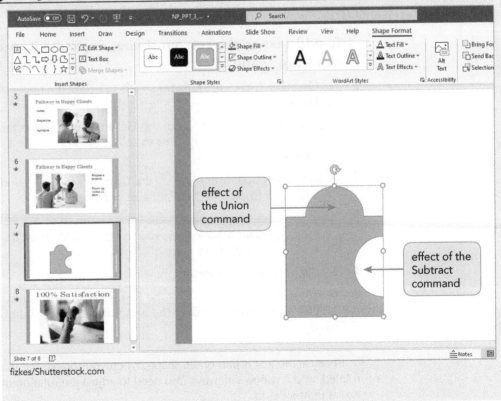

fizkes/Shutterstock.com

Now that the puzzle piece is created, Kavita wants you to save it as a picture so that she can reuse it in the future. You'll do that now.

### To save the custom shape as a picture:

**1.** Right-click the puzzle piece shape. A shortcut menu opens.

**2.** On the shortcut menu, click **Save as Picture**. The Save as Picture dialog box opens. It is very similar to the Save As dialog box you use when you save a presentation with a new name. In the Save as type box, PNG Portable Network Graphics Format is selected. This is one of the file types that pictures are saved as. The temporary file name is selected in the File name box.

**3.** Type **NP_PPT_3_Puzzle**, navigate to the location where you are saving your files, and then click **Save**. The dialog box closes, and the puzzle shape is saved as a picture in a file.

# Rotating Shapes with Text

You already know that when you rotate a shape that contains text, the text rotates with the shape. There are times when you need to adjust the rotation of the text so that it appears right-side up even after the shape is rotated.

Kavita wants you to add text to the puzzle shape, duplicate the shape so that there are four puzzle piece shapes, and then arrange them so it looks like you put the puzzle together. When you are finished with this slide, there will be four puzzle pieces and each piece will have different text on it.

First, you will add text to the first shape, duplicate the shape, and then rotate it so it is in the correct position to "attach" the original puzzle piece.

### To add text to the custom shape, duplicate it, and rotate the duplicate shape:

**1.** On Slide 7, click the custom shape to select it if necessary, and then type **Listen**.

**2.** Move the pointer on top of the **Listen** shape so that the pointer changes to the move pointer ✛, click to select the entire shape, and then click the **Home** tab.

**3.** In the Clipboard group, click the **Copy arrow** 🗐 ˅, and then click **Duplicate**. You need to edit the text in the duplicated shape.

**4.** In the duplicate shape, double-click **Listen** to select the entire word, and then type **Empathize**. Now you need to rotate the duplicated shape so that it will fit on top of the original shape.

**5.** Click the **Shape Format** tab.

**6.** In the Arrange group, click the **Rotate** button, and then click **Rotate Right 90°**. The shape, including the text, rotates to the right by 90 degrees.

Because the text is part of the shape, when you rotated the shape, the text also rotated, and it is now sideways. You need to adjust the rotation of the text so that the text is right-side-up.

## To adjust the rotation of the text in the rotated shape:

1. On the Shape Format tab, in the Arrange group, click the **Rotate** button, and then click **More Rotation Options**. The Format Shape pane opens with the Shape Options tab selected, the Size & Properties button selected, and the Size section expanded. In the Rotation box, 90° appears. See Figure 3–33. This is because the shape was already rotated once.

| Figure 3–33 | Empathize shape rotated right 90 degrees |
| --- | --- |

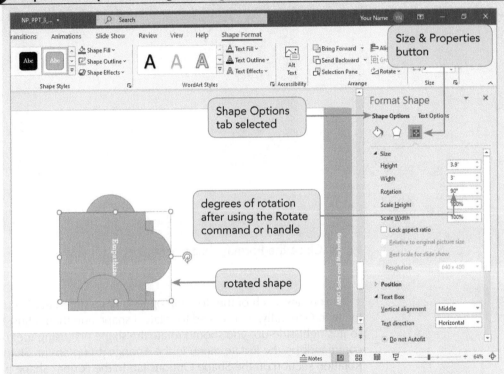

2. In the Format Shape pane, click the **Text Options** tab, click the **Text Effects** button [A], and then click **3-D Rotation** to expand that section, if necessary.

3. To the right of Z Rotation, click the **Counter-clockwise** button [C]. The text in the Empathize shape rotates five degrees in a counter-clockwise direction. In the Format Shape pane, the number in the Z Rotation box changes to 5°. You need to rotate the text by 90 degrees.

4. In the Z Rotation box, click after 5°, press **BACKSPACE** twice, and then type **90**. The text rotates 90 degrees in a counter-clockwise direction and is now right-side up.

5. Drag the **Empathize** shape above the "Listen" shape, and then place it so that the two puzzle pieces fit together, using the smart guides to ensure that the shapes are exactly aligned with one another. See Figure 3–34.

**Figure 3–34**    Empathize shape positioned to fit in the puzzle

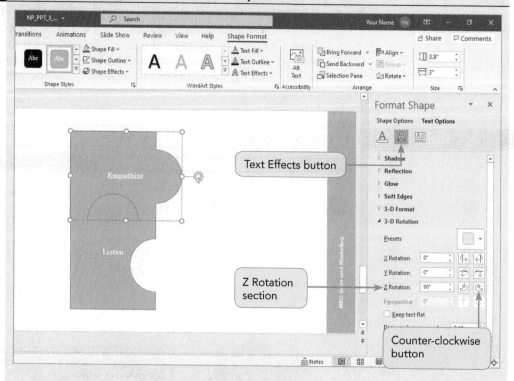

▶ **6.** Close the Format Shape pane.

As you saw, each of the Rotation options has a different effect on the shape and the text. Generally, if you need to rotate a shape and then adjust the text in the shape so it is right-side-up, you should rotate the shape first using the rotate handle ⟳ , the commands on the Rotate menu in the Arrange group on the Shape Format tab, or the Rotation section on the Shape Options tab in the Format Shape pane when the Size & Properties button ▦ is selected. Then, you can rotate the text using the Z Rotation command on the Text Options tab in the Format Shape pane when the Text Effects Ⓐ button is selected.

Although this method works, editing and formatting the text in the shapes is going to get more difficult because when you are editing, the text flips back to its original rotation. Instead, you can create text boxes to contain the text for each shape. You will remove the text from the two puzzle pieces on the slide and add text boxes instead. Then, you will create the other two missing puzzle pieces.

### To delete the text in the shapes and add text boxes:

▶ **1.** Click **Empathize**. The text rotates to its original position.

▶ **2.** Double-click **Empathize** to select the entire word, and then press **DELETE**.

▶ **3.** Double-click **Listen**, and then press **DELETE**. Now you will add text boxes to label the two puzzle pieces.

▶ **4.** Click the **Insert** tab.

▶ **5.** In the **Text** group, click the **Text Box** button, and then click a blank area of the slide. A text box is inserted.

6. Type **Listen**. As you type, the width of the text box expands to accommodate the text you type. This is because the Wrap Text option is not selected when you click (instead of drag) to insert a text box.

7. Drag the **Listen** text box on top of the bottom puzzle piece so it is approximately centered in the piece.

8. Insert another text box without wrapping the text, type **Empathize**, and then drag the **Empathize** text box onto the top puzzle piece so it is approximately centered in the shape. Now you need to create the final two puzzle pieces.

9. Duplicate the **Empathize** puzzle piece, rotate the duplicate shape, rotate it to the right by 90 degrees, and then position the duplicate shape to the right of the Empathize shape.

10. Duplicate the **Listen** shape, rotate the duplicate shape to the left by 90 degrees, and then position the duplicate shape to the right of the Listen shape.

11. Create a text box that does not wrap, type **Apologize**, and then position the **Apologize** text box so it is approximately centered on the shape to the right of the Empathize shape.

12. Create one more text box that does not wrap, type **Solve**, and then position the **Solve** text box so it is approximately centered on the shape to the right of the Listen shape.

Next you need to adjust the formatting of the text in the puzzle pieces. You will change the color and font size of the text.

### To format and reposition the text boxes:

1. Click **Empathize**, press and hold **SHIFT**, click each of the other three text boxes, and then release **SHIFT**. The four text boxes are selected.

2. Click the **Home** tab if necessary, and then in the Font group, click the **Increase Font Size** button four times. The text in all of the shapes changes to 32 points.

3. In the Font group, click the **Font Color arrow**, and then click the **White, Background 1** color. All of the text changes to white. Now you need to reposition the shapes.

4. Click a blank area of the slide to deselect all of the text boxes, and then position the **Empathize** text box so that its right edge aligns with the straight edge on the right side of the shape and so its middle aligns with the middle of the shape.

5. Drag the **Apologize** text box so it aligns horizontally with the Empathize text box and just fits between the sides of the piece.

6. Position the **Listen** text box so its left edge aligns with the left edge of the Empathize text box and its middle aligns with the middle of the shape.

7. Position the **Solve** text box so it horizontally aligns with the Listen text box and its left edge aligns with the left edge of the Apologize text box. Compare your screen to Figure 3–35.

**Figure 3–35**    **Final puzzle pieces**

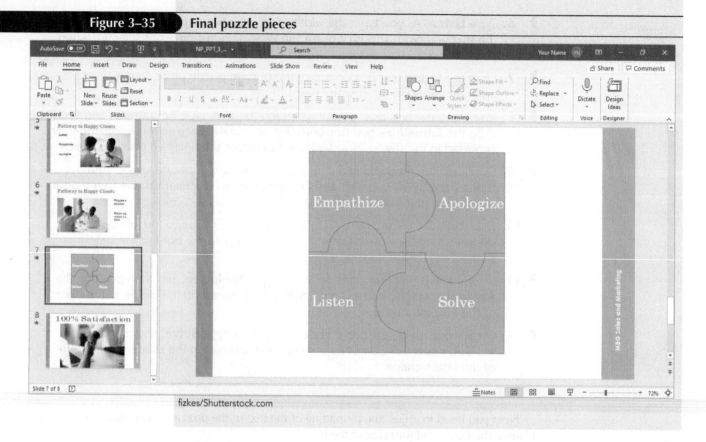

fizkes/Shutterstock.com

Now that the puzzle pieces are created, you need to use the Morph transition so that it looks like the pieces appear on the screen during the slide show and fit together. The first thing you need to do is group each shape and its text box. Then you need to copy the pieces and place the copies on Slide 6.

### To copy the puzzle pieces, place them around Slide 6, and apply the Morph transition:

1. Click **Listen**, press and hold **SHIFT**, click the **Listen** shape, and then release **SHIFT**.

2. On the Home tab, in the Drawing group, click the **Arrange** button, and then click **Group**. The Listen text box and the shape it is on are grouped into one object.

3. Group each of the remaining text boxes and their shapes so that there are four grouped objects.

4. Select the four puzzle pieces, and then on the Home tab, in the Clipboard group, click the **Copy** button ⌧. The four shapes are copied to the Clipboard.

5. Display Slide 6 (the second "Pathway to Happy Clients" slide), and then in the Clipboard group, click the **Paste** button. The four shapes are pasted on top of the Slide 6 content.

6. On the status bar, click the **Zoom Out** button ⊟ as many times as needed to change the zoom percentage to 40%.

**7.** Click a blank area of the slide to deselect the shapes, and then drag each of the puzzle pieces off the slide and position them so they are off the slide near each corner of the slide. See Figure 3–36.

**Figure 3–36**   Copies of the puzzle pieces placed next to Slide 6

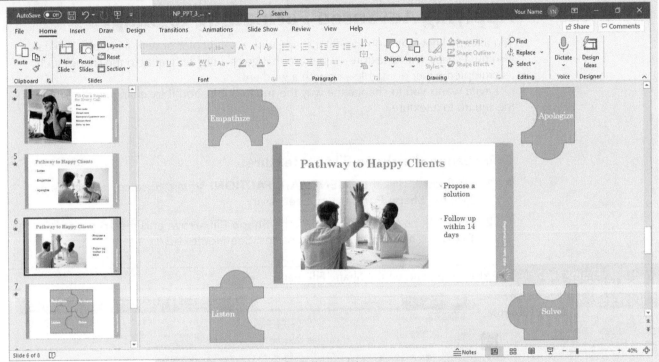

Jacob Lund/Shutterstock.com; fizkes/Shutterstock.com

**8.** On the status bar, click the **Fit slide to current window** button 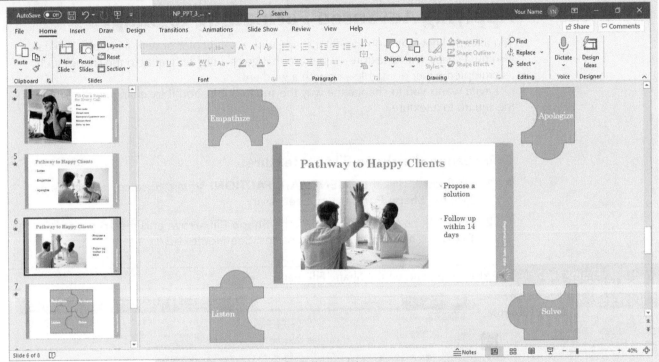, display Slide 7, and then apply the **Morph** transition to Slide 7. Now the puzzle pieces will move onto the screen when you display Slide 7 during the slide show.

Finally, Kavita wants the puzzle pieces to appear to change to a solid square that contains the text "Client Satisfaction!" You will create the shape for that next.

**To draw a square on top of the puzzle pieces:**

**1.** With Slide 7 (the slide containing the four puzzle pieces) displayed, click the **Insert** tab, in the Illustrations group, click the **Shapes** button, click the **Rectangle** shape, and then click anywhere on Slide 7. A one-inch square is added to the slide and the Shape Format tab is selected.

**2.** In the Size group, click in the **Shape Height** box, type **6**, click in the **Shape Width** box, type **6**, and then press **ENTER**. The shape you added is now six inches square.

**3.** Drag the shape you added directly on top of the four puzzle pieces, using the smart guides to align it.

**Tip**

To precisely position an object, select it. On the Shape or Picture Format tab, click the Dialog Box Launcher in the Size group to open the Format Shape or Format Picture pane with the Size & Properties button selected, and then adjust the values in the Position section.

▶  **4.** Type **CLIENT SATISFACTION!** in the square, change the font size of this
text to **32** points, and then change the color of the text to **Gray, Accent 6,
Darker 50%**.

▶  **5.** Save the changes to the presentation.

# Applying Advanced Formatting to Shapes

You already know that you can fill a shape with a solid color or with a picture. You can
also fill a shape with a texture—a pattern that gives a tactile quality to the shape, such
as crumpled paper or marble—or with a gradient.

Kavita wants you to change the way the square looks. You'll try changing the fill of
the square to a texture.

### To change the shape fill to a texture:

▶  **1.** On Slide 7, click the **CLIENT SATISFACTION!** square to select it, and then
click the **Shape Format** tab if necessary.

▶  **2.** In the Shape Styles group, click the **Shape Fill arrow**, and then point to
**Texture**. The Texture submenu opens. See Figure 3–37.

**Figure 3–37**    Texture submenu on the Shape Fill menu

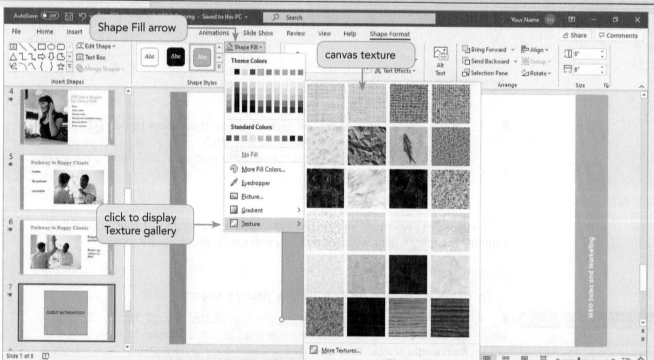

Jacob Lund/Shutterstock.com; fizkes/Shutterstock.com

▶  **3.** Click the **Canvas** texture (the second texture in the first row). The custom
shape is filled with a texture resembling canvas.

The texture did not achieve the effect Kavita wanted for the shape. She asks you to simulate the look of metal or silver. To create this effect, you will use a gradient. You can apply gradients on the Shape Fill menu that use shades of the Accent 1 color in the theme color palette. You can also create a custom gradient using the options in the Format Shape pane. To create a custom gradient, you select a gradient stop, which is a position in the shape at which point the color changes. Then you can change the color and the position in the shape where the color will change. You can also change the direction of the gradient in the shape. If you need to add or remove gradient stops, you can click the Add gradient stop button or the Remove gradient stop button in the Format Shape pane. Refer to the Session 3.2 Visual Overview for more information about using the Format Shape pane to create a custom gradient.

## Reference

### Creating a Custom Gradient in a Shape

- Select the shape.
- Click the Shape Format tab.
- In the Shape Styles group, click the Shape Fill arrow, point to Gradient, and then click More Gradients to open the Format Shape pane with the Fill & Line button selected and the Fill section expanded.
- In the Format Shape pane, click the Gradient fill option button.
- To change the position of a gradient stop, click a tab on the Gradient stops slider, and then drag it to the desired position on the slider or change the value in the Position box.
- To change the color of a gradient stop, select the tab on the Gradient stops slider, click the Color button, and then select a color.
- To add a new gradient stop, click the Add gradient stop button; to remove a gradient stop, click it, and then click the Remove gradient stop button.
- Click the Type arrow, and then click the type of gradient you want to use.
- Click the Direction button, and then click the direction of the gradient.

You will change the fill of the square to a custom gradient. You could remove the texture by clicking No Fill on the Shape Fill menu, but there is no need because you will replace the texture fill with the gradient.

### To create a custom gradient fill for the square:

1. On the Shape Format tab, in the Shape Styles group, click the **Shape Fill arrow**, and then point to **Gradient**. The gradients on the submenu that appears use shades of the Ice Blue, Accent 1 color.

2. In the Dark Variations section, click the **From Center** gradient. The shape fill is changed to a gradient of blues. To create a custom gradient, you need to open the Format Shape pane.

3. In the Shape Styles group, click the **Shape Fill arrow**, point to **Gradient**, and then click **More Gradients**. The Format Shape pane opens with the Fill & Line button [⬧] selected on the Shape Options tab and with the Fill section expanded. In the Fill section, the Gradient fill option button is selected because the shape is currently filled with a gradient. Under Gradient stops, the first tab on the slider is selected, and its value in the Position box is 0%. You will change the position and color of the second tab on the slider.

4. On the Gradient stops slider, click the **Stop 1 of 3** tab (the first tab), and then click the **Color** button. The color palette opens.

5. Click the **Gray, Accent 6** color.

6. On the Gradient stops slider, drag the **Stop 2 of 3** tab to the left until the value in the Position box is 40%.

   **Trouble?** If you can't position the slider exactly, click the Stop 2 of 3 tab, type 40 in the Position box, and then press ENTER.

7. With the Stop 2 of 3 tab selected, click the **Color** button, and then click the **White, Background 1, Darker 5%** color.

8. Click the **Stop 3 of 3** tab, click the **Color** button, and then click the **Gray, Accent 6, Lighter 60%** color.

9. To the right of the slider, click the **Add gradient stop** button 🔲. A new tab stop is added to the slider in the third position and is selected.

10. Change the color of the **Stop 3 of 4** tab to **White, Background 1, Darker 35%**. Next you will change the gradient type. Above the Gradient stops slider, in the Type box, Radial is selected. This means that the shading varies from the center out in a circle towards the edges. You will change the type to Linear so that the gradient will change linearly—that is, top to bottom, side to side, or diagonally.

11. Click the **Type** arrow, and then click **Linear**. Next you will change the direction of the gradient.

12. Click the **Direction** button. A gallery of gradient options opens.

13. Click the **Linear Diagonal – Top Right to Bottom Left** direction. The shading in the shape changes so it varies diagonally from the top-right corner to the bottom-left corner. Finally, Kavita wants this shape to look slightly three-dimensional, so you will apply a bevel effect. You could use the Shape Effects button on the Shape Format tab, but you will use a command in the Format Shape pane instead.

14. In the Format Shape pane, click the **Effects** button 🔲, and then click **3-D Format**, if necessary, to expand that section.

15. Click the **Top bevel** button, and then click the **Angle** bevel (first bevel in the second row in the Bevel section). The bevel effect is applied. Compare your screen to Figure 3–38.

**Figure 3–38** Shape with modified gradient fill and bevel

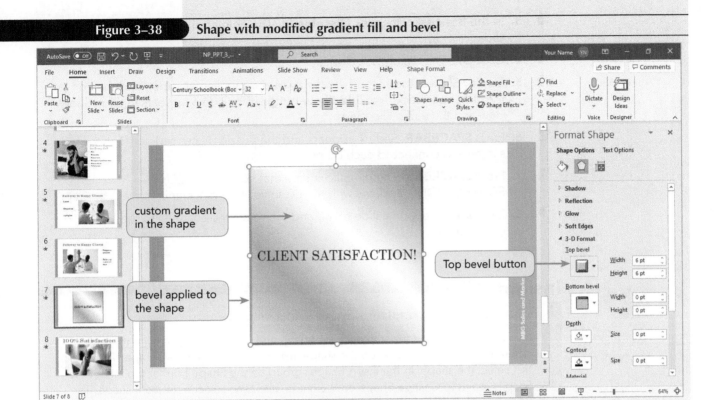

Jacob Lund/Shutterstock.com; fizkes/Shutterstock.com

▶ **16.** Close the Format Shape pane.

Now you will apply an entrance animation to the shape with the gradient fill on Slide 7. Then you will examine Slides 6 and 7 in Slide Show view.

### To animate the shape filled with a gradient:

▶ **1.** Click the Animations tab, and then in the Animation group, click the **More** button ⊽.

▶ **2.** At the bottom of the gallery, click **More Entrance Effects**. The Change Entrance Effects dialog box opens. See Figure 3–39.

**Figure 3–39** Change Entrance Effect dialog box

▶ **3.** In the Basic section, click **Dissolve In**. The animation previews on the slide.

▶ **4.** Click **OK**. The dialog box closes.

▶ **5.** Display Slide 6 (the second "Pathway to Happy Clients" slide), and then on the status bar, click the **Slide Show** button 🖵. Slide 6 appears in Slide Show view and the audio clip plays.

▶ **6.** Press **SPACEBAR**. Slide 7 appears and the puzzle pieces slide onto the screen and connect to each other.

▶ **7.** Press **SPACEBAR**. The metallic square that contains "CLIENT SATISFACTION!" appears with the Dissolve In entrance animation.

▶ **8.** Press **ESC** to end the slide show, and then save the changes to the presentation.

## Insight

### Changing and Formatting Shapes and Pictures

If you insert a shape, format it, and position it, and then decide you want to use a different shape you can change the shape instead of creating a new shape. To do this, first select the shape. In the Insert Shapes group on the Shape Format tab, click Edit Shapes, point to Change Shape on the menu, and then select a different shape. The new shape will replace the existing shape, but the formatting you applied and the shape's position will be the same. Likewise, you can change a picture that you have resized and repositioned. To change a picture, right-click it, point to Change Picture on the shortcut menu, and then click a command on the submenu to replace the picture with one stored in a file on your computer or network, a picture you find online, or an object stored on the Clipboard. You can also change a picture to an icon (also called a scalable vector graphic).

# Making Presentations Accessible

People with physical impairments or disabilities use assistive technology to help them when using computers. For example, people who cannot use their arms or hands can use foot, head, or eye movements to control the pointer. One of the most common assistive technologies is the screen reader. The screen reader identifies objects on the screen and produces an audio of the text in the objects or alt text describing the objects for those with visual impairments.

Graphics and tables cause problems for users of screen readers unless they have alt text. When a screen reader encounters an object that has alt text, it announces that an object is on the slide, and then it reads the alt text. You already know how to add alt text to pictures. Other types of graphics, such as shapes, SmartArt graphics, and charts need alt text as well. You can add alt text to shapes or a SmartArt graphic by clicking the Alt Text button in the Accessibility group on the Format tab for shapes or SmartArt.

After she gives her presentation orally to her team, Kavita plans to post the PowerPoint file on the company server so that others can read it. She asks you to add missing alt text and fix, or at least identify, other issues that might cause accessibility issues. You will use the Accessibility Checker to do this.

## Checking for Accessibility Issues

The Accessibility Checker identifies possible problems on slides that might prevent a presentation from being completely accessible. The Accessibility Checker classifies potential problems into three categories—errors, warnings, and tips. Content flagged as an error is content that people with disabilities cannot access at all or only with great difficulty. Content flagged with a warning is content that is difficult for many people with disabilities to access. Content flagged with a tip isn't necessarily impossible for people with disabilities to access, but the content could possibly be reorganized in a way that would make it easier to access.

You will use the Accessibility Checker to see what adjustments you should consider to make the presentation accessible.

**To use the Accessibility Checker:**

▶ 1. Display Slide 1 (the title slide), click the **Review** tab, and then in the Accessibility group, click the **Check Accessibility** button. The Accessibility pane opens. See Figure 3–40. At the top of the pane is the list of Inspection Results. At the bottom is the Additional Information section where details about the issues in the Inspection Results list will appear.

| Figure 3–40 | Accessibility pane listing potential issues |
| --- | --- |

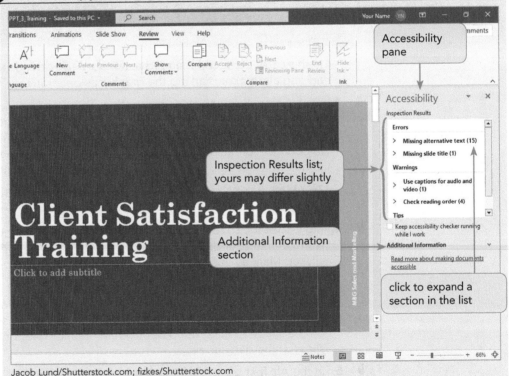

Jacob Lund/Shutterstock.com; fizkes/Shutterstock.com

The Errors section is the first section listed, and the first type of error is "Missing alternative text".

▶ 2. In the Errors section, click **Missing alternative text** to expand the issue, click **Content Placeholder 6**, and then click the **arrow** ☑. Slide 2 ("Client Satisfaction Scores") appears, and in the Accessibility pane, a menu listing Recommended Actions and Other Suggestions opens. At the bottom of the pane, the Additional Information section changes to describe the selected problem. See Figure 3–41. Note that the numbers after the word "Group" might be different on your screen.

**Figure 3–41** **Menu listing recommended actions for missing alt text**

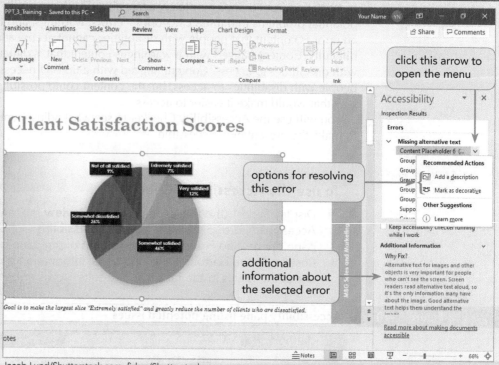

Jacob Lund/Shutterstock.com; fizkes/Shutterstock.com

In this case, the recommended actions are to add a description (which is adding alt text) or marking the graphic as decorative.

3. On the menu, click **Mark as decorative**. The chart is marked as decorative—that is, an object that does not need alt text—and Content Placeholder 6 is removed from the list in the Accessibility pane. However, because the chart conveys important information, Kavita wants you to add alt text to the chart. You could undo the last action, or you can just open the Alt Text pane for the chart.

   **Trouble?** If the Notes pane opens, click the Notes button on the status bar to close it.

4. Right-click the shaded background of the chart area, and then on the shortcut menu, click **Edit Alt Text**. The Alt Text pane opens. Because you clicked Mark as decorative on the menu in the Accessibility pane, the Mark as decorative check box is selected.

   **Trouble?** If the Edit Alt Text command is not on the shortcut menu, click anywhere on the slide, and then repeat Step 4 making sure you right-click on the shaded background of the chart area, but not on any of the pie chart slices or the data labels.

5. In the Alt Text pane, click the **Mark as decorative** check box to deselect it, click in the white box, and then type **Pie chart showing that almost half of MBG's clients are only somewhat satisfied, 26% are somewhat dissatisfied, and only 7% are extremely satisfied.** (including the period). It is difficult to create alt text that adequately describes charts. The description you typed isn't perfect, but it conveys Kavita's biggest concerns, and will be more meaningful than a recitation of the chart data.

   In the Accessibility pane, the next five items listed as missing alt text are all on Slide 3.

6. Close the Alt Text pane, and then, in the Accessibility pane, click **Group X (Slide 3)** (where "X" is the number after the word "Group"). Slide 3 ("Handling Client Complaints") is displayed. The Follow Up grouped object on the slide is selected. Each of the five grouped objects on the slide are graphics that need alt text. Kavita decides that she will keep Slide 3 as is for her presentation to her team, but before she posts the presentation on the company server, she will recreate the SmartArt graphic and add alt text to it by clicking the Alt Text button in the Accessibility group on the Format tab.

   The next item in the "Missing alternative text" section is the audio file on Slide 6.

7. In the Accessibility pane, click **Support_PPT_3_Comment**, click the **arrow** ⌄ that appears, and then click **Add a description**. Slide 6 is displayed, the speaker icon is selected, and the Alt Text pane opens.

8. In the Alt Text pane, click in the white box, type **Audio object for audio that will play during the slide show.**, and then close the Alt Text pane. This alt text describes the object on the slide. The next four items listed as missing alt text are on Slide 6, and the last four items listed as missing alt text are on Slide 7.

9. In the Accessibility pane, click the first object on Slide 6. Slide 6 appears.

10. Click to the left of the scroll box in the horizontal scroll bar. The slide scrolls right and the Listen grouped shape and text box is selected. The four grouped shapes on Slide 6 can be marked as decorative.

11. In the Accessibility pane, click the **arrow** ⌄ next to the first object on Slide 6, click **Mark as Decorative**, and then mark the other three items on Slide 6 as decorative also. The next four items on Slide 7 are the grouped puzzle piece shapes on that slide. Kavita will add alt text for these shapes before she posts the file. The next issue listed is in the Errors section. It identifies a missing slide title on Slide 7.

12. In the Accessibility pane, scroll down, click **Missing slide** title to expand that issue, and then click **Slide 7**. Slide 7 is displayed in Outline view. Like the graphic on Slide 3, Kavita will leave this slide as is (without a title) for her presentation, but she will modify it by adding a slide title before she posts the presentation on the company server.

**Tip**

To add closed captions to a video object, click the Insert Captions button in the Caption Options group on the Playback tab for video or audio, locate the WebVTT file containing the captions, select it, and then click Insert.

13. In the Accessibility pane, scroll the list of Inspection Results down until the Warnings section is at the top. At the top of the Warnings list, click the first warning about audio and video using closed captions to display the audio clip on Slide 6 again. Kavita will create captions for the audio clip using another app, and then she will add them to the audio object.

14. Scroll the list of Inspection Results to the Tips section, click **Duplicate slide title**, scroll down again, and then click **Pathway to Happy Clients**. Slide 6 appears. This Tip tells you that this slide title is the same as another slide title in the presentation. The title of Slide 5 is also "Pathway to Happy Clients". Kavita wants you to change the titles of Slides 5 and 6.

15. On Slide 6, change the title text to **Become Happy Clients**.

16. Switch to Normal view, display Slide 5, delete the title text, and then type **Unhappy Clients...** in the title text placeholder. The Tip section disappears from the list of Inspection Results in the Accessibility pane.

You skipped the "Check reading order" list in the Warning section in the Accessibility pane. You will examine this issue next.

## Checking the Order Objects Will Be Read by a Screen Reader

When a person uses a screen reader to access a presentation, the screen reader selects and describes the elements on the slides in the order they were added. In PowerPoint, most screen readers first explain that a slide is displayed. After the user signals to the screen reader that the user is ready for the next piece of information (for example, by pressing the Tab key), the reader identifies the first object on the slide. For most slides, this is the title text box. The second object is usually the content placeholder on the slide.

To check the order in which a screen reader will describe objects on a slide, you can press TAB or open the Reading Order. You'll start by opening the Reading Order pane using the Accessibility Checker. You can also use the Selection pane by clicking the Select button in the Editing group on the Home tab, and then clicking Selection Pane, or by clicking the Selection Pane button in the Arrange group on the Shape or Picture Format tab.

If an object is listed in the wrong order in the Reading Order pane—for example, if the content placeholder was identified first and the title second—you could change this in the Reading Order pane. To do this, click the object you want to move, and then at the top of the pane, click the Move Up or Move Down buttons at the top of the Selection pane to move the selected object up or down in the list.

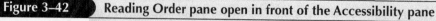

### To identify the order of objects on slides:

1. In the Accessibility pane, click **Check reading order** to display a list of errors in that section, click **Slide 5**, and then click the arrow ⌄ that appears. The only option on the menu to address the problem is "Verify object order."

2. On the menu, click **Verify object order**. The Reading Order pane opens. See Figure 3–42. In the Reading Order pane, the first object added to the slide appears at the top of the list, and the last object added appears at the bottom of the list. (The blue bar on the right side of the slide and the gray bar on the left side of the slide aren't listed in the Reading Order pane because they are part of the slide background.)

**Figure 3–42**   Reading Order pane open in front of the Accessibility pane

Jacob Lund/Shutterstock.com; fizkes/Shutterstock.com

3. Click a blank area of the slide, and then press **TAB**. On the slide, the title text box is selected. In the Reading Order pane, Title 1 is selected at the top of the list.

4. Press **TAB** three more times. On the slide, the content placeholder with the picture is selected, then the content placeholder with the bulleted list, and finally, the footer on the right. In the Reading Order pane, the items in the list are selected when they are selected on the slide. The reading order of objects on Slide 5 is correct. Slide 7 is the next slide listed in the "Check reading order" section of the Accessibility pane.

5. Display Slide 7 (the untitled slide with the "Client Satisfaction" shape). In the Reading Order pane, **Footer Placeholder 1** is listed first, but it was listed last on Slide 5. It would be best if the footer placeholder was consistently placed in the same position on each slide, so Kavita wants you to make it the last object selected. Click Footer Placeholder 1, and then at the top of the pane, click the **Move Down** button ⌄ five times. The Footer Placeholder 1 object moves down the list in the Reading Order pane, and the footer will now be read last on the slide.

6. Display Slide 8 ("100% Satisfaction"), the next slide listed in the "Check reading order" section of the Accessibility pane. The order of objects on Slide 8 is correct, except Footer Placeholder 2 is in the middle of the list in the Reading Order pane. Click **Footer Placeholder 2**, and then at the top of the pane, click the **Move Down** button ⌄. The Footer Placeholder 2 object moves to the end of the list. Although Slides 2, 3, 4, and 6 may not be listed in the Check reading order section of the Accessibility pane, you should check the reading order on these slides as well.

7. Display Slide 2 ("Client Satisfaction Scores"). Move Footer Placeholder 3 to the bottom of the list in the Reading Order pane.

8. Display Slide 3 ("Handling Client Complaints"), examine the order of the objects in the Reading Order pane, display Slide 4 ("Fill Out a Report for Every Call"), and then examine the order of the objects in the Reading Order pane. On both slides, the footer placeholder appears at the bottom of the list in the Reading Order pane.

9. Display Slide 6 ("Become Happy Clients"). Footer Placeholder 2 appears in the middle of the list in the Reading Order pane.

10. In the Reading Order pane, click **Footer Placeholder 2**, and then at the top of the pane, click the **Move Down** button ⌄ to move it below the Support_PPT_3_Comment audio object. You don't need to move it below the grouped objects because they are marked as decorative.

11. To the right of the Reading Order pane, click the **Accessibility** button ▯ to redisplay the Accessibility pane if necessary. Close the Accessibility pane, and then, if the Notes pane is open below the slide, click the Notes button on the status bar to close it.

You have addressed all of the issues listed in the Accessibility pane. There is one issue that was not flagged by the Accessibility Checker. On Slide 8, you duplicated the picture before you removed the background from the duplicate. This means the alt text was copied. You should edit the alt text so that one of the images is marked as decorative.

**To rename objects in the Reading Order pane and mark an object as decorative:**

1. Display Slide 8 ("100% Satisfaction"), then in the Reading Order pane, click **Picture 3**, and then click **Picture 4**. On the slide, a selection box appears around the pictures, but you can't tell which picture is Picture 3 and which one is Picture 4.

2. On the slide, click the picture, and then drag it to the left about one inch. The picture you dragged is the version of the picture with the background removed. In the Reading Order pane, Picture 4 is selected. To avoid confusion in the future, you will rename these objects in the Selection pane.

3. In the Reading Order pane, click **Picture 4**. Because it was already selected, it changes to a text box displaying a description of the picture.

4. Press **DELETE** as many times as needed to delete all of the text, type **Picture with background removed**, and then press **ENTER**.

5. In the Reading Order pane, click **Picture 3**, click it again to display a text box with a description of the picture, delete all of the text, type **Picture with artistic effect**, and then press **ENTER**.

6. On the slide, drag the picture with the background removed back on top of the other picture. Now that you know which picture is which, you will mark the picture with the artistic effect applied as decorative.

7. In the Reading Order pane, click **Picture 3: Picture with artistic effect**, click the **Picture Format** tab, and then in the Accessibility group, click the **Alt Text** button. The Alt Text pane opens.

8. In the Alt Text pane, click the **Mark as decorative** check box to select it.

9. Close the Alt Text pane, and then close the Reading Order pane.

10. **sam** ⬆ Display Slide 1 (the title slide), add your name as the subtitle, and then save and close the presentation.

You have created and saved a custom shape and used advanced formatting techniques for shapes and photos in the presentation. You also checked the presentation for accessibility and corrected the issues that Kavita wanted you to correct.

# Review

## Session 3.2 Quick Check

1. What happens when you use the Remove Background command?

2. What are artistic effects?

3. What happens when you merge shapes?

4. When you create a custom gradient, how do you change the colors used?

5. What feature can you use to check a file for accessibility issues?

6. What is the Reading Order pane?

# Practice

## Review Assignments

**Data Files needed for the Review Assignments: NP_PPT_3-2.pptx, Support_PPT_3_Compliment.mp3, Support_PPT_3_FollowUp.jpg, Support_PPT_3_Form.jpg, Support_PPT_3_Respect.jpg**

Three months after Kavita Goyal, a client operations manager for MBG Sales and Marketing, created a new training program for her customer service team, the percentage of clients who are extremely or very satisfied has increased and the percentage of clients who are only somewhat satisfied or who are somewhat dissatisfied has decreased. Kavita is very pleased with her team, although they still have room for improvement. She wants to congratulate them, but also point out some areas where there is still room for improvement. She asks you to help her create a presentation she can use when she meets with her team. Complete the following:

1. Open the presentation **NP_PPT_3-2.pptx**, located in the PowerPoint3 > Review folder included with your Data Files, add your name as the Slide 1 subtitle, and then save it as **NP_PPT_3_FollowUp** to the location where you are storing your files.

2. On Slide 2 ("Improved Client Satisfaction Scores"), add a pie chart. Change the width of column A so that the ScreenTip indicates that column A is 145 pixels wide. In cells A2 through A6, type **Extremely satisfied**, **Very satisfied**, **Somewhat satisfied**, **Somewhat dissatisfied**, and **Not at all satisfied**. In cell B1, type **Number**. In cells B2 through B6, type **5700**, **7668**, **5047**, **3419**, and **2250**.

3. Apply Layout 6 to the chart.

4. Apply Style 6 to the chart.

5. Change the number of clients who are Not at all satisfied to **1650**.

6. Remove the title and the legend from the chart, and then change the position of the data labels to the Data Callout option. Change the font size of the data labels to 16 points, and then format them as bold.

7. On Slide 2, add a text box approximately 2 inches wide and one-half inch high. Type **"Extremely satisfied" increased from 7% to 24% and "Very satisfied" increased from 12% to 33%.** (including the period). Change the format of the text box so the text doesn't wrap and so that the left margin is zero. Format the text in the text box with italics and change the font size to 16 points.

8. Align the left edge of the text box with the left edge of the chart, and align it vertically so that there is the same amount of space between the text box and the bottom of the chart as there is between the top of the chart and the bottom of the title text box.

9. On Slide 3, duplicate the square shape. Change the size of the duplicate square so it is 3 inches high and wide, and then move the duplicate shape to the side of the original shape. Insert an oval shape, and then resize it so it is 1.5 inches high and wide. Position the circle on the top edge of the three-inch square so that its center is aligned with the center of the square and so that its middle is aligned with the top edge of the square.

10. Duplicate the circle. Position the duplicate circle on the right edge of the three-inch square so that its middle is aligned with the middle of the square and its left edge is aligned with the right edge of the circle on the top edge of the square.

11. Create two more identical circles and position them on the bottom and left edges of the three-inch square so they are aligned with the circles on the opposite edge. Make sure the right edge of the circle on the left edge of the three-inch square is aligned with the left edges of the circles on the top and bottom edges of the three-inch square.

12. Use the Union command to merge the two side circles with the three-inch square, and then use the Subtract command to remove the top and bottom circles from the square. Make sure to select the square first each time so that the color of the final shape is the same color as the square. The final shape is shown in Figure 3–43.

Figure 3–43    Custom shape on Slide 3

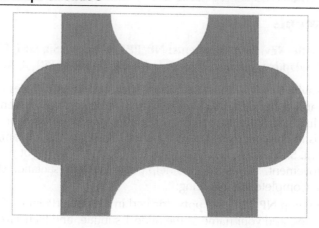

13. On Slide 3, duplicate the merged shape you created, and then place the duplicate on top of the original square in the center of the slide. Make sure it is aligned so that its middle and center are aligned with the middle and the center of the original square. Use the Subtract command to remove the duplicate puzzle piece from the original square.

14. Select the original puzzle piece you created, and then type **YOU!**. Change the font size of this text to 44 points and format it as bold. Move the YOU! puzzle piece above and a little to the left of the slide (zoom out if necessary), and then rotate it to the left about 160 degrees so that 200° appears in the Rotation box in the Size section on the Shape Options tab in the Format Shape pane.

15. Duplicate Slide 3. On the new Slide 4, move the YOU! shape onto the slide, rotate it so the text is right-side up, and then position it on top of the square in the empty space. Apply the Morph transition to Slide 4 and change the speed of this transition to 1.5 seconds.

16. On Slide 4, insert a rectangle shape that is 5 inches high and wide. Position it directly on top of the square with the filled-in puzzle piece. Fill the shape with the From Center gradient in the Dark Variations section on the Shape Fill menu.

17. Customize the gradient in the square by changing the color of the Stop 1 of 3 tab to Gold, Accent 4, Darker 50%. Position the Step 2 of 3 tab at 33% and change its color to Gold, Accent 4, Lighter 40%. Change the color of the Stop 3 of 3 tab to Gold, Accent 4, Lighter 80%. Add a new tab stop at the 66% position and change its color to Gold, Accent 4. Change the Type to Linear, and then change the Direction to Linear Diagonal–Bottom Right to Top Left.

18. Type **Problem Solved!** in the square with the gradient. Change the font size to 40 points and format the text as bold. Apply the Zoom entrance animation to the square with the gradient. (*Hint*: Make sure you apply the animation to the square and not to the text.)

19. On Slide 4, add the audio clip **Support_PPT_3_Compliment.mp3**, located in the PowerPoint3 > Review folder. Hide the icon during the slide show. Position the icon centered below the square so its top edge is aligned with the bottom edge of the vertical Footer text box in the blue bar. Change the order of animations on Slide 4 so that the audio clip plays first.

20. On Slide 5 ("Room for Improvement"), create a SmartArt graphic using the Picture Accent Process layout, which is a Process type graphic. From left to right, replace the first-level placeholder text in the shapes with **Follow up**, **Call sheets**, and **Solve**.

21. Add a new first-level shape as the rightmost shape in the SmartArt graphic, and then replace the placeholder text in it with **Respect**. Move the Respect shape up so it is the second shape in the graphic.

22. Delete the entire Solve shape from the SmartArt graphic.

23. In the Follow Up shape, add **Follow up within two weeks!** as second-level text, and then delete the other second-level item. In the Respect shape, add **Listen respectfully to the client.** as second-level text. In the Call sheets shape, add **Fill out call sheets completely.** as second-level text, and then delete the other second-level item.

24. In the SmartArt graphic, above the Follow Up shape, insert the picture **Support_PPT_3_FollowUp.jpg**, and then increase the brightness of the picture by 10% and increase its contrast by 40%. Above the Respect shape, insert the picture **Support_PPT_3_Respect.jpg**, sharpen it by 50%, and then change its tone by changing the temperature to 5900K. (*Hint*: If you use the Format Picture pane instead of the command on the ribbon to change the temperature, you cannot type the letter "K" in the Temperature box.) Above the Call sheets shape, insert the picture **Support_PPT_3_Form.jpg**, and then decrease its saturation to 66%.

25. Animate the SmartArt graphic with the Wipe entrance animation. Change the effect options to One by One and From Top.

26. Change the style of the SmartArt graphic to the Intense Effect style, and then change the color to the Colored Fill – Accent 2 colors.

27. Convert the SmartArt graphic to shapes. Ungroup the shapes, and then delete the two arrows. Group each picture and its corresponding shape containing text. Apply the Wipe animation to each grouped shape with the From Top effect. Make sure the grouped shapes animate in order from left to right, and that the start setting of each animation is On Click.

28. On Slide 6, format the title as WordArt using the Fill: Green, Accent color 5; Outline: White, Background color 1; Hard Shadow: Green, Accent color 5 style.

29. Change the Text fill color of the WordArt text to Orange, Accent 2, Darker 25%, and then change the font size of the text to 66 points. Apply the Chevron: Down transform effect to the text box.

30. Move the title text box that contains the WordArt down so its bottom is aligned with the bottom of the vertical footer text box in the blue box on the right. Resize the picture on the slide so it is 5 inches high (maintaining the aspect ratio), and then position the picture so it is horizontally centered on the slide and so that its top edge is aligned with the top of the slide.

31. On Slide 6, remove the background of the picture (keep all the people and the monitor on the right). It doesn't need to be perfect. Next, apply the Photocopy artistic effect to the picture.

32. Run the Accessibility Checker.

33. On Slide 2 ("Improved Client Satisfaction Scores"), add the following as alt text for the chart: **Pie chart showing that 24% of MBG's clients are extremely satisfied, 33% are very satisfied, 21% are somewhat satisfied, 15% are somewhat dissatisfied, and only 7% are not at all satisfied.** (including the period).

34. On Slide 4, resolve the duplicate slide title by first changing the title to **YOU!**. Because this title does not need to be seen during the slide show, select the title text box, and then change the text color to White, Background 1.

35. On every slide, the Footer Placeholder object should be the last object selected. Move it to the bottom of the list in the Reading Order pane on each slide if necessary. On Slide 4, select the Rectangle 2 shape and edit the Rectangle 2 shape name in the Reading Order pane to **Problem Solved shape**. (Do not include the period).

36. If necessary, close the Notes pane. View the presentation as a slide show, and then save and close it.

# Apply

## Case Problem 1

Data Files needed for this Case Problem: NP_PPT_3-3.pptx, Support_PPT_Recovery.mp3

**Springfield Hospital** Jake Cohen is the director of the physical therapy clinic at Springfield Hospital in Springfield, Georgia. The clinic has a good reputation because their patients have faster recovery times than average. The staff at the clinic has also consistently received positive reviews from their patients. The board of directors asked Jake to talk about the clinic's success at their next meeting. Jake prepared a PowerPoint presentation and asked you to finish it for him. Complete the following steps:

1. Open the presentation **NP_PPT_3-3.pptx**, located in the PowerPoint3 > Case1 folder included with your Data Files, add your name as the subtitle, and then save the presentation as **NP_PPT_3_Therapy** to the location where you are storing your files.

2. On Slide 2 ("Our Clinic"), add a text box, and type ***American Board of Physical Therapy Specialties** in the text box. Turn off the Wrap text option, change the right margin to 0, and then right-align the text in the text box by clicking the Align Right button in the Paragraph group on the Home tab. Position the text box so that its right edge is aligned with the right edge of the bulleted list text box and its top edge is aligned with the bottom edge of the bulleted list text box.

3. On Slide 3 ("Recovery Time Examples in Weeks"), add a clustered bar chart in the content placeholder. In the spreadsheet, change the width of column A so that the ScreenTip indicates it is 157 pixels wide, and then enter the data shown in Figure 3–44 to create the chart.

**Figure 3–44**    Data for Slide 4

|  | Industry Average | Clinic at Springfield Hospital |
|---|---|---|
| Rotator cuff injuries | 35 | 26 |
| Meniscus tear | 8 | 5 |
| Achilles tendon rupture | 24 | 18 |

4. Drag the small blue box in the lower-right corner of cell D5 up and to the left so that the blue border surrounds cells B2 through C4 and the data in column D and in row 5 is removed from the chart. Close the spreadsheet.

5. Change the style of the chart to Style 7, and then change the colors of the chart to the Colorful Palette 2 palette.

6. Reposition the legend so it is at the top of the chart.

7. Add data labels to the outside end of the bars.

8. Change the font size of the data labels to 16 points and make them bold. Make sure you format the data labels for both the green bars and the red bars.

9. Change the font size of the text in the legend to 14 points, and then change the font size of the labels on the vertical axis to 14 points.

10. Remove the chart title.

11. On Slide 3, insert the audio clip **Support_PPT_3_Recovery.mp3**, located in the PowerPoint3 > Case1 folder. Hide the speaker icon during a slide show and set it to start automatically. Position the speaker icon so it is centered below the slide title and so its bottom edge is aligned with the bottom of the chart.

12. On Slide 4 ("We Love Our Patients"), increase the brightness of the photo by 5% and the contrast by 20%. Sharpen the photo by 25%.

13. On Slide 5 ("Questions?"), change the color saturation of the photo to 66%, and then change its tone to a temperature of 5300K. (*Hint*: If you use the Format Picture pane instead of the command on the ribbon to change the temperature, you cannot type the letter "K" in the Temperature box.)

14. Check the accessibility of the presentation. Add **Audio object for audio that will play during the slide show.** as alt text for the audio icon. Then add **Chart showing that recovery times for certain injuries is faster at our clinic than the industry average.** as alt text for the chart.

15. Check the reading order on all of the slides. Make sure the Title object on each slide is selected first. On Slide 5, move the Text Placeholder so it is selected second.

16. Save and close the presentation.

# Challenge

## Case Problem 2

**Data Files needed for this Case Problem: NP_PPT_3-4.pptx**

**Keystone State Elder Services**  Kelly Lewis is the associate director of the Executive Office of Elder Affairs (EOEA) in Massachusetts. The EOEA contracts with home care agencies across the state to provide services for elderly and disabled people so that they can continue to live at home rather than in a nursing home. Kelly was asked to prepare a presentation to explain how people obtain services. She started creating a PowerPoint presentation and asked you to help complete it by correcting photos and adding SmartArt. She also created a design similar to a logo that she wants you to place on the first and last slides. Complete the following steps:

1. Open the file named **NP_PPT_3-4.pptx**, located in the PowerPoint3 > Case2 folder included with your Data Files, add your name as the subtitle on Slide 1, and then save it as **NP_PPT_3_Elder** to the location where you are storing your files.

2. On Slide 2, duplicate the square shape three times. These are the four squares behind the center square in Figure 3–45. Arrange them as shown in Figure 3–45 so that there is about one-quarter inch of space between each square. Merge the four squares using the Union command.

| Figure 3–45 | Kelly's design |
| --- | --- |

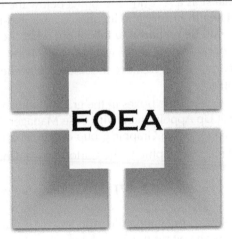

3. Apply the From Center Gradient style in the Dark Variations set of gradient styles to the merged square. Customize this gradient by changing the Stop 2 of 3 tab to the Bright Green, Accent 4, Darker 25% color, and changing its position to 60%. Then change the gradient Type to Rectangular and the direction to From Center.

4. Create a text box, and then type **EOEA** in it.

5. Turn off the Wrap text option in the text box, if necessary.

⊕ **Explore**  6. Turn on the Do not Autofit option in the Format Shape pane.

7. Change the size of the text box to 1.5" square.

8. Change the font to Copperplate Gothic Bold, and change the font size to 32 points.

9. Use the Center button in the Paragraph group on the Home tab to center the text in the box horizontally, and then use the Align Text button in the Paragraph group to center the text vertically in the middle of the text box.

10. Fill the text box shape with the White, Background 1 color.

11. Position the text box so it is centered over the custom shape, using the smart guides to assist you.

12. Group the custom shape and the text box.

13. Save the final grouped shape as a picture named **NP_PPT_3_EOEA** to the location where you are storing your files.

14. Delete Slide 2, and then insert the picture **NP_PPT_3_EOEA.png** on Slide 1 (the title slide). Position it to the left of the title so that its bottom edge is aligned with the top of the subtitle text box and so that there is approximately the same amount of space between the picture and the slide title and the picture and the left side of the slide.

15. On Slide 2 ("Services Provided by Home Care Agencies"), decrease the brightness of the picture by -10% and increase the contrast by 20%. Change the color tone to a temperature of 7200K. (*Hint*: If you use the Format Picture pane instead of the command on the ribbon to change the temperature, you cannot type the letter "K" in the Temperature box.)

16. On Slide 3 ("What Is Case Management?"), sharpen the picture by 25%, and change the color saturation to 66%.

17. On Slide 4 ("How Does a New Client Get Services?"), insert a SmartArt graphic using the Horizontal Bullet List layout (in the List category). Type the following as first-level items in the graphic, adding first-level shapes if needed:

**Schedule Services**

**Set Up Appointment with Case Manager**

**Answer Intake Questions**

**Call Elder Line**

18. Add **Talk to Intake Specialist** as a second-level bullet below the Call Elder Line shape. Add **Answer questions about health history and income** as a second-level bullet below the Answer Intake Questions shape. Add **Be prepared to talk about what the client needs** as a second-level bullet below the Set Up Appointment with Case Manager shape.

19. Delete the Schedule Services shape. Remove the unused placeholder text and second-level bullets in the rest of the shapes.

⊕ **Explore** 20. Reverse the order of the boxes in the graphic so that the Call Elder Line shape is the leftmost shape and the Set Up Appointment with Case Manager shape is the rightmost shape. (*Hint*: Use a command in the Create Graphic group on the SmartArt Design tab.)

21. Change the style of the SmartArt graphic to the Cartoon style. Change the color to Colorful – Accent Colors.

22. On Slide 5 ("Questions?"), insert the **NP_PPT_3_EOEA.png** file you created in the content placeholder on the left.

23. Check the accessibility of the presentation file. Add **SmartArt graphic listing the three steps to take to receive services.** as alt text for the SmartArt graphic. Mark the pictures you inserted on Slides 1 and 5 as decorative. On Slide 3 ("What Is Case Management?"), change the selection order of the objects so that the title is selected first, the bulleted list is selected second, and the picture last.

24. Save and close the presentation.

# Advanced Animations and Distributing Presentations

Creating an Advanced Presentation for Agricultural Development

## OBJECTIVES

**Session 4.1**
- Use guides to place objects
- Add more than one animation to an object
- Set animation triggers
- Change the slide background
- Create and edit links and action buttons
- Create slide zooms
- Hide slides during a slide show

**Session 4.2**
- Create a self-running presentation
- Rehearse slide timings
- Record slide timings and narration
- Set up a presentation for kiosk browsing
- Inspect a presentation for private information
- Save a presentation in other formats

## Case | Pennsylvania Department of Agriculture

Jack Chu works in the Agricultural Commodity Marketing Division in the Pennsylvania Department of Agriculture. Over the past few years, small family-owned farms have contacted his office requesting suggestions and assistance in expanding and extending their cash flow into the fall and early winter seasons. In response, Jack will begin presenting on this topic at agricultural fairs and trade shows across the state. He wants your help in finishing the presentation he has created.

In this module, you will enhance Jack's presentation by adding multiple animations to objects and setting triggers for animations. You'll also add a picture as the slide background, create links, and create a self-running presentation that includes narration. Finally, you'll save the presentation in other formats for distribution.

## Starting Data Files

**PowerPoint4** → **Module**

NP_PPT_4-1.pptx
NP_PPT_4-2.pptx
Support_PPT_4_Light.png
Support_PPT_4_Tractor.png

**Review**

NP_PPT_4-3.pptx
NP_PPT_4-4.pptx
Support_PPT_4_Corn.png

**Case1**

NP_PPT_4-5.pptx
Support_PPT_4_Waves.jpg

**Case2**

NP_PPT_4-6.pptx
Support_PPT_4_Bacteria.png
Support_PPT_4_Isopropanol.3mf

# Session 4.1 Visual Overview:

When multiple animations are applied to an object, select one of the animation sequence icons to display its associated animation in the Animation gallery.

To add a second animation to an object, click the Add Animation button in the Advanced Animation group on the Animations tab.

If the second animation applied to an object is set to With Previous or After Previous, the animation sequence icons are stacked on top of one another.

The motion path is indicated by a dashed line. To modify it, click it, and then drag the green circle that indicates the beginning of the path or the red circle indicating the ending of the path.

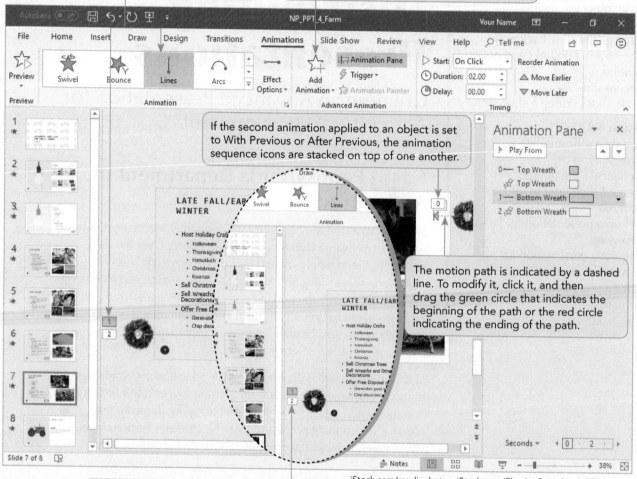

When you add a second animation to an object, a second animation sequence icon appears next to the object.

# Understanding Advanced Animations

When an animation has a trigger, the number in the animation sequence icon is replaced with a lightning bolt. This is because the animation is no longer part of a sequence; it will occur only when the trigger is clicked.

The list of objects on the "On Click of" submenu corresponds to the objects on the slide. You can also see this list of objects in the Selection pane.

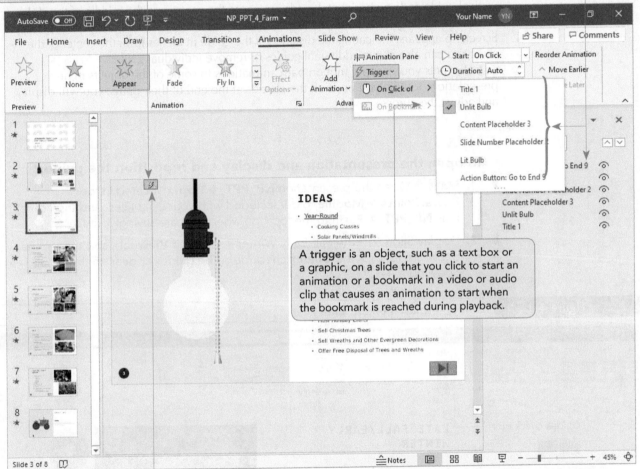

A **trigger** is an object, such as a text box or a graphic, on a slide that you click to start an animation or a bookmark in a video or audio clip that causes an animation to start when the bookmark is reached during playback.

The Play/Pause animation automatically applied to a video when a video is added to a slide is triggered by clicking the video object itself. That is why the animation sequence icon for the Play/Pause animation contains a lightning bolt.

# Using Guides

You are already familiar with three tools that help you align objects as you drag them. Smart guides are the dashed red lines that appear when you drag objects on a slide. Gridlines are evenly spaced horizontal and vertical lines that you can display on slides. You also have used the horizontal and vertical rulers. In addition to these tools, you can use **guides**, which are dashed vertical and horizontal lines you display and position on the slide, to help you precisely position objects. When you first display guides, one vertical guide and one horizontal guide appear in the center and the middle of the slide. To reposition the guides, you drag them to a new location on the slide. As you drag, a ScreenTip appears, indicating the distance of the guide in inches from the center of the slide. You can also create additional guides or remove individual guides.

Jack wants you to apply motion path animations to some of the objects in his presentation. To help you position the objects at the end of their paths, you will display and adjust the guides.

### To open the presentation and display and reposition the guides:

1. **sam** ↓ Open the presentation **NP_PPT_4-1.pptx**, located in the **PowerPoint4 > Module** folder included with your Data Files, and then save it as **NP_PPT_4_Farm** to the location where you are saving your files.

2. Display Slide 6 ("Late Fall/Early Winter"), click the **View** tab, and then in the Show group, click the **Guides** check box. The guides appear on the slide. See Figure 4–1.

**Figure 4–1**  Guides displayed on the slide

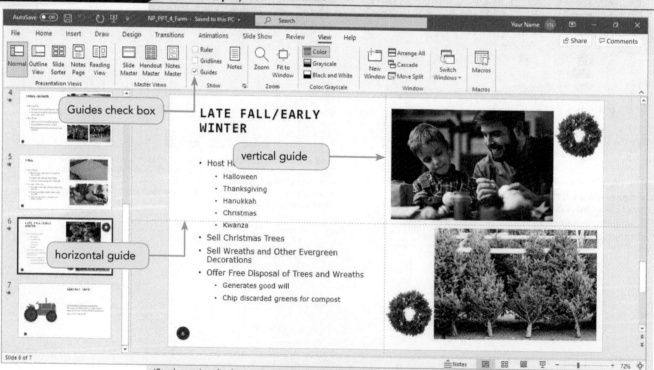

iStock.com/mediaphotos; iStock.com/FlamingPumpkin; ND700/Shutterstock.com; iStock.com/AzmanJaka; Vicki L. Miller/Shutterstock.com; gvictoria/Shutterstock.com; iStock.com/BanksPhotos; Jack Frog/Shutterstock.com; Heather Stokes/Shutterstock.com

3. In a blank area of the slide, position the pointer on top of the horizontal guide so that the pointer changes to the move horizontal guide pointer ⊕, and then press and hold the mouse button. The pointer disappears, and a ScreenTip appears in its place displaying 0.00. This indicates that the horizontal guide is in the middle of the slide.

   **Trouble?** If the pointer doesn't change, you are pointing to the bulleted list text box or a photo. Repeat Step 3, this time positioning the pointer on top of the guide in a blank area of the slide so that the pointer changes to the move horizontal guide pointer.

4. Drag the guide up until the ScreenTip displays 2.71, and then release the mouse button. The horizontal guide now intersects the middle of the wreath at the top of the slide. Next, you will create a second horizontal guide.

5. Position the pointer on top of the horizontal guide so that the pointer changes to the move horizontal guide pointer ⊕, press and hold **CTRL**, press and hold the mouse button, and then start dragging the guide down. A second horizontal guide is created and moves down with the mouse pointer.

6. Continue dragging down past the middle of the slide until the ScreenTip displays 2.67, release the mouse button, and then release **CTRL**. The horizontal guide you created is aligned with the middle of the wreath at the bottom of the slide.

7. Position the pointer on top of the vertical guide so that the pointer changes to the move vertical guide pointer +‖+, press and hold **CTRL**, drag the vertical guide to the right until the ScreenTip displays 0.75, and then release **CTRL** and the mouse button. The copy of the vertical guide is aligned with the center of the wreath at the bottom of the slide.

8. Drag another copy of the vertical guide to the right until the ScreenTip displays 5.92. The second copy of the vertical guide is aligned with the center of the wreath at the top of the slide. You don't need the original vertical guide that is positioned in the center of the slide.

9. Right-click the vertical guide that is positioned in the center of the slide on a part of the guide that is not inside the title text box. A shortcut menu that includes the Delete command appears. See Figure 4–2.

Figure 4–2     **Shortcut menu for deleting a guide**

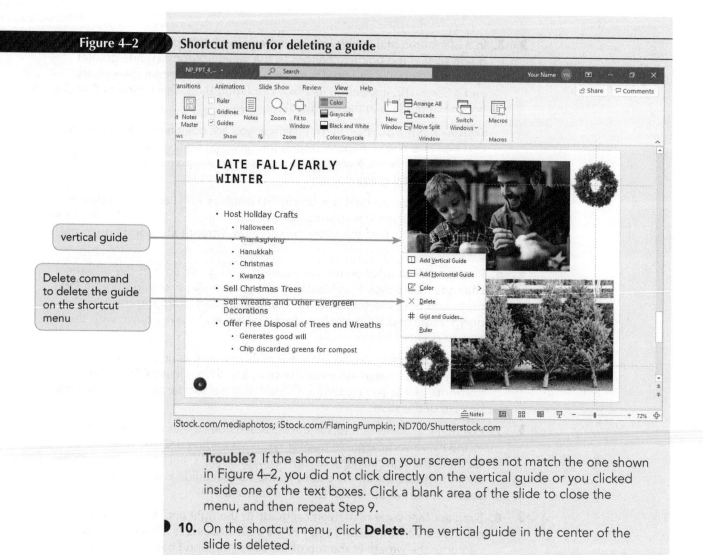

iStock.com/mediaphotos; iStock.com/FlamingPumpkin; ND700/Shutterstock.com

**Trouble?** If the shortcut menu on your screen does not match the one shown in Figure 4–2, you did not click directly on the vertical guide or you clicked inside one of the text boxes. Click a blank area of the slide to close the menu, and then repeat Step 9.

▶ **10.** On the shortcut menu, click **Delete**. The vertical guide in the center of the slide is deleted.

# Adding More Than One Animation to an Object

You can apply more than one animation to an object. For example, you can apply an entrance animation to an object by having it fly into a slide, and then once the object is on the slide, you can animate it a second time to further emphasize a bullet point on the slide or to show a relationship between the object and another object on the slide.

On Slide 6 in the presentation, Jack wants you to add animations to the photos of wreaths to add interest. He wants the wreaths to roll onto the slide.

**To add a motion path animation to the top wreath on Slide 6:**

▶ **1.** Click the wreath at the top of the slide, and then on the ribbon, click the **Animations** tab.

▶ **2.** In the Animation group, click the **More** button ⬛, scroll down to locate the Motion Paths section, and then click the **Lines** animation. The animation previews, and the wreath moves down the slide. After the preview, the motion path appears below the wreath, and a faint image of the wreath appears at the end of the path. At the beginning of the path, the green circle indicates the path's starting point, and at the end of the path, the red circle indicates the path's ending point. See Figure 4–3.

| Figure 4–3 | Wreath with Lines motion path animation applied |

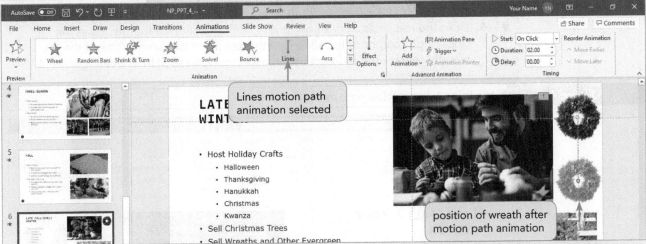

iStock.com/mediaphotos; iStock.com/FlamingPumpkin; ND700/Shutterstock.com; iStock.com/AzmanJaka; Vicki L. Miller/Shutterstock.com; gvictoria/Shutterstock.com; iStock.com/BanksPhotos; Jack Frog/Shutterstock.com

To have the wreath roll onto the slide, you will position the wreath to the right of the slide, and then change the direction of the Lines animation so that the wreath moves to the left instead of down. Then you will adjust the ending point of the motion path so that the wreath ends up in the upper-right corner of the slide when the animation is finished.

### To move the top wreath off the slide and modify the motion path animation:

1. Click the wreath at the top of the slide. The faint image of the wreath at the end of the motion path disappears, and the end points of the motion path change from circles to arrows.

2. Press and hold **SHIFT**, drag the wreath to the right until it is completely off the slide, and then release **SHIFT**. Pressing SHIFT while you drag an object forces the object to move in a straight line. The center of the wreath is still aligned with the horizontal guide.

3. In the Animation group, click the **Effect Options** button, and then click **Left**. The motion path changes to a horizontal line, and the wreath moves to the left as the animation previews. You need to reposition the end point of the motion path so that the wreath ends up to the right of the picture of the man and boy after the animation is finished. First you need to select the motion path. To do this, you click the motion path or the starting or ending point. Because the motion path is aligned with the horizontal guide, you will click the red ending point.

**4.** Click the red ending arrow. The arrows on the ends of the motion path change to circles, and a faint copy of the image appears at the end of the motion path. Now you can drag the start and end points to new locations.

**5.** Position the pointer on top of the red circle so that it changes to the double-headed diagonal pointer ⤢ , press and hold **SHIFT**, and then press and hold the mouse button. The pointer changes to the thin cross pointer ╋ .

**6.** Drag the red circle to the right until the intersection of the guides in the upper-right corner of the slide is in the center of the faint image of the wreath, release the mouse button, and then release **SHIFT**. See Figure 4–4.

| Figure 4–4 | Modified Lines motion path animation |
|---|---|

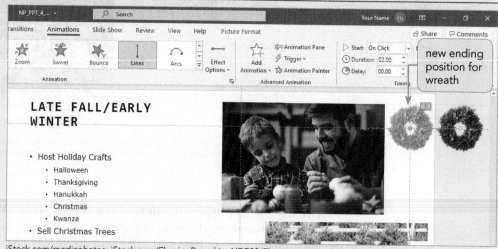

iStock.com/mediaphotos; iStock.com/FlamingPumpkin; ND700/Shutterstock.com

**Trouble?** If the path is slanted, you released SHIFT before you released the mouse button when you were dragging the wreath or the end point of the motion path. Click the Undo button ⟲ on the Quick Access Toolbar, and then repeat Steps 4 through 6, this time making sure you release the mouse button before you release SHIFT.

Jack wants the wreath to look like it is rolling onto the slide. To create this effect, you need to add a second animation to the wreath. To add a second animation to an object, you must use the Add Animation button in the Advanced Animation group on the Animations tab. If you try to add a second animation to an object by clicking an animation in the gallery in the Animation group, you will simply replace the animation already applied to the object.

### To add a second animation to the top wreath on Slide 6:

**1.** Click the wreath positioned to the right of the slide to select it, and then click the **Animations** tab, if necessary.

**2.** In the Advanced Animation group, click the **Add Animation** button.

The same gallery of animations that is in the Animation group appears.

Make sure you do not click another animation in the Animation group.

> **3.** In the Emphasis section of the gallery, click the **Spin** animation. Nothing happens for a moment, and then the animations preview very quickly. Next to the top wreath, a second animation sequence icon appears and is selected. In the Animation group, the Spin animation is selected, which means that the 2 animation sequence icon corresponds to the Spin animation. To see both animations, you need to preview them.

> **4.** In the Preview group, click the **Preview** button. The wreath moves left onto the slide, stops to the right of the picture of the man and boy, and then spins once in a clockwise direction.

To make the wreath look like it is rolling onto the slide, you need to change the start setting of the Spin animation to With Previous so that it happens at the same time as the Lines animation. Because two animations are applied to the object, you need to make sure that the correct animation sequence icon and the correct animation in the Animation group on the Animations tab are selected before you make any changes.

### To modify the start setting of the Spin animation applied to the wreath:

> **1.** Click the top wreath. In the Animation gallery, Multiple is selected. This indicates that more than one animation is applied to the selected object.

> **2.** Next to the top wreath, click the **2** animation sequence icon to select it. In the Animation gallery, Spin is selected. This is the animation that corresponds to the selected animation sequence icon.

> **3.** In the Timing group, click the **Start** arrow, and then click **With Previous**. The two animation sequence icons are now stacked on top of the other and they are both selected.

> **4.** In the Preview group, click the **Preview** button. Because the Lines motion path and the Spin animation happen at the same time, the wreath appears to roll as it moves onto the slide. However, it rolls in the wrong direction. Because the wreath starts from the right side of the slide, it should roll onto the slide in a counter-clockwise direction.

> **5.** With the Spin animation selected in the Animation group, click the **Effect Options** button, click **Counterclockwise**, and then in the Preview group, click the **Preview** button. The wreath rolls onto the slide in a counterclockwise direction.

Next, you need to apply the same animations to the wreath that is positioned at the bottom of the slide. You can follow the same steps you took when you applied the animations to the first wreath, or you can copy the animations and then modify them. You will copy the animations.

### To copy and modify the animations:

> **1.** Click the top wreath, and then in the Advanced Animation group, click the **Animation Painter** button.

2. Click the wreath at the bottom of the slide. The animations are copied and preview. Now you need to move the bottom wreath to the left of the slide, and then adjust its motion path.

3. Drag the bottom wreath off the slide to the left in a straight line, keeping its center aligned with the horizontal guide at the bottom of the slide. Now you need to change the direction and the end position of the motion path so that the wreath stops in the correct position on the slide.

4. Scroll left if necessary, and then click one of the end points on the motion path applied to the wreath at the bottom of the slide to select the motion path.

5. In the Animation group, click the **Effect Options** button, and then click **Right**. The end point of the motion path moves so it is below the bulleted list.

6. Select the motion path again, press and hold **SHIFT**, drag the red circle that indicates the end of the motion path to the right until the intersection of the guides to the left of the picture of the trees is in the center of the faint image of the wreath, release the mouse button, and then release **SHIFT**.

7. In the Preview group, click the **Preview** button. The wreath at the top of the slide rolls onto the slide, then the wreath at the bottom of the slide rolls onto the slide. The wreath at the bottom rolls in the wrong direction, but you will fix this in the next section. You are finished using the guides, so you can hide them.

8. Click the **View** tab, and then in the Show group, click the **Guides** check box. The guides no longer appear on the screen.

9. Click a blank area of the slide, and then save the changes to the presentation.

## Using the Animation Pane

On Slide 6, the bottom wreath rolled onto the slide in a counterclockwise direction. Since it rolls from the left, it should roll in a clockwise direction. But when more than one animation is applied to an object and the Start setting of one of the animations is set to With Previous or After Previous, you can't select only one of the animation sequence icons because they are stacked on top of one another. To select one animation when the animation sequence icons are stacked, you need to open the Animation pane.

### To examine the animations on Slide 6 in the Animation pane:

1. To the left of the slide, click the bottom wreath, click the Animations tab, and then in the Advanced Animation group, click the **Animation Pane** button. The Animation pane opens and Multiple is selected in the Animation group on the Animations tab. In the Advanced Animation group, the Animation Pane button is selected. See Figure 4–5.

**Figure 4–5**     **Animation pane listing the animations on Slide 6**

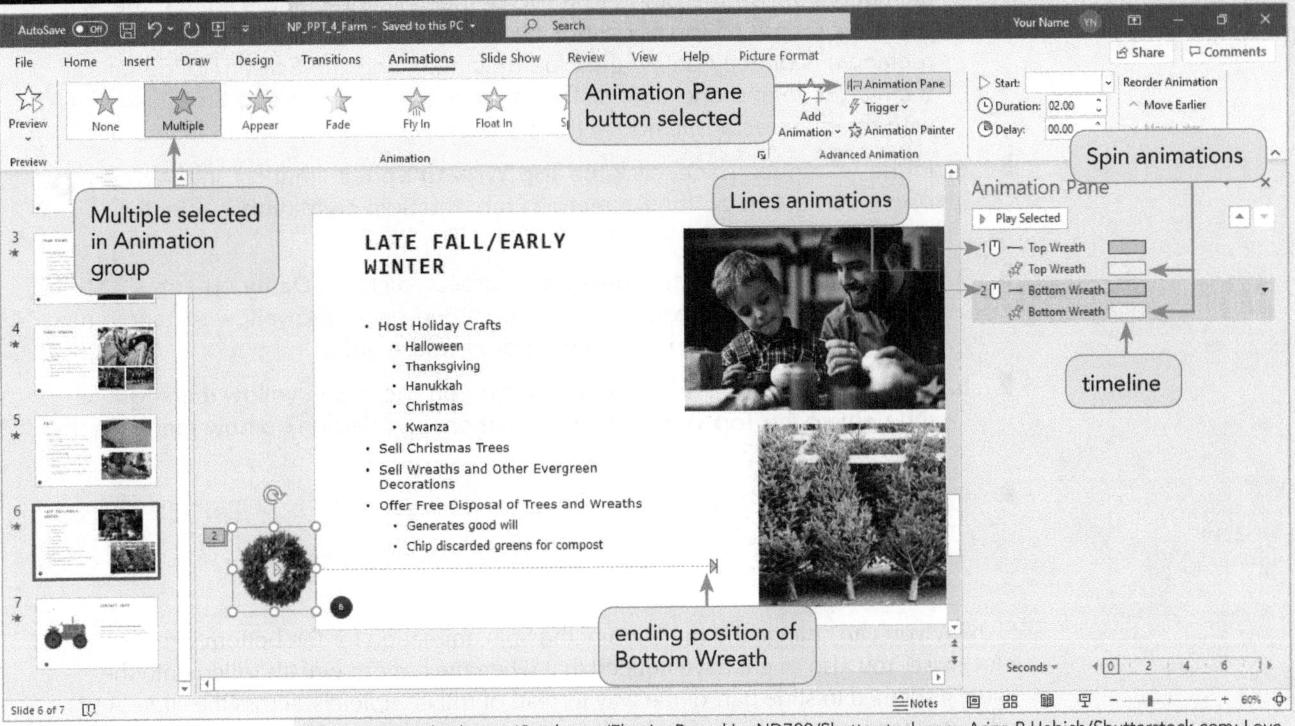

iStock.com/mediaphotos; iStock.com/FlamingPumpkin; ND700/Shutterstock.com; Arina P Habich/Shutterstock.com; Love Silhouette/Shutterstock.com; fokke baarssen/Shutterstock.com; iStock.com/AzmanJaka; Vicki L. Miller/Shutterstock.com; gvictoria/Shutterstock.com; iStock.com/BanksPhotos; Jack Frog/Shutterstock.com; Heather Stokes/Shutterstock.com

**Trouble?** If Lines is selected in the Animation group, click a blank area of the slide, and then click the bottom wreath.

2. In the Animation pane, move the pointer on top of the first animation in the list, **Top Wreath**. A ScreenTip appears, identifying the start setting (On Click), the type of animation (Motion Paths), the direction of the animation (Left), and the full name of the object (Top Wreath). This is the Lines animation applied to the wreath that ends up in the upper-right corner of the slide. The horizontal line to the left of the object name indicates that this is a motion path animation. The number 1 to the left of the object name is the same number that appears in the animation sequence icon for this animation.

3. In the Animation pane, move the pointer on top of the second animation in the list, the second **Top Wreath**. This is the Spin animation applied to the wreath that ends up in the upper-right corner of the slide. There is no number to the left of this animation because this animation occurs automatically (With Previous), not when the slide show is advanced (On Click). The yellow star to the left of the object name indicates that this is an emphasis animation. (Entrance animations are indicated with a green star, and exit animations are indicated with a red star.)

4. To the right of the Top Wreath Line animation (the first Top Wreath animation), move the pointer on top of the blue rectangle so that the pointer changes to the horizontal two-headed arrow pointer ↔. The rectangle indicates the length of the animation. The ScreenTip identifies the start time as 0s (zero seconds), which means it starts immediately after the slide show is advanced. The animation takes two seconds to complete so the ending time in the ScreenTip is 2s.

**Tip**

The entrance animation Appear and the exit animation Disappear have no length, so an arrow appears in the Animation Pane instead of a rectangle and the ScreenTip displays only a start time.

5. To the right of the Top Wreath Spin animation (the second Top Wreath animation), move the pointer on top of the yellow rectangle so that the pointer changes to the horizontal two-headed arrow pointer ↔. The yellow rectangle is directly below the blue rectangle, and the ScreenTip identifies the start time and end time as the same as the start and end times associated with the blue rectangle above it (0s and 2s).

6. In the Animation pane, click the **Top Wreath Spin** animation. In the Animation group on the Animations tab, the Spin animation is selected instead of Multiple.

7. On the Animations tab, in the Timing group, click the **Delay** up arrow once to set a delay of 0.25 seconds. In the Animation pane, the yellow rectangle next to the Top Wreath Spin animation moves to the right.

8. In the Animation pane, move the pointer on top of the yellow rectangle to the right of the Top Wreath Spin animation. The ScreenTip now identifies the start time as 0.25s.

9. In the Timing group, click the **Delay** down arrow once to change the Delay back to 0.00 seconds.

Now you can change the direction of the Spin animation for the bottom wreath to clockwise. You also might have noticed that when the bottom wreath rolled onto the slide, it seemed to slide part of the way instead of roll completely across the slide. And when the top wreath rolled onto the slide, it continued rolling after it was in position in the upper-right corner of the slide. To make the rolling effects appear more realistic, you will change the number of revolutions each wreath makes.

### To select the Spin animations in the Animation pane and modify them:

1. In the Animation pane, click the **Bottom Wreath Spin** animation. First, you will change the direction of the animation.

2. On the Animations tab, in the Animation group, click the **Effect Options** button, and then click **Clockwise**.

3. Click the **Effect Options** button again. In the Amount section, Full Spin is selected. Because this wreath needs to travel all the way across the slide, two spins would look better.

4. On the Effect Options menu, click **Two Spins**. As the animation previews (which you can't see because the wreath is not on the slide), only the Bottom Wreath Spin animation is shown in the Animation Pane, and a vertical line moves across the pane. You need to preview both animations applied to the bottom wreath.

5. Press and hold **SHIFT**, in the Animation pane click the **Bottom Wreath Lines** animation, and then release **SHIFT**. The two Bottom Wreath animations are selected. The button at the top of the Animation Pane changes to the Play Selected button.

6. Click the **Play Selected** button. The two selected animations preview, with the bottom wreath rolling onto the slide while spinning twice. Now you need to adjust the number of spins for the top wreath.

7. In the Animation Pane, click the **Top Wreath Spin** animation (the second animation in the list). On the Animations tab, in the Animation group, the Spin animation is selected.

8. In the Animation group, click the **Effect Options** button. In the Amount section, Full Spin is selected. Because this wreath needs to travel only a short distance, a half spin might look better.

9. On the Effect Options menu, click **Half Spin**. The menu closes, and the Spin animation applied to the top wreath previews. Again, you can't see this because the wreath is spinning to the right of the slide.

10. In the Animation Pane, click the **Top Wreath Lines** animation, and then at the top of the pane, click the **Play From** button. The four animations preview by starting with the selected animation and playing each animation in the pane.

When the bottom wreath animates, it continues to roll after it is in position. To fix this problem, you will slightly speed up the Spin animation applied to it by shortening its duration. The top wreath seems to roll more slowly than the first wreath. To fix that issue, you will speed up both animations applied to the top wreath.

### To modify the duration of the animations applied to the wreaths:

1. Make sure the Top Wreath Lines animation is selected in the Animation pane, press and hold **SHIFT**, click the **Top Wreath Spin** animation, and then release **SHIFT**.

2. On the Animations tab, in the Timing group, change the value in the Duration box to **0.75**.

3. In the Animation pane, click the **Bottom Wreath Spin** animation.

4. Change the duration of the Bottom Wreath Spin animation to **1.75** seconds.

5. On the status bar, click the **Slide Show** button 🖵, and then press **SPACEBAR**. The top wreath rolls onto the slide faster than before.

6. Press **SPACEBAR** again. The second wreath rolls on and no longer has an extra spin at the end.

7. Press **ESC** to end the slide show and return to Normal view.

Jack wants the wreaths to roll onto the slide automatically after the slide transitions onto the screen during a slide show. In order for this to happen, the start timing of both Lines animations need to be set to After Previous.

### To change the start timing of the Lines animations:

1. In the Animation Pane, click the **Top Wreath Lines** animation. An arrow ▾ appears to the right of the blue rectangle.

2. Click the **arrow** ▾ to the right of the blue rectangle. A menu appears. The first three commands are the same commands that appear when you click the Start arrow in the Timing group on the Animations tab. See Figure 4–6.

**Figure 4–6** Menu in the Animation pane for the selected Top Wreath Lines animation

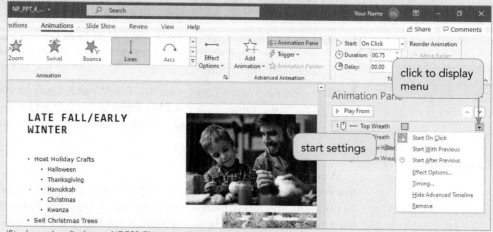

iStock.com/mediaphotos; ND700/Shutterstock.com

3. Click **Start After Previous**. Now the first wreath will roll onto the slide after the slide transitions. Notice that the number 1 that had been next to the animation changes to zero.

4. Click the **Bottom Wreath Lines** animation, click the arrow that appears, and then click **Start After Previous**. The blue and yellow rectangles next to the Bottom Wreath animations shift right to indicate that they won't start until after the previous animations finish. See Figure 4–7.

**Figure 4–7** Modified timeline in the Animation pane

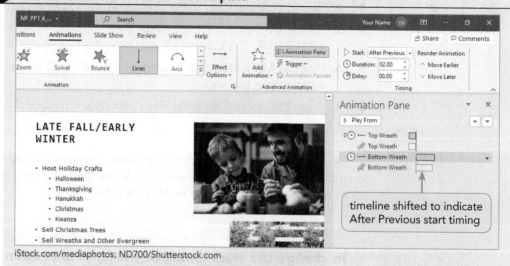

iStock.com/mediaphotos; ND700/Shutterstock.com

5. Point to the blue rectangle to the right of the Bottom Wreath Lines animation. The ScreenTip indicates that the animation will start 0.75 seconds after the slide show is advanced and will end 2.75 seconds after the slide show was advanced. Now preview the animations in Slide Show view.

6. On the status bar, click the **Slide Show** button 🖵. Slide 6 appears in Slide Show view, the top wreath rolls onto the slide, and then the bottom wreath rolls on.

7. Press **ESC** to end the slide show.

On each of the four slides that contain the ideas for generating income, Jack wants the bulleted lists to appear with an entrance animation and for the pictures to appear with the bulleted item they are illustrating. You'll start with Slide 4.

**To animate the bulleted list and pictures on Slide 4:**

1. Display Slide 4 ("Three-Season"), click the bulleted list, press and hold **SHIFT**, click the picture of the boy feeding the goat, click the picture of the red tractor, click the picture of the horses pulling a wagon, and then release **SHIFT**. The four objects you clicked are selected.

2. On the Animations tab, in the Animation group, click the **Fade** entrance animation. The Fade animation is applied to all four objects. In the Animation pane, the bulleted list appears first. The bulleted list animation is collapsed so you can see only the name of the entire object.

3. In the Animation pane, move the pointer on top of the first item in the list. The ScreenTip identifies this item as Content Placeholder 2: Petting Zoo. This is the name of the bulleted list object.

4. In the Animation pane, click the **Click to expand contents** button ⯆. The list expands and instead of "Content Placeholder 2," the first item is the same as the first item in the bulleted list, the second item is the next item in the bulleted list, and so on. See Figure 4–8.

Figure 4–8    Expanded bulleted list in the Animation pane

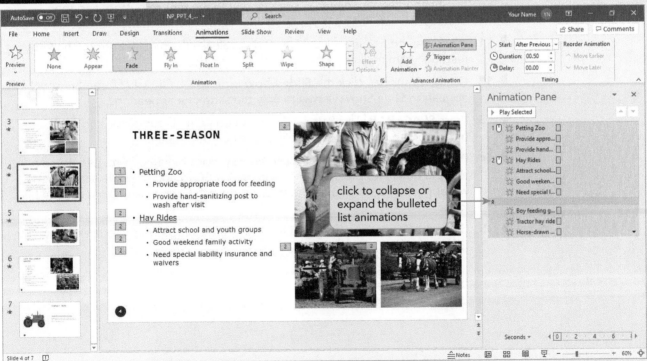

Jack wants the Petting Zoo bulleted item and its subitems to appear first, and he wants the picture of the little boy feeding the goat to appear at the same time. Then he wants the Hay Rides bulleted item and its subitems to appear along with the other two pictures.

5.  Move the pointer on top of each bulleted list item in the Animation pane to see how it starts. The Petting Zoo and Hay Rides items are set to start On Click. These two items are first-level bulleted items in the list. All of the other items (the subitems in the bulleted list and the pictures) are set to start With Previous.

6.  In the Animation pane, near the bottom of the list, move the pointer on top of **Boy feeding**. The ScreenTip for the "Boy feeding" item shows that the full name of this item is "Boy feeding goat." This picture needs to move up in the list so that it animates at the same time as the Petting Zoo item.

7.  On the slide, click the **2** animation sequence icon next to the picture of the boy feeding a goat. In the Animation pane, "Boy feeding," which is just below the "Need special" subbullet near the bottom of the list, is selected.

8.  On the Animations tab, in the Timing group, click the **Move Earlier** button. In the Animation pane, the "Boy feeding" item moves up one spot and is now above the "Need special" item. On the slide however, it looks as if nothing has changed—the animation sequence icon next to the picture is still 2. The Animation pane gives you a more complete picture.

9.  At the top of the Animation pane, click the up arrow ⌃. The "Boy feeding" item moves up one more position.

10. Move the pointer on top of **Boy feeding** so that the pointer changes to the two-headed arrow pointer ↕, press and hold the mouse button, and then drag up the list. As you drag, a red line follows the pointer.

11. When the red line is above 2 Hay Rides, release the mouse button. The "Boy feeding" item now appears above the Hay Rides item.

12. On the status bar, click the **Slide Show** button 🖵. Slide 4 ("Three-Season") appears in Slide Show view with only the slide title appearing.

13. Press **SPACEBAR**. The Petting Zoo bulleted item, its subitems, and the picture of the boy feeding a goat appear on the screen.

14. Press **SPACEBAR** again to display the Hay Rides bulleted item, its subitems, and the other two pictures, and then press **ESC** to end the slide show. Jack will apply the same animation effects to the other three slides that contain his ideas later.

15. Close the Animation pane, and then save the changes to the presentation.

**Proskills**

### Problem Solving: Solving Animation Problems

Sometimes animations do not work as you expect, especially if you combine triggers, multiple animations, and the Morph transition. This is why you should periodically preview your animations in Slide Show view as you create them. First, make sure that the effect you are trying to create actually enhances your message and does not distract from it. Before fixing the animation, duplicate the slide so that you can return to the original version if you want. On the copy of the slide, open the Animation pane and examine the animations. Make sure objects animate in the correct order and that each animation has the correct start setting. In the Animation pane, click an animation, click the arrow that appears, and then click Effect Options to open a dialog box that offers more options for modifying the selected animation. With a little detective work, you should be able to solve most of your problems. Sometimes, you might decide that you have too many animations occurring on one slide. The solution in that case might be to create two slides instead of just one, and then use a transition to help you create the effect you want.

# Setting Animation Triggers

Jack created an overview slide listing his suggestions for increasing the cash flow for farms in the fall and early winter months. He included a graphic of an unlit light bulb on the slide, and he wants to be able to click it during his presentation to cause a lit light bulb image to appear so it looks like he turned the light on. To do this, you will make the unlit bulb a trigger for that entrance animation. Refer to the Session 4.1 Visual Overview for more information about triggers.

### To set a trigger for an animation on Slide 2:

1. Display Slide 2 ("Ideas"), and then, on the ribbon, click the **Home** tab. Slide 2 contains a title, a light bulb graphic, and a bulleted list. The white light bulb is a little hard to see because the background on the left side of the slide is very light blue.

2. In the Editing group, click the **Select** button, and then click **Selection Pane**. The Selection pane opens.

3. On the slide, click the light bulb. In the Selection pane, Content Placeholder 5 is selected.

4. In the Selection pane, click **Content Placeholder 5**, drag across **Content Placeholder 5** to select the text, type **Unlit Bulb**, and then press **ENTER**.

5. Insert the picture **Support_PPT_4_Light.png**, located in the PowerPoint 4 > Module folder. Another light bulb graphic is added to the slide, but this one looks like the light bulb is turned on. In the Selection pane, Picture 6 is added to the top of the list.

6. In the Selection pane, rename Picture 6 so it is **Lit Bulb**.

7. On the slide, drag the lit version of the light bulb graphic directly on top of the unlit version, using the smart guides to make sure the two graphics are perfectly aligned.

> **8.** Click the **Animations** tab, and then in the Animation group, click the **Appear** entrance animation. The Appear animation is applied to the lit bulb. Now you need to make the unlit bulb the trigger for this animation.

> **9.** In the Advanced Animation group, click the **Trigger** button, and then point to **On Click of**. The same list of objects that appears in the Selection pane appears on the submenu, but in reverse order.

> **10.** Click **Unlit Bulb**. The animation sequence icon next to the light changes to a lightning bolt. This means the animation applied to the lit bulb will not occur until the trigger happens—in this case, until the unlit bulb is clicked during a slide show.

Next, you will test the trigger. You'll view Slide 2 in Slide Show view and click the unlit bulb to make sure the lit bulb appears.

### To test the animation trigger in Slide Show view:

> **1.** On the status bar, click the **Slide Show** button 🖵. Slide 2 appears in Slide Show view displaying the slide title, the bulleted list, and the unlit version of the light bulb graphic.

> **2.** Click the unlit bulb. The light bulb appears to turn on as the lit version of the light bulb graphic appears on top of the unlit version.
>
> **Trouble?** If Slide 3 ("Year-Round") appears instead of the lit bulb appearing on Slide 2, you clicked the slide area instead of clicking the light bulb. Press the Backspace key to redisplay Slide 2, and then click the unlit bulb graphic.

> **3.** Press **ESC** to end the presentation.

> **4.** In the Selection pane, click the **Close** button ☒, and then save the changes to the presentation.

**Tip**

To remove a trigger, select the animated object, click the Trigger button, and then click the checked object on the menu.

## Insight

### Using Bookmarks as Triggers and Using the Seek Animation

When you add bookmarks to video and audio objects, you can click the bookmarks to jump to that point in the clip or set the bookmark to trigger an animation. For example, if you want to skip the first part of a clip, but you don't want to trim the clip, you can click the bookmark to start playback at a point in the middle of the clip. Another example is if you add a video with a bookmark and a text box containing the title of the video to a slide, you could set the bookmark to be a trigger for an entrance animation applied to the text box containing the title. To add a bookmark, first identify the pointer where you want to insert the bookmark by clicking the video or audio toolbar, or by playing the clip and then clicking the Pause button when it reaches the point where you want the bookmark inserted. Then, on the Playback tab for the object, in the Bookmarks group, click the Add Bookmark button. The Remove Bookmark button is in the same group if you no longer need the bookmark.

When a video or audio object has a bookmark, the Seek animation in the Media section is available on the Animations tab. You can use this if you want to play the beginning and end of a clip but skip the middle. To use the Seek animation, insert bookmarks at the beginning and end of the section you want to skip. Select the bookmark at the end of the section you want to clip, and then apply the Seek animation to it. Then set the bookmark at the beginning of the section that you want to clip as a trigger for the Seek animation.

# Changing the Slide Background

The background of a slide can be as important as the foreground when you are creating a presentation with a strong visual impact. To change the background, you use the Format Background pane. When you change the background, you are essentially changing the fill of the background. The commands are the same as the commands you use when you change the fill of a shape. For example, you can change the color, add a gradient or a pattern, or fill it with a texture or a picture.

## Reference

### Modify the Slide Background

- On the Design tab, in the Variants group, click the More button, point to Background styles, and then click a style to apply that background to all of the slides in the presentation.

*or*

- On the Design tab, in the Customize group, click the Format Background button to open the Format Background pane with the Fill button selected and the Fill section expanded.
- Click one of the fill option buttons to select the type of fill you want to use.
- Use the option buttons, menus, and sliders that appear to customize the selected fill option.
- To apply the background to all the slides in the presentation, click Apply to All.

The entire background of Slide 1 is light blue. The layout applied to the rest of the slides includes a white box below the text or pictures in the content placeholder on the right side of the slide. On those slides, the light blue background shows only on the left side of the slide.

On Slide 2, the light blue background makes it difficult to see the unlit light bulb. Jack wants you to change the color of the slide background so that this is not a problem. Then he wants you to apply that background to all of the slides to give the presentation a consistent look.

### To change the fill of the slide background:

▶ **1.** With Slide 2 ("Ideas") displayed, click the **Design** tab.

▶ **2.** In the Variants group, click the **More** button ⬇, and then on the menu, point to **Background Styles**. A gallery of color choices appears. See Figure 4–9.

**Figure 4–9**     **Background Styles gallery**

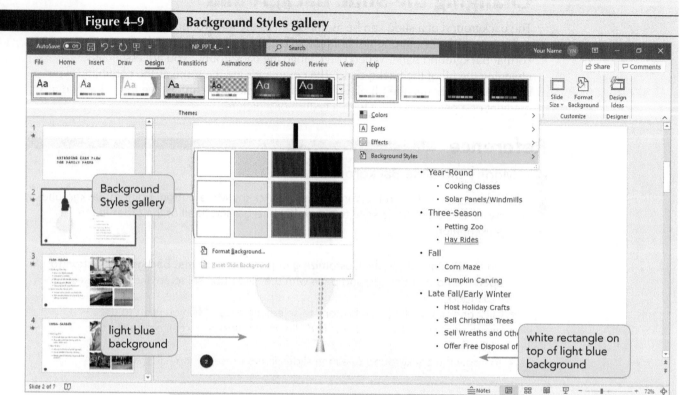

Arina P Habich/Shutterstock.com; Love Silhouette/Shutterstock.com; fokke baarssen/Shutterstock.com; iStock.com/AzmanJaka; Vicki L. Miller/Shutterstock.com; gvictoria/Shutterstock.com

3. On the menu, click **Style 2** (the second style in the first row). The light blue background on the slides changes to the style you selected. Slide 2 is one of the slides that has a layout with a white rectangle on the right, so only the left side of this slide changed color. Jack thinks this color is a little dark.

4. On the Design tab, in the Customize group, click the **Format Background** button. The Format Background pane opens. See Figure 4–10. This pane has only one button—the Fill button—and one section of commands—the Fill section. It contains the same commands as the Fill section in the Format Shape pane. The Solid fill option button is selected, indicating that the current background has a solid fill.

**Figure 4–10**     **Format Background pane**

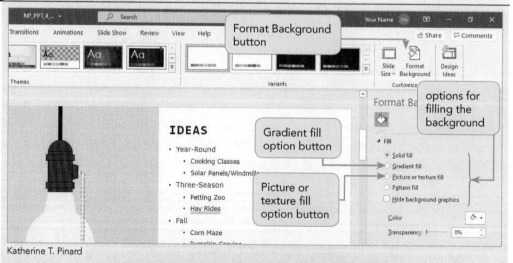

Katherine T. Pinard

5. In the pane, click the **Gradient fill** option button. The background of Slide 2 changes to a gradient fill with the color varying from green to a light yellow orange. Jack wants the background to be a solid green color, but a little lighter than the color that was applied when you changed the background style.

6. In the pane, click the **Solid fill** option button, click the **Color** button, and then click the **Light Green, Background 2, Lighter 40%** color. The background of Slide 2 changes to the green color you selected.

7. At the bottom of the Format Background pane, click **Apply to All**. The light green background is applied to all of the slides in the presentation.

Jack wants the title slide to have a different background than the rest of the slides. You can fill the slide background with a picture, or you can tile the picture, which means to make the picture appear as repeating images across the slide. When you set an image to tile across the background, you can make the tiles smaller so that more tiles appear on the background.

You can also change the offset of a picture in the slide background. This means you can move the picture horizontally or vertically in the background.

You'll add a picture of a tractor as the slide background of Slide 1, and then you will tile it.

### To tile a picture in the background of Slide 1:

1. Display **Slide 1** (the title slide), and then in the Format Background pane, click the **Picture or texture fill** option button. The default texture is applied to the current slide background and the Format Background pane changes to include commands for inserting pictures. Below the Transparency slider, the Tile picture as texture check box is selected. Textures are made up of a picture that is sized much smaller than the slide and then repeated across and up and down the slide.

2. Click the **Tile picture as texture** check box. The check box is deselected, and the texture picture changes to fill the slide. The original picture that was tiled to create the texture background is very small, so when you deselect the Tile picture as texture option, the small image enlarges to fill the screen and is now blurry.

3. In the Picture source section of the pane, click the **Insert** button. The Insert Pictures dialog box opens. Click **From a File**. The Insert Picture dialog box opens.

4. Navigate to the **PowerPoint 4 > Module** folder, click **Support_PPT_4_Tractor.png**, and then click **Insert**. A picture of a tractor fills the slide background of Slide 1. See Figure 4–11.

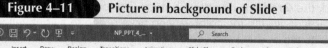

Figure 4-11      Picture in background of Slide 1

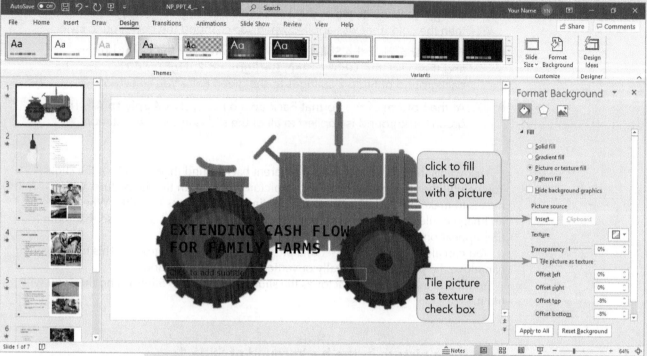

Heather Stokes/Shutterstock.com; Arina P Habich/Shutterstock.com; Love Silhouette/Shutterstock.com; fokke baarssen/Shutterstock.com; iStock.com/AzmanJaka; Vicki L. Miller/Shutterstock.com; gvictoria/Shutterstock.com; iStock.com/BanksPhotos; Jack Frog/Shutterstock.com; iStock.com/mediaphotos

5. In the pane, click the **Tile picture as texture** check box to select it. The picture changes to a series of tiles on the slide in three rows. You want four rows of tiles to appear, so you will change the scale.

6. To the right of **Scale Y** box, click the down arrow on the box until there are four rows of tractors on the slide and the box contains the value **80%**. Each tile was resized smaller vertically to fit the extra row of tractors on the slide. The aspect ratio was not maintained, but for this picture, that is fine. (If you needed to maintain the aspect ratio, you would change the Scale X value to the same percentage as the Scale Y value.) Now you will move the pictures sideways by changing the horizontal offset.

7. Click in the **Offset X** box, delete the value in it, type **85**, and then press **ENTER**. The tiles on the slide shift sideways so that the front half of a tractor appears on the left and the back half appears on the right.

8. Scroll to the bottom of the Format Background pane, click the **Mirror type** arrow, and then click **Horizontal**. Every other image is flipped horizontally to create mirror images. See Figure 4-12.

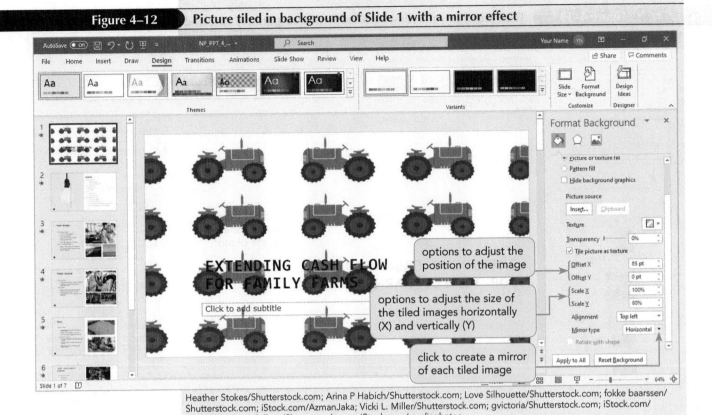

**Figure 4–12**    **Picture tiled in background of Slide 1 with a mirror effect**

Heather Stokes/Shutterstock.com; Arina P Habich/Shutterstock.com; Love Silhouette/Shutterstock.com; fokke baarssen/
Shutterstock.com; iStock.com/AzmanJaka; Vicki L. Miller/Shutterstock.com; gvictoria/Shutterstock.com; iStock.com/
BanksPhotos; Jack Frog/Shutterstock.com; iStock.com/mediaphotos

The text on the slide is hard to see on the picture background. You could adjust the brightness and the contrast of the photo, or you could make the photo more transparent. You'll adjust the transparency of the photo now.

### To change the transparency of the background picture:

1. In the Format Background pane, drag the **Transparency** slider to the right until the value in the Transparency box is 85%. Compare your screen to Figure 4–13.

| Figure 4–13 | Tiled picture in slide background with transparency adjusted |

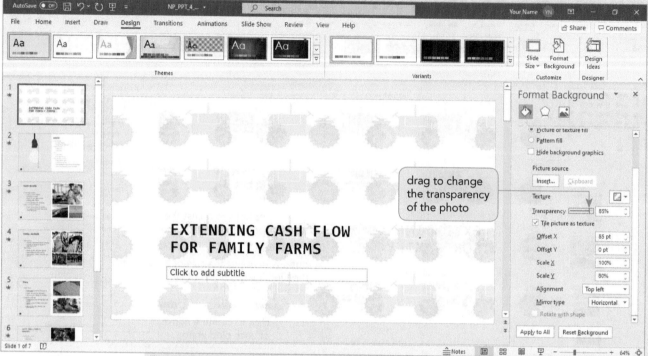

Heather Stokes/Shutterstock.com; Arina P Habich/Shutterstock.com; Love Silhouette/Shutterstock.com; fokke baarssen/Shutterstock.com; iStock.com/AzmanJaka; Vicki L. Miller/Shutterstock.com; gvictoria/Shutterstock.com; iStock.com/BanksPhotos; Jack Frog/Shutterstock.com; iStock.com/mediaphotos

**Trouble?** If you can't position the slider so that 85% appears in the Transparency box, click the up or down arrows in the Transparency box as needed to change the value.

The slide appears somewhat gray. This is because the Office theme is set to Colorful. When the slide is displayed during a slide show, the space between the images will be white.

2. On the status bar, click the **Slide Show** button 🖵. Slide 1 appears in Slide Show view, and the space between the images is white, not gray. The text is easy to read in Slide Show view.

3. Press **ESC** to end the slide show, and then close the Format Background pane.

4. Save the changes to the presentation.

# Insight

## Hiding Background Graphics

Some themes include graphics as part of the slide background. If you need to print slides with graphics in the background in black and white or grayscale, you might want to remove those graphics before printing the slides because the graphics could make the text difficult to read. To hide graphics in the background, select the Hide background graphics check box in the Format Background pane. Note that selecting this option will not hide anything you use as a fill for the background, such as the picture you added as the background in this module.

# Creating and Editing Links

If you've visited webpages on the Internet, you have clicked links (sometimes called "hyperlinks") to "jump to"—or display—other webpages or files. In PowerPoint, a link on a slide accomplishes the same thing. You can convert any text or object on a slide to a link to another slide in the same presentation, to a different file, or to a webpage. A link can be customized to do several other actions as well.

To create a link from text or a shape, you use the Link button or the Action button in the Links group on the Insert tab. You can use either button to create most types of links; however, the Action Settings dialog box allows you to also run a macro (which is a predefined set of instructions). In addition, when you use the Action button, you can create a link that responds when you simply point to it rather than click it, plays a sound when you click it or point to it, and highlights the link in some way when you click it or point to it.

## Creating and Editing Text Links

As you know, when you type a webpage or an email address, it is automatically converted to a link. If you want, you can change the text that appears on the slide. For example, if you type a webpage address and it is converted to a link, you can change the text of the link to the name of the webpage.

You can also convert any text on a slide to a link. Text links are usually underlined and a different color than the rest of the text on a slide. After you click a text link during a slide show, the link changes to another color to indicate that it has been clicked, or followed.

Slide 7 contains Jack's email address formatted as a link. You can edit this link so that the text displayed on the slide is Jack's name instead of his email address.

### To change the text displayed for a link:

1. Display Slide 7 ("Contact Info"), and then move the pointer on top of the email address. The ScreenTip that appears shows the "mailto" instruction followed by Jack's email address. (The "mailto" instruction causes your email app to start and create a new email message addressed to the email address when you click the link.)

2. Click anywhere in the email address link on the slide, click the **Insert** tab, and then in the Links group, click the **Link** button. The Edit Hyperlink dialog box opens. In the Link to list on the left, the E-mail Address option is selected. The email address, preceded by the "mailto" instruction, appears in the E-mail address box. In addition, the email address that appears on the slide is in the Text to display box at the top of the dialog box. See Figure 4–14.

**Figure 4–14**    **Edit Hyperlink dialog box for a link to an email address**

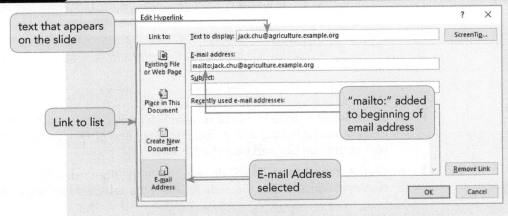

> **3.** Click in the **Text to display** box, delete all the text, and then type **Jack Chu**.
>
> **4.** Click **OK**. The dialog box closes, and the email address on Slide 7 changes to the text you typed in the Edit Hyperlink dialog box, Jack Chu.
>
> **5.** Move the pointer on top of **Jack Chu**. The ScreenTip that appears still shows Jack's email address.

Slide 2 in Jack's presentation is an overview slide. Each first-level bulleted item on this slide names another slide in the presentation. Jack wants you to convert each first-level bulleted item to a link that links to the related slide. One way to create links is to use the Insert Hyperlink dialog box.

### To create a link using the Insert Hyperlink dialog box:

> **1.** Display Slide 2 ("Ideas"), and then in the first bulleted item, drag across the text **Year-Round**. The text is selected.

**Tip**

If you open a file stored on OneDrive, you can click the Link arrow, and then click the file name of a recently opened file in the menu to insert a link to that file.

> **2.** Click the **Insert** tab, if necessary, and then in the Links group, click the **Link** button. The Insert Hyperlink dialog box opens. In the Link to list on the left, the E-mail Address option is selected. You need to identify the file or location to which you want to link. In this case, you're going to link to a slide in the current presentation. If you wanted to link to another file on your computer or network, you would click the Existing File or Web Page button. If you wanted to create a new PowerPoint file when you clicked the link, you would click the Create New Document button.
>
> **3.** In the Link to list on the left, click **Place in This Document**. The dialog box changes to show the Select a place in this document box, listing all the slides in the presentation. See Figure 4–15.

| **Figure 4–15** | **Insert Hyperlink dialog box with list of slides in this presentation** |

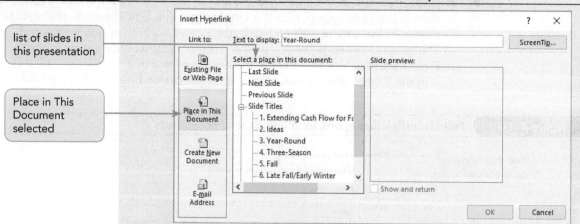

list of slides in this presentation

Place in This Document selected

> **4.** In the Select a place in this document list, scroll up to the top of the list. Commands for linking to the first, last, next, and previous slides are listed, as well as the number and title of each slide.
>
> **5.** Click **3. Year-Round**. The Slide preview on the right side of the dialog box displays Slide 3. This is the slide to which the selected text will be linked.

6. Click **OK**, and then click a blank area of the slide to deselect the text. The text of the first bullet is now a link and is formatted as light-blue and underlined.

You can also create a link using the Action Settings dialog box. You'll create the link to the Three-Season slide using the Action button on the Insert tab.

### To create a link using the Action Settings dialog box:

1. Drag across the text **Three-Season** to select it.

2. On the Insert tab, in the Links group, click the **Action** button. The Action Settings dialog box opens with the Mouse Click tab selected. See Figure 4–16.

**Figure 4–16** | Action Settings dialog box

Hyperlink to option button

select to play a sound when the link is clicked

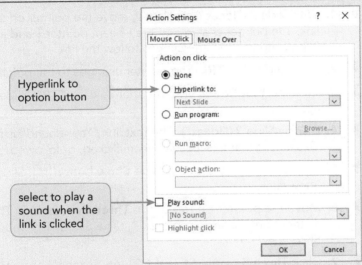

**Tip**

Click the Mouse Over tab to create a link that you only need to point to in order to display the linked slide or file.

3. In the Action on click section, click the **Hyperlink to** option button. The Hyperlink to box becomes available, and lists the default option, Next Slide.

4. Click the **Hyperlink to** arrow. The commands on the list allow you to create links to the same things you can link to using the Insert Hyperlink dialog box. You want to link to a specific slide in the current presentation.

5. Click **Slide**. The Hyperlink to Slide dialog box opens listing all the slides in the presentation. See Figure 4–17.

**Figure 4–17** | Hyperlink to Slide dialog box

Slide title list

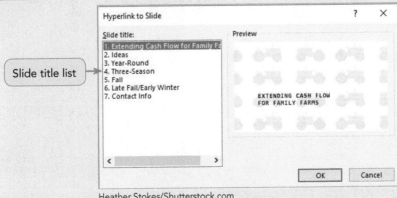

Heather Stokes/Shutterstock.com

6. Click **4. Three-Season**, and then click **OK**. The Hyperlink to Slide dialog box closes and "Three-Season" appears in the Hyperlink to box.

7. Click **OK**. The dialog box closes, and the second bulleted item is formatted as a link.

8. Change the next two first-level bulleted items to links to Slides 5 and 6 respectively, using either the Link or the Action button.

Now you need to test the text links you created. You can press and hold CTRL while you click a text link in Normal view, or you can switch to Slide Show view and then just click the text link.

### To test the links:

1. With Slide 2 ("Ideas") displayed, move the pointer on top of the Year-Round link. The pointer changes to the I-beam pointer $\mathrm{I}$ and a ScreenTip appears instructing you to Ctrl+Click to follow the link.

2. Press and hold **CTRL**. The pointer changes to the pointing finger pointer ᕦ.

3. Click the **Year-Round** link, and then release **CTRL**. Slide 3 ("Year-Round") appears.

4. Display Slide 2 ("Ideas"). The text link "Year-Round" is now grayish-green. This means that this link has been clicked, or followed.

5. On the status bar, click the **Slide Show** button 🖵. Slide 2 appears in Slide Show view.

6. Move the pointer on top of the **Three-Season** link. The pointer changes to the pointing finger pointer ᕦ. The ScreenTip does not appear in Slide Show view.

7. Click **Three-Season**. Slide 4 ("Three-Season") appears in Slide Show view using the Push transition. (The bulleted list and the pictures do not appear on the slide because you applied entrance animations whose start setting is On Click.)

8. Right-click anywhere on the slide, and then on the shortcut menu, click **Last Viewed**. Slide 2 ("Ideas") appears in Slide Show view also using the Push transition. The first two bulleted items are now grayish-green, indicating that the links have been followed. See Figure 4–18.

**Tip**

To show a ScreenTip in Slide Show view, click the ScreenTip button in the Insert Hyperlink dialog box, and then type the ScreenTip in the box.

Figure 4–18     **Followed and unfollowed links on Slide 2 in Slide Show view**

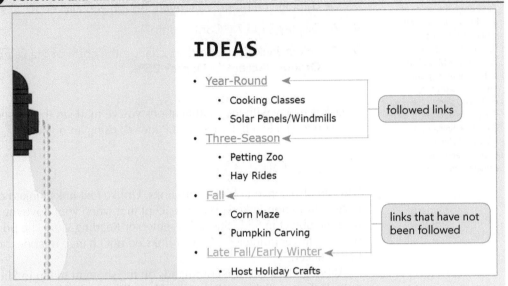

9. Click each of the other two links to verify that they link to the correct slides, using the Last Viewed command on the shortcut menu to return to Slide 2 each time.

10. Press **ESC** to end the slide show. Slide 2 appears in Normal view. The links are now all grayish-green. They changed color because they have been clicked—followed—during a slide show. They will reset to the light-blue color when you close and reopen the presentation.

   **Trouble?** If Slide 2 is not displayed, you did not return to Slide 2 in the Slide Show after clicking the last link. Display Slide 2.

## Changing the Color of Text Links

You can change the color of text links in the same manner you change the color of any text. If you do this, however, the color of followed links will be the same color you choose for the color of unfollowed links.

   Jack thinks that both the light-blue color of unfollowed links and the grayish-green color of followed links are hard to see. You'll change the color of the links.

### To change the color of text links:

1. On Slide 2 ("Ideas"), select the text **Year-Round**, press and hold **CTRL**, select **Three-Season**, **Fall**, and **Late Fall/Early Winter**, and then release **CTRL**. All of the text links are selected.

2. Click the **Home** tab, and then in the Font group, click the **Font color arrow** [A ·]. The palette of colors applied to this presentation appears.

3. On the menu, click the **Orange, Accent 3, Darker 25%**, and then click a blank area of the slide. The four text links are now the orange color you selected.

4. Click a blank area of the slide, press and hold **CTRL**, and then click the **Year-Round** link. Slide 3 ("Year-Round") appears.

**Tip**

To change the color of a followed link as well, you need to customize the color palette by clicking the More button in the Variants group on the Design tab, clicking Colors, clicking Customize Colors, clicking the Hyperlink and the Followed Hyperlink buttons, and then selecting new colors.

5. Display Slide 2 ("Ideas"). On Slide 2, the Year-Round link is still the same color as the other links, even though you clicked it.

6. Display Slide 7 ("Contact Info").

7. Select **Jack Chu**, and then change the color of the selected link text to **Orange, Accent 3, Darker 25%**.

Jack is happy with the modifications you've made to the presentation so far. Next he asks you to create a link to Slide 2 ("Ideas") using an object.

## Creating Object Links

You can also convert objects into links. Unlike text links, linked objects are not visually distinct from non-linked objects, except that when you move the mouse pointer over the object in Slide Show, Presenter, or Reading view, the pointer changes to the pointing finger pointer 🖑. Object links do not change in appearance after they have been clicked.

Although Jack can use commands on the shortcut menu in Slide Show view to return to Slide 2 after clicking a link to another slide, it would be easier for him to navigate during the slide show if you added a link to Slide 2 on each slide. You'll do this now by adding a shape that you format as a link on Slides 3 through 6.

**To create a shape and format it as a link:**

1. Display **Slide 3** ("Year-Round"), and then click the **Insert** tab.

2. In the Illustrations group, click the **Shapes** button, and then in the Rectangles group, click the **Rectangle: Rounded Corners** shape.

3. Click below the bulleted list to insert the shape, resize it so it is one-half inch high and 1.2 inches wide, and then using the smart guides that appear, position it so that the shape's right edge aligns with the right edge of the bulleted list text box and its bottom edge aligns with the bottom edge of the slide number.

4. With the shape selected, type **IDEAS**, and then format the text as bold.

5. Click the outside of the shape to select the entire shape, then, on the ribbon, click the **Shape Format** tab if necessary.

6. In the Shape Styles group, click the **More** button ⤓, and then in the Presets section, click the **Transparent, Colored Outline – Orange, Accent 3** style. See Figure 4–19.

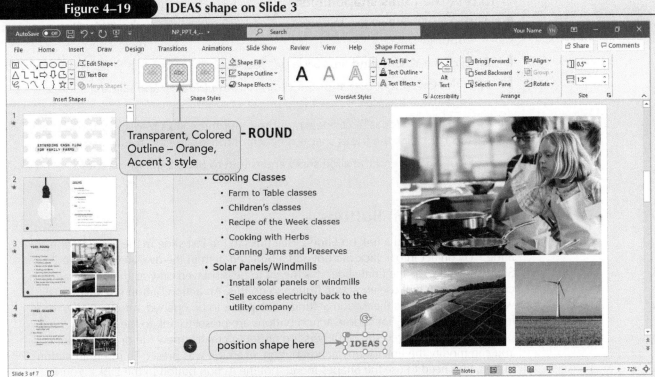

**Figure 4–19    IDEAS shape on Slide 3**

Arina P Habich/Shutterstock.com; Love Silhouette/Shutterstock.com; fokke baarssen/Shutterstock.com; Heather Stokes/Shutterstock.com; iStock.com/AzmanJaka; Vicki L. Miller/Shutterstock.com; gvictoria/Shutterstock.com

7. On the ribbon, click the **Insert** tab.

8. With the shape selected, in the Links group, click the **Link** button. The Insert Hyperlink dialog box opens. Because Slide 2 is the previous slide, you could select the Previous Slide location instead of clicking the slide number. However, you will be copying this link to other slides, so you will link specifically to Slide 2.

9. With Place in This Document selected in the Link to list, click **2. Ideas** in the Select a place in this document list, and then click **OK**. The shape does not look any different now that it is a link. You want the same link to appear on Slides 4, 5, and 6. You can insert a shape on each slide and format it as a link, or you can copy the shape on Slide 3 and paste it on each slide.

10. With the **IDEAS** shape selected, click the **Home** tab, and then in the Clipboard group, click the **Copy** button.

11. Display **Slide 4** ("Three-Season"), and then in the Clipboard group, click the **Paste** button. A copy of the IDEAS link appears in the lower-right corner of the slide—the same position it was in on Slide 3.

12. Paste the IDEAS link onto Slide 5 ("Fall") and Slide 6 ("Late Fall/Early Winter").

You need to test the Ideas links. As with text links, you can test object links in Normal or Slide Show view.

**To test the Ideas shape links:**

1. Display Slide 2 ("Ideas"), and then on the status bar, click the **Slide Show** button 🖵.

2. Click the **Year-Round** link. Slide 3 ("Year-Round") appears in Slide Show view.

3. In the lower-right corner of the slide, click the **Ideas** shape. Slide 2 ("Ideas") appears on the screen.

4. On Slide 2 ("Ideas"), click each of the other three links to display those slides, and then click the Ideas shape on each of those slides to return to Slide 2.

5. Press **ESC** to end the slide show and return to Slide 2 in Normal view.

## Inserting Action Buttons

Jack wants you to add a link on Slide 2 that links to the last slide in the presentation, Slide 7 ("Contact Info"). Jack did not add a bulleted item in the overview on Slide 2 for Slide 7 because, as the final slide, it is meant to be displayed only as the presentation is concluding. You will use an action button to do this. An action button is a shape that, when inserted, causes the Action Settings dialog box to be opened automatically, ready for you to specify the link. Some action buttons are preset to link to the first, last, next, previous, or last viewed slides. Others are preset to create a new file or play a sound. You can modify the link for any action button, even if it was preset. To insert an action button, you need to use the Shapes menu, not the Action button in the Links group.

**To insert an action button on Slide 2:**

1. With Slide 2 ("Ideas") displayed, on the ribbon, click the **Insert** tab.

2. In the Illustrations group, click the **Shapes** button, scroll to the bottom of the gallery, and then in the Action Buttons section, click the **Action Button: Go to End** shape.

3. Click near the bottom-right corner of the slide. The action button is inserted, and the Action Settings dialog box opens. The Hyperlink to option button is selected, and Last Slide appears in the Hyperlink to box.

4. Click **OK**. On the Shape Format tab, in the Shape Styles group, the Colored Fill – Gold, Accent 1 style is selected.

5. Resize the action button so it is one-half inch high and one inch wide, position it in the lower-right corner of the slide so its right edge aligns with the right edge of the bulleted list text box and its bottom edge aligns with the bottom of the slide number, and then click a blank area of the slide to deselect the button. Compare your screen to Figure 4–20.

Figure 4–20 | Action button on Slide 2

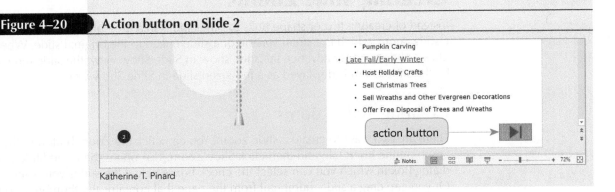

Katherine T. Pinard

Now you need to test the new link. Unlike the other links you have created, you can test action buttons only in Slide Show view.

### To test the action button:

1. On Slide 2 ("Ideas"), move the pointer on top of the action button. The pointer changes to the move pointer ⁺, not the I-beam pointer I or the pointing finger pointer ⏱. This means that you cannot click it to follow the link.

2. On the status bar, click the **Slide Show** button 🖵. Slide 2 ("Ideas") appears in Slide Show view.

3. Move the pointer on top of the action button. The pointer changes to the pointing finger pointer ⏱.

4. Click the action button. Slide 7 ("Contact Info") appears.

5. Press **ESC** to end the slide show. Slide 7 appears in Normal view.

6. Save the changes to the presentation.

## Insight

### Linking to Another File

You can create a link to another file so that when you click the link during a slide show, the other file opens. The other file can be any file type; it doesn't need to be a PowerPoint file. To create a link to another file, open the Insert Hyperlink dialog box, click Existing File or Web Page in the Link to list, and then click the Browse for File button. To change the link destination of an action button to another file, open the Action Settings dialog box, click the Hyperlink to option button, click the Hyperlink to arrow, and then click Other PowerPoint Presentation or Other File. For either type of link, a dialog box opens in which you can navigate to the location of the file.

When you create a link to another file, the linked file is not included within the PowerPoint file; only the original path and filename to the files on the computer where you created the links are stored in the presentation. Therefore, if you need to show the presentation on another computer, you must copy linked files as well as the PowerPoint presentation file to the other computer, and then you need to edit the path to the linked file so that PowerPoint can find the file in its new location. To update the path for a link or action button, right-click it, and then click Edit Link on the shortcut menu to open the Edit Hyperlink or the Action Settings dialog box.

# Creating Slide Zooms

Instead of creating text or shape links to other slides in a presentation, you can create a **slide zoom**, which is a small version of a slide linked to the original slide. When you click a slide zoom or advance the slide show in Slide Show view, the slide represented by the slide zoom is displayed as a full-sized slide in Slide Show view.

## Creating Slide Zooms

There are two ways to create a slide zoom. You can click the Zoom button in the Links group on the Insert tab, and then click Slide Zoom. This opens the Insert Slide Zoom dialog box in which you can select the check boxes below the slides you want to insert. Or you can drag a slide thumbnail from the pane that contains the thumbnails onto a slide in Normal view.

When you select a slide zoom, the Zoom contextual tab appears on the ribbon. This tab contains many of the same commands as the Picture Format tab. For example, you can resize a slide zoom or apply a style, border, or effect to it. In addition, you can use the Zoom Background command to remove the background of the slide zoom so that you see the background of the slide that the slide zoom is on.

## Reference

### Inserting Slide Zooms

- Display the slide you want to insert the slide zooms on, and then click the Insert tab.
- In the Links group, click the Zoom button, and then click Slide Zoom.
- In the Insert Slide Zoom dialog box, click the check boxes below the slides you want to create a slide zoom for, and then click Insert.

or

- Display the slide you want to insert the slide zooms on, and then in Normal view, drag a thumbnail from the pane on the left onto the slide.

Jack wants you to create another version of the "Ideas" slide that contains slide zooms of the same four slides that the bulleted items on Slide 2 link to.

### To create slide zooms:

1. Duplicate Slide 2 ("Ideas"). A copy of Slide 2 is inserted as a new Slide 3 and is the current slide. Jack wants you to keep Slide 3 as it is and add the slide zooms to Slide 2.

2. Display Slide 2, click anywhere on the bulleted list, click the text box outline, and then press **DELETE**. The text is deleted, and the content placeholder text and icons appear.

3. Click the border of the content placeholder, press **DELETE**, and then click the **Insert** tab. Now you will insert the slide zooms.

4. In the Links group, click the **Zoom** button, and then click **Slide Zoom**. The Insert Slide Zoom dialog box appears. See Figure 4–21.

| Figure 4–21 | Insert Slide Zoom dialog box |

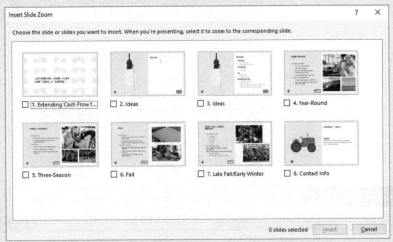

Heather Stokes/Shutterstock.com; Arina P Habich/Shutterstock.com; Love Silhouette/Shutterstock.com; fokke baarssen/ Shutterstock.com; iStock.com/AzmanJaka; Vicki L. Miller/Shutterstock.com; gvictoria/Shutterstock.com; iStock.com/ BanksPhotos; Jack Frog/Shutterstock.com; iStock.com/mediaphotos; iStock.com/FlamingPumpkin; ND700/Shutterstock.com/ Katherine T. Pinard

5. In the dialog box, click the **5. Three-Season** check box, the **6. Fall** check box, and the **7. Late Fall/Early Winter** check box. The three check boxes you clicked are selected.

6. Click **Insert**. The dialog box closes, and three slides you selected appear in the center of Slide 2 as slide zooms. On the ribbon, the Zoom contextual tab appears.

7. Click the **Zoom** tab. The Size group shows that the height of each selected slide zoom is 1.88 inches, and the width is 3.33 inches.

**Tip**

To unlock or lock the aspect ratio of objects, click the Dialog Box launcher in the Size group on the object's contextual Format tab, and then in the Format pane that opens, click the Lock aspect ratio check box.

8. In the Size group, click in the **Height** box, type **1.7**, and then press **ENTER**. The height changes to the measurement you typed. The width also changed. This is because the aspect ratio is locked for slide zooms.

9. Click a blank area of the slide to deselect the slide zooms, and then display the gridlines and the ruler.

10. Drag the slide zoom on the top of the stack down and to the right so that its top edge aligns with the gridline at the negative 1-inch mark on the vertical ruler and its right edge aligns with the right edge of the title text box and the action button.

    **Trouble?** If you have trouble aligning the top of the slide zoom with the gridline, press and hold ALT while you are positioning the slide zoom.

11. Drag the next slide zoom on the stack down and position it to the left of the first slide zoom that you positioned so that its top edge aligns with the negative 1-inch mark on the vertical ruler and so that its right edge is one gridline dot away from the slide zoom you already positioned.

12. Drag the third slide zoom to the right so its left and right edges align with the left and right edges of the slide zoom on the bottom-right and so its top edge aligns with the gridline at the 2-inch mark on the vertical ruler. You still need to add a slide zoom of Slide 4. You will insert the last slide zoom by dragging the thumbnail of Slide 4 onto Slide 2.

**13.** In the pane containing the slide thumbnails, move the pointer on top of the Slide 4 thumbnail, press and hold the mouse button, drag the thumbnail onto the slide, and then release the mouse button.

**Trouble?** If Slide 4 is displayed, you clicked the Slide 4 thumbnail before you tried to drag it. Display Slide 2, and then repeat Step 13.

**14.** Change the height of the Slide 4 slide zoom to **1.7** inches, and then position it to the left of the Slide 5 slide zoom so that its top and bottom align with the top and bottom of the slide zoom to its right and its left and right edges align with the left and right edges of the slide zoom below it. When the Zoom tab is selected, the slide number of each slide is in the lower-right corner of each slide zoom. Compare your screen to Figure 4–22.

**Figure 4–22** Resized and repositioned slide zooms on Slide 2

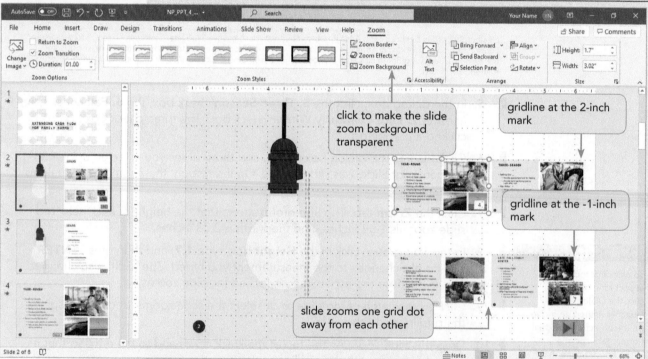

Heather Stokes/Shutterstock.com; Arina P Habich/Shutterstock.com; Love Silhouette/Shutterstock.com; fokke baarssen/Shutterstock.com; iStock.com/AzmanJaka; Vicki L. Miller/Shutterstock.com; gvictoria/Shutterstock.com; iStock.com/BanksPhotos; Jack Frog/Shutterstock.com; iStock.com/mediaphotos; iStock.com/FlamingPumpkin; ND700/Shutterstock.com/Katherine T. Pinard

**15.** Hide the gridlines and the ruler.

Now you will test the slide zoom links. Slide zooms are similar to action buttons in that you cannot test them in Normal view. You need to switch to Slide Show view.

## To test the slide zooms:

**1.** On Slide 2 (the "Ideas" slide with the slide zooms), move the pointer on top of one of the slide zooms. The pointer changes to the move pointer ✛. This is because you cannot test the link in Normal view.

2. On the Quick Access Toolbar, click the **Start from Beginning** button 🖵 . Slide 1 (the title slide) appears in Slide Show view with the Push transition.

3. Click anywhere on the slide to display Slide 2 (the "Ideas" slide with the zoom slides), and then move the pointer on top of the **Year-Round** slide zoom (the first slide zoom in the first row). The pointer changes to the pointing finger pointer 🖑 .

4. Click the **Year-Round** zoom slide. The slide zoom you clicked zooms larger and fills the screen.

5. Press **SPACEBAR**. The view slides out, sideways, and then back in so that the Slide 5 ("Three-Season") slide zoom fills the screen. As Slide 5 slides onto the screen, the bulleted list and images fade away because they have entrance animations applied.

6. Click twice anywhere on the slide except on the IDEAS link to display the slide content, and then click one more time to move to the next slide. The view shifts down and to the left so that the Slide 6 ("Fall") slide zoom fills the screen.

7. Press **SPACEBAR** to slide the view sideways so that Slide 7 ("Late Fall/Early Winter") slide zoom fills the screen. This is the last slide zoom.

8. Press **SPACEBAR**. Slide 8 ("Contact Info") appears with the Push transition.

9. Press **BACKSPACE**. Slide 7 ("Late Fall/Early Winter") appears on the screen with the Push transition. This is the actual Slide 7, not the linked slide zoom on Slide 3.

10. Press **SPACEBAR** to display Slide 8, press **SPACEBAR** again to display the black slide that signals the end of the slide show, and then press **SPACEBAR** one more time to display Slide 8 in Normal view.

## Modifying Slide Zooms

As you saw, the default transition for slide zooms is for the slide zoom to slide into view based on where it is located on the slide that contains the slide zooms. This is what happened when you tested the slide zooms you inserted on Slide 3. You can change this so that clicking a slide zoom will display the slide using whatever transition is applied to that slide instead of the slide zoom transition.

Another setting you can change is what happens when you advance the slide show when a slide zoom is displayed. The default is for the next slide to appear when you advance the slide show. You can change this so that after you click the slide zoom to display it, the next click or pressing SPACEBAR causes the slide that contains the slide zoom to reappear.

Finally, you can change the speed with which the next slide zoom or slide appears by changing the duration of the zoom. You will change some of the settings applied to the slide zooms on Slide 2.

### To modify the slide zooms on Slide 2:

1. Display Slide 2 (the "Ideas" slide with the slide zooms) if necessary, click the **Slide 4** ("Year-Round") slide zoom, and then click the **Zoom** tab. See Figure 4–23.

**Figure 4–23**    **Zoom Options group on the Zoom contextual tab**

click to have the selected slide zoom return to this slide instead of moving to the next slide zoom or slide

click to change the image used for the slide zoom

when Zoom Transition is selected, use this to change the speed of the zoom effect

IDEAS

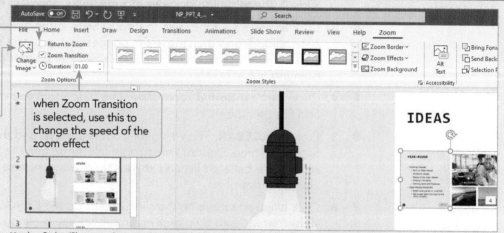

Heather Stokes/Shutterstock.com; Arina P Habich/Shutterstock.com; Love Silhouette/Shutterstock.com; fokke baarssen/ Shutterstock.com; iStock.com/AzmanJaka; Vicki L. Miller/Shutterstock.com; gvictoria/Shutterstock.com; iStock.com/BanksPhotos; Jack Frog/Shutterstock.com; iStock.com/mediaphotos; iStock.com/FlamingPumpkin; ND700/Shutterstock.com/Katherine T. Pinard

**Tip**

To change the image used for a zoom slide, in the Zoom Options group, click the Change Image button to open the Insert Pictures window. The image you select replaces the image shown as the zoom slide, but when you zoom into that slide, you will see the slide contents.

2. In the Zoom Options group, click the **Zoom Transition** check box to deselect it.

3. Click the **Slide 5** ("Three-Season") slide zoom, and then in the Zoom Options group, click the **Duration** box down arrow to change the value to **0.75** seconds.

4. Click the **Slide 6** ("Fall") slide zoom, and then in the Zoom Options group, click the **Return to Zoom** check box to select it. An arrow appears next to the slide number on the slide zoom to indicate that advancing the slide show after displaying this slide zoom will cause Slide 2 to reappear.

5. On the status bar, click the **Slide Show** button 🖵. Slide 2 appears in Slide Show view.

6. Click the **Slide 4** ("Year-Round") slide zoom. Because you deselected the Zoom Transition check box for this slide zoom, Slide 4 ("Year-Round") appears on the screen with the Push transition.

7. Press **SPACEBAR**. Because the Zoom Transition check box is still selected for the Slide 5 ("Three-Season") slide zoom, this slide appears using the zoom transition. It appears a little faster than it did in the last set of steps because you changed the time from one second to three-quarters of a second.

8. Press **SPACEBAR** three times to display Slide 6 ("Fall") with the zoom transition, and then press **SPACEBAR** again. Slide 2 (the "Ideas" slide with the slide zooms on it) appears. This is because you selected the Return to Zoom check box for the Slide 6 ("Fall") slide zoom.

9. Press **ESC** to end the slide show. Now that you've seen how the different zoom options affect the slide show, you will adjust them so that they are the same.

10. Click the **Slide 4** ("Year-Round") slide zoom, click the **Zoom** tab, click the **Zoom Transition** check box in the Zoom Options group to select it, and then change the duration to **0.75** seconds.

11. Click the **Slide 6** ("Fall") slide zoom, click the **Return to Zoom** check box to deselect it, and then change the duration to **0.75** seconds. You will apply the same settings to the Slide 7 slide zoom, except you will also select the Return to Zoom check box. This is because the Slide 7 slide zoom is the last slide zoom and Jack wants to provide the opportunity to display any of the four idea slides again.

12. Click the **Slide 7** ("Late Fall/Early Winter") slide zoom, change the duration to **0.75** seconds, and then click the **Return to Zoom** check box to select it.

13. Start the slide show from Slide 2 (the "Ideas" slide with the slide zooms), click the **Slide 4** ("Year-Round") slide zoom, press the **SPACEBAR** five times to display Slide 7 ("Late Fall/Early Winter"), wait for the wreaths to roll onto the slide, and then press **SPACEBAR** again. Slide 2 appears again.

14. On Slide 2, click the action button in the lower-right corner of the slide. Slide 8 ("Contact Info") appears.

15. Press **ESC**, and then save the changes to the presentation.

# Hiding a Slide

There are now two slides titled "Ideas" in the presentation and both contain a way to jump to the same slides. Jack wants to keep both slides in the presentation, but for now, he wants to use the Ideas slide that contains the zoom slides. He asks you to hide the other "Ideas" slide. When you hide a slide, you can still see it and edit it in Normal view, but it will not appear in Slide Show view.

**To hide Slide 3:**

**Tip**
You can also right-click a slide thumbnail, and then click Hide Slide on the shortcut menu.

1. Display Slide 3 (the "Ideas" slide with the text links).

2. Click the **Slide Show** tab, and then in the Set Up group, click the **Hide Slide** button. The Hide Slide button is selected. In the pane containing the slide thumbnails, a slash appears through the slide number for Slide 3 and that thumbnail appears somewhat faded. See Figure 4–24.

**Figure 4–24**   **Slide 3 hidden**

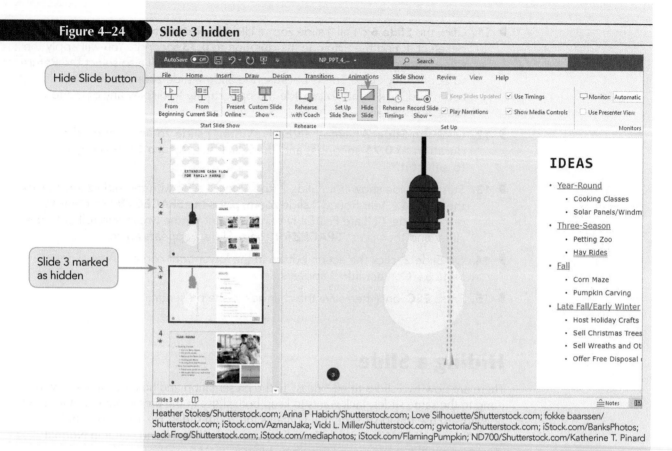

Heather Stokes/Shutterstock.com; Arina P Habich/Shutterstock.com; Love Silhouette/Shutterstock.com; fokke baarssen/
Shutterstock.com; iStock.com/AzmanJaka; Vicki L. Miller/Shutterstock.com; gvictoria/Shutterstock.com; iStock.com/BanksPhotos;
Jack Frog/Shutterstock.com; iStock.com/mediaphotos; iStock.com/FlamingPumpkin; ND700/Shutterstock.com/Katherine T. Pinard

3. On the Quick Access Toolbar, click the **Start from Beginning** button 📺.
   Slide 1 (the title slide) appears in Slide Show view.

4. Press **SPACEBAR** to display Slide 2 (the "Ideas" slide with the zoom slides),
   and then press **SPACEBAR** again. Slide 4 ("Year-Round") appears. Slide 3,
   the hidden slide, was skipped.

5. Press **ESC** to end the slide show.

6. **sam** ⬆ On Slide 1 (the title slide), add your name as the subtitle, save the
   changes to the presentation, and then close it.

Jack is happy with the modifications you've made to the presentation so far.
You modified motion path animations. You applied two animations to objects and
selected and modified one of them using the Animation pane. You set a trigger
for an animation. You also changed the fill of slide backgrounds and filled the
title slide background with a tiled picture that you made somewhat transparent.
You converted text and a shape to links and added an action button. You changed
the color of text links so that they can be more easily distinguished on the slides.
Finally, you created slide zooms to link to slides.

In the next session, you will create a self-running presentation by setting
slide timings. You will then record a narration to accompany the self-running
presentation. You also will save the presentation in other formats so it can be
more easily distributed.

# Review

## Session 4.1 Quick Check

1. What happens if you try to add a second animation by using the Animation gallery instead of the Add Animation button?
2. What is a trigger?
3. When you change the background of a slide, can you apply that change to all of the slides in a presentation?
4. What items on a slide can be a link?
5. What is an action button?
6. What is a slide zoom?

# Session 4.2 Visual Overview:

To set automatic timings manually, select the After check box. During a slide show, the slides will advance automatically after the time displayed in the After box.

When the On Mouse Click check box is selected, the slide show can be advanced by clicking the slide, even if there are saved slide timings. If the On Mouse Click check box is deselected, the slide show cannot be advanced by clicking a slide, although users can still use the keyboard or click links to display other slides.

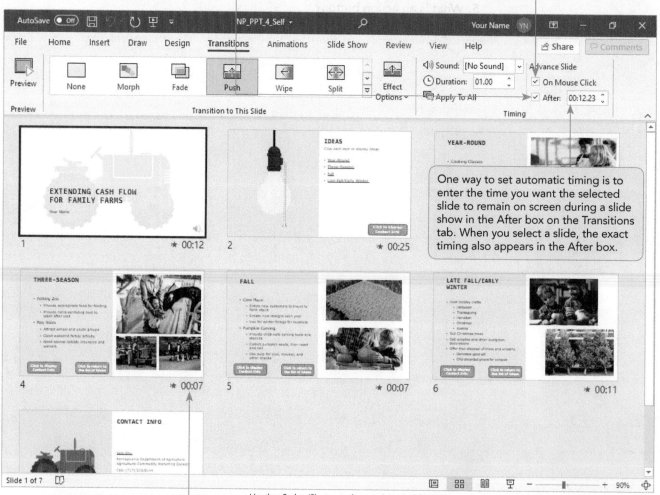

One way to set automatic timing is to enter the time you want the selected slide to remain on screen during a slide show in the After box on the Transitions tab. When you select a slide, the exact timing also appears in the After box.

Automatic timings indicate how many seconds a slide will stay on the screen before transitioning to the next slide during a slide show.

Heather Stokes/Shutterstock.com; Arina P Habich/Shutterstock.com; Love Silhouette/Shutterstock.com; fokke baarssen/Shutterstock.com; iStock.com/AzmanJaka; Vicki L. Miller/Shutterstock.com; gvictoria/Shutterstock.com; iStock.com/BanksPhotos; Jack Frog/Shutterstock.com; iStock.com/mediaphotos; iStock.com/FlamingPumpkin; ND700/Shutterstock.com/Katherine T. Pinard

# Automatic Slide Timings

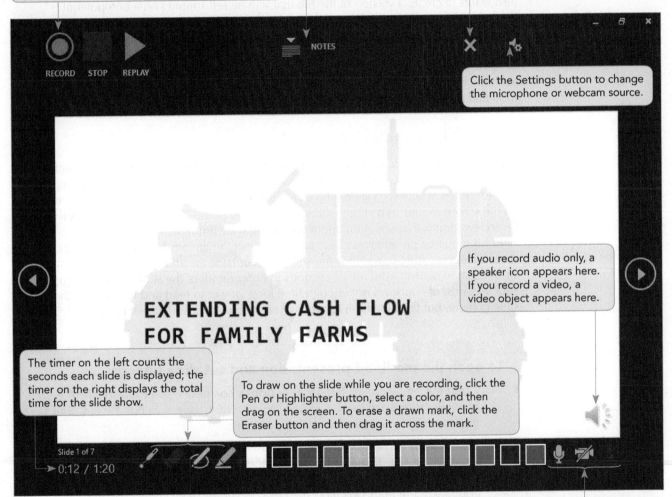

Click the Record button to start recording the slide show. Click the Stop button to stop recording. Click the Replay button to watch the recording of the slide. After you start recording, the Record button changes to the Pause button. You can click the Pause button to pause the recording without stopping it.

If the slide includes speaker notes, you can click the NOTES button to display the notes on the screen. The notes will not be part of the slide show recording.

Click the Clear button to delete the recording from the current slide or from all the slides.

Click the Settings button to change the microphone or webcam source.

If you record audio only, a speaker icon appears here. If you record a video, a video object appears here.

The timer on the left counts the seconds each slide is displayed; the timer on the right displays the total time for the slide show.

To draw on the slide while you are recording, click the Pen or Highlighter button, select a color, and then drag on the screen. To erase a drawn mark, click the Eraser button and then drag it across the mark.

EXTENDING CASH FLOW FOR FAMILY FARMS

Keep the Microphone button selected to record audio. Keep the Camera button selected to record video. Keep the Camera Preview button selected to see a preview of your webcam recording on the screen while you are recording.

Heather Stokes/Shutterstock.com

# Creating Self-Running Presentations

A self-running presentation advances without a presenter or viewer doing anything. Self-running presentations include settings that specify the amount of time each slide is displayed as well as the time at which animations occur. Some self-running presentations include audio that takes the place of the presenter's oral explanations or gives the viewer instructions for watching the slide show. To give the user more control over the viewing experience, you can include links on the slides or allow the user to advance the slide show manually using the mouse or keyboard.

Jack intends to use his PowerPoint file when he gives oral presentations, but he also wants to create a version of the file that will be self-running on a computer at agricultural fairs and trade shows for people who are unable to attend his presentation. Jack made several modifications to the presentation including removing the slide zooms, modifying the links, and removing the trigger from the lit light bulb. This is because in a self-running presentation, trigger animations do not occur automatically, so the lit bulb would never appear unless the viewer knew to click the unlit bulb. This modified presentation can now be set up as a self-running presentation.

## Setting Slide Timings Manually

When setting up a slide show to be self-running, you need to specify how long each slide remains on the screen. The amount of time each slide stays on the screen might vary for different slides—a slide with only three bullet points might not need to remain on the screen as long as a slide containing six bullet points. See the Session 4.2 Visual Overview for more information about specifying slide timings.

In his modified presentation, Jack asks you to set the timings to four seconds per slide, except for Slide 6, which is the slide that contains the animated wreaths. That slide needs to be displayed for 10 seconds in order for all of the slide content to appear. Four seconds, of course, is not enough time for a viewer to read and understand the slide content, but the slide timings are kept short here for instructional purposes.

### To open the modified presentation and set slide timings:

1. Open the presentation **NP_PPT_4-2.pptx**, located in the **PowerPoint4 > Module** included with your Data Files, and then save it as **NP_PPT_4_Self** to the location where you are saving your files.

2. Display Slide 2 ("Ideas"), click the lit bulb graphic, and then click the **Animations** tab. The animation sequence icon does not contain a lightning bolt because Jack removed the trigger. In the timing group, After Previous appears in the Start box, and the delay is set for one-quarter second.

3. Display Slide 3 ("Year-Round"). Jack modified the four slides that contain the ideas so that the first bulleted item animates automatically along with the picture that goes along with that item, and then after a second or two, the next item and its associated picture animates.

4. Display Slide 7 ("Contact Info"), and then click each item in the unnumbered list. You can see that in the Animation group, the Fade entrance animation is selected and the start setting is On Click for each of the three items.

5. On the status bar, click the **Slide Sorter** button to switch to Slide Sorter view. Slide 7 is selected.

6. Press and hold **SHIFT**, scroll up if necessary, click the **Slide 1** (the title slide) thumbnail, and then release **SHIFT**. All of the slides are selected.

7. On the ribbon, click the **Transitions** tab. In the Timing group, the On Mouse Click check box is selected in the Advance Slide section. This means that the viewer can take an action to advance the slide show.

8. In the Timing group, click the **After** check box. The check box is selected, and 00:00 appears below each slide thumbnail. See Figure 4–25.

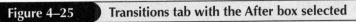

| Figure 4–25 | Transitions tab with the After box selected |

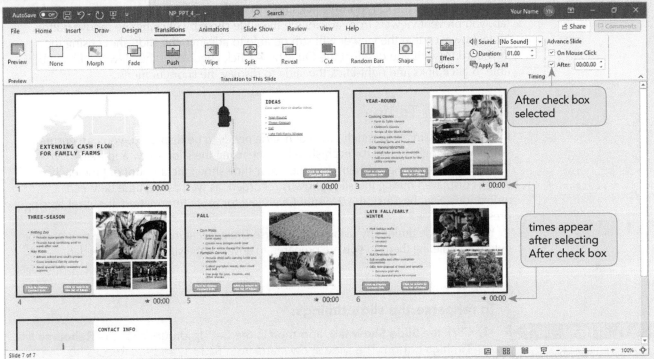

Heather Stokes/Shutterstock.com; Arina P Habich/Shutterstock.com; Love Silhouette/Shutterstock.com; fokke baarssen/ Shutterstock.com; iStock.com/AzmanJaka; Vicki L. Miller/Shutterstock.com; gvictoria/Shutterstock.com; iStock.com/BanksPhotos; Jack Frog/Shutterstock.com; iStock.com/mediaphotos; iStock.com/FlamingPumpkin; ND700/Shutterstock.com/Katherine T. Pinard

**Tip**

If you want to remove slide timings, select all the slides in Slide Sorter view, click the Transitions tab, and then click the After check box in the Timing group to deselect it.

9. In the Timing group, click the **After up** arrow four times to change the time to four seconds per slide. Under each slide thumbnail, the time changes to 00:04.00. Because Slide 6 contains more information and more animations than the other slides, that slide needs to be displayed longer.

10. Click the **Slide 6** ("Late Fall/Early Winter") thumbnail, and then in the Timing group, click the **After up** arrow six times to change the time for Slide 6 to 10 seconds.

11. On the Quick Access Toolbar, click the **Start From Beginning** button. Watch as Slide 1 appears, then after four seconds, Slide 2 ("Ideas") appears. After a brief pause, the lit bulb appears, and then after four seconds, Slide 3 ("Year Round") appears.

12. Immediately after Slide 3 appears, click the mouse button twice to display the bulleted list and the pictures, and then click it again to display Slide 4 ("Three-Season"). You are able to advance the slide show by clicking the mouse button because you left the On Mouse Click check box on the Transitions tab selected.

**13.** Watch as the slide show advances through the rest of the slides. When Slide 7 appears, watch as the unnumbered list appears automatically, even though the animation is set to start On Click. This is because the automatic slide timing overrides the animation's On Click start setting.

**14.** When the black slide that indicates the end of the slide show appears, press **SPACEBAR**. The presentation appears in Slide Sorter view.

If you deselect the On Mouse Click check box in the Timing group on the Transitions tab, you prevent viewers from advancing the slide show by clicking the mouse button. Note, however, that the viewer will still be able to advance the slide show using the keyboard. Also, if you deselect the On Mouse Click check box, the viewer will still be able to click links and right-click the slide to display the shortcut menu.

## Rehearsing Timings

Instead of guessing how much time each slide needs to be displayed, you can ensure you have the right timing for each slide by rehearsing the slide show and then saving the slide timings. When you rehearse a slide show, the amount of time each slide is displayed during the slide show is recorded, as well as the time between animations. See the Session 4.2 Visual Overview for more information about rehearsing presentations.

You'll set slide timings by using the Rehearse Timings feature. Read the next set of steps before completing them so you are prepared to advance the slide show as needed.

**To rehearse the slide timings:**

> **Tip**
> Click the Pause Recording button on the Recording toolbar to pause the timer; click the Repeat button to restart the timer for the current slide.

**1.** Click the **Slide Show** tab, and then in the Set Up group, click the **Rehearse Timings** button. The slide show starts from Slide 1, and the Recording toolbar appears on the screen in the upper-left corner. The toolbar includes a timer on the left that indicates the number of seconds the slide is displayed and a timer on the right that tracks the total time for the slide show.

**2.** Leave Slide 1 on the screen for about five seconds, and then advance the slide show. Slide 2 ("Ideas") appears with the bulleted list and the unlit light bulb, then the lit bulb appears.

**3.** Leave Slide 2 on the screen for about five seconds, and then advance to Slide 3 ("Year-Round").

**4.** On Slides 3 ("Year-Round") through 5 ("Fall"), wait for the bulleted lists and pictures to appear, and then wait for about three more seconds on each slide so that the timer indicates 6 seconds.

**5.** On Slide 6 ("Late Fall/Early Winter"), wait for the bulleted lists and pictures to appear, and then wait for about two to three more seconds so that the timer indicates 10 seconds.

**6.** On Slide 7 ("Contact Info"), wait two seconds, advance the slide three times to display the three items in the unnumbered list, and then advance the slide show once more when the timer indicates 10 seconds. A dialog box opens asking if you want to save the timings.

**7.** Click **Yes**. The presentation appears in Slide Sorter view. The rehearsed time appears below each slide thumbnail. You can also see the timing assigned to the slides on the Transitions tab.

▶ 8. Click the **Transitions** tab, and then click the **Slide 1** thumbnail. In the Timing group, the recorded timing to the hundredth of a second for the selected slide appears in the After box. The rehearsed timing replaced the four-second slide timing you set previously.

After you rehearse a slide show, you should run it to evaluate the timings. If a slide stays on the screen for too much or too little time, stop the slide show, and then change that slide's time in the After box in the Timing group on the Transitions tab.

### To play the slide show using the rehearsed slide timings:

▶ 1. On the Quick Access Toolbar, click the **Start From Beginning** button ▣. The slide show starts and Slide 1 appears on the screen. The slide show advances to Slide 2 ("Ideas") automatically after the saved rehearsal timing for Slide 1 elapses. When Slide 7 ("Contact Info") appears, the animation occurs automatically after the two seconds you waited before you advanced the slide show.

▶ 2. When the final black slide appears, advance the slide show to end it.

Jack wants you to see what happens if the viewer tries to interact with the slide show and clicks one of the shapes that links to the last slide.

### To interact with the self-running presentation:

▶ 1. Click the **Slide 2** thumbnail, and then on the status bar, click the **Slide Show** button ▣. Slide 2 ("Ideas") appears in Slide Show view.

▶ 2. Move the mouse to display the pointer, and then in the lower-right corner, click the **Click to display Contact Info** shape. Slide 7 ("Contact Info") appears.

▶ 3. Press **BACKSPACE** as many times as needed to display Slide 5 ("Fall"), and then wait. After about six seconds, the slide show advances automatically to Slide 6 ("Late Fall/Early Winter").

▶ 4. Right-click a blank area of the slide, and then on the shortcut menu, click **See All Slides**. The slides appear as thumbnails, similar to Slide Sorter view.

▶ 5. Click the **Slide 3** thumbnail. Slide 3 ("Year-Round") appears in Slide Show view. After about six seconds, the slide show advances.

▶ 6. Press **S**. The slide show stops advancing automatically.

▶ 7. Press **S** again. The slide show resumes advancing automatically.

▶ 8. Press **ESC** to end the slide show and display the presentation in Slide Sorter view.

**Tip**

You can also right-click a blank area of the screen, and then click Pause to stop the automatic slide advancement or click Resume to resume the automatic advancement.

## Recording a Slide Show

When you use the Rehearse Timings command, only the amount of time a slide is displayed during the slide show and the time when animations occur are saved. In addition to just recording timings, you can record a slide show by recording video of yourself or just narration to give viewers more information about your presentation's content.

To record video or narration to play while a slide is displayed, you use the Record Slide Show command. When you record video, the recorded video for each slide is inserted on the slide as a video object. If you record narration only, the recorded audio is inserted on each slide as an audio object. Refer to the Session 4.2 Visual Overview for more information about recording video or narration.

When you record video or narration for a slide, you should not read the text on the slide—the viewers can read that for themselves. You should provide additional information about the slides or instructions for the viewers as they watch the self-running presentation. For example, you can tell viewers that they can click action buttons to manually advance the presentation.

When you record a slide show, you can also draw on the slides. The default color is red, but you can change this. Or you can use the highlighter tool to draw a thick, transparent line across items on the slide.

## Reference

### Recording Narration

- Click the Slide Show tab, and then in the Set Up group, click the Record Slide Show button.
- In the recording window, click the Microphone, Camera Off/Camera On, and Camera Preview buttons to select or deselect these options.
- Click the Pen or Highlighter button to select that tool, and then click the color you want to use to draw on the slides.
- At the top of the window, click the RECORD button, and then after the three-second countdown, speak into the microphone to record the narration for the current slide.
- After the desired amount of time, advance the slide show, record the narration for the next slide, and then continue, as desired, to other slides.
- End the slide show after recording the last narration; or continue displaying all the slides in the presentation for the appropriate amount of time, even if you do not add narration to each slide, and then end the slide show as you normally would.
- Click the Close button in the upper-right corner to close the recording window.

Jack wants viewers to have some guidance in navigating through the presentation. You will record narration for Slides 1 and 2 and record new timings for these two slides.

1. Make sure your computer is equipped with a microphone.

   **Trouble?** If your computer doesn't have a microphone, connect one, or check with your instructor or technical support person. If you can't connect a microphone, read the following steps but do not complete them. If your computer has a webcam, it probably includes a microphone.

2. Click the Slide 3 thumbnail to select it, if necessary, and then on the ribbon, click the **Slide Show** tab.

**Tip**

You can also right-click a tab on the ribbon, click Customize the Ribbon, and then in the Customize the Ribbon list in the PowerPoint Options dialog box, click the Recording check box. Click OK, and then on the new Recording tab on the ribbon, in the Record group, click the Record Slide Show button.

3. In the Set Up group, click the **Record Slide Show** button. The recording window appears with Slide 3 displayed. If your computer has a microphone and a camera, and if they are turned on, and the camera preview is turned on. The camera preview is the small square at the bottom right of the slide. It shows you how you look as your camera is recording you. In these steps, the camera will be turned off.

4. At the bottom right of the screen, click the **Turn Camera Off** button 📷. Both the camera and the camera preview are turned off.

   **Trouble?** If the camera button is the Turn Camera On button 📷, do not click it or you will turn the camera back on.

5. At the top of the screen click the **Settings** button, and then point to the microphone name listed below the label "Microphone." If the selected microphone is not the one you are using, click the microphone you are using. If there is only one microphone listed, it is probably the built-in microphone.

6. Below the slide, in the Inking section, click the **Pen** button ✏️. The Pen button is selected. In the row of color squares, the red color is selected. (It is the only color square without a white outline.)

The information below the bottom left of a slide tells you which slide is displayed and how many slides are in the presentation. It also tells you the timing set for the current slide and how long the entire presentation takes to view in Slide Show view if the slide timings are used.

Now that the recording options are set up, you can start recording. To do this, you click the Record button ⏺ at the top of the window. You want to start recording from Slide 1.

1. To the left of the slide, click the **Return to the previous slide** button ◀ twice. Slide 1 appears.

2. At the top of the screen, click the **RECORD** button. The RECORD button changes to the PAUSE button, and after a three-second countdown, Slide 1 reappears on the screen with the Push transition. The timer below the slide that had indicated the rehearsed timing for Slide 1 starts over at zero.

3. Speak the following into the microphone: "**This presentation describes several ideas for increasing cash flow at your farm. The presentation will advance automatically from one slide to the next.**"

4. Wait for a moment, click the **Advance to the next slide button** ⏭ to the right of the slide to advance to Slide 2, wait for the light to "turn on," and then say into the microphone, "**To go to a specific slide, click its name in this list. Or right-click a blank area of a slide, click See All Slides, and then click the slide you want to view. To pause or resume the slide show, press S on the keyboard. You can also click the buttons at the bottom of the slides.**"

5. Wait five seconds, and then at the top of the window, click the **STOP** button. The timer below the slide stops, and the Pause button changed back to the Record button. A speaker icon appears in the bottom-right corner of Slide 2.

**Tip**

Another way to remove a recording on a slide is to delete the speaker icon in Normal view.

6. To the left of the slide, click the **Return to the previous slide** button ◉ to display Slide 1. A speaker icon appears on this slide as well.

   **Trouble?** If you made a mistake and want to re-record, click the Clear button at the top of the window, and then click the command to clear the recording on either the current slide or on all the slides. Next, display the slide that you want to record again, click the Record button, and then click the Stop button when you are finished.

7. In the upper-right corner of the window, click the **Close** button ☒. The recording window closes, and the presentation appears in Slide Sorter view.

8. Double-click the **Slide 1** thumbnail to display it in Normal view, and then click the speaker icon in the lower-right corner. This is the narration you recorded on Slide 1.

9. On the ribbon, click the **Playback** tab. In the Audio Options group, note that the start timing is set to Automatically (not In Click Sequence), and the Hide During Show check box is selected.

10. On the Quick Access Toolbar, click the **Start From Beginning** button 🖵. The slide show starts, the recording that you made for Slide 1 plays, and then the slide show advances to Slide 2 a few seconds after the recording ends. Five seconds after the recording on Slide 2 finishes playing, the slide show advances automatically to display Slide 3. The rest of the slides will continue to appear using the timings you set when you rehearsed the presentation.

11. Press **ESC** to end the slide show, and then save your changes.

## Insight

### Creating a Screen Recording and Inserting Screenshots

In addition to creating a recording of a slide show, you can record your actions on a screen or take a screenshot and insert it on a slide. The commands for both of these actions are on both the Insert tab and the Recording tab.

To create a recording of your actions on the screen, first open the window in which you want to record your actions. Then in the window containing your PowerPoint presentation, click the Screen Recording button in the Media group on the Insert tab. The PowerPoint window you are working in minimizes, the Screen Recording toolbar appears, the pointer changes to the thin cross pointer, and the entire screen is dimmed. Drag the pointer from one corner to the other of the window in which you want to record your actions. The Record button on the toolbar turns red, indicating that you can click it to begin recording. Click the Record button, do the actions you want to record, speaking to record audio if you want. When you are finished, click the Stop button. The screen recording is added to the current slide in the PowerPoint presentation as a video object.

To add a screenshot of a window to a presentation, make sure the window is open. Then click the Screenshot button in the Images group on the Insert tab. This opens a menu. Click one of the windows shown in the menu to insert a screenshot of that window, or click Screen Clipping to drag on the part of the screen that you want to insert as an image on a slide.

## Applying Kiosk Browsing

Jack wants you to set the presentation so that after the last slide appears, it will restart. He also doesn't want the viewer to be able to do anything other than click the links and press ESC to end the slide show. To do this, you'll set up the slide show to be browsed at a kiosk. If you apply kiosk browsing, every slide must have a link or timing assigned to it. Otherwise, after Slide 1 appears, the viewer will be unable to advance the slide show.

### To set up the presentation for browsing at a kiosk:

▶ **1.** Click the **Slide Show** tab, and then in the Set Up group, click the **Set Up Slide Show** button. The Set Up Show dialog box opens. See Figure 4–26.

| Figure 4–26 | Set Up Show dialog box |

select for kiosk browsing

will be selected automatically when kiosk browsing is selected

select to disable narration

select to disable animations

options for advancing slides; these are not available for kiosk browsing

The Advance slides section in the Set Up Show dialog box is similar to the options in the Timing group on the Transitions tab. However, the options in this dialog box take precedence. For example, if the After check box is selected on the Transitions tab, but you select the Manually option button in this dialog box, the slide show will not advance automatically.

**Tip**

To change the resolution of the slide show, click the Slide show monitor arrow, click the monitor on which the slide show will run, click the Resolution arrow, and then click the resolution you want to use.

▶ **2.** In the Show type section, click the **Browsed at a kiosk (full screen)** option button. In the Show options section, the Loop continuously until 'Esc' check box becomes selected. That option has also changed to light gray, indicating that you cannot deselect it. The options under Advance slides also cannot be changed now.

▶ **3.** Click **OK**. The dialog box closes, and the presentation is set up for kiosk browsing.

▶ **4.** Display Slide 2 ("Ideas"), and then on the status bar, click the **Slide Show** button 🖵. Slide 2 appears in Slide Show view.

▶ **5.** Click the **Click to display Contact Info** shape. Slide 7 ("Contact Info") appears.

▶ **6.** Press **SPACEBAR**. The slide show does not advance. Instead, Slide 7 remains on the screen until the saved timing for Slide 7 elapses, and then the slide show automatically starts over with Slide 1.

**7.** After Slide 1 (the title slide) appears on the screen, press **ESC** to end the slide show.

**8.** Save the changes to the presentation.

## Proskills

Written Communication: Preparing a PowerPoint Presentation for People to View on Their Own

You have learned that when you prepare a PowerPoint presentation to use while you are presenting a topic in front of an audience, the PowerPoint file should only contain content that enhances your oral presentation to keep the audience focused on you. However, when you prepare a PowerPoint presentation for others to view on their own, you need to make sure the slides contain enough content so that anyone viewing it will understand it without you standing in front of them to clarify your message. This usually means you need to add more text than you would if you were presenting orally, use complete sentences rather than one-word bullets, or add narration to explain visuals. Keep in mind that PowerPoint is not just an alternative to a word processor. Unlike a printed document, a PowerPoint presentation can help present your information in a visual manner. People understand and remember information presented graphically better than information presented as text. Take advantage of the many tools available in PowerPoint to display or enhance the content of the slides with graphics.

## Using the Document Inspector

The Document Inspector is a tool you can use to check a presentation for hidden data that you might not want others to see, such as the author's name and other personal information, objects that are in the presentation but are hidden or placed in the area next to a slide instead of on the slide, and speaker notes.

Jack wants to be able to send the presentation to small farmers who call into his office looking for information on expanding their selling season and offerings. Before doing so, he wants to ensure there is no hidden data he wouldn't want to distribute. You will check the presentation for hidden data.

### To check the presentation using the Document Inspector:

**1.** With Slide 1 (the title slide) displayed, on the status bar, click the **Notes** button. There is a note on this slide that Jack added before he gave you the presentation to work with. Jack created this note to remind him to create a self-running presentation. The audience doesn't need to see this note. When you use the Document Inspector, you will remove notes.

**2.** On the ribbon, click the **File** tab, and then click **Info**. The Info screen in Backstage view appears. On the right, file properties are listed, including the number of slides in the presentation and the author name. On the left, next to the Check for Issues button, a bulleted list informs you that the presentation contains document properties that you might want to delete, off-slide objects, presentation notes, and content that people with disabilities are unable to read. See Figure 4–27.

Figure 4–27    Info screen in Backstage view

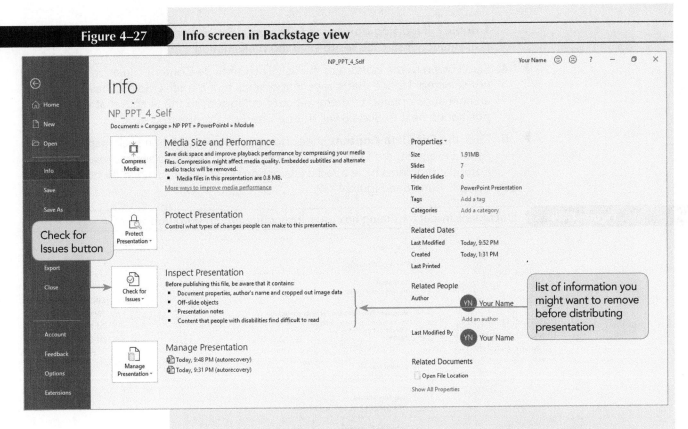

3. Click the **Check for Issues** button, and then click **Inspect Document**. The Document Inspector dialog box opens. All of the visible check boxes are selected. Each section is a category of issues that will be examined. See Figure 4–28.

Figure 4–28    Document Inspector dialog box

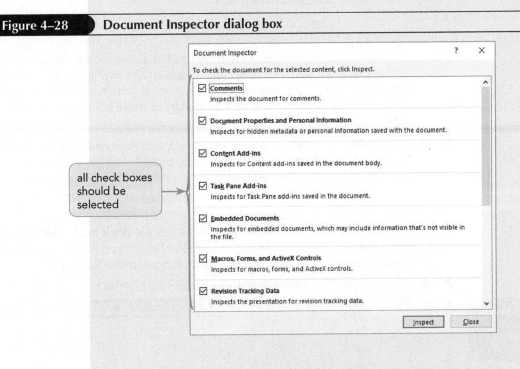

**Trouble?** If a dialog box opens telling you that you need to save the presentation first, click Yes to save the presentation.

4. Scroll down to the bottom of the list. The Off-Slide Content check box is not selected. Notice that it says that objects that are off-slide and have an animation applied to them will not be flagged, so the wreath that is positioned next to Slide 8 will not be listed as a problem.

5. Click the **Off-Slide Content** check box to select it, and then click **Inspect**. After a moment, the Document Inspector dialog box displays the results. Potential problems have a red exclamation point and a Remove All button next to them. See Figure 4–29.

| Figure 4–29 | Document Inspector dialog box after inspecting the presentation |
| --- | --- |

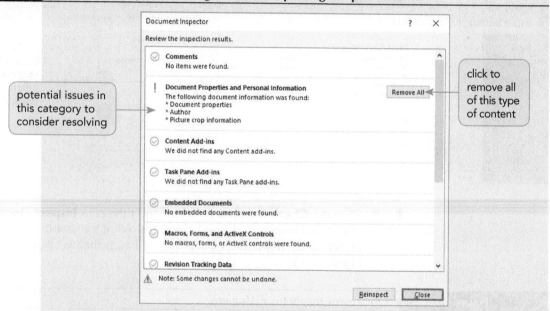

potential issues in this category to consider resolving

click to remove all of this type of content

Jack doesn't mind that he is identified as the author of the presentation or that other document properties are saved with the file, so you will not remove the document properties and personal information. You should, however, scroll the Document Inspector dialog to make sure no other potential problems are identified.

6. In the dialog box, scroll down if necessary, and then next to Presentation Notes, click the **Remove All** button. The button disappears, a green checkmark replaces the red exclamation point next to Presentation Notes, and a message appears in that section telling you that all presentation notes were removed.

7. In the dialog box, click **Close**, and then click the **Back** button ⬅ to return to the presentation with Slide 1 (the title slide) displayed in Normal view. The speaker note that Jack had added is no longer in the Notes pane.

8. On the status bar, click the **Notes** button to close the Notes pane.

9. On **Slide 1** (the title slide), add your name as the subtitle, and then save the changes to the presentation.

Save the changes now because next you will be saving the presentation in a different format.

# Saving a Presentation in Other Formats

PowerPoint lets you save presentations in several formats that allow others to view the presentation without allowing them to make any changes to it. Figure 4–30 lists several of the file formats you can save a PowerPoint presentation as.

| Figure 4–30 | File formats that PowerPoint presentations can be saved as |
| --- | --- |

| File Format | Description |
| --- | --- |
| MPEG-4 Video<br>Windows Media Video | A video created from the slides in the presentation. |
| PNG Portable Network Graphics<br>JPEG File Interchange Format | One or all of the slides saved as individual graphic files in the PNG or JPG graphic format. |
| PowerPoint Picture Presentation | Each slide is saved as a graphic object (as if you took a photo of each slide) and then each graphic object is placed on a slide in a new PowerPoint presentation. |
| PDF | Portable Document File format, a file format shows a document as it looks in the app that created it and that can be opened on any make or model of computer, as long as a free PDF reader program is installed, such as the Reader app included with Windows 10. |
| XPS | XML Paper Specification, a file format that lists the content of a document and describes how it should look and that can be opened on any make or model of computer |
| PowerPoint Show | A PowerPoint format that automatically opens in Slide Show view if you double-click the file in a File Explorer window. |
| PowerPoint 97-2003 | A PowerPoint format that can be opened in earlier versions of PowerPoint, specifically, PowerPoint 97, PowerPoint 2000, PowerPoint 2002, and PowerPoint 2003. |
| Outline/RTF | The text of the presentation saved in a Word document. |

Jack wants to be able to post the presentation to his department's website and email the presentation to small farmers when they contact him for information about expanding their season or services. To ensure that the presentation can be opened and viewed by anyone, regardless of the type of computer they have and the programs they have access to, he asked you to save it in several formats.

To save the file in different formats, you can use the Export screen in Backstage view or the Save As dialog box. You'll save the presentation in several different formats now.

**Tip**

In addition to using the Export screen, you can click Save As in Backstage view, and then click Browse to open the Save As dialog box. Click the Save as type arrow, and then click the file type you want to save the presentation as.

## Saving a Presentation as a Video

You can create a video of your presentation that can be viewed the same way you view any digital video, in an app such as the Movies & TV app included with Windows 10. You can save a presentation as a video in either the MPEG-4 or Windows Media Video file format. When you do this using the command on the Export screen in Backstage view, you can choose the resolution of the video, whether to use recorded narrations and timings, or, if you choose not to use saved timings, how long each slide will appear on the screen. After you have created the video, you can play it in any video player.

Jack wants you to save the presentation as a video. When he posts it, he will include instructions to let viewers know that despite the narration on Slide 2, because it is a video and not a PowerPoint file, they will not be able to click the links to control the progression of the slides.

## To save the presentation as a video:

1. On the ribbon, click the **File** tab, and then in the navigation bar, click **Export** to display the Export screen in Backstage view.

2. In the Export list on the left, click **Create a Video**. Options for saving the presentation as a video appear on the right. See Figure 4–31. The options shown are the default options and are how the video would be created if you used the Save As dialog box to save the presentation as video.

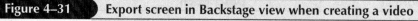

**Figure 4–31** Export screen in Backstage view when creating a video

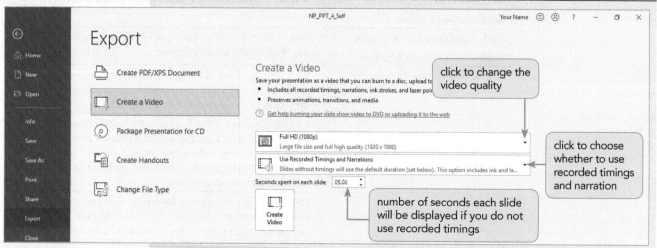

First, you need to select the quality of the video you want to create. Jack wants people to be able to play this presentation on smartphones, tablets, or other mobile devices, so you will create a video with the smallest possible file size.

3. Click the **Full HD (1080p)** button. The menu that opens lists four options for selecting the quality of the video. The highest quality—and therefore the largest file size—is Ultra HD (4K), and the lowest quality is Standard (480p).

4. Click **Standard (480p)**.

5. Click the **Use Recorded Timings and Narrations** button. The menu that opens allows you to choose to use or not use the recorded narrations and timings. You can also preview the timings or record new timings. If you choose to not use the recorded narrations and timings, you could adjust the number of seconds for each slide to be displayed in the Seconds to spend on each slide box.

6. Click **Use Recorded Timings and Narrations**.

7. Click the **Create Video** button. Backstage view closes and the Save As dialog box opens with MPEG-4 Video selected in the Save as type box and the filename of the presentation in the File name box. If you wanted, you could change the file type by clicking the Save as type arrow and then clicking Windows Media Video. The folder where you are storing your files should be the current folder.

8. Change the name in the File name box to **NP_PPT_4_Video**, and then click **Save**. The dialog box closes, and in the status bar, a progress bar labeled Creating video NP_PPT_4_Video.mp4 appears. After a moment, the progress bar disappears, which means the video has been created.

Now that you've created the video, you can watch it.

### To watch the video:

1. Open a File Explorer folder window, and then navigate to the folder where you are storing your files. The NP_PPT_4_Video file is included in the file list.

   Double-click the **NP_PPT_4_Video** file. Your video player starts and the video you created starts playing. The narrations and timings you recorded are retained. After the last slide appears, the video ends.

2. Close the video player.

3. On the Windows taskbar, click the **PowerPoint** button [P]. The PowerPoint window appears with the NP_PPT_4_Self presentation displayed.

## Saving Slides as Pictures and a Presentation as a Picture Presentation

If you want to distribute your presentation to others so they can see it but prevent them from modifying it or copying complex animations, backgrounds, or other features, you can save individual slides as graphic files. You can choose the type of graphic file you want to save the slides as. The most common choices are PNG or JPEG. You can also save slides in the TIF, BMP, and other graphic file formats.

When you save slides as graphic files, you can choose to save only the current slide or all of the slides in the presentation. If you save only the current slide, the file is saved in the folder you choose. If you save all of the slides in the presentation as graphic files, a new folder is automatically created with the same name as the presentation file name. Each slide is saved as a graphic file in this new folder. The file name of each file is SlideX where "X" is the slide number in the presentation.

Jack asks you to save the title slide as a graphic file in the PNG format.

### To save a slide as a picture:

1. Display Slide 1 (the title slide) if necessary.

2. On the ribbon, click the **File** tab, and then in the navigation bar, click **Export**.

3. On the Export screen, click **Change File Type**. The right side of the screen changes to list various file type options that you can save the presentation as. See Figure 4–32. You will save Slide 1 as a PNG file.

**Figure 4–32** | **Export screen in Backstage view with Change File Type selected**

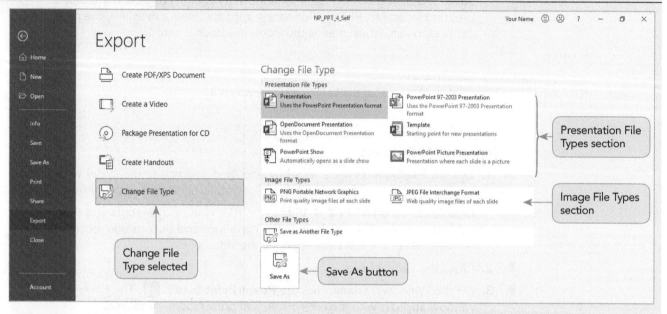

**Tip**

If you want to choose a different file format, click the Save as type arrow, and then click the file format you want to use.

4. In the Image File Types section in the right pane, click **PNG Portable Network Graphics**, and then click the **Save As** button. The Save As dialog box opens with PNG Portable Network Graphics Format in the Save as type box. The name in the File name box is the same as the presentation filename, and the current folder is the folder in which you are storing your files.

5. Change the filename to **NP_PPT_4_PNG**, and then click **Save**. The Save As dialog box closes and another dialog box opens asking which slides you want to export. You can choose to export all of the slides or just the current slide.

6. In the dialog box, click **Just This One**. The dialog box closes and Slide 1 is saved as a PNG file.

7. On the Windows taskbar, click the **File Explorer** button 🗔. The NP_PPT_4_PNG file is included in the file list.

8. Double-click the **NP_PPT_4_PNG** file. The Photos app opens and Slide 1 of the presentation appears as a picture.

   **Trouble?** If a dialog box opens asking how you want to open this file, click the app you want to use, and then click OK.

9. Close the Photos app window, and then on the Windows taskbar, click the **PowerPoint** button 📄. The PowerPoint window appears with the NP_PPT_4_Self presentation displayed.

You can also save the entire presentation as a picture presentation. When you save a presentation as a picture presentation, each slide is saved as an image file in the JPEG format, and then that image is placed on a slide in a new presentation so that it fills the entire slide. If there are timings assigned to the slides, the timings will be preserved.

Jack asks you to save the presentation as a picture presentation.

## To save the presentation as a picture presentation:

▶ 1. On the ribbon, click the **File** tab, and then in the navigation bar, click **Export**.

▶ 2. On the Export screen, click **Change File Type**, and then in the Presentation File Types section in the right pane, click **PowerPoint Picture Presentation**.

▶ 3. Click the **Save As** button. The Save As dialog box opens with PowerPoint Picture Presentation in the Save as type box. The name in the File name box is the same as the presentation filename, and the current folder is the folder in which you are storing your files.

▶ 4. Change the filename to **NP_PPT_4_PicturePres**, and then click **Save**. The Save As dialog box closes and, after a moment, another dialog box opens telling you that a copy of the presentation has been saved.

▶ 5. Click **OK**. You can open the picture presentation in the same way you normally open a presentation.

▶ 6. On the ribbon, click the **File** tab, and then in the navigation bar, click **Open**. The Open screen appears in Backstage view.

▶ 7. Navigate to the folder where you are storing your files, if necessary, click **NP_PPT_4_PicturePres**, and then click **Open**. The presentation opens in Normal view, displaying Slide 1 (the title slide).

▶ 8. Click anywhere on the slide. Sizing handles appear around the edges of the slide in the Slide pane and the Picture Format tab appears on the ribbon. This is because all of the objects in the original slide were converted to a single JPEG file and this picture is sized to fill the entire slide. See Figure 4–33.

| Figure 4–33 | Image of Slide 1 selected in the picture presentation |

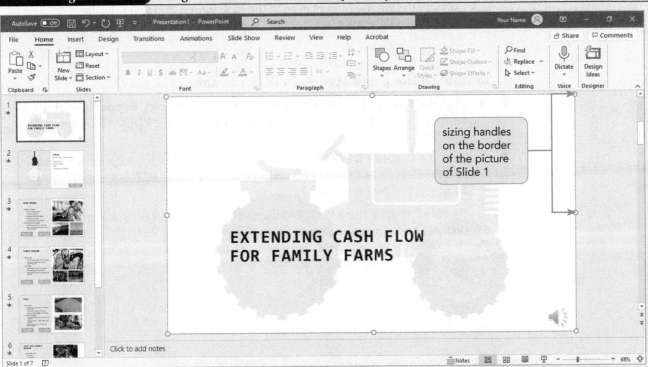

Heather Stokes/Shutterstock.com; Arina P Habich/Shutterstock.com; Love Silhouette/Shutterstock.com; fokke baarssen/ Shutterstock.com; iStock.com/AzmanJaka; Vicki L. Miller/Shutterstock.com; gvictoria/Shutterstock.com; iStock.com/BanksPhotos; Jack Frog/Shutterstock.com; iStock.com/mediaphotos

9. Display **Slide 3** ("Year-Round") in the Slide pane, and then click the "Click to display Contact Info" shape. The shape is not selected. Instead, the entire image of Slide 3 is selected.

10. On the status bar, click the **Slide Show button** 🖵. Slide 3 appears in Slide Show view.

11. Click the "Click to display Contact Info" shape. Nothing happens. The links do not function because each slide is just a picture of the original slide.

12. Wait several more seconds. After about eight seconds, Slide 4 ("Three-Season") appears.

13. Press **ESC** to end the slide show, and then click the Transitions tab. The After check box in the Timing group is selected, and the timing you set is in the After box.

14. Close the **NP_PPT_4_PicturePres** file. The original NP_PPT_4_Self presentation appears again.

## Save a Presentation as a PDF

The PDF file format is a format that can be opened on any make or model of computer, as long as a free PDF reader program is installed. It is a good format to choose if you don't know whether the people to whom you distribute the presentation have PowerPoint available. In addition, recipients cannot edit the presentation when it is saved as a PDF. When you save a presentation as a PDF, you can choose the number of slides to include on each page, similar to choosing the number of slides per handout when you print handouts.

Jack asks you to save the presentation in the PDF format. You will save the presentation in the PDF format as a handout with all seven slides on a page.

### To publish the presentation in PDF format:

1. Click the **File** tab to open Backstage view, and then click **Export** in the navigation bar. The Export screen appears with Create PDF/XPS Document selected.

2. Click the **Create PDF/XPS** button in the right pane. Backstage view closes, and the Publish as PDF or XPS dialog box opens with PDF listed in the Save as type box. See Figure 4–34.

   **Trouble?** If the Create PDF/XPS button is not selected on the Export screen, click it, and then continue with Step 2.

**Figure 4–34**    Publish as PDF or XPS dialog box

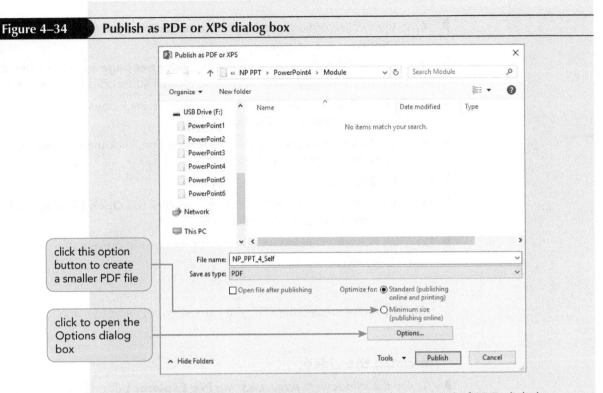

click this option button to create a smaller PDF file

click to open the Options dialog box

**Trouble?** If XPS appears in the Save as type box instead of PDF, click the Save as type arrow, and then click PDF.

3. Navigate to the location where you are storing your files, if necessary, and then change the filename to **NP_PPT_4_PDF**. You want to create a small file size suitable for attaching to an email message.

4. Click the **Minimum size (publishing online)** option button. Now you need to set the option to save it as a handout.

5. Click the **Options** button. The Options dialog box opens. See Figure 4–35.

**Figure 4–35**    Options dialog box for saving a presentation as a PDF

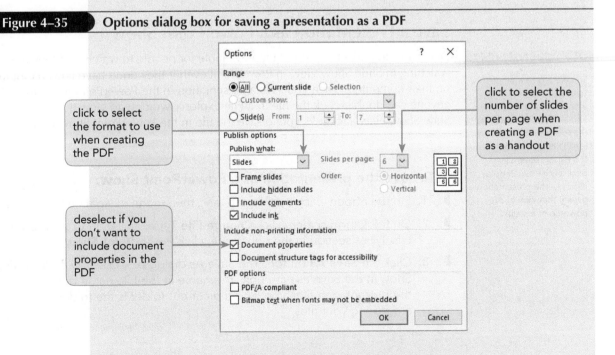

click to select the format to use when creating the PDF

click to select the number of slides per page when creating a PDF as a handout

deselect if you don't want to include document properties in the PDF

6. In the Publish options section, click the **Publish what** arrow, and then click **Handouts**.

7. In the Publish options section, click the **Slides per page** arrow, and then click **9**. The slides have a light background, so you will add a border around each slide.

8. Click the **Frame slides** check box to select it. Jack doesn't want the document properties to be included.

9. In the Include non-printing information section, click the **Document properties** check box to deselect it.

10. Click **OK**.

11. In the Publish as PDF or XPS dialog box, click the **Open file after publishing** check box to deselect it, if necessary.

12. Click **Publish**. A dialog box briefly appears as the presentation is saved in PDF format.

Now that you've created the PDF, you can use your PDF reader app to view it.

### To watch the video:

1. On the Windows taskbar, click the **File Explorer** button ▣. The NP_PPT_4_ PDF file is included in the file list.

2. Double-click the **NP_PPT_4_PDF** file. The PDF reader app on your computer starts and the PDF file you created opens. Each slide in the presentation appears as an image on the page. There is a border around each image.

3. Close the PDF reader app.

4. On the Windows taskbar, click the **PowerPoint** button ▣. The PowerPoint window appears with the NP_PPT_4_Self presentation displayed.

## Save a Presentation as a PowerPoint Show

Jack wants to make the presentation available for people to watch as if they are watching in Slide Show view in PowerPoint even if they don't have PowerPoint installed on their computer. When you save a presentation in the PowerPoint Show format, anyone can double-click the file in a File Explorer window to view the presentation in Slide Show view. Jack asks you to save the file in the PowerPoint Show format.

### To save the presentation as a PowerPoint Show:

1. On the ribbon, click the **File** tab, and then in the navigation bar, click **Export**.

2. On the Export screen, click **Change File Type**, and then in the Presentation File Types section in the right pane, click **PowerPoint Show**.

3. Click the **Save As** button. The Save As dialog box opens with PowerPoint Show in the Save as type box. The name in the File name box is the same as the presentation filename, and the current folder is the folder in which you are storing your files.

▶ **4.** Change the filename to **NP_PPT_4_Show**, and then click **Save**. The Save As dialog box closes and the file is saved as a PowerPoint show. The PowerPoint show presentation file you just created is the currently open presentation.

▶ **5.** Close the NP_PPT_4_Show presentation file.

# Insight

### Checking a Presentation for Compatibility with Earlier Versions of PowerPoint

If you want to save a presentation in a format compatible with earlier versions of PowerPoint, you should first use the Compatibility Checker to identify features in the presentation that are incompatible with earlier versions of PowerPoint so that you can decide whether to modify the presentation. To do this, click the File tab, click Info, and then on the Info screen in Backstage view, click the Check for Issues button, and then click Check Compatibility. When you save a presentation in the PowerPoint 97-2003 format, the compatibility checker runs automatically.

In this session, you set slide timings manually, rehearsed slide timings, recorded a slide show, and set up the show to be viewed at a kiosk. You also inspected the file for hidden information and saved the file in other formats. Jack has the presentation in all the formats he needs.

# Review

### Session 4.2 Quick Check

1. How do you manually change the amount of time a slide stays on the screen during Slide Show view in a self-running presentation?
2. Do links work in a self-running presentation?
3. How do you prevent viewers from advancing the slide show by clicking the mouse during a self-running presentation?
4. When you record a slide show, can you save audio or video along with the presentation?
5. What does the Document Inspector reveal?
6. What are the two types of file formats you can save a presentation as when you save it as a video?
7. What file format should you save a presentation in if you want to make sure that almost anyone with a computer can view the contents of the slides?
8. What file format should you save a presentation in if you want to allow anyone to double-click the file to view it in Slide Show view even if they don't have PowerPoint installed?

# Practice

## Review Assignments

**Data Files needed for the Review Assignments: NP_PPT_4-3.pptx, NP_PPT_4-4.pptx, Support_PPT_4_Corn.png**

Some owners of small farms have asked Jack Chu for suggestions on how to create a corn maze. Specifically, farmers have asked about how to design and build the maze, how to monitor customers in the maze, how to advertise the attraction, and how to set ticket prices. Jack created a presentation that he plans to use when he describes building a corn maze, and he wants your help to finish it. Complete the following steps:

1. Open the file **NP_PPT_4-3.pptx**, located in the PowerPoint4 > Review folder included with your Data Files, add your name as the subtitle, and then save the presentation as **NP_PPT_4_Maze** to the location where you are saving your files.

2. Add a gradient fill to the background of Slide 1. Change the color of the Stop 4 of 4 tab to Brown, Accent 4, Lighter 40%. Change the color of the Stop 3 of 4 tab to Brown, Accent 4, Lighter 60% and change its position to 90%. Change the color of the Stop 2 of 4 tab to Brown, Accent 4, Lighter 80% and change its position to 85%. Change the color of the Stop 1 of 4 tab to White, Background 1 and change its position to 75%. Change the Type to Linear and change the Direction to Linear Down.

3. Apply the gradient background to all of the slides in the presentation.

4. On Slide 1 (the title slide), add the photo **Support_PPT_4_Corn.png**, located in the PowerPoint4 > Review folder included with your Data Files as the background fill. Tile the picture as texture, and then change the horizontal offset (Offset X) to 120 pt. Change the transparency of the photo background on Slide 1 to 50%.

5. On Slide 2, display the guides. Reposition the vertical guide at 2.17 inches to the right of center. Reposition the horizontal guide at 0.17 inches above the middle.

6. On Slide 2, move the maze off of the slide to the left, keeping its center aligned with the horizontal guide. (Remember to press and hold SHIFT to move an object in a straight line. Zoom out if necessary.) Apply the Lines motion path animation with the Right effect to the maze. Adjust the ending of the Lines motion path so that the center of the maze ends on the intersection of the guides and so that the maze will travel in a straight line.

7. Add the Spin emphasis animation to the maze. Change the start setting of the Spin animation to With Previous, and then change its duration to 1.75 seconds.

8. Change the start setting of the Lines animation to After Previous.

9. On Slide 2 ("Plan"), format each of the unnumbered list items to links to the corresponding slides.

10. Change the color of the links on Slide 2 ("Plan") to Light Yellow, Background 2, Darker 75%.

11. On Slide 9 ("Questions?"), change the text displayed for the link to **Jack Chu**, and then change the color of the link to the same color as the text links on Slide 2 (Light Yellow, Background 2, Darker 75%).

12. Insert a new Slide 3 using the Title Only layout. Type **Plan** as the slide title. Add Slides 4 through 8 as slide zooms on the new Slide 3. Resize the slide zooms so they are 1.5 inches high.

13. Reposition the vertical guide so it is 4.33 inches to the right of center. Make a copy of the vertical guide and reposition the copy 4.33 inches to the left of center. Make another copy of the vertical guide, and then position it so it is centered on the slide at 0.00 inches. Reposition the horizontal guide so it is in the middle of the slide at 0.00 inches. Make a copy of the horizontal guide and reposition the copy at 1.75 inches below the middle.

14. Position the slide zooms as follows:

    a.  Position the "Pricing" slide zoom so the right edge aligns with the vertical guide on the right side of the slide and the bottom edge aligns with the horizontal guide at 1.75 inches below the middle.

    b.  Position the "Liability" slide zoom so the center aligns with the guide at the center of the slide and the top and bottom edges align with the top and bottom edges of the "Pricing" slide zoom.

    c. Position the "Marketing" slide zoom so the left edge aligns with the vertical guide positioned 4.33 inches to the left of center and the top and bottom edges align with the top and bottom edges of the "Liability" and "Pricing" slide zooms.

    d. Position the "Operation" slide zoom so the bottom edge aligns with the horizontal guide in the middle of the slide (at 0.00 inches) and so the center approximately aligns with the center of the space between the "Liability" and "Pricing" slide zooms.

    e. Position the "Design and Build" slide zoom so the top and bottom edges align with the top and bottom edges of the "Operation" slide zoom and so the center approximately aligns with the center of the space between the "Marketing" and "Liability" slide zooms.

15. Change the duration of the zoom transitions applied to each of the slide zooms to 1.25 seconds. Change the setting of the "Pricing" slide zoom so that after the slide is displayed, Slide 3 (the "Plan" slide with the slide zooms) reappears.

16. On Slide 4 ("Design and Build"), insert the Arrow: Left shape, and then type **Plan** in the shape. Change the font size to 20 points. Resize the shape so it is 0.5 inches high and 0.9 inches wide. Apply the Intense Effect – Orange, Accent 1 shape style in the Theme Styles section, and then position the shape in the lower-left corner of the slide so that the top of the shape aligns with the bottom of the bulleted list and so its center aligns with the guide 4.33 inches to the left of center.

17. Format the Plan shape as a link to Slide 3 (the "Plan" slide with the slide zooms).

18. Copy the Plan shape on Slide 4 ("Design and Build") to Slide 5 ("Operation"), Slide 6 ("Marketing"), Slide 7 ("Liability"), and Slide 8 ("Pricing").

19. On Slide 3 ("Plan"), insert the Blank action button, and then set it to link to Slide 9 ("Tips"). Enter **TIPS** in the action button, and then format the action button with the Semitransparent – Black, Dark 1, No Outline shape style in the Presets section. Resize the action button so it is one-half inch high and 0.7 inches wide. Position the action button in the upper-right corner of the slide so that the bottom aligns with the bottom of the title text and the center aligns with the right edge of the Slide 8 ("Pricing") slide zoom and the vertical guide at 4.33 inches right of center. Hide the guides.

20. On Slide 6 ("Marketing"), modify the animation of the bulleted list so that the first item ("Put up road signs") animates after the previous action. Then change the start settings of the other three first-level bulleted items so that they animate after the previous action with a delay of one second. Keep the start setting of the animations of the second-level items below "Conventional ads" as With Previous and add a delay of one second if necessary so that their animations start at the same time as the animation applied to the "Conventional ads" bulleted item.

21. On Slide 6, change the start setting of the animation applied to the picture of the corn maze sign to With Previous, and then change the order of the animations so that the animation of the corn maze sign occurs at the same time as the animation of the first-level item "Put up road signs." Preview the animations on Slide 6.

22. Hide Slide 2 (the "Plan" slide with the text links) during a slide show.

23. Save the presentation and close it.

24. Open the presentation **NP_PPT_4-4.pptx**, add your name as the subtitle, and then save it as **NP_PPT_4-MazeSelf** to the location where you are saving your files.

25. Rehearse the timings, displaying the content of Slide 1 for four seconds, and displaying the content of each of the rest of the slides for about one second after the last bulleted item appears, except Slide 2. Display Slide 2 long enough to watch the maze morph onto the screen and the path animate through the maze, and then wait five seconds.

26. Change the timing of Slide 9 ("Questions?") to eight seconds.

27. Record the slide show starting on Slide 2 ("Plan"). After the path through the maze animates, say, **"To skip to the last slide, which contains tips for running the corn maze attraction, click the button in the lower-right corner."** Wait five seconds, and then stop the recording.

28. Set up the show to be browsed at a kiosk.

29. Run the Document Inspector and then remove anything found, except do not remove document properties and personal information.

30. Save the changes to the presentation. Make sure you do this before you continue with the rest of the steps.

31. Save the presentation as an MPEG-4 video at the Standard (480p) size and using the recorded timings and narration. Name the video file **NP_PPT_4_MazeVideo** and save it in the location where you are saving your files.

32. Save Slide 1 of the presentation as a PNG file named **NP_PPT_4_MazeSlide1** to the location where you are saving your files.

33. Save the entire presentation as a picture presentation named **NP_PPT_4_MazePic** to the location where you are saving your files.

34. Save the presentation file as a PDF named **NP_PPT_4_MazePDF** in the location where you are saving your files. Use the Minimum size option, do not include the document properties, and create a handout with nine slides per page with each slide framed.

35. Save the presentation in the PowerPoint Show format with the name **NP_PPT_4_MazeShow**.

36. Close the file.

# Apply

## Case Problem 1

**Data Files needed for this Case Problem: NP_PPT_4-5.pptx, Support_PPT_4_Waves.jpg**

**Shoreside Realty**: Julia Moreno owns Shoreside Realty, a real estate company in Scarborough, Maine, that specializes in selling and renting homes in local beach communities. As part of her marketing, she attends local events, such as the farmer's market, weekly summer concerts, and Chamber of Commerce events, and shows photos of houses near beaches for sale or rent. She created a presentation with slides containing the addresses and brief descriptions of several newly listed properties. She asks you to finish the presentation by adding formatting to the title slide background, and by adding animations to highlight the fact that two of the properties can fit a large number of people. Then she wants you to make the presentation self-running and save it as other file types. Complete the following steps:

1. Open the file **NP_PPT_4-5.pptx**, located in the PowerPoint 4 > Case1 folder included with your Data Files, add your name as the subtitle on the title slide, and then save it as **NP_PPT_4_Realty** in the location where you are saving your files.

2. Apply the Style 6 Background style to all of the slides in the presentation.

3. On Slide 1 (the title slide), fill the background with the picture **Support_PPT_4_Waves.jpg**, located in the PowerPoint 4 > Case1 folder.

4. On Slide 2 ("Available Properties"), change each address to a link to the corresponding slide. Change the color of the links to Ice Blue, Background 2, Darker 75%.

5. On Slide 3 ("18 Oceanside Road"), insert the Rectangle: Rounded Corners shape and resize it so it is 0.7 inches high and 2.5 inches wide. Type **Click here to find out how to contact us!** in the shape, and then apply the Gradient Fill – Brown, Accent 6, No Outline shape style in the Presets section. Position the shape so it is centered below the text boxes in the darker area on the left side of the slide and so the top edge aligns with the bottom edge of the picture of the cottage.

6. On Slide 3, format the shape you drew as a link to Slide 8 ("Schedule an Appointment Today"). Copy this shape link and paste it on Slides 4, 5, 6, and 7.

7. Display Slide 3 ("18 Oceanside Road"), and then display the guides. Drag the horizontal guide up to 2.58 inches above the middle, and then drag the vertical guide to 1.75 inches to the right.

8. On Slide 3, insert a Rectangle shape. Resize it so it is 0.7 inches high and 2.4 inches wide. Fill the shape with the Light Blue color in the Standard Colors section, remove the shape outline, and then insert the text **Sleeps 10!** in the shape. Position the shape so it is centered on top of the intersection of the horizontal and vertical guides. Apply the Wipe entrance animation to the shape, and then change its direction effect to From Left.

9. On Slide 3, insert the Double Wave shape in the Stars and Banners section of the Shapes menu. Resize the shape so it is 0.3 inches high and 2.5 inches wide. Duplicate the shape, and then

position the copy of the shape to the right of the original shape so that the two shapes are aligned horizontally and the ends are touching. Group the two wave shapes.

10. Position the grouped shape above the Sleeps 10! shape so that the top edge of the grouped shape aligns with the top edge of the slide and so it is centered horizontally above the Sleeps 10! shape.

11. Apply the Lines motion path to the grouped shape. Change the direction effect to Right. Move the start point of the motion path in a straight line so it is approximately aligned with the left edge of the Sleeps 10! shape, and then move the end point of the motion path so it is approximately aligned with the right edge of the Sleeps 10! shape.

12. Duplicate the grouped shape. Position the copy of the grouped shape so that it is below the Sleeps 10! shape with the bottom of the grouped shape touching but not overlapping the picture of the cottage, and so it is vertically aligned with the original grouped shape.

13. Change the start setting of the animation applied to the Sleeps 10! shape to After Previous. Make sure the animation applied to the grouped shapes above and below the Sleeps 10! shape occur after the animation applied to the Sleeps 10! shape, and then change the start setting of both animations to With Previous.

14. On Slide 3, select the two grouped shapes and the Sleeps 10! shape, and then copy them. Display Slide 5 ("4 West Beach Road"), and then paste the shapes you copied to this slide. Click a blank area of the slide to deselect the pasted shapes. Click the Sleeps 10! shape, select "10", and then type **14** to change the text to "Sleeps 14!"

15. On Slide 5 ("4 West Beach Road"), select both grouped shapes and fill them with the Ice Blue, Background 2 color (this is the same color as the background fill color). Remove the outline of the grouped shapes. The shapes are now the same color as the slide background and you cannot see them. Preview the animations on the slide.

16. Display Slide 3, and then fill both grouped shapes with the Ice Blue, Background 2 color and remove their outlines.

17. Hide the guides.

18. On Slide 8 ("Schedule an Appointment Today"), edit the link to the website so that the text on the slide is **Click to visit us online!**

19. On Slide 8, change the color of the link text to Ice Blue, Background 2, Darker 75%.

20. Rehearse the timings. Leave Slide 1 (the title slide) and Slide 2 ("Available Properties") displayed for five seconds. Leave Slide 3 ("18 Oceanside Road") through Slide 7 ("31 Island View Road") displayed for four seconds each. Leave the last slide—Slide 8 ("Schedule an Appointment Today") displayed for 10 seconds.

21. Record the presentation starting at Slide 1. After Slide 1 appears, say, **"Shoreside Realty is the answer to your vacation needs."** Wait five seconds, and then stop the recording.

22. Use the Transitions tab to change the timing of Slide 2 ("Available Properties") to 10 seconds.

23. Set up the slide show to be browsed at a kiosk.

24. Run the Document Inspector to remove the note on Slide 2.

25. Save the changes to the presentation.

26. Save the presentation as an MPEG-4 video named **NP_PPT_4_RealtyVideo** using the Standard (480p) option and the recorded timings. Because only two slides have timings assigned, the rest of the slides will be displayed for five seconds each—the time listed in the Seconds spent on each slide box in the Create a Video section of the Export screen in Backstage view.

27. Save the presentation as a picture presentation named **NP_PPT_4_RealtyPic**.

28. Save the presentation as a PDF named **NP_PPT_4_RealtyPDF** in the location where you are saving your files. Use the Minimum size option, do not include the document properties, and create a handout with nine slides per page.

29. Close the presentation.

# Challenge

## Case Problem 2

Data Files needed for this Case Problem: **NP_PPT_4-6.pptx**, **Support_PPT_4_Bacteria.png**, **Support_PPT_4_Isopropanol.3mf**

**Northwest Biotech** NMW Medical Manufacturing in Tacoma, Washington, manufactures medical devices. They have recently started helping hospitals reprocess single-use medical devices. They hired Northwest Biotech to advise them so that they can meet FDA guidelines. Ben Yeung is the department head of Vitro Services at Northwest Biotech. Ben has set up a series of meetings at NMW to help them set up their validation process. He created a presentation for his first meeting and he asks you to help him complete it. Complete the following steps:

1. Open the file **NP_PPT_4-6.pptx**, located in the PowerPoint 4 > Case2 folder included with your Data Files, add your name as the subtitle on the title slide, and then save it as **NP_PPT_4_Reprocess** in the location where you are saving your files.

2. Insert a new Slide 2 with the Blank layout. Add Slides 3 through 11 as slide zooms on the new Slide 2. Resize the slide zooms so they are 1.8 inches high. Arrange them on the side in three rows with the slide zooms for Slides 3 through 5 in the first row, Slides 6 through 8 in the second row, and Slides 9 through 11 in the third row.

3. Change the zoom options for Slides 3, 4, 6, 9, and 10 so that Slide 2 reappears after displaying those slides during a slide show.

⊕ **Explore** 4. On Slide 3 ("Terms"), select "Single-Use Medical Device" and then use the Search button on the Review tab to search for information about this term on the web. Click one of the results to open that webpage in your browser.

⊕ **Explore** 5. Click once in the address bar in the browser to select the entire webpage address, and then press CTRL+C to copy the webpage address. Change the selected text on the slide to a link to the webpage address. Change the text color of the link to Aqua, Accent 1, Darker 50%.

⊕ **Explore** 6. On Slide 5 ("Clean"), insert the Get Information action button. Set it so that if you move the pointer on top of the shape, it will display Slide 3 ("Terms") and so it will play the Click sound when you do this.

7. Resize the action button so it is one-inch square. Position it in the upper-right corner of the slide so the middle aligns with the middle of the title text box and the right edge aligns with the right edge of the picture. Copy the action button and paste it onto Slides 4, 6, 7, 9, and 10.

8. On Slide 8 ("One Bacteria Can Multiply Quickly and Infect Patient"), insert the picture **Support_PPT_4_Bacteria.png**, located in the PowerPoint 4 > Case2 folder. Resize it so it is two inches high, rotate it 180 degrees, and position it above the slide so it aligns with the top and right edge of the slide.

9. Apply the Lines motion path animation to the picture of the bacteria. Drag the ending point of the animation so it is approximately centered on the picture of the medical tubing on the slide.

10. Add the Pulse emphasis animation to the picture of the bacteria. Change the start setting to After Previous, and change the duration to 0.25 seconds.

⊕ **Explore** 11. Change the number of times the picture pulses to three. (*Hint*: Click the arrow for the animation in the Animation pane, and then click Effect Options.)

12. Insert another copy of the picture **Support_PPT_4_Bacteria.png**, and resize it so it is two inches high. Apply the Appear entrance animation to this image. Change its start setting to After Previous and add a delay of 0.50 seconds. Position this image on top of the picture of the tubing near the top-left of the image.

13. Copy the picture of the bacteria that you placed near the top-left of the image, and then paste the copy on the slide. Position the copied image somewhere else on top of the picture of the tubing. Change the delay of the Appear animation to 0.25 seconds. Rotate this image about 45 degrees in either direction.

14. Make a copy of the image that has the Appear animation with a delay of 0.25 seconds. Paste this copy on the slide. Position it on a part of the picture of the tubing that does not already have a picture of the bacteria. Rotate it slightly in any direction.

15. Paste the copied image 10 more times. Arrange the pasted images so they are scattered on top of the picture of the tubing. Rotate the pictures of the bacteria to different orientations.

✦ **Explore** 16. On Slide 9 ("Isopropanol Alcohol—Common Disinfectant"), insert the 3D model **Support_PPT_4_Isopropanol.3mf**, located in the PowerPoint4 > Case2 folder. Resize the image so it is 3.8 inches high. This is a molecular model of isopropanol alcohol. Use the handle in the middle of the image to rotate and tilt the image in all directions until you can see all of the molecules on the slide at once. Position it so its top edge aligns with the top edge of the bulleted list text box and its left edge aligns with the left edge of the title text box.

17. On Slide 11 ("For More Information"), change the text displayed for Sean's email address to **Sean McLaughlin Email**. Then change the color of the text of both links on Slide 11 to Aqua, Accent 1, Darker 50%.

18. Save the changes to the presentation.

✦ **Explore** 19. Save all of the slides as PNG files to a folder named **NP_PPT_4_ReprocessAll**.

# INDEX